Media and Cultural Studies

KeyWorks in Cultural Studies

As cultural studies powers ahead to new intellectual horizons, it becomes increasingly important to chart the discipline's controversial history. This is the object of an exciting new series, KeyWorks in Cultural Studies. By showcasing the best that has been thought and written on the leading themes and topics constituting the discipline, KeyWorks in Cultural Studies provides an invaluable genealogy for students striving to better understand the contested space in which cultural studies takes place and is practiced.

Media and Cultural Studies

KeyWorks

Revised Edition

Edited by

Meenakshi Gigi Durham and
Douglas M. Kellner

Blackwell
Publishing

BLACKWELL PUBLISHING
350 Main Street, Malden, MA 02148-5020, USA
9600 Garsington Road, Oxford OX4 2DQ, UK
550 Swanston Street, Carlton, Victoria 3053, Australia

First published 2001
This revised edition published 2006 by Blackwell Publishing Ltd

5   2008

Library of Congress Cataloging-in-Publication Data

Media and cultural studies : keyworks / edited by Meenakshi Gigi Durham and Douglas M.
Kellner. — Rev. ed.
     p. cm. — (Keyworks in cultural studies)
   Includes bibliographical references and index.
   ISBN: 978-1-4051-3258-9 (pbk.)
   1. Mass media and culture.   2. Popular culture.   I. Durham, Meenakshi Gigi.   II.
Kellner, Douglas, 1943–   III. Series.

   P94.6.M424 2006
   302.23—dc22

                                                                                                    2005014104

A catalogue record for this title is available from the British Library.

Set in 10/12.5pt Galliard
by Graphicraft Limited, Hong Kong
Printed and bound in Singapore
by C.O.S. Printers Pte Ltd

The publisher's policy is to use permanent paper from mills that operate a sustainable
forestry policy, and which has been manufactured from pulp processed using acid-free and
elementary chlorine-free practices. Furthermore, the publisher ensures that the text paper
and cover board used have met acceptable environmental accreditation standards.

For further information on
Blackwell Publishing, visit our website:
www.blackwellpublishing.com

Contents

Preface to the Revised Edition

We have produced a revised edition of KeyWorks to collect some of the new material that has appeared since the first edition and have also included material that colleagues have urged would be important additions to the Reader. We are grateful to Blackwell for allowing us to select eight new essays and to offer a section on globalization. With the constant proliferation of new media, there is a growing amount of analyses, debates, and conflicting positions and we attempt to capture some of the ferment in media and cultural studies today by including fresh material. These changes are reflected in the expanded and revised introduction to the KeyWorks.

Choices were extremely difficult and we were forced to exclude much important material. We appreciate comments by readers and users of the text that have helped with the revision, and the support of our Blackwell editors Jayne Fargnoli and Elizabeth Swayze. Thanks, as well, to Cameron Laux and Erin Pfaff. We also gratefully acknowledge the ongoing support and encouragement of our spouses and families; heartfelt thanks to Rhonda Hammer, and Frank, Sonali and Maya Durham.

MGD & DMK

About the Editors

Meenakshi Gigi Durham is Associate Professor of Journalism and Mass Communication at the University of Iowa. She has published widely on feminist media studies and related critical approaches, especially those of race, class, and sexuality.

Douglas M. Kellner is George F. Kneller Chair in the Philosophy of Education at UCLA and is the author of many books on social theory, politics, history, and culture, including *Television and the Crisis of Democracy* (1990), *The Persian Gulf TV War* (1992), *Media Culture* (1995), *Media Spectacle* (2003), and *From September 11 to Terror War* (2003).

Adventures in Media and Cultural Studies: Introducing the KeyWorks

Douglas M. Kellner and Meenakshi Gigi Durham

It is increasingly clear that media and culture today are of central importance to the maintenance and reproduction of contemporary societies. Societies, like species, need to reproduce to survive, and culture cultivates attitudes and behavior that predispose people to consent to established ways of thought and conduct, thus integrating individuals into a specific socio-economic system. Forms of media culture like television, film, popular music, magazines, and advertising provide role and gender models, fashion hints, lifestyle images, and icons of personality. The narratives of media culture offer patterns of proper and improper behavior, moral messages, and ideological conditioning, sugar-coating social and political ideas with pleasurable and seductive forms of popular entertainment. Likewise, media and consumer culture, cyberculture, sports, and other popular activities engage people in practices which integrate them into the established society, while offering pleasures, meanings, and identities. Various individuals and audiences respond to these texts disparately, negotiating their meanings in complex and often paradoxical ways.

With media and culture playing such important roles in contemporary life, it is obvious that we must come to understand our cultural environment if we want control over our lives. Yet there are many approaches to the study of media, culture, and society in separate disciplines and academic fields. Often critics take a single perspective and use a specific method and theory to understand, make sense of, interpret, or criticize media and cultural texts. Others eschew all methodological and theoretical critical strategies in favor of empirical description and analysis.

We would advocate the usefulness of a wide range of theoretical and methodological approaches to the study of media, culture, and society. Yet we do not believe that any one theory or method is adequate to engage the richness, complexity, variety, and novelty displayed in contemporary constellations of rapidly proliferating cultural forms and new media. We have therefore assembled what we consider some KeyWorks of current theories and methods for the study of the abundance and diversity of culture and media in the present age. The texts we have chosen are "*Key*" because we believe that the perspectives and theorists which we have included in this volume are among the most significant and serviceable for engaging the forms and influences of contemporary media and culture.

The material in this reader provides "keys" which help unlock the domain of meaning, value, politics, and ideology in familiar forms of cultural artifacts and practices. They furnish prisms which enable critical readers to see cultural texts and phenomena in a new light, generating insight into the sometimes hidden production processes and ideological constraints of media culture. Key theories and methods help unlock and unveil structural codes and organizing conventions of media texts, their meanings and values, and often contradictory social and political effects. Understanding culture critically also provides insight into the ways that media and culture construct gender and role models, and even identities, as the populace come to pattern their lives on the celebrities and stars of media culture. These readings are also "key" in that they open novel theoretical directions and formulations of culture and society; at the time of their writing, they presented inventive and sometimes revolutionary directions in the study of media and culture.

The texts selected are "works" in that their methods and theories enable media-involved readers to engage in the activity of analysis, interpretation, criticism, and making sense of their cultural and social worlds and experiences. The theories and methods presented provide tools for critical vision and practice, helping to produce active creators of meaning and interpretation, rather than merely passive audiences. The KeyWorks thus empower those who wish to gain skills of media literacy, providing instruments of criticism and interpretation. They provide essential elements of becoming intelligent and resourceful cultural subjects, discriminating readers, and creative users and producers of contemporary culture.

The texts assembled in this book can therefore help cultural consumers to become critics and creators. Our introduction will accordingly attempt to demonstrate how the diverse approaches and texts that we have assembled provide valuable keys to cultural criticism and interpretation, helping to produce more competent and discriminating critics. We discuss below how the specific groupings of the KeyWorks provide different approaches to the study of media and culture and point to the contributions and limitations of each perspective. In this opening introduction, we accordingly furnish overviews of each distinctive way of seeing and engaging culture and media. More detailed presentation of the theorists and critics we have chosen, along with explications of the key concepts, theories, and methods selected, will head each of the five sections we have delineated.

Theory/Method/Critique: A Multiperspectival Approach

There is *only* a perspective seeing, *only* a perspective "knowing"; and the *more* affects we allow to speak about one thing, the more complete will our "concept" of this thing, our "objectivity," be.

– Friedrich Nietzsche

Our opening discussion will also give the reader a sense of current debates and issues within cultural and media theory, emphasizing which issues and controversies are of crucial importance in the contemporary era. Our narrative will track salient developments in the study of culture and media, supplying a mapping of the prevailing fields of theories and methods which have proliferated especially since the 1960s. Indeed, to pursue our KeyWorks metaphor, each perspective provides an opening into the complex terrain of contemporary media and culture, furnishing access to understanding the world in which we live. Each "key" will open doors to new domains, such as ideology, the politics of representations, and cultural studies. They provide novel ways of seeing and understanding the flora and fauna of images, symbols, and messages through which we wander, trying to make sense and give shape to our lives.

The terrain of contemporary culture, however, is so vast, the maze of theories is so complex, and the debates over media and culture are so intense and convoluted, that we have necessarily had to choose some perspectives and theorists to the exclusion of others. In fact, there are many forms of media that saturate our everyday lives and the cultural change of the current technological revolution is so turbulent that it is becoming increasingly difficult to map the transformations and to keep up with the cultural discourses and theories that attempt to make sense of it all. Culture today is both ordinary and complex, encompassing multiple realms of everyday life. We – and many of the theorists assembled in this volume – employ the term "culture" broadly to signify types of cultural artifacts (i.e. TV, CDs, newspapers, paintings, opera, journalism, cyberculture, DVDs, and so on), as well as discourses about these phenomena. Since culture is bound up with both forms, like film or sports, and discourses, it is both a space of interpretation and debate as well as a subject matter and domain of inquiry. Theories and writings like this introduction are themselves modes of culture, spaces that attempt to make sense of particular phenomena and subject matter, and a part of a contemporary cultural field.

A theory is a way of seeing, an optic, that focuses on a specific subject matter. The Greek word *theoria* signifies perspective and vision which centers upon specific topics, processes, and attributes, as a theory of the state focuses on how the government works. Theories are also modes of explanation and interpretation that construct connections and illuminate sociocultural practices and structures, thus helping to make sense of our everyday life, as an analysis of how Microsoft dominates the computer software field would indicate what particular issues are at stake. Thus, cultural and social theories are descriptive and interpretive; they highlight specific topics, make connections, contextualize, provide interpretations, and offer explanations. There is also a narrative component to theory, as in Adam Smith's or Karl Marx's theories of capitalism, which tell of the origin and genesis of the market economy as well as describing how it works, and in Marx's case offering a critique and proposals of revolutionary transformation.

All social theories are perspectives that center attention on phenomena and their connections to the broader society and a wide range of institutions, discourses, and practices. As optics, or ways of seeing, they illuminate part of the social and cultural field, but may ignore or leave in darkness other dimensions. Consequently, constantly expanding one's theoretical perspectives and horizons helps to illuminate multiple dimensions of our cultural environment, providing richer and more complex understandings of our sociocultural life. Multiplying theories and methods at one's disposal aids in grasping diverse dimensions of an object, in making more and better connections, and thus provides richer and more comprehensive understanding of cultural artifacts or practices under scrutiny.

It is therefore our conviction that no one approach contributes *the* key to cultural and media criticism, that all given theories and methods have their limitations as well as strengths, their blindspots as well as illuminating perspectives. Hence, in our view, no one theory, method, or thinker dispenses privileged access to the truth of our culture and society; there is no magical formula or hermeneutic key to unlock the hidden secrets of cultural meaning and effects. Rather, we believe that the categories, theories, and texts presented as KeyWorks provide tools for making sense of our life, or to switch the metaphor, weapons of critique which enable individuals to engage in discriminating practice in distinct contexts.

Furthermore, some of the theoretical perspectives offered will furnish useful material for some tasks, while others will prove more valuable for different projects. Someone might choose, for instance, to do a feminist reading of a cultural text, while at another time the category of race or class may be most salient to one's critical intentions. Analyses will necessarily often involve the confluence of these and other vectors. Likewise, one critical exercise might focus on the ideology of the text and the ways that texts legitimate and reproduce dominant forms of oppression, while another reading might emphasize the ways that specific texts resist dominant institutions and ideologies – or show how certain texts both legitimate and contest the established culture and society at the same time and are thus markedly ambiguous.

Viewing culture from political economy, from the perspective of analysis of the system of production and distribution, may disclose how the culture industries reproduce the dominant corporate and commercial culture, excluding discourses and images that contest the established social system. Closer reading of media texts can reveal a wealth of meanings, values, and messages, often contradictory. Examining how people engage cultural texts, however, may reveal that audiences refuse dominant meanings and offer their own, sometimes surprising, interpretations. Conjoining production/text/audience perspectives can accordingly help provide a more complex sense of how culture and media actually operate in everyday life.

It is our conviction that competent and critical cultural consumers and commentators need to be able to examine media, culture, and society from a variety of perspectives, in order to cultivate critical vision and understanding of the nature and effects of cultural production and the artifacts with which we interact. Each new approach, each emergent theory, equips the budding critic with a different way of seeing and interpreting, thus creating a more diverse perspective for understanding media and culture. Hence, the many concepts, theories, and methods embedded in the texts in KeyWorks will enable readers to engage themselves in cultural and media criticism, and consequently to become competent critics and consumers.

The texts and approaches we have chosen for KeyWorks are foundational in the sense that they provide building-blocks for constructing analyses, interpretations, and criticisms of cultural texts and the societies in which they originate and operate. Most of the selections are "radical" in the sense that they go to the roots of the situation (the meaning of the Latin term *radix*), showing, for example, how media and culture are grounded in a social system and its conflicts. All of the perspectives we have selected are "sociological" in the sense that they show, in varying ways, how media and cultural texts are rooted in a particular system of political economy like capitalism, or in the dominant media and cultural forms of a particular social order based on relations of domination and subordination in the arenas of gender, race, and class. The roots of media and cultural texts are consequently embedded in social reproduction and conflict, part and parcel of our social life.

The theorists and writings chosen accordingly provide critical understandings and interpretations of media and culture, showing how they are often constructed to serve specific social interests and functions – and yet can be read, enjoyed, and interpreted in a multiplicity of ways. We conceive of KeyWorks as a toolkit that enables individuals to produce their own understandings, meanings, and critiques of contemporary culture, media, and society. We will try to make these often complex perspectives on media and culture accessible and to make our text "user-friendly" by, first, explaining in the sections that follow the key concepts and methods deployed in the leading competing approaches to the study of media and culture, and by introducing the theorists presented in our reader. And then, before each section, we provide more detailed contextualizing of both the particular topics through which we have organized the collection and the theorists and texts chosen. While the book was designed to be employed in classroom situations, we also hope that enterprising readers will use it on their own to become more competent cultural consumers and critics; hence, we also hope that it will prove valuable to people who wish to educate themselves in the theories and methods of cultural and media criticism. Consequently, we begin with discussion of the origins and meanings of some key concepts, to start the trek toward a more empowering cultural and media literacy that will enable people to make better sense of their world and to become more competent actors within it.

Culture, Ideology, and Hegemony

The ideas of the ruling class are in every epoch the ruling ideas; i.e., the class which is the ruling *material* force of society, is at the same time its ruling *intellectual* force. The class which has the means of material production at its disposal, has control at the same time over the means of mental production, so that thereby, generally speaking, the ideas of those who lack the means of mental production are subject to it.

– Karl Marx and Friedrich Engels

Contemporary criticism has forced students and teachers to see that there are no innocent texts, that all artifacts of the established culture and society are laden with

meaning, values, biases, and messages that advance relations of power and subordination. There is no pure entertainment that does not contain representations, often
extremely prejudicial, of class, gender, race, sexuality, and myriad social categories and
groupings. Cultural texts are saturated with social meanings, they generate political
effects, reproducing or opposing governing social institutions and relations of domination and subordination. Culture can also embody specific political discourses –
liberal, conservative, oppositional, or mixed – advancing competing political positions
on issues like the family and sexuality, masculinity or femininity, or violence and war.
Cultural representations often transcode major political discourses and perspectives
presenting, for instance, an array of positions on topics like sexuality, the state, or
religion.

Culture in today's societies thus constitutes a set of discourses, stories, images,
spectacles, and varying cultural forms and practices that generate meaning, identities, and political effects. Culture includes artifacts such as newspapers, television
programs, movies, and popular music, but also practices like shopping, watching
sports events, going to a club, or hanging out in the local coffee shop. Culture is
ordinary, a familiar part of everyday life, yet special cultural artifacts are extraordinary, helping people to see and understand things they've never quite perceived, like
certain novels or films that change your view of the world. Or, we would hope that
some of the challenging theoretical texts included here will provide novel and
transformative understandings of culture, media, and society.

The concept of *ideology*, for example, forces readers to perceive that all cultural
texts have distinct biases, interests, and embedded values, reproducing the point of
view of their producers and often the values of the dominant social groups. Karl
Marx and Friedrich Engels coined the term "ideology" in the 1840s to describe the
dominant ideas and representations in a given social order. On their analysis, during
the feudal period, ideas of piety, honor, valor, and military chivalry were the ruling
ideas of the hegemonic aristocratic classes. During the capitalist era, values of individualism, profit, competition, and the market became dominant, articulating the
ideology of the emergent bourgeois class which was consolidating its class power.
Today, in our high-tech and global capitalism, ideas that promote globalization,
digital technologies, and an unrestrained market society are becoming the prevailing
ideas – conceptions that further the interests of the governing elites in the global
economy.

As we note below, feminists, multiculturalists, and members of a wide range of
subordinate groups, detected that ideologies also reproduced relations of domination
in the arenas of gender, race, ethnicity, sexuality, and further domains of everyday
life. Feminists, for example, criticized sexist ideologies that advanced the domination
of women by men and social institutions and practices that propagated male supremacy. Racist ideologies were criticized that furthered the subordination of specific
races and ethnicities. In a broad sense, therefore, ideologies reproduce social domination, they legitimate rule by the prevailing groups over subordinate ones, and help
replicate the existing inequalities and hierarchies of power and control.

Ideologies appear natural, they seem to be common sense, and are often invisible
and elude criticism. Marx and Engels began a critique of ideology, attempting to

show how ruling ideas reproduce dominant societal interests serving to naturalize, idealize, and legitimate the existing society and its institutions and values. In a competitive and atomistic capitalist society, it appears natural to assert that human beings are primarily self-interested and competitive by nature, just as in a communist society it is natural to assert that people are cooperative by nature. In fact, human beings and societies are extremely complex and contradictory, but ideology smoothes over conflicts and negative features, idealizing human or social traits like individuality and competition which are elevated into governing conceptions and values.

For classical Marxism, the ruling classes employ intellectuals and cultural producers who both produce ideas that glorify the dominant institutions and ways of life, and propagate these governing ideas in cultural forms like literature, the press, or, in our day, film and television. The concept of ideology accordingly makes us question the naturalness of cultural texts and to see that prevailing ideas are not self-evident and obvious, but are constructed, biased, and contestable. This notion makes us suspicious and critical, putting into question regnant ideas which often serve the interests of governing groups. Moreover, the more one studies cultural forms and representations, the more one sees the presence of ideologies that support the interests of the reigning economic, gender, race, or social groups who are presented positively and idealized, while subordinate groups are often presented negatively and prejudicially.

The Italian Marxian thinker Antonio Gramsci developed these ideas further, arguing that diverse social groups attained "hegemony," or dominance, at different times through inducing the consent of the majority of subaltern, or subordinate, groups to a given sociopolitical constellation. He points out that while the unity of prevailing groups is usually created through the state (as in the American revolution, or unification of Italy in the nineteenth century), the institutions of "civil society" also play a role in establishing hegemony. Civil society, in this discourse, involves institutions of the church, schooling, the media and forms of popular culture, among others. It mediates between the private sphere of personal economic interests and the family and the public authority of the state, serving as the locus of what Habermas described as "the public sphere."

For Gramsci, societies maintained their stability through a combination of "domination," or force, and "hegemony," defined as consent to "intellectual and moral leadership." In this conception, social orders are founded and reproduced with some institutions and groups violently exerting power and domination to maintain social boundaries and rules (i.e. the police, military, vigilante groups, etc.), while other institutions (like religion, schooling, or the media) induce consent to the dominant order through establishing the hegemony, or ideological dominance, of a distinctive type of social order (i.e. market capitalism, fascism, communism, and so on). In addition, societies establish the hegemony of males and certain races through the institutionalizing of male dominance or the rule of a specific race or ethnicity over subordinate groups.

Hegemony theory for Gramsci involves both analysis of current forces of domination and the ways that particular political forces achieved hegemonic authority, *and* the delineation of counterhegemonic forces, groups, and ideas that could contest and overthrow the existing hegemony. An analysis, for instance, of how the conservative regimes of Margaret Thatcher in England and Ronald Reagan in the United States in the late 1970s and early 1980s won power would dissect how conservative groups gained dominance through control of the state, and the use of media, new technologies, and cultural institutions such as think-tanks and fund-raising and political action groups. Explaining the Thatcher–Reagan conservative hegemony of the 1980s would require analysis of how conservative ideas became dominant in the media, schools, and culture at large. It would discuss how on a global level the market rather than the state was seen as the source of all wealth and solution to social problems, while the state was pictured as a source of excessive taxation, overregulation, and bureaucratic inertia.

A cultural hegemony analysis would therefore show how particular media, technologies, or institutions contributed to a broader sociopolitical domination by forces like fascism, communism, or market capitalism. A Gramscian theory would also discuss how a hegemonic social order is always contested by counterhegemonic forces, such as during the 1980s, when conservative rule was contested, and the 1990s, when it was in part overthrown with a resurgence of liberalism and social-democratic movements and regimes, as well as an upsurge of oppositional social movements. Such analysis, however, would also have to show how the more liberal hegemonic groups compromised with the dominant conservative forces, whereby liberal democrats like Bill Clinton, or social democrats like Tony Blair, would themselves take conservative positions in curbing welfare, cutting social spending, or unleashing military intervention.

Hegemony theory thus calls for historically specific sociocultural analysis of particular contexts and forces, requiring dissection of how culture and a variety of social institutions from the media to the university facilitate broader social and political ends. Analyses of hegemony emphasize that a wide array of cultural institutions function within social reproduction including the church, schools, traditional and elite culture, sports, and the entertainment media. The approach requires social contextualization of all ideas, representations, and cultural forms; it enjoins seeing societies as a locus of social contestation between competing groups who seek dominance and who manipulate reigning institutions and culture to promote their ends.

Theories of hegemony and ideology were further developed by a group of thinkers who were organized around the German Institute for Social Research in Frankfurt in the 1930s. Their core members were Jewish radicals who later went into exile to the United States after Hitler's rise to power. Establishing themselves in a small institute in New York affiliated with Columbia University, the Institute for Social Research, they developed analyses of the culture industries which had emerged as key institutions of social hegemony in the era that they called state-monopoly capitalism. Max Horkheimer, Theodor W. Adorno, Herbert Marcuse, and Walter Benjamin, who was loosely affiliated with the Institute, analyzed the new forms of corporate and state power during a time in which giant corporations ruled the capitalist economies and the might of the state grew significantly under the guise of fascism, Russian communism, and the state capitalism of Roosevelt's New Deal which required a sustained government response to the crisis of the economic

Depression in the 1930s. In this conjuncture, ideology played an increasingly important role in inducing consent to a diversity of social systems.

To a large extent, the Frankfurt school inaugurated critical studies of mass communication and culture, showing in detail how the media were controlled by groups who employed them to further their own interests and domination. They were the first social theorists to see the importance of what they called the "culture industries" in the reproduction of contemporary societies, in which so-called mass culture and communications stand in the center of leisure activity, are important agents of socialization and mediators of political reality, and should be seen as primary institutions of contemporary societies with a variety of economic, political, cultural, and social effects.

Having experienced the rise of fascism and fascist use of the media in Germany in the 1930s, they noted during their exile in the United States how the culture industry was controlled by predominant capitalist economic interests and functioned to reproduce the established market society and democratic polity. The Frankfurt school developed a critical and transdisciplinary approach to cultural and communications studies, combining critique of political economy of the media, analysis of texts, and audience reception studies of the social and ideological effects of mass culture and communications. They coined the term "culture industry" to signify the process of the industrialization of mass-produced culture and the commercial imperatives which drove the system. The critical theorists analyzed all mass-mediated cultural artifacts within the context of industrial production, in which the commodities of the culture industries exhibited the same features as other products of mass production: commodification, standardization, and massification. The culture industries had the singular function, however, of providing ideological legitimation of the existing capitalist societies and of integrating individuals into the framework of the capitalist system.

Furthermore, the critical theorists investigated the cultural industries in a political context as a form of the integration of the working class into capitalist societies. The Frankfurt school were one of the first neo-Marxian groups to examine the effects of mass culture and the rise of the consumer society on the working classes which were to be vehicles of revolution in the classical Marxian scenario. They also analyzed the ways that the culture industries were stabilizing contemporary capitalism, and accordingly they sought new strategies for political change, agencies of social transformation, and models for human emancipation that could serve as norms of social critique and goals for political struggle.

Thus, in their theories of the culture industries and critiques of mass culture, the Frankfurt school were the first to systematically analyze and criticize mass-mediated culture and communications within critical social theory. Their approach suggests that to properly understand any specific form of media or culture, one must understand how it is produced and distributed in a given society and how it is situated in relation to the dominant social structure. The Frankfurt school thought, for the most part, that media culture simply reproduced the existing society and manipulated mass audiences into obedience.

One of their members, however, Walter Benjamin, had a more optimistic and activist view of the potential of media, such as film, to promote progressive political ends than his colleagues Horkheimer and Adorno. In "The Work of Art in the Age of Mechanical Reproduction," Benjamin argued that film, sports, and other forms of mass entertainment were creating a new kind of spectator, able to critically dissect cultural forms and to render intelligent judgment on them. For Benjamin, the decline of the aura of the work of art – the sense of originality, uniqueness, and authenticity – under the pressures of mechanical reproduction helped produce a public able to more actively engage a wide range of cultural phenomena. He argued that, for instance, the spectators of sports events were discriminating judges of athletic activity, able to criticize and analyze plays, athletes, strategies, and so on. Likewise, Benjamin postulated that film audiences as well can become experts of criticism and ably dissect the construction, meanings, and ideologies of film.

Benjamin saw that politics were being aestheticized in the contemporary era, deploying techniques of mystification and cultural manipulation to produce media spectacles to gain mass assent to specific political candidates and groups. He was one of the first to dissect the new public spheres that were emerging in the period when the fascist party and state used organs of public communication like the film, radio, or political rally to promote their ends. Moreover, Benjamin's work is also important for focusing on the technology of cultural reproduction, seeing the changes in new media techniques, and carrying out political critique, while calling for democratic transformation of media technology and institutions.

A second-generation member of the Frankfurt school, Jürgen Habermas, grew up under German fascism, found it repellent, and undertook life-long investigations of contemporary society and culture, in part motivated by desire to prevent the recurrence of fascism. After studying with Horkheimer and Adorno in Frankfurt, Germany, in the 1950s, Habermas investigated in his early work the ways that a new public sphere emerged during the time of the Enlightenment and the American and French revolutions, and how it promoted political discussion and debate. Habermas's concept of the public sphere described a space of institutions and practices between private and public interests. The public sphere mediated for Habermas between the domains of the family and the workplace (where private interests prevail), and the state, which often exerts arbitrary forms of power and domination. What Habermas called the "bourgeois public sphere" consisted of the realm of public assemblies, pubs and coffee houses, literary salons, and meeting halls where citizens gathered to discuss their common public affairs and to organize against arbitrary and oppressive forms of social and public authority. The public sphere was nurtured by newspapers, journals, pamphlets, and books which were read and discussed in social sites like pubs and coffee houses.

Habermas notes that newspapers were initially commercial sheets that disseminated "news" (i.e. what was novel and contemporary), but then were transformed into instruments of political debate under the pressures of the American and French Revolutions and the organization of political groups to revolutionize society. Yet newspapers also fell prey to commercial imperatives and often put profit and business interests above political opinion, selling advertising and papers via tabloid sensationalism and entertainment rather than disseminating political information and ideas. Moreover, as the society became more dominated by mass media, powerful corporations came to control major institutions like newspapers, radio, film, and television. These arms of the culture industry served the interests of the media conglomerates and the corporations and advertisers who financed them. In this conjuncture, the public sphere was colonized by big media which came to dominate public life and which recast the public sphere from a locus of information and debate to a site of manipulation by corporate powers.

In retrospect, the theorists discussed so far articulate ascending stages of modern Western societies. While Habermas's theory of the public sphere describes the earlier phase of liberal bourgeois society, Marx and Engels analyze the consolidation of the class rule of the bourgeoisie and hegemony of capitalism during the mid-nineteenth century. Gramsci in turn presents the transition from liberal capitalism to fascism in Italy in the 1930s, while the work of Horkheimer and Adorno can be read as an articulation of a theory of the state and monopoly capitalism which became domin-ant throughout the world during the 1930s. This era constituted a form of "organized capitalism," in which the state and mammoth corporations managed the economy and in which individuals submitted to state and corporate control.

The period is often described as "Fordism" to designate the system of mass pro-duction and the homogenizing regime of capital which sought to produce mass desires, tastes, and behavior. The culture industries discussed by Horkheimer and Adorno were the form of cultural organization parallel to Fordism as a mode of industrial production. Just as American automobiles were produced on assembly lines accord-ing to a well-organized plan and division of labor, so too were film, broadcasting, magazines, and assorted forms of media culture generated according to types and with a well-organized division of labor.

The decades following the Second World War were a period of mass production and consumption characterized by uniformity and homogeneity of needs, thought, and behavior, constituting a "mass society" and what the Frankfurt school described as "the end of the individual." No longer was personal thought and action the motor of social and cultural progress; instead gigantic organizations and institutions overpowered individuals. The period corresponds to the staid, ascetic, conformist, and conservative world of corporate capitalism that was dominant in the 1950s with its organization men, its conspicuous consumption, and its mass culture.

During this period, mass culture and communication were essential in generating the modes of thought and behavior appropriate to a highly organized and homo-genized social order. Hence, the Frankfurt-school theory of "the culture industries" articulates a vital historical shift to an epoch in which mass consumption and culture were indispensable to producing a consumer society based on uniform needs and desires for mass-produced products and a mass society based on social organization and conformity. It is culturally the time in the United States of strongly controlled net-work radio and television, insipid top-40 pop music, glossy Hollywood films, national magazines, largely conservative newspapers, and other mass-produced cultural artifacts. In the Soviet communist bloc, and other sectors where state-controlled broadcast-ing prevailed, systems of broadcasting were intended to reproduce the dominant national culture or state ideology, while serving as instruments of social integration and conformity.

Of course, media culture was never as massified and homogeneous as in the Frankfurt-school model, and one could argue that the model was flawed even during its time of origin and influence and that other models were preferable (such as those of Walter Benjamin, Siegfried Kracauer, Ernst Bloch, and others of the Weimar generation and, later, British cultural studies, as we suggest below). Yet the original Frankfurt-School theory of the culture industry articulated the important social roles of media culture during a particular sociohistorical epoch and provided a model, still of use, of an exceedingly commercial and technologically advanced culture that promotes the needs of dominant corporate interests, plays a principal role in ideological reproduction, and enculturates the populace into the dominant system of needs, thought, and behavior.

With the economic boom of the 1960s and proliferation of new products and ideas, structuralism became the intellectual vogue in France. Theories of structure (linguistic, anthropological, social) emerged from an age of burgeoning technology and influenced the Marxist revisionism of French philosopher Louis Althusser. Beginning with Marx's thesis that the mode of production determines the character of social, intellectual, and cultural life, Althusser sees ideology as an effect of the structure of society, a force in which economic, political-legal, cultural, and ideological practices are interrelated to shape social consciousness. In Althusser's version of "structural Marxism," "ideological state apparatuses" (schooling, media, the judiciary, etc.) "interpellated" individuals into preconceived forms of subjectivity that left no space for opposition or resistance. On this account, subjects were constructed as pre-constituted individuals, men or women, members of a specific class, and were induced to identify with the roles, behavior, values, and practices of the existing state-capitalist society. In fact, it is Althusser who advanced the idea that ideology operates via everyday practices, rather than through some form of externally imposed doctrine. Combining psychoanalysis, Marxism, and structuralism, Althusser thus analyzed how individuals were incorporated into specific social systems and functioned to reproduce contemporary capitalist societies. A strain of Althusserian structural Marxism is evident in the early period of British cultural studies.

Following the lines of this narrative, we will argue through the Introduction that the subsequent forms of cultural and media analysis respond to developments within Western capitalist societies from the end of the Second World War until the present. Cultural theories analyze historical metamorphosis and novelties, and articulate sociohistorical conditions, practices, and transformations. Theories provide maps of social orders and tools to understand and transform them. The proliferation of theories in the past two decades itself highlights the increasing differentiation and fragmentation of Western societies during an epoch of intense social struggle and turbulent change. Accordingly, we will map the vicissitudes of theory in the post-Second World War conjuncture in the remainder of the introduction, providing an overview of the emergence of leading theories, methods, and themes within the terrain of media and cultural studies.

Social Life and Cultural Studies

But certainly for the present age, which prefers the sign to the thing signified, the copy to the original, fancy to reality, the appearance to the essence, . . . illusion only is sacred, truth profane. Nay, sacredness is held to be enhanced in proportion as truth decreases and illusion increases, so that the highest degree of illusion comes to be the highest degree of sacredness.

– Ludwig Feuerbach

Culture is produced and consumed within social life. Hence, particular cultural artifacts and practices must be situated within the social relations of production and reception in which culture is produced, distributed, and consumed in order to be properly understood and interpreted. Contextualizing cultural forms and audiences in historically specific situations helps illuminate how cultural artifacts reflect or reproduce concrete social relations and conditions – or oppose and attempt to transform them. The foundational writings that we discussed in the previous section provide concepts for situating culture and media within distinctive social and historical contexts. Likewise, in our introduction, we are positioning the emergence of theories of media and culture within determinate sociohistorical circumstances, and are thus engaging in social contextualization ourselves.

After the Second World War, the consumer society emerged throughout the Western world. Whereas the primary US corporations were developing systems of mass production and consumption in the 1920s, which saw the rise of media industries like broadcasting, advertising, and mass publications to promote consumer goods, the 1930s depression and then the Second World War prevented the introduction of the consumer society. As we observed above, the Frankfurt school, living in exile in the United States, were among the first to theorize this new configuration of society and culture in their critique of the culture industry, the integrative role of mass consumer society, and the new values and personality structures being developed. By the 1950s, theorists throughout the more evolved capitalist countries were producing theories of consumption, the media, and the changed conditions of everyday life to respond to the changes and transformations in the emergent consumer and media society.

In the United States, marketing research for big corporations and advertising agencies took up broadcasting research, and out of this process a certain model of "mass communication" studies emerged. Paul Lazarsfeld and his colleagues at the Princeton Radio Research Institute, which included Frankfurt-school member T. W. Adorno, began researching which programs audiences regularly tuned into, studied audience taste, and accordingly advised corporations concerning consumer demand for broadcasting product and what sort of programming was most popular. Hence, mass communications research emerged as an off-shoot of consumer research in the 1940s and 1950s, producing a tradition of empirical study of the established forms of culture and communications.

Rapid modernization in France after the Second World War and the introduction of the consumer society in the 1950s provoked much debate and contributed to constructing a variety of discourses on the media and consumer society in France, inspiring Roland Barthes, Henri Lefebvre, Guy Debord, Jean Baudrillard, and their contemporaries to develop novel analyses of the emerging forms of society and culture. It was clear that the consumer society was multiplying images, spectacle, and new cultural forms and modes of everyday life. The leading French theorists of the period attempted to explain, make sense of, and in many cases criticize the novelties of the era.

Roland Barthes applied the emergent theories of structuralism and semiology to make sense of the expansion of media culture and its important social functions. Structuralism was developed in the 1950s by the French anthropologist Claude Lévi-Strauss to articulate the basic structures of culture and society. Semiology, created earlier in the century by the Swiss linguist Ferdinand de Saussure, analyzed the fundamental rules, codes, and practices of language usage. In the hands of Barthes, semiology assumed that society and culture were texts that could be analyzed for their structures, significance, and effects.

Barthes's *Mythologies* employed both methods to analyze the codes and meanings embedded in artifacts of popular culture ranging from wrestling to soap ads, while dissecting their social functions. The "mythologies" Barthes studied functioned to naturalize and eternalize the historically contingent forms of French bourgeois culture that he analyzed. In his famous reading of a picture of a Black African soldier saluting the French flag, for example, Barthes claimed that the image erased the horrors of French imperialism, presenting a sanitized portrait of a French soldier that made it appear natural that an African should salute the French flag and exhibit the proper signs of military behavior.

A very different historical and cultural approach to the study of media and culture was developed in North America in the 1950s and 1960s by Marshall McLuhan. In his distinguished and influential work *Understanding Media*, McLuhan described a paradigm shift from earlier print culture to the new media culture. Whereas print culture, McLuhan argued, produced rational, literate, and individualist subjects, who followed the linear and logical form of print media in thought and reasoning, the proliferating media culture produced more fragmentary, nonrational, and aestheticized subjects, immersed in the sights, sounds, and spectacles of media like film, radio, television, and advertising. The new media culture was, McLuhan argued, "tribal," sharing collective ideas and behavior. It was generating an expanding global culture and consciousness that he believed would overcome the individualism and nationalism of the previous modern era.

McLuhan aroused a generation to take seriously media as an active agent of fundamental historical change and media culture as an important terrain of study. In his groundbreaking work *Society of the Spectacle*, Guy Debord described the proliferation of commodities and the "immense accumulation of spectacles" that characterized the new consumer society. Grocery, drug, and department stores were exhibiting a dazzling profusion of commodities and things to purchase which in turn were celebrated in advertising campaigns that inscribed the seductive consumer items with an aura of magic and divinity. The media themselves are spectacles in Debord's sense with MTV, for example, broadcasting a collage of dazzling music videos, ads, and sequences that attempt to capture the dynamics and attractions of contemporary youth culture. Films provide larger-than-life spectacle replete with special effects, snappy editing, and intense sound.

Hence, the "society of the spectacle" refers to a media and consumer society, organized around the consumption of images, commodities, and spectacles. In our day, malls, the cyberspectacle of the internet, and emerging virtual-reality devices proliferate the realm of the spectacle, providing new relevance to Debord's analysis. Moreover, the "society of the spectacle" also refers to the vast institutional and technical apparatus of contemporary societies which produce commodities and media events. The concept encompasses all the means and methods ruling powers employ, outside of direct force, which subject individuals to societal manipulation, while obscuring the nature and effects of operations of domination and subordination. Under this broader definition, the education system and the institutions of representative democracy, as well as the endless inventions of consumer gadgets, sports, media culture, and urban and suburban architecture and design are all integral components of the spectacular society. Schooling, for example, involves sports, fraternity and sorority rituals, bands and parades, and various public assemblies that indoctrinate individuals into dominant ideologies and practices. Contemporary politics is also saturated with spectacles, ranging from daily "photo opportunities," to highly orchestrated special events which dramatize state power, to TV ads and image management for prepackaged candidates during election campaigns.

In the post-Second World War conjuncture, the spectacle became globalized as corporations like Coke and Pepsi, sundry national automobile corporations, IBM and the nascent computer industry, and subsequently McDonald's, Nike, Microsoft, and a cornucopia of global products circulated throughout the world. Ariel Dorfman and Armand Mattelart record the response of Third World activists to the saturation of their Latin American culture with products from the Walt Disney corporation. In their controversial *How to Read Donald Duck*, they provide critical dissection of the meanings, messages, and ideologies in artifacts as seemingly harmless as comic books. The authors explain that these popular comics contained a wealth of images and stories that naturalized capitalism and imperialism, much like the "mythologies" which Barthes criticized in France.

Critical approaches to society and culture were proliferating throughout the world by the 1960s. All of the theories we have discussed so far can be seen as providing models of media and cultural studies, but the school of cultural studies that has become a global phenomenon of great importance over the last decades was inaugurated by the University of Birmingham Centre for Contemporary Cultural Studies in 1964. Under its director Richard Hoggart, and his successor Stuart Hall, who directed the Centre from 1968 to 1979, the Birmingham groups developed a variety of critical perspectives for the analysis, interpretation, and criticism of cultural artifacts, combining sociological theory and contextualization with literary analysis of cultural texts. The now classical period of British cultural studies from the early 1960s to the early 1980s adopted a Marxian approach to the study of culture, one especially influenced by Althusser and Gramsci. Through a set of internal debates, and responding to social conflicts and movements of the 1960s and the 1970s, the Birmingham group came to concentrate on the interplay of representations and ideologies of class, gender, race, ethnicity, and nationality in cultural texts, especially concentrating on media culture. They were among the first to study the effects of newspapers, radio, television, film, and other popular cultural forms on audiences. They also engaged how assorted audiences interpreted and deployed media culture in varied ways and contexts, analyzing the factors that made audiences respond in contrasting manners to media texts.

From the beginning, British cultural studies systematically rejected high/low culture distinctions and took seriously the artifacts of media culture, thus surpassing the elitism of dominant literary approaches to culture. Likewise, British cultural studies overcame the limitations of the Frankfurt-school notion of a passive audience in their conceptions of an active audience that creates meanings and the popular. Reproducing the activism of oppositional groups in the 1960s and 1970s, the Birmingham school was engaged in a project aimed at a comprehensive criticism of the present configuration of culture and society, attempting to link theory and practice to orient cultural studies toward fundamental social transformation. British cultural studies situated culture within a theory of social production and reproduction, specifying the ways that cultural forms served either to further social control, or to enable people to resist. It analyzed society as a hierarchical and antagonistic set of social relations characterized by the oppression of subordinate class, gender, race, ethnic, and national strata. Employing Gramsci's model of hegemony and counter-hegemony, British cultural studies sought to analyze "hegemonic," or ruling, social and cultural forces of domination and to locate "counterhegemonic" forces of resistance and contestation.

British cultural studies aimed at a political goal of social transformation in which location of forces of domination and resistance would aid the process of political transformation. From the beginning, the Birmingham group was oriented toward the crucial political problems of their age and milieu. Their early spotlight on class and ideology derived from an acute sense of the oppressive and systemic effects of class in British society and the movements of the 1960s against class inequality and oppression. The work of the late 1950s and early 1960s Williams/Hoggart/Hall stage of cultural studies emphasized the potential of working-class cultures; then began in the 1960s and 1970s appraising the potential of youth subcultures to resist the hegemonic forms of capitalist domination. Unlike the classical Frankfurt school (but similar to Herbert Marcuse), British cultural studies looked to youth cultures as providing potentially potent forms of opposition and social change. Through studies of youth subcultures, British cultural studies demonstrated how culture came to constitute distinct forms of identity and group membership and appraised the oppositional potential of diverse youth subcultures.

Cultural studies came to center attention on how subcultural groups resist dominant forms of culture and identity, creating their own style and identities. Individuals who conform to hegemonic dress and fashion codes, behavior, and political ideologies produce their identities within mainstream groups, as members of particular social groupings (such as white, middle-class, conservative Americans). Individuals who identify with subcultures, like punk or hip hop, look and act differently from those in the mainstream, and create oppositional identities, defining themselves against standard models.

As it developed into the 1970s and 1980s, British cultural studies successively appropriated emerging analyses of gender, race, sexuality, and a wide range of critical theories. They developed ways to examine and critique how the established society and culture promoted sexism, racism, homophobia, and additional forms of oppression – or helped to generate resistance and struggle against domination and injustice. This approach implicitly contained political critique of all cultural forms that promoted oppression, while positively affirming texts and representations that produced a potentially more just and egalitarian social order.

Developments within British cultural studies have been in part responses to con-testation by a multiplicity of distinct groups that have produced new methods and voices within cultural studies (such as a variety of feminisms, gay and lesbian studies, many multiculturalisms, critical pedagogies, and projects of critical media literacy). Hence, the center and fulcrum of British cultural studies at any given moment was determined by the struggles in the present political conjuncture, and their major work was conceived as political interventions. Their studies of ideology and the politics of culture directed the Birmingham group toward analyzing cultural arti-facts, practices, and institutions within existing networks of power. In this context, they attempted to show how culture both provided tools and forces of domination and resources for resistance and opposition. This political optic valorized studying the effects of culture and audience use of cultural artifacts, which provided an extremely productive focus on audiences and reception, topics that had been neglected in most previous text-based methods. Yet recent developments in the field of cul-tural studies have arguably vitiated and depoliticized the enterprise, as we shall note in the conclusion to the introduction.

British cultural studies, then, in retrospect, emerges in a later era of capital follow-ing the stage of state and monopoly capitalism analyzed by the Frankfurt school into a more variegated, globalized, and conflicted cultural formation. The forms of culture described by the earliest phase of British cultural studies in the 1950s and early 1960s articulated conditions in an era in which there were still significant tensions in England and much of Europe between an older working-class-based culture and the newer mass-produced culture whose models and exemplars were the products of American culture industries. The initial stage of cultural studies developed by Richard Hoggart, Raymond Williams, and E. P. Thompson attempted to preserve working-class culture against onslaughts of mass culture produced by the culture industries. Thompson's historical inquiries into the history of British working-class institutions and struggles, the defenses of working-class culture by Hoggart and Williams, and their attacks on mass culture were part of a socialist and working-class-oriented project which assumed that the industrial working class was an agent of progressive social change and that it could be mobilized and organized to resist the inequalities of the existing capitalist societies and work for a more egalitarian one. Williams and Hoggart were deeply involved in activities of working-class education and oriented toward socialist working-class politics, seeing their form of cultural studies as an instrument of progressive social change.

The initial critiques in the first wave of British cultural studies of Americanism and mass culture in Hoggart, Williams, and the Birmingham center paralleled to some extent the earlier critique of the Frankfurt school, yet celebrated a working class that the Frankfurt school saw as defeated in Germany and much of Europe during the period of fascism and which they never saw as a strong resource for emancipatory social change. The early work of the Birmingham school was continuous with the radicalism of the first wave of British cultural studies (the Hoggart–Thompson–Williams "culture and society" tradition). The post-1980s work inspired by British cultural studies became global in impact and responded to the new cultural and political conditions described in postmodern theory which we discuss below.

As we shall see, many forms of the study of culture and media preceded and accompanied the development of British cultural studies. In the following sections, we will observe examples of European and North American cultural studies and developments within the field throughout the world. We will also present a range of perspectives, often critical of the Frankfurt school, British cultural studies, and the other theories that we have so far examined. Next, however, we will introduce an approach to media and culture which focuses on the system and practices of production and distribution. This "political economy" perspective is sometimes taken as antithetical to cultural studies, and representatives of each position often attack each other, claiming their approach is superior. We, however, will argue that cultural studies and political economy viewpoints can be integrated, and that both are key parts of a more inclusive critical media and cultural theory.

Political Economy and Globalization

The anatomy of civil society is to be sought in political economy.

– Karl Marx

A political economy approach to media and culture centers more on the production and distribution of culture than on interpreting texts or studying audiences. The references to the terms "political" and "economy" call attention to the fact that the production and distribution of culture takes place within a specific economic and political system, constituted by relations between the state, the economy, social institutions and practices, culture, and organizations like the media. Political economy thus encompasses economics and politics, and the relations between them and the other central structures of society and culture. With regard to media institutions, for instance, in Western democracies, a capitalist economy dictates that cultural production is governed by laws of the market, but the democratic imperatives mean that there is some regulation of culture by the state. There are often tensions within a given society concerning which activities should be governed by the imperatives of the market, or economics, alone, and how much state regulation or intervention is desirable to assure a wider diversity of broadcast programming, or the prohibition of phenomena agreed to be harmful, such as cigarette advertising or pornography.

Political economy highlights that capitalist societies are organized according to a dominant mode of production that structures institutions and practices according to the logic of commodification and capital accumulation. Cultural production and distribution is accordingly profit- and market-oriented in such a system. Forces of production (such as media technologies and creative practice) are shaped according to dominant relations of production (such as the profit imperative, the maintenance of hierarchical control, and relations of domination). Hence, the system of production (e.g. market or state oriented) is important, as suggested below, in determining what sort of cultural artifacts are produced and how they are consumed. Hence, "political economy" does not merely pertain solely to economics, but to the relations between the economic, political, technological, and cultural dimensions of social reality. The structure of political economy links culture to its political and economic context and opens up cultural studies to history and politics. It refers to a field of contestation and antagonism and not an inert structure as caricatured by some of its opponents.

Political economy should also discern and analyze the role of technology in cultural production and distribution, seeing, as in McLuhan, how technology and forms of media structure economic, social, and cultural practices and forms of life. In our era, the proliferation of new technologies and multimedia – ranging from computers to DVDs to new types of digitized film and music – call attention to the key role of technology in the economy and everyday life and make clear that technological and economic factors are often deeply interconnected. In a time of technological revolution, the role of technology is especially important, and so political economy must engage the dominant forms of technology in its analysis.

In the present stage of capitalist hegemony, political economy grounds its approach within empirical analysis of the actual system of cultural production, investigating the constraints and structuring influence of the dominant capitalist economic system and a commercialized cultural system controlled by powerful corporations. Inserting texts into the system of culture within which they are produced and distributed can help elucidate features and effects of the texts that textual analysis alone might miss or downplay. Rather than being antithetical to approaches to culture, political economy can contribute to textual analysis and critique. The system of production often determines what type of artifacts will be produced, what structural limits there will be as to what can and cannot be said and shown, and what kind of audience effects cultural artifacts may generate.

Study of the codes of television, film, or popular music, for instance, is enhanced by examining the formulas and conventions of media culture production. These cultural forms are structured by well-defined rules and conventions, and investigation of the production of culture can help elucidate the codes actually in play. Because of the demands of the format of radio or music television, for instance, most popular songs are three to five minutes, fitting into the format of the distribution system. Because of their control by giant media corporations oriented primarily toward profit, film and television production in the US is dominated by specific genres such as talk and game shows, soap operas, situation comedies, action/adventure shows, and so on. This economic factor explains why there are cycles of certain genres and subgenres, sequelmania in the film industry, crossovers of popular films into television series. Seeing how competition for audiences decides what shows are produced also helps explain why there is homogeneity in products constituted within systems of production with established generic codes, formulaic conventions, and well-defined ideological boundaries.

Furthermore, one cannot really discern the role of the media in events like the Gulf War without analyzing the production and political economy of news and information, as well as the actual text of the Gulf War and its reception by its audience. Or, one cannot fully grasp the Madonna phenomenon without discussing her marketing strategies, her political environment, her cultural artifacts, and their effects. Likewise, in appraising the full social impact of pornography, one needs to be aware of the sex industry and the production process of, say, pornographic films, and not just on the texts themselves and their effects on audiences.

In addition, study of political economy can help ascertain the limits and range of political and ideological discourses and effects. Study of television and politics in the United States, for instance, suggests that takeover of the television networks by leading transnational corporations and communications conglomerates was part of a "right turn" within US society in the 1980s whereby powerful corporate groups won control of the state and the mainstream media. For example, during the 1980s all three networks were taken over by leading corporate conglomerates: ABC was purchased by Capital Cities, NBC merged with GE, and CBS was bought by the Tisch Financial Group. Both ABC and NBC sought corporate mergers, and this motivation, along with other benefits derived from the Reagan administration, might well have influenced them to downplay criticisms of Reagan and to generally support his conservative programs, military adventures, and simulated presidency.

In the current conjuncture that is exhibiting a crossing of boundaries and synergy between information and entertainment industries, there have been significant mergers between the immense corporations. Previous forms of entertainment are rapidly being absorbed within the internet, and the computer is coming to be a major household appliance and source of entertainment, information, play, communication, and connection with the outside world. As clues to the immensity of the transformation going on, and as indicators of the syntheses of information and entertainment in the emerging infotainment society, one might reflect on the massive mergers of the primary information and entertainment conglomerates that have taken place in the United States during the past years which have seen the most extensive concentration and conglomeration of information and entertainment industries in history, including:

Time Warner and Turner	$7.5 billion
Disney/Capital Cities/ABC	$19 billion
NBC and Microsoft	$20 billion
Viacom and CBS	$37 billion.

Dwarfing all previous information/entertainment corporation mergers, Time Warner and America On-Line (AOL) proposed a $163.4 billion amalgamation in January 2000. These fusions bring together corporations involved in TV, film, magazines, newspapers, books, information data bases, computers, and other media, suggesting a coming implosion of media and computer culture, of entertainment and information in a new communications/infotainment society. The merger mania is now global in scale, pointing to an ever more intricately connected global economy. Accordingly, there have been massive mergers in the telecommunications industry, as well as between cable and satellite industries with major entertainment and corporate conglomerates. By 2003, ten gigantic multinational corporations, including AOL Time Warner, Disney–ABC, General Electric–NBC, Viacom–CBS, News Corporation, Vivendi, Sony, Bertelsmann, AT&T, and Liberty Media, controlled most of the production of information and entertainment throughout the globe. The result is less competition and diversity, and more corporate control of newspapers and journalism, television, radio, film, and other media of information and entertainment.

The corporate media, communications, and information industries are frantically scrambling to provide delivery for the wealth of information, entertainment, and further services that will include increased internet access, cellular telephones and satellite personal communication devices, and computerized video, film, and information on demand, as well as internet shopping and more unsavory services like pornography and gambling. Hence, study of the political economy of media can be immensely useful for describing the infrastructure of the media, information, and communications industry and their effects on culture and society. Yet political economy alone does not hold the key to cultural studies, and important as it is, it has limitations as a single perspective.

Some political economy analyses reduce the meanings and effects of texts to rather circumscribed and reductive ideological functions, arguing that media culture merely reflects the ideology of the ruling economic elite that controls the culture industries and is nothing more than a vehicle for the dominant ideology. It is true that media culture overwhelmingly supports capitalist values, but it is also a site of intense conflict between different races, classes, gender, and social groups. Thus, in order to fully grasp the nature and effects of media culture, one should see contemporary society and culture as contested terrains and media and cultural forms as spaces in which particular battles over gender, race, sexuality, political ideology, and values are fought.

Feminist political economy involves domestic activities like cleaning, child-rearing, shopping, and additional forms of consumption. Feminist critics contend that activities of packaging, marketing, and display are important dimensions of the capitalist economy and that therefore study of consumption is as significant as production in constructing political economy. As feminist political economists point out, questions of economic power extend to issues of social power. At the heart of studies of political economy lies the question of how social resources are controlled and by whom – a question that lays open issues of race, gender, sexual orientation, and other social groupings that underpin economic privilege and power (or the lack thereof).

As Eileen Meehan observes, patriarchy and capitalism are historically intertwined; her analysis brings to the surface the ways in which the media industries's commodification of audiences rests on the intersecting dynamics of these parallel vectors of power. Media artifacts operate simultaneously on economic and cultural levels, with one circumscribing the other. Her analysis elucidates the way that societal divisions of labor based on gender, coupled with prejudices about gender, play a significant role in defining and differentiating the media's commodity audience.

Political economy today necessarily involves discussion of a global capitalist world economy in an era marked by the fall of communism in 1989, technological revolution, and emergence of a "new economy" based on computer and communication networks. The term "globalization" is often deployed as a cover concept for the new world economy, but as Herbert Schiller argues, its continuities with the old world-system of market capitalism should not be ignored. In fact, globalization is a contested term with some identifying it with new forms of imperialism, and seeing it as predominantly negative, while others equate it with modernization and the proliferation of novel products, cultural forms, and identities. In fact, it is best to see it as an extremely complex and ambiguous phenomenon that contains both exciting and progressive forms like the internet, novel terrains of cyberculture, and emergent economic and political actors and groups in the world economy – combined with the growing strength of transnational institutions, intensified competition on a global level, heightened exploitation, corporate downsizing, and greater levels of unemployment, economic inequality, and insecurity.

The conception of political economy that we are proposing goes beyond traditional, sometimes excessively economistic approaches that focus on more strictly economic issues such as ownership, gate-keeping, and the production and distribution of culture. Instead, we are suggesting that it involves relations between economy and polity, culture and people, as well as the interconnection between production and consumption, distribution and use. Although some conceptions of political economy are reductive, focusing solely on the economic dimension, we believe that far richer notions of political economy are possible.

In addition, we would argue that both political economy and more sociologically and culturally oriented approaches to the study of media culture should be combined. For some decades now, however, advocates of media and cultural studies based in textual or audience analysis have been at war with those who advocate a political economy optic. The hostility between political economy and cultural studies, in our view, reproduces a great divide within the field of communication and cultural studies between two competing approaches with different methodologies, objects of study, and, by now, bodies of texts that represent the opposing schools. This dichotomization pits social-science-based approaches that take media and communications as their object against a humanities- and text-based view that focuses on culture.

A largely textual approach centers on the analysis and criticism of texts as cultural artifacts, employing methods primarily derived from the humanities. The methods of political economy and empirical communications research, by contrast, utilize more social-science-based research strategies, ranging from straight quantitative analysis to more qualitative empirical studies of specific cases or topics, structural analysis of media institutions, or historical research. Topics in this area include analysis of ownership patterns within the political economy of the media, empirical studies of audience reception and media effects, or structural analysis of the impact of media institutions in the economy, politics, or everyday life.

Consequently, the seemingly never-ending hostility between political economy and cultural studies replicates a bifurcation within the fields of communications and culture between competing paradigms. In our view, the divide is an artificial one, rooted in an arbitrary academic division of labor. These conflicting approaches point to a splintering of the field of media communications into specialized subareas with competing models and methods, and, ironically, to a lack of communication in the field of communications. The split reproduces an academic division of labor which – beginning early in the century and intensifying since the end of the Second World War – followed the trend toward specialization and differentiation symptomatic of the capitalist economy. The university has followed this broader trend which some theorists equate with the dynamics of modernity itself, interpreted as a process of ever-greater differentiation and thus specialization in all fields from business to education. This trend toward specialization has undermined the power and scope of cultural and media studies and should be replaced, as we are arguing, by a more transdisciplinary position.

Moreover, in the present configuration of the emergence of a new global economy, a critical cultural and media studies needs to grasp the global, national, and local systems of media production and distribution. In the 1960s, critics of the global capitalist system described the domination of the world economy by transnational – mostly American and European – corporations as "imperialism" or "neo-imperialism," while its supporters celebrated "modernization." Today, the term "globalization" is the standard concept used to describe the new global economy and culture. One of the features of globalization is the proliferation of new voices and perspectives on culture and society and the politicization and contestation of forms of culture previously taken for granted. In a global culture, the proliferation of dif-ference and new actors are part of the landscape and the question of representation becomes intensely politicized and contested, as we see in the next section.

The Politics of Representation

Representation in the mediated "Reality" of our mass culture is in itself Power.
– Larry Gross

Whereas political economy approaches to the media and culture derive from a social sciences tradition, analysis of the politics of representation in media texts derives from a humanities-based textual approach. Earlier, mass communications approaches to media content ranged from descriptive content analysis to quantitative analysis of references, figures, or images in media texts. The more sophisticated methods of textual analysis, however, derive from more advanced understandings of texts, narratives, and representation, as well as the contributions of critical concepts such as ideology and hegemony.

The idea that all cultural representations are political is one of the major themes of media and cultural theory of the past several decades. In the 1960s, feminist, African American, Latino, gay and lesbian, and diverse oppositional movements attacked the stereotypes and biased images of cultural representations of their groups. These critiques of sexism, racism, homophobia, and other biases made it clear that cultural representations are never innocent or pure, that they contain positive, negative, or ambiguous representations of diverse social groups, that they can serve pernicious interests of cultural oppression by positioning certain groups as inferior, thus pointing to the superiority of dominant social groups. Studies of representations of women or blacks on American television, for instance, would catalogue negative representations and show how they produce sexism or racism, or would champion more positive representations.

Early interventions in the politics of representation concentrated on primarily "images of" particular social groups, decrying negative images and affirming more constructive ones. The limitations of such approaches were quickly apparent, and already by the 1970s more sophisticated analyses began emerging of how texts position audiences, of how narratives, scenes, and images produce biased representations. There emerged, then, more sophisticated understanding of how textual mechanisms help construct social meanings and representations of specific social groups. Exclusions of groups like Latinos, as well as negative stereotypes, were emphasized, as were the ways framing, editing, subtexts, and the construction of pictorial images produced culturally loaded and biased representations of subordinate groups. The narratives of media culture were scrutinized to discern how certain (usually socially dominant) forces were represented more affirmatively than subordinate groups, and there was a search for narratives and representations that more positively represented social types that had been excluded or negatively presented in mainstream culture (i.e. various ethnic groups, gays and lesbians, or members of the deaf community).

The turn toward study of audiences in the 1980s, as we have noted, also created more complex notions of the politics of representation and construction of meaning by stressing how audiences could perform oppositional readings, reacting negatively to what they perceived as prejudiced representations of their own social groups, thus showing themselves to be active creators of meaning, and not just passive victims of manipulation. Reading culture was seen as a political event, in which one looked for negative or positive representations, learned how narratives were constructed, and discerned how image and ideology functioned with media and culture to reproduce social domination and discrimination.

The debates over the politics of representation and how best to analyze and criticize offensive images of subordinate groups provided a wealth of insights into the nature and effects of culture and media. Culture was now conceived as a field of representation, as a producer of meaning that provided negative and positive depictions of gender, class, race, sexuality, religion, and further key constituents of identity. The media were interpreted as potent creators of role models, gender identity, norms, values, and appropriate and inappropriate behavior, positioning audiences to behave in diverging ways. Audiences, however, were eventually able to perceive themselves as active and creative, able to construct meanings and identities out of the materials of their culture.

Culture and identity were regarded as constructed, as artificial, malleable, and contestable artifacts, and not as natural givens. Representations in turn were interpreted not just as replications of the real, reproductions of natural objects, but as constructions of complex technical, narrative, and ideological apparatuses. The emphasis on the politics of representation called attention to media technologies, as well as narrative forms, conventions, and codes. It was determined that formal aspects of media texts, such as framing, editing, or special effects, could help construct specific representations and that different technologies produced different products and effects.

In addition, the growing emphasis on the active role of audiences from the 1980s to the present suggested that people could creatively construct cultural meanings, contest dominant forms, and create alternative readings and interpretations. Audiences could be empowered to reject prejudicial or stereotyped representations of specific groups and individuals, and could affirm positive ones. The politics of representation focused on both encoding and decoding, texts and audiences, and called for more critical and discriminating responses to the products of media production.

Consequently, cultural representations were perceived to be subject to political critique and culture itself was conceived as a contested terrain. Film, television, music, and assorted cultural forms were interpreted as an arena of struggle in which representations transcode the discourses of conflicting social movements. Beginning in the 1960s, alternative representations of gender, race, class, the family, the state, the corporation, and additional dominant forces and institutions began appearing in a sustained fashion. More complex and engaging representations of women, for instance, transcoded the critiques of negative stereotypes and sexist representations, as well as the demand for more active and positive representations. Calls for alternative voices and the creation of oppositional subcultures were met by increased cultural production by women, people of color, sexual minorities, and others excluded from cultural debate and creation. Giving voice to alternative visions, telling more complex stories from the perspective of subordinate groups, and presenting works of marginalized people shook up dominant systems of cultural production and representation. The process created more variety and diversity but also intensified cultural resistance, as a backlash against oppositional groups of women, people of color, gays and lesbians, and various marginalized subcultures inevitably began.

The Postmodern Turn

It seems that to talk seriously about postmodernism today, one is still by definition being defensive. This is because postmodernism has become everybody's favorite *bête noire*, while at the same time not only generously providing something solid to argue against, when so many other things have been "melting in the air," but also, in some mysterious way, being a concept in the right place at the right moment. Postmodernism has therefore served the function of shifting the paradigms in cultural studies and sociology, doing that kind of intellectual work which inevitably provokes controversy and protest, all the more so when what seems to be at stake are precisely those terms like history, society and politics that have given substance and direction to the kind of work we do as teachers and researchers and the reasons why we do it.

– Angela McRobbie

The notion of the postmodern implies a fundamental rupture in culture and history. It suggests that there are important changes in the economy, society, culture, the arts, and our everyday life which require new theories, ways of perceiving the world, and forms of discourse and practice. Yet as the above quotation indicates, postmodernism is extremely controversial, with discourses and practices of the "post" attracting some and repelling others.

To make sense of the bewildering variety of uses of the family of terms within the field of the postmodern, we would propose distinguishing between modernity and postmodernity as epochs or stages of history; modernism and postmodernism as developments within art; and modern and postmodern theory as opposed to modes of theoretical discourse and intellectual orientations toward the world. In terms of the narrative of our Introduction, a postmodern turn in culture and society would correspond to an emergent stage of global capitalism, characterized by new multimedia, exciting computer and informational technology, and a proliferation of novel forms of politics, society, culture, and everyday life.

From this perspective, postmodern theorists like Jean Baudrillard, Jean-François Lyotard, Michel Foucault, Fredric Jameson, Angela McRobbie, Mark Poster, and others are attempting to engage the new technologies, the emergent forms of culture and identity, the innovative modes of theory and discourse, and the ascendant forms of global capitalism that are shaping the contemporary era. Just as previous theories and methods responded to the emergent historical conditions of their era, so too do the postmodern theories attempt to engage novel and original contemporary conditions. But just as previous theories and methods had their limitations and blindspots, postmodern theory also has its omissions and deficiencies. Hence, we would caution our readers, who are perhaps eager to embrace the latest theories and approaches, to be alert to drawbacks, as well as the benefits of the postmodern turn.

French theorist Jean Baudrillard was one of the first to engage the novel forms of culture in theorizing the modes of simulation and hyperreality by which he described the emergent media and cyberspaces of the new technologies. While he was prescient in perceiving the importance of new forms of culture and fields of cultural experience, by declaring "the end of political economy" and by claiming that simulation, hyperreality, and nascent modes of media and computer culture are autonomous organizing forces of the contemporary world, he forfeits insight into the connections between new technologies and form of culture and the restructuring of global capitalism.

North American cultural theorist Fredric Jameson, by contrast, in his famous article "Postmodernism, or the Cultural Logic of Late Capitalism," interprets the emergent forms of postmodern culture within the context of contemporary capitalism, thus connecting the economy and culture. For Jameson, postmodernism is a form of culture appropriate to the glitzy surfaces, culture of image and spectacle, and high-intensity emphasis on appearance, style, and look found in contemporary consumer and media culture. Theorizing postmodernism, for Jameson, requires understanding the new forms of global capitalism and culture that are emerging, of which postmodernism is a symptomatic form.

Seen in retrospect, the cultural populism, turn to the audience, and fetishism of the popular that emerged in British cultural studies during the 1980s and 1990s can be read as part of a postmodern turn in cultural studies which corresponds to a new stage of consumer and global capitalism. The Frankfurt school described a mass society and culture that sought to incorporate individuals into a more homogenized culture, controlled by big corporations, the state, and centralized media. By contrast, the current form of consumer capitalism is more fragmented, specialized, aestheticized and eroticized, and celebratory of difference, choice, and individual freedom than the previous stage.

The postmodern turn has generated a great variety and diversity of novel forms of cultural studies and approaches to the study of media and culture. At their most extreme, postmodern theories erase the economic, political, and social dimensions of cultural production and reception, engage in a type of cultural and technological determinism, indulge in theoreticist blather, and renounce the possibility of textual interpretation, social criticism, and political struggle. In a more dialectical and political version, postmodern theory is used to rethink cultural criticism and politics in the contemporary era. In addition, postmodern theory can be effective in calling attention to innovative configurations and functions of culture, as it charts the trajectories and impacts of new technologies, the emergent global economy and culture, and the novel political terrain and movements, without losing sight of questions of political power, domination, and resistance. In addition, some versions of postmodern theory provide extremely useful transdisciplinary perspectives, as did the Frankfurt school, British cultural studies, feminist, and diverse critical theories at their best.

Globalization and Social Movements

Postmodern, as well as modern, theorists recognize that the world is increasingly marked by transnational cross-currents and flows which on the one hand are destabilizing traditional concepts of the nation-state as they become supplanted by multinational corporations and cross-border affiliations, and on the other hand are reasserting the dominance of Western capitalism. As Arjun Appadurai argues, the "global processes involving mobile texts and migrant audiences" cross and trouble the borders of the modernist nation-state, unlocking a global imagination that opens up the possibilities of new forms of identity, solidarity, and politics. Yet Appadurai does not present an uncritical and idealizing vision: the flows that crosscut the globe xxxvi Douglas M. Kellner and Meenakshi Gigi Durham

are sometimes violent and repressive, at other times democratic and progressive. Globalization is a contested term with some identifying it with new forms of imperialism, and seeing it as predominantly negative, while others equate it with modernization and the proliferation of innovative products, cultural forms, and identities. For example, Douglas Kellner and Richard Kahn identify the uses of the internet in creating alternative public spheres that foster political activism and progressive, emancipatory sodalities formed through the use of blogs and other virtual networking tools.

In fact, it is best to see globalization as an extremely complex and ambiguous phenomenon that contains both exciting and progressive forms like the internet, novel terrains of cyberculture, and emergent economic and political actors and groups in the world economy – combined with the growing strength of transnational institutions, intensified competition on a global level, heightened exploitation, corporate downsizing, and greater levels of unemployment, economic inequality, insecurity, terrorism, and war. Jan Nederveen Pieterse acknowledges the ambiguity of globalization as a concept and argues for a recognition of plural forms of globalization that give rise to new modes of sociopolitical organizing and "hybrid spaces," such as cities of peasants or ethnically mixed neighborhoods and cultures.

Globalization is connected with scientific-technological-economic revolution which involves the advent of emergent forms of labor, politics, culture, and everyday life. The networked global economy contains economic opportunities, openings for political transformation, and a wealth of innovative products and technologies which might improve the human condition. Yet it also threatens to increase divisions between haves and have-nots, deplete diminishing resources, undermine union and labor rights, and circulate novel forms of war and terrorism. Hence, globalization is highly ambiguous, with both promising and threatening features. The internet, for example, can aid progressive political struggles and movements, or be used by corporations to enforce their hegemony and control. Globalization is always proliferating new forms of media and culture. In addition, global forces are both creating novel modes of cultural homogenization and proliferating cultural differences and hybridities. It is advancing the interests of major US and other transnational corporations, as well as providing openings for new economic forms and players. Global processes are producing proliferating transnational institutions and forces, while challenging the state to strengthen its authority and regulatory powers. And as globalization comes ever more to the fore, the importance of the local is highlighted and dramatized. Globalization is thus one of the dominant forces of our era and has expanded the terrain and scope of media and cultural studies.

Concluding Remarks

Despite their dissimilarity, many of the theories and methods that we have discussed in this Introduction, ranging from the Frankfurt school to British cultural studies to French postmodern theory, are transdisciplinary in terms of their metatheory and practice. Standard academic approaches are discipline oriented, with English

Departments typically analyzing cultural forms as literary texts, Sociology Departments focusing on the social dimension of culture, Political Science Departments highlighting the politics of culture, and so on. By contrast, transdisciplinary perspectives subvert existing academic boundaries by combining social theory, cultural analysis, and political critique. Such transdisciplinary theory requires knowledge of a multiplicity of methods and theories that we have indeed attempted to assemble in our reader.

While our multiperspectivist approach might suggest to the reader a liberal pluralist tolerance of disparate theories and methods, we want to advance more systematic and critical perspectives. Against pluralism and eclecticism, we believe that it is important to challenge the established academic division of labor and to develop a transdisciplinary approach that contests both the bifurcation of the field of media and cultural studies and the society that produces it. A critical media and cultural studies will overcome the boundaries of academic disciplines and will combine political economy, social theory and research, and cultural criticism in its project that aims at critique of domination and social transformation.

Such a critical venture must also engage the emergent cultural, political, and social forms of the present era. Confronting new technologies, multimedia, and modes of experience such as cyberspace creates a variety of challenges for media and cultural studies, ranging from the need to chart the emergent cultural terrains and experiences to producing multiple literacies to analyze and evaluate these spheres and their forms. Since media and culture are themselves a type of pedagogy, one needs to create a counterpedagogy to question and critically analyze the often distorted forms of knowledge, misinformation, deceptive images, and seductive spectacles of the media and consumer society. Cultivating critical media literacy to analyze intelligently contemporary forms of culture calls for advancement of a new postmodern pedagogy that takes seriously image, spectacle, and narrative, and thus promotes visual and media literacy, the ability to read, analyze, and evaluate images, stories, and spectacles of media culture. Yet a postmodern pedagogy is concerned to develop multiple literacies, to rethink literacy itself in relation to new technologies and cultural forms, and to create a cultural studies that encompasses a wide array of fields, texts, and practices, extending from popular music to poetry and painting to cyberspace and multimedia like DVDs or iPods.

The particular pedagogy employed, however, should be contextual, depending on the concrete situation, interests, and problems within the specific site in which cultural studies is taught or carried out. Yet the pedagogy must address salient general issues. Media culture is produced in a context of asymmetries of race, class, and gender and concrete relations of domination and subordination that must be accounted for in any critical analysis. For us, a postmodern pedagogy does not elide or occlude issues of power; rather, it allows for a contemporary understanding of current social and cultural configurations of culture, power, and domination. While the distinctive situation and interests of the teachers, students, or critics help decide what precise artifacts are engaged, what methods will be employed, and what pedagogy will be deployed, the sociocultural environment in which cultural production, reception, and education occurs must be scrutinized as well.

Hence, a transdisciplinary cultural and media studies would productively engage postmodern theory and emergent interpretive discourses and methods while maintaining important traditional goals like cultivating literacy, critical thinking, and the art of interpretation. We are currently living in a proliferating image and media culture in which new technologies are changing every dimension of life from the economy to personal identity. In a postmodern media and computer culture, fresh critical strategies are needed to read cultural texts, to interpret the conjunctions of sight and sound, words and images, that are producing seductive cultural spaces, forms, and experiences. This undertaking also involves exploration of the emergent cyberspaces and modes of identities, interaction, and production that are taking place in the rapidly exploding computer culture, as well as exploring the new public spaces where myriad forms of political debate and contestation are evolving. Yet engaging the fresh forms of culture requires using the tools and insights already gained, rather than simply rejecting all "modern" concepts and theories as irrelevant to the new "postmodern" condition. As we have argued, adequately understanding postmodern phenomena requires contextualization in terms of the way that novel cultural artifacts are produced by the dominant mode of production and are used to reproduce – or contest – existing figurations of class, race, gender, and other forms of power and domination.

Indeed, a future-oriented cultural and media studies should look closely at the development of the entertainment and information technology industries, the mergers and synergies taking place, the syntheses of computer and media culture that are being planned and already implemented, and emergent wireless technologies. A global media and cyberculture is our life-world and fate, and we need to be able to chart and map it accordingly to survive the dramatic changes currently taking place and the even more transformative novelties of the rapidly approaching future.

Part I

Culture, Ideology, and Hegemony

Introduction to Part I

This section contains a set of key texts which introduce some of the fundamental concepts of cultural and media criticism. For the theorists whom we have selected here, culture always arises in specific historical situations, serving particular socio-economic interests, and carrying out important social functions. For Marx and Engels, the cultural ideas of an epoch serve the interests of the ruling class, providing ideologies that legitimate class domination. We have selected a famous text on ideology written for their unpublished work *The German Ideology* in 1845. Here for the first time, Marx and Engels presented their materialist theory of history whereby material interests and class struggles are conceived as the ruling forces of history – as opposed to the actions of great individuals, ideas, and cultural forces, or political events like elections and wars.[1]

The economic base of society for Marx and Engels consisted of the forces and relations of production in which culture and ideology are constructed to help secure the dominance of ruling social groups. This influential "base/superstructure" model considers the economy the base, or foundation, of society, and cultural, legal, political, and other forms of life are conceived as "superstructures" which grow out of and serve to reproduce the economic base. Many of the theorists in this book develop, revise, and in some cases contest this model, attempting to theorize, for example, more precisely how culture and media function within contemporary societies and everyday life.

For the Italian Marxist theorist, Antonio Gramsci, the ruling intellectual and cultural forces of the era constitute a form of hegemony, or domination by ideas and cultural forms which induce consent to the rule of the leading groups in a society. Gramsci's example in his *Prison Notebooks*, from which we reproduce a selection defining his concept of hegemony, is Italian fascism, which supplanted the previous liberal bourgeois regime in Italy through its control of the state and multiplied, often repressive, influence over schooling, the media, and other cultural, social, and political institutions. Gramsci himself was imprisoned for his opposition to Mussolini's fascist regime, and while in prison he sketched out criticism of the ways that fascism became the ruling force in Italy, an analysis through which he developed more general accounts of how ruling social groups and institutions attain social dominance or hegemony.[2]

Gramsci defined ideology as the ruling ideas which present the "social cement" which unifies and holds together the dominant social order. He described his own "philosophy of praxis" as a mode of thought opposed to ideology, which includes, among other things, a critical analysis of ruling ideas. In a short passage we have included on "Cultural Themes:

Ideological Material," Gramsci notes that in his day the press was the dominant instrument of producing ideological legitimation of the existing institutions and social order, but that many other institutions such as the church, schools, and different associations and groups also played a role. He proposed developing a critique of these institutions and the ideologies that legitimate them, accompanied by development of counterinstitutions and ideas that would produce alternatives to the existing system.

Members of the Institute for Social Research, established in the 1920s in Frankfurt, Germany, developed some of the first critical perspectives on mass culture and communication in their famous studies of the culture industries.[3] T. W. Adorno's analyses of popular music and culture (1978 [1932], 1941, 1982, 1989, and 1991), Leo Lowenthal's studies of popular demagogues, literature, and magazines (1949, 1957, and 1961), Herta Herzog's studies of radio soap operas (1941), and the perspectives and critiques of mass culture developed in Horkheimer and Adorno's famous study of the culture industries (1972 and Adorno, 1991) provide many examples of the value of what became known as the "Frankfurt school" approach.

As victims of European fascism, members of the Institute for Social Research experienced first-hand the ways that the Nazis used the instruments of mass culture to induce submission to fascist culture and society. While in exile in the United States, the group came to believe that American media culture was also highly ideological and worked to promote the interests of US capitalism. Controlled by giant corporations, the culture industries were organized according to the structures of mass production, churning out mass-produced products that generated a highly commercial system of culture which in turn sold the values, lifestyles, and institutions of American capitalism.

The work of the Frankfurt School provided what Paul Lazarsfeld, one of the originators of modern communications studies, called a critical approach, which he distinguished from the "administrative research," which served the interests of dominant corporations and institutions. The views of Adorno, Lowenthal, and other members of the inner circle of the Institute for Social Research were contested by Walter Benjamin, an idiosyncratic theorist loosely affiliated with the Institute. Benjamin, writing in Paris during the 1930s, discerned progressive aspects in new technologies of cultural production such as photography, film, and radio. In "The Work of Art in the Age of Mechanical Reproduction" (1969), Benjamin noted how new mass media were supplanting older forms of culture whereby the mass reproduction of photography, film, recordings, and publications replaced the emphasis on the originality and "aura" of the work of art in an earlier era. Freed from the mystification of high culture, Benjamin believed that mass culture could cultivate more critical individuals able to judge and analyze their culture, just as sports fans could dissect and evaluate athletic activities. In addition, processing the rush of images of cinema created, Benjamin believed, subjectivities better able to parry the flux and turbulence of experience in industrialized, urbanized societies.

Himself a collaborator of the prolific German artist Bertolt Brecht, Benjamin worked with Brecht on films, created radio plays, and attempted to utilize the media as organs of social progress. In the essay "The Artist as Producer" (1999 [1934]), Benjamin argued that progressive cultural creators should "refunction" the apparatus of cultural production, turning theater and film, for instance, into a forum of political enlightenment and discussion rather than a medium of "culinary" audience pleasure. Both Brecht and Benjamin wrote radio plays and were interested in film as an instrument of progressive social change. In an essay on radio theory, Brecht anticipated the internet in his call for reconstructing the apparatus of broadcasting from one-way transmission to a more interactive form of two-way, or multiple, communication (in Silberman 2000: 41ff.) – a form first realized in CB radio and then electronically mediated computer communication.[4]

Moreover, Benjamin wished to promote a radical cultural and media politics concerned with the development of alternative oppositional cultures. Yet he recognized that media such as film could have conservative effects. While he thought it was progressive that mass-produced works were losing their "aura," their magical force, and were opening cultural artifacts for more critical and political discussion, he recognized that film could create a new kind of ideological magic and aura through the cult of celebrity and techniques like the close-up that fetishized certain stars or images via the technology of the cinema. His work is also important therefore for focusing on the technology of cultural reproduction, seeing the changes in new media techniques, and carrying out political critique while calling for democratic transformation of media technology and institutions.

Max Horkheimer and T. W. Adorno answered Benjamin's optimism in a highly influential analysis of the culture industry published in their book *Dialectic of Enlightenment*, which first appeared in 1948 and was translated into English in 1972. They argued that the system of cultural production dominated by film, radio broadcasting, newspapers, and magazines was controlled by advertising and commercial imperatives, and served to create subservience to the system of consumer capitalism. While later critics pronounced their approach too manipulative, reductive, and elitist, it is important to note that Horkheimer and Adorno combine analysis of the system of cultural production, distribution, and consumption with analysis of some of the sorts of texts of the culture industry, and thus provide a model of a critical and multidimensional mode of cultural criticism that overcomes the divide between approaches that solely focus on political economy, texts, or audiences.[5]

In an encyclopedia article on the public sphere which we have included in KeyWorks, the German social theorist Jürgen Habermas summarizes the ideas in his path-breaking book *The Structural Transformation of the Public Sphere*. Providing historical background to the triumph of what Horkheimer and Adorno described as the culture industry, Habermas notes how bourgeois society was distinguished by the rise of a public sphere which stood between civil society and the state and which mediated between public and private interests. For the first time in history, individuals and groups could shape public opinion, giving direct expression to their needs and interests while influencing political practice. The bourgeois public sphere made it possible to form a realm of public opinion that opposed state power and the powerful interests that were coming to shape bourgeois society.

Yet Habermas also notes a transition from the liberal public sphere which originated in the Enlightenment and the American and French Revolution to a media-dominated public sphere in the current era of what he calls "welfare state capitalism and mass democracy." This historical transformation is grounded in Horkheimer and Adorno's analysis of the culture industry, in which giant corporations have taken over the public sphere and transformed it from a sphere of rational debate into one of manipulative consumption and passivity. In this transformation, "public opinion" shifts from rational consensus emerging from debate, discussion, and reflection to the manufactured opinion of polls or media experts. In this analysis, the interconnection between a sphere of public debate and individual participation has thus been fractured and transmuted into that of a realm of political manipulation and spectacle, in which citizen-consumers passively ingest and absorb entertainment and information. "Citizens" thus become spectators of media presentations and discourse which arbitrate public discussion and thus reduce its audiences to objects of news, information, and public affairs. In Habermas's words: "Inasmuch as the mass media today strip away the literary husks from the kind of bourgeois self-interpretation and utilize them as marketable forms for the public services provided in a culture of consumers, the original meaning is reversed" (1989a, p. 171).

Habermas's critics, however, contend that he idealizes the earlier bourgeois public sphere by presenting it as a forum of rational discussion and debate when in fact certain groups were excluded. While the concepts of the public sphere and democracy assume a liberal and populist celebration of diversity, tolerance, debate, and consensus, in actuality, the bourgeois public sphere was dominated by white, property-owning males. As Habermas's critics have documented, working-class, plebeian, and women's public spheres developed alongside of the bourgeois public sphere to represent voices and interests excluded in this forum.[6]

Nonetheless, Habermas is right that in the era of the democratic revolutions a public sphere emerged in which for the first time in history ordinary citizens could participate in political discussion and debate, organize, and struggle against unjust authority. Habermas's account also points to the increasingly important role of the media in politics and everyday life and the ways that corporate interests have colonized this sphere, using the media and culture to promote their own interests.

The issue of ideology as a colonizing force is a prevalent theme in the work of the French philosopher Louis Althusser, whose ideas were enormously influential in the 1970s, especially shaping early British cultural studies and the work of postmodern Marxist Fredric Jameson. As Stuart Hall has pointed out, "Althusser's interventions and their consequent development are enormously formative for the field of cultural studies" (1978). Althusser drew on the vogue of structuralism in postwar France, amalgamating Barthesian semiotics, Lévi-Strauss's structural anthropology, psychoanalytic theory, and a revisionist Marxism to develop a conceptualization of "ideology" that rested on a notion of a social formation composed of economic, social, and ideological practices.

Indeed, it is Althusser who shifted the discussion of "ideology" to focus on everyday practices and rituals organized via social institutions he designated as "Ideological State Apparatuses" (schools, religion, the family, the media, and others). These material practices, he argued, were part of a closed system in which individuals were constantly "interpellated" into a social order, becoming constituted as subjects unconsciously by the dominant social institutions and discourses. His most widely-read essay, "Ideology and Ideological State Apparatuses," outlines his basic assumption that experience, consciousness, and subjectivity itself, is an effect of an imaginary relationship between an individual and his/her real conditions of existence, a relationship that is constructed by the ISAs, reifies social hierarchies, and induces people to consent to systems of oppression. As he writes, "[A]ll ideology has the function (which defines it) of 'constructing' concrete individuals as subjects" (Althusser, 1971, p. 171).

In later sections, we will see how a variety of other theorists and groups have analyzed current configurations of culture, ideology, and hegemony and how the positions presented in this section have been developed in a variety of fashions and have been often sharply contested as new political and theoretical impulses and movements have come to the fore. Hence, whereas a critical cultural and media studies emerged in the 1960s during an era strongly influenced by Marxism, later theoretical developments would contest Marxian positions and develop a wide variety of approaches to culture and media.

Notes

1 *The German Ideology* is published in vol. 5 of Karl Marx and Frederick Engels, *Collected Works* (New York: International Publishers). On Marxism, see Marx and Engels (1978). On the concept of ideology, see Thompson (1991).
2 See Gramsci (1971); on Gramsci, see Boggs (1984).
3 On the Frankfurt-school theory of the cultural industries, see Horkheimer and Adorno (1972); Adorno (1991); the anthology edited by Rosenberg and White (1957); the readers edited by Arato

and Gebhardt (1982) and Bronner and Kellner (1989); the discussions of the history of the Frankfurt school in Jay (1971) and Wiggershaus (1994); and the discussion of the Frankfurt-school combination of social theory and cultural criticism in Kellner (1989a); Steinert (2003), and Gunster (2004).

4   Silberman (2000) collects a wealth of Brecht's texts on radio, film, and the construction of alternative media and culture. Enzensberger (1974) provides a highly influential updating of Brecht's and Benjamin's media activism in his call for a progressive media politics in the contemporary era.

5   For further discussion of the Frankfurt-school culture industry analysis, see Kellner (1989 and 1997); for more primary texts on the debates between Benjamin and the Frankfurt school, see the collection in Bloch et al. (1977).

6   For a discussion of the first sets of critiques of Habermas's work on the public sphere see Hohendahl (1979); for a bibliography of writings on the topic, see Görtzen (1981); and for a set of contemporary English-language discussions of the work, after it was finally translated in 1989, see Calhoun (1992). To get a sense of the astonishingly productive impact of the work in encouraging research and reflection on the public sphere, see the studies in Calhoun (1992) and Habermas's "Further Reflections on the Public Sphere" (1992), which cite a striking number of criticisms or developments of his study.

References

Adorno, T. W. (1941) "On Popular Music" (with G. Simpson), *Studies in Philosophy and Social Science* 9(1): 17–48.

—— (1978 [1932]) "On the Social Situation of Music," *Telos* 35 (Spring): 129–65.

—— (1982) "On the Fetish Character of Music and the Regression of Hearing," in Arato and Gebhardt 1982: 270–99.

—— (1989) "On Jazz," in Bronner and Kellner 1989: 199–209.

—— (1991) *The Culture Industry*. London: Routledge.

Althusser, Louis (1971) "Ideology and ideological state apparatuses (Notes toward an investigation)," in *Lenin and Philosophy and Other Essays*. London and New York: Monthly Review Books, 127–86.

Arato, Andrew and Gebhardt, Eike (1982) *The Essential Frankfurt School Reader*. New York: Continuum.

Benjamin, Walter (1969) "The Work of Art in the Age of Mechanical Reproduction," in *Illuminations*. New York: Shocken.

Bloch, E., et al. (1977) *Aesthetics and Politics*. London: Verso.

Bronner, Stephen and Kellner, Douglas (1989) *Critical Theory and Society: A Reader*. New York: Routledge.

Calhoun, Craig (1992) *Habermas and the Public Sphere*. Cambridge, MA: MIT Press.

Enzensberger (1974) ???

Görtzen, R. (1981) *J. Habermas: Eine Bibliographie seiner Schriften und der Sekundärliteratur, 1952–1981*. Frankfurt: Suhrkamp.

Gramsci, Antonio (1971) "History of the Subaltern Classes," and "The Concept of 'Ideology,'" in *Selections from the Prison Notebooks of Antonio Gramsci*, eds. and trans. Quintin Hoare and Geoffrey Nowell-Smith. New York: International Publishers, 52–3, 57–8, 375–7.

—— (1985) "Cultural Themes: Ideological Material," in *Selections from Cultural Writings*, eds. David Forgacs and Geoffrey Nowell-Smith, trans. William Boelhower. London: Lawrence and Wishart, 389–90.

Gunster, Shane (2004) *Capitalizing Culture: Critical Theory for Cultural Studies*. Toronto: University of Toronto Press.

Habermas, Jürgen (1989a) *Structural Transformation of the Public Sphere*. Cambridge, MA: MIT Press.

—— (1989b) "The Public Sphere: An Encyclopedia Article," in Bronner and Kellner 1989: 136–42.

—— (1992) "Further Reflections on the Public Sphere," in Calhoun 1992: 421–61.

—— (1998) *Between Facts and Norms*. Cambridge, MA: MIT Press.

Hall, Stuart (1978) "Some Paradigms in Cultural Studies," *Annali* 3: 21.

Herzog, Herta (1941) "On Borrowed Experience. An Analysis of Listening to Daytime Sketches," *Studies in Philosophy and Social Science* 9(1): 65–95.

Hohendahl, Peter (1979) "Critical Theory, Public Sphere and Culture: Habermas and His Critics," *New German Critique* 16 (Winter): 89–118.

Horkheimer, Max and Adorno, T. W. (1972) *Dialectic of Enlightenment*. New York: Herder and Herder.

Jay, Martin (1971) *The Dialectical Imagination*. Boston: Little, Brown, & Co.

Kellner, Douglas (1987) "Critical Theory and British Cultural Studies: The Missed Articulation," in *Cultural Methodologies*, ed. Jim McGuigan. London: Sage, 12–41.

—— (1989) *Critical Theory, Marxism, and Modernity*. Cambridge and Baltimore: Polity and John Hopkins University Press.

Lazarsfeld, Paul (1941) "Administrative and Critical Communications Research," *Studies in Philosophy and Social Science* 9(1): 2–16.

Lowenthal, Leo (with Norbert Guttermann) (1949) *Prophets of Deceit*. New York: Harper.

—— (1957) *Literature and the Image of Man*. Boston: Beacon Press.

—— (1961) *Literature, Popular Culture and Society*. Englewood Cliffs, NJ: Prentice-Hall.

Marx, Karl, and Engels, Friedrich (1976) "The Ruling Class and the Ruling Ideas," in Karl Marx and Friedrich Engels, *Collected Works*, vol. 5, trans. Richard Dixon. New York: International Publishers, 59–62.

—— and —— (1978) *The Marx–Engels Reader*. New York: Norton.

Rosenberg, Bernard and White, David Manning (eds.) (1957) *Mass Culture*. Glencoe, IL: The Free Press.

Silberman, Marc (ed.) (2000) *Brecht on Film and Radio*. London: Methuen.

Steinert, Heinz (2003) *Culture Industry*. Cambridge: Polity Press.

Wiggershaus, Rolf (1994) *The Frankfurt School*. Cambridge: Polity Press.

1

The Ruling Class and the Ruling Ideas

Karl Marx and Friedrich Engels

1. The Ruling Class and the Ruling Ideas: How the Hegelian Conception of the Domination of the Spirit in History Arose

[30] The ideas of the ruling class are in every epoch the ruling ideas: i.e., the class which is the ruling *material* force of society is at the same time its ruling *intellectual* force. The class which has the means of material production at its disposal, consequently also controls the means of mental production, so that the ideas of those who lack the means of mental production are on the whole subject to it. The ruling ideas are nothing more than the ideal expression of the dominant material relations, the dominant material relations grasped as ideas; hence of the relations which make the one class the ruling one, therefore, the ideas of its dominance. The individuals composing the ruling class possess among other things consciousness, and therefore think. Insofar, therefore, as they rule as a class and determine the extent and compass of an historical epoch, it is self-evident that they do this in its whole range, hence among other things rule also as thinkers, as producers of ideas, and regulate the production and distribution of the ideas of their age: thus their ideas are the ruling ideas of the epoch. For instance, in an age and in a country where royal power, aristocracy and bourgeoisie are contending for domination and where, therefore, domination is shared, the doctrine of the separation of powers proves to be the dominant idea and is expressed as an "eternal law".

The division of labour, which we already saw above (pp. [15–18])[a] as one of the chief forces of history up till now, manifests itself also in the ruling class as the division of mental and [31] material labour, so that inside this class one part appears

---

[a] See *Karl Marx, Friedrich Engels: Collected Works*, vol. 5, 1976, pp. 44–8. [Editor's note to that volume]

From Karl Marx and Friedrich Engels, "The ruling class and the ruling ideas." In *Karl Marx, Friedrich Engels: Collected Works*, vol. 5, pp. 59–62. Translated by Richard Dixon. New York: International Publishers, 1976.

as the thinkers of the class (its active, conceptive ideologists, who make the formation of the illusions of the class about itself their chief source of livelihood), while
the others' attitude to these ideas and illusions is more passive and receptive, because
they are in reality the active members of this class and have less time to make up
illusions and ideas about themselves. Within this class this cleavage can even develop
into a certain opposition and hostility between the two parts, but whenever a
practical collision occurs in which the class itself is endangered they automatically
vanish, in which case there also vanishes the appearance of the ruling ideas being not
the ideas of the ruling class and having a power distinct from the power of this class.
The existence of revolutionary ideas in a particular period presupposes the existence
of a revolutionary class; about the premises of the latter sufficient has already been
said above (pp. [18–19, 22–23]).[b]

If now in considering the course of history we detach the ideas of the ruling class
from the ruling class itself and attribute to them an independent existence, if we
confine ourselves to saying that these or those ideas were dominant at a given time,
without bothering ourselves about the conditions of production and the producers
of these ideas, if we thus ignore the individuals and world conditions which are the
source of the ideas, then we can say, for instance, that during the time the aristocracy was dominant, the concepts honour, loyalty, etc., were dominant, during the
dominance of the bourgeoisie the concepts freedom, equality, etc. The ruling class
itself on the whole imagines this to be so. This conception of history, which is
common to all historians, particularly since the eighteenth century, will necessarily
come up against [32] the phenomenon that ever more abstract ideas hold sway, i.e.,
ideas which increasingly take on the form of universality. For each new class which
puts itself in the place of one ruling before it is compelled, merely in order to carry
through its aim, to present its interest as the common interest of all the members of
society, that is, expressed in ideal form: it has to give its ideas the form of universality, and present them as the only rational, universally valid ones. The class making a
revolution comes forward from the very start, if only because it is opposed to a *class*,
not as a class but as the representative of the whole of society, as the whole mass of
society confronting the one ruling class.[1] It can do this because initially its interest
really is as yet mostly connected with the common interest of all other non-ruling
classes, because under the pressure of hitherto existing conditions its interest has not
yet been able to develop as the particular interest of a particular class. Its victory,
therefore, benefits also many individuals of other classes which are not winning a
dominant position, but only insofar as it now enables these individuals to raise
themselves into the ruling class. When the French bourgeoisie overthrew the rule of
the aristocracy, it thereby made it possible for many proletarians to raise themselves
above the proletariat, but only insofar as they became bourgeois. Every new class,
therefore, achieves domination only on a broader basis than that of the class ruling
previously; on the other hand the opposition of the non-ruling class to the new

---

[b] See *Karl Marx, Friedrich Engels: Collected Works*, vol. 5, 1976, pp. 48–9 and 52–3. [Editor's
note to that volume]

ruling class then develops all the more sharply and profoundly. Both these things determine the fact that the struggle to be waged against this new ruling class, in its turn, has as its aim a more decisive and more radical negation of the previous conditions of society than [33] all previous classes which sought to rule could have.

This whole appearance, that the rule of a certain class is only the rule of certain ideas, comes to a natural end, of course, as soon as class rule in general ceases to be the form in which society is organised, that is to say, as soon as it is no longer necessary to represent a particular interest as general or the "general interest" as ruling.

Once the ruling ideas have been separated from the ruling individuals and, above all, from the relations which result from a given stage of the mode of production, and in this way the conclusion has been reached that history is always under the sway of ideas, it is very easy to abstract from these various ideas "the Idea", the thought, etc., as the dominant force in history, and thus to consider all these separate ideas and concepts as "forms of self-determination" of the Concept developing in history. It follows then naturally, too, that all the relations of men can be derived from the concept of man, man as conceived, the essence of man, Man. This has been done by speculative philosophy. Hegel himself confesses at the end of the *Geschichtsphilosophie*[c] that he "has considered the progress of *the concept* only" and has represented in history the "true *theodicy*" (p. 446). Now one can go back again to the producers of "the concept", to the theorists, ideologists and philosophers, and one comes then to the conclusion that the philosophers, the thinkers as such, have at all times been dominant in history: a conclusion, as we see, already expressed by Hegel.

The whole trick of proving the hegemony of the spirit in history (hierarchy Stirner calls it) is thus confined to the following three attempts.

[34] No. 1. One must separate the ideas of those ruling for empirical reasons, under empirical conditions and as corporeal individuals, from these rulers, and thus recognise the rule of ideas or illusions in history.

No. 2. One must bring an order into this rule of ideas, prove a mystical connection among the successive ruling ideas, which is managed by regarding them as "forms of self-determination of the concept" (this is possible because by virtue of their empirical basis these ideas are really connected with one another and because, conceived as *mere* ideas, they become self-distinctions, distinctions made by thought).

No. 3. To remove the mystical appearance of this "self-determining concept" it is changed into a person – "self-consciousness" – or, to appear thoroughly materialistic, into a series of persons, who represent the "concept" in history, into the "thinkers", the "philosophers", the ideologists, who again are understood as the manufacturers of history, as the "council of guardians", as the rulers.[2] Thus the whole body of materialistic elements has been eliminated from history and now full rein can be given to the speculative steed.

This historical method which reigned in Germany, and especially the reason why, must be explained from its connection with the illusion of ideologists in general,

---

[c] G. W. F. Hegel, *Vorlesungen über die Philosophie der Geschichte*. [Editor's note to *Collected Works*]

e.g., the illusions of the jurists, politicians (including the practical statesmen), from the dogmatic dreamings and distortions of these fellows; this is explained perfectly easily from their practical position in life, their job, and the division of labour.

[35] Whilst in ordinary life every shopkeeper[d] is very well able to distinguish between what somebody professes to be and what he really is, our historiography has not yet won this trivial insight. It takes every epoch at its word and believes that everything it says and imagines about itself is true.

Notes

1   [Marginal note by Marx:] (Universality corresponds to 1) the class versus the estate, 2) the competition, world intercourse, etc., 3) the great numerical strength of the ruling class, 4) the illusion of the *common* interests, in the beginning this illusion is true, 5) the delusion of the ideologists and the division of labour.)
2   [Marginal note by Marx:] Man=the "thinking human spirit".

---

[d] This word is in English in the manuscript. [Editor's note to *Collected Works*]

(i) History of the Subaltern Classes; (ii) The Concept of "Ideology"; (iii) Cultural Themes: Ideological Material

Antonio Gramsci

(i) History of the Subaltern Classes

Methodological Criteria

The historical unity of the ruling classes is realised in the State, and their history is essentially the history of States and of groups of States. But it would be wrong to think that this unity is simply juridical and political (though such forms of unity do have their importance too, and not in a purely formal sense); the fundamental historical unity, concretely, results from the organic relations between State or political society and "civil society".[1]

The subaltern classes, by definition, are not unified and cannot unite until they are able to become a "State": their history, therefore, is intertwined with that of civil society, and thereby with the history of States and groups of States. Hence it is necessary to study: 1. the objective formation of the subaltern social groups, by the developments and transformations occurring in the sphere of economic production; their quantitative diffusion and their origins in pre-existing social groups, whose mentality, ideology and aims they conserve for a time; 2. their active or passive affiliation to the dominant political formations, their attempts to influence the programmes of these formations in order to press claims of their own, and the

---

(i and ii) From Antonio Gramsci, "History of the subaltern classes" and "The concept of 'ideology.'" In Quintin Hoare and Geoffrey Nowell Smith (eds. and trans.), *Selections from the Prison Notebooks of Antonio Gramsci*, pp. 52–3, 57–8, and 375–7. New York: International Publishers, 1971. (iii) From Antonio Gramsci, "Cultural themes: Ideological material." In David Forgacs and Geoffrey Nowell-Smith (eds.), *Antonio Gramsci: Selections from Cultural Writings*, pp. 389–90. Translated by William Boelhower. London: Lawrence and Wishart, 1985. © 1985 by Lawrence and Wishart.

consequences of these attempts in determining processes of decomposition, renovation or neo-formation; 3. the birth of new parties of the dominant groups, intended
to conserve the assent of the subaltern groups and to maintain control over them;
4. the formations which the subaltern groups themselves produce, in order to press
claims of a limited and partial character; 5. those new formations which assert the
autonomy of the subaltern groups, but within the old framework; 6. those formations which assert the integral autonomy, . . . etc.[2]

The list of these phases can be broken down still further, with intermediate phases
and combinations of several phases. The historian must record, and discover the
causes of, the line of development towards integral autonomy, starting from the
most primitive phases; he must note every manifestation of the Sorelian "spirit of
cleavage".[3] Therefore, the history of the parties of the subaltern groups is very
complex too. It must include all the repercussions of party activity, throughout the
area of the subaltern groups themselves taken globally, and also upon the attitudes
of the dominant group; it must include as well the repercussions of the far more
effective actions (effective because backed by the State) of the dominant groups
upon the subaltern groups and their parties. Among the subaltern groups, one will
exercise or tend to exercise a certain hegemony through the mediation of a party;
this must be established by studying the development of all the other parties too, in
so far as they include elements of the hegemonic group or of the other subaltern
groups which undergo such hegemony. . . .

The methodological criterion on which our own study must be based is the
following: that the supremacy of a social group manifests itself in two ways, as
"domination" and as "intellectual and moral leadership". A social group dominates
antagonistic groups, which it tends to "liquidate", or to subjugate perhaps even by
armed force; it leads kindred and allied groups. A social group can, and indeed must,
already exercise "leadership" before winning governmental power (this indeed is one
of the principal conditions for the winning of such power); it subsequently becomes
dominant when it exercises power, but even if it holds it firmly in its grasp, it must
continue to "lead" as well. . . .

(ii) The Concept of "Ideology"

"Ideology" was an aspect of "sensationalism", i.e. eighteenth-century French
materialism. Its original meaning was that of "science of ideas", and since analysis
was the only method recognised and applied by science it means "analysis of ideas",
that is, "investigation of the origin of ideas". Ideas had to be broken down into
their original "elements", and these could be nothing other than "sensations". Ideas
derived from sensations. But sensationalism could be associated, without too much
difficulty, with religious faith and with the most extreme beliefs in the "power of the
Spirit" and its "immortal destinies", so that Manzoni,[4] even after his conversion and
return to Catholicism, even at the time when he wrote the *Inni sacri*, continued to
adhere in principle to the theory of sensationalism, until he learnt about the philosophy of Rosmini.[5]

How the concept of Ideology passed from meaning "science of ideas" and "analysis of the origin of ideas" to meaning a specific "system of ideas" needs to be examined historically. In purely logical terms the process is easy to grasp and understand.

It could be asserted that Freud is the last of the Ideologues, and that De Man is also an "ideologue". This makes the "enthusiasm" of Croce and the Croceans for De Man even more curious – or would if there wasn't a "practical" justification for their enthusiasm.[6] One should examine the way in which the author of the *Popular Manual* [Bukharin][7] has remained trapped in Ideology; whereas the philosophy of praxis represents a distinct advance and historically is precisely in opposition to Ideology. Indeed the meaning which the term "ideology" has assumed in Marxist philosophy implicitly contains a negative value judgment and excludes the possibility that for its founders the origin of ideas should be sought for in sensations, and therefore, in the last analysis, in physiology. "Ideology" itself must be analysed historically, in the terms of the philosophy of praxis, as a superstructure.

It seems to me that there is a potential element of error in assessing the value of ideologies, due to the fact (by no means casual) that the name ideology is given both to the necessary superstructure of a particular structure and to the arbitrary elucubrations of particular individuals. The bad sense of the word has become widespread, with the effect that the theoretical analysis of the concept of ideology has been modified and denatured. The process leading up to this error can be easily reconstructed:

1. ideology is identified as distinct from the structure, and it is asserted that it is not ideology that changes the structures but vice versa;
2. it is asserted that a given political solution is "ideological" – i.e. that it is not sufficient to change the structure, although it thinks that it can do so; it is asserted that it is useless, stupid, etc.;
3. one then passes to the assertion that every ideology is "pure" appearance, useless, stupid, etc.

One must therefore distinguish between historically organic ideologies, those, that is, which are necessary to a given structure, and ideologies that are arbitrary, rationalistic, or "willed". To the extent that ideologies are historically necessary they have a validity which is "psychological"; they "organise" human masses, and create the terrain on which men move, acquire consciousness of their position, struggle, etc. To the extent that they are arbitrary they only create individual "movements", polemics and so on (though even these are not completely useless, since they function like an error which by contrasting with truth, demonstrates it).

It is worth recalling the frequent affirmation made by Marx on the "solidity of popular beliefs" as a necessary element of a specific situation. What he says more or less is "when this way of conceiving things has the force of popular beliefs", etc. Another proposition of Marx is that a popular conviction often has the same energy as a material force or something of the kind, which is extremely significant. The analysis of these propositions tends, I think, to reinforce the conception of *historical bloc* in which precisely material forces are the content and ideologies are the form, though this distinction between form and content has purely didactic value, since the material forces would be inconceivable historically without form and the ideologies would be individual fancies without the material forces.

(iii) Cultural Themes: Ideological Material

A study of how the ideological structure of a dominant class is actually organized: namely the material organization aimed at maintaining, defending and developing the theoretical or ideological "front". Its most prominent and dynamic part is the press in general: publishing houses (which have an implicit and explicit programme and are attached to a particular tendency), political newspapers, periodicals of every kind, scientific, literary, philological, popular, etc., various periodicals down to parish bulletins. If this kind of study were conducted on a national scale it would be gigantic: one could therefore do a series of studies for one city or for a number of cities. A news editor of a daily newspaper should have this study as a general outline for his work: indeed, he should make his own version of it. Think of all the wonderful leading articles one could write on the subject!

The press is the most dynamic part of this ideological structure, but not the only one. Everything which influences or is able to influence public opinion, directly or indirectly, belongs to it: libraries, schools, associations and clubs of various kinds, even architecture and the layout and names of streets. It would be impossible to explain the position retained by the Church in modern society if one were unaware of the constant and patient efforts it makes to develop continuously its particular section of this material structure of ideology.[8] Such a study, done seriously, would be very important. Besides providing a living historical model of such a structure, it would accustom one to a more cautious and exact estimate of the forces acting in society. What resources can an innovative class set against this formidable complex of trenches and fortification of the dominant class? The spirit of scission,[9] in other words the progressive acquisition of the consciousness of its own historical personality, a spirit of scission that must aim to spread itself from the protagonist class to the classes that are its potential allies – all this requires a complex ideological labour, the first condition of which is an exact knowledge of the field that must be cleared of its element of human "mass".

Notes

1 For Gramsci's use of the term "civil society", see introduction to *State and Civil Society*, pp. 206–9.
2 The last three categories refer presumably to trade unions, reformist parties, and communist parties respectively.
3 See note 4 on p. 126.
4 Alessandro Manzoni (1785–1873), Italian novelist and poet, brought up on the ideas of the French and Italian Enlightenment but converted to Catholicism in or about 1810.

His major work is the historical novel *I promessi sposi* (The Betrothed) (1827: revised and partly rewritten 1840) in which Enlightenment ideas co-exist uneasily with Catholic Quietism. The *Inni sacri* (Sacred Hymns, or Songs) date from 1812–22.

5   The most effective literary propagator of ideology was Destutt de Tracy 1754–1836), because of the ease and popularity of his exposition. Another was Dr. Cabanis with his *Rapport du Physique et du Moral*. (Condillac, Helvétius, etc., are more strictly speaking philosophers.) Link between Catholicism and ideology: Manzoni, Cabanis, Bourget, Taine (Taine is the *chef d'école* for Maurras and others of a Catholic tendency); also the "psycho-logical novel" (Stendhal was a pupil of De Tracy, etc.). Destutt de Tracy's main work is the *Eléments d'Idéologie* (Paris, 1817–18). The Italian translation is more complete (*Elementi di Ideologia del Conte Destutt de Tracy*, translated by G. Compagnoni, Milan, Stamperia di Giambattista Sonzogno, 1819). In the French text a whole section is missing, I think the one on Love, which Stendhal knew and used from the Italian translation.

6   Henri De Man, Belgian Social-Democrat, was the author of a book *Au delà du Marxisme* (Beyond Marxism), frequently referred to and criticised in the *Quaderni* (see in particular MS, pp. 111–14). Croce's "practical" reason for enthusiasm for De Man lies in their shared opposition to revolutionary Marxism, although strictly speaking Crocean philosophy denies a serious theoretical role to ideological and instrumental thought such as De Man's.

7   For Gramsci's criticism of Bukharin's *Popular Manual*, see *Selections from the Prison Notebooks of Antonio Gramsci*, pp. 419–72.

8   In 1916 Gramsci had written of the array of titles in a Catholic bookshop window in Turin: "I admire and envy the priests who succeed in obtaining such visible results with their cultural propaganda. In reality, we do not pay much attention to this slow process of intellectual stagnation by the clergy. It is something impalpable, which slides along like an eel, limp, which does not seem solid, and yet it is like the mattress that resists cannonades better than the walls of Liège" (CT, p. 132; SM, pp. 39–40).

9   The term "scission" (sometimes translated as "cleavage") is drawn from Sorel, who wrote in the *Reflexions on Violence* (Chapter 6 § 1) of "the scission between classes, the basis of all socialism". It derives from his analogy between socialism and primitive Christianity. For Sorel, Christianity made a distinct "scission" or "rupture" from Judaism while at the same time inheriting its compatible elements. In the same way socialism, in its scission from capitalism, would keep the heritage both of capitalist science and technology and of the "morality of the producers" (i.e. the proletariat), formed through trade union solidarity and struggles (see *Le Système historique de Renan*, Paris 1905, p. 71). Compare Gramsci's statement of 1920: "Every revolution which, like the Christian and the Communist revolutions, comes about and can only come about through a stirring within the deepest and broadest popular masses, cannot help but smash and destroy the existing system of social organization" (SPWI, p. 331).

3

The Work of Art in the Age of Mechanical Reproduction

Walter Benjamin

Our fine arts were developed, their types and uses were established, in times very different from the present, by men whose power of action upon things was insignificant in comparison with ours. But the amazing growth of our techniques, the adaptability and precision they have attained, the ideas and habits they are creating, make it a certainty that profound changes are impending in the ancient craft of the Beautiful. In all the arts there is a physical component which can no longer be considered or treated as it used to be, which cannot remain unaffected by our modern knowledge and power. For the last twenty years neither matter nor space nor time has been what it was from time immemorial. We must expect great innovations to transform the entire technique of the arts, thereby affecting artistic invention itself and perhaps even bringing about an amazing change in our very notion of art.[1]

– Paul Valéry, "La Conquète de l'ubiquité"

Preface

When Marx undertook his critique of the capitalistic mode of production, this mode was in its infancy. Marx directed his efforts in such a way as to give them prognostic value. He went back to the basic conditions underlying capitalistic production and through his presentation showed what could be expected of capitalism in the future. The result was that one could expect it not only to exploit the proletariat with increasing intensity, but ultimately to create conditions which would make it possible to abolish capitalism itself.

The transformation of the superstructure, which takes place far more slowly than that of the substructure, has taken more than half a century to manifest in all areas

From Walter Benjamin, "The work of art in the age of mechanical reproduction." In *Illuminations*, pp. 217–51. New York: Schocken Books, 1969.

of culture the change in the conditions of production. Only today can it be indicated what form this has taken. Certain prognostic requirements should be met by
these statements. However, theses about the art of the proletariat after its assumption of power or about the art of a classless society would have less bearing on these
demands than theses about the developmental tendencies of art under present conditions of production. Their dialectic is no less noticeable in the superstructure than
in the economy. It would therefore be wrong to underestimate the value of such
theses as a weapon. They brush aside a number of outmoded concepts, such as
creativity and genius, eternal value and mystery – concepts whose uncontrolled (and
at present almost uncontrollable) application would lead to a processing of data in
the Fascist sense. The concepts which are introduced into the theory of art in what
follows differ from the more familiar terms in that they are completely useless for the
purposes of Fascism. They are, on the other hand, useful for the formulation of
revolutionary demands in the politics of art.

I

In principle a work of art has always been reproducible. Man-made artifacts could
always be imitated by men. Replicas were made by pupils in practice of their craft, by
masters for diffusing their works, and, finally, by third parties in the pursuit of gain.
Mechanical reproduction of a work of art, however, represents something new.
Historically, it advanced intermittently and in leaps at long intervals, but with accelerated intensity. The Greeks knew only two procedures of technically reproducing
works of art: founding and stamping. Bronzes, terra cottas, and coins were the only
art works which they could produce in quantity. All others were unique and could
not be mechanically reproduced. With the woodcut graphic art became mechanically
reproducible for the first time, long before script became reproducible by print. The
enormous changes which printing, the mechanical reproduction of writing, has
brought about in literature are a familiar story. However, within the phenomenon
which we are here examining from the perspective of world history, print is merely
a special, though particularly important, case. During the Middle Ages engraving
and etching were added to the woodcut; at the beginning of the nineteenth century
lithography made its appearance.

   With lithography the technique of reproduction reached an essentially new stage.
This much more direct process was distinguished by the tracing of the design on a
stone rather than its incision on a block of wood or its etching on a copperplate and
permitted graphic art for the first time to put its products on the market, not only in
large numbers as hitherto, but also in daily changing forms. Lithography enabled
graphic art to illustrate everyday life, and it began to keep pace with printing. But
only a few decades after its invention, lithography was surpassed by photography.
For the first time in the process of pictorial reproduction, photography freed the
hand of the most important artistic functions which henceforth devolved only upon
the eye looking into a lens. Since the eye perceives more swiftly than the hand can
draw, the process of pictorial reproduction was accelerated so enormously that it

could keep pace with speech. A film operator shooting a scene in the studio captures the images at the speed of an actor's speech. Just as lithography virtually implied the illustrated newspaper, so did photography foreshadow the sound film. The technical reproduction of sound was tackled at the end of the last century. These convergent endeavors made predictable a situation which Paul Valéry pointed up in this sentence: "Just as water, gas, and electricity are brought into our houses from far off to satisfy our needs in response to a minimal effort, so we shall be supplied with visual or auditory images, which will appear and disappear at a simple movement of the hand, hardly more than a sign" (*op. cit.*, p. 226). Around 1900 technical reproduction had reached a standard that not only permitted it to reproduce all transmitted works of art and thus to cause the most profound change in their impact upon the public; it also had captured a place of its own among the artistic processes. For the study of this standard nothing is more revealing than the nature of the repercussions that these two different manifestations – the reproduction of works of art and the art of the film – have had on art in its traditional form.

II

Even the most perfect reproduction of a work of art is lacking in one element: its presence in time and space, its unique existence at the place where it happens to be. This unique existence of the work of art determined the history to which it was subject throughout the time of its existence. This includes the changes which it may have suffered in physical condition over the years as well as the various changes in its ownership.[2] The traces of the first can be revealed only by chemical or physical analyses which it is impossible to perform on a reproduction; changes of ownership are subject to a tradition which must be traced from the situation of the original.

The presence of the original is the prerequisite to the concept of authenticity. Chemical analyses of the patina of a bronze can help to establish this, as does the proof that a given manuscript of the Middle Ages stems from an archive of the fifteenth century. The whole sphere of authenticity is outside technical – and, of course, not only technical – reproducibility.[3] Confronted with its manual reproduction, which was usually branded as a forgery, the original preserved all its authority; not so *vis à vis* technical reproduction. The reason is twofold. First, process reproduction is more independent of the original than manual reproduction. For example, in photography, process reproduction can bring out those aspects of the original that are unattainable to the naked eye yet accessible to the lens, which is adjustable and chooses its angle at will. And photographic reproduction, with the aid of certain processes, such as enlargement or slow motion, can capture images which escape natural vision. Secondly, technical reproduction can put the copy of the original into situations which would be out of reach for the original itself. Above all, it enables the original to meet the beholder halfway, be it in the form of a photograph or a phonograph record. The cathedral leaves its locale to be received in the studio of a lover of art; the choral production, performed in an auditorium or in the open air, resounds in the drawing room.

The situations into which the product of mechanical reproduction can be brought may not touch the actual work of art, yet the quality of its presence is always depreciated. This holds not only for the art work but also, for instance, for a landscape which passes in review before the spectator in a movie. In the case of the art object, a most sensitive nucleus – namely, its authenticity – is interfered with whereas no natural object is vulnerable on that score. The authenticity of a thing is the essence of all that is transmissible from its beginning, ranging from its substantive duration to its testimony to the history which it has experienced. Since the historical testimony rests on the authenticity, the former, too, is jeopardized by reproduction when substantive duration ceases to matter. And what is really jeopardized when the historical testimony is affected is the authority of the object.[4]

One might subsume the eliminated element in the term "aura" and go on to say: that which withers in the age of mechanical reproduction is the aura of the work of art. This is a symptomatic process whose significance points beyond the realm of art. One might generalize by saying: the technique of reproduction detaches the reproduced object from the domain of tradition. By making many reproductions it substitutes a plurality of copies for a unique existence. And in permitting the reproduction to meet the beholder or listener in his own particular situation, it reactivates the object reproduced. These two processes lead to a tremendous shattering of tradition which is the obverse of the contemporary crisis and renewal of mankind. Both processes are intimately connected with the contemporary mass movements. Their most powerful agent is the film. Its social significance, particularly in its most positive form, is inconceivable without its destructive, cathartic aspect, that is, the liquidation of the traditional value of the cultural heritage. This phenomenon is most palpable in the great historical films. It extends to ever new positions. In 1927 Abel Gance exclaimed enthusiastically: "Shakespeare, Rembrandt, Beethoven will make films . . . all legends, all mythologies and all myths, all founders of religion, and the very religions . . . await their exposed resurrection, and the heroes crowd each other at the gate."[5] Presumably without intending it, he issued an invitation to a far-reaching liquidation.

III

During long periods of history, the mode of human sense perception changes with humanity's entire mode of existence. The manner in which human sense perception is organized, the medium in which it is accomplished, is determined not only by nature but by historical circumstances as well. The fifth century, with its great shifts of population, saw the birth of the late Roman art industry and the Vienna Genesis, and there developed not only an art different from that of antiquity but also a new kind of perception. The scholars of the Viennese school, Riegl and Wickhoff, who resisted the weight of classical tradition under which these later art forms had been buried, were the first to draw conclusions from them concerning the organization of perception at the time. However far-reaching their insight, these scholars limited themselves to showing the significant, formal hallmark which characterized perception in late Roman times. They did not attempt – and, perhaps, saw no way – to show the social transformations expressed by these changes of perception. The conditions for an analogous insight are more favorable in the present. And if changes in the medium of contemporary perception can be comprehended as decay of the aura, it is possible to show its social causes.

The concept of aura which was proposed above with reference to historical objects may usefully be illustrated with reference to the aura of natural ones. We define the aura of the latter as the unique phenomenon of a distance, however close it may be. If, while resting on a summer afternoon, you follow with your eyes a mountain range on the horizon or a branch which casts its shadow over you, you experience the aura of those mountains, of that branch. This image makes it easy to comprehend the social bases of the contemporary decay of the aura. It rests on two circumstances, both of which are related to the increasing significance of the masses in contemporary life. Namely, the desire of contemporary masses to bring things "closer" spatially and humanly, which is just as ardent as their bent toward overcoming the uniqueness of every reality by accepting its reproduction.[6] Every day the urge grows stronger to get hold of an object at very close range by way of its likeness, its reproduction. Unmistakably, reproduction as offered by picture magazines and newsreels differs from the image seen by the unarmed eye. Uniqueness and permanence are as closely linked in the latter as are transitoriness and reproducibility in the former. To pry an object from its shell, to destroy its aura, is the mark of a perception whose "sense of the universal equality of things" has increased to such a degree that it extracts it even from a unique object by means of reproduction. Thus is manifested in the field of perception what in the theoretical sphere is noticeable in the increasing importance of statistics. The adjustment of reality to the masses and of the masses to reality is a process of unlimited scope, as much for thinking as for perception.

IV

The uniqueness of a work of art is inseparable from its being imbedded in the fabric of tradition. This tradition itself is thoroughly alive and extremely changeable. An ancient statue of Venus, for example, stood in a different traditional context with the Greeks, who made it an object of veneration, than with the clerics of the Middle Ages, who viewed it as an ominous idol. Both of them, however, were equally confronted with its uniqueness, that is, its aura. Originally the contextual integration of art in tradition found its expression in the cult. We know that the earliest art works originated in the service of a ritual – first the magical, then the religious kind. It is significant that the existence of the work of art with reference to its aura is never entirely separated from its ritual function.[7] In other words, the unique value of the "authentic" work of art has its basis in ritual, the location of its original use value. This ritualistic basis, however remote, is still recognizable as secularized ritual even in the most profane forms of the cult of beauty.[8] The secular cult of beauty, developed during the Renaissance and prevailing for three centuries, clearly showed that ritualistic basis in its decline and the first deep crisis which befell it. With the advent of the first truly revolutionary means of reproduction, photography, simultan-eously with the rise of socialism, art sensed the approaching crisis which has become evident a century later. At the time, art reacted with the doctrine of *l'art pour l'art*, that is, with a theology of art. This gave rise to what might be called a negative theology in the form of the idea of "pure" art, which not only denied any social function of art but also any categorizing by subject matter. (In poetry, Mallarmé was the first to take this position.)

An analysis of art in the age of mechanical reproduction must do justice to these relationships, for they lead us to an all-important insight: for the first time in world history, mechanical reproduction emancipates the work of art from its parasitical dependence on ritual. To an ever greater degree the work of art reproduced becomes the work of art designed for reproducibility.[9] From a photographic negative, for example, one can make any number of prints; to ask for the "authentic" print makes no sense. But the instant the criterion of authenticity ceases to be applicable to artistic production, the total function of art is reversed. Instead of being based on ritual, it begins to be based on another practice – politics.

V

Works of art are received and valued on different planes. Two polar types stand out: with one, the accent is on the cult value; with the other, on the exhibition value of the work.[10] Artistic production begins with ceremonial objects destined to serve in a cult. One may assume that what mattered was their existence, not their being on view. The elk portrayed by the man of the Stone Age on the walls of his cave was an instrument of magic. He did expose it to his fellow men, but in the main it was meant for the spirits. Today the cult value would seem to demand that the work of art remain hidden. Certain statues of gods are accessible only to the priest in the cella; certain Madonnas remain covered nearly all year round; certain sculptures on medieval cathedrals are invisible to the spectator on ground level. With the emancipa-tion of the various art practices from ritual go increasing opportunities for the exhibition of their products. It is easier to exhibit a portrait bust that can be sent here and there than to exhibit the statue of a divinity that has its fixed place in the interior of a temple. The same holds for the painting as against the mosaic or fresco that preceded it. And even though the public presentability of a mass originally may have been just as great as that of a symphony, the latter originated at the moment when its public presentability promised to surpass that of the mass.

With the different methods of technical reproduction of a work of art, its fitness for exhibition increased to such an extent that the quantitative shift between its two poles turned into a qualitative transformation of its nature. This is comparable to the situation of the work of art in prehistoric times when, by the absolute emphasis on its cult value, it was, first and foremost, an instrument of magic. Only later did it come to be recognized as a work of art. In the same way today, by the absolute emphasis on its exhibition value the work of art becomes a creation with entirely new functions, among which the one we are conscious of, the artistic function, later may be recognized as incidental.[11] This much is certain: today photography and the film are the most serviceable exemplifications of this new function.

VI

In photography, exhibition value begins to displace cult value all along the line. But cult value does not give way without resistance. It retires into an ultimate retrenchment: the human countenance. It is no accident that the portrait was the focal point of early photography. The cult of remembrance of loved ones, absent or dead, offers a last refuge for the cult value of the picture. For the last time the aura emanates from the early photographs in the fleeting expression of a human face. This is what constitutes their melancholy, incomparable beauty. But as man withdraws from the photographic image, the exhibition value for the first time shows its superiority to the ritual value. To have pinpointed this new stage constitutes the incomparable significance of Atget, who, around 1900, took photographs of deserted Paris streets. It has quite justly been said of him that he photographed them like scenes of crime. The scene of a crime, too, is deserted; it is photographed for the purpose of establishing evidence. With Atget, photographs become standard evidence for historical occurrences, and acquire a hidden political significance. They demand a specific kind of approach; free-floating contemplation is not appropriate to them. They stir the viewer; he feels challenged by them in a new way. At the same time picture magazines begin to put up signposts for him, right ones or wrong ones, no matter. For the first time, captions have become obligatory. And it is clear that they have an altogether different character than the title of a painting. The directives which the captions give to those looking at pictures in illustrated magazines soon become even more explicit and more imperative in the film where the meaning of each single picture appears to be prescribed by the sequence of all preceding ones.

VII

The nineteenth-century dispute as to the artistic value of painting versus photography today seems devious and confused. This does not diminish its importance, however; if anything, it underlines it. The dispute was in fact the symptom of a historical transformation the universal impact of which was not realized by either of the rivals. When the age of mechanical reproduction separated art from its basis in cult, the semblance of its autonomy disappeared forever. The resulting change in the function of art transcended the perspective of the century; for a long time it even escaped that of the twentieth century, which experienced the development of the film.

Earlier much futile thought had been devoted to the question of whether photography is an art. The primary question – whether the very invention of photography had not transformed the entire nature of art – was not raised. Soon the film theoreticians asked the same ill-considered question with regard to the film. But the difficulties which photography caused traditional aesthetics were mere child's play as compared to those raised by the film. Whence the insensitive and forced character of early theories of the film. Abel Gance, for instance, compares the film with hieroglyphs: "Here, by a remarkable regression, we have come back to the level of expression of the Egyptians. . . . Pictorial language has not yet matured because our eyes have not yet adjusted to it. There is as yet insufficient respect for, insufficient cult of, what it expresses."[12] Or, in the words of Séverin-Mars: "What art has been granted a dream more poetical and more real at the same time! Approached in this fashion the film might represent an incomparable means of expression. Only the most high-minded persons, in the most perfect and mysterious moments of their lives, should be allowed to enter its ambience."[13] Alexandre Arnoux concludes his fantasy about the silent film with the question: "Do not all the bold descriptions we have given amount to the definition of prayer?"[14] It is instructive to note how their desire to class the film among the "arts" forces these theoreticians to read ritual elements into it – with a striking lack of discretion. Yet when these speculations were published, films like *L'Opinion publique* and *The Gold Rush* had already appeared. This, however, did not keep Abel Gance from adducing hieroglyphs for purposes of comparison, nor Séverin-Mars from speaking of the film as one might speak of paintings by Fra Angelico. Characteristically, even today ultrareactionary authors give the film a similar contextual significance – if not an outright sacred one, then at least a supernatural one. Commenting on Max Reinhardt's film version of *A Midsummer Night's Dream*, Werfel states that undoubtedly it was the sterile copying of the exterior world with its streets, interiors, railroad stations, restaurants, motorcars, and beaches which until now had obstructed the elevation of the film to the realm of art. "The film has not yet realized its true meaning, its real possibilities . . . these consist in its unique faculty to express by natural means and with incomparable persuasiveness all that is fairylike, marvelous, supernatural."[15]

VIII

The artistic performance of a stage actor is definitely presented to the public by the actor in person; that of the screen actor, however, is presented by a camera, with a twofold consequence. The camera that presents the performance of the film actor to the public need not respect the performance as an integral whole. Guided by the cameraman, the camera continually changes its position with respect to the performance. The sequence of positional views which the editor composes from the material supplied him constitutes the completed film. It comprises certain factors of movement which are in reality those of the camera, not to mention special camera angles, close-ups, etc. Hence, the performance of the actor is subjected to a series of optical tests. This is the first consequence of the fact that the actor's performance is presented by means of a camera. Also, the film actor lacks the opportunity of the stage actor to adjust to the audience during his performance, since he does not present his performance to the audience in person. This permits the audience to take the position of a critic, without experiencing any personal contact with the actor. The audience's identification with the actor is really an identification with the camera. Consequently the audience takes the position of the camera; its approach is that of testing.[16] This is not the approach to which cult values may be exposed.

IX

For the film, what matters primarily is that the actor represents himself to the public before the camera, rather than representing someone else. One of the first to sense the actor's metamorphosis by this form of testing was Pirandello. Though his remarks on the subject in his novel *Si Gira* were limited to the negative aspects of the question and to the silent film only, this hardly impairs their validity. For in this respect, the sound film did not change anything essential. What matters is that the part is acted not for an audience but for a mechanical contrivance – in the case of the sound film, for two of them. "The film actor," wrote Pirandello, "feels as if in exile – exiled not only from the stage but also from himself. With a vague sense of discomfort he feels inexplicable emptiness: his body loses its corporeality, it evaporates, it is deprived of reality, life, voice, and the noises caused by his moving about, in order to be changed into a mute image, flickering an instant on the screen, then vanishing into silence. . . . The projector will play with his shadow before the public, and he himself must be content to play before the camera."[17] This situation might also be characterized as follows: for the first time – and this is the effect of the film – man has to operate with his whole living person, yet forgoing its aura. For aura is tied to his presence; there can be no replica of it. The aura which, on the stage, emanates from Macbeth, cannot be separated for the spectators from that of the actor. However, the singularity of the shot in the studio is that the camera is substituted for the public. Consequently, the aura that envelops the actor vanishes, and with it the aura of the figure he portrays.

It is not surprising that it should be a dramatist such as Pirandello who, in characterizing the film, inadvertently touches on the very crisis in which we see the theater. Any thorough study proves that there is indeed no greater contrast than that of the stage play to a work of art that is completely subject to or, like the film, founded in, mechanical reproduction. Experts have long recognized that in the film "the greatest effects are almost always obtained by 'acting' as little as possible. . . ." In 1932 Rudolf Arnheim saw "the latest trend . . . in treating the actor as a stage prop chosen for its characteristics and . . . inserted at the proper place."[18] With this idea something else is closely connected. The stage actor identifies himself with the character of his role. The film actor very often is denied this opportunity. His creation is by no means all of a piece; it is composed of many separate performances. Besides certain fortuitous considerations, such as cost of studio, availability of fellow players, décor, etc., there are elementary necessities of equipment that split the actor's work into a series of mountable episodes. In particular, lighting and its installation require the presentation of an event that, on the screen, unfolds as a rapid and unified scene, in a sequence of separate shootings which may take hours at the studio; not to mention more obvious montage. Thus a jump from the window can be shot in the studio as a jump from a scaffold, and the ensuing flight, if need be, can be shot weeks later when outdoor scenes are taken. Far more paradoxical cases can easily be construed. Let us assume that an actor is supposed to be startled by a knock at the door. If his reaction is not satisfactory, the director can resort to an expedient: when the actor happens to be at the studio again he has a shot fired behind him without his being forewarned of it. The frightened reaction can be shot now and be cut into the screen version. Nothing more strikingly shows that art has left the realm of the "beautiful semblance" which, so far, had been taken to be the only sphere where art could thrive.

X

The feeling of strangeness that overcomes the actor before the camera, as Pirandello describes it, is basically of the same kind as the estrangement felt before one's own image in the mirror. But now the reflected image has become separable, transportable. And where is it transported? Before the public.[19] Never for a moment does the screen actor cease to be conscious of this fact. While facing the camera he knows that ultimately he will face the public, the consumers who constitute the market. This market, where he offers not only his labor but also his whole self, his heart and soul, is beyond his reach. During the shooting he has as little contact with it as any article made in a factory. This may contribute to that oppression, that new anxiety which, according to Pirandello, grips the actor before the camera. The film responds to the shriveling of the aura with an artificial build-up of the "personality" outside the studio. The cult of the movie star, fostered by the money of the film industry, preserves not the unique aura of the person but the "spell of the personality," the phony spell of a commodity. So long as the movie-makers' capital sets the fashion, as a rule no other revolutionary merit can be accredited to today's film than the promotion of a revolutionary criticism of traditional concepts of art. We do not deny that in some cases today's films can also promote revolutionary criticism of social conditions, even of the distribution of property. However, our present study is no more specifically concerned with this than is the film production of Western Europe.

It is inherent in the technique of the film as well as that of sports that everybody who witnesses its accomplishments is somewhat of an expert. This is obvious to anyone listening to a group of newspaper boys leaning on their bicycles and discussing the outcome of a bicycle race. It is not for nothing that newspaper publishers arrange races for their delivery boys. These arouse great interest among the participants, for the victor has an opportunity to rise from delivery boy to professional racer. Similarly, the newsreel offers everyone the opportunity to rise from passer-by to movie extra. In this way any man might even find himself part of a work of art, as witness Vertoff's *Three Songs About Lenin* or Ivens' *Borinage*. Any man today can lay claim to being filmed. This claim can best be elucidated by a comparative look at the historical situation of contemporary literature.

For centuries a small number of writers were confronted by many thousands of readers. This changed toward the end of the last century. With the increasing extension of the press, which kept placing new political, religious, scientific, professional, and local organs before the readers, an increasing number of readers became writers – at first, occasional ones. It began with the daily press opening to its readers space for "letters to the editor." And today there is hardly a gainfully employed European who could not, in principle, find an opportunity to publish somewhere or other comments on his work, grievances, documentary reports, or that sort of thing. Thus, the distinction between author and public is about to lose its basic character. The difference becomes merely functional; it may vary from case to case. At any moment the reader is ready to turn into a writer. As expert, which he had to become willy-nilly in an extremely specialized work process, even if only in some minor respect, the reader gains access to authorship. In the Soviet Union work itself is given a voice. To present it verbally is part of a man's ability to perform the work. Literary license is now founded on polytechnic rather than specialized training and thus becomes common property.[20]

All this can easily be applied to the film, where transitions that in literature took centuries have come about in a decade. In cinematic practice, particularly in Russia, this change-over has partially become established reality. Some of the players whom we meet in Russian films are not actors in our sense but people who portray *themselves* – and primarily in their own work process. In Western Europe the capitalistic exploitation of the film denies consideration to modern man's legitimate claim to being reproduced. Under these circumstances the film industry is trying hard to spur the interest of the masses through illusion-promoting spectacles and dubious speculations.

XI

The shooting of a film, especially of a sound film, affords a spectacle unimaginable anywhere at any time before this. It presents a process in which it is impossible to assign to a spectator a viewpoint which would exclude from the actual scene such extraneous accessories as camera equipment, lighting machinery, staff assistants, etc. – unless his eye were on a line parallel with the lens. This circumstance, more than any other, renders superficial and insignificant any possible similarity between a scene in the studio and one on the stage. In the theater one is well aware of the place from which the play cannot immediately be detected as illusionary. There is no such place for the movie scene that is being shot. Its illusionary nature is that of the second degree, the result of cutting. That is to say, in the studio the mechanical equipment has penetrated so deeply into reality that its pure aspect freed from the foreign substance of equipment is the result of a special procedure, namely, the shooting by the specially adjusted camera and the mounting of the shot together with other similar ones. The equipment-free aspect of reality here has become the height of artifice; the sight of immediate reality has become an orchid in the land of technology.

Even more revealing is the comparison of these circumstances, which differ so much from those of the theater, with the situation in painting. Here the question is:

How does the cameraman compare with the painter? To answer this we take recourse to an analogy with a surgical operation. The surgeon represents the polar opposite of the magician. The magician heals a sick person by the laying on of hands; the surgeon cuts into the patient's body. The magician maintains the natural distance between the patient and himself; though he reduces it very slightly by the laying on of hands, he greatly increases it by virtue of his authority. The surgeon does exactly the reverse; he greatly diminishes the distance between himself and the patient by penetrating into the patient's body, and increases it but little by the caution with which his hand moves among the organs. In short, in contrast to the magician – who is still hidden in the medical practitioner – the surgeon at the decisive moment abstains from facing the patient man to man; rather, it is through the operation that he penetrates into him.

Magician and surgeon compare to painter and cameraman. The painter maintains in his work a natural distance from reality, the cameraman penetrates deeply into its web.[21] There is a tremendous difference between the pictures they obtain. That of the painter is a total one, that of the cameraman consists of multiple fragments which are assembled under a new law. Thus, for contemporary man the representation of reality by the film is incomparably more significant than that of the painter, since it offers, precisely because of the thoroughgoing permeation of reality with mechanical equipment, an aspect of reality which is free of all equipment. And that is what one is entitled to ask from a work of art.

XII

Mechanical reproduction of art changes the reaction of the masses toward art. The reactionary attitude toward a Picasso painting changes into the progressive reaction toward a Chaplin movie. The progressive reaction is characterized by the direct, intimate fusion of visual and emotional enjoyment with the orientation of the expert. Such fusion is of great social significance. The greater the decrease in the social significance of an art form, the sharper the distinction between criticism and enjoyment by the public. The conventional is uncritically enjoyed, and the truly new is criticized with aversion. With regard to the screen, the critical and the receptive attitudes of the public coincide. The decisive reason for this is that individual reactions are predetermined by the mass audience response they are about to produce, and this is nowhere more pronounced than in the film. The moment these responses become manifest they control each other. Again, the comparison with painting is fruitful. A painting has always had an excellent chance to be viewed by one person or by a few. The simultaneous contemplation of paintings by a large public, such as developed in the nineteenth century, is an early symptom of the crisis of painting, a crisis which was by no means occasioned exclusively by photography but rather in a relatively independent manner by the appeal of art works to the masses.

Painting simply is in no position to present an object for simultaneous collective experience, as it was possible for architecture at all times, for the epic poem in the past, and for the movie today. Although this circumstance in itself should not lead one to conclusions about the social role of painting, it does constitute a serious threat as soon as painting, under special conditions and, as it were, against its nature, is confronted directly by the masses. In the churches and monasteries of the Middle Ages and at the princely courts up to the end of the eighteenth century, a collective reception of paintings did not occur simultaneously, but by graduated and hierarchized mediation. The change that has come about is an expression of the particular conflict in which painting was implicated by the mechanical reproducibility of paintings. Although paintings began to be publicly exhibited in galleries and salons, there was no way for the masses to organize and control themselves in their reception.[22] Thus the same public which responds in a progressive manner toward a grotesque film is bound to respond in a reactionary manner to surrealism.

XIII

The characteristics of the film lie not only in the manner in which man presents himself to mechanical equipment but also in the manner in which, by means of this apparatus, man can represent his environment. A glance at occupational psychology illustrates the testing capacity of the equipment. Psychoanalysis illustrates it in a different perspective. The film has enriched our field of perception with methods which can be illustrated by those of Freudian theory. Fifty years ago, a slip of the tongue passed more or less unnoticed. Only exceptionally may such a slip have revealed dimensions of depth in a conversation which had seemed to be taking its course on the surface. Since the *Psychopathology of Everyday Life* things have changed. This book isolated and made analyzable things which had heretofore floated along unnoticed in the broad stream of perception. For the entire spectrum of optical, and now also acoustical, perception the film has brought about a similar deepening of apperception. It is only an obverse of this fact that behavior items shown in a movie can be analyzed much more precisely and from more points of view than those presented on paintings or on the stage. As compared with painting, filmed behavior lends itself more readily to analysis because of its incomparably more precise statements of the situation. In comparison with the stage scene, the filmed behavior item lends itself more readily to analysis because it can be isolated more easily. This circumstance derives its chief importance from its tendency to promote the mutual penetration of art and science. Actually, of a screened behavior item which is neatly brought out in a certain situation, like a muscle of a body, it is difficult to say which is more fascinating, its artistic value or its value for science. To demonstrate the identity of the artistic and scientific uses of photography which heretofore usually were separated will be one of the revolutionary functions of the film.[23]

By close-ups of the things around us, by focusing on hidden details of familiar objects, by exploring commonplace milieus under the ingenious guidance of the camera, the film, on the one hand, extends our comprehension of the necessities which rule our lives; on the other hand, it manages to assure us of an immense and unexpected field of action. Our taverns and our metropolitan streets, our offices and furnished rooms, our railroad stations and our factories appeared to have us locked up hopelessly. Then came the film and burst this prison-world asunder by the dynamite of the tenth of a second, so that now, in the midst of its far-flung ruins and debris, we calmly and adventurously go traveling. With the close-up, space expands; with slow motion, movement is extended. The enlargement of a snapshot does not simply render more precise what in any case was visible, though unclear: it reveals entirely new structural formations of the subject. So, too, slow motion not only presents familiar qualities of movement but reveals in them entirely unknown ones "which, far from looking like retarded rapid movements, give the effect of singularly gliding, floating, supernatural motions."[24] Evidently a different nature opens itself to the camera than opens to the naked eye – if only because an unconsciously penetrated space is substituted for a space consciously explored by man. Even if one has a general knowledge of the way people walk, one knows nothing of a person's posture during the fractional second of a stride. The act of reaching for a lighter or a spoon is familiar routine, yet we hardly know what really goes on between hand and metal, not to mention how this fluctuates with our moods. Here the camera intervenes with the resources of its lowerings and liftings, its interruptions and isolations, its extensions and accelerations, its enlargements and reductions. The camera introduces us to unconscious optics as does psychoanalysis to unconscious impulses.

XIV

One of the foremost tasks of art has always been the creation of a demand which could be fully satisfied only later.[25] The history of every art form shows critical epochs in which a certain art form aspires to effects which could be fully obtained only with a changed technical standard, that is to say, in a new art form. The extravagances and crudities of art which thus appear, particularly in the so-called decadent epochs, actually arise from the nucleus of its richest historical energies. In recent years, such barbarisms were abundant in Dadaism. It is only now that its impulse becomes discernible: Dadaism attempted to create by pictorial – and literary – means the effects which the public today seeks in the film.

Every fundamentally new, pioneering creation of demands will carry beyond its goal. Dadaism did so to the extent that it sacrificed the market values which are so characteristic of the film in favor of higher ambitions – though of course it was not conscious of such intentions as here described. The Dadaists attached much less importance to the sales value of their work than to its uselessness for contemplative immersion. The studied degradation of their material was not the least of their means to achieve this uselessness. Their poems are "word salad" containing obscenities and every imaginable waste product of language. The same is true of their paintings, on which they mounted buttons and tickets. What they intended and achieved was a relentless destruction of the aura of their creations, which they branded as reproductions with the very means of production. Before a painting of Arp's or a poem by August Stramm it is impossible to take time for contemplation and evaluation as one would before a canvas of Derain's or a poem by Rilke. In the decline of middle-class society, contemplation became a school for asocial behavior; it was countered by distraction as a variant of social conduct.[26] Dadaistic activities actually assured a rather vehement distraction by making works of art the center of scandal. One requirement was foremost: to outrage the public.

From an alluring appearance or persuasive structure of sound the work of art of the Dadaists became an instrument of ballistics. It hit the spectator like a bullet, it happened to him, thus acquiring a tactile quality. It promoted a demand for the film, the distracting element of which is also primarily tactile, being based on changes of place and focus which periodically assail the spectator. Let us compare the screen on which a film unfolds with the canvas of a painting. The painting invites the spectator to contemplation; before it the spectator can abandon himself to his associations. Before the movie frame he cannot do so. No sooner has his eye grasped a scene than it is already changed. It cannot be arrested. Duhamel, who detests the film and knows nothing of its significance, though something of its structure, notes this circumstance as follows: "I can no longer think what I want to think. My thoughts have been replaced by moving images."[27] The spectator's process of association in view of these images is indeed interrupted by their constant, sudden change. This constitues the shock effect of the film, which, like all shocks, should be cushioned by heightened presence of mind.[28] By means of its technical structure, the film has taken the physical shock effect out of the wrappers in which Dadaism had, as it were, kept it inside the moral shock effect.[29]

XV

The mass is a matrix from which all traditional behavior toward works of art issues today in a new form. Quantity has been transmuted into quality. The greatly increased mass of participants has produced a change in the mode of participation. The fact that the new mode of participation first appeared in a disreputable form must not confuse the spectator. Yet some people have launched spirited attacks against precisely this superficial aspect. Among these, Duhamel has expressed himself in the most radical manner. What he objects to most is the kind of participation which the movie elicits from the masses. Duhamel calls the movie "a pastime for helots, a diversion for uneducated, wretched, worn-out creatures who are consumed by their worries . . . , a spectacle which requires no concentration and presupposes no intelligence . . . , which kindles no light in the heart and awakens no hope other than the ridiculous one of someday becoming a "star" in Los Angeles."[30] Clearly, this is at bottom the same ancient lament that the masses seek distraction whereas art demands concentration from the spectator. That is a commonplace. The question remains whether it provides a platform for the analysis of the film. A closer look is needed here. Distraction and concentration form polar opposites which may be stated as follows: A man who concentrates before a work of art is absorbed by it. He enters into this work of art the way legend tells of the Chinese painter when he viewed his finished painting. In contrast, the distracted mass absorbs the work of art. This is most obvious with regard to buildings. Architecture has always represented the prototype of a work of art the reception of which is consummated by a collectivity in a state of distraction. The laws of its reception are most instructive.

Buildings have been man's companions since primeval times. Many art forms have developed and perished. Tragedy begins with the Greeks, is extinguished with them, and after centuries its "rules" only are revived. The epic poem, which had its origin in the youth of nations, expires in Europe at the end of the Renaissance. Panel painting is a creation of the Middle Ages, and nothing guarantees its uninterrupted existence. But the human need for shelter is lasting. Architecture has never been idle. Its history is more ancient than that of any other art, and its claim to being a living force has significance in every attempt to comprehend the relationship of the masses to art. Buildings are appropriated in a twofold manner: by use and by perception – or rather, by touch and sight. Such appropriation cannot be understood in terms of the attentive concentration of a tourist before a famous building. On the tactile side there is no counterpart to contemplation on the optical side. Tactile appropriation is accomplished not so much by attention as by habit. As regards architecture, habit determines to a large extent even optical reception. The latter, too, occurs much less through rapt attention than by noticing the object in incidental fashion. This mode of appropriation, developed with reference to architecture, in certain circumstances acquires canonical value. For the tasks which face the human apparatus of perception at the turning points of history cannot be solved by optical means, that is, by contemplation, alone. They are mastered gradually by habit, under the guidance of tactile appropriation.

The distracted person, too, can form habits. More, the ability to master certain tasks in a state of distraction proves that their solution has become a matter of habit. Distraction as provided by art presents a covert control of the extent to which new tasks have become soluble by apperception. Since, moreover, individuals are tempted to avoid such tasks, art will tackle the most difficult and most important ones where it is able to mobilize the masses. Today it does so in the film. Reception in a state of distraction, which is increasing noticeably in all fields of art and is symptomatic of profound changes in apperception, finds in the film its true means of exercise. The film with its shock effect meets this mode of reception half-way. The film makes the cult value recede into the background not only by putting the public in the position of the critic, but also by the fact that at the movies this position requires no attention. The public is an examiner, but an absent-minded one.

Epilogue

The growing proletarianization of modern man and the increasing formation of masses are two aspects of the same process. Fascism attempts to organize the newly created proletarian masses without affecting the property structure which the masses strive to eliminate. Fascism sees its salvation in giving these masses not their right, but instead a chance to express themselves.[31] The masses have a right to change property relations; Fascism seeks to give them an expression while preserving property. The logical result of Fascism is the introduction of aesthetics into political life.

The violation of the masses, whom Fascism, with its *Führer* cult, forces to their knees, has its counterpart in the violation of an apparatus which is pressed into the production of ritual values.

All efforts to render politics aesthetic culminate in one thing: war. War and war only can set a goal for mass movements on the largest scale while respecting the traditional property system. This is the political formula for the situation. The technological formula may be stated as follows: Only war makes it possible to mobilize all of today's technical resources while maintaining the property system. It goes without saying that the Fascist apotheosis of war does not employ such arguments. Still, Marinetti says in his manifesto on the Ethiopian colonial war: "For twenty-seven years we Futurists have rebelled against the branding of war as antiaesthetic. . . . Accordingly we state: . . . War is beautiful because it establishes man's dominion over the subjugated machinery by means of gas masks, terrifying megaphones, flame throwers, and small tanks. War is beautiful because it initiates the dreamt-of metalization of the human body. War is beautiful because it enriches a flowering meadow with the fiery orchids of machine guns. War is beautiful because it combines the gunfire, the cannonades, the cease-fire, the scents, and the stench of putrefaction into a symphony. War is beautiful because it creates new architecture, like that of the big tanks, the geometrical formation flights, the smoke spirals from burning villages, and many others. . . . Poets and artists of Futurism! . . . remember these principles of an aesthetics of war so that your struggle for a new literature and a new graphic art . . . may be illumined by them!"

The manifesto has the virtue of clarity. Its formulations deserve to be accepted by dialecticians. To the latter, the aesthetics of today's war appears as follows: If the natural utilization of productive forces is impeded by the property system, the increase in technical devices, in speed, and in the sources of energy will press for an unnatural utilization, and this is found in war. The destructiveness of war furnishes proof that society has not been mature enough to incorporate technology as its organ, that technology has not been sufficiently developed to cope with the elemental forces of society. The horrible features of imperialistic warfare are attributable to the discrepancy between the tremendous means of production and their inadequate utilization in the process of production – in other words, to unemployment and the lack of markets. Imperialistic war is a rebellion of technology which collects, in the form of "human material," the claims to which society has denied its natural material. Instead of draining rivers, society directs a human stream into a bed of trenches; instead of dropping seeds from airplanes, it drops incendiary bombs over cities; and through gas warfare the aura is abolished in a new way.

"*Fiat ars – pereat mundus*," says Fascism, and, as Marinetti admits, expects war to supply the artistic gratification of a sense perception that has been changed by technology. This is evidently the consummation of "*l'art pour l'art.*" Mankind, which in Homer's time was an object of contemplation for the Olympian gods, now is one for itself. Its self-alienation has reached such a degree that it can experience its own destruction as an aesthetic pleasure of the first order. This is the situation of politics which Fascism is rendering aesthetic. Communism responds by politicizing art.

Notes

1   Quoted from Paul Valéry, *Aesthetics*, "The Conquest of Ubiquity," translated by Ralph Manheim, p. 225. Pantheon Books, Bollingen Series, New York, 1964.

2   Of course, the history of a work of art encompasses more than this. The history of the "Mona Lisa," for instance, encompasses the kind and number of its copies made in the 17th, 18th, and 19th centuries.

3   Precisely because authenticity is not reproducible, the intensive penetration of certain (mechanical) processes of reproduction was instrumental in differentiating and grading authenticity. To develop such differentiations was an important function of the trade in works of art. The invention of the woodcut may be said to have struck at the root of the quality of authenticity even before its late flowering. To be sure, at the time of its origin a medieval picture of the Madonna could not yet be said to be "authentic." It became "authentic" only during the succeeding centuries and perhaps most strikingly so during the last one.

4   The poorest provincial staging of *Faust* is superior to a Faust film in that, ideally, it competes with the first performance at Weimar. Before the screen it is unprofitable to remember traditional contents which might come to mind before the stage – for instance, that Goethe's friend Johann Heinrich Merck is hidden in Mephisto, and the like.

5   Abel Gance, "Le Temps de l'image est venu," *L'Art cinématographique*, vol. 2, pp. 94 f, Paris, 1927.

6   To satisfy the human interest of the masses may mean to have one's social function removed from the field of vision. Nothing guarantees that a portraitist of today, when painting a famous surgeon at the breakfast table in the midst of his family, depicts his social function more precisely than a painter of the 17th century who portrayed his medical doctors as representing this profession, like Rembrandt in his "Anatomy Lesson."

7   The definition of the aura as a "unique phenomenon of a distance however close it may be" represents nothing but the formulation of the cult value of the work of art in categories of space and time perception. Distance is the opposite of closeness. The essentially distant object is the unapproachable one. Unapproachability is indeed a major quality of the cult image. True to its nature, it remains "distant, however close it may be." The closeness which one may gain from its subject matter does not impair the distance which it retains in its appearance.

8   To the extent to which the cult value of the painting is secularized the ideas of its fundamental uniqueness lose distinctness. In the imagination of the beholder the uniqueness of the phenomena which hold sway in the cult image is more and more displaced by the empirical uniqueness of the creator or of his creative achievement. To be sure, never completely so; the concept of authenticity always transcends mere genuineness. (This is particularly apparent in the collector who always retains some traces of the fetishist and who, by owning the work of art, shares in its ritual power.) Nevertheless, the function of the concept of authenticity remains determinate in the evaluation of art; with the secularization of art, authenticity displaces the cult value of the work.

9   In the case of films, mechanical reproduction is not, as with literature and painting, an external condition for mass distribution. Mechanical reproduction is inherent in the very technique of film production. This technique not only permits in the most direct way but virtually causes mass distribution. It enforces distribution because the production of a film is so expensive that an individual who, for instance, might afford to buy a painting no longer can afford to buy a film. In 1927 it was calculated that a major film, in order

to pay its way, had to reach an audience of nine million. With the sound film, to be sure, a setback in its international distribution occurred at first: audiences became limited by language barriers. This coincided with the Fascist emphasis on national interests. It is more important to focus on this connection with Fascism than on this setback, which was soon minimized by synchronization. The simultaneity of both phenomena is attributable to the depression. The same disturbances which, on a larger scale, led to an attempt to maintain the existing property structure by sheer force led the endangered film capital to speed up the development of the sound film. The introduction of the sound film brought about a temporary relief, not only because it again brought the masses into the theaters but also because it merged new capital from the electrical industry with that of the film industry. Thus, viewed from the outside, the sound film promoted national interests, but seen from the inside it helped to internationalize film production even more than previously.

10 This polarity cannot come into its own in the aesthetics of Idealism. Its idea of beauty comprises these polar opposites without differentiating between them and consequently excludes their polarity. Yet in Hegel this polarity announces itself as clearly as possible within the limits of Idealism. We quote from his *Philosophy of History*:

> Images were known of old. Piety at an early time required them for worship, but it could do without *beautiful* images. These might even be disturbing. In every beautiful painting there is also something nonspiritual, merely external, but its spirit speaks to man through its beauty. Worshipping, conversely, is concerned with the work as an object, for it is but a spiritless stupor of the soul. . . . Fine art has arisen . . . in the church . . . , although it has already gone beyond its principle as art.

Likewise, the following passage from *The Philosophy of Fine Art* indicates that Hegel sensed a problem here.

> We are beyond the stage of reverence for works of art as divine and objects deserving our worship. The impression they produce is one of a more reflective kind, and the emotions they arouse require a higher test. . . . (G. W. F. Hegel, *The Philosophy of Fine Art*, trans., with notes, by F. P. B. Osmaston, vol. I, p. 12, London, 1920.)

The transition from the first kind of artistic reception to the second characterizes the history of artistic reception in general. Apart from that, a certain oscillation between these two polar modes of reception can be demonstrated for each work of art. Take the Sistine Madonna. Since Hubert Grimme's research it has been known that the Madonna originally was painted for the purpose of exhibition. Grimme's research was inspired by the question: What is the purpose of the molding in the foreground of the painting which the two cupids lean upon? How, Grimme asked further, did Raphael come to furnish the sky with two draperies? Research proved that the Madonna had been commissioned for the public lying-in-state of Pope Sixtus. The Popes lay in state in a certain side chapel of St. Peter's. On that occasion Raphael's picture had been fastened in a nichelike background of the chapel, supported by the coffin. In this picture Raphael portrays the Madonna approaching the papal coffin in clouds from the background of the niche, which was demarcated by green drapes. At the obsequies of Sixtus a pre-eminent exhibition value of Raphael's picture was taken advantage of. Some time later it was placed on the high altar in the church of the Black Friars at Piacenza. The reason for this exile is to be found in the Roman rites which forbid the use of paintings exhibited at obsequies as cult objects on the high altar. This regulation devalued Raphael's picture to some degree. In order to obtain an adequate price nevertheless, the Papal See resolved to add to the bargain the tacit toleration of the picture above the high altar. To avoid attention the picture was given to the monks of the far-off provincial town.

11 Bertolt Brecht, on a different level, engaged in analogous reflections: "If the concept of "work of art" can no longer be applied to the thing that emerges once the work is transformed into a commodity, we have to eliminate this concept with cautious care but without fear, lest we liquidate the function of the very thing as well. For it has to go through this phase without mental reservation, and not as noncommittal deviation from the straight path; rather, what happens here with the work of art will change it fundamentally and erase its past to such an extent that should the old concept be taken up again – and it will, why not? – it will no longer stir any memory of the thing it once designated."

12 Abel Gance, *op. cit.*, pp. 100–1.

13 Séverin-Mars, quoted by Abel Gance, *op. cit.*, p. 100.

14 Alexandre Arnoux, *Cinéma pris*, 1929, p. 28.

15 Franz Werfel, "Ein Sommernachtstraum, Ein Film von Shakespeare und Reinhardt," *Neues Wiener Journal*, cited in *Lu* 15, November, 1935.

16 "The film . . . provides – or could provide – useful insight into the details of human actions. . . . Character is never used as a source of motivation; the inner life of the persons never supplies the principal cause of the plot and seldom is its main result." (Bertolt Brecht, *Versuche*, "Der Dreigroschenprozess," p. 268.) The expansion of the field of the testable which mechanical equipment brings about for the actor corresponds to the extraordinary expansion of the field of the testable brought about for the individual through economic conditions. Thus, vocational aptitude tests become constantly more important. What matters in these tests are segmental performances of the individual. The film shot and the vocational aptitude test are taken before a committee of experts. The camera director in the studio occupies a place identical with that of the examiner during aptitude tests.

17 Luigi Pirandello, *Si Gira*, quoted by Léon Pierre-Quint, "Signification du cinéma," *L'Art cinématographique, op. cit.*, pp. 14–15.

18 Rudolf Arnheim, *Film als Kunst*, Berlin, 1932, pp. 176 f. In this context certain seemingly unimportant details in which the film director deviates from stage practices gain in interest. Such is the attempt to let the actor play without make-up, as made among others by Dreyer in his *Jeanne d'Arc*. Dreyer spent months seeking the forty actors who constitute the Inquisitors' tribunal. The search for these actors resembled that for stage properties that are hard to come by. Dreyer made every effort to avoid resemblances of age, build, and physiognomy. If the actor thus becomes a stage property, this latter, on the other hand, frequently functions as actor. At least it is not unusual for the film to assign a role to the stage property. Instead of choosing at random from a great wealth of examples, let us concentrate on a particularly convincing one. A clock that is working will always be a disturbance on the stage. There it cannot be permitted its function of measuring time. Even in a naturalistic play, astronomical time would clash with theatrical time. Under these circumstances it is highly revealing that the film can, whenever appropriate, use time as measured by a clock. From this more than from many other touches it may clearly be recognized that under certain circumstances each and every prop in a film may assume important functions. From here it is but one step to Pudovkin's statement that "the playing of an actor which is connected with an object and is built around it . . . is always one of the strongest methods of cinematic construction." (W. Pudovkin, *Filmregie und Filmmanuskript*, Berlin, 1928, p. 126.) The film is the first art form capable

of demonstrating how matter plays tricks on man. Hence, films can be an excellent means of materialistic representation.

19   The change noted here in the method of exhibition caused by mechanical reproduction applies to politics as well. The present crisis of the bourgeois democracies comprises a crisis of the conditions which determine the public presentation of the rulers. Democracies exhibit a member of government directly and personally before the nation's representatives. Parliament is his public. Since the innovations of camera and recording equipment make it possible for the orator to become audible and visible to an unlimited number of persons, the presentation of the man of politics before camera and recording equipment becomes paramount. Parliaments, as much as theaters, are deserted. Radio and film not only affect the function of the professional actor but likewise the function of those who also exhibit themselves before this mechanical equipment, those who govern. Though their tasks may be different, the change affects equally the actor and the ruler. The trend is toward establishing controllable and transferable skills under certain social conditions. This results in a new selection, a selection before the equipment from which the star and the dictator emerge victorious.

20   The privileged character of the respective techniques is lost. Aldous Huxley writes:

> Advances in technology have led . . . to vulgarity. . . . Process reproduction and the rotary press have made possible the indefinite multiplication of writing and pictures. Universal education and relatively high wages have created an enormous public who know how to read and can afford to buy reading and pictorial matter. A great industry has been called into existence in order to supply these commodities. Now, artistic talent is a very rare phenomenon; whence it follows . . . that, at every epoch and in all countries, most art has been bad. But the proportion of trash in the total artistic output is greater now than at any other period. That it must be so is a matter of simple arithmetic. The population of Western Europe has a little more than doubled during the last century. But the amount of reading – and seeing – matter has increased, I should imagine, at least twenty and possibly fifty or even a hundred times. If there were n men of talent in a population of x millions, there will presumably be 2n men of talent among 2x millions. The situation may be summed up thus. For every page of print and pictures published a century ago, twenty or perhaps even a hundred pages are published today. But for every man of talent then living, there are now only two men of talent. It may be of course that, thanks to universal education, many potential talents which in the past would have been stillborn are now enabled to realize themselves. Let us assume, then, that there are now three or even four men of talent to every one of earlier times. It still remains true to say that the consumption of reading – and seeing – matter has far outstripped the natural production of gifted writers and draughtsmen. It is the same with hearing-matter. Prosperity, the gramophone and the radio have created an audience of hearers who consume an amount of hearing-matter that has increased out of all proportion to the increase of population and the consequent natural increase of talented musicians. It follows from all this that in all the arts the output of trash is both absolutely and relatively greater than it was in the past; and that it must remain greater for just so long as the world continues to consume the present inordinate quantities of reading-matter, seeing-matter, and hearing-matter. (Aldous Huxley, *Beyond the Mexique Bay. A Traveller's Journal*, London, 1949, pp. 274 ff. First published in 1934.)

This mode of observation is obviously not progressive.

21   The boldness of the cameraman is indeed comparable to that of the surgeon. Luc Durtain lists among specific technical sleights of hand those "which are required in surgery in the case of certain difficult operations. I choose as an example a case from otorhinolaryngology; . . . the so-called endonasal perspective procedure; or I refer to the acrobatic tricks of larynx surgery which have to be performed following the reversed picture in the laryngoscope. I might also speak of ear surgery which suggests the precision work of watchmakers. What range of the most subtle muscular acrobatics is required from the man who wants to repair or save the human body! We have only to think of the couching of a cataract where there is virtually a debate of steel with nearly fluid tissue, or of the major abdominal operations (laparotomy)." – Luc Durtain, *op. cit.*

22   This mode of observation may seem crude, but as the great theoretician Leonardo has shown, crude modes of observation may at times be usefully adduced. Leonardo compares painting and music as follows: "Painting is superior to music because, unlike unfortunate music, it does not have to die as soon as it is born. . . . Music which is consumed in the very act of its birth is inferior to painting which the use of varnish has rendered eternal." (Trattato I, 29.)

23   Renaissance painting offers a revealing analogy to this situation. The incomparable development of this art and its significance rested not least on the integration of a number of new sciences, or at least of new scientific data. Renaissance painting made use of anatomy and perspective, of mathematics, meteorology, and chromatology. Valéry writes: "What could be further from us than the strange claim of a Leonardo to whom painting was a supreme goal and the ultimate demonstration of knowledge? Leonardo was convinced that painting demanded universal knowledge, and he did not even shrink from a theoretical analysis which to us is stunning because of its very depth and precision. . . ." – Paul Valéry, *Pièces sur l'art*, "Autour de Corot," Paris, p. 191.

24   Rudolf Arnheim, *loc. cit.*, p. 138.

25   "The work of art," says André Breton, "is valuable only in so far as it is vibrated by the reflexes of the future." Indeed, every developed art form intersects three lines of development. Technology works toward a certain form of art. Before the advent of the film there were photo booklets with pictures which flitted by the onlooker upon pressure of the thumb, thus portraying a boxing bout or a tennis match. Then there were the slot machines in bazaars; their picture sequences were produced by the turning of a crank.

    Secondly, the traditional art forms in certain phases of their development strenuously work toward effects which later are effortlessly attained by the new ones. Before the rise of the movie the Dadaists' performances tried to create an audience reaction which Chaplin later evoked in a more natural way.

    Thirdly, unspectacular social changes often promote a change in receptivity which will benefit the new art form. Before the movie had begun to create its public, pictures that were no longer immobile captivated an assembled audience in the so-called *Kaiserpanorama*. Here the public assembled before a screen into which stereoscopes were mounted, one to each beholder. By a mechanical process individual pictures appeared briefly before the stereoscopes, then made way for others. Edison still had to use similar devices in presenting the first movie strip before the film screen and projection were known. This strip was presented to a small public which stared into the apparatus in which the succession of pictures was reeling off. Incidentally, the institution of the *Kaiserpanorama* shows very clearly a dialectic of the development. Shortly before the movie turned the reception of pictures into a collective one, the individual viewing of pictures in these swiftly outmoded establishments came into play once more with an intensity comparable to that of the ancient priest beholding the statue of a divinity in the cella.

26   The theological archetype of this contemplation is the awareness of being alone with one's God. Such awareness, in the heyday of the bourgeoisie, went to strengthen the freedom to shake off clerical tutelage. During the decline of the bourgeoisie this awareness had to take into account the hidden tendency to withdraw from public affairs those forces which the individual draws upon in his communion with God.

27   Georges Duhamel, *Scènes de la vie future*, Paris, 1930, p. 52.

28   The film is the art form that is in keeping with the increased threat to his life which modern man has to face. Man's need to expose himself to shock effects is his adjustment to the dangers threatening him. The film corresponds to profound changes in the apperceptive apparatus – changes that are experienced on an individual scale by the man in the street in big-city traffic, on a historical scale by every present-day citizen.

29   As for Dadaism, insights important for Cubism and Futurism are to be gained from the movie. Both appear as deficient attempts of art to accommodate the pervasion of reality by the apparatus. In contrast to the film, these schools did not try to use the apparatus as such for the artistic presentation of reality, but aimed at some sort of alloy in the joint presentation of reality and apparatus. In Cubism, the premonition that this apparatus will be structurally based on optics plays a dominant part; in Futurism, it is the premonition of the effects of this apparatus which are brought out by the rapid sequence of the film strip.

30   Duhamel, *op. cit.*, p. 58.

31   One technical feature is significant here, especially with regard to newsreels, the propagandist importance of which can hardly be overestimated. Mass reproduction is aided especially by the reproduction of masses. In big parades and monster rallies, in sports events, and in war, all of which nowadays are captured by camera and sound recording, the masses are brought face to face with themselves. This process, whose significance need not be stressed, is intimately connected with the development of the techniques of reproduction and photography. Mass movements are usually discerned more clearly by a camera than by the naked eye. A bird's-eye view best captures gatherings of hundreds of thousands. And even though such a view may be as accessible to the human eye as it is to the camera, the image received by the eye cannot be enlarged the way a negative is enlarged. This means that mass movements, including war, constitute a form of human behavior which particularly favors mechanical equipment.

4

The Culture Industry: Enlightenment as Mass Deception

Max Horkheimer and Theodor W. Adorno

The sociological view that the loss of support from objective religion and the disintegration of the last precapitalist residues, in conjunction with technical and social differentiation and specialization, have given rise to cultural chaos is refuted by daily experience. Culture today is infecting everything with sameness. Film, radio, and magazines form a system. Each branch of culture is unanimous within itself and all are unanimous together. Even the aesthetic manifestations of political opposites proclaim the same inflexible rhythm. The decorative administrative and exhibition buildings of industry differ little between authoritarian and other countries. The bright monumental structures shooting up on all sides show off the systematic ingenuity of the state-spanning combines, toward which the unfettered entrepreneurial system, whose monuments are the dismal residential and commercial blocks in the surrounding areas of desolate cities, was already swiftly advancing. The older buildings around the concrete centers already look like slums, and the new bungalows on the outskirts, like the flimsy structures at international trade fairs, sing the praises of technical progress while inviting their users to throw them away after short use like tin cans. But the town-planning projects, which are supposed to perpetuate individuals as autonomous units in hygienic small apartments, subjugate them only more completely to their adversary, the total power of capital. Just as the occupants of city centers are uniformly summoned there for purposes of work and leisure, as producers and consumers, so the living cells crystallize into homogenous, well-organized complexes. The conspicuous unity of macrocosm and microcosm confronts human beings

From Max Horkheimer and Theodor W. Adorno, "The culture industry: Enlightenment as mass deception." In Gunzelin Schmid Noerr (ed.), *Dialectic of Enlightenment: Philosophical Fragments*, pp. 94–136. Translated by Edmund Jephcott. Stanford, CA: Stanford University Press, 2002. Original German version © 1944 by Social Studies Association, NY; new edition © 1969 by S. Fischer Verlag GmbH, Frankfurt am Main. English translation © 2002 by Board of Trustees of Leland Stanford Jr. University. All rights reserved. Used with the permission of Stanford University Press, www.sup.org.

with a model of their culture: the false identity of universal and particular. All mass culture under monopoly is identical, and the contours of its skeleton, the conceptual armature fabricated by monopoly, are beginning to stand out. Those in charge no longer take much trouble to conceal the structure, the power of which increases the more bluntly its existence is admitted. Films and radio no longer need to present themselves as art. The truth that they are nothing but business is used as an ideology to legitimize the trash they intentionally produce. They call themselves industries, and the published figures for their directors' incomes quell any doubts about the social necessity of their finished products.

Interested parties like to explain the culture industry in technological terms. Its millions of participants, they argue, demand reproduction processes which inevitably lead to the use of standard products to meet the same needs at countless locations. The technical antithesis between few production centers and widely dispersed reception necessitates organization and planning by those in control. The standardized forms, it is claimed, were originally derived from the needs of the consumers: that is why they are accepted with so little resistance. In reality, a cycle of manipulation and retroactive need is unifying the system ever more tightly. What is not mentioned is that the basis on which technology is gaining power over society is the power of those whose economic position in society is strongest. Technical rationality today is the rationality of domination. It is the compulsive character of a society alienated from itself. Automobiles, bombs, and films hold the totality together until their leveling element demonstrates its power against the very system of injustice it served. For the present the technology of the culture industry confines itself to standardization and mass production and sacrifices what once distinguished the logic of the work from that of society. These adverse effects, however, should not be attributed to the internal laws of technology itself but to its function within the economy today. Any need which might escape the central control is repressed by that of individual consciousness. The step from telephone to radio has clearly distinguished the roles. The former liberally permitted the participant to play the role of subject. The latter democratically makes everyone equally into listeners, in order to expose them in authoritarian fashion to the same programs put out by different stations. No mechanism of reply has been developed, and private transmissions are condemned to unfreedom. They confine themselves to the apocryphal sphere of "amateurs," who, in any case, are organized from above. Any trace of spontaneity in the audience of the official radio is steered and absorbed into a selection of specializations by talent-spotters, performance competitions, and sponsored events of every kind. The talents belong to the operation long before they are put on show; otherwise they would not conform so eagerly. The mentality of the public, which allegedly and actually favors the system of the culture industry, is a part of the system, not an excuse for it. If a branch of art follows the same recipe as one far removed from it in terms of its medium and subject matter; if the dramatic denouement in radio "soap operas"[1] is used as an instructive example of how to solve technical difficulties – which are mastered no less in "jam sessions" than at the highest levels of jazz – or if a movement from Beethoven is loosely "adapted" in the same way as a Tolstoy novel is adapted for film, the pretext of meeting the public's spontaneous wishes is mere hot air. An explanation in terms of the specific interests of the technical apparatus and its personnel would be closer to the truth, provided that apparatus were understood in all its details as a part of the economic mechanism of selection. Added to this is the agreement, or at least the common determination, of the executive powers to produce or let pass nothing which does not conform to their tables, to their concept of the consumer, or, above all, to themselves.

If the objective social tendency of this age is incarnated in the obscure subjective intentions of board chairmen, this is primarily the case in the most powerful sectors of industry: steel, petroleum, electricity, chemicals. Compared to them the culture monopolies are weak and dependent. They have to keep in with the true wielders of power, to ensure that their sphere of mass society, the specific product of which still has too much of cozy liberalism and Jewish intellectualism about it, is not subjected to a series of purges. The dependence of the most powerful broadcasting company on the electrical industry, or of film on the banks, characterizes the whole sphere, the individual sectors of which are themselves economically intertwined. Everything is so tightly clustered that the concentration of intellect reaches a level where it overflows the demarcations between company names and technical sectors. The relentless unity of the culture industry bears witness to the emergent unity of politics. Sharp distinctions like those between A and B films, or between short stories published in magazines in different price segments, do not so much reflect real differences as assist in the classification, organization, and identification of consumers. Something is provided for everyone so that no one can escape; differences are hammered home and propagated. The hierarchy of serial qualities purveyed to the public serves only to quantify it more completely. Everyone is supposed to behave spontaneously according to a "level" determined by indices and to select the category of mass product manufactured for their type. On the charts of research organizations, indistinguishable from those of political propaganda, consumers are divided up as statistical material into red, green, and blue areas according to income group.

The schematic nature of this procedure is evident from the fact that the mechanically differentiated products are ultimately all the same. That the difference between the models of Chrysler and General Motors is fundamentally illusory is known by any child, who is fascinated by that very difference. The advantages and disadvantages debated by enthusiasts serve only to perpetuate the appearance of competition and choice. It is no different with the offerings of Warner Brothers and Metro Goldwyn Mayer. But the differences, even between the more expensive and cheaper products from the same firm, are shrinking – in cars to the different number of cylinders, engine capacity, and details of the gadgets, and in films to the different number of stars, the expense lavished on technology, labor and costumes, or the use of the latest psychological formulae. The unified standard of value consists in the level of conspicuous production, the amount of investment put on show. The budgeted differences of value in the culture industry have nothing to do with actual differences, with the meaning of the product itself. The technical media, too, are being engulfed by an insatiable uniformity. Television aims at a synthesis of radio and film, delayed only for as long as the interested parties cannot agree. Such a synthesis, with its unlimited possibilities, promises to intensify the impoverishment of the aesthetic material so radically that the identity of all industrial cultural products, still scantily disguised today, will triumph openly tomorrow in a mocking fulfillment of Wagner's dream of the total art work. The accord between word, image, and music is achieved so much more perfectly than in *Tristan* because the sensuous elements, which compliantly document only the surface of social reality, are produced in principle within the same technical work process, the unity of which they express as their true content. This work process integrates all the elements of production, from the original concept of the novel, shaped by its side-long glance at film, to the last sound effect. It is the triumph of invested capital. To impress the omnipotence of capital on the hearts of expropriated job candidates as the power of their true master is the purpose of all films, regardless of the plot selected by the production directors.

Even during their leisure time, consumers must orient themselves according to the unity of production. The active contribution which Kantian schematism still expected of subjects – that they should, from the first, relate sensuous multiplicity to fundamental concepts – is denied to the subject by industry. It purveys schematism as its first service to the customer. According to Kantian schematism, a secret mechanism within the psyche preformed immediate data to fit them into the system of pure reason. That secret has now been unraveled. Although the operations of the mechanism appear to be planned by those who supply the data, the culture industry, the planning is in fact imposed on the industry by the inertia of a society irrational despite all its rationalization, and this calamitous tendency, in passing through the agencies of business, takes on the shrewd intentionality peculiar to them. For the consumer there is nothing left to classify, since the classification has already been preempted by the schematism of production. This dreamless art for the people fulfils the dreamy idealism which went too far for idealism in its critical form. Everything comes from consciousness – from that of God for Malebranche and Berkeley, and from earthly production management for mass art. Not only do hit songs, stars, and soap operas conform to types recurring cyclically as rigid invariants, but the specific content of productions, the seemingly variable element, is itself derived from those types. The details become interchangeable. The brief interval sequence which has proved catchy in a hit song, the hero's temporary disgrace which he accepts as a "good sport," the wholesome slaps the heroine receives from the strong hand of the male star, his plain-speaking abruptness toward the pampered heiress, are, like all the details, ready-made clichés, to be used here and there as desired and always completely defined by the purpose they serve within the schema. To confirm the schema by acting as its constituents is their sole *raison d'être*. In a film, the outcome can invariably be predicted at the start – who will be rewarded, punished, forgotten – and in light music the prepared ear can always guess the continuation after the first bars of a hit song and is gratified when it actually occurs. The average choice of words in a short story must not be tampered with. The gags and effects are no less calculated than their framework. They are managed by special experts, and their slim variety is specifically tailored to the office pigeonhole. The culture industry has developed in conjunction with the predominance of the effect, the tangible performance, the technical detail, over the work, which once carried the idea and was liquidated with it. By emancipating itself, the detail had become refractory; from Romanticism to Expressionism it had rebelled as unbridled expression, as the agent of opposition, against organization. In music, the individual harmonic effect had obliterated awareness of the form as a whole; in painting the particular detail had obscured the overall composition; in the novel psychological penetration had blurred the architecture. Through totality, the culture industry is putting an end to all that. Although operating only with effects, it subdues their unruliness and subordinates them to the formula which supplants the work. It crushes equally the whole and the parts. The whole confronts the details in implacable detachment: somewhat like the career of a successful man, in which everything serves to illustrate and demonstrate a success which, in fact, it is no more than the sum of those idiotic events. The so-called leading idea is a filing compartment which creates order, not connections. Lacking both contrast and relatedness, the whole and the detail look alike. Their harmony, guaranteed in advance, mocks the painfully achieved harmony of the great bourgeois works of art. In Germany even the most carefree films of democracy were overhung already by the graveyard stillness of dictatorship.

The whole world is passed through the filter of the culture industry. The familiar experience of the moviegoer, who perceives the street outside as a continuation of the film he has just left, because the film seeks strictly to reproduce the world of everyday perception, has become the guideline of production. The more densely and completely its techniques duplicate empirical objects, the more easily it creates the illusion that the world outside is a seamless extension of the one which has been revealed in the cinema. Since the abrupt introduction of the sound film, mechanical duplication has become entirely subservient to this objective. According to this tendency, life is to be made indistinguishable from the sound film. Far more strongly than the theatre of illusion, film denies its audience any dimension in which they might roam freely in imagination – contained by the film's framework but unsuper-vised by its precise actualities – without losing the thread; thus it trains those exposed to it to identify film directly with reality. The withering of imagination and spon-taneity in the consumer of culture today need not be traced back to psychological mechanisms. The products themselves, especially the most characteristic, the sound film, cripple those faculties through their objective makeup. They are so constructed that their adequate comprehension requires a quick, observant, knowledgeable cast of mind but positively debars the spectator from thinking, if he is not to miss the fleeting facts. This kind of alertness is so ingrained that it does not even need to be activated in particular cases, while still repressing the powers of imagination. Anyone who is so absorbed by the world of the film, by gesture, image, and word, that he or she is unable to supply that which would have made it a world in the first place, does not need to be entirely transfixed by the special operations of the machinery at the moment of the performance. The required qualities of attention have become so familiar from other films and other culture products already known to him or her that they appear automatically. The power of industrial society is imprinted on people once and for all. The products of the culture industry are such that they can be alertly consumed even in a state of distraction. But each one is a model of the gigantic economic machinery, which, from the first, keeps everyone on their toes, both at work and in the leisure time which resembles it. In any sound film or any radio broadcast something is discernible which cannot be attributed as a social effect to any one of them, but to all together. Each single manifestation of the culture industry inescapably reproduces human beings as what the whole has made them. And all its agents, from the producer to the women's organizations, are on the alert to ensure that the simple reproduction of mind does not lead on to the expansion of mind.

The complaints of art historians and cultural attorneys over the exhaustion of the energy which created artistic style in the West are frighteningly unfounded. The routine translation of everything, even of what has not yet been thought, into the schema of mechanical reproducibility goes beyond the rigor and scope of any true style – the concept with which culture lovers idealize the precapitalist past as an organic era. No Palestrina could have eliminated the unprepared or unresolved dissonance more puristically than the jazz arranger excludes any phrase which does not exactly fit the jargon. If he jazzes up Mozart, he changes the music not only where it is too difficult or serious but also where the melody is merely harmonized differently, indeed, more simply, than is usual today. No medieval patron of architecture can have scrutinized the subjects of church windows and sculptures more suspiciously than the studio hierarchies examine a plot by Balzac or Victor Hugo before it receives the imprimatur of feasibility. No cathedral chapter could have assigned the grimaces and torments of the damned to their proper places in the order of divine love more scrupulously than production managers decide the position of the torture of the hero or the raised hem of the leading lady's dress within the litany of the big film. The explicit and implicit, exoteric and esoteric catalog of what is forbidden and what is tolerated is so extensive that it not only defines the area left free but wholly controls it. Even the most minor details are modeled according to this lexicon. Like its adversary, avant-garde art, the culture industry defines its own language positively, by means of prohibitions applied to its syntax and vocabulary. The permanent compulsion to produce new effects which yet remain bound to the old schema, becoming additional rules, merely increases the power of the tradition which the individual effect seeks to escape. Every phenomenon is by now so thoroughly imprinted by the schema that nothing can occur that does not bear in advance the trace of the jargon, that is not seen at first glance to be approved. But the true masters, as both producers and reproducers, are those who speak the jargon with the same free-and-easy relish as if it were the language it has long since silenced. Such is the industry's ideal of naturalness. It asserts itself more imperiously the more the perfected technology reduces the tension between the culture product and everyday existence. The paradox of routine travestied as nature is detectable in every utterance of the culture industry, and in many is quite blatant. A jazz musician who has to play a piece of serious music, Beethoven's simplest minuet, involuntarily syncopates and condescends to start on the beat only with a superior smile. Such "naturalness," complicated by the ever more pervasive and exorbitant claims of the specific medium, constitutes the new style, "a system of nonculture to which one might even concede a certain 'unity of style' if it made any sense to speak of a stylized barbarism."[2]

The general influence of this stylization may already be more binding than the official rules and prohibitions; a hit song is treated more leniently today if it does not respect the thirty-two bars or the compass of the ninth than if it includes even the most elusive melodic or harmonic detail which falls outside the idiom. Orson Welles is forgiven all his offences against the usages of the craft because, as calculated rudeness, they confirm the validity of the system all the more zealously. The compulsion of the technically conditioned idiom which the stars and directors must produce as second nature, so that the nation may make it theirs, relates to nuances so fine as to be almost as subtle as the devices used in a work of the avant-garde, where, unlike those of the hit song, they serve truth. The rare ability to conform punctiliously to the obligations of the idiom of naturalness in all branches of the culture industry becomes the measure of expertise. As in logical positivism, what is said and how it is said must be verifiable against everyday speech. The producers are experts. The idiom demands the most prodigious productive powers, which it absorbs and squanders. Satanically, it has rendered cultural conservatism's distinction between genuine and artificial style obsolete. A style might possibly be called artificial if it had been imposed from outside against the resistance of the intrinsic tendencies of form. But in the culture industry the subject matter itself, down to its smallest elements, springs from the same apparatus as the jargon into which it is absorbed. The deals struck between the art specialists and the sponsor and censor over some all-too-unbelievable lie tell us less about internal, aesthetic tensions than about a divergence of interests. The reputation of the specialist, in which a last residue of actual autonomy still occasionally finds refuge, collides with the business policy of the church or the industrial combine producing the culture commodity. By its own nature, however, the matter has already been reified as negotiable even before the various agencies come into conflict. Even before Zanuck[3] acquired her, Saint Bernadette gleamed in the eye of her writer as an advert aimed at all the relevant consortia. To this the impulses of form have been reduced. As a result, the style of the culture industry, which has no resistant material to overcome, is at the same time the negation of style. The reconciliation of general and particular, of rules and the specific demands of the subject, through which alone style takes on substance, is nullified by the absence of tension between the poles: "the extremes which touch" have become a murky identity in which the general can replace the particular and vice versa.

Nevertheless, this caricature of style reveals something about the genuine style of the past. The concept of a genuine style becomes transparent in the culture industry as the aesthetic equivalent of power. The notion of style as a merely aesthetic regularity is a retrospective fantasy of Romanticism. The unity of style not only of the Christian Middle Ages but of the Renaissance expresses the different structures of social coercion in those periods, not the obscure experience of the subjects, in which the universal was locked away. The great artists were never those whose works embodied style in its least fractured, most perfect form but those who adopted style as a rigor to set against the chaotic expression of suffering, as a negative truth. In the style of these works expression took on the strength without which existence is dissipated unheard. Even works which are called classical, like the music of Mozart, contain objective tendencies which resist the style they incarnate. Up to Schönberg and Picasso, great artists have been mistrustful of style, which at decisive points has guided them less than the logic of the subject matter. What the Expressionists and Dadaists attacked in their polemics, the untruth of style as such, triumphs today in the vocal jargon of the crooner, in the adept grace of the film star, and even in the mastery of the photographic shot of a farm laborer's hovel. In every work of art, style is a promise. In being absorbed through style into the dominant form of universality; into the current musical, pictorial, or verbal idiom, what is expressed seeks to be reconciled with the idea of the true universal. This promise of the work of art to create truth by impressing its unique contours on the socially transmitted forms is as necessary as it is hypocritical. By claiming to anticipate fulfillment through their aesthetic derivatives, it posits the real forms of the existing order as absolute. To this extent the claims of art are always also ideology. Yet it is only in its struggle with tradition, a struggle precipitated in style, that art can find expression for suffering. The moment of the work of art by which it transcends reality cannot, indeed, be severed from style; that moment, however, does not consist in achieved harmony, in the questionable unity of form and content, inner and outer, individual and society, but in those traits in which the discrepancy emerges, in the necessary failure of the passionate striving for identity. Instead of exposing itself to this failure, in which the style of the great work of art has always negated itself, the inferior work has relied on its similarity to others, the surrogate of identity. The culture industry has finally posited this imitation as absolute. Being nothing other than style, it divulges style's secret: obedience to the social hierarchy. Aesthetic barbarism today is accomplishing what has threatened intellectual formations since they were brought together as culture and neutralized. To speak about culture always went against the grain of culture. The general designation "culture" already contains, virtually, the process of identifying, cataloging, and classifying which imports culture into the realm of administration. Only what has been industrialized, rigorously subsumed, is fully adequate to this concept of culture. Only by subordinating all branches of intellectual production equally to the single purpose of imposing on the senses of human beings, from the time they leave the factory in the evening to the time they clock on in the morning, the imprint of the work routine which they must sustain throughout the day, does this culture mockingly fulfill the notion of a unified culture which the philosophers of the individual personality held out against mass culture.

The culture industry, the most inflexible style of all, thus proves to be the goal of the very liberalism which is criticized for its lack of style. Not only did its categories and contents originate in the liberal sphere, in domesticated naturalism no less than in the operetta and the revue, but the modern culture combines are the economic area in which a piece of the circulation sphere otherwise in the process of disintegration, together with the corresponding entrepreneurial types, still tenuously survives. In that area people can still make their way, provided they do not look too closely at their true purpose and are willing to be compliant. Anyone who resists can survive only by being incorporated. Once registered as diverging from the culture industry, they belong to it as the land reformer does to capitalism. Realistic indignation is the trademark of those with a new idea to sell. Public authority in the present society allows only those complaints to be heard in which the attentive ear can discern the prominent figure under whose protection the rebel is suing for peace. The more immeasurable the gulf between chorus and leaders, the more certainly is there a place among the latter for anyone who demonstrates superiority by well-organized dissidence. In this way liberalism's tendency to give free rein to its ablest members survives in the culture industry. To open that industry to clever people is the function of the otherwise largely regulated market, in which, even in its heyday, freedom was the freedom of the stupid to starve, in art as elsewhere. Not for nothing did the system of the culture industry originate in the liberal industrial countries, just as all its characteristic media, especially cinema, radio, jazz, and magazines, also triumph there. Its progress, however, stems from the general laws of capital. Gaumont and Pathé,[4] Ullstein and Hugenberg[5] did not follow the international trend to their own disadvantage; Europe's economic dependence on the USA after the war and the inflation also made its contribution. The belief that the barbarism of the culture industry is a result of "cultural lag," of the backwardness of American consciousness in relation to the state of technology, is quite illusory. Prefascist Europe was backward in relation to the monopoly of culture. But it was precisely to such backwardness that intellectual activity owed a remnant of autonomy, its last exponents their livelihood, however meager. In Germany the incomplete permeation of life by democratic control had a paradoxical effect. Many areas were still exempt from the market mechanism which had been unleashed in Western countries. The German educational system, including the universities, the artistically influential theatres, the great orchestras, and the museums were under patronage. The political powers, the state and the local authorities who inherited such institutions from absolutism, had left them a degree of independence from the power of the market as the princes and feudal lords had done up to the nineteenth century. This stiffened the backbone of art in its late phase against the verdict of supply and demand, heightening its resistance far beyond its actual degree of protection. In the market itself the homage paid to not yet marketable artistic quality was converted into purchasing power, so that reputable literary and musical publishers could support authors who brought in little more than the respect of connoisseurs. Only the dire and incessant threat of incorporation into commercial life as aesthetic experts finally brought the artists to heel. In former times they signed their letters, like Kant and Hume, "Your most obedient servant," while undermining the foundations of throne and altar. Today they call heads of government by their first names and are subject, in every artistic impulse, to the judgment of their illiterate principals. The analysis offered by de Tocqueville a hundred years ago has been fully borne out in the meantime. Under the private monopoly of culture tyranny does indeed "leave the body free and sets to work directly on the soul. The ruler no longer says: 'Either you think as I do or you die.' He says: 'You are free not to think as I do; your life, your property – all that you shall keep. But from this day on you will be a stranger among us.'"[6] Anyone who does not conform is condemned to an economic impotence which is prolonged in the intellectual powerlessness of the eccentric loner. Disconnected from the mainstream, he is easily convicted of inadequacy. Whereas the mechanism of supply and demand is today disintegrating in material production, in the superstructure it acts as a control on behalf of the rulers. The consumers are the workers and salaried employees, the farmers and petty bourgeois. Capitalist production hems them in so tightly, in body and soul, that they unresistingly succumb to whatever is proffered to them. However, just as the ruled have always taken the morality dispensed to them by the rulers more seriously than the rulers themselves, the defrauded masses today cling to the myth of success still more ardently than the successful. They, too, have their aspirations. They insist unwaveringly on the ideology by which they are enslaved. The pernicious love of the common people for the harm done to them outstrips even the cunning of the authorities. It surpasses the rigor of the Hays Office,[7] just as, in great epochs, it has inspired renewed zeal in greater agencies directed against it, the terror of the tribunals. It calls for Mickey Rooney rather than the tragic Garbo, Donald Duck rather than Betty Boop. The industry bows to the vote it has itself rigged. The incidental costs to the firm which cannot turn a profit from its contract with a declining star are legitimate costs for the system as a whole. By artfully sanctioning the demand for trash, the system inaugurates total harmony. Connoisseurship and expertise are proscribed as the arrogance of those who think themselves superior, whereas culture distributes its privileges democratically to all. Under the ideological truce between them, the conformism of the consumers, like the shamelessness of the producers they sustain, can have a good conscience. Both content themselves with the reproduction of sameness.

Unending sameness also governs the relationship to the past. What is new in the phase of mass culture compared to that of late liberalism is the exclusion of the new. The machine is rotating on the spot. While it already determines consumption, it rejects anything untried as a risk. In film, any manuscript which is not reassuringly based on a best-seller is viewed with mistrust. That is why there is incessant talk of ideas, novelty and surprises, of what is both totally familiar and has never existed before. Tempo and dynamism are paramount. Nothing is allowed to stay as it was, everything must be endlessly in motion. For only the universal victory of the rhythm of mechanical production and reproduction promises that nothing will change, that nothing unsuitable will emerge. To add anything to the proven cultural inventory would be too speculative. The frozen genres – sketch, short story, problem film, hit song – represent the average of late liberal taste threateningly imposed as a norm. The most powerful of the culture agencies, who work harmoniously with others of their kind as only managers do, whether they come from the ready-to-wear trade or college, have long since reorganized and rationalized the objective mind. It is as if some omnipresent agency had reviewed the material and issued an authoritative catalog tersely listing the products available. The ideal forms are inscribed in the cultural heavens where they were already numbered by Plato – indeed, were only numbers incapable of increase or change.

Amusement and all the other elements of the culture industry existed long before the industry itself. Now they have been taken over from above and brought fully up to date. The culture industry can boast of having energetically accomplished and elevated to a principle the often inept transposition of art to the consumption sphere, of having stripped amusement of its obtrusive naiveties and improved the quality of its commodities. The more all-embracing the culture industry has become, the more pitilessly it has forced the outsider into either bankruptcy or a syndicate; at the same time it has become more refined and elevated, becoming finally a synthesis of Beethoven and the Casino de Paris.[8] Its victory is twofold: what is destroyed as truth outside its sphere can be reproduced indefinitely within it as lies. "Light" art as such, entertainment, is not a form of decadence. Those who deplore it as a betrayal of the ideal of pure expression harbor illusions about society. The purity of bour-geois art, hypostatized as a realm of freedom contrasting to material praxis, was bought from the outset with the exclusion of the lower class; and art keeps faith with the cause of that class, the true universal, precisely by freeing itself from the purposes of the false. Serious art has denied itself to those for whom the hardship and oppression of life make a mockery of seriousness and who must be glad to use the time not spent at the production line in being simply carried along. Light art has accompanied autonomous art as its shadow. It is the social bad conscience of serious art. The truth which the latter could not apprehend because of its social premises gives the former an appearance of objective justification. The split between them is itself the truth: it expresses at least the negativity of the culture which is the sum of both spheres. The antithesis can be reconciled least of all by absorbing light art into serious or vice versa. That, however, is what the culture industry attempts. The eccentricity of the circus, the peep show, or the brothel in relation to society is as embarrassing to it as that of Schönberg and Karl Kraus. The leading jazz musician Benny Goodman therefore has to appear with the Budapest String Quartet, more pedantic rhythmically than any amateur clarinetist, while the quartet play with the saccharine monotony of Guy Lombardo.[9] What is significant is not crude ignorance, stupidity or lack of polish. The culture industry has abolished the rubbish of former times by imposing its own perfection, by prohibiting and domesticating dilettantism, while itself incessantly committing the blunders without which the elevated style cannot be conceived. What is new, however, is that the irreconcilable elements of culture, art, and amusement have been subjected equally to the concept of purpose and thus brought under a single false denominator: the totality of the culture industry. Its element is repetition. The fact that its characteristic innovations are in all cases mere improvements to mass production is not extraneous to the system. With good reason the interest of countless consumers is focused on the technology, not on the rigidly repeated, threadbare and half-abandoned content. The social power revered by the spectators manifests itself more effectively in the technically enforced ubiquity of stereotypes than in the stale ideologies which the ephemeral contents have to endorse.

Nevertheless, the culture industry remains the entertainment business. Its control of consumers is mediated by entertainment, and its hold will not be broken by outright dictate but by the hostility inherent in the principle of entertainment to anything which is more than itself. Since the tendencies of the culture industry are turned into the flesh and blood of the public by the social process as a whole, those tendencies are reinforced by the survival of the market in the industry. Demand has not yet been replaced by simple obedience. The major reorganization of the film industry shortly before the First World War, the material precondition for its expansion, was a deliberate adaptation to needs of the public registered at the ticket office, which were hardly thought worthy of consideration in the pioneering days of the screen. That view is still held by the captains of the film industry, who accept only more or less phenomenal box-office success as evidence and prudently ignore the counterevidence, truth. Their ideology is business. In this they are right to the extent that the power of the culture industry lies in its unity with fabricated need and not in simple antithesis to it – or even in the antithesis between omnipotence and powerlessness. Entertainment is the prolongation of work under late capitalism. It is sought by those who want to escape the mechanized labor process so that they can cope with it again. At the same time, however, mechanization has such power over leisure and its happiness, determines so thoroughly the fabrication of entertainment commodities, that the off-duty worker can experience nothing but after-images of the work process itself. The ostensible content is merely a faded foreground; what is imprinted is the automated sequence of standardized tasks. The only escape from the work process in factory and office is through adaptation to it in leisure time. This is the incurable sickness of all entertainment. Amusement congeals into boredom, since, to be amusement, it must cost no effort and therefore moves strictly along the well-worn grooves of association. The spectator must need no thoughts of his own: the product prescribes each reaction, not through any actual adherence – which collapses once exposed to thought – but through signals. Any logical connection presupposing mental capacity is scrupulously avoided. Developments are to emerge from the directly preceding situation, not from the idea of the whole. There is no plot which could withstand the screenwriters' eagerness to extract the maximum effect from the individual scene. Finally, even the schematic formula seems dangerous, since it provides some coherence of meaning, however meager, when only meaninglessness is acceptable. Often the plot is willfully denied the development called for by characters and theme under the old schema. Instead, the next step is determined by what the writers take to be their most effective idea. Obtusely ingenious surprises disrupt the plot. The product's tendency to fall back perniciously on the pure nonsense which, as buffoonery and clowning, was a legitimate part of popular art up to Chaplin and the Marx brothers, emerges most strikingly in the less sophisticated genres. Whereas the films of Greer Garson and Bette Davis can still derive some claim to a coherent plot from the unity of the socio-psychological case represented, the tendency to subvert meaning has taken over completely in the text of novelty songs,[10] suspense films, and cartoons. The idea itself, like objects in comic and horror films, is massacred and mutilated. Novelty songs have always lived on contempt for meaning, which, as both ancestors and descendants of psychoanalysis, they reduce to the monotony of sexual symbolism. In crime and adventure films the spectators are begrudged even the opportunity to witness the resolution. Even in nonironic examples of the genre they must make do with the mere horror of situations connected in only the most perfunctory way.

Cartoon and stunt films were once exponents of fantasy against rationalism. They allowed justice to be done to the animals and things electrified by their technology, by granting the mutilated beings a second life. Today they merely confirm the victory of technological reason over truth. A few years ago they had solid plots which were resolved only in the whirl of pursuit of the final minutes. In this their procedure resembled that of slapstick comedy. But now the temporal relations have shifted. The opening sequences state a plot motif so that destruction can work on it throughout the action: with the audience in gleeful pursuit the protagonist is tossed about like a scrap of litter. The quantity of organized amusement is converted into the quality of organized cruelty. The self-elected censors of the film industry, its accomplices, monitor the duration of the atrocity prolonged into a hunt. The jollity dispels the joy supposedly conferred by the sight of an embrace and postpones satisfaction until the day of the pogrom. To the extent that cartoons do more than accustom the senses to the new tempo, they hammer into every brain the old lesson that continuous attrition, the breaking of all individual resistance, is the condition of life in this society. Donald Duck in the cartoons and the unfortunate victim in real life receive their beatings so that the spectators can accustom themselves to theirs.

The enjoyment of the violence done to the film character turns into violence against the spectator; distraction becomes exertion. No stimulant concocted by the experts may escape the weary eye; in face of the slick presentation no one may appear stupid even for a moment; everyone has to keep up, emulating the smartness displayed and propagated by the production. This makes it doubtful whether the culture industry even still fulfils its self-proclaimed function of distraction. If the majority of radio stations and cinemas were shut down, consumers probably would not feel too much deprived. In stepping from the street into the cinema, they no longer enter the world of dream in any case, and once the use of these institutions was no longer made obligatory by their mere existence, the urge to use them might not be so overwhelming.[11] Shutting them down in this way would not be reactionary machine-wrecking. Those who suffered would not be the film enthusiasts but those who always pay the penalty in any case, the ones who had lagged behind. For the housewife, despite the films which are supposed to integrate her still further, the dark of the cinema grants a refuge in which she can spend a few unsupervised hours, just as once, when there were still dwellings and evening repose, she could sit gazing out of the window. The unemployed of the great centers find freshness in summer and warmth in winter in these places of regulated temperature. Apart from that, and even by the measure of the existing order, the bloated entertainment apparatus does not make life more worthy of human beings. The idea of "exploiting" the given technical possibilities, of fully utilizing the capacities for aesthetic mass consumption, is part of an economic system which refuses to utilize capacities when it is a question of abolishing hunger.

The culture industry endlessly cheats its consumers out of what it endlessly promises. The promissory note of pleasure issued by plot and packaging is indefinitely prolonged: the promise, which actually comprises the entire show, disdainfully intimates that there is nothing more to come, that the diner must be satisfied with reading the menu. The desire inflamed by the glossy names and images is served up finally with a celebration of the daily round it sought to escape. Of course, genuine works of art were not sexual exhibitions either. But by presenting denial as negative, they reversed, as it were, the debasement of the drive and rescued by mediation what had been denied. That is the secret of aesthetic sublimation: to present fulfillment in its brokenness. The culture industry does not sublimate: it suppresses. By constantly exhibiting the object of desire, the breasts beneath the sweater, the naked torso of the sporting hero, it merely goads the unsublimated anticipation of pleasure, which through the habit of denial has long since been mutilated as masochism. There is no erotic situation in which innuendo and incitement are not accompanied by the clear notification that things will never go so far. The Hays Office merely confirms the ritual which the culture industry has staged in any case: that of Tantalus. Works of art are ascetic and shameless; the culture industry is pornographic and prudish. It reduces love to romance. And, once reduced, much is permitted, even libertinage as a marketable specialty, purveyed by quota with the trade description "daring." The mass production of sexuality automatically brings about its repression. Because of his ubiquity, the film star with whom one is supposed to fall in love is, from the start, a copy of himself. Every tenor now sounds like a Caruso record, and the natural faces of Texas girls already resemble those of the established models by which they would be typecast in Hollywood. The mechanical reproduction of beauty – which, admittedly, is made only more inescapable by the reactionary culture zealots with their methodical idolization of individuality – no longer leaves any room for the unconscious idolatry with which the experience of beauty has always been linked. The triumph over beauty is completed by humor, the malicious pleasure elicited by any successful deprivation. There is laughter because there is nothing to laugh about. Laughter, whether reconciled or terrible, always accompanies the moment when a fear is ended. It indicates a release, whether from physical danger or from the grip of logic. Reconciled laughter resounds with the echo of escape from power; wrong laughter copes with fear by defecting to the agencies which inspire it. It echoes the inescapability of power. Fun is a medicinal bath which the entertainment industry never ceases to prescribe. It makes laughter the instrument for cheating happiness. To moments of happiness laughter is foreign; only operettas, and now films, present sex amid peals of merriment. But Baudelaire is as humorless as Hölderlin. In wrong society laughter is a sickness infecting happiness and drawing it into society's worthless totality. Laughter about something is always laughter at it, and the vital force which, according to Bergson, bursts through rigidity in laughter is, in truth, the irruption of barbarity, the self-assertion which, in convivial settings, dares to celebrate its liberation from scruple. The collective of those who laugh parodies humanity. They are monads, each abandoning himself to the pleasure – at the expense of all others and with the majority in support – of being ready to shrink from nothing. Their harmony presents a caricature of solidarity. What is infernal about wrong laughter is that it compellingly parodies what is best, reconciliation. Joy, however, is austere: *res severa verum gaudium*.[12] The ideology of monasteries, that it is not asceticism but the sexual act which marks the renunciation of attainable bliss, is negatively confirmed by the gravity of the lover who presciently pins his whole life to the fleeting moment. The culture industry replaces pain, which is present in ecstasy no less than in asceticism, with jovial denial. Its supreme law is that its consumers shall at no price be given what they desire: and in that very deprivation they must take their laughing satisfaction. In each performance of the culture industry the permanent denial imposed by civilization is once more inflicted on and unmistakably demonstrated to its victims. To offer them something and to withhold it is one and the same. That is what the erotic commotion achieves. Just because it can never take place, everything revolves around the coitus. In film, to allow an illicit relationship without due punishment of the culprits is even more strictly tabooed than it is for the future son-in-law of a millionaire to be active in the workers' movement. Unlike that of the liberal era, industrial no less than nationalist culture can permit itself to inveigh against capitalism, but not to renounce the threat of castration. This threat constitutes its essence. It outlasts the organized relaxation of morals toward the wearers of uniforms, first in the jaunty films produced for them and then in reality. What is decisive today is no longer Puritanism, though it still asserts itself in the form of women's organizations, but the necessity, inherent in the system, of never releasing its grip on the consumer, of not for a moment allowing him or her to suspect that resistance is possible. This principle requires that while all needs should be presented to individuals as capable of fulfillment by the culture industry, they should be so set up in advance that individuals experience themselves through their needs only as eternal consumers, as the culture industry's object. Not only does it persuade them that its fraud is satisfaction; it also gives them to understand that they must make do with what is offered, whatever it may be. The flight from the everyday world, promised by the culture industry in all its branches, is much like the abduction of the daughter in the American cartoon: the father is holding the ladder in the dark. The culture industry presents that same everyday world as paradise. Escape, like elopement, is destined from the first to lead back to its starting point. Entertainment fosters the resignation which seeks to forget itself in entertainment.

Amusement, free of all restraint, would be not only the opposite of art but its complementary extreme. Absurdity in the manner of Mark Twain, with which the American culture industry flirts from time to time, could be a corrective to art. The more seriously art takes its opposition to existence, the more it resembles the seriousness of existence, its antithesis: the more it labors to develop strictly according to its own formal laws, the more labor it requires to be understood, whereas its goal had been precisely to negate the burden of labor. In some revue films, and especially in grotesque stories and "funnies,"[13] the possibility of this negation is momentarily glimpsed. Its realization, of course, cannot be allowed. Pure amusement indulged to the full, relaxed abandon to colorful associations and merry nonsense, is cut short by amusement in its marketable form: it is disrupted by the surrogate of a coherent meaning with which the culture industry insists on endowing its products while at the same time slyly misusing them as pretexts for bringing on the stars. Biographies and other fables stitch together the scraps of nonsense into a feeble-minded plot. It is not the bells on the fool's cap that jingle but the bunch of keys of capitalist reason, which even in its images harnesses joy to the purpose of getting ahead. Every kiss in the revue film must contribute to the career of the boxer or hit-song expert whose success is being glorified. The deception is not that the culture industry serves up amusement but that it spoils the fun by its business-minded attachment to the ideological clichés of the culture which is liquidating itself. Ethics and taste suppress unbridled amusement as "naïve" – naivety being rated no more highly than intellectualism – and even restrict its technical possibilities. The culture industry is corrupt, not as a sink of iniquity but as the cathedral of higher gratification. At all its levels, from Hemingway to Emil Ludwig,[14] from Mrs. Miniver[15] to the Lone Ranger,[16] from Toscanini to Guy Lombardo, intellectual products drawn ready-made from art and science are infected with untruth. Traces of something better persist in those features of the culture industry by which it resembles the circus – in the stubbornly purposeless expertise of riders, acrobats, and clowns, in the "defense and justification of physical as against intellectual art."[17] But the hiding places of mindless artistry, which represents what is human against the social mechanism, are being relentlessly ferreted out by organizational reason, which forces everything to justify itself in terms of meaning and effect. It is causing meaninglessness to disappear at the lowest level of art just as radically as meaning is disappearing at the highest.

The fusion of culture and entertainment is brought about today not only by the debasement of culture but equally by the compulsory intellectualization of amusement. This is already evident in the fact that amusement is now experienced only in facsimile, in the form of cinema photography or the radio recording. In the age of liberal expansion amusement was sustained by an unbroken belief in the future: things would stay the same yet get better. Today, that belief has itself been intellectualized, becoming so refined as to lose sight of all actual goals and to consist only in a golden shimmer projected beyond the real. It is composed of the extra touches of meaning – running exactly parallel to life itself – applied in the screen world to the good guy, the engineer, the decent girl, and also to the ruthlessness disguised as character, to the sporting interest, and finally to the cars and cigarettes, even where the entertainment does not directly serve the publicity needs of the manufacture concerned but advertises the system as a whole. Amusement itself becomes an ideal, taking the place of the higher values it eradicates from the masses by repeating them in an even more stereotyped form than the advertising slogans paid for by private interests. Inwardness, the subjectively restricted form of truth, was always more beholden to the outward rulers than it imagined. The culture industry is perverting it into a barefaced lie. It appears now only as the high-minded prattle tolerated by consumers of religious bestsellers, psychological films, and women's serials as an embarrassingly agreeable ingredient, so that they can more reliably control their own human emotions. In this sense entertainment is purging the affects in the manner once attributed by Aristotle to tragedy and now by Mortimer Adler[18] to film. The culture industry reveals the truth not only about style but also about catharsis.

The more strongly the culture industry entrenches itself, the more it can do as it chooses with the needs of consumers – producing, controlling, disciplining them; even withdrawing amusement altogether: here, no limits are set to cultural progress. But the tendency is immanent in the principle of entertainment itself, as a principle of bourgeois enlightenment. If the need for entertainment was largely created by industry, which recommended the work to the masses through its subject matter, the oleograph through the delicate morsel it portrayed and, conversely, the pudding mix through the image of a pudding, entertainment has always borne the trace of commercial brashness, of sales talk, the voice of the fairground huckster. But the original affinity between business and entertainment reveals itself in the meaning of entertainment itself: as society's apologia. To be entertained means to be in agreement. Entertainment makes itself possible only by insulating itself from the totality of the social process, making itself stupid and perversely renouncing from the first the inescapable claim of any work, even the most trivial: in its restrictedness to reflect the whole. Amusement always means putting things out of mind, forgetting suffering, even when it is on display. At its root is powerlessness. It is indeed escape, but not, as it claims, escape from bad reality but from the last thought of resisting that reality. The liberation which amusement promises is from thinking as negation. The shamelessness of the rhetorical question "What do people want?" lies in the fact that it appeals to the very people as thinking subjects whose subjectivity it specifically seeks to annul. Even on those occasions when the public rebels against the pleasure industry it displays the feebleness systematically instilled in it by that industry. Nevertheless, it has become increasingly difficult to keep the public in submission. The advance of stupidity must not lag behind the simultaneous advance of intelligence. In the age of statistics the masses are too astute to identify with the millionaire on the screen and too obtuse to deviate even minutely from the law of large numbers. Ideology hides itself in probability calculations. Fortune will not smile on all – just on the one who draws the winning ticket or, rather, the one designated to do so by a higher power – usually the entertainment industry itself, which presents itself as ceaselessly in search of talent. Those discovered by the talent scouts and then built up by the studios are ideal types of the new, dependent middle classes. The female starlet is supposed to symbolize the secretary, though in a way which makes her seem predestined, unlike the real secretary, to wear the flowing evening gown. Thus she apprises the female spectator not only of the possibility that she, too, might appear on the screen but still more insistently of the distance between them. Only one can draw the winning lot, only one is prominent, and even though all have mathematically the same chance, it is so minimal for each individual that it is best to write it off at once and rejoice in the good fortune of someone else, who might just as well be oneself but never is. Where the culture industry still invites naïve identification, it immediately denies it. It is no longer possible to lose oneself in others. Once, film spectators saw their own wedding in that of others. Now the happy couple on the screen are specimens of the same species as everyone in the audience, but the sameness posits the insuperable separation of its human elements. The perfected similarity is the absolute difference. The identity of the species prohibits that of the individual cases. The culture industry has sardonically realized man's species being. Everyone amounts only to those qualities by which he or she can replace everyone else: all are fungible, mere specimens. As individuals they are absolutely replaceable, pure nothingness, and are made aware of this as soon as time deprives them of their sameness. This changes the inner composition of the religion of success, which they are sternly required to uphold. The path *per aspera ad astra*, which presupposes need and effort, is increasingly replaced by the prize. The element of blindness in the routine decision as to which song is to be a hit, which extra a heroine, is celebrated by ideology. Films emphasize chance. By imposing an essential sameness on their characters, with the exception of the villain, to the point of excluding any faces which do not conform – for example, those which, like Garbo's, do not look as if they would welcome the greeting "Hello, sister" – the ideology does, it is true, make life initially easier for the spectators. They are assured that they do not need to be in any way other than they are and that they can succeed just as well without having to perform tasks of which they know themselves incapable. But at the same time they are given the hint that effort would not help them in any case, because even bourgeois success no longer has any connection to the calculable effect of their own work. They take the hint. Fundamentally, everyone recognizes chance, by which someone is sometimes lucky, as the other side of planning. Just because society's energies have developed so far on the side of rationality that anyone might become an engineer or a manager, the choice of who is to receive from society the investment and confidence to be trained for such functions becomes entirely irrational. Chance and planning become identical since, given the sameness of people, the fortune or misfortune of the individual, right up to the top, loses all economic importance. Chance itself is planned; not in the sense that it will affect this or that particular individual but in that people believe in its control. For the planners it serves as an alibi, giving the impression that the web of transactions and measures into which life has been transformed still leaves room for spontaneous, immediate relationships between human beings. Such freedom is symbolized in the various media of the culture industry by the arbitrary selection of average cases. In the detailed reports on the modestly luxurious pleasure trip organized by the magazine for the lucky competition winner – preferably a shorthand typist who probably won through contacts with local powers-that-be – the powerlessness of everyone is reflected. So much are the masses mere material that those in control can raise one of them up to their heaven and cast him or her out again: let them go hang with their justice and their labor. Industry is interested in human beings only as its customers and employees and has in fact reduced humanity as a whole, like each of its elements, to this exhaustive formula. Depending on which aspect happens to be paramount at the time, ideology stresses plan or chance, technology or life, civilization or nature. As employees people are reminded of the rational organization and must fit into it as common sense requires. As customers they are regaled, whether on the screen or in the press, with human interest stories demonstrating freedom of choice and the charm of not belonging to the system. In both cases they remain objects.

The less the culture industry has to promise and the less it can offer a meaningful explanation of life, the emptier the ideology it disseminates necessarily becomes. Even the abstract ideals of the harmony and benevolence of society are too concrete in the age of the universal advertisement. Abstractions in particular are identified as publicity devices. Language which appeals to mere truth only arouses impatience to get down to the real business behind it. Words which are not a means seem meaningless, the others seem to be fiction, untruth. Value judgments are perceived either as advertisements or as mere chatter. The noncommittal vagueness of the resulting ideology does not make it more transparent, or weaker. Its very vagueness, the quasiscientific reluctance to be pinned down to anything which cannot be verified,

functions as an instrument of control. Ideology becomes the emphatic and systematic proclamation of what is. Through its inherent tendency to adopt the tone of the
factual report, the culture industry makes itself the irrefutable prophet of the existing
order. With consummate skill it maneuvers between the crags of demonstrable
misinformation and obvious truth by faithfully duplicating appearances, the density
of which blocks insight. Thus the omnipresent and impenetrable world of appearances is set up as the ideal. Ideology is split between the photographing of brute
existence and the blatant lie about its meaning, a lie which is not articulated directly
but drummed in by suggestion. The mere cynical reiteration of the real is enough to
demonstrate its divinity. Such photological proof[19] may not be stringent, but it is
overwhelming. Anyone who continues to doubt in face of the power of monotony is
a fool. The culture industry sweeps aside objections to itself along with those to the
world it neutrally duplicates. One has only the choice of conforming or being
consigned to the backwoods: the provincials who oppose cinema and radio by falling
back on eternal beauty and amateur theatricals have already reached the political
stance toward which the members of mass culture are still being driven. This culture
is hardened enough either to poke fun at the old wishful dreams, the paternal ideal
no less than unconditional feeling, or to invoke them as ideology, as the occasion
demands. The new ideology has the world as such as its subject. It exploits the cult
of fact by describing bad existence with utmost exactitude in order to elevate it into
the realm of facts. Through such elevation existence itself becomes a surrogate of
meaning and justice. Beauty is whatever the camera reproduces. The disappointed hope
that one might oneself be the employee who won the world trip is matched by the
disappointing appearance of the exactly photographed regions through which
the journey might have led. What is offered is not Italy but evidence that it exists.
The film can permit itself to show the Paris in which the young American woman
hopes to still her longing as a desolately barren place, in order to drive her all the
more implacably into the arms of the smart American boy she might equally well
have met at home. That life goes on at all, that the system, even in its most recent
phase, reproduces the lives of those who constitute it instead of doing away with
them straight away, is even credited to the system as its meaning and value. The
ability to keep going at all becomes the justification for the blind continuation of the
system, indeed, for its immutability. What is repeated is healthy – the cycle in nature
as in industry. The same babies grin endlessly from magazines, and endlessly the jazz
machine pounds. Despite all the progress in the techniques of representation, all the
rules and specialties, all the gesticulating bustle, the bread on which the culture
industry feeds humanity, remains the stone of stereotype. It lives on the cyclical, on
the admittedly well-founded amazement that, in spite of everything, mothers still
give birth to children, that the wheels have not yet come completely to a halt. All
this consolidates the immutability of the existing circumstances. The swaying corn-
fields at the end of Chaplin's film on Hitler give the lie to the anti-fascist speech
about freedom. They resemble the blond tresses of the German maidens whose
outdoor life in the summer wind is photographed by Ufa. Nature, in being presented by society's control mechanism as the healing antithesis of society, is itself
absorbed into that incurable society and sold off. The solemn pictorial affirmation

that the trees are green, the sky is blue, and the clouds are sailing overhead already
makes them cryptograms for factory chimneys and gasoline stations. Conversely,
wheels and machine parts are made to gleam expressively, debased as receptacles of
that leafy, cloudy soul. In this way both nature and technology are mobilized against
the alleged stuffiness, the faked recollection of liberal society as a world in which
people idled lasciviously in plush-lined rooms instead of taking wholesome open-air
baths as they do today, or suffered breakdowns in antediluvian Benz models instead
of traveling at rocket speed from where they are in any case to where it is no different. The triumph of the giant corporation over entrepreneurial initiative is celebrated
by the culture industry as the perpetuity of entrepreneurial initiative. The fight is
waged against an enemy who has already been defeated, the thinking subject. The
resurrection of *Hans Sonnenstößer*,[20] the enemy of bourgeois philistines, in Germany,
and the smug coziness of *Life with Father*[21] have one and the same meaning.

On one matter, however, this hollow ideology is utterly serious: everyone is
provided for. "No one must be hungry or cold. Anyone failing to comply goes to a
concentration camp." The joke from Hitler's Germany might well shine out as a
maxim above all the portals of the culture industry. With naïve shrewdness it anticipates the situation characteristic of the latest society: that it knows how to identify its
true supporters. Formal freedom is guaranteed for everyone. No one has to answer
officially for what he or she thinks. However, all find themselves enclosed from early
on within a system of churches, clubs, professional associations, and other relationships which amount to the most sensitive instrument of social control. Anyone who
wants to avoid ruin must take care not to weigh too little in the scales of this
apparatus. Otherwise he will fall behind in life and finally go under. The fact that in
every career, and especially in the liberal professions, specialist knowledge as a rule
goes hand in hand with a prescribed set of attitudes easily gives the misleading
impression that expert knowledge is all that counts. In reality, it is a feature of the
irrationally systematic nature of this society that it reproduces, passably, only the
lives of its loyal members. The gradations in the standard of living correspond very
precisely to the degree by which classes and individuals inwardly adhere to the
system. Managers can be relied on; even the minor employee Dagwood,[22] who lives
in reality no less than in the comic strip, is reliable. But anyone who goes hungry
and suffers from cold, especially if he once had good prospects, is a marked man. He
is an outsider, and – with the occasional exception of the capital crime – to be an
outsider is the gravest guilt. In films such a person is, at best, an eccentric, an object
of maliciously indulgent humor; but mostly he is a villain and is identified as such on
his very first appearance, long before the action requires it, to forestall even the
momentary misapprehension that society turns against those of good will. In fact, a
kind of welfare state on a higher level is being established today. To assert their
positions people keep in motion an economy in which the extreme development of
technology has made the masses in principle superfluous as producers in their own
country. According to the ideological illusion, the workers, the true providers, are
fed by the leaders of industry, whom they feed. Thus the position of the individual
becomes precarious. Under liberalism the poor were regarded as lazy; today they are

automatically suspect. Anyone who is not provided for outside the concentration camp belongs inside it, or at any rate in the hell of the most demeaning labor and the slums. The culture industry, however, reflects society's positive and negative provision for those it administers as direct human solidarity in the world of honest folk. No one is forgotten, everywhere are neighbors, social welfare officers, Dr Gillespies, and armchair philosophers with their hearts in the right place who, with their kindly man-to-man interventions, turn the socially perpetuated wretchedness into remediable individual cases, unless even that is ruled out by the personal depravity of those concerned. The managed provision of friendly care, administered by every factory as a means of increasing production, brings the last private impulse under social control; by being given the appearance of immediacy, the relationships of people within production are returned to the private sphere. Such "winter aid"[23] casts its conciliatory shadow over the films and broadcasts of the culture industry long before such care is transferred in totalitarian style from the factory to society itself. The great helpers and benefactors of humanity, whose scholarly and scientific achievements have to be embellished by scriptwriters as simple acts of compassion to wring from them a fictitious human interest, function as stand-ins for the leaders of nations who ultimately decree the abolition of compassion and succeed in preventing all infections by exterminating the last of the sick.

The emphasis on the heart of gold is society's way of admitting the suffering it creates: everyone knows that they are helpless within the system, and ideology must take account of this. Far from merely concealing the suffering under the cloak of improvised comradeship, the culture industry stakes its company pride on looking it manfully in the eye and acknowledging it with unflinching composure. This posture of steadfast endurance justifies the world which that posture makes necessary. Such is the world – so hard, yet therefore so wonderful, so healthy. The lie does not shrink back even from tragedy. Just as totalitarian society does not abolish the suffering of its members, but registers and plans it, mass culture does the same with tragedy. Hence the persistent borrowings from art. Art supplies the tragic substance which pure entertainment cannot provide on its own yet which it needs if it is to adhere to its principle of meticulously duplicating appearance. Tragedy, included in society's calculations and affirmed as a moment of the world, becomes a blessing. It deflects the charge that truth is glossed over, whereas in fact it is appropriated with cynical regret. It imparts an element of interest to the insipidity of censored happiness and makes that interest manageable. To the consumer who has seen culturally better days it offers the surrogate of long-abolished depth, and to regular moviegoers the veneer of culture they need for purposes of prestige. To all it grants the solace that human fate in its strength and authenticity is possible even now and its unflinching depiction inescapable. The unbroken surface of existence, in the duplication of which ideology consists solely today, appears all the more splendid, glorious, and imposing the more it is imbued with necessary suffering. It takes on the aspect of fate. Tragedy is leveled down to the threat to destroy anyone who does not conform, whereas its paradoxical meaning once lay in hopeless resistance to mythical threat. Tragic fate becomes the just punishment into which bourgeois aesthetics has always longed to transform it. The morality of mass culture has come down to it from yesterday's children's books. In the first-class production the villain is dressed up as the hysteric who, in a study of ostensibly clinical exactitude, seeks to trick her more realistic rival out of her life's happiness and who herself suffers a quite untheatrical death. To be sure, only at the top are things managed as scientifically as this. Further down, the resources are scarcer. There tragedy has its teeth drawn without social psychology. Just as any honest Hungarian-Viennese operetta must have its tragic finale in the second act, leaving nothing for the third but the righting of misunderstandings, mass culture gives tragedy permanent employment as routine. The obvious existence of a formula is enough in itself to allay the concern that tragedy might still be untamed. The housewife's description of the recipe for drama as "getting into trouble and out again" encompasses the whole of mass culture from the weak-minded women's serial to its highest productions. Even the worst outcome, which once had better intentions, still confirms the established order and corrupts tragedy, whether because the irregular lover pays for her brief happiness with death or because the sad end in the picture makes the indestructibility of actual life shine all the more brightly. Tragic cinema is becoming truly a house of moral correction. The masses, demoralized by existence under the pressure of the system and manifesting civilization only as compulsively rehearsed behavior in which rage and rebelliousness everywhere show through, are to be kept in order by the spectacle of implacable life and the exemplary conduct of those it crushes. Culture has always contributed to the subduing of revolutionary as well as of barbaric instincts. Industrial culture does something more. It inculcates the conditions on which implacable life is allowed to be lived at all. Individuals must use their general satiety as a motive for abandoning themselves to the collective power of which they are sated. The permanently hopeless situations which grind down filmgoers in daily life are transformed by their reproduction, in some unknown way, into a promise that they may continue to exist. One needs only to become aware of one's nullity, to subscribe to one's own defeat, and one is already a party to it. Society is made up of the desperate and thus falls prey to rackets. In a few of the most significant German novels of the prefascistic era, such as *Berlin Alexanderplatz* and *Kleiner Mann, was nun?*, this tendency was as vividly evident as in the mediocre film and in the procedures of jazz. Fundamentally, they all present the self-mockery of man. The possibility of becoming an economic subject, an entrepreneur, a proprietor, is entirely liquidated. Right down to the small grocery, the independent firm on the running and inheriting of which the bourgeois family and the position of its head were founded, has fallen into hopeless dependence. All have become employees, and in the civilization of employees the dignity of the father, dubious in any case, ceases to be. The behavior of the individual toward the racket, whether commercial, professional, or political, both before and after admittance to it; the gestures of the leader before the masses, of the lover before the woman he woos, are taking on peculiarly masochistic traits. The attitude all are forced to adopt in order to demonstrate ever again their moral fitness for this society is reminiscent of that of boys during admission to a tribe; circling under the blows of the priest, they wear stereotypical smiles. Existence in late capitalism is a permanent rite of initiation. Everyone must show that they identify wholeheartedly with the power which beats them. This is inherent in the principle of syncopation in jazz, which mocks the act of stumbling while elevating it to the norm. The eunuch-like voice of the radio crooner, the handsome suitor of the heiress, who falls into the swimming pool wearing his tuxedo, are models for those who want to make themselves into that to which the system breaks them. Everyone can be like the omnipotent society, everyone can be happy if only they hand themselves over to it body and soul and relinquish their claim to happiness. In their weakness society recognizes its own strength and passes some of it back to them. Their lack of resistance certifies them as reliable customers. Thus is tragedy abolished. Once, the antithesis between individual and society made up its substance. Tragedy glorified "courage and freedom of feeling in face of a mighty foe, sublime adversity, a problem which awakened dread.[24] Today tragedy has been dissipated in the void of the false identity of society and subject, the horror of which is still just fleetingly visible in the vacuous semblance of the tragic. But the miracle of integration, the permanent benevolence of those in command, who admit the unresisting subject while he chokes down his unruliness – all this signifies fascism. Fascism lurks in the humaneness with which Döblin allows his protagonist Biberkopf to find refuge, no less than in films with a social slant. The ability to slip through, to survive one's own ruin, which has superseded tragedy, is ingrained in the new generation; its members are capable of any work, since the work process allows them to become attached to none. One is reminded of the sad pliability of the soldier returning home, unaffected by the war, of the casual laborer who finally joins the clandestine groups and the paramilitary organizations. The liquidation of tragedy confirms the abolition of the individual.

It is not only the standardized mode of production of the culture industry which makes the individual illusory in its products. Individuals are tolerated only as far as their wholehearted identity with the universal is beyond question. From the standardized improvisation in jazz to the original film personality who must have a lock of hair straying over her eyes so that she can be recognized as such, pseudoindividuality reigns. The individual trait is reduced to the ability of the universal so completely to mold the accidental that it can be recognized as accidental. The sulky taciturnity or the elegant walk of the individual who happens to be on show is serially produced like the Yale locks which differ by fractions of a millimeter. The peculiarity of the self is a socially conditioned monopoly commodity misrepresented as natural. It is reduced to the moustache, the French accent, the deep voice of the prostitute, the "Lubitsch touch" – like a fingerprint on the otherwise uniform identity cards to which the lives and faces of all individuals, from the film star to the convict, have been reduced by the power of the universal. Pseudoindividuality is a precondition for apprehending and detoxifying tragedy: only because individuals are none but mere intersections of universal tendencies is it possible to reabsorb them smoothly into the universal. Mass culture thereby reveals the fictitious quality which has characterized the individual throughout the bourgeois era and is wrong only in priding itself on this murky harmony between universal and particular. The principle of individuality was contradictory from the outset. First, no individuation was ever really achieved. The class-determined form of self preservation maintained everyone at the level of mere species being. Every bourgeois character expressed the same thing, even and especially when deviating from it: the harshness of competitive society. The individual, on whom society was supported, itself bore society's taint; in the individual's apparent freedom he was the product of society's economic and social apparatus. Power has always invoked the existing power relationships when seeking the approval of those subjected to power. At the same time, the advance of bourgeois society has promoted the development of the individual. Against the will of those controlling it, technology has changed human beings from children into persons. But all such progress of individuation has been at the expense of the individuality in whose name it took place, leaving behind nothing except individuals' determination to pursue their own purposes alone. The citizens whose lives are split between business and private life, their private life between ostentation and intimacy, their intimacy between the sullen community of marriage and the bitter solace of being entirely alone, at odds with themselves and with everyone, are virtually already Nazis, who are at once enthusiastic and fed up, or the city dwellers of today, who can imagine friendship only as "social contact" between the inwardly unconnected. The culture industry can only manipulate individuality so successfully because the fractured nature of society has always been reproduced within it. In the ready-made faces of film heroes and private persons fabricated according to magazine-cover stereotypes, a semblance of individuality – in which no one believes in any case – is fading, and the love for such hero-models is nourished by the secret satisfaction that the effort of individuation is at last being replaced by the admittedly more breathless one of imitation. The hope that the contradictory, disintegrating person could not survive for generations, that the psychological fracture within it must split the system itself, and that human beings might refuse to tolerate the mendacious substitution of the stereotype for the individual – that hope is vain. The unity of the personality has been recognized as illusory since Shakespeare's Hamlet. In the synthetically manufactured physiognomies of today the fact that the concept of human life ever existed is already forgotten. For centuries society has prepared for Victor Mature and Mickey Rooney. They come to fulfill the very individuality they destroy.

The heroizing of the average forms part of the cult of cheapness. The highest-paid stars resemble advertisements for unnamed merchandise. Not for nothing are they often chosen from the ranks of commercial models. The dominant taste derives its ideal from the advertisement, from commodified beauty. Socrates' dictum that beauty is the useful has at last been ironically fulfilled. The cinema publicizes the cultural conglomerate as a totality, while the radio advertises individually the products for whose sake the cultural system exists. For a few coins you can see the film which cost millions, for even less you can buy the chewing gum behind which stand the entire riches of the world, and the sales of which increase those riches still further. Through universal suffrage the vast funding of armies is generally known and approved, if *in absentia*, while prostitution behind the lines is not permitted. The best orchestras in the world, which are none, are delivered free of charge to the home. All this mockingly resembles the land of milk and honey as the national community apes the human one. Something is served up for everyone. A provincial visitor's comment on the old Berlin Metropoltheater that "it is remarkable what can be done for the money" has long since been adopted by the culture industry and elevated to the substance of production itself. Not only is a production always accompanied by triumphant celebration that it has been possible at all, but to a large extent it is that triumph itself. To put on a show means to show everyone what one has and can do. The show is still a fairground, but one incurably infected by culture. Just as people lured by the fairground crier overcame their disappointment inside the booths with a brave smile, since they expected it in any case, the movie-goer remains tolerantly loyal to the institution. But the cheapness of mass-produced luxury articles, and its complement, universal fraud, are changing the commodity character of art itself. That character is not new: it is the fact that art now dutifully admits to being a commodity, abjures its autonomy and proudly takes its place among consumer goods, that has the charm of novelty. Art was only ever able to exist as a separate sphere in its bourgeois form. Even its freedom, as negation of the social utility which is establishing itself through the market, is essentially conditioned by the commodity economy. Pure works of art, which negated the commodity character of society by simply following their own inherent laws, were at the same time always commodities. To the extent that, up to the eighteenth century, artists were protected from the market by patronage, they were subject to the patrons and their purposes instead. The purposelessness of the great modern work of art is sustained by the anonymity of the market. The latter's demands are so diversely mediated that the artist is exempted from any particular claim, although only to a certain degree, since his autonomy, being merely tolerated, has been attended throughout bourgeois history by a moment of untruth, which has culminated now in the social liquidation of art. The mortally sick Beethoven, who flung away a novel by Walter Scott with the cry: "The fellow writes for money," while himself proving an extremely experienced and tenacious businessman in commercializing the last quartets – works representing the most extreme repudiation of the market – offers the most grandiose example of the unity of the opposites of market and autonomy in bourgeois art. The artists who succumb to ideology are precisely those who conceal this contradiction instead of assimilating it into the consciousness of their own production, as Beethoven did: he improvised on "Rage over a Lost Penny" and derived the metaphysical injunction "It must be," which seeks aesthetically to annul the world's compulsion by taking that burden onto itself, from his housekeeper's demand for her monthly wages. The principle of idealist aesthetics, purposiveness without purpose, reverses the schema socially adopted by bourgeois art: purposelessness for purposes dictated by the market. In the demand for entertainment and relaxation, purpose has finally consumed the realm of the purposeless. But as the demand for the marketability of art becomes total, a shift in the inner economic composition of cultural commodities is becoming apparent. For the use which is made of the work of art in antagonistic society is largely that of confirming the very existence of the useless, which art's total subsumption under usefulness has abolished. In adapting itself entirely to need, the work of art defrauds human beings in advance of the liberation from the principle of utility which it is supposed to bring about. What might be called use value in the reception of cultural assets is being replaced by exchange value; enjoyment is giving way to being there and being in the know, connoisseurship by enhanced prestige.

The consumer becomes the ideology of the amusement industry, whose institutions he or she cannot escape. One has to have seen Mrs. Miniver, just as one must subscribe to *Life* and *Time*. Everything is perceived only from the point of view that it can serve as something else, however vaguely that other thing might be envisaged. Everything has value only in so far as it can be exchanged, not in so far as it is something in itself. For consumers the use value of art, its essence, is a fetish, and the fetish – the social valuation which they mistake for the merit of works of art – becomes its only use value, the only quality they enjoy. In this way the commodity character of art disintegrates just as it is fully realized. Art becomes a species of commodity, worked up and adapted to industrial production, saleable and exchangeable; but art as the species of commodity which exists in order to be sold yet not for sale becomes something hypocritically unsaleable as soon as the business transaction is no longer merely its intention but its sole principle. The Toscanini performance on the radio is, in a sense, unsaleable. One listens to it for nothing, and each note of the symphony is accompanied, as it were, by the sublime advertisement that the symphony is not being interrupted by advertisements – "This concert is brought to you as a public service." The deception takes place indirectly *via* the profit of all the united automobile and soap manufacturers, on whose payments the stations survive, and, of course, *via* the increased sales of the electrical industry as the producer of the receiver sets. Radio, the progressive latecomer to mass culture, is drawing conclusions which film's pseudomarket at present denies that industry. The technical structure of the commercial radio system makes it immune to liberal deviations of the kind the film industry can still permit itself in its own preserve. Film is a private enterprise which already represents the sovereign whole, in which respect it has some advantages over the other individual combines. Chesterfield is merely the nation's cigarette, but the radio is its mouthpiece. In the total assimilation of culture products into the commodity sphere radio makes no attempt to purvey its products as commodities. In America it levies no duty from the public. It thereby takes on the deceptive form of a disinterested, impartial authority, which fits fascism like a glove. In fascism radio becomes the universal mouthpiece of the *Führer*; in the loudspeakers on the street his voice merges with the howl of sirens proclaiming panic, from which modern propaganda is hard to distinguish in any case. The National Socialists knew that broadcasting gave their cause stature as the printing press did to the Reformation. The *Führer*'s metaphysical charisma, invented by the sociology of religion,[25] turned out finally to be merely the omnipresence of his radio addresses, which demonically parodies that of the divine spirit. The gigantic fact that the speech penetrates everywhere replaces its content, as the benevolent act of the Toscanini broadcast supplants its content, the symphony. No listener can apprehend the symphony's true coherence, while the *Führer*'s address is in any case a lie. To posit the human word as absolute, the false commandment, is the immanent tendency of radio. Recommendation becomes command. The promotion of identical commodities under different brand names, the scientifically endorsed praise of the laxative in the slick voice of the announcer between the overtures of *La Traviata* and *Rienzi*, has become untenable if only for its silliness. One day the *Diktat* of production, the specific advertisement, veiled by the semblance of choice, can finally become the

Führer's overt command. In a society of large-scale fascistic rackets which agree among themselves on how much of the national product is to be allocated to providing for the needs of the people, to invite the people to use a particular soap powder would, in the end, seem anachronistic. In a more modern, less ceremonious style, the *Führer* directly orders both the holocaust and the supply of trash.

Today works of art, suitably packaged like political slogans, are pressed on a reluctant public at reduced prices by the culture industry; they are opened up for popular enjoyment like parks. However, the erosion of their genuine commodity character does not mean that they would be abolished in the life of a free society but that the last barrier to their debasement as cultural assets has now been removed. The abolition of educational privilege by disposing of culture at bargain prices does not admit the masses to the preserves from which they were formerly excluded but, under the existing social conditions, contributes to the decay of education and the progress of barbaric incoherence. Someone who in the nineteenth or early twentieth century spent money to attend a drama or a concert, paid the performance at least as much respect as the money spent. The citizen who wanted a return for his outlay might occasionally try to establish some connection to the work. The guidebooks to Wagner's music dramas or the commentaries on *Faust* bear witness to this. They form a transition to the biographical glaze applied to works of art and the other practices to which works of art are subjected today. Even when the art business was in the bloom of youth, use value was not dragged along as a mere appendage by exchange value but was developed as a precondition of the latter, to the social benefit of works of art. As long as it was expensive, art kept the citizen within some bounds. That is now over. Art's unbounded proximity to those exposed to it, no longer mediated by money, completes the alienation between work and consumer, which resemble each other in triumphant reification. In the culture industry respect is vanishing along with criticism: the latter gives way to mechanical expertise, the former to the forgetful cult of celebrities. For consumers, nothing is expensive any more. Nevertheless, they are dimly aware that the less something costs, the less it can be a gift to them. The twofold mistrust of traditional culture as ideology mingles with that of industrialized culture as fraud. Reduced to mere adjuncts, the degraded works of art are secretly rejected by their happy recipients along with the junk the medium has made them resemble. The public should rejoice that there is so much to see and hear. And indeed, everything is to be had. The "screenos"[26] and cinema vaudevilles, the competitions in recognizing musical extracts, the free magazines, rewards, and gift articles handed out to the listeners of certain radio programs are not mere accidents, but continue what is happening to the culture products themselves. The symphony is becoming the prize for listening to the radio at all, and if the technology had its way the film would already be delivered to the apartment on the model of the radio.[27] It is moving towards the commercial system. Television points the way to a development which easily enough could push the Warner brothers[28] into the doubtless unwelcome position of little theatre performers and cultural conservatives. However, the pursuit of prizes has already left its imprint on consumer behavior. Because culture presents itself as a bonus, with unquestioned private and social benefits, its reception has become a matter of taking one's chances. The public crowds forward for fear of missing something. What that might be is unclear, but, at any rate, only those who join in have any chance. Fascism, however, hopes to reorganize the gift-receivers trained by the culture industry into its enforced adherents.

Culture is a paradoxical commodity. It is so completely subject to the law of exchange that it is no longer exchanged; it is so blindly equated with use that it can no longer be used. For this reason it merges with the advertisement. The more meaningless the latter appears under monopoly, the more omnipotent culture becomes. Its motives are economic enough. That life could continue without the whole culture industry is too certain; the satiation and apathy it generates among consumers are too great. It can do little to combat this from its own resources. Advertising is its elixir of life. But because its product ceaselessly reduces the pleasure it promises as a commodity to that mere promise, it finally coincides with the advertisement it needs on account of its own inability to please. In the competitive society advertising performed a social service in orienting the buyer in the market, facilitating choice and helping the more efficient but unknown supplier to find customers. It did not merely cost labor time, but saved it. Today, when the free market is coming to an end, those in control of the system are entrenching themselves in advertisng. It strengthens the bond which shackles consumers to the big combines. Only those who can keep paying the exorbitant fees charged by the advertising agencies, and most of all by radio itself, that is, those who are already part of the system or are co-opted into it by the decisions of banks and industrial capital, can enter the pseudomarket as sellers. The costs of advertising, which finally flow back into the pockets of the combines, spare them the troublesome task of subduing unwanted outsiders; they guarantee that the wielders of influence remain among their peers, not unlike the resolutions of economic councils which control the establishment and continuation of businesses in the totalitarian state. Advertising today is a negative principle, a blocking device: anything which does not bear its seal of approval is economically suspect. All-pervasive advertising is certainly not needed to acquaint people with the goods on offer, the varieties of which are limited in any case. It benefits the selling of goods only directly. The termination of a familiar advertising campaign by an individual firm represents a loss of prestige, and is indeed an offence against the discipline which the leading clique imposes on its members. In wartime, commodities which can no longer be supplied continue to be advertised merely as a display of industrial power. At such times the subsidizing of the ideological media is more important than the repetition of names. Through their ubiquitous use under the pressure of the system, advertising techniques have invaded the idiom, the "style" of the culture industry. So complete is their triumph that in key positions it is no longer even explicit: the imposing buildings of the big companies, floodlit advertisements in stone, are free of advertising, merely displaying the illuminated company initials on their pinnacles, with no further need of self-congratulation. By contrast, the buildings surviving from the nineteenth century, the architecture of which still shamefully reveals their utility as consumer goods, their function as accommodation, are covered from basement to above roof level with hoardings and banners: the landscape becomes a mere background for sign-boards and symbols.

Advertising becomes simply the art with which Goebbels presciently equated it, *l'art pour l'art*, advertising for advertising's sake, the pure representation of social power. In the influential American magazines *Life* and *Fortune* the images and texts of advertisements are, at a cursory glance, hardly distinguishable from the editorial section. The enthusiastic and unpaid picture story about the living habits and personal grooming of celebrities, which wins them new fans, is editorial, while the advertising pages rely on photographs and data so factual and lifelike that they represent the ideal of information to which the editorial section only aspires. Every film is a preview of the next, which promises yet again to unite the same heroic couple under the same exotic sun: anyone arriving late cannot tell whether he is watching the trailer or the real thing. The montage character of the culture industry, the synthetic, controlled manner in which its products are assembled – factory-like not only in the film studio but also, virtually, in the compilation of the cheap biographies, journalistic novels, and hit songs – predisposes it to advertising: the individual moment, in being detachable, replaceable, estranged even technically from any coherence of meaning, lends itself to purposes outside the work. The special effect, the trick, the isolated and repeatable individual performance have always conspired with the exhibition of commodities for advertising purposes, and today every close-up of a film actress is an advert for her name, every hit song a plug for its tune. Advertising and the culture industry are merging technically no less than economically. In both, the same thing appears in countless places, and the mechanical repetition of the same culture product is already that of the same propaganda slogan. In both, under the dictate of effectiveness, technique is becoming psychotechnique, a procedure for manipulating human beings. In both, the norms of the striking yet familiar, the easy but catchy, the worldly wise but straightforward hold good; everything is directed at overpowering a customer conceived as distracted or resistant.

Through the language they speak, the customers make their own contribution to culture as advertising. For the more completely language coincides with communication, the more words change from substantial carriers of meaning to signs devoid of qualities; the more purely and transparently they communicate what they designate, the more impenetrable they become. The demythologizing of language, as an element of the total process of enlightenment, reverts to magic. In magic word and content were at once different from each other and indissolubly linked. Concepts like melancholy, history, indeed, life, were apprehended in the word which both set them apart and preserved them. Its particular form constituted and reflected them at the same time. The trenchant distinction which declares the word itself fortuitous and its allocation to its object arbitrary does away with the superstitious commingling of word and thing. Anything in a given sequence of letters which goes beyond the correlation to the event designated is banished as unclear and as verbal metaphysics. As a result, the word, which henceforth is allowed only to designate something and not to mean it, becomes so fixated on the object that it hardens to a formula. This affects language and subject matter equally. Instead of raising a matter to the level of experience, the purified word exhibits it as a case of an abstract moment, and everything else, severed from now defunct expression by the demand for pitiless clarity, therefore withers in reality also. The outside-left in football, the blackshirt,[29] the Hitler Youth member, and others of their kind are no more than what they are called. If, before its rationalization, the word had see free not only longing but lies, in its rationalized form it has become a straightjacket more for longing than for lies. The blindness and muteness of the data to which positivism reduces the world passes over into language itself, which is limited to registering those data. Thus relationships themselves become impenetrable, taking on an impact, a power of adhesion and repulsion which makes them resemble their extreme antithesis, spells. They act once more like the practices of a kind of sorcery, whether the name of a diva is concocted in the studio on the basis of statistical data, or welfare government is averted by the use of taboo-laden words such as "bureaucracy" and "intellectuals," or vileness exonerates itself by invoking the name of a homeland. The name, to which magic most readily attaches, is today undergoing a chemical change. It is being transformed into arbitrary, manipulable designations, the power of which, although calculable, is for that reason as willful as that of archaic names. First names, the archaic residues, have been brought up to date either by stylizing them into advertising brands – film stars' surnames have become first names – or by standardizing them collectively. By contrast, the bourgeois, family name which, instead of being a trademark, individualized its bearers by relating them to their own prehistory, sounds old-fashioned. In Americans it arouses a curious unease. To conceal the uncomfortable distance existing between particular people they call themselves Bob and Harry, like replaceable members of teams. Such forms of interaction reduce human beings to the brotherhood of the sporting public, which protects them from true fraternity. Signification, the only function of the word admitted by semantics, is consummated in the sign. Its character as sign is reinforced by the speed with which linguistic models are put into circulation from above. Whether folksongs are rightly or wrongly called upper-class culture which has come down in the world, their elements have at least taken on their popular form in a long, highly mediated process of experience. The dissemination of popular songs, by contrast, is practically instantaneous. The American term "fad" for fashions which catch on epidemically – inflamed by the action of highly concentrated economic powers – referred to this phenomenon long before totalitarian advertising bosses had laid down the general lines of culture in their countries. If the German fascists launch a word like "intolerable" [*Untragbar*] over the loudspeakers one day, the whole nation is saying "intolerable" the next. On the same pattern, the nations against which the German *Blitzkrieg* was directed have adopted it in their own jargon. The universal repetition of the term denoting such measures makes the measures, too, familiar, just as, at the time of the free market, the brand name on everyone's lips increased sales. The blind and rapidly spreading repetition of designated words links advertising to the totalitarian slogan. The layer of experience which made words human like those who spoke them has been stripped away and in its prompt appropriation language takes on the coldness which hitherto was peculiar to billboards and the advertising sections of newspapers. Countless people use words and expressions which they either have ceased to understand at all or use only according to their behavioral functions, just as trademarks adhere all the more compulsively to their objects the less their linguistic meaning is apprehended. The

Minister of Public Education speaks ignorantly of "dynamic forces," and the hit songs sing endlessly of "reverie" and "rhapsody," hitching their popularity to the magic of the incomprehensible as if to some deep intimation of a higher life. Other stereotypes, such as "memory," are still partly comprehended, but become detached from the experience which might fulfill them. They obtrude into the spoken language like enclaves. On the German radio of Flesch and Hitler they are discernible in the affected diction of the announcer, who pronounces phrases like "Goodnight, listeners," or "This is the Hitler Youth speaking," or even "the *Führer*" with an inflection which passes into the mother tongue of millions. In such turns of phrase the last bond between sedimented experience and language, which still exerted a reconciling influence in dialect in the nineteenth century, is severed. By contrast, in the hands of the editor whose supple opinions have promoted him to the status of *Schriftleiter*,[30] German words become petrified and alien. In any word one can distinguish how far it has been disfigured by the fascist "folk" community. By now, of course, such language has become universal, totalitarian. The violence done to words is no longer audible in them. The radio announcer does not need to talk in an affected voice; indeed, he would be impossible if his tone differed from that of his designated listeners. This means, however, that the language and gestures of listeners and spectators are more deeply permeated by the patterns of the culture industry than ever before, in nuances still beyond the reach of experimental methods. Today the culture industry has taken over the civilizing inheritance of the frontier and entrepreneurial democracy, whose receptivity to intellectual deviations was never too highly developed. All are free to dance and amuse themselves, just as, since the historical neutralization of religion, they have been free to join any of the countless sects. But freedom to choose an ideology, which always reflects economic coercion, everywhere proves to be freedom to be the same. The way in which the young girl accepts and performs the obligatory date, the tone of voice used on the telephone and in the most intimate situations, the choice of words in conversation, indeed, the whole inner life compartmentalized according to the categories of vulgarized depth psychology, bears witness to the attempt to turn oneself into an apparatus meeting the requirements of success, an apparatus which, even in its unconscious impulses, conforms to the model presented by the culture industry. The most intimate reactions of human beings have become so entirely reified, even to themselves, that the idea of anything peculiar to them survives only in extreme abstraction: personality means hardly more than dazzling white teeth and freedom from body odor and emotions. That is the triumph of advertising in the culture industry: the compulsive imitation by consumers of cultural commodities which, at the same time, they recognize as false.

Notes

1   "Soap operas": alludes to the fact that such programs were originally broadcast at times when housewives were at home doing their washing.
2   Nietzsche, *Unzeitgemässe Betrachtungen. Werke*, Leipzig 1917, Vol. I, p. 187. [Adorno and Horkheimer's note.]

3   "Zanuck": Film producer, cofounder of 20th Century Pictures.

4   "Pathé": French film magnates.

5   "Hugenberg": Founders of German publishing combines.

6   A. de Tocqueville, *De la Démocratie en Amérique*, Paris 1864, Vol. II, p. 151. [Adorno and Horkheimer's note.]

7   "Hays Office": Voluntary censorship agency, set up in 1934 in Hollywood.

8   "Casino de Paris": Music hall in Paris, famous for its luxurious furnishings.

9   "Lombardo": Orchestra leader especially known for his annual musical broadcasts on New Year's Eve.

10   "novelty songs": Hit songs with comic elements.

11   ". . . overwhelming": The idea expressed here dates from a time when television was not in widespread use.

12   "*res . . . gaudium*": Seneca, Letter 23; letters to Lucilius (*Letters from a Stoic*, trans. Robin Campbell, Harmondsworth 1969).

13   "funnies": Amusement pages in newspapers with jokes and comic strips.

14   "Ludwig": Primarily a writer of popular biographies.

15   "Mrs. Miniver": Leading role in a radio family serial; also filmed.

16   "Lone Ranger": Title figure in a radio western serial, the type of the lone cowboy fighting for the good; also filmed.

17   Frank Wedekind, *Gesammelte Werke*, Munich 1921, Vol. IX, p. 426. [Adorno and Horkheimer's note.]

18   "Adler": Neo-Thomist popular philosopher who defended film with arguments from scholastic philosophy (It. tr.) – Cf. Horkheimer, "Neue Kunst und Massenkultur," in *Gesammelte Schriften*, Vol. 4.

19   "proof": A play on the various philosophical-theological (ontological, cosmological, etc.) proofs of the existence of God.

20   *Hans Sonnenstößers Höllenfahrt. Ein heiteres Traumspiel.* Radio play by Paul Apel (1931), revised version by Gustaf Gründgens (1937).

21   "*Life with Father*": Popular American radio family serial after a stage play by Clarence Day.

22   "Dagwood": Character in the comic strip *Blondie*.

23   "winter aid": *Winterhilfswerk*: National Socialist organization to support the unemployed and other needy persons under the direction of the Ministry of Propaganda.

24   Nietzsche, *Götzendämmerung, Werke, op. cit.*, Vol. VIII, p. 136. [Adorno and Horkheimer's note.]

25   "invented by the sociology of religion": Allusion to Max Weber's concept of charismatic authority: cf. *Economy and Society*, Vol. I, ed. Guenther Roth and Claus Wittich, Berkeley 1978, pp. 241ff.

26   "screenos": Bingo games played by the audience between pictures.

27   "radio": Television was still in its infancy when the authors were writing (It. tr.).

28   "the Warner brothers": Owners of large film studios.

29   "blackshirt": A term for fascists, after the black shirts of their uniforms, especially in Italy but also in other countries.

30   "*Schriftleiter*": The term *Schriftleiter* [lit. director of writing] was preferred by the National Socialists to the "foreign" word *Redakteur*.

5

The Public Sphere: An Encyclopedia Article

Jürgen Habermas

The Concept. By "the public sphere" we mean first of all a realm of our social life in which something approaching public opinion can be formed. Access is guaranteed to all citizens. A portion of the public sphere comes into being in every conversation in which private individuals assemble to form a public body.[1] They then behave neither like business or professional people transacting private affairs, nor like members of a constitutional order subject to the legal constraints of a state bureaucracy. Citizens behave as a public body when they confer in an unrestricted fashion – that is, with the guarantee of freedom of assembly and association and the freedom to express and publish their opinions – about matters of general interest. In a large public body, this kind of communication requires specific means for transmitting information and influencing those who receive it. Today, newspapers and magazines, radio and television are the media of the public sphere. We speak of the political public sphere in contrast, for instance, to the literary one, when public discussion deals with objects connected to the activity of the state. Although state authority is, so to speak, the executor of the political public sphere, it is not a part of it.[2] To be sure, state authority is usually considered "public" authority, but it derives its task of caring for the well-being of all citizens primarily from this aspect of the public sphere. Only when the exercise of political control is effectively subordinated to the democratic demand that information be accessible to the public, does the political public sphere win an institutionalized influence over the government through the instrument of law-making bodies. The expression *public opinion* refers to the tasks of criticism and control which a public body of citizens informally – and, in periodic elections, formally as well – practices vis-à-vis the ruling structure organized in the form of a state. Regulations demanding that certain proceedings be public [*Publizitätsvorschriften*] – for example, those providing for open court hearings – are also related to this function of public opinion. The public sphere as a sphere which

From Jürgen Habermas, "The public sphere: An encyclopedia article." In Stephen Eric Bronner and Douglas M. Kellner (eds.), *Critical Theory and Society: A Reader*, pp. 136–42. Translated by Sara Lennox and Frank Lennox. New York and London: Routledge, 1989.

mediates between society and state, in which the public organizes itself as the bearer of public opinion, accords with the principle of the public sphere[3] – that principle of public information which once had to be fought for against the arcane policies of monarchies and which since that time has made possible the democratic control of state activities.

It is no coincidence that these concepts of the public sphere and public opinion arose for the first time only in the eighteenth century. They acquire their specific meaning from a concrete historical situation. It was at that time that the distinction of "opinion" from "opinion publique" and "public opinion" came about. Though mere opinions (cultural assumptions, normative attitudes, collective prejudices and values) seem to persist unchanged in their natural form as a kind of sediment of history, public opinion can by definition come into existence only when a reasoning public is presupposed. Public discussions about the exercise of political power which are both critical in intent and institutionally guaranteed have not always existed – they grew out of a specific phase of bourgeois society and could enter into the order of the bourgeois constitutional state only as a result of a particular constellation of interests.

History. There is no indication that European society of the high Middle Ages possessed a public sphere as a unique realm distinct from the private sphere. Nevertheless, it was not coincidental that during that period symbols of sovereignty, for instance, the princely seal, were deemed "public." At that time there existed a public representation of power. The status of the feudal lord, at whatever level of the feudal pyramid, made it unnecessary to employ the categories "public" and "private." The holder of the position represented it publicly; he showed himself, presented himself as the embodiment of an ever-present "higher" power. The concept of this representation has been maintained up to the most recent constitutional history. Regardless of the degree to which it has loosened itself from the old base, the authority of political power today still demands a representation at the highest level by a head of state. Such elements, however, derive from a prebourgeois social structure. Representation in the sense of a bourgeois public sphere,[4] for instance, the representation of the nation or of particular mandates, has nothing to do with the medieval representative public sphere – a public sphere directly linked to the concrete existence of a ruler. As long as the prince and the estates of the realm still "are" the land, instead of merely functioning as deputies for it, they are able to "represent"; they represent their power "before" the people, instead of for the people.

The feudal authorities (Church, princes, and nobility), to which the representative public sphere was first linked, disintegrated during a long process of polarization. By the end of the eighteenth century they had broken apart into private elements on the one hand, and into public elements on the other. The position of the Church changed with the Reformation: the link to divine authority which the Church represented, that is, religion, became a private matter. So-called religious freedom came to insure what was historically the first area of private autonomy. The Church itself continued its existence as one public and legal body among others. The corresponding polarization within princely authority was visibly manifested in the separation of the public budget from the private household expenses of a ruler. The institutions of public authority, along with the bureaucracy and the military, and in part also with the legal institutions, asserted their independence from the privatized sphere of the princely court. Finally, the feudal estates were transformed as well: the nobility became the organs of public authority, parliament, and the legal institutions; while those occupied in trades and professions, insofar as they had already established urban corporations and territorial organizations, developed into a sphere of bourgeois society which would stand apart from the state as a genuine area of private autonomy.

The representative public sphere yielded to that new sphere of "public authority" which came into being with national and territorial states. Continuous state activity (permanent administration, standing army) now corresponded to the permanence of the relationships which with the stock exchange and the press had developed within the exchange of commodities and information. Public authority consolidated into a concrete opposition for those who were merely subject to it and who at first found only a negative definition of themselves within it. These were the "private individuals" who were excluded from public authority because they held no office. "Public" no longer referred to the "representative" court of a prince endowed with authority, but rather to an institution regulated according to competence, to an apparatus endowed with a monopoly on the legal exertion of authority. Private individuals subsumed in the state at whom public authority was directed now made up the public body.

Society, now a private realm occupying a position in opposition to the state, stood on the one hand as if in clear contrast to the state. On the other hand, that society had become a concern of public interest to the degree that the production of life in the wake of the developing market economy had grown beyond the bounds of private domestic authority. *The bourgeois public sphere* could be understood as the sphere of private individuals assembled into a public body, which almost immediately laid claim to the officially regulated "intellectual newspapers" for use against the public authority itself. In those newspapers, and in moralistic and critical journals, they debated that public authority on the general rules of social intercourse in their fundamentally privatized yet publicly relevant sphere of labor and commodity exchange.

The Liberal Model of the Public Sphere. The medium of this debate – public discussion – was unique and without historical precedent. Hitherto the estates had negotiated agreements with their princes, settling their claims to power from case to case. This development took a different course in England, where the parliament limited royal power, than it did on the Continent, where the monarchies mediatized the estates. The Third Estate then broke with this form of power arrangement, since it could no longer establish itself as a ruling group. A division of power by means of the delineation of the rights of the nobility was no longer possible within an exchange economy – private authority over capitalist property is, after all, unpolitical. Bourgeois individuals are private individuals. As such, they do not "rule." Their claims to power vis-à-vis public authority were thus directed not against the concentration of power, which was to be "shared." Instead, their ideas infiltrated the very principle on which the existing power is based. To the principle of existing power, the bourgeois public opposed the principle of supervision – that very principle which demands that proceedings be made public [*Publizität*]. The principle of supervision is thus a means of transforming the nature of power, not merely one basis of legitimation exchanged for another.

In the first modern constitutions, the catalogues of fundamental rights were a perfect image of the liberal model of the public sphere: they guaranteed the society as a sphere of private autonomy and the restriction of public authority to a few functions. Between these two spheres, the constitutions further insured the existence of a realm of private individuals assembled into a public body who as citizens transmit the needs of bourgeois society to the state, in order, ideally, to transform political into "rational" authority within the medium of this public sphere. The general interest, which was the measure of such rationality, was then guaranteed, according to the presuppositions of a society of free commodity exchange, when the activities of private individuals in the marketplace were freed from social compulsion and from political pressure in the public sphere.

At the same time, daily political newspapers assumed an important role. In the second half of the eighteenth century, literary journalism created serious competition for the earlier news sheets, which were mere compilations of notices. Karl Bücher characterized this great development as follows: "Newspapers changed from mere institutions for the publication of news into bearers and leaders of public opinion – weapons of party politics. This transformed the newspaper business. A new element emerged between the gathering and publication of news: the editorial staff. But for the newspaper publisher it meant that he changed from a vendor of recent news to a dealer in public opinion." The publishers insured the newspapers a commercial basis, yet without commercializing them as such. The press remained an institution of the public itself, effective in the manner of a mediator and intensifier of public discussion, no longer a mere organ for the spreading of news but not yet the medium of a consumer culture.

This type of journalism can be observed above all during periods of revolution, when newspapers of the smallest political groups and organizations spring up – for instance, in Paris in 1789. Even in the Paris of 1848 every half-way eminent politician organized his club, every other his journal: 450 clubs and over 200 journals were established there between February and May alone. Until the permanent legalization of a politically functional public sphere, the appearance of a political newspaper meant joining the struggle for freedom and public opinion, and thus for the public sphere as a principle. Only with the establishment of the bourgeois constitutional state was the intellectual press relieved of the pressure of its convictions. Since then it has been able to abandon its polemical position and take advantage of the earning possibilities of a commercial undertaking. In England, France, and the United States, the transformation from a journalism of conviction to one of commerce began in the 1830s at approximately the same time. In the transition from the literary journalism of private individuals to the public services of the mass media, the public sphere was transformed by the influx of private interests, which received special prominence in the mass media.

The Public Sphere in the Social Welfare State Mass Democracy. Although the liberal model of the public sphere is still instructive today with respect to the normative claim that information be accessible to the public,[5] it cannot be applied to the actual conditions of an industrially advanced mass democracy organized in the form of the social welfare state. In part, the liberal model had always included ideological components, but it is also in part true that the social preconditions, to which the ideological elements could at one time at least be linked, had been fundamentally transformed. The very forms in which the public sphere manifested itself, to which supporters of the liberal model could appeal for evidence, began to change with the Chartist movement in England and the February revolution in France. Because of the diffusion of press and propaganda, the public body expanded beyond the bounds of the bourgeoisie. The public body lost not only its social exclusivity; it lost in addition the coherence created by bourgeois social institutions and a relatively high standard of education. Conflicts hitherto restricted to the private sphere now intrude into the public sphere. Group needs which can expect no satisfaction from a self-regulating market now tend toward a regulation by the state. The public sphere, which must now mediate these demands, becomes a field for the competition of interests, competitions which assume the form of violent conflict. Laws which obviously have come about under the "pressure of the street" can scarcely still be understood as arising from the consensus of private individuals engaged in public discussion. They correspond in a more or less unconcealed manner to the compromise of conflicting private interests. Social organizations which deal with the state act in the political public sphere, whether through the agency of political parties or directly in connection with the public administration. With the interweaving of the public and private realms, not only do the political authorities assume certain functions in the sphere of commodity exchange and social labor, but, conversely, social powers now assume political functions. This leads to a kind of "refeudalization" of the public sphere. Large organizations strive for political compromises with the state and with one another, excluding the public sphere whenever possible. But at the same time the large organizations must assure themselves of at least plebiscitary support from the mass of the population through an apparent display of openness [*demonstrative Publizität*].[6]

The political public sphere of the social welfare state is characterized by a peculiar weakening of its critical functions. At one time the process of making proceedings public [*Publizität*] was intended to subject persons or affairs to public reason, and to make political decisions subject to appeal before the court of public opinion. But often enough today the process of making public simply serves the arcane policies of special interests; in the form of "publicity" it wins public prestige for people or affairs, thus making them worthy of acclamation in a climate of nonpublic opinion. The very words "public relations work" [*Öffentlichkeitsarbeit*] betray the fact that a public sphere must first be arduously constructed case by case, a public sphere which earlier grew out of the social structure. Even the central relationship of the public, the parties, and the parliament is affected by this change in function.

Yet this trend towards the weakening of the public sphere as a principle is opposed by the extension of fundamental rights in the social welfare state. The demand that information be accessible to the public is extended from organs of the state to all organizations dealing with the state. To the degree that this is realized, a public body of organized private individuals would take the place of the now-defunct public body of private individuals who relate individually to each other. Only these organized individuals could participate effectively in the process of public communication; only they could use the channels of the public sphere which exist within parties and associations and the process of making proceedings public [*Publizität*] which was established to facilitate the dealings of organizations with the state. Political compromises would have to be legitimized through this process of public communication. The idea of the public sphere, preserved in the social welfare state mass democracy, an idea which calls for a rationalization of power through the medium of public discussion among private individuals, threatens to disintegrate with the structural transformation of the public sphere itself. It could only be realized today, on an altered basis, as a rational reorganization of social and political power under the mutual control of rival organizations committed to the public sphere in their internal structure as well as in their relations with the state and each other.

Notes

1   Habermas's concept of the public sphere is not to be equated with that of "the public," i.e., of the individuals who assemble. His concept is directed instead at the institution, which to be sure only assumes concrete form through the participation of people. It cannot, however, be characterized simply as a crowd. (This and the following notes by Peter Hohendahl.)

2   The state and the public sphere do not overlap, as one might suppose from casual language use. Rather, they confront one another as opponents. Habermas designates that sphere as public which antiquity understood to be private, i.e., the sphere of nongovernmental opinion making.

3   The principle of the public sphere could still be distinguished from an institution which is demonstrable in social history. Habermas thus would mean a model of norms and modes of behavior by means of which the very functioning of public opinion can be guaranteed for the first time. These norms and modes of behavior include: a) general accessibility, b) elimination of all privileges, and c) discovery of general norms and rational legitimations.

4   The expression *represent* is used in a very specific sense in the following section, namely, to "present oneself." The important thing to understand is that the medieval public sphere, if it even deserves this designation, is tied to the *personal*. The feudal lord and estates create the public sphere by means of their very presence.

5   Here it should be understood that Habermas considers the principle behind the bourgeois public sphere, but not its historical form, as indispensable.

6   One must distinguish between Habermas's concept of "making proceedings public" [*Publizität*] and the "public sphere" [*Öffentlichkeit*]. The term *Publizität* describes the degree of public effect generated by a public act. Thus, a situation can arise in which the form of public opinion making is maintained, while the substance of the public sphere has long ago been undermined.

6

Ideology and Ideological State Apparatuses (Notes Towards an Investigation)

Louis Althusser

The State Ideological Apparatuses

In order to advance the theory of the State it is indispensable to take into account not only the distinction between *State power* and *State apparatus*, but also another reality which is clearly on the side of the (repressive) State apparatus, but must not be confused with it. I shall call this reality by its concept: *the ideological State apparatuses*.

What are the ideological State apparatuses (ISAs)?

They must not be confused with the (repressive) State apparatus. Remember that in Marxist theory, the State Apparatus (SA) contains: the Government, the Administration, the Army, the Police, the Courts, the Prisons, etc., which constitute what I shall in future call the Repressive State Apparatus. Repressive suggests that the State Apparatus in question "functions by violence" – at least ultimately (since repression, e.g. administrative repression, may take non-physical forms).

I shall call Ideological State Apparatuses a certain number of realities which present themselves to the immediate observer in the form of distinct and specialized institutions. I propose an empirical list of these which will obviously have to be examined in detail, tested, corrected and reorganized. With all the reservations implied by this requirement, we can for the moment regard the following institutions as Ideological State Apparatuses (the order in which I have listed them has no particular significance):

From Louis Althusser, "Ideology and ideological state apparatuses (Notes towards an investigation)." In *Lenin and Philosophy and Other Essays*, pp. 142–7, 166–76. Translated by Ben Brewster. New York and London: Monthly Review Press, 1971. © 1971 by Monthly Review Press. Reprinted by permission of Monthly Review Press.

- the religious ISA (the system of the different Churches),
- the educational ISA (the system of the different public and private "Schools"),
- the family ISA,[1]
- the legal ISA,[2]
- the political ISA (the political system, including the different Parties),
- the trade-union ISA,
- the communications ISA (press, radio and television, etc.),
- the cultural ISA (Literature, the Arts, sports, etc.).

I have said that the ISAs must not be confused with the (Repressive) State Apparatus. What constitutes the difference?

As a first moment, it is clear that while there is *one* (Repressive) State Apparatus, there is a *plurality* of Ideological State Apparatuses. Even presupposing that it exists, the unity that constitutes this plurality of ISAs as a body is not immediately visible.

As a second moment, it is clear that whereas the – unified – (Repressive) State Apparatus belongs entirely to the *public* domain, much the larger part of the Ideological State Apparatuses (in their apparent dispersion) are part, on the contrary, of the *private* domain. Churches, Parties, Trade Unions, families, some schools, most newspapers, cultural ventures, etc., etc., are private.

We can ignore the first observation for the moment. But someone is bound to question the second, asking me by what right I regard as Ideological *State* Apparatuses, institutions which for the most part do not possess public status, but are quite simply *private* institutions. As a conscious Marxist, Gramsci already forestalled this objection in one sentence. The distinction between the public and the private is a distinction internal to bourgeois law, and valid in the (subordinate) domains in which bourgeois law exercises its "authority". The domain of the State escapes it because the latter is "above the law": the State, which is the State *of* the ruling class, is neither public nor private; on the contrary, it is the precondition for any distinction between public and private. The same thing can be said from the starting-point of our State Ideological Apparatuses. It is unimportant whether the institutions in which they are realized are "public" or "private". What matters is how they function. Private institutions can perfectly well "function" as Ideological State Apparatuses. A reasonably thorough analysis of any one of the ISAs proves it.

But now for what is essential. What distinguishes the ISAs from the (Repressive) State Apparatus is the following basic difference: the Repressive State Apparatus functions "by violence", whereas the Ideological State Apparatuses *function "by ideology"*.

I can clarify matters by correcting this distinction. I shall say rather that every State Apparatus, whether Repressive or Ideological, "functions" both by violence and by ideology, but with one very important distinction which makes it imperative not to confuse the Ideological State Apparatuses with the (Repressive) State Apparatus.

This is the fact that the (Repressive) State Apparatus functions massively and predominantly *by repression* (including physical repression), while functioning secondarily by ideology. (There is no such thing as a purely repressive apparatus.) For example, the Army and the Police also function by ideology both to ensure their own cohesion and reproduction, and in the "values" they propound externally.

In the same way, but inversely, it is essential to say that for their part the Ideological State Apparatuses function massively and predominantly *by ideology*, but they also function secondarily by repression, even if ultimately, but only ultimately, this is very attenuated and concealed, even symbolic. (There is no such thing as a purely ideological apparatus.) Thus Schools and Churches use suitable methods of punishment, expulsion, selection, etc., to "discipline" not only their shepherds, but also their flocks. The same is true of the Family. . . . The same is true of the cultural IS Apparatus (censorship, among other things), etc.

Is it necessary to add that this determination of the double "functioning" (predominantly, secondarily) by repression and by ideology, according to whether it is a matter of the (Repressive) State Apparatus or the Ideological State Apparatuses, makes it clear that very subtle explicit or tacit combinations may be woven from the interplay of the (Repressive) State Apparatus and the Ideological State Apparatuses? Everyday life provides us with innumerable examples of this, but they must be studied in detail if we are to go further than this mere observation.

Nevertheless, this remark leads us towards an understanding of what constitutes the unity of the apparently disparate body of the ISAs. If the ISAs "function" massively and predominantly by ideology, what unifies their diversity is precisely this functioning, insofar as the ideology by which they function is always in fact unified, despite its diversity and its contradictions, *beneath the ruling ideology*, which is the ideology of "the ruling class". Given the fact that the "ruling class" in principle holds State power (openly or more often by means of alliances between classes or class fractions), and therefore has at its disposal the (Repressive) State Apparatus, we can accept the fact that this same ruling class is active in the Ideological State Apparatuses insofar as it is ultimately the ruling ideology which is realized in the Ideological State Apparatuses, precisely in its contradictions. Of course, it is a quite different thing to act by laws and decrees in the (Repressive) State Apparatus and to "act" through the intermediary of the ruling ideology in the Ideological State Apparatuses. We must go into the details of this difference – but it cannot mask the reality of a profound identity. To my knowledge, *no class can hold State power over a long period without at the same time exercising its hegemony over and in the State Ideological Apparatuses.* I only need one example and proof of this: Lenin's anguished concern to revolutionize the educational Ideological State Apparatus (among others), simply to make it possible for the Soviet proletariat, who had seized State power, to secure the future of the dictatorship of the proletariat and the transition to socialism.[3]

This last comment puts us in a position to understand that the Ideological State Apparatuses may be not only the *stake*, but also the *site* of class struggle, and often of bitter forms of class struggle. The class (or class alliance) in power cannot lay down the law in the ISAs as easily as it can in the (repressive) State apparatus, not only because the former ruling classes are able to retain strong positions there for a long time, but also because the resistance of the exploited classes is able to find means and occasions to express itself there, either by the utilization of their contradictions, or by conquering combat positions in them in struggle.[4] [. . .]

While discussing the ideological State apparatuses and their practices, I said that each of them was the realization of an ideology (the unity of these different regional ideologies – religious, ethical, legal, political, aesthetic, etc. – being assured by their subjection to the ruling ideology). I now return to this thesis: an ideology always exists in an apparatus, and its practice, or practices. This existence is material.

Of course, the material existence of the ideology in an apparatus and its practices does not have the same modality as the material existence of a paving-stone or a rifle. But, at the risk of being taken for a Neo-Aristotelian (NB Marx had a very high regard for Aristotle), I shall say that "matter is discussed in many senses", or rather that it exists in different modalities, all rooted in the last instance in "physical" matter.

Having said this, let me move straight on and see what happens to the "individuals" who live in ideology, i.e. in a determinate (religious, ethical, etc.) representation of the world whose imaginary distortion depends on their imaginary relation to their conditions of existence, in other words, in the last instance, to the relations of production and to class relations (ideology = an imaginary relation to real relations). I shall say that this imaginary relation is itself endowed with a material existence.

Now I observe the following.

An individual believes in God, or Duty, or Justice, etc. This belief derives (for everyone, i.e. for all those who live in an ideological representation of ideology, which reduces ideology to ideas endowed by definition with a spiritual existence) from the ideas of the individual concerned, i.e. from him as a subject with a consciousness which contains the ideas of his belief. In this way, i.e. by means of the absolutely ideological "conceptual" device (*dispositif*) thus set up (a subject endowed with a consciousness in which he freely forms or freely recognizes ideas in which he believes), the (material) attitude of the subject concerned naturally follows.

The individual in question behaves in such and such a way, adopts such and such a practical attitude, and, what is more, participates in certain regular practices which are those of the ideological apparatus on which "depend" the ideas which he has in all consciousness freely chosen as a subject. If he believes in God, he goes to Church to attend Mass, kneels, prays, confesses, does penance (once it was material in the ordinary sense of the term) and naturally repents and so on. If he believes in Duty, he will have the corresponding attitudes, inscribed in ritual practices "according to the correct principles". If he believes in Justice, he will submit unconditionally to the rules of the Law, and may even protest when they are violated, sign petitions, take part in a demonstration, etc.

Throughout this schema we observe that the ideological representation of ideology is itself forced to recognize that every "subject" endowed with a "consciousness" and believing in the "ideas" that his "consciousness" inspires in him and freely accepts, must "*act* according to his ideas", must therefore inscribe his own ideas as a free subject in the actions of his material practice. If he does not do so, "that is wicked".

Indeed, if he does not do what he ought to do as a function of what he believes, it is because he does something else, which, still as a function of the same idealist scheme, implies that he has other ideas in his head as well as those he proclaims, and that he acts according to these other ideas, as a man who is either "inconsistent" ("no one is willingly evil") or cynical, or perverse.

In every case, the ideology of ideology thus recognizes, despite its imaginary distortion, that the "ideas" of a human subject exist in his actions, or ought to exist in his actions, and if that is not the case, it lends him other ideas corresponding to the actions (however perverse) that he does perform. This ideology talks of actions: I shall talk of actions inserted into *practices. And* I shall point out that these practices are governed by the *rituals* in which these practices are inscribed, within the *material existence of an ideological apparatus*, be it only a small part of that apparatus: a small mass in a small church, a funeral, a minor match at a sports' club, a school day, a political party meeting, etc.

Besides, we are indebted to Pascal's defensive "dialectic" for the wonderful formula which will enable us to invert the order of the notional schema of ideology. Pascal says more or less: "Kneel down, move your lips in prayer, and you will believe." He thus scandalously inverts the order of things, bringing, like Christ, not peace but strife, and in addition something hardly Christian (for woe to him who brings scandal into the world!) – scandal itself. A fortunate scandal which makes him stick with Jansenist defiance to a language that directly names the reality.

I will be allowed to leave Pascal to the arguments of his ideological struggle with the religious ideological State apparatus of his day. And I shall be expected to use a more directly Marxist vocabulary, if that is possible, for we are advancing in still poorly explored domains.

I shall therefore say that, where only a single subject (such and such an individual) is concerned, the existence of the ideas of his belief is material in that *his ideas are his material actions inserted into material practices governed by material rituals which are themselves defined by the material ideological apparatus from which derive the ideas of that subject.* Naturally, the four inscriptions of the adjective "material" in my proposition must be affected by different modalities: the materialities of a displacement for going to mass, of kneeling down, of the gesture of the sign of the cross, or of the *mea culpa*, of a sentence of a prayer, of an act of contrition, of a penitence, of a gaze, of a hand-shake, of an external verbal discourse or an "internal" verbal discourse (consciousness), are not one and the same materiality. I shall leave on one side the problem of a theory of the differences between the modalities of materiality.

It remains that in this inverted presentation of things, we are not dealing with an "inversion" at all, since it is clear that certain notions have purely and simply disappeared from our presentation, whereas others on the contrary survive, and new terms appear.

Disappeared: the term *ideas.*

Survive: the terms *subject, consciousness, belief, actions.*

Appear: the terms *practices, rituals, ideological apparatus.*

It is therefore not an inversion or overturning (except in the sense in which one might say a government or a glass is overturned), but a reshuffle (of a non-ministerial type), a rather strange reshuffle, since we obtain the following result.

Ideas have disappeared as such (insofar as they are endowed with an ideal or spiritual existence), to the precise extent that it has emerged that their existence is inscribed in the actions of practices governed by rituals defined in the last instance by an ideological apparatus. It therefore appears that the subject acts insofar as he is acted by the following system (set out in the order of its real determination): ideology existing in a material ideological apparatus, prescribing material practices governed by a material ritual, which practices exist in the material actions of a subject acting in all consciousness according to his belief.

But this very presentation reveals that we have retained the following notions: subject, consciousness, belief, actions. From this series I shall immediately extract the decisive central term on which everything else depends: the notion of the *subject*.

And I shall immediately set down two conjoint theses:

1. there is no practice except by and in an ideology;
2. there is no ideology except by the subject and for subjects.

I can now come to my central thesis.

Ideology Interpellates Individuals as Subjects

This thesis is simply a matter of making my last proposition explicit: there is no ideology except by the subject and for subjects. Meaning, there is no ideology except for concrete subjects, and this destination for ideology is only made possible by the subject: meaning, *by the category of the subject* and its functioning.

By this I mean that, even if it only appears under this name (the subject) with the rise of bourgeois ideology, above all with the rise of legal ideology,[5] the category of the subject (which may function under other names: e.g., as the soul in Plato, as God, etc.) is the constitutive category of all ideology, whatever its determination (regional or class) and whatever its historical date – since ideology has no history.

I say: the category of the subject is constitutive of all ideology, but at the same time and immediately I add that *the category of the subject is only constitutive of all ideology insofar as all ideology has the function (which defines it) of "constituting" concrete individuals as subjects*. In the interaction of this double constitution exists the functioning of all ideology, ideology being nothing but its functioning in the material forms of existence of that functioning.

In order to grasp what follows, it is essential to realize that both he who is writing these lines and the reader who reads them are themselves subjects, and therefore ideological subjects (a tautological proposition), i.e. that the author and the reader of these lines both live "spontaneously" or "naturally" in ideology in the sense in which I have said that "man is an ideological animal by nature".

That the author, insofar as he writes the lines of a discourse which claims to be scientific, is completely absent as a "subject" from "his" scientific discourse (for all scientific discourse is by definition a subject-less discourse, there is no "Subject of science" except in an ideology of science) is a different question which I shall leave on one side for the moment.

As St Paul admirably put it, it is in the "Logos", meaning in ideology, that we "live, move and have our being". It follows that, for you and for me, the category of the subject is a primary "obviousness" (obviousnesses are always primary): it is clear that you and I are subjects (free, ethical, etc. . . .). Like all obviousnesses, including those that make a word "name a thing" or "have a meaning" (therefore including the obviousness of the "transparency" of language), the "obviousness" that you and I are subjects – and that that does not cause any problems – is an ideological effect, the elementary ideological effect.[6] It is indeed a peculiarity of ideology that it imposes (without appearing to do so, since these are "obviousnesses") obviousnesses as obviousnesses, which we cannot *fail to recognize* and before which we have the inevitable and natural reaction of crying out (aloud or in the "still, small voice of conscience"): "That's obvious! That's right! That's true!"

At work in this reaction is the ideological *recognition* function which is one of the two functions of ideology as such (its inverse being the function of *misrecognition* – *méconnaissance*).

To take a highly "concrete" example, we all have friends who, when they knock on our door and we ask, through the door, the question "Who's there?", answer (since "it's obvious") "It's me". And we recognize that "it is him", or "her". We open the door, and "it's true, it really was she who was there". To take another example, when we recognize somebody of our (previous) acquaintance ((*re*)-*connaissance*) in the street, we show him that we have recognized him (and have recognized that he has recognized us) by saying to him "Hello, my friend", and shaking his hand (a material ritual practice of ideological recognition in everyday life – in France, at least; elsewhere, there are other rituals).

In this preliminary remark and these concrete illustrations, I only wish to point out that you and I are *always already* subjects, and as such constantly practice the rituals of ideological recognition, which guarantee for us that we are indeed concrete, individual, distinguishable and (naturally) irreplaceable subjects. The writing I am currently executing and the reading you are currently[7] performing are also in this respect rituals of ideological recognition, including the "obviousness" with which the "truth" or "error" of my reflections may impose itself on you.

But to recognize that we are subjects and that we function in the practical rituals of the most elementary everyday life (the hand-shake, the fact of calling you by your name, the fact of knowing, even if I do not know what it is, that you "have" a name of your own, which means that you are recognized as a unique subject, etc.) – this recognition only gives us the "consciousness" of our incessant (eternal) practice of ideological recognition – its consciousness, i.e. its *recognition* – but in no sense does it give us the (scientific) *knowledge* of the mechanism of this recognition. Now it is this knowledge that we have to reach, if you will, while speaking in ideology, and from within ideology we have to outline a discourse which tries to break with ideology, in order to dare to be the beginning of a scientific (i.e. subject-less) discourse on ideology.

Thus in order to represent why the category of the "subject" is constitutive of ideology, which only exists by constituting concrete subjects as subjects, I shall employ a special mode of exposition: "concrete" enough to be recognized, but abstract enough to be thinkable and thought, giving rise to a knowledge.

As a first formulation I shall say: *all ideology hails or interpellates concrete individuals as concrete subjects*, by the functioning of the category of the subject.

This is a proposition which entails that we distinguish for the moment between concrete individuals on the one hand and concrete subjects on the other, although at this level concrete subjects only exist insofar as they are supported by a concrete individual.

I shall then suggest that ideology "acts" or "functions" in such a way that it "recruits" subjects among the individuals (it recruits them all), or "transforms" the individuals into subjects (it transforms them all) by that very precise operation which I have called *interpellation* or hailing, and which can be imagined along the lines of the most commonplace everyday police (or other) hailing: "Hey, you there!"[8]

Assuming that the theoretical scene I have imagined takes place in the street, the hailed individual will turn round. By this mere one-hundred-and-eighty-degree physical conversion, he becomes a *subject*. Why? Because he has recognized that the hail was "really" addressed to him, and that "it was *really him* who was hailed" (and not someone else). Experience shows that the practical telecommunication of hailings is such that they hardly ever miss their man: verbal call or whistle, the one hailed always recognizes that it is really him who is being hailed. And yet it is a strange phenomenon, and one which cannot be explained solely by "guilt feelings", despite the large numbers who "have something on their consciences".

Naturally for the convenience and clarity of my little theoretical theatre I have had to present things in the form of a sequence, with a before and an after, and thus in the form of a temporal succession. There are individuals walking along. Somewhere (usually behind them) the hail rings out: "Hey, you there!" One individual (nine times out of ten it is the right one) turns round, believing/suspecting/knowing that it is for him, i.e. recognizing that "it really is he" who is meant by the hailing. But in reality these things happen without any succession. The existence of ideology and the hailing or interpellation of individuals as subjects are one and the same thing.

I might add: what thus seems to take place outside ideology (to be precise, in the street), in reality takes place in ideology. What really takes place in ideology seems therefore to take place outside it. That is why those who are in ideology believe themselves by definition outside ideology: one of the effects of ideology is the practical *denegation* of the ideological character of ideology by ideology: ideology never says, "I am ideological". It is necessary to be outside ideology, i.e. in scientific knowledge, to be able to say: I am in ideology (a quite exceptional case) or (the general case): I was in ideology. As is well known, the accusation of being in ideology only applies to others, never to oneself (unless one is really a Spinozist or a Marxist, which, in this matter, is to be exactly the same thing). Which amounts to saying that ideology *has no outside* (for itself), but at the same time *that it is nothing but outside* (for science and reality).

Spinoza explained this completely two centuries before Marx, who practised it but without explaining it in detail. But let us leave this point, although it is heavy with consequences, consequences which are not just theoretical, but also directly political, since, for example, the whole theory of criticism and self-criticism, the golden rule of the Marxist-Leninist practice of the class struggle, depends on it.

Thus ideology hails or interpellates individuals as subjects. As ideology is eternal, I must now suppress the temporal form in which I have presented the functioning of ideology, and say: ideology has always-already interpellated individuals as subjects, which amounts to making it clear that individuals are always-already interpellated by ideology as subjects, which necessarily leads us to one last proposition: *individuals are always-already subjects*. Hence individuals are "abstract" with respect to the subjects which they always-already are.

Notes

1   The family obviously has other "functions" than that of an ISA. It intervenes in the reproduction of labour power. In different modes of production it is the unit of production and/or the unit of consumption.

2   The "Law" belongs both to the (Repressive) State Apparatus and to the system of the ISAs.

3   In a pathetic text written in 1937, Krupskaya relates the history of Lenin's desperate efforts and what she regards as his failure.

4   What I have said in these few brief words about the class struggle in the ISAs is obviously far from exhausting the question of the class struggle.

   To approach this question, two principles must be borne in mind:

   The first principle was formulated by Marx in the Preface to *A Contribution to the Critique of Political Economy*: "In considering such transformations [a social revolution] a distinction should always be made between the material transformation of the economic conditions of production, which can be determined with the precision of natural science, and the legal, political, religious, aesthetic or philosophic – in short, ideological forms in which men become conscious of this conflict and fight it out." The class struggle is thus expressed and exercised in ideological forms, thus also in the ideological forms of the ISAs. But the class struggle *extends far beyond* these forms, and it is because it extends beyond them that the struggle of the exploited classes may also be exercised in the forms of the ISAs, and thus turn the weapon of ideology against the classes in power.

   This by virtue of the *second principle*: the class struggle extends beyond the ISAs because it is rooted elsewhere than in ideology, in the Infrastructure, in the relations of production, which are relations of exploitation and constitute the base for class relations.

5   Which borrowed the legal category of "subject in law" to make an ideological notion: man is by nature a subject.

6   Linguists and those who appeal to linguistics for various purposes often run up against difficulties which arise because they ignore the action of the ideological effects in all discourses – including even scientific discourses.

7   NB: this double "currently" is one more proof of the fact that ideology is "eternal", since these two "currentlys" are separated by an indefinite interval; I am writing these lines on 6 April 1969, you may read them at any subsequent time.

8   Hailing as an everyday practice subject to a precise ritual takes a quite "special" form in the policeman's practice of "hailing" which concerns the hailing of "suspects".

Part II

Social Life and Cultural Studies

Introduction to Part II

As we noted in our introduction, "Adventures in Media and Cultural Studies," a tradition of social-science based empirical research into mass communications and culture emerged in the United States during the 1940s and 1950s. The empirical methods of determining consumer demand, taste, opinions, and the effects of mass media were applied to a wide range of issues by Paul Lazarsfeld and a group of colleagues in the Bureau for Applied Social Research which Lazarsfeld founded at Columbia University. This project provided ground-breaking studies of the media and their effects, inaugurating debates that are still raging. In addition, communication departments were being established in the United States and elsewhere during the 1940s and 1950s which for the most part deployed empirical methods of communications research and made the study of mass communications a branch of academic inquiry.

Opposed to what were seen as overly empiricist and conformist approaches to the study of communication and culture, more critical approaches emerged. Within the traditions of critical media and cultural criticism, there are many models of social approaches to culture and what has become known as cultural studies. In a sense, every essay in this reader can be seen as an example of a social-contextualizing approach, which sees culture as a form of social life, and thus as a type of cultural studies. This perspective situates cultural and media artifacts within the social relations of production and reception in which culture is produced, distributed, and consumed. It analyzes media and culture as part of society and relates text to context in order to properly analyze, interpret, or criticize meaning and effect.

In *Mythologies*, Roland Barthes critically dissects a wide range of contemporary forms of culture, producing a unique method of cultural interpretation and critique. One of the selections we have chosen, "Operation Margarine," embodies the fundamental rhetorical and ideological operations that Barthes dissects in the conclusion to *Mythologies* ("Myth Today") that we also include. Margarine, on Barthes's account, is a highly artificial substance transfigured by advertising as natural, beneficial, and acceptable as a substitution for butter, as if they were identical. Analyzing ads which admit its deficiencies and then trumpet its benefits, Barthes claims that such operations provide an "inoculation" against criticism of its imperfections. A similar operation, he claims, is typical in discourses on topics like the military, church, or capitalism, in which their limitations are mentioned, to highlight their necessity and importance for the social order.

Likewise, mythologies "disappear" history, transforming contingent factors into natural essences, as if it were natural that an African soldier salute the French flag, in Barthes's famous example that erases all of the evils of French colonization in an idealized image. Constructing an argument that anticipates postmodern emphasis on difference and otherness, Barthes points out how myths also erase what is different and dissimilar, assimilating otherness to nature, as when the image of the French soldier folds the African into the French empire, or margarine ads assimilate an artificial substance to the order of culinary appropriateness.

Myths, Barthes argues, also use the rhetorical figure of tautology, incorporating in the examples given above African blacks to France or margarine to natural substances like butter. Myths may deploy as well the figure of what Barthes calls "neither-norism," a liberal device that enjoins rejecting extremes to identify with common sense – which usually means conforming to existing attitudes and behavior. Translating quality into quantity sometimes takes the form of holding certain qualities (high art, religion, or the state) as impossible to grasp, as ineffable, and thus above criticism. Or it may take the form of reducing discussion of business or politics to quantity alone, as in lists of the most profitable corporations or most valuable stocks in business publications; political discussions that focus on polls or ratings of candidates as opposed to more substantive and qualitative features also embody this operation. Such devices lend themselves to what Barthes calls "statements of fact," proverbial wisdom like "What's good for General Motors is Good for America" or "God Save the Queen," in which a contingent and problematic institution is identified with the country itself.

Barthes thus developed a method of analyzing rhetorical strategies of media culture, taking apart the mythologies that colonize social life and helping produce a critical consciousness on behalf of the reader. In *Understanding Media*, Marshall McLuhan taught his readers to take media seriously as important agents of change in the contemporary era. In the selection we have included, McLuhan sketches out his famous dictum, "the medium is the message." As a salient example, McLuhan appeals to the electric light bulb: it was the medium of electricity that profoundly changed social life, making possible new activities, creating novel cultural spaces, and overcoming the limitations of darkness. Likewise, McLuhan asserts, it is the formal effects of new media like radio or television that are crucial: television, for instance, appeals to a private citizen's viewing in a domestic space, and thus is part of a colonization of leisure by media corporations. And while radio appeals to the ear, television, McLuhan suggests, is more synaesthetic, bringing into play a wide range of senses and thus producing a more sensual and tribal culture than previous book culture.

Media are thus, for McLuhan, "translators" which provide access to a wide range of social experience. New media often transpose the old media in novel forms, as television absorbed the formats of radio, translating radio genres or forms into a new medium. In our day, everything is becoming digitized, translated into the language and form of computers. McLuhan was a prophet of both the media and computer age, noting how more and more forms of culture and our own consciousness are being rendered into the form of information. Think of how our personalities are translated into data in computer chatrooms, or email discussions, and of how the computer is transforming more and more modes of culture from print material to music to visual media into its own digital form and technology. Reflecting on the growth and power of electronic and digital culture helps one grasp that McLuhan was a prophet of the computer age as well as provocative analyst of media culture.

McLuhan himself also became an apologist for the media and consumer society, advising corporations and giving advice to governments (often ironically). A group in Europe, called the "Situationist International," theorized the latest developments in the media and consumer society in the 1950s and 1960s and developed oppositional practices to use the media against existing society. One of its key members, the French theorist and artist Guy Debord, described the contemporary scene as "the society of the spectacle." Debord and his comrades were themselves initially part of a French avant-garde artist milieu that was shaped by Dada, surrealism, lettrism, and other attempts to merge art and politics (see Marcus, 1989; Plant, 1992; and Wollen, 1993).[1] Influenced by Jean-Paul Sartre and his concept that human existence is always lived within a particular context or situation and that individuals can create their own situations – as well as Lefebvre's concept of everyday life and demand to radically transform it – Debord and his colleagues began devising strategies to construct new "situations" (see the 1957 Debord text in Knabb, 1981, pp. 17ff). This project would merge art and everyday life in the spirit of the radical avant-garde, and would require a revolution of both art and life.

For Debord, the spectacle is a tool of pacification and depoliticization; it is a "permanent opium war" (Debord, 1977, sec. 44) which stupefies social subjects and distracts them from the most urgent task of real life – recovering the full range of their human powers through creative practice. In Debord's formulation, the concept of the spectacle is integrally connected to the concept of separation, for in passively consuming spectacles, one is separated from actively producing one's life. Capitalist society separates workers from the product of their labor, art from life, and spheres of production from consumption, which involve spectators passively observing the products of social life. Debord and his group, the Situationist International, promoted an overcoming of all forms of separation against this passivity, in which individuals would directly produce their own life and modes of self-activity and collective practice.

Debord dissects a society saturated with spectacle which advertises its products, promotes its politicians, and reproduces its social life. Consumers of the spectacle, Debord argues, are separated from the process of production of everyday life, lost in consumerist fantasies, media phantasmagoria, and in our day the transformative media of cyberspace and computer technology. "Real life" is unreal, unglamorous, and boring in this world, while the spectacle is exciting and enthralling. Yet, Debord warns, the spectacle is entangling its devotees in the clutches of consumer capitalism, replicating consumption fetishism, and helping capital to commodify all domains of social and everyday life.

Walt Disney was perhaps the master of the spectacle during his day, and Ariel Dorfman and Armand Mattelart demystify the Disney spectacle. Reading Walt Disney comic books in the specific conjuncture of intense cultural struggle in Chile during the early 1970s, they unveil its ideological messages and conservative subtext. Both writers were political émigrés to Chile who were participating in the attempt to construct a socialist society when Salvador Allende was elected president – and eventually overthrown and murdered in 1973. In this highly charged political situation, Dorfman and Mattelart see Walt Disney comic books as agents of American imperialism, attempting to inculcate values of capitalism, patriarchy, and social conformity into readers of seemingly harmless cultural artifacts.

Adopting a satiric and mocking tone in the introduction to their book that we include here, Dorfman and Mattelart make fun of those academics who would ignore the artifacts of media culture as beneath their dignity. They also poke fun at themselves as "subversive" critics of the highly popular Walt Disney comics. Yet the issues they are dealing with are highly important and involve the early socialization of the child and creation of its imagination and fantasy life. Mass culture, the authors contend, plays a key role in this domain in the contemporary era, and is not always beneficent. Children's literature and media can, as we now are aware, cultivate violence, provide dubious role models, and teach problematic values and behavior.

Combining approaches of the humanities and social sciences (Dorfman has emerged as a major writer and cultural critic, while Mattelart is a world-renowned communications researcher), the authors contextualize Disney comic books as effective purveyors of capitalist ideology and Disney's American middle-class values. Pointing out that there are no fathers in the Donald Duck comics, Disney himself, in the authors' view, emerges as a surrogate father, teaching proper (conservative) values through his figures, images, and stories. Relentlessly scrutinizing the world of Disney, the authors detect conservative values and messages saturating the seemingly harmless and innocent "entertainment." Their work thus embodies an ideological critique that sees media culture as a crucial site of the ideological reproduction of the status quo.

In the article which we include here, Raymond Williams develops his own interpretation of "Base and Superstructure in Marxist Cultural Theory." Williams provides a clear and penetrating analysis of key concepts in Marxian theory including base and superstructure, determination, totality, hegemony, ideology, class, and practice. The selection provides a useful reprise of many of the key concepts introduced already by other theorists and adds some concepts to the critical arsenal. His discussion of "The Complexity of Hegemony" is especially interesting and points to his connections with British cultural studies.

Indeed, Williams is often interpreted as one of the precursors and key sources of the British cultural studies that first emerged in the early 1960s and since has become a global phenomenon.[2] Developing an expanded conception of culture that went beyond the literary conceptions dominant in the British academy, Williams conceptualized culture as "a whole way of life," that encompasses cultural artifacts, modes of sensibility, values, and practices (1958 and 1961). Arguing for the need to think together "culture and society," seeing the importance of media culture, and overcoming the division between "high" and "low" culture, Williams produced an impressive series of publications that deeply influenced the trajectory of British cultural studies. He polemicized against the concept of the masses which he claimed was condescending, elitist, and overly homogenizing, covering over real and important differences. This theme in turn came to run through the cultural populism which helped shape and distinguish British cultural studies.

The immediate precursors of British cultural studies created a critique of mass culture in some ways parallel to the work of the Frankfurt School, while more positively evaluating traditions of working-class culture and resistance. Richard Hoggart, Raymond Williams, and E. P. Thompson sought to affirm working-class culture against onslaughts of media culture produced by the culture industries. Richard Hoggart's *The Uses of Literacy* (1957) contrasted the vitality of British working-class institutions and life with the artificiality of the products of the culture industry, that were seen as a banal homogenization of British life and a colonization of its culture by heavily American-influenced institutions and capitalist ideology.

British cultural studies was also shaped by E. P. Thompson's studies of English working-class culture and celebration of forms of resistance (1963). Like Williams and Hoggart, Thompson interpreted the vicissitudes of English culture as a response to industrialization and urbanization; all three affirmed cultural values that criticized the excesses and horrors of urban-industrial development, and all saw culture as a potentially positive force, that could uplift and improve people. They were also strong democrats, seeing culture as an important force of democracy, and were anti-elitist, opposing conservative traditions of cultural criticism in England. Williams and Hoggart were deeply involved in projects of working-class education and oriented toward socialist politics, seeing their form of cultural studies as an instrument of progressive social change. Their critiques of Americanism and mass culture paralleled to some extent the earlier critique of the Frankfurt school, yet valorized a working class that the Frankfurt school saw as defeated in Germany and much of Europe during the era of fascism, and which they never saw as a strong resource for emancipatory social change.

The democratic and socialist humanism of Thompson, Williams, and Hoggart influenced the early Birmingham project that would continue their critique of modern culture and would seek forms of resistance to capitalist modernization. Resisting distinctions between high and low culture, Birmingham cultural studies valorized popular culture and active audiences, able to produce their own readings and meanings. Building on semiotic conceptions developed by Roland Barthes and Umberto Eco, Stuart Hall argued that a distinction must be made between the encoding of media texts by producers and the decoding by consumers in a study of "Encoding/Decoding" which we include below.[3] This distinction highlighted the ability of audiences to produce their own readings and meanings, to decode texts in aberrant or oppositional ways, as well as the "preferred" ways in tune with the dominant ideology.

In an article "On the Politics of Empirical Audience Research" which appears below, Ien Ang distinguishes the "new audience research" undertaken by British cultural studies and their followers from a more liberal-pluralist view of the active audience associated with "uses and gratifications" theory and mainstream communication research. While the latter adopts empiricist models to gain more accurate scientific knowledge to learn how audiences use and enjoy media like television, the more critical cultural studies approach adopts "self-reflexive" and "interpretive" methods, critically reflecting on the presuppositions of audience research and the actual studies undertaken; it also employs a more explicitly interpretive methodology to make sense of the results of inquiry, wishing to learn more about the contextual situation of audiences, their social relations, and how they both use and resist dominant cultures.

Hence, whereas empiricist approaches to the audience strive for pure knowledge, cultural studies aims at social critique and transformation, stressing the conflictual elements of audience reception and how audiences oppose the dominant social order rather than simply being absorbed and integrated. Thus, whereas uses and gratification theory reproduces a liberal-pluralist perspective, emphasizing consumer sovereignty, freedom of choice, and the individual creation of meaning, cultural studies adopts a more oppositionalist position, showing how audiences negotiate a complex relation to dominant institutions and forms of power. Hence, although institutional power disappears or is ignored by empiricist approaches to the audience, cultural studies describes a complex interaction between audiences and dominant institutions and forces.

The British cultural studies notion of the active audience has also been criticized by political economists as well as others who are skeptical about the unreserved celebration of audience agency and textual polysemy. Herbert Schiller (1989), for instance, sharply critiques the notion of "limited effects" and its contemporary corollary, "the active audience." The rhetoric of pluralism and diversity in the media pivots on the celebration of multiple channels and increasingly fragmented and individualized media offerings. Yet as Schiller points out, this impression of multiplicity diverts attention from the concentration of ownership behind the apparent diversity. Any potential for social transformation is impeded by, as he says, "a very considerable 'if' – if the instrumentation had different controllers" (p. 148). His analysis of the idea of an "active" audience is more pointed, as it engages questions of power between viewer and text as well as the complex relationships among media and other "cultural means that together provide the apparatus of domination and the conditions of dependency" (p. 151).

British cultural studies, however, insists that individuals use media culture to generate potentially oppositional readings, fashion identities, and subcultures. In his book *Subculture: The Meaning of Style*, selections from which we are including here, Dick Hebdige analyzes the ways in which individuals and groups mobilize style and subcultures to produce their own often oppositional identities and groups. The introduction to his book draws on many of the figures that we have included in our reader – Gramsci, Barthes, Raymond Williams, British cultural studies, etc. Hebdige applies their positions in studies of various English subcultures, including mods, rockers, and punks. In the passage that we have chosen for inclusion, he discusses how subcultures break with the mainstream culture and provide alternatives for their members.

Hebdige highlights the transgressive and potentially oppositional dimension of subcultures. But he also analyzes how subcultures can be incorporated back into mainstream cultures, or effectively marginalized. Subcultures can be commodified, as sex, drugs, music, and fashion of the counterculture of the 1960s were successfully marketed after the initial shock of an oppositional culture was absorbed. Ideologically, subcultures can be trivialized, in which differences are minimized and denied with the mainstream, or they can be exoticized, presented as marginal freaks – as the mainstream tried to accomplish with the more extreme Yippies in the 1960s or punks of the 1970s.

British cultural studies was thus engaged in a sustained quest for political agency and new oppositional political subjects and movements when they discerned that the working class was integrated into existing capitalist societies. Their studies were highly political in nature and stressed the potentials for resistance in oppositional subcultures. The development of cultural studies and search for new political agents were influenced by 1960s struggles and political movements. The move toward feminism, often conflictual, was shaped by the feminist movement, while the turn toward race as a significant factor of study was fueled by the antiracist struggles of the day. The focus in British cultural studies on education was related to political concern with the role of schooling in the continuing bourgeois hegemony despite the struggles of the 1960s – as well as a return to a pedagogical concern that was at the origins of the work of the Birmingham group. The right turn in British politics with Thatcher's victory led in the late 1970s to concern with understanding the authoritarian populism of the new conservative hegemony.

Moreover, British cultural studies developed an approach that avoided cutting up the field of culture into high and low, popular vs. elite, and saw all forms of culture as worthy of scrutiny and criticism. It advocated approaches to culture that appraised the politics of culture and made political discriminations between different types of culture and their vary-ing political effects. Bringing the study of race, gender, and class into the center of the study of culture and communications, the Birmingham Centre adopted a critical approach that, like the Frankfurt school, but without some of its flaws, interpreted culture within society and situated the study of culture within the field of contemporary social theory and oppositional politics.

Yet the Birmingham project also paved the way, as we suggest in a later section, for a postmodern populist turn in cultural studies, which responds to a later stage of capitalism. Emphasis on consumption, on audience creation of meaning, on difference and heterogen-eity, corresponds to the contemporary stage of global capitalism in which consumer sover-eignty is celebrated, more differences are tolerated and marketed, and audiences are enjoined to embrace new products, technology, and to produce novel identities. Hence, cultural studies today is extremely variegated on a global scale with a wealth of different perspectives, topics, and projects.

Notes

1   On Debord and the Situationist International see Marcus (1989); Plant (1992), Wollen (1993), and the material in Substance 90 (1999).

2   For accounts of origins and genesis of British cultural studies, see Hall (1980); Johnson (1985/86); Fiske (1986); O'Conner (1989); Turner (1990); Agger (1992); McGuigan (1992); Kellner (1995); Dworkin (1997); and Grossberg (1997a, b). More polemical, alternative genealogies of cultural

studies stress the broader historical antecedents, and include Davies (1995) who points to the origins of the problematic of British cultural studies in debates around the journals *University Review* and *New Left Review*. Steele (1997) wishes to go back and retrieve the roots of British cultural studies in an earlier adult education movement that he thinks provides important resources for cultural studies today that have been covered over in the narratives of the progressive appropriations of theory that characterize most genealogies of cultural studies. He argues that the long and heroic march of the "theory express" of European Marxism and post-Marxism may have dumped "an extremely ripe mound of manure on the seedling of British cultural studies, only to bury some of their more fragile shoots" (1997: 205). And Ang and Stratton (1996) argue that identification of cultural studies with the British model perpetuates an imperialist ideology that identifies all-important cultural creation with the imperial power, relegating broader international developments in cultural studies to the margins. On earlier traditions of US cultural studies, see Ross (1989) and Aronowitz (1993). For readers which document the positions of British cultural studies, see the articles collected in Grossberg, Nelson, and Triechler (1992) and During (1993).

3   It might be pointed out that Walter Benjamin – loosely affiliated with the Frankfurt School, but not part of their inner circle – also took seriously media culture, saw its emancipatory potential, and posited the possibility of an active audience. Likewise T. W. Adorno and Leo Lowenthal focused attention on audience use and reception of artifacts of media culture, so there are precedents to the Birmingham focus on the audience and the reception and decoding of cultural texts. On Benjamin, see Buck-Morss (1989).

References

Agger, Ben (1992) *Cultural Studies*. London: Falmer Press.

Ang, Ien (1985) *Watching Dallas*. New York: Metheun.

—— (1991) "On the Politics of Empirical Audience Research," in *Living Room Wars: Rethinking Media Audiences for a Postmodern World*, 35–52. New York and London: Routledge.

—— (1991) *Desperately Seeking the Audience*. London and New York: Routledge.

Ang, Ien and J. Stratton (1996) "Asianing Australia: Notes Towards a Critical Transnational in Cultural Studies," *Cultural Studies* (10/1).

Aronowitz, Stanley (1993) *Roll Over Beethoven*. Hanover, NH: University Press of New England.

Barthes, Roland (1983) "Operation Margarine" and "Myth Today," in *Mythologies*, 41–2 and 150–9. Translated by Annette Lavers. New York: Hill and Wang.

Buck-Morss, Susan (1989) *The Dialectics of Seeing*. Cambridge, MA: MIT Press.

Davies, Ioan (1995) *Cultural Studies and After*. London and New York: Routledge.

Debord, Guy (1977) "The Consumption as Spectacle," in *Society of the Spectacle*, nos. 1–18 and 42. Detroit: Black & Red.

Dorfman, Ariel, and Armand Mattelart (1971) "Introduction: Instructions on How to Become a General in the Disneyland Club," in *How to Read Donald Duck*: 25–32. New York: International General.

During, Simon (ed.) (1993) *The Cultural Studies Reader*. London and New York: Routledge.

Dworkin, Dennis (1997) *Cultural Marxism in Postwar Britain: History, the New Left, and the Origins of Cultural Studies*. Durham, NC: Duke University Press.

Fiske, John (1986) "British Cultural Studies and Television," in *Channels of Discourse*, ed. R. C. Allen: 254–89. Chapel Hill: University of North Carolina Press.

—— (1989) *Reading the Popular*. Boston, MA: Unwin Hyman.

—— (1993) *Power Plays: Power Works*. New York and London: Verso.

Grossberg, Lawrence (1997a) *Bringing It All Back Home: Essays on Cultural Studies*. Durham, NC, and London: Duke University Press.

—— (1997b) *Dancing in Spite of Myself: Essays on Popular Culture*. Durham, NC, and London: Duke University Press.

Grossberg, Lawrence, Nelson, Cary and Paula Treichler (1992) *Cultural Studies*. New York: Routledge.

Hall, Stuart (1980) "Encoding/Decoding," in *Culture, Media, Language*: 128–38, op. cit.

Hebdige, Dick (1979) *Subculture: The Meaning of Style*. New York and London: Routledge.

Hoggart, Richard (1957) *The Uses of Literacy*. New York: Oxford University Press.

Jefferson, Tony (ed.) (1976) *Resistance through Rituals*. London: Hutchinson.

Johnson, Richard (1985/6) "What is Cultural Studies Anyway?" *Social Text*, 16: 38–80.

Kellner, Douglas (1995) *Media Culture: Cultural Studies, Identity, and Politics Between the Modern and the Postmodern*. London and New York: Routledge.

—— (1997) "Critical Theory and British Cultural Studies: The Missed Articulation," in *Cultural Methodologies*, ed. Jim McGuigan: 12–41. London: Sage.

Knabb, Ken (1981) *Situationist International Anthology*. Berkeley: Bureau of Public Secrets.

Lazarsfeld, Paul (1993) *On Social Research and its Language*, ed. Raymond Boudon. Chicago: University of Chicago Press.

Marcus, Greil (1989) *Lipstick Traces*. Cambridge, MA: Harvard University Press.

Marx, Karl and Engels, Friedrich (1978). *The Marx–Engels Reader*, ed. Robert Tucker. New York: Norton.

McGuigan, Jim (1992) *Cultural Populism*. London and New York: Routledge.

McLuhan, Marshall (1961) *The Gutenberg Galaxy*. New York: Signet.

—— (1964) *Understanding Media: The Extensions of Man*. New York: Signet.

Merton, Robert (1980) *Qualitative and Quantitive Social Research: Papers in Honor of Paul F. Lazarsfeld*. New York: Free Press.

O'Connor, Alan (1989) "The Problem of American Cultural Studies," *Critical Studies in Mass Communication* (December), 405–13.

Plant, Sadie (1992) *The Most Radical Gesture*. London and New York: Routledge.

Ross, Andrew (1989) *No Respect: Intellectuals and Popular Culture*. London and New York: Routledge.

Schiller, Herbert (1980) *Culture, Inc*. New York: Oxford University Press.

Schramm, Wilbur (1997) *The Beginnings of Communication Study in America: A Personal Memoir*. Altamira.

Steele, Tom (1997) *The Emergence of Cultural Studies 1945–65: Adult Education, Cultural Politics and the English Question*. London: Lawrence & Wishart.

Thompson, E. P. (1963) *The Making of the English Working Class*. New York: Pantheon.

Thompson, John (1991) *Ideology and Modern Culture*. Cambridge: Polity Press.

Turner, Graeme (1990) *British Cultural Studies: An Introduction*. New York: Unwin Hyman.

Williams, Raymond (1958) *Culture and Society*. New York: Columbia University Press.

—— (1961) *The Long Revolution*. London: Chatto & Windus.

—— (1962) *Communications*. London: Penguin.

—— (1980) *Problems in Materialism and Culture: Selected Essays*. London: Verso.

Wollen, Peter (1993) *Raiding the Icebox: Reflections on Twentieth Century Culture*. Bloomington, IN: Indiana University Press.

(i) Operation Margarine; (ii) Myth Today

Roland Barthes

(i) Operation Margarine

To instil into the Established Order the complacent portrayal of its drawbacks has nowadays become a paradoxical but incontrovertible means of exalting it. Here is the pattern of this new-style demonstration: take the established value which you want to restore or develop, and first lavishly display its pettiness, the injustices which it produces, the vexations to which it gives rise, and plunge it into its natural imperfection; then, at the last moment, save it *in spite of*, or rather *by* the heavy curse of its blemishes. Some examples? There is no lack of them.

Take the army; show without disguise its chiefs as martinets, its discipline as narrow-minded and unfair, and into this stupid tyranny immerse an average human being, fallible but likeable, the archetype of the spectator. And then, at the last moment, turn over the magical hat, and pull out of it the image of an army, flags flying, triumphant, bewitching, to which, like Sganarelle's wife,[1] one cannot but be faithful although beaten (*From here to eternity*).

Take the Army again: lay down as a basic principle the scientific fanaticism of its engineers, and their blindness; show all that is destroyed by such a pitiless rigour: human beings, couples. And then bring out the flag, save the army in the name of progress, hitch the greatness of the former to the triumph of the latter (*Les Cyclones*, by Jules Roy).

Finally, the Church: speak with burning zeal about its self-righteousness, the narrow-mindedness of its bigots, indicate that all this can be murderous, hide none of the weaknesses of the faith. And then, *in extremis*, hint that the letter of the law, however unattractive, is a way to salvation for its very victims, and so justify moral austerity by the saintliness of those whom it crushes (*The Living Room*, by Graham Greene).

From Roland Barthes, "Operation margarine" and "Myth today." In *Mythologies*, pp. 41–2 and 150–9. Translated by Annette Lavers. New York: Hill and Wang, 1983.

It is a kind of homeopathy: one cures doubts about the Church or the Army by the very ills of the Church and the Army. One inoculates the public with a contingent evil to prevent or cure an essential one. To rebel against the inhumanity of the Established Order and its values, according to this way of thinking, is an illness which is common, natural, forgivable; one must not collide with it head-on, but rather exorcize it like a possession: the patient is made to give a representation of his illness, he is made familiar with the very appearance of his revolt, and this revolt disappears all the more surely since, once at a distance and the object of a gaze, the Established Order is no longer anything but a Manichaean compound and therefore inevitable, one which wins on both counts, and is therefore beneficial. The imminent evil of enslavement is redeemed by the transcendent good of religion, fatherland, the Church, etc. A little "confessed" evil saves one from acknowledging a lot of hidden evil.

One can trace in advertising a narrative pattern which clearly shows the working of this new vaccine. It is found in the publicity for *Astra* margarine. The episode always begins with a cry of indignation against margarine: "A mousse? Made with margarine? Unthinkable!" "Margarine? Your uncle will be furious!" And then one's eyes are opened, one's conscience becomes more pliable, and margarine is a delicious food, tasty, digestible, economical, useful in all circumstances. The moral at the end is well known: "Here you are, rid of a prejudice which cost you dearly!" It is in the same way that the Established Order relieves you of your progressive prejudices. The Army, an absolute value? It is unthinkable: look at its vexations, its strictness, the always possible blindness of its chiefs. The Church, infallible? Alas, it is very doubtful: look at its bigots, its powerless priests, its murderous conformism. And then common sense makes its reckoning: what is this trifling dross of Order, compared to its advantages? It is well worth the price of an immunization. What does it matter, *after all*, if margarine is just fat, when it goes further than butter, and costs less? What does it matter, *after all*, if Order is a little brutal or a little blind, when it allows us to live cheaply? Here we are, in our turn, rid of a prejudice which cost us dearly, too dearly, which cost us too much in scruples, in revolt, in fights and in solitude. [. . .]

(ii) Myth Today

Since we cannot yet draw up the list of the dialectal forms of bourgeois myth, we can always sketch its rhetorical forms. One must understand here by *rhetoric* a set of fixed, regulated, insistent figures, according to which the varied forms of the mythical signifier arrange themselves. These figures are transparent inasmuch as they do not affect the plasticity of the signifier; but they are already sufficiently conceptualized to adapt to an historical representation of the world (just as classical rhetoric can account for a representation of the Aristotelian type). It is through their rhetoric that bourgeois myths outline the general prospect of this *pseudo-physis* which defines the dream of the contemporary bourgeois world. Here are its principal figures:

1. *The inoculation.*   I have already given examples of this very general figure, which consists in admitting the accidental evil of a class-bound institution the better to conceal its principal evil. One immunizes the contents of the collective imagination by means of a small inoculation of acknowledged evil; one thus protects it against the risk of a generalized subversion. This *liberal* treatment would not have been possible only a hundred years ago. Then, the bourgeois Good did not compromise with anything, it was quite stiff. It has become much more supple since: the bourgeoisie no longer hesitates to acknowledge some localized subversions: the avant-garde, the irrational in childhood, etc. It now lives in a balanced economy: as in any sound joint-stock company, the smaller shares – in law but not in fact – compensate the big ones.

2. *The privation of history.*   Myth deprives the object of which it speaks of all History.[2] In it, history evaporates. It is a kind of ideal servant: it prepares all things, brings them, lays them out, the master arrives, it silently disappears: all that is left for one to do is to enjoy this beautiful object without wondering where it comes from. Or even better: it can only come from eternity: since the beginning of time, it has been made for bourgeois man, the Spain of the *Blue Guide* has been made for the tourist, and "primitives" have prepared their dances with a view to an exotic festivity. We can see all the disturbing things which this felicitous figure removes from sight: both determinism and freedom. Nothing is produced, nothing is chosen: all one has to do is to possess these new objects from which all soiling trace of origin or choice has been removed. This miraculous evaporation of history is another form of a concept common to most bourgeois myths: the irresponsibility of man.

3. *Identification.*   The petit-bourgeois is a man unable to imagine the Other.[3] If he comes face to face with him, he blinds himself, ignores and denies him, or else transforms him into himself. In the petit-bourgeois universe, all the experiences of confrontation are reverberating, any otherness is reduced to sameness. The spectacle or the tribunal, which are both places where the Other threatens to appear in full view, become mirrors. This is because the Other is a scandal which threatens his essence. Dominici cannot have access to social existence unless he is previously reduced to the state of a small simulacrum of the President of the Assizes or the Public Prosecutor: this is the price one must pay in order to condemn him justly, since Justice is a weighing operation and since scales can only weigh like against like. There are, in any petit-bourgeois consciousness, small simulacra of the hooligan, the parricide, the homosexual, etc., which periodically the judiciary extracts from its brain, puts in the dock, admonishes and condemns: one never tries anybody but analogues *who have gone astray*: it is a question of direction, not of nature, for *that's how men are.* Sometimes – rarely – the Other is revealed as irreducible: not because of a sudden scruple, but because *common sense* rebels: a man does not have a white skin, but a black one, another drinks pear juice, not *Pernod.* How can one assimilate the Negro, the Russian? There is here a figure for emergencies: exoticism. The Other becomes a pure object, a spectacle, a clown. Relegated to the confines of humanity, he

no longer threatens the security of the home. This figure is chiefly petit-bourgeois. For, even if he is unable to experience the Other in himself, the bourgeois can at least imagine the place where he fits in: this is what is known as liberalism, which is a sort of intellectual equilibrium based on recognized places. The petit-bourgeois class is not liberal (it produces Fascism, whereas the bourgeoisie uses it): it follows the same route as the bourgeoisie, but lags behind.

4. *Tautology.* Yes, I know, it's an ugly word. But so is the thing. Tautology is this verbal device which consists in defining like by like (*"Drama is drama"*). We can view it as one of those types of magical behaviour dealt with by Sartre in his *Outline of a Theory of the Emotions*: one takes refuge in tautology as one does in fear, or anger, or sadness, when one is at a loss for an explanation: the accidental failure of language is magically identified with what one decides is a natural resistance of the object. In tautology, there is a double murder: one kills rationality because it resists one; one kills language because it betrays one. Tautology is a faint at the right moment, a saving aphasia, it is a death, or perhaps a comedy, the indignant "representation" of the *rights* of reality over and above language. Since it is magical, it can of course only take refuge behind the argument of authority: thus do parents at the end of their tether reply to the child who keeps on asking for explanations: "*because that's how it is*", or even better: "*just because, that's all*" – a magical act ashamed of itself, which verbally makes the gesture of rationality, but immediately abandons the latter, and believes itself to be even with causality because it has uttered the word which introduces it. Tautology testifies to a profound distrust of language, which is rejected because it has failed. Now any refusal of language is a death. Tautology creates a dead, a motionless world.

5. *Neither-Norism.* By this I mean this mythological figure which consists in stating two opposites and balancing the one by the other so as to reject them both. (I want *neither* this *nor* that.) It is on the whole a bourgeois figure, for it relates to a modern form of liberalism. We find again here the figure of the scales: reality is first reduced to analogues; then it is weighed; finally, equality having been ascertained, it is got rid of. Here also there is magical behaviour: both parties are dismissed because it is embarrassing to choose between them; one flees from an intolerable reality, reducing it to two opposites which balance each other only inasmuch as they are purely formal, relieved of all their specific weight. Neither-Norism can have degraded forms: in astrology, for example, ill-luck is always followed by equal good-luck; they are always predicted in a prudently compensatory perspective: a final equilibrium immobilizes values, life, destiny, etc.: one no longer needs to choose, but only to endorse.

6. *The quantification of quality.* This is a figure which is latent in all the preceding ones. By reducing any quality to quantity, myth economizes intelligence: it understands reality more cheaply. I have given several examples of this mechanism which bourgeois – and especially petit-bourgeois – mythology does not hesitate to apply to aesthetic realities which it deems on the other hand to partake of an immaterial essence. Bourgeois theatre is a good example of this contradiction: on

the one hand, theatre is presented as an essence which cannot be reduced to any language and reveals itself only to the heart, to intuition. From this quality, it receives an irritable dignity (it is forbidden as a crime of "lese-essence" to speak about the theatre *scientifically*: or rather, any intellectual way of viewing the theatre is discredited as scientism or pedantic language). On the other hand, bourgeois dramatic art rests on a pure quantification of effects: a whole circuit of computable appearances establishes a quantitative equality between the cost of a ticket and the tears of an actor or the luxuriousness of a set: what is currently meant by the "naturalness" of an actor, for instance, is above all a conspicuous quantity of effects.

7. *The statement of fact.*   Myths tend towards proverbs. Bourgeois ideology invests in this figure interests which are bound to its very essence: universalism, the refusal of any explanation, an unalterable hierarchy of the world. But we must again distinguish the language-object from the metalanguage. Popular, ancestral proverbs still partake of an instrumental grasp of the world as object. A rural statement of fact, such as "*the weather is fine*" keeps a real link with the usefulness of fine weather. It is an implicitly technological statement; the word, here, in spite of its general, abstract form, paves the way for actions, it inserts itself into a fabricating order: the farmer does not speak *about* the weather, he "acts it", he draws it into his labour. All our popular proverbs thus represent active speech which has gradually solidified into reflexive speech, but where reflection is curtailed, reduced to a statement of fact, and so to speak timid, prudent, and closely hugging experience. Popular proverbs foresee more than they assert, they remain the speech of a humanity which is making itself, not one which is. Bourgeois aphorisms, on the other hand, belong to metalanguage; they are a second-order language which bears on objects already prepared. Their classical form is the maxim. Here the statement is no longer directed towards a world to be made; it must overlay one which is already made, bury the traces of this production under a self-evident appearance of eternity: it is a counter-explanation, the decorous equivalent of a tautology, of this peremptory *because* which parents in need of knowledge hang above the heads of their children. The foundation of the bourgeois statement of fact is *common sense*, that is, truth when it stops on the arbitrary order of him who speaks it.

I have listed these rhetorical figures without any special order, and there may well be many others: some can become worn out, others can come into being. But it is obvious that those given here, such as they are, fall into two great categories, which are like the Zodiacal Signs of the bourgeois universe: the Essences and the Scales. Bourgeois ideology continuously transforms the products of history into essential types. Just as the cuttlefish squirts its ink in order to protect itself, it cannot rest until it has obscured the ceaseless making of the world, fixated this world into an object which can be for ever possessed, catalogued its riches, embalmed it, and injected into reality some purifying essence which will stop its transformation, its flight towards other forms of existence. And these riches, thus fixated and frozen, will at last become computable: bourgeois morality will essentially be a weighing operation, the essences will be placed in scales of which bourgeois man will remain the motionless beam. For the very end of myths is to immobilize the world: they must suggest and mimic a universal order which has fixated once and for all the hierarchy of possessions. Thus, every day and everywhere, man is stopped by myths, referred by them to this motionless prototype which lives in his place, stifles him in the manner of a huge internal parasite and assigns to his activity the narrow limits within which he is allowed to suffer without upsetting the world: bourgeois pseudo-physis is in the fullest sense a prohibition for man against inventing himself. Myths are nothing but this ceaseless, untiring solicitation, this insidious and inflexible demand that all men recognize themselves in this image, eternal yet bearing a date, which was built of them one day as if for all time. For the Nature, in which they are locked up under the pretext of being eternalized, is nothing but an Usage. And it is this Usage, however lofty, that they must take in hand and transform.

Necessity and Limits of Mythology

I must, as a conclusion, say a few words about the mythologist himself. This term is rather grand and self-assured. Yet one can predict for the mythologist, if there ever is one, a few difficulties, in feeling if not in method. True, he will have no trouble in feeling justified: whatever its mistakes, mythology is certain to participate in the making of the world. Holding as a principle that man in a bourgeois society is at every turn plunged into a false Nature, it attempts to find again under the assumed innocence of the most unsophisticated relationships, the profound alienation which this innocence is meant to make one accept. The unveiling which it carries out is therefore a political act: founded on a responsible idea of language, mythology thereby postulates the freedom of the latter. It is certain that in this sense mythology *harmonizes* with the world, not as it is, but as it wants to create itself (Brecht had for this an efficiently ambiguous word: *Einverstandnis*, at once an understanding of reality and a complicity with it).

This harmony justifies the mythologist but does not fulfil him: his status still remains basically one of being excluded. Justified by the political dimension, the mythologist is still at a distance from it. His speech is a metalanguage, it "acts" nothing; at the most, it unveils – or does it? To whom? His task always remains ambiguous, hampered by its ethical origin. He can live revolutionary action only vicariously: hence the self-conscious character of his function, this something a little stiff and pains-taking, muddled and excessively simplified which brands any intellectual behaviour with an openly political foundation ("uncommitted" types of literature are infinitely more "elegant"; they are in their place in metalanguage).

Also, the mythologist cuts himself off from all the myth-consumers, and this is no small matter. If this [is] applied to a particular section of the collectivity, well and good.[4] But when a myth reaches the entire community, it is from the latter that the mythologist must become estranged if he wants to liberate the myth. Any myth with some degree of generality is in fact ambiguous, because it represents the very humanity of those who, having nothing, have borrowed it. To decipher the Tour de France or the "good French Wine" is to cut oneself off from those who are entertained or warmed up by them. The mythologist is condemned to live in a theoretical sociality; for him, to be in society is, at best, to be truthful: his utmost sociality dwells in his utmost morality. His connection with the world is of the order of sarcasm.

One must even go further: in a sense, the mythologist is excluded from this history in the name of which he professes to act. The havoc which he wreaks in the language of the community is absolute for him, it fills his assignment to the brim: he must live this assignment without any hope of going back or any assumption of payment. It is forbidden for him to imagine what the world will concretely be like, when the immediate object of his criticism has disappeared. Utopia is an impossible luxury for him: he greatly doubts that tomorrow's truths will be the exact reverse of today's lies. History never ensures the triumph pure and simple of something over its opposite: it unveils, while making itself, unimaginable solutions, unforeseeable syntheses. The mythologist is not even in a Moses-like situation: he cannot see the Promised Land. For him, tomorrow's positivity is entirely hidden by today's negativity. All the values of his undertaking appear to him as acts of destruction: the latter accurately cover the former, nothing protrudes. This subjective grasp of history in which the potent seed of the future *is nothing but* the most profound apocalypse of the present has been expressed by Saint-Just in a strange saying: "*What constitutes the Republic is the total destruction of what is opposed to it.*" This must not, I think, be understood in the trivial sense of: "One has to clear the way before reconstructing." The copula has an exhaustive meaning: there is for some men a subjective dark night of history where the future becomes an essence, the essential destruction of the past.

One last exclusion threatens the mythologist: he constantly runs the risk of causing the reality which he purports to protect, to disappear. Quite apart from all speech, the *D.S.19* is a technologically defined object: it is capable of a certain speed, it meets the wind in a certain way, etc. And this type of reality cannot be spoken of by the mythologist. The mechanic, the engineer, even the user, "*speak* the object"; but the mythologist is condemned to metalanguage. This exclusion already has a name: it is what is called ideologism. Zhdanovism has roundly condemned it (without proving, incidentally, that it was, *for the time being*, avoidable) in the early Lukács, in Marr's linguistics, in works like those of Bénichou or Goldmann, opposing to it the reticence of a reality inaccessible to ideology, such as that of language according to Stalin. It is true that ideologism resolves the contradiction of alienated reality by an amputation, not a synthesis (but as for Zhdanovism, it does not even resolve it): wine is objectively good, and *at the same time*, the goodness of wine is a myth: here is the aporia. The mythologist gets out of this as best he can: he deals with the goodness of wine, not with the wine itself, just as the historian deals with Pascal's ideology, not with the *Pensées* in themselves.[5]

It seems that this is a difficulty pertaining to our times: there is as yet only one possible choice, and this choice can bear only on two equally extreme methods: either to posit a reality which is entirely permeable to history, and ideologize; or, conversely, to posit a reality which is *ultimately* impenetrable, irreducible, and, in this case, poetize. In a word, I do not yet see a synthesis between ideology and poetry (by poetry I understand, in a very general way, the search for the inalienable meaning of things).

The fact that we cannot manage to achieve more than an unstable grasp of reality doubtless gives the measure of our present alienation: we constantly drift between the object and its demystification, powerless to render its wholeness. For if we penetrate the object, we liberate it but we destroy it; and if we acknowledge its full weight, we respect it, but we restore it to a state which is still mystified. It would seem that we are condemned for some time yet always to speak *excessively* about reality. This is probably because ideologism and its opposite are types of behaviour which are still magical, terrorized, blinded and fascinated by the split in the social world. And yet, this is what we must seek: a reconciliation between reality and men, between description and explanation, between object and knowledge.

Notes

1   In Molière's *Médecin malgré lui*.
2   Marx: ". . . we must pay attention to this history, since ideology boils down to either an erroneous conception of this history, *or to a complete abstraction from it*" (*The German Ideology*).
3   Marx: ". . . what makes them representative of the petit-bourgeois class, is that their minds, their consciousnesses, do not extend beyond the limits which this class has set to its activities" (*The Eighteenth Brumaire*). And Gorki: "the petit-bourgeois is the man who has preferred himself to all else."
4   It is not only from the public that one becomes estranged; it is sometimes also from the very object of the myth. In order to demystify Poetic Childhood, for instance, I have had, so to speak, *to lack confidence* in Minou Drouet the child. I have had to ignore, in her, under the enormous myth with which she is cumbered, something like a tender, open, possibility. It is never a good thing to speak *against* a little girl.
5   Even here, in these mythologies, I have used trickery: finding it painful constantly to work on the evaporation of reality, I have started to make it excessively dense, and to discover in it a surprising compactness which I savoured with delight, and I have given a few examples of "substantial psycho-analysis" about some mythical objects.

8

The Medium is the Message

Marshall McLuhan

In a culture like ours, long accustomed to splitting and dividing all things as a means of control, it is sometimes a bit of a shock to be reminded that, in operational and practical fact, the medium is the message. This is merely to say that the personal and social consequences of any medium – that is, of any extension of ourselves – result from the new scale that is introduced into our affairs by each extension of ourselves, or by any new technology. Thus, with automation, for example, the new patterns of human association tend to eliminate jobs, it is true. That is the negative result. Positively, automation creates roles for people, which is to say depth of involvement in their work and human association that our preceding mechanical technology had destroyed. Many people would be disposed to say that it was not the machine, but what one did with the machine, that was its meaning or message. In terms of the ways in which the machine altered our relations to one another and to ourselves, it mattered not in the least whether it turned out cornflakes or Cadillacs. The restructuring of human work and association was shaped by the technique of fragmentation that is the essence of machine technology. The essence of automation technology is the opposite. It is integral and decentralist in depth, just as the machine was fragmentary, centralist, and superficial in its patterning of human relationships.

The instance of the electric light may prove illuminating in this connection. The electric light is pure information. It is a medium without a message, as it were, unless it is used to spell out some verbal ad or name. This fact, characteristic of all media, means that the "content" of any medium is always another medium. The content of writing is speech, just as the written word is the content of print, and print is the content of the telegraph. If it is asked, "What is the content of speech?," it is necessary to say, "It is an actual process of thought, which is in itself nonverbal." An abstract painting represents direct manifestation of creative thought processes as

From Marshall McLuhan, "The medium is the message." In *Understanding Media: The Extensions of Man*, pp. 23–35, 63–7. New York: Signet, 1964.

they might appear in computer designs. What we are considering here, however, are the psychic and social consequences of the designs or patterns as they amplify or accelerate existing processes. For the "message" of any medium or technology is the change of scale or pace or pattern that it introduces into human affairs. The railway did not introduce movement or transportation or wheel or road into human society, but it accelerated and enlarged the scale of previous human functions, creating totally new kinds of cities and new kinds of work and leisure. This happened whether the railway functioned in a tropical or a northern environment, and is quite independent of the freight or content of the railway medium. The airplane, on the other hand, by accelerating the rate of transportation, tends to dissolve the railway form of city, politics, and association, quite independently of what the airplane is used for.

Let us return to the electric light. Whether the light is being used for brain surgery or night baseball is a matter of indifference. It could be argued that these activities are in some way the "content" of the electric light, since they could not exist without the electric light. This fact merely underlines the point that "the medium is the message" because it is the medium that shapes and controls the scale and form of human association and action. The content or uses of such media are as diverse as they are ineffectual in shaping the form of human association. Indeed, it is only too typical that the "content" of any medium blinds us to the character of the medium. It is only today that industries have become aware of the various kinds of business in which they are engaged. When IBM discovered that it was not in the business of making office equipment or business machines, but that it was in the business of processing information, then it began to navigate with clear vision. The General Electric Company makes a considerable portion of its profits from electric light bulbs and lighting systems. It has not yet discovered that, quite as much as A.T.&T., it is in the business of moving information.

   The electric light escapes attention as a communication medium just because it has no "content." And this makes it an invaluable instance of how people fail to study media at all. For it is not till the electric light is used to spell out some brand name that it is noticed as a medium. Then it is not the light but the "content" (or what is really another medium) that is noticed. The message of the electric light is like the message of electric power in industry, totally radical, pervasive, and decentralized. For electric light and power are separate from their uses, yet they eliminate time and space factors in human association exactly as do radio, telegraph, telephone, and TV, creating involvement in depth.

   A fairly complete handbook for studying the extensions of man could be made up from selections from Shakespeare. Some might quibble about whether or not he was referring to TV in these familiar lines from *Romeo and Juliet*:

> But soft! what light through yonder window breaks?
> It speaks, and yet says nothing.

In *Othello*, which, as much as *King Lear*, is concerned with the torment of people transformed by illusions, there are these lines that bespeak Shakespeare's intuition of the transforming powers of new media:

> Is there not charms
> By which the property of youth and maidhood
> May be abus'd? Have you not read, Roderigo,
> Of some such thing?

In Shakespeare's *Troilus and Cressida*, which is almost completely devoted to both a psychic and social study of communication, Shakespeare states his awareness that true social and political navigation depend upon anticipating the consequences of innovation:

> The providence that's in a watchful state
> Knows almost every grain of Plutus' gold,
> Finds bottom in the uncomprehensive deeps,
> Keeps place with thought, and almost like the gods
> Does thoughts unveil in their dumb cradles.

The increasing awareness of the action of media, quite independently of their "content" or programming, was indicated in the annoyed and anonymous stanza:

> In modern thought, (if not in fact)
> Nothing is that doesn't act,
> So that is reckoned wisdom which
> Describes the scratch but not the itch.

The same kind of total, configurational awareness that reveals why the medium is socially the message has occurred in the most recent and radical medium theories. In his *Stress of Life*, Hans Selye tells of the dismay of a research colleague on hearing of Selye's theory:

> When he saw me thus launched on yet another enraptured description of what I had observed in animals treated with this or that impure, toxic material, he looked at me with desperately sad eyes and said in obvious despair: "But Selye, try to realize what you are doing before it is too late! You have now decided to spend your entire life studying the pharmacology of dirt!" (Hans Selye, *The Stress of Life*)

As Selye deals with the total environmental situation in his "stress" theory of disease, so the latest approach to media study considers not only the "content" but the medium and the cultural matrix within which the particular medium operates. The older unawareness of the psychic and social effects of media can be illustrated from almost any of the conventional pronouncements.

   In accepting an honorary degree from the University of Notre Dame a few years ago, General David Sarnoff made this statement: "We are too prone to make technological instruments the scapegoats for the sins of those who wield them. The products of modern science are not in themselves good or bad; it is the way they are used that determines their value." That is the voice of the current somnambulism. Suppose we were to say, "Apple pie is in itself neither good nor bad; it is the way it is used that determines its value." Or, "The small-pox virus is in itself neither good nor bad; it is the way it is used that determines its value." Again, "Firearms are in themselves neither good nor bad; it is the way they are used that determines their value." That is, if the slugs reach the right people firearms are good. If the TV tube fires the right ammunition at the right people it is good. I am not being perverse. There is simply nothing in the Sarnoff statement that will bear scrutiny, for it ignores the nature of the medium, of any and all media, in the true Narcissus style of one hypnotized by the amputation and extension of his own being in a new technical form. General Sarnoff went on to explain his attitude to the technology of print, saying that it was true that print caused much trash to circulate, but it had also disseminated the Bible and the thoughts of seers and philosophers. It has never occurred to General Sarnoff that any technology could do anything but *add* itself on to what we already are.

Such economists as Robert Theobald, W. W. Rostow, and John Kenneth Galbraith have been explaining for years how it is that "classical economics" cannot explain change or growth. And the paradox of mechanization is that although it is itself the cause of maximal growth and change, the principle of mechanization excludes the very possibility of growth or the understanding of change. For mechanization is achieved by fragmentation of any process and by putting the fragmented parts in a series. Yet, as David Hume showed in the eighteenth century, there is no principle of causality in a mere sequence. That one thing follows another accounts for nothing. Nothing follows from following, except change. So the greatest of all reversals occurred with electricity, that ended sequence by making things instant. With instant speed the causes of things began to emerge to awareness again, as they had not done with things in sequence and in concatenation accordingly. Instead of asking which came first, the chicken or the egg, it suddenly seemed that a chicken was an egg's idea for getting more eggs.

Just before an airplane breaks the sound barrier, sound waves become visible on the wings of the plane. The sudden visibility of sound just as sound ends is an apt instance of that great pattern of being that reveals new and opposite forms just as the earlier forms reach their peak performance. Mechanization was never so vividly fragmented or sequential as in the birth of the movies, the moment that translated us beyond mechanism into the world of growth and organic interrelation. The movie, by sheer speeding up the mechanical, carried us from the world of sequence and connections into the world of creative configuration and structure. The message of the movie medium is that of transition from lineal connections to configurations. It is the transition that produced the now quite correct observation: "If it works, it's obsolete." When electric speed further takes over from mechanical movie sequences, then the lines of force in structures and in media become loud and clear. We return to the inclusive form of the icon.

To a highly literate and mechanized culture the movie appeared as a world of triumphant illusions and dreams that money could buy. It was at this moment of the movie that cubism occurred, and it has been described by E. H. Gombrich (*Art and Illusion*) as "the most radical attempt to stamp out ambiguity and to enforce one reading of the picture – that of a man-made construction, a colored canvas." For cubism substitutes all facets of an object simultaneously for the "point of view" or facet of perspective illusion. Instead of the specialized illusion of the third dimension on canvas, cubism sets up an interplay of planes and contradiction or dramatic conflict of patterns, lights, textures that "drives home the message" by involvement. This is held by many to be an exercise in painting, not in illusion.

In other words, cubism, by giving the inside and outside, the top, bottom, back, and front and the rest, in two dimensions, drops the illusion of perspective in favor of instant sensory awareness of the whole. Cubism, by seizing on instant total awareness, suddenly announced that *the medium is the message.* Is it not evident that the moment that sequence yields to the simultaneous, one is in the world of the structure and of configuration? Is that not what has happened in physics as in painting, poetry, and in communication? Specialized segments of attention have shifted to total field, and we can now say, "The medium is the message" quite naturally. Before the electric speed and total field, it was not obvious that the medium is the message. The message, it seemed, was the "content," as people used to ask what a painting was *about.* Yet they never thought to ask what a melody was about, nor what a house or a dress was about. In such matters, people retained some sense of the whole pattern, of form and function as a unity. But in the electric age this integral idea of structure and configuration has become so prevalent that educational theory has taken up the matter. Instead of working with specialized "problems" in arithmetic, the structural approach now follows the linea of force in the field of number and has small children meditating about number theory and "sets."

Cardinal Newman said of Napoleon, "He understood the grammar of gunpowder." Napoleon had paid some attention to other media as well, especially the semaphore telegraph that gave him a great advantage over his enemies. He is on record for saying that "Three hostile newspapers are more to be feared than a thousand bayonets."

Alexis de Tocqueville was the first to master the grammar of print and typography. He was thus able to read off the message of coming change in France and America as if he were reading aloud from a text that had been handed to him. In fact, the nineteenth century in France and in America was just such an open book to de Tocqueville because he had learned the grammar of print. So he, also, knew when that grammar did not apply. He was asked why he did not write a book on England, since he knew and admired England. He replied:

> One would have to have an unusual degree of philosophical folly to believe oneself able to judge England in six months. A year always seemed to me too short a time in which to appreciate the United States properly, and it is much easier to acquire clear and precise notions about the American Union than about Great Britain. In America all laws derive in a sense from the same line of thought. The whole of society, so to speak, is founded upon a single fact; everything springs from a simple principle. One could compare America to a forest pierced by a multitude of straight roads all converging on the same point. One has only to find the center and everything is revealed at a glance. But in England the paths run criss-cross, and it is only by travelling down each one of them that one can build up a picture of the whole.

De Tocqueville, in earlier work on the French Revolution, had explained how it was the printed word that, achieving cultural saturation in the eighteenth century, had homogenized the French nation. Frenchmen were the same kind of people from north to south. The typographic principles of uniformity, continuity, and lineality had overlaid the complexities of ancient feudal and oral society. The Revolution was carried out by the new literati and lawyers.

In England, however, such was the power of the ancient oral traditions of common law, backed by the medieval institution of Parliament, that no uniformity or continuity of the new visual print culture could take complete hold. The result was that the most important event in English history has never taken place; namely, the English Revolution on the lines of the French Revolution. The American Revolution had no medieval legal institutions to discard or to root out, apart from monarchy. And many have held that the American Presidency has become very much more personal and monarchical than any European monarch ever could be.

De Tocqueville's contrast between England and America is clearly based on the fact of typography and of print culture creating uniformity and continuity. England, he says, has rejected this principle and clung to the dynamic or oral common-law tradition. Hence the discontinuity and unpredictable quality of English culture. The grammar of print cannot help to construe the message of oral and nonwritten culture and institutions. The English aristocracy was properly classified as barbarian by Matthew Arnold because its power and status had nothing to do with literacy or with the cultural forms of typography. Said the Duke of Gloucester to Edward Gibbon upon the publication of his *Decline and Fall*: "Another damned fat book, eh, Mr. Gibbon? Scribble, scribble, scribble, eh, Mr. Gibbon?" De Tocqueville was a highly literate aristocrat who was quite able to be detached from the values and assumptions of typography. That is why he alone understood the grammar of typography. And it is only on those terms, standing aside from any structure or medium, that its principles and lines of force can be discerned. For any medium has the power of imposing its own assumption on the unwary. Prediction and control consist in avoiding this subliminal state of Narcissus trance. But the greatest aid to this end is simply in knowing that the spell can occur immediately upon contact, as in the first bars of a melody.

A Passage to India by E. M. Forster is a dramatic study of the inability of oral and intuitive oriental culture to meet with the rational, visual European patterns of experience. "Rational," of course, has for the West long meant "uniform and continuous and sequential." In other words, we have confused reason with literacy, and rationalism with a single technology. Thus in the electric age man seems to the conventional West to become irrational. In Forster's novel the moment of truth and dislocation from the typographic trance of the West comes in the Marabar Caves. Adela Quested's reasoning powers cannot cope with the total inclusive field of resonance that is India. After the Caves: "Life went on as usual, but had no consequences, that is to say, sounds did not echo nor thought develop. Everything seemed cut off at its root and therefore infected with illusion."

A Passage to India (the phrase is from Whitman, who saw America headed Eastward) is a parable of Western man in the electric age, and is only incidentally related to Europe or the Orient. The ultimate conflict between sight and sound, between written and oral kinds of perception and organization of existence is upon us. Since understanding stops action, as Nietzsche observed, we can moderate the fierceness of this conflict by understanding the media that extend us and raise these wars within and without us.

Detribalization by literacy and its traumatic effects on tribal man is the theme of a book by the psychiatrist J. C. Carothers, *The African Mind in Health and Disease* (World Health Organization, Geneva, 1953). Much of his material appeared in an article in *Psychiatry* magazine, November, 1959: "The Culture, Psychiatry, and the Written Word." Again, it is electric speed that has revealed the lines of force operating from Western technology in the remotest areas of bush, savannah, and desert. One example is the Bedouin with his battery radio on board the camel. Submerging natives with floods of concepts for which nothing has prepared them is the normal action of all of our technology. But with electric media Western man himself experiences exactly the same inundation as the remote native. We are no more prepared to encounter radio and TV in our literate milieu than the native of Ghana is able to cope with the literacy that takes him out of his collective tribal world and beaches him in individual isolation. We are as numb in our new electric world as the native involved in our literate and mechanical culture.

Electric speed mingles the cultures of prehistory with the dregs of industrial marketeers, the nonliterate with semiliterate and the postliterate. Mental breakdown of varying degrees is the very common result of uprooting and inundation with new information and endless new patterns of information. Wyndham Lewis made this a theme of his group of novels called *The Human Age*. The first of these, *The Childermass*, is concerned precisely with accelerated media change as a kind of massacre of the innocents. In our own world as we become more aware of the effects of technology on psychic formation and manifestation, we are losing all confidence in our right to assign guilt. Ancient prehistoric societies regard violent crime as pathetic. The killer is regarded as we do a cancer victim. "How terrible it must be to feel like that," they say. J. M. Synge took up this idea very effectively in his *Playboy of the Western World*.

If the criminal appears as a nonconformist who is unable to meet the demand of technology that we behave in uniform and continuous patterns, literate man is quite inclined to see others who cannot conform as somewhat pathetic. Especially the child, the cripple, the woman, and the colored person appear in a world of visual and typographic technology as victims of injustice. On the other hand, in a culture that assigns roles instead of jobs to people – the dwarf, the skew, the child create their own spaces. They are not expected to fit into some uniform and repeatable niche that is not their size anyway. Consider the phrase "It's a man's world." As a quantitative observation endlessly repeated from within a homogenized culture, this phrase refers to the men in such a culture who have to be homogenized Dagwoods in order to belong at all. It is in our I.Q. testing that we have produced the greatest flood of misbegotten standards. Unaware of our typographic cultural bias, our testers assume that uniform and continuous habits are a sign of intelligence, thus eliminating the ear man and the tactile man.

C. P. Snow, reviewing a book of A. L. Rowse (*The New York Times Book Review*, December 24, 1961) on *Appeasement* and the road to Munich, describes the top level of British brains and experience in the 1930s. "Their I.Q.'s were much higher than usual among political bosses. Why were they such a disaster?" The view of Rowse, Snow approves: "They would not listen to warnings because they did not wish to hear." Being anti-Red made it impossible for them to read the message of Hitler. But their failure was as nothing compared to our present one. The American stake in literacy as a technology or uniformity applied to every level of education, government, industry, and social life is totally threatened by the electric technology. The threat of Stalin or Hitler was external. The electric technology is within the gates, and we are numb, deaf, blind, and mute about its encounter with the Gutenberg technology, on and through which the American way of life was formed. It is, however, no time to suggest strategies when the threat has not even been acknowledged to exist. I am in the position of Louis Pasteur telling doctors that their greatest enemy was quite invisible, and quite unrecognized by them. Our conventional response to all media, namely that it is how they are used that counts, is the numb stance of the technological idiot. For the "content" of a medium is like the juicy piece of meat carried by the burglar to distract the watchdog of the mind. The effect of the medium is made strong and intense just because it is given another medium as "content." The content of a movie is a novel or a play or an opera. The effect of the movie form is not related to its program content. The "content" of writing or print is speech, but the reader is almost entirely unaware either of print or of speech.

Arnold Toynbee is innocent of any understanding of media as they have shaped history, but he is full of examples that the student of media can use. At one moment he can seriously suggest that adult education, such as the Workers' Educational Association in Britain, is a useful counterforce to the popular press. Toynbee considers that although all of the oriental societies have in our time accepted the industrial technology and its political consequences: "On the cultural plane, however, there is no uniform corresponding tendency." (Somervell, I. 267) This is like the voice of the literate man, floundering in a milieu of ads, who boasts, "Personally, I pay no attention to ads." The spiritual and cultural reservations that the oriental peoples may have toward our technology will avail them not at all. The effects of technology do not occur at the level of opinions or concepts, but alter sense ratios or patterns of perception steadily and without any resistance. The serious artist is the only person able to encounter technology with impunity, just because he is an expert aware of the changes in sense perception.

The operation of the money medium in seventeenth-century Japan had effects not unlike the operation of typography in the West. The penetration of the money economy, wrote G. B. Sansom (in *Japan*, Cresset Press, London, 1931) "caused a slow but irresistible revolution, culminating in the breakdown of feudal government and the resumption of intercourse with foreign countries after more than two hundred years of seclusion." Money has reorganized the sense life of peoples just because it is an *extension* of our sense lives. This change does not depend upon approval or disapproval of those living in the society.

Arnold Toynbee made one approach to the transforming power of media in his concept of "etherialization," which he holds to be the principle of progressive simplification and efficiency in any organization or technology. Typically, he is ignoring the *effect* of the challenge of these forms upon the response of our senses. He imagines that it is the response of our opinions that is relevant to the effect of media and technology in society, a "point of view" that is plainly the result of the typographic spell. For the man in a literate and homogenized society ceases to be sensitive to the diverse and discontinuous life of forms. He acquires the illusion of the third dimension and the "private point of view" as part of his Narcissus fixation, and is quite shut off from Blake's awareness or that of the Psalmist, that we become what we behold.

Today when we want to get our bearings in our own culture, and have need to stand aside from the bias and pressure exerted by any technical form of human expression, we have only to visit a society where that particular form has not been felt, or a historical period in which it was unknown. Professor Wilbur Schramm made such a tactical move in studying *Television in the Lives* of *Our Children*. He found areas where TV had not penetrated at all and ran some tests. Since he had made no study of the peculiar nature of the TV image, his tests were of "content" preferences, viewing time, and vocabulary counts. In a word, his approach to the problem was a literary one, albeit unconsciously so. Consequently, he had nothing to report. Had his methods been employed in 1500 A.D. to discover the effects of the printed book in the lives of children or adults, he could have found out nothing of the changes in human and social psychology resulting from typography. Print created individualism and nationalism in the sixteenth century. Program and "content" analysis offer no clues to the magic of these media or to their subliminal charge.

Leonard Doob, in his report *Communication in Africa*, tells of one African who took great pains to listen each evening to the BBC news, even though he could understand nothing of it. Just to be in the presence of those sounds at 7 p.m. each day was important for him. His attitude to speech was like ours to melody – the resonant intonation was meaning enough. In the seventeenth century our ancestors still shared this native's attitude to the forms of media, as is plain in the following sentiment of the Frenchman Bernard Lam expressed in *The Art of Speaking* (London, 1696):

> 'Tis an effect of the Wisdom of God, who created Man to be happy, that whatever is useful to his conversation (way of life) is agreeable to him . . . because all victual that conduces to nourishment is relishable, whereas other things that cannot be assimilated and be turned into our substance are insipid. A Discourse cannot be pleasant to the Hearer that is not easie to the Speaker; nor can it be easily pronounced unless it be heard with delight.

Here is an equilibrium theory of human diet and expression such as even now we are only striving to work out again for media after centuries of fragmentation and specialism.

Pope Pius XII was deeply concerned that there be serious study of the media today. On February 17, 1950, he said:

It is not an exaggeration to say that the future of modern society and the stability of its inner life depend in large part on the maintenance of an equilibrium between the strength of the techniques of communication and the capacity of the individual's own reaction.

Failure in this respect has for centuries been typical and total for mankind. Subliminal and docile acceptance of media impact has made them prisons without walls for their human users. As A. J. Liebling remarked in his book *The Press*, a man is not free if he cannot see where he is going, even if he has a gun to help him get there. For each of the media is also a powerful weapon with which to clobber other media and other groups. The result is that the present age has been one of multiple civil wars that are not limited to the world of art and entertainment. In *War and Human Progress*, Professor J. U. Nef declared: "The total wars of our time have been the result of a series of intellectual mistakes . . ."

If the formative power in the media are the media themselves, that raises a host of large matters that can only be mentioned here, although they deserve volumes. Namely, that technological media are staples or natural resources, exactly as are coal and cotton and oil. Anybody will concede that society whose economy is dependent upon one or two major staples like cotton, or grain, or lumber, or fish, or cattle is going to have some obvious social patterns of organization as a result. Stress on a few major staples creates extreme instability in the economy but great endurance in the population. The pathos and humor of the American South are embedded in such an economy of limited staples. For a society configured by reliance on a few commodities accepts them as a social bond quite as much as the metropolis does the press. Cotton and oil, like radio and TV, become "fixed charges" on the entire psychic life of the community. And this pervasive fact creates the unique cultural flavor of any society. It pays through the nose and all its other senses for each staple that shapes its life.

That our human senses, of which all media are extensions, are also fixed charges on our personal energies, and that they also configure the awareness and experience of each one of us, may be perceived in another connection mentioned by the psychologist C. G. Jung:

> Every Roman was surrounded by slaves. The slave and his psychology flooded ancient Italy, and every Roman became inwardly, and of course unwittingly, a slave. Because living constantly in the atmosphere of slaves, he became infected through the unconscious with their psychology. No one can shield himself from such an influence. (*Contributions to Analytical Psychology*, London, 1928)

The Commodity as Spectacle

Guy Debord

1

In societies where modern conditions of production prevail, all of life presents itself as an immense accumulation of *spectacles*. Everything that was directly lived has moved away into a representation.

2

The images detached from every aspect of life fuse in a common stream in which the unity of this life can no longer be reestablished. Reality considered *partially* unfolds, in its own general unity, as a pseudo-world *apart*, an object of mere contemplation. The specialization of images of the world is completed in the world of the autonomous image, where the liar has lied to himself. The spectacle in general, as the concrete inversion of life, is the autonomous movement of the nonliving.

3

The spectacle presents itself simultaneously as all of society, as part of society, and as *instrument of unification*. As a part of society it is specifically the sector which concentrates all gazing and all consciousness. Due to the very fact that this sector is *separate*, it is the common ground of the deceived gaze and of false consciousness, and the unification it achieves is nothing but an official language of generalized separation.

From Guy Debord, "The commodity as spectacle." In *Society of the Spectacle*, paras. 1–18 and 42. Detroit: Black & Red Books, 1977 revised edition.

4

The spectacle is not a collection of images, but a social relation among people, mediated by images.

5

The spectacle cannot be understood as an abuse of the world of vision, as a product of the techniques of mass dissemination of images. It is, rather, a *Weltanschauung* which has become actual, materially translated. It is a world vision which has become objectified.

6

The spectacle, grasped in its totality, is both the result and the project of the existing mode of production. It is not a supplement to the real world, an additional decoration. It is the heart of the unrealism of the real society. In all its specific forms, as information or propaganda, as advertisement or direct entertainment consumption, the spectacle is the present *model* of socially dominant life. It is the omnipresent affirmation of the choice *already made* in production and its corollary consumption. The spectacle's form and content are identically the total justification of the existing system's conditions and goals. The spectacle is also the *permanent presence* of this justification, since it occupies the main part of the time lived outside of modern production.

7

Separation is itself part of the unity of the world, of the global social praxis split up into reality and image. The social practice which the autonomous spectacle confronts is also the real totality which contains the spectacle. But the split within this totality mutilates it to the point of making the spectacle appear as its goal. The language of the spectacle consists of *signs* of the ruling production, which at the same time are the ultimate goal of this production.

8

One cannot abstractly contrast the spectacle to actual social activity: such a division is itself divided. The spectacle which inverts the real is in fact produced. Lived reality is materially invaded by the contemplation of the spectacle while simultaneously absorbing the spectacular order, giving it positive cohesiveness. Objective reality is present on both sides. Every notion fixed this way has no other basis than its passage into the opposite: reality rises up within the spectacle, and the spectacle is real. This reciprocal alienation is the essence and the support of the existing society.

9

In a world which *really is topsy-turvy*, the true is a moment of the false.

10

The concept of "spectacle" unifies and explains a great diversity of apparent phenomena. The diversity and the contrasts are appearances of a socially organized appearance, the general truth of which must itself be recognized. Considered in its own terms, the spectacle is *affirmation* of appearance and affirmation of all human life, namely social life, as mere appearance. But the critique which reaches the truth of the spectacle exposes it as the visible *negation* of life, as a negation of life which *has become visible*.

11

To describe the spectacle, its formation, its functions and the forces which tend to dissolve it, one must artificially distinguish certain inseparable elements. When *analyzing* the spectacle one speaks, to some extent, the language of the spectacular itself in the sense that one moves through the methodological terrain of the very society which expresses itself in the spectacle. But the spectacle is nothing other than the *sense* of the total practice of a social-economic formation, its *use of time*. It is the historical movement in which we are caught.

12

The spectacle presents itself as something enormously positive, indisputable and inaccessible. It says nothing more than "that which appears is good, that which is good appears." The attitude which it demands in principle is passive acceptance which in fact it already obtained by its manner of appearing without reply, by its monopoly of appearance.

13

The basically tautological character of the spectacle flows from the simple fact that its means are simultaneously its ends. It is the sun which never sets over the empire of modern passivity. It covers the entire surface of the world and bathes endlessly in its own glory.

14

The society which rests on modern industry is not accidentally or superficially spec-tacular, it is fundamentally *spectaclist*. In the spectacle, which is the image of the ruling economy, the goal is nothing, development everything. The spectacle aims at nothing other than itself.

15

As the indispensable decoration of the objects produced today, as the general exposé of the rationality of the system, as the advanced economic sector which directly shapes a growing multitude of image-objects, the spectacle is the *main production* of present-day society.

16

The spectacle subjugates living men to itself to the extent that the economy has totally subjugated them. It is no more than the economy developing for itself. It is the true reflection of the production of things, and the false objectification of the producers.

17

The first phase of the domination of the economy over social life brought into the definition of all human realization the obvious degradation of *being* into *having*. The present phase of total occupation of social life by the accumulated results of the economy leads to a generalized sliding of *having* into *appearing*, from which all actual "having" must draw its immediate prestige and its ultimate function. At the same time all individual reality has become social reality directly dependent on social power and shaped by it. It is allowed to appear only to the extent that it *is not*.

18

Where the real world changes into simple images, the simple images become real beings and effective motivations of hypnotic behavior. The spectacle, as a tendency to *make one see* the world by means of various specialized mediations (it can no longer be grasped directly), naturally finds vision to be the privileged human sense which the sense of touch was for other epochs; the most abstract, the most mystifiable sense corresponds to the generalized abstraction of present-day society. But the spectacle is not identifiable with mere gazing, even combined with hearing. It is that which escapes the activity of men, that which escapes reconsideration and correction by their work. It is the opposite of dialogue. Wherever there is independent *representation*, the spectacle reconstitutes itself. [. . .]

42

The spectacle is the moment when the commodity has attained the *total occupation* of social life. Not only is the relation to the commodity visible but it is all one sees: the world one sees is its world. Modern economic production extends its dictatorship extensively and intensively. In the least industrialized places, its reign is already attested by a few star commodities and by the imperialist domination imposed by regions which are ahead in the development of productivity. In the advanced regions, social space is invaded by a continuous superimposition of geological layers of commodities. At this point in the "second industrial revolution," alienated consumption becomes for the masses a duty supplementary to alienated production. It is *all the sold labor* of a society which globally becomes the *total commodity* for which the cycle must be continued. For this to be done, the total commodity has to return as a fragment to the fragmented individual, absolutely separated from the productive forces operating as a whole. Thus it is here that the specialized science of domination must in turn specialize: it fragments itself into sociology, psychotechnics, cybernetics, semiology, etc., watching over the self-regulation of every level of the process.

10

Introduction: Instructions on How to Become a General in the Disneyland Club

Ariel Dorfman and Armand Mattelart

My dog has become a famous lifeguard and my nephews will be brigadier-generals. To what greater honor can one aspire?

(Donald Duck, D 422)[1]

Baby frogs will be *big* frogs someday, which bring high prices on the market ... I'm going to fix some special *frog food* and speed up the growth of those little hoppers!

(Donald Duck, D 451, CS 5/60)

It would be wrong to assume that Walt Disney is merely a business man. We are all familiar with the massive merchandising of his characters in films, watches, umbrellas, records, soaps, rocking chairs, neckties, lamps, etc. There are Disney strips in five thousand newspapers, translated into more than thirty languages, spread over a hundred countries. According to the magazine's own publicity puffs, in Chile alone, Disney comics reach and delight each week over a million readers. The former Zig-Zag Company, now bizarrely converted into Pinsel Publishing Enterprise (Juvenile Publications Company Ltd.), supplies them to a major part of the Latin American continent. From their national base of operations, where there is so much screaming about the trampling underfoot (the suppression, intimidation, restriction, repression, curbing, etc.) of the liberty of the press, this consortium, controlled by financiers and "philanthropists" of the previous Christian Democrat regime (1964–70), has just permitted itself the luxury of converting several of its publications from biweeklies to weekly magazines.

From Ariel Dorfman and Armand Mattelart, "Introduction: Instructions on how to become a general in the Disneyland Club." In *How to Read Donald Duck*, pp. 25–32. New York: International General, 1971.

Apart from his stock exchange rating, Disney has been exalted as the inviolable common cultural heritage of contemporary man; his characters have been incorporated into every home, they hang on every wall, they decorate objects of every kind; they constitute a little less than a social environment inviting us all to join the great universal Disney family, which extends beyond all frontiers and ideologies, transcends differences between peoples and nations, and particularities of custom and language. Disney is the great supranational bridge across which all human beings may communicate with each other. And amidst so much sweetness and light, the registered trademark becomes invisible.

Disney is part – an immortal part, it would seem – of our common collective vision. It has been observed that in more than one country Mickey Mouse is more popular than the national hero of the day.

In Central America, AID (the U.S. Agency for International Development) – sponsored films promoting contraception featuring the characters from "Magician of Fantasy." In Chile, after the earthquake of July 1971, the children of San Bernardo sent Disneyland comics and sweets to their stricken fellow children of San Antonio. And the year before, a Chilean women's magazine proposed giving Disney the Nobel Peace Prize.[2]

We need not be surprised, then, that any innuendo about the world of Disney should be interpreted as an affront to morality and civilization at large. Even to whisper anything against Walt is to undermine the happy and innocent palace of childhood, for which he is both guardian and guide.

No sooner had the first children's magazine been issued by the Chilean Popular Unity Government publishing house Quimantú, than the reactionary journals sprang to the defense of Disney:

> The voice of a newscaster struck deep into the microphone of a radio station in the capital. To the amazement of his listeners he announced that Walt Disney is to be banned in Chile. The government propaganda experts have come to the conclusion that Chilean children should not think, feel, love or suffer through animals.
>
> So, in place of Scrooge McDuck, Donald and nephews, instead of Goofy and Mickey Mouse, we children and grownups will have to get used to reading about our own society, which, to judge from the way it is painted by the writers and panegyrists of our age, is rough, bitter, cruel and hateful. It was Disney's magic to be able to stress the happy side of life, and there are always, in human society, characters who resemble those of Disney comics.
>
> Scrooge McDuck is the miserly millionaire of any country in the world, hoarding his money and suffering a heart attack every time someone tries to pinch a cent off him, but in spite of it all, capable of revealing human traits which redeem him in his nephews' eyes.
>
> Donald is the eternal enemy of work and lives dependent upon his powerful uncle. Goofy is the innocent and guileless common man, the eternal victim of his own clumsiness, which hurts no one and is always good for a laugh.
>
> Big Bad Wolf and Little Wolf are masterly means of teaching children pleasantly, not hatefully, the difference between good and evil. For Big Bad Wolf himself, when he gets a chance to gobble up the Three Little Pigs, suffers pangs of conscience and is unable to do his wicked deed.

And finally, Mickey Mouse is Disney in a nutshell. What human being over the last forty years, at the mere presence of Mickey, has not felt his heart swell with emotion? Did we not see him once as the "Sorcerer's Apprentice" in an unforgettable cartoon which was the delight of children and grownups, which preserved every single note of the masterly music of Prokoviev [a reference no doubt to the music of Paul Dukas]. And what of *Fantasia*, that prodigious feat of cinematic art, with musicians, orchestras, decorations, flowers, and every animate being moving to the baton of Leopold Stokowski? And one scene, of the utmost splendor and realism, even showed elephants executing the most elegant performance of "The Dance of the Dragonflies" [a reference no doubt to the "Dance of the hours"].

How can one assert that children do not learn from talking animals? Have they not been observed time and again engaging in tender dialogues with their pet dogs and cats, while the latter adapt to their masters and show with a purr or a twitch of the ears their understanding of the orders they are given? Are not fables full of valuable lessons in the way animals can teach us how to behave under the most difficult circumstances?

There is one, for instance, by Tomas de Iriarte which serves as a warning against the danger of imposing too stringent principles upon those who work for the public. The mass does not always blindly accept what is offered to them.[3]

This pronouncement parrots some of the ideas prevailing in the media about childhood and children's literature. Above all, there is the implication that politics cannot enter into areas of "pure entertainment," especially those designed for children of tender years. Children's games have their own rules and laws, they move, supposedly, in an autonomous and asocial sphere like the Disney characters, with a psychology peculiar to creatures at a "privileged" age. Inasmuch as the sweet and docile child can be sheltered effectively from the evils of existence, from the petty rancors, the hatreds, and the political or ideological contamination of his elders, any attempt to politicize the sacred domaine of childhood threatens to introduce perversity where there once reigned happiness, innocence and fantasy. Since animals are also exempt from the vicissitudes of history and politics, they are convenient symbols of a world beyond socio-economic realities, and the animal characters can represent ordinary human types, common to all classes, countries and epochs. Disney thus establishes a moral background which draws the child down the proper ethical and aesthetic path. It is cruel and unnecessary to tear it away from its magic garden, for it is ruled by the Laws of Mother Nature; children *are* just like that and the makers of comic books, in their infinite wisdom, understand their behavior and their biologically-determined need for harmony. Thus, to attack Disney is to reject the unquestioned stereotype of the child, sanctified as the law in the name of the immutable human condition.

There are *automagic*[4] antibodies in Disney. They tend to neutralize criticism because they are the same values already instilled into people, in the tastes, reflexes and attitudes which inform everyday experience at all levels. Disney manages to subject these values to the extremest degree of commercial exploitation. The potential assailer is thus condemned in advance by what is known as "public opinion," that is, the thinking of people who have already been conditioned by the Disney message and have based their social and family life upon it.

The publication of this book will of course provoke a rash of hostile comment against the authors. To facilitate our adversaries' task, and in order to lend uniformity to their criteria, we offer the following model, which has been drawn up with due consideration for the philosophy of the journals to which the gentlemen of the press are so attached:

Instructions on How to Expel Someone from the Disneyland Club

1.   The authors of this book are to be defined as follows: indecent and immoral (while Disney's world is pure); hyper-complicated and hyper-sophisticated (while Walt is simple, open and sincere); members of a sinister elite (while Disney is the most popular man in the world); political agitators (while Disney is non-partisan, above politics); calculating and embittered (while Walt D. is spontaneous, emotional, loves to laugh and make laughter); subverters of youth and domestic peace (while W. D. teaches respect for parents, love of one's fellows and protection of the weak); unpatriotic and antagonistic to the national spirit (while Mr Disney, being international, represents the best and dearest of our native traditions); and finally, cultivators of "Marxism-fiction," a theory imported from abroad by "wicked foreigners"[5] (while Unca Walt is against exploitation and promotes the classless society of the future).

2.   Next, the authors of this book are to be accused of the very lowest of crimes: of daring to raise doubts about the child's imagination, that is, O horror!, to question the right of children to have a literature of their own, which interprets them so well, and is created on their behalf.

3.   FINALLY, TO EXPEL SOMEONE FROM THE DISNEYLAND CLUB, ACCUSE HIM REPEATEDLY OF TRYING TO BRAINWASH CHILDREN WITH THE DOCTRINE OF COLORLESS SOCIAL REALISM, IMPOSED BY POLITICAL COMMISSARS.

There can be no doubt that children's literature is a genre like any other, monopolized by specialized subsectors within the culture industry. Some dedicate themselves to the adventure story, some to mystery, others to the erotic novel, etc. But at least the latter are directed towards an amorphous public, which buys at random. In the case of the children's genre, however, there is a virtually biologically captive, predetermined audience.

Children's comics are devised by adults, whose work is determined and justified by their idea of what a child is or should be. Often, they even cite "scientific" sources or ancient traditions ("it is popular wisdom, dating from time immemorial") in order to explain the nature of the public's needs. In reality, however, these adults are not about to tell stories which would jeopardize the future they are planning for their children.

So the comics show the child as a miniature adult, enjoying an idealized, gilded infancy which is really nothing but the adult projection of some magic era beyond the reach of the harsh discord of daily life. It is a plan for salvation which presupposes a primal stage within every existence, sheltered from contradictions and permitting imaginative escape. Juvenile literature, embodying purity, spontaneity, and natural virtue, while lacking in sex and violence, represents earthly paradise. It guarantees man's own redemption as an adult: as long as there are children, he will have the pretext and means for self-gratification with the spectacle of his own dreams. In his children's reading, man stages and performs over and over again the supposedly unproblematical scenes of his inner refuge. Regaling himself with his own legend, he falls into tautology; he admires himself in the mirror, thinking it to be a window. But the child playing down there in the garden is the purified adult looking back at himself.

So it is the adult who produces the comics, and the child who consumes them. The role of the apparent child actor, who reigns over this uncontaminated world, is at once that of audience and dummy for his father's ventriloquism. The father denies his progeny a voice of his own, and as in any authoritarian society, he establishes himself as the other's sole interpreter and spokesman. All the little fellow can do is to let his father represent him.

But wait a minute, gentlemen! Perhaps children really *are* like that?

Indeed, the adults set out to prove that this literature is essential to the child, satisfying his eager demands. But this is a closed circuit: children have been conditioned by the magazines and the culture which spawned them. They tend to reflect in their daily lives the characteristics they are supposed to possess, in order to win affection, acceptance, and rewards; in order to grow up properly and integrate into society. The Disney world is sustained by rewards and punishments; it hides an iron hand with the velvet glove. Considered, by definition, unfit to choose from the alternatives available to adults, the youngsters intuit "natural" behavior, happily accepting that their imagination be channeled into incontestable ethical and aesthetic ideals. Juvenile literature is justified by the children it has generated through a vicious circle.

Thus, adults create for themselves a childhood embodying their own angelical aspirations, which offer consolation, hope and a guarantee of a "better," but unchanging, future. This "new reality," this autonomous realm of magic, is artfully isolated from the reality of the everyday. Adult values are projected onto the child, as if childhood was a special domaine where these values could be protected uncritically. In Disney, the two strata – adult and child – are not to be considered as antagonistic; they fuse in a single embrace, and history becomes biology. The identity of parent and child inhibits the emergence of true generational conflicts. The pure child will replace the corrupt father, preserving the latter's values. The future (the child) reaffirms the present (the adult), which, in turn, transmits the past. The apparent independence which the father benevolently bestows upon this little territory of his creation, is the very means of assuring his supremacy.

But there is more: this lovely, simple, smooth, translucent, chaste and pacific region, which has been promoted as Salvation, is unconsciously infiltrated by a multiplicity of adult conflicts and contradictions. This transparent world is designed both to conceal and reveal latent traces of real and painful tensions. The parent suffers this split consciousness without being aware of his inner turmoil. Nostalgically, he appropriates the "natural disposition" of the child in order to conceal the guilt arising from his own fall from grace; it is the price of redemption for his own condition. By the standards of his angelic model, he must judge himself guilty; as much as he needs this land of enchantment and salvation, he could never imagine it with the necessary purity. He could never turn into his own child. But this salvation only offers him an imperfect escape; it can never be so pure as to block off all his real life problems.

In juvenile literature, the adult, corroded by the trivia of everyday life blindly defends his image of youth and innocence. Because of this, it is perhaps the best (and least expected) place to study the disguises and truths of contemporary man. For the adult, in protecting his dream-image of youth, hides the fear that to penetrate it would destroy his dreams and reveal the reality it conceals.

Thus, *the imagination of the child is conceived as the past and future utopia of the adult*. But set up as an inner realm of fantasy, this model of his Origin and his Ideal Future Society lends itself to the free assimilation of all his woes. It enables the adult to partake of his own demons, provided they have been coated in the syrup of paradise, and that they travel there with the passport of innocence.

Mass culture has granted to contemporary man, in his constant need to visualize the reality about him, the means of feeding on his own problems without having to encounter all the difficulties of form and content presented by the modern art and literature of the elite. Man is offered knowledge without commitment, a self-colonization of his own imagination. By dominating the child, the father dominates himself. The relationship is a sado-masochistic one, not unlike that established between Donald and his nephews. Similarly, readers find themselves caught between their desire and their reality, and in their attempt to escape to a purer realm, they only travel further back into their own traumas.

Mass culture has opened up a whole range of new issues. While it certainly has had a levelling effect and has exposed a wider audience to a broader range of themes, it has simultaneously generated a cultural elite which has cut itself off more and more from the masses. Contrary to the democratic potential of mass culture, this elite has plunged mass culture into a suffocating complexity of solutions, approaches and techniques, each of which is comprehensible only to a narrow circle of readers. The creation of children's culture is part of this specialization process.

Child fantasy, although created by adults, becomes the exclusive reserve of children. The self-exiled father, once having created this specialized imaginary world, then revels in it through the keyhole. The father must be absent, and without direct jurisdiction, just as the child is without direct obligations. Coercion melts away in the magic palace of sweet harmony and repose – the palace raised and administered at a distance by the father, whose physical absence is designed to avoid direct confrontation with his progeny. This absence is the prerequisite of his omnipresence, his total invasion. Physical presence would be superfluous, even counterproductive, since the whole magazine is already his projection. He shows up instead as a favorite uncle handing out free magazines. Juvenile literature is a father surrogate. The model of paternal authority is at every point immanent, the implicit basis of its structure and very existence. The natural creativity of the child, which no one in his right mind can deny, is channelled through the apparent absence of the father into an adult-authoritarian vision of the real world. Paternalism *in absentia* is the indispensable vehicle for the defense and invisible control of the ostensibly autonomous childhood model. The comics, like television, in all vertically structured societies, rely upon distance as a means of authoritarian reinforcement.

The authoritarian relationship between the real life parent and child is repeated and reinforced within the fantasy world itself, and is the basis for all relations in the entire world of the comics. Later, we shall show how the relationship of child-readers to the magazine they consume is generally based on and echoed in the way the characters experience their own fantasy world within the comic. Children will not only identify with Donald Duck because Donald's situation relates to their own life, but also because the way they read or the way they are exposed to it, imitates and prefigures the way Donald Duck lives out his own problems. Fiction reinforces, in a circular fashion, the manner in which the adult desires the comic be received and read.

Now that we have peeked into the parent–child relationship, let us be initiated into the Disney world, beginning with the great family of ducks and mice.

Notes

1   We use the following abbreviations: D = *Disneylandia* F = *Fantasias*, TR = *Tio Rico* (Scrooge McDuck), TB = *Tribilin* (Goofy). These magazines are published in Chile by Empresa Editorial Zig-Zag (now Pinsel), with an average of two to four large-and medium-sized stories per issue. We obtained all available back issues and purchased current issues during the months following March 1971. Our sample is thus inevitably somewhat random:

    Disneylandia: 185, 192, 210, 281, 292, 294, 297, 303, 329, 342, 347, 357, 364, 367, 370, 376, 377, 379, 381, 382, 383, 393, 400, 401, 421, 422, 423, 424, 431, 432, 433, 434, 436, 437, 439, 440, 441, 443, 444, 445, 446, 447, 448, 449, 451, 452, 453, 454, 455, 457.

    Tio Rico: 40, 48, 53, 57, 61, 96, 99, 106, 108, 109, 110, 111, 113, 115, 116, 117, 119, 120, 128.

    Fantasias: 57, 60, 68, 82, 140, 155, 160, 165, 168, 169, 170, 173, 174, 175, 176, 177, 178.

    Tribilin: 62, 65, 78, 87, 92, 93, 96, 99, 100, 101, 103, 104, 106, 107.

    (Translator's Note: Stories for which I have been able to locate the U.S. originals are coded thus: CS = (*Walt Disney's*) *Comics and Stories*; DA = *Duck Album*; DD = *Donald Duck*; GG = *Gyro Gearloose*; HDL = *Huey, Dewey and Louie, Junior Woodchucks*; and US = *Uncle Scrooge*.

    The figures following represent the original date of issue; thus 7/67 means July 1967. Sometimes, however, when there is no monthly date, the issue number appears followed by the year.)

2   "At the time of his death (1966), a small, informal but worldwide group was promoting – with the covert assistance of his publicity department – his nomination for the Nobel

Peace prize" (from Richard Schickel, *The Disney Version*, New York, 1968, p. 303). San Bernardo is a working-class suburb of greater Santiago; San Antonio a port in the central zone. (Trans.)

3   *La Segunda* (Santiago), July 20, 1971, p. 3. This daily belongs to the Mercurio group, which is controlled by Augustin Edwards, the major press and industrial monopolist in Chile. The writer of the article quoted worked as Public Relations officer for the American copper companies Braden and Kennecott. (cf. A. Mattelart, "Estructura del poder informativo y dependencia" in "Los Medios de Communicación de Masas: La Ideologia de la Prensa Liberal en Chile" *Cuadernos de la Realidad Nacional* (CEREN, Santiago), 3, Marzo de 1970).

4   A word-play on the advertising slogan for a washing machine, which cleans "auto-magicamente" (automatically and magically) – Trans.

5   Actual words of Little Wolf (D 210).

Base and Superstructure in Marxist Cultural Theory

Raymond Williams

Any modern approach to a Marxist theory of culture must begin by considering the proposition of a determining base and a determined superstructure. From a strictly theoretical point of view this is not, in fact, where we might choose to begin. It would be in many ways preferable if we could begin from a proposition which originally was equally central, equally authentic: namely the proposition that social being determines consciousness. It is not that the two propositions necessarily deny each other or are in contradiction. But the proposition of base and superstructure, with its figurative element, with its suggestion of a fixed and definite spatial relationship, constitutes, at least in certain hands, a very specialized and at times unacceptable version of the other proposition. Yet in the transition from Marx to Marxism, and in the development of mainstream Marxism itself, the proposition of the determining base and the determined superstructure has been commonly held to be the key to Marxist cultural analysis.

It is important, as we try to analyse this proposition, to be aware that the term of relationship which is involved, that is to say "determines", is of great linguistic and theoretical complexity. The language of determination and even more of determinism was inherited from idealist and especially theological accounts of the world and man. It is significant that it is in one of his familiar inversions, his contradictions of received propositions, that Marx uses the word which becomes, in English translation, "determines" (the usual but not invariable German word is *bestimmen*). He is opposing an ideology that had been insistent on the power of certain forces outside man, or, in its secular version, on an abstract determining consciousness. Marx's own proposition explicitly denies this, and puts the origin of determination in men's own activities. Nevertheless, the particular history and continuity of the term serves to remind us that there are, within ordinary use – and this is true of most of the major European languages – quite different possible meanings and implications of

From Raymond Williams, "Base and superstructure in Marxist cultural theory." In *Problems in Materialism and Culture: Selected Essays*, pp. 31–49. London: Verso and NLB, 1980.

the word "determine". There is, on the one hand, from its theological inheritance, the notion of an external cause which totally predicts or prefigures, indeed totally controls a subsequent activity. But there is also, from the experience of social practice, a notion of determination as setting limits, exerting pressures.[1]

Now there is clearly a difference between a process of setting limits and exerting pressures, whether by some external force or by the internal laws of a particular development, and that other process in which a subsequent content is essentially prefigured, predicted and controlled by a pre-existing external force. Yet it is fair to say, looking at many applications of Marxist cultural analysis, that it is the second sense, the notion of prefiguration, prediction or control, which has often explicitly or implicitly been used.

Superstructure: Qualifications and Amendments

The term of relationship is then the first thing that we have to examine in this proposition, but we have to do this by going on to look at the related terms themselves. "Superstructure" (*Überbau*) has had most attention. In common usage, after Marx, it acquired a main sense of a unitary "area" within which all cultural and ideological activities could be placed. But already in Marx himself, in the later correspondence of Engels, and at many points in the subsequent Marxist tradition, qualifications were made about the determined character of certain superstructural activities. The first kind of qualification had to do with delays in time, with complications, and with certain indirect or relatively distant relationships. The simplest notion of a superstructure, which is still by no means entirely abandoned, had been the reflection, the imitation or the reproduction of the reality of the base in the superstructure in a more or less direct way. Positivist notions of reflection and reproduction of course directly supported this. But since in many real cultural activities this relationship cannot be found, or cannot be found without effort or even violence to the material or practice being studied, the notion was introduced of delays in time, the famous lags; of various technical complications; and of indirectness, in which certain kinds of activity in the cultural sphere – philosophy, for example – were situated at a greater distance from the primary economic activities. That was the first stage of qualification of the notion of superstructure: in effect, an operational qualification. The second stage was related but more fundamental, in that the process of the relationship itself was more substantially looked at. This was the kind of reconsideration which gave rise to the modern notion of "mediation", in which something more than simple reflection or reproduction – indeed something radically different from either reflection or reproduction – actively occurs. In the later twentieth century there is the notion of "homologous structures", where there may be no direct or easily apparent similarity, and certainly nothing like reflection or reproduction, between the superstructural process and the reality of the base, but in which there is an essential homology or correspondence of structures, which can be discovered by analysis. This is not the same notion as "mediation", but it is the same kind of amendment in that the relationship between the base and the superstructure is not supposed to be direct, nor simply operationally subject to lags and complications and indirectnesses, but that of its nature it is not direct reproduction.

These qualifications and amendments are important. But it seems to me that what has not been looked at with equal care is the received notion of the "base" (*Basis, Grundlage*). And indeed I would argue that the base is the more important concept to look at if we are to understand the realities of cultural process. In many uses of the proposition of base and superstructure, as a matter of verbal habit, "the base" has come to be considered virtually as an object, or in less crude cases, it has been considered in essentially uniform and usually static ways. "The base" is the real social existence of man. "The base" is the real relations of production corresponding to a stage of development of the material productive forces. "The base" is a mode of production at a particular stage of its development. We make and repeat propositions of this kind, but the usage is then very different from Marx's emphasis on productive activities, in particular structural relations, constituting the foundation of all other activities. For while a particular stage of the development of production can be discovered and made precise by analysis, it is never in practice either uniform or static. It is indeed one of the central propositions of Marx's sense of history that there are deep contradictions in the relationships of production and in the consequent social relationships. There is therefore the continual possibility of the dynamic variation of these forces. Moreover, when these forces are considered, as Marx always considers them, as the specific activities and relationships of real men, they mean something very much more active, more complicated and more contradictory than the developed metaphorical notion of "the base" could possibly allow us to realize.

The Base and the Productive Forces

So we have to say that when we talk of "the base", we are talking of a process and not a state. And we cannot ascribe to that process certain fixed properties for subsequent translation to the variable processes of the superstructure. Most people who have wanted to make the ordinary proposition more reasonable have concentrated on refining the notion of superstructure. But I would say that each term of the proposition has to be revalued in a particular direction. We have to revalue "determination" towards the setting of limits and the exertion of pressure, and away from a predicted, prefigured and controlled content. We have to revalue "superstructure" towards a related range of cultural practices, and away from a reflected, reproduced or specifically dependent content. And, crucially, we have to revalue "the base" away from the notion of a fixed economic or technological abstraction, and towards the specific activities of men in real social and economic relationships, containing fundamental contradictions and variations and therefore always in a state of dynamic process.

It is worth observing one further implication behind the customary definitions. "The base" has come to include, especially in certain twentieth-century developments, a strong and limiting sense of basic industry. The emphasis on heavy industry, even, has played a certain cultural role. And this raises a more general problem, for we find ourselves forced to look again at the ordinary notion of "productive forces". Clearly what we are examining in the base is primary productive forces. Yet some very crucial distinctions have to be made here. It is true that in his analysis of capitalist production Marx considered "productive work" in a very particular and specialized sense corresponding to that mode of production. There is a difficult passage in the *Grundrisse* in which he argues that while the man who makes a piano is a productive worker, there is a real question whether the man who distributes the piano is also a productive worker; but he probably is, since he contributes to the realization of surplus value. Yet when it comes to the man who plays the piano, whether to himself or to others, there is no question: he is not a productive worker at all. So piano-maker is base, but pianist superstructure. As a way of considering cultural activity, and incidentally the economics of modern cultural activity, this is very clearly a dead-end. But for any theoretical clarification it is crucial to recognize that Marx was there engaged in an analysis of a particular kind of production, that is capitalist commodity production. Within his analysis of this mode, he had to give to the notion of "productive labour" and "productive forces" a specialized sense of primary work on materials in a form which produced commodities. But this has narrowed remarkably, and in a cultural context very damagingly, from his more central notion of *productive forces*, in which, to give just brief reminders, the most important thing a worker ever produces is himself, himself in the fact of that kind of labour, or the broader historical emphasis of men producing themselves, themselves and their history. Now when we talk of the base, and of primary productive forces, it matters very much whether we are referring, as in one degenerate form of this proposition became habitual, to primary production within the terms of capitalist economic relationships, or to the primary production of society itself, and of men themselves, the material production and reproduction of real life. If we have the broad sense of productive forces, we look at the whole question of the base differently, and we are then less tempted to dismiss as superstructural, and in that sense as merely secondary, certain vital productive social forces, which are in the broad sense, from the beginning, basic.

Uses of Totality

Yet, because of the difficulties of the ordinary proposition of base and superstructure, there was an alternative and very important development, an emphasis primarily associated with Lukács, on a social "totality". The totality of social practices was opposed to this layered notion of base and a consequent superstructure. This concept of a totality of practices is compatible with the notion of social being determining consciousness, but it does not necessarily interpret this process in terms of a base and a superstructure. Now the language of totality has become common, and it is indeed in many ways more acceptable than the notion of base and superstructure. But with one very important reservation. It is very easy for the notion of totality to empty of its essential content the original Marxist proposition. For if we come to say that society is composed of a large number of social practices which form a concrete social whole, and if we give to each practice a certain specific recognition, adding only that they interact, relate and combine in very complicated ways, we are at one level much more obviously talking about reality, but we are at another level withdrawing from the claim that there is any process of determination. And this I, for one, would be very unwilling to do. Indeed, the key question to ask about any notion of totality in cultural theory is this: whether the notion of totality includes the notion of intention.

If totality is simply concrete, if it is simply the recognition of a large variety of miscellaneous and contemporaneous practices, then it is essentially empty of any content that could be called Marxist. Intention, the notion of intention, restores the key question, or rather the key emphasis. For while it is true that any society is a complex whole of such practices, it is also true that any society has a specific organization, a specific structure, and that the principles of this organization and structure can be seen as directly related to certain social intentions, intentions by which we define the society, intentions which in all our experience have been the rule of a particular class. One of the unexpected consequences of the crudeness of the base/superstructure model has been the too easy acceptance of models which appear less crude – models of totality or of a complex whole – but which exclude the facts of social intention, the class character of a particular society and so on. And this reminds us of how much we lose if we abandon the superstructural emphasis altogether. Thus I have great difficulty in seeing processes of art and thought as superstructural in the sense of the formula as it is commonly used. But in many areas of social and political thought – certain kinds of ratifying theory, certain kinds of law, certain kinds of institution, which after all in Marx's original formulations were very much part of the superstructure – in all that kind of social apparatus, and in a decisive area of political and ideological activity and construction, if we fail to see a superstructural element we fail to recognize reality at all. These laws, constitutions, theories, ideologies, which are so often claimed as natural, or as having universal validity or significance, simply have to be seen as expressing and ratifying the domination of a particular class. Indeed the difficulty of revising the formula of base and superstructure has had much to do with the perception of many militants – who have to fight such institutions and notions as well as fighting economic battles – that if these institutions and their ideologies are not perceived as having that kind of dependent and ratifying relationship, if their claims to universal validity or legitimacy are not denied and fought, then the class character of the society can no longer be seen. And this has been the effect of some versions of totality as the description of cultural process. Indeed I think we can properly use the notion of totality only when we combine it with that other crucial Marxist concept of "hegemony".

The Complexity of Hegemony

It is Gramsci's great contribution to have emphasized hegemony, and also to have understood it at a depth which is, I think, rare. For hegemony supposes the existence of something which is truly total, which is not merely secondary or superstructural, like the weak sense of ideology, but which is lived at such a depth, which saturates the society to such an extent, and which, as Gramsci put it, even constitutes the substance and limit of common sense for most people under its sway, that it corresponds to the reality of social experience very much more clearly than any notions derived from the formula of base and superstructure. For if ideology were merely some abstract, imposed set of notions, if our social and political and cultural ideas and assumptions and habits were merely the result of specific manipulation, of a kind of overt training which might be simply ended or withdrawn, then the society would be very much easier to move and to change than in practice it has ever been or is. This notion of hegemony as deeply saturating the consciousness of a society seems to me to be fundamental. And hegemony has the advantage over general notions of totality, that it at the same time emphasizes the facts of domination.

Yet there are times when I hear discussions of hegemony and feel that it too, as a concept, is being dragged back to the relatively simple, uniform and static notion which "superstructure" in ordinary use had become. Indeed I think that we have to give a very complex account of hegemony if we are talking about any real social formation. Above all we have to give an account which allows for its elements of real and constant change. We have to emphasize that hegemony is not singular; indeed that its own internal structures are highly complex, and have continually to be renewed, recreated and defended; and by the same token, that they can be continually challenged and in certain respects modified. That is why instead of speaking simply of "the hegemony", "a hegemony", I would propose a model which allows for this kind of variation and contradiction, its sets of alternatives and its processes of change.

For one thing that is evident in some of the best Marxist cultural analysis is that it is very much more at home in what one might call *epochal* questions than in what one has to call *historical* questions. That is to say, it is usually very much better at distinguishing the large features of different epochs of society, as commonly between feudal and bourgeois, than at distinguishing between different phases of bourgeois society, and different moments within these phases: that true historical process which demands a much greater precision and delicacy of analysis than the always striking epochal analysis which is concerned with main lineaments and features.

The theoretical model which I have been trying to work with is this. I would say first that in any society, in any particular period, there is a central system of practices, meanings and values, which we can properly call dominant and effective. This implies no presumption about its value. All I am saying is that it is central. Indeed I would call it a corporate system, but this might be confusing, since Gramsci uses "corporate" to mean the subordinate as opposed to the general and dominant elements of hegemony. In any case what I have in mind is the central, effective and dominant system of meanings and values, which are not merely abstract but which are organized and lived. That is why hegemony is not to be understood at the level of mere opinion or mere manipulation. It is a whole body of practices and expectations; our assignments of energy, our ordinary understanding of the nature of man and of his world. It is a set of meanings and values which as they are experienced as practices appear as reciprocally confirming. It thus constitutes a sense of reality for most people in the society, a sense of absolute because experienced reality beyond which it is very difficult for most members of the society to move, in most areas of their lives. But this is not, except in the operation of a moment of abstract analysis, in any sense a static system. On the contrary we can only understand an effective and dominant culture if we understand the real social process on which it depends: I mean the process of incorporation. The modes of incorporation are of great social significance. The educational institutions are usually the main agencies of the transmission of an effective dominant culture, and this is now a major economic as well as a cultural activity; indeed it is both in the same moment. Moreover, at a philosophical level, at the true level of theory and at the level of the history of various practices, there is a process which I call the *selective tradition*: that which, within the terms of an effective dominant culture, is always passed off as "*the* tradition", "*the* significant past". But always the selectivity is the point; the way in which from a whole possible area of past and present, certain meanings and practices are chosen for emphasis, certain other meanings and practices are neglected and excluded. Even more crucially, some of these meanings and practices are reinterpreted, diluted, or put into forms which support or at least do not contradict other elements within the effective dominant culture. The processes of education; the processes of a much wider social training within institutions like the family; the practical definitions and organization of work; the selective tradition at an intellectual and theoretical level: all these forces are involved in a continual making and remaking of an effective dominant culture, and on them, as experienced, as built into our living, its reality depends. If what we learn there were merely an imposed ideology, or if it were only the isolable meanings and practices of the ruling class, or of a section of the ruling class, which gets imposed on others, occupying merely the top of our minds, it would be – and one would be glad – a very much easier thing to overthrow.

It is not only the depths to which this process reaches, selecting and organizing and interpreting our experience. It is also that it is continually active and adjusting; it isn't just the past, the dry husks of ideology which we can more easily discard. And this can only be so, in a complex society, if it is something more substantial and more flexible than any abstract imposed ideology. Thus we have to recognize the alternative meanings and values, the alternative opinions and attitudes, even some alternative senses of the world, which can be accommodated and tolerated within a particular effective and dominant culture. This has been much under-emphasized in our notions of a superstructure, and even in some notions of hegemony. And the under-emphasis opens the way for retreat to an indifferent complexity. In the practice of politics, for example, there are certain truly incorporated modes of what are nevertheless, within those terms, real oppositions, that are felt and fought out. Their existence within the incorporation is recognizable by the fact that, whatever the degree of internal conflict or internal variation, they do not in practice go beyond the limits of the central effective and dominant definitions. This is true, for example, of the practice of parliamentary politics, though its internal oppositions are real. It is true about a whole range of practices and arguments, in any real society, which can by no means be reduced to an ideological cover, but which can nevertheless be properly analysed as in my sense corporate, if we find that, whatever the degree of internal controversy and variation, they do not in the end exceed the limits of the central corporate definitions.

But if we are to say this, we have to think again about the sources of that which is not corporate; of those practices, experiences, meanings, values which are not part of the effective dominant culture. We can express this in two ways. There is clearly something that we can call alternative to the effective dominant culture, and there is something else that we can call oppositional, in a true sense. The degree of existence of these alternative and oppositional forms is itself a matter of constant historical variation in real circumstances. In certain societies it is possible to find areas of social life in which quite real alternatives are at least left alone. (If they are made available, of course, they are part of the corporate organization.) The existence of the possibility of opposition, and of its articulation, its degree of openness, and so on, again depends on very precise social and political forces. The facts of alternative and oppositional forms of social life and culture, in relation to the effective and dominant culture, have then to be recognized as subject to historical variation, and as having sources which are very significant as a fact about the dominant culture itself.

Residual and Emergent Cultures

I have next to introduce a further distinction, between *residual* and *emergent* forms, both of alternative and of oppositional culture. By "residual" I mean that some experiences, meanings and values, which cannot be verified or cannot be expressed in terms of the dominant culture, are nevertheless lived and practised on the basis of the residue – cultural as well as social – of some previous social formation. There is a real case of this in certain religious values, by contrast with the very evident incorporation of most religious meanings and values into the dominant system. The same is true, in a culture like Britain, of certain notions derived from a rural past, which have a very significant popularity. A residual culture is usually at some distance from the effective dominant culture, but one has to recognize that, in real cultural activities, it may get incorporated into it. This is because some part of it, some version of it – and especially if the residue is from some major area of the past – will in many cases have had to be incorporated if the effective dominant culture is to make sense in those areas. It is also because at certain points a dominant culture cannot allow too much of this kind of practice and experience outside itself, at least without risk. Thus the pressures are real, but certain genuinely residual meanings and practices in some important cases survive.

By "emergent" I mean, first, that new meanings and values, new practices, new significances and experiences, are continually being created. But there is then a much earlier attempt to incorporate them, just because they are part – and yet not a defined part – of effective contemporary practice. Indeed it is significant in our own period how very early this attempt is, how alert the dominant culture now is to anything that can be seen as emergent. We have then to see, first, as it were a temporal relation between a dominant culture and on the one hand a residual and on the other hand an emergent culture. But we can only understand this if we can make distinctions, that usually require very precise analysis, between residual-incorporated and residual not incorporated. It is an important fact about any particular society, how far it reaches into the whole range of human practices and experiences in an attempt at incorporation. It may be true of some earlier phases of bourgeois society, for example, that there were some areas of experience which it was willing to dispense with, which it was prepared to assign as the sphere of private or artistic life, and as being no particular business of society or the state. This went along with certain kinds of political tolerance, even if the reality of that tolerance was malign neglect. But I am sure it is true of the society that has come into existence since the last war, that progressively, because of developments in the social character of labour, in the social character of communications, and in the social character of decision, it extends much further than ever before in capitalist society into certain hitherto resigned areas of experience and practice and meaning. Thus the effective decision, as to whether a practice is alternative or oppositional, is often now made within a very much narrower scope. There is a simple theoretical distinction between alternative and oppositional, that is to say between someone who simply finds a different way to live and wishes to be left alone with it, and someone who finds a different way to live and wants to change the society in its light. This is usually the difference between individual and small-group solutions to social crisis and those solutions which properly belong to political and ultimately revolutionary practice. But it is often a very narrow line, in reality, between alternative and oppositional. A meaning or a practice may be tolerated as a deviation, and yet still be seen only as another particular way to live. But as the necessary area of effective dominance extends, the same meanings and practices can be seen by the dominant culture, not merely as disregarding or despising it, but as challenging it.

Now it is crucial to any Marxist theory of culture that it can give an adequate explanation of the sources of these practices and meanings. We can understand, from an ordinary historical approach, at least some of the sources of residual meanings and practices. These are the results of earlier social formations, in which certain real meanings and values were generated. In the subsequent default of a particular phase of a dominant culture, there is then a reaching back to those meanings and values which were created in real societies in the past, and which still seem to have some significance because they represent areas of human experience, aspiration and achievement, which the dominant culture under-values or opposes, or even cannot recognize. But our hardest task, theoretically, is to find a non-metaphysical and non-subjectivist explanation of emergent cultural practice. Moreover, part of our answer to this question bears on the process of persistence of residual practices.

Class and Human Practice

We have indeed one source to hand from the central body of Marxist theory. We have the formation of a new class, the coming to consciousness of a new class. This remains, without doubt, quite centrally important. Of course, in itself, this process of formation complicates any simple model of base and superstructure. It also complicates some of the ordinary versions of hegemony, although it was Gramsci's whole purpose to see and to create by organization that hegemony of a proletarian kind which would be capable of challenging the bourgeois hegemony. We have then one central source of new practice, in the emergence of a new class. But we have also to recognize certain other kinds of source, and in cultural practice some of these are very important. I would say that we can recognize them on the basis of this proposition: that no mode of production, and therefore no dominant society or order of society, and therefore no dominant culture, in reality exhausts the full range of human practice, human energy, human intention (this range is not the inventory of some original "human nature" but, on the contrary, is that extraordinary range of variations, both practised and imagined, of which human beings are and have shown themselves to be capable). Indeed it seems to me that this emphasis is not merely a negative proposition, allowing us to account for certain things which happen outside the dominant mode. On the contrary, it is a fact about the modes of domination that they select from and consequently exclude the full range of actual and possible human practice. The difficulties of human practice outside or against the dominant mode are, of course, real. It depends very much whether it is in an area in which the dominant class and the dominant culture have an interest and a stake. If the interest and the stake are explicit, many new practices will be reached for, and if possible incorporated, or else extirpated with extraordinary vigour. But in certain areas, there will be in certain periods practices and meanings which are not reached for. There will be areas of practice and meaning which, almost by definition from its own limited character, or in its profound deformation, the dominant culture is unable in any real terms to recognize. This gives us a bearing on the observable difference between, for example, the practices of a capitalist state and a state like the contemporary Soviet Union in relation to writers. Since from the whole Marxist tradition literature was seen as an important activity, indeed a crucial activity, the Soviet state is very much sharper in investigating areas where different versions of practice, different meanings and values, are being attempted and expressed. In capitalist practice, if the thing is not making a profit, or if it is not being widely circulated, then it can for some time be overlooked, at least while it remains alternative. When it becomes oppositional in an explicit way, it does, of course, get approached or attacked.

I am saying then that in relation to the full range of human practice at any one time, the dominant mode is a conscious selection and organization. At least in its fully formed state it is conscious. But there are always sources of actual human practice which it neglects or excludes. And these can be different in quality from the developing and articulate interests of a rising class. They can include, for example, alternative perceptions of others, in immediate personal relationships, or new perceptions of material and media, in art and science, and within certain limits these new perceptions can be practised. The relations between the two kinds of source – the emerging class and either the dominatively excluded or the more generally new practices – are by no means necessarily contradictory. At times they can be very close, and on the relations between them much in political practice depends. But culturally and as a matter of theory the areas can be seen as distinct.

Now if we go back to the cultural question in its most usual form – what are the relations between art and society, or literature and society? – in the light of the preceding discussion, we have to say first that there are no relations between literature and society in that abstracted way. The literature is there from the beginning as a practice in the society. Indeed until it and all other practices are present, the society cannot be seen as fully formed. A society is not fully available for analysis until each of its practices is included. But if we make that emphasis we must make a corresponding emphasis: that we cannot separate literature and art from other kinds of social practice, in such a way as to make them subject to quite special and distinct laws. They may have quite specific features as practices, but they cannot be separated from the general social process. Indeed one way of emphasizing this is to say, to insist, that literature is not restricted to operating in any one of the sectors I have been seeking to describe in this model. It would be easy to say, it is a familiar rhetoric, that literature operates in the emergent cultural sector, that it represents the new feelings, the new meanings, the new values. We might persuade ourselves of this theoretically, by abstract argument, but when we read much literature, over the whole range, without the sleight-of-hand of calling Literature only that which we have already selected as embodying certain meanings and values at a certain scale of intensity, we are bound to recognize that the act of writing, the practices of discourse in writing and speech, the making of novels and poems and plays and theories, all this activity takes place in all areas of the culture.

Literature appears by no means only in the emergent sector, which is always, in fact, quite rare. A great deal of writing is of a residual kind, and this has been deeply true of much English literature in the last half-century. Some of its fundamental meanings and values have belonged to the cultural achievements of long-past stages of society. So widespread is this fact, and the habits of mind it supports, that in many minds "literature" and "the past" acquire a certain identity, and it is then said that there is now no literature: all that glory is over. Yet most writing, in any period, including our own, is a form of contribution to the effective dominant culture. Indeed many of the specific qualities of literature – its capacity to embody and enact and perform certain meanings and values, or to create in single particular ways what would be otherwise merely general truths – enable it to fulfil this effective function with great power. To literature, of course, we must add the visual arts and music, and in our own society the powerful arts of film and of broadcasting. But the general theoretical point should be clear. If we are looking for the relations between literature and society, we cannot either separate out this one practice from a formed body of other practices, nor when we have identified a particular practice can we give it a uniform, static and ahistorical relation to some abstract social formation. The arts of writing and the arts of creation and performance, over their whole range, are parts of the cultural process in all the different ways, the different sectors, that I have been seeking to describe. They contribute to the effective dominant culture and are a central articulation of it. They embody residual meanings and values, not all of which are incorporated, though many are. They express also and significantly some emergent practices and meanings, yet some of these may eventually be incorporated, as they reach people and begin to move them. Thus it was very evident in the sixties, in some of the emergent arts of performance, that the dominant culture reached out to transform, or seek to transform, them. In this process, of course, the dominant culture itself changes, not in its central formation, but in many of its articulated features. But then in a modern society it must always change in this way, if it is to remain dominant, if it is still to be felt as in real ways central in all our many activities and interests.

Critical Theory as Consumption

What then are the implications of this general analysis for the analysis of particular works of art? This is the question towards which most discussion of cultural theory seems to be directed: the discovery of a method, perhaps even a methodology, through which particular works of art can be understood and described. I would not myself agree that this is the central use of cultural theory, but let us for a moment consider it. What seems to me very striking is that nearly all forms of contemporary critical theory are theories of *consumption*. That is to say, they are concerned with understanding an object in such a way that it can profitably or correctly be consumed. The earliest stage of consumption theory was the theory of "taste", where the link between the practice and the theory was direct in the metaphor. From taste there came the more elevated notion of "sensibility", in which it was the consumption by sensibility of elevated or insightful works that was held to be the essential practice of reading, and critical activity was then a function of this sensibility. There were then more developed theories, in the 1920s with I. A. Richards, and later in New Criticism, in which the effects of consumption were studied directly. The language of the work of art as object then became more overt. "What effect does this work ('the poem' as it was ordinarily described) have on me?" Or, "what impact does it have on me?", as it was later to be put in a much wider area of communication studies. Naturally enough, the notion of the work of art as *object*, as *text*, as an isolated artefact, became central in all these later consumption theories. It was not only that the practices of *production* were then overlooked, though this fused with the notion that most important literature anyway was from the past. The real social conditions of production were in any case neglected because they were believed to be at best secondary. The true relationship was seen always as between the taste, the sensibility or the training of the reader and this isolated work, this object "as in itself it really is", as most people came to put it. But the notion of the work of art as object had a further large theoretical effect. If you ask questions about the work of art seen as object, they may include questions about the components of its production. Now, as it happened, there was a use of the formula of base and superstructure which was precisely in line with this. The components of a work of art were the real activities of the base, and you could study the object to discover these components. Sometimes you even studied the components and then projected the object. But in any case the relationship that was looked for was one between an object and its components. But this was not only true of Marxist suppositions of a base and a superstructure. It was true also of various kinds of psychological theory, whether in the form of archetypes, or the images of the collective unconscious, or the myths and symbols which were seen as the *components* of particular works of art. Or again there was biography, or psychobiography and its like, where the components were in the man's life and the work of art was an object in which components of this kind were discovered. Even in some of the more rigorous forms of New Criticism and of structuralist criticism, this essential procedure of regarding the work as an object which has to be reduced to its components, even if later it may be reconstituted, came to persist.

Objects and Practices

Now I think the true crisis in cultural theory, in our own time, is between this view of the work of art as object and the alternative view of art as a practice. Of course it is at once argued that the work of art *is* an object: that various works have survived from the past, particular sculptures, particular paintings, particular buildings, and these are objects. This is of course true, but the same way of thinking is applied to works which have no such singular existence. There is no *Hamlet*, no *Brothers Karamazov*, no *Wuthering Heights*, in the sense that there is a particular great painting. There is no *Fifth Symphony*, there is no work in the whole area of music and dance and performance, which is an object in any way comparable to those works in the visual arts which have survived. And yet the habit of treating all such works as objects has persisted because this is a basic theoretical and practical presupposition. But in literature (especially in drama), in music and in a very wide area of the performing arts, what we permanently have are not objects but *notations*. These notations have then to be interpreted in an active way, according to the particular conventions. But indeed this is true over an even wider field. The relationship between the making of a work of art and its reception is always active, and subject to conventions, which in themselves are forms of (changing) social organization and relationship, and this is radically different from the production and consumption of an object. It is indeed an activity and a practice, and in its accessible forms, although it may in some arts have the character of a singular object, it is still only accessible through active perception and interpretation. This makes the case of notation, in arts like drama and literature and music, only a special case of a much wider truth. What this can show us here about the practice of analysis is that we have to break from the common procedure of isolating the object and then discovering its components. On the contrary we have to discover the nature of a practice and then its conditions.

Often these two procedures may in part resemble each other, but in many other cases they are of radically different kinds, and I would conclude with an observation on the way this distinction bears on the Marxist tradition of the relation between primary economic and social practices, and cultural practices. If we suppose that what is produced in cultural practice is a series of objects, we shall, as in most current forms of sociological-critical procedure, set about discovering their components. Within a Marxist emphasis these components will be from what we have been in the habit of calling the base. We then isolate certain features which we can so to say recognize *in component form*, or we ask what processes of transformation or mediation these components have gone through before they arrived in this accessible state.

But I am saying that we should look not for the components of a product but for the conditions of a practice. When we find ourselves looking at a particular work, or group of works, often realizing, as we do so, their essential community as well as their irreducible individuality, we should find ourselves attending first to the reality of their practice and the conditions of the practice as it was then executed. And from this I think we ask essentially different questions. Take for example the way in which an object – "a text" – is related to a genre, in orthodox criticism. We identify it by certain leading features, we then assign it to a larger category, the genre, and then we may find the components of the genre in a particular social history (although in some variants of criticism not even that is done, and the genre is supposed to be some permanent category of the mind).

It is not that way of proceeding that is now required. The recognition of the relation of a collective mode and an individual project – and these are the only categories that we can initially presume – is a recognition of related practices. That is to say, the irreducibly individual projects that particular works are, may come in experience and in analysis to show resemblances which allow us to group them into collective modes. These are by no means always genres. They may exist as resemblances within and across genres. They may be the practice of a group in a period, rather than the practice of a phase in a genre. But as we discover the nature of a particular practice, and the nature of the relation between an individual project and a collective mode, we find that we are analysing, as two forms of the same process, both its active composition and its conditions of composition, and in either direction this is a complex of extending active relationships. This means, of course, that we have no built-in procedure of the kind which is indicated by the fixed character of an object. We have the principles of the relations of practices, within a discoverably intentional organization, and we have the available hypotheses of dominant, residual and emergent. But what we are actively seeking is the true practice which has been alienated to an object, and the true conditions of practice – whether as literary conventions or as social relationships – which have been alienated to components or to mere background.

As a general proposition this is only an emphasis, but it seems to me to suggest at once the point of break and the point of departure, in practical and theoretical work, within an active and self-renewing Marxist cultural tradition.

Note

1   For a further discussion of the range of meanings in "determine" see Raymond Williams, *Keywords* (London, 1976), pp. 87–91.

(i) From Culture to Hegemony; (ii) Subculture: The Unnatural Break

Dick Hebdige

(i) From Culture to Hegemony

Culture

Culture: cultivation, tending, in Christian authors, worship; the action or practice of cultivating the soil; tillage, husbandry; the cultivation or rearing of certain animals (e.g. fish); the artificial development of microscopic organisms, organisms so produced; the cultivating or development (of the mind, faculties, manners), improvement or refinement by education and training; the condition of being trained or refined; the intellectual side of civilization; the prosecution or special attention or study of any subject or pursuit.

— *Oxford English Dictionary*

Culture is a notoriously ambiguous concept as the above definition demonstrates. Refracted through centuries of usage, the word has acquired a number of quite different, often contradictory, meanings. Even as a scientific term, it refers both to a process (artificial development of microscopic organisms) and a product (organisms so produced). More specifically, since the end of the eighteenth century, it has been used by English intellectuals and literary figures to focus critical attention on a whole range of controversial issues. The "quality of life", the effects in human terms of mechanization, the division of labour and the creation of a mass society have all been discussed within the larger confines of what Raymond Williams has called the "Culture and Society" debate (Williams, 1961). It was through this tradition of dissent and criticism that the dream of the "organic society" – of society as an integrated, meaningful whole – was largely kept alive. The dream had two basic

From Dick Hebdige, "From culture to hegemony" and "Subculture: The unnatural break." In *Subculture: The Meaning of Style*, pp. 5–19 and 90–9. New York and London: Routledge, 1979.

trajectories. One led back to the past and to the feudal ideal of a hierarchically ordered community. Here, culture assumed an almost sacred function. Its "harmonious perfection" (Arnold, 1868) was posited against the Wasteland of contemporary life.

The other trajectory, less heavily supported, led towards the future, to a socialist Utopia where the distinction between labour and leisure was to be annulled. Two basic definitions of culture emerged from this tradition, though these were by no means necessarily congruent with the two trajectories outlined above. The first – the one which is probably most familiar to the reader – was essentially classical and conservative. It represented culture as a standard of aesthetic excellence: "the best that has been thought and said in the world" (Arnold, 1868), and it derived from an appreciation of "classic" aesthetic form (opera, ballet, drama, literature, art). The second, traced back by Williams to Herder and the eighteenth century (Williams, 1976), was rooted in anthropology. Here the term "culture" referred to a

> particular way of life which expresses certain meanings and values not only in art and learning, but also in institutions and ordinary behaviour. The analysis of culture, from such a definition, is the clarification of the meanings and values implicit and explicit in a particular way of life, a particular culture. (Williams, 1965)

This definition obviously had a much broader range. It encompassed, in T. S. Eliot's words,

> all the characteristic activities and interests of a people. Derby Day, Henley Regatta, Cowes, the 12th of August, a cup final, the dog races, the pin table, the dart-board, Wensleydale cheese, boiled cabbage cut into sections, beetroot in vinegar, 19th Century Gothic churches, the music of Elgar. . . . (Eliot, 1948)

As Williams noted, such a definition could only be supported if a new theoretical initiative was taken. The theory of culture now involved the "study of relationships between elements in a whole way of life" (Williams, 1965). The emphasis shifted from immutable to historical criteria, from fixity to transformation:

> an emphasis [which] from studying particular meanings and values seeks not so much to compare these, as a way of establishing a scale, but by studying their modes of change to discover certain general causes or "trends" by which social and cultural developments as a whole can be better understood. (Williams, 1965)

Williams was, then, proposing an altogether broader formulation of the relationships between culture and society, one which through the analysis of "particular meanings and values" sought to uncover the concealed fundamentals of history; the "general causes" and broad social "trends" which lie behind the manifest appearances of an "everyday life".

In the early years, when it was being established in the universities, Cultural Studies sat rather uncomfortably on the fence between these two conflicting definitions – culture as a standard of excellence, culture as a "whole way of life" – unable to determine which represented the most fruitful line of enquiry. Richard Hoggart and Raymond Williams portrayed working-class culture sympathetically in wistful accounts of prescholarship boyhoods – Leeds for Hoggart (1958), a Welsh mining village for Williams (1960) – but their work displayed a strong bias towards literature and literacy[1] and an equally strong moral tone. Hoggart deplored the way in which the traditional working-class community – a community of tried and tested values despite the dour landscape in which it had been set – was being undermined and replaced by a "Candy Floss World" of thrills and cheap fiction which was somehow bland *and* sleazy. Williams tentatively endorsed the new mass communications but was concerned to establish aesthetic and moral criteria for distinguishing the worthwhile products from the "trash"; the jazz – "a real musical form" – and the football – "a wonderful game" – from the "rape novel, the Sunday strip paper and the latest Tin Pan drool" (Williams, 1965). In 1966 Hoggart laid down the basic premises upon which Cultural Studies were based:

> First, without appreciating good literature, no one will really understand the nature of society, second, literary critical analysis can be applied to certain social phenomena other than "academically respectable" literature (for example, the popular arts, mass communications) so as to illuminate their meanings for individuals and their societies. (Hoggart, 1966)

The implicit assumption that it still required a literary sensibility to "read" society with the requisite subtlety, and that the two ideas of culture could be ultimately reconciled was also, paradoxically, to inform the early work of the French writer, Roland Barthes, though here it found validation in a method – semiotics – a way of reading signs (Hawkes, 1977).

Barthes: Myths and Signs

Using models derived from the work of the Swiss linguist Ferdinand de Saussure[2] Barthes sought to expose the *arbitrary* nature of cultural phenomena, to uncover the latent meanings of an everyday life which, to all intents and purposes, was "perfectly natural". Unlike Hoggart, Barthes was not concerned with distinguishing the good from the bad in modern mass culture, but rather with showing how *all* the apparently spontaneous forms and rituals of contemporary bourgeois societies are subject to a systematic distortion, liable at any moment to be dehistoricized, "naturalized", converted into myth:

> The whole of France is steeped in this anonymous ideology: our press, our films, our theatre, our pulp literature, our rituals, our Justice, our diplomacy, our conversations, our remarks about the weather, a murder trial, a touching wedding, the cooking we dream of, the garments we wear, everything in everyday life is dependent on the representation which the bourgeoisie *has and makes us have* of the relations between men and the world. (Barthes, 1972)

Like Eliot, Barthes' notion of culture extends beyond the library, the opera-house and the theatre to encompass the whole of everyday life. But this everyday life is for

Barthes overlaid with a significance which is at once more insidious and more systematically organized. Starting from the premise that "myth is a type of speech", Barthes set out in *Mythologies* to examine the normally hidden set of rules, codes and conventions through which meanings particular to specific social groups (i.e. those in power) are rendered universal and "given" for the whole of society. He found in phenomena as disparate as a wrestling match, a writer on holiday, a tourist-guide book, the same artificial nature, the same ideological core. Each had been exposed to the same prevailing rhetoric (the rhetoric of common sense) and turned into myth, into a mere element in a "second-order semiological system" (Barthes, 1972). (Barthes uses the example of a photograph in *Paris-Match* of a Negro soldier saluting the French flag, which has a first and second order connotation: (1) a gesture of loyalty, but also (2) "France is a great empire, and all her sons, without colour discrimination, faithfully serve under her flag".)

Barthes' application of a method rooted in linguistics to other systems of discourse outside language (fashion, film, food, etc.) opened up completely new possibilities for contemporary cultural studies. It was hoped that the invisible seam between language, experience and reality could be located and prised open through a semiotic analysis of this kind: that the gulf between the alienated intellectual and the "real" world could be rendered meaningful and, miraculously, at the same time, be made to disappear. Moreover, under Barthes' direction, semiotics promised nothing less than the reconciliation of the two conflicting definitions of culture upon which Cultural Studies was so ambiguously posited – a marriage of moral conviction (in this case, Barthes' Marxist beliefs) and popular themes: the study of a society's total way of life.

This is not to say that semiotics was easily assimilable within the Cultural Studies project. Though Barthes shared the literary preoccupations of Hoggart and Williams, his work introduced a new Marxist "problematic"[3] which was alien to the British tradition of concerned and largely untheorized "social commentary". As a result, the old debate seemed suddenly limited. In E. P. Thompson's words it appeared to reflect the parochial concerns of a group of "gentlemen amateurs". Thompson sought to replace Williams' definition of the theory of culture as "a theory of relations between elements in a whole way of life" with his own more rigorously Marxist formulation: "the study of relationships in a whole way of *conflict*". A more analytical framework was required; a new vocabulary had to be learned. As part of this process of theorization, the word "ideology" came to acquire a much wider range of meanings than had previously been the case. We have seen how Barthes found an "anonymous ideology" penetrating every possible level of social life, inscribed in the most mundane of rituals, framing the most casual social encounters. But how can ideology be "anonymous", and how can it assume such a broad significance? Before we attempt any reading of subcultural style, we must first define the term "ideology" more precisely.

Ideology: A Lived *Relation*

In *The German Ideology*, Marx shows how the basis of the capitalist economic structure (surplus value, neatly defined by Godelier as "Profit . . . is unpaid work")

(Godelier, 1970)) is hidden from the consciousness of the agents of production. The failure to see through appearances to the real relations which underlie them does not occur as the direct result of some kind of masking operation consciously carried out by individuals, social groups or institutions. On the contrary, ideology by definition thrives *beneath* consciousness. It is here, at the level of "normal common sense", that ideological frames of reference are most firmly sedimented and most effective, because it is here that their ideological nature is most effectively concealed. As Stuart Hall puts it:

> It is precisely its "spontaneous" quality, its transparency, its "naturalness", its refusal to be made to examine the premises on which it is founded, its resistance to change or to correction, its effect of instant recognition, and the closed circle in which it moves which makes common sense, at one and the same time, "spontaneous", ideological and *unconscious*. You cannot learn, through common sense, *how things are*: you can only discover *where they fit* into the existing scheme of things. In this way, its very taken-for-grantedness is what establishes it as a medium in which its own premises and presuppositions are being rendered *invisible* by its apparent transparency. (Hall, 1977)

Since ideology saturates everyday discourse in the form of common sense, it cannot be bracketed off from everyday life as a self-contained set of "political opinions" or "biased views". Neither can it be reduced to the abstract dimensions of a "world view" or used in the crude Marxist sense to designate "false consciousness". Instead, as Louis Althusser has pointed out:

> ideology has very little to do with "consciousness". . . . It is profoundly *unconscious*. . . . Ideology is indeed a system of representation, but in the majority of cases these representations have nothing to do with "consciousness": they are usually images and occasionally concepts, but it is above all as *structures* that they impose on the vast majority of men, not via their "consciousness". They are perceived-accepted-suffered cultural objects and they act functionally on men via a process that escapes them. (Althusser, 1969)

Although Althusser is here referring to structures like the family, cultural and political institutions, etc., we can illustrate the point quite simply by taking as our example a physical structure. Most modern institutes of education, despite the apparent neutrality of the materials from which they are constructed (red brick, white tile, etc.) carry within themselves implicit ideological assumptions which are literally structured into the architecture itself. The categorization of knowledge into arts and sciences is reproduced in the faculty system which houses different disciplines in different buildings, and most colleges maintain the traditional divisions by devoting a separate floor to each subject. Moreover, the hierarchical relationship between teacher and taught is inscribed in the very lay-out of the lecture theatre where the seating arrangements – benches rising in tiers before a raised lectern – dictate the flow of information and serve to "naturalize" professorial authority. Thus, a whole range of decisions about what is and what is not possible within education have been made, however unconsciously, before the content of individual courses is even decided.

These decisions help to set the limits not only on what is taught but on *how* it is taught. Here the buildings literally *reproduce* in concrete terms prevailing (ideological) notions about what education is and it is through this process that the educational structure, which can, of course, be altered, is placed beyond question and appears to us as a "given" (i.e. as immutable). In this case, the frames of our thinking have been translated into actual bricks and mortar.

Social relations and processes are then appropriated by individuals only through the forms in which they are represented to those individuals. These forms are, as we have seen, by no means transparent. They are shrouded in a "common sense" which simultaneously validates and mystifies them. It is precisely these "perceived-accepted-suffered cultural objects" which semiotics sets out to "interrogate" and decipher. All aspects of culture possess a semiotic value, and the most taken-for-granted phenomena can function as signs: as elements in communication systems governed by semantic rules and codes which are not themselves directly apprehended in experience. These signs are, then, as opaque as the social relations which produce them and which they re-present. In other words, there is an ideological dimension to every signification:

> A sign does not simply exist as part of reality – it reflects and refracts another reality. Therefore it may distort that reality or be true to it, or may perceive it from a special point of view, and so forth. Every sign is subject to the criteria of ideological evaluation. . . . The domain of ideology coincides with the domain of signs. They equate with one another. Whenever a sign is present, ideology is present too. Everything ideological possesses a semiotic value. (Volosinov, 1973)

To uncover the ideological dimension of signs we must first try to disentangle the codes through which meaning is organized. "Connotative" codes are particularly important. As Stuart Hall has argued, they ". . . cover the face of social life and render it classifiable, intelligible, meaningful" (Hall, 1977). He goes on to describe these codes as "maps of meaning" which are of necessity the product of selection. They cut across a range of potential meanings, making certain meanings available and ruling others out of court. We tend to live inside these maps as surely as we live in the "real" world: they "think" us as much as we "think" them, and this in itself is quite "natural". All human societies *reproduce* themselves in this way through a process of "naturalization". It is through this process – a kind of inevitable reflex of all social life – that *particular* sets of social relations, *particular* ways of organizing the world appear to us as if they were universal and timeless. This is what Althusser (1971a) means when he says that "ideology has no history" and that ideology in this general sense will always be an "essential element of every social formation" (Althusser and Balibar, 1968).

However, in highly complex societies like ours, which function through a finely graded system of divided (i.e. specialized) labour, the crucial question has to do with which specific ideologies, representing the interests of which specific groups and classes will prevail at any given moment, in any given situation. To deal with this question, we must first consider how power is distributed in our society. That is, we must ask which groups and classes have how much say in defining, ordering and classifying out the social world. For instance, if we pause to reflect for a moment, it should be obvious that access to the means by which ideas are disseminated in our society (i.e. principally the mass media) is *not* the same for all classes. Some groups have more say, more opportunity to make the rules, to organize meaning, while others are less favourably placed, have less power to produce and impose their definitions of the world on the world.

Thus, when we come to look beneath the level of "ideology-in-general" at the way in which specific ideologies work, how some gain dominance and others remain marginal, we can see that in advanced Western democracies the ideological field is by no means neutral. To return to the "connotative" codes to which Stuart Hall refers we can see that these "maps of meaning" are charged with a potentially explosive significance because they are traced and re-traced along the lines laid down by the *dominant* discourses about reality, the *dominant* ideologies. They thus tend to represent, in however obscure and contradictory a fashion, the interests of the *dominant* groups in society.

To understand this point we should refer to Marx:

> The ideas of the ruling class are in every epoch the ruling ideas, i.e. the class which is the ruling *material* force of society is at the same time its ruling *intellectual* force. The class which has the means of material production at its disposal, has control at the same time over the means of mental production, so that generally speaking, the ideas of those who lack the means of mental production are subject to it. The ruling ideas are nothing more than the ideal expression of the dominant material relationships grasped as ideas; hence of the relationships which make the one class the ruling class, therefore the ideas of its dominance. (Marx and Engels, 1970)

This is the basis of Antonio Gramsci's theory of *hegemony* which provides the most adequate account of how dominance is sustained in advanced capitalist societies.

Hegemony: The Moving Equilibrium

Society cannot share a common communication system so long as it is split into warring classes.

– Brecht, *A Short Organum for the Theatre*

The term hegemony refers to a situation in which a provisional alliance of certain social groups can exert "total social authority" over other subordinate groups, not simply by coercion or by the direct imposition of ruling ideas, but by "winning and shaping consent so that the power of the dominant classes appears both legitimate and natural" (Hall, 1977). Hegemony can only be maintained so long as the dominant classes "succeed in framing all competing definitions within their range" (Hall, 1977), so that subordinate groups are, if not controlled; then at least contained within an ideological space which does not seem at all "ideological": which appears instead to be permanent and "natural", to lie outside history, to be beyond particular interests (see *Social Trends*, no. 6, 1975).

This is how, according to Barthes, "mythology" performs its vital function of naturalization and normalization and it is in his book *Mythologies* that Barthes demonstrates most forcefully the full extension of these normalized forms and meanings. However, Gramsci adds the important proviso that hegemonic power, precisely *because* it requires the consent of the dominated majority, can never be permanently exercised by the same alliance of "class fractions". As has been pointed out, "Hegemony . . . is not universal and 'given' to the continuing rule of a particular class. It has to be won, reproduced, sustained. Hegemony is, as Gramsci said, a 'moving equilibrium' containing relations of forces favourable or unfavourable to this or that tendency" (Hall et al., 1976a).

In the same way, forms cannot be permanently normalized. They can always be deconstructed, demystified, by a "mythologist" like Barthes. Moreover commodities can be symbolically "repossessed" in everyday life, and endowed with implicitly oppositional meanings, by the very groups who originally produced them. The symbiosis in which ideology and social order, production and reproduction, are linked is then neither fixed nor guaranteed. It can be prised open. The consensus can be fractured, challenged, overruled, and resistance to the groups in dominance cannot always be lightly dismissed or automatically incorporated. Although, as Lefebvre has written, we live in a society where ". . . objects in practice become signs and signs objects and a second nature takes the place of the first – the initial layer of perceptible reality" (Lefebvre, 1971), there are, as he goes on to affirm, always "objections and contradictions which hinder the closing of the circuit" between sign and object, production and reproduction.

We can now return to the meaning of youth subcultures, for the emergence of such groups has signalled in a spectacular fashion the breakdown of consensus in the postwar period. In the following chapters we shall see that it is precisely objections and contradictions of the kind which Lefebvre has described that find expression in subculture. However, the challenge to hegemony which subcultures represent is not issued directly by them. Rather it is expressed obliquely, in style. The objections are lodged, the contradictions displayed (and, as we shall see, "magically resolved") at the profoundly superficial level of appearances: that is, at the level of signs. For the sign-community, the community of myth-consumers, is not a uniform body. As Volosinov has written, it is cut through by class:

> Class does not coincide with the sign community, i.e. with the totality of users of the same set of signs of ideological communication. Thus various different classes will use one and the same language. As a result, differently oriented accents intersect in every ideological sign. Sign becomes the arena of the class struggle. (Volosinov, 1973)

The struggle between different discourses, different definitions and meanings within ideology is therefore always, at the same time, a struggle within signification: a struggle for possession of the sign which extends to even the most mundane areas of everyday life. To turn once more to the examples used in the Introduction, to the safety pins and tubes of vaseline, we can see that such commodities are indeed open to a double inflection: to "illegitimate" as well as "legitimate" uses. These "humble objects" can be magically appropriated; "stolen" by subordinate groups and made to carry "secret" meanings: meanings which express, in code, a form of resistance to the order which guarantees their continued subordination.

Style in subculture is, then, pregnant with significance. Its transformations go "against nature", interrupting the process of "normalization". As such, they are gestures, movements towards a speech which offends the "silent majority", which challenges the principle of unity and cohesion, which contradicts the myth of consensus. Our task becomes, like Barthes', to discern the hidden messages inscribed in code on the glossy surfaces of style, to trace them out as "maps of meaning" which obscurely re-present the very contradictions they are designed to resolve or conceal.

Academics who adopt a semiotic approach are not alone in reading significance into the loaded surfaces of life. The existence of spectacular subcultures continually opens up those surfaces to other potentially subversive readings. Jean Genet, the archetype of the "unnatural" deviant, again exemplifies the practice of resistance through style. He is as convinced in his own way as is Roland Barthes of the ideological character of cultural signs. He is equally oppressed by the seamless web of forms and meanings which encloses and yet excludes him. His reading is equally partial. He makes his own list and draws his own conclusions:

> I was astounded by so rigorous an edifice whose details were united against me. Nothing in the world is irrelevant: the stars on a general's sleeve, the stock-market quotations, the olive harvest, the style of the judiciary, the wheat exchange, the flower-beds, . . . Nothing. This order . . . had a meaning – my exile. (Genet, 1967)

It is this alienation from the deceptive "innocence" of appearances which gives the teds, the mods, the punks and no doubt future groups of as yet unimaginable "deviants" the impetus to move from man's second "false nature" (Barthes, 1972) to a genuinely expressive artifice; a truly subterranean style. As a symbolic violation of the social order, such a movement attracts and will continue to attract attention, to provoke censure and to act, as we shall see, as the fundamental bearer of significance in subculture.

No subculture has sought with more grim determination than the punks to detach itself from the taken-for-granted landscape of normalized forms, nor to bring down upon itself such vehement disapproval. We shall begin therefore with the moment of punk and we shall return to that moment throughout the course of this book. It is perhaps appropriate that the punks, who have made such large claims for illiteracy, who have pushed profanity to such startling extremes, should be used to test some of the methods for "reading" signs evolved in the centuries-old debate on the sanctity of culture. [. . .]

(ii)   Subculture: The Unnatural Break

I felt unclean for about 48 hours.
> – G.L.C. councillor after seeing a concert by the Sex Pistols,
> reported *New Musical Express*, 18 July 1977

[Language is] of all social institutions, the least amenable to initiative. It blends with the life of society, and the latter, inert by nature, is a prime conservative force.

– Saussure, 1974

Subcultures represent "noise" (as opposed to sound): interference in the orderly sequence which leads from real events and phenomena to their representation in the media. We should therefore not underestimate the signifying power of the spectacular subculture not only as a metaphor for potential anarchy "out there" but as an actual mechanism of semantic disorder: a kind of temporary blockage in the system of representation. As John Mepham (1972) has written:

> Distinctions and identities may be so deeply embedded in our discourse and thought about the world whether this be because of their role in our practical lives, or because they are cognitively powerful and are an important aspect of the way in which we appear to make sense of our experience, that the theoretical challenge to them can be quite startling.

Any elision, truncation or convergence of prevailing linguistic and ideological categories can have profoundly disorienting effects. These deviations briefly expose the arbitrary nature of the codes which underlie and shape all forms of discourse. As Stuart Hall (1974) has written (here in the context of explicitly political deviance):

> New . . . developments which are both dramatic and "meaningless" within the consensually validated norms, pose a challenge to the normative world. They render problematic not only how the . . . world is defined, but how it ought to be. They "breach our expectancies". . . .

Notions concerning the sanctity of language are intimately bound up with ideas of social order. The limits of acceptable linguistic expression are prescribed by a number of apparently universal taboos. These taboos guarantee the continuing "transparency" (the taken-for-grantedness) of meaning.

Predictably then, violations of the authorized codes through which the social world is organized and experienced have considerable power to provoke and disturb. They are generally condemned, in Mary Douglas' words (1967), as "contrary to holiness" and Lévi-Strauss has noted how, in certain primitive myths, the mispronunciation of words and the misuse of language are classified along with incest as horrendous aberrations capable of "unleashing storm and tempest" (Lévi-Strauss, 1969). Similarly, spectacular subcultures express forbidden contents (consciousness of class, consciousness of difference) in forbidden forms (transgressions of sartorial and behavioural codes, law breaking, etc.). They are profane articulations, and they are often and significantly defined as "unnatural". The terms used in the tabloid press to describe those youngsters who, in their conduct or clothing, proclaim subcultural membership ("freaks", "animals . . . who find courage, like rats, in hunting in packs"[4]) would seem to suggest that the most primitive anxieties concerning the sacred distinction between nature and culture can be summoned up by the emergence of such a group. No doubt, the breaking of rules is confused with the "absence of rules" which, according to Lévi-Strauss (1969), "seems to provide the surest criteria for distinguishing a natural from a cultural process". Certainly, the official reaction to the punk subculture, particularly to the Sex Pistols' use of "foul language" on television[5] and record[6], and to the vomiting and spitting incidents at Heathrow Airport[7] would seem to indicate that these basic taboos are no less deeply sedimented in contemporary British society.

Two Forms of Incorporation

Has not this society, glutted with aestheticism, already integrated former romanticisms, surrealism, existentialism and even Marxism to a point? It has, indeed, through trade, in the form of commodities. That which yesterday was reviled today becomes cultural consumer-goods, consumption thus engulfs what was intended to give meaning and direction.

– Lefebvre, 1971

We have seen how subcultures "breach our expectancies", how they represent symbolic challenges to a symbolic order. But can subcultures always be effectively incorporated and if so, how? The emergence of a spectacular subculture is invariably accompanied by a wave of hysteria in the press. This hysteria is typically ambivalent: it fluctuates between dread and fascination, outrage and amusement. Shock and horror headlines dominate the front page (e.g. "Rotten Razored", *Daily Mirror*, 28 June 1977) while, inside the editorials positively bristle with "serious" commentary[8] and the centrespreads or supplements contain delirious accounts of the latest fads and rituals (see, for example, *Observer* colour supplements 30 January, 10 July 1977, 12 February 1978). Style in particular provokes a double response: it is alternately celebrated (in the fashion page) and ridiculed or reviled (in those articles which define subcultures as social problems).

In most cases, it is the subculture's stylistic innovations which first attract the media's attention. Subsequently deviant or "anti-social" acts – vandalism, swearing, fighting, "animal behaviour" – are "discovered" by the police, the judiciary, the press; and these acts are used to "explain" the subculture's original transgression of sartorial codes. In fact, either deviant behaviour or the identification of a distinctive uniform (or more typically a combination of the two) can provide the catalyst for a moral panic. In the case of the punks, the media's sighting of punk style virtually coincided with the discovery or invention of punk deviance. The *Daily Mirror* ran its first series of alarmist centrespreads on the subculture, concentrating on the bizarre clothing and jewellery during the week (29 Nov–3 Dec 1977) in which the Sex Pistols exploded into the public eye on the Thames *Today* programme. On the other hand, the mods, perhaps because of the muted character of their style, were not identified as a group until the Bank Holiday clashes of 1964, although the subculture was, by then, fully developed, at least in London. Whichever item opens the amplifying sequence, it invariably ends with the simultaneous diffusion and defusion of the subcultural style.

As the subculture begins to strike its own eminently marketable pose, as its vocabulary (both visual and verbal) becomes more and more familiar, so the referential context to which it can be most conveniently assigned is made increasingly apparent. Eventually, the mods, the punks, the glitter rockers can be incorporated, brought back into line, located on the preferred "map of problematic social reality" (Geertz, 1964) at the point where boys in lipstick are "just kids dressing up", where girls in rubber dresses are "daughters just like yours" (see pp. 98–9; 158–9, n. 8). The media, as Stuart Hall (1977) has argued, not only record resistance, they "situate it within the dominant framework of meanings" and those young people who choose to inhabit a spectacular youth culture are simultaneously *returned*, as they are represented on T.V. and in the newspapers, to the place where common sense would have them fit (as "animals" certainly, but also "in the family", "out of work", "up to date", etc.). It is through this continual process of recuperation that the fractured order is repaired and the subculture incorporated as a diverting spectacle within the dominant mythology from which it in part emanates: as "folk devil", as Other, as Enemy. The process of recuperation takes two characteristic forms:

1. the conversion of subcultural signs (dress, music, etc.) into mass-produced objects (i.e. the commodity form);
2. the "labelling" and re-definition of deviant behaviour by dominant groups – the police, the media, the judiciary (i.e. the ideological form).

The Commodity Form

The first has been comprehensively handled by both journalists and academics. The relationship between the spectacular subculture and the various industries which service and exploit it is notoriously ambiguous. After all, such a subculture is concerned first and foremost with consumption. It operates exclusively in the leisure sphere ("I wouldn't wear my punk outfit for work – there's a time and a place for everything" (see note 11)). It communicates through commodities even if the meanings attached to those commodities are purposefully distorted or overthrown. It is therefore difficult in this case to maintain any absolute distinction between commercial exploitation on the one hand and creativity/originality on the other, even though these categories are emphatically opposed in the value systems of most subcultures. Indeed, the creation and diffusion of new styles is inextricably bound up with the process of production, publicity and packaging which must inevitably lead to the defusion of the subculture's subversive power – both mod and punk innovations fed back directly into high fashion and mainstream fashion. Each new subculture establishes new trends, generates new looks and sounds which feed back into the appropriate industries. As John Clarke (1976b) has observed:

> The diffusion of youth styles from the subcultures to the fashion market is not simply a "cultural process", but a real network or infrastructure of new kinds of commercial and economic institutions. The small-scale record shops, recording companies, the boutiques and one- or two-woman manufacturing companies – these versions of artisan capitalism, rather than more generalised and unspecific phenomena, situate the dialectic of commercial "manipulation".

However, it would be mistaken to insist on the absolute autonomy of "cultural" and commercial processes. As Lefebvre (1971) puts it: "Trade is . . . both a social and an intellectual phenomenon", and commodities arrive at the market-place already laden with significance. They are, in Marx's words (1970), "social hieroglyphs"[9] and their meanings are inflected by conventional usage.

Thus, as soon as the original innovations which signify "subculture" are translated into commodities and made generally available, they become "frozen". Once removed from their private contexts by the small entrepreneurs and big fashion interests who produce them on a mass scale, they become codified, made comprehensible, rendered at once public property and profitable merchandise. In this way, the two forms of incorporation (the semantic/ideological and the "real"/commercial) can be said to converge on the commodity form. Youth cultural styles may begin by issuing symbolic challenges, but they must inevitably end by establishing new sets of conventions; by creating new commodities, new industries or rejuvenating old ones (think of the boost punk must have given haberdashery!). This occurs irrespective of the subculture's political orientation: the macrobiotic restaurants, craft shops and "antique markets" of the hippie era were easily converted into punk boutiques and record shops. It also happens irrespective of the startling content of the style: punk clothing and insignia could be bought mail-order by the summer of 1977, and in September of that year *Cosmopolitan* ran a review of Zandra Rhodes' latest collection of couture follies which consisted entirely of variations on the punk theme. Models smouldered beneath mountains of safety pins and plastic (the pins were jewelled, the "plastic" wet-look satin) and the accompanying article ended with an aphorism – "To shock is chic" – which presaged the subculture's imminent demise.

The Ideological Form

The second form of incorporation – the ideological – has been most adequately treated by those sociologists who operate a transactional model of deviant behaviour. For example, Stan Cohen has described in detail how one particular moral panic (surrounding the mod–rocker conflict of the mid-60s) was launched and sustained.[10] Although this type of analysis can often provide an extremely sophisticated explanation of why spectacular subcultures consistently provoke such hysterical outbursts, it tends to overlook the subtler mechanisms through which potentially threatening phenomena are handled and contained. As the use of the term "folk devil" suggests, rather too much weight tends to be given to the sensational excesses of the tabloid press at the expense of the ambiguous reactions which are, after all, more typical. As we have seen, the way in which subcultures are represented in the media makes them both more *and less* exotic than they actually are. They are seen to contain both dangerous aliens and boisterous kids, wild animals and wayward pets. Roland Barthes furnishes a key to this paradox in his description of "identification" – one of the seven rhetorical figures which, according to Barthes, distinguish the meta-language of bourgeois mythology. He characterizes the petit-bourgeois as a person ". . . unable to imagine the Other . . . the Other is a scandal which threatens his existence" (Barthes, 1972).

Two basic strategies have been evolved for dealing with this threat. First, the Other can be trivialized, naturalized, domesticated. Here, the difference is simply denied ("Otherness is reduced to sameness"). Alternatively, the Other can be trans-formed into meaningless exotica, a "pure object, a spectacle, a clown" (Barthes, 1972). In this case, the difference is consigned to a place beyond analysis. Spectacu-lar subcultures are continually being defined in precisely these terms. Soccer hooli-gans, for example, are typically placed beyond "the bounds of common decency" and are classified as "animals". ("These people aren't human beings", football club manager quoted on the *News at Ten*, Sunday, 12 March 1977.) (See Stuart Hall's treatment of the press coverage of football hooligans in *Football Hooliganism* (edited by Roger Ingham, 1978).) On the other hand, the punks tended to be resituated by the press in the family, perhaps because members of the subculture deliberately obscured their origins, refused the family and willingly played the part of folk devil, presenting themselves as pure objects, as villainous clowns. Certainly, like every other youth culture, punk was perceived as a threat to the family. Occasionally this threat was represented in literal terms. For example, the *Daily Mirror* (1 August 1977) carried a photograph of a child lying in the road after a punk–ted confronta-tion under the headline "VICTIM OF THE PUNK ROCK PUNCH-UP: THE BOY WHO FELL FOUL OF THE MOB". In this case, punk's threat to the family was made "real" (that could be my child!) through the ideological framing of photographic evidence which is popularly regarded as unproblematic.

None the less, on other occasions, the opposite line was taken. For whatever reason, the inevitable glut of articles gleefully denouncing the latest punk outrage was counterbalanced by an equal number of items devoted to the small details of punk family life. For instance, the 15 October 1977 issue of *Woman's Own* carried an article entitled "Punks and Mothers" which stressed the classless, fancy dress aspects of punk.[11] Photographs depicting punks with smiling mothers, reclining next to the family pool, playing with the family dog, were placed above a text which dwelt on the ordinariness of individual punks: "It's not as rocky horror as it appears" . . . "punk can be a family affair" . . . "punks as it happens are non-political", and, most insidiously, albeit accurately, "Johnny Rotten is as big a house-hold name as Hughie Green". Throughout the summer of 1977, the *People* and the *News of the World* ran items on punk babies, punk brothers, and punk–ted weddings. All these articles served to minimize the Otherness so stridently proclaimed in punk style, and defined the subculture in precisely those terms which it sought most vehemently to resist and deny.

Once again, we should avoid making any absolute distinction between the ideo-logical and commercial "manipulations" of subculture. The symbolic restoration of daughters to the family, of deviants to the fold, was undertaken at a time when the widespread "capitulation" of punk musicians to market forces was being used throughout the media to illustrate the fact that punks were "only human after all". The music papers were filled with the familiar success stories describing the route from rags to rags and riches – of punk musicians flying to America, of bank clerks become magazine editors or record producers, of harassed seamstresses turned overnight into successful business women. Of course, these success stories had ambiguous implications. As with every other "youth revolution" (e.g., the beat boom, the mod explosion and the Swinging Sixties) the relative success of a few individuals created an impression of energy, expansion and limitless upward mobility. This ultimately reinforced the image of the open society which the very presence of the punk subculture – with its rhetorical emphasis on unemployment, high-rise living and narrow options – had originally contradicted. As Barthes (1972) has written: "myth can always, as a last resort, signify the resistance which is brought to bear against it" and it does so typically by imposing its own ideological terms, by substituting in this case "the fairy tale of the artist's creativity"[12] for an art form "within the compass of every consciousness",[13] a "music" to be judged, dismissed or marketed for "noise" – a logically consistent, self-constituted chaos. It does so finally by replacing a subculture engendered by history, a product of real historical contradictions, with a handful of brilliant nonconformists, satanic geniuses who, to use the words of Sir John Read, Chairman of EMI "become in the fullness of time, wholly acceptable and can contribute greatly to the development of modern music".[14]

Notes

1   Although Williams had posited a new, broader definition of culture, he intended this to complement rather than contradict earlier formulations:

> It seems to me that there is value in each of these kinds of definition . . . the degree to which we depend, in our knowledge of many past societies and past stages of our own, on the body of intellectual and imaginative work which has retained its major communicative power, makes the description of culture in these terms if not complete, then at least reasonable . . . there are elements in the "ideal" definition which . . . seem to me valuable. (Williams, 1965)

2   In his *Course in General Linguistics* (1974), Saussure stressed the arbitrary nature of the linguistic sign. For Saussure, language is a system of mutually related values, in which arbitrary "signifiers" (e.g., words) are linked to equally arbitrary "signifieds" ("concepts . . . negatively defined by their relations with other terms in the system") to form signs. These signs together constitute a system. Each element is defined through its position within the relevant system – its relation to other elements – through the dialectics of identity and difference. Saussure postulated that other systems of significance (e.g., fashion, cookery) might be studied in a similar way, and that eventually linguistics would form part of a more general science of signs – a semiology.

3   The fashionable status of this word has in recent years contributed to its indiscriminate use. I intend here the very precise meaning established by Louis Althusser: "the *problematic* of a word or concept consists of the theoretical or ideological framework within

which that word or concept can be used to establish, determine and discuss a particular range of issues and a particular kind of problem" (Althusser and Balibar, 1968; see also Bennett, 1979).

4   This was part of a speech made by Dr George Simpson, a Margate magistrate, after the mod–rocker clashes of Whitsun 1964. For sociologists of deviance, this speech has become *the* classic example of rhetorical overkill and deserves quoting in full: "These long-haired, mentally unstable, petty little hoodlums, these sawdust Caesars who can only find courage like rats, in hunting in packs" (quoted in Cohen, 1972).

5   On 1 December 1976 the Sex Pistols appeared on the Thames twilight programme *Today*. During the course of the interview with Bill Grundy they used the words "sod", "bastard" and "fuck". The papers carried stories of jammed switchboards, shocked parents, etc., and there were some unusual refinements. The *Daily Mirror* (2 December) contained a story about a lorry driver who had been so incensed by the Sex Pistols' performance that he had kicked in the screen of his colour television: "I can swear as well as anyone, but I don't want this sort of muck coming into my home at teatime."

6   The police brought an unsuccessful action for obscenity against the Sex Pistols after their first LP *Never Mind the Bollocks* was released in 1977.

7   On 4 January 1977 the Sex Pistols caused an incident at Heathrow Airport by spitting and vomiting in front of airline staff. The *Evening News* quoted a check-in desk girl as saying: "The group are the most revolting people I have ever seen in my life. They were disgusting, sick and obscene." Two days after this incident was reported in the newspapers, EMI terminated the group's contract.

8   The 1 August 1977 edition of the *Daily Mirror* contained just such an example of dubious editorial concern. Giving "serious" consideration to the problem of ted–punk violence along the King's Road, the writer makes the obvious comparison with the seaside disturbances of the previous decade: "[The clashes] must not be allowed to grow into the pitched battles like the mods and rockers confrontations at several seaside towns a few years back." Moral panics can be recycled; even the same events can be recalled in the same prophetic tones to mobilise the same sense of outrage.

9   "The characters that stamp products as commodities, and whose establishment is a necessary preliminary to the circulation of commodities, have already acquired the stability of natural, self-understood forms of social life before man seeks to decipher, not their historical character, for in his eyes they are immutable, but their meaning" (Marx and Engels, 1970).

10   The definitive study of a moral panic is Cohen's *Folk Devils and Moral Panics*. The mods and rockers were just two of the "folk devils" – "the gallery of types that society erects to show its members which roles should be avoided" – which periodically become the centre of a "moral panic".

> Societies appear to be subject, every now and then, to periods of moral panic. A condition, episode, person or group of persons emerges to become defined as a threat to societal values and interests; its nature is presented in a stylised and stereotypical fashion by the mass media; the moral barricades are manned by editors, bishops, politicians and other right-thinking people; socially accredited experts pronounce their diagnoses and solutions; ways of coping are evolved or (more often) resorted to; the condition then disappears, submerges or deteriorates and becomes more visible. (Cohen, 1972)

Official reactions to the punk subculture betrayed all the classic symptoms of a moral panic. Concerts were cancelled; clergymen, politicians and pundits unanimously denounced the degeneracy of youth. Among the choicer reactions, Marcus Lipton, the late MP for Lambeth North, declared: "If pop music is going to be used to destroy our established institutions, then it ought to be destroyed first." Bernard Brook-Partridge, MP for Havering-Romford, stormed, "I think the Sex Pistols are absolutely bloody revolting. I think their whole attitude is calculated to incite people to misbehaviour. . . . It is a deliberate incitement to anti-social behaviour and conduct" (quoted in *New Musical Express*, 15 July 1977).

11   See also "Punks have Mothers Too: They tell us a few home truths" in *Woman* (15 April 1978) and "Punks and Mothers" in *Woman's Own* (15 October 1977). These articles draw editorial comment (a sign of recognition on the part of the staff of the need to reassure the challenged expectations of the reader?). The following anecdote appeared beneath a photograph showing two dancing teddy boys:

> The other day I overheard two elderly ladies, cringing as a gang of alarming looking punks passed them, say in tones of horror: "Just imagine what their children will be like". I'm sure a lot of people must have said exactly the same about the Teddy Boys, like the ones pictured . . . and Mods and Rockers. That made me wonder what had happened to them when the phase passed. I reckon they put away their drape suits or scooters and settled down to respectable, quiet lives, bringing up the kids and desperately hoping they won't get involved in any of these terrible Punk goings-on.

12   "The fairy-tale of the artist's creativity is western culture's last superstition. One of Surrealism's first revolutionary acts was to attack this myth . . ." (Max Ernst, "What is Surrealism?" quoted in Lippard, 1970).

13   "Surrealism is within the compass of every consciousness" (surrealist tract quoted in Lippard, 1970). See also Paul Eluard (1933): "We have passed the period of individual exercises".

  The solemn and extremely reverential exhibition of Surrealism, mounted at London's Hayward Gallery in 1978 ironically sought to establish the reputation of individual surrealists as artists and was designed to win public recognition of their "genius". It is fitting that punk should be absorbed into high fashion at the same time as the first major exhibition of Dada and surrealism in Britain was being launched.

14   On 7 December one month before EMI terminated its contract with the Sex Pistols, Sir John Read, the record company's Chairman, made the following statement at the annual general meeting:

> Throughout its history as a recording company, EMI has always sought to behave within contemporary limits of decency and good taste – taking into account not only the traditional rigid conventions of one section of society, but also the increasingly liberal attitudes of other (perhaps larger) sections . . . at any given time . . . What is decent or in good taste compared to the attitudes of, say, 20 or even 10 years ago?
>
>   It is against this present-day social background that EMI has to make value judgements about the content of records . . . Sex Pistols is a pop group devoted to a new form of music known as "punk rock". It was contracted for recording purposes by EMI . . . in October, 1976 . . . In this context, it must be remembered that the recording industry has signed many pop groups, initially controversial, who have in the fullness of time become wholly acceptable and contributed greatly

to the development of modern music . . . EMI should not set itself up as a public censor, but it does seek to encourage restraint. (Quoted in Vermorel and Vermorel, 1978)

Despite the eventual loss of face (and some £40,000 paid out to the Pistols when the contract was terminated) EMI and the other record companies tended to shrug off the apparent contradictions involved in signing up groups who openly admitted to a lack of professionalism, musicianship, and commitment to the profit motive. During the Clash's famous performance of "White Riot" at the Rainbow in 1977 when seats were ripped out and thrown at the stage, the last two rows of the theatre (left, of course, intact) were occupied almost exclusively by record executives and talent scouts: CBS paid for the damage without complaint. There could be no clearer demonstration of the fact that symbolic assaults leave real institutions intact. Nonetheless, the record companies did not have everything their own way. The Sex Pistols received five-figure sums in compensation from both A & M and EMI and when their LP (recorded at last by Virgin) finally did reach the shops, it contained a scathing attack on EMI delivered in Rotten's venomous nasal whine:

> You thought that we were faking
> That we were all just money-making
> You don't believe that we're for real
> Or you would lose your cheap appeal.
> Who?
> EMI – EMI
>
> Blind acceptance is a sign
> Of stupid fools who stand in line
> Like EMI – EMI
>
> ("EMI", Virgin, 1977)

References

Althusser, L. (1969), *For Marx*, Allen Lane.
—— (1971a), *Lenin and Philosophy and Other Essays*, New Left Books.
Althusser, L. and Balibar, E. (1968), *Reading Capital*, New Left Books.
Arnold, M. (1868), *Culture and Anarchy*.
Barthes, R. (1972), *Mythologies*, Paladin.
Bennett, T. (1979), *Formalism and Marxism*, Methuen.
Clarke, J. (1976a), "The Skinheads and the Magical Recovery of Working Class Community", in S. Hall et al. (eds.), *Resistance Through Rituals*, Hutchinson.
—— (1976b), "Style", in S. Hall et al. (eds.), *Resistance Through Rituals*, Hutchinson.
Cohen, S. (1972), *Folk Devils and Moral Panics*, MacGibbon & Kee.
Douglas, M. (1967), *Purity and Danger*, Penguin.
Eluard, P. (1933), *Food for Vision*, Editions Galliard.
Geertz, C. (1964), "Ideology as a Cultural System", in D. E. Apter (ed.), *Ideology and Discontent*, Free Press.
—— (1967), *The Thief's Journal*, Penguin.

Godelier, M. (1970), "Structure and Contradiction in 'Capital'", in M. Lane (ed.), *Structuralism: A Reader*, Cape.

Hall, S. (1974), "Deviancy, Politics and the Media", in P. Rock and M. McIntosh (eds.), *Deviance and Social Control*, Tavistock.

—— (1977), "Culture, the Media and the 'Ideological Effect'", in J. Curran et al. (eds.), *Mass Communication and Society*, Arnold.

Hall, S., Clarke, J., Jefferson, T. and Roberts, B. (eds.) (1976a), *Resistance Through Rituals*, Hutchinson.

Hawkes, T. (1977), *Structuralism and Semiotics*, Methuen.

Hoggart, R. (1958), *The Uses of Literacy*, Penguin.

—— (1966), "Literature and Society", *American Scholar*, Spring.

Ingham, R. (ed.) (1977), *Football Hooliganism*, Inter-action Imprint.

Lefebvre, H. (1971), *Everyday Life in the Modern World*, Allen Lane.

—— (1969), *The Elementary Structures of Kinship*, Eyre & Spottiswoode.

Lippard, L. (ed.) (1970), *Surrealists on Art*, Spectrum.

Marx, K. and Engels, F. (1970), *The German Ideology*, Lawrence & Wishart.

Mepham, J. (1972), "The Structuralist Sciences and Philosophy", in D. Robey (ed.), *Structuralism: The Wolfson College Lectures 1972*, Cape, 1973.

Saussure, F. de (1974), *Course in General Linguistics*, Fontana.

Vermorel, F. and Vermorel, J. (1978), *The Sex Pistols*, Tandem.

Volosinov, V. N. (1973), *Marxism and the Philosophy of Language*, Seminar Press.

Williams, R. (1960), *Border Country*, Penguin.

—— (1961), *Culture and Society*, Penguin.

—— (1965), *The Long Revolution*, Penguin.

—— (1976), *Keywords*, Fontana.

13

Encoding/Decoding

Stuart Hall

Traditionally, mass-communications research has conceptualized the process of communication in terms of a circulation circuit or loop. This model has been criticized for its linearity – sender/message/receiver – for its concentration on the level of message exchange and for the absence of a structured conception of the different moments as a complex structure of relations. But it is also possible (and useful) to think of this process in terms of a structure produced and sustained through the articulation of linked but distinctive moments – production, circulation, distribution/consumption, reproduction. This would be to think of the process as a "complex structure in dominance", sustained through the articulation of connected practices, each of which, however, retains its distinctiveness and has its own specific modality, its own forms and conditions of existence. This second approach, homologous to that which forms the skeleton of commodity production offered in Marx's *Grundrisse* and in *Capital*, has the added advantage of bringing out more sharply how a continuous circuit – production–distribution–production – can be sustained through a "passage of forms".[1] It also highlights the specificity of the forms in which the product of the process "appears" in each moment, and thus what distinguishes discursive "production" from other types of production in our society and in modern media systems.

The "object" of these practices is meanings and messages in the form of sign-vehicles of a specific kind organized, like any form of communication or language, through the operation of codes within the syntagmatic chain of a discourse. The apparatuses, relations and practices of production thus issue, at a certain moment (the moment of "production/circulation") in the form of symbolic vehicles constituted within the rules of "language". It is in this discursive form that the circulation of the "product" takes place. The process thus requires, at the production end, its material instruments – its "means" – as well as its own sets of social (production) relations – the organization and combination of practices within media apparatuses. But it is in the

From Stuart Hall, "Encoding/decoding." In Stuart Hall, Dorothy Hobson, Andrew Love, and Paul Willis (eds.), *Culture, Media, Language*, pp. 128–38. London: Hutchinson, 1980.

discursive form that the circulation of the product takes place, as well as its distribution to different audiences. Once accomplished, the discourse must then be translated – transformed, again – into social practices if the circuit is to be both completed and effective. If no "meaning" is taken, there can be no "consumption". If the meaning is not articulated in practice, it has no effect. The value of this approach is that while each of the moments, in articulation, is necessary to the circuit as a whole, no one moment can fully guarantee the next moment with which it is articulated. Since each has its specific modality and conditions of existence, each can constitute its own break or interruption of the "passage of forms" on whose continuity the flow of effective production (that is, "reproduction") depends.

Thus while in no way wanting to limit research to "following only those leads which emerge from content analysis",[2] we must recognize that the discursive form of the message has a privileged position in the communicative exchange (from the viewpoint of circulation), and that the moments of "encoding" and "decoding", though only "relatively autonomous" in relation to the communicative process as a whole, are *determinate* moments. A "raw" historical event cannot, *in that form*, be transmitted by, say, a television newscast. Events can only be signified within the aural-visual forms of the televisual discourse. In the moment when a historical event passes under the sign of discourse, it is subject to all the complex formal "rules" by which language signifies. To put it paradoxically, the event must become a "story" before it can become a *communicative event*. In that moment the formal sub-rules of discourse are "in dominance", without, of course, subordinating out of existence the historical event so signified, the social relations in which the rules are set to work or the social and political consequences of the event having been signified in this way. The "message form" is the necessary "form of appearance" of the event in its passage from source to receiver. Thus the transposition into and out of the "message form" (or the mode of symbolic exchange) is not a random "moment", which we can take up or ignore at our convenience. The "message form" is a determinate moment; though, at another level, it comprises the surface movements of the communications system only and requires, at another stage, to be integrated into the social relations of the communication process as a whole, of which it forms only a part.

From this general perspective, we may crudely characterize the television communicative process as follows. The institutional structures of broadcasting, with their practices and networks of production, their organized relations and technical infrastructures, are required to produce a programme. Using the analogy of *Capital*, this is the "labour process" in the discursive mode. Production, here, constructs the message. In one sense, then, the circuit begins here. Of course, the production process is not without its "discursive" aspect: it, too, is framed throughout by meanings and ideas: knowledge-in-use concerning the routines of production, historically defined technical skills, professional ideologies, institutional knowledge, definitions and assumptions, assumptions about the audience and so on frame the constitution of the programme through this production structure. Further, though the production structures of television originate the television discourse, they do not constitute a closed system. They draw topics, treatments, agendas, events, personnel, images of the audience, "definitions of the situation" from other sources and other discursive formations within the wider socio-cultural and political structure of which they are a differentiated part. Philip Elliott has expressed this point succinctly, within a more traditional framework, in his discussion of the way in which the audience is both the "source" and the "receiver" of the television message. Thus – to borrow Marx's terms – circulation and reception are, indeed, "moments" of the production process in television and are reincorporated, via a number of skewed and structured "feedbacks", into the production process itself. The consumption or reception of the television message is thus also itself a "moment" of the production process in its larger sense, though the latter is "predominant" because it is the "point of departure for the realization" of the message. Production and reception of the television message are not, therefore, identical, but they are related: they are differentiated moments within the totality formed by the social relations of the communicative process as a whole.

At a certain point, however, the broadcasting structures must yield encoded messages in the form of a meaningful discourse. The institution-societal relations of production must pass under the discursive rules of language for its product to be "realized". This initiates a further differentiated moment, in which the formal rules of discourse and language are in dominance. Before this message can have an "effect" (however defined), satisfy a "need" or be put to a "use", it must first be appropriated as a meaningful discourse and be meaningfully decoded. It is this set of decoded meanings which "have an effect", influence, entertain, instruct or persuade, with very complex perceptual, cognitive, emotional, ideological or behavioural consequences. In a "determinate" moment the structure employs a code and yields a "message": at another determinate moment the "message", via its decodings, issues into the structure of social practices (see figure 13.1). We are now fully aware that this re-entry into the practices of audience reception and "use" cannot be understood in simple behavioural terms. The typical processes identified in positivistic

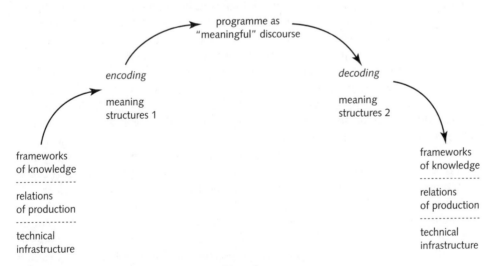

Figure 13.1   Encoding and decoding of broadcast structures

research on isolated elements – effects, uses, "gratifications" – are themselves framed by structures of understanding, as well as being produced by social and economic relations, which shape their "realization" at the reception end of the chain and which permit the meanings signified in the discourse to be transposed into practice or consciousness (to acquire social use value or political effectivity).

Clearly, what we have labelled in figure 13.1 "meaning structures 1" and "meaning structures 2" may not be the same. They do not constitute an "immediate identity". The codes of encoding and decoding may not be perfectly symmetrical. The degrees of symmetry – that is, the degrees of "understanding" and "misunderstanding" in the communicative exchange – depend on the degrees of symmetry/asymmetry (relations of equivalence) established between the positions of the "personifications", encoder-producer and decoder-receiver. But this in turn depends on the degrees of identity/non-identity between the codes which perfectly or imperfectly transmit, interrupt or systematically distort what has been transmitted. The lack of fit between the codes has a great deal to do with the structural differences of relation and position between broadcasters and audiences, but it also has something to do with the asymmetry between the codes of "source" and "receiver" at the moment of trans-formation into and out of the discursive form. What are called "distortions" or "mis-understandings" arise precisely from the *lack of equivalence* between the two sides in the communicative exchange. Once again, this defines the "relative autonomy", but "determinateness", of the entry and exit of the message in its discursive moments.

The application of this rudimentary paradigm has already begun to transform our understanding of the older term, television "content". We are just beginning to see how it might also transform our understanding of audience reception, "reading" and response as well. Beginnings and endings have been announced in communica-tions research before, so we must be cautious. But there seems some ground for thinking that a new and exciting phase in so-called audience research, of a quite new kind, may be opening up. At either end of the communicative chain the use of the semiotic paradigm promises to dispel the lingering behaviourism which has dogged mass-media research for so long, especially in its approach to content. Though we know the television programme is not a behavioural input, like a tap on the knee cap, it seems to have been almost impossible for traditional researchers to conceptualize the communicative process without lapsing into one or other variant of low-flying behaviourism. We know, as Gerbner has remarked, that representations of violence on the TV screen "are not violence but messages about violence":[3] but we have continued to research the question of violence, for example, as if we were unable to comprehend this epistemological distinction.

The televisual sign is a complex one. It is itself constituted by the combination of two types of discourse, visual and aural. Moreover, it is an iconic sign, in Peirce's terminology, because "it possesses some of the properties of the thing represented".[4] This is a point which has led to a great deal of confusion and has provided the site of intense controversy in the study of visual language. Since the visual discourse translates a three-dimensional world into two-dimensional planes, it cannot, of course, *be* the referent or concept it signifies. The dog in the film can bark but it cannot bite! Reality exists outside language, but it is constantly mediated by and through language: and what we can know and say has to be produced in and through discourse. Discursive "knowledge" is the product not of the transparent representation of the "real" in language but of the articulation of language on real relations and conditions. Thus there is no intelligible discourse without the operation of a code. Iconic signs are therefore coded signs too – even if the codes here work differently from those of other signs. There is no degree zero in language. Naturalism and "realism" – the apparent fidelity of the representation to the thing or concept represented – is the result, the effect, of a certain specific articulation of language on the "real". It is the result of a discursive practice.

Certain codes may, of course, be so widely distributed in a specific language community or culture, and be learned at so early an age, that they appear not to be constructed – the effect of an articulation between sign and referent – but to be "naturally" given. Simple visual signs appear to have achieved a "near-universality" in this sense: though evidence remains that even apparently "natural" visual codes are culture-specific. However, this does not mean that no codes have intervened; rather, that the codes have been profoundly *naturalized*. The operation of naturalized codes reveals not the transparency and "naturalness" of language but the depth, the habituation and the near-universality of the codes in use. They produce apparently "natural" recognitions. This has the (ideological) effect of concealing the practices of coding which are present. But we must not be fooled by appearances. Actually, what naturalized codes demonstrate is the degree of habituation produced when there is a fundamental alignment and reciprocity – an achieved equivalence – between the encoding and decoding sides of an exchange of meanings. The functioning of the codes on the decoding side will frequently assume the status of naturalized perceptions. This leads us to think that the visual sign for "cow" actually *is* (rather than *represents*) the animal, cow. But if we think of the visual representation of a cow in a manual on animal husbandry – and, even more, of the linguistic sign "cow" – we can see that both, in different degrees, are *arbitrary* with respect to the concept of the animal they represent. The articulation of an arbitrary sign – whether visual or verbal – with the concept of a referent is the product not of nature but of convention, and the conventionalism of discourses requires the intervention, the support, of codes. Thus Eco has argued that iconic signs "look like objects in the real world because they reproduce the conditions (that is, the codes) of perception in the viewer".[5] These "conditions of perception" are, however, the result of a highly coded, even if virtually unconscious, set of operations – decodings. This is as true of the photographic or televisual image as it is of any other sign. Iconic signs are, however, particularly vulnerable to being "read" as natural because visual codes of perception are very widely distributed and because this type of sign is less arbitrary than a linguistic sign: the linguistic sign, "cow" possesses *none* of the properties of the thing represented, whereas the visual sign appears to possess *some* of those properties.

This may help us to clarify a confusion in current linguistic theory and to define precisely how some key terms are being used in this article. Linguistic theory frequently employs the distinction "denotation" and "connotation". The term "denotation" is widely equated with the literal meaning of a sign: because this literal meaning is almost universally recognized, especially when visual discourse is being employed, "denotation" has often been confused with a literal transcription of "reality" in language – and thus with a "natural sign", one produced without the intervention of a code. "Connotation", on the other hand, is employed simply to refer to less fixed and therefore more conventionalized and changeable, associative meanings, which clearly vary from instance to instance and therefore must depend on the intervention of codes.

We do *not* use the distinction – denotation/connotation – in this way. From our point of view, the distinction is an *analytic* one only. It is useful, in analysis, to be able to apply a rough rule of thumb which distinguishes those aspects of a sign which appear to be taken, in any language community at any point in time, as its "literal" meaning (denotation) from the more associative meanings for the sign which it is possible to generate (connotation). But analytic distinctions must not be confused with distinctions in the real world. There will be very few instances in which signs organized in a discourse signify *only* their "literal" (that is, near-universally consensualized) meaning. In actual discourse most signs will combine both the denotative and the connotative *aspects* (as redefined above). It may, then, be asked why we retain the distinction at all. It is largely a matter of analytic value. It is because signs appear to acquire their full ideological value – appear to be open to articulation with wider ideological discourses and meanings – at the level of their "associative" meanings (that is, at the connotative level) – for here "meanings" are *not* apparently fixed in natural perception (that is, they are not fully naturalized), and their fluidity of meaning and association can be more fully exploited and transformed.[6] So it is at the connotative *level* of the sign that situational ideologies alter and transform signification. At this level we can see more clearly the active intervention of ideologies in and on discourse: here, the sign is open to new accentuations and, in Vološinov's terms, enters fully into the struggle over meanings – the class struggle in language.[7] This does not mean that the denotative or "literal" meaning is outside ideology. Indeed, we could say that its ideological value is strongly *fixed* – because it has become so fully universal and "natural". The terms "denotation" and "connotation", then, are merely useful analytic tools for distinguishing, in particular contexts, between not the presence/absence of ideology in language but the different levels at which ideologies and discourses intersect.[8]

The level of connotation of the visual sign, of its contextual reference and positioning in different discursive fields of meaning and association, is the point where *already coded* signs intersect with the deep semantic codes of a culture and take on additional, more active ideological dimensions. We might take an example from advertising discourse. Here, too, there is no "purely denotative", and certainly no "natural", representation. Every visual sign in advertising connotes a quality, situation, value or inference, which is present as an implication or implied meaning, depending on the connotational positioning. In Barthes's example, the sweater always signifies a "warm garment" (denotation) and thus the activity/value of "keeping warm". But it is also possible, at its more connotative levels, to signify "the coming of winter" or "a cold day". And, in the specialized sub-codes of fashion, sweater may also connote a fashionable style of *haute couture* or, alternatively, an informal style of dress. But set against the right visual background and positioned by the romantic sub-code, it may connote "long autumn walk in the woods".[9] Codes of this order clearly contract relations for the sign with the wider universe of ideologies in a society. These codes are the means by which power and ideology are made to signify in particular discourses. They refer signs to the "maps of meaning" into which any culture is classified; and those "maps of social reality" have the whole range of social meanings, practices, and usages, power and interest "written in" to them. The connotative levels of signifiers, Barthes remarked, "have a close communication with culture, knowledge, history, and it is through them, so to speak, that the environmental world invades the linguistic and semantic system. They are, if you like, the fragments of ideology".[10]

The so-called denotative *level* of the televisual sign is fixed by certain, very complex (but limited or "closed") codes. But its connotative *level*, though also bounded, is more open, subject to more active *transformations*, which exploit its polysemic values. Any such already constituted sign is potentially transformable into more than one connotative configuration. Polysemy must not, however, be confused with pluralism. Connotative codes are *not* equal among themselves. Any society/culture tends, with varying degrees of closure, to impose its classifications of the social and cultural and political world. These constitute a *dominant cultural order*, though it is neither univocal nor uncontested. This question of the "structure of discourses in dominance" is a crucial point. The different areas of social life appear to be mapped out into discursive domains, hierarchically organized into *dominant or preferred meanings*. New, problematic or troubling events, which breach our expectancies and run counter to our "common-sense constructs", to our "taken-for-granted" knowledge of social structures, must be assigned to their discursive domains before they can be said to "make sense". The most common way of "mapping" them is to assign the new to some domain or other of the existing "maps of problematic social reality". We say *dominant*, not "determined", because it is always possible to order, classify, assign and decode an event within more than one "mapping". But we say "dominant" because there exists a pattern of "preferred readings"; and these both have the institutional/political/ideological order imprinted in them and have themselves become institutionalized.[11] The domains of "preferred meanings" have the whole social order embedded in them as a set of meanings, practices and beliefs: the everyday knowledge of social structures, of "how things work for all practical purposes in this culture", the rank order of power and interest and the structure of legitimations, limits and sanctions. Thus to clarify a "misunderstanding" at the connotative level, we must refer, *through* the codes, to the orders of social life, of economic and political power and of ideology. Further, since these mappings are "structured in dominance" but not closed, the communicative process consists not in the unproblematic assignment of every visual item to its given position within a set of prearranged codes, but of *performative rules* – rules of competence and use, of logics-in-use – which seek actively to *enforce* or *pre-fer* one semantic domain over another and rule items into and out of their appropriate meaning-sets. Formal semiology has too often neglected this practice of *interpretative work*, though this constitutes, in fact, the real relations of broadcast practices in television.

In speaking of *dominant meanings*, then, we are not talking about a one-sided process which governs how all events will be signified. It consists of the "work" required to enforce, win plausibility for and command as legitimate a *decoding* of the event within the limit of dominant definitions in which it has been connotatively signified. Terni has remarked:

> By the word *reading* we mean not only the capacity to identify and decode a certain number of signs, but also the subjective capacity to put them into a creative relation between themselves and with other signs: a capacity which is, by itself, the condition for a complete awareness of one's total environment.[12]

Our quarrel here is with the notion of "subjective capacity", as if the referent of a televisional discourse were an objective fact but the interpretative level were an individualized and private matter. Quite the opposite seems to be the case. The televisual practice takes "objective" (that is, systemic) responsibility precisely for the relations which disparate signs contract with one another in any discursive instance, and thus continually rearranges, delimits and prescribes into what "awareness of one's total environment" these items are arranged.

This brings us to the question of misunderstandings. Television producers who find their message "failing to get across" are frequently concerned to straighten out the kinks in the communication chain, thus facilitating the "effectiveness" of their communication. Much research which claims the objectivity of "policy-oriented analysis" reproduces this administrative goal by attempting to discover how much of a message the audience recalls and to improve the extent of understanding. No doubt misunderstandings of a literal kind do exist. The viewer does not know the terms employed, cannot follow the complex logic of argument or exposition, is unfamiliar with the language, finds the concepts too alien or difficult or is foxed by the expository narrative. But more often broadcasters are concerned that the audience has failed to take the meaning as they – the broadcasters – intended. What they really mean to say is that viewers are not operating within the "dominant" or "preferred" code. Their ideal is "perfectly transparent communication". Instead, what they have to confront is "systematically distorted communication".[13]

In recent years discrepancies of this kind have usually been explained by reference to "selective perception". This is the door via which a residual pluralism evades the compulsions of a highly structured, asymmetrical and non-equivalent process. Of course, there will always be private, individual, variant readings. But "selective perception" is almost never as selective, random or privatized as the concept suggests. The patterns exhibit, across individual variants, significant clusterings. Any new approach to audience studies will therefore have to begin with a critique of "selective perception" theory.

It was argued earlier that since there is no necessary correspondence between encoding and decoding, the former can attempt to "pre-fer" but cannot prescribe or guarantee the latter, which has its own conditions of existence. Unless they are wildly aberrant, encoding will have the effect of constructing some of the limits and parameters within which decodings will operate. If there were no limits, audiences could simply read whatever they liked into any message. No doubt some total mis-understandings of this kind do exist. But the vast range must contain *some* degree of reciprocity between encoding and decoding moments, otherwise we could not speak of an effective communicative exchange at all. Nevertheless, this "correspondence" is not given but constructed. It is not "natural" but the product of an articulation between two distinct moments. And the former cannot determine or guarantee, in a simple sense, which decoding codes will be employed. Otherwise communication would be a perfectly equivalent circuit, and every message would be an instance of "perfectly transparent communication". We must think, then, of the variant articula-tions in which encoding/decoding can be combined. To elaborate on this, we offer a hypothetical analysis of some possible decoding positions, in order to reinforce the point of "no necessary correspondence".[14]

We identify *three* hypothetical positions from which decodings of a televisual discourse may be constructed. These need to be empirically tested and refined. But the argument that decodings do not follow inevitably from encodings, that they are not identical, reinforces the argument of "no necessary correspondence". It also helps to deconstruct the common-sense meaning of "misunderstanding" in terms of a theory of "systematically distorted communication".

The first hypothetical position is that of the *dominant-hegemonic position*. When the viewer takes the connoted meaning from, say, a television newscast or current affairs programme full and straight, and decodes the message in terms of the refer-ence code in which it has been encoded, we might say that the viewer *is operating inside the dominant code*. This is the ideal-typical case of "perfectly transparent communication" – or as dose as we are likely to come to it "for all practical pur-poses". Within this we can distinguish the positions produced by the *professional code*. This is the position (produced by what we perhaps ought to identify as the operation of a "metacode") which the professional broadcasters assume when encoding a message which has *already* been signified in a hegemonic manner. The professional code is "relatively independent" of the dominant code, in that it applies criteria and transformational operations of its own, especially those of a technico-practical nature. The professional code, however, operates *within* the "hegemony" of the dominant code. Indeed, it serves to reproduce the dominant definitions precisely by bracketing their hegemonic quality and operating instead with displaced professional codings which foreground such apparently neutral-technical questions as visual quality, news and presentational values, televisual quality, "professionalism" and so on. The hegemonic interpretations of, say, the politics of Northern Ireland, or the Chilean *coup* or the Industrial Relations Bill are principally generated by political and military elites: the particular choice of presentational occasions and formats, the selection of personnel, the choice of images, the staging of debates are selected and combined through the operation of the professional code. How the broadcasting professionals are able *both* to operate with "relatively autonomous" codes of their own *and* to act in such a way as to reproduce (not without contradic-tion) the hegemonic signification of events is a complex matter which cannot be further spelled out here. It must suffice to say that the professionals are linked with the defining elites not only by the institutional position of broadcasting itself as an "ideological apparatus",[15] but also by the structure of *access* (that is, the systematic "over-accessing" of selective elite personnel and their "definition of the situation" in television). It may even be said that the professional codes serve to reproduce hegemonic definitions specifically by *not overtly* biasing their operations in a dominant direction: ideological reproduction therefore takes place here inadvertently, unconsciously, "behind men's backs".[16] Of course, conflicts, contradictions and even misunderstandings regularly arise between the dominant and the professional significations and their signifying agencies.

The second position we would identify is that of the *negotiated code* or position. Majority audiences probably understand quite adequately what has been dominantly defined and professionally signified. The dominant definitions, however, are hegemonic precisely because they represent definitions of situations and events which are "in dominance", (*global*). Dominant definitions connect events, implicitly or explicitly, to grand totalizations, to the great syntagmatic views-of-the-world: they take "large views" of issues: they relate events to the "national interest" or to the level of geopolitics, even if they make these connections in truncated, inverted or mystified ways. The definition of a hegemonic viewpoint is (a) that it defines within its terms the mental horizon, the universe, of possible meanings, of a whole sector of relations in a society or culture; and (b) that it carries with it the stamp of legitimacy – it appears coterminous with what is "natural", "inevitable", "taken for granted" about the social order. Decoding within the *negotiated version* contains a mixture of adaptive and oppositional elements: it acknowledges the legitimacy of the hegemonic definitions to make the grand significations (abstract), while, at a more restricted, situational (situated) level, it makes its own ground rules – it operates with exceptions to the rule. It accords the privileged position to the dominant definitions of events while reserving the right to make a more negotiated application to "local conditions", to its own more *corporate* positions. This negotiated version of the dominant ideology is thus shot through with contradictions, though these are only on certain occasions brought to full visibility. Negotiated codes operate through what we might call particular or situated logics: and these logics are sustained by their differential and unequal relation to the discourses and logics of power. The simplest example of a negotiated code is that which governs the response of a worker to the notion of an Industrial Relations Bill limiting the right to strike or to arguments for a wages freeze. At the level of the "national interest" economic debate the decoder may adopt the hegemonic definition, agreeing that "we must all pay ourselves less in order to combat inflation". This, however, may have little or no relation to his/her willingness to go on strike for better pay and conditions or to oppose the Industrial Relations Bill at the level of shop-floor or union organization. We suspect that the great majority of so-called "misunderstandings" arise from the contradictions and disjunctures between hegemonic-dominant encodings and negotiated-corporate decodings. It is just these mismatches in the levels which most provoke defining elites and professionals to identify a "failure in communications".

Finally, it is possible for a viewer perfectly to understand both the literal and the connotative inflection given by a discourse but to decode the message in a *globally* contrary way. He/she detotalizes the message in the preferred code in order to retotalize the message within some alternative framework of reference. This is the case of the viewer who listens to a debate on the need to limit wages but "reads" every mention of the "national interest" as "class interest". He/she is operating with what we must call an *oppositional code*. One of the most significant political moments (they also coincide with crisis points within the broadcasting organizations themselves, for obvious reasons) is the point when events which are normally signified and decoded in a negotiated way begin to be given an oppositional reading. Here the "politics of signification" – the struggle in discourse – is joined.

Notes

1   For an explication and commentary on the methodological implications of Marx's argument, see S. Hall, "A reading of Marx's 1857 *Introduction to the Grundrisse*", in *WPCS*, 6 (1974).

2   J. D. Halloran, "Understanding television", paper for the Council of Europe Colloquy on "Understanding Television" (University of Leicester, 1973).

3   G. Gerbner et al., *Violence in TV Drama: A Study of Trends and Symbolic Functions* (The Annenberg School, University of Pennsylvania, 1970).

4   Charles Peirce, *Speculative Grammar*, in *Collected Papers* (Cambridge, Mass.: Harvard University Press, 1931–58).

5   Umberto Eco, "Articulations of the cinematic code", in *Cinemantics*, no. 1.

6   See the argument in S. Hall, "Determinations of news photographs", in *WPCS*, 3 (1972).

7   Vološinov, *Marxism and the Philosophy of Language* (London: The Seminar Press, 1973).

8   For a similar clarification, see Marina Camargo Heck, "Ideological dimensions of media messages", in Stuart Hall, Dorothy Hobson, Andrew Lowe and Paul Willis (eds.), *Culture, Media, Language* (London: Hutchinsen, 1980), pp. 122–7.

9   Roland Barthes, "Rhetoric of the image", in *WPCS*, 1 (1971).

10   Roland Barthes, *Elements of Semiology* (London: Jonathan Cape, 1967).

11   For an extended critique of "preferred reading", see Alan O'Shea, "Preferred reading" (unpublished paper, CCCS, University of Birmingham).

12   P. Terni, "Memorandum", paper for the Council of Europe Colloquy on "Understanding Television" (University of Leicester, 1973).

13   The phrase is Habermas's, in "Systematically distorted communications", in P. Dretzel (ed.), *Recent Sociology*, vol. 2 (London: Collier-Macmillan, 1970). It is used here, however, in a different way.

14   For a sociological formulation which is close, in some ways, to the positions outlined here but which does not parallel the argument about the theory of discourse, see Frank Parkin, *Class Inequality and Political Order* (London: MacGibon and Kee, 1971).

15   See Louis Althusser, "Ideology and ideological state apparatuses", in *Lenin and Philosophy and Other Essays* (London: New Left Books, 1971).

16   For an expansion of this argument, see Stuart Hall, "The external/internal dialectic in broadcasting", *4th Symposium on Broadcasting* (University of Manchester, 1972), and "Broadcasting and the state: the independence/impartiality couplet", AMCR Symposium, University of Leicester, 1976 (CCCS unpublished paper).

14

On the Politics of Empirical Audience Research

Ien Ang

In his pioneering book *The "Nationwide" Audience*, David Morley situates his research on which the book reports as follows:

> The relation of an audience to the ideological operations of television remains in principle an empirical question: the challenge is the attempt to develop appropriate methods of empirical investigation of that relation. (Morley 1980a: 162)

Although this sentence may initially be interpreted as a call for a methodological discussion about empirical research techniques, its wider meaning should be sought in the theoretical and political context of Morley's work. To me, the importance of *The "Nationwide" Audience* does not so much reside in the fact that it offers an empirically validated, and thus "scientific", account of "the ideological operations of television", nor merely in its demonstration of some of the ways in which the television audience is "active". Other, more wide-ranging issues are at stake – issues related to the *politics* of research.

Since its publication in 1980, *The "Nationwide" Audience* has played an important role in media studies. The book occupies a key strategic position in the study of media audiences – a field of study that went through a rapid development in the 1980s. It seems fair to say that this book forms a major moment in the growing popularity of an "ethnographic" approach on media audiences – Morley himself has termed his project an "ethnography of reading" (1981: 13). This type of qualitative empirical research, usually carried out in the form of in-depth interviews with a small number of people (and at times supplemented with some form of participant observation), is now recognized by many as one of the best ways to learn about the differentiated subtleties of people's engagements with television and other media.

This "ethnographic" approach has gained popularity in both "critical" media studies and "mainstream" mass communications research (see, e.g., Hobson 1980

From Ien Ang, "On the politics of empirical audience research." In *Living Room Wars: Rethinking Media Audiences for a Postmodern World*, pp. 35–52. New York and London: Routledge, 1991.

and 1982; Lull 1980 and 1988; Radway 1984; Ang 1985; Jensen 1986; Lindlof 1987; Liebes and Katz 1990). A sort of methodological consensus has emerged, a common ground in which scholars from divergent epistemological backgrounds can thrive. On the one hand, qualitative methods of empirical research seem to be more acceptable than quantitative ones because they offer the possibility to avoid what C. Wright Mills (1970) has termed abstracted empiricism – a tendency often levelled at the latter by "critical" scholars. On the other hand, some "mainstream" audience researchers are now acknowledging the limitations on the kind of data that can be produced by large-scale, quantitative survey work, and believe that ethnographically oriented methods can overcome the shortcomings observed. Given this enthusiastic, rather new interest in qualitative research methods, I would like to reflect upon its general implications for our understanding of television audiences. What kind of knowledge does it produce? What can this manner of doing empirical research on audiences mean? In short, what are the politics of audience "ethnography"?[1]

In exploring these questions, I want to clarify some of the issues that are at stake in developing a *critical* perspective in empirical audience studies. The term "critical" as I would like to use it here refers first of all to a certain intellectual-political *orientation* towards academic practice: whatever its subject matter or methodology, essential to doing "critical" research would be the adoption of a self-reflective perspective, one that is, first, conscious of the social and discursive nature of any research practice, and, second, takes seriously the Foucauldian reminder that the production of knowledge is always bound up in a network of power relations (Foucault 1979). By characterizing "critical" research in this way, that is, as an orientation rather than as a fixed "paradigm", I aim to relativize the more rigid ways in which "critical" and "mainstream" research have often been opposed to one another.

Formally speaking, positions can only be "critical" or "mainstream" in relation to other positions within a larger discursive field. The two terms thus do not primarily signify fixed contents of thought, but their status within a whole, often dispersed, field of statements, claims and knowledges, what Foucault calls a "regime of truth". The relations of force in that field can change over time: what was once "critical" (or marginal) can become part of the "mainstream"; what was once "mainstream" (or dominant) can lose its power and be pushed aside to a marginal(ized) position. Furthermore, as Larry Grossberg (1987) has usefully remarked, the term "critical" can bear uneasy arrogant connotations: after all, is there any scholar whose work is not "critical" in some sense?

This does not mean, of course, that the distinction is totally devoid of any substantive bearings. In media studies, for instance, the "critical" tradition, whose beginnings can be located in the work of the Frankfurt School, has generally derived its philosophical and political inspiration from European schools of thought such as Marxism and (post)structuralism. In terms of research problematics, "critical" media researchers have mainly been concerned with the analysis of the ideological and/or economic role of the media in capitalist and patriarchal society. Furthermore, the epistemological underpinnings of this kind of work are generally characterized by a strident anti-positivist and anti-empiricist mentality.[2]

This distrust of positivist empiricism on the part of "critical" theorists, however, does not necessarily imply an *inherent* incompatibility between "critical" and empirical research, as is often contended by "mainstream" scholars.[3] Indeed, if doing "critical" research is more a matter of intellectual-political orientation than of academic para-digm building, then no fixed, universal yardstick, theoretical or methodological, for what constitutes "critical" knowledge is possible. On the contrary, in my view what it means to be critical needs to be assessed and constantly reassessed in every concrete conjuncture, with respect to the concrete issues and directions that are at stake in any concrete research field. In other words, I am proposing an *open* and *contextual* definition of "critical" research, one that does not allow itself to rest easily on pre-existent epistemological foundations but, on the contrary, is reassessed continuously according to the ways in which it contributes to our understanding of the world. In the following, I hope to clarify some of the implications of this perspective on doing "critical" research for an evaluation of the current developments in audience studies as I indicated above.

More concretely, what I will discuss and try to elaborate in this chapter is what I take as the political and theoretical specificity of the *cultural studies* approach as a "critical" perspective, from which David Morley, coming from the Birmingham Centre for Contemporary Cultural Studies, has developed his work (see Hall et al. 1980; Streeter 1984; Fiske 1987b). I will set this perspective on audience studies against some developments in and around the uses and gratifications approach, where an interest in "ethnographic" methods has been growing recently. In doing this I will not be able to discuss the wide range of concrete studies that have been made in this area. Rather I will restrict myself, somewhat schematically and all too briefly, to the more programmatic statements and proposals pertaining to the identity and the future development of the field, and evaluate them in the light of what I see as important for a critical cultural studies approach. Furthermore, it is not my intention to construct an absolute antagonism between the two approaches. Rather, I would like to highlight some of the differences in preoccupation and perspective, in order to specify how ethnographic or ethnographically oriented studies of media audiences can contribute to a "critical" approach in the sense I have outlined. Before doing this, I will first give a short sketch of the intellectual arena in which Morley intervened.

The Problem of the Disappearing Audience

The "Nationwide" Audience appeared at a time when critical discourse about film and television in Britain was heavily preoccupied with what Morley (1980a: 161), following Steve Neale, calls an "abstract text/subject relationship", formulated within a generally (post)structuralist and psychoanalytic theoretical framework. In this dis-course, primarily developed in the journal *Screen*, film and television spectatorship is almost exclusively theorized from the perspective of the "productivity of the text". As a consequence, the role of the viewer was conceived in purely formalist terms: as a position inscribed in the text. Here, the subject-in-the-text tends to collapse with "real" social subjects. In this model, there is no space for a dialogical relation-ship between texts and social subjects. Texts are assumed to be the only source of meaning; they construct subject positions which viewers are bound to take up if they are to make sense of the text. In other words, the reading of texts is conceived in "*Screen* theory" as entirely dictated by textual structures.

It is this model's textual determinism that fuelled Morley's dissatisfaction. Theoretically, it implied an ahistorical, asocial and generalist conception of film and TV spectatorship. Methodologically, the analysis of textual structures alone was considered to be sufficient to comprehend how viewers are implicated in the texts they encounter. Politically, this model left no room for manoeuvre for television viewers. They are implicitly conceived as "prisoners" of the text. It was against this background that Morley decided to undertake an empirical investigation of how groups of viewers with different social positions read or interpret one particular text: an episode of the British TV magazine programme *Nationwide*. One of the most important motivations of Morley's intervention, then, was to overcome the textualism of *Screen* theory's discourse, in which the relation of text and subject is dealt with "as an *a priori* question to be deduced from a theory of the ideal spectator 'inscribed' in the text" (Morley 1980a: 162). By looking at how one text could be decoded in different ways by different groups of social subjects, Morley's intention, in which he was successful, was to demonstrate that encounters between texts and viewers are far more complex than the textualist theory would suggest; they are overdetermined by the operation of a multiplicity of forces – certain historical and social structures, but also other texts – that simultaneously act upon the subjects concerned.[4] What *The "Nationwide" Audience* explores is the notion that the moment of decoding should be considered as a relatively autonomous process in which a constant struggle over the meaning of the text is fought out. Textual meanings do not reside in the texts themselves: a certain text can come to mean different things depending on the interdiscursive context in which viewers interpret it.

The significance of Morley's turn towards empirical research of the television audience should be assessed against this critical background. It is first of all a procedure that is aimed at opening up a space in which watching television can begin to be understood as a complex cultural practice full of dialogical negotiations and contestations, rather than as a singular occurrence whose meaning can be determined once and for all in the abstract. Doing empirical research, then, is here used as a strategy to break out of a hermetically closed theoreticism in which an absolute certainty about the ideological effectivity of television is presumed. Thus, when Morley says that the relation of an audience to television "remains an empirical question", what he is basically aiming at is to open up critical discourse on television audiences, and to sensitize it for the possibility of struggle in the practices of television use and consumption – a struggle whose outcome cannot be known in advance, for the simple reason that encounters between television and audiences are always historically specific and context-bound.

Academic Convergence?

The "Nationwide" Audience has generally been received as an innovative departure within cultural studies, both theoretically and methodologically. If *Screen* theory can be diagnosed as one instance in which critical discourse on television suffered from "the problem of the disappearing audience" (Fejes 1984), Morley's project represents an important acknowledgement within cultural studies that television viewing is a practice that involves the active production of meanings by viewers. But the book has not only made an impact in cultural studies circles. Curiously, but not surprisingly, it has also been welcomed by adherents of the uses and gratifications approach, one of the most influential "mainstream" strands of audience research in mass communication scholarship. These scholars see books such as Morley's as an important step on the part of "critical" scholars in their direction, that is, as a basic acceptance of, and possible contribution to, a refinement of their own basic axiomatic commitment to "the active audience". At the same time, some uses and gratifications researchers, for their part, have now incorporated some of the insights developed within the "critical" perspective into their own paradigm. For example, they have adopted semiologically informed cultural studies concepts such as "text" and "reader" in their work. This move indicates an acknowledgement of the symbolic nature of negotiations between media texts and their readers which they, in their narrow functionalist interest in the multiple relationships between audience "needs" and media "uses", had previously all but ignored. As Jay Blumler, Michael Gurevitch and Elihu Katz admit:

> Gratifications researchers, in their paradigmatic personae, have lost sight of what the media are purveying, in part because of an over-commitment to the endless freedom of the audience to reinvent the text, in part because of a too rapid leap to mega-functions, such as surveillance or self-identity. (Blumler et al. 1985: 272)

On top of this conceptual rapprochement, they have also expressed their delight in noticing a methodological "concession" among "critical" scholars: at last, so they exclaim, some "critical" scholars have dropped their suspicion of doing empirical research. In a benevolent, rather fatherly tone, Blumler, Gurevitch and Katz, three senior ambassadors of the uses and gratifications approach, have thus proclaimed a gesture of "reaching out" to the other "camp" (1985: 275). Therefore the prospect is evoked of a merger of the two approaches, to the point that they may ultimately fuse into a happy common project in which the perceived hostility between the two "camps" will have been unmasked as academic "pseudo-conflicts". As one leading gratifications researcher, Karl Erik Rosengren, optimistically predicts: "To the extent that the same problematics are empirically studied by members of various schools, the present sharp differences of opinion will gradually diminish and be replaced by a growing convergence of perspectives" (1983: 203).[5]

However, to interpret these recent developments in audience studies in terms of such a convergence is to simplify and even misconceive what is at stake in the "ethnographic turn" within cultural studies. For one thing, I would argue that cultural studies and uses and gratifications research only superficially share "the same problematics", as Rosengren would have it. Also, what separates a "critical" from a "mainstream" perspective is more than merely some "differences of opinion", sharp or otherwise. Rather, it concerns fundamental differences not only in epistemological but also in theoretical and political attitudes towards the aim and status of doing empirical work in the first place.

The academic idealization of joining forces in pursuit of a supposedly common goal as if it were a neutral, scientific project is a particularly depoliticizing strategy, because it tends to neutralize all antagonism and disagreement in favour of a forced consensus. If I am cautious and a little wary about this euphoria around the prospect of academic convergence, it is not my intention to impose a rigid and absolute, eternal dichotomy between "critical" and "mainstream" research. Nor would I want to assert that Morley's project is entirely "critical" and the uses and gratifications approach completely "mainstream". As I have noted before, the relationship between "critical" and "mainstream" is not a fixed one; it does not concern two mutually exclusive, antagonistic sets of knowledge, as some observers would imply by talking in terms of "schools", "paradigms" or even "camps". In fact, many assumptions and ideas do not, in themselves, intrinsically belong to one or the other perspective. For example, the basic assumption that the audience is "active" (rather than passive) and that watching television is a social (rather than an individual) practice is currently accepted in both perspectives. There is nothing spectacular about that.[6] What matters is how this idea of "activeness" is articulated with a more general theory of social agency and power. Also, I would suggest that the idea that texts can generate multiple meanings because readers/viewers can "negotiate" textual meanings is not in itself a sufficient condition for the declared convergence. For example, Tamar Liebes has suggested that "the focus of the convergence is on the idea that the interaction between messages and receivers takes on the form of negotiation, and is not predetermined" (1986: 1). However, as I will try to show below, what makes all the difference is the way in which "negotiation" is conceived. After all, "not pre-determined" does not mean "undetermined"; on the contrary.

While uses and gratifications researchers generally operate within a liberal pluralist conception of society where individuals are seen as ideally free, that is, unhindered by external powers, in cultural studies, following Marxist/(post)structuralist assumptions, people are conceived as always-already implicated in, and necessarily constrained by, the web of relationships and structures which constitute them as social subjects. This doesn't mean that they are stripped of agency like preprogrammed automatons, but that that agency itself, or the "negotiations" subjects undertake in constructing their lives, is *over*determined (i.e. neither predetermined nor undetermined) by the concrete conditions of existence they find themselves in. Following Hall (1986b: 46), "determinacy" here is understood in terms of the setting of limits, the establishment of parameters, the defining of the space of operations, rather than in terms of the absolute predictability of particular outcomes. This is what Hall (1986c) calls a "Marxism without guarantees", a non-determinist theory of determination, or, to put it simply, a recognition of the virtual truism that "people make their own history but under conditions not of their own making".

How complex structural and conjunctural determinations of viewership and audiencehood should be conceived remains therefore an important point of divergence between "critical" and "mainstream" studies. Finally, it is also noteworthy to point out that, while uses and gratifications researchers now seem to be "rediscovering the text", researchers working within a cultural studies perspective seem to be moving away from the text. This is very clear in Morley's second book, *Family Television* (1986), on which I will comment later. In fact, it becomes more and more difficult to delineate what "the television text" is in a media-saturated world.

In other words, in evaluating whether we can really speak of a paradigmatic convergence, it is not enough to establish superficially similar research questions, nor to take at face value a shared acknowledgement of the usefulness of certain methods of inquiry. Of course, such commonalities are interesting enough and it would be nonsense to categorically discard them. I do think it is important to avoid a dogmatism or antagonism-for-the-sake-of-it, and to try to learn from others wherever that is possible. But at the same time we should not lose sight of the fact that any call for a convergence itself is not an innocent gesture. It tends to be done from a certain point of view, and therefore necessarily involves a biased process in which certain issues and themes are highlighted and others suppressed. And it is my contention that an all too hasty declaration of convergence could lead to neglecting some of the most important distinctive features of cultural studies as a critical intellectual enterprise.

A difference in conceptualizing the object of study is a first issue that needs to be discussed here. As I have already suggested, in a cultural studies perspective "audience activity" cannot and should not be studied nominalistically, decontextualized from the larger network of social relationships in which it occurs. The aim of cultural studies is not a matter of dissecting "audience activity" in ever more refined variables and categories so that we can ultimately have a complete and generalizable formal "map" of all dimensions of "audience activity" (which seems to be the drive behind the uses and gratifications project; e.g. Levy and Windahl 1984, 1986). Rather, the aim, as I see it, is to arrive at a more historicized and contextualized insight into the ways in which "audience activity" is articulated within and by a complex set of social, political, economic and cultural forces. In other words, what is at stake is not the understanding of "audience activity" as such as an isolated and isolatable object of research, but the embeddedness of "audience activity" in a complex network of ongoing cultural practices and relationships.

As a result, an audience researcher working within a cultural studies sensibility cannot restrict herself or himself to "just" studying audiences and their activities (and, for that matter, relating those activities with other variables such as gratifications sought or obtained, dependencies, effects, and so on). She or he will also engage herself/himself with the structural and cultural *processes* through which the audiences she or he is studying are constituted and being constituted. Thus, one essential theoretical point of the cultural studies approach of the television audience is its foregrounding of the notion that the dynamics of watching television, no matter how heterogeneous and seemingly free, are always related to the operations of forms of social power. It is in this light that we should see Morley's decision to do research on viewers' decodings: it was first of all motivated by an interest in what he in the quote at the beginning of this chapter calls "the ideological operations of television".

It is important then to emphasize that the reference to "the active audience" does not occupy the same theoretical status in the two approaches. From a cultural studies point of view, evidence that audiences are "active" cannot simply be equated with the rather triumphant, liberal pluralist conclusion, often displayed by gratificationists, that media consumers are "free" or even "powerful" – a conclusion which allegedly undercuts the idea of "media hegemony". The question for cultural studies is not simply one of "where the power lies in media systems" (Blumler et al. 1985: 260) – i.e. with the audience or with the media producers – but rather how relations of power are organized within the heterogeneous practices of media use and consumption. In other words, rather than constructing an opposition between "the" media and "the" audience, as if these were separate ontological entities, and, along with it, the application of a distributional theory of power – i.e. power conceived as a "thing" that can be attributed to either side of the opposing entities – cultural studies is interested in understanding media consumption as a site of cultural struggle, in which a variety of forms of power are exercised, with different sorts of effects.[7] Thus if, as Morley's study has shown, viewers decode a text in different ways and sometimes even give oppositional meanings to it, this should be understood not as an example of "audience freedom", but as a moment in that cultural struggle, an ongoing struggle over meaning and pleasure which is central to the fabric(ation) of everyday life.

I hope to have made it clear by now that in evaluating the possibility or even desirability of a paradigmatic convergence, it is important to look at how "audience activity" is theorized or interpreted, and how research "findings" are placed in a wider theoretical framework. So, if one type of "audience activity" which has received much attention in both approaches has been the "interpretive strategies" used by audiences to read media texts (conceptualized in terms of decoding structures, interpretive communities, patterns of involvement, and so on), how are we to make sense of those interpretive strategies? The task of the cultural studies researcher, I would suggest, is to develop *strategic interpretations* of them, different not only in form and content but also in scope and intent from those offered in more "mainstream" accounts.[8] I will return to this central issue of interpretation below.

Beyond Methodology

A troubling aspect about the idea of (and desire for) convergence, then, is that it tends to be conceptualized as an exclusively "scientific" enterprise. Echoing the tenets of positivism, its aim seems to be the gradual accumulation of scientifically confirmed "findings". It is propelled by the hope that by seeking a shared agreement on what is relevant to study and by developing shared methodological skills, the final scientific account of "the audience" can eventually be achieved. In this framework, audience research is defined as a specialized niche within an academic discipline (e.g. "mass communication"), in which it is assumed that "the audience" is a proper object of study whose characteristics can be ever more accurately observed, described, categorized, systematized and explained until the whole picture is "filled in". In other words, this scientific project implicitly claims in principle (if not in practice) to be able to produce total knowledge, to reveal the full and objective "truth" about "the audience". The audience here is imagined as, and turned into, an object with researchable attributes and features (be it described in terms of preferences, uses, effects, decodings, interpretive strategies, or whatever) that can be definitively known – if only researchers of different breeding would stop quarrelling with each other and unite to work harmoniously together to accomplish the task.[9]

From such a point of view, the question of *methodology* becomes a central issue. After all, rigour of method has traditionally been seen as the guarantee *par excellence* for the "scientific" status of knowledge. In positivist social science, the hypothetico-deductive testing of theory through empirical research, quantitative in form, is cherished as the cornerstone of the production of "scientific" knowledge. Theory that is not empirically tested or that is too complex to be moulded into empirically testable hypotheses has to be dismissed as "unscientific". These assumptions, which are more or less central to the dominant version of the uses and gratifications approach as it was established in the 1970s, are now contested by a growing number of researchers who claim that reality cannot be grasped and explained through quantitative methods alone. Stronger still, they forcefully assert that to capture the multidimensionality and complexity of audience activity the use of qualitative methods – and thus a move towards the "ethnographic" – is desperately called for (cf. Lull 1986; Jensen 1987; Lindlof and Meyer 1987).

From a "scientific" point of view, it is this methodological challenge that forms the condition of possibility of the perceived convergence. However, although I think that the struggle for legitimization of qualitative research is a very important one, I do believe that it is not the central point for critical cultural studies. This is the case because, as the struggle is defined as a matter of methodology, its relevance is confined to the development of audience research as an *academic* enterprise. Of course, this development is in itself interesting given the decades-long hegemony of positivism and the quantifying attitude in audience research. Furthermore, the growing influence of alternative "paradigms" such as ethnomethodology and symbolic interactionism should certainly be welcomed. The problem with many "mainstream" claims about the usefulness of qualitative methods, however, is that they are put forward in the name of "scientific progress", without questioning the epistemological distinction between Science and commonsense which lies at the heart of positivism. The aim still seems to be the isolation of a body of knowledge that can be recognized as "scientific" (in its broadest meaning), the orientation being one towards the advancement of an academic discipline, and, concomitantly, the technical improvement of its instruments of analysis.

A cultural studies perspective on audience research cannot stop short at this level of debate. For critical cultural studies, it is not questions of methodology, nor "scientific progress" that prevail. On the contrary, we should relativize the academic commitment to increasing knowledge *per se*, and resist the temptation of what Stuart Hall (1986b: 56) has called the "codification" of cultural studies into a stable realm of established theories and canonized methodologies. In this respect, the territorial conflict between "mainstream" and "critical" research, quantitative and qualitative methods, humanistic and social-scientific disciplines, and so on, should perhaps not bother us too much at all in the first place. As James Carey once remarked, "[p]erhaps all the talk about theory, method, and other such things prevents us from raising, or permits us to avoid raising, deeper and disquieting questions about the purposes of our scholarship" (1983: 5). And indeed: why are we so interested in knowing about audiences in the first place? In empirical audience research, especially, it is important to reflect upon the politics of the knowledge produced. After all, scrutinizing media audiences is not an innocent practice. It does not take place in a social and institutional vacuum. As we all know, historically, the hidden agenda of audience research, even when it presents itself as pure and object-ive, has all too often been its commercial or political usefulness. In other words, what we should reflect upon is the *political* interventions we make when studying audiences – political not only in the sense of some external societal goal, but, more importantly, in that we cannot afford to ignore the political dimensions of the process and practice of the production of knowledge itself. What does it mean to subject audiences to the researcher's gaze? How can we develop insights that do not reproduce the kind of objectified knowledge served up by, say, market research or empiricist effects research? How is it possible to do audience research which is "on the side" of the audience?[10] These are nagging political questions which can-not be smoothed out by the comforting canons of epistemology, methodology and Science.

Of course it is not easy to pin down what such considerations would imply in concrete terms. But it could at least be said that we should try to avoid a stance in which "the audience" is relegated to the status of exotic "other" – merely interest-ing in so far as "we", as researchers, can turn "them" into "objects" of study, and about whom "we" have the privileged position of acquiring "scientific" knowledge.[11] To begin with, I think, critical audience studies should not strive and pretend to tell "the truth" about "the audience". Its ambitions should be much more modest. As Grossberg has suggested, "the goal of [critical research] is to offer not a polished representation of the truth, but simply a little help in our efforts to better under-stand the world" (1987: 89). This modesty has less to do with some sort of false humility than with the basic acknowledgement that every research practice unavoid-ably takes place in a particular historical situation, and is therefore in principle of a partial nature. As Hammersley and Atkinson have provocatively put it, "all social research takes the form of participant observation: it involves participating in the social world, in whatever role, and reflecting on the products of that participation" (1983: 16). The collection of data, either quantitative or qualitative in form, can never be separated from its interpretation; it is only through practices of interpretive theorizing that unruly social experiences and events related to media consumption become established as meaningful "facts" about audiences. Understanding "audi-ence activity" is thus caught up in the discursive representation, not the transparent reflection, of diverse realities pertaining to people's engagements with media.

These considerations lead to another, more politicized conception of doing research. It is not the search for (objective, scientific) Truth in which the researcher is engaged, but the construction of *interpretations*, of certain ways of understanding the world, always historically located, subjective and relative. It is the decisive import-ance of this interpretive moment that I would like to highlight in exploring the possibilities of critical audience studies.[12]

In positivism, the necessarily worldly nature of interpretation is repressed, relegated to the refuted realm of "bias". It is assumed to follow rather automatically – i.e. without the intervention of the subjective "whims" of the researcher – from the controlled process of "empirical testing of theory". An apparent innocence of interpretation is then achieved, one that is seemingly grounded in "objective social reality" itself. In fact, the very term "interpretation" would seem to have definite negative connotations for positivists because of its connection with "subjectivism". And even within those social science approaches in which the interpretive act of the researcher – i.e. the moment of data analysis that comes after data collection – is taken more seriously, interpretation is more often than not problematized as a technical rather than a political matter, defined in terms of careful inference making rather than in terms of discursive constructions of reality.

It should be recognized, however, that because interpretations always inevitably involve the construction of certain representations of reality (and not others), they can never be "neutral" and merely "descriptive". After all, the "empirical", captured in either quantitative or qualitative form, does not yield self-evident meanings; it is only through the interpretive framework constructed by the researcher that understandings of the "empirical" come about. No "theory" brought to bear on the "empirical" can ever be "value-neutral"; it is always "interested" in the strong sense of that word. Here, then, the thoroughly political nature of any research practice manifests itself. What is at stake is a *politics of interpretation*: "[T]o advance an interpretation is to insert it into a network of power relations" (Pratt 1986: 52).

Of course, this also implies a shift in the position of the researcher. She or he is no longer a bearer of the truth, but occupies a "partial" position in two senses of the word. On the one hand, she or he is no longer the neutral observer, but is someone whose job it is to produce historically and culturally specific knowledges that are the result of equally specific discursive encounters between researcher and informants, in which the subjectivity of the researcher is not separated from the "object" s/he is studying. The interpretations that are produced in the process can never claim to be definitive: on the contrary, they are necessarily incomplete (for they always involve simplification, selection and exclusion) and temporary. "If neither history nor politics ever comes to an end, then theory (as well as research) is never completed and our accounts can never be closed or totalized" (Grossberg 1987: 89). On the other hand, and even more important, the position of the researcher is also more than that of the professional scholar: beyond being a capable interpreter she or he is also inherently a political and moral subject. As an intellectual s/he is responsible not only to the Academy, but to the social world s/he lives in as well, consciously or unconsciously so. It is at the interface of "ethics" and "scholarship" that the researcher's interpretations take on their distinctive political edge (cf. Rabinow 1986).

Of course, all this entails a different status for empirical research. Material obtained by ethnographic fieldwork or depth-interviews with audience members cannot simply be treated as direct slices of reality, as in naturalist conceptions of ethnography. Viewers' statements about their relation to television cannot be regarded as self-evident facts. Nor are they immediate, transparent reflections of those viewers' "lived realities" that can speak for themselves. What is of critical importance, therefore, is the way in which those statements are made sense of, that is, interpreted. Here lies the ultimate political responsibility of the researcher. The comfortable assumption that it is the reliability and accuracy of the methodologies being used that will ascertain the validity of the outcomes of research, thereby reducing the researcher's responsibility to a technical matter, is rejected. In short, to return to Morley's opening statement, audience research is undertaken because the relation between television and viewers is an empirical *question*. But the empirical is not the privileged domain where the *answers* should be sought. Answers – partial ones, to be sure, that is, both provisional and committed – are to be constructed, in the form of interpretations.[13]

Towards Interpretive Ethnography

I would now like to return to Morley's work, and evaluate its place in the research field in the light of my reflections above. To be sure, Morley himself situates his work firmly within the academic context. And parallel to the recent calls for convergence and cross-fertilization of diverse perspectives, Morley seems to have dropped his original antagonistic posture. For example, while in *The "Nationwide" Audience* he emphasizes that "we need to break fundamentally with the 'uses and gratifications' approach" (1980a: 14),[14] in *Family Television*, he simply states that this new piece of research draws "upon some of the insights" of this very approach (1986: 15). The latter book is also in a more general sense set in a less polemical tone than the first one: rather than taking up a dissident's stance against other theoretical perspectives, which is a central attribute of *The "Nationwide" Audience*, *Family Television* is explicitly presented as a study that aims to combine the perspectives of separate traditions in order to overcome what Morley calls an "unproductive form of segregation" (ibid.: 13). Furthermore, both books have been written in a markedly conventional style of academic social science, structured according to a narrative line which starts out with their contextualization within related academic research trends, followed by a methodological exposition and a description of the findings, and rounded off with a chapter containing an interpretation of the results and some more general conclusions. In both books Morley's voice is exclusively that of the earnest researcher; the writer's "I", almost completely eliminated from the surface of the text, is apparently a disembodied subject solely driven by a disinterested wish to contribute to "scientific progress".[15]

Morley's academistic inclination tends to result in a lack of clarity about the critical import and political relevance of his analyses. For example, the relevance of *Family Television* as a project designed to investigate at the same time two different types of questions regarding television consumption – questions of television use, on the one hand, and questions of textual interpretation, on the other – is simply asserted by the statement that these are "urgent questions about the television audience" (Morley 1986: 13). But why? What kind of urgency is being referred to here? Morley goes on to say that it is the analysis of the domestic viewing context as such which is his main interest, and that he wishes to identify the multiple meanings hidden behind the catch-all phrase "watching television". Indeed, central to *Family Television*'s discourse are, as Hall remarks in his introduction to the book, the notions of variability, diversity and difference:

> We are all, in our heads, several different audiences at once, and can be constituted as such by different programmes. We have the capacity to deploy different levels and modes of attention, to mobilise different competences in our viewing. At different times of the day, for different family members, different patterns of viewing have different "saliences". Here the monolithic conceptions of the viewer, the audience or of television itself have been displaced – one hopes forever – before the new emphasis on difference and variation. (Hall 1986a: 10)

Yet when taken in an unqualified manner it is exactly this stress on difference that essentially connects Morley's project with the preoccupations of the gratificationists. After all, it is their self-declared distinctive mission to get to grips with "the gamut of audience experience" (Blumler et al. 1985: 271). For them too, the idea of plurality and diversity is pre-eminently the guiding principle for research. A convergence of perspectives after all?

Despite all the agreements that are certainly there, however, a closer look at the ramifications of Morley's undertaking reveals other concerns than merely the characterization and categorizing of varieties within viewers' readings and uses of television. Ultimately, it is not difference as such that is of main interest in Morley's work. To be sure, differences are not just simple facts that emerge more or less spontaneously from the empirical interview material; it is a matter of interpretation what are established as *significant* differences – significant not in the formal, statistical sense of that word, but in a culturally meaningful, interpretive sense. In cultural studies, then, it is the meanings of differences that matter – something that can only be grasped, interpretively, by looking at their contexts, social and cultural bases, and impacts. Thus, rather than the classification of differences and varieties in all sorts of typologies, which is a major preoccupation of a lot of uses and gratifications work, cultural studies would be oriented towards more specific and conjunctural understandings of how and why varieties in experience occur – a venture, to be sure, that is a closer approach to the ethnographic spirit.

In *Family Television*, for example, Morley has chosen to foreground the pattern of differences in viewing habits that are articulated with gender. What Morley emphasizes is that men and women clearly relate in contrasting ways to television, not only as to programme preferences, but also in, for example, viewing styles. The wives interviewed by Morley tend to watch television less attentively, at the same time doing other things such as talking or doing some housework. The husbands, in contrast, state a clear preference for viewing attentively, in silence, without interruption, "in order not to miss anything" (Morley 1986: chapter 6). These differences are substantiated and highlighted by Morley's research as empirical facts, but he is careful to avoid considering these as *essential* differences between men and women. As Charlotte Brunsdon has noted, it seems possible.

to differentiate a male – fixed, controlling, uninterrupted gaze – and a female – distracted, obscured, already busy – manner of watching television. There is some empirical truth in these characterizations, but to take this empirical truth for explanation leads to a theoretical short-circuit. (Brunsdon 1986: 105)

Indeed, in mainstream sociological accounts, gender would probably be treated as a self-evident pregiven factor that can be used as "independent variable" to explain these differences. Male and female modes of watching television would then be constituted as two separate, discrete types of experience, clearly defined, fixed, static "objects" in themselves as it were.[16] Such an empiricist account not only essentializes gender differences, but also fails to offer an understanding of how and why differentiations along gender lines take the very forms they do.

In contrast to this, both Morley and Brunsdon start out to construct a tentative interpretation which does not take the difference between male and female relations to television as an empirical given. Neither do they take recourse to psychological notions such as "needs" or "socialization" – as is often done in accounts of gender differences, as well as in uses and gratifications research – to try to understand why men and women tend to watch and talk about television in the disparate ways they do. In their interpretive work Morley and Brunsdon emphasize the structure of domestic power relations as constitutive for the differences concerned. The home generally has different meanings for men and women living in nuclear family arrangements: for husbands it is the site of leisure, for wives it is the site of work. Therefore, television as a domestic cultural form tends to be invested with different meanings for men and women. Television has for men become a central symbol for relaxation; women's relation to television, on the other hand, is much more contradictory. Brunsdon has this to say on Morley's research:

> The social relations between men and women appear to work in such a way that although the men feel ok about imposing their choice of viewing on the whole of the family, the women do not. The women have developed all sorts of strategies to cope with television viewing they don't particularly like. The men in most cases appear to feel it would be literally unmanning for them to sit quiet during the women's programmes. However, the women in general seem to find it almost impossible to switch into the silent communion with the television set that characterises so much male viewing. (Brunsdon 1986: 104)

Women's distracted mode of watching television, then, does not have something to do with some essential femininity, but is a result of a complex of cultural and social arrangements which makes it difficult for them to do otherwise, even though they often express a longing to be able to watch their favourite programmes without being disturbed. Men, on the other hand, can watch television in a concentrated manner because they control the conditions to do so. Their way of watching television, Brunsdon concludes, "seems not so much a masculine mode, but a mode of power" (1986: 106).

What clearly emerges here is the beginning of an interpretive framework in which differences in television-viewing practices are not just seen as expressions of different needs, uses or readings, but are connected with the way in which particular social subjects are structurally positioned in relation to each other. In the context of the nuclear family home, women's viewing patterns can only be understood in relation to men's patterns; the two are in a sense constitutive of each other. Thus, if watching television is a social and even collective practice, it is not a harmonious practice.[17] Because subjects are positioned in different ways towards the set, they engage in a continuing struggle over programme choice and programme interpretation, styles of viewing and textual pleasure. What kind of viewer they become can be seen as the outcome of this struggle, an outcome, however, that is never definitive because it can always be contested and subverted. What we call "viewing habits" are thus not a more or less static set of behaviours inhabited by an individual or group of individuals; rather they are the temporary result of a neverending, dynamic and conflictual process in which "the fine-grained interrelationships between meaning, pleasure, use and choice" are shaped (Hall 1986a: 10).

Morley's empirical findings, then, acquire their relevance and critical value in the context of this emerging theoretical understanding. And of course it could only have been carried out from a specific interpretive point of view. Needless to say, the point of view taken up by Morley and Brunsdon is a feminist one, that is, a worldly intellectual position that is sensitive to the micro-politics of male/female relationships. Television consumption, so we begin to understand, contributes to the everyday construction of male and female subjectivities through the relations of power, contradiction and struggle that men and women enter into in their daily engagements with the TV sets in their homes. At this point, we can also see how Morley's research enables us to begin to conceive of "the ideological operations of television" in a much more radical way than has hitherto been done. The relation between television and audiences is not just a matter of discrete "negotiations" between texts and viewers. In a much more profound sense the process of television consumption – and the positioning of television as such in the culture of modernity – has created new areas of constraints and possibilities for structuring social relationships, identities and desires. If television is an "ideological apparatus", to use that oldfashioned-sounding term, then this is not so much because its texts transmit certain "messages", but because it is a cultural form through which those constraints are negotiated and those possibilities take shape.

But, one might ask, do we need empirical research, or, more specifically, ethnographic audience research, to arrive at such theoretical understandings? Why examine audiences empirically at all? After all, some critical scholars still dismiss the idea of doing empirical audience research altogether, because, so they argue, it would necessarily implicate the researcher with the strategies and aims of the capitalist culture industry (e.g. Modleski 1986: xi–xii). Against this background, I would like to make one last comment on Morley's work here. Due to his academistic posture Morley has not deemed it necessary to reflect upon his own position as a researcher. We do not get to know how he found and got on with his interviewees, nor are we informed about the way in which the interviews themselves took place. One of the very few things we learn about this in *Family Television* is that he gave up interviewing the adults and the young children at the same time, reportedly "because after an initial period of fascination the young children quite quickly got bored" (Morley 1986: 174)! But what about the adults? What were the reasons for their willingness to talk at such length to an outsider (or was David Morley not an outsider to them)? And how did the specific power relationship pervading the interview situation affect not only the families, but also the researcher himself? These are problems inherent to conducting ethnographic research that are difficult to unravel. But that does not mean that audience researchers should not confront them, and, eventually, draw the radical and no doubt uncomfortable conclusions that will emerge from that confrontation. We can think of Valerie Walkerdine's provocative and disturbing query:

> Much has been written about the activity of watching films in terms of scopophilia. But what of that other activity, [. . .] this activity of research, of trying so hard to understand what people see in films? Might we not call this the most perverse voyeurism? (Walkerdine 1986: 166)

It is, of course, important for us to recognize the inherent symbolic violence of any kind of research. However, we cannot renounce our inevitable complicity simply by not doing research at all, empirical or otherwise. Indeed, such a retreat would only lead to the dangerous illusion of our own exemption from the realities under scrutiny, including the realities of living with the media – as if it were possible to keep our hands clean in a fundamentally dirty world. It is precisely for this reason that I believe that, in the expanding field of audience studies, an ethnographic approach can and does have a distinct critical value. Ethnographic work, in the sense of drawing on what we can perceive and experience in everyday settings, acquires its critical edge when it functions as a reminder that reality is always more complicated and diversified than our theories can represent, and that there is no such thing as "audience" whose characteristics can be set once and for all.[18] The critical promise of the ethnographic attitude resides in its potential to make and keep our interpretations sensitive to concrete specificities, to the unexpected, to history; it is a commitment to submit ourselves to the possibility of, in Paul Willis's words, "being 'surprised', of reaching knowledge not prefigured in one's starting paradigm" (1980: 90). What matters is not the certainty of knowledge about audiences, but an ongoing critical and intellectual engagement with the multifarious ways in which we constitute ourselves through media consumption. Or, as in the words of Stuart Hall: "I am not interested in Theory, I am interested in going on theorizing" (1986b: 60).

Notes

1   It should be noted that the term "ethnography" is somewhat misplaced in this context. Within anthropology, ethnography refers to an in-depth field study of a culture and its inhabitants in their natural location, which would require the researcher to spend a fair amount of time in that location, allowing her/him to acquire a nuanced and comprehensive insight into the dynamics of the social relationships in the culture under study, and enabling her/him to produce a "thick description" of it. Most qualitative studies of

media audiences do not meet these requirements. In Morley's *Nationwide* study, for example, the informants were extracted from their natural viewing environment and interviewed in groups that were put together according to socio-economic criteria. In a looser sense, however, the use of the term "ethnographic" can be justified here in so far as the approach is aimed at getting a thorough insight into the "lived experience" of media consumption.

2   It should be stressed, however, that the "critical" tradition is not a monolithic whole: there is not one "critical theory" with generally shared axioms, but many different, and often conflicting, "critical perspectives", e.g. political economy and cultural studies.

3   Thus, the dichotomization of "critical" and "empirical" schools in communication studies, particularly in the United States, should be considered with some flexibility. See, e.g., the famous "Ferment in the Field" issue of the *Journal of Communication* (1983).

4   The direct theoretical inspiration of Morley's research was the so-called encoding/decoding model as launched by Stuart Hall, which presented a theoretical intervention against "*Screen* theory". See Hall (1980a, 1980b). Morley himself has elaborated on the "interdiscursive" nature of encounters between text and subjects. See Morley (1980b).

5   See also Tamar Liebes (1986) and Kim Christian Schrøder (1987). Such an insistence upon convergence is not new among "mainstream" communication researchers. For example, Jennifer Slack and Martin Allor have recalled how in the late 1930s Lazarsfeld hired Adorno in the expectation that the latter's critical theory could be used to "revitalize" American empiricist research by supplying it with "new research ideas". The collaboration ended only one year later because it proved to be impossible to translate Adorno's critical analysis into the methods and goals of Lazarsfeld's project. Lazarsfeld has never given up the idea of a convergence, however (Slack and Allor 1983: 210).

6   Note, for instance, the striking similarities between the following two sentences, one from a uses and gratifications source, the other from a cultural studies one: "There seems to be growing support for that branch of communications research which asserts that television viewing is an active and social process" (Katz and Liebes 1985: 187); "Television viewing, the choices which shape it and the many social uses to which we put it, now turn out to be an irrevocably active and social process" (Hall 1986a: 8).

7   In stating this I do not want to suggest that cultural studies is a closed paradigm, nor that all cultural studies scholars share one – say, Foucauldian – conception of power. For example, the Birmingham version of cultural studies, with its distinctly Gramscian inflection, has been criticized by Lawrence Grossberg for its lack of a theory of pleasure. An alternative, postmodernist perspective on cultural studies is developed in Grossberg (1983).

8   Strategic interpretations, that is, interpretations that are "political" in the sense that they are aware of the fact that interpretations are always concrete interventions into an already existing discursive field. They are therefore always partial in both senses of the word (i.e. partisan and incomplete), and involved in making sense of the world in specific, power-laden ways. See Mary Louise Pratt (1986).

9   Rosengren expresses this view in very clearcut terms, where he reduces the existence of disagreements between "critical" and "mainstream" researchers to "psychological reasons" (1983: 191).

10   I have borrowed this formulation from Virginia Nightingale (1986: 21–2). Nightingale remarks that audience research has generally been "on the side" of those with vested interests in influencing the organization of the mass-media in society, and that it is important to develop a research perspective that is "on the side" of the audience. However, it is far from simple to work out exactly what such a perspective would mean.

The notion of the "active audience", for example, often put forward by uses and gratifications researchers not just as an object of empirical investigation but also as an article of faith, as an axiom to mark the distinctive identity of the "paradigm", is not in itself a guarantee of a stance "on the side of the audience". In fact, the whole passive/active dichotomy in accounts of audiences has now become so ideologized that it all too often serves as a mystification of the real commitments behind the research at stake.

11 Reflections on the predicaments and politics of research on and with living historical subjects have already played an important role in, for example, feminist studies and anthropology, particularly ethnography. At least two problems are highlighted in these reflections. First, there is the rather awkward but seldom discussed concrete relation between researcher and researched as concrete subjects occupying differential social positions, more and less invested with power; second, there is the problem of the discursive form in which the cultures of "others" can be represented in non-objectifying (or, better, less objectifying) ways. See, e.g., Angela McRobbie (1982); James Clifford (1983); James Clifford and George Marcus (1986); Lila Abu-Lughold (1991). Researchers of media audiences have, as far as I know, generally been silent about these issues. However, for a thought-provoking engagement with the problem, see Valerie Walkerdine (1986).

12 See, for a more general overview of the interpretive or hermeneutic turn in the social sciences, Paul Rabinow and William M. Sullivan (1979). A more radical, Foucauldian conception of what they call "interpretive analytics" is developed by Hubert Dreyfuss and Paul Rabinow (1982).

13 A concise and useful criticism of empiricist mass communication research is offered by Robert C. Allen (1985: chapter 2).

14 Morley's main objection to the uses and gratifications approach concerns "its psychologistic problematic and its emphasis on individual differences of interpretation" (1983: 117). Elsewhere Morley even more emphatically expresses his distance from the uses and gratifications approach: "Any superficial resemblance between this study of television audience and the 'uses and gratifications' perspective in media research is misleading" (ibid.).

15 Note that in positivist epistemology intersubjectivity is considered as one of the main criteria for scientific "objectivity". One of the myths by which the institution of Science establishes itself is that scientific discourse is a process without a subject. Hence the normative rule that the concrete historical subject of scientific practice, the researcher, should be interchangeable with any other so as to erase all marks of idiosyncratic subjectivity.

16 All sorts of cautious qualifications as to the generalizability of such "findings", so routinely put forward in research reports so that the validity of the given typifications are said to be limited to certain demographic or subcultural categories (e.g. the urban working class), do not in principle affect this reification of experiential structures.

17 An image of the television audience as consisting of harmonious collectivities is suggested by Elihu Katz and Tamar Liebes, when they describe the process of decoding a television programme as an activity of "mutual aid" (1985). While this idea is useful in that it highlights the social nature of processes of decoding, it represses the possibility of tension, conflict and antagonism between different decodings within the same group.

18 For epistemological deconstructions of the category of "audience" as object of power/knowledge, see Briankle G. Chang (1987); Martin Allor (1988); Ang (1991).

References

Abu-Lughold, L. (1991) "Writing against culture", in R. G. Fox (ed.), *Recapturing Anthropology*, Santa Fe, NM: School of American Research Press.

Allen, R. C. (1985) *Speaking of Soap Operas*, Chapel Hill/London: University of North Carolina Press.

Allor, M. (1988) "Relocating the site of the audience", *Critical Studies in Mass Communication*, 5(3): 217–33.

Ang, I. (1985) *Watching Dallas: Soap Opera and the Melodramatic Imagination*, London/ New York: Methuen.

—— (1991) *Desperately Seeking the Audience*, London/New York: Routledge.

Blumler, J. G., Gurevitch, M. and Katz, E. (1985) "Reaching out: a future for gratifications research", in K. E. Rosengren, L. A. Wenner and P. Palmgreen (eds.), *Media Gratifications Research: Current Perspectives*, Beverly Hills, CA: Sage.

Brunsdon, C. (1986) "Women watching television", *MedieKultur*, 4.

Carey, J. (1983) "Introduction", in M. S. Mander (ed.), *Communications in Transition*, New York: Praeger.

Chang, B. G. (1987) "Deconstructing the audience: who are they and what do we know about them?", in M. L. McLaughlin (ed.), *Communication Yearbook*, 10, Beverly Hills CA: Sage.

Clifford, J. (1983) "On ethnographic authority", *Representations*, 1 (Spring) 2: 118–46.

Clifford, J. and Marcus, G. E. (eds.) (1986) *Writing Culture: The Poetics and Politics of Ethnography*, Berkeley/Los Angeles/London: University of California Press.

Dreyfuss, H. and Rabinow, P. (1982) *Michel Foucault: Beyond Structuralism and Hermeneutics*, Chicago: University of Chicago Press.

Fejes, F. (1984) "Critical communications research and media effects: the problem of the disappearing audience", *Media, Culture and Society*, 6: 219–32.

Fiske, J. (1987) "British cultural studies and television", in R. C. Allen (ed.), *Channels of Discourse*, Chapel Hill/London: University of North Carolina Press.

Foucault, M. (1979) *Discipline and Punishment*, trans. A. Sheridan, Harmondsworth: Penguin.

Grossberg, L. (1983) "Cultural studies revisited and revised", in M. S. Mander (ed.), *Communications in Transition*, New York: Praeger.

—— (1987) "Critical theory and the politics of empirical research", in M. Gurevitch and M. R. Levy (eds.), *Mass Communication Review Yearbook* 6, Newbury Park, CA: Sage.

Hall, S. (1980a) "Encoding/decoding", in S. Hall, D. Hobson, A. Lowe and P. Willis (eds.), *Culture, Media, Language*, London: Hutchinson.

—— (1980b) "Recent developments in theories of language and ideology: a critical note", in S. Hall, D. Hobson, A. Lowe and P. Willis (eds.), *Culture, Media, Language*, London: Hutchinson.

—— (1986a) "Introduction", in D. Morley, *Family Television: Cultural Power and Domestic Leisure*, London: Comedia/Routledge.

—— (1986b) "On postmodernism and articulation: an interview with Stuart Hall", *Journal of Communication Inquiry*, 10(2): 45–60.

—— (1986c) "The problem of ideology – Marxism without Guarantees", *Journal of Communication Inquiry*, 10(2): 5–27.

Hall, S., Hobson, D., Lowe, A. and Willis, P. (eds.) (1980) *Culture, Media, Language*, London: Hutchinson.

Hammersley, M. and Atkinson, P. (1983) *Ethnography: Principles in Practice*, London/New York: Tavistock.

Hobson, D. (1980) "Housewives and the mass media", in S. Hall, D. Hobson, A. Lowe and P. Willis (eds.), *Culture, Media, Language*, London: Hutchinson.

—— (1982) *Crossroads: The Drama of a Soap Opera*, London: Methuen.

Jensen, K. B. (1986) *Making Sense of the News*, Århus: University of Århus Press.

—— (1987) "Qualitative audience research: towards an integrative approach to reception", *Critical Studies in Mass Communication*, 4: 21–36.

Katz, E. and Liebes, T. (1985) "Mutual aid in the decoding of *Dallas*: preliminary notes from a cross-cultural study", in P. Drummond and R. Paterson (eds.), *Television in Transition*, London: BFI.

Levy, M. R. and Windahl, S. (1984) "Audience activity and gratifications: a conceptual clarification and exploration", *Communication Research*, 11: 51–78.

—— (1986) "The concept of audience activity", in K. E. Rosengren, L. Wenner and P. Palmgreen (eds.), *Media Gratifications Research*, Beverly Hills, CA: Sage.

Liebes, T. (1986) "On the convergence of theories of mass communication and literature regarding the role of the reader", paper presented to the Sixth International Conference on Culture and Communication, October.

Liebes, T. and Katz, E. (1990) *The Export of Meaning: Cross-Cultural Readings of Dallas*, New York: Oxford University Press.

Lindlof, T. R. (ed.) (1987) *Natural Audiences*, Norwood, NJ: Ablex Publishing Company.

Lindlof, T. R. and Meyer, T. P. (1987) "Mediated communication as ways of seeing, acting, and constructing culture: the tools and foundations of qualitative research", in T. R. Lindlof (ed.), *Natural Audiences*, Norwood, NJ: Ablex Publishing Company.

Lull, J. (1980) "The social uses of television", *Human Communication Research*, 6(3): 198–209.

—— (1986) "The naturalistic study of media use and youth culture", in K. E. Rosengren, L. A. Wenner and P. Palmgreen (eds.), *Media Gratifications Research: Current Perspectives*, Beverly Hills, CA: Sage.

—— (ed.) (1988) *World Families Watch Television*, Newbury Park, CA: Sage.

McRobbie, A. (1982) "The politics of feminist research: between talk, text and action", *Feminist Review*, 12 (October): 46–57.

Mills, C. W. (1970) *The Sociological Imagination*, Harmondsworth: Penguin.

—— (1986) "Introduction", in T. Modleski (ed.), *Studies in Entertainment: Critical Approaches to Mass Culture*, Bloomington/Indianapolis: Indiana University Press.

Morley, D. (1980a) *The "Nationwide" Audience: Structure and Decoding*, London: BFI.

—— (1980b) "Texts, readers, subjects", in S. Hall, D. Hobson, A. Lowe and P. Willis (eds.), *Culture, Media, Language*, London: Hutchinson.

—— (1981) "'The Nationwide Audience' – A Critical Postscript", *Screen Education*, 39 (Summer): 3–14.

—— (1983) "Cultural transformations: the politics of resistance", in H. Davies and P. Walton (eds.), *Language, Image, Media*, Oxford: Basil Blackwell.

—— (1986) *Family Television: Cultural Power and Domestic Leisure*, London: Comedia/Routledge.

Nightingale, V. (1986) "What's happening to audience research?", *Media Information Australia*, 39 (February): 21–2.

Pratt, M. L. (1986) "Interpretive strategies/strategic interpretations: on Anglo-American reader-response criticism", in J. Arac (ed.), *Postmodernism and Politics*, Minneapolis: University of Minnesota Press.

Rabinow, P. (1986) "Representations are social facts: modernity and post-modernity in anthropology", in J. Clifford and G. E. Marcus (eds.), *Writing Culture: The Poetics and Politics of
Ethnography*, Berkeley/Los Angeles/London: University of California Press.

Rabinow, P. and Sullivan, W. M. (eds.) (1979) *Interpretive Social Science*, Berkeley/Los
Angeles/London: University of California Press.

Radway, J. (1984) *Reading the Romance: Women, Patriarchy, and Popular Literature*, Chapel
Hill: University of North Carolina Press.

Rosengren, K. E. (1983) "Communication research: one paradigm, or four?", *Journal of
Communication*, 33: 185–207.

Schrøder, K. C. (1987) "Convergence of antagonistic traditions? the case of audience research", *European Journal of Communication*, 2(1): 7–31.

Slack, J. D. and Allor, M. (1983) "The Political and Epistemological Constituents of Critical
Communication Research", *Journal of Communication*, 33(3): 208–18.

Streeter, T. (1984) "An alternative approach to television research: developments in British
cultural studies in Birmingham", in W. D. Rowland Jr and B. Watkins (eds.), *Interpreting
Television*, Beverly Hills, CA: Sage.

Walkerdine, V. (1986) "Video replay: families, films and fantasy", in V. Burgin, J. Donald and
C. Kaplan (eds.), *Formations of Fantasy*, London/New York: Methuen.

Part III

Political Economy

Introduction to Part III

The essays selected in this section of the reader highlight some of the important developments in the study of the political economy of the mass media – now a robust school of critical communication scholarship, but one that broke sharply with prevailing academic trends when it emerged in the 1960s. Scholars such as Harold Innis, Ben Bagdikian, Dallas Smythe, and Herbert Schiller in North America, and Nicholas Garnham, Peter Golding, Graham Murdock, and others in Great Britain, began to consider issues of the nature and effects of the system of production of media and information. The focus in US-based political economy of communication tends to emphasize the economic side of the equation with focus on ownership, corporatization, and consumption, while in Britain there has been a spotlighting of the political dimension, with emphasis on public service broadcasting, the importance of state-supported and regulated communications, and the politics of broadcasting.[1]

Even today, the place of political economy in critical cultural studies is a contested area. Advocates of British cultural studies have been emphatic in positioning their work in opposition to political economy approaches, emphasizing that cultural studies originated and developed through the critique of the Marxist base/superstructure model and its "reductionist" economic determinism. Rather than affirm one side or another in this ongoing debate, we would suggest that the texts offered in KeyWorks can be used to overcome the divide between political economy and cultural analysis rather than pitting one side against the other.

The London-based communication scholar Nicholas Garnham attempted to counter charges of economic reductionism and determinism by offering a revision of the much-maligned base/superstructure model in an attempt to connect media and culture with developments within industrial capitalism, and thus rethink relations between economics and culture. In the essay included here (from 1986), Garnham's revamped model moves away from what he calls "the twin traps of economic reductionism and of the idealist autonomization of the ideological level" toward a more complex, relational design that seeks to address the issues raised by cultural studies regarding ideology and autonomy, while retaining its engagement with classical Marxism. His most significant intervention is the idea that cultural artifacts are social and materialist phenomena articulated to specific historical moments in capitalist development and thus variable and shifting. Garnham's core point is that the production and dissemination of mass culture is rooted in the material dimension: the pressing need, he writes, is "to distinguish between the media as processes of material production on the one hand, and as sites of ideological struggle on the other, and the relationship between those two levels or instances." That relationship, he argues, is vital to a complete understanding of contemporary culture. In his essay, Garnham offers a useful map of the terrain of the political economy of the mass media, areas of which are further explored in the other selections included here.[2]

Garnham's call for more concrete analysis of the economics of media production is illustrated by Canadian communications researcher Dallas Smythe's innovative reconceptualization of a political economy of the media which focuses on media consumption – but with a new critical twist. In Smythe's view, the audience of media in the act of consumption constitutes "exchange value." As Smythe points out, none of the literature on economics or political economy deals with "the role of the markets for audiences, produced by the mass media, bought and used by advertisers." Smythe revisions the audience's role in the system as unpaid work in the service of the advertising industry. He was among the first to examine the connection between the apparently nonadvertising content of the media with the paid advertisements, noting the symbiotic relationship between these two purportedly separate functions. Smythe's "audience consumption" is much different from the "active audience" of British cultural studies, and it is still a potent challenge to the myths and claims of an uncritical celebration of audience empowerment.

In *Manufacturing Consent: The Political Economy of the Mass Media* (1988), Noam Chomsky and Edward Herman present a more traditional analysis in their examination of the influence of market forces on media content, developing what they term a "propaganda model" of the news that connects corporate and state power in a regulatory nexus. Exploding prevailing myths of US journalism that rest on ideas of pluralism and free agency in a democratic society, Herman and Chomsky demonstrate that the free-market economics model of media leads inevitably to normative and narrow reportorial frames. In the chapter included here, they detail the five "filters" on which their propaganda model is based: media ownership and profit orientation, the influence of advertising, the role of experts, "flak" as a means of disciplining the media, and the rhetorical strategy of anticommunism.

Herman and Chomsky's central point is that the media tend to "marginalize dissent and allow the government and dominant private interests to get their messages across to the public" in ways that promote hegemonic constructions and suppress oppositional voices. Herman and Chomsky have together, individually, and with other collaborators, developed a large body of work critical of US foreign policy and the role of the media in promoting state and corporate interests.[3] Their work is highly controversial – it has been methodologically challenged, dismissed as derivative, and derided as a "conspiracy theory." We include a selection from *Manufacturing Consent* here in the belief that it can be viewed as a theoretical "key" that opens up a radical critique of the media by integrating certain significant themes into a critical heuristic that encourages readers to analyze the frames and discourse within which political events are presented by mainstream media. Most notably, Herman and Chomsky remind us that in a nominal democracy with serious inequities of wealth and power, the media can function to "manufacture consent" to policies that rarely represent the voices or interests of the majority of readers and citizens.

This idea is echoed in the work of Herbert Schiller, who also addresses an aspect of Nicholas Garnham's "map" of political economy – "the industrialization of culture," where culture is construed as an arm of the industrial-business sector, combined with the "corporate takeover of public expression" whereby corporations come to control the media, education, public spaces, and cultural creation. Teaching for some decades at the University of California at San Diego before his death in May 2000, Schiller was a pioneer in analyzing the role of media and culture in the world economy, forging theoretical linkages of communication and information with political economy. His early work – starting with 1969's *Mass Communications and American Empire* – revealed the role of the media industries in the military-industrial complex and the interconnected power structures that shape the function-ing and content of the mass media. The critical lens that Schiller applied to the examination of the role of popular culture in the spread of American corporate dominance illuminated the links between cultural and economic hegemonic processes.

We are including a text by Schiller in *KeyWorks* that contains an early critique of the emerging concept of globalization (1991). Recognizing that the collapse of the system of Soviet communism and triumph of the capitalist market system on a global scale represented a striking difference from the post-Second World War geopolitical system, Schiller insists that the expansion of the capitalist market is a metamorphosis and expansion of the system of economic domination and consumption. Arguing against the claim that the new global culture represents a field of diversity, heterogeneity, and difference, in an article titled "Not Yet the Post-Imperialist Era," Schiller argues that US media cultural dominance continues apace and that corporate transnationalism and not an amorphous "globalism" is the dominant economic force of the present moment.

The significance of Schiller's critique is that it does not allow the question of power to be elided. The underlying thesis of his analyses is humanitarian and politically progressive: he reminds us that people (especially in Asia, Latin America, and Africa) have vast unmet needs, yet these are consistently supplanted by the imperatives for profit of multinational US and European corporations. From this optic, the mass media are agents in an ongoing process of marginalization and displacement of people's genuine needs in favor of the consumption of global culture that narcotizes its audiences and induces conformity to the existing system.

The question of who constitutes those media audiences offers another glimpse into the politico-economic functioning of the cultural industries. Eileen Meehan revisits, from a feminist perspective, the concept of the "commodity audience" that underpins all media conglomer-ates's decision-making tactics. As she points out, the definition of the "commodity audience" for broadcasting corporations has nothing to do with the people watching television – or even the people purchasing the goods advertised on TV. Rather, the audience is a construc-tion whose definition is tied to controlling costs of production and advertising prices. But as she notes, "[S]ocietal divisions of labor based on gender, plus prejudicial assumptions about gender, [have] played a significant role in defining and differentiating the commodity audience." Unspoken racist and sexist biases shaped the delineation of the most desirable audience as white males between 18 and 34, a privileging that, as Meehan asserts, "makes little economic sense" and rests on an inherently contradictory stereotyping of gender roles, wherein men are assumed to be both higher wage-earners and frequent shoppers. The quest for this young, white, male audience affects the ideological content of programming and renders television an instrument of oppression of women, people of color, and the working classes.

The argument underpinning her position, and indeed that of the others in this section, is that there cannot be an engagement with cultural products without a consideration of the material realities of the context in which they are produced and consumed. Political economy is thus a vital part of any useful critique of the media and mass culture, offering a space in which the material and the symbolic can converge. But more importantly, it brings us back to the essentially progressive nature of media criticism, the understanding that real lives and real human conditions are impacted by these systems of cultural production and distribution, and that improving media and culture are a crucial part of social transformation.

Perhaps the French sociologist Pierre Bourdieu brought these issues to light most clearly in his wide-ranging body of work spanning the disciplines of anthropology, philosophy, art criticism, media studies, Marxist analysis, postmodernism, poststructuralism, and sociology. Bourdieu's central concern was with the relationship between class and cultural consumption, a relationship most intricately analyzed in his book *Distinction* (1984). For Bourdieu, the economy of cultural goods is motivated by an inherent "practical logic" that positions some aesthetic objects and their appreciation above others in a social and material hierarchy. But the ability to distinguish artistic merit, to exhibit an aesthetic sense or "good taste," is an outcome of class position – "of early immersion into a world of cultivated people, practices and objects" (Bourdieu, 1984, p. 75). The acquisition of such "cultural capital" plays out on a field of antagonistic struggle between classes, wherein elites defend themselves against the "vulgar" or "common" tastes of the working classes, and middle-class people seek to gain status while fending off the pretentiousness of the upper echelons as well as the perceived boorishness of the peasantry. Bourdieu makes a distinction between economic capital and cultural capital, but argues that they are deeply mutually imbricated; he sees "all practices, including those purporting to be disinterested or gratuitous, and hence non-economic, as economic practices directed towards the maximizing of material or symbolic profit" (Bourdieu, 1977, p. 183). In Bourdieu's view, the role of symbolic, or cultural, capital in society serves to legitimize and reproduce the material conditions of existence.

Political economy, then, involves a complex interaction between the economy, state, social movements, and popular participation in social and cultural processes. It encompasses analysis of production and consumption of media, goods, and services which incorporate individuals in a modern consumer and media society. Yet, political economies are historically specific, with differences between countries like the United States and Britain in terms of ownership patterns of the media and such things as television consumer practices. Important differences also exist between the Western and non-Western countries in terms of how they appropriate the products of Western transnational media industries and create their own local cultural forms and meanings. Moreover, globalization and new technologies are so dramatically altering the world economy that constant updating and rethinking of the political economy of communication is now more important than ever, as we show in Part VI of this Reader.

Notes

1   Of course, various practitioners of the political economy of communication have mixed their focus on the economic and political sides of the field. For useful overviews of the field of political economy of communication see Mosco (1996) and Calabrese and Sparks (2003).
2   Ironically, in some ways his vision of relating culture to an economic base in a nonreductionist way echoes the themes in Stuart Hall's theory of articulation; although these theoreticians (and other scholars in the two schools of thought) locate themselves in opposition to one another, their positions in some areas reveal more parallels than the writers themselves might care to admit.
3   Chomsky has published by now a small library of books criticizing US media and foreign policy; see *The Chomsky Reader* (1987) for selections and the documentary film *Manufacturing Consent* for an overview.

References

Bourdieu, Pierre (1977) *Outline of a Theory of Practice*, trans. R. Nice. Cambridge: Cambridge University Press.
—— (1984) *Distinction*, trans. R. Nice. Cambridge, MA: Harvard University Press.
Calabrese, Andrew and Sparks, Colin (eds.) (2003) *Toward a Political Economy of Culture: Capitalism and Communication in the Twenty-First Century*. Lanham, MD: Rowman & Littlefield.
Chomsky, Noam (1987) *The Chomsky Reader*, ed. J. Peck. New York: Pantheon.
Mosco, Vincent (1996) *The Political Economy of Communication*. London: Sage.

15

Contribution to a Political Economy of Mass-Communication

Nicholas Garnham

Introduction

The major modern communication systems are now so evidently key institutions in advanced capitalist societies that they require the same kind of attention, at least initially, that is given to the institutions of industrial production and distribution. Studies of the ownership and control of the capitalist press, the capitalist cinema, and capitalist and state capitalist radio and television interlock, historically and theoretically, with wider analysis of capitalist society, capitalist economy and the neo-capitalist state. Further, many of the same institutions require analysis in the context of modern imperialism and neo-colonialism, to which they are crucially relevant.

Over and above their empirical results, these analyses force theoretical revision of the formula of base and superstructure and of the definition of productive forces, in a social area in which large scale capitalist economic activity and cultural production are now inseparable. Unless this theoretical revision is made, even the best work of the radical and anti-capitalist empiricists is in the end overlaid or absorbed by the specific theoretical structures of bourgeois cultural sociology.

– R. Williams, 1977: 136

The purpose of this article is to support this call for a major revision within cultural theory, to explain why such a revision is necessary and to begin to explore some of its consequences.

From Nicholas Garnham,."Contribution to a political economy of mass-communication." In Richard Collins, et al. (eds.), *Media, Culture & Society: A Critical Reader*, pp. 9–32. London: Sage, 1986.

The fact that Williams's own call for this theoretical revision is hidden, gnomically, in a book of literary theory, and has thus not received the attention it deserves within mass-media research, is itself symptomatic of the existing ideological resistances to such a revision, not only within "bourgeois cultural theory", but also within what pass for Marxist alternatives. Indeed, I will go on to argue that in his effort to break with this all pervasive idealism, Williams, in formulating his own "cultural material-ism", has reacted by taking too materialist a stance.

What this article calls for, therefore, is the elaboration of a political economy of culture with a political economy of mass-communication taking its subsidiary place within that wider framework as the analysis of an important, but historically specific mode of the wider process of cultural production and reproduction. The need to elaborate such a political economy is intensely practical. It stems from actual changes in the structure of contemporary capitalism as they effect what has been dubbed "The Culture Industry" and the relationship of that industry to the State. Symptoms of the urgent political problems raised by these changes can be observed throughout the developed, capitalist world. They can be seen in a whole range of Government Reports and interventions of which, in Britain, the most obvious recent examples are the Royal Commission on the Press, the Annan Committee Report and the subsequent White Paper on Broadcasting, the Prime Minister's Working Party on the Film Industry and its proposals for a British Film Authority. They can be seen underlying the present dispute at Times Newspapers, the debate over the allocation of the fourth TV channel and the present financial problems of the BBC. Parallels to these reports, problems and debates can be found in all the member countries of OECD. At an international level, recent debates in UNESCO and the continuing diplomatic activity surrounding the concept of a New World Information Order can only be properly understood in this context. In the face of such developments most current mass-media research and theorizing is demonstrably inadequate.

Before moving on to examine some of the theoretical problems raised by this shift in research emphasis, let me give just one concrete example of the kind of informa-tion to which it gives privileged attention and why. During the last few weeks in Britain we have witnessed the failure of the Government to provide the BBC with adequate finance, a matter of great and ill-understood strategic significance in the whole development of British broadcasting and a subject that will repay substantive analysis from the perspective I am here outlining in a future edition of this journal. We have also witnessed the reactivation of the debate on TV and Violence by the publication of Dr Belson's study, a matter of undoubted importance to anyone concerned with mass-media research in Britain. Nonetheless, in my view the most significant development of the period was hidden away on the financial pages, namely the take-over of British Relay Wireless by the Electronic Rental Group, making ERG the second largest TV rental group in the UK. The significance of this take-over is that it was financed by a £10 million loan from ERG's controlling share-holder Philips Electronic. Now Philips is one of the firms involved in the audio-visual sector of the culture industry, in terms of total sales the world's third largest after General Electric and ITT and in terms of the proportion of its business related to electronic audio-visual manufacture and production it is the world leader by some way. The next phase of development of the culture industry will involve the attempt to develop and exploit the domestic entertainment market, particularly through video. Control of a rental network will be one of the keys to success in the competitive struggle for this market for two reasons: firstly, as has been true for domestic TV receivers, because the necessary hardware can only be sold in sufficient quantity on credit, but secondly, and here we have a crucial distinction between the new developments and the rental of TV receivers, because there is no internationally agreed technical standard for video recorders and players (whether of cassettes or discs) with the result that the decision on the choice of hardware limits the consumer's subsequent choice of software. Now since, of all the world's major electronic companies, only Philips is already in a position to develop co-ordinated software production (through such subsidiaries as Polygram and Phonogram) control of tied rental outlets for their hardware would give them a vertically integrated international cultural monopoly of a scale and type not yet seen in this sector and with cultural consequences over the medium term (10 to 20 years) that make our petty domestic disputes over the allocation of the fourth channel pale into insignificance (see *Financial Times*, 19 December 1978).

A Necessary Return to Fundamentals

Before returning to further concrete examples of the problems a political economy of mass-communication tries to analyse, it is necessary, precisely because of the dominance of idealism within the analysis of culture and of the mass-media, to make an unavoidable theoretical digression in order to base subsequent discussion firmly within the necessary historical materialist perspective. In asking for a shift within mass-media research towards historical materialism, one is asserting an order of priorities which is both a hierarchy of concrete historical and material determinants in the real world as well as an order of research priorities. That is to say, we are faced with the problem of understanding an actual historical process which itself concretely exhibits structurally ordered determinants within which material production is ultimately determinant, which is what makes our theory materialist, while at the same time there are a limited number of researchers with limited material resources among which I include time, who must thus choose, from within the complex totality of the historical social process, to examine those aspects of the process which are likely to lead to the clearest understanding of the dynamics of that process and through that understanding to its human control. It is this question of choice which underlies Marx's own mode of abstraction. Thus, in opposition to that post-Althusserian/Lacanian current which has been dangerously dominant within recent British Marxist research in the area of mass-media, a current of which *Screen* is a representative example, one asserts, not that the problem of subjectivity for instance is of no interest, but that it is of less interest than that of class or capital accumulation. Moreover, one is not asserting that such a hierarchy of historical determinants of research concerns is universal, that there is A theory of mass-media, but that they correspond to the actual historically specific hierarchy of a particular social formation. Or as Marx himself put it,

> my analytical method . . . does not start out from man, but from the analytically given social period.[1]

That is to say the economic is determinant under capitalism, because capitalism is a mode of social organization characterized by the domination of an abstract system of exchange relations. Further the particular relationship between the abstract and the concrete or between "phenomenal forms" and "real relations" or between ideas and matter, which is appropriate to historical materialism as a mode of analysis of capitalism, stems from the real relation between the abstract (exchange relations) and the concrete (individual lived experience, real labour etc.) within the social formation itself. In a social formation in which social relations were not abstracted into a relation of exchange a different theoretical relationship between the abstract and the concrete would hold.

Moreover, the abstract should not be opposed to the concrete, just as the phenomenal forms should not be opposed to the real relations. One is precisely a form of the other. That is to say, the exchange relation has a concrete material reality in the form of money, bills of exchange, credit cards, banks etc., but its mode of operation and with it the reproduction of the capitalist social formation depends upon its abstraction, the fact that it works "behind men's backs" and thus "can be determined with the precision of natural science". It can only be determined with such precision so long as it is a supra-individual social process. This is both a methodological and historical postulate. That is to say, the necessary condition for a capitalist social formation is the existence of a more or less universal domination of social relations by the exchange relation, i.e. a market economy. Wherever such domination is challenged (and we do not and never have seen, in this sense, an "ideal" capitalist social formation) by explicit political action, by human will and reason, the logic of capital is challenged. It is for this reason that the State is a necessarily contradictory form.

This leads us to the concept of ideology which so dominates our field of study and to the central problem within cultural theory, namely the base/superstructure relationship. The central postulate of historical materialism is that man as a biological organism must undertake a constant material exchange with nature and it is this exchange that is named labour. Within history the labour/nature relationship has become increasingly mediated through specific modes of production, thus making the links more difficult to analyse. Because of this difficulty the possibility of error and thus of ideology enters. But it remains a material fact that, ultimately, material production in this direct sense is determinate in that it is only the surplus produced by this labour that enables other forms of human activity to be pursued. Thus the superstructure remains dependent upon and determined by the base of material production in that very fundamental sense.

Clearly the greater the surplus to immediate physical reproductive needs the greater the autonomy of the superstructure and indeed the greater the possible variation and diversity within superstructural organization, always providing of course that the mode of material production is such as to guarantee the necessary surplus. In this important sense the superstructure/culture is and remains subordinate and secondary and the crucial questions are the relationship between, on the one hand, the mode of extraction and distribution of the material surplus, e.g. class relations and, on the other, the allocation of this material surplus within the superstructure, for instance, the problem of public expenditure among others. But while, historically, the super-structure has become more autonomous, there still remain direct, narrow material constraints upon individuals even within developed, industrial societies. Everyone has to eat and sleep and be maintained at a given body temperature in determinate temporal cycles. Thus, as Marx himself noted, every economy is an economy of time (Marx, 1973), which is why labour-time is so crucial an analytical concept. Cultural reproduction is still directly governed by these material determinants in the sense that the time and resources available to those who have to sell their labour power to capital, within labour-time constraints largely imposed by capital, remain limited and they still use the most significant proportion of their available time and material resources in order to ensure material, biological reproduction.

It is at this primary level both theoretically and actually that social being determines social consciousness. Thus economism, the concern for immediate physical survival and reproduction within the dominant relations of exchange is an immediate and rational response to the determinants of social being. What E. P. Thompson has recently dubbed "lumped bourgeois intellectuals" (Thompson, 1978) too easily forget this, both because their material conditions of existence are often less imme-diately determinate and also because of a guilty conscience concerning the subjective relationship of exploitation in which they stand *vis-à-vis* productive material labour.

The Material, the Economic and the Ideological

No political economy of culture can avoid discussion of the base/superstructure relationship, but in so doing it needs to avoid the twin traps of economic reduction-ism and of the idealist autonomization of the ideological level. The central problem with the base/superstructure metaphor as with the related culture/society dichotomy is that being a metaphor of polarity, essentially binary in form, it is unable adequately to deal with the number of distinctions that are necessary, in this instance between the material, the economic and the ideological. These should be seen not as three levels, but as analytically distinct, but coterminous moments both of concrete social practices and of concrete analysis. Furthermore, any political economy needs to hold constantly to the historicity of the specific articulations between these moments. There is a sense in which the base/superstructure metaphor always does imply a notion of expressive totality, a totality in which either the superstructure is express-ive of an economic base (under capitalism of a capitalist economic base) or, on the other hand, a tautological sense of expressive totality by which all phenomena of a social formation are expressive of that social formation. That is to say, the notion of expressive totality can be used either deterministically or relationally. For me at least it is clear that the analysis in *Capital* is of the latter type. That is to say what is being analysed is not, as Mandel (1975) has stressed, a social formation in equilibrium but in disequilibrium; an uncompleted at the time Marx wrote, and still incomplete, process of capitalist development, a development which was marked not by the total domination and determinacy of capitalist economic forms, an expressive totality in that sense, but on the contrary by a series of shifting relationships between the economic and other instances each interacting with the other in a process of uneven and contradictory development, so that the totality of the social formation at any historic moment was only expressive of the actual state of those shifting interrelationships.

Thus the pertinence or meaning of any analytical category, such as base and superstructure, expressing as it does a relationship, will shift as the historical reality it is used to explain shifts. Similarly, we could say that the purpose of a political economy of culture is to elucidate what Marx and Engels meant in *The German Ideology* by "control of the means of mental production", while stressing that the meaning that they gave to the term was quite clearly historical and therefore shifting and was never meant to be frozen into some simple dichotomy as it has so often been in subsequent Marxist writing. Further the political economy of mass-media is the analysis of a specific historical phase of this general development linked to historically distinct modalities of cultural production and reproduction.

In his discussion of base and superstructure in *Marxism and Literature*, Williams points out that, although, in stressing the determinacy of the base against bourgeois idealism, one version of Marxist cultural theory has been accused, both by bourgeois and Marxist critics, of "vulgar materialism", "the truth is that it was never materialist enough". And he continues:

> What any notion of a "self-subsistent order" suppresses is the material character of the productive forces which produce such a version of production. Indeed it is often a way of suppressing full consciousness of the very nature of such a society. If "production", in capitalist society, is the production of commodities for a market, then different but misleading terms are found for every other kind of production and productive force. What is most often suppressed is the direct material production of "politics". Yet any ruling class devotes a significant part of material production to establishing a political order. The social and political order which maintains a capitalist market, like the social and political struggle that created it, is necessarily a material production. From castles and palaces and churches to prisons and workhouses and schools; from weapons of war to a controlled press: any ruling class, in variable ways though always materially, produces a social and political order. These are never superstructural activities. They are the necessary material production within which an apparently self-subsistent mode of production can alone be carried on. The complexity of the process is especially remarkable in advanced capitalist societies, where it is wholly beside the point to isolate "production" and "industry" from the comparable material production of "defence", "law and order", "welfare", "entertainment" and "public opinion". In failing to grasp the material character of the production of a social and political order, this specialised (and bourgeois) materialism failed also, but even more conspicuously, to understand the material character of the production of a cultural order. The concept of the superstructure was then not a reduction but an evasion. (Williams, 1977: 92–3)

Williams's stress here on the materiality of the cultural process is a necessary correction to both bourgeois idealism and its post-Althusserian Marxist variants. But this formulation also suffers from a misleading reductionism by failing to distinguish between the material and the economic. It is in fact a materialist rather than a historical materialist formulation. The absence of this necessary distinction is contained in the apparently insignificant but crucial phrase "in variable ways though always materially", for it is precisely the specific articulations of these variable ways that characterize various stages of pre-capitalist and capitalist development, that characterize the shifting meaning of what Marx and Engels called "control of the means of mental production", shifts which it is the central purpose of a political economy of mass-communication to map and analyse. Certainly a licensed press and a commercial, "free" press are both material, but the economic differences between these two forms of "political" control are precisely what differentiates a capitalist from a pre-capitalist form. Similarly, the difference between the economic structure of private and public education constitutes within the same materiality, the substance of "political" struggle. While the materiality of politics, i.e. its maintenance out of the total social surplus of material production, is a general, universal phenomenon, the ways in which that surplus is extracted and distributed and the relation of that economic form to the political are historically distinct and specific, so that, at present, the matter of subsidies to political parties or to the Press becomes an object of "political" struggle to change economic forms and by so doing to change "political" structures.

Similarly, while Williams is correct to stress the materiality of all social practices it cannot be said, from an economic perspective, that it is wholly beside the point to isolate "production" and "industry" from the material production of "defence", etc., when what is often in question when considering the relation between these various social practices is not their shared materiality, but on the contrary their significantly different economic articulation, for instance the variance between those practices carried on by private capital for profit, the publication of a newspaper for instance, and those practices carried on by the State outside direct commodity production, e.g. the BBC or the State education system. To collapse all this into a general category of "material" production is precisely an "evasion", both of the differing and developing economic articulations between various forms of material production and also of the amount of cultural production and reproduction that takes place within the industrial sphere as narrowly defined, in the organizations of the labour process with its industrial psychologists, its labour relations experts, its time and motion study experts, its production engineers and its personnel managers, in the structures of employer paternalism, in the organization of the market itself, etc. To take one example of such an articulation one might hypothesize that the relationship between the male predominance in newspaper readership compared with TV was not unconnected with the contrast between the culture of work as against the culture of home and has important political consequences.

This confusion between the material and the economic is common and it is worth dwelling briefly on the nature of the distinction. Insofar as historical materialism is materialist, it is based upon the postulates that Williams outlines. But insofar as it is historical, it is concerned to analyse the specific and shifting modes of this funda-mental material relation, all of which are forms of that relation. In particular, it is postulated that any form of extended social relationship depends upon the extrac-tion and distribution of material surplus and the means by which this is achieved is thus the central determining characteristic of any social formation. Such modes of social production and exchange are cultural, hence the very real problem of making a society/culture differentiation without narrowing the definition of culture to include only those elements of social interaction which involve a secondary level of abstraction, namely the representation of concrete, material relations in *symbolic* forms. Thus we must distinguish two types of form, a social form which is a series of material relations that, insofar as they operate unconsciously, can be abstractly analysed and determined with the precision of natural science, and a cultural form which, while it entails a material support, is not itself material and which has an essentially mediated relationship with the material reality it represents. Indeed, there is an essential divide between these distinct formal realms, the existence of which allows ideology to enter, because it allows denial and the lie, both of which depend upon a relationship which is not determinant. However, this autonomy is bought at the cost of a loss of real or material effectivity. Cultural forms only become effective when they are translated into social forms which do have material effectivity. Thus there is a constant dialectic at the cultural level between autonomy and effectivity and it is at the level of social effectivity that material production is ultimately determinant.

However, to return to the level of social forms, the economic is a specific histor-ical form of the social relations of production and distribution. It is the form these relations take in a social formation within which commodity exchange is dominant. Thus, it is possible to argue that the economic is superstructural in relation to the material base or structure, that it could in fact be seen as the dominant level of the superstructure. For what Marx argues in *Capital* is that the real historical transition to capitalism involves a move from a system of social relations and domination based upon the direct physical control of landed property and people to one based upon the increasingly indirect control through commodity exchange and, in particular, through the exchange of the commodity of labour power, and that this real histor-ical process is a real process of social abstraction which thus requires appropriate theoretical abstraction for its analysis. It is because the economic is the most abstract and fundamental form of the social relation within capitalism that it is primary both theoretically and actually, but as a historically specific representation of a predetermin-ate material relationship.

It is the real existence of this abstract economic level of extended commodity production that allows for the development of an increasing division of labour and thus for the development of the specific superstructural forms of capitalism. Thus the relative autonomy of the superstructure is a real and increasingly central charac-teristic of capitalism, but it is itself determined at the level of the economic and ultimately it is a form, at two levels of mediation, of a material relation which also remains determinant in and through the economic.

The Inadequacies of Existing Marxist Theory

From this perspective available historical materialist theories are inadequate to deal with the real practical challenges they face largely because they offer reductionist explanations which favour either a simple economic determinism or an ideological autonomy, thus failing to analyse and explain precisely that which makes the object of analysis centrally significant, namely the relationship between the economic and the ideological. Thus we are offered the following.

(a)   An unproblematic acceptance of the base/superstructure model drawn from a partial reading of *The German Ideology* which, unargued, simply states that the mass-media are ideological tools of ruling-class domination either through direct ownership or, as in the case of broadcasting, via ruling-class control of the State. Such a position neglects both the specific effects of subordinating cultural production and reproduction to the general logic of capitalist commodity production and the specificities of the varying and shifting relationships between economic, ideological and political levels within actual concrete historical moments. Miliband in *Marxism and Politics* expresses a classic version of this theory:

> Whatever else the immense output of the mass media is intended to achieve, it is *also* intended to help prevent the development of class-consciousness in the working class and to reduce as much as possible any hankering it might have for a radical alternative to capitalism. The ways in which this is attempted are endlessly different; and the degree of success achieved varies considerably from country to country and from one period to another – there are other influences at work. But the fact remains that "the class which has the means of material production at its disposal" does have, "control at the same time of the means of mental production": and that it does seek to use them for the weakening of opposition to the established order. Nor is the point much affected by the fact that the state in almost all capitalist countries "owns" the radio and television – its purpose is identical. (Miliband, 1977: 50)

It should be noted here that for all its philosophical sophistication the Althusserian position on ISA represents little if any advance on this position, as indeed Simon Clarke (1977) has correctly noted with respect to the Miliband/Poulantzas controversy.

(b)   Secondly, and in partial reaction against this classic Marxist explanation of the role of the mass-media, we are offered an elaboration of the relative autonomy of the superstructure and within the superstructure of the ideological and political levels. All such theories in their effort to reject economism or, as Althusser puts it, "the idea of a 'pure and simple' non-overdetermined contradiction", to a greater or lesser extent have also removed economic determinacy, i.e. as Althusser again puts it, in such theories "the lonely hour of the 'last instance' never comes" (Althusser, 1969: 113). This general position has rightly developed the insights of the Frankfurt School into the importance of the superstructure and of mediation, while damagingly neglecting a crucial component of the Frankfurt School's original position, namely the fact that under monopoly capitalism the superstructure becomes precisely industrialized; it is invaded by the base and the base/superstructure distinction breaks down but via a collapse into the base rather than, as is the tendency with the post-Althusserian position, via the transformation of the base into another autonomous superstructural discourse.

> In our age the objective social tendency is incarnate in the hidden subjective purpose of company directors, the foremost among whom are in the most powerful sectors of industry – steel, petroleum, electricity and chemicals. Culture monopolies are weak and dependant in comparison. They cannot afford to neglect their appeasement of the real holders of power if their sphere of activity in mass-society is not to undergo a series of purges. (Adorno and Horkheimer, 1977: 351)

The truth of this original insight is demonstrated monthly as firms in the cultural sector are absorbed into large industrial conglomerates and brought under the sway of their business logic. Indeed, the real weakness of the Frankfurt School's original position was not their failure to realize the importance of the base or the economic, but insufficiently to take account of the economically contradictory nature of the process they observed and thus to see the industrialization of culture as unproblematic and irresistible. Those who have come after, while rightly criticizing the Frankfurt School for its absence of concrete class analysis, an absence stemming precisely from their insufficiently nuanced analysis of the economic level, in developing their theories of the effectivity of the superstructure have, ironically, massively compounded the original error.

The most distinguished exponent of the post-Althusserian position in Britain, Stuart Hall, in his essay "Culture, the Media and the Ideological Effect" (Curran et al., 1977), recognizes that there is a decisive relationship between the growth of the mass-media and "everything that we now understand as characterizing 'monopoly capitalism'", but at the same time refuses an analysis of this decisive relationship claiming that "these aspects of the growth and expansion of the media historically have to be left to one side by the exclusive attention given here to media as 'ideological apparatuses'." Murdoch and Golding (1979) rightly criticize Hall and claim that "on the contrary the ways in which the mass-media function as 'ideological apparatuses' can only be adequately understood when they are systematically related to their position as large scale commercial enterprises in a capitalist economic system and if these relations are examined historically". Hall's failure to do this leads him to explain the ideological effect in terms of pre-existent and ideologically predetermined communicators or encoders choosing from a pre-existent and ideologically predetermined set of codes so that there is a systematic tendency of the media to reproduce the ideological field of society in such a way as to reproduce also its structure of domination. That is to say he offers the description of an ideological process, but not an explanation of why or how it takes place, except in tautological terms.

Moreover, he is led by his mode of analysis, as again Murdoch and Golding rightly point out, to favour a specific and atypical instance of media practice, namely public service broadcasting and indeed within that, an atypical form, namely informational broadcasting. While stressing that the production of the ideological effect requires work and struggle, his mode of analysis does not allow him to deal, for instance, with an important and developing moment in that struggle within the Press caused by a contradiction between the crucial underpinning idea of a "free press" and the economic pressures towards monopoly or the relationship precisely between the ideological effect of broadcasting and the fact that it is perceived by its audience to be under State control as opposed to the biased privately owned press.

(c)   A further elaboration of the post-Althusserian position, popular within film studies leads in its elaboration of a theory of autonomous discourses effectively to an evacuation of the field of historical materialism, whatever its materialistic rhetoric, placing its determinacy in the last instance on the unconscious as theorized within an essentially idealist, indeed Platonist, problematic. Such idiocies need detain us no further.[2]

(d)   Finally, Dallas Smythe, identifying the excessive stress on the autonomy of the ideological level within Western Marxism as its "Blind-spot", rightly redirects our attention away from the mass-media as ideological apparatuses and back to their economic function within capitalism. But in so doing, he proposes an extreme reductionist theory. For Smythe, any political economy of mass-media must be based upon an analysis of its commodity form and for him the commodity form specific to the mass-media is the Audience, that is to say, for Smythe, the crucial function of the mass-media is not to sell packages of ideology to consumers, but audiences to advertisers. Now it is undoubtedly important to focus attention upon the ways in which the mass-media manufacture and sell audiences as one moment in the complex circuit of capital that structures the operation of the mass-media economically. Moreover, to stress this moment as the crucial one and to concentrate on the mass-media's directly functional role for capital as advertising vehicles is undoubtedly a more plausible reflection of reality in the North American context than it would be in Europe. However, Smythe's theory misunderstands the function of the commodity form as an abstraction within Marxist economic theory and thus neglects the relationship between specific forms of the commodity, in this case the audience, and the commodity form in general. As a result, his theory lacks any sense of contradiction, failing to account for the function of those cultural commodities directly exchanged, failing to account for the role of the State, failing sufficiently to elaborate the function for capital of advertising itself and, perhaps most crucially of all, failing to relate the process of audience production by the mass-media to determinants of class and to class-struggle.[3]

The Ideological Level

What problems is it, then, that a political economy of mass-communication attempts to analyse? The research perspective, whose theoretical and historical basis I have briefly outlined, attempts to shift attention away from the conception of the mass-media as

ISAs and sees them first as economic entities with both a direct economic role as creators of surplus value through commodity production and exchange and an indirect role, through advertising, in the creation of surplus value within other sectors of commodity production. Indeed, a political economy of mass-communication in part chooses its object of study precisely because it offers a challenge to the Althusser/ Poulantzas theorization of the social formation as structured into the relatively autonomous levels of the economic, the ideological and the political. For the major institutions of mass-communication, the press and broadcasting, although, as will be analysed later, displaying notable differences of articulation, both at the same time display the close inter-weaving within concrete institutions and within their specific commodity forms of the economic, the ideological and the political. When we buy a newspaper we participate simultaneously in an economic exchange, in subjection to or reaction against an ideological formation and often in a quite specific act of political identification or at least involvement. We also know from historical analysis of the development of the press that the nature of the political involvement is quite specifically economically conditioned. Similarly, TV news is economically determined within commodity production in general, performs an ideological function and explicitly operates within politics, in terms of balance, etc.

While accepting that the mass media can be and are politically and ideologically over-determined within many specific conjunctures, a political economy, as I understand it, rests upon ultimate determination by the economic (a level that itself always remains problematic and to be defined in the process of analysis).

Indeed, one of the key features of the mass media within monopoly capitalism has been the exercise of political, and ideological domination through the economic.[4] What concerns us in fact is firstly to stress, from the analytical perspective, the validity of the base/superstructure model while at the same time pointing to and analysing the ways in which the development of monopoly capitalism has industrialized the superstructure. Indeed Marx's own central insight into the capitalist mode of production stressed its generalizing, abstracting drive; the pressure to reduce everything to the equivalence of exchange value.

Before going on to examine the economic level and its specific articulations within the cultural sphere, let us look at the relationship between the material conditions of production (not, as we have seen, to be confused with the economic far less the capitalist modes of such production, which are specific forms) on the one hand and ideological forms on the other. That is to say how do we relate Williams's correct stress, within the limits indicated, upon the materiality of cultural production, to Marx's famous distinction "between the material transformations of the economic conditions of production, which can be determined with the precision of natural science, and the legal, political, aesthetic or philosophic – in short, ideological – forms in which men become conscious of this conflict and fight it out" (Marx, 1859).

What the quotation from Marx underlines is the importance of the distinction between the two levels, a distinction focused upon the difference between the *unconscious* forces governing material production "beyond our will", etc. and the conscious form of ideology. If we follow the Althusserians and make ideology an unconscious process this crucial distinction is lost.

As far as the mass-media specifically are concerned this distinction points to the need to distinguish between the media as processes of material production (whether capitalist or not is precisely a question for analysis) on the one hand, and as sites of ideological struggle on the other and the relationship between those two levels or instances.

There are here two distinctions to be made. I think we can liken ideological practice to what Marx called the "real labour process".

> Looking at the process of production from its real side, i.e. as a process which creates new use-values by performing useful labour with existing use-values, we find it to be a *real labour process*. As such its element, its conceptually specific components, are those of the labour process itself, of any labour process, irrespective of the mode of production or the stage of economic development in which they find themselves. (Marx, 1976)

That is to say the processes of consciousness and of representation, for instance, language, are real processes by which human beings socially appropriate their environment (nature) which pre-exist and continue to exist within specifically capitalist modes of ideological production and indeed upon which these capitalist modes rest.

The materiality of such ideological production *qua* ideology rests upon the fact that consciousness is a human transformation of "real" experience, it is in that sense "practical knowledge". Clearly therefore, the relationship of any particular instance of ideological production to the totality of social experience will depend upon an analysis of the experiential position of the human consciousness in question, e.g. the conventional and simple definition of class consciousness as based upon the direct experience of a given position within the capital/labour relationship. Of course in any complex society such direct experience becomes highly mediated both diachronically and synchronically. But its translation into forms of representation is nonetheless a process of consciousness which is different from and in its forms has no necessary correspondence with, the economic processes to which it relates or of which it is a representation. Indeed as a representation it is precisely by definition distinct from those processes which it represents.

Moreover ideological forms can never be simply collapsed into a system of exchange values, i.e. the specifically capitalist mode of production, precisely because ideological forms, forms of consciousness, are concerned with difference, with distinction; they are by definition heterogeneous (as Marx himself remarked when discussing the limited possibilities for the subsumption of ideological production under capitalism, "I want the doctor and not his errand boy"). Whereas exchange value is precisely the realm of equivalence.[5]

Material and Mental Production

In order to study the connection between intellectual and material production it is above all essential to conceive the latter in its determined historical form and not as a general category. For example, there corresponds to the capitalist mode of production a type of intellectual production quite different from that which corresponded to the mediaeval mode of production. Unless material production itself is understood in its specific historical form, it is impossible to grasp the characteristics of the intellectual production which corresponds to it or the reciprocal action between the two.

– Marx, 1963: 96–7

We need to lay stress on and distinguish two distinct but related moments in a historical materialist analysis of intellectual production.

(a)   Culture as a superstructural phenomenon in relation to non-cultural modes of material production, i.e. on the one hand, the dominant or hegemonic cultural production paid for out of capitalist *revenue* and, on the other, a subordinate working class or oppositional culture paid for out of wages. Cultural production in this sense and its articulations with the sphere of material production involves one specific interpretation of the meaning in *The German Ideology* of "control of the means of mental production", i.e. through the direct payment of ideologists and the necessary maintenance of the physical instruments of their ideological production. It is within that analytical perspective that we need to analyse the historical development of the "historically specific needs" of the working class and their sustenance of "organic intellectuals" and of specific instruments of cultural production such as trade-unions.

(b)   Culture as part of material production itself, directly subordinate to or at least in a closely determined articulation with the laws of development of capital. This is both a latter historical phase, part of developing monopoly capitalism, the phenomenon dubbed "the industrialization of culture", but it also lives alongside the other moment and in specific instances we need to analyse the interrelationship between these two distinct modes of intellectual production within intellectual production (Culture in its narrow sense) in general.

What, in general, has been lost in Marxist studies of the mass media is the precise historical elaboration of what Marx and Engels meant in *The German Ideology* by "control of the means of mental production".

In general it is clear, I think, in *The German Ideology* that, reflecting the contemporary stage of capitalist development, Marx and Engels were concerned with the payment of ideologists, of intellectuals, out of capitalist revenue. It is this perspective that Raymond Williams picks up in the passage already cited. That is to say they rightly saw that superstructural activities require a cohort of mental workers who were not directly economically or materially productive and thus whose price of reproduction must be borne by the sphere of material production. Since under capitalism it was capitalists who were extracting this surplus, it was they who could redistribute this surplus into superstructural activities of their choosing and by so doing exert direct economic pressures on the ideologists who were their hired servants.

The creation of surplus labour on the one side corresponds to the creation of minus labour, relative idleness (or non-productive labour at best) on the other. This goes without saying as regards capital itself; but holds then also for the classes with which it shares; hence of paupers, flunkeys, lick-spittles, etc. living from the surplus product, in short, the whole train of retainers; the part of the *servant* class which lives not from capital but from revenue. (Marx, 1973: 401)

This direct relationship remains important and should not be forgotten. That is to say the working class also developed, out of its wages, a subordinate or counter culture with its own "organic intellectuals" such as paid trade-union officials, co-operative organizers, journalists, etc., but the surplus available for this purpose was exiguous both really and comparatively, so that this direct ideological power was decisively weighted in favour of capital and remains so. Compare a small organization like Counter Information Services with the public relations and research investment of a major company. Look at the way in which large companies manipulate the legal system by their ability to sustain expensive, long drawn out actions (e.g. the Thalidomide case). Look at the way media research itself has been and is significantly influenced by the flow of funds from vested commercial interests.

There now exists of course, as the division of labour has developed further, a more mediated version of this employment of ideologists out of revenue, namely, as Bourdieu has analysed, the creation of a subordinate fraction of the capitalist class who possess cultural capital (Bourdieu and Passeron, 1977). Just as younger sons of the aristocracy went into Church and army, so now a section of the capitalist class occupies key positions in the cultural sector. The class origins of ideological workers remains an important but neglected aspect of media analysis. This does not of course mean that such people necessarily reproduce ruling class ideology (see Engels and William Morris for obvious counter-examples). It does mean that there is a structural tendency so to do.

Neglect of this aspect of direct economic control of ideologists is reflected in current discussion of the ideological role of the media where there is much sophisticated discussion of professionalization, of hierarchies of discourse, of hegemonic and subordinate codes, etc. discussions which often serve to mask a reality which is ever present to those actually working in the media, namely the possibility of losing one's job. This economic reality is of course often internalized by both employee and employer in the form of the ideologies of professionalism or managerialism but it remains nonetheless potent for that, indeed is the underpinning which professionalism requires. Once again, this was a fact that Adorno and Horkheimer did not make the mistake of forgetting:

Under the private culture monopoly it is a fact that "tyranny leaves the body free and directs its attack at the soul". The ruler no longer says, "You must think as I do, or die". He says, "You are free not to think as I do, your life, your property, everything shall remain yours, but from this day on you are a stranger among us". Not to conform means to be rendered powerless, economically and therefore, spiritually – to be "self-employed". When the outsider is excluded from the concern, he can only too easily be accused of incompetence. Whereas today in material production the mechanism of supply and demand is disintegrating in the superstructure it still operates as a check in the ruler's favour.[6]

The second moment, upon which of course increasingly in the actual historical development the former moment has come to depend, is the actual control by capital within the process of commodity production of the means of cultural production. This moment was clearly under-developed at the time when *The German Ideology* was written but, while not entirely superceding the other moment as I have indicated, it is this moment that has become crucial for an analysis of cultural reproduction under monopoly capitalism.[7] Within the sphere of cultural production the development of specifically economic, industrial forms was in part possible precisely because of the effect of the other moment, i.e. working class powers of cultural resistance were weakened. A good example of this is R. Williams's suggestion that the popular success of ITV and of the general invasion of American commercialized cultural forms was a reaction on the part of the working class to the liberating overthrow of a particular hegemonic cultural formation represented by the BBC. It is in particular on the implications of this second moment that I wish to concentrate, i.e. the effects of the imposition of capital logic upon cultural production.

As I have indicated there has been a tendency to see such an imposition as ideologically non-contradictory. One must stress at the outset that this is not so. Because capital controls the means of cultural production in the sense that the production and exchange of cultural commodities become the dominant forms of cultural relationship, it does not follow that these cultural commodities will necessarily support, either in their explicit content or in their mode of cultural appropriation, the dominant ideology. Indeed as Terry Lovell has recently stressed and as, once again, Adorno and Horkheimer made clear, the cultural commodity possesses an inherent contradiction, a contradiction which, as with the other contradictions within the capitalist mode of production, may be profoundly subversive.[8] Whether it is or not depends upon a concrete analysis of a specific conjuncture. Before turning to the general implications of the proposition that one definition of the control of the means of mental production is the take-over of large areas of cultural production and reproduction by capitalist commodity production, what the proposition leads one to question is that stress on intentionality which we find in theories such as that of Miliband. It is quite clear in Marx's analysis of *Capital* that he wished to distinguish firmly between the logic of capital and the intention of individual capitalists, even at the economic, let alone the ideological, level:

> The fact that baking, shoemaking, etc. are only just being put on a capitalist basis in England is entirely due to the circumstances that English capital cherished feudal preconceptions of "respectability". It was "respectable" to sell Negroes into slavery, but it was not respectable to make sausages, shoes or bread. (Marx, 1976: 1014, footnote)

It is perhaps worth noting in passing that this characteristic of British capital still operates with respect to the media, which still carry a certain bohemian, mountebank and marginal reputation. Hence the characteristics of the particular capitals who started ITV for instance or who developed the British film industry in the 1930s or the role of colonial capital via Beaverbrook and Murdoch in the British Press. Such attitudes still affect the Tory party in its ambivalent relation to commercial broadcasting.

> The function fulfilled by the capitalist is no more than the function of capital – viz. the valorization of value by absorbing living labour – executed *consciously* and *willingly*. The capitalist functions only as personified capital, capital as a person, just as the worker is no more than *labour* personified. (Marx, 1976: 989)

What this quotation points to is the importance of not viewing capitalists, for analytical purposes, as unified subjects. That is to say a given person or group can only be described as capitalist in those moments when s/he or they are acting in conscious and willed accord with the logic of capital accumulation. Thus there may well be many such conscious, willed actions, never mind unconscious actions, that are contradictory to the logic of capital, of course always within determinate limits. There may be therefore a clear divergence between the functions of capital within the material process of mental production and the conscious, willed intentions of the capitalist or of their ideologues. We cannot predict *a priori* which at any time will be predominant, e.g. how long a Harmsworth, a Beaverbrook or a Thomson will keep a loss-making newspaper going for reasons of social prestige or political power, although clearly the outer limits of such possibilities of deviation by the individual capitalist will be determined by the norms of capital's logic.

There is then, and this cannot be sufficiently stressed, no necessary coincidence between the effects of the capitalist process proper and the ideological needs of the dominant class. On the contrary the entire thesis of capital points to the opposite conclusion.

This, for instance, affects assumptions concerning the relationship between capital and the State. To take one example, the proportion of the budget of the COI that has to be devoted to paid access to the media, i.e. the use of paid advertising for Government propaganda or information, has risen in the last decade from 20 per cent to 50 per cent. Such evidence can be interpreted in two ways. Either there is an observable conflict between the ideological needs of the State and the accumulation process within the media sector (leaving aside the question of whether the State is in fact the representative of capital or of the dominant class and therefore whether such a conflict would represent a contradiction between the economic and ideological needs of that class in general or whether it represents a contradiction between the ideological needs of capital in general versus the economic needs of a class fraction who control the media sector). Alternatively, this evidence can be interpreted to show the increasing sway of capitalist logic over the political and ideological level, i.e. forcing it to work increasingly through direct exchange relations within the economic.

This question of intentionality within ideological production is, of course, central to the media debate, within both the bourgeois and Marxist problematic. That is to say one argument runs, for instance the Frankfurt School tradition, that the mass media are important because monopoly capitalism has moved from direct coercion of the working class, for instance within the labour process, to ideological coercion as its preferred method of domination and the mass-media or ISA's are crucial in this process.

But do we in fact require this shift onto the terrain of ideology in order to explain the absence of direct coercion. Marx himself on the contrary saw the avoidance of such coercion as central to the economic mechanism of capitalism. That is to say the abstraction of exchange value, the wage-form, etc. were in themselves quite powerful enough to explain the dominance of capital and indeed that this non-coercive dominance was both historically necessary and progressive. Bourdieu has developed this general proposition.[9]

> Thus at the level of material production, of the life process in the realm of the social – for that is what the process of production is – we find the *same* situation that we find in *religion* at the ideological level, namely the inversion of subject into object and vice-versa. Viewed *historically* this inversion is the indispensable transition without which wealth as such, i.e. the relentless productive forces of social labour, which alone can form the material base of a free human society, could not possibly be created by force at the expense of the majority. (Marx, 1976: 990)

Mental Production and Capitalist Commodity Production

Let us now turn back to look at mental production, of which the mass media are an example, as processes of capitalist production and at the implications for our modes of social communication of the subsumption by capital of the real forms of ideological production.

This needs to be looked at historically, i.e. unlike the capital logic or capital derivation school we must not see capitalism as a mode of production which arrives *sui generis* and then sprouts a social formation like dragon's teeth. It is rather a specific form which grew within a pre-existing social formation and is involved in a process of expansion and conquest of non-capitalist sectors, a process which is incomplete and contradictory. This process of expansion involves both the subsumption of other areas of material production and pre-capitalist forms of economic organisation and also of non-economic activity under the sway of the economic in its capitalist form.

When examining mass communication within predominantly capitalist social formations we must not make the mistake of assuming that they are therefore necessarily capitalist, i.e. we cannot make the easy elision Miliband makes between those sectors controlled by private capital and those controlled by the State. Nor can we assume that all non-State sectors are in fact capitalist. Indeed the relationship between pre-capitalist and capitalist forms within the media sector is a significant feature both economically and ideologically, i.e. the relationship between notions of creative freedom, freedom of the Press, the Fourth Channel debate, community communication, etc. This relationship significantly determines the forms of the struggle within the media over the labour process.

Thus artisanal modes of labour organization ranging from individual craft production, i.e. the authorship of a book, to the small group, i.e. the independent film company or record producer, remain common and important within the cultural sphere. Such residues have been the focus for struggle against the logic of capital and have produced a powerful anti-economic cultural ideology (see the whole culture/society tradition). Nonetheless in certain instances such artisanal organization may be functional for capital so long as capital controls the means of mass reproduction of the authorial product and of the means of mass distribution, because it ensures the necessary production of a range of heterogeneous cultural artefacts from which capital can choose for further exploitation without capital having to bear the risks and overheads for this production which are born directly by labour. Indeed, the ideology of creative freedom can be used by capital to keep their labour force divided and weak and with no control over the strategic moments of the total labour process. Thus, for instance, while the Open Broadcasting Authority will be fought for by cultural workers under the banner of creative freedom and against the apparent interests of capital in the form of ITV, such a structure of small-scale freelance production, if it were to be realized, would be more functional for capital in general than an extension of the present structure, because it would open British broadcasting more fully both to advertising and to the pressures of the international market.[10]

Nor must we make the mistake of assuming an easy equation between private ownership and capitalism.

> Where capital still appears only in its elementary forms such as commodities . . . or money, the capitalist manifests himself in the already familiar character of the owner of money or commodities. But such a person is no more a capitalist in himself than money or commodities are capital in themselves. They become translated into capital only in certain specific circumstances and their owners likewise become capitalist only when these circumstances obtain. (Marx, 1976: 976)

What then are these circumstances? The central characteristic of capital is growth or accumulation.

> In itself the sum of money may only be defined as capital if it is employed, spent, with the aim of increasing it, if it is spent expressly in order to increase it. In the case of the sum of value or money this phenomenon is its destiny, its inner law, its tendency, while to the capitalist, i.e. the owner of the sum of money, in whose hands it shall acquire its function, it appears as intention, purpose. (Marx, 1976: 976)

Thus to examine the specifically capitalist mode of media production we need to see the ways in which capital uses the real process of media production in order to increase its value, in order to grow, and the barriers which are placed in the way of this process either by the inherent contradictions of the process itself or by external forces.

At a minimum in order to accumulate capital must bring living labour into the production process by exchanging in the sphere of circulation through the wage bargain. It must combine this living labour in a determinate manner with objectified labour as means of production (raw materials and instruments) in the production of a commodity in the exchange of which surplus value will be realized.

In a fully constituted capitalist mode based upon relative surplus value and competition between capitals this process of growth requires ever increased productivity and ever widening markets.

Historically the sphere of mental production or non-material production presented and continues to present important barriers to this process and the forms and dynamics of the mass media can in part be understood as resulting from a continuous attempt to surmount those barriers and from the concretely various successes and failures of this attempt.

We thus start from the historical materialist assumption that the development of capitalism or the capitalist mode of production is:

(a)   a contradictory process;
(b)   not yet complete.

The contradictory nature of the process is in part intrinsic, i.e. the conflict between capital and labour, the conflict between capital accumulation and the socialization of the forces and relations of production, the conflict between the drive to accumulate through the extraction of relative surplus value and labour power as the creator of surplus value, a contradiction expressed in the tendency of the rate of profit to fall.

In part the contradictions are extrinsic, that is to say related precisely to the relationship between developing capitalism and the non-capitalist areas of the social formation. The necessary expansion of the valorization process is not a process of automatic expansion; it comes up against social and political barriers; it needs to conquer physical barriers, e.g. communication and transport; it requires the necessary accumulation of capital, etc.

We see these contradictions in the field of mass-media:

(a)   in resistances both actual and ideological to the industrialization of the artisanal modes of cultural production;
(b)   in the conflicts between national and international capitals, sometimes mediated through the State and sometimes direct, e.g. the split in the Tory party over the original introduction of commercial broadcasting – or the developing struggle over national versus supra-national control of European satellite broadcasting – or the existence of quotas on the importation of foreign film and TV material;
(c)   growing Third World demand for a New World Information Order.

The problem with cultural and informational goods is that, because their use value is almost limitless, i.e. cannot be destroyed or consumed by use, it is extremely difficult to attach an exchange value to them. They are in fact, in general, classic public goods. What we are considering is what Marx called "non-material production". Marx discusses such production in the context of a discussion of the distinction between productive and non-productive labour (whether such a distinction can be maintained and, if so, its analytical significance, is a matter of general importance within the field of the political economy of culture which we cannot pursue further here). In brief, Marx clearly foresaw difficulties in subsuming non-material production under capitalism. He identified two possible forms of such production:

> (1) It results in commodities which exist separately from the producer, i.e. they can circulate in the interval between production and consumption as commodities, e.g. books, paintings and all products of art as distinct from the artistic achievement of the practising artist. Here capitalist production is possible only within very narrow limits. Apart from such cases as, say, sculptors who employ assistants, these people (where they are not independent) mainly work for merchants capital, e.g. booksellers, a pattern that is only transitional in itself and can only lead to a capitalist mode of production in the formal sense. Nor is the position altered by the fact that exploitation is at its greatest precisely in these transitional forms.
>
> (2) The product is not separable from the act of producing. Here too the capitalist mode of production occurs only on a limited scale and in the nature of the case it can only operate in certain areas (I want the doctor not his errand boy). For example, in teaching institutions the teacher can be no more than wage-labour for the entrepreneur of the learning factory. Such peripheral phenomena can be ignored when considering capitalist production as a whole. (Marx, 1976: 1047–8)

This passage would be worth lengthy analysis. At this stage I would only like to point to the following.

(a) The relevance of example (1) for the debate between Marcuse and Benjamin concerning the role of the aura of a work of art and the effect on that aura of the attempt to subject culture production to at least the forces of capitalist production.[11]

(b) The need to look, with reference to the observation concerning the degree of exploitation in this field, at the evidence of the persistent low pay of cultural workers and the extent to which even the most advanced sectors of capitalist cultural production depend upon drawing relative surplus value from sectors which still operate a pre-capitalist artisanal mode of economic organization.[12]

(c) The above relates to the need to examine the relationship between Marx's belief that capitalist production of cultural goods was possible only within very narrow limits, the phenomenon of Baumol's disease (Baumol and Bouran, 1976) and the ever increasing pressure on the State to intervene in the cultural sector.

(d) Similar considerations are raised by Marx's second example where the product is not separable from the act of producing, thus raising strict limits to productivity and thus raising relative costs.

The economic contradictions that arise from the nature of cultural commodities takes different forms within different sectors of the media and at different historical moments.

Five main ways have been adopted in an attempt to circumvent the problem.

(a)   Copyright. This is in effect an attempt to commoditize information via the uniqueness of authorship or by turning the author into a commodity. But this only works if you either then make the commodity scarce, i.e. stress its uniqueness. We see this in the economics of the art market. Or if you control supply, i.e. control access to the means of reproduction such as printing presses and film laboratories. However, if such control is used to over-price it will encourage the development of pirating alternatives. This is now a major problem internationally for the cultural industries in records, books, films and even TV programmes.

(b)   Control of access to consumption through a box-office mechanism at the point of sale and/or through economic control of the channels of distribution, i.e. newspapers and cinema. The problem here is that such control is resistant to economies of scale and as the theatre found when faced by the cinema and the cinema when faced by broadcasting, is highly susceptible to competition from more efficient technologies of reproduction and distribution. However, as broadcasting demonstrates, the massive economies of scale produced by these more efficient means of distribution by destroying the box office, i.e. by making access open, create major problems of creating the necessary moment of exchange.

(c)   Built-in obsolescence through the manipulation of time. This was the great achievement of the newspaper which, by creating rapidly decaying information, created thereby a constant need to re-consume. But this manipulation of time has its limits since consumption time is physically limited. (The central importance of time within the economics of the mass-media is a subject to which I intend to give substantive treatment in a subsequent article.)

(d)   The creation, packaging and sale, not of cultural and informational goods to direct consumers, but of audiences to advertisers (Smythe, 1977).

(e)   State patronage. The inherent tendency towards the socialization of cultural and informational goods has always given the State an important role in this field from the days of direct patronage of cultural workers by King, Aristocracy and Church via the early subsidy of newspapers by governments and political parties, through public libraries and public education, to the key contemporary example of broadcasting.

In brief therefore, the specific nature of the commodity form within cultural production leads to a constant problem of realization and thus to a two-way pressure either towards advertising finance or towards State finance. We find these pressures quite clearly at the moment in the growing controversy over sponsorship in sport and the arts.[13]

The question these pressures raise is in what ways (a) advertising and (b) State intervention in this sphere is functional or dysfunctional for capitalism in general on the one hand and on the other the effect of such pressures upon cultural production itself.

The Modes of Extraction and Distribution of the Cultural Surplus

Since all cultural forms are material in the sense that they take time which will only be available after the needs of physical reproduction are satisfied, the material requirements of the cultural process must be extracted as surplus from direct material production. As we have seen this can be done by paying for cultural production directly out of revenue. But as Marx remarked of capitalism in general, it has found it more efficient as a means of control to extract surpluses directly by means of economic processes. Thus the developments of the capitalist mode of production and its associated division of mental and manual labour have led to the development of the extraction of the necessary surplus for the maintenance of cultural production and reproduction directly via the commodity and exchange form. But this process will only take place to the extent that:

(a)   there is surplus capital searching for opportunities for valorization;
(b)   the anticipated rate of profit in the chosen sphere of cultural production is at least as high as that available elsewhere.

Where these conditions do not exist cultural processes will have to continue to be undertaken by the direct transfer of resources, i.e. by the expenditure of surplus. This may take place under the following conditions.

(a)   By capitalists as individuals or groups funding such activities, e.g. the classic model of arts patronage. Such a form may be sustained within the contemporary capitalist social formation by means of tax concessions. It may be channelled through charitable foundations, etc.

Such funding leads to direct ideological control, legitimated as the cultural extension of private property, namely personal taste. This sphere can give rise to significant political battles, e.g. the wealth tax/national heritage debate.

But examples within the media field are the direct subsidy of newspapers by political parties or by politically ambitious individuals, e.g. Beaverbrook, Goldsmith and possibly now Broakes and Matthews, the new owners of the *Express* Group and Morgan-Grampian.

(b)   Via the State. Here electronic communication is the key case. The exact mix in the field of both telephonic and broadcast communication between the State and capital needs examination state by state. As any superficial examination will show, key differences between Western Europe and the United States give the lie to any simple capital logic explanation of how the particular economic and institutional forms, within which electronic communication has developed, have arisen.

The explanation of such differences and the present conjunctural relations between national capitals and the State, between states and between international capital and states in this area would have to take account of the following.

(1)   The structures of national capitals.
(2)   The existing State structure, i.e. federal structure of US and Germany as opposed to centralized structure of Britain and even more, France.
(3)   The strategic requirements of the State, e.g. the State-inspired creation of RCA as the first step in a long history of the US government's explicit geo-political involvement in communication, the clearest case of which is satellites, such a policy requiring intervention to restructure national capitals.
(4)   The balance of forces between sections of capital and the relations of that balance of force to the State's assessment of both economic and strategic requirements, e.g. the foundation of the BBC in which we see an interaction between the needs of the nascent British electronic industry, which the State wished to foster both for strategic and economic reasons, but which was only interested in the sales of hardware and was able to shift the expense and ideological problems of programme production onto the State, because the State needed also to take account both of the economically and politically powerful British press, which was opposed to competition for advertising and of a culturally conservative and elitist ruling class fraction.[14]

To sum up, historically the development of the material process known as the superstructure depended upon the availability of a surplus in the sphere of direct material production, i.e. the sphere of the extraction, shaping and consumption of nature. Historically the shape of that superstructure is determined by the social relations of production, because it is these social relations that determine the distribution of that surplus. For example, Athenian democracy as a form of political practice depends directly materially upon the slave economy that supported it by making time available for political activity to a non-productive class. Such directly material considerations remain important, i.e. in a planned economy like the Soviet Union direct choices have to be made between for instance producing more shoes or the paper for more newspapers. Such considerations may be acute in the planning of media systems in Third World countries and indeed it is the influencing of such decisions in the interest not of the indigenous economy or social formation but of a foreign high surplus economy that is one of the matters at issue in the media imperialism debate. It is a less obvious form of the starvation caused in some countries by the development of industrialized agriculture serving a world market. Under developing capitalism the means of cultural production may be provided either in commodity form as part of the accumulation process, e.g. records or as part of the realization process of other sectors of the capitalist economy, e.g. advertising or directly out of capitalist revenue, e.g. arts patronage or the Thompson family and *The Times* or through the State.

Each of the above means of surplus distribution to the cultural sphere will differentially affect the ways in which the dominant class controls the means of cultural production. Different contradictions will come into play, contradictions which need to be specifically analysed in each conjunctural case. Not only are these contradictions intrinsic to each subsidiary mode of cultural production but there are also contradictions which arise because of conflicts between them, e.g. between broadcasting whether state or private and the press, a conflict in its turn differentially mediated through competition for readers/viewers and through competition for advertising.

The Industrialization of Culture

While drawing different conclusions as to the significance of the phenomenon both bourgeois and Marxist economists agree that the current phase of capitalist development is characterized by the following.

(a)   Unprecedented capital concentration in all the key traditional manufacturing sectors accompanied in general by a rising surplus.
(b)   A resulting problem of valorization which drives surplus capital in search of other areas of investment.
(c)   An associated development of the so-called service sector characterized by the industrialization of sectors which were either more primitively organized or, as in the sphere of domestic labour, altogether outside the market.

These tendencies are now rapidly affecting the whole cultural, mass-media sector. This has been extensively documented by A. Mattelart in his recent "Multi-nationales et systeme de communication" and, for France, by A. Huet et al. in their "Capitalisme et industries culturelles". So all I wish to do here, is point out certain key aspects and examples of this tendency.

This absorption of the sphere of reproduction into full-scale commodity production is characterized by the following.

(a)   Increased international competition and the resulting take-over of domestic, national publishing companies, advertising agencies, private broadcasting stations etc. by multinational companies. See, for instance, the example of Philips given at the start of this piece. This competition also leads to increasing penetration by international media products, particularly Anglo-Saxon.[15]
(b)   A sharpening struggle within cultural production over the labour process in an attempt by capital to increase productivity in a sector which is notoriously resistant to such increases. This struggle has been most marked recently in the newspaper industry with the present dispute at Times Newspapers being the most notorious and current example in Britain.
(c)   Increasingly persistent attempts to open up new markets in order to absorb excess capital. The most obvious example of this is the increasing pressure throughout Western Europe to privatize public broadcasting. See, for instance, the case of Italy, but the current crisis in the financing of the BBC and Annan's proposals for an advertising financed O.B.A. must be seen in this light.
(d)   Attempts to open up new markets for both cultural hard-ware and soft-ware by introducing new communication technologies, such as cable TV, satellites, Teletext, etc. Because of the huge infrastructural investments involved and the comparatively low rate of return on such investments these moves involve close

alliances between capital and the State in an attempt to get the tax-payer to carry the cost of the distribution system, while private capital takes the profits from the sale of hardware and from the subsequent development of a consumer durable market in such items as teletext decoders and of a software market, e.g. Pay TV. The full development of this push into new technologies has undoubtedly been slowed down significantly by the current recession in the Western economies, but the long-term implications for national cultures, for class cultures and for freedom of expression of all these trends, not only in the Third World where the problem is dramatized as media imperialism, but in the capitalist heartlands, are profoundly significant.

Thus I return to where I started by reiterating that the development of political economy in the cultural sphere is not a mere matter of theoretical interest but of urgent practical political priority. So long as Marxist analysis concentrates on the ideological content of the mass media it will be difficult to develop coherent political strategies for resisting the underlying dynamics of development in the cultural sphere in general which rest firmly and increasingly upon the logic of generalized commodity production. In order to understand the structure of our culture, its production, consumption and reproduction and of the role of the mass media in that process, we increasingly need to confront some of the central questions of political economy in general, the problem of productive and non-productive labour, the relation between the private and public sectors and the role of the State in capitalist accumulation, the role of advertising within late capitalism, etc.

As long ago as 1960, Asa Briggs wrote in his Fisher Memorial Lecture:

> The provision of entertainment has never been a subject of great interest either to economists or to economic historians – at least in their working hours. Yet in 20th century conditions it is proper to talk of a highly organized entertainment industry, to distinguish within it between production and distribution, to examine forces making for competition, integration, concentration and control and to relate such study to the statistics of national income and output, the development of advertising, international economic relations and – not least – to the central economic concept of the market which, in the 20th century, is as much concerned with leisure as it is with work. (Briggs, 1960)

Nearly two decades later that research gap remains and there has been little coherent effort to understand the process known as "the industrialization of culture", a process by which, as Briggs put it, "Massive market interests have come to dominate an area of life which, until recently, was dominated by individuals themselves" (Briggs, 1960).

Notes

1   See Marx, "Notes on Adolph Wagner" in Marx (1975). Quoted in Corrigan and Singer (1978). Here Corrigan and Singer present an extended version of this methodological argument. See also Sayer (forthcoming).

2   We intend to publish a detailed critique of this position in a forthcoming issue. In the meantime, see Thompson (1978), Williams (1977) and Corrigan and Singer (1978). [Editorial note to original.]

3   See Smythe (1977), Murdoch (1978), Smythe (1978) and Levant (1978).

4   See J. Curran, "Capitalism and Control of the Press 1800–1979", in Curran et al. (1977).

5   For a detailed discussion of this problem see Baudrillard (1972, 1975).

6   Adorno and Horkheimer, "The Dialectic of Enlightenment", in Curran et al. (1977: 133, 358–9).

7   But note Marx's own comments in the *Grundrisse*, p. 532: "The highest development of capital exists when the general conditions of the process of social production are not paid out of *deduction from the social revenue*, the state's taxes – where revenue and not capital appears as the labour fund, and where the worker, although he is a free wage worker like any other, nevertheless stands economically in a different relation – but rather out of *capital as capital*. This shows the degree to which capital has subjugated all conditions of social production to itself, on the one side; and, on the other side, hence, the extent to which social reproduction wealth has been *capitalised* and all needs are satisfied through the exchange form" (Marx's italics).

8   See T. Lovell (1979) and Adorno and Horkheimer: "Nevertheless the culture industry remains the entertainment business. Its influence over the consumer is established by entertainment; that will ultimately be broken not by an outright decree, but by the hostility inherent in the principle of entertainment to what is greater than itself" (in Curran et al., 1977: 361).

9   See Bourdieu (1971: 183–97): "It is in the degree of objectification of the accumulated social capital that one finds the basis of all pertinent differences between the modes of domination . . . Objectification guarantees the permanence and cumulativity of material and symbolic acquisition which can thus subsist without agents having to recreate them continously and in their entirety by deliberate action; but, because the profits of their institutions are the object of differential appropriation, objectification also and insepar- ably ensures the reproduction of the structure of distribution of the capital which, in its various forms, is the precondition for such appropriation, and in so doing, reproduces the structure of the relation of dominance and dependence" (p. 184).

10 For a fuller elaboration of the modes of labour organization within capitalist cultural industries, see Huet et al. (1978).

11 See Benjamin (1977) for the positive view and Marcuse (1972) for the negative view.

12 See Huet et al. (1978) for theoretical elaboration and Krust (1977) for data. See also discussion in Owen, Beebe and Manning (1974), which shows, from a neo-classical perspective that the so-called economic efficiency of US TV depends upon high un- employment in Hollywood.

13 See, for instance, P. Harland (1978) and recent correspondence in *The Times* concerning the Arts Council's expression of disapproval of its grant recipients giving too large a billing to commercial sponsors at the expense of itself.

14 For a discussion of the relationship between the French State and private capital in the development of the electronic audio-visual field in general, see Flichy (1978) and Huet et al. (1978).

15 It should be noted that from this point of view the UK is in a privileged position since it is second only to the USA as a media exporter.

References

Adorno, T. and Horkheimer, M. (1977). The culture industry (abridged), in J. Curran et al., (eds.), *Mass Communication and Society*, Edward Arnold, London.

Althusser, L. (1969). *Contradiction and Over-determination*, Allen Lane, London.

Baudrillard, J. (1972). *Pour une Critique de l'Economic Politique du Signe*, Gallimard, Paris.

Baudrillard, J. (1975). *The Mirror of Production*, Tela Press, St. Louis.

Baumol, W. J. and Bouran, W. G. (1976). On the performing arts: the anatomy of their economic problems, in M. Blang, (ed.), *The Economics of the Arts*, Martin Robertson, London.

Benjamin, W. (1977). The work of art in the age of mechanical reproduction, in Curran et al., op. cit.

Bottomore, T. and Rubel, M. (1963). Theories of surplus value, in *K. Marx on Sociology and Social Philosophy*, pp. 96, 97, Pelican.

Bourdieu, P. (1971). *Outline of a Theory of Practice*, CUP.

Bourdieu, P. and Passeron, J. L. (1977). *Reproduction*, Sage, London.

Briggs, A. (1960). Fisher Memorial Lecture, University of Adelaide.

Clarke, S. (1977). Marxism, sociology and Poulantzas's theory of the state, *Capital and Class*, no. 2, Summer.

Corrigan, P. and Singer, D. (1978). Hindess and Hirst: a critical review, *Socialist Register*, Merlin, London.

Curran, J. et al., (eds.) (1977). *Mass-Communication and Society*, Edward Arnold, London.

Financial Times (1978). Electronic Rentals ups its ratings, 19 December.

Flichy, P. (1978). *Contribution à une Étude du Industries de l'Audiovisual*, Institut National de l'Audiovisual.

Harland, P. (1978). Enter the money men, stage right, *Sunday Times*, 11 June.

Huet, A. et al. (1978). *Capitalisme et Industries Culturelles*, University of Grenoble Press.

Krust, M. (1977). *Droit au Travail et Problems d'Emploi du Travailleur Culturels du Spectacle et de l'Interpretation Musicale dans la Communante Economique Europeenne*, CCE.

Levant, P. (1978). The audience commodity: on the blindspot debate, *Canadian Journal of Political and Social Theory*.

Lovell, T. (1979). *Realism, Ideology and Film*, British Film Institute, London (forthcoming).

Mandel, E. (1975). *Late Capitalism*, ch. 1, NLB, London.

Marcuse, H. (1972). Art as a form of reality, *New Left Review* 74.

Marx, K. (1859). Preface to a contribution to a critique of political economy, in Marx, K. and Engels, F., (eds.), *Selected Works*, vol. 1, p. 364, Lawrence and Wishart, London (1962).

Marx, K. (1973). *Grundrisse*, Pelican, London.

Marx, K. (1975). Notes on Adolph Wagner, in T. Carver, (ed.), *Texts on Method*, p. 201, Blackwell, Oxford.

Marx, K. (1976). Results of the immediate process of production, in *Capital*, vol. 1, Pelican.

Miliband, R. R. (1977). *Marxism and Politics*, p. 50, OUP.

Murdoch, G. (1978). Blindspots about Western Marxism: a reply to Dallas Smythe, *Canadian Journal of Political and Social Theory*, vol. 2, no. 2.

Murdoch, G. and Golding, P. (1979). Ideology and the mass media: the question of determination, in M. Barrett et al. (eds.) *Ideology and Cultural Production*, Croom-Helm, London.

Owen, B., Beebe, J. and Manning, W. (1974). *TV Economics*, D. C. Heath, London.

Sayer, D. (1979). *Marx's Method*, Harvester Press, forthcoming.

Smythe, D. (1977). Communication: blindspot of Western Marxism, *Canadian Journal of Political and Social Theory*, vol. 1, no. 3.

Smythe, D. (1978). Rejoinder to Graham Murdoch, *Canadian Journal of Political and Social Theory*, vol. 2, no. 2.

Thompson, E. P. (1978). *The Poverty of Theory*, Merlin, London.

Williams, R. (1977). *Marxism and Literature*, OUP, London.

16

On the Audience Commodity and its Work

Dallas W. Smythe

Obviously communications and their equipment, and labor and its equipment
are inseparable except in the mind. Both complexes are useful and marketable,
therefore commodities, whatever the theoretical assumptions may be.
                    – M. M. Knight, letter to author, 23 Jan. 1978

To suggest that the mass media audience is a commodity and that audiences "work" is
to raise many questions which unsettle established ways of thinking. As most audience
"work" centers in the home, all the other functions of the family become involved
in considering the implications of the proposition. Marital relations, child care and
development, leisure time activities, consumer expenditure, decision making – all
these functions are somehow involved with audience work. Beyond these, for possible
consideration, are the relations of family life and of audience work to alcoholism, drug
and tranquilizer addiction, crime and violence – all of which in one way or another
focus on the family. In raising these issues in the context of the North American
capitalist core, I cannot answer many of the significant questions which are generated. Indeed, so complex and unanalyzed are the issues I shall be discussing that it
may be as much as can be done on this occasion to try to pose the "right" questions.
Traditional behavioral research (and its popular handmaiden, market research) is
simply tangential, self-interested, and irrelevant to the complex dialectical processes
of contradictions which are working before our eyes. In order to analyze our largely
commoditized society, we must beware thinking of people and commodities as
disconnected things and see them as relationships in a social process.
    What is the principal product of the mass media? To answer this central question
one needs tools – theories. There may be two modes of theory: subjective, idealist
concepts, or objective and realistic concepts. Until now, all theory relevant to our

From Dallas W. Smythe, "On the audience commodity and its work." In *Dependency Road:
Communications, Capitalism, Consciousness, and Canada*, pp. 22–51. Norwood, NJ: Ablex, 1981.

principal question has been subjective and idealist. My argument is that this is so and that an objective and realistic theory is needed. Before entering into explanation of such a realistic theory, it is necessary to state why theory concerning the mass media and their principal product has been subjective and idealist. It is easy to see why conventional, bourgeois theory about communication is idealist. The entire literature – bourgeois and Marxist alike – about mass communications has defined the principal product of the mass media as "messages," "information," "images," "meaning," "entertainment," "education," "orientation," "manipulation," etc. *All* these concepts are subjective mental entities; all deal with superficial appearances, divorced from real life processes. The concepts of entertainment, education, orientation, and manipulation do not even refer to any aspects of mass media content but to its *effects, or purpose.*

Of course, this is not to say that abstract, subjective processes are not real. Much of the work that audience power does for advertisers takes place in the heads of audience members. My argument, however, is that there is a material base of work which people must do under monopoly capitalism. Food, clothing, etc., must be bought, and it is this aspect of audience work which "pays off" for the advertiser. At the same time, with inadequate income to meet the demands on the family budget, sacrifices must be made in order that the values of family life may be achieved. Parents postpone some expenditures on their own needs in order that the children or grandma may receive dental care. There is a dialectical tension between the work for advertisers and the effort necessary to put into practice the values which people believe are necessary to make a home, a community, and a nation of which they can be proud. Practical consciousness (awareness of what it means to live – to put it briefly) is objectively and realistically powerfully affected by the outcome of this dialectical contradictory process. (See chapter 11 [Smythe, 1981].)

Naturally, the general literature about economics has, for the past century, had opportunity to recognize and analyze the significance of the mass media, advertising, audiences, and Consciousness Industry. None of it deals with the role of the markets for audiences, produced by the mass media, bought and used by advertisers. It is not surprising that this is true of neoclassical marginal utility economists whose interest concerns imaginary competitive models which correspond to nothing significant in the real world of oligopolistic reality. Those in the Keynesian tradition do notice advertising but only in subjective psychological terms as aimed at "control of the buyer's consciousness" (Chamberlin, 1931, pp. 113–34). But having noticed it they then disregard it. Some bourgeois economists, increasingly since the 1960s, have shown interest in developing theories of taste and buying behavior, joining in management's interest in market research or in efforts to enforce antimonopoly laws. Without exception, they ignore the role of demand management by monopoly capitalism and the role of the mass media in producing the marketing agent (the audience) for it. Instead they treat advertising expenditures in relation to firm profitability in purely statistical terms as if nothing real was being purchased or used.[1] Among institutional economists, J. K. Galbraith alone has pursued the matter of demand management by giant corporations by means of advertising but stops short at the brink of discovering the audience market:

The present disposition of conventional economic theory to write off annual outlays of tens of billions of dollars of advertising and similar sales costs by the industrial system as without purpose or consequence is, to say the least, drastic. No other legal economic activity is subject to similar rejection. The discovery that sales and advertising expenditures have an organic role in the system will not, accordingly, seem wholly implausible. (Galbraith, 1967, p. 205)

Unfortunately he does not explore that "organic role," nor describe and analyze the relation of mass media, audiences, and advertisers to each other (Smythe, 1980).

How does it happen that Marxists have not pursued a materialist, realistic theory of communications? Marxists from Marx down to about 1920, and including Lenin, could hardly be expected to recognize and deal with the demand-management function of advertising and mass communication on behalf of monopoly capitalism because it was hardly evident until after World War I. In the period of newspaper and magazine development before the 1880s, the press was mostly supported by money and influence from political parties – not advertisers. The press which politicians subsidized thus seemed to influence audiences toward the point of view of the subsidizer through the editorial content (everything but the relatively insignificant advertisements). Because the only market substantially involved in the sale of newspapers and magazines was that in which people bought them, it was easy for them to fall into a psychological, subjective answer to the question, what does the press produce. It produced newspapers and magazines and sold them; no organized market for the production and sale of audiences then existed. So for Marxists the press was lumped together with educational and other high culture institutions of the state as part of its "superstructure," while productive *work* took place at the base – the "infrastructure" – where people were paid for working. After 1920, Marxists continued to assume that the principal product of the mass media is influence.

Gramsci, the Frankfurt School (Adorno, Horkheimer, Lowenthal, Marcuse, Habermas), Raymond Williams, Poulantzas, Althusser, and Marxists concerned particularly with the problems of countries peripheral to the capitalist core (e.g., Samir Amin, Clive Y. Thomas) – none addresses the Consciousness Industry from the standpoint of its historical-materialist role in making monopoly capitalism function through demand management (advertising, marketing, and mass media).[2] Baran and Sweezy in *Monopoly Capital* (1966) do indeed emphasize the importance of demand management by monopoly capitalism but they unfortunately stop short of analyzing realistically *how* it takes place, contenting themselves with a manipulative assumption about the mass media and advertising. The same blind spot afflicts communications scholars who take a more or less Marxist view of communications (Nordenstreng, Enzensberger, Hamelink, Schiller, Murdock, Golding, and me until recently). Because they do not take account of how the mass media under monopoly capitalism produce audiences to market commodities, candidates, and issues to themselves, theory and practice regarding the production of ideology continues on a subjective, unrealistic, and essentially ahistorical basis. *Why* they continue to suffer this blind spot it is not my present task to determine.[3]

The answer given in chapter 1 [Smythe, 1981] to the question, what is the principal function which the commercial mass media perform for the capitalist system was essentially to set an agenda for the production of consciousness with two mutually reinforcing objectives: (1) to mass market the mass-produced consumer goods and services generated by monopoly capitalism by using audience power to accomplish this end; (2) to mass market legitimacy of the state and its strategic and tactical policies and actions, such as election of government officers, military thrusts against states which show signs of moving toward socialism (Vietnam, Korea, Cuba, Chile, Dominican Republic, etc.), and policies against youthful dissent ("Middle America"). The answer to the question, what is the principal product of the commercial mass media in monopoly capitalism was simple: audience power. *This* is the concrete product which is used to accomplish the economic and political tasks which are the reason for the existence of the commercial mass media. Let us consider this strange commodity, audience power.

Because audience power is produced, sold, purchased and consumed, it commands a price and is a commodity. Like other "labor power" it involves "work." So at the outset let us consider what we mean by *work*. By common usage under capitalism, *work* may be defined as whatever one does for which one receives pay (wages, salaries, etc.). (Let us defer for the moment the fact that audience members do not get paid for the use of their audience power.) As such it has come to be regarded generally as doing something which you would prefer not to do, something unpleasant, alienating, and frustrating. It also is thought of as something linked with a job, a factory, an office, or a store. It was not always this way. At its base, work is doing something creative, something distinctively human – for the capacity to work is one of the things which distinguishes human beings from other animals. "By changing the world they live in through labor, human beings *at the same time* alter their own nature, for the lives of people *are influenced both by what they* produce and how they produce" (Rinehart, 1975; emphasis added).

It seems that with other animals (e.g., beavers, ants, bees) work skills are programmed through the genes, whereas with human beings, they are learned after birth – i.e., are social products. This fact conceals a secret which explains both the unlimited creativity of which human beings are capable in their work and their alienation in the processes of work under capitalism. The secret is that for human beings, work involves both thinking and the application or testing of ideas in practice. The link between thinking and practice (or theory and practice) – that *thinking may be joined to, or separated from, practice* – is basic to the power struggle between capital and labor. (Parenthetically, it is the grasp of this fact which gives the thought of Mao Zedong and the Chinese people the basis of their amazing accomplishments.) (Mao Zedong, 1968) The revolutionary success of capitalism as a system rests on the division of labor and its command of capital to multiply the "productivity" of work using ever more sophisticated machines, at the human cost of effectively denying the creative process by fragmenting workers' practice and divorcing it from the interaction of thought and practice. This is the practical effect of "scientific management" (see Smythe, 1981).

Let us pose and answer some questions which should serve to identify and describe the audience commodity more precisely:

What do advertisers buy with their advertising expenditures? As hardnosed businessmen they are not paying for advertising for nothing, nor from altruism. What they buy are the services of audiences with predictable specifications which will pay attention in predictable numbers and at particular times to particular means of communication (television, radio, newspapers, magazines, billboards, and third-class mail) in particular market areas.[4] As collectivities these audiences are commodities. As commodities they are dealt with in markets by producers and buyers (the latter being advertisers). Such markets establish prices in the familiar mode of monopoly capitalism. Both these markets and the audience commodities traded in are specialized. The audience commodities bear specifications known in the business as "the demographics." The specifications for the audience commodities include age, sex, income level, family composition, urban or rural location, ethnic character, ownership of home, automobile, credit card status, social class, and, in the case of hobby and fan magazines, a dedication to photography, model electric trains, sports cars, philately, do-it-yourself crafts, foreign travel, kinky sex, etc.

Are audiences homogeneous? By no means, although all of them have the common features of being produced by mass media and priced and sold in oligopolistic markets to advertisers for whom they perform services which earn their keep, i.e., keep advertisers advertising because the expenditure is productive from the advertisers' standpoint. Audiences produced for sale to advertisers fall into two groups: those produced in connection with marketing consumers' goods and those for producers' goods. The latter are typically produced by trade or business media (magazines, newspapers, or direct mail). The buyers of producers' goods are typically institutions (government, in the case of the "military sales effort," or private corporations) which presumably buy on specifications of objective qualities. Moreover, such advertising is a relatively small part of the total; hence, the following analysis disregards this category of audience. The second and strategically most important class of audiences is produced for advertisers marketing consumers' goods. Again, these audiences fall into two classes: The first of these are for producers of what Julian L. Simon (1970, p. 71) calls *homogenous package goods* (HPG) which have certain common features:

(1) Slight or no objective physical difference between the brands, (2) Low unit cost, (3) Short time period between repeated purchases, (4) Large total dollar volume for each product industry, (5) Except for liquor, heavy use of television as an advertising medium, and (6) Large proportions of sales spent for advertising.

In the HPG category are soft drinks, gum, candy, soaps, cleaners, waxes, etc., tobacco products, beer, wine, liquor, gasoline, patent drugs, perfumes, cosmetics, deodorants, razor blades, etc., as well as fast foods and restaurants. The second subclass of audiences for consumers' goods is that for durable consumer goods. Here are automobiles, snowmobiles, clothes, boats, shoes, hobby equipment (e.g., cameras, sports equipment, household tools), household appliances, etc. Although objective qualitative characteristics are ascertainable, annual style changes dominate them. It is the consumer goods advertisers whose audiences are produced by the mass media to generate the "demand" which can increase GNP.

How are advertisers assured that they are getting what they pay for when they buy audience power? After all, the skeptic asks, how does the advertiser know that I am in his audience? And even if I am in the room when the television set is on, why does he think that I am paying attention to the commercials (I may time my visits to the refrigerator or toilet to coincide with the appearance of the commercials)? The answer is simple. The advertiser is assured that he/she gets the audience power that is paid for in just the same way that an insurance company profits by insuring your life. You may drop dead the day after taking out the policy, or you may pay premiums for 50 years. The insurance company "gambles" on the probability of your living a certain number of years. Probability, working with large numbers, removes the risk from the gamble. Similarly with advertising, the assurance lies in the law of large numbers and the experience with audience probabilities which yields the basis for prediction on which the price of audience power is based. So it matters not if some audience members withdraw their attention; that is expected and discounted in advance by the advertiser.

As to the statistical basis of the experience and prediction of audience size: that is the specialized business of a subindustry sector of the Consciousness Industry which checks to determine audience size. The behavior of the members of the audience under the impact of advertising and the other content of the mass media is the object of market research by a large number of independent market research agencies as well as by similar staffs in advertising agencies, in the corporations which advertise, and in media enterprises. The raw data for their demographic and psychographic research are gathered by intensive interview studies and extrapolated to estimates of total audiences, using reports from A. C. Nielsen and a host of competitors who specialize in rapid assessment of the delivered audience commodity. Scientific sampling yields results as reliable for audiences as it does for grain, sugar, and other basic commodities which also can be "graded" only on the basis of probability and experience.

What institutions produce the commodity which advertisers buy with their advertising expenditures? There seem to be two levels to the answer to this question. The first, immediate level is the media enterprises and the family which is the nexus of audiences. Media enterprises include those which operate commercial television and radio stations (and networks of such stations), newspapers, magazines and which produce billboard and third-class mail advertising. The second, deeper level is that of the factor supply services for the media. Feeding these media enterprises with what might be thought of as the producers' goods which support the commercial media "side" of the production process are all the advertising agencies, talent agencies, package program producers, specialist firms in producing commercial announcements, film producers, the wire services (AP, UPI, Reuters, Canadian Press, etc.), "syndicators" of news columns, writers' agents, book publishers, motion picture producers and distributors.

But powerful institutions feed the audience production process from the family or audience side as well. Here the role of the educational institutions, especially at the primary and secondary levels, is important. Preparation of children for their role in audiences in those institutions is both explicit in classroom experience which "educates" children as to how media and business function (e.g., classes in business English or other vocational skills related to salesmanship, advertising, etc.) and implicit in the submissiveness to authority which the schools impart. Obviously, underlying both the media side and the audience side of the process of producing audiences is the electronics-photography industry complex which conceives, produces, and markets both the "software" (package programs, wire service copy, for example) and the hardware (high-speed presses, porto-pak television cameras, home receivers for television, radio, etc.).

How are prices for audience power determined? Monopoly and oligopoly characterize the supply of audiences produced by the newspaper industry. Single newspaper ownership is practically universal in American and Canadian urban areas, and the only effective ceiling on audience prices demanded by newspaper publishers is the opportunity cost to the advertiser of using alternative media (direct mail, billboards, radio and television). Cross-ownership of radio and television stations by newspaper publishers is so common as to inhibit intermedia competition in the sale of audience power. Moreover oligopolistic price setting is supported by long-established trade associations for each of the media. Prices are differentiated according to types of demand for audience power. Basic to newspaper pricing is the separation of "national" from "retail" advertisers, with the former being charged substantially higher rates than the latter. A separate price schedule governs sales to "classified" advertisers. Within the retail category, different prices are commonly charged for different classes of advertisers, e.g., on "business pages" – main financial pages, notices of dividends, corporate meetings, etc. – or listings of restaurants, amusements, books, resorts, etc. Quantity reductions are commonly granted for larger spaces; frequency discounts, for multiple exposures over time. The levels of rates are set on the basis of ability to pay (Simon, 1970, pp. 146–7). Magazine prices for audiences are classified as "national" for magazines producing nationwide audiences, and "local," for magazines with more limited geographic scope.

The markets for radio and television audiences, except for the relatively small proportion served only by single stations, display more competition for the advertisers' expenditures than do those of newspapers. For television audiences, the competition between networks is intense. Audiences for television (and radio before radio networks atrophied after television was innovated) command different prices according to whether they are priced as a network package or the product of a single station. They were originally priced differently if they were sold as produced by a "sponsored program," or as spot announcements *between* programs. By the 1970s, few "sponsored" programs were broadcast (mostly soap operas and one-time "specials" in prime time); the great bulk of audience time on both television and radio is now sold via spot announcements – mostly those sold by networks, but some directly by stations through "station representatives" to advertisers.

Erik Barnouw (1978, pp. 69–70) describes the television market for audience power in terms analogous to markets for spot and future transactions in commodities like wheat or copper:

A central point was that a sale designated a particular *program* – not merely a time period. The advertiser had taken the position that he must have program settings suitable to his messages and purposes, and the networks had accepted this as reasonable. From this flowed many consequences.

One was the disappearance of fixed prices. The rate card became virtually obsolete. A slot in a program that had, at the moment, a top Nielsen or Arbitron rating could be sold for a higher price than a slot in a program with a lower rating. Thus the business gravitated toward endless bargaining. Prices fluctuated as on a stock market.

A sharp rise in ratings brought a rise in asking price. When NBC decided in 1970 to schedule a series around the comedian Flip Wilson – then a relatively unknown quantity – network time salesmen began by selling 30-second slots for about $35,000 each. As the program won unexpected success and climbing ratings, the asking price went to $40,000, $45,000, $50,000 and beyond. On a single broadcast, one slot might have been sold at the lowest, earliest price; others at later prices. On some series, ratings and prices went down instead of up.

The buying and selling was generally done in clusters or packages. In view of the staggering number of spots involved, this seemed inevitable. For the sponsor it was also a way to hedge his bets. Unexpected failures could be balanced by unexpected successes. There was a safety in this "scatter" buying.

In the bargaining process, a sponsor might indicate through his advertising agency that he was ready to invest $1,400,000 in time purchases for Mouthwash X; the network was asked to provide a suggested list of available slots. Some would be rejected as unsuitable, others accepted. Eventually there would be agreement on a spectrum of spots, and on a package price. A specific dollar value would be assigned to each spot; this was essential because a program cancellation would require the network to make a refund, or provide a comparable spot. The spots in a package might have wildly diverse price tags, reflecting their ratings and other bargaining factors. They might include 30-second slots in a football bowl game at $90,000 each; in a popular mystery series at $55,000 each; in an evening news series at $18,000 each; in a documentary prime time special at $14,000 each; and in an early morning show at $4,000 each.

A documentary special, even in prime time, was likely to go at a "bargain price" unless some sensational element was involved. A special could not have a track record, so its ratings could only be guessed at. And most sponsors were in any case reluctant to consider a slot in what might prove controversial; some flatly refused to take the risk.

To see that audience power is literally a commodity, consider the following packages of audience power available in the Vancouver, British Columbia, area for local television advertisers in May 1978:

For One 30-Second Spot on Bulk Basis
(Dollar cost per 1,000 persons)

	M*A*S*H (prime time)	Hockey Night in Canada (prime time)	Batman (Saturday AM)
Total viewers	2.32	1.99	0.96
Adults, total	3.00	2.29	—
Men	5.84	3.45	—
Women	5.13	5.98	7.35
Teenagers	25.39	42.44	3.85
Children	50.78	50.78	1.89

If the demographic and psychographic characteristics of women in these audiences in this market fitted the demand-management needs of an advertiser, M∗A∗S∗H would be a better buy than either of the other programs. Similarly, if the advertiser's marketing strategy was aimed at children, the best buy of the three would be the Batman program on Saturday morning.

These audience power markets establish prices in the familiar oligopolistic mode of monopoly capitalism. And an advertiser's power in the audience market has been a significant factor in building monopoly corporate empires. A sympathetic expert on advertising, Julian Simon (1970, pp. 222–3) says:

> At the corporate level, advertising sometimes has led to increased concentration by diversification because of multiproduct volume discounts on advertising time and space. For example, the FTC record revealed that Procter & Gamble could buy television time for 5 percent less than could the Clorox Company and this was an admitted motivation in Procter & Gamble's purchase. . . . Blake and Blum (1965) have compiled their relevant data on these volume discounts and provide compelling analysis to show that they must have been an important reason for firms that advertise heavily to seek mergers and reduce the cost of advertising.
>
> This effect is illustrated by a recent trade-paper story: "The proposed Cadbury-Schweppes merger, which sees economies in advertising and overseas expansion as its chief benefits, will create (if the Board of Trade permits) the United Kingdom's fourth largest food group, with estimated sales of $600,000,000. Savings would come from the group buying of television time, which accounts for at least 75 percent of the companies' joint budget in that medium. In 1968, the two companies put out $13,650,000 for advertising, the second largest in the country. . . ." (*Advertising Age*, March 3, 1969, p. 26)

Simon also points out that the better the advertiser's ability to measure the productivity of his purchased audience power, the more sensitive the advertiser will be to rate changes. And he uses as example, the case of mail order advertisers who buy magazine audience power:

> Mail order advertisers have an almost perfect measure of the effect of their advertising, and they receive sharp discounts below the rates paid by general advertisers. (Simon, 1970, p. 146)

Who pays how much for the production of audience power? On the surface it seems as if the exchange of audience power for commercial media content is equal or perhaps is even tilted in favour of the audience. You audience members contribute your unpaid work time and in exchange you receive the program material and the explicit advertisements. What better way to spend those "leisure hours" anyway? Especially if, as audience research suggests, television audience behavior since the mid-1960s increasingly tends to treat television as aural-visual wallpaper: the set is left on and audience members either attend to it or drift between the television room and adjacent (or remote) rooms, "glimpsing" the television set in passing and monitoring it auditorily all the while (Lyle, 1972, p. 23). Is there inconsistency between the concept of audience power as a commodity and such disrespectful behavior? Of course not. Is the tendency of workers on the production line to skimp or sabotage their work processes inconsistent with the fact that they have sold their labor power to the boss?

If we would understand the full audience contribution to producing their own audience power in a capitalist system, we must start by asking what value the system places on that audience power. And we shall find (in the next two chapters) that it is of vital importance to the system which could not survive without it. But, and the contradiction is significant, the system gets it "dirt-cheap."

Regarding television and radio broadcasting, advertisers spent in Canada in 1976 about $417 million on television and $279 million on radio.[5] For the 6,684,000 Canadian households with television sets in 1976 (and they were 97 percent of all households), advertisers spent $62 per household. Assuming a 23-hour week for television viewing per household (a very conservative figure), advertisers paid 5.2 cents an hour for the audience power of the average television household in 1976. Similarly, the 6,918,000 Canadian households with radio (100 percent saturation) cost the advertisers an average of $40 per household per annum. Assuming 18 hours per week of radio listening per household, this equaled 4.2 cents per household per hour of radio listening. Even without sophisticated productivity analysis of these costs, it is evident that the productivity of audience power need not be very high for all the individuals in the audience in order for it to be profitable for advertisers to recoup the costs – to them – of putting audience power to work.

From the standpoint of the audience, however, it bears much heavier costs than the advertisers. For what? For the privilege of working without pay as audience members, marketing consumer goods and services to themselves. And these heavier costs ignore the hidden costs they incur through commodity purchases. Table 16.1 compares the direct cost to audiences in Canada and the United States of commercial television and radio programming. It shows that, in 1976, Canadian audience members paid $2.188 billion as the direct cost of owning and operating their television receivers, whereas advertisers spent a mere $417 million. In other words, for every dollar spent by advertisers to buy media-produced television audiences, Canadian householders spent five. And whereas the depreciated investment in property, plant, and equipment of the combined over-the-air and cable television industry and the over-the-air radio broadcast industry in Canada was $645 million in 1976, the audience's depreciated investment in television and radio receivers was $3.905 billion. (Because CBC does not report investment in television and radio property separately, it is necessary to combine them.) In other words, for every dollar invested by the television-cable and radio broadcast industry in plant and equipment, Canadian householders had invested more than six dollars in their television and radio receivers.

In the United States, audience members paid $21.949 billion to own and operate their television receivers in 1976; advertisers spent $6.721 billion to buy the television audiences – a ratio of three dollars spent by the audience to one by the advertisers. A similar ratio of three to one existed between costs for radio receivers ($2.330 billion) and advertiser expenditures to buy radio audiences ($8.040 billion).

Table 16.1 Comparative cost of television and radio in Canada and the United States, 1976

	Canada		USA	
	TV	Radio	TV	Radio
Audience Costs, Direct:				
Basic Data:				
Number of receivers (000)[a]	9,895	23,400	121,000	402,000
Average purchase price (est. $)	600	80	540	72
Average useful life (est. years)	7	7	7	7
Average remaining useful life (est. years)	3.5	3.5	3.5	3.5
Interest rate on investment (est. %)	10	10	8	8
Average cost of power (est. $)	15	4	15	4
Average cost of repairs (est. $)	70	3	60	3
Annual Costs per Set ($):				
Depreciation (1/7 of price)	86	11	77	10
Interest (on 1/2 of price)	30	4	22	3
Power	15	4	15	4
Repairs	70	3	60	3
Total	201	22	174	20
Total Audience Cost (total cost per set times number of receivers/million $ per year)	1,989	515	21,054	8,040
Add cable costs for cabled households (million $ per year)[b]	199	—	895	—
Total Audience Cost (million $)	2,188	515	21,949	8,040
Advertiser Costs (million $ per year)[c]	417	279	6,721	2,330
Audience and Industry Investment:				
Depreciated audience investment (1/2 original cost, million $)	2,969	936	32,670	14,472
Depreciated investment in broadcast property, plant and equipment (million $):				
Over-air industry (except CBC)[d]	101	56	850	504
Over-air industry (including CBC)[d]		409	—	—
Cable industry	236	—	?	—
Total Cable and Over-Air (Canada)		645		
Profitability of Industry:				
Net profit before taxes (million $):				
Over-air industry[d]	60	36	1,546	158
Cable (Canada)[b]	36	—	—	—
Rate of return (%)				
Over-air industry	59	65	182	31
Cable (Canada)	15	—	—	—

[a] UNESCO *Statistical Yearbook*, 1997, pp. 996, 1016.
[b] Statistics Canada, *Cable Television*, Cat. 56, 205, 1976; United States Bureau of the Census, *Statistical Abstract*, 1978. Aspen Institute, *The Mass Media*, 1978, p. 215.
[c] For Canada, see footnote 5 (in text); for United States, Aspen Institute, *The Mass Media*, 1978, p. 203.
[d] For Canada, Statistics Canada, *Television and Radio Broadcasting*, Cat. 56, 204,1976; for United States, Federal Communications Commission, *Annual Report*, 1976, pp. 130, 141; Aspen Institute.

Curiously, although these ratios for operating costs were lower in the United States than in Canada, the ratios for depreciated investment by audiences were higher. Thus for television, audience investment was $32.670 billion, but over-the-air television depreciated investment was $850 million – a ratio of 33 to 1. And for radio broadcasting, audience investment was $14.472 billion as against $504 million by the radio broadcast networks and stations – a ratio of 33 to 1.

If one examines the basic data on audience receiver costs in Table 16.1 closely, it is evident that I have had to make rough estimates for all of them. The estimates appear to be conservative. At any event, the gross imbalance between audience costs and investment on the one hand, and expenditures by advertisers and investment by television and radio broadcast industries is obvious. Even if the real costs of depreciation, interest, power, repairs were a third less than my estimates suggest, television audiences in Canada and the United States would still be paying twice as much as advertisers.

What seems surprising from this analysis is that this preponderant investment and expense by audience members is virtually unnoticed by them and by scholars working in the mass media field. By what magicians term *misdirection*, attention is so focused on the exotic performances and lives of media stars and the showbiz glamor of program production and network and station operations that the real situation is mystified out of existence, as far as popular consciousness is concerned.

Who pays how much for the production of audience power other than via television-radio? For newspapers and magazines, advertisers pay the great bulk of the cost – typically from 70 to 90 percent. Audience subscription and newsstand purchase payments cover approximately only the delivery cost of the newspapers and magazines. "Community" and "shopping" newspapers which have no subscription price are paid for entirely by advertisers. Direct mail advertising materials are at the expense of advertisers, subsidized by heavy drains on revenues from first class mail and general tax revenues through below-cost postal rates. A similar postal subsidy for magazines and newspapers has shifted substantial portions of the costs of magazines and newspapers to the postal service in Canada and the United States since the last quarter of the nineteenth century.

What is the nature of the content of the commercial mass media under monopoly capitalism? In chapter 1 [Smythe, 1981], we considered the many ways in which there is unity between the apparently advertising and the apparently nonadvertising content of the commercial mass media. Both types have the same features. But it would be a serious error to ignore the importance of the formal difference between the "advertising" and the "program" or "editorial" content. The fiction that the advertising supports or makes possible the news, entertainment, or "educational" content has been a public relations mainstay of the commercial mass media. The professional *esprit de corps* of journalists hinges on it. And the textbooks, courses of instruction, teachers, and researchers in the mass media accept this fiction as defining the boundaries of their concerns. Either they deal with editorial content (in the case of newspapers and magazines) or program content, or they are hived off into textbooks, research, etc., about advertising. The only connection commonly made between advertising and the nonadvertising content of the media is to raise and dispel the suspicion that advertisers commonly tell the editorial departments of news-papers and magazines or the program producers of television and radio what *not* to say in the nonadvertising portions. (Of course, they seldom do this; it is not neces-sary, because the editorial policy of the media selects people for employment and predetermines the limits of what is "acceptable" noneditorial content.)

As a necessary consequence of the prevalence of this fiction, audience members and social scientists have come to regard the nonadvertising content as the sufficient attraction which warrants audiences spending time attending to the whole media product. So A. J. Liebling's (1961) point that the nonadvertising content is the "free lunch" does have a solid basis in public consciousness, a basis cynically rein-forced by the newspapers' practice of referring to the space between the advertise-ments as the *holes* which must be filled with appropriately sized chunks of "news." The appropriateness of the analogy is manifest. As with the *hors d'oeuvres* or potato chips and peanuts given to the customers of the pub, bar, or cocktail lounge, the function of the free lunch is to whet the appetite. In this case, to whet the prospect-ive audience members' appetites and thus (1) attract and keep them attending to the program, newspaper, or magazine; (2) cultivate a mood conducive to favorable reaction to the advertisers' explicit and implicit messages.

In the policy of the mass media, the characteristics of the free lunch must always be subordinated to those of the formal advertisements, because the purpose of the mass media is to produce audiences to sell to the advertisers. Therefore a program which is more arousing than the adjacent advertisements will not survive; it could survive the preliminary screening only because of faulty judgment on part of the media management and advertisers. The cost per unit of time or space of producing an explicit advertisement is many times the cost per unit of time or space of pro-ducing the free lunch (in a ratio of 8 or 10 to 1 in television) which is a rough index of the relative attention paid to the arousal qualities of the two.

There is, of course, a market for the free lunch, and this market spans not only the totally advertiser-dependent media (television and radio) but also the cinema, maga-zines, newspapers, and book industries. A particular commodity in the free lunch market (*Roots*, for example) will appear in more than one of these media, sometimes simultaneously (as with the book and film *China Syndrome*), often successively, in each case appropriately edited to fit the media's needs.

Qualification is necessary regarding the free lunch. On the one hand, in the case of newspapers and magazines, many readers buy the publication *because* they want the advertisements. This is especially true with classified advertisements and display advertising of products and prices by local merchants in newspapers. It is also true of most "hobby" magazines where the product information in advertisements may be as much an inducement as the free lunch to prospective readers. On the other hand, cable television, coupled with commercial television broadcasting, results in audi-ence members paying directly for *both* the free lunch *and* the advertisements, as inescapably they will for pay-television – if and when that becomes widespread and able to preempt mass appeal free lunch programs, such as championship sports events.

By emphasizing the economic role of the free lunch in media content, I by no means wish to minimize its importance in its own right. As a social institution with the agenda-setting role which it has, the mass media free lunch puts into words and images the view of events in the local community, the region, the country, and the world which journalists produce and media entrepreneurs publish. That the mass media in Canada and the United States on occasion expose and attack corruption and otherwise critically examine the working of the present social system is undeniable. We need not expand on that here because the literature on the mass media amply celebrates these efforts. But as is demonstrated in chapter 11 [Smythe, 1981], the overwhelming tendency of the free lunch is to reaffirm the status quo and retard change.

Nor should one minimize the propaganda value of the free lunch. Its production by Consciousness Industry is a process of interpreting and homogenizing the entire cultural heritage in current commoditized terms. (A sign over a Hollywood publicity agent's desk reads, "You never lose money by underestimating the level of popular taste.") As and when bourgeois literature, drama, art, and music, and traditional folk cultural materials (e.g., Calypso music) provide profitable opportunities, it all becomes raw material for commercial media free lunch and advertising content. The ideological basis of it all is possessive individualism with the corollaries described in Chapter 1. Beginnings are being made in the exploration of the concrete reality of how the process works (Dorfman and Mattelart, 1975; Schiller, 1969, 1973, 1976; Kellner, 1979; Gitlin, 1979). The range and subtlety of the propaganda is evidenced by the following testimony before a United States congressional subcommittee, "On Winning the Cold War," by Dr. Joseph Klapper. Although it is an evaluation of a form of propaganda addressed to foreigners, it is equally applicable to domestic media content:

> Now, of course the broadcasting of popular music is not likely to have an immediate effect on the audience's political attitude, but this kind of communication nevertheless provides a sort of entryway of Western ideas and Western concepts, even though these concepts may not be explicitly and completely stated at any one particular moment in the communication. In addition, and simply because the communication does fill a need which the audience enjoys having filled, it probably serves to build up a certain credibility and respect for the source of that communication. . . . And this building of source credibility is one of the numerous possible preparatory steps toward the eventual clinching moment of persuasion. (U.S. Congress, House, 1967, pp. 64–5)

The free lunch thus provides material which, taken jointly with the explicit advertising, gives the audience material to work on.

What is the nature of the service performed for the advertiser by the members of the purchased audience? In economic terms, the audience commodity is a nondurable producer's good which is bought and used in the marketing of the advertiser's product. The work which audience members perform for the advertiser to whom they have been sold is learning to buy goods and to spend their income accordingly. Sometimes, it is to buy any of the class of goods (e.g., an aircraft manufacturer is selling air transport in general, or the dairy industry, all brands of milk) but most often it is a particular "brand" of consumer goods. In short, they work to create the demand for advertised goods which is the purpose of the monopoly-capitalist advertisers. Audience members may resist, but the advertiser's expectations are realized sufficiently that the results perpetuate the system of demand management.

People in audiences, we should remember, have had a rich history of education for their work as audience members. As children, teenagers, and adults they have observed old and new models of particular brands of products on the street, in homes of friends, at school, at the job front, etc. Much time will have been spent in discussing the "good" and "bad" features of brands of commodities in hundreds of contexts. A constant process of direct experience with commodities goes on and blends into all aspects of people's lives all the time. Advertisers get this huge volume of audience work (creation of consumer consciousness) as a bonus even before a specific media free-lunch-advertising program appears on the tube face and initiates a new episode in audience work (See Smythe, 1981).

While people do their work as audience members they are simultaneously reproducing their own labor power. In this respect, we may avoid the trap of a manipulation-explanation by noting that if such labor power is, in fact, loyally attached to the monopoly-capitalist system, this would be welcome to the advertisers whose existence depends on the maintenance of that system. But in reproducing their labor power, workers respond to other realistic conditions which may on occasion surprise and disappoint the advertisers.

The nature of audience work may best be approached through successive approximations. At a superficial level it looks like this: "Customers do not buy things. They buy tools to solve problems," according to Professor T. N. Levitt (1976, p. 73) of Harvard Business School. The nature of the work done by audience power thus seems to be to use the advertising free lunch combination of sensory stimuli to determine whether s/he (1) has the "problem" the advertiser is posing (e.g., loneliness, sleeplessness, prospective economic insecurity for loved ones after the bread-winner's death, etc.), (2) is aware that there is a class of commodities which, if purchased and used will "solve" that problem (e.g., shampoo, nonprescription sleeping drugs, life insurance) and that people like him/her use this class of commodity for this purpose, (3) ought to add brand ZX of that class of commodities to the mental or physical shopping list for the next trip to the store. This is the advertisers' rational basis. For audience members, however, their work is not so rational.

There is an *ever-increasing* number of decisions forced on audience members by new commodities and their related advertising. In addition to the many thousands of different items stocked by a typical supermarket at any one time, more than a thousand new consumer commodities appear each year. Literally millions of possible comparative choices face the audience member who goes shopping. As a long line of books stretching back to the 1920s has argued (for example, Chase and Schlink, 1927), the consumer is totally unable to *know* either the craftsman's sense of quality or the "scientific" basis of quality as built into consumers goods by modern mass production techniques. Imagine yourself entering a toilet-goods section of a modern department store in which every product was in a similar glass container and the containers bore only the chemical description of the contents and the price. Unless you were a very experienced chemist specializing in cosmetics and other toiletries (and even then you would have to do a lot of thinking), how could you know which was a "best buy," or even what the product was intended to do: be it a shampoo, deodorant, skin-care cream, or what? Lacking the product brand name, the shape and symbolic decoration of the package, you would be helpless.[6]

It must be assumed that when most people go shopping, even for H.P.G., there is real necessity moving them. The refrigerator needs restocking. Soap is needed for washing, and so on. And that they are increasingly aware of the squeeze of increasing cost of living versus inadequate income. The recent appearance of "no-name brand" commodities is a response of monopoly capitalism to consumer resistance to the usual brand pricing practice. In the 1950s there was a flurry of "discount stores" where "standard" brand merchandise (acquired from bankrupt stores, from usual sources, or from thieves) was sold at substantial discounts. This was a tactical response of the system to consumer resistance. And with the artificial prosperity of the Vietnam war period these stores disappeared. It is probable that "no-name brand" merchandise is a similar, temporary tactical concession. In any event, "no-name brands" amount in fact to new "house brands" with, for the present, reduced prices.

Your work, as audience member, has to do with how your life's problems interact with the advertising-free-lunch experience. But how? How, in light of that experience do you decide whether you really have the "problem" to which the advertiser has sought to sensitize you? And if the answer to this question be affirmative, how do you decide that the class of commodities which have been produced to cope with that problem will really serve their advertised purpose? And if the answer to that question be affirmative, how do you decide whether to buy brand A, B, or n? *The process contains a monstrous contradiction. It is totally rational from the advertisers' perspective and totally irrational from the audience members'.*

Faced with the necessity to make some decisions as to what classes and what brands of commodities to put on the shopping list (if only to preserve a shred of self-respect as one capable of making one's own decisions), it seems that Staffen B. Linder (1970, p. 59) may be correct in saying that the most important way by which consumers can cope with commodities and advertising is to limit the time spent per purchase in thinking about what to buy:

> Reduced time for reflection previous to a decision would apparently entail a growing irrationality. However, since it is extremely rational to consider less and less per decision there exists a rationale of irrationality.

"Impulse purchasing" has increasingly become the practice of Consciousness Industry, as market researchers have studied the effect of store layout, shelf-level display, and commodity package design and artwork on customers pushing their basket-carts through supermarket aisles. Studies of eye-blink rates indicate that a semihypnotic condition of the customer results in impulse purchases for which no rationale can be remembered when the customer returns home. "Consumers" produced and delivered by Consciousness Industry are in the position of trying to cope with a giant con game. They know that they do not really have all the problems which advertisers press them to solve by buying their products. Placed in a time- and income-spending bind, the impossibility of making rational shopping decisions forces consumers to "take a chance." The lottery is perhaps the best model for explaining what happens at the moment of truth when the customer reaches for the package from the shelf. And it is perhaps significant that lotteries, so long excluded from socially sanctioned practice, have recently become legal and generally used in North America. For consumers accustomed to taking a chance on a $9.99 item on the supermarket shelf, the option of a statistically sheer random "chance" to win a million dollars can be very attractive and compelling. Yet the rationale of irrationality (Linder's) is unsatisfactory as an explanation of audience work. It may serve as a first approximation to an explanation. But we must dig deeper into the process of which audience work is a part.

How can audience power be "work" when it takes place in "free" or "leisure" time? What becomes of the labor theory of value if audiences are working? Is it not true that what people do when not working at the job front (where they are paid money for their work) is their free or leisure time by definition? Is it not true that "you can do as you please" in this "free" time? Have not "modern" household appliances relieved women of household work?

At the outset it is important to note that the idea of such free or leisure time is a hand-me-down from the upper classes in bourgeois society. It derives from the upper-class notion of leisure for the enjoyment of "official culture" (see chapter 9 [Smythe, 1981]). At the height of imperialist power toward the end of the nineteenth century, it took the form of emulating the *conspicuous* consumption of the rich and powerful, as Veblen so bitingly revealed in *The Theory of the Leisure Class* (1899). As transformed by monopoly capitalism, it meant the imitation of *expensive* consumption, for, as Veblen also pointed out, the policy of monopoly capitalism was to be "a competition in publicity and scarcity" (Smythe, 1981). David Riesman (1950) and Stuart Ewen (1976) focused on the illusory semblance of reality in such "leisure" and "free time."

It is necessary to state clearly that just as people are rarely totally controlled by Consciousness Industry, so marketed commodities rarely have absolutely no use value. Repeatedly, in different ways I emphasize that most people embody a dialectical tension: they feel it necessary to cooperate with the monopoly-capitalist system in a variety of ways and for a variety of reasons; yet at the same time, as human beings they resist such cooperation in a variety of ways, for a variety of reasons. An analogous internal dialectical tension seems to exist *within* most commodities under capitalism. The gas-guzzling, overpowered, dangerous private automobile *also* transports you from home to work and back again; when suitably "hotted up," it may even lure into a lasting relationship a commoditized person of the opposite sex, just as the advertisements promise. The relative strength of the repressive and emancipatory ingredients in a commodity obviously differs greatly as between different commodities, e.g., an adulterated drug as against ordinary packaged milk. As we shall see in chapter 10 [Smythe, 1981], this dialectical conflict within commodities exists within producer goods as well as consumer goods, which is the reason that the term *technology*, with its assumed neutral quality, is dangerously misleading. For most people in the core area today, leisure or free time, like technology, are propaganda devices which obscure and confuse the real contradictions between the respects in which people cooperate with and resist the monopoly-capitalist system and its commodities.

Except for those people who have been so rich that they did not have to work, all people have always had to work – one way or another – when not at the job in order to prepare themselves to work *tomorrow*. *Before* the mass production of consumer goods – roughly before 1875 – in capitalist core countries, people's work to prepare themselves to work tomorrow (e.g., to reproduce their labor power) was done under conditions of cottage industry. For example they baked their own bread using flour which they might have ground themselves and yeast which they cultured for themselves. But with the mass production of consumer goods, their work to reproduce their labor power depends on buying and using consumer goods *in end-product form*. They have become dependent on factory-baked bread. And if sophisticated durable goods, e.g., vacuum cleaners, have relieved them of the necessity to sweep with brooms, it has required them to spend time buying filters and other equipment and arranging for maintenance of such equipment by "service men." And the end-less proliferation of new commodities which clamor for their place in household consumption (e.g., electric can openers, electric carving knives, power lawn mowers, etc.) demands so much of so-called free time to buy, use, and maintain them that the idea of "free time" has become ridiculous. Consider what has happened to the time available to workers and the way it is used in the past century.

In 1850, under conditions of cottage industry, i.e., unbranded consumer goods, the average work week of employed men was about 70 hours per week in the United States.[7] The average worker could devote about 42 hours per week to such cottage industry types of reproduction of his labor power. By 1960, the time spent on the job was about 39.5 hours per week – an apparent reduction in time spent on the job of about 30 hours per week (to which should be added 2.5 hours as a generous estimate of the weekly equivalent of paid vacations).

Advertisers and home economists regularly argued that the apparent reduction in "work" hours created new leisure time for workers and housewives between 1910 and 1940, as Stuart Ewen's *Captains of Consciousness* (1976) demonstrated. Con-sumer durable goods like washing machines, vacuum cleaners, etc., were said to *free* housekeepers from work. Some time was indeed freed from drudgery in this way, but the illusion that most people had large blocks of free time was a myth created by Consciousness Industry. Upon close inspection, as we shall argue, leisure time for most people is work time. As Marylee Stephenson (1977, p. 32) puts it: "over 90 percent of 51 percent of the adult population is engaged in . . . wageless labor (known as housework) for their entire adult life. . . ."

In fact, the meaning of the almost 30 hours per week by which the *job* work week shrank between 1850 and 1960 was transformed doubly by monopoly capitalism. One transformation removed huge chunks of people's time from their discretion by metropolitan sprawl and by the nature of unpaid work which workers were obligated to perform. For example, recently travel time to and from the job has been estimated at 8.5 hours per week; "moonlighting" employment at a minimum of one hour per week; repair work around the home at another five hours per week; and men's work on household chores and shopping at another 2.3 hours per week. As I write this the postman drops through the slot a piece of direct mail advertising for a *Do-It-Yourself* manual. It tells me that owning this manual:

> . . . is like having the experts at your side . . . but without having to pay for them! You can save the expense of countless calls for cabinetmaker, carpenter, decorator, electrician, heating expert, locksmith, mason, painter, paper-hanger, plasterer, plumber, roofer, rug cleaner, tile layer.

And it lists more than 50 "projects you can build for your home or garden" with the manual.

A total of 16.8 hours per week of the roughly 32 hours of time suposedly "freed" as a result of "modernization" is thus anything but free. A further 7 hours of the 32 hours of "freed" time disappears when a correction for part-time female employment is made in the reported hours per week in 1960.[8]

A second transformation involved the pressure placed by the system on the remaining hours of the week. If sleeping is estimated at 8 hours a day, the remainder of the 168 hours in the week after subtracting sleeping time and the unfree work time identified earlier was 42 hours in 1850 and 49 hours in 1960. The apparent increase in "free" time has thus shrunk to 7 hours per week (instead of about 30 hours). We lack systematic information about the use of this increased free time for both dates. We do know that certain types of activities were common to both dates: personal care, making love, visiting with relatives and friends, preparing and eating meals, attending union, church, and other associative institutions, including saloons. We also know that in 1960 (but not in 1850) there was a vast array of *branded* consumer goods and services pressed on workers through advertising, retail establishment displays, and peer group influence. Attendance at spectator sports and participation in such activities as little leagues, bowling, camping, and "pleasure driving" of the automobile or snowmobile – all promoted for the sake of equipment and energy sales by the Consciousness Industry – now takes time that was devoted to noncommercial activities in 1850. In-house time must now be devoted to deciding whether to buy and to use (by whom, where, under what conditions, and why) an endless proliferation of goods for personal care, household furnishings, clothing, music reproduction equipment, etc. And thus far we have not mentioned mass media *use*, although it should be noted that workers are guided in all income and time expenditures by the mass media – through the blend of explicit advertising and advertising implicit in the program content.

Let us now introduce mass media use as it relates to the seven hours of "free" time thus far identified (ignoring the pressures on the audience to use its time and income referred to in the preceding paragraph). How much time do most people spend as part of the audience product of the mass media – their time which is sold by the media to advertisers? David Blank, economist for the Columbia Broadcasting System, found in 1970 that the average person watched television for 3.3 hours per day (23 hours per week) on an annual basis, listened to radio for 2.5 hours per day (18 hours per week), and read newspapers and magazines for 1 hour per day

(7 hours per week) (Blank, 1970). Recent years show similar magnitudes. If we look at the audience product in terms of families rather than individuals, we find that in 1973 advertisers in the United States purchased television audiences for an average of a little more than 43 hours per home per week.[9] By industry usage, this lumps together specialized audience commodities sold independently as "housewives," "children," and "families." In the prime time evening hours (7:00 PM to 11:00 PM), the television audience commodity consisted of a daily average of 83.8 million people, with an average of two persons viewing per home. Women were a significantly higher proportion of this prime time audience than men (42 percent as against 32 percent; children were 16 percent; teenagers 10 percent).

Let us sum up these figures. Television, radio, and newspapers plus magazines take up 48 hours per week, for the average American! And they have only seven hours more free time than in 1850! Obviously some doubling up takes place. So let us estimate that half of the radio listening takes place while traveling to or from work; perhaps another quarter while doing the personal care chores at the beginning and end of the day. As for television, perhaps a fourth of it (on average) is glimpsed while preparing meals, eating, washing dishes, or doing other household tasks or repair/construction work. Estimate half of newspaper and magazine reading as taking place while traveling between home and job, while eating, etc. Our reduced exclusive audience time with the four commercial media is now down to 22 hours per week. Obviously more doubling takes place between audience time and other activities, and the reader is invited to make more precise estimates based on (perhaps) some empirical research. On television broadcasts of commercial sports events in the United States one sees some spectators *in the stadia* who are simultaneously watching the live event and portable television sets (for the "instant replay" in stadia not blessed with huge overhead television screens for that purpose), or listening to the radio (for the sportscaster's instant comments on the play just completed).

Perhaps the only conclusion to be drawn at this time on this point is that there is no free time devoid of audience activity which is not preempted by other activities which are market-related (including sleep which is necessary if you are to be fit to meet your market tests on the morrow). In *any* society, sleep and other nonwork activities are necessary to restore and maintain life and labor power. Work itself is not intrinsically oppressive. It is the inclusion in so-called leisure time of commodity-producing work under monopoly capitalism which creates the contradiction between oppressive liberating activity in time for which people are not paid.

The bitter reality for most Canadians and Americans is that the commodity rat race – as they call it – makes a mockery of free time and leisure, both during their years at the job and after retirement.

What time is *not* work time in the mature capitalist core area? For the great majority of the population – all except those who are so rich that they can afford to have their shopping done by servants – 24 hours a day is work time. Modern machinery requires maintenance when idle between shifts. The human body requires rest, time for reflection, time for the cultivation of the arts (see chapter 9 [Smythe, 1981), time for the subtleties of raising children, time for community activities, etc. But the pressures for audience-oriented work exerted by Consciousness Industry are relentless. George Allen, famous American football coach, tells his players, "Nobody should work all the time. Leisure time is the five or six hours you sleep at night. You can combine two good things at once, sleep and leisure" (quoted in Terkel, 1974, p. 389).

How does the view that all the time of most of the people in the capitalist core countries is work time relate to Karl Marx's theory of labor power? As Bill Livant puts it, the power of the concept of surplus value ". . . rests wholly on the way Marx solved the great value problems of classical political economy, by *splitting the notion of labour in two*, into labour in productive use and labour power (the capacity to labor)."[10]

Labor in productive use in the production of commodities-in-general was Marx's concern in the three volumes of *Capital* (except for vol. 1, chap. 6) and scattered passages in the *Grundrisse*. It is clear from those exceptions that Marx assumed that labor power is produced by the laborer and by his or her immediate family, i.e., under the conditions of handicraft production prevailing when he wrote. In a word, labor power was "home made" (in the absence of dominant brand name commodities, mass advertising, and the mass media which monopoly capitalism had not yet invented). In Marx's period and in his analysis, the principal aspect of capitalist production was the alienation of workers from the means of producing commodities-in-general. Today and for some time past, the principal aspect of capitalist production has been the alienation of workers from the means of producing and reproducing themselves.

The prevailing Western Marxist view today still holds the incorrect assumption that the laborer is an *independent* commodity producer of labor power *which is his to sell*. But

> What often escapes attention is that just because the labourer sells it (his or her labour power) does not mean that he or she produces it. We are misled by fixating on the true fact that a human must eat and sleep into thinking that therefore the seller of labour power must also be the producer. Again the error of two combines into one (Livant, 1975b).

> Livant goes on to say that a Marxist view: . . . sees leisure time correctly as time of production, reproduction and repair of labour power. This production, reproduction and repair are activities. They are things people must do. As such they require labour power. To be sure, this latter labour power you do not have to sell directly to capital. But you do have to use it to produce labour power in the form you do have to sell.

(Chapters 3 and 4 [Smythe, 1981] discuss just how the contradictions within capitalism produced monopoly capitalism, Consciousness Industry, and the mass media.)

Under capitalism your labor power becomes a personal possession. It seems that you can do what you want with it. If you work at a job where you are paid, you sell it. Away from the job, it seems that your work is something you do not sell. But there is common misunderstanding at this point. At the job you are not paid for all the labor time you do sell (otherwise interest, profits, and management salaries could not be paid). And away from the job, your labor time *is* sold (through the audience commodity), although you do not sell it. What is produced at the job where you get paid are commodities used for consumption or for further production. And what is produced by you away from the job is your labor power for tomorrow and for the next generation: ability to work and to live (Livant, 1975a).

The point to be pursued here is that the ruling groups cultivated "high" or bourgeois culture (in the fine arts) both for their own enjoyment and as an invaluable ideological feature of monopoly capitalism (itself dealt with in chapter 9 [Smythe, 1981]). Liberal notions about "leisure" to which a substantial amount of effort by bourgeois sociologists has been devoted (see, for example, Kaplin, 1960, 1975) perpetuate the mystification of leisure, treating it "apolitically." In fact, the system used labor unions, religious organizations, and community arts organizations (musical, painting, sculpture, literary, poetic, etc.), to turn the "high culture" from Greece on down into a means of attaching workers loyally to the system. A considerable literature about "popular culture" and "mass culture" deals with this relationship, which is also dealt with in chapter 9 [Smythe, 1981] (see, for example, Garnham, 1977). The unrelenting pressures of Consciousness Industry, however, reveal the yawning gap between high culture notions of leisure, which are the stuff of establishment propaganda regarding "national identity," and the vulgar, atomized, and capitalized exploitation of leisure as a cover for an ever-expanding range of commodity markets.

Audiences for the commercial mass media are a strange type of institution. They are more a statistical abstraction than are, for example, the audience of the live or motion picture theater because they have no possibility of simultaneously and totally interacting internally to create an audience mood or affect. Yet we know that they are far from merely being statistical abstractions. Orson Welles' "Invasion from Mars" radio broadcast precipitated mass hysteria (Cantril et al., 1940). And the record industry depends on radio stations to produce "hit parades" which mobilize fans of popular music stars to buy records on a mass scale. We are far from having a full understanding of the audience commodity, but there is no doubt that it is a qualitatively new major social institution, a collectivity, and a commodity. As Bill Livant (1979a, p. 103) says:

> Virtually everyone is organized into the complex tapestry of these audiences, whose underlying properties we are just beginning to understand. For one thing, the production, destruction, division and recombination of audiences is a vast and turbulent motion. For another, the Audience Commodity is a multipurpose capacity. It is the other side of the labour power that Marx discovered in the production of commodities-in-general, and it is as Protean in its capacities.
>
> The *first* great form of the organization of this commodity [is] the Audience Commodity as a Market. This form emerged first historically and with the greatest clarity in the United States. . . . This form is the first, *but not the last.*

We can already observe that the audience commodity has changed the social form for political party electoral behavior in the capitalist world. Murdock (1978, p. 117) refers to the changing form of social conflict in Europe:

The expansion of consumerism was accompanied by a dampening down of industrial conflict and class struggle. The contradiction between capital and labor receded from the centre of attention and its place was taken by conflicts grounded in age, in gender, in nationality, in race, and above all in the yawning gap between the developed and underdeveloped worlds, between the colonizers and the colonized.

The rationalization by Consciousness Industry of the process of conducting elections through mass media "pseudo events" and advertising is, through the telltale demographics, evidence of the audience commodity, having been produced for the election market and paid for by the parties, at work in ways quite familiar in the North American scene. Richeri (1978) has linked the rapid transformation of the Italian political constituency system to the rapid introduction of the production of audiences by commercial television and radio stations in recent years. An analogous transformation of the electoral process took place in the United States and Canada between the mid-1930s and 1960s as political campaigning/advertising via radio broadcasting, public opinion polling, and interlocking ownership interests in radio (and later television) stations between politicians and newspaper publishers were substituted for nineteenth-century modes of mobilizing people for elections. Richard Nixon's flat statement in 1957 that political candidates must now be merchandised like any other consumer product recognized the reality. Europe, lagged by a decade or so, has now experienced the same transformation more quickly.

The work of the audience commodity poses severe problems for Marxist theory derived from Europe and based upon the analysis of competitive capitalism, nineteenth-century style. The *base* or *infrastructure* in that theory was defined as the job front where pay was received for productive work. There were two main reasons for this: (1) The factory system of nineteenth-century capitalism embodied mass production of (almost all unbranded) commodities with all the improved efficiency traceable to the Industrial Revolution. (2) The tradition in economic theory begun by the Physiocrats and running through Marx that production was closely allied to natural resources and especially agriculture. The superstructure in that theory was where the ruling class in the state inculcated ideology by its press, its educational and religious institutions, and its monopoly of force (police and military).

The clear dichotomy between base and superstructure was no longer possible under monopoly capitalism, with Consciousness Industry buying audiences comprising virtually the whole population to aid it in managing demand for its commodity output. For the audiences are engaged in production which is an essential to the capitalist system as was the production at the job front in the early nineteenth century. Perhaps the audience market even takes priority away from the job front because the former "beckons" the latter into action very directly through the mode of operation of giant integrated corporations. The superstructure (in nineteenth-century terms) is thus decisively engaged in production. And increasingly, as welfare programs of employers have engaged people at the job front in all manner of popular cultural activities and vocational training, it seems as if the old "infrastructure" has taken on in part the ideological training functions previously associated with the old "superstructure." (See chapters 3 and 4 [Smythe, 1981].) It is not clear now how Marxists will resolve the anomalies in their theory as it applies to core area monopoly capitalism, especially because current Marxist theorists do not recognize that the audience commodity even exists.

It appears, as will be argued further in chapters 11 and 12 [Smythe, 1981], that in seeming to perfect its system for managing demand through producing and consuming audiences in order to market its products, monopoly capital has produced its principal antagonist in the core area: people commodified in audience markets who are consciously seeking noncommodified group relations. A symptom may be apparent in a downward trend in television viewing in 1977 and 1979 in the United States after 30 years of rising viewing.[11]

It has long been noticed that all traditional social institutions (family, church, labor union, political party, etc.) have been stripped of much of their traditional purpose by the impact of mass-produced communications. The mysticism attached to technique (and "technology") has incorrectly assumed that the medium basically defines the audience. But as a historical analysis of the rise of the mass media will show, the opposite has been true: the availability and actions of the audience is the basic feature in the definition of the media, singly and collectively. By placing the contradiction between advertisers/media on the one hand and audiences on the other on the level of social relations we are on solid ground and can repudiate the mysticism of the technological trap by which audiences are tied to hardware, software, and technique (as in Innis, McLuhan, and others).

In order to dig deeper into the process of which audience work is a part, it is necessary to consider how we got this way. In other words, we must review some history of monopoly capitalism. This will be the burden of chapters 3 and 4 [Smythe, 1981].

Notes

1 This literature is reviewed in Simon (1970); Schmalensee (1972); also, Pollak (1978); Pessemier (1978); and Marschak (1978).

2 Raymond Williams comes closer than many Marxists to a realistic treatment of communications and may be singled out for comment. In his *Marxism and Literature* (1978) he sees the full range of "cultural industry," including entertainment, as "necessary material production." He does not include advertising in cultural industry and is vague as to what, if any, activities besides official "culture" are included in it. He criticizes the base–superstructure dichotomy in twentieth-century Marxism and shows that it derived from Plekhanov, not Marx. Williams' *Television: Technology and Cultural Form* (1975) is disappointing. Broadcasting was called into existence by "a new way of life." The innovation of broadcasting is similarly mystified. It is traced to "no more than a set of particular social decisions, in particular circumstances, which were then so widely if imperfectly ratified that it is now difficult to see them as decisions rather than as (retrospectively) inevitable results" (p. 23). By whom, why, in what circumstances, the decisions were

made he doesn't say. "Ideological control" was vaguely a purpose, again with no indication of how or who was involved. He never defines "technology" and uses the term as politically neutral. He sees broadcasting in technical terms, worldwide in scope, and advertising as ". . . a feature not of broadcasting itself but of its uses in a specific society [unnamed]" (p. 68). He does a fair critical analysis of McLuhan, not noticing that he himself had given us a line from McLuhan (". . . the means of communication preceded their content," p. 25). In reality, of course, it was the prospective audience which beckoned both the means and the content into existence. In neither book does he recognize the media as producing audiences for sale to advertisers or that advertisers use the audience power to complete the marketing of their consumer goods production. In neither does he recognize demand management by TNCs in monopoly capitalism – terms strangely lacking from his books.

3   I first addressed this criticism to Marxist theories in "Communications: Blindspot of Western Marxism" (1977). Also see Murdock, Graham, "Blindspots about Western Marxism: A Reply to Dallas Smythe" (1978) and my "Rejoinder to Graham Murdock" (Smythe, 1978), and Livant (1979a).

4   One of my critics argues that a better term for what advertisers buy would be *attention*. At our present naive stage concerning the matter, it does *seem* as if attention is indeed what is bought. But where people are paid for working on the job, should one say that what the employer buys is "labor power" or "the manual dexterity and attention necessary for tending machines?" Where I refer to audiences as being produced, purchased, and used, let it be understood that I mean "audience power," however it may turn out upon further realistic analysis to be exercised.

5   These estimates are made by applying to Canadian time sales by television and radio the same ratio which such time sales bear to total advertising expenditures on television and radio in the United States. In the United States in 1976, 77 percent of advertising expenditures on television went for network and station time ($5.198 billion), and 22 percent for production of program and advertising content; in radio 87 percent ($2.019 billion) went to network and station time and 13 percent to program and advertising content. In Canada the official statistics are nonsensical. Statistics Canada reported total advertising expenditures on television of $341.8 million; time sales of networks and stations to advertisers were given as $322.6 million. For radio, $111.1 million advertising expenditures were reported; time sales of networks and stations to advertisers (which represent only part of advertising expenditures) were given as $241.8 million. I have assumed that Canadian practice followed the United States model.

6   I am indebted to William Leiss for this hypothetical and chastening idea. See his *The Limits to Satisfaction* (1976, p. 81).

7   The following analysis of time use is based on de Grazia (1964).

8   Part-time workers (probably more female than male) amounted in 1960 to 19 percent of the employed labor force in the United States and they worked an average of 19 hours weekly. If we exclude such workers in order to get a figure comparable to the 70 hours in 1850, we consider the weekly hours worked by the average American male who worked at least 35 hours per week. We then find that they averaged 46.4 hours (as against 39.5 hours for all workers). For the sake of brevity, I omit the counterpart calculation of "free time" for women jobholders. No sexist implications are intended.

9   *Broadcasting Yearbook*, 1974, p. 69.

10   Livant (1975c); Bill Livant, University of Regina, has helped to develop the analysis of the audience commodity and I acknowledge this emphatically.

11   *Time*, 12 March 1979, p. 57.

References

Baran, P. T., and Sweezy, P. (1966) *Monopoly Capital*. New York: Monthly Review.

Barnouw, Erik (1978) *The Sponsor*. New York: Oxford University Press.

Blank, David M. (1970) "Pleasurable Pursuits – The Changing Structure of Leisure Time Spectator Activities," National Association of Business Economists, Annual Meeting, September (unpublished paper).

Cantril, Hadley, Gaudet, Hazel, and Herzog, Herta (1940) *Invasion from Mars*. Princeton: Princeton University Press.

Chamberlin, E. H. (1931) *The Theory of Monopolistic Competition*. Cambridge: Harvard University Press.

Chase, Stuart, and Schlink, F. J. (1927) *Your Money's Worth: A Study in the Waste of the Consumer's Dollar*. New York: Macmillan.

de Grazia, Sebastian (1964) *Of Time, Work and Leisure*. New York: Anchor.

Dorfman, Ariel, and Mattelart, Armand (1975) *How to Read Donald Duck: Imperialist Ideology in the Disney Comic*. New York: International General.

Ewen, Stuart (1976) *Captains of Consciousness*. New York: McGraw-Hill.

Galbraith, J. K. (1967) *The New Industrial State*. Boston: Houghton Mifflin.

Garnham, Nicholas (1977) "Towards a Political Economy of Culture," *NUQ*, Summer, pp. 341–57.

Citlin, Todd (1979) "Prime Time Ideology: The Hegemonic Process in Television Entertainment," *Social Problems*, vol. 26, no. 3, pp. 257–66.

Kaplin, Max (1960) *Leisure in America: A Social Inquiry*. New York: Wiley.

—— (1975) *Leisure: Theory and Policy*. New York: Wiley.

Kellner, Douglas (1979) "TV, Ideology and Emancipatory Popular Culture," *Socialist Review*, vol. 9, no. 3, May–June, pp. 13–53.

Leiss, William (1976) *The Limits to Satisfaction: An Essay on the Problems of Needs and Commodities*. Toronto: University of Toronto Press.

Levitt, T. N. (1976) "The Industrialization of Service," *Harvard Business Review*, September–October, pp. 63–74.

Liebling, A. J. (1961) *The Press*. New York: Ballantine.

Linder, Staffen B. (1970) *The Harried Leisure Class*. New York: Columbia University Press.

Livant, Bill (1975a) "The Communication Commodity," University of Regina, 25 December (unpublished paper).

—— (1975b) "More on the Production of Damaged Labour Power," 1 April (unpublished paper).

—— (1975c) "Notes on the Development of the Production of Labour Power" (unpublished paper).

Lyle, Jack (1972) "Television in Daily Life: Patterns of Use," in Rubenstein, E. A., Comstock, G. H., and Murray, J. P. (eds.), *Television and Social Behaviour*, vol. IV, pp. 1–32. Rockville, MD., National Institute of Mental Health.

Mao Zedong (1968) *Four Essays on Philosophy*. Beijing: Foreign Language Press.

Marschak, T. A. (1978) "On the Study of Taste-Changing Policies," *American Economic Review*, vol. 68, no. 2, pp. 386–91.

Murdock, Graham (1978) "Blindspots about Western Marxism: A Reply to Dallas Smythe," *Canadian Journal of Political and Social Theory*, vol. 2, no. 2, pp. 109–19.

Pessemier, Edgar A. (1978) "Stochastic Properties of Changing Preferences," *American Economic Review*, vol. 68, no. 2, pp. 380–5.

Pollak, Robert A. (1978) "Endogenous Taste in Demand and Welfare Analysis," *American Economic Review*, vol. 68, no. 2, pp. 374–9.

Richeri, Giuseppe (1978) "Italy: A Democratization of the Media," paper at Congress of International Association for Mass Communication Research, Warsaw, Poland.

Riesman, David (1950) *The Lonely Crowd*. New Haven: Yale University Press.

Rinchart, James W. (1975) *The Tyranny of Work*. Don Mills, Ontario: General Publishing.

Schiller, Herbert I. (1969) *Mass Communications and American Empire*. New York: A. M. Kelley.

—— (1973) *The Mind Managers*. Boston: Beacon Press.

Schiller, Herbert, I., and Phillips, J. D. (1976) *Superstate*. Urbana: University of Illinois Press.

Schmalensee, R. (1972) *The Economics of Advertising*. Amsterdam: North Holland.

Simon, Julian L. (1970) *Issues in the Economics of Advertising*. Urbana: University of Illinois Press.

Smythe, Dallas W. (1977) "Communications: Blindspot of Western Marxism," *Canadian Journal of Political and Social Theory*, vol. 1, no. 3, pp. 1–28.

—— (1978) "Rejoinder to Graham Murdock," *Canadian Journal of Political and Social Theory*, vol. 2, no. 2, pp. 120–7.

—— (1980) "Communications: Blindspot of Economics," in Melody, W. (ed.), *Culture, Communication and Dependency: The Tradition of H. A. Innis*. Norwood, NJ: Ablex.

—— (1981) *Dependency Road: Communications, Capitalism, Consciousness Canada*. Norwood, NJ: Ablex.

Stephenson, Marylee (1977) "Never Done, Never Noticed: Women's Work in Canada," *This Magazine*, vol. 11, no. 6, pp. 31–3.

Terkel, Louis (1974) *Working*. New York: Pantheon.

US Congress (1967) House of Representatives. Subcommittee on International Organizations and Movements. Committee on Foreign Affairs, Report no. 5, *Winning the Cold War: The United States Ideological Offensive*. 90th Congress, 1st Session, House of Representatives.

Veblen, Thorstein (1927 [1899]) *The Theory of the Leisure Class*. New York: Macmillan.

Williams, Raymond (1975) *Television: Technology and Cultural Form*. New York: Schocken Books.

—— (1978) *Marxism and Literature*. Oxford: Oxford University Press.

17

A Propaganda Model

Edward Herman and Noam Chomsky

The mass media serve as a system for communicating messages and symbols to the general populace. It is their function to amuse, entertain, and inform, and to inculcate individuals with the values, beliefs, and codes of behavior that will integrate them into the institutional structures of the larger society. In a world of concentrated wealth and major conflicts of class interest, to fulfil this role requires systematic propaganda.[1]

In countries where the levers of power are in the hands of a state bureaucracy, the monopolistic control over the media, often supplemented by official censorship, makes it clear that the media serve the ends of a dominant elite. It is much more difficult to see a propaganda system at work where the media are private and formal censorship is absent. This is especially true where the media actively compete, periodically attack and expose corporate and governmental malfeasance, and aggressively portray themselves as spokesmen for free speech and the general community interest. What is not evident (and remains undiscussed in the media) is the limited nature of such critiques, as well as the huge inequality in command of resources, and its effect both on access to a private media system and on its behavior and performance.

A propaganda model focuses on this inequality of wealth and power and its multi-level effects on mass-media interests and choices. It traces the routes by which money and power are able to filter out the news fit to print, marginalize dissent, and allow the government and dominant private interests to get their messages across to the public. The essential ingredients of our propaganda model, or set of news "filters," fall under the following headings: (1) the size, concentrated ownership, owner wealth, and profit orientation of the dominant mass-media firms; (2) advertising as the primary income source of the mass media; (3) the reliance of the media on information provided by government, business, and "experts" funded and approved

From Edward Herman and Noam Chomsky, "A propaganda model." In *Manufacturing Consent: The Political Economy of the Mass Media*, pp. 1–35. New York: Pantheon, 1988.

by these primary sources and agents of power; (4) "flak" as a means of disciplining the media; and (5) "anticommunism" as a national religion and control mechanism. These elements interact with and reinforce one another. The raw material of news must pass through successive filters, leaving only the cleansed residue fit to print. They fix the premises of discourse and interpretation, and the definition of what is newsworthy in the first place, and they explain the basis and operations of what amount to propaganda campaigns.

The elite domination of the media and marginalization of dissidents that results from the operation of these filters occurs so naturally that media news people, frequently operating with complete integrity and goodwill, are able to convince themselves that they choose and interpret the news "objectively" and on the basis of professional news values. Within the limits of the filter constraints they often are objective; the constraints are so powerful, and are built into the system in such a fundamental way, that alternative bases of news choices are hardly imaginable. In assessing the newsworthiness of the U.S. government's urgent claims of a shipment of MIGs to Nicaragua on November 5, 1984, the media do not stop to ponder the bias that is inherent in the priority assigned to government-supplied raw material, or the possibility that the government might be manipulating the news,[2] imposing its own agenda, and deliberately diverting attention from other material.[3] It requires a macro, alongside a micro- (story-by-story), view of media operations, to see the pattern of manipulation and systematic bias.

Let us turn now to a more detailed examination of the main constituents of the propaganda model, which will be applied and tested in the chapters that follow.

Size, Ownership, and Profit Orientation of the Mass Media: The First Filter

In their analysis of the evolution of the media in Great Britain, James Curran and Jean Seaton describe how, in the first half of the nineteenth century, a radical press emerged that reached a national working-class audience. This alternative press was effective in reinforcing class consciousness: it unified the workers because it fostered an alternative value system and framework for looking at the world, and because it "promoted a greater collective confidence by repeatedly emphasizing the potential power of working people to effect social change through the force of "combination" and organized action."[4] This was deemed a major threat by the ruling elites. One MP asserted that the working-class newspapers "inflame passions and awaken their selfishness, contrasting their current condition with what they contend to be their future condition – a condition incompatible with human nature, and those immutable laws which Providence has established for the regulation of civil society."[5] The result was an attempt to squelch the working-class media by libel laws and prosecutions, by requiring an expensive security bond as a condition for publication, and by imposing various taxes designed to drive out radical media by raising their costs. These coercive efforts were not effective, and by mid-century they had been abandoned in favor of the liberal view that the market would enforce responsibility.

Curran and Seaton show that the market *did* successfully accomplish what state intervention failed to do. Following the repeal of the punitive taxes on newspapers between 1853 and 1869, a new daily local press came into existence, but not one new local working-class daily was established through the rest of the nineteenth century. Curran and Seaton note that

> Indeed, the eclipse of the national radical press was so total that when the Labour Party developed out of the working-class movement in the first decade of the twentieth century, it did not obtain the exclusive backing of a single national daily or Sunday paper.[6]

One important reason for this was the rise in scale of newspaper enterprise and the associated increase in capital costs from the mid-nineteenth century onward, which was based on technological improvements along with the owners' increased stress on reaching large audiences. The expansion of the free market was accompanied by an "industrialization of the press." The total cost of establishing a national weekly on a profitable basis in 1837 was under a thousand pounds, with a break-even circulation of 6,200 copies. By 1867, the estimated start-up cost of a new London daily was 50,000 pounds. The *Sunday Express*, launched in 1918, spent over two million pounds before it broke even with a circulation of over 250,000.[7]

Similar processes were at work in the United States, where the start-up cost of a new paper in New York City in 1851 was $69,000; the public sale of the *St. Louis Democrat* in 1872 yielded $456,000; and city newspapers were selling at from $6 to $18 million in the 1920s.[8] The cost of machinery alone, of even very small newspapers, has for many decades run into the hundreds of thousands of dollars; in 1945 it could be said that "Even small-newspaper publishing is big business . . . [and] is no longer a trade one takes up lightly even if he has substantial cash – or takes up at all if he doesn't."[9]

Thus the first filter – the limitation on ownership of media with any substantial outreach by the requisite large size of investment – was applicable a century or more ago, and it has become increasingly effective over time.[10] In 1986 there were some 1,500 daily newspapers, 11,000 magazines, 9,000 radio and 1,500 TV stations, 2,400 book publishers, and seven movie studios in the United States – over 25,000 media entities in all. But a large proportion of those among this set who were news dispensers were very small and local, dependent on the large national companies and wire services for all but local news. Many more were subject to common ownership, sometimes extending through virtually the entire set of media variants.[11]

Ben Bagdikian stresses the fact that despite the large media numbers, the twenty-nine largest media systems account for over half of the output of newspapers, and most of the sales and audiences in magazines, broadcasting, books, and movies. He contends that these "constitute a new Private Ministry of Information and Culture" that can set the national agenda.[12]

Actually, while suggesting a media autonomy from corporate and government power that we believe to be incompatible with structural facts (as we describe below), Bagdikian also may be understating the degree of effective concentration in news manufacture. It has long been noted that the media are tiered, with the top tier – as measured by prestige, resources, and outreach – comprising somewhere between ten and twenty-four systems.[13] It is this top tier, along with the government and wire services, that defines the news agenda and supplies much of the national and international news to the lower tiers of the media, and thus for the general public.[14] Centralization within the top tier was substantially increased by the post-World War II rise of television and the national networking of this important medium. Pre-television news markets were local, even if heavily dependent on the higher tiers and a narrow set of sources for national and international news; the networks provide national and international news from three national sources, and television is now the principal source of news for the public.[15] The maturing of cable, however, has resulted in a fragmentation of television audiences and a slow erosion of the market share and power of the networks.

Table 17.1 provides some basic financial data for the twenty-four media giants (or their controlling parent companies) that make up the top tier of media companies in the United States.[16] This compilation includes: (1) the three television networks: ABC (through its parent, Capital Cities), CBS, and NBC (through its ultimate parent, General Electric [GE]); (2) the leading newspaper empires: *New York Times, Washington Post, Los Angeles Times* (Times-Mirror), *Wall Street Journal* (Dow Jones), Knight-Ridder, Gannett, Hearst, Scripps-Howard, Newhouse (Advance Publications), and the Tribune Company; (3) the major news and general-interest magazines: *Time, Newsweek* (subsumed under *Washington Post*), *Reader's Digest, TV Guide* (Triangle), and *U.S. News & World Report*; (4) a major book publisher (McGraw-Hill); and (5) other cable-TV systems of large and growing importance: those of Murdoch, Turner, Cox, General Corp., Taft, Storer,[17] and Group W (Westinghouse). Many of these systems are prominent in more than one field and are only arbitrarily placed in a particular category (Time, Inc., is very important in cable as well as magazines; McGraw-Hill is a major publisher of magazines; the Tribune Company has become a large force in television as well as newspapers; Hearst is important in magazines as well as newspapers; and Murdoch has significant newspaper interests as well as television and movie holdings).

These twenty-four companies are large, profit-seeking corporations, owned and controlled by quite wealthy people. It can be seen in Table 17.1 that all but one of the top companies for whom data are available have assets in excess of $1 billion, and the median size (middle item by size) is $2.6 billion. It can also be seen in the table that approximately three-quarters of these media giants had after-tax profits in excess of $100 million, with the median at $183 million.

Many of the large media companies are fully integrated into the market, and for the others, too, the pressures of stockholders, directors, and bankers to focus on the bottom line are powerful. These pressures have intensified in recent years as media stocks have become market favorites, and actual or prospective owners of newspapers and television properties have found it possible to capitalize increased audience size and advertising revenues into multiplied values of the media franchises – and great wealth.[18] This has encouraged the entry of speculators and increased the pressure and temptation to focus more intensively on profitability. Family owners have been

Table 17.1 Financial data for 24 large media corporations (or their parent firms), December 1986

Company	Total assets ($ millions)	Profits before taxes ($ millions)	Profits after taxes ($ millions)	Total revenue ($ millions)
Advance Publications (Newhouse)[a]	2,500	NA	NA	2,200
Capital Cities/ABC	5,191	688	448	4,124
CBS	3,370	470	370	4,754
Cox Communications[b]	1,111	170	87	743
Dow Jones & Co.	1,236	331	183	1,135
Gannett	3,365	540	276	2,801
General Electric (NBC)	34,591	3,689	2,492	36,725
Hearst[c]	4,040	NA	215 (1983)	2,100 (1983)
Knight-Ridder	1,947	267	140	1,911
McGraw-Hill	1,463	296	154	1,577
News Corp. (Murdoch)[d]	8,460	377	170	3,822
New York Times	1,405	256	132	1,565
Reader's Digest[e]	NA	75–110 (1985)	NA	1,400 (1985)
Scripps-Howard[f]	NA	NA	NA	1,062
Storer[g]	1,242	68	(–17)	537
Taft	1,257	(–11)	(–53)	500
Time, Inc.	4,230	626	376	3,762
Times-Mirror	2,929	680	408	2,948
Triangle[h]	NA	NA	NA	730
Tribune Co.	2,589	523	293	2,030
Turner Broadcasting	1,904	(–185)	(–187)	570
U.S. News & World Report[i]	200+	NA	NA	140
Washington Post	1,145	205	100	1,215
Westinghouse	8,482	801	670	10,731

NA = not available

[a] The asset total is taken from *Forbes* magazine's wealth total for the Newhouse family for 1985; the total revenue is for media sales only, as reported in *Advertising Age*, June 29, 1987.

[b] Cox Communications was publicly owned until 1985, when it was merged into another Cox family company, Cox Enterprises. The data presented here are for year-end 1984, the last year of public ownership and disclosure of substantial financial information.

[c] Data compiled in William Barrett, "Citizens Rich," *Forbes*, Dec. 14, 1987.

[d] These data are in Australian dollars and are for June 30, 1986; at that date the Australian dollar was worth 68 /100 of a U.S. dollar.

[e] Data for 1985, as presented in the *New York Times*, Feb. 9, 1986.

[f] Total revenue for media sales only, as reported in *Advertising Age*, June 29, 1987.

[g] Storer came under the control of the Wall Street firm Kohlberg Kravis Roberts & Co. in 1985; the data here are for December 1984, the last period of Storer autonomy and publicly available information.

[h] Total revenue for media sales only; from *Advertising Age*, June 29, 1987.

[i] Total assets as of 1984–5, based on "Mort Zuckerman, Media's New Mogul," *Fortune*, Oct. 14, 1985; total revenue from *Advertising Age*, June 29, 1987.

increasingly divided between those wanting to take advantage of the new opportunities and those desiring a continuation of family control, and their splits have often precipitated crises leading finally to the sale of the family interest.[19]

This trend toward greater integration of the media into the market system has been accelerated by the loosening of rules limiting media concentration, cross-ownership, and control by non-media companies.[20] There has also been an abandonment of restrictions – previously quite feeble anyway – on radio–TV commercials, entertainment-mayhem programming, and "fairness doctrine" threats, opening the door to the unrestrained commercial use of the airwaves.[21]

The greater profitability of the media in a deregulated environment has also led to an increase in takeovers and takeover threats, with even giants like CBS and Time, Inc., directly attacked or threatened. This has forced the managements of the media giants to incur greater debt and to focus ever more aggressively and unequivocally on profitability, in order to placate owners and reduce the attractiveness of their properties to outsiders.[22] They have lost some of their limited autonomy to bankers, institutional investors, and large individual investors whom they have had to solicit as potential "white knights."[23]

While the stock of the great majority of large media firms is traded on the securities markets, approximately two-thirds of these companies are either closely held or still controlled by members of the originating family who retain large blocks of stock. This situation is changing as family ownership becomes diffused among larger numbers of heirs and the market opportunities for selling media properties continue to improve, but the persistence of family control is evident in the data shown in Table 17.2. Also evident in the table is the enormous wealth possessed by the controlling families of the top media firms. For seven of the twenty-four, the market value of the media properties owned by the controlling families in the mid-1980s exceeded a billion dollars, and the median value was close to half a billion dollars.[24] These control groups obviously have a special stake in the status quo by virtue of their wealth and their strategic position in one of the great institutions of society. And they exercise the power of this strategic position, if only by establishing the general aims of the company and choosing its top management.[25]

The control groups of the media giants axe also brought into close relationships with the mainstream of the corporate community through boards of directors and social links. In the cases of NBC and the Group W television and cable systems, their respective parents, GE and Westinghouse, are themselves mainstream corporate giants, with boards of directors that are dominated by corporate and banking executives. Many of the other large media firms have boards made up predominantly of insiders, a general characteristic of relatively small and owner-dominated companies. The larger the firm and the more widely distributed the stock, the larger the number and proportion of outside directors. The composition of the outside directors of the media giants is very similar to that of large non-media corporations. Table 17.3 shows that active corporate executives and bankers together account for a little over half the total of the outside directors of ten media giants; and the lawyers and corporate-banker retirees (who account for nine of the thirteen under "Retired") push the corporate total to about two-thirds of the outside-director aggregate.

Table 17.2 Wealth of the control groups of 24 large media corporations (or their parent companies), February 1986

Company	Controlling family or group	Percentage of voting stock by control group (%)	Value of controlling stock interest ($ millions)
Advance Publications	Newhouse family	Closely held	2,200[F]
Capital Cities	Officers and directors (ODs)	20.7 (Warren Buffett, 17.8)	711[P]
CBS	ODs	20.6[a]	551[P]
Cox Communications	Cox family	36	1,900[F]
Dow Jones & Co.	Bancroft-Cox families	54	1,500[P]
Gannett	ODs	1.9	95[P]
General Electric	ODs	Under 1	171[P]
Hearst	Hearst family	33	1,500[F]
Knight-Ridder	Knight and Ridder families	18	447[P]
McGraw-Hill	McGraw family	c.20	450[F]
News Corp.	Murdoch family	49	300[F]
New York Times	Sulzberger family	80	450[F]
Reader's Digest	Wallace estate managed by trustees; no personal beneficiaries	NA	NA
Scripps-Howard	Scripps heirs	NA	1,400[F]
Storer	ODs	8.4	143[P]
Taft	ODs	4.8	37[P]
Time, Inc.	ODs	10.7 (Luce 4.6, Temple 3.2)	406[P]
Times-Mirror	Chandlers	35	1,200[P]
Triangle	Annenbergs	Closely held	1,600[F]
Tribune Co.	McCormick heirs	16.6	273[P]
Turner Broadcasting	Turner	80	222[P]
U.S. News & World Report	Zuckerman	Closely held	176[b]
Washington Post	Graham family	50+	350[F]
Westinghouse	ODs	Under 1	42[P]

[a] These holdings include William Paley's 8.1 percent and a 12.2 percent holding of Laurence Tisch through an investment by Loews. Later in the year, Loews increased its investment to 24.9 percent, and Laurence Tisch soon thereafter became acting chief executive officer.

[b] This is the price paid by Zuckerman when he bought *U.S. News* in 1984. See Gwen Kinkead, "Mort Zuckerman, Media's New Mogul," *Fortune*, Oct. 14, 1985, p. 196.

Sources: P means taken from proxy statements and computed from stock values as of February 1986; F. means taken from *Forbes* magazine's annual estimate of wealth holdings of the very rich.

Table 17.3 Affiliations of the outside directors of ten large media companies (or their parents) in 1986[a]

Primary affiliation	Number	Percent
Corporate executive	39	41.1
Lawyer	8	8.4
Retired (former corporate executive or banker)	13 (9)	13.7 (9.5)
Banker	8	8.4
Consultant	4	4.2
Nonprofit organization	15	15.8
Other	8	8.4
Total	95	100.0
Other relationships		
Other directorships (bank directorships)	255 (36)	
Former government officials	15	
Member of Council on Foreign Relations	20	

[a] Dow Jones & Co.; Washington Post; New York Times; Time, Inc.; CBS; Times-Mirror; Capital Cities; General Electric; Gannett; and Knight-Ridder.

These 95 outside directors had directorships in an additional 36 banks and 255 other companies (aside from the media company and their own firm of primary affiliation).[26]

In addition to these board linkages, the large media companies all do business with commercial and investment bankers, obtaining lines of credit and loans, and receiving advice and service in selling stock and bond issues and in dealing with acquisition opportunities and takeover threats. Banks and other institutional investors are also large owners of media stock. In the early 1980s, such institutions held 44 percent of the stock of publicly owned newspapers and 35 percent of the stock of publicly owned broadcasting companies.[27] These investors are also frequently among the largest stockholders of individual companies. For example, in 1980–1, the Capital Group, an investment company system, held 7.1 percent of the stock of ABC, 6.6 percent of Knight-Ridder, 6 percent of Time, Inc., and 2.8 percent of Westinghouse.[28] These holdings, individually and collectively, do not convey control, but these large investors can make themselves heard, and their actions can affect the welfare of the companies and their managers.[29] If the managers fail to pursue actions that favor shareholder returns, institutional investors will be inclined to sell the stock (depressing its price), or to listen sympathetically to outsiders contemplating takeovers. These investors are a force helping press media companies toward strictly market (profitability) objectives.

So is the diversification and geographic spread of the great media companies. Many of them have diversified out of particular media fields into others that seemed like growth areas. Many older newspaper-based media companies, fearful of the power of television and its effects on advertising revenue, moved as rapidly as they could into broadcasting and cable TV. Time, Inc., also, made a major diversification move into cable TV, which now accounts for more than half its profits. Only a small minority of the twenty-four largest media giants remain in a single media sector.[30]

The large media companies have also diversified beyond the media field, and non-media companies have established a strong presence in the mass media. The most important cases of the latter are GE, owning RCA, which owns the NBC network, and Westinghouse, which owns major television-broadcasting stations, a cable network, and a radio-station network. GE and Westinghouse are both huge, diversified multinational companies heavily involved in the controversial areas of weapons production and nuclear power. It may be recalled that from 1965 to 1967, an attempt by International Telephone and Telegraph (ITT) to acquire ABC was frustrated following a huge outcry that focused on the dangers of allowing a great multinational corporation with extensive foreign investments and business activities to control a major media outlet.[31] The fear was that ITT control "could compromise the independence of ABC's news coverage of political events in countries where ITT has interests."[32] The soundness of the decision disallowing the acquisition seemed to have been vindicated by the later revelations of ITT's political bribery and involvement in attempts to overthrow the government of Chile. RCA and Westinghouse, however, had been permitted to control media companies long before the ITT case, although some of the objections applicable to ITT would seem to apply to them as well. GE is a more powerful company than ITT, with an extensive international reach, deeply involved in the nuclear power business, and far more important than ITT in the arms industry. It is a highly centralized and quite secretive organization, but one with a vast stake in "political" decisions.[33] GE has contributed to the funding of the American Enterprise Institute, a right-wing think tank that supports intellectuals who will get the business message across. With the acquisition of ABC, GE should be in a far better position to assure that sound views are given proper attention.[34] The lack of outcry over its takeover of RCA and NBC resulted in part from the fact that RCA control over NBC had already breached the gate of separateness, but it also reflected the more pro-business and *laissez-faire* environment of the Reagan era.

The non-media interests of most of the media giants are not large and, excluding the GE and Westinghouse systems, they account for only a small fraction of their total revenue. Their multinational outreach, however, is more significant. The television networks, television syndicators, major news magazines, and motion-picture studios all do extensive business abroad, and they derive a substantial fraction of their revenues from foreign sales and the operation of foreign affiliates. *Reader's Digest* is printed in seventeen languages and is available in over 160 countries. The Murdoch empire was originally based in Australia, and the controlling parent company is still an Australian corporation; its expansion in the United States is funded by profits from Australian and British affiliates.[35]

Another structural relationship of importance is the media companies' dependence on and ties with government. The radio-TV companies and networks all require government licenses and franchises and are thus potentially subject to government control or harassment. This technical legal dependency has been used as a club to discipline the media, and media policies that stray too often from an establishment orientation could activate this threat.[36] The media protect themselves from this contingency by lobbying and other political expenditures, the cultivation of political relationships, and care in policy. The political ties of the media have been impressive. Table 17.3 shows that fifteen of ninety-five outside directors of ten of the media giants are former government officials, and Peter Dreier gives a similar proportion in his study of large newspapers.[37] In television, the revolving-door flow of personnel between regulators and the regulated firms was massive during the years when the oligopolistic structure of the media and networks was being established.[38]

The great media also depend on the government for more general policy support. All business firms are interested in business taxes, interest rates, labor policies, and enforcement and nonenforcement of the antitrust laws. GE and Westinghouse depend on the government to subsidize their nuclear power and military research and development, and to create a favorable climate for their overseas sales. The *Reader's Digest, Time, Newsweek,* and movie- and television-syndication sellers also depend on diplomatic support for their rights to penetrate foreign cultures with U.S. commercial and value messages and interpretations of current affairs. The media giants, advertising agencies, and great multinational corporations have a joint and close interest in a favorable climate of investment in the Third World, and their interconnections and relationships with the government in these policies are symbiotic.[39]

In sum, the dominant media firms are quite large businesses; they are controlled by very wealthy people or by managers who are subject to sharp constraints by owners and other market-profit-oriented forces;[40] and they are closely interlocked, and have important common interests, with other major corporations, banks, and government. This is the first powerful filter that will affect news choices.

The Advertising License to do Business: The Second Filter

In arguing for the benefits of the free market as a means of controlling dissident opinion in the mid-nineteenth century, the Liberal chancellor of the British exchequer, Sir George Lewis, noted that the market would promote those papers "enjoying the preference of the advertising public."[41] Advertising did, in fact, serve as a powerful mechanism weakening the working-class press. Curran and Seaton give the growth of advertising a status comparable with the increase in capital costs as a factor allowing the market to accomplish what state taxes and harassment failed to do, noting that these "advertisers thus acquired a de facto licensing authority since, without their support, newspapers ceased to be economically viable."[42]

Before advertising became prominent, the price of a newspaper had to cover the costs of doing business. With the growth of advertising, papers that attracted ads could afford a copy price well below production costs. This put papers lacking in advertising at a serious disadvantage: their prices would tend to be higher, curtailing sales, and they would have less surplus to invest in improving the salability of the paper (features, attractive format, promotion, etc.). For this reason, an advertising-based system will tend to drive out of existence or into marginality the media companies and types that depend on revenue from sales alone. With advertising, the free market does not yield a neutral system in which final buyer choice decides. The *advertisers'* choices influence media prosperity and survival.[43] The ad-based media receive an advertising subsidy that gives them a price-marketing-quality edge, which allows them to encroach on and further weaken their ad-free (or ad-disadvantaged) rivals.[44] Even if ad-based media cater to an affluent ("upscale") audience, they easily pick up a large part of the "down-scale" audience, and their rivals lose market share and are eventually driven out or marginalized.

In fact, advertising has played a potent role in increasing concentration even among rivals that focus with equal energy on seeking advertising revenue. A market share and advertising edge on the part of one paper or television station will give it additional revenue to compete more effectively – promote more aggressively, buy more salable features and programs – and the disadvantaged rival must add expenses it cannot afford to try to stem the cumulative process of dwindling market (and revenue) share. The crunch is often fatal, and it helps explain the death of many large-circulation papers and magazines and the attrition in the number of newspapers.[45]

From the time of the introduction of press advertising, therefore, working-class and radical papers have been at a serious disadvantage. Their readers have tended to be of modest means, a factor that has always affected advertiser interest. One advertising executive stated in 1856 that some journals are poor vehicles because "their readers are not purchasers, and any money thrown upon them is so much thrown away."[46] The same force took a heavy toll of the post-World War II social-democratic press in Great Britain, with the *Daily Herald, News Chronicle,* and *Sunday Citizen* failing or absorbed into establishment systems between 1960 and 1967, despite a collective average daily readership of 9.3 million. As James Curran points out, with 4.7 million readers in its last year, "the *Daily Herald* actually had almost double the readership of *The Times,* the *Financial Times* and the *Guardian* combined." What is more, surveys showed that its readers "thought more highly of their paper than the regular readers of any other popular newspaper," and "they also read more in their paper than the readers of other popular papers despite being overwhelmingly working class. . . ."[47] The death of the *Herald,* as well as of the *News Chronicle* and *Sunday Citizen,* was in large measure a result of progressive strangulation by lack of advertising support. The *Herald,* with 8.1 percent of national daily circulation, got 3.5 percent of net advertising revenue; the *Sunday Citizen* got one-tenth of the net advertising revenue of the *Sunday Times* and one-seventh that of the *Observer* (on a per-thousand-copies basis). Curran argues persuasively that the loss of these three papers was an important contribution to the declining fortunes of the Labour party, in the case of the *Herald* specifically removing a mass-circulation institution that provided "an alternative framework of analysis and understanding that contested the dominant systems of representation in both broadcasting and the mainstream press."[48] A mass movement without any major media support, and subject to a great deal of active press hostility, suffers a serious disability, and struggles against grave odds.

The successful media today are fully attuned to the crucial importance of audience "quality": CBS proudly tells its shareholders that while it "continuously seeks to maximize audience delivery," it has developed a new "sales tool" with which it approaches advertisers: "Client Audience Profile, or CAP, will help advertisers optimize the effectiveness of their network television schedules by evaluating audience segments in proportion to usage levels of advertisers' products and services."[49] In short, the mass media are interested in attracting audiences with buying power, not audiences per se; it is affluent audiences that spark advertiser interest today, as in the nineteenth century. The idea that the drive for large audiences makes the mass media "democratic" thus suffers from the initial weakness that its political analogue is a voting system weighted by income!

The power of advertisers over television programming stems from the simple fact that they buy and pay for the programs – they are the "patrons" who provide the media subsidy. As such, the media compete for their patronage, developing specialized staff to solicit advertisers and necessarily having to explain how their programs serve advertisers' needs. The choices of these patrons greatly affect the welfare of the media, and the patrons become what William Evan calls "normative reference organizations,"[50] whose requirements and demands the media must accommodate if they are to succeed.[51]

For a television network, an audience gain or loss of one percentage point in the Nielsen ratings translates into a change in advertising revenue of from $80 to $100 million a year, with some variation depending on measures of audience "quality." The stakes in audience size and affluence are thus extremely large, and in a market system there is a strong tendency for such considerations to affect policy profoundly.

This is partly a matter of institutional pressures to focus on the bottom line, partly a matter of the continuous interaction of the media organization with patrons who supply the revenue dollars. As Grant Tinker, then head of NBC-TV, observed, television "is an advertising-supported medium, and to the extent that support falls out, programming will change."[52]

Working-class and radical media also suffer from the political discrimination of advertisers. Political discrimination is structured into advertising allocations by the stress on people with money to buy. But many firms will always refuse to patronize ideological enemies and those whom they perceive as damaging their interests, and cases of overt discrimination add to the force of the voting system weighted by income. Public-television station WNET lost its corporate funding from Gulf + Western in 1985 after the station showed the documentary "Hungry for Profit," which contains material critical of multinational corporate activities in the Third World. Even before the program was shown, in anticipation of negative corporate reaction, station officials "did all we could to get the program sanitized" (according to one station source).[53] The chief executive of Gulf + Western complained to the station that the program was "virulently anti-business if not anti-American," and that the station's carrying the program was not the behavior "of a friend" of the corporation. The London *Economist* says that "Most people believe that WNET would not make the same mistake again."[54]

In addition to discrimination against unfriendly media institutions, advertisers also choose selectively among programs on the basis of their own principles. With rare exceptions these are culturally and politically conservative.[55] Large corporate advertisers on television will rarely sponsor programs that engage in serious criticisms of corporate activities, such as the problem of environmental degradation, the workings of the military-industrial complex, or corporate support of and benefits from Third World tyrannies. Erik Barnouw recounts the history of a proposed documentary series on environmental problems by NBC at a time of great interest in these issues. Barnouw notes that although at that time a great many large companies were spending money on commercials and other publicity regarding environmental problems, the documentary series failed for want of sponsors. The problem was one of excessive objectivity in the series, which included suggestions of corporate or systemic failure, whereas the corporate message "was one of reassurance."[56]

Television networks learn over time that such programs will not sell and would have to be carried at a financial sacrifice, and that, in addition, they may offend powerful advertisers.[57] With the rise in the price of advertising spots, the forgone revenue increases; and with increasing market pressure for financial performance and the diminishing constraints from regulation, an advertising-based media system will gradually increase advertising time and marginalize or eliminate altogether programming that has significant public-affairs content.[58]

Advertisers will want, more generally, to avoid programs with serious complexities and disturbing controversies that interfere with the "buying mood." They seek programs that will lightly entertain and thus fit in with the spirit of the primary purpose of program purchases – the dissemination of a selling message. Thus over time, instead of programs like "The Selling of the Pentagon," it is a natural evolution of a market seeking sponsor dollars to offer programs such as "A Bird's-Eye View of Scotland," "Barry Goldwater's Arizona," "An Essay on Hotels," and "Mr. Rooney Goes to Dinner" – a CBS program on "how Americans eat when they dine out, where they go and why."[59] There are exceptional cases of companies willing to sponsor serious programs, sometimes a result of recent embarrassments that call for a public-relations offset.[60] But even in these cases the companies will usually not want to sponsor close examination of sensitive and divisive issues – they prefer programs on Greek antiquities, the ballet, and items of cultural and national history and nostalgia. Barnouw points out an interesting contrast: commercial-television drama "deals almost wholly with the here and now, as processed via advertising budgets," but on public television, culture "has come to mean 'other cultures.' . . . American civilization, here and now, is excluded from consideration."[61]

Television stations and networks are also concerned to maintain audience "flow" levels, i.e., to keep people watching from program to program, in order to sustain advertising ratings and revenue. Airing program interludes of documentary-cultural matter that cause station switching is costly, and over time a "free" (i.e., ad-based) commercial system will tend to excise it. Such documentary-cultural-critical materials will be driven out of secondary media vehicles as well, as these companies strive to qualify for advertiser interest, although there will always be some cultural-political programming trying to come into being or surviving on the periphery of the main-stream media.

Sourcing Mass-Media News: The Third Filter

The mass media are drawn into a symbiotic relationship with powerful sources of information by economic necessity and reciprocity of interest. The media need a steady, reliable flow of the raw material of news. They have daily news demands and imperative news schedules that they must meet. They cannot afford to have reporters and cameras at all places where important stories may break. Economics dictates that they concentrate their resources where significant news often occurs, where import-ant rumors and leaks abound, and where regular press conferences are held. The White House, the Pentagon, and the State Department, in Washington, D.C., are central nodes of such news activity. On a local basis, city hall and the police depart-ment are the subject of regular news "beats" for reporters. Business corporations and trade groups are also regular and credible purveyors of stories deemed newsworthy. These bureaucracies turn out a large volume of material that meets the demands of news organizations for reliable, scheduled flows. Mark Fishman calls this "the prin-ciple of bureaucratic affinity: only other bureaucracies can satisfy the input needs of a news bureaucracy."[62]

Government and corporate sources also have the great merit of being recogniz-able and credible by their status and prestige. This is important to the mass media. As Fishman notes,

> Newsworkers are predisposed to treat bureaucratic accounts as factual because news personnel participate in upholding a normative order of authorized knowers in the society. Reporters operate with the attitude that officials ought to know what it is their job to know. . . . In particular, a newsworker will recognize an official's claim to know-ledge not merely as a claim, but as a credible, competent piece of knowledge. This amounts to a moral division of labor: officials have and give the facts; reporters merely get them.[63]

Another reason for the heavy weight given to official sources is that the mass media claim to be "objective" dispensers of the news. Partly to maintain the image of objectivity, but also to protect themselves from criticisms of bias and the threat of libel suits, they need material that can be portrayed as presumptively accurate.[64] This is also partly a matter of cost: taking information from sources that may be presumed credible reduces investigative expense, whereas material from sources that are not prima facie credible, or that will elicit criticism and threats, requires careful checking and costly research.

The magnitude of the public-information operations of large government and corporate bureaucracies that constitute the primary news sources is vast and ensures special access to the media. The Pentagon, for example, has a public-information service that involves many thousands of employees, spending hundreds of millions of dollars every year and dwarfing not only the public-information resources of any dissenting individual or group but the *aggregate* of such groups. In 1979 and 1980, during a brief interlude of relative openness (since closed down), the U.S. Air Force revealed that its public-information outreach included the following:

140 newspapers, 690,000 copies per week
Airman magazine, monthly circulation 125,000
34 radio and 17 TV stations, primarily overseas
45,000 headquarters and unit news releases
615,000 hometown news releases
6,600 interviews with news media
3,200 news conferences
500 news media orientation flights
50 meetings with editorial boards
11,000 speeches[65]

This excludes vast areas of the air force's public-information effort. Writing back in 1970, Senator J. W. Fulbright had found that the air force public-relations effort in 1968 involved 1,305 full-time employees, exclusive of additional thousands that "have public functions collateral to other duties."[66] The air force at that time offered a weekly film-clip service for TV and a taped features program for use three times a week, sent to 1,139 radio stations; it also produced 148 motion pictures, of which 24 were released for public consumption.[67] There is no reason to believe that the air force public-relations effort has diminished since the 1960s.[68]

Note that this is just the air force. There are three other branches with massive programs, and there is a separate, overall public-information program under an assistant secretary of defense for public affairs in the Pentagon. In 1971, an *Armed Forces Journal* survey revealed that the Pentagon was publishing a total of 371 magazines at an annual cost of some $57 million, an operation sixteen times larger than the nation's biggest publisher. In an update in 1982, the *Air Force Journal International* indicated that the Pentagon was publishing 1,203 periodicals.[69] To put this into perspective, we may note the scope of public-information operations of the American Friends Service Committee (AFSC) and the National Council of the Churches of Christ (NCC), two of the largest of the nonprofit organizations that offer a consistently challenging voice to the views of the Pentagon. The AFSC's main office information-services budget in 1984–85 was under $500,000, with eleven staff people.[70] Its institution-wide press releases run at about two hundred per year, its press conferences thirty a year, and it produces about one film and two or three slide shows a year. It does not offer film clips, photos, or taped radio programs to the media. The NCC Office of Information has an annual budget of some $350,000, issues about a hundred news releases per year, and holds four press conferences annually.[71] The ratio of air force news releases and press conferences to those of the AFSC and NCC taken together are 150 to 1 (or 2,200 to 1 if we count hometown news releases of the air force), and 94 to 1 respectively. Aggregating the other services would increase the differential by a large factor.

Only the corporate sector has the resources to produce public information and propaganda on the scale of the Pentagon and other government bodies. The AFSC and NCC cannot duplicate the Mobil Oil company's multimillion-dollar purchase of newspaper space and other corporate investments to get its viewpoint across.[72] The number of individual corporations with budgets for public information and lobbying in excess of those of the AFSC and NCC runs into the hundreds, perhaps even the thousands. A corporate *collective* like the U.S. Chamber of Commerce had a 1983 budget for research, communications, and political activities of $65 million.[73] By 1980, the chamber was publishing a business magazine (*Nation's Business*) with a circulation of 1.3 million and a weekly newspaper with 740,000 subscribers, and it was producing a weekly panel show distributed to 400 radio stations, as well as its own weekly panel-discussion programs carried by 128 commercial television stations.[74]

Besides the U.S. Chamber, there are thousands of state and local chambers of commerce and trade associations also engaged in public-relations and lobbying activities. The corporate and trade-association lobbying network community is "a network of well over 150,000 professionals,"[75] and its resources are related to corporate income, profits, and the protective value of public-relations and lobbying outlays. Corporate profits before taxes in 1985 were $295.5 billion. When the corporate community gets agitated about the political environment, as it did in the 1970s, it obviously has the wherewithal to meet the perceived threat. Corporate and trade-association image and issues advertising increased from $305 million in 1975 to $650 million in 1980.[76] So did direct-mail campaigns through dividend and other mail stuffers, the distribution of educational films, booklets and pamphlets, and outlays on initiatives and referendums, lobbying, and political and think-tank contributions. Aggregate corporate and trade-association political advertising and grassroots outlays were estimated to have reached the billion-dollar-a-year level by 1978, and to have grown to $1.6 billion by 1984.[77]

To consolidate their preeminent position as sources, government and business-news promoters go to great pains to make things easy for news organizations. They provide the media organizations with facilities in which to gather; they give journalists advance copies of speeches and forthcoming reports; they schedule press conferences at hours well-geared to news deadlines;[78] they write press releases in usable language; and they carefully organize their press conferences and "photo opportunity" sessions.[79] It is the job of news officers "to meet the journalist's scheduled needs with material that their beat agency has generated at its own pace."[80]

In effect, the large bureaucracies of the powerful *subsidize* the mass media, and gain special access by their contribution to reducing the media's costs of acquiring the raw materials of, and producing, news. The large entities that provide this subsidy become "routine" news sources and have privileged access to the gates. Non-routine sources must struggle for access, and may be ignored by the arbitrary decision of the gatekeepers. It should also be noted that in the case of the largesse of the Pentagon and the State Department's Office of Public Diplomacy,[81] the subsidy is at the taxpayers' expense, so that, in effect, the citizenry pays to be propagandized in the interest of powerful groups such as military contractors and other sponsors of state terrorism.

Because of their services, continuous contact on the beat, and mutual dependency, the powerful can use personal relationships, threats, and rewards to further influence and coerce the media. The media may feel obligated to carry extremely dubious stories and mute criticism in order not to offend their sources and disturb a close relationship.[82] It is very difficult to call authorities on whom one depends for daily news liars, even if they tell whoppers. Critical sources may be avoided not only because of their lesser availability and higher cost of establishing credibility, but also because the primary sources may be offended and may even threaten the media using them.

Powerful sources may also use their prestige and importance to the media as a lever to deny critics access to the media: the Defense Department, for example, refused to participate in National Public Radio discussions of defense issues if experts from the Center for Defense Information were on the program; Elliott Abrams refused to appear on a program on human rights in Central America at the Kennedy School of Government, at Harvard University, unless the former ambassador, Robert White, was excluded as a participant;[83] Claire Sterling refused to participate in television-network shows on the Bulgarian Connection where her critics would appear.[84] In the last two of these cases, the authorities and brand-name experts were successful in monopolizing access by coercive threats.

Perhaps more important, powerful sources regularly take advantage of media routines and dependency to "manage" the media, to manipulate them into following a special agenda and framework (as we will show in detail in the chapters that follow).[85] Part of this management process consists of inundating the media with stories, which serve sometimes to foist a particular line and frame on the media (e.g., Nicaragua as illicitly supplying arms to the Salvadoran rebels), and at other times to help chase unwanted stories off the front page or out of the media altogether (the alleged delivery of MIGs to Nicaragua during the week of the 1984 Nicaraguan election). This strategy can be traced back at least as far as the Committee on Public Information, established to coordinate propaganda during World War I, which "discovered in 1917–18 that one of the best means of controlling news was flooding news channels with 'facts,' or what amounted to official information."[86]

The relation between power and sourcing extends beyond official and corporate provision of day-to-day news to shaping the supply of "experts." The dominance of official sources is weakened by the existence of highly respectable unofficial sources that give dissident views with great authority. This problem is alleviated by "co-opting the experts"[87] – i.e., putting them on the payroll as consultants, funding their research, and organizing think tanks that will hire them directly and help disseminate their messages. In this way bias may be structured, and the supply of experts may be skewed in the direction desired by the government and "the market."[88] As Henry Kissinger has pointed out, in this "age of the expert," the "constituency" of the expert is "those who have a vested interest in commonly held opinions; elaborating and defining its consensus at a high level has, after all, made him an expert."[89] It is therefore appropriate that this restructuring has taken place to allow the commonly held opinions (meaning those that are functional for elite interests) to continue to prevail.

This process of creating the needed body of experts has been carried out on a deliberate basis and a massive scale. Back in 1972, Judge Lewis Powell (later elevated to the Supreme Court) wrote a memo to the U.S. Chamber of Commerce urging business "to buy the top academic reputations in the country to add credibility to corporate studies and give business a stronger voice on the campuses."[90] One buys them, and assures that – in the words of Dr. Edwin Feulner, of the Heritage Foundation – the public-policy area "is awash with in-depth academic studies" that have the proper conclusions. Using the analogy of Procter & Gamble selling toothpaste, Feulner explained that "They sell it and resell it every day by keeping the product fresh in the consumer's mind." By the sales effort, including the dissemination of the correct ideas to "thousands of newspapers," it is possible to keep debate "within its proper perspective."[91]

In accordance with this formula, during the 1970s and early 1980s a string of institutions was created and old ones were activated to the end of propagandizing the corporate viewpoint. Many hundreds of intellectuals were brought to these institutions, where their work was funded and their outputs were disseminated to the media by a sophisticated propaganda effort.[92] The corporate funding and clear ideological purpose in the overall effort had no discernible effect on the credibility of the intellectuals so mobilized; on the contrary, the funding and pushing of their ideas catapaulted them into the press.

As an illustration of how the funded experts preempt space in the media, Table 17.4 describes the "experts" on terrorism and defense issues who appeared on the "McNeil–Lehrer News Hour" in the course of a year in the mid-1980s. We can see that, excluding journalists, a majority of the participants (54 percent) were present or former government officials, and that the next highest category (15.7 percent) was drawn from conservative think tanks. The largest number of appearances in the latter category was supplied by the Georgetown Center for Strategic and International Studies (CSIS), an organization funded by conservative foundations and corporations, and providing a revolving door between the State Department and CIA and a nominally private organization.[93] On such issues as terrorism and the Bulgarian Connection, the CSIS has occupied space in the media that otherwise might have been filled by independent voices.[94]

The mass media themselves also provide "experts" who regularly echo the official view. John Barron and Claire Sterling are household names as authorities on the KGB and terrorism because the *Reader's Digest* has funded, published, and publicized their work; the Soviet defector Arkady Shevchenko became an expert on Soviet arms and intelligence because *Time*, ABC-TV, and the *New York Times* chose to feature him (despite his badly tarnished credentials).[95] By giving these purveyors of the preferred view a great deal of exposure, the media confer status and make them the obvious candidates for opinion and analysis.

Another class of experts whose prominence is largely a function of serviceability to power is former radicals who have come to "see the light." The motives that cause these individuals to switch gods, from Stalin (or Mao) to Reagan and free enterprise, is varied, but for the establishment media the reason for the change is simply that the ex-radicals have finally seen the error of their ways. In a country whose citizenry

Table 17.4   Experts on terrorism and defense on the "McNeil–Lehrer News Hour," January 14, 1985, to January 27, 1986[a]

Category of expert	No.	%	No. excluding journalists	% Excluding journalists
Government official	24	20	24	27
Former government official	24	20	24	27
Conservative think tank	14	11.7	14	15.7
Academic	12	10	12	13.5
Journalist	31	25.8	—	—
Consultant	3	2.5	3	3.4
Foreign government official	5	4.2	5	5.6
Other	7	5.8	7	7.8
Totals	120	100	89	100

[a] This is a compilation of all appearances on the news hour concerning the Bulgarian Connection (3), the shooting down of the Korean airliner KAL 007 (5), and terrorism, defense, and arms control (33), from January 14, 1985, through January 27, 1986.

values acknowledgement of sin and repentance, the turncoats are an important class of repentant sinners. It is interesting to observe how the former sinners, whose previous work was of little interest or an object of ridicule to the mass media, are suddenly elevated to prominence and become authentic experts. We may recall how, during the McCarthy era, defectors and ex-Communists vied with one another in tales of the imminence of a Soviet invasion and other lurid stories.[96] They found that news coverage was a function of their trimming their accounts to the prevailing demand. The steady flow of ex-radicals from marginality to media attention shows that we are witnessing a durable method of providing experts who will say what the establishment wants said.[97]

Flak and the Enforcers: The Fourth Filter

"Flak" refers to negative response to a media statement or program. It may take the form of letters, telegrams, phone calls, petitions, lawsuits, speeches and bills before Congress, and other modes of complaint, threat, and punitive action. It may be organized centrally or locally, or it may consist of the entirely independent actions of individuals.

If flak is produced on a large scale, or by individuals or groups with substantial resources, it can be both uncomfortable and costly to the media. Positions have to be defended within the organization and without, sometimes before legislatures and possibly even in courts. Advertisers may withdraw patronage. Television advertising is mainly of consumer goods that are readily subject to organized boycott. During the McCarthy years, many advertisers and radio and television stations were effectively coerced into quiescence and blacklisting of employees by the threats of determined Red hunters to boycott products. Advertisers are still concerned to avoid offending constituencies that might produce flak, and their demand for suitable programming is a continuing feature of the media environment.[98] If certain kinds of fact, position, or program are thought likely to elicit flak, this prospect can be a deterrent.

The ability to produce flak, and especially flak that is costly and threatening, is related to power. Serious flak has increased in close parallel with business's growing resentment of media criticism and the corporate offensive of the 1970s and 1980s. Flak from the powerful can be either direct or indirect. The direct would include letters or phone calls from the White House to Dan Rather or William Paley, or from the FCC to the television networks asking for documents used in putting together a program, or from irate officials of ad agencies or corporate sponsors to media officials asking for reply time or threatening retaliation.[99] The powerful can also work on the media indirectly by complaining to their own constituencies (stock-holders, employees) about the media, by generating institutional advertising that does the same, and by funding right-wing monitoring or think-tank operations designed to attack the media. They may also fund political campaigns and help put into power conservative politicians who will more directly serve the interests of private power in curbing any deviationism in the media.

Along with its other political investments of the 1970s and 1980s, the corporate community sponsored the growth of institutions such as the American Legal Foundation, the Capital Legal Foundation, the Media Institute, the Center for Media and Public Affairs, and Accuracy in Media (AIM). These may be regarded as institutions organized for the specific purpose of producing flak. Another and older flak-producing machine with a broader design is Freedom House. The American Legal Foundation, organized in 1980, has specialized in Fairness Doctrine complaints and libel suits to aid "media victims." The Capital Legal Foundation, incorporated in 1977, was the Scaife vehicle for Westmoreland's $120-million libel suit against CBS.[100]

The Media Institute, organized in 1972 and funded by corporate-wealthy patrons, sponsors monitoring projects, conferences, and studies of the media. It has focused less heavily on media failings in foreign policy, concentrating more on media portrayals of economic issues and the business community, but its range of interests is broad. The main theme of its sponsored studies and conferences has been the failure of the media to portray business accurately and to give adequate weight to the business point of view,[101] but it underwrites works such as John Corry's exposé of the alleged left-wing bias of the mass media.[102] The chairman of the board of trustees of the institute in 1985 was Steven V. Seekins, the top public-relations officer of the American Medical Association; chairman of the National Advisory Council was Herbert Schmertz, of the Mobil Oil Corporation.

The Center for Media and Public Affairs, run by Linda and Robert Lichter, came into existence in the mid-1980s as a "non-profit, non-partisan" research institute, with warm accolades from Patrick Buchanan, Faith Whittlesey, and Ronald Reagan himself, who recognized the need for an objective and fair press. Their *Media Monitor* and research studies continue their earlier efforts to demonstrate the liberal bias and anti-business propensities of the mass media.[103]

AIM was formed in 1969, and it grew spectacularly in the 1970s. Its annual income rose from $5,000 in 1971 to $1.5 million in the early 1980s, with funding mainly from large corporations and the wealthy heirs and foundations of the corporate system. At least eight separate oil companies were contributors to AIM in the early 1980s, but the wide representation in sponsors from the corporate community is impressive.[104] The function of AIM is to harass the media and put pressure on them to follow the corporate agenda and a hard-line, right-wing foreign policy. It presses the media to join more enthusiastically in Red-scare bandwagons, and attacks them for alleged deficiencies whenever they fail to toe the line on foreign policy. It conditions the media to expect trouble (and cost increases) for violating right-wing standards of bias.[105]

Freedom House, which dates back to the early 1940s, has had interlocks with AIM, the World Anticommunist League, Resistance International, and U.S. government bodies such as Radio Free Europe and the CIA, and has long served as a virtual propaganda arm of the government and international right wing. It sent election monitors to the Rhodesian elections staged by Ian Smith in 1979 and found them "fair," whereas the 1980 elections won by Mugabe under British supervision it found dubious. Its election monitors also found the Salvadoran elections of 1982 admirable.[106] It has expended substantial resources in criticizing the media for insufficient sympathy with U.S. foreign-policy ventures and excessively harsh criticism of U.S. client states. Its most notable publication of this genre was Peter Braestrup's *Big Story*, which contended that the media's negative portrayal of the Tet offensive helped lose the war. The work is a travesty of scholarship, but more interesting is its premise: that the mass media not only should support any national venture abroad, but should do so with enthusiasm, such enterprises being by definition noble (see the extensive review of the Freedom House study in chapter 5 and appendix 3 [Herman and Chomsky 1988]). In 1982, when the Reagan administration was having trouble containing media reporting of the systematic killing of civilians by the Salvadoran army, Freedom House came through with a denunciation of the "imbalance" in media reporting from El Salvador.[107]

Although the flak machines steadily attack the mass media, the media treat them well. They receive respectful attention, and their propagandistic role and links to a larger corporate program are rarely mentioned or analyzed. AIM head, Reed Irvine's diatribes are frequently published, and right-wing network flaks who regularly assail the "liberal media," such as Michael Ledeen,[108] are given Op-Ed column space, sympathetic reviewers, and a regular place on talk shows as experts. This reflects the power of the sponsors, including the well-entrenched position of the right wing in the mass media themselves.[109]

The producers of flak add to one another's strength and reinforce the command of political authority in its news-management activities. The government is a major producer of flak, regularly assailing, threatening, and "correcting" the media, trying to contain any deviations from the established line. News management itself is designed to produce flak. In the Reagan years, Mr. Reagan was put on television to exude charm to millions, many of whom berated the media when they dared to criticize the "Great Communicator."[110]

Anticommunism as a Control Mechanism

A final filter is the ideology of anticommunism. Communism as the ultimate evil has always been the specter haunting property owners, as it threatens the very root of their class position and superior status. The Soviet, Chinese, and Cuban revolutions were traumas to Western elites, and the ongoing conflicts and the well-publicized abuses of Communist states have contributed to elevating opposition to communism to a first principle of Western ideology and politics. This ideology helps mobilize the populace against an enemy, and because the concept is fuzzy it can be used against anybody advocating policies that threaten property interests or support accommodation with Communist states and radicalism. It therefore helps fragment the left and labor movements and serves as a political-control mechanism. If the triumph of communism is the worst imaginable result, the support of fascism abroad is justified as a lesser evil. Opposition to social democrats who are too soft on Communists and "play into their hands" is rationalized in similar terms.

Liberals at home, often accused of being pro-Communist or insufficiently anti-Communist, are kept continuously on the defensive in a cultural milieu in which anticommunism is the dominant religion. If they allow communism, or something that can be labeled communism, to triumph in the provinces while they are in office, the political costs are heavy. Most of them have fully internalized the religion anyway, but they are all under great pressure to demonstrate their anti-Communist credentials. This causes them to behave very much like reactionaries. Their occasional support of social democrats often breaks down where the latter are insufficiently harsh on their own indigenous radicals or on popular groups that are organizing among generally marginalized sectors. In his brief tenure in the Dominican Republic, Juan Bosch attacked corruption in the armed forces and government, began a land-reform program, undertook a major project for mass education of the populace, and maintained a remarkably open government and system of effective civil liberties. These policies threatened powerful internal vested interests, and the United States resented his independence and the extension of civil liberties to Communists and radicals. This was carrying democracy and pluralism too far. Kennedy was "extremely disappointed" in Bosch's rule, and the State Department "quickly soured on the first democratically elected Dominican President in over thirty years." Bosch's overthrow by the military after nine months in office had at least the tacit support of the United States.[111] Two years later, by contrast, the Johnson administration invaded the Dominican Republic to make sure that Bosch did not resume power.

The Kennedy liberals were enthusiastic about the military coup and displacement of a populist government in Brazil in 1964.[112] A major spurt in the growth of neo-Fascist national-security states took place under Kennedy and Johnson. In the cases of the U.S. subversion of Guatemala, 1947–54, and the military attacks on Nicaragua, 1981–7, allegations of Communist links and a Communist threat caused many liberals to support counterrevolutionary intervention, while others lapsed into silence, paralyzed by the fear of being tarred with charges of infidelity to the national religion.

It should be noted that when anti-Communist fervor is aroused, the demand for serious evidence in support of claims of "communist" abuses is suspended, and charlatans can thrive as evidential sources. Defectors, informers, and assorted other opportunists move to center stage as "experts," and they remain there even after exposure as highly unreliable, if not downright liars.[113] Pascal Delwit and Jean-Michel Dewaele point out that in France, too, the ideologues of anticommunism "can do and say anything."[114] Analyzing the new status of Annie Kriegel and Pierre Daix, two former passionate Stalinists now possessed of a large and uncritical audience in France,[115] Delwit and Dewaele note:

> If we analyse their writings, we find all the classic reactions of people who have been disappointed in love. But no one dreams of criticising them for their past, even though it has marked them forever. They may well have been converted, but they have not changed. . . . no one notices the constants, even though they are glaringly obvious. Their best sellers prove, thanks to the support of the most indulgent and slothful critics anyone could hope for, that the public can be fooled. No one denounces or even notices the arrogance of both yesterday's eulogies and today's diatribes; no one cares that there is never any proof and that invective is used in place of analysis. Their inverted hyper-Stalinism – which takes the usual form of total manicheanism – is whitewashed simply because it is directed against Communism. The hysteria has not changed, but it gets a better welcome in its present guise.[116]

The anti-Communist control mechanism reaches through the system to exercise a profound influence on the mass media. In normal times as well as in periods of Red scares, issues tend to be framed in terms of a dichotomized world of Communist and anti-Communist powers, with gains and losses allocated to contesting sides, and rooting for "our side" considered an entirely legitimate news practice. It is the mass media that identify, create, and push into the limelight a Joe McCarthy, Arkady Shevchenko, and Claire Sterling and Robert Leiken, or an Annie Kriegel and Pierre Daix. The ideology and religion of anticommunism is a potent filter.

Dichotomization and Propaganda Campaigns

The five filters narrow the range of news that passes through the gates, and even more sharply limit what can become "big news," subject to sustained news campaigns. By definition, news from primary establishment sources meets one major filter requirement and is readily accommodated by the mass media. Messages from and about dissidents and weak, unorganized individuals and groups, domestic and foreign, are at an initial disadvantage in sourcing costs and credibility, and they often do not comport with the ideology or interests of the gatekeepers and other powerful parties that influence the filtering process.[117]

Thus, for example, the torture of political prisoners and the attack on trade unions in Turkey will be pressed on the media only by human-rights activists and groups that have little political leverage. The U.S. government supported the Turkish martial-law government from its inception in 1980, and the U.S. business community has been warm toward regimes that profess fervent anticommunism, encourage foreign investment, repress unions, and loyally support U.S. foreign policy (a set of virtues that are frequently closely linked). Media that chose to feature Turkish violence against their own citizenry would have had to go to extra expense to find and check out information sources; they would elicit flak from government, business, and organized rightwing flak machines, and they might be looked upon with disfavor by the corporate community (including advertisers) for indulging in such a quixotic interest and crusade. They would tend to stand alone in focusing on victims that from the standpoint of dominant American interests were *unworthy*.[118]

In marked contrast, protest over political prisoners and the violation of the rights of trade unions in Poland was seen by the Reagan administration and business elites in 1981 as a noble cause, and, not coincidentally, as an opportunity to score political points. Many media leaders and syndicated columnists felt the same way. Thus information and strong opinions on human-rights violations in Poland could be obtained from official sources in Washington, and reliance on Polish dissidents would not elicit flak from the U.S. government or the flak machines. These victims would be generally acknowledged by the managers of the filters to be *worthy*. The mass media never explain *why* Andrei Sakharov is worthy and José Luis Massera, in Uruguay, is unworthy – the attention and general dichotomization occur "naturally" as a result of the working of the filters, but the result is the same as if a commissar had instructed the media: "Concentrate on the victims of enemy powers and forget about the victims of friends."[119]

Reports of the abuses of worthy victims not only pass through the filters; they may also become the basis of sustained propaganda campaigns. If the government or corporate community and the media feel that a story is useful as well as dramatic, they focus on it intensively and use it to enlighten the public. This was true, for example, of the shooting down by the Soviets of the Korean airliner KAL 007 in early September 1983, which permitted an extended campaign of denigration of an official enemy and greatly advanced Reagan administration arms plans. As Bernard Gwertzman noted complacently in the *New York Times* of August 31, 1984, U.S. officials "assert that worldwide criticism of the Soviet handling of the crisis has strengthened the United States in its relations with Moscow." In sharp contrast, the shooting down by Israel of a Libyan civilian airliner in February 1973 led to no outcry in the West, no denunciations for "cold-blooded murder,"[120] and no boycott. This difference in treatment was explained by the *New York Times* precisely on the grounds of utility: "No useful purpose is served by an acrimonious debate over the assignment of blame for the downing of a Libyan airliner in the Sinai peninsula last week."[121] There was a very "useful purpose" served by focusing on the Soviet act, and a massive propaganda campaign ensued.[122]

Propaganda campaigns in general have been closely attuned to elite interests. The Red scare of 1919–20 served well to abort the union-organizing drive that followed World War I in the steel and other industries. The Truman–McCarthy Red scare helped inaugurate the Cold War and the permanent war economy, and it also served to weaken the progressive coalition of the New Deal years. The chronic focus on the plight of Soviet dissidents, on enemy killings in Cambodia, and on the Bulgarian

Connection helped weaken the Vietnam syndrome, justify a huge arms buildup and a more aggressive foreign policy, and divert attention from the upward redistribution of income that was the heart of Reagan's domestic economic program.[123] The recent propaganda–disinformation attacks on Nicaragua have been needed to avert eyes from the savagery of the war in El Salvador and to justify the escalating U.S. investment in counterrevolution in Central America.

Conversely, propaganda campaigns will *not* be mobilized where victimization, even though massive, sustained, and dramatic, fails to meet the test of utility to elite interests. Thus, while the focus on Cambodia in the Pol Pot era (and thereafter) was exceedingly serviceable, as Cambodia had fallen to the Communists and useful lessons could be drawn by attention to their victims, the numerous victims of the U.S. bombing *before* the Communist takeover were scrupulously ignored by the U.S. elite press. After Pol Pot's ouster by the Vietnamese, the United States quietly shifted support to this "worse than Hitler" villain, with little notice in the press, which adjusted once again to the national political agenda.[124] Attention to the Indonesian massacres of 1965–6, or the victims of the Indonesian invasion of East Timor from 1975 onward, would also be distinctly unhelpful as bases of media campaigns, because Indonesia is a U.S. ally and client that maintains an open door to Western investment, and because, in the case of East Timor, the United States bears major responsibility for the slaughter. The same is true of the victims of state terror in Chile and Guatemala, U.S. clients whose basic institutional structures, including the state terror system, were put in place and maintained by, or with crucial assistance from, U.S. power, and who remain U.S. client states. Propaganda campaigns on behalf of these victims would conflict with government–business–military interests and, in our model, would not be able to pass through the filtering system.[125]

Propaganda campaigns may be instituted either by the government or by one or more of the top media firms. The campaigns to discredit the government of Nicaragua, to support the Salvadoran elections as an exercise in legitimizing democracy, and to use the Soviet shooting down of the Korean airliner KAL 007 as a means of mobilizing public support for the arms buildup, were instituted and propelled by the government. The campaigns to publicize the crimes of Pol Pot and the alleged KGB plot to assassinate the pope were initiated by the *Reader's Digest*, with strong follow-up support from NBC-TV, the *New York Times*, and other major media companies.[126] Some propaganda campaigns arc jointly initiated by government and media; all of them require the collaboration of the mass media. The secret of the unidirectionality of the politics of media propaganda campaigns is the multiple filter system discussed above: the mass media will allow any stories that are hurtful to large interests to peter out quickly, if they surface at all.[127]

For stories that are *useful*, the process will get under way with a series of government leaks, press conferences, white papers, etc., or with one or more of the mass media starting the ball rolling with such articles as Barron and Paul's "Murder of a Gentle Land" (Cambodia), or Claire Sterling's "The Plot to Kill the Pope," both in the *Reader's Digest*. If the other major media like the story, they will follow it up with their own versions, and the matter quickly becomes newsworthy by familiarity.

If the articles are written in an assured and convincing style, are subject to no criticisms or alternative interpretations in the mass media, and command support by authority figures, the propaganda themes quickly become established as true even without real evidence. This tends to close out dissenting views even more comprehensively, as they would now conflict with an already established popular belief. This in turn opens up further opportunities for still more inflated claims, as these can be made without fear of serious repercussions. Similar wild assertions made in contradiction of official views would elicit powerful flak, so that such an inflation process would be controlled by the government and the market. No such protections exist with system-supportive claims; there, flak will tend to press the media to greater hysteria in the face of enemy evil. The media not only suspend critical judgment and investigative zeal, they compete to find ways of putting the newly established truth in a supportive light. Themes and facts – even careful and well-documented analyses – that are incompatible with the now institutionalized theme are suppressed or ignored. If the theme collapses of its own burden of fabrications, the mass media will quietly fold their tents and move on to another topic.[128]

Using a propaganda model, we would not only anticipate definitions of worth based on utility, and dichotomous attention based on the same criterion, we would also expect the news stories about worthy and unworthy victims (or enemy and friendly states) to differ in *quality*. That is, we would expect official sources of the United States and its client regimes to be used heavily – and uncritically – in connection with one's own abuses and those of friendly governments, while refugees and other dissident sources will be used in dealing with enemies.[129] We would anticipate the uncritical acceptance of certain premises in dealing with self and friends – such as that one's own state and leaders seek peace and democracy, oppose terrorism, and tell the truth – premises which will not be applied in treating enemy states. We would expect different criteria of evaluation to be employed, so that what is villainy in enemy states will be presented as an incidental background fact in the case of oneself and friends.[130] What is on the agenda in treating one case will be off the agenda in discussing the other.[131] We would also expect great investigatory zeal in the search for enemy villainy and the responsibility of high officials for abuses in enemy states, but diminished enterprise in examining such matters in connection with one's own and friendly states.

The quality of coverage should also be displayed more directly and crudely in placement, headlining, word usage, and other modes of mobilizing interest and outrage. In the opinion columns, we would anticipate sharp restraints on the range of opinion allowed expression. Our hypothesis is that worthy victims will be featured prominently and dramatically, that they will be humanized, and that their victimization will receive the detail and context in story construction that will generate reader interest and sympathetic emotion. In contrast, unworthy victims will merit only slight detail, minimal humanization, and little context that will excite and enrage.

Meanwhile, because of the power of establishment sources, the flak machines, and anti-Communist ideology, we would anticipate outcries that the worthy victims are being sorely neglected, that the unworthy are treated with excessive and uncritical generosity,[132] that the media's liberal, adversarial (if not subversive) hostility to government explains our difficulties in mustering support for the latest national venture in counterrevolutionary intervention.

In sum, a propaganda approach to media coverage suggests a systematic and highly political dichotomization in news coverage based on serviceability to important domestic power interests. This should be observable in dichotomized choices of story and in the volume and quality of coverage. In the chapters that follow we will see that such dichotomization in the mass media is massive and systematic: not only are choices for publicity and suppression comprehensible in terms of system advantage, but the modes of handling favored and inconvenient materials (placement, tone, context, fullness of treatment) differ in ways that serve political ends.

Notes

1   See note 4 of the Preface [to Herman and Chomsky's *Manufacturing Consent*].
2   Media representatives claim that what the government says is "newsworthy" in its own right. If, however, the government's assertions are transmitted without context or evaluation, and without regard to the government's possible manipulative intent, the media have set themselves up to be "managed." Their objectivity is "nominal," not substantive.

In early October 1986, memos were leaked to the press indicating that the Reagan administration had carried out a deliberate campaign of disinformation to influence events in Libya. The mass media, which had passed along this material without question, expressed a great deal of righteous indignation that they had been misled. To compound the absurdity, five years earlier the press had reported a CIA-run "disinformation program designed to embarrass Qaddafi and his government," along with terrorist operations to overthrow Qaddafi and perhaps assassinate him (*Newsweek*, Aug. 3, 1981; P. Edward Haley, *Qaddafi and the United States since 1969* [New York: Praeger, 1984], p. 272). But no lessons were learned. In fact, the mass media are gulled on an almost daily basis, but rarely have to suffer the indignity of government *documents* revealing their gullibility. With regard to Libya, the media have fallen into line for each propaganda ploy, from the 1981 "hit squads" through the Berlin discothèque bombing, swallowing each implausible claim, failing to admit error in retrospect, and apparently unable to learn from successive entrapment – which suggests willing error. See Noam Chomsky, *Pirates & Emperors* (New York: Claremont, 1986), chapter 3. As we show throughout the present book, a series of lies by the government, successively exposed, never seems to arouse skepticism in the media regarding the next government claim.
3   For a description of the government's strategy of deflecting attention away from the Nicaraguan election by the fabricated MIG story, and the media's service in this government program, see chapter 3 [of Herman and Chomsky's *Manufacturing Consent*], under "The MIG Crisis Staged during the Nicaraguan Election Week."
4   James Curran and Jean Seaton, *Power without Responsibility: The Press and Broadcasting in Britain*, 2d ed. (London: Methuen, 1985), p. 24.
5   Quoted in ibid., p. 23.
6   Ibid., p. 34.
7   Ibid., pp. 38–9.
8   Alfred McClung Lee, *The Daily Newspaper in America* (New York: Macmillan, 1937), pp. 166, 173.

9   Earl Vance, "Freedom of the Press for Whom," *Virginia Quarterly Review* (Summer 1945), quoted in *Survival of a Free, Competitive Press: The Small Newspaper: Democracy's Grass Roots*, Report of the Chairman, Senate Small Business Committee, 80th Cong., 1st session, 1947, p. 54.

10   Note that we are speaking of media with substantial outreach – mass media. It has always been possible to start small-circulation journals and to produce mimeographed or photocopied newsletters sent around to a tiny audience. But even small journals in the United States today typically survive only by virtue of contributions from wealthy financial angels.

11   In 1987, the Times–Mirror Company, for example, owned newspapers in Los Angeles, Baltimore, Denver, and Hartford, Connecticut, had book publishing and magazine subsidiaries, and owned cable systems and seven television stations.

12   Ben Bagdikian, *The Media Monopoly*, 2nd ed. (Boston, Mass.: Beacon Press, 1987), p. xvi.

13   David L. Paletz and Robert M. Entman, *Media, Power, Politics* (New York: Free Press, 1981), p. 7; Stephen Hess, *The Government/Press Connection: Press Officers and Their Offices* (Washington: Brookings, 1984), pp. 99–100.

14   The four major Western wire services – Associated Press, United Press International, Reuters, and Agence-France-Presse – account for some 80 percent of the international news circulating in the world today. AP is owned by member newspapers; UPI is privately owned; Reuters was owned mainly by the British media until it went public in 1984, but control was retained by the original owners by giving lesser voting rights to the new stockholders; Agence-France-Presse is heavily subsidized by the French government. As is pointed out by Jonathan Fenby, the wire services "exist to serve markets," and their prime concern, accordingly, "is with the rich media markets of the United States, Western Europe, and Japan, and increasingly with the business community. . . ." They compete fiercely, but AP and UPI "are really U.S. enterprises that operate on an international scale. . . . Without their domestic base, the AP and UPI could not operate as international agencies. With it, they must be American organizations, subject to American pressures and requirements" (*The International News Services* [New York: Schocken, 1986], pp. 7, 9, 73–4). See also Anthony Smith, *The Geopolitics of Information: How Western Culture Dominates the World* (New York: Oxford University Press, 1980), chapter 3.

15   The fourteenth annual Roper survey, "Public Attitudes toward Television and Other Media in a Time of Change" (May 1985), indicates that in 1984, 64 percent of the sample mentioned television as the place "where you usually get most of your news about what's going on in the world today" (p. 3). It has often been noted that the television networks themselves depend heavily on the prestige newspapers, wire services, and government for their choices of news. Their autonomy as newsmakers can be easily exaggerated.

16   The members of the very top tier qualify by audience outreach, importance as setters of news standards, and asset and profit totals. The last half dozen or so in our twenty-four involve a certain amount of arbitrariness of choice, although audience size is still our primary criterion. McGraw-Hill is included because of its joint strength in trade books and magazines of political content and outreach.

17   As noted earlier, Storer came under the temporary control of the securities firm Kohlberg Kravis Roberts & Co. in 1985. As its ultimate fate was unclear at the time of writing, and as financial data were no longer available after 1984, we have kept Storer on the table and list it here, despite its uncertain status.

18   John Kluge, having taken the Metromedia system private in a leveraged buyout in 1984 worth $1.1 billion, sold off various parts of this system in 1985–6 for $5.5 billion, at a personal profit of some $3 billion (Gary Hector, "Are Shareholders Cheated by LBOs?" *Fortune*, Jan. 17, 1987, p. 100). Station KDLA-TV, in Los Angeles, which had been bought by a management-outsider group in a leveraged buyout in 1983 for $245 million, was sold to the Tribune Company for $510 million two years later (Richard Stevenson, "Tribune in TV Deal for $510 Million," *New York Times*, May 7, 1985). See also "The Media Magnates: Why Huge Fortunes Roll Off the Presses," *Fortune*, October 12, 1987.

19   A split among the heirs of James E. Scripps eventually resulted in the sale of the *Detroit Evening News*. According to one news article, "Daniel Marentette, a Scripps family member and a self described 'angry shareholder,' says family members want a better return on their money. 'We get better yields investing in a New York checking account,' says Mr. Marentette, who sells race horses" (Damon Darlin, "Takeover Rumors Hit Detroit News Parent," *Wall Street Journal*, July 18, 1985). The Bingham family division on these matters led to the sale of the *Louisville Courier-Journal*; the New Haven papers of the Jackson family were sold after years of squabbling, and "the sale price [of the New Haven papers], $185 million, has only served to publicize the potential value of family holdings of family newspapers elsewhere" (Geraldine Fabrikant, "Newspaper Properties, Hotter than Ever," *New York Times*, Aug. 17, 1986).

20   The Reagan administration strengthened the control of existing holders of television-station licenses by increasing their term from three to five years, and its FCC made renewals essentially automatic. The FCC also greatly facilitated speculation and trading in television properties by a rule change reducing the required holding period before sale of a newly acquired property from three years to one year.

   The Reagan era FCC and Department of Justice also refused to challenge mergers and takeover bids that would significantly increase the concentration of power (GE–RCA) or media concentration (Capital Cities–ABC). Furthermore, beginning April 2, 1985, media owners could own as many as twelve television stations, as long as their total audience didn't exceed 25 percent of the nation's television households; and they could also hold twelve AM and twelve FM stations, as the 1953 "7-7-7 rule" was replaced with a "12-12-12 rule." See Herbert H. Howard, "Group and Cross-Media Ownership of Television Stations: 1985" (Washington: National Association of Broadcasters, 1985).

21   This was justified by Reagan-era FCC chairman Mark Fowler on the grounds that market options are opening up and that the public should be free to choose. Criticized by Fred Friendly for doing away with the law's public-interest standard, Fowler replied that Friendly "distrusts the ability of the viewing public to make decisions on its own through the marketplace mechanism. I do not" (Jeanne Saddler, "Clear Channel: Broadcast Takeovers Meet Less FCC Static, and Critics Are Upset," *Wall Street Journal*, June 11, 1985). Among other problems, Fowler ignores the fact that true freedom of choice involves the ability to select options that may not be offered by an oligopoly selling audiences to advertisers.

22   CBS increased its debt by about $1 billion in 1985 to finance the purchase of 21 percent of its own stock, in order to fend off a takeover attempt by Ted Turner. The *Wall Street Journal* noted that "With debt now standing at 60 percent of capital, it needs to keep advertising revenue up to repay borrowings and interest" (Peter Barnes, "CBS Profit Hinges on Better TV Ratings," June 6, 1986). With the slowed-up growth

of advertising revenues, CBS embarked on an employment cutback of as many as six hundred broadcast division employees, the most extensive for CBS since the loss of cigarette advertising in 1971 (Peter Barnes, "CBS Will Cut up to 600 Posts in Broadcasting," *Wall Street Journal*, July 1, 1986). In June 1986, Time, Inc., embarked on a program to buy back as much as 10 million shares, or 16 percent of its common stock, at an expected cost of some $900 million, again to reduce the threat of a hostile takeover (Laura Landro, "Time Will Buy as Much as 16 percent of Its Common," *Wall Street Journal*, June 20, 1986).

23   In response to the Jesse Helms and Turner threats to CBS, Laurence Tisch, of Loews Corporation, was encouraged to increase his holdings in CBS stock, already at 11.7 percent. In August 1986, the Loews interest was raised to 24.9 percent, and Tisch obtained a position of virtual control. In combination with William Paley, who owned 8.1 percent of the shares, the chief executive officer of CBS was removed and Tisch took over that role himself, on a temporary basis (Peter Barnes, "Loews Increases Its Stake in CBS to Almost 25 percent," *Wall Street Journal*, Aug. 12, 1986).

24   The number would be eight if we included the estate of Lila Wallace, who died in 1984, leaving the controlling stock interest in *Reader's Digest* to the care of trustees.

25   As we noted in the preface, the neoconservatives speak regularly of "liberal" domination of the media, assuming or pretending that the underlings call the shots, not the people who own or control the media. These data, showing the wealth position of media owners, are understandably something they prefer to ignore. Sometimes, however, the neoconservatives go "populist," and – while financed by Mobil Oil Corporation and Richard Mellon Scaife – pretend to be speaking for the "masses" in opposition to a monied elite dominating the media. For further discussion, see Edward S. Herman's review of *The Spirit of Democratic Capitalism*, "Michael Novak's Promised Land: Unfettered Corporate Capitalism," *Monthly Review* (October 1983).

26   Similar results are found in Peter Dreier, "The Position of the Press in the U.S. Power Structure," *Social Problems* (February 1982), pp. 298–310.

27   Benjamin Compaine et al., *Anatomy of the Communications Industry: Who Owns the Media?* (White Plains, N.Y.: Knowledge Industry Publications, 1982), p. 463.

28   Ibid., pp. 458–60.

29   See Edward S. Herman, *Corporate Control, Corporate Power* (New York: Cambridge University Press, 1981), pp. 26–54.

30   For the interests of fifteen major newspaper companies in other media fields, and a checklist of other fields entered by leading firms in a variety of media industries, see Compaine, *Anatomy of the Communications Industry*, tables 2.19 and 8.1, pp. 11 and 452–3.

31   The merger had been sanctioned by the FCC but was stymied by intervention of the Department of Justice. See "A broken engagement for ITT and ABC," *Business Week*, January 6, 1967.

32   Ibid.

33   On the enormous and effective lobbying operations of GE, see Thomas B. Edsall, "Bringing Good Things to GE: Firm's Political Savvy Scores in Washington," *Washington Post*, April 13, 1985.

34   The widely quoted joke by A. J. Liebling – that if you don't like what your newspaper says you are perfectly free to start or buy one of your own – stressed the impotence of the individual. In a favorable political climate such as that provided by the Reagan administration, however, a giant corporation not liking media performance *can* buy its own, as exemplified by GE.

35 Allan Sloan, "Understanding Murdoch – The Numbers Aren't What Really Matters," *Forbes*, March 10, 1986, pp. 114ff.

36 On the Nixon–Agnew campaign to bully the media by publicity attacks and threats, see Marilyn Lashner, *The Chilling Effect in TV News* (New York: Praeger, 1984). Lashner concluded that the Nixon White House's attempt to quiet the media "succeeded handily, at least as far as television is concerned" (p. 167). See also Fred Powledge, *The Engineering of Restraint: The Nixon Administration and the Press* (Washington: Public Affairs Press, 1971), and William E. Porter, *Assault on the Media: The Nixon Years* (Ann Arbor: University of Michigan Press, 1976).

37 Of the 290 directors in his sample of large newspapers, 36 had high-level positions – past or present – in the federal government (Dreier, "The Position of the Press," p. 303).

38 One study showed that out of sixty-five FCC commissioners and high-level staff personnel who left the FCC between 1945 and 1970, twelve had come out of the private-communications sector before their FCC service, and thirty-four went into private-firm service after leaving the commission (Roger Noll et al., *Economic Aspects of Television Regulation* [Washington: Brookings, 1973], p. 123).

39 "The symbolic growth of American television and global enterprise has made them so interrelated that they cannot be thought of as separate. They are essentially the same phenomenon. Preceded far and wide by military advisers, lobbyists, equipment salesmen, advertising specialists, merchandising experts, and telefilm salesmen as advance agents, the enterprise penetrates much of the non-socialist world. Television is simply its most visible portion" (Erik Barnouw, *The Sponsor* [New York: Oxford University Press, 1978], p. 158). For a broader picture, see Herbert I. Schiller, *Communication and Cultural Domination* (White Plains, N.Y.: International Arts and Sciences Press, 1976), especially chapters 3–4.

40 Is it not possible that if the populace "demands" program content greatly disliked by the owners, competition and the quest for profits will cause them to offer such programming? There is some truth in this, and it, along with the limited autonomy of media personnel, may help explain the "surprises" that crop up occasionally in the mass media. One limit to the force of public demand, however, is that the millions of customers have no means of registering their demand for products that are not offered to them. A further problem is that the owners' class interests are reinforced by a variety of other filters that we discuss below.

41 Quoted in Curran and Seaton, *Power without Responsibility*, p. 31.

42 Ibid., p. 41.

43 "Producers presenting patrons [advertisers] with the greatest opportunities to make a profit through their publics will receive support while those that cannot compete on this score will not survive" (Joseph Turow, *Media Industries: The Production of News and Entertainment* [New York: Longman, 1984], p. 52).

44 Noncommercial television is also at a huge disadvantage for the same reason, and will require a public subsidy to be able to compete. Because public television does not have the built-in constraints of ownership by the wealthy, and the need to appease advertisers, it poses a threat to a narrow elite control of mass communications. This is why conservatives struggle to keep public television on a short leash, with annual funding decisions, and funding at a low level (see Barnouw, *The Sponsor*, pp. 179–82). Another option pursued in the Carter–Reagan era has been to force it into the commercial nexus by sharp defunding.

45 Bagdikian, *Media Monopoly*, pp. 118–26. " 'The dominant paper ultimately thrives,' Gannett Chairman Allen H. Neuharth says. 'The weaker paper ultimately dies' " (Joseph B. White, "Knight-Ridder's No-Lose Plan Backfires," *Wall Street Journal*, Jan. 4, 1988).

46 Quoted in Curran and Seaton, *Power without Responsibility*, p. 43.
47 "Advertising and the Press," in James Curran (ed.), *The British Press: A Manifesto* (London: Macmillan, 1978), pp. 252–5.
48 Ibid., p. 254.
49 *1984 CBS Annual Report*, p. 13. This is a further refinement in the measurement of "efficiency" in "delivering an audience." In the magazine business, the standard measure is CPM, or "costs per thousand," to an advertiser to reach buyers through a full-page, black-and-white ad. Recent developments, like CBS's CAP, have been in the direction of identifying the special characteristics of the audience delivered. In selling itself to advertisers, the *Soap Opera Digest* says: "But you probably want to know about our first milestone: today *Soap Opera Digest* delivers more women in the 18–49 category at the lowest CPM than any other women's magazine" (quoted in Turow, *Media Industries*, p. 55).
50 William Evan, *Organization Theory* (New York: Wiley, 1976), p. 123.
51 Turow asserts that "The continual interaction of producers and primary patrons plays a dominant part in setting the general boundary conditions for day-to-day production activity" (*Media Industries*, p. 51).
52 Quoted in Todd Gitlin, *Inside Prime Time* (New York: Pantheon, 1983), p. 253.
53 Pat Aufderheide, "What Makes Public TV Public?" *The Progressive* (January 1988).
54 "Castor oil or Camelot?" December 5, 1987. For further information on such interventions, see Harry Hammitt, "Advertising Pressures on Media," Freedom of Information Center Report no. 367 (School of Journalism, University of Missouri at Columbia, February 1977). See also James Aronson, *Deadline for the Media* (New York: Bobbs-Merrill, 1972), pp. 261–3.
55 According to Procter & Gamble's instructions to their ad agency, "There will be no material on any of our programs which could in any way further the concept of business as cold, ruthless, and lacking in all sentiment or spiritual motivation." The manager of corporate communications for General Electric has said: "We insist on a program environment that reinforces our corporate messages" (quoted in Bagdikian, *Media Monopoly*, p. 160). We may recall that GE now owns NBC-TV.
56 Barnouw, *The Sponsor*, p. 135.
57 Advertisers may also be offended by attacks on themselves or their products. On the tendency of the media to avoid criticism of advertised products even when very important to consumer welfare [e.g., the effects of smoking], see Bagdikian, *Media Monopoly*, pp. 168–73.
58 This is hard to prove statistically, given the poor data made available by the FCC over the years. The long-term trend in advertising time/programming time is dramatically revealed by the fact that in 1929 the National Association of Broadcasting adopted as a standard of commercial practice on radio the following: "Commercial announcements . . . shall not be broadcast between 7 and 11 P.M." William Paley testified before the Senate Commerce Committee in 1930 that only 22 percent of CBS's time was allocated to commercially sponsored programs, with the other 78 percent sustaining; and he noted that advertising took up only "seven-tenths of 1 percent of all our time" (quoted in *Public Service Responsibility of Broadcast Licenses*, FCC [Washington: GPO, March 7, 1946], p. 42). Frank Wolf states in reference to public-affairs programming: "That such programs were even shown at all on commercial television may have been the result of FCC regulation" (*Television Programming for News and Public Affairs* [New York: Praeger, 1972], p. 138; see also pp. 99–139).
59 Barnouw, *The Sponsor*, p. 134.

60 For Alcoa's post-antitrust-suit sponsorship of Edward R. Murrow, and ITT's post-early-1970s-scandals sponsorship of "The Big Blue Marble," see Barnouw, *The Sponsor*, ibid., pp. 51–2, 84–6. Barnouw shows that network news coverage of ITT was sharply constrained during the period of ITT program sponsorship.

61 Barnouw, *The Sponsor*, p. 150.

62 Mark Fishman, *Manufacturing the News* (Austin: University of Texas Press, 1980), p. 143.

63 Ibid., pp. 144–5.

64 Gaye Tuchman, "Objectivity as Strategic Ritual: An Examination of Newsmen's Notions of Objectivity," *American Journal of Sociology*, 77, no. 2 (1972), pp. 662–4.

65 United States Air Force, "Fact Sheet: The United States Air Force Information Program" (March 1979); "News Releases: 600,000 in a Year," *Air Force Times*, April 28, 1980.

66 J. W. Fulbright, *The Pentagon Propaganda Machine* (New York: H. Liveright, 1970), p. 88.

67 Ibid., p. 90.

68 An Associated Press report on "Newspapers Mustered as Air Force Defends BiB," published in the *Washington Post*, April 3, 1987, indicates that the U.S. Air Force had 277 newspapers in 1987, as compared with 140 in 1979.

69 "DOD Kills 205 Periodicals; Still Publishes 1,203 Others," *Armed Forces Journal International* (August 1982), p. 16.

70 Its nine regional offices also had some public-information operations, but personnel and funding are not readily allocatable to this function. They are smaller than the central office aggregate.

The AFSC aggregate public-information budget is about the same size as the contract given by the State Department to International Business Communications (IBC) for lobbying on behalf of the contras ($419,000). This was only one of twenty-five contracts investigated by the GAO that "the Latin American Public Diplomacy office awarded to individuals for research and papers on Central America, said a GAO official involved in the investigation" (Rita Beamish, "Pro-contra Contracts are Probed," *Philadelphia Inquirer*, July 22, 1987, p. 4A).

71 The NCC's news services are concentrated in the Office of Information, but it has some dispersed staff in communications functions elsewhere in the organization that produce a few newsletters, magazines, and some videotapes and filmstrips.

72 In 1980, Mobil Oil had a public-relations budget of $21 million and a public-relations staff of seventy-three. Between 1976 and 1981 it produced at least a dozen televised special reports on such issues as gasoline prices, with a hired television journalist interviewing Mobil executives and other experts, that are shown frequently on television, often without indication of Mobil sponsorship. See A. Kent MacDougall, *Ninety Seconds To Tell It All* (Homewood, Ill.: Dow Jones–Irwin, 1981), pp. 117–20.

73 John S. Saloma III, *Ominous Politics: The New Conservative Labyrinth* (New York: Hill & Wang, 1984), p. 79.

74 MacDougall, *Ninety Seconds*, pp. 116–17.

75 Thomas B. Edsall, *The New Politics of Inequality* (New York: Norton, 1984), p. 110.

76 Peggy Dardenne, "Corporate Advertising," *Public Relations Journal* (November 1982), p. 36.

77 S. Prakash Sethi, *Handbook of Advocacy Advertising: Strategies and Applications* (Cambridge, Mass.: Ballinger, 1987), p. 22. See also Edsall, *New Politics*, chapter 3, "The Politicization of the Business Community"; and Saloma, *Ominous Politics*, chapter 6, "The Corporations: Making Our Voices Heard."

78 The April 14, 1986, U.S. bombing of Libya was the first military action timed to preempt attention on 7 P.M. prime-time television news. See Chomsky, *Pirates & Emperors*, p. 147.

79 For the masterful way the Reagan administration used these to manipulate the press, see "Standups," *The New Yorker*, December 2, 1985, pp. 81ff.

80 Fishman, *Manufacturing the News*, p. 153.

81 See note 70.

82 On January 16, 1986, the American Friends Service Committee issued a news release, based on extended Freedom of Information Act inquiries, which showed that there had been 381 navy nuclear-weapons accidents and "incidents" in the period 1965–77, a figure far higher than that previously claimed. The mass media did not cover this hot story directly but through the filter of the navy's reply, which downplayed the significance of the new findings and eliminated or relegated to the background the AFSC's full range of facts and interpretation of the meaning of what they had uncovered. A typical heading: "Navy Lists Nuclear Mishaps: None of 630 Imperilled Public, Service Says," *Washington Post*, January 16, 1986.

83 The Harvard professor in charge of the program, Harvey Mansfield, stated that the invitation to White had been a mistake anyway, as he "is a representative of the far left," whereas the forum was intended to involve a debate "between liberals and conservatives" (*Harvard Crimson*, May 14, 1986).

84 See Edward S. Herman and Frank Brodhead, *The Rise and Fall of the Bulgarian Connection* (New York: Sheridan Square Publications, 1986), pp. 123–4.

85 Mark Hertsgaard, "How Reagan Seduced Us: Inside the President's Propaganda Factory," *Village Voice*, September 18, 1984; see also "Standups," cited in note 79 above.

86 Stephen L. Vaughn, *Holding Fast the Inner Lines* (Chapel Hill: University of North Carolina Press, 1980), p. 194.

87 Bruce Owen and Ronald Braeutigam, *The Regulation Game: Strategic Use of the Administrative Process* (Cambridge, Mass.: Ballinger, 1978), p. 7.

88 See Edward S. Herman, "The Institutionalization of Bias in Economics," *Media, Culture and Society* (July 1982), pp. 275–91.

89 Henry Kissinger, *American Foreign Policy* (New York: Norton, 1969), p. 28.

90 Quoted in Alex Carey, "Managing Public Opinion: The Corporate Offensive" (University of New South Wales, 1986, mimeographed), p. 32.

91 Ibid., pp. 46–7, quoting Feulner papers given in 1978 and 1985.

92 For a good discussion of many of these organizations and their purpose, funding, networking, and outreach programs, see Saloma, *Ominous Politics*, chapters 4, 6, and 9.

93 See Herman and Broadhead, *Bulgarian Connection*, p. 259; Fred Landis, "Georgetown's Ivory Tower for Old Spooks," *Inquiry*, September 30, 1979, pp. 7–9.

94 The CSIS's expert on terrorism, Robert Kupperman, was probably the most widely used participant on radio and television talk shows on terrorism in the last several years.

95 On Sterling's qualifications as an expert, see Herman and Broadhead, *Bulgarian Connection*, pp. 125–46; on Shevchenko, see Edward J. Epstein, "The Invention of Arkady Shevchenko, Supermole: The Spy Who Came in to be Sold," *New Republic*, July 15–22, 1985.

96 See David Caute, *The Great Fear: The Anti-Communist Purge under Truman and Eisenhower* (New York: Simon & Schuster, 1978), pp. 114–38, who stresses the importance of the *lying* informer. This McCarthyite pathology was replicated in Robert Leiken's 1982 book on "Soviet hegemonism" – the standard Maoist phrase – which conjures up a Soviet strategy of taking over the Western hemisphere by means of Cuba and the

Sandinistas, and guerrilla movements elsewhere (Leiken, *Soviet Strategy in Latin America* [New York: Praeger, 1982]).

97   Then and now, former dissidents are portrayed as especially valuable experts for the seeming authenticity they can bring to the mistakes of their former associates. The fact that their claims are often fraudulent is not a problem because the mass media refuse to point this out. Thus Jean Lacouture lent credence to his criticisms of the Khmer Rouge by claiming to have been a former sympathizer – not only a falsehood, as he was pro-Sihanouk, but an absurdity, as nothing had been known about the the Khmer Rouge. David Horowitz added to his value as a born-again patriot by claiming that along with protesters against the Vietnam War generally, he came "to acquire a new appreciation for foreign tyrants like Kim Il Sung of North Korea" (Peter Collier and David Horowitz, "Confessions of Two New-Left Radicals: Why We Voted for Reagan," *Washington Post National Weekly Edition*, April 8, 1985). Robert Leiken became more potent as a critic of the Sandinistas as an alleged former peace-movement activist and early supporter of the Sandinistas. Each of these claims was a fabrication, but this fact went unmentioned in the mass media. On Leiken's claims, and the "special force" his anti-Sandinista writings gained by his alleged conversion from "fan of the Sandinistas," see Michael Massing, "Contra Aides," *Mother Jones* (October 1987). While dismissing this pretense, Massing credits Leiken's claim that he "was active in the antiwar movement," but that is highly misleading. Activists in the Boston area, where he claims to have been an antiwar organizer, recall no participation by Leiken until about 1970 – at which time McGeorge Bundy could also have been described as an activist leader.

98   See above, note 55.

99   See "The Business Campaign Against 'Trial by TV,'" *Business Week*, June 22, 1980, pp. 77–9; William H. Miller, "Fighting TV Hatchet Jobs," *Industry Week*, January 12, 1981, pp. 61–4.

100 See Walter Schneir and Miriam Schneir, "Beyond Westmoreland: The Right's Attack on the Press," *The Nation*, March 30, 1985.

101 An ad widely distributed by United Technologies Corporation, titled "Crooks and Clowns on TV," is based on the Media Institute's study entitled *Crooks, Conmen and Clowns: Businessmen in TV Entertainment*, which contends that businessmen are treated badly in television entertainment programs.

102 John Corry, *TV News and the Dominant Culture* (Washington: Media Institute), 1986.

103 See S. Robert Lichter, Stanley Rothman, and Linda Lichter, *The Media Elite* (Bethesda, MD: Adler & Adler, 1986). For a good discussion of the Lichters' new center, see Alexander Cockburn, "Ashes and Diamonds," *In These Times*, July 8–21, 1987.

104 Louis Wolf, "Accuracy in Media Rewrites News and History," *Covert Action Information Bulletin* (Spring 1984), pp. 26–9.

105 AIM's impact is hard to gauge, but it must be recognized as only a part of a larger corporate right-wing campaign of attack. It has common funding sources with such components of the conservative labyrinth as AEI, Hoover, the Institute for Contemporary Studies, and others (see Saloma, *Ominous Politics*, esp. chapters 2, 3, and 6), and has its own special role to play. AIM's head, Reed Irvine, is a frequent participant in television talk shows, and his letters to the editor and commentary are regularly published in the mass media. The media feel obligated to provide careful responses to his detailed attacks on their news and documentaries, and the Corporation for Public Broadcasting even helped fund his group's reply to the PBS series on Vietnam. His ability to get the publisher of the *New York Times* to meet with him personally once a year – a first objective of any lobbyist – is impressive testimony to influence. On his contribution to

the departure of Raymond Bonner from the *Times*, see Wolf, "Accuracy in Media Rewrites News and History," pp. 32–3.

106   For an analysis of the bias of the Freedom House observers, see Edward S. Herman and Frank Brodhead, *Demonstration Elections: U.S.-Staged Elections in the Dominican Republic, Vietnam, and El Salvador* (Boston: South End Press, 1984), appendix I, "Freedom House Observers in Zimbabwe Rhodesia and El Salvador."

107   R. Bruce McColm, "El Salvador: Peaceful Revolution or Armed Struggle?" *Perspectives on Freedom* I (New York: Freedom House, 1982); James Nelson Goodsell, "Freedom House Labels US Reports on Salvador Biased," *Christian Science Monitor*, February 3, 1982.

108   For a discussion of Ledeen's views on the media, see Herman and Brodhead, *Bulgarian Connection*, pp. 166–70.

109   Among the contributors to AIM have been the Reader's Digest Association and the DeWitt Wallace Fund, Walter Annenberg, Sir James Goldsmith (owner of the French *L'Express*), and E. W. Scripps II, board chairman of a newspaper-television-radio system.

110   George Skelton, White House correspondent for the *Los Angeles Times*, noted that in reference to Reagan's errors of fact, "You write the stories once, twice, and you get a lot of mail saying, 'You're picking on the guy, you guys in the press make mistakes too.' And editors respond to that, so after a while the stories don't run anymore. We're intimidated" (quoted in Hertsgaard, "How Reagan Seduced Us").

111   Piero Gleijeses, *The Dominican Crisis* (Baltimore: Johns Hopkins University Press, 1978), pp. 95–9.

112   Jan K. Black, *United States Penetration of Brazil* (Philadelphia: University of Pennsylvania Press, 1977), pp. 39–56.

113   See above, pp. 24–5; below, pp. 157–61.

114   "The Stalinists of Anti-Communism," in Ralph Miliband, John Saville, and Marcel Liebman, *Socialist Register, 1984: The Uses of Anticommunism* (London: Merlin Press, 1984), p. 337.

115   Daix, in 1949, referred to the Stalin concentration camps as "one of the Soviet Union's most glorious achievements," displaying "the complete suppression of man's exploitation of man" (quoted in Miliband et al., *Socialist Register*, p. 337). Kriegel, formerly a hard-line Communist party functionary, was the author of a 1982 book explaining that the KGB organized the Sabra–Shatila massacres, employing German terrorists associated with the PLO and with the tacit cooperation of the CIA, in order to defame Israel as part of the Soviet program of international terrorism. For more on this profound study, and its influence, see Noam Chomsky, *Fateful Triangle* (Boston: South End Press, 1983), pp. 291–2, 374–5.

116   *Socialist Register*, p. 345.

117   Where dissidents are prepared to denounce official enemies, of course, they can pass through the mass-media filtering system, in the manner of the ex-Communist experts described in "Anticommunism as a Control Mechanism" (p. 29).

118   See chapter 2 [of Herman and Chomsky's *Manufacturing Consent*]: "Worthy and Unworthy Victims." Of interest in the Turkish case is the Western press's refusal to publicize the Turkish government's attacks on the press, including the U.S. press's own reporters in that country. UPI's reporter Ismet Ismet, beaten up by the Turkish police and imprisoned under trumped-up charges, was warned by UPI not to publicize the charges against him, and UPI eventually fired him for criticizing their badly compromised handling of his case. See Chris Christiansen, "Keeping in with the Generals," *New Statesman*, January 4, 1985.

119 We believe that the same dichotomization applies in the domestic sphere. For example, both British and American analysts have noted the periodic intense focus on – and indignation over – "welfare chiselers" by the mass media, and the parallel de-emphasis of and benign attitudes toward the far more important fraud and tax abuses of business and the affluent. There is also a deep-seated reluctance on the part of the mass media to examine the structural causes of inequality and poverty. Peter Golding and Sue Middleton, after an extensive discussion of the long-standing "criminalization of poverty" and incessant attacks on welfare scroungers in Britain, point out that tax evasion, by contrast; is "acceptable, even laudable," in the press, that the tax evader "is not merely a victim but a hero." They note, also, that "The supreme achievement of welfare capitalism" has been to render the causes and condition of poverty almost invisible (*Images of Welfare: Press and Public Attitudes to Poverty* [Oxford: Martin Robertson, 1982], pp. 66–7, 98–100, 186, 193).

In a chapter entitled "The Deserving Rich," A. J. Liebling pointed out that in the United States as well, "The crusade against the destitute is the favorite crusade of the newspaper publisher," and that "There is no concept more generally cherished by publishers than that of the Undeserving Poor" (*The Press* [New York: Ballantine, 1964], pp. 78–9). Liebling went into great detail on various efforts of the media to keep welfare expenses and taxes down "by saying that they [the poor] have concealed assets, or bad character, or both" (p. 79). These strategies not only divert, they also help split the employed working class from the unemployed and marginalized, and make these all exceedingly uncomfortable about participating in a degraded system of scrounging. See Peter Golding and Sue Middleton, "Attitudes to Claimants: A Culture of Contempt," in *Images of Welfare*, pp. 169ff. President Reagan's fabricated anecdotes about welfare chiselers, and his complete silence on the large-scale chiseling of his corporate sponsors, have fitted into a long tradition of cynical and heartless greed.

120 For a full discussion of this dichotomized treatment, see Edward S. Herman, "Gatekeeper versus Propaganda Models: A Critical American Perspective," in Peter Golding, Graham Murdock and Philip Schlesinger (eds.), *Communicating Politics* (New York: Holmes & Meier, 1986), pp. 182–94.

121 Editorial, March 1, 1973. The Soviets apparently didn't know that they were shooting down a civilian plane, but this was covered up by U.S. officials, and the false allegation of a knowing destruction of a civilian aircraft provided the basis for extremely harsh criticism of the Soviets for barbaric behavior. The Israelis openly admitted knowing that they were shooting down a civilian plane, but this point was of no interest in the West in this particular case.

122 The *New York Times Index*, for example, has seven full pages of citations to the KAL 007 incident for September 1983 alone.

123 Patriotic orgies, such as the 1984 Olympic Games in Los Angeles, the space-shuttle flights, and "Liberty Weekend," perform a similar function in "bringing us all together." See Elayne Rapping, *The Looking Glass World of Nonfiction TV* (Boston: South End Press, 1987), chapter 5, "National Rituals."

124 See below [see chapter 6 of Herman and Chomsky's *Manufacturing Consent*].

125 On issues where the elite is seriously divided, there will be dissenting voices allowed in the mass media, and the inflation of claims and suspension of critical judgment will be subject to some constraint. See the discussion of this point in the preface, and examples in the case studies that follow.

126 The role of the government in these cases cannot be entirely discounted, given the close ties of the *Reader's Digest* to the CIA and the fact that Paul Henze, one of the

primary sources and movers in the Bulgarian Connection campaign, was a longtime CIA official. On the CIA–*Reader's Digest* connection, see Epstein, "The Invention of Arkady Shevchenko," pp. 40–1. On Henze, see below, chapter 4. On the strong likelihood that an influential *Reader's Digest* best seller on Cambodia was in part a CIA disinformation effort, see below [see chapter 6 of Herman and Chomsky's *Manufacturing Consent*] and sources cited.

127   We provide many illustrations of these points in the chapters that follow. Watergate and, more recently, the late-Reagan-era exposures of Iran-Contragate, which are put forward as counterexamples, are discussed below.

128   These points apply clearly to the case of the alleged Bulgarian Connection in the plot to assassinate the pope. See below.

129   We have noted elsewhere that the *New York Times* regularly relied upon Indonesian officials in "presenting the facts" about East Timor, which was being invaded by Indonesia, and ignored refugees, church sources, etc. In contrast, refugees, not state officials, were the prime source in the *Times*'s reporting on postwar events in Vietnam and Cambodia (*The Washington Connection and Third World Fascism* [Boston: South End Press, 1979], pp. 151–2, 169–76, 184–7). On attempts to evade the obvious implications, see chapter 6 [of Herman and Chomsky's *Manufacturing Consent*], under "The Pol Pot Era" (pp. 284–5).

130   Thus when the CIA directs Nicaraguan contras to attack such "soft targets" as farming cooperatives, with explicit State Department approval, the media commentators, including doves, either applaud or offer philosophical disquisitions on whether such targets are legitimate, given that they are defended by lightly armed militia. Terrorist attacks on Israeli kibbutzim, also defended by armed settlers, are regarded somewhat differently. For details, see Noam Chomsky, *The Culture of Terrorism* (Boston: South End Press, 1988).

131   The variable use of agendas and frameworks can be seen with great clarity in the treatment of Third World elections supported and opposed by the United States.

132   Classic in their audacity are Michael Ledeen's assertions that: (1) Qaddafi's word is given more credence in the mass media than that of the U.S. government; and (2) "Relatively minor human rights transgressions in a friendly country (especially if ruled by an authoritarian government of the Right) are given far more attention and more intense criticism than far graver sins of countries hostile to us." (*Grave New World* [New York: Oxford University Press, 1985], p. 131; Qaddafi's superior credence is described on pp. 132–3) See chapter 2 [of Herman and Chomsky's *Manufacturing Consent*], for documentation on the reality of mass-media treatment of abuses by clients and enemy states.

18

Not Yet the Post-Imperialist Era

Herbert I. Schiller

Apart from the persistent explanatory and semantic efforts in recent years to minimize or discredit the idea of cultural domination (Ang, 1985; Liebes & Katz, 1990), changing conditions make it desirable to reassess the original thesis.

Two governing circumstances strongly influenced the early elaboration of the theory of cultural dominance in the mid-1960s. The first was the then-existing world balance of forces.

Twenty-five years ago, the international order could be divided into three major groups. The most powerful of these was the so-called First World, including essentially those countries that were grounded in private propertied relations and whose production was undertaken by capitalist enterprise. The Second World comprised those nations that were organized along state ownership of property lines and that called themselves socialist. The last category (in every sense) was the Third World, containing those countries that had just emerged from the collapsed European colonial empires. In the case of Latin America, these nations continued to suffer economic exploitation although they had been nominally independent for over a century. In most of the Third World states, national liberation movements still existed, and the social structures had not yet been completely captured by new, privileged elites.

In this general map, the United States was by far the most powerful individual state in the First World and in the other two categories as well. Although the Soviet Union, after the Second World War, claimed superpower status on the basis of possessing nuclear weapons, its economic and technological position was decidedly subordinate.

The other determining feature of this period in the cultural realm was the rapid development of television and its capability for transmitting compelling imagery and messages to vast audiences.

These geopolitical and technological conditions provided the social landscape for the era's cultural domination perspective. The essential assumptions undergirding it

From Herbert I. Schiller, "Not yet the post-imperialist era." In *Critical Studies in Mass Communication*, 8 (1991), pp. 13–28. © 1991 by the National Communications Association.

were (and are) few and relatively straightforward: Media-cultural imperialism is a subset of the *general* system of imperialism. It is not freestanding; the media-cultural component in a developed, corporate economy supports the economic objectives of the decisive industrial-financial sectors (i.e., the creation and extension of the consumer society); the cultural and economic spheres are indivisible. Cultural, no less than automobile, production has its political economy. Consequently, what is regarded as cultural output also is ideological and profit-serving to the system at large. Finally, in its latest mode of operation, in the late twentieth century, the corporate economy is increasingly dependent on the media-cultural sector.

The thesis assumed that the state socialist (Second) World was, if not immune to Western cultural-informational pressure, at least to some degree insulated from it and would, under certain circumstances, support limits on its advance. The Third World, in contrast, was seen as an extremely vulnerable and deliberate target of American cultural exports. At the same time, it also was viewed as a potentially organizable force – not yet frozen in class relationships – that might give leadership to a comprehensive restructuring of the world information system. The movement for a new international information order was one vehicle for such a mobilization.

The charge that American-produced cultural commodities – television programs in particular – were overwhelming a good part of the world hardly needed documentation. But the data were there (Nordenstreng & Varis, 1974).

Changes in the International Geopolitical Arena

Twenty-five years later, some of this map has changed. Most importantly, the Second World (the socialist "camp") has all but disappeared. With the (temporary?) exceptions of China, Albania, North Korea, Vietnam, and Cuba, there is no longer a state socialist sphere in the global arena.

The Eastern European states, along with the Soviet Union, are in varying stages of capitalist restoration. Rather than providing an oppositional pole to the First World, they are now eager adherents to that world, as well as its supplicants. They offer national space to the marketing and ideological message flows of their former adversaries.

In a material sense, the strength and influence of the First World, especially that of its most powerful members, are less restrained than they were in the preceding period. This is observable not only with regard to the erstwhile socialist bloc but even more so with respect to the people and nations of Africa, Asia, and Latin America.

Actually, the condition of the Third World vis-à-vis the North (Western Europe, Japan, and the United States) is one of near-desperation. Now under the control of elites that accept and benefit from the workings of the world market economy, the African, Asian, and Latin American nations are deeply in debt and stalled for the most part in efforts for improvement. Most of the Third World nations seem more helpless than ever to resist the demands of their creditors and overseers. Despite some variability in this condition and occasional balking by a recalcitrant ruling group, the general situation reveals practically an abandonment of the challenging economic and cultural positions this group advanced not so long ago.

The role of television in the global arena of cultural domination has not diminished in the 1990s. Reinforced by new delivery systems – communication satellites and cable networks – the image flow is heavier than ever. Its source of origin also has not changed that much in the last quarter of a century. There is, however, one significant difference. Today, television is but one element, however influential, in an all-encompassing cultural package.

The corporate media-cultural industries have expanded remarkably in recent decades and now occupy most of the global social space. For this reason alone, cultural domination today cannot be measured by a simple index of exposure to American television programming. The cultural submersion now includes the English language itself, shopping in American-styled malls, going to theme parks (of which Disney is the foremost but not exclusive example), listening to the music of internationally publicized performers, following news agency reports or watching the Cable News Network in scores of foreign locales, reading translations of commercial best sellers, and eating in franchised fast-food restaurants around the world. Cultural domination means also adopting broadcasting systems that depend on advertising and accepting deregulatory practices that transform the public mails, the telephone system, and cable television into private profit centers (Engelhardt, 1990).

Alongside this all-service-supplying cultural-media environment, the relative economic and political power of the United States continues to diminish. This suggests that American cultural domination is not guaranteed in perpetuity. Yet irrefutably that domination has been preeminent for the last four decades and remains so to this date, though subsumed increasingly under transnational corporate capital and control. The cultural primacy that the ruling national power in the world economy historically exercised may now be changing.

The commanding position of American media products in the post-World War II era, the expertise derived from more than a century of successful marketing activity, and the now near-universal adoption of English as the international lingua franca still confer extraordinary influence on U.S.-produced cultural commodities. How long this influence can be sustained while American systemic power declines is an open question. But in any case, American *national* power no longer is an exclusive determinant of cultural domination.

The domination that exists today, though still bearing a marked American imprint, is better understood as *transnational corporate cultural domination*. Philips of the Netherlands, Lever Brothers of Britain, Daimler-Benz of Germany, Samson of Korea, and Sony of Japan, along with some few thousand other companies, are now the major players in the international market. The media, public relations, advertising, polling, cultural sponsorship, and consultants these industrial giants use and support hardly are distinguishable from the same services at the disposal of

American-owned corporations. Still, a good fraction of these informational-cultural activities continue to be supplied by American enterprises.

These developments leave most of the peoples and nations in the world more vulnerable than ever to domination – cultural, military, and economic. Former oppositional forces have collapsed.

Unsurprisingly, at this moment, there seems a barely contained euphoria in Washington and other centers where capital rules. George Bush, speaking at the United Nations General Assembly in New York in October 1990, proclaimed "a new era of peace and competition and freedom." He saw "a world of open borders, open trade and, most importantly, open minds" (Transcript of President's address to U.N. General Assembly, 1990, p. A-6).

How aptly expressed are the current objectives of the for-the-moment unrestrained global corporate order – open borders, which can be transgressed; open trade, which enables the most powerful to prevail; open minds, which are at the mercy of the swelling global flows of the cultural industries. At least for now, the celebratory mood seems justified. Still, the currently triumphant corporate juggernaut is not on an open freeway with no stop lights and road checks. Possible sources of slowdown will be considered later.

Cheerful Surveyors of the Current Scene

Not all view the developments described above with skepticism or dismay. Indeed, some see the phenomena that now characterize daily life in a very large, and growing, part of the world as evidence that cultural domination no longer exists, or that what appears as domination actually fosters resistance to itself.

The idea of cultural diversity, for example, enjoys great popularity among many cultural observers. The central assumption – that many diverse cultural tendencies and movements operate, with no one element dominating – is the familiar pluralist argument, now applied to the cultural field. A more recent construct is the notion of "globalization." In this proposition, the world is moving, however haltingly, toward a genuinely global civilization. There is also the very widely accepted hypothesis of an "active audience," one in which viewers, readers, and listeners make their own meaning from the messages that come their way, often to the point of creating resistance to hegemonic meanings. Most comprehensive of all is the postmodern perspective. Whatever else this approach offers, it insists that systemic explanations of social phenomena are futile and wrong-headed. Mike Featherstone, editor of *Global Culture*, writes:

> Postmodernism is both a symptom and a powerful cultural image of the swing away from the conceptualization of global culture less in terms of alleged homogenizing processes (e.g. theories which present cultural imperialism, Americanization, and mass consumer culture as a proto-universal culture riding on the back of Western economic and political domination) and more in terms of the diversity, variety and richness of popular and local discourses, codes and practices which resist and play-back systemicity and order. (Featherstone, 1990, p. 2)

Each of these presently prevailing ideas asserts that:

1. Imperialism no longer exists. (A variant is that U.S. imperialism, in particular, is a spent force.)
2. A new global community is now emerging – global civil society, so to speak – that is independent of the interstate system. It is busily constructing alternative linkages and networks that provide space for new cultural environments.
3. Finally, it is of little consequence if cultural outputs from one source occupy a preponderant share of an audience's attention, because individuals reshape the material to their own tastes and needs. In this schema, the individual receptor takes precedence over the cultural producer.

How do these propositions stand up when examined against the actual context of observable conditions?

Imperialism's Vital Signs are Unimpaired

Is imperialism dead? Is the United States a declining imperialist power? These are two separate though connected questions.

Imperialism, understood as a system of exploitative control of people and resources, is alive and well. At the same time, opposition and resistance to imperialism are far more intense now than at the end of the nineteenth century. The existence of 125 new nations testifies to the fact that many relations of domination have been broken. But powerful means of control still exist. Most of the African, Asian, and Latin American nations continue to experience economic, financial, and even military domination.

Although the term "imperialism" rarely appears in Western media, the word seems to befit the deployment of more than 400,000 U.S. troops in Saudi Arabia. It is also a signal that people's efforts to arrange their affairs without regard for the interests of current controllers (of oil, real estate, or good geographical bases) will be met with overpowering force. Moreover, the Middle East situation reveals another aspect of contemporary imperialist strategy: the ability to mobilize international organizations – now that the Soviet presence has been integrated into the West – for imperialist aims. President Bush explained it this way: "Not since 1945 have we seen the real possibility of using the United Nations as it was designed, as a center for international collective security" (Transcript of President's address to U.N. General Assembly, 1990, p. A-6).

A good part of the world's population lives in desperation, often below the subsistence level. A recent dispatch from Mexico City starkly described the appalling conditions in the capital city of the country directly south of the United States (Guillermoprieto, 1990). Hundreds of millions of people on all continents are similarly affected.

When efforts are made – as they continuously are – to radically change these awful conditions, invariably there is foreign intervention to maintain the arrangements that offer advantage to one or another global governor and their local surrogates, the so-called national elites. In recent years, Central and South America serve as models of this process. Chile, Guatemala, El Salvador, the Dominican Republic, Nicaragua, and Cuba have felt the force of U.S. intervention – economic, military, ideological – when they have tried to create new living conditions. Similar treatment has been meted out across Africa – e.g., Angola, Mozambique, Zaire – and Asia as well – e.g., Vietnam, Afghanistan.

The U.S. military deployment in Saudi Arabia is only the most recent instance of imperialism. This action takes place amidst growing contradictions, however. The relative position of the United States in the world economy seems to be declining, yet it embarks on a costly and potentially disastrous adventure to maintain control of an economically and strategically valuable region and a source of colossal profitability.

One explanation, one most pleasing to officialdom, is that American power is still dominant. It is expressed best by Joseph Nye, a former top-level State Department official and currently a professor of international relations at Harvard University:

> Obviously, we have strengths and weaknesses. . . . But the mistake many analysts were making was to take a single anecdote illustrating American weakness, such as a decline in auto sales or the fact that the Germans concluded a deal with Gorbachev, and extrapolating from that to some very broad general conclusions that we were going down the tubes. We still have a lot more strengths than weaknesses. (Nye, 1990, p. 1)

Interestingly, Nye finds some of these strengths in what he calls "soft power." "Soft power – the ability to co-opt rather than command – rests on intangible resources: culture, ideology, the ability to use international institutions to determine the frame-work of debate" (p. A-33). Soft power, as Nye defines it, is essentially the control of communications and definitional power. This is cultural imperialism with a semantic twist.

Nye may be overly sanguine about the capabilities of "soft power" to do the job, but he is not totally off the mark, especially with respect to "hard power." *Fortune*'s 1990 list of "The Global 500," the 500 biggest industrial corporations in the world reveals that "The U.S. leads all countries, with 167 companies on the list. That's more than Japan, West Germany, and Canada combined. . . . Americans are No. 1 in 14 of the 25 industries on the Global 500." Still, the magazine notes, "Impressive as these figures are, U.S. dominance is slowly giving way. In 1980, 23 U.S. companies made the top 50, compared with only 5 Japanese. Now there are 17 American and 10 Japanese."

But other factors must be considered in evaluating the present strength or weakness of the American global imperial position. One momentous development is the break-up of Communist Eastern Europe and the accelerating restoration of capitalist forms and practices there and in the Soviet Union. Removed thereby is an oppositional pole that served to severely limit, though not fully check, the exercise of American power in the postwar years. One (possibly too extravagant) reading of this situation is that "Washington may enjoy a greater freedom of action in foreign affairs than at any time since the end of World War II" (Toth, 1990, p. A-6).

Certainly, the Saudi Arabian intervention would have been inconceivable a few years ago. In any case, whatever the extent of the expanded range of American power, for the poorer people and countries in the world, the new situation is a disaster (Ramirez, 1990). The unrestrained use of what is called "low intensity warfare," against desperate people, now moves closer to realization as American military power no longer has to be concerned with Soviet counterforce (Klare, 1990). Whether it can disregard the financial cost of such undertakings is another matter.

Domination is further strengthened by the enfeeblement of the Non-Aligned Movement of the nations of Africa, Asia, and Latin America, established in Belgrade in 1961. Its present weakness can be attributed, in large part, to the enormous growth of transnational corporate power in the last twenty years, the collapse of the nonmarket sector of the world, and its own internal class stratification. Today, the ruling strata in the periphery have nowhere to turn except to the reservoirs of corporate capital. And they are doing just that.

Once assertive and insisting on national sovereignty, governments on all continents – Brazil, India, Mexico – headed by their dominant classes are enlisting the support of Western banks and the flow of Western-Japanese capital. One-time stalwarts of independence have demonstrated their new accommodationist outlook by engaging in sweeping denationalizations and privatizations.

Some still believe that these vast regions soon will be the vanguard of a new revolutionary upsurge (Amin, 1990). Perhaps, if the time frame is long enough, this will prove true. But in the meantime, their integration into the world market economy moves ahead. As part of their integration, the people are exposed to the drumbeat of corporate consumerism, no matter how limited the ordinary individual's spending power. The consumerist virus is an inseparable element in the rising global volume of marketing messages. This virus will impair the ability of leaders, still unborn, to act for the national community's social benefit.

A new hope for overcoming the deepening economic and social disparities around the world is seen in what is called the trend to globalization. This development, according to Featherstone (1990), one of its proponents, "emphasizes the autonomy of the globalization process, which should be seen not as the outcome of inter-state processes, but to operate in *relative* independence of conventionally designated societal and social-cultural processes." Contributing to this movement are "the increase in the number of international agencies and institutions, the increasing global forms of communication, the acceptance of unified global time, the development of standard notions of citizenship, rights and conception of humankind" (p. 6). It is emphasized that "the focus on the globe is to suggest that a new level of conceptualization is necessary." This new conceptualization can be comprehended in what it wants to dispose of: the center–periphery model of analysis and the very notion of intense social conflict. "From the vantage point of the late twentieth century it seems that the era of revolution is now finally over" (p. 4).

In short, globalization is defined to exclude domination, cultural control (soft or hard), and social revolution. The growth of the global institutions enumerated above is supposed to make these relationships and processes irrelevant, if not obsolete.

Globalism or Corporate Transnationalism?

It is indisputable that extranational cultural and political relationships have expanded spectacularly in recent decades. But what has been the engine of this growth? Is it a multifaceted outpouring of impulses toward a still-distant but slowly emerging world order? Do the forms and structures, however embryonic, indicate a looming era of universality?

It would be comforting to believe this. It would also be profoundly delusionary. The genuine character of the globalization drive can be appreciated by examining the fate of United Nations structures in the last fifteen years and the apparent reversal of their prospects since the Iraq–Kuwait imbroglio.

Until the fall of 1990, the experiences of the World Health Organization (WHO), the Food and Agriculture Organization (FAO), and, especially, the United Nations Educational, Scientific and Cultural Organization (UNESCO) – the entity established to encourage education, science, and culture on a world scale – tell a uniform story. Each of these organizations, as well as the United Nations itself, has been harshly attacked by the U.S. government and the American media. Each has been financially disabled for pursuing goals unacceptable to powerful American interests, i.e., the media, right-wring anti-abortion and anti-environmental groups, and the military-industrial complex. In mid-1990, the United States owed $750 million to the U.N. overall, exclusive of unpaid dues to WHO and FAO (*The New York Times*, September 13, 1990, p. A-10).

Such massive withholding of funds has crippled major health, agricultural, and educational programs worldwide. UNESCO has been a special target of Washington's anger because it served as a forum – nothing more – to express the complaints of 125 nations against the prevailing international information order. The United States withdrew from UNESCO in 1984 and has remained outside that organization since (Preston, Herman & Schiller, 1989).

Now, however, a new era seems to be opening up. It was inaugurated with U.N. support (thus far) for the U.S.-initiated embargo of Iraq and the American military deployment in Saudi Arabia. A newfound appreciation of the international organization has emerged in Washington and across the American media.

Does this suggest a better-late-than-never response to global organization and international cooperation? More realistically, what the new spirit reveals is the current U.S.–U.S.S.R. accommodation, achieved on the collapse of the Soviet economy and consequent Soviet eagerness to acquiesce in whatever initiatives its former adversary may propose – embargoes, aid termination to Angola and Cuba, unification of Germany and its adherence to NATO.

Equally important in this era of seemingly widespread international agreement is the indebtedness and paralyzing weakness of the Third World and its resultant inability to express any serious opposition to current developments. This species of "internationalism", based on either the weakness or the opportunism of most of the participants, can hardly be viewed as a movement toward global equilibrium and social peace.

The actual sources of what is being called globalization are not to be found in a newly achieved harmony of interests in the international arena. To the contrary, the infrastructure of what is hopefully seen as the first scaffolding of universalism is supplied by the transnational corporate business order, actively engaged on all continents, in all forms of economic and cultural organization, production, and distribution. Many of the actual international structures that monitor these activities are staffed and managed or advised by personnel on leave from the major (mostly American) companies in the system (D. Schiller, 1985).

This worldwide system now enlists American, Japanese, German, Korean, Brazilian, English, and other nationally based but globally engaged corporations. These private giant economic enterprises pursue – sometimes competitively, sometimes cooperatively – historical capitalist objectives of profit making and capital accumulation in continuously changing market and geopolitical conditions.

The actual practices of individual companies vary from one national setting to another, and there is no general coordination of the system at large. (This does not mean that there is an absence of uncoordinated ensemble action. Capital flight, for example, demonstrates how many groups and companies, acting independently when there is a perceived threat to their interests, can cripple the economy from which the capital flows). Still, with different specific interests and objectives, and often rival aims, harmonization of the global business system is out of the question. Yet the *generalized interest* of some thousands of super-companies is not that different. In their quest for both markets and consumers, they adopt fairly similar practices and institutional processes – technological, economic, political, and cultural. They are at one in maintaining the existing global hierarchy of power, though individual positions in that hierarchy constantly change. They utilize the communication and telecommunication systems, locally and globally, to direct their complex and geographically dispersed operations. They have pressed for and obtained privatization of communication facilities in one national locale after another, enabling them to have the greatest possible flexibility of decision making and allowing them a maximum of social unaccountability. They fill the media circuits with their marketing messages. Their combined efforts in the places they exercise the greatest influence have produced the consumer society, of which the United States stands as model.

Although the super-companies are owned for the most part by national groups of investors and are based in specific national settings, national concerns are not necessarily primary in the calculations and decisions of these enterprises. As the chief executive of Fiat, Italy's largest industrial corporation, pointed out: "Reasoning in nationalist terms does not make sense anymore" (Greenhouse, 1990, p. C-11). This seems to be the case for at least some of the transnational corporate companies.

How this works itself out in the world-at-large is still unclear, and not all transnationals behave identically. Still, the question of national sovereignty has become quite murky in the intersection of national interest and the profit-driven activities of these economic colossuses.

Insofar as the visible slippage of the U.S. economy in the global hierarchy of advantage is concerned, American companies' constant search for low-cost sites of production has contributed considerably to this condition. Yet there is one sector in which American dominance remains, if not intact, at least very considerable: the media-cultural arena.

U.S. Media-Cultural Dominance

American films, TV programs, music, news, entertainment, theme parks, and shopping malls set the standard for worldwide export and imitation. How long this dominance can endure alongside a receding economic primacy is uncertain. Already, many U.S. media enterprises have been acquired by Japanese (film and TV), German (publishing and music distribution), British (advertising), and other competing groups. Yet even when this occurs, the new owners, at least for the time being, usually are intent on keeping American creative and managerial media people in executive positions.

American cultural domination remains forceful in a rapidly changing international power scene. It is also undergoing transformation. This occurs by acquisition and, more importantly, by its practices being adopted by the rest of the transnational corporate system. What is emerging, therefore, is a world where alongside the American output of cultural product are the practically identical items marketed by competing national and transnational groups.

For some time, critics of media-imperialism theory have offered, as evidence of the doctrine's fatal flaw, the emergence of new centers of media production. Brazil, in particular, is hailed as a strikingly successful example of this development. Its achievement in television production and export is supposed to demolish the notion of a single center of cultural domination (Rogers & Antola, 1985; Straubhaar, 1989; Tracy, 1988).

In reality, according to the work of Brazilian researcher Omar Souki Oliveira (1990), Brazilian TV now broadcasts a minimum of U.S. programming. The biggest audiences watch and prefer Brazilian shows, which are widely exported abroad. Globo, the main Brazilian private TV network, currently exports shows to 128 countries. "Its productions outnumber those of any other station [sic] in the world." Oliveira writes that one American researcher (Straubhaar, 1989) has concluded that Brazilian television programs have been "Brazilianized almost beyond (American) recognition." Other U.S. researchers (Rogers & Antola, 1985) see Brazil's exports as "reverse media imperialism." A third observer (Tracy, 1988) writes that "in Brazil one sees a television devoted to national culture."

In Oliveira's reading of the same evidence, Brazilian programming is "the creolization of U.S. cultural products. It is the spiced up Third World copy of Western values, norms, patterns of behavior and models of social relations." He states that "the over whelming majority of Brazilian soaps have the same purpose as their U.S. counterparts, i.e., to sell products" – and, it should be emphasized, to sell goods made by the same transnational corporations who advertise in Brazil as well as in the United States. The "local" sponsors are Coca-Cola, Volkswagen, General Motors, Levi's, etc.

"In most Brazilian soaps," Oliveira finds, "the American lifestyle portrayed by Hollywood production reappears with a "brazilianized face." Now we don't see wealthy Anglos any more, but rich white Brazilians enjoying standards of living that would make any middle class American envious." Oliveira concludes: "Glamorous as they [TV series] are – even outshining Hollywood – their role within Brazilian society isn't different from that of U.S. imports. Unfortunately, the refinements applied to the genre were not to enhance diversity, but domination."

Domination is precisely what cultural imperialism is all about. With that domination comes the definitional power, Nye's "soft power," that sets the boundaries for national discourse.

Meanwhile, despite the developments already noted, the global preeminence of American cultural product is being not only maintained but extended to new locales. U.S. media incursions into Eastern Europe and the Soviet Union are assuming the dimension of a full-scale takeover, albeit shared with German and British media conglomerates.

American-owned and -styled theme parks, with their comprehensive ideological assumptions literally built into the landscape and architecture, are being staked out across Europe and Japan. "Euro-Disneyland will open its first park at Marne la Vallee in 1992, with a second possible in 1996. Anheuser-Busch [the second-largest theme park owner after Disney] has launched a theme park development in Spain, and other U.S. corporations are exploring projects elsewhere in Europe" (Sloan, 1990, p. D-3).

It must be emphasized that the corporate takeover of (popular) culture for marketing and ideological control is not a patented American practice, limited exclusively to U.S. companies. It is, however, carried to its fullest development in the United States. Cultural-recreational activity is now the very active site for spreading the transnational corporate message, especially in professional sports, where American practice again provides the basic model.

In the United States, practically no sports activity remains outside the interest and sponsorship of the big national advertisers. The irresistible lure of big sponsorship money has become the lubricant for a sport's national development. Accordingly, sports events and games have become multi-billion-dollar businesses, underwritten by the major corporations who stake out huge TV audiences. The hunt for sports events that can be made available to advertisers now includes university and, in increasing instances, high-school games. Assuming the mantle of moral concern, *The New York Times* editorialized: "College athletic departments have abandoned any pretense of representing cap and gown and now they roam the country in naked pursuit of hundreds of millions of television dollars" (Bright lights, big college money, 1990, p. A-22).

Unsurprisingly, the practice has become internationalized. A report from Italy describes the frenzied pursuit, by the largest Italian corporations, to own soccer and basketball franchises. "A growing trend in Italy . . . [is] the wholesale takeover of a sport by the captains of industry in search of new terrain from which to promote a corporate product or image" (Agnew, 1990, p. 14). The new patrons of Italian sports include the agro-chemicals giant Montedison, which also owns the widely read Rome daily *Il Mesaggero*; the Agnelli family, owners of the giant Fiat company, who also own the successful Juventus soccer club; and Silvio Berlusconi, the Italian TV and film mogul, who owns the AC Milan soccer club and other teams.

Recent developments in East Germany illustrate the extent to which sports have become a venue of corporate image promotion and an aggressive marketing instrument. *Business Week* ("Look Out" Wimbleton [sic], 1990) reports that

> the women's Grand Prix tennis tournament scheduled for the final week of September [1990] is moving from Mahwah, New Jersey to Leipzig, East Germany. . . . the tournament [is] the first successful effort to lure big corporate sponsors into a major tourney behind the old Iron Curtain. . . . a number of heavyweight sponsors . . . include Volkswagen, Isostar, Sudmilch, Kraft-General Foods and American Airlines.

Major sports are now transmitted by satellite to global audiences. The commercial messages accompanying the broadcast, ringing the stadia, and often worn on the uniforms of the athletes constitute a concerted assault of corporate marketing values on global consciousness.

The Total Cultural Package and the "Active Audience"

The envelopment of professional and amateur sports for transnational corporate marketing objectives and ideological pacification is a good point at which to return to another one of the arguments contradicting the cultural imperialist concept. This is the belief in the existence of an "active audience," a view supported by a good number of Anglo-U.S. communications researchers.

According to this view, the audience is supposed to make its own meaning of the messages and images that the media disseminate, thereby playing a relatively autonomous role that is often interpreted as resistance to these messages and meanings (see Budd, Entman, & Steinman, 1990; H. Schiller, 1989). Active-audience theorizing has been largely preoccupied with the analysis of individual cultural products – a program or a TV series, a movie, or a genre of fiction. The theory follows closely in the tradition of "effects" research, though not necessarily coming to the same conclusions.

Leaving specific studies aside, it can be argued that one overarching condition invalidates, or at least severely circumscribes, the very idea of an active audience, to say nothing of one resisting a flow of messages. This is the current state – impossible to miss – of Western cultural enterprise. How can one propose to extract *one* TV show, film, book, or even a group, from the now nearly seamless media-cultural environment, and examine it (them) for specific effects? This is not say there are no *generalized* effects – but these are not what the reception theorists seem to be concerned with.

Cultural/media production today has long left the cottage industry stage. Huge conglomerates like Time-Warner, with nearly $20 billion in assets, sit astride publishing, TV production, film making, and music recording, as well as book publishing and public classroom education. Theme park construction and ownership, shopping malls, and urban architectural design also are the domain of the same or related interests.

In this totalizing cultural space, who is able to specify the individual source of an idea, value, perspective, or reaction? A person's response, for example, to the TV series *Dallas* may be the outcome of half-forgotten images from a dozen peripheral encounters in the cultural supermarket. Who is to say what are the specific sites from which individual behavior and emotions now derive?

In 1990, even actual war locales become the setting for the marketing message. *Business Week* ("Publicity?" 1990) announces: "Welcome to the New World Order, Marketing Dept. Where companies are using history-making events as occasions to promote their products." The magazine explains: "With U.S. troops digging in their heels in Saudi Arabia, companies all around the country are vying to supply them with everything from nonalcoholic beer to video cassettes. . . . if a soldier is going to be photographed sipping a cold drink or playing poker, most marketers agree that he or she might as well be using their product." In this new world of pervasive corporate message making, the dispatch of over 450,000 troops provides an opportunity to cultivate this or that taste for consumption, along with a powerful patriotic backdrop for the company and the product. How does the audience engage this spectacle of democracy and consumption?

There is much to be said for the idea that people don't mindlessly absorb everything that passes before their eyes. Yet much of the current work on audience reception comes uncomfortably close to being apologetics for present-day structures of cultural control.

Meaningful Resistance to the Cultural Industries

There is good reason to be skeptical about the resistance of an audience, active or not, to its menu of media offerings. Yet this does not mean that the cultural conglomerates and the social system they embody are without an opposition. It is a resistance, however, that differs enormously from the kind of opposition that is supposed to occur in reinterpreting the message of a TV sitcom.

Some may believe in the end of history and others may insist that the era of revolution is finally over and that social (class) conflict is obsolete. The daily newspaper headlines tell a different story (though of course they don't explain it). What *is* apparent is that aroused people, if not their leaderships, all around the world are protesting their existing living conditions.

In the United States itself, still the most influential single unit of the world market economy, numerous oppositional elements force at least minimal acknowledgment, and some limited accommodation, from the governing crowd. For example, the congressional fight over the national budget in the fall of 1990 was essentially a class conflict, however obscured this was in its media coverage. To be sure, the class most directly affected – the working people – was largely absent from the deliberations. But the main question at issue was which class would be compelled to shoulder the burden of America's deepening crisis. This debate, and others underway, reveal the fragile condition of the dominating power in the country.

Between 1980 and 1990, the wealthiest 1 percent saw their incomes rise by 75 percent, while the income of the bottom 20 percent actually declined. The richest 2.5 million Americans' combined income nearly equaled that of the 100 million Americans at the bottom of the pyramid (Meisler, 1990).

It is the still growing disparities between the advantaged and the disadvantaged countries, as well as the widening gap *inside* the advantaged and disadvantaged societies, that constitute the fault line of the still seemingly secure world market economy. To this may be added the ecological disaster in the making, which is the inevitable accompaniment of the market forces that are roaring triumphantly across the continents.

A routine headline in the Western media reads: "Indonesia: The Hottest Spot in Asia." Elaborating, *Business Week* ("Indonesia: The Hottest Spot," 1990) rhapsodizes: "With a 7 percent growth rate, a population of 182 million – the world's fifth largest – and a wealth of natural resources, Indonesia is poised to be the region's new success story." As the twentieth century winds down, success presumably is achieved by adopting the long-standing Western industrialization model, profligate with resource use and wastage, and exploiting the work force to satisfy foreign capital's search for the maximum return.

Indonesia, with an average wage of $1.25 *a day*, is an irresistible site. The chairman of the American Chamber of Commerce in Indonesia explains: "Indonesia will have a cheap labor supply well into the 21st century. . . . Nobody else in Asia except China can offer that." Not unexpectedly, "The income gap between affluent business people and the millions of impoverished who eke out a living in the villages and Jakarta's teeming slums is widening" (p. 45).

The Indonesian "success story," and others like it, are hardly confirmation for the end-of-social-conflict perspective. Much more convincing is the expectation that the next century will be the truly revolutionary era, accomplishing what the twentieth began but could not finish. In any case, communication theory, tied to the assumptions of political or cultural pluralism, harmonization of interests between the privileged and the deprived, resistance to domination residing in individualized interpretation of TV or film shows, or, overall, the long-term viability of capitalist institutions, is and will be unable to explain the looming social turbulence.

Certainly, there are no grounds for complacency about the prospects of the First and Third Worlds (the latter now including the once-Second World states) in the years ahead. Yet Western communication researchers seem intent on holding on to these assumptions. James Curran, surveying the English and continental research scene over the last fifteen years, concludes that

> a major change has taken place. The most important and significant overall shift has been the steady advance of pluralist themes within the radical tradition, in particular, the repudiation of the totalizing, explanatory framework of Marxism, the reconceptualization of the audience as creative and active and the shift from the political to a popular aesthetic. . . . A sea change has occurred in the field, and this will reshape – for better or worse – the development of media and cultural studies in Europe. (1990, pp. 157–8)

The same tendencies are well advanced, if not dominant, in the United States, though they have not totally swept the field as they seem to have done in England. There is still more than a little life left in those who look at the material side of the economy in general and the cultural industries in particular. Expressing this perspective is David Harvey, in his comprehensive approach to *The Condition of Postmodernity* (1989). Reviewing the same years that Curran surveyed, from the 1970s on, and relying on many of the same basic sources (though not as focused on the field of communication research), Harvey also finds that "there has been a sea-change in cultural as well as in political-economic practices since around 1972" (p. vii). He concludes that these changes, and the rise of postmodernist cultural forms, "when set against the basic rules of capitalist accumulation, appear more as shifts in surface appearance rather than as signs of the emergence of some entirely new post-capitalist or even post-industrial society" (p. vii).

Yet these "shifts in surface appearance" have contributed greatly to the capability of the corporate business system to maintain, and expand, its global reach. For this reason, the acknowledgement of and the struggle against cultural imperialism are more necessary than ever if the general system of domination is to be overcome.

References

Agnew, P. (1990, September 4). "Italy's sport madness has a very business like basis." *International Herald Tribune*, p. 14.

Amin, S. (1990). "The future of socialism." *Monthly Review, 42*(3), 10–29.

Ang, I. (1985). *Watching "Dallas": Soap Opera and the Melodramatic Imagination.* London: Methuen.

"Bright lights, big college money." (1990, September 13). *The New York Times*, p. A-22.

Budd, M., Entman, R. M., & Steinman, C. (1990). "The affirmative character of U.S. cultural studies." *Critical Studies in Mass Communication, 7,* 169–84.

Curran, J. (1990). "The new revisionism in mass communication research." *European Journal of Communication, 5,* 135–64.

Engelhardt, T. (1990). "Bottom line dreams and the end of culture." *The Progressive, 54*(10), 30–5.

Featherstone, M. (ed.). (1990). *Global Culture.* London: Sage.

"The global 500, the world's biggest industrial corporations." (1990, July 30). *Fortune,* p. 265.

Greenhouse, S. (1990, October 5). "Alliance is formed by Fiat and French company." *The New York Times.* p. C-11.

Guillermoprieto, A. (1990, September 17). "Letter from Mexico City." *The New Yorker,* 93–104.

Harvey, D. (1989). *The Condition of Postmodernity.* Oxford: Basil Blackwell.

"Indonesia:" The hottest spot in Asia. (1990, August 27). *Business Week,* pp. 44–5.

Klare, M. T. (1990). "Policing the gulf – and the world." *The Nation, 251*(12), 1, 416, 418, 420.

Liebes, T., & Katz, E. (1990). *The Export of Meaning: Cross-cultural Readings of "Dallas."* New York: Oxford University Press.

"Look out Wimbleton [sic], here comes Leipzig." (1990, September 24). *Business Week,* p. 54.

Meisler, S. (1990, July 24). "Rich-poor gap held widest in 40 years." *Los Angeles Times*, p. A-11.

Nordenstreng, K., & Varis, T. (1974). "Television traffic – A one-way street." *Reports and Papers on Mass Communication*, No. 70. Paris: UNESCO.

Nye, J. S., Jr. (1990, October 3). "No, the U.S. isn't in decline." *The New York Times*, p. A-33.

Oliveira, O. S. (1990, October 8–10). *Brazilian Soaps Outshine Hollywood: Is cultural Imperialism Fading Out?* Paper presented at the meetings of the Deutsche Gesellschaft für Semiotik, Internationaler Kongress, Universität Passau.

Preston, W., Jr., Herman, E., & Schiller, H. (1989). *Hope & Folly. The United States and Unesco, 1945–1985.* Minneapolis: University of Minnesota Press.

"Publicity? Why it never even occurred to us." (1990, September 24). *Business Week*, p. 46.

Ramirez, A. (1990, September 14). "2 American makers agree to sell Soviets 34 billion cigarettes." *The New York Times*, p. A-14.

Rogers, E., & Antola, L. (1985). "*Telenovelas*: A Latin American success story." *Journal of Communication*, *35*(4), 24–35.

Schiller, D. (1985). "The emerging global grid: Planning for what?" *Media, Culture and Society*, 7, 105–25.

Schiller, H. I. (1989). *Culture, Inc.: The Corporate Takeover of Public Expression.* New York: Oxford University Press.

Sloan, A. K. (1990, August 22). "Europe is ripe for theme parks." *Los Angeles Times*, p. D-3.

Straubhaar, J. (1989, May 25–9). *Change in Assymetrical Interdependence in Culture: The Brazilianization of Television in Brazil.* Paper presented at the International Communication Association, San Francisco.

Toth, R. C. (1990, September 12). "With Moscow crippled, U.S. emerges as top power." *Los Angeles Times*, p. D-3.

Tracy, M. (1988, March). "Popular culture and the economics of global television." *Intermedia*, 19–25.

Transcript of President's address to U.N. General Assembly. (1990, October 2). *The New York Times*, p. A-6.

19

Gendering the Commodity Audience: Critical Media Research, Feminism, and Political Economy

Eileen R. Meehan

Throughout the 1970s and 1980s, media scholars sorted the field into the categories of "mainstream" versus "critical" research. These adjectives instantly communicated where one stood in terms of the root assumptions and valuations undergirding one's work – as well as which side you rooted for at the staged debates where administrative researchers like Elihu Katz or Wilbur Schramm debated some representative of the opposition – perhaps James Carey, or Herbert Schiller, or Stuart Hall (Meehan 1999; see Poole and Schiller 1981). At the time, the administrative paradigm so dominated the field that its practitioners often assumed it was the only way to do research, rejecting other approaches as subjective, unsystematic, and impractical – as "armchair theorizing" little better than wishful thinking. Thus George Gerbner underplayed the intellectual hostility associated with the paradigmatic debates when he titled his special 1983 issue of the *Journal of Communication* "Ferment in the Field." Glancing back, I am struck by the "mainstream" paradigm's ability to unify its opposition – to place Carey, Schiller, and Hall on the same side. But I am also struck by the absence of feminist work in that benchmark publication, despite the *Journal*'s openness to feminist work under Gerbner's editorship (e.g., Busby 1975; Cantor 1977, 1979; Lemon 1977; Poe 1976; Streicher 1974) as well as the tremendous outpouring of feminist research across media studies in the 1970s generally (e.g., Arnold 1976; Brabant 1976; Holly 1979; Janus 1978; Marzoff, Rush, and Stern 1974–5; Morris 1973; Ogan and Weaver 1978–9; St. John 1978; Tuchman et al. 1978).

One decade later, in two issues of the same journal, Michael Gurevitch and Mark Levy published essays addressing "the future of the field," which were republished under the title *Defining Media Studies: Reflections on the Future of the Field* (1994). The book organized its forty-eight contributions into seven categories (disciplinarity, new directions, influencing public policy, audiences and institutions, critical research, history of the field, and academic curriculum and legitimacy). Administrative research dominated the volume and critical scholarship was sprinkled across four of the categories. In the critical category, two essays focused on political economy (Meehan, Mosco, and Wasko 1994; Schiller 1994); the other two on cultural studies (Grossberg 1994; McChesney 1994). Overall, only one essay offered a feminist perspective. H. Leslie Steeves's "Creating Imagined Communities: Development Communication and the Challenge of Feminism" (1994) in the public policy category. Yet, in describing the collection, Gurevitch and Levy state:

> The paradigmatic debate (or "dialogue") that dominated communication scholarship in the '70s and early '80s has been replaced by new and different intellectual nudgings, by the injection into communication scholarship of *recently emergent perspectives such as feminism,* post-modernism, and neofunctionalism. (1994, 7, emphasis mine)

As a political economist, trained during the period leading up to "Ferment," and as a coauthor of an essay in *Defining,* I find this all rather disturbing, yet oddly unsurprising.

That contradictory reaction motivates this essay. As a political economist, I have focused my research mainly on the internal structures of media-based corporations – which shape the form and content of cultural commodities (e.g., Meehan 1991) – and the external relationships between such corporations – which also shape cultural commodities and which construct media markets (e.g., Meehan 1990). Working at this level of abstraction generally has meant treating large-scale, impersonal institutions as agents with little reference to the actions, struggles, or alliances of human beings. Much of the feminist scholarship in communications takes a less abstracted point of entry: women working in the industries (Martin 1991); women's use of mediated artifacts (Radway 1984; Steeves et al. 1988); the fictional men and women offered as role models by the media (Byars 1991; Byars and Dell 1992); or some combination of these concerns (Andersen 1995; Stabile 1995).

Connections between feminist lines of research and institutional lines of research may not be readily apparent. The conditions of people's work and leisure, and the artifacts that they employ in each sphere, may seem fairly remote from the impact of transindustrial conglomeration on blockbuster films or the structure of markets in the broadcasting industry. Yet political economists and feminist scholars understand that patriarchy and capitalism have been historically intertwined in the United States from the nation's founding. This suggests that important connections between patriarchy and capitalism can be discovered by scholars who synthesize feminist and political-economic approaches to media research. It also suggests that our research heritages can be taken as one starting point from which to articulate that synthesis.

To test this, I return to a defining moment in political economy – the Blindspot Debate over the commodity audience, which raged in print in the *Canadian Journal of Political and Social Theory* (Smythe 1977, 1978; Murdock 1978; Livant 1979) and in person (Smythe, Murdock, Garnham) at the 1978 conference of the International Association for Mass Communication Research in Poland. After summarizing the Blindspot Debate, I then return to my own analysis of the commodity audience in national television. I review that work to tease out the dynamics of patriarchy and capitalism that undergird the markets for commodity ratings and commodity audiences. This particular intersection of feminism and political economy suggests that much can be gained by such revisionist exercises, which, in concert with new syntheses and new approaches to research, may generate an intellectual rapprochement between feminism and political economy in media studies.

What Do the Media Make?

This seemingly innocent question drove the Blindspot Debate. Having posed the question, Smythe (1977) suggested that most critical researchers of the period would respond thus: the media were consciousness industries that made texts (films, television shows, etc.) embodying the dominant ideology, which was absorbed by the average audience member as naturalized, common sense. Hence, media were best studied by decoding texts to uncover the ideology that produced consciousness. Smythe dismissed this as a blindspot of Western Marxism, caused by academic Marxists' overriding concern with ideology and their rejection of both political economy and political action. Smythe next posed his own, then-startling, answer: the media manufactured only one commodity – audiences. By this, Smythe meant that all media assembled, packaged, and sold audiences to advertisers. Content was secondary – a free lunch at best. Media industries were neither dream factories nor consciousness industries: they were hunter-gatherers of the audience.

These bold claims generated considerable debate, with Murdock (1978) taking the lead. Murdock offered a series of differentiations to scale back Smythe's claims. For Murdock, media earning revenues from advertisers were clearly different from media earning revenues directly from audience members. This separated movie studios, book publishers, and recording labels from television networks, newspapers, and magazines. Only advertiser-supported media produced commodity audiences but, for Murdock, even those media could not be reduced to transactions between corporations. He argued that any media artifact operated at two levels: economic and cultural. While the economic level was of greatest interest to media companies, it was less relevant to audiences being processed for sale. The images, ideas, visions, narratives, characters, and performances embodied in the media artifact, and the people comprising the audiences for such artifacts, also needed study. Murdock called for research recognizing the economic and cultural dimensions of commercial media.

Smythe responded by critiquing Murdock and reasserting his central claims. Over the years, other scholars engaged these issues, shifting the focus and testing the claims of the original debate (D'Acci 1994; Jhally 1982; Livant 1982; McCormack

1983; Meehan 1984; Wasko et al. 1993). The phrases "audience commodity" and "commodity audience" entered the critical lexicon. That such a commodity existed and played a crucial role in advertiser-supported media generally became axiomatic in political-economic research on media. Further, as advertising ("product placement") increasingly shaped content in movies and books, the demarcation between advertiser-supported and audience-supported media artifacts thinned. However, for scholars working on reception or representation, the significance of the audience commodity in their decoding of texts or reconstruction of readers' reactions was little appreciated, as pointed out by such critical cultural scholars as Stabile (1995) or Budd, Entman, and Steinem (1990).

Case Study: Broadcasting and Ratings

As Smythe's notion of the audience commodity became established, it also became a focus for research. In my case, that meant exploring the audience commodity in the U.S. system of national broadcasting. My research focused on the corporations that oligopolized network broadcasting (RCA's NBC and CBS in radio; RCA's NBC, CBS, and ABC in television) and in the market where those networks sold and advertisers bought the audience commodity. These transactions were highly routinized. The employees who made the deals relied entirely on the ratings book, which specified the number of people in the audience and described them in rough demographic categories. These employees were not executives; they were relatively low-paid and generally female. Yet their labor put together the basic transactions from which networks earned revenues.

These crucial transactions were routinized through dependence on the ratings. This suggested a structural dependence between the market for the audience commodity and the market for ratings. From 1929 to the present, advertisers and networks had typically purchased ratings from a single provider. The buyers' apparent willingness to allow a monopoly suggested that the dynamics in this market deserved closer inspection. Rather than rehearse my research into the history of the ratings industry and the rating market's structuration, I will focus on the results of that research. Four elements that emerged from it are relevant for this discussion.

The first element was shared demand: advertisers and networks demanded measurements of bona fide consumers. Bona fide consumers had the disposable income, access, and desire to loyally purchase brand names and to habitually make impulse purchases. This consumerist caste expanded and contracted in response to capitalism's boom-and-bust cycle. To accommodate the shared demand for consumers, the ratings monopolist selected methods that discriminated against mere listeners or viewers. For example, during the Great Depression, the C. E. Hooper Company used telephone interviews to measure the commodity audience; in the 1975–80 recession, the A. C. Nielsen Company (ACN) based its sample on cable households. In both cases, the measurement method ensured that the sampled households had the funds, desire, and location that allowed them to subscribe to nonessential services. This clearly differentiated the methods and reports of such ratings "research" from social-scientific studies of audience behavior. In ratings, unified demand for the con-sumerist caste shaped measurement practices.

The second element was the connection between demand and price, which revealed a discontinuity between advertisers' and networks' interests in the size of the commodity audience. The larger the number of bona fide consumers viewing, the higher the price charged by networks. Conversely, the smaller the number, the lower the price. This discontinuity allowed the ratings monopolist to play networks against advertisers, and corporations to form alliances across industries. During the early 1960s, NBC tried to restructure the market by persuading advertisers to shift demand from "how many viewers overall" to "how many viewers between 18 and 34." ABC joined in the campaign and the two networks persuaded advertisers that 18- to 34-year-olds were better consumers. By 1963, ACN was shifting its sample to emphasize the new demographic; the networks followed by replacing "old favorites" like *The Beverly Hillbillies* and *Petticoat Junction* with "youth-oriented" and "socially relevant" programs like *Mod Squad* and *Storefront Lawyers*. Similarly, in the early 1970s, cable channels used this discontinuity to insert themselves into the rela-tionships among advertisers and networks, and to persuade ACN to measure cable audiences. Discontinuity in demand, then, was used by "players" to renegotiate relationships and restructure the market, thereby changing how the commodity audience was defined and measured.

The third element to emerge was the cybernetic nature of the commodity audi-ence (Mosco, 1996). The commodity audience was knowable only through the ratings that measured it and those ratings were the outcome of corporate rivalries, alliances, and manipulations.

This led to the fourth and last element: television's commodity audience had nothing to do with the people who watched television.[1]

These four claims emerged from my institutional analysis of the long-term, impersonal relationships between corporations constituting the markets for com-modity ratings and commodity audiences. Building on these claims, I then organized "television" into three markets. The market for commodity ratings served as the fundamental market that set the parameters within which the market for the com-modity audience and the market for programming worked.

Three of the Markets Constituting Broadcast Television

The ratings monopolist balanced continuities and discontinuities in demand through its selection of measurement practices. The monopolist responded to continuities in demand by targeting the bona fide consumers demanded by advertisers and broad-casters; unless demanded, the rest of the viewership was unimportant. Discontinuities meant that either the ratings monopolist or blocs of buyers could attempt restruc-turation of the marker for commodity ratings; the monopolist's methods and its definition of the commodity audience responded to shifts in market structuration and participants' power.[2] Given its monopoly position and the pricing conflict that separated advertisers and networks, the ratings monopolist exercised some agency in selecting its methods, thereby controlling costs of production. All of these economic concerns shaped the ratings reports and ensured that they were commodities – not research.

Based on the ratings commodity, advertisers and networks set to work low-paid, female employees relying on ratings to conduct the transactions in which networks sell their portions of the commodity audience to advertisers. This market and the routinization of its transactions depended entirely on the power relations embodied in the market for commodity ratings. Ratings became the proverbial floor upon which this market rested. And, although ratings were widely dismissed as misleading or inadequate in the trade press, they were treated as absolute truths in this market.

Upon that market was erected yet another structure: the market for programs in which networks, their internal production units, and independent producers negotiated over programs. Decisions here relied on track record, that is, on previous success in the ratings. A proven track record meant either that the production unit's previous series had earned high ratings or that elements of the proposed show had been featured in last year's top-rated programs. Elements included the proposed stars, type of cast, typical plot, genre, and "twist" in the genre's formula.[3] Networks assumed that past success was a predictor of future success – always defining success in terms of the ratings. The ratings, then, shaped decisions about contracts for new series and employment, about casting and plots, about routine and innovative representations.

With track record as the main prognosticator of success, no network would accept – and no producer would propose – a series without a track record.[4] But even the best prognostications go wrong. Historically, most new series are canceled due to poor ratings. Indeed, a tenth of a rating point can mean the difference between retention and cancellation. Thus, commodity ratings set the limits of broadcast programming in the present and the future.

Engendering Markets

For broadcasting, then, Smythe was both correct and incorrect. His analysis revealed that the main product manufactured by networks and sold to advertisers was the commodity audience. But his belief that the ratings monopolist exercised no agency misled him. The political economy of ratings, as summarized above, demonstrated the key role played by the market for commodity ratings and traced the structural forces that constructed ratings as truly *manufactured* commodities whose content depended on changing power relations within that market.

Returning to the main concern of this essay, I now ask: what does a feminist perspective illuminate about these ungendered markets and the ungendered corporations operating within them? My answer is twofold: taking a feminist perspective reveals that societal divisions of labor based on gender, plus prejudicial assumptions about gender, played a significant role in defining and differentiating the commodity audience. To see this, let us return to industrial concerns about the demographics of the commodity audience.

Although age grade became a central concern in the 1960s, the demographic category of gender was an industrial concern for the rating monopolist, advertisers, and broadcasters from at least 1929. Indeed, the female commodity audience had a special place in network schedules: in the daytime, doing housework, listening to talk shows and episodic serials. Both forms of programming were geared toward advertising, whether indirectly using product placements in the script or directly as commercial interruptions. Episodic serials were called soap operas as much for their content as their ownership: soap manufacturers produced the shows and contracted for broadcast time on NBC or CBS to run them. The ratings monopolist[5] treated female audiences as the normal, naturally occurring listenership for daytime programming. During the Great Depression, there was no interest in households without telephones, women who worked outside the home, or men who did not. This carried over into the 1960s and was reflected in Nielsen reports on daytime viewership by women, which carried such titles as *Where the Girls Are*.

Opposite daytime and its female commodity audience was "prime time" and its highly prized male commodity audience. However, prime time was not "where the boys were" but rather where *the* audience was. Networks that couldn't draw *the* audience counterprogrammed for niche audiences, meaning women, or women and children, or African Americans, or Hispanic Americans, or some combination thereof.[6] This subtle shift in language gendered the commodity audience as male and assumed its descent line to be European. Thus the commodity audience was differentiated into the valuable and desired audience of white men produced by the network that won the ratings contest versus the niche audiences begrudgingly produced by networks that lost the ratings contest. As *the* audience, the white male commodity audience had a "higher quality" for which advertisers willingly paid.

The industrial definition of "higher quality" shifted when NBC and ABC succeeded in joining age to gender as the crucial markers of *the* audience. That commodity audience narrowed to the white men aged 18 to 34 within the ACN sample. As cable channels squirmed their way into the mix, cable subscription was added to the industrial definition of *the* audience, yet again narrowing the commodity audience, this time to white male cable subscribers 18 to 34.

With two further modifications in this industrial definition, ACN adjusted its ratings to take into account social status and women's employment outside the home. The long recessionary cycle that spanned 1975–89 coincided with second-wave feminism. Through the same period, the Reagan and Bush administrations' monetarist policies effectively transferred wealth from the general population to the elite, promoted the exportation of heavy industrial operations, discouraged wage increases for workers of middle or lower social status, and encouraged companies to replace employees with temporary contractees (Bluestone and Harrison 1982). Among other things, these synergistic policies brought more women generally, and more college-educated women specifically, into the documented workforce. In such two-income households may be seen one effect of second-wave feminism: these women generally retained some control over their earnings.

In any case, ACN expanded its demographic categories to include "working women" as well as the terms "upscale" and "downscale" to identify the social status attached to occupation and income. For advertisers, upscale white male cable sub-scribers aged 18 to 34 watching television during prime time became the most valued and demanded commodity audience. Daytime remained women's time, although upscale women 18 to 34 and upscale working women 18 to 34 using video-cassette recorders to tape programs were more highly valued than mere house-wives. Among the new niche audiences for prime time, the category of upscale white working women aged 18 to 34 and subscribing to cable had sufficient attraction for advertisers that networks designed programs blending elements of soap operas into action–adventure programs.[7]

This periodic narrowing of *the* audience demonstrates the difference between the commodity audience and the people who actually watch television. It also suggests that noneconomic assumptions undergird beliefs about what sorts of people *ought* to be *the* audience and that those assumptions follow familiar patterns of discrimination on the grounds of gender, race, social status, sexual orientation, and age. Given limitations of space, I will discuss only the assumptions about gender.

Such institutionalized sexism might be dismissed as pragmatic given certain assumptions about gender and money: most of the workforce was male; men earned more than women; thus more men had more to spend than women regardless of women's occupations. Advertisers wanted spenders, so networks and cable channels had to target men to meet advertisers' demand for spenders.

According to these assumptions, the three markets operated rationally by discrim-inating against women. The market for commodity ratings necessarily placed greater value on measurements of males than on measurements of females. The market for the commodity audience rationally preferred buying the male commodity audience in prime time and treated the female commodity audience as a special niche with limited and time-specific appeal. When some of that latter commodity audience gained and controlled income, they become a very special niche – one that could be attracted through the manipulation of subtexts in male-oriented programming. That left the market for prime-time programming gearing production for the male com-modity audience, but with female-friendly elements to attract the subniche of upscale women. Television was largely in the business of men – counting them, characteriz-ing them, selling them, and programming for them. As long as "society" defined men as the proverbial breadwinners, that social reality governed the decisions of advertisers, networks, and the ratings monopolist.

Of course, that argument could be countered on its own stereotypical grounds: a sexist society may have defined men as breadwinners, but it also defined women as spenders. In the patriarchal division of domestic labor, woman's work included shopping for the household's general needs, for her own needs, and for the man's needs. The idealized version of that division of labor sent men outside the home to work for wages and women to spend those wages by shopping. Through their shopping, women assembled the materials necessary for men to rest and recuperate. If advertisers wanted to reach spenders, then they needed to target that category of people socially designated as spenders: women. Could advertisers have been blinded by sexism?

That question, posed ironically, has played out concretely in the history of two cable channels: ESPN and Lifetime. ESPN was launched in 1979 as a twenty-four-hour sports channel. It quickly gained acceptance from advertisers and cable operators. Now 80 percent owned by the Walt Disney Company, ESPN has added three more sports channels (ESPN-2, ESPN Classic, and ESPN News) and a chain of restaurant/entertainment complexes called ESPNZone. While ESPN attracts mostly male viewers, it has not been categorized as a narrowcaster – that is, a channel serving a niche audience with highly defined and delimited tastes (Disney 1998).

In contrast, since its launch in 1984, Lifetime has consistently been treated as a narrowcaster reaching a small niche audience – women. As part of ABC's and Hearst's joint ventures in cable (A&E, Lifetime), the channel enjoyed success in terms of inclusion on cable systems but struggled to attract advertisers (Byars and Meehan 1994). Eventually, Lifetime reorganized its prime time schedule in an attempt to attract upscale heterosexual couples.[8] That seemed to turn the trick for Lifetime, which now carries extensive advertising for everything from aspirin to cars.

With Disney's acquisition of ABC, Lifetime seemed poised to launch a second channel targeting women in their teens and twenties, but nothing came of it.[9] Although Disney's 1998 annual report extolled the transformation of ESPN from cable channel into franchise, no similar plans seem to be on the horizon for Lifetime (Disney 1998). While audience gender is not the only variable differentiating the corporate histories of these two channels, this sketch suggests that being a "channel for men who love sports" places a company in a position significantly different from being "television for women."

Feminism and Political Economy

When reanalyzed from a feminist perspective, my case study of broadcast ratings yielded an unexpected finding: a structural contradiction between patriarchy and capitalism embodied in a fundamental market in the television industry, and effecting the structure of two derivative markets. The structure of the market for commodity ratings assumed that men controlled both wages and spending, making them *the* audience. But the market structure ignored similarly patriarchal assumptions about the domestic division of labor that assigned the household's shopping to women. While men as breadwinners and women as shoppers fits into the patriarchal division of labor that was idealized in the 1950s, the fact remains that women have always worked in this country. Not only have women been allotted a considerable share of the caretaking and household purchasing, but women have sought and secured paid work.

Paralleling the social status of men's blue-collar occupations have been women's pink-collar jobs: grocery clerk, secretary, domestic worker, telephone operator, nurse, farm worker, court reporter, teacher, etc. These occupations typically offered lower wages than those paid for blue-collar jobs, regardless of the levels of skill – suggesting that the patriarchal devaluation of women was echoed in capitalism's wage structure. For the market in commodity audiences, that would make male earners a better buy, but only if they adhered to a nonpatriarchal division of domestic labor. With a patriarchal division, an audience of female shoppers was the better buy. Because this contradiction was not articulated in the demand for commodity ratings, the ratings monopolist had no reason to investigate or to resolve it.

One might expect that contradiction to emerge and be resolved in the 1980s as political-economic changes forced more women into the workplace and into white-collar occupations. As women achieved greater – though not perfect – economic equality, they would seem likely candidates for inclusion in *the* audience. Yet, despite the ratings monopolist's adoption of categories to sort viewers by occupational status, women remained marginalized as niches. Males remained the object of the rating firm's art, with upscale males the most prized trophies.

This makes little economic sense. In capitalism, money is supposed to be the great leveler. Arbitrary social distinctions that unfairly oppress individuals are supposed to evaporate when people enter the market for goods and services as consumers, or when they offer themselves as labor. The logic of profit should drive advertisers to demand shoppers regardless of the gender, social status, race, age, ethnicity, sexual orientation, etc., of the particular people buying the bars of soap, rolls of toilet paper, or cans of beans. Why, then, do such distinctions persist in the markets for commodity ratings and commodity audiences – in markets where companies essentially trade in people?

A feminist political economy allows us to answer that question in terms of both gender and social status. The overvaluing of a male audience reflects the sexism of patriarchy as surely as the overvaluing of an upscale audience reflects the classism of capitalism. Each practice is rooted in the illogic of prejudice, that is, in the ideologies naturalizing the oppression of women and of working people.[10] Those ideologies shape corporate decisions such that corporations structure markets as instruments of oppression and not as liberatory spaces. Indeed, restructuring markets to foster the liberation of women and working people would actually undermine the interests of individual capitalists and of capitalism, which profit from disparities in income and oppressive social relations. From this perspective, television is structured to discriminate against anyone outside the commodity audience of white, 18- to 34-year-old, heterosexual, English-speaking, upscale men. This recognition is crucial to scholarly work on television. Whatever amenities or pleasures television offers to viewers outside *the* commodity audience, television is an instrument of oppression.

Notes

1 Because Smythe assumed that the audience commodity and the viewership were identical, I use commodity audience to differentiate the manufactured audience from the viewership.
2 Other possibilities may exist; these are the two that I have identified.
3 "Twists" are minor innovations in plot, character, props, setting, etc., that are used to differentiate among series building on similar track records. Twists and track record are

typically balanced. For example, the more recent series *Nash Bridges* was derived from *Miami Vice*. Both starred Don Johnson; both were crime dramas about an ensemble of undercover police officers who wore stylish outfits, talked tough, raced about in luxury cars, and were frequently lectured by a senior officer. In *Miami Vice*, the authority figure was the unit's enigmatic captain; in *Nash Bridges*, an internal affairs officer investigating the unit. Here the twist is gender: the investigator was cast as a stylishly dressed woman who also served as Bridges's love interest. Where officers in *Miami Vice* experienced considerable moral ambiguity, *Nash Bridges* maintained a clear division between cops and robbers. Where *Miami Vice* specialized in a brooding, enigmatic atmosphere, *Nash Bridges* struck an upbeat note through the use of bright lighting for indoor scenes. Where Johnson's character and his partner drove through Miami at night, Nash and his partner raced around an eternally sunny San Francisco. On *Miami Vice*, Johnson's character lacked stable and fulfilling relationships outside his work. On *Nash Bridges*, Johnson's character had good relationships at work and at home: he easily led his unit, had established a personal friendship with his investigator, acted as a loving and protective father to his daughter, and seemed to be a dutiful, if skeptical, son to his father.

4 This has encouraged producers "pitching" innovative shows in terms of old shows; the best-known example, perhaps, being Gene Roddenberry's attempt to persuade network executives that a science fiction drama targeting adults should be thought of as a Western: *Star Trek* was really *Wagon Train* set in outer space.

5 The American Association of Advertising Agencies and the Association of National Advertisers owned the Cooperative Analysis of Broadcasting, which provided ratings only to those AAAA and ANA members that subscribed to the service. CAB conducted telephone surveys with a long list of questions asking respondents to recount every fifteen minutes of radio listening done the day prior to contact. Unsurprisingly, CAB reported low ratings. The C. E. Hooper Company capitalized on the networks' discontent while offering advertisers and agencies results from telephone surveys that asked for a report of current listening and of listening during the previous fifteen minutes. Greater accuracy combined with a lower cost from expanding the buyer base worked: CEH monopolized broadcast ratings throughout the "golden age" of radio. ACN achieved monopolistic control over network radio and television in the 1950s. It maintains its monopoly over television ratings to the present day and has extended operations into web site ratings.

6 Little if any interest has been expressed in Native Americans or viewers descended from immigrants from Asia or the Pacific Rim.

7 For example, in *Miami Vice*, the melodrama centered on whether Johnson's character would recover from the death of his previous partner, form a bond with his current partner, and sort out his love life. In *Nash Bridges*, the melodrama focuses on the continuing story of one man's family. Johnson's character must deal with the romance between his daughter and one of his subordinates, maintain his relationship with his father, and transform the woman investigating his operations from antagonist to friend and, perhaps, lover.

8 Personal interview with Judy Girard, head of programming, Lifetime, New York, 1995.

9 Personal interview with Douglas McCormack, Chief Executive Officer, Lifetime, New York, 1995.

10 Although the particular dynamics shift as demographic categories shift, I believe that the basic analysis holds for people of color, speakers of languages other than English, people younger or older than the valued age grade, gay men, lesbians, etc. One would look for dynamics rooted in colonialism, ageism, heterosexism, etc., and trace the connections to patriarchy and/or capitalism.

(i) Introduction; (ii) The Aristocracy of Culture

Pierre Bourdieu

(i) Introduction

You said it, my good knight! There ought to be laws to protect the body of acquired knowledge.

Take one of our good pupils, for example: modest and diligent, from his earliest grammar classes he's kept a little notebook full of phrases.

After hanging on the lips of his teachers for twenty years, he's managed to build up an intellectual stock in trade; doesn't it belong to him as if it were a house, or money?

– Paul Claudel, *Le soulier de satin*, Day III, Scene ii

There is an economy of cultural goods, but it has a specific logic. Sociology endeavours to establish the conditions in which the consumers of cultural goods, and their taste for them, are produced, and at the same time to describe the different ways of appropriating such of these objects as are regarded at a particular moment as works of art, and the social conditions of the constitution of the mode of appropriation that is considered legitimate. But one cannot fully understand cultural practices unless "culture", in the restricted, normative sense of ordinary usage, is brought back into "culture" in the anthropological sense, and the elaborated taste for the most refined objects is reconnected with the elementary taste for the flavours of food.

Whereas the ideology of charisma regards taste in legitimate culture as a gift of nature, scientific observation shows that cultural needs are the product of upbringing

From Pierre Bourdieu, "Introduction" and "The aristocracy of culture." In *Distinction: A Social Critique of the Judgement of Taste*, pp. 1–3, 5–7, and 11–13. Translated by Richard Nice. Cambridge, Mass.: Harvard University Press, 1984. © 1984 by the President and Fellows of Harvard College and Routledge and Kegan Paul, Ltd. Reprinted by permission of Harvard University Press, Taylor & Francis Books Ltd, Georges Borchardt, Inc and Les Editions de Minuit.

and education: surveys establish that all cultural practices (museum visits, concert-going, reading etc.), and preferences in literature, painting or music, are closely linked to educational level (measured by qualifications or length of schooling) and secondarily to social origin.[1] The relative weight of home background and of formal education (the effectiveness and duration of which are closely dependent on social origin) varies according to the extent to which the different cultural practices are recognized and taught by the educational system, and the influence of social origin is strongest – other things being equal – in "extra-curricular" and avant-garde culture. To the socially recognized hierarchy of the arts, and within each of them, of genres, schools or periods, corresponds a social hierarchy of the consumers. This predisposes tastes to function as markers of "class". The manner in which culture has been acquired lives on in the manner of using it: the importance attached to manners can be understood once it is seen that it is these imponderables of practice which distinguish the different – and ranked – modes of culture acquisition, early or late, domestic or scholastic, and the classes of individuals which they characterize (such as "pedants" and *mondains*). Culture also has its titles of nobility – awarded by the educational system – and its pedigrees, measured by seniority in admission to the nobility.

The definition of cultural nobility is the stake in a struggle which has gone on unceasingly, from the seventeenth century to the present day, between groups differing in their ideas of culture and of the legitimate relation to culture and to works of art, and therefore differing in the conditions of acquisition of which these dispositions are the product.[2] Even in the classroom, the dominant definition of the legitimate way of appropriating culture and works of art favours those who have had early access to legitimate culture in a cultured household, outside of scholastic disciplines, since even within the educational system it devalues scholarly knowledge and interpretation as "scholastic" or even "pedantic" in favour of direct experience and simple delight.

The logic of what is sometimes called, in typically "pedantic" language, the "reading" of a work of art, offers an objective basis for this opposition. Consumption is, in this case, a stage in a process of communication, that is, an act of deciphering, decoding, which presupposes practical or explicit mastery of a cipher or code. In a sense, one can say that the capacity to see (*voir*) is a function of the knowledge (*savoir*), or concepts, that is, the words, that are available to name visible things, and which are, as it were, programmes for perception. A work of art has meaning and interest only for someone who possesses the cultural competence, that is, the code, into which it is encoded. The conscious or unconscious implementation of explicit or implicit schemes of perception and appreciation which constitutes pictorial or musical culture is the hidden condition for recognizing the styles characteristic of a period, a school or an author, and, more generally, for the familiarity with the internal logic of works that aesthetic enjoyment presupposes. A beholder who lacks the specific code feels lost in a chaos of sounds and rhythms, colours and lines, without rhyme or reason. Not having learnt to adopt the adequate disposition, he stops short at what Erwin Panofsky calls the "sensible properties", perceiving a skin as downy or lace-work as delicate, or at the emotional resonances aroused by these properties, referring to "austere" colours or a "joyful" melody. He cannot move from the "primary stratum of the meaning we can grasp on the basis of our ordinary experience" to the "stratum of secondary meanings", i.e., the "level of the meaning of what is signified", unless he possesses the concepts which go beyond the sensible properties and which identify the specifically stylistic properties of the work.[3] Thus the encounter with a work of art is not "love at first sight" as is generally supposed, and the act of empathy, *Einfüblung*, which is the art-lover's pleasure, presupposes an act of cognition, a decoding operation, which implies the implementation of a cognitive acquirement, a cultural code.[4]

This typically intellectualist theory of artistic perception directly contradicts the experience of the art-lovers closest to the legitimate definition; acquisition of legitimate culture by insensible familiarization within the family circle tends to favour an enchanted experience of culture which implies forgetting the acquisition.[5] The "eye" is a product of history reproduced by education. [...]

In fact, through the economic and social conditions which they presuppose, the different ways of relating to realities and fictions, of believing in fictions and the realities they simulate, with more or less distance and detachment, are very closely linked to the different possible positions in social space and, consequently, bound up with the systems of dispositions (habitus) characteristic of the different classes and class fractions. Taste classifies, and it classifies the classifier. Social subjects, classified by their classifications, distinguish themselves by the distinctions they make, between the beautiful and the ugly, the distinguished and the vulgar, in which their position in the objective classifications is expressed or betrayed. And statistical analysis does indeed show that oppositions similar in structure to those found in cultural practices also appear in eating habits. The antithesis between quantity and quality, substance and form, corresponds to the opposition – linked to different distances from necessity – between the taste of necessity, which favours the most "filling" and most economical foods, and the taste of liberty – or luxury – which shifts the emphasis to the manner (of presenting, serving, eating etc.) and tends to use stylized forms to deny function.

The science of taste and of cultural consumption begins with a transgression that is in no way aesthetic: it has to abolish the sacred frontier which makes legitimate culture a separate universe, in order to discover the intelligible relations which unite apparently incommensurable "choices", such as preferences in music and food, painting and sport, literature and hairstyle. This barbarous reintegration of aesthetic consumption into the world of ordinary consumption abolishes the opposition, which has been the basis of high aesthetics since Kant, between the "taste of sense" and the "taste of reflection", and between facile pleasure, pleasure reduced to a pleasure of the senses, and pure pleasure, pleasure purified of pleasure, which is predisposed to become a symbol of moral excellence and a measure of the capacity for sublimation which defines the truly human man. The culture which results from this magical division is sacred. Cultural consecration does indeed confer on the objects, persons and situations it touches, a sort of ontological promotion akin to a transubstantiation. Proof enough of this is found in the two following quotations, which might almost have been written for the delight of the sociologist:

"What struck me most is this: nothing could be obscene on the stage of our premier theatre, and the ballerinas of the Opera, even as naked dancers, sylphs, sprites or Bacchae, retain an inviolable purity."[6]

"There are obscene postures: the stimulated intercourse which offends the eye. Clearly, it is impossible to approve, although the interpolation of such gestures in dance routines does give them a symbolic and aesthetic quality which is absent from the intimate scenes the cinema daily flaunts before its spectators' eyes . . . As for the nude scene, what can one say, except that it is brief and theatrically not very effective? I will not say it is chaste or innocent, for nothing commercial can be so described. Let us say it is not shocking, and that the chief objection is that it serves as a box-office gimmick. . . . In *Hair*, the nakedness fails to be symbolic."[7]

The denial of lower, coarse, vulgar, venal, servile – in a word, natural – enjoyment, which constitutes the sacred sphere of culture, implies an affirmation of the superiority of those who can be satisfied with the sublimated, refined, disinterested, gratuitous, distinguished pleasures forever closed to the profane. That is why art and cultural consumption are predisposed, consciously and deliberately or not, to fulfil a social function of legitimating social differences.

(ii)   The Aristocracy of Culture

Sociology is rarely more akin to social psychoanalysis than when it confronts an object like taste, one of the most vital stakes in the struggles fought in the field of the dominant class and the field of cultural production. This is not only because the judgement of taste is the supreme manifestation of the discernment which, by reconciling reason and sensibility, the pedant who understands without feeling and the *mondain* who enjoys without understanding, defines the accomplished individual. Nor is it solely because every rule of propriety designates in advance the project of defining this indefinable essence as a clear manifestation of philistinism – whether it be the academic propriety which, from Alois Riegl and Heinrich Wölfflin to Elie Faure and Henri Focillon, and from the most scholastic commentators on the classics to the avant-garde semiologist, insists on a formalist reading of the work of art; or the upperclass propriety which treats taste as one of the surest signs of true nobility and cannot conceive of referring taste to anything other than itself.

Here the sociologist finds himself in the area par excellence of the denial of the social. It is not sufficient to overcome the initial self-evident appearances, in other words, to relate taste, the uncreated source of all "creation", to the social conditions of which it is the product, knowing full well that the very same people who strive to repress the clear relation between taste and education, between culture as the state of that which is cultivated and culture as the process of cultivating, will be amazed that anyone should expend so much effort in scientifically proving that self-evident fact. He must also question that relationship, which only appears to be self-explanatory, and unravel the paradox whereby the relationship with educational capital is just as strong in areas which the educational system does not teach. And he must do this without ever being able to appeal unconditionally to the positivistic arbitration of what are called facts. Hidden behind the statistical relationships between educational capital or social origin and this or that type of knowledge or way of applying it, there are relationships between groups maintaining different, and even antagonistic, relations to culture, depending on the conditions in which they acquired their cultural capital and the markets in which they can derive most profit from it. But we have not yet finished with the self-evident. The question itself has to be questioned – in other words, the relation to culture which it tacitly privileges – in order to establish whether a change in the content and form of the question would not be sufficient to transform the relationships observed. There is no way out of the game of culture; and one's only chance of objectifying the true nature of the game is to objectify as fully as possible the very operations which one is obliged to use in order to achieve that objectification. *De te fabula narratur.* The reminder is meant for the reader as well as the sociologist. Paradoxically, the games of culture are protected against objectification by all the partial objectifications which the actors involved in the game perform on each other: scholarly critics cannot grasp the objective reality of society aesthetes without abandoning their grasp of the true nature of their own activity; and the same is true of their opponents. The same law of mutual lucidity and reflexive blindness governs the antagonism between "intellectuals" and "bourgeois" (or their spokesmen in the field of production). And even when bearing in mind the function which legitimate culture performs in class relations, one is still liable to be led into accepting one or the other of the self-interested representations of culture which "intellectuals" and "bourgeois" endlessly fling at each other. Up to now the sociology of the production and producers of culture has never escaped from the play of opposing images, in which "right-wing intellectuals" and "left-wing intellectuals" (as the current taxonomy puts it) subject their opponents and their strategies to an objectivist reduction which vested interests make that much easier. The objectification is always bound to remain partial, and therefore false, so long as it fails to include the point of view from which it speaks and so fails to construct the game as a whole. Only at the level of the field of positions is it possible to grasp both the generic interests associated with the fact of taking part in the game and the specific interests attached to the different positions, and, through this, the form and content of the self-positionings through which these interests are expressed. Despite the aura of objectivity they like to assume, neither the "sociology of the intellectuals", which is traditionally the business of "right-wing intellectuals", nor the critique of "right-wing thought", the traditional speciality of "left-wing intellectuals", is anything more than a series of symbolic aggressions which take on additional force when they dress themselves up in the impeccable neutrality of science. They tacitly agree in leaving hidden what is essential, namely the structure of objective positions which is the source, inter alia, of the view which the occupants of each position can have of the occupants of the other positions and which determines the specific form and force of each group's propensity to present and receive a group's partial truth as if it were a full account of the objective relations between the groups.

Notes

1   Bourdieu et al., *Un art moyen: essai sur les usages sociaux de la photographie* (Paris, Ed. de Minuit, 1965); P. Bourdieu and A. Darbel, *L'Amour de l'art: les musées et leur public* (Paris, Ed. de Minuit, 1966).

2   The word *disposition* seems particularly suited to express what is covered by the concept of habitus (defined as a system of dispositions) – used later in this chapter. It expresses first the *result of an organizing action*, with a meaning close to that of words such as structure; it also designates a way of being, a habitual state (especially of the body) and, in particular, a *predisposition, tendency, propensity* or *inclination*. [The semantic cluster of "disposition" is rather wider in French than in English, but as this note – translated literally – shows, the equivalence is adequate. Translator.] P. Bourdieu, *Outline of a Theory of Practice* (Cambridge, Cambridge University Press, 1977), p. 214, n. 1.

3   E. Panofsky, "Iconography and Iconology: An Introduction to the Study of Renaissance Art", *Meaning in the Visual Arts* (New York, Doubleday, 1955), p. 28.

4   It will be seen that this internalized code called culture functions as cultural capital owing to the fact that, being unequally distributed, it secures profits of distinction.

5   The sense of familiarity in no way excludes the ethnocentric misunderstanding which results from applying the wrong code. Thus, Michael Baxandall's work in historical ethnology enables us to measure all that separates the perceptual schemes that now tend to be applied to Quattrocento paintings and those which their immediate addressees applied. The "moral and spiritual eye" of Quattrocento man, that is, the set of cognitive and evaluative dispositions which were the basis of his perception of the world and his perception of pictorial representation of the world, differs radically from the "pure" gaze (purified, first of all, of reference to economic value) with which the modern cultivated spectator looks at works of art. As the contracts show, the clients of Filippo Lippi, Domenico Ghirlandaio or Piero della Francesca were concerned to get "value for money". They approached works of art with the mercantile dispositions of a businessman who can calculate quantities and prices at a glance, and they applied some surprising criteria of appreciation, such as the expense of the colours, which sets gold and ultramarine at the top of the hierarchy. The artists, who shared this world view, were led to include arithmetical and geometrical devices in their compositions so as to flatter this taste for measurement and calculation; and they tended to exhibit the technical virtuosity which, in this context, is the most visible evidence of the quantity and quality of the labour provided; M. Baxandall, *Painting and Experience in Fifteenth-Century Italy: A Primer in the Social History of Pictorial Style* (Oxford, Oxford University Press, 1972).

6   O. Merlin, "Mlle. Thibon dans la vision de Marguerite", *Le Monde*, 9 December 1965.

7   F. Chenique, "*Hair* est-il immoral?" *Le Monde*, 28 January 1970.

21

On Television

Pierre Bourdieu

Making Everything Ordinary

Television's power of diffusion means that it poses a terrible problem for the print media and for culture generally. Next to it, the mass circulation press that sent so many shudders up educated spines in earlier times doesn't seem like much at all. (Raymond Williams argued that the entire romantic revolution in poetry was brought about by the horror that English writers felt at the beginnings of the mass circulation press.[1]) By virtue of its reach and exceptional power, television produces effects which, though not without precedent, are completely original.

For example, the evening news on French TV brings together more people than all the French newspapers together, morning and evening editions included. When the information supplied by a single news medium becomes a universal source of news, the resulting political and cultural effects are clear. Everybody knows the "law" that if a newspaper or other news vehicle wants to reach a broad public, it has to dispense with sharp edges and anything that might divide or exclude readers (just think about *Paris-Match* or, in the U.S., *Life* magazine). It must attempt to be inoffensive, not to "offend anyone," and it must never bring up problems – or, if it does, only problems that don't pose any problem. People talk so much about the weather in day-to-day life because it's a subject that cannot cause trouble. Unless you're on vacation and talking with a farmer who needs rain, the weather is the absolutely ideal *soft* subject. The farther a paper extends its circulation, the more it favors such topics that interest "everybody" and don't raise problems. The object – news – is constructed in accordance with the perceptual categories of the receiver.

The collective activity I've described works so well precisely because of this homogenization, which smoothes over things, brings them into line, and depoliticizes them. And it works even though, strictly speaking, this activity is without a subject,

From Pierre Bourdieu, *On Television*, pp. 44–56 and 66–7. Translated by Priscilla Parkhurst Ferguson. New York: The New Press, 1998. © 1998 by Pierre Bourdieu.

that is, no one ever thought of or wished for it as such. This is something that is observed frequently in social life. Things happen that nobody wants but seem somehow to have been willed. Herein lies the danger of simplistic criticism. It takes the place of the work necessary to understand phenomena such as the fact that, even though no one really wished it this way, and without any intervention on the part of the people actually paying for it, we end up with this very strange product, the "TV news." It suits everybody because it confirms what they already know and, above all, leaves their mental structures intact. There are revolutions, the ones we usually talk about, that aim at the material bases of a society – take the nationalization of Church property after 1789 – and then there are symbolic revolutions effected by artists, scholars, or great religious or (sometimes, though less often) political prophets. These affect our mental structures, which means that they change the ways we see and think. Manet is an example: his painting upset the fundamental structure of all academic teaching of painting in the nineteenth century, the opposition between the contemporary and the traditional.[2] If a vehicle as powerful as television were oriented even slightly toward this kind of symbolic revolution, I can assure you that everyone would be rushing to put a stop to it. . . .

But it turns out that, without anyone having to ask television to work this way, the model of competition and the mechanisms outlined above ensure that television does nothing of the sort. It is perfectly adapted to the mental structures of its audience. I could point to television's moralizing, telethon side, which needs to be analyzed from this perspective. André Gide used to say that worthy sentiments make bad literature. But worthy sentiments certainly make for good audience ratings. The moralizing bent of television should make us wonder how cynical individuals are able to make such astoundingly conservative, moralizing statements. Our news anchors, our talk show hosts, and our sports announcers have turned into two-bit spiritual guides, representatives of middle-class morality. They are always telling us what we "should think" about what they call "social problems," such as violence in the inner city or in the schools. The same is true for art and literature, where the best-known of the so-called literary programs serve the establishment and ever-more obsequiously promote social conformity and market values.[3]

Journalists – we should really say the journalistic field – owe their importance in society to their de facto monopoly on the large-scale informational instruments of production and diffusion of information. Through these, they control the access of ordinary citizens but also of other cultural producers such as scholars, artists, and writers, to what is sometimes called "public space," that is, the space of mass circulation. (This is the monopoly that blocks the way whenever an individual or member of a group tries to get a given piece of news into broad circulation.) Even though they occupy an inferior, dominated position in the fields of cultural production, journalists exercise a very particular form of domination, since they control the means of public expression. They control, in effect, public existence, one's ability to be recognized as a *public figure*, obviously critical for politicians and certain intellectuals. This position means that at least the most important of these figures are treated with a respect that is often quite out of proportion with their intellectual merits . . . Moreover, they are able to use part of this power of consecration to their own benefit. Even the best-known journalists occupy positions of structural inferior-ity vis-à-vis social categories such as intellectuals or politicians – and journalists want nothing so much as to be part of the intellectual crowd. No doubt, this structural inferiority goes a long way to explain their tendency toward anti-intellectualism. Nevertheless, they are able to dominate members of these "superior" categories on occasion.

Above all, though, with their permanent access to public visibility, broad circula-tion, and mass diffusion – an access that was completely unthinkable for any cultural producer until television came into the picture – these journalists can impose on the whole of society their vision of the world, their conception of problems, and their point of view. The objection can be raised that the world of journalism is divided, differentiated, and diversified, and as such can very well represent all opinions and points of view or let them be expressed. (It is true that to break through journal-ism's protective shield, you can to a certain extent and provided you possess a minimum of symbolic capital on your own, play journalists and media off against one another.) Yet it remains true that, like other fields, the journalistic field is based on a set of shared assumptions and beliefs, which reach beyond differences of position and opinion. These assumptions operate within a particular set of mental categories; they reside in a characteristic relationship to language, and are visible in everything implied by a formulation such as "it's just *made* for television." These are what supplies the principle that determines what journalists select both within social reality and among symbolic productions as a whole. There is no discourse (scientific analysis, political manifesto, whatever) and no action (demonstration, strike) that doesn't have to face this trial of journalistic selection in order to catch the public eye. The effect is *censorship*, which journalists practice without even being aware of it. They retain only the things capable of *interesting* them and "keeping their atten-tion," which means things that fit their categories and mental grid; and they reject as insignificant or remain indifferent to symbolic expressions that ought to reach the population as a whole.

Another consequence, one more difficult to grasp, of television's increased (relative) power in the space of the means of diffusion and of the greater market pressures on this newly dominant medium, shows up in the shift from a national cultural policy, which once worked through television, to a sort of spontaneistic demagoguery. While this change affects television in particular, it has also contaminated supposedly serious newspapers – witness the greater and greater space given over to letters to the editor and op-ed pieces. In the 1950s, television in France was openly "cul-tural": it used its monopoly to influence virtually every product that laid claim to high cultural status (documentaries, adaptations of the classics, cultural debates, and so forth) and to raise the taste of the general public. In the 1990s, because it must reach the largest audience possible, television is intent on exploiting and pandering to these same tastes. It does so by offering viewers what are essentially raw products, of which the paradigmatic program is the talk show with its "slices of life." These lived experiences come across as unbuttoned exhibitions of often extreme behavior aimed at satisfying a kind of voyeurism and exhibitionism. (TV game shows, which people are dying to get on, if only as a member of the studio audience, just to have a moment of visibility, are another example.) That said, I don't share the nostalgia professed by some people for the paternalistic-pedagogical television of the past, which I see as no less opposed to a truly democratic use of the means of mass circulation than populist spontaneism and demagogic capitulation to popular tastes.

Struggles Settled by Audience Ratings

So you have to look beyond appearances, beyond what happens in the studio, and even beyond the competition inside the journalistic field. To the extent that it decides the very form of onscreen interactions, one must understand the power relationship between the different news media. To understand why we continually see the same debates between the same journalists, we have to consider the position of the various media that these journalists represent and their position within those media. Similarly, both of these factors have to be kept in mind if we want to understand what a reporter for *Le Monde* can and cannot write. What are actually positional pressures are experienced as ethical interdictions or injunctions: "that's not the practice at *Le Monde*" or "that doesn't fit with *Le Monde*'s culture," or again, "that just isn't done here," and so on. All these experiences, presented as ethical precepts, translate the structure of the field through an individual who occupies a particular position in this space.

Competitors within a given field often have polemical images of one another. They produce stereotypes about one another and insults as well. (In the world of sports, for example, rugby players routinely refer to soccer players as "armless wonders.") These images are often strategies that take into account and make use of power relationships, which they aim to transform or preserve. These days, print journalists, in particular those who occupy a dominated position within this sphere (that is, those who write for lesser newspapers and are in lesser positions) are elaborating a discourse that is highly critical of television.

In fact, these images themselves take a stand, which essentially gives expression to the position occupied by the individual who, with greater or lesser disclaimers, articulates the view in question. At the same time, these strategies aim to transform the position this individual occupies in the field. Today, the struggle over television is central to the journalistic milieu, and its centrality makes it very difficult to study. Much pseudo-scholarly discourse on television does no more than record what TV people say about TV. (Journalists are all the more inclined to say that a sociologist is good when what he says is close to what they think. Which means – and it's probably a good thing, too – that you haven't a prayer of being popular with TV people if you try to tell the truth about television.) That said, there are indicators that, relative to television, print journalism is in gradual retreat. Witness the increasing space given to TV listings in newspapers, or the great store set by journalists in having their stories picked up by television, as well as, obviously, being seen on television. Such visibility gives them greater status in their newspaper or journal. Any journalist who wants power or influence has to have a TV program. It is even possible for television journalists to get important positions in the printed press. This calls into question the specificity of writing, and, for that matter, the specificity of the entire profession. The fact that a television news anchor can become the editor of a newspaper or news magazine from one day to the next makes you wonder just what the specific competence required of a journalist might be.

Then there is the fact that television more and more defines what Americans call the *agenda* (the issues up for discussion, the subjects of the editorials, important problems to be covered). In the circular circulation of information I've described, television carries decisive weight. If the printed press should happen to raise an issue – a scandal or a debate – it becomes central only when television takes it up and gives it full orchestration, and, thereby, political impact. This dependence on television threatens the position of print journalists, and this too calls the specificity of the profession into question. Of course, all of this needs to be documented and verified. What I'm giving here is simultaneously a balance sheet based on a number of studies and a program for further research. These are very complicated matters about which knowledge cannot really advance without significant empirical work. This doesn't prevent the practitioners of "mediology," self-designated specialists in a science that doesn't exist, from drawing all sorts of peremptory conclusions about the state of media in the world today before any study has been conducted.

But the most important point is that through the increased symbolic power of television overall, and, among the competing kinds of television, the increased influence of the most cynical and most successful seekers after anything sensational, spectacular, or extraordinary, a certain vision of the news comes to take over the whole of the journalistic field. Until recently, this conception of the news had been relegated to the tabloids specializing in sports and human interest stories. Similarly, a certain category of journalists, recruited at great cost for their ability immediately to fulfill the expectations of the public that expects the least – journalists who are necessarily the most cynical, the most indifferent to any kind of structural analysis, and even more reluctant to engage in any inquiry that touches on politics – tends to impose on all journalists its "values," its preferences, its ways of being and speaking, its "human ideal." Pushed by competition for marketshare, television networks have greater and greater recourse to the tried and true formulas of tabloid journalism, with emphasis (when not the entire newscast) devoted to human interest stories or sports. No matter what has happened in the world on a given day, more and more often the evening news begins with French soccer scores or another sporting event, interrupting the regular news. Or it will highlight the most anecdotal, ritualized political event (visits of foreign heads of state, the president's trips abroad, and so on), or the natural disasters, accidents, fires and the like. In short, the focus is on those things which are apt to arouse curiosity but require no analysis, especially in the political sphere.

As I've said, human interest stories create a political vacuum. They depoliticize and reduce what goes on in the world to the level of anecdote or scandal. This can occur on a national or international scale, especially with film stars or members of royal families, and is accomplished by fixing and keeping attention fixed on events without political consequences, but which are nonetheless dramatized so as to "draw a lesson" or be transformed into illustrations of "social problems." This is where our TV philosophers are called in to give meaning to the meaningless, anecdotal, or fortuitous event that has been artificially brought to stage center and given significance – a headscarf worn to school, an assault on a school-teacher or any other "social fact" tailor-made to arouse the pathos and indignation of some commentators or the tedious moralizing of others. This same search for sensational news, and hence market success, can also lead to the selection of stories that give free rein to the unbridled constructions of demagoguery (whether spontaneous or intentional) or can stir up great excitement by catering to the most primitive drives and emotions (with stories of kidnapped children and scandals likely to arouse public indignation). Purely sentimental and therapeutic forms of mobilizing feelings can come into play, but, with murders of children or incidents tied to stigmatized groups, other forms of mobilization can also take place, forms that are just as emotional but aggressive enough almost to qualify as symbolic lynching.

It follows that the printed press today faces a choice: Should it go in the direction of the dominant model, which means publishing newspapers that resemble TV news, or should it emphasize its difference and engage instead in a strategy of product differentiation? Should it compete, and run the risk of losing on both fronts, not reaching a mass public while losing the one that remains faithful to the strict definition of the cultural message? Or, once again, should it stress its difference? The same problem exists inside the television field itself, which is, of course, a subfield within the larger journalistic field. From my observations so far, I think that, unconsciously, those in charge, who are themselves victims of the "audience ratings mindset," don't really choose. (It is regularly observed that major social decisions aren't made by anyone. If sociologists always disturb things, it's because they force us to make conscious things that we'd rather leave unconscious.) I think that the general trend is for old-style means of cultural production to lose their specificity and move onto a terrain where they can't win. Thus, the cultural network Channel 7 (now Arte) moved from a policy of intransigent, even aggressive, esotericism to a more or less disreputable compromise with audience ratings. The result is programming that makes concessions to facile, popular programming during prime time and keeps the esoteric fare for late at night. *Le Monde* (like other serious newspapers throughout the world) currently faces the same choice. I think I've said enough to show the move from the analysis of invisible structures – a bit like the force of gravity, things that nobody sees but have to be accepted for us to understand what's going on – to individual experience, and how the invisible power relations are translated into personal conflicts and existential choices.

The journalistic field has one distinguishing characteristic: it is much more dependent on external forces than the other fields of cultural production, such as mathematics, literature, law, science, and so on. It depends very directly on demand, since, and perhaps even more than the political field itself, it is subject to the decrees of the market and the opinion poll. The conflict of "pure" versus "market" can be seen in every field. In the theater, for example, it turns up in the opposition between big, popular shows and avant-garde theater, between Broadway musicals and off-Broadway experimental theater. In the media, it's the difference between TF1 and *Le Monde*. All reflect the same opposition between catering to a public that is more educated, on the one hand, less so on the other, with more students for the one, more businessmen for the other. But if this opposition is ubiquitous, it's particularly brutal in the journalistic field, where the market weighs particularly heavily. Its intensity is unprecedented and currently without equal. Furthermore, the journalistic field has no equivalent of the sort of immanent justice in the scientific world that censures those individuals who break certain rules and rewards those who abide by them with the esteem of their peers (as manifested most notably in citations and references). Where are the positive or negative sanctions for journalism? The only criticism consists of satirical spoofs such as that on the Puppets.[4] As for the rewards, there is little more than the possibility of having one's story "picked up" (copied by another journalist), but this indicator is infrequent, not very visible, and ambiguous.

The Power of Television

The world of journalism in itself is a field, but one that is subject to great pressure from the economic field via audience ratings. This very heteronomous field, which is structurally very strongly subordinated to market pressures, in turn applies pressure to all other fields. This structural, objective, anonymous and invisible effect has nothing to do with what is visible or with what television usually gets attacked for, namely, the direct intervention of one or another individual . . . It is not enough, it should not be enough, to attack the people in charge. For example, Karl Kraus, the great Viennese satirist early in this century, launched violent attacks on a man who was the equivalent of the editor of *Le Nouvel Observateur*. He denounced the cultural conformism so destructive of culture and the complacency of minor or measly writers whom he saw as discrediting pacifist ideas by championing them hypocritically . . . As a general rule, critics are concerned with individuals. But when you do sociology, you learn that men and women are indeed responsible, but that what they can or cannot do is largely determined by the structure in which they are placed and by the positions they occupy within that structure. So polemical attacks on this or that journalist, philosopher, or philosopher-journalist are not enough . . . Everyone has a favorite whipping boy, and I'm no exception. Bernard-Henri Lévy has become something of a symbol of the writer-journalist and the philosopher-journalist. But no sociologist worthy of the name talks about Bernard-Henri Lévy.[5] It is vital to understand that he is only a sort of structural epiphenomenon, and that, like an electron, he is the expression of a field. You can't understand anything if you don't understand the field that produces him and gives him his parcel of power.

This understanding is important both to remove the analysis from the level of drama and to direct action rationally. I am in fact convinced (and this presentation on television bears witness to this conviction) that analyses like this can perhaps help to change things. Every science makes this claim. Auguste Comte, the founder of sociology, proclaimed that "science leads to foresight, and foresight leads to action." Social science has as much right to this aspiration as any other science. By describing a space such as journalism, investing it from the beginning with drives, feelings, and emotions – emotions and drives that are glossed over by the work of analysis –

sociologists can hope to have some effect. Increasing awareness of the mechanisms at work, for example, can help by offering a measure of freedom to those manipulated by these mechanisms, whether they are journalists or viewers. Another aside: I think (or at least I hope) that if they really listen to what I am saying, journalists who might initially feel attacked will feel that, by spelling out things they know vaguely but don't really want to know too much about, I am giving them instruments of freedom with which to master the mechanisms I discuss.

In fact, it might be possible to create alliances between news media that could cancel out certain of the structural effects of competition that are most pernicious, such as the race for the scoop. Some of these dangerous effects derive from the structural effects shaping the competition, which produces a sense of urgency and leads to the race for the scoop. This means that news which might prove dangerous to those involved can be broadcast simply to beat out a competitor, with no thought given to the danger. To the extent that this is true, making these mechanisms conscious or explicit could lead to an arrangement that would neutralize competition. In a scenario somewhat like what sometimes happens now in extreme cases, as when children are kidnapped, for example, one could imagine – or dream – that journalists might agree to forget about audience ratings for once and refuse to open their talk shows to political leaders known for and by their xenophobia. Further, they could agree not to broadcast what these characters say. (This would be infinitely more effective than all the so-called refutations put together.)

All of this is utopian, and I know it. But to those who always tax the sociologist with determinism and pessimism, I will only say that if people became aware of them, conscious action aimed at controlling the structural mechanisms that engender moral failure would be possible. As we have seen, this world characterized by a high degree of cynicism has a lot of talk about morality. As a sociologist, I know that morality only works if it is supported by structures and mechanisms that give people an interest in morality. And, for something like a moral anxiety to occur, that morality has to find support, reinforcement, and rewards in this structure. These rewards could also come from a public more enlightened and more aware of the manipulations to which it is subject.

I think that all the fields of cultural production today are subject to structural pressure from the journalistic field, and not from any one journalist or network executive, who are themselves subject to control by the field. This pressure exercises equivalent and systematic effects in every field. In other words, this journalistic field, which is more and more dominated by the market model, imposes its pressures more and more on other fields. Through pressure from audience ratings, economic forces weigh on television, and through its effect on journalism, television weighs on newspapers and magazines, even the "purest" among them. The weight then falls on individual journalists, who little by little let themselves be drawn into television's orbit. In this way, through the weight exerted by the journalistic field, the economy weighs on all fields of cultural production. [. . .]

The audience rating system can and should be contested in the name of democracy. This appears paradoxical, because those who defend audience ratings claim that nothing is more democratic (this is a favorite argument of advertisers, which has been picked up by certain sociologists, not to mention essayists who've run out of ideas and are happy to turn any criticism of opinion polls – and audience ratings – into a criticism of universal suffrage). You must, they declare, leave people free to judge and to choose for themselves ("all those elitist intellectual prejudices of yours make you turn your nose up at all this"). The audience rating system is the sanction of the market and the economy, that is, of an external and purely market law. Submission to the requirements of this marketing instrument is the exact equivalent for culture of what poll-based demagogy is for politics. Enslaved by audience ratings, television imposes market pressures on the supposedly free and enlightened consumer. These pressures have nothing to do with the democratic expression of enlightened collective opinion or public rationality, despite what certain commentators would have us believe. The failure of critical thinkers and organizations charged with articulating the interests of dominated individuals to think clearly about this problem only reinforces the mechanisms I have described.

Notes

1   [See Raymond Williams, *Culture and Society, 1780–1950* (New York: Columbia University Press, 1958). – Tr.]
2   [See Pierre Bourdieu, "The Institutionalization of Anomie," in Randal Johnson, ed., *The Field of Cultural Production: Essays on Art and Literature* (New York: Columbia University Press, 1993), pp. 238–53. – Tr.]
3   For example, the long-running show of Bernard Pivot (see note 17, below). The American equivalents are found on PBS. – Tr.]
4   [The Puppets [*Les Guignols*] is a weekly satirical program where prominent political figures are represented by marionettes with exaggerated features and such. – Tr.]
5   [Bernard-Henri Lévy is one of the most prominent of contemporary journalist-philosophers, so well known in fact that he is often referred simply as "BHL." Besides his many books and essays, he has written plays and directed films (and has acted in television drama). Lévy has also taken a particularly active stand in favor of Bosnia (see his film from 1992, *La Mort de Sarajevo*). – Tr.]

Part IV

The Politics of Representation

Introduction to Part IV

The ground-breaking work of critical media theorists such as those in the Frankfurt School, British cultural studies, and French structuralism and poststructuralism revealed that culture is a social construct, intrinsically linked to the vicissitudes of the social and historically specific milieu in which it is conceived. Media and cultural studies unavoidably had to engage the politics of representation, which drew upon feminist approaches and multicultural theories to fully analyze the functions of gender, class, race, ethnicity, nationality, sexual preference and so on – social dimensions that are vital to the constitution of cultural texts and their effects, as well as being constitutive of audiences who appropriate and use texts. British cultural studies, for instance, progressively adopted a feminist dimension, paid greater attention to race, ethnicity and nationality, and concentrated on sexuality, as various discourses of race, gender, sex, nationality, and so on circulated in response to social struggles and movements (see Gilroy 1991; McRobbie, 1994; and Ang 1998). An increasingly complex, culturally hybrid, and diasporic world calls for sophisticated understandings of the interplay of representations, politics, and the forms of media, and the readings in this section were ground-breaking in offering new perspectives on these problematics.

Laura Mulvey's essay "Visual Pleasure and Narrative Cinema" has now achieved the status of a "classic" in critical cultural studies. Contested, challenged, and reworked over the years since its first appearance in *Screen* in 1975, its significance lies in the original theoretical framework it offered for considering the relationship between the viewer – or the viewing subject – and the cinematic text. Using psychoanalytic conceptions of the subject, Mulvey's analysis explores the ways in which cinematic techniques interpellate the viewer as subject and articulate the spectator's "look" at the screen with the intra-diegetic "looks" of a film. Mulvey provides a feminist inflection, as the viewer's "look" is construed in her analysis as male. Mulvey contends that the cinematic apparatus legitimates and perpetuates a patriarchal order in which the object of the look is female and the subject of the look – the active "looker" – is male. At the time of its publication, her article offered a radical tool for analyzing the representation of sexual difference and desire in cinema. In the more than 20 years since it first appeared, critics have questioned the binarism of its argument and the fixity of its constructions of gender; a spate of scholarship has emerged as a result of questions and challenges raised by this piece (see Dyer, 1982; Doane, 1982; Willemen, 1994, for example), thus signaling its position as a theoretical "key" in media and cultural studies.

Sexuality and representation are also the focus of Richard Dyer's essay, "Stereotyping." Dyer's essay engages the problem of ideology at work in conventional representations of sexual and various minorities in film and other media, identifying stereotyping as a hegemonic process by which dominance is maintained by ruling groups. Yet he complicates the obvious issues of misrepresentation and distortion by questioning whether more "realistic" images are in fact preferable to the stereotypes. Dyer identifies strategies or "short cuts" by which stereotyping is accomplished, such as through the use of iconography, narrative structures, individuation, and member types, concluding with the suggestion that certain modes of "typing" are "linked to historically and culturally specific and determined groups or classes and their praxes" (Dyer, 1984, p. 37) which in fact speak to a collective identity, political solidarity, and communal struggle. Though dated, this essay is included here because it raised issues previously ignored pertaining to sexuality and the media, and, as such, was a "key" that unlocked certain core aspects of gay/lesbian media studies.

Relations of looking, sexuality, and desire are further taken up by bell hooks in her essay "Eating the Other," drawn from *Black Looks: Race and Representation*. hooks was among the first African American feminist scholars to call attention to the interlockings of race, class, gender, and other markers of identity in the constitution of subjectivity – early in her career she challenged feminists to recognize and confront the ways in which race and class inscribe women's (and men's) experiences. A hallmark of hooks's work is its admixture of mature theoretical analysis with everyday language and sensibilities. Her goal is to make social and cultural criticism accessible to people beyond the halls of academe, and to combine intellectual energy with activism. The essay included here is representative of her unique approach to critical studies. In this essay, hooks explores cultural constructions of the "Other" as object of desire, tying such positioning to consumerism and commodification as well as to issues of racial domination and subordination. Cautioning against the seductiveness of celebrating "Otherness," hooks uses various media cultural artifacts – clothing catalogs, films, rap music – to debate issues of cultural appropriation versus cultural appreciation, and to uncover the personal and political cross-currents at work in mass-media representation.

Paul Gilroy's prolific writings on race, diaspora, and national identity can be traced to an intense critical engagement with "the canon" of British cultural studies. In the essay presented here, Gilroy observes that the current popularity of the concept of "identity" in academic work has its roots in early cultural studies. He highlights the ways in which the theme of identity was a subtext in such seminal works as E. P. Thompson's *Making of the English Working Class* and Richard Hoggart's *Uses of Literacy*, which provided models for thinking identity in relation to issues of class and nation. But Gilroy also notes that race was an aporia in this work, and that the absence of race as a vector of class identity marks a deliberate political choice on the part of these early writers. He concludes his essay by calling for theorizations of identity, culture, and nation that take into account the history of colonialism and migration, transnational economics, and the new multiculturalism. This essay is a first step toward the highly sophisticated and complex engagements with race and nation that mark the later work of Gilroy and other European, American, and a wide range of global cultural studies scholars.

Chandra Mohanty also engages key issues of nation, identity, and power in her often-cited essay, "Under Western Eyes." While this essay does not specifically address media culture, it offers a critique that must be taken into consideration in a sustained discussion of the politics of representation. Mohanty challenges the appropriation and coding of "Third World women" in Western feminist scholarship, reminding us that the Third World is more complex, diverse, and multiform than dominant constructions allow. Even the supposedly progressive discourses of feminism often end up being reductive and ahistorical in terms of what Mohanty calls "Third World difference." Mohanty, like hooks, poses an important challenge to the notion that the category of "woman" can be considered without acknowledging class, ethnic, and racial locations. Her objection is to "the elision . . . between 'women' as a discursively constructed group and 'women' as material subjects of their own history." In arguing for historically and culturally grounded understandings of women's multiple experiences, Mohanty presents important theoretical and methodological issues that impel us to challenge hegemonies and asymmetries of power in critical cultural studies as well as in mainstream scholarship.

Mohanty's work reminds us that social and political changes have implications far beyond a single nation's borders. Just as Mulvey, hooks, and Gilroy recognize the multilayered, intertextual, and heterogeneous character of racial and gendered representation in the United States, Néstor García Canclini grapples with the theoretical consequences of the decentering of the nation-state and the impact of postmodern, postnational, and global cultures on Latin American cultural production. In traditional media studies, Latin America's "Third World" status of economic dependency on the US led to theories of "cultural imperialism" wherein the US was perceived to have a hegemonic and monolithically destructive impact on the indigenous cultural production of its neighbors to the south. Yet more recent work by Latin American scholars identifies transnationalism as a force calling for fresh research perspectives; new technologies and new markets have impacts that are not simply oppressive, they argue, but rather make way for local and regional cultural production that has progressive potential.

This revisionist "escape from dependency" thesis is fleshed out by García Canclini in the essay "Hybrid Cultures, Oblique Powers." While still taking into account the exercise of power between "First" and "Third" world nations, García Canclini argues that the mass media have not erased traditional Latin American forms of cultural expression, but rather that they have contributed to a reshaping that has displaced established modes of thinking about culture. This reconfiguration, however, is tied to various other social shifts, including the expansion of metropolitan areas, the decrease in collective public action, and the unfinished projects of political change in many Latin American countries. The mass media constitute a new kind of public sphere as they simulate the integration of a disintegrated society. Contrasting media culture with traditional symbols of modernity – monuments and museums – García Canclini focuses on the central question of how the new, dense networks of economic and ideological crossings, and the deterritorializations and hybridities born of them, reconfigure power relations.

Focus on the politics of representation thus calls attention to the fact that culture is produced within relationships of domination and subordination and tends to reproduce or resist existing structures of power. Such a perspective also provides tools for cultural studies whereby the critic can denounce aspects of cultural texts that reproduce class, gender, racial, and other forms of domination, and positively valorize aspects that subvert existing dominations, or depict forms of resistance and struggle against them.

References

Doane, Mary Ann (1982) "Film and the Masquerade: Theorizing the Female Spectator," *Screen* 23 (3/4): 74–87.

Dyer, Richard (1982) "Don't Look Now: The Male Pin-Up," *Screen* 23 (3/4): 61–73.

Gilroy, Paul (1991) *There Ain't No Black in the Union Jack*. Chicago: University of Chicago Press.

Gross, Larry, and Woods, James D. (1999) "Introduction: Being Gay in American Media and Society," in *The Columbia Reader on Lesbians and Gay Men in Media, Society, and Politics*. New York: Columbia University Press, 3–22.

McRobbie, Angela (1994) *Postmodernism and Popular Culture*. New York and London: Routledge.

Willemen, Paul (1994) "The Fourth Look," in *Looks and Frictions: Essays in Cultural Studies and Film Theory*. Bloomington: Indiana University Press, 99–110.

22

Visual Pleasure and Narrative Cinema

Laura Mulvey

Introduction

A political use of psychoanalysis

This paper intends to use psychoanalysis to discover where and how the fascination of film is reinforced by pre-existing patterns of fascination already at work within the individual subject and the social formations that have moulded him. It takes as starting point the way film reflects, reveals and even plays on the straight, socially established interpretation of sexual difference which controls images, erotic ways of looking and spectacle. It is helpful to understand what the cinema has been, how its magic has worked in the past, while attempting a theory and a practice which will challenge this cinema of the past. Psychoanalytic theory is thus appropriated here as a political weapon, demonstrating the way the unconscious of patriarchal society has structured film form.

The paradox of phallocentrism in all its manifestations is that it depends on the image of the castrated woman to give order and meaning to its world. An idea of woman stands as linchpin to the system: it is her lack that produces the phallus as a symbolic presence, it is her desire to make good the lack that the phallus signifies. Recent writing in *Screen* about psychoanalysis and the cinema has not sufficiently brought out the importance of the representation of the female form in a symbolic order in which, in the last resort, it speaks castration and nothing else. To summarize briefly: the function of woman in forming the patriarchal unconscious is twofold, she first symbolizes the castration threat by her real absence of a penis and second thereby raises her child into the Symbolic. Once this has been achieved, her meaning in the process is at an end, it does not last into the world of law and language except as a memory which oscillates between memory of maternal plenitude and memory of lack. Both are posited on nature (or on anatomy in Freud's famous phrase).

From Laura Mulvey, "Visual pleasure and narrative cinema." In *The Sexual Subject: A Screen Reader in Sexuality*, pp. 22–34. New York and London: Routledge, 1992.

Woman's desire is subjected to her image as bearer of the bleeding wound, she can exist only in relation to castration and cannot transcend it. She turns her child into the signifier of her own desire to possess a penis (the condition, she imagines, of entry into the Symbolic). Either she must gracefully give way to the word, the Name of the Father and the Law, or else struggle to keep her child down with her in the half-light of the Imaginary. Woman then stands in patriarchal culture as signifier for the male other, bound by a symbolic order in which man can live out his phantasies and obsessions through linguistic command by imposing them on the silent image of woman still tied to her place as bearer of meaning, not maker of meaning.

There is an obvious interest in this analysis for feminists, a beauty in its exact rendering of the frustration experienced under the phallocentric order. It gets us nearer to the roots of our oppression, it brings an articulation of the problem closer, it faces us with the ultimate challenge: how to fight the unconscious structured like a language (formed critically at the moment of arrival of language) while still caught within the language of the patriarchy. There is no way in which we can produce an alternative out of the blue, but we can begin to make a break by examining patriarchy with the tools it provides, of which psychoanalysis is not the only but an important one. We are still separated by a great gap from important issues for the female unconscious which are scarcely relevant to phallocentric theory: the sexing of the female infant and her relationship to the Symbolic, the sexually mature woman as non-mother, maternity outside the signification of the phallus, the vagina. . . . But, at this point, psychoanalytic theory as it now stands can at least advance our understanding of the status quo, of the patriarchal order in which we are caught.

Destruction of Pleasure as a Radical Weapon

As an advanced representation system, the cinema poses questions of the ways the unconscious (formed by the dominant order) structures ways of seeing and pleasure in looking. Cinema has changed over the last few decades. It is no longer the monolithic system based on large capital investment exemplified at its best by Hollywood in the 1930s, 1940s and 1950s. Technological advances (16mm, etc.) have changed the economic conditions of cinematic production, which can now be artisanal as well as capitalist. Thus it has been possible for an alternative cinema to develop. However self-conscious and ironic Hollywood managed to be, it always restricted itself to a formal *mise-en-scène* reflecting the dominant ideological concept of the cinema. The alternative cinema provides a space for a cinema to be born which is radical in both a political and an aesthetic sense and challenges the basic assumptions of the mainstream film. This is not to reject the latter moralistically, but to highlight the ways in which its formal preoccupations reflect the psychical obsessions of the society which produced it, and, further, to stress that the alternative cinema must start specifically by reacting against these obsessions and assumptions. A politically and aesthetically avant-garde cinema is now possible, but it can still only exist as a counterpoint.

The magic of the Hollywood style at its best (and of all the cinema which fell within its sphere of influence) arose, not exclusively, but in one important aspect, from its skilled and satisfying manipulation of visual pleasure. Unchallenged, mainstream film coded the erotic into the language of the dominant patriarchal order. In the highly developed Hollywood cinema it was only through these codes that the alienated subject, torn in his imaginary memory by a sense of loss, by the terror of potential lack in phantasy, came near to finding a glimpse of satisfaction: through its formal beauty and its play on his own formative obsessions. This article will discuss the interweaving of that erotic pleasure in film, its meaning, and in particular the central place of the image of woman. It is said that analysing pleasure, or beauty, destroys it. That is the intention of this article. The satisfaction and reinforcement of the ego that represent the high point of film history hitherto must be attacked. Not in favour of a reconstructed new pleasure, which cannot exist in the abstract, nor of intellectualized unpleasure, but to make way for a total negation of the ease and plenitude of the narrative fiction film. The alternative is the thrill that comes from leaving the past behind without rejecting it, transcending outworn or oppressive forms, or daring to break with normal pleasurable expectations in order to conceive a new language of desire.

Pleasure in Looking/Fascination with the Human Form

A

The cinema offers a number of possible pleasures. One is scopophilia. There are circumstances in which looking itself is a source of pleasure, just as, in the reverse formation, there is pleasure in being looked at. Originally, in his "Three Essays on the Theory of Sexuality", Freud isolated scopophilia as one of the component instincts of sexuality which exist as drives quite independently of the erotogenic zones. At this point he associated scopophilia with taking other people as objects, subjecting them to a controlling and curious gaze. His particular examples centre around the voyeuristic activities of children, their desire to see and make sure of the private and the forbidden (curiosity about other people's genital and bodily functions, about the presence or absence of the penis and, retrospectively, about the primal scene). In this analysis scopophilia is essentially active. (Later, in "Instincts and their Vicissitudes", Freud developed his theory of scopophilia further, attaching it initially to pre-genital auto-eroticism, after which the pleasure of the look is transferred to others by analogy. There is a close working here of the relationship between the active instinct and its further development in a narcissistic form.) Although the instinct is modified by other factors, in particular the constitution of the ego, it continues to exist as the erotic basis for pleasure in looking at another person as object. At the extreme, it can become fixated into a perversion, producing obsessive voyeurs and Peeping Toms, whose only sexual satisfaction can come from watching, in an active controlling sense, an objectified other.

At first glance, the cinema would seem to be remote from the undercover world of the surreptitious observation of an unknowing and unwilling victim. What is seen of the screen is so manifestly shown. But the mass of mainstream film, and the conventions within which it has consciously evolved, portray a hermetically sealed world which unwinds magically, indifferent to the presence of the audience, producing for them a sense of separation and playing on their voyeuristic phantasy. Moreover, the extreme contrast between the darkness in the auditorium (which also isolates the spectators from one another) and the brilliance of the shifting patterns of light and shade on the screen helps to promote the illusion of voyeuristic separation. Although the film is really being shown, is there to be seen, conditions of screening and narrative conventions give the spectator an illusion of looking in on a private world. Among other things, the position of the spectators in the cinema is blatantly one of repression of their exhibitionism and projection of the repressed desire on to the performer.

B

The cinema satisfies a primordial wish for pleasurable looking, but it also goes further, developing scopophilia in its narcissistic aspect. The conventions of mainstream film focus attention on the human form. Scale, space, stories are all anthropomorphic. Here, curiosity and the wish to look intermingle with a fascination with likeness and recognition: the human face, the human body, the relationship between the human form and its surroundings, the visible presence of the person in the world. Jacques Lacan has described how the moment when a child recognizes its own image in the mirror is crucial for the constitution of the ego. Several aspects of this analysis are relevant here. The mirror phase occurs at a time when the child's physical ambitions outstrip his motor capacity, with the result that his recognition of himself is joyous in that he imagines his mirror image to be more complete, more perfect than he experiences his own body. Recognition is thus overlaid with misrecognition: the image recognized is conceived as the reflected body of the self, but its misrecognition as superior projects this body outside itself as an ideal ego, the alienated subject, which, re-introjected as an ego ideal, gives rise to the future generation of identification with others. This mirror moment predates language for the child.

Important for this article is the fact that it is an image that constitutes the matrix of the imaginary, of recognition/misrecognition and identification, and hence of the first articulation of the "I", of subjectivity. This is a moment when an older fascination with looking (at the mother's face, for an obvious example) collides with the initial inklings of self-awareness. Hence it is the birth of the long love affair/despair between image and self-image which has found such intensity of expression in film and such joyous recognition in the cinema audience. Quite apart from the extraneous similarities between screen and mirror (the framing of the human form in its surroundings, for instance), the cinema has structures of fascination strong enough to allow temporary loss of ego while simultaneously reinforcing the ego. The sense of forgetting the world as the ego has subsequently come to perceive it (I forgot who I am and where I was) is nostalgically reminiscent of that pre-subjective moment of image recognition. At the same time the cinema has distinguished itself in the production of ego ideals as expressed in particular in the star system, the stars centring both screen presence and screen story as they act out a complex process of likeness and difference (the glamorous impersonates the ordinary).

C

Subsections A and B above have set out two contradictory aspects of the pleasurable structures of looking in the conventional cinematic situation. The first, scopophilic, arises from pleasure in using another person as an object of sexual stimulation through sight. The second, developed through narcissism and the constitution of the ego, comes from identification with the image seen. Thus, in film terms, one implies a separation of the erotic identity of the subject from the object on the screen (active scopophilia), the other demands identification of the ego with the object on the screen through the spectator's fascination with and recognition of his like. The first is a function of the sexual instincts, the second of ego libido. This dichotomy was crucial for Freud. Although he saw the two as interacting and overlaying each other, the tension between instinctual drives and self-preservation continues to be a dramatic polarization in terms of pleasure. Both are formative structures, mechanisms not meaning. In themselves they have no signification, they have to be attached to an idealization. Both pursue aims in indifference to perceptual reality, creating the imagized, eroticized concept of the world that forms the perception of the subject and makes a mockery of empirical objectivity.

During its history, the cinema seems to have evolved a particular illusion of reality in which this contradiction between libido and ego has found a beautifully complementary phantasy world. In *reality* the phantasy world of the screen is subject to the law which produces it. Sexual instincts and identification processes have a meaning within the symbolic order which articulates desire. Desire, born with language, allows the possibility of transcending the instinctual and the imaginary, but its point of reference continually returns to the traumatic moment of its birth: the castration complex. Hence the look, pleasurable in form, can be threatening in content, and it is woman as representation/image that crystallizes this paradox.

Woman as Image, Man as Bearer of the Look

A

In a world ordered by sexual imbalance, pleasure in looking has been split between active/male and passive/female. The determining male gaze projects its phantasy on to the female figure which is styled accordingly. In their traditional exhibitionist role women are simultaneously looked at and displayed, with their appearance coded for strong visual and erotic impact so that they can be said to connote *to-be-looked-at-ness.* Woman displayed as sexual object is the leitmotif of erotic spectacle: from pin-ups to striptease, from Ziegfeld to Busby Berkeley, she holds the look, plays to and signifies male desire. Mainstream film neatly combined spectacle and narrative. (Note, however, how in the musical song-and-dance numbers break the flow of the diegesis.) The presence of woman is an indispensable element of spectacle in normal narrative film, yet her visual presence tends to work against the development of a story line, to freeze the flow of action in moments of erotic contemplation. This alien presence then has to be integrated into cohesion with the narrative. As Budd Boetticher has put it:

What counts is what the heroine provokes, or rather what she represents. She is the one, or rather the love or fear she inspires in the hero, or else the concern he feels for her, who makes him act the way he does. In herself the woman has not the slightest importance.

(A recent tendency in narrative film has been to dispense with this problem altogether; hence the development of what Molly Haskell has called the "buddy movie", in which the active homosexual eroticism of the central male figures can carry the story without distraction.) Traditionally, the woman displayed has functioned on two levels: as erotic object for the characters within the screen story, and as erotic object for the spectator within the auditorium, with a shifting tension between the looks on either side of the screen. For instance, the device of the showgirl allows the two looks to be unified technically without any apparent break in the diegesis. A woman performs within the narrative: the gaze of the spectator and that of the male characters in the film are neatly combined without breaking narrative verisimilitude. For a moment the sexual impact of the performing woman takes the film into a no man's land outside its own time and space. Thus Marilyn Monroe's first appearance in *The River of No Return* and Lauren Bacall's songs in *To Have or Have Not*. Similarly, conventional close-ups of legs (Dietrich, for instance) or a face (Garbo) integrate into the narrative a different mode of eroticism. One part of a fragmented body destroys the Renaissance space, the illusion of depth demanded by the narrative, it gives flatness, the quality of a cutout or icon rather than verisimilitude to the screen.

B

An active/passive heterosexual division of labour has similarly controlled narrative structure. According to the principles of the ruling ideology and the psychical structures that back it up, the male figure cannot bear the burden of sexual objectification. Man is reluctant to gaze at his exhibitionist like. Hence the split between spectacle and narrative supports the man's role as the active one of forwarding the story, making things happen. The man controls the film phantasy and also emerges as the representative of power in a further sense: as the bearer of the look of the spectator, transferring it behind the screen to neutralize the extra-diegetic tendencies represented by woman as spectacle. This is made possible through the processes set in motion by structuring the film around a main controlling figure with whom the spectator can identify. As the spectator identifies with the main male[1] protagonist, he projects his look on to that of his like, his screen surrogate, so that the power of the male protagonist as he controls events coincides with the active power of the erotic look, both giving a satisfying sense of omnipotence. A male movie star's glamorous characteristics are thus not those of the erotic object of the gaze, but those of the more perfect, more complete, more powerful ideal ego conceived in the original moment of recognition in front of the mirror. The character in the story can make things happen and control events better than the subject/spectator, just as the image in the mirror was more in control of motor co-ordination. In contrast to woman as icon, the active male figure (the ego ideal of the identification process) demands a three-dimensional space corresponding to that of the mirror-recognition in which the alienated subject internalized his own representation of this imaginary existence. He is a figure in a landscape. Here the function of film is to reproduce as accurately as possible the so-called natural conditions of human perception. Camera technology (as exemplified by deep focus in particular) and camera movements (determined by the action of the protagonist), combined with invisible editing (demanded by realism) all tend to blur the limits of screen space. The male protagonist is free to command the stage, a stage of spatial illusion in which he articulates the look and creates the action.

C1

Subsections A and B immediately above have set out a tension between a mode of representation of woman in film and conventions surrounding the diegesis. Each is associated with a look: that of the spectator in direct scopophilic contact with the female form displayed for his enjoyment (connoting male phantasy) and that of the spectator fascinated with the image of his like set in an illusion of natural space, and through him gaining control and possession of the woman within the diegesis. (This tension and the shift from one pole to the other can structure a single text. Thus both in *Only Angels Have Wings* and in *To Have and Have Not*, the film opens with the woman as object of the combined gaze of spectator and all the male protagonists in the film. She is isolated, glamorous, on display, sexualized. But as the narrative progresses she falls in love with the main male protagonist and becomes his property, losing her outward glamorous characteristics, her generalized sexuality, her showgirl connotations; her eroticism is subjected to the male star alone. By means of identi- fication with him, through participation in his power, the spectator can indirectly possess her too.)

But in psychoanalytic terms, the female figure poses a deeper problem. She also connotes something that the look continually circles around but disavows: her lack of a penis, implying a threat of castration and hence unpleasure. Ultimately, the meaning of woman is sexual difference, the absence of the penis as visually ascertain- able, the material evidence on which is based the castration complex essential for the organization of entrance to the Symbolic order and the Law of the Father. Thus the woman as icon, displayed for the gaze and enjoyment of men, the active controllers of the look, always threatens to evoke the anxiety it originally signified. The male unconscious has two avenues of escape from this castration anxiety: preoccupation with the re-enactment of the original trauma (investigating the woman, demystify- ing her mystery), counterbalanced by the devaluation, punishment or saving of the guilty object (an avenue typified by the concerns of the *film noir*); or else complete disavowal of castration by the substitution of a fetish object or turning the repres- ented figure itself into a fetish so that it becomes reassuring rather than dangerous (hence overvaluation, the cult of the female star). This second avenue, fetishistic scopophilia, builds up the physical beauty of the object, transforming it into something satisfying in itself. The first avenue, voyeurism, on the contrary, has associations with sadism: pleasure lies in ascertaining guilt (immediately associated with castration), asserting control and subjecting the guilty person through punishment or forgiveness. This sadistic side fits in well with narrative. Sadism demands a story, depends on making something happen, forcing a change in another person, a battle of will and strength, victory/defeat, all occurring in a linear time with a beginning and an end. Fetishistic scopophilia, on the other hand, can exist outside linear time as the erotic instinct is focused on the look alone. These contradictions and ambiguities can be illustrated more simply by using works by Hitchcock and Sternberg, both of whom take the look almost as the content or subject matter of many of their films. Hitchcock is the more complex, as he uses both mechanisms. Sternberg's work, on the other hand, provides many pure examples of fetishistic scopophilia.

C2

It is well known that Sternberg once said he would welcome his films being projected upside down so that story and character involvement would not interfere with the spectator's undiluted appreciation of the screen image. This statement is revealing but ingenuous. Ingenuous in that his films do demand that the figure of the woman (Dietrich, in the cycle of films with her, as the ultimate example) should be identifiable. But revealing in that it emphasizes the fact that for him the pictorial space enclosed by the frame is paramount rather than narrative or identification processes. While Hitchcock goes into the investigative side of voyeurism, Sternberg produces the ultimate fetish, taking it to the point where the powerful look of the male protagonist (characteristic of traditional narrative film) is broken in favour of the image in direct erotic rapport with the spectator. The beauty of the woman as object and the screen space coalesce; she is no longer the bearer of guilt but a perfect product, whose body, stylized and fragmented by close-ups, is the content of the film and the direct recipient of the spectator's look. Sternberg plays down the illusion of screen depth; his screen tends to be one-dimensional, as light and shade, lace, steam, foliage, net, streamers, etc. reduce the visual field. There is little or no mediation of the look through the eyes of the main male protagonist. On the contrary, shadowy presences like La Bessière in *Morocco* act as surrogates for the director, detached as they are from audience identification. Despite Sternberg's insistence that his stories are irrelevant, it is significant that they are concerned with situation, not suspense, and cyclical rather than linear time, while plot complications revolve around misunderstanding rather than conflict. The most important absence is that of the controlling male gaze within the screen scene. The high point of emotional drama in the most typical Dietrich films, her supreme moments of erotic meaning, take place in the absence of the man she loves in the fiction. There are other witnesses, other spectators watching her on the screen, their gaze is one with, not standing in for, that of the audience. At the end of *Morocco*, Tom Brown has already disappeared into the desert when Amy Jolly kicks off her gold sandals and walks after him. At the end of *Dishonoured*, Kranau is indifferent to the fate of Magda. In both cases, the erotic impact, sanctified by death, is displayed as a spectacle for the audience. The male hero misunderstands and, above all, does not see.

In Hitchcock, by contrast, the male hero does see precisely what the audience sees. However, in the films I shall discuss here, he takes fascination with an image through scopophilic eroticism as the subject of the film. Moreover, in these cases the hero portrays the contradictions and tensions experienced by the spectator. In *Vertigo* in particular, but also in *Marnie* and *Rear Window*, the look is central to the plot, oscillating between voyeurism and fetishistic fascination. As a twist, a further manipulation of the normal viewing process which in some sense reveals it, Hitchcock uses the process of identification normally associated with ideological correctness and the recognition of established morality and shows up its perverted side. Hitchcock has never concealed his interest in voyeurism, cinematic and non-cinematic. His heroes are exemplary of the symbolic order and the law – a policeman (*Vertigo*), a dominant male possessing money and power (*Marnie*) – but their erotic drives lead them into compromised situations. The power to subject another person to the will sadistically or to the gaze voyeuristically is turned on to the woman as the object of both. Power is backed by a certainty of legal right and the established guilt of the woman (evoking castration, psychoanalytically speaking). True perversion is barely concealed under a shallow mask of ideological correctness – the man is on the right side of the law, the woman on the wrong. Hitchcock's skilful use of identification processes and liberal use of subjective camera from the point-of-view of the male protagonist draw the spectators deeply into his position, making them share his uneasy gaze. The audience is absorbed into a voyeuristic situation within the screen scene and diegesis which parodies his own in the cinema. In his analysis of *Rear Window*, Douchet takes the film as a metaphor for the cinema. Jeffries is the audience, the events in the apartment block opposite correspond to the screen. As he watches, an erotic dimension is added to his look, a central image to the drama. His girlfriend Lisa had been of little sexual interest to him, more or less a drag, so long as she remained on the spectator side. When she crosses the barrier between his room and the block opposite, their relationship is reborn erotically. He does not merely watch her through his lens, as a distant meaningful image, he also sees her as a guilty intruder exposed by a dangerous man threatening her with punishment, and thus finally saves her. Lisa's exhibitionism has already been established by her obsessive interest in dress and style, in being a passive image of visual perfection; Jeffries's voyeurism and activity have also been established through his work as a photo-journalist, a maker of stories and captor of images. However, his enforced inactivity, binding him to his seat as a spectator, puts him squarely in the phantasy position of the cinema audience.

In *Vertigo*, subjective camera predominates. Apart from one flashback from Judy's point-of-view, the narrative is woven around what Scottie sees or fails to see. The audience follows the growth of his erotic obsession and subsequent despair precisely from his point-of-view. Scottie's voyeurism is blatant: he falls in love with a woman he follows and spies on without speaking to. Its sadistic side is equally blatant: he has chosen (and freely chosen, for he had been a successful lawyer) to be a policeman, with all the attendant possibilities of pursuit and investigation. As a result, he follows, watches and falls in love with a perfect image of female beauty and mystery. Once he actually confronts her, his erotic drive is to break her down and force her to tell by persistent cross-questioning. Then, in the second part of the film, he re-enacts his obsessive involvement with the image he loved to watch secretly. He reconstructs Judy as Madeleine, forces her to conform in every detail to the actual physical appearance of his fetish. Her exhibitionism, her masochism, make her an ideal passive counterpart to Scottie's active sadistic voyeurism. She knows her part is to perform, and only by playing it through and then replaying it can she keep Scottie's erotic interest. But in the repetition he does break her down and succeeds in exposing her guilt. His curiosity wins through and she is punished. In *Vertigo*, erotic involvement with the look is disorientating: the spectator's fascination is turned against him as the narrative carries him through and entwines him with the pro- cesses that he is himself exercising. The Hitchcock hero here is firmly placed within the symbolic order, in narrative terms. He has all the attributes of the patriarchal superego. Hence the spectator, lulled into a false sense of security by the apparent legality of his surrogate, sees through his look and finds himself exposed as complicit, caught in the moral ambiguity of looking. Far from being simply an aside on the perversion of the police, *Vertigo* focuses on the implications of the active/looking, passive/looked-at split in terms of sexual difference and the power of the male Symbolic encapsulated in the hero. Marnie, too, performs for Mark Rutland's gaze and masquerades as the perfect to-be-looked-at image. He, too, is on the side of the law until, drawn in by obsession with her guilt, her secret, he longs to see her in the act of committing a crime, make her confess and thus save her. So he, too, becomes complicit as he acts out the implications of his power. He controls money and words, he can have his cake and eat it.

Summary

The psychoanalytic background that has been discussed in this article is relevant to the pleasure and unpleasure offered by traditional narrative film. The scopophilic instinct (pleasure in looking at another person as an erotic object), and, in con- tradistinction, ego libido (forming identification processes) act as formations, mechanisms, which this cinema has played on. The image of woman as (passive) raw material for the (active) gaze of man takes the argument a step further into the structure of representation, adding a further layer demanded by the ideology of the patriarchal order as it is worked out in its favourite cinematic form – illusionistic narrative film. The argument returns again to the psychoanalytic background in that woman as representation signifies castration, inducing voyeuristic or fetishistic mechan- isms to circumvent her threat. None of these interacting layers is intrinsic to film, but it is only in the film form that they can reach a perfect and beautiful contradic- tion, thanks to the possibility in the cinema of shifting the emphasis of the look. It is the place of the look that defines cinema, the possibility of varying it and exposing it. This is what makes cinema quite different in its voyeuristic potential from, say, striptease, theatre, shows, etc. Going far beyond highlighting a woman's to-be- looked-at-ness, cinema builds the way she is to be looked at into the spectacle itself. Playing on the tension between film as controlling the dimension of time (editing, narrative) and film as controlling the dimension of space (changes in distance, editing), cinematic codes create a gaze, a world and an object, thereby producing an illusion cut to the measure of desire. It is these cinematic codes and their relationship to formative external structures that must be broken down before mainstream film and the pleasure it provides can be challenged.

To begin with (as an ending), the voyeuristic-scopophilic look that is a crucial part of traditional filmic pleasure can itself be broken down. There are three different looks associated with cinema: that of the camera as it records the profilmic event, that of the audience as it watches the final product, and that of the characters at each other within the screen illusion. The conventions of narrative film deny the first two and subordinate them to the third, the conscious aim being always to eliminate intrusive camera presence and prevent a distancing awareness in the audience. Without these two absences (the material existence of the recording process, the critical reading of the spectator), fictional drama cannot achieve reality, obviousness and truth. Nevertheless, as this article has argued, the structure of looking in narrative fiction film contains a contradiction in its own premises: the female image as a castration threat constantly endangers the unity of the diegesis and bursts through the world of illusion as an intrusive, static, one-dimensional fetish. Thus the two looks materially present in time and space are obsessively subordinated to the neurotic needs of the male ego. The camera becomes the mechanism for producing an illusion of Renaissance space, flowing movements compatible with the human eye, an ideology of representation that revolves around the perception of the subject; the camera's look is disavowed in order to create a convincing world in which the spectator's surrogate can perform with verisimilitude. Simultaneously, the look of the audience is denied an intrinsic force: as soon as fetishistic representation of the female image threatens to break the spell of illusion, and the erotic image on the screen appears directly (without mediation) to the spectator, the fact of fetishization, concealing as it does castration fear, freezes the look, fixates the spectator and prevents him from achieving any distance from the image in front of him.

This complex interaction of looks is specific to film. The first blow against the monolithic accumulation of traditional film conventions (already undertaken by radical filmmakers) is to free the look of the camera into its materiality in time and space and the look of the audience into dialectics, passionate detachment. There is no doubt that this destroys the satisfaction, pleasure and privilege of the "invisible guest", and highlights how film has depended on voyeuristic active/passive mechanisms. Women, whose image has continually been stolen and used for this end, cannot view the decline of the traditional film form with anything much more than sentimental regret.

Note

1 There are films with a woman as the main protagonist, of course. To analyse this phenomenon seriously here would take me too far afield. Pam Cook and Claire Johnston's study of *The Revolt of Mamie Stover* in Phil Hardy (ed.), *Raoul Walsh*, Edinburgh, Edinburgh Film Festival (1974), shows in a striking case how the strength of this female protagonist is more apparent than real.

23

Stereotyping

Richard Dyer

Gay people, whether activists or not, have resented and attacked the images of homo-sexuality in films (and the other arts and media) for as long as we have managed to achieve any self-respect. (Before that, we simply accepted them as true and inevitable). The principal line of attack has been on stereotyping.

The target is a correct one. There is plenty of evidence[1] to suggest that stereotypes are not just put out in books and films, but are widely agreed upon and believed to be right. Particularly damaging is the fact that many gay people believe them, lead-ing on the one hand to the self-oppression so characteristic of gay people's lives,[2] and on the other to behaviour in conformity with the stereotypes which of course only serves to confirm their truth. Equally, there can be no doubt that most stereotypes of gays in films are demeaning and offensive. Just think of the line-up – the butch dyke and the camp queen, the lesbian vampire and the sadistic queer, the predatory schoolmistress and the neurotic faggot, and all the rest. The amount of hatred, fear, ridicule and disgust packed into those images is unmistakable.

But we cannot leave the question of stereotyping at that. Just as recent work on images of blacks and women has done,[3] thinking about images of gayness needs to go beyond simply dismissing stereotypes as wrong and distorted. Righteous dismissal does not make the stereotypes go away, and tends to prevent us from understanding just what stereotypes are, how they function, ideologically and aesthetically, and why they are so resilient in the face of our rejection of them. In addition, there is a real problem as to just what we would put in their place. It is often assumed that the aim of character construction should be the creation of "realistic individuals", but, as I will argue, this may have as many drawbacks as its apparent opposite, "unreal" stereotypes, and some form of typing may actually be preferable to it. These then are the issues that I want to look at in this article – the definition and function of stereotyping and what the alternatives to it are.

From Richard Dyer, "Stereotyping." In *Gays and Film*, pp. 27–39. New York: Zoetrope, 1984.

Ideology and Types

How do we come to our "understanding" of the people we encounter, in fiction as in life? We get our information about them partly from what other people tell us – although we may not necessarily trust this – and, in fiction, from narrators and from the "thoughts" of the characters, but most of our knowledge about them is based on the evidence in front of us: what they do and how they do it, what they say and how they say it, dress, mannerisms, where they live and so on. That is where the information comes from – but how do we make sense of it? Sociological theory suggests four different, though inter-related, ways of organising this information: *role, individual, type and member.*[4] When we regard a person in their *role*, we are thinking of them purely in terms of the particular set of actions (which I take to include dress, speech and gesture) that they are performing at the moment we encounter them. Thus I may walk down the street and see a road-sweeper, a house-wife, a child, an OAP, a milkman. I know from what they are doing what their social role is, and I know, because I live in this society, that that role is defined by what sociologists call "variables" of occupation, gender, age and kinship. Although this notion of role has developed within a tradition of sociology that views social structure as neutral (not founded upon power and inequality), it is nonetheless valuable because it allows us to distinguish, theoretically at least, between what people do and what they are. However we seldom in practice stop at that, and role usually forms the basis for other inferences we make about people we encounter. We can see a person in the totality of her/his roles – their sum total, specific combination and interaction – a totality that we call an *individual*, complex, specific, unique. Or we can see a person according to a logic that assumes a certain kind-of-person performs a given role, hence is a *type*. Both individual and type relate the information that has been coded into roles to a notion of "personality" – they are psychological, or social psychological, inferences. The last inference we can make, however, is based on the realisation that roles are related not just to abstract, neutral structures but to divisions in society, to groups that are in struggle with each other, primarily along class and gender lines but also along racial and sexual lines. In this perspective, we can see the person – or character, if we're dealing with a novel or film – as a *member* of a given class or social group.

One of the implications of this break-down is that there is no way of making sense of people, or of constructing characters, that is somehow given, natural or correct. Role, individual, type and member relate to different, wider, and politically significant ways of understanding the world – the first to a reified view of social structures as things that exist independently of human praxis, the second and third to explanations of the world in terms of personal dispositions and individual psychologies, and the fourth to an understanding of history in terms of class struggle (though I extend the traditional concept of class here to include race, gender and sex caste). Since the main focus of this article is stereotyping, I shall deal first and at greatest length with the question of type, but I also want to go on to deal with the two chief alternatives to it, individuals and members.

When discussing modes of character construction, it is I think better to use the broad term type and then to make distinctions within it. A type is any simple, vivid, memorable, easily-grasped and widely recognised characterisation in which a few traits are foregrounded and change or "development" is kept to a minimum. Within this, however, we may make distinctions between social types, stereotypes and member types. (I leave out of account here typing from essentially earlier forms of fiction – *e.g.* archetypes and allegorical types – where the type is linked to metaphysical or moral principles rather than social or personal ones.) I shall deal with the first two now, and member types in the last section, since they are in important ways different from social and stereotypes.

The distinction between social type and stereotype I take from Orrin E. Klapp's book *Heroes, Villains and Fools.* The general aim of this book is to describe the social types prevalent in American society at the time at which Klapp was writing (pre-1962), that is to say, the range of kinds-of-people that, Klapp claims, Americans would expect to encounter in day-to-day life. Like much mainstream sociology Klapp's book is valuable not so much for what it asserts as for what it betrays about that which is "taken for granted" in an established intellectual discourse. Klapp's distinction between a social type and a stereotype is very revealing in its implications:

> . . . stereotypes refer to things outside one's social world, whereas social types refer to things with which one is familiar; stereotypes tend to be conceived as functionless or dysfunctional (or, if functional, serving prejudice and conflict mainly), whereas social types serve the structure of society at many points.[6]

The point is not that Klapp is wrong – on the contrary, this is a very useful distinction – but that he is so unaware of the political implications of it that he does not even try to cover himself. For we have to ask – who is the "one" referred to? and whom does the social structure itself serve? As Klapp proceeds to describe the American social types (*i.e.* those within "one's social world"), the answer becomes clear – for nearly all his social types turn out to be white, middle-class, heterosexual and male. One might expect this to be true of the heroes, but it is also largely true of the villains and fools as well. That is to say that there are accepted, even recognised, ways of being bad or ridiculous, ways that "belong" to "one's social world". And there are also ways of being bad, ridiculous and even heroic that do not "belong".

In other words, a system of social- and stereotypes refers to what is, as it were, within and beyond the pale of normalcy. Types are instances which indicate those who live by the rules of society (social types) and those whom the rules are designed to exclude (stereotypes). For this reason, stereotypes are also more rigid than social types. The latter are open-ended, more provisional, more flexible, to create the sense of freedom, choice, self-definition for those within the boundaries of normalcy. These boundaries themselves, however, must be clearly delineated, and so stereotypes, one of the mechanisms of boundary maintenance, are characteristically fixed, clear-cut, unalterable. You appear to choose your social type in some measure, whereas you are condemned to a stereotype. Moreover, the dramatic, ridiculous or horrific quality of stereotypes, as Paul Rock argues, serves to show how important it is to live by the rules:

> It is plausible that much of the expensive drama and ritual which surround the apprehension and denunciation of the deviant are directed at maintaining the daemonic and isolated character of deviancy. Without these demonstrations, typifications would be weakened and social control would suffer correspondingly."

It is not surprising then that the *genres* in which gays most often appear are horror films and comedy.

The establishment of normalcy through social- and stereotypes is one aspect of the habit of ruling groups – a habit of such enormous political consequences that we tend to think of it as far more premeditated than it actually is – to attempt to fashion the whole of society according to their own world-view, value-system, sensibility and ideology. So right is this world-view for the ruling groups, that they make it appear (as it does to them) as "natural" and "inevitable" – and for everyone – and, in so far as they succeed, they establish their hegemony. However, and this cannot be stressed too emphatically, hegemony is an *active* concept – it is something that must be ceaselessly built and rebuilt in the face of both implicit and explicit challenges to it. The subcultures of subordinated groups are implicit challenges to it, recuperable certainly but a nuisance, a thorn in the flesh; and the political struggles that are built within these sub-cultures are directly and explicitly about who shall have the power to fashion the world.

The establishment of hegemony through stereotyping has then two principal features which Roger Brown has termed ethnocentrism, which he defines as thinking "of the norms of one's group as right for men [sic] everywhere", and the assumption that given social groups "have inborn and unalterable psychological characteristics".[5] Although Brown is writing in the context of cross-cultural and inter-racial stereotyping, what he says seems to me eminently transferable to the stereotyping of gays. Let me illustrate this from *The Killing of Sister George*.

By ethnocentrism, Brown means the application of the norms appropriate to one's own culture to that of others. Recasting this politically (within a culture rather than between cultures), we can say that in stereotyping the dominant groups apply their norms to subordinated groups, find the latter wanting, hence inadequate, inferior, sick or grotesque and hence reinforcing the dominant groups' own sense of the legitimacy of their domination. One of the modes of doing this for gays is casting gay relationships and characters in terms of heterosexual sex roles. Thus in *The Killing of Sister George*, George and Childie are very much presented as the man and woman respectively of the relationship, with George's masculinity expressed in her name, gruff voice, male clothes and by association with such icons of virility as horse brasses, pipes, beer and tweeds. However, George is not a man, and is "therefore" inadequate to the role. Her "masculinity" has to be asserted in set pieces of domination (shot to full dramatic hilt, with low angles, chiaroscuro lighting and menacing music), and her straining after male postures is a source of humour. *Sister George* emphasises the absence of men in the lesbian milieu, by structuring Childie and George's quarrels around the latter's fears of any man with whom Childie has dealings and by the imagery of dolls as surrogate children which are used in a cumulatively horrific way (analogous to some to her horror films, including the director's [Robert Aldrich] earlier *Whatever Happened to Baby Jane?* [1962]) to suggest the grotesque sterility of a woman loving another woman (and so denying herself the chance of truly being a woman, *i.e.* a heterosexual mother).

The idea that this image of lesbianism indicates an inborn trait (hence reinforcing the idea that the way the dominant culture defines gays is the way we must always be) is enforced in *Sister George* partly through dialogue to that effect and partly through a chain of imagery linking lesbianism with the natural, bestial or low – the lingered-over *cigar-butt eating* episode, the emphasis on their relationship as founded on *physical domination* rather than affection, George's close friendship with a *prosti-tute* (someone who lives off her natural functions), the *descent* into the Gateways club, the important scene in a *lavatory*, the end of the film with George *mooing* to a deserted studio. The link between lesbians and animals is a strong feature of the iconography of gay women in films-they often wear furs, suede or feather (*e.g. The Haunting, Ann and Eve, Once is not Enough*), are interested in horses or dogs (*e.g. The Fox, La fiancée du pirate*), or are connected, through composition, montage or allusion, with animals (*e.g. Les biches, Lilith*, the cut from two women kissing to a back projection of a tarantula in the "hippie" club in *Coogan's Bluff* [1969]).

What is wrong with these stereotypes is not that they are inaccurate. The implica-tions of attacking them on that ground (one of the most common forms of attack) raise enormous problems for gay politics – first of all, it flies in the face of the actual efficacy of the hegemonic definitions enshrined in stereotypes, that is to say, gay people often believe (I did) that the stereotypes are accurate and act accordingly in line with them; and second, one of the things the stereotypes are onto is the fact that gay people do cross the gender barriers, so that many gay women do refuse to be typically "feminine" just as many gay men refuse to be typically "masculine" and we must beware of getting ourselves into a situation where we cannot defend, still less applaud, such sex-caste transgressions. What we should be attacking in stereo-types is the attempt of heterosexual society to define us for ourselves, in terms that inevitably fall short of the "ideal" of heterosexuality (that is, taken to be the norm of being human), and to pass this definition off as necessary and natural. Both these simply bolster heterosexual hegemony, and the task is to develop our own alternat-ive and challenging definitions of ourselves.

Stereotyping Through Iconography

In a film, one of the methods of stereotyping is through iconography. That is, films use a certain set of visual and aural signs which immediately bespeak homosexuality and connote the qualities associated, stereotypically, with it.

The opening of *The Boys in the Band* shows this very clearly. In a series of brief shots or scenelets, each of the major characters in the subsequent film is introduced and their gay identity established. This can be quite subtle. For instance, while there is the "obvious" imagery of Emory – mincing walk, accompanied by a poodle, shutting up an over-chic, over-gilded furniture store – there is also, cross cut with it, and with shots of the other "boys", Michael going shopping. He wears a blue blazer and slacks, we do not see what he buys. It is a plain image. Except that the blazer, a sports garment, is too smart, the slacks too well pressed – the casualness of the garment type is belied by the fastidiousness of the grooming style. When he signs a cheque, at chic store Gucci's, we get a close-up of his hand, with a large, elaborate ring on it. Thus the same stereotypical connotations are present, whether obviously or mutedly, in the iconography of both Emory and Michael – over-concern with appearance, association with a "good taste" that is just shading into decadence. The other "boys" are similarly signalled, and although there is a range of stereotypes, nearly all of them carry this connotation of fastidiousness and concern with appearance. This observation can be extended to most gay male iconography – whether it be the emphasis on the grotesque artifices of make-up and obvious wigs (*e.g. Death in Venice*), body-building (*e.g. The Detective*), or sickliness of features, connoting not only depravity and mental illness but also the primped, unexposed face of the indoors (non-active, non-sporting) man (*e.g. The Eiger Sanction*).

Iconography is a kind of short-hand – it places a character quickly and economically. This is particularly useful for gay characters, for, short of showing physical gayness or having elaborate dialogue to establish it in the first few minutes, some means of communicating immediately that a character is gay has to be used. This of course is not a problem facing other stereotyped groups such as women or blacks (but it may include the working class), since the basis of their difference (gender, colour) shows whereas ours does not. However, while this is true, and, as I want to argue later, some kind of typing has positive value, it does seem that there may be a further ideological function to the gay iconography. Why, after all, is it felt so necessary to establish from the word go that a character is gay? The answer lies in one of the prime mechanisms of gay stereotyping, synechdoche – that is, taking the part for the whole. It is felt necessary to establish the character's gayness, because that one aspect of her or his personality is held to give you, and explain, the rest of the personality. By signalling gayness from the character's first appearance, all the character's subsequent actions and words can be understood, explained, and explained away, as those of a gay person. Moreover, it seems probable that gayness is, as a material category, far more fluid than class, gender or race – that is, most people are not either gay or non-gay, but have, to varying degrees, the capacity for both. However, this fluidity is unsettling both to the rigidity of social categorisation and to the maintenance of heterosexual hegemony. What's more, the invisibility of gayness may come creeping up on heterosexuality unawares and, fluid-like, seep into the citadel. It is therefore reassuring to have gayness firmly categorised and kept separate from the start through a widely known iconography.

Stereotyping Through Structure

Stereotypes are also established by the function of the character in the film's structures (whether these be static structures, such as the way the film's world is shown to be organised, materially and ideologically, or dynamic ones, such as plot). I'd like here to look at a group of French films with lesbian characters – *Les biches, La chatte sans pudeur, Emmanuelle, La fiancée du pirate, La fille aux yeux d'or, Les garces* and *La religieuse*. Others could have been used, but I am restricting myself to films I have seen relatively recently. I suspect that the vast majority of films with lesbian characters in them are built on the structures I'm about to suggest, but that would require further work. There is no particular reason for picking a group of French films rather than, say, American or Swedish, although lesbian characters have been relatively common in French cinema since the late forties (*e.g. Quai des Orfèvres, Au royaume des cieux, Olivia, Huis clos, Thérèse Desqueyroux, La fille aux yeux d'or* etc.). There is also some polemical intent in the choice – I have deliberately made no distinction between the high-class porn of *Emmanuelle*, the critically acclaimed *auteurist* films *Les biches* and *La religieuse*, the commercial soft porn of *La chatte sans pudeur* and *Les garces*, the quasi-feminist *La fiancée du pirate*, and the chicly decadent *La fille aux yeux d'or*. The point is that lesbian stereotyping is no respecter of artistic merit or intellectual ambition. Whatever the ultimate merits of these films, in terms of lesbianism there is little to choose between them.

There is some iconographic stereotyping in these films. The chief lesbian characters are usually considerably smarter than the other female character(s) – they are often associated with the older world of *haute couture* (older in the sense both of a previous age and of being for older women), their clothes more expertly cut, their appearance always showing greater signs of thought and care, smart coiffure, use of unflashy, quality jewellery, and a taste for clothes made from animal skins. Mannish clothes are also found – jodhpurs and hacking jacket for Irène in *La fiancée du pirate*, khaki shirt and trousers for Bee in *Emmanuelle* – though this never goes so far as actually wearing men's clothes. Rather they are well coutured women's versions of men's clothing. What both types of clothing emphasise are hard, precise lines, never disguising the female form, but presenting it conspicuously without frills or fussiness or any sort of softness – in a word, without "femininity". (The exception here is the Mother Superior in *La religieuse*, who deliberately softens the lines of her habit with frills.) However, the full significance of this, especially as it compares to the rather dressed-down appearance of the central female protagonist, only becomes clear from a consideration of the films' structures.

In terms of the structure of the lesbian relationships as the films show them, it seems that the films always feel a need to recreate the social inequality of heterosexuality within homosexuality. By this I mean that whereas heterosexual relationships involve people defined as social unequals (or oppressor and oppressed, men and women) – an inequality that while not insuperable is always there as a problem in heterosexual relationships – homosexual relationships involve two people who, in terms of sex caste, are equals (both women or both men). Films, however, are seldom happy to acknowledge this and so introduce other forms of social inequality which are seen as having a primary role in defining the nature of the gay relationship. In the case of the films under consideration, this is done primarily through age, but with strong underpinnings of money and class. Thus Leo (*La fille aux yeux d'or*), Elaine (*Les garces*), Bee (*Emmanuelle*), and Frédérique (*Les biches*) are older than "the girl", Juliette, Emmanuelle and Why respectively, while Leo and Frédérique, as well as Irène (*La fiancée du pirate*) are also richer. (This of course in turn relates to the ideological connection of gayness with the idle sexual experimentation of the rich and the mistaken belief that there is no such thing as a working-class gay.) This inequality is more clear-cut between the Mother Superior and Suzanne in *La religieuse*. In the films under discussion, only Martina in *La chatte sans pudeur* is no older or richer than Julie. But it is clear that she, like Leo, Elaine, Bee, Frédérique, Irène and the Mother Superior, is the stronger of the lesbian pair. This is partly because she, like them, is shown to take initiative and precipitate various events in the plot; and partly because, like them, she is involved in the central structure of the film, which we may characterise as a struggle for control.

This struggle is for control over the central female character. Control here means, as much as anything, definition, for what characterises these central figures is that they are without character, they are unformed. (Hence their dress is iconographically almost striking in its non-descriptness.) They are not just passive, they are nothing, an absence. Suzanne takes no decisions after her initial (defeated) stand against taking holy orders – things happen to her, people struggle to make her what they want her to be. The same negative function holds for the others. Why does not even have a name – she is just a question mark. And similarly we never get to know the name of the girl with golden eyes.

In this struggle it is the lesbian who must be defeated. The central character is sexually malleable to a degree – she will be had by anyone, not because she is voracious but because her sexuality is undefined. But defeat of the lesbian by the man signals that the true sexual definition of a woman is heterosexual and that she gets that definition from a man. This is clearest in *Emmanuelle*, where there is not so much a struggle between a lesbian and a heterosexual male protagonist as a progression for Emmanuelle from vaguely unsatisfactory marital sex through lesbianism (with Bee) to relations with Mario. (In this *Emmanuelle* is following the plot structure of very many recent soft pornography films.) After her affair with Bee, Emmanuelle says "I'm not grown up yet" (*i.e.* that relationship was not an "adult" one), while Mario is explicitly introduced as a philosopher-tutor in sexuality. The filming further reflects this progression – where the lesbianism takes place out of doors and is suffused with light, white, the later sex scenes, presided over by Mario, are indoors, dark with patches of deep rich colours. The open air purity and simplicity of lesbianism ("pretty enough in its way", the film grants), is replaced by the dark, vibrant secrets of "mature" sexuality.

There are variations on this structure. In *La religieuse* the opposite of lesbianism is asexuality – but that is defined and demanded by priests, and throughout the film men are seen as sources of rationality set against the various insanities of convent life. In *La fille aux yeux d'or* the lesbian gets her revenge by murdering the girl. In *Les biches*, Why herself murders Frédérique and probably Paul, who, having "defined" her, have now both let her down. In all cases, the "committed" lesbian (as opposed to the "undefined" girl) is seen as a perverse rival to the man (or men), condemned for trying to do what only a man can – or should – really do, that is, define and control women.

The only exception is *La fiancée du pirate*, where Maria rejects both Irène and the men, and leaves the town. Yet despite the wonderful élan of the film's ending,[10] it is still based on the same structure, with the lesbian character playing the same pred-atory, competitive role as in the other films. In other words, even in a film of great feminist appeal, heterosexual thought and feeling structures remain intact. And the gayness is there to reinforce the sense of rightness of those structures.

Individuals

The alternative to character construction through types is often held to be the creation of "individuals". Indeed, in certain usages, this is what the word "charac-ter" means – thus Robert Scholes and Robert Kellogg can remark, "in so far as a character is a type, he [sic] is less a character.[11]

This approach to character construction derives from the novel. As Ian Watt has shown, the novel made a decisive break with previous modes of fiction – in terms of character construction, it replaced historical, mythic or archetypal personages with particular, individuated characters situated in time and space; it introduced the elements of time and memory, and with them changes of personality and con-sciousness of those changes. Watt argues that these developments in fiction went hand in hand with the development of "realist" philosophy (*e.g.* Descartes, Locke), although not necessarily through any direct influence of the one on the other. Rather:

> . . . both the philosophical and the literary innovations must be seen as parallel manifes-tations of larger change – that vast transformation of Western civilisation since the Renaissance which has replaced the unified world picture of the Middle Ages with another very different one – one which presents us, essentially, with a developing but unplanned aggregate of particular individuals having particular experiences at particular times and at particular places.[12]

In other words, capitalism and its peculiar conception of the individual.

In the cinema, character construction in terms of individuality draws on several aspects of the medium – "invisible" photography, which places characters in a definite time and space; stars, whose particularity and real existence outside the film fiction "guarantees" the "uniqueness" of the characters they portray; linear narrative which permits the showing of change over time; acting and scripting traditions which signal the notion of individuality; and, very often, a deliberate "going against" types of the kind analysed by Christine Geraghty in her article on *Alice Doesn't Live Here Any More*.[13]

All of these features are evident in such individuated characterisations as those played by Dorothea Wieck and Hertha Thiele in *Mädchen in Uniform*, Danielle Darrieux in *Olivia*, Dirk Bogarde in *Victim*, Shirley MacLaine in *The Loudest Whisper*, Peter Finch in *Sunday Bloody Sunday*, and Al Pacino in *Dog Day Afternoon*. All avoid the more "expressionist" modes of photography available in their period (*Mädchen in Uniform*) or genre (*Victim*, *Dog Day Afternoon*). All are stars who also have a reputation for being "actors" – *i.e.* not just embodiments of modes of being but also interpreters of roles, fixing character with nuances of gesture, attention to the details of performance etc. Personal change and consciousness of change become key elements in the narrative development – for instance, Shirley MacLaine realises that perhaps after all she did love Audrey Hepburn "like that", and hangs herself; Dirk Bogarde accepts his gayness and resolves to fight blackmail openly in the courts. Stereotypes of gays are shown in *Victim* and *Dog Day Afternoon*, the better to distinguish Bogarde and Pacino from them. (Pacino becomes a hero for the crowd outside the bank, but the film never allows this to become identification with the painted gay activists who turn up to support him.) Going against stereotypes can also operate at the structural level – thus triangle situations like those in the French films (two people of opposite sex in love with the same person) are set up in *The Loudest Whisper* and *Sunday Bloody Sunday*, but Shirley MacLaine and Peter Finch do not fight to control the ones they love but rather insist on granting them autonomy. They even get on with their rivals – James Garner and Glenda Jackson, respectively.

There is no doubt that these performances had a progressive impact. They showed that gays are human – that is, that gays can be portrayed according to the norms of what it is to be human in this society. The problem is that these norms themselves, by their focus on uniqueness and inner growth, tend to prevent people from seeing themselves in terms of class, sex group or race. The very density, richness, refinement and "roundness" of these characterisations, and especially the device of setting up the individual gays over against the stereotypes, make it very difficult to think of there being solidarity, sisterhood or brotherhood, collective identity and action between the gay protagonist and her/his sex caste.[14] The net result is that these films tend to stress gayness as a personality issue, a problem to which there are only individual solutions – suicide (*Mädchen in Uniform*, *The Loudest Whisper*), bank-robbing (*Dog Day Afternoon*), mature resignation (*Sunday Bloody Sunday*) and so on.

This does not mean that individual character construction is unable to deal with social issues, with the determinations that act on a human life. For instance, *Mädchen in Uniform*, as Janet Meyers writes, brings out:

> . . . the causal connection . . . between the control and repression of feelings between women and the maintenance of fascist values.[15]

Equally, *Victim* makes clear how the law operates on the lives of gay men. Yet in both cases the central articulation is still the individual versus society as a whole, not the individual as a member of an oppressed group. This becomes quite clear if one considers *Victim*, the film amongst this group which gets closest to seeing gays as oppressed – but it does that not through Bogarde, who keeps his distance from the other gays, even when he embarks on his personal crusade for law reform, but through the cross-section of gay types that are set over against him (who perhaps come close to being member types rather than stereotypes).

Member Types

Member types are not, in their mode of construction (*i.e.* use of vivid, recognisable icons, lack of development etc.), different from social- and stereotypes. Where they differ is in the correlation made between the type and social reality. Social- and stereotypes are linked to psychological categories, sorts of personality, within or without a cultural hegemony. Member types, on the other hand, are linked to historically and culturally specific and determined social groups or classes and their praxes, which are almost bound to be outside the present cultural hegemony (in so far as it has so much invested in the notion of individuality).

Member types may, for now, be achieved by strategies such as more "obvious" typing, melodrama, fantasy and montage, which, as Pam Cook writes of Dorothy Arzner's films, "denaturalise" the stereotypes, and allow for an understanding of the concrete and ideological forces that determine them.[16] I'd like to suggest how this may happen from an account of *Some of my Best Friends Are...*

Best Friends is obviously similar to *The Boys in the Band* – a single evening in a single setting, with some claim to presenting an anatomy of male gay life. There is not much to choose between them in terms of the particular gallery of types they choose to present. But *Boys* is more subtle and individualising (*i.e.* it is a mixture of type and individual character construction). Its narrative centres on character development (*e.g.* Larry and Hank come to see more clearly the nature of the problems of their relationship and resolve to work at improving it; Alan realises he does love his wife; Michael comes face to face with his own self-disgust, and this brings out reserves of strength in the insecure Donald; and so on). By setting it in a private home and excluding non-gay characters (except Alan) and women, the drama is located in individual personalities, personal strengths and weaknesses. By using loose pacing, allowing for *longueurs* and the illusion of randomness, and eschewing non-naturalistic devices such as non-eye-level camera angles, inserts, varieties of editing rhythm and so on, it conforms to the perceptual conventions of realism. Point for point, *Best Friends* is different.

The narrative is organised around a multiplicity of strands, none of which can be developed in terms of exploration of character, and which usually come to a head in a series of melodramatic or comic set pieces – Terry's mother denouncing him, and Scott insisting he stay with him rather than go and beg her forgiveness; Cheri/Philip, realising Tom cannot accept him (because he's a man), suddenly hoisted above everyone's heads, with wings and wand, to the chant of "We believe in fairies!" – set pieces which orchestrate, respectively, the opposed loyalties of family and sexuality, and the possibility of gay solidarity. That is to say, this organisation of types permits a certain generalising force about the gay *situation*. Particularly interesting here is the way the exaggeratedly heterosexual role-play of the hustler, fag-hag Lita and transvestite Karen (which in the case of the first two is also intended by them as a taunt to the gay characters) is exposed as factitious, inappropriate and masking profound insecurities, alongside the low key style of the couples and the freely embraced camping about of Cheri and the rest.

Where *Boys* is set in a private home, *Best Friends* is set in a gay club, which is controlled by straight society. This allows it to show the operation of oppression on the lives, life-styles (and hence life-types) of gay people. The enclosedness of *Boys* can only be seen as a function of the characters' own cliqueishness, whereas *Best Friends* shows that this banding together (with which straights often reproach gays) is a product of ghettoisation. The song, *Where Do You Go?*, and much of the dialogue, emphasises this. The economics of the ghetto – the straight owner's recognition of the club as "a gravy train", his mock friendly relations with the police to whom he is paying protection – are clearly located in non-gay interests; and the fact that the policeman who collects the protection turns out to be the transvestite Karen's boyfriend reinforces the notion that gay people work in the interests of straight society (often against themselves). The oppressiveness of the ghetto is finally made clear by the end of the film, where our hoped-for romantic moment – Barrett coming back for Michel to commit himself to him rather than clinging on to his empty heterosexual marriage – is denied us because the straight owners cannot be bothered to open up the club for Barrett. We know Michel is inside. As they drive away, one of the barmen remarks that there is still someone in the club asleep, but they decide to leave him – "He'll still be there in the morning – where else has a faggot got to go?" Thus the control of the ghetto – by straights – is shown, schematically perhaps but chillingly too, as destructive of gay relationships.

Best Friends maintains a tight, even old-fashioned, control on the narrative, building to melodramatic climaxes and wringing all the emotion out of them. It makes free use of camera angles and composition to stress the characters' relatedness to the specific environment of the club (thereby reinforcing the notion of a social situation). Cutting in of events from the characters' pasts make connections – of tension and release, of conflicting demands – between how they are placed within the dominant straight culture and the brief, concentrated moment of gayness permitted them in ghetto life. Cut-in fantasy sequences, such as Karen's vision of herself dressed and beautiful as Lita, dancing with the hustler in tie and tails; Howard's daydream of the club members dressed as choristers (thus reintegrating for him his gayness and his religious beliefs) – suggest the gap between aspiration and reality in gay lives.

In all these ways then *Some of My Best Friends Are . . .* suggests the possibility of a mode of representation that does not dissolve concrete social distinctions into psychologistic ones (whether these be individualised or social/stereotypical), but emphasises such distinctions as the basis of collective identity and the heart of historical struggle. It would be absurd to maintain that *Best Friends* actually achieved this (and much more so that it was consciously aiming to). And there is the additional problem that we are brought up to "read" types in the psychologistic ways I've suggested, so that it is doubtful if the majority of cinema-goers would actually construct from *Best Friends* the kind of anatomy of ghetto oppression that I've just done. What I hope to have brought out, however, is the importance of holding on to some concept of typing (in the way we make films, as producers or audience) at the same time as we are exposing the reactionary political force of most social and stereotyping.

Notes

1   See Ken Plummet, *Sexual Stigma*, Tavistock, London, 1974.

2   The concept of self-oppression is crucial to an understanding of the politics of homo-sexuality. It is excellently examined in Andrew Hodges and David Hutter, *With Down-cast Gays*, Pomegranate Press, London, 1974.

3   *E.g.* Jim Pines, *Blacks in Films*, Studio Vista, London, 1975; Claire Johnston (ed.), *Notes on Women's Cinema*, SEFT, London, 1973).

4   Classic texts this in this area include G. H. Mead, *Mind, Self and Society*, University of Chicago Press, 1934; Alfred Schutz in M. Natanson (ed.), *Collected Papers*, Martinus Nijhoff. The Hague, 1967; Peter Berger and Thomas Luckman, *The Social Construction of Reality*, Allen Lane, London, 1967; Talcott Parsons, *The Social System*, Free Press, New York, 1951; Elizabeth Burns, *Theatricality*, Longman, London, 1972. The termi-nology used is my own.

5   A view stemming ultimately from Durkheim but detectable in most mainstream sociology.

6   Orrin E. Klapp, *Heroes, Villains and Fools*, Prentice-Hall, Englewood Cliffs, 1962, p. 16.

7   Paul Rock, *Deviant Behaviour*, Hutchinson, London, 1973, pp. 34–5.

8   Roger Brown, *Social Psychology*, Macmillan, New York & London, 1965, p. 183.

9   *La chatte sans pudeur* and *Les garces* were distributed in this country with the titles *Sexy Lovers and Love Hungry Girls* respectively.

10 The ending of *La fiancée* is a problem, I think. She is probably on her way to join a man who runs a travelling cinema; one of the films he shows, a poster for which she passes on her way out of the village, has the same title as the film we are watching. In a sense then, his film defines her . . .

11 Robert Scholes and Robert Kellogg, *The Nature of Narrative*, OUP, Oxford, 1966, p. 204.

12 Ian Watt, *The Rise of the Novel*, Penguin, 1963, p. 32.

13 Christine Geraghty, "*Alice Doesn't Live Here Any More*", *Movie* (London), No. 22, pp. 39–42.

14 This is perhaps further enforced by the fact that the stars playing the parts are assumed not to be gay – were when the film was made.

15 Janet Meyers, "Dyke Goes to the Movies", *Dyke* (New York), Spring 1976, p. 38.

16 Pam Cook, "Approaching the work of Dorothy Arzner", in Claire Johnson (ed.). *The Work of Dorothy Arzner*, BFI, London, 1974.

24

Eating the Other:
Desire and Resistance

bell hooks

This is theory's acute dilemma: that desire expresses itself most fully where only those absorbed in its delights and torments are present, that it triumphs most completely over other human preoccupations in places sheltered from view. Thus it is paradoxically in hiding that the secrets of desire come to light, that hegemonic impositions and their reversals, evasions, and subversions are at their most honest and active, and that the identities and disjunctures between felt passion and established culture place themselves on most vivid display.

      – Joan Cocks, *The Oppositional Imagination*

Within current debates about race and difference, mass culture is the contemporary location that both publicly declares and perpetuates the idea that there is pleasure to be found in the acknowledgment and enjoyment of racial difference. The commodification of Otherness has been so successful because it is offered as a new delight, more intense, more satisfying than normal ways of doing and feeling. Within commodity culture, ethnicity becomes spice, seasoning that can liven up the dull dish that is mainstream white culture. Cultural taboos around sexuality and desire are transgressed and made explicit as the media bombards folks with a message of difference no longer based on the white supremacist assumption that "blondes have more fun." The "real fun" is to be had by bringing to the surface all those "nasty" unconscious fantasies and longings about contact with the Other embedded in the secret (not so secret) deep structure of white supremacy. In many ways it is a contemporary revival of interest in the "primitive," with a distinctly postmodern slant. As Marianna Torgovnick argues in *Gone Primitive: Savage Intellects, Modern Lives*:

From bell hooks, "Eating the other: Desire and resistance." In *Black Looks: Race and Representation*, pp. 21–39. Boston: South End Press, 1992.

What is clear now is that the West's fascination with the primitive has to do with its own crises in identity, with its own need to clearly demarcate subject and object even while flirting with other ways of experiencing the universe.

Certainly from the standpoint of white supremacist capitalist patriarchy, the hope is that desires for the "primitive" or fantasies about the Other can be continually exploited, and that such exploitation will occur in a manner that reinscribes and maintains the *status quo*. Whether or not desire for contact with the Other, for connection rooted in the longing for pleasure, can act as a critical intervention challenging and subverting racist domination, inviting and enabling critical resistance, is an unrealized political possibility. Exploring how desire for the Other is expressed, manipulated, and transformed by encounters with difference and the different is a critical terrain that can indicate whether these potentially revolutionary longings are ever fulfilled.

Contemporary working-class British slang playfully converges the discourse of desire, sexuality, and the Other, evoking the phrase getting "a bit of the Other" as a way to speak about sexual encounter. Fucking is the Other. Displacing the notion of Otherness from race, ethnicity, skin-color, the body emerges as a site of contestation where sexuality is the metaphoric Other that threatens to take over, consume, transform *via* the experience of pleasure. Desired and sought after, sexual pleasure alters the consenting subject, deconstructing notions of will, control, coercive domination. Commodity culture in the United States exploits conventional thinking about race, gender, and sexual desire by "working" both the idea that racial difference marks one as Other and the assumption that sexual agency expressed within the context of racialized sexual encounter is a conversion experience that alters one's place and participation in contemporary cultural politics. The seductive promise of this encounter is that it will counter the terrorizing force of the *status quo* that makes identity fixed, static, a condition of containment and death. And that it is this willingness to transgress racial boundaries within the realm of the sexual that eradicates the fear that one must always conform to the norm to remain "safe." Difference can seduce precisely because the mainstream imposition of sameness is a provocation that terrorizes. And as Jean Baudrillard suggests in *Fatal Strategies*:

> Provocation – unlike seduction, which allows things to come into play and appear in secret, dual and ambiguous – does not leave you free to be; it calls on you to reveal yourself as you are. It is always blackmail by identity (and thus a symbolic murder, since you are never that, except precisely by being condemned to it).

To make one's self vulnerable to the seduction of difference, to seek an encounter with the Other, does not require that one relinquish forever one's mainstream positionality. When race and ethnicity become commodified as resources for pleasure, the culture of specific groups, as well as the bodies of individuals, can be seen as constituting an alternative playground where members of dominating races, genders, sexual practices affirm their power-over in intimate relations with the Other. While teaching at Yale, I walked one bright spring day in the downtown area of New

Haven, which is close to campus and invariably brings one into contact with many of the poor black people who live nearby, and found myself walking behind a group of very blond, very white, jock type boys. (The downtown area was often talked about as an arena where racist domination of blacks by whites was contested on the sidewalks, as white people, usually male, often jocks, used their bodies to force black people off the sidewalk, to push our bodies aside, without ever looking at us or acknowledging our presence.) Seemingly unaware of my presence, these young men talked about their plans to fuck as many girls from other racial/ethnic groups as they could "catch" before graduation. They "ran" it down. Black girls were high on the list, Native American girls hard to find, Asian girls (all lumped into the same category), deemed easier to entice, were considered "prime targets." Talking about this over-heard conversation with my students, I found that it was commonly accepted that one "shopped" for sexual partners in the same way one "shopped" for courses at Yale, and that race and ethnicity was a serious category on which selections were based.

To these young males and their buddies, fucking was a way to confront the Other, as well as a way to make themselves over, to leave behind white "innocence" and enter the world of "experience." As is often the case in this society, they were confident that non-white people had more life experience, were more worldly, sensual, and sexual because they were different. Getting a bit of the Other, in this case engaging in sexual encounters with non-white females, was considered a ritual of transcendence, a movement out into a world of difference that would transform, an acceptable rite of passage. The direct objective was not simply to sexually possess the Other; it was to be changed in some way by the encounter. "Naturally," the pres-ence of the Other, the body of the Other, was seen as existing to serve the ends of white male desires. Writing about the way difference is recouped in the West in "The 'Primitive' Unconscious of Modern Art, or White Skin, Black Masks," Hal Foster reminds readers that Picasso regarded the tribal objects he had acquired as "witnesses" rather than as "models." Foster critiques this positioning of the Other, emphasizing that this recognition was "contingent upon instrumentality": "In this way, through affinity and use, the primitive is sent up into the service of the Western tradition (which is then seen to have partly produced it)." A similar critique can be made of contemporary trends in inter-racial sexual desire and contact initiated by white males. They claim the body of the colored Other instrumentally, as unexplored terrain, a symbolic frontier that will be fertile ground for their reconstruction of the masculine norm, for asserting themselves as transgressive desiring subjects. They call upon the Other to be both witness and participant in this transformation.

For white boys to openly discuss their desire for colored girls (or boys) publicly announces their break with a white supremacist past that would have such desire articulated only as taboo, as secret, as shame. They see their willingness to openly name their desire for the Other as affirmation of cultural plurality (its impact on sexual preference and choice). Unlike racist white men who historically violated the bodies of black women/women of color to assert their position as colonizer/ conqueror, these young men see themselves as non-racists, who choose to transgress racial boundaries within the sexual realm not to dominate the Other, but rather so that they can be acted upon, so that they can be changed utterly. Not at all attuned to those aspects of their sexual fantasies that irrevocably link them to collective white racist domination, they believe their desire for contact represents a progressive change in white attitudes towards non-whites. They do not see themselves as perpetuating racism. To them the most potent indication of that change is the frank expression of longing, the open declaration of desire, the need to be intimate with dark Others. The point is to be changed by this convergence of pleasure and Otherness. One dares – acts – on the assumption that the exploration into the world of difference, into the body of the Other, will provide a greater, more intense pleasure than any that exists in the ordinary world of one's familiar racial group. And even though the conviction is that the familiar world will remain intact even as one ventures outside it, the hope is that they will reenter that world no longer the same.

The current wave of "imperialist nostalgia" (defined by Renato Rosaldo in *Culture and Truth* as "nostalgia, often found under imperialism, where people mourn the passing of what they themselves have transformed" or as "a process of yearning for what one has destroyed that is a form of mystification") often obscures contemporary cultural strategies deployed not to mourn but to celebrate the sense of a continuum of "primitivism." In mass culture, imperialist nostalgia takes the form of reenacting and reritualizing in different ways the imperialist, colonizing journey as narrative fantasy of power and desire, of seduction by the Other. This longing is rooted in the atavistic belief that the spirit of the "primitive" resides in the bodies of dark Others whose cultures, traditions, and lifestyles may indeed be irrevocably changed by imperialism, colonization, and racist domination. The desire to make contact with those bodies deemed Other, with no apparent will to dominate, assuages the guilt of the past, even takes the form of a defiant gesture where one denies accountability and historical connection. Most importantly, it establishes a contemporary narrative where the suffering imposed by structures of domination on those designated Other is deflected by an emphasis on seduction and longing where the desire is not to make the Other over in one's image but to become the Other.

Whereas mournful imperialist nostalgia constitutes the betrayed and abandoned world of the Other as an accumulation of lack and loss, contemporary longing for the "primitive" is expressed by the projection onto the Other of a sense of plenty, bounty, a field of dreams. Commenting on this strategy in "Readings in Cultural Resistance," Hal Foster contends, "Difference is thus used productively; indeed, in a social order which seems to know no outside (and which must contrive its own transgressions to redefine its limits), difference is often fabricated in the interests of social control as well as of commodity innovation." Masses of young people dissatisfied by U.S. imperialism, unemployment, lack of economic opportunity, afflicted by the postmodern malaise of alienation, no sense of grounding, no redemptive identity, can be manipulated by cultural strategies that offer Otherness as appeasement, particularly through commodification. The contemporary crises of identity in the west, especially as experienced by white youth, are eased when the "primitive" is recouped *via* a focus on diversity and pluralism which suggests the Other can provide life-sustaining alternatives. Concurrently, diverse ethnic/racial groups can also embrace this sense of specialness, that histories and experience once seen as worthy only of disdain can be looked upon with awe.

Cultural appropriation of the Other assuages feelings of deprivation and lack that assault the psyches of radical white youth who choose to be disloyal to western civilization. Concurrently, marginalized groups, deemed Other, who have been ignored, rendered invisible, can be seduced by the emphasis on Otherness, by its commodification, because it offers the promise of recognition and reconciliation. When the dominant culture demands that the Other be offered as sign that progressive political change is taking place, that the American Dream can indeed be inclusive of difference, it invites a resurgence of essentialist cultural nationalism. The acknowledged Other must assume recognizable forms. Hence, it is not African American culture formed in resistance to contemporary situations that surfaces, but nostalgic evocation of a "glorious" past. And even though the focus is often on the ways that this past was "superior" to the present, this cultural narrative relies on stereotypes of the "primitive," even as it eschews the term, to evoke a world where black people were in harmony with nature and with one another. This narrative is linked to white western conceptions of the dark Other, not to a radical questioning of those representations.

Should youth of any other color not know how to move closer to the Other, or how to get in touch with the "primitive," consumer culture promises to show the way. It is within the commercial realm of advertising that the drama of Otherness finds expression. Encounters with Otherness are clearly marked as more exciting, more intense, and more threatening. The lure is the combination of pleasure and danger. In the cultural marketplace the Other is coded as having the capacity to be more alive, as holding the secret that will allow those who venture and dare to break with the cultural anhedonia (defined in Sam Keen's *The Passionate Life* as "the insensitivity to pleasure, the incapacity for experiencing happiness") and experience sensual and spiritual renewal. Before his untimely death, Michel Foucault, the quintessential transgressive thinker in the west, confessed that he had real difficulties experiencing pleasure:

> I think that pleasure is a very difficult behavior. It's not as simple as that to enjoy one's self. And I must say that's my dream. I would like and I hope I die of an overdose of pleasure of any kind. Because I think it's really difficult and I always have the feeling that I do not feel *the* pleasure, the complete total pleasure and, for me, it's related to death. Because I think that the kind of pleasure I would consider as *the* real pleasure, would be so deep, so intense, so overwhelming that I couldn't survive it. I would die.

Though speaking from the standpoint of his individual experience, Foucault voices a dilemma felt by many in the west. It is precisely that longing for *the* pleasure that has led the white west to sustain a romantic fantasy of the "primitive" and the concrete search for a real primitive paradise, whether that location be a country or a body, a dark continent or dark flesh, perceived as the perfect embodiment of that possibility.

Within this fantasy of Otherness, the longing for pleasure is projected as a force that can disrupt and subvert the will to dominate. It acts to both mediate and challenge. In Lorraine Hansberry's play *Les Blancs*, it is the desire to experience closeness and community that leads the white American journalist Charles to make contact and attempt to establish a friendship with Tshembe, the black revolutionary. Charles struggles to divest himself of white supremacist privilege, eschews the role of colonizer, and refuses racist exoticization of blacks. Yet he continues to assume that he alone can decide the nature of his relationship to a black person. Evoking the idea of a universal transcendent subject, he appeals to Tshembe by repudiating the role of oppressor, declaring, "I am a man who feels like talking." When Tshembe refuses to accept the familiar relationship offered him, refuses to satisfy Charles' longing for camaraderie and contact, he is accused of hating white men. Calling attention to situations where white people have oppressed other white people, Tshembe challenges Charles, declaring that "race is a device – no more, no less," that "it explains nothing at all." Pleased with this disavowal of the importance of race, Charles agrees, stating "race hasn't a thing to do with it." Tshembe then deconstructs the category "race" without minimizing or ignoring the impact of racism, telling him:

> I believe in the recognition of devices as *devices* – but I also believe in the reality of those devices. In one century men choose to hide their conquests under religion, in another under race. So you and I may recognize the fraudulence of the device in both cases, but the fact remains that a man who has a sword run through him because he will not become a Moslem or a Christian – or who is lynched in Mississippi or Zatembe because he is black – is suffering the utter reality of that device of conquest. And it is pointless to pretend that it doesn't *exist* – merely because it is a lie . . .

Again and again Tshembe must make it clear to Charles that subject to subject contact between white and black which signals the absence of domination, of an oppressor/oppressed relationship, must emerge through mutual choice and negotiation. That simply by expressing their desire for "intimate" contact with black people, white people do not eradicate the politics of racial domination as they are made manifest in personal interaction.

Mutual recognition of racism, its impact both on those who are dominated and those who dominate, is the only standpoint that makes possible an encounter between races that is not based on denial and fantasy. For it is the ever present reality of racist domination, of white supremacy, that renders problematic the desire of white people to have contact with the Other. Often it is this reality that is most masked when representations of contact between white and non-white, white and black, appear in mass culture. One area where the politics of diversity and its concomitant insistence on inclusive representation have had serious impact is advertising. Now that sophisticated market surveys reveal the extent to which poor and materially underprivileged people of all races/ethnicities consume products, sometimes in a quantity disproportionate to income, it has become more evident that these markets can be appealed to with advertising. Market surveys revealed that black people buy more Pepsi than other soft drinks and suddenly we see more Pepsi commercials with black people in them.

The world of fashion has also come to understand that selling products is heightened by the exploitation of Otherness. The success of Benetton ads, which with their racially diverse images have become a model for various advertising strategies, epitomize this trend. Many ads that focus on Otherness make no explicit comments, or rely solely on visual messages, but the recent fall *Tweeds* catalogue provides an excellent example of the way contemporary culture exploits notions of Otherness with both visual images and text. The catalogue cover shows a map of Egypt. Inserted into the heart of the country, so to speak, is a photo of a white male (an *Out of Africa* type) holding an Egyptian child in his arms. Behind them is not the scenery of Egypt as modern city, but rather shadowy silhouettes resembling huts and palm trees. Inside, the copy quotes Gustave Flaubert's comments from *Flaubert in Egypt*. For seventy-five pages Egypt becomes a landscape of dreams, and its darker-skinned people background, scenery to highlight whiteness, and the longing of whites to inhabit, if only for a time, the world of the Other. The front page copy declares:

> We did not want our journey to be filled with snapshots of an antique land. Instead, we wanted to rediscover our clothing in the context of a different culture. Was it possible, we wondered, to express our style in an unaccustomed way, surrounded by Egyptian colors, Egyptian textures, even bathed in an ancient Egyptian light?

Is this not imperialist nostalgia at its best – potent expression of longing for the "primitive"? One desires "a bit of the Other" to enhance the blank landscape of whiteness. Nothing is said in the text about Egyptian people, yet their images are spread throughout its pages. Often their faces are blurred by the camera, a strategy which ensures that readers will not become more enthralled by the images of Otherness than those of whiteness. The point of this photographic attempt at defamiliarization is to distance us from whiteness, so that we will return to it more intently.

In most of the "snapshots," all carefully selected and posed, there is no mutual looking. One desires contact with the Other even as one wishes boundaries to remain intact. When bodies contact one another, touch, it is almost always a white hand doing the touching, white hands that rest on the bodies of colored people, unless the Other is a child. One snapshot of "intimate" contact shows two women with their arms linked, the way close friends might link arms. One is an Egyptian woman identified by a caption that reads "with her husband and baby, Ahmedio A'bass, 22, leads a gypsy's life"; the second woman is a white-skinned model. The linked hands suggest that these two women share something, have a basis of contact and indeed they do, they resemble one another, look more alike than different. The message again is that "primitivism," though more apparent in the Other, also resides in the white self. It is not the world of Egypt, of "gypsy" life, that is affirmed by this snapshot, but the ability of white people to roam the world, making contact. Wearing pants while standing next to her dark "sister" who wears a traditional skirt, the white woman appears to be cross-dressing (an ongoing theme in *Tweeds*). Visually the image suggests that she and first world white women like her are liberated, have greater freedom to roam than darker women who live peripatetic lifestyles.

Significantly, the catalogue that followed this one focused on Norway. There the people of Norway are not represented, only the scenery. Are we to assume that white folks from this country are as at "home" in Norway as they are here so there is no need for captions and explanations? In this visual text, whiteness is the unifying feature – not culture. Of course, for *Tweeds* to exploit Otherness to dramatize "whiteness" while in Egypt, it cannot include darker-skinned models since the play on contrasts that is meant to highlight "whiteness" could not happen nor could the exploitation that urges consumption of the Other whet the appetite in quite the same way; just as inclusion of darker-skinned models in the Norway issue might suggest that the west is not as unified by whiteness as this visual text suggests. Essentially speaking, both catalogues evoke a sense that white people are homogeneous and share "white bread culture."

Those progressive white intellectuals who are particularly critical of "essentialist" notions of identity when writing about mass culture, race, and gender have not focused their critiques on white identity and the way essentialism informs representations of whiteness. It is always the non-white, or in some cases the non-heterosexual Other, who is guilty of essentialism. Few white intellectuals call attention to the way in which the contemporary obsession with white consumption of the dark Other has served as a catalyst for the resurgence of essentialist based racial and ethnic nationalism. Black nationalism, with its emphasis on black separatism, is resurging as a response to the assumption that white cultural imperialism and white yearning to possess the Other are invading black life, appropriating and violating black culture. As a survival strategy, black nationalism surfaces most strongly when white cultural appropriation of black culture threatens to decontextualize and thereby erase knowledge of the specific historical and social context of black experience from which cultural productions and distinct black styles emerge. Yet most white intellectuals writing critically about black culture do not see these constructive dimensions of black nationalism and tend to see it instead as naive essentialism, rooted in notions of ethnic purity that resemble white racist assumptions.

In the essay "Hip, and the Long Front of Color," white critic Andrew Ross interprets Langston Hughes' declaration ("You've taken my blues and gone – You sing 'em on Broadway – And you sing 'em in Hollywood Bowl – And you mixed 'em up with symphonies – And you fixed 'em – So they don't sound like me. Yet, you done taken my blues and gone.") as a "complaint" that "celebrates . . . folk purism." Yet Hughes' declaration can be heard as a critical comment on appropriation (not a complaint). A distinction must be made between the longing for ongoing cultural recognition of the creative source of particular African American cultural productions that emerge from distinct black experience, and essentialist investments in notions of ethnic purity that undergird crude versions of black nationalism.

Currently, the commodification of difference promotes paradigms of consumption wherein whatever difference the Other inhabits is eradicated, *via* exchange, by a consumer cannibalism that not only displaces the Other but denies the significance of that Other's history through a process of decontextualization. Like the "primitivism" Hal Foster maintains "absorbs the primitive, in part *via* the concept of affinity" contemporary notions of "crossover" expand the parameters of cultural production to enable the voice of the non-white Other to be heard by a larger audience even as it denies the specificity of that voice, or as it recoups it for its own use.

This scenario is played out in the film *Heart Condition* when Mooney, a white racist cop, has a heart transplant and receives a heart from Stone, a black man he has been trying to destroy because Stone has seduced Chris, the white call girl that Mooney loves. Transformed by his new "black heart," Mooney learns how to be more seductive, changes his attitudes towards race, and, in perfect Hollywood style, wins the girl in the end. Unabashedly dramatizing a process of "eating the Other" (in ancient religious practices among so called "primitive" people, the heart of a person may be ripped out and eaten so that one can embody that person's spirit or special characteristics), a film like *Heart Condition* addresses the fantasies of a white audience. At the end of the film, Mooney, reunited with Chris through marriage and surrounded by Stone's caring black kin, has become the "father" of Chris and Stone's bi-racial baby who is dark-skinned, the color of his father. Stone, whose ghost has haunted Mooney, is suddenly "history" – gone. Interestingly, this main-stream film suggests that patriarchal struggle over "ownership" (i.e., sexual posses-sion of white women's bodies) is the linchpin of racism. Once Mooney can accept and bond with Stone on the phallocentric basis of their mutual possession and "desire" for Chris, their homosocial bonding makes brotherhood possible and eradic-ates, the racism that has kept them apart. Significantly, patriarchal bonding mediates and becomes the basis for the eradication of racism.

In part, this film offers a version of racial pluralism that challenges racism by suggesting that the white male's life will be richer, more pleasurable, if he accepts diversity. Yet it also offers a model of change that still leaves a white supremacist capitalist patriarchy intact, though no longer based on coercive domination of black people. It insists that white male desire must be sustained by the "labor" (in this case the heart) of a dark Other. The fantasy, of course, is that this labor will no longer be exacted *via* domination, but will be given willingly. Not surprisingly, most black folks talked about this film as "racist." The young desirable handsome intelligent black male (who we are told *via* his own self-portrait is "hung like a shetland pony") must die so that the aging white male can both restore his potency (he awakens from the transplant to find a replica of a huge black penis standing between his legs) and be more sensitive and loving. Torgovnick reminds readers in *Gone Primitive* that a central element in the western fascination with primitivism is its focus on "overcoming alienation from the body, restoring the body, and hence the self, to a relation of full and easy harmony with nature or the cosmos." It is this concep-tualization of the "primitive" and the black male as quintessential representative that is dramatized in *Heart Condition*. One weakness in Torgovnick's work is her refusal to recognize how deeply the idea of the "primitive" is entrenched in the psyches of everyday people, shaping contemporary racist stereotypes, perpetuating racism. When she suggests, "our own culture by and large rejects the association of blackness with rampant sexuality and irrationality, with decadence and corruption, with disease and death," one can only wonder what culture she is claiming as her own.

Films like *Heart Condition* make black culture and black life backdrop, scenery for narratives that essentially focus on white people. Nationalist black voices critique this cultural crossover, its decentering of black experience as it relates to black people, and its insistence that it is acceptable for whites to explore blackness as long as their ultimate agenda is appropriation. Politically "on the case" when they critique white cultural appropriation of black experience that reinscribes it within a "cool" narrative of white supremacy, these voices can not be dismissed as naive. They are misguided when they suggest that white cultural imperialism is best critiqued and resisted by black separatism, or when they evoke outmoded notions of ethnic purity that deny the way in which black people exist in the west, are western, and are at times positively influenced by aspects of white culture.

Steve Perry's essay "The Politics of Crossover" deconstructs notions of racial purity by outlining the diverse inter-cultural exchanges between black and white musicians, yet he seems unable to acknowledge that this reality does not alter the fact that white cultural imperialist appropriation of black culture maintains white supremacy and is a constant threat to black liberation. Even though Perry can admit that successful black crossover artists, such as Prince, carry the "crossover impulse" to the point where it "begins to be a denial of blackness," he is unable to see this as threatening to black people who are daily resisting racism, advocating ongoing decolonization, and in need of an effective black liberation struggle.

Underlying Perry's condescension, and at times contemptuous attitude towards all expressions of black nationalism, is a traditional leftist insistence on the primacy of class over race. This standpoint inhibits his capacity to understand the specific political needs of black people that are addressed, however inadequately, by essentialist-based black separatism. As Howard Winant clarifies in "Postmodern Racial Politics in the United States: Difference and Inequality," one must understand race to understand class because "in the postmodern political framework of the contemporary United States, hegemony is determined by the articulation of race and class." And most importantly it is the "ability of the right to represent class issues in racial terms" that is "central to the current pattern of conservative hegemony." Certainly an essentialist-based black nationalism imbued with and perpetuating many racial stereotypes is an inadequate and ineffective response to the urgent demand that there be renewed and viable revolutionary black liberation struggle that would take radical politicization of black people, strategies of decolonization, critiques of capitalism, and ongoing resistance to racist domination as its central goals.

Resurgence of black nationalism as an expression of black people's desire to guard against white cultural appropriation indicates the extent to which the commodi-fication of blackness (including the nationalist agenda) has been reinscribed and marketed with an atavistic narrative, a fantasy of Otherness that reduces protest to spectacle and stimulates even greater longing for the "primitive." Given this cultural context, black nationalism is more a gesture of powerlessness than a sign of critical resistance. Who can take seriously Public Enemy's insistence that the dominated and their allies "fight the power" when that declaration is in no way linked to a collect-ive organized struggle. When young black people mouth 1960s black nationalist rhetoric, don Kente cloth, gold medallions, dread their hair, and diss the white folks they hang out with, they expose the way meaningless commodification strips these signs of political integrity and meaning, denying the possibility that they can serve as a catalyst for concrete political action. As signs, their power to ignite critical con-sciousness is diffused when they are commodified. Communities of resistance are replaced by communities of consumption. As Stuart and Elizabeth Ewen emphasize in *Channels of Desire*:

> The politics of consumption must be understood as something more than what to buy, or even what to boycott. Consumption is a social relationship, the dominant relationship in our society – one that makes it harder and harder for people to hold together, to create community. At a time when for many of us the possibility of meaningful change seems to elude our grasp, it is a question of immense social and political proportions. To establish popular initiative, consumerism must be transcended – a difficult but central task facing all people who still seek a better way of life.

Work by black artists that is overtly political and radical is rarely linked to an oppositional political culture. When commodified it is easy for consumers to ignore political messages. And even though a product like rap articulates narratives of coming to critical political consciousness, it also exploits stereotypes and essentialist notions of blackness (like black people have natural rhythm and are more sexual). The television show *In Living Color* is introduced by lyrics that tell listeners "do what you wanna do." Positively, this show advocates transgression, yet it negatively promotes racist stereotypes, sexism, and homophobia. Black youth culture comes to stand for the outer limits of "outness." The commercial nexus exploits the culture's desire (expressed by whites and blacks) to inscribe blackness as "primitive" sign, as wildness, and with it the suggestion that black people have secret access to intense pleasure, particularly pleasures of the body. It is the young black male body that is seen as epitomizing this promise of wildness, of unlimited physical prowess and unbridled eroticism. It was this black body that was most "desired" for its labor in slavery, and it is this body that is most represented in contemporary popular culture as the body to be watched, imitated, desired, possessed. Rather than a sign of pleasure in daily life outside the realm of consumption, the young black male body is represented most graphically as the body in pain.

Regarded fetishisticly in the psycho-sexual racial imagination of youth culture, the real bodies of young black men are daily viciously assaulted by white racist violence, black on black violence, the violence of overwork, and the violence of addiction and disease. In her introduction to *The Body in Pain*, Elaine Scarry states that "there is ordinarily no language for pain," that "physical pain is difficult to express; and that this inexpressibility has political consequences." This is certainly true of black male pain. Black males are unable to fully articulate and acknowledge the pain in their lives. They do not have a public discourse or audience within racist society that enables them to give their pain a hearing. Sadly, black men often evoke racist rhetoric that identifies the black male as animal, speaking of themselves as "endangered species," as "primitive," in their bid to gain recognition of their suffering.

When young black men acquire a powerful public voice and presence *via* cultural production, as has happened with the explosion of rap music, it does not mean that they have a vehicle that will enable them to articulate that pain. Providing narratives that are mainly about power and pleasure, that advocate resistance to racism yet support phallocentrism, rap denies this pain. True, it was conditions of suffering and survival, of poverty, deprivation, and lack that characterized the marginal locations from which breakdancing and rap emerged. Described as "rituals" by participants in the poor urban non-white communities where they first took place, these practices offered individuals a means to gain public recognition and voice. Much of the psychic pain that black people experience daily in a white supremacist context is caused by dehumanizing oppressive forces, forces that render us invisible and deny us recognition. Michael H. (commenting on style in Stuart Ewen's book *All Consuming Images*) also talks about this desire for attention, stating that breakdancing and rap are a way to say "listen to my story, about myself, life, and romance." Rap music provides a public voice for young black men who are usually silenced and overlooked. It emerged in the streets – outside the confines of a domesticity shaped and informed by poverty, outside enclosed spaces where young male bodies had to be contained and controlled.

In its earliest stages, rap was "a male thing." Young black and brown males could not breakdance and rap in cramped living spaces. Male creativity, expressed in rap and dancing, required wide-open spaces, symbolic frontiers where the body could do its thing, expand, grow, and move, surrounded by a watching crowd. Domestic space, equated with repression and containment, as well as with the "feminine" was resisted and rejected so that an assertive patriarchal paradigm of competitive masculinity and its concomitant emphasis on physical prowess could emerge. As a result, much rap music is riddled with sexism and misogyny. The public story of black male lives narrated by rap music speaks directly to and against white racist domination, but only indirectly hints at the enormity of black male pain. Constructing the black male body as site of pleasure and power, rap and the dances associated with it suggest vibrancy, intensity, and an unsurpassed joy in living. It may very well be that living on the edge, so close to the possibility of being "exterminated" (which is how many young black males feel) heightens one's ability to risk and make one's pleasure more intense. It is this charge, generated by the tension between pleasure and danger, death and desire, that Foucault evokes when he speaks of that *complete total pleasure* that is related to death. Though Foucault is speaking as an individual, his words resonate in a culture affected by anhedonia – the inability to feel pleasure. In the United States, where our senses are daily assaulted and bombarded to such an extent that an emotional numbness sets in, it may take being "on the edge" for individuals to feel intensely. Hence the overall tendency in the culture is to see young black men as both dangerous and desirable.

Certainly the relationship between the experience of Otherness, of pleasure and death, is explored in the film *The Cook, the Thief, His Wife and Her Lover*, which critiques white male imperialist domination even though this dimension of the movie was rarely mentioned when it was discussed in this country. Reviewers of the film did not talk about the representation of black characters, one would have assumed from such writing that the cast was all white and British. Yet black males are a part of the community of subordinates who are dominated by one controlling white man. After he has killed her lover, his blonde white wife speaks to the dark-skinned cook, who clearly represents non-white immigrants, about the links between death and pleasure. It is he who explains to her the way blackness is viewed in the white imagination. The cook tells her that black foods are desired because they remind those who eat them of death, and that this is why they cost so much. When they are eaten (in the film, always and only by white people), the cook as native informant tells us it is a way to flirt with death, to flaunt one's power. He says that to eat black food is a way to say "death, I am eating you" and thereby conquering fear and acknowledging power. White racism, imperialism, and sexist domination prevail by courageous consumption. It is by eating the Other (in this case, death) that one asserts power and privilege.

A similar confrontation may be taking place within popular culture in this society as young white people seek contact with dark Others. They may long to conquer their fear of darkness and death. On the reactionary right, white youth may be simply seeking to affirm "white power" when they flirt with having contact with the Other. Yet there are many white youths who desire to move beyond whiteness. Critical of white imperialism and "into" difference, they desire cultural spaces where boundaries can be transgressed, where new and alternative relations can be formed. These desires are dramatized by two contemporary films, John Waters' *Hairspray* and the more recent film by Jim Jarmusch, *Mystery Train*. In *Hairspray*, the "cool" white people, working-class Traci and her middle-class boyfriend, transgress class and race boundaries to dance with black folks. She says to him as they stand in a rat-infested alley with winos walking about, "I wish I was dark-skinned." And he replies, "Traci, our souls are black even though our skin is white." Blackness – the culture, the music, the people – is once again associated with pleasure as well as death and decay. Yet their recognition of the particular pleasures and sorrows black folks experience does not lead to cultural appropriation but to an appreciation that extends into the realm of the political – Traci dares to support racial integration. In this film, the longing and desire whites express for contact with black culture is coupled with the recognition of the culture's value. One does not transgress boundaries to stay the same, to reassert white domination. *Hairspray* is nearly unique in its attempt to construct a fictive universe where white working class "undesirables" are in solidarity with black people. When Traci says she wants to be black, blackness becomes a metaphor for freedom, an end to boundaries. Blackness is vital not because it represents the "primitive" but because it invites engagement in a revolutionary ethos that dares to challenge and disrupt the *status quo*. Like white rappers MC Search and Prime Minister Pete Nice who state that they "want to bring forth some sort of positive message to black people, that there are white people out there who understand what this is all about, who understand we have to get past all the hatred," Traci shifts her positionality to stand in solidarity with black people. She is concerned about her freedom and sees her liberation linked to black liberation and an effort to end racist domination.

Expressing a similar solidarity with the agenda of "liberation," which includes freedom to transgress, Sandra Bernhard, in her new film *Without You I'm Nothing*, also associates blackness with this struggle. In the March issue of *Interview* she says that the movie has "this whole black theme, which is like a personal metaphor for being on the outside." This statement shows that Bernhard's sense of blackness is both problematic and complex. The film opens with her pretending she is black.

Dressed in African clothing, she renders problematic the question of race and identity, for this representation suggests that racial identity can be socially constructed even as it implies that cultural appropriation falls short because it is always imitation, fake. Conversely, she contrasts her attempt to be a black woman in drag with the black female's attempt to imitate a white female look. Bernhard's film suggests that alternative white culture derives its standpoint, its impetus from black culture. Identifying herself with marginalized Others, Bernhard's Jewish heritage as well as her sexually ambiguous erotic practices are experiences that already place her outside the mainstream. Yet the film does not clarify the nature of her identification with black culture. Throughout the film, she places herself in a relationship of comparison and competition with black women, seemingly exposing white female envy of black women and their desire to "be" imitation black women; yet she also pokes fun at black females. The unidentified black woman who appears in the film, like a phantom, looking at herself in the mirror has no name and no voice. Yet her image is always contrasted with that of Bernhard. Is she the fantasy Other Bernhard desires to become? Is she the fantasy Other Bernhard desires? The last scene of the film seems to confirm that black womanhood is the yardstick Bernhard uses to measure herself. Though she playfully suggests in the film that the work of black women singers like Nina Simone and Diana Ross is derivative, "stolen" from her work, this inversion of reality ironically calls attention to the way white women have "borrowed" from black women without acknowledging the debt they owe. In many ways, the film critiques white cultural appropriation of "blackness" that leaves no trace. Indeed, Bernhard identifies that she had her artistic beginnings working in black clubs, among black people. Though acknowledging where she is coming from, the film shows Bernhard clearly defining an artistic performance space that only she as a white woman can inhabit. Black women have no public, paying audience for our funny imitations of white girls. Indeed, it is difficult to imagine any setting other than an all black space where black women could use comedy to critique and ridicule white womanhood in the way Bernhard mocks black womanhood.

Closing the scene shrouded in a cloak that resembles an American flag, Bernhard unveils her nearly nude body. The film ends with the figure of the black woman, who has heretofore only been in the background, foregrounded as the only remaining audience watching this seductive performance. As though she is seeking acknowledgment of her identity, her power, Bernhard stares at the black woman, who returns her look with a contemptuous gaze. As if this look of disinterest and dismissal is not enough to convey her indifference, she removes a tube of red lipstick from her purse and writes on the table "fuck Sandra Bernhard." Her message seems to be: "you may need black culture since without us you are nothing, but black women have no need of you." In the film, all the white women strip, flaunt their sexuality, and appear to be directing their attention to a black male gaze. It is this standpoint that the film suggests may lead them to ignore black women and only notice what black women think of them when we are "right up in their face."

Bernhard's film walks a critical tightrope. On one hand it mocks white appropriation of black culture, white desire for black (as in the scene where Bernhard with a blonde white girl persona is seen being "boned" by a black man whom we later find is mainly concerned about his hair – i.e., his own image) even as the film works as spectacle largely because of the clever ways Bernhard "uses" black culture and standard racial stereotypes. Since so many of the representations of blackness in the film are stereotypes it does not really go against the Hollywood cinematic grain. And like the *Tweeds* catalogue on Egypt, ultimately black people are reduced, as Bernhard declares in *Interview*, to "a personal metaphor." Blackness is the backdrop of Otherness she uses to insist on and clarify her status as Other, as cool, hip, and transgressive. Even though she lets audiences know that as an entertainment "rookie" she had her start working in close association with black people, the point is to name where she begins to highlight how far she has come. When Bernhard "arrives," able to exploit Otherness in a big time way, she arrives alone, not in the company of black associates. They are scenery, backdrop, background. Yet the end of the film problematizes this leave-taking. Is Bernhard leaving black folks or has she been rejected and dismissed? Maybe it's mutual. Like her entertainment cohort Madonna, Bernhard leaves her encounters with the Other richer than she was at the onset. We have no idea how the Other leaves her.

When I began thinking and doing research for this piece, I talked to folks from various locations about whether they thought the focus on race, Otherness, and difference in mass culture was challenging racism. There was overall agreement that the message that acknowledgment and exploration of racial difference can be pleasurable represents a breakthrough, a challenge to white supremacy, to various systems of domination. The over-riding fear is that cultural, ethnic, and racial differences will be continually commodified and offered up as new dishes to enhance the white palate – that the Other will be eaten, consumed, and forgotten. After weeks of debating with one another about the distinction between cultural appropriation and cultural appreciation, students in my introductory course on black literature were convinced that something radical was happening, that these issues were "coming out in the open." Within a context where desire for contact with those who are different or deemed Other is not considered bad, politically incorrect, or wrong-minded, we can begin to conceptualize and identify ways that desire informs our political choices and affiliations. Acknowledging ways the desire for pleasure, and that includes erotic longings, informs our politics, our understanding of difference, we may know better how desire disrupts, subverts, and makes resistance possible. We cannot, however, accept these new images uncritically.

25

British Cultural Studies and the Pitfalls of Identity

Paul Gilroy

It is only in the last phase of British imperialism that the labouring classes of the satellites and the labouring classes of the metropolis have confronted one another directly "on native ground". But their fates have long been indelibly intertwined. The very definition of "what it is to be British" – the centrepiece of that culture now to be preserved from racial dilution – has been articulated around this absent/present centre. If their blood has not mingled extensively with yours, their labour power has long since entered your economic blood-stream. It is in the sugar you stir: it is in the sinews of the infamous British "sweet tooth": it *is* the tea leaves at the bottom of the "British cuppa".

– Stuart Hall

Whenever I felt an inclination to national enthusiasm I strove to suppress it as being harmful and wrong, alarmed by the warning examples of the peoples among whom we Jews live. But plenty of other things remained over to make the attraction of Jewry and Jews irresistible – many obscure emotional forces, which were the more powerful the less they could be expressed in words, as well as clear consciousness of inner identity, the safe privacy of a common mental construction. And beyond this there was a perception that it was to my Jewish nature alone that I owed two characteristics that had become indispensable to me in the difficult course of my life. Because I was a Jew I found myself free from many prejudices which restricted others in the use of their intellect; and as a Jew I was prepared to join the Opposition and to do without agreement with the "compact majority".

– Freud

From Paul Gilroy, "British cultural studies and the pitfalls of identity." In James Curran, David Morley, and Valerie Walkerdine (eds.), *Cultural Studies and Communications*, pp. 35–49. London: Arnold, 1996. © 1996 by Paul Gilroy. Reprinted by permission of the author.

This short piece cannot hope to provide a comprehensive exposition of the concept of identity, its surrogates and kin terms in the diverse writings of cultural studies. Indeed, if the discrepant practices that take place under the tattered banners of British cultural studies can be unified at all, and that must remain in doubt, exploring the concept of identity and its changing resonance in critical scholarship is not the best way to approach the prospect of their unity. Reflecting upon identity seems to unleash a power capable of dissolving those tentative projects back into the contradictory components from which they were first assembled. Highlighting the theme of identity readily flushes out disagreements over profound political and intellectual problems. It can send the aspirant practitioners of cultural studies scuttling back towards the quieter sanctuaries of their old disciplinary affiliations, where the problems and the potential pleasures of thinking through identity are less formidable and engaging. Anthropologists utter sighs of relief, psychologists rub their hands with glee, philosophers relax confident that their trials are over, sociologists mutter discontentedly about the illegitimate encroachments of post-modernism while literary critics look blank and perplexed. Historians remain silent. These characteristic reactions from the more secure positions of closed disciplines underline that few words in the conceptual vocabulary of contemporary cultural analysis have been more flagrantly contested and more thoroughly abused than "identity".

The history of the term, which has a lengthy presence in social thought, and a truly complex philosophical lineage that goes back to the pre-Socratics, is gradually becoming better known (Gleason 1983; Hall 1992a; Calhoun 1994). However, though it has received some attention in debates over modernity and its anxieties, little critical attention has been directed towards the specific puzzle involved in accounting for identity's contemporary popularity. Though the philosophical pedigree of the term is usually appreciated by today's users, identity is invoked more often in arguments that are primarily political rather than philosophical. The popular currency of the term may itself be a symptom of important political conflicts and a signal of the altered character of post-modern politics especially in the overdeveloped countries. Another clue to this change is provided by the frequency with which the noun "identity" appears coupled with the adjective "cultural". This timely pairing is only the most obvious way in which the concept "identity" directs attention towards a more elaborate sense of the power of culture and the relationship of culture to power. It introduces a sense of *cultural* politics as something more substantial than a feeble echo of the *political* politics of days gone by. This cultural politics applies both to the increased salience of identity as a problem played out in everyday life, and to identity as it is managed and administered in the cultural industries of mass communication that have transformed understanding of the world and the place of individual possessors of identity within it.

The stability and coherence of the self has been placed in jeopardy in these overlapping settings. This may help to explain why identity has become a popular, valuable and useful concept. Though the currency of identity circulates far outside the walls of the academy, much of its appeal derives from a capacity to make supply connections between scholarly and political concerns. These days, especially when an unsavoury climate created by the unanswerable accusation of "political correctness" makes too many critical scholars, political thinkers and cultural activists hypersensitive about professional standards and the disciplinary integrity of their embattled work, identity has become an important idea precisely because of these bridging qualities. It is a junction or hinge concept that can help to maintain the connective tissue that articulates political and cultural concerns. It has also provided an important means to both rediscover and preserve an explicitly political dynamic in serious interdisciplinary scholarship.

It would be wrong, however, to imagine that the concept of identity belongs exclusively to *critical* thought, let alone to the emancipatory intellectual and political projects involved in enhancing democracy and extending tolerance. Identity's passage into vogue has also been mirrored in conservative, authoritarian and rightwing thought, which has regularly attempted to use both enquiries into identity and spurious certainty about its proper boundaries to enhance their own interests, to improve their capacity to explain the world and to legitimate the austere social patterns that they favour. The crisis involved in acquiring and maintaining an appropriate form of *national* identity has appeared repeatedly as the principal focus of this activity. It too makes a special investment in the idea of culture, for nations are presented as entirely homogeneous cultural units staffed by people whose hyper-similarity renders them interchangeable.

Apart from these obviously political claims on identity, the concept has also provided an important site for the erasure and abandonment of *any* political aspirations. Clarion calls to comprehend identity and set it to work often suggest that mere politics has been exhausted and should now be left behind in favour of more authentic and powerful forms of self-knowledge and consciousness that are coming into focus. Thus, if the idea of identity has been comprehensively politicized it has also become an important intellectual resource for those who have sought an emergency exit from what they see as the barren world of politics. Identity becomes a means to open up those realms of being and acting in the world which are prior to and somehow more fundamental than political concerns. Any lingering enthusiasm for the supposedly trivial world of politics is misguided, untimely and therefore doomed to be frustrating. It also corrodes identity and can profitably be replaced by the open-ended processes of self-exploration and reconstruction that take shape where politics gives way to more glamorous and avowedly therapeutic alternatives.

This type of reorientation has occurred most readily where reflection on individual identity has been debased by simply being equated with the stark question "who am I?" This deceptively simple question has been used to promote an inward turn away from the profane chaos of an imperfect world. It is a problematic gesture that all too often culminates in the substitution of an implosive and therefore anti-social form of *self*-scrutiny for the discomfort and the promise of public political work which does not assume either solidarity or community but works instead to bring them into being and then to make them democratic. That memorable question ends with a fateful and emphatically disembodied "I". It refers to an entity, that is represented as both the subject of knowing and a privileged location of being. When it sets out in pursuit of truth, this "I" can be made to speak authoritatively from everywhere while being nowhere if only the right methods are brought to bear upon its deployment. This fateful fiction has a long and important history in the modern world, its thinking and its thinking about thinking (Taylor 1989; Haraway 1991). This "I" can readily become a signature and cipher for numerous other problems to which the sign "identity" can help to supply the answers. For example, if we are committed to changing and hopefully improving the world rather than simply analysing it, will political agency be possible if the certainty and integrity of that "I" have been compromised by its unconscious components, by tricks played upon it by the effects of the language through which it comes to know itself or by the persistent claims of the body that will not easily accept being devalued in relation to the mind and the resulting banishment to the domain of unreason? Is the "I" and the decidedly modern subjects and subjectives to which it points, a product or symptom of some underlying history, an effect of individual insertion into and constitution by society and culture? At what point or under what conditions might that "I" bring forth a collective counterpart, a "we"? These are some of the troubling questions that spring to mind in a period when the previously rather contradictory idea of "identity politics" has suddenly begun to make sense.

This is a time in which *what* (no longer even *who*) you are can count for a great deal more than anything that you might do, for yourself and for others. The slippage from "who" to "what" is absolutely crucial. It expresses a reification (thingification) and fetishization of self that might once have been captured by the term "alienation", which was itself a significant attempt to account for the relationship between the subject and the world outside it upon which it relied. Today, social processes have assumed more extreme and complex forms. They construct a radical estrangement that draws its energy from the reification of culture and the fetishization of absolute cultural difference. In other words, identity is inescapably political, especially where its social workings – patterns of identification – precipitate the retreat and contraction of politics.

No inventory currently exists – either inside or outside the flimsy fortifications of existing cultural studies – of the ways in which identity operates politically and how it can change political culture, stretching political thinking so that modern secular distinctions between private and public become blurred and the boundaries formed by and through the exercise of power on both sides of that line are shown to be permeable. Before the preparation of that precious inventory can proceed, we must face how the concept of identity tangles together three overlapping but basically different concerns. This suggestion involves a degree of over-simplification, but it is instructive to try and separate out these tangled strands before we set about making their symptomatic interlinkage a productive feature of our own thinking and writing. Each cluster of issues under the larger constellation of identity has an interesting place in the chequered history of the scholarly and political movement that has come to be known as cultural studies.

The concept of identity points initially towards the question of the self. This is an issue that has usually been approached in the emergent canon of cultural studies via histories of the subject and subjectivity.[1] We should note, however, that it has not been the exclusive property of cultural studies' more theoretically inclined affiliates. These ideas and the characteristic language of inwardness in which they have been expressed are extremely complex and immediately require us to enter the wild frontier between psychological and sociological domains. On this contested terrain we must concede immediately that human agents are made and make themselves rather than being born in some already finished form. The force of this observation has had a special significance in the development of modernity's oppositional movements. Their moral and political claims have arisen from a desire to estrange social life from natural processes and indeed from quarrels over the status of nature and its power to determine history.

Feminist thought and critical analyses of racism have made extensive use of the concept of identity in exploring how "subjects" bearing gender and racial characteristics are constituted in social processes that are amenable to historical explanation and political struggle. The production of the figures "woman" and "Negro" has been extensively examined from this point of view (de Beauvoir 1960; Fanon 1986; Schiebinger 1993). The emergence of these durable but fictive creations has been understood in relation to the associated development of categories of humanity from which women and blacks have been routinely excluded. This kind of critical investigation has endowed strength in contemporary political thinking about the modern self and its contingencies. This is not solely a matter of concern to the "minorities" who have not so far enjoyed the dubious privileges of inclusion in this official humanism.

The obligation to operate historically and thereby to undermine the idea of an invariant human nature that determines social life has been readily combined with psychological insights. This blend provided not only a means to trace something of the patterned processes of individual becoming but to grasp, through detailed accounts of that variable process, the kind of protean entity that a human agent might be (Geertz 1985). The endlessly mutable nature of unnatural humanity can be revealed in conspicuous contrast between different historically and culturally specific versions of the boundedness of the human person. Labour, language and lived interactive culture have been identified as the principal media for evaluating this social becoming.

Each of these options stages the dramas of identity in a contrasting manner. Each, for example, materializes the production and reproduction of gender differences and resolves the antagonistic relationship between men and women differently. All raise the question of hierarchy and the status of visible differences, whether they are based on signs like age and generation, or the modern, secular semiotics of "race" and ethnicity. The ideal of universal humanity certainly appears in a less attractive light once the unsavoury exclusionary practices that have surrounded its coronation at the centre of bourgeois political culture are placed on display. Nietzsche showed long ago how an archaeological investigation of the modern self could lead towards this goal.

Identity can be used to query the quality of relations established between superficial and underlying similarities in human beings, between their similar insides and dissimilar outsides. By criticizing the compromised authority invested in that suspect, transcendent humanity, identity – understood here as subjectivity – presents another issue: the agent's reflexive qualities and unreliable consciousness of its own operations and limits. Posed in this way, the theoretical coherence of identity unravels almost immediately. The concept is revealed to be little more than a name given to one important element in the interminable struggle to impose order on the flux of painful social life.

The impossible modern quest for stable and integral selfhood points towards the second theme that has been (con)fused in the compound inner logic of identity. This is the equally complicated question of sameness. It too has psychological and psychoanalytic aspects. In this second incarnation, identity becomes visible as the point where a concern with individual subjectivity opens out into an expansive engagement with the dynamics of identification: how one subject or agent may come to see itself in others, to be itself through its mediated relationships with others and to see others in itself. Dealing with an agent's consciousness of sameness unavoidably raises the fact of otherness and the phenomenon of difference. Politics enters here as well. Difference should not be confined exclusively to the gaps we imagine between whole, stable subjects. One lesson yielded up by the initial approach to identity as subjectivity is that difference exists within identities – within selves – as well as between them. This means that the longed-for integrity and unity of subjects is always fragile.

In many of the political movements where the idea of a common identity has become a principle of organization and mobilization, there is an idea of interplay between "inner" and "outer" differences that must be systematically orchestrated if their goals are to be achieved. For example, differences within a group can be minimized so that differences between that group and others appear greater. Identity can emerge from the very operations it is assumed to precede and facilitate. The investment in ideas of essential difference that emerges from several different kinds of feminist thinking, as well as from many movements of the racially oppressed and immiserated, confirms that deeper connections have been supposed to reside unseen, hidden beneath or beyond the superficial, non-essential differences that they may or may not regulate.

Identity as sameness can be distinguished from identity as subjectivity because it moves on from dealing with the formation and location of subjects and their historical individuality into thinking about collective or communal identities: nations, genders, classes, generational, "racial" and ethnic groups. Identity can be traced back towards its sources in the institutional patterning of identification. Spoken and written languages, memory, ritual and governance have all been shown to be important identity-producing mechanisms in the formation and reproduction of imagined community. The technological and technical processes that create and reproduce mentalities of belonging in which sameness features have also come under critical scrutiny. Exploring the link between these novel forms of identification and the unfolding of modernity has also provided a significant stimulus to politically engaged interdisciplinary research (Gillis 1994). So far, Benedict Anderson's ground-breaking discussion of the role of print cultures in establishing new ways of relating to the power of the nation-state and experiencing nationality has not acquired a postmodern equivalent. The mediation and reproduction of national and postnational identities in cyberspace and on virtual paper await a definitive interpretation. The changing resonance of nationality and the intermittent allure of subnational and supranational identities demand that we note how theorizing identity as sameness unfolds in turn into a concern with identifications and the technologies that mediate and circulate them. We must acknowledge the difficult work involved in thinking about how understanding identification might transform and enrich political thought and action.

Analysis of communal and collective identity thus leads into the third issue encompassed by identity: the question of solidarity. This aspect of identity concerns how both connectedness and difference become bases on which social action can be produced. This third element moves decisively away from the subject-centred approach that goes with the first approach and the intersubjective dynamic that takes shape when the focus is on the second. Instead, where the relationship between identity and solidarity moves to the centre-stage, another issue, that of the social constraints upon the agency of individuals and groups, must also be addressed. To what extent can we be thought of as making ourselves? How do we balance a desire to affirm the responsibility that goes with accepting self-creation as a process and the altogether different obligation to recognize the historical limits within which individual and collective subjects materialize and act? This reconciliation usually proceeds through an appeal to supra-individual identity-making structures. These may be material, discursive or some heuristic and unstable combination of them both. Attention to identity as a principle of solidarity asks us to comprehend identity as an effect mediated by historical and economic structures, instantiated in the signifying practices through which they operate and arising in contingent institutional settings that both regulate and express the coming together of individuals in patterned social processes.

Apart from its extensive contributions to the analysis of nationality, "race" and ethnicity, the term "identity" has been used to discern and evaluate the institution of gender difference and of differences constituted around sexualities. These unsynchronized critical projects have sometimes coexisted under the ramshackle protection that cultural studies has been able to construct. Conflicts between them exist in latent and manifest forms and have been identified by several authoritative commentators as a key source of the intellectual energy (and perversely as a sign of the seriousness) in some cultural studies writing (Hall 1992b). These tensions have also been presented as part of a corrective counternarrative that has been pitched against some inappropriately heroic accounts of political scholarship and pedagogy in the institutional wellspring of cultural studies: the Centre for Contemporary Cultural Studies at Birmingham University. Undermining those overly pastoral accounts of the Birmingham experience that might obstruct the development of today's cultural studies by mystifying it and sanitizing its embattled origins may be useful. However, those conflicts – which are usually presented as phenomena that arose where the unity of class-oriented work supposedly crumbled under the impact of feminisms and anti-racist scholarship – are only half the story.

In assessing the importance of the concept of identity to the development of cultural studies, it is important to ponder whether that concept – and the agenda of difficulties for which it supplies a valuable shorthand – might have played a role in establishing the parameters within which those conflicts were contained and some-times made useful. I am not suggesting that the term "identity" was used from the start in a consistent, rigorous or self-conscious way to resolve disagreements or to synchronize common problems and problematics. But rather that, with the benefit of hindsight, it is possible to imagine a version of the broken evolution of cultural studies in which thinking about identity – as subjectivity and sameness – can be shown to have been a significant factor in the continuity and integrity of the project as a whole. It may be that an interest in identity and its political workings in a variety of different social and historical sites provided a point of intersection between the divergent intellectual interests from which a self-conscious cultural studies was gradu-ally born. I will suggest below that a tacit intellectual convergence around problems of identity and identification was indeed an important catalyst for cultural studies, and by implication, that identity's capacity to synthesize and connect various enquir-ies into political cultures and cultural politics is something that makes it a valuable asset even now – something worth struggling with and struggling over.

There is an elaborate literature surrounding all three aspects of identity sketched above. It includes work in and around the Marxist traditions that contributed so much to the vision, verve and ethical commitments demonstrated in British cultural studies' early interventionist ambitions. Much feminist writing has also made use of the concept of identity and generated a rich discussion of the political consequences of its deployment (Fuss 1990; Haraway 1990; Riley 1990). But before that genera-tion of feminist scholar-activists was allowed to find its voice, the themes of identity as sameness and solidarity emerged in the political testing ground provided by the urgent commentary on the changing nature of class relations: conflict, solidarity and what we would now call identity. A new understanding of these questions was being produced as new social and cultural movements appeared to eclipse the labour movement, and old political certainties evaporated under pressure from the manifest barbarity of classless societies, a technological revolution and a transformed under-standing of the relationship between the overdeveloped and underdeveloped parts of the planet that had been underlined by decolonization and mass migration. These half-forgotten debates over class are a good place to consider subjectivity, sameness and solidarity because they took place beyond the grasp of body-coded difference in a happy interlude when biology was not supposed, mechanically, to be destiny and classes were not understood to be discrete bio-social units. No one dreamed back then of genes that could predispose people to homelessness or drug abuse.

If a deceptive oblique stroke was sometimes placed between the words "culture" and "identity", this was done to emphasize that the latter was a product of the former – a consequence of anthropological variation. This literature on class encompassed research into both historical and contemporary social relations. It was governed by political impulses that were not born from complacent application of anachronistic Marxist formulae but rather from an acute comprehension of the political limits and historical specificity of Marxist theory. This stance suggested that class relations were an integral part of capitalist societies but that they were not, in themselves, sufficient to generate a complete explanation of any political situation. Insights drawn from other sources were needed to illuminate the process in which the English working class had been born and in order to comprehend the more recent circumstances in which it might be supposed to be undergoing a protracted death. The subtle and thoughtful concern with class and its dynamics yielded slowly and only partially to different agendas set by interpretation of countercultural movements and oppositional practices that had constituted new social actors and consequently new politicized identities. Women, youth, "races" and sexualities: under each of these headings interest in subjectivity, sameness and solidarity developed the order of priorities that had taken shape as a result of exploring class. Partly, this was because an important divergence existed between political movements and consciousness in which the body was an immediate and inescapable issue and those where the relationship to phenotypical variation, though certainly present, was more attenuated, arising, as it were, at one remove.

Historical materialism as a political and philosophical doctrine was strongest where the politicization of the body and the consequent grasp of embodiment as the guarantor of shared identity were weakest. The reluctance to engage biology or the semiotics of the body produced a heavy theoretical investment in the idea of labour as a universal category that could transcend particularity and dissolve differences. Willingness to accept the exclusion of the body from the domains of rational cognition and scientific inquiry was thought to establish the hallmark of intellectual enterprise. The abstraction "labour power" was offered as a means to connect the actions and experiences of different people in ways that made the kind of body in which they found themselves a secondary and often superficial issue. Marx's cryptic observation that there is a "historical and moral element" that affects the differential price paid for the labour power of different social groups suggests otherwise and is an important clue to comprehending how these superficial differences could resist the embrace of a higher unity. This unity was situational. Consciousness of solidarity and sameness as well as collective class-based subjectivity grew from common submission to the regime of production and its distinctive conceptions of time, right and property.

Edward Thompson's 1963 *Making of the English Working Class* broke with the complacent moods of mechanical materialism and productivism and reformulated class analysis in an English idiom that supplied later cultural studies with vital political energy and a distinctive ethical style. Recognizing the strongly masculinist flavour of this important intervention should take nothing away from contemporary attempts to comprehend how it could have grown as much from the context supplied by CND, the New Left and "practical political activity of several kinds, [that] undoubtedly prompted me [Thompson] to see the problems of political consciousness and organisation in certain ways." (Thompson 1980: 14). Thompson's famous statement of the dynamics of class formation is relevant here:

We cannot have love without lovers, nor deference without squires and labourers. And class happens when some men, as a result of common experiences (inherited or shared), feel and articulate the identity of their interests as between themselves, and against other men whose interests are different from (and usually opposed to) theirs. (pp. 8–9)

This is not the place to attempt some hasty resolution of the difficult issues implicit in this formulation, such as the base and superstructure relationship, the tension between different forms of consciousness and the epistemological valency of immediate experience. Nor is this an appropriate moment in which to try and chart the convoluted debates arising from the need to conceptualize the material effects of ideology and the materializing capacities of discourse (Butler 1993). Thompson's celebrated formulation links identity to selfhood, self-interests and political agency. To say that his politicized notion of identity derived from an engagement with powers which operate outside of and sometimes in opposition to those rooted in production, for example, in the residential community, would be too simple. An interest in identity was not injected into the thinking of the labour movement and its scholarly advocates by an alternative feminist historiography. An explicit and implicit concern with the political mechanisms of identity emerged directly if not spontaneously from complex analyses of past class relations. This work by Thompson and others was produced in a continuous dialogue with the urgent obligation to understand the present by seeking its historical precedents. Almost without being aware of the fact, these analyses reached beyond themselves, not towards an all-encompassing holy totality but, in the name of discomforting complexity, towards deeply textured accounts of bounded and conflictual consciousness that could illuminate contemporary antagonisms.

Though he makes use of the idea of identification rather than the concept of identity, something of the same political and imaginative enterprise can be detected in the closing pages of Raymond Williams's *The Long Revolution* (1961: 354). Grasping for the "new creative definitions" through which that oppositional process might be maintained if not completed, Williams wrote of "structures of feeling – the meanings and values which are lived in world and relationships" and "the essential language – the created and creative meanings – which our inherited reality teaches and through which new reality forms and is negotiated (p. 293). Williams's conclusion seeks to make the individualization effect of contemporary society into a problem. It is not therefore surprising that he avoids the ambiguities of identity – a term which has a strongly individualistic undertone. However the theme of political identity as an outcome of conflictual social and cultural processes rather than some fixed invariant condition is clearly present:

> the reasonable man . . . who is he exactly? And then who is left for that broad empty margin, the "public opinion of the day"?
> I think we are all in this margin: it is what we have learned and where we live. But unevenly, tentatively, we get a sense of movement, and the meanings and values extend. (pp. 354–5)

It took me a long time to appreciate how the founding texts of my own encounter with English cultural studies could be seen to converge around the thematics of identity. The key to appreciating this architecture lay in the ideas of nationality and national identity and the related issues of ethnicity and local and regional identity. Structures of feeling and the forms of consciousness that they fostered were nationally bounded. Similarly, for Thompson, the magical happening of class was something that could only be apprehended on a national basis. Along with Thompson's *Making of the English Working Class* and Williams's *The Long Revolution*, Richard Hoggart's *The Uses of Literacy* (1957) can be positioned so that it triangulates the rather ethnocentric space in which cultural development and cultural politics came to be configured as exclusively English national phenomena. Though each of these critical thinkers had his own subnational, regional and local sensitivities and obligations, culture and its political forms were comprehended by all of them on the basis that nationality supplied. To be sure, the nation was often recognized as riven with the antagonist relations that characterized the struggle to create and maintain the domination of one group by others. But the boundaries of the nation formed the essential parameters in which these conflicts took shape. Though by no means always celebratory in tone, none of these important texts conveyed a sense of Britain and British identity being formed by forces, processes that overflowed from the imperial crucible of the nation-state. Williams's fleeting mentions of jazz or Hoggart's scarcely disguised apprehension about the catastrophic consequences of uniform "faceless" internationalism (his code for the levelling effects of American culture) suggest other conclusions and reveal their authors' direct interest in what might be worth protecting and maintaining amidst the turmoil of the post-war reconstruction of British social life.

Each of these founding texts in the cultural studies canon can be read as a study of becoming: as an examination of class-based identity in process – transformed by historical forces that exceed their inscription in individual lives or consciousness and, at the same time, resisting that inevitable transformation.

This often unspoken fascination with the workings of identity has several additional facets. It does not always initiate the tacit collusion with Englishness that has been the festive site of cultural studies' reconciliation to a bunting-bedecked structure of feeling that its democratic, libertarian and reconstructive aspirations once threatened to contextualize if not exactly overturn.

The significantly different political alignments and hopes of these writers, as well as their contrasting stances within the generative political context that the New Left supplied for their attempts to grapple with class, popular culture and communications (Thompson 1981), should not be played down. That the direction of Hoggart's investigations was parallel to those of Thompson and Williams was signalled in the force of his opening question "Who are the working classes?". His thoughtful and stimulating book elaborated the distinguishing features of working-class English cultural identity. They were apprehended with special clarity even as they were assailed by the insidious forces of Americanism and commercialism: as they yielded "place to new" in a process he understood exclusively in terms of diminution and loss: "the debilitating mass trends of the day". The diseased organs of a vanishing working-class culture were anatomized in a sympathetic conservationist spirit. This mournful operation captured the pathological character of their extraordinary post-1945 transformation.

Hoggart's interest in the class-based division of the social world into "them" and "us" and his enthusiasm for the "live and let live" vernacular tolerance that thrived there could not be sustained once the insertion of post-colonial settler-citizens was recognized as a fundamental element in the transformation of Britain that alarmed and excited him. Immigration would become something that tested out the integrity and character of national and class identities in ways that he was not able to imagine. Hoggart's interesting speculations about the lack of patriotism in the working class, their spontaneous anti-authoritarianism and "rudimentary internationalism" sounded hollow. This was not only because complications introduced into the analysis of class and nationalism by the existence of a "domestic" fascism (Mosley 1946) were somewhat brushed over but, more importantly, because he was entirely silent about the social and political problems that mass black settlement was thought to be introducing into the previously calm and peaceable urban districts of England and Wales. It is not illegitimate to point to the narrowness of Hoggart's concerns or, in the light of the subsequent patterning of British racial politics, to remind ourselves that his enigmatic silences on that subject could be used to undermine the authority of his pronouncements overall.

This is not just a question of hindsight. Before Hoggart's great book was published, Kenneth Little's *Negroes in Britain* (1947) had included a section entitled "the coloured man through modern English eyes" (pp. 240–68). Michael Banton's *The Coloured Quarter* (1955) – which had preceded Hoggart into print by some two years – had drawn explicit attention to the problems precipitated by large-scale "Negro immigration" into "the large industrial cities of the North and the Midlands in particular Leeds, Sheffield and Birmingham" (p. 69). By this time, the morality and injustices of the British colour bar had been extensively discussed in a wide range of publications including the *Picture Post* (Kee 1949). The moral and physical health status of "colonial coloured people" had been given a good public airing by this time and associated panics over the proliferation of half-caste children, Negro criminality and vice were all established media themes when Hoggart's book was published.[2]

Learie Constantine (1955) attempted to sum up the situation when, as Harold Macmillan has revealed, the Conservative government discussed the possibility of using "keep Britain white" as its electoral slogan (Macmillan 1973: 73–4). Constantine's insightful view of the class and gender topology of English racism in the same period that produced *The Uses of Literacy* is worth quoting at length. It is a valuable reminder to anyone who would suggest that a sensitivity to the destructive effects of racism did not arise until after the 1958 "race riots" in London's Notting Hill and Nottingham (see Pilkington 1988):

> After practically twenty-five years' residence in England, where I have made innumerable white friends, I still think it would be just to say that almost the entire population of Britain really expect the coloured man to live in an inferior area devoted to coloured people, and not to have free and open choice of a living place. Most British people would be quite unwilling for a black man to enter their home, nor would they wish to work with one as a colleague, nor to stand shoulder to shoulder with one at a factory bench. This intolerance is far more marked in lower grades of English society than in higher, and perhaps it disfigures the lower middle classes most of all, possibly because respectability is so dear to them. Hardly any Englishwomen and not more than a small

proportion of Englishmen would sit at a restaurant table with a coloured man or woman, and inter-racial marriage is considered almost universally to be out of the question. (Constantine 1955: 67)

Repositioned against the backdrop of this minoritarian history, it seems impossible to deny that Hoggart's comprehensive exclusion of "race" from his discussion of postwar class and culture represented clear political choices. His work certainly exemplifies a wider tendency to render those uncomfortable political issues invisible. The same fate awaited the unwanted "coloured immigrants" to whose lives the problems of "race" in Britain became perversely attached. It may be too harsh to judge his inability to perceive the interrelation of "race", nationality and class as a form of myopia induced by an indifferent ethnocentrism and complacent crypto-nationalism, but that is exactly how it seemed to me as a student of cultural studies on the twentieth anniversary of the publication of *The Uses of Literacy*.

What is more important to me now, almost twenty years later still, is the possibility that the distinctive sense of cultural politics created by those precious New Left initiatives supplied critical resources to the investigation of identity. And further, that mingled with insights drawn from other standpoints, these very resources encouraged us to see and to transcend the limits of the quietly nationalistic vision advanced by British cultural studies' imaginary founding fathers.

Thankfully these days, the writing of contemporary cultural history has become a less self-consciously ethnocentric affair than it was in the 1950s. Stuart Hall uncompromisingly insisted that, contrary to appearances, "race" was an integral and absolutely internal feature of British political culture and national consciousness; Hall made a solid bridge not so much from scholarly nationalism to internationalism but towards a more open, global understanding of where Britain might be located in a decolonized and post-imperial world order defined by the cold war. Hall's consistent political engagements with the identity-(re)producing actions of Britain's mass media allocated substantial space to the issue of racism and used it as a magnifying glass through which to consider the unfolding of authoritarian forms that masked their grim and joyless character with a variety of populist motifs.

Particularly when appreciated in concert with the interventions of Edward Said, whose study of the Orient as an object of European knowledge and power endowed cultural studies with new heart in the late 1970s, Hall's work has supplied an invigorating corrective to the morbidity and implosiveness of figures like Williams, Thompson and Hoggart. Said and Hall are both thinkers whose critiques of power and grasp of modern history have been enriched by their own experiences of migration and some ambivalent personal intimacies with the distinctive patterns of colonial social life in Palestine and Jamaica. Both draw explicitly upon the work of Antonio Gramsci and implicitly on the legacy of the itinerant anglophile Trinidadian Marxist C. L. R. James. With the supplementary input of these intellectual but non-academic figures, cultural studies' evaluations of identity were comprehensively complicated by colonialism as well as the enduring power of a different, non-European or marginal modernity that had been forged amidst the cultures of terror that operate at the limits of a belligerent imperial system.

The nation-state could not remain the central legitimizing principle brought to bear upon the analysis of the cultural relations and forms that subsumed identity. It was not only that core units of modern government and production had been constituted from their external activities and in opposition to forces and flows acting upon them from the outside. Henceforth, identities deriving from the nation could be shown to be competing with subnational (local or regional) and supranational (diaspora) structures of belonging and kinship.

The main purpose of this inevitably cursory and oversimplified genealogy of identity is not to rake over the fading embers of the "Birmingham School" or to endorse a specific canon for cultural studies' institutional expansion. It has been to prompt enquiries into what cultural studies' committed scholarship might have to offer to contemporary discussions, not of culture, but of multiculture and multicultural*ism*. Today, the volatile concept of identity belongs above all to the important debate in which multicultural*ism* is being redefined outside the outmoded conventions that governed its earlier incarnations, especially in the educational system. The obvious reply to this demand – for a new theory of multicultural society that can yield a timely strategy for enhancing tolerance and respect – renounces innocent varieties of orthodox pluralism and starts afresh by rethinking cultural difference through notions of hierarchy and hegemony. This is surely valuable but can only be a beginning. Multiculturalism in both Britain and the United States has retreated from re-examining the concept of culture in any thoroughgoing manner and drifted towards a view of "separate but equal" cultures. These parcels of incompatible activity may need to be rearranged in some new compensatory hierarchy or better still, positioned in wholesome relations of reciprocal recognition and mutual equivalence that have been denied hitherto by the unjust operations of power which is not itself comprehended in cultural terms. In this approach, power exists outside of cultures and is therefore able to distort the proper relationship between them. The best remedy for this unhappy state of affairs is supposedly to be found in strengthening political processes and modernity's neutral civic identities so that cultural particularity can be confined and regulated in appropriately private places from which the spores of destructive incommensurability cannot contaminate the smooth functioning of always imperfect democracy. A political understanding of identity and identification – emphatically not a reified identity politics – points to other more radical possibilities in which we can begin to imagine ways for reconciling the particular and the general. We can build upon the contributions of cultural studies to dispose of the idea that identity is an absolute and to find the courage necessary to argue that identity formation – even body-coded ethnic and gender identity – is a chaotic process that can have no end. In this way, we may be able to make cultural identity a premise of political action rather than a substitute for it.

Notes

1   This was a strong component of the early analyses of subculture produced by Paul Willis, Iain Chambers, Dick Hebdige and Angela McRobbie. See also Probyn (1994).
2   For a preliminary survey of the English political discussion of race during this period, see Carter et al. (1987). See also Smith (1986) and Rich (1986).

References

Banton, M., 1955: *The Coloured Quarter*. London: Jonathan Cape.
Butler, J., 1993: *Bodies that Matter*. New York: Routledge.
Calhoun, C. (ed.), 1994: *Social Theory and the Politics of Identity*. Oxford: Basil Blackwell.
Carter, B., Harris, C. and Joshi, S., 1987: "The 1951–55 Conservative Government and the Racialization of Black Immigration", *Immigrants and Minorities*, 6(3).
Constantine, L., 1955: *Colour Bar*. London: Stanley Paul.
De Beauvoir, S., 1960: *The Second Sex*. London: Four Square Books.
Fanon, F., 1986: *Black Skin, White Masks*. London: Pluto Press.
Fuss, D., 1990: *Essentially Speaking*. New York: Routledge.
Geertz, C., 1985: "The Uses of Diversity", *Michigan Quarterly Review*.
Gillis, J. R. (ed.), 1994: *Commemorations: The Politics of National Identity*. Princeton, NJ: Princeton University Press.
Gleason, P., 1983: "Identifying Identity: A Semantic History", *Journal of American History*, 69.
Hall, S., 1992a: In L. Grossberg, et al. (eds.) *Cultural Studies*. New York: Routledge.
Hall, S., 1992b: "The Question of Cultural Identity", in S. Hall, C. Nelson and P. Treichler (eds.) *Modernity and Its Futures*. Oxford: Polity Press.
Haraway, D., 1990: *Simians, Cyborgs and Women*. London: Free Association Books.
Haraway, D., 1991: "Situated Knowledges".
Hoggart, R., 1957: *The Uses of Literacy*. London: Chatto & Windus.
Kee, R., 1949: "Is There a British Colour Bar?", *Picture Post*, 2 July.
Little, K., 1947: *Negroes in Britain*. London: Routledge & Kegan Paul.
Macmillan, H., 1973: *At the End of the Day, 1961–63*. Basingstoke: Macmillan.
Mosley, O., 1946: *My Answer*. Horley: Mosley Publications/Invicta Press.
Pilkington, E., 1988: *Beyond the Mother Country*. London: I. B. Tauris.
Probyn, E., 1994: *Sexing the Self*. Routledge.
Rich, P. B., 1986: "Blacks in Britain: Response and Reaction, 1945–62", *History Today*, 36 (January).
Riley, D., 1990: *Am I That Name?*. Basingstoke: Macmillan.
Schiebinger, L., 1993: *Nature's Body*. Boston, MA: Beacon Press.
Smith, G., 1986: *When Jim Crow Met John Bull: Black American Soldiers in World War II Britain*. London: I. B. Tauris.
Taylor, C., 1989: *Sources of the Self*. Cambridge: Cambridge University Press.
Thompson, E. P., 1980: *The Making of the English Working Class*. Harmondsworth: Penguin
Thompson, E. P., 1981: "Culturalism", in R. Samuel (ed.) *People's History and Socialist Theory*. London: Routledge.
Williams, R., 1961: *The Long Revolution*. London: Chatto & Windus.

26

Under Western Eyes: Feminist Scholarship and Colonial Discourses

Chandra Talpade Mohanty

Any discussion of the intellectual and political construction of "third world feminisms" must address itself to two simultaneous projects: the internal critique of hegemonic "Western" feminisms, and the formulation of autonomous, geographically, historically, and culturally grounded feminist concerns and strategies. The first project is one of deconstructing and dismantling; the second, one of building and constructing. While these projects appear to be contradictory, the one working negatively and the other positively, unless these two tasks are addressed simultaneously, "third world" feminisms run the risk of marginalization or ghettoization from both mainstream (right and left) and Western feminist discourses.

It is to the first project that I address myself. What I wish to analyze is specifically the production of the "third world woman" as a singular monolithic subject in some recent (Western) feminist texts. The definition of colonization I wish to invoke here is a predominantly *discursive* one, focusing on a certain mode of appropriation and codification of "scholarship" and "knowledge" about women in the third world by particular analytic categories employed in specific writings on the subject which take as their referent feminist interests as they have been articulated in the U.S. and Western Europe. If one of the tasks of formulating and understanding the locus of "third world feminisms" is delineating the way in which it resists and *works against* what I am referring to as "Western feminist discourse," an analysis of the discursive construction of "third world women" in Western feminism is an important first step.

Clearly Western feminist discourse and political practice is neither singular nor homogeneous in its goals, interests, or analyses. However, it is possible to trace a coherence of *effects* resulting from the implicit assumption of "the West" (in all its complexities and contradictions) as the primary referent in theory and praxis. My

From Chandra Talpade Mohanty, "Under Western eyes: Feminist scholarship and colonial discourse." In Chandra Talpade Mohanty, Ann Russo, and Lourdes Torres (eds.), *Third World Women and the Politics of Feminism*, pp. 51–80. Bloomington: Indiana University Press, 1991.

reference to "Western feminism" is by no means intended to imply that it is a monolith. Rather, I am attempting to draw attention to the similar effects of various textual strategies used by writers which codify Others as non-Western and hence themselves as (implicitly) Western. It is in this sense that I use the term *Western feminist*. Similar arguments can be made in terms of middle-class urban African or Asian scholars producing scholarship on or about their rural or working-class sisters which assumes their own middle-class cultures as the norm, and codifies working-class histories and cultures as Other. Thus, while this essay focuses specifically on what I refer to as "Western feminist" discourse on women in the third world, the critiques I offer also pertain to third world scholars writing about their own cultures, which employ identical analytic strategies.

It ought to be of some political significance, at least, that the term *colonization* has come to denote a variety of phenomena in recent feminist and left writings in general. From its analytic value as a category of exploitative economic exchange in both traditional and contemporary Marxisms (cf. particularly contemporary theorists such as Baran 1962, Amin 1977, and Gunder-Frank 1967) to its use by feminist women of color in the U.S. to describe the appropriation of their experiences and struggles by hegemonic white women's movements (cf. especially Moraga and Anzaldúa 1983; Smith 1983; Joseph and Lewis 1981; and Moraga 1984), colonization has been used to characterize everything from the most evident economic and political hierarchies to the production of a particular cultural discourse about what is called the "third world."[1] However sophisticated or problematical its use as an explanatory construct, colonization almost invariably implies a relation of structural domination, and a suppression – often violent – of the heterogeneity of the subject(s) in question.

My concern about such writings derives from my own implication and investment in contemporary debates in feminist theory, and the urgent political necessity (especially in the age of Reagan/Bush) of forming strategic coalitions across class, race, and national boundaries. The analytic principles discussed below serve to distort Western feminist political practices, and limit the possibility of coalitions among (usually white) Western feminists and working-class feminists and feminists of color around the world. These limitations are evident in the construction of the (implicitly consensual) priority of issues around which apparently *all* women are expected to organize. The necessary and integral connection between feminist scholarship and feminist political practice and organizing determines the significance and status of Western feminist writings on women in the third world, for feminist scholarship, like most other kinds of scholarship, is not the mere production of knowledge about a certain subject. It is a directly political and discursive *practice* in that it is purposeful and ideological. It is best seen as a mode of intervention into particular hegemonic discourses (for example, traditional anthropology, sociology, literary criticism, etc.); it is a political praxis which counters and resists the totalizing imperative of age-old "legitimate" and "scientific" bodies of knowledge. Thus, feminist scholarly practices (whether reading, writing, critical, or textual) are inscribed in relations of power – relations which they counter, resist, or even perhaps implicitly support. There can, of course, be no apolitical scholarship.

The relationship between "Woman" – a cultural and ideological composite Other constructed through diverse representational discourses (scientific, literary, juridical, linguistic, cinematic, etc.) – and "women" – real, material subjects of their collective histories – is one of the central questions the practice of feminist scholarship seeks to address. This connection between women as historical subjects and the re-presentation of Woman produced by hegemonic discourses is not a relation of direct identity, or a relation of correspondence or simple implication.[2] It is an arbitrary relation set up by particular cultures. I would like to suggest that the feminist writings I analyze here discursively colonize the material and historical heterogeneities of the lives of women in the third world, thereby producing/re-presenting a composite, singular "third world woman" – an image which appears arbitrarily constructed, but nevertheless carries with it the authorizing signature of Western humanist discourse.[3]

I argue that assumptions of privilege and ethnocentric universality, on the one hand, and inadequate self-consciousness about the effect of Western scholarship on the "third world" in the context of a world system dominated by the West, on the other, characterize a sizable extent of Western feminist work on women in the third world. An analysis of "sexual difference" in the form of a cross-culturally singular, monolithic notion of patriarchy or male dominance leads to the construction of a similarly reductive and homogeneous notion of what I call the "third world difference" – that stable, ahistorical something that apparently oppresses most if not all the women in these countries. And it is in the production of this "third world difference" that Western feminisms appropriate and "colonize" the constitutive complexities which characterize the lives of women in these countries. It is in this process of discursive homogenization and systematization of the oppression of women in the third world that power is exercised in much of recent Western feminist discourse, and this power needs to be defined and named.

In the context of the West's hegemonic position today, of what Anouar Abdel-Malek (1981) calls a struggle for "control over the orientation, regulation and decision of the process of world development on the basis of the advanced sector's monopoly of scientific knowledge and ideal creativity," Western feminist scholarship on the third world must be seen and examined precisely in terms of its inscription in these particular relations of power and struggle. There is, it should be evident, no universal patriarchal framework which this scholarship attempts to counter and resist – unless one posits an international male conspiracy or a monolithic, ahistorical power structure. There is, however, a particular world balance of power within which any analysis of culture, ideology, and socioeconomic conditions necessarily has to be situated. Abdel-Malek is useful here, again, in reminding us about the inherence of politics in the discourses of "culture":

> Contemporary imperialism is, in a real sense, a hegemonic imperialism, exercising to a maximum degree a rationalized violence taken to a higher level than ever before – through fire and sword, but also through the attempt to control hearts and minds. For its content is defined by the combined action of the military-industrial complex and the hegemonic cultural centers of the West, all of them founded on the advanced levels of

development attained by monopoly and finance capital, and supported by the benefits
of both the scientific and technological revolution and the second industrial revolution
itself. (145–6)

Western feminist scholarship cannot avoid the challenge of situating itself and
examining its role in such a global economic and political framework. To do any less
would be to ignore the complex interconnections between first and third world
economies and the profound effect of this on the lives of women in all countries.
I do not question the descriptive and informative value of most Western feminist
writings on women in the third world. I also do not question the existence of
excellent work which does not fall into the analytic traps with which I am concerned. In fact I deal with an example of such work later on. In the context of an
overwhelming silence about the experiences of women in these countries, as well as
the need to forge international links between women's political struggles, such work
is both pathbreaking and absolutely essential. However, it is both to the *explanatory
potential* of particular analytic strategies employed by such writing, and to their
political effect in the context of the hegemony of Western scholarship that I want to
draw attention here. While feminist writing in the U.S. is still marginalized (except
from the point of view of women of color addressing privileged white women),
Western feminist writing on women in the third world must be considered in the
context of the global hegemony of Western scholarship – i.e., the production,
publication, distribution, and consumption of information and ideas. Marginal or
not, this writing has political effects and implications beyond the immediate feminist
or disciplinary audience. One such significant effect of the dominant "representations" of Western feminism is its conflation with imperialism in the eyes of particular
third world women.[4] Hence the urgent need to examine the *political* implications of
our *analytic* strategies and principles.

My critique is directed at three basic analytic principles which are present in
(Western) feminist discourse on women in the third world. Since I focus primarily
on the Zed Press Women in the Third World series, my comments on Western
feminist discourse are circumscribed by my analysis of the texts in this series.[5] This is
a way of focusing my critique. However, even though I am dealing with feminists
who identify themselves as culturally or geographically from the "West," as mentioned earlier, what I say about these presuppositions or implicit principles holds for
anyone who uses these methods, whether third world women in the West, or third
world women in the third world writing on these issues and publishing in the West.
Thus, I am not making a culturalist argument about ethnocentrism; rather, I am
trying to uncover how ethnocentric universalism is produced in certain analyses. As
a matter of fact, my argument holds for any discourse that sets up its own authorial
subjects as the implicit referent, i.e., the yardstick by which to encode and represent
cultural Others. It is in this move that power is exercised in discourse.

The first analytic presupposition I focus on is involved in the strategic location of
the category "women" vis-à-vis the context of analysis. The assumption of women as
an already constituted, coherent group with identical interests and desires, regardless
of class, ethnic or racial location, or contradictions, implies a notion of gender or

sexual difference or even patriarchy which can be applied universally and cross-culturally. (The context of analysis can be anything from kinship structures and the organization of labor to media representations.) The second analytical presupposition is evident on the methodological level, in the uncritical way "proof" of universality and cross-cultural validity are provided. The third is a more specifically political presupposition underlying the methodologies and the analytic strategies, i.e., the model of power and struggle they imply and suggest. I argue that as a result of the two modes – or, rather, frames – of analysis described above, a homogeneous notion of the oppression of women as a group is assumed, which, in turn, produces the image of an "average third world woman." This average third world woman leads an essentially truncated life based on her feminine gender (read: sexually constrained) and her being "third world" (read: ignorant, poor, uneducated, tradition-bound, domestic, family-oriented, victimized, etc.). This, I suggest, is in contrast to the (implicit) self-representation of Western women as educated, as modern, as having control over their own bodies and sexualities, and the freedom to make their own decisions.

The distinction between Western feminist re-presentation of women in the third world and Western feminist self-presentation is a distinction of the same order as that made by some Marxists between the "maintenance" function of the housewife and the real "productive" role of wage labor, or the characterization by developmentalists of the third world as being engaged in the lesser production of "raw materials" in contrast to the "real" productive activity of the first world. These distinctions are made on the basis of the privileging of a particular group as the norm or referent. Men involved in wage labor, first world producers, and, I suggest, Western feminists who sometimes cast third world women in terms of "ourselves undressed" (Michelle Rosaldo's [1980] term), all construct themselves as the normative referent in such a binary analytic.

"Women" as Category of Analysis, or:
We Are All Sisters in Struggle

By women as a category of analysis, I am referring to the crucial assumption that all of us of the same gender, across classes and cultures, are somehow socially constituted as a homogeneous group identified prior to the process of analysis. This is an assumption which characterizes much feminist discourse. The homogeneity of women as a group is produced not on the basis of biological essentials but rather on the basis of secondary sociological and anthropological universals. Thus, for instance, in any given piece of feminist analysis, women are characterized as a singular group on the basis of a shared oppression. What binds women together is a sociological notion of the "sameness" of their oppression. It is at this point that an elision takes place between "women" as a discursively constructed group and "women" as material subjects of their own history.[6] Thus, the discursively consensual homogeneity of "women" as a group is mistaken for the historically specific material reality of groups of women. This results in an assumption of women as an always already constituted group, one which has been labeled "powerless," "exploited," "sexually harassed," etc., by feminist scientific, economic, legal, and sociological discourses. (Notice that this is quite similar to sexist discourse labeling women weak, emotional, having math anxiety, etc.) This focus is not on uncovering the material and ideological specificities that constitute a particular group of women as "powerless" in a particular context. It is, rather, on finding a variety of cases of "powerless" groups of women to prove the general point that women as a group are powerless.

In this section I focus on five specific ways in which "women" as a category of analysis is used in Western feminist discourse on women in the third world. Each of these examples illustrates the construction of "third world women" as a homogeneous "powerless" group often located as implicit *victims* of particular socioeconomic systems. I have chosen to deal with a variety of writers – from Fran Hosken, who writes primarily about female genital mutilation, to writers from the Women in International Development school, who write about the effect of development policies on third world women for both Western and third world audiences. The similarity of assumptions about "third world women" in all these texts forms the basis of my discussion. This is not to equate all the texts that I analyze, nor is it to equalize their strengths and weaknesses. The authors I deal with write with varying degrees of care and complexity; however, the *effect* of their representation of third world women is a coherent one. In these texts women are defined as victims of male violence (Fran Hosken); victims of the colonial process (Maria Cutrufelli); victims of the Arab familial system (Juliette Minces); victims of the economic development process (Beverley Lindsay and the [liberal] WID School); and finally, victims of *the* Islamic code (Patricia Jeffery). This mode of defining women primarily in terms of their *object status* (the way in which they are affected or not affected by certain institutions and systems) is what characterizes this particular form of the use of "women" as a category of analysis. In the context of Western women writing/studying women in the third world, such objectification (however benevolently motivated) needs to be both named and challenged. As Valerie Amos and Pratibha Parmar argue quite eloquently, "Feminist theories which examine our cultural practices as "feudal residues" or label us "traditional," also portray us as politically immature women who need to be versed and schooled in the ethos of Western feminism. They need to be continually challenged . . ." (1984, 7).

Women as Victims of Male Violence

Fran Hosken, in writing about the relationship between human rights and female genital mutilation in Africa and the Middle East, bases her whole discussion/ condemnation of genital mutilation on one privileged premise: that the goal of this practice is "to mutilate the sexual pleasure and satisfaction of woman" (1981: 11). This, in turn, leads her to claim that woman's sexuality is controlled, as is her reproductive potential. According to Hosken, "male sexual politics" in Africa and around the world "share the same political goal: to assure female dependence and subservience by any and all means" (14). Physical violence against women (rape, sexual assault, excision, infibulation, etc.) is thus carried out "with an astonishing consensus among men in the world" (14). Here, women are defined consistently as the *victims* of male control – the "sexually oppressed."[7] Although it is true that the potential of male violence against women circumscribes and elucidates their social position to a certain extent, defining women as archetypal victims freezes them into "objects-who-defend-themselves," men into "subjects-who-perpetrate-violence," and (every) society into powerless (read: women) and powerful (read: men) groups of people. Male violence must be theorized and interpreted *within* specific societies, in order both to understand it better and to effectively organize to change it.[8] Sisterhood cannot be assumed on the basis of gender; it must be forged in concrete historical and political practice and analysis.

Women as Universal Dependants

Beverly Lindsay's conclusion to the book *Comparative Perspectives of Third World Women: The Impact of Race, Sex and Class* (1983: 298, 306) states: "dependency relationships, based upon race, sex and class, are being perpetuated through social, educational, and economic institutions. These are the linkages among Third World Women." Here, as in other places, Lindsay implies that third world women constitute an identifiable group purely on the basis of shared dependencies. If shared dependencies were all that was needed to bind us together as a group, third world women would always be seen as an apolitical group with no subject status. Instead, if anything, it is the *common context* of political struggle against class, race, gender, and imperialist hierarchies that may constitute third world women as a strategic group at this historical juncture. Lindsay also states that linguistic and cultural differences exist between Vietnamese and black American women, but "both groups are victims of race, sex, and class." Again black and Vietnamese women are characterized by their victim status.

Similarly, examine statements such as "My analysis will start by stating that all African women are politically and economically dependent" (Cutrufelli 1983: 13), "Nevertheless, either overtly or covertly, prostitution is still the main if not the only source of work for African women" (Cutrufelli 1983: 33). *All* African women are dependent. Prostitution is the only work option for African women as a *group*. Both statements are illustrative of generalizations sprinkled liberally through a recent Zed Press publication, *Women of Africa: Roots of Oppression*, by Maria Rosa Cutrufelli, who is described on the cover as an Italian writer, sociologist, Marxist, and feminist. In the 1980s, is it possible to imagine writing a book entitled *Women of Europe: Roots of Oppression*? I am not objecting to the use of universal groupings for descriptive purposes. Women from the continent of Africa can be descriptively characterized as "women of Africa." It is when "women of Africa" becomes a homogeneous sociological grouping characterized by common dependencies or powerlessness (or even strengths) that problems arise – we say too little and too much at the same time.

This is because descriptive gender differences are transformed into the division between men and women. Women are constituted as a group via dependency relationships vis-à-vis men, who are implicitly held responsible for these relationships. When "women of Africa" as a group (versus "men of Africa" as a group?) are seen as a group precisely because they are generally dependent and oppressed, the analysis of specific historical differences becomes impossible, because reality is always apparently structured by divisions – two mutually exclusive and jointly exhaustive groups, the victims and the oppressors. Here the sociological is substituted for the biological, in order, however, to create the same – a unity of women. Thus, it is not the descriptive potential of gender difference but the privileged positioning and explanatory potential of gender difference as the *origin* of oppression that I question. In using "women of Africa" (as an already constituted group of oppressed peoples) as a category of analysis, Cutrufelli denies any historical specificity to the location of women as subordinate, powerful, marginal, central, or otherwise, vis-à-vis particular social and power networks. Women are taken as a unified "powerless" group prior to the analysis in question. Thus, it is then merely a matter of specifying the context *after the fact*. "Women" are now placed in the context of the family, or in the workplace, or within religious networks, almost as if these systems existed outside the relations of women with other women, and women with men.

The problem with this analytic strategy, let me repeat, is that it assumes men and women are already constituted as sexual-political subjects prior to their entry into the arena of social relations. Only if we subscribe to this assumption is it possible to undertake analysis which looks at the "effects" of kinship structures, colonialism, organization of labor, etc., on women, who are defined in advance as a group. The crucial point that is forgotten is that women are produced through these very relations as well as being implicated in forming these relations. As Michelle Rosaldo argues, "woman's place in human social life is not in any direct sense a product of the things she does (or even less, a function of what, biologically, she is) but the meaning her activities acquire through concrete social interactions" (1980: 400). That women mother in a variety of societies is not as significant as the value attached to mothering in these societies. The distinction between the act of mothering and the status attached to it is a very important one – one that needs to be stated and analyzed contextually.

Married Women as Victims of the Colonial Process

In Lévi-Strauss's theory of kinship structure as a system of the exchange of women, what is significant is that exchange itself is not constitutive of the subordination of women; women are not subordinate because of the *fact* of exchange, but because of the *modes* of exchange instituted, and the values attached to these modes. However, in discussing the marriage ritual of the Bemba, a Zambian matrilocal, matrilineal people, Cutrufelli in *Women of Africa* focuses on the fact of the marital exchange of women before and after Western colonization, rather than the value attached to this exchange in this particular context. This leads to her definition of Bemba women as a coherent group affected in a particular way by colonization. Here again, Bemba women are constituted rather unilaterally as victims of the effects of Western colonization.

Cutrufelli cites the marriage ritual of the Bemba as a multistage event "whereby a young man becomes incorporated into his wife's family group as he takes up residence with them and gives his services in return for food and maintenance" (43). This ritual extends over many years, and the sexual relationship varies according to the degree of the girl's physical maturity. It is only after she undergoes an initiation ceremony at puberty that intercourse is sanctioned, and the man acquires legal rights over her. This initiation ceremony is the more important act of the consecration of women's reproductive power, so that the abduction of an uninitiated girl is of no consequence, while heavy penalty is levied for the seduction of an initiated girl. Cutrufelli asserts that the effect of European colonization has changed the whole marriage system. Now the young man is entitled to take his wife away from her people in return for money. The implication is that Bemba women have now lost the protection of tribal laws. However, while it is possible to see how the structure of the traditional marriage contract (versus the postcolonial marriage contract) offered women a certain amount of control over their marital relations, only an analysis of the political significance of the actual practice which privileges an initiated girl over an uninitiated one, indicating a shift in female power relations as a result of this ceremony, can provide an accurate account of whether Bemba women were indeed protected by tribal laws *at all times*.

However, it is not possible to talk about Bemba women as a homogeneous group within the traditional marriage structure. Bemba women *before* the initiation are constituted within a different set of social relations compared to Bemba women *after* the initiation. To treat them as a unified group characterized by the fact of their "exchange" between male kin is to deny the sociohistorical and cultural specificities of their existence, and the differential *value* attached to their exchange before and after their initiation. It is to treat the initiation ceremony as a ritual with no political implications or effects. It is also to assume that in merely describing the *structure* of the marriage contract, the situation of women is exposed. Women as a group are positioned within a given structure, but there is no attempt made to trace the effect of the marriage practice in constituting women within an obviously changing network of power relations. Thus, women are assumed to be sexual-political subjects prior to entry into kinship structures.

Women and Familial Systems

Elizabeth Cowie (1978), in another context, points out the implications of this sort of analysis when she emphasizes the specifically political nature of kinship structures which must be analyzed as ideological practices which designate men and women as father, husband, wife, mother, sister, etc. Thus, Cowie suggests, women as women are not *located* within the family. Rather, it is *in* the family, as an effect of kinship structures, that women as women are *constructed*, defined within and by the group. Thus, for instance, when Juliette Minces (1980) cites *the* patriarchal family as the basis for "an almost identical vision of women" that Arab and Muslim societies have, she falls into this very trap (see especially p. 23). Not only is it problematical to speak of a vision of women shared by Arab and Muslim societies (i.e., over twenty different countries) without addressing the particular historical, material, and ideological power structures that construct such images, but to speak of the patriarchal family or the tribal kinship structure as the origin of the socioeconomic status of women is to again assume that women are sexual-political subjects prior to their entry into the family. So while on the one hand women attain value or status within the family, the assumption of a singular patriarchal kinship system (common to all Arab and Muslim societies) is what apparently structures women as an oppressed group in these societies! This singular, coherent kinship system presumably influences another separate and given entity, "women." Thus, all women, regardless of class and cultural differences, are affected by this system. Not only are *all* Arab and Muslim women seen to constitute a homogeneous oppressed group, but there is no discussion of the specific *practices* within the family which constitute women as mothers, wives, sisters, etc. Arabs and Muslims, it appears, don't change at all. Their patriarchal family is carried over from the times of the prophet Mohammed. They exist, as it were, outside history.

Women and Religious Ideologies

A further example of the use of "women" as a category of analysis is found in cross-cultural analyses which subscribe to a certain economic reductionism in describing the relationship between the economy and factors such as politics and ideology. Here, in reducing the level of comparison to the economic relations between "developed and developing" countries, any specificity to the question of women is denied. Mina Modares (1981), in a careful analysis of women and Shi'ism in Iran, focuses on this very problem when she criticizes feminist writings which treat Islam as an ideology separate from and outside social relations and practices, rather than a discourse which includes rules for economic, social, and power relations within society. Patricia Jeffery's (1979) otherwise informative work on Pirzada women in purdah considers Islamic ideology a partial explanation for the status of women in that it provides a justification for the purdah. Here, Islamic ideology is reduced to a set of ideas whose internalization by Pirzada women contributes to the stability of the system. However, the primary explanation for purdah is located in the control that Pirzada men have over economic resources, and the personal security purdah gives to Pirzada women.

By taking a specific version of Islam as *the* Islam, Jeffery attributes a singularity and coherence to it. Modares notes, "'Islamic Theology' then becomes imposed on a separate and given entity called 'women.' A further unification is reached: Women (meaning *all women*), regardless of their differing positions within societies, come to be affected or not affected by Islam. These conceptions provide the right ingredients for an unproblematic possibility of a cross-cultural study of women" (63). Marina Lazreg makes a similar argument when she addresses the reductionism inherent in scholarship on women in the Middle East and North Africa:

A ritual is established whereby the writer appeals to religion as *the* cause of gender inequality just as it is made the source of underdevelopment in much of modernization theory. In an uncanny way, feminist discourse on women from the Middle East and North Africa mirrors that of theologians' own interpretation of women in Islam. . . .

The overall effect of this paradigm is to deprive women of self-presence, of being. Because women are subsumed under religion presented in fundamental terms, they are inevitably seen as evolving in nonhistorical time. They virtually have no history. Any analysis of change is therefore foreclosed. (1988: 87)

While Jeffery's analysis does not quite succumb to this kind of unitary notion of religion (Islam), it does collapse all ideological specificities into economic relations, and universalizes on the basis of this comparison.

Women and the Development Process

The best examples of universalization on the basis of economic reductionism can be found in the liberal "Women in Development" literature. Proponents of this school seek to examine the effect of development on third world women, sometimes from self-designated feminist perspectives. At the very least, there is an evident interest in and commitment to improving the lives of women in "developing" countries. Scholars such as Irene Tinker and Michelle Bo Bramsen (1972), Ester Boserup (1970), and Perdita Huston (1979) have all written about the effect of development policies on women in the third world.[9] All three women assume "development" is synonymous with "economic development" or "economic progress." As in the case of Minces's patriarchal family, Hosken's male sexual control, and Cutrufelli's Western colonization, development here becomes the all-time equalizer. Women are affected positively or negatively by economic development policies, and this is the basis for cross-cultural comparison.

For instance, Perdita Huston (1979) states that the purpose of her study is to describe the effect of the development process on the "family unit and its individual members" in Egypt, Kenya, Sudan, Tunisia, Sri Lanka, and Mexico. She states that the "problems" and "needs" expressed by rural and urban women in these countries all center around education and training, work and wages, access to health and other services, political participation, and legal rights. Huston relates all these "needs" to the lack of sensitive development policies which exclude women as a group or category. For her, the solution is simple: implement improved development policies which emphasize training for women fieldworkers, use women trainees, and women rural development officers, encourage women's cooperatives, etc. Here again, women are assumed to be a coherent group or category prior to their entry into "the development process." Huston assumes that all third world women have similar problems and needs. Thus, they must have similar interests and goals. However, the interests of urban, middle-class, educated Egyptian housewives, to take only one instance, could surely not be seen as being the same as those of their uneducated, poor maids. Development policies do not affect both groups of women in the same way. Practices which characterize women's status and roles vary according to class.

Women are constituted as women through the complex interaction between class, culture, religion, and other ideological institutions and frameworks. They are not "women" – a coherent group – solely on the basis of a particular economic system or policy. Such reductive cross-cultural comparisons result in the colonization of the specifics of daily existence and the complexities of political interests which women of different social classes and cultures represent and mobilize.

Thus, it is revealing that for Perdita Huston, women in the third world countries she writes about have "needs" and "problems," but few if any have "choices" or the freedom to act. This is an interesting representation of women in the third world, one which is significant in suggesting a latent self-presentation of Western women which bears looking at. She writes, "What surprised and moved me most as I listened to women in such very different cultural settings was the striking common-ality – whether they were educated or illiterate, urban or rural – of their most basic values: the importance they assign to family, dignity, and service to others" (1979: 115). Would Huston consider such values unusual for women in the West?

What is problematical about this kind of use of "women" as a group, as a stable category of analysis, is that it assumes an ahistorical, universal unity between women based on a generalized notion of their subordination. Instead of analytically *demon-strating* the production of women as socioeconomic political groups within particu-lar local contexts, this analytical move limits the definition of the female subject to gender identity, completely bypassing social class and ethnic identities. What charac-terizes women as a group is their gender (sociologically, not necessarily biologically, defined) over and above everything else, indicating a monolithic notion of sexual difference. Because women are thus constituted as a coherent group, sexual differ-ence becomes coterminous with female subordination, and power is automatically defined in binary terms: people who have it (read: men), and people who do not (read: women). Men exploit, women are exploited. Such simplistic formulations are historically reductive; they are also ineffectual in designing strategies to combat oppressions. All they do is reinforce binary divisions between men and women.

What would an analysis which did not do this look like? Maria Mies's work illustrates the strength of Western feminist work on women in the third world which does not fall into the traps discussed above. Mies's study of the lace makers of Narsapur, India (1982), attempts to carefully analyze a substantial household indus-try in which "housewives" produce lace doilies for consumption in the world mar-ket. Through a detailed analysis of the structure of the lace industry, production and reproduction relations, the sexual division of labor, profits and exploitation, and the overall consequences of defining women as "non-working housewives" and their work as "leisure-time activity." Mies demonstrates the levels of exploitation in this industry and the impact of this production system on the work and living conditions of the women involved in it. In addition, she is able to analyze the "ideology of the housewife," the notion of a woman sitting in the house, as providing the necessary subjective and sociocultural element for the creation and maintenance of a produc-tion system that contributes to the increasing pauperization of women, and keeps them totally atomized and disorganized as workers. Mies's analysis shows the effect of a certain historically and culturally specific mode of patriarchal organization, an organization constructed on the basis of the definition of the lace makers as "non-working housewives" at familial, local, regional, statewide, and international levels. The intricacies and the effects of particular power networks not only are emphasized, but they form the basis of Mies's analysis of how this particular group of women is situated at the center of a hegemonic, exploitative world market.

This is a good example of what careful, politically focused, local analyses can accomplish. It illustrates how the category of women is constructed in a variety of political contexts that often exist simultaneously and overlaid on top of one another. There is no easy generalization in the direction of "women" in India, or "women in the third world"; nor is there a reduction of the political construction of the exploitation of the lace makers to cultural explanations about the passivity or obedience that might characterize these women and their situation. Finally, this mode of local, political analysis which generates theoretical categories from within the situation and context being analyzed, also suggests corresponding effective strategies for organizing against the exploitation faced by the lace makers. Narsapur women are not mere victims of the production process, because they resist, challenge, and subvert the process at various junctures. Here is one instance of how Mies delineates the connections between the housewife ideology, the self-consciousness of the lace makers, and their interrelationships as contributing to the latent resistances she perceives among the women:

> The persistence of the housewife ideology, the self-perception of the lace makers as petty commodity producers rather than as workers, is not only upheld by the structure of the industry as such but also by the deliberate propagation and reinforcement of reactionary patriarchal norms and institutions. Thus, most of the lace makers voiced the same opinion about the rules of *purdah* and seclusion in their communities which were also propagated by the lace exporters. In particular, the *Kapu* women said that they had never gone out of their houses, that women of their community could not do any other work than housework and lace work etc. but in spite of the fact that most of them still subscribed fully to the patriarchal norms of the *gosha* women, there were also contradictory elements in their consciousness. Thus, although they looked down with contempt upon women who were able to work outside the house – like the untouchable *Mala* and *Madiga* women or women of other lower castes, they could not ignore the fact that these women were earning more money precisely because they were *not* respectable housewives but workers. At one discussion, they even admitted that it would be better if they could also go out and do coolie work. And when they were asked whether they would be ready to come out of their houses and work in one place in some sort of a factory, they said they would do that. This shows that the *purdah* and housewife ideology, although still fully internalized, already had some cracks, because it has been confronted with several contradictory realities. (157)

It is only by understanding the *contradictions* inherent in women's location within various structures that effective political action and challenges can be devised. Mies's study goes a long way toward offering such analysis. While there are now an increasing number of Western feminist writings in this tradition,[10] there is also, unfortunately, a large block of writing which succumbs to the cultural reductionism discussed earlier.

Methodological Universalisms, or:
Women's Oppression is a Global Phenomenon

Western feminist writings on women in the third world subscribe to a variety of methodologies to demonstrate the universal cross-cultural operation of male dominance and female exploitation. I summarize and critique three such methods below, moving from the simplest to the most complex.

First, proof of universalism is provided through the use of an arithmetic method. The argument goes like this: the greater the number of women who wear the veil, the more universal is the sexual segregation and control of women (Deardon 1975: 4–5). Similarly, a large number of different, fragmented examples from a variety of countries also apparently add up to a universal fact. For instance, Muslim women in Saudi Arabia, Iran, Pakistan, India, and Egypt all wear some sort of a veil. Hence, this indicates that the sexual control of women is a universal fact in those countries in which the women are veiled (Deardon 1975: 7, 10). Fran Hosken writes, "Rape, forced prostitution, polygamy, genital mutilation, pornography, the beating of girls and women, purdah (segregation of women) are all violations of basic human rights" (1981: 15). By equating purdah with rape, domestic violence, and forced prostitution, Hosken asserts its "sexual control" function as the primary explanation for purdah, whatever the context. Institutions of purdah are thus denied any cultural and historical specificity, and contradictions and potentially subversive aspects are totally ruled out.

In both these examples, the problem is not in asserting that the practice of wearing a veil is widespread. This assertion can be made on the basis of numbers. It is a descriptive generalization. However, it is the analytic leap from the practice of veiling to an assertion of its general significance in controlling women that must be questioned. While there may be a physical similarity in the veils worn by women in Saudi Arabia and Iran, the specific meaning attached to this practice varies according to the cultural and ideological context. In addition, the symbolic space occupied by the practice of purdah may be similar in certain contexts, but this does not automatically indicate that the practices themselves have identical significance in the social realm. For example, as is well known, Iranian middle-class women veiled themselves during the 1979 revolution to indicate solidarity with their veiled working-class sisters, while in contemporary Iran, mandatory Islamic laws dictate that all Iranian women wear veils. While in both these instances, similar reasons might be offered for the veil (opposition to the Shah and Western cultural colonization in the first case, and the true Islamicization of Iran in the second), the concrete *meanings* attached to Iranian women wearing the veil are clearly different in both historical contexts. In the first case, wearing the veil is both an oppositional and a revolutionary gesture on the part of Iranian middle-class women; in the second case, it is a coercive, institutional mandate (see Tabari 1980 for detailed discussion). It is on the basis of such context-specific differentiated analysis that effective political strategies can be generated. To assume that the mere practice of veiling women in a number of Muslim countries indicates the universal oppression of women through sexual segregation not only is analytically reductive, but also proves quite useless when it comes to the elaboration of oppositional political strategy.

Second, concepts such as reproduction, the sexual division of labor, the family, marriage, household, patriarchy, etc., are often used without their specification in local cultural and historical contexts. Feminists use these concepts in providing explanations for women's subordination, apparently assuming their universal applicability. For instance, how is it possible to refer to "the" sexual division of labor when the *content* of this division changes radically from one environment to the next, and from one historical juncture to another? At its most abstract level, it is the fact of the differential assignation of tasks according to sex that is significant; however, this is quite different from the *meaning* or *value* that the content of this sexual division of labor assumes in different contexts. In most cases the assigning of tasks on the basis of sex has an ideological origin. There is no question that a claim such as "women are concentrated in service-oriented occupations in a large number of countries around the world" is descriptively valid. Descriptively, then, perhaps the existence of a similar sexual division of labor (where women work in service occupations such as nursing, social work, etc., and men in other kinds of occupations) in a variety of different countries can be asserted. However, the concept of the "sexual division of labor" is more than just a descriptive category. It indicates the differential *value* placed on "men's work" versus "women's work."

Often the mere existence of a sexual division of labor is taken to be proof of the oppression of women in various societies. This results from a confusion between and collapsing together of the descriptive and explanatory potential of the concept of the sexual division of labor. Superficially similar situations may have radically different, historically specific explanations, and cannot be treated as identical. For instance, the rise of female-headed households in middle-class America might be construed as a sign of great independence and feminist progress, whereby women are considered to have *chosen* to be single parents, there are increasing numbers of lesbian mothers, etc. However, the recent increase in female-headed households in Latin America,[11] where women might be seen to have more decision-making power, is concentrated among the poorest strata, where life choices are the most constrained economically. A similar argument can be made for the rise of female-headed families among black and Chicana women in the U.S. The positive correlation between this and the level of poverty among women of color and white working-class women in the U.S. has now even acquired a name: the feminization of poverty. Thus, while it is possible to state that there is a rise in female-headed households in the U.S. and in Latin America, this rise cannot be discussed as a universal indicator of women's independence, nor can it be discussed as a universal indicator of women's impoverishment. The *meaning* of and *explanation* for the rise obviously vary according to the sociohistorical context.

Similarly, the existence of a sexual division of labor in most contexts cannot be sufficient explanation for the universal subjugation of women in the work force. That the sexual division of labor does indicate a devaluation of women's work must be shown through analysis of particular local contexts. In addition, devaluation of *women* must also be shown through careful analysis. In other words, the "sexual division of labor" and "women" are not commensurate analytical categories. Concepts such as the sexual division of labor can be useful only if they are generated through local, contextual analyses (see Eldhom, Harris, and Young 1977). If such concepts are assumed to be universally applicable, the resultant homogenization of class, race, religious, and daily material practices of women in the third world can create a false sense of the commonality of oppressions, interests, and struggles between and among women globally. Beyond sisterhood there are still racism, colonialism, and imperialism!

Finally, some writers confuse the use of gender as a superordinate category of organizing analysis with the universalistic proof and instantiation of this category. In other words, empirical studies of gender differences are confused with the analytical organization of cross-cultural work. Beverly Brown's (1983) review of the book *Nature, Culture and Gender* (Strathern and McCormack 1980) best illustrates this point. Brown suggests that nature:culture and female:male are superordinate categories which organize and locate lesser categories (such as wild/domestic and biology/technology) within their logic. These categories are universal in the sense that they organize the universe of a system of representations. This relation is totally independent of the universal substantiation of any particular category. Her critique hinges on the fact that rather than clarify the generalizability of nature:culture :: female:male as subordinate organization categories, *Nature, Culture and Gender* construes the universality of this equation to lie at the level of empirical truth, which can be investigated through fieldwork. Thus, the usefulness of the nature:culture :: female:male paradigm as a universal mode of the organization of representation within any particular sociohistorical system is lost. Here, methodological universalism is assumed on the basis of the reduction of the nature:culture :: female:male analytic categories to a demand for empirical proof of its existence in different cultures. Discourses of representation are confused with material realities, and the distinction made earlier between "Woman" and "women" is lost. Feminist work which blurs this distinction (which is, interestingly enough, often present in certain Western feminists' self-representation) eventually ends up constructing monolithic images of "third world women" by ignoring the complex and mobile relationships between their historical materiality on the level of specific oppressions and political choices, on the one hand, and their general discursive representations, on the other.

To summarize: I have discussed three methodological moves identifiable in feminist (and other academic) cross-cultural work which seeks to uncover a universality in women's subordinate position in society. The next and final section pulls together the previous sections, attempting to outline the political effects of the analytical strategies in the context of Western feminist writing on women in the third world. These arguments are not against generalization as much as they are for careful, historically specific generalizations responsive to complex realities. Nor do these arguments deny the necessity of forming strategic political identities and affinities. Thus, while Indian women of different religions, castes, and classes might forge a political unity on the basis of organizing against police brutality toward women (see Kishwar and Vanita 1984), an *analysis* of police brutality must be contextual. Strategic coalitions which construct oppositional political identities for themselves are based on generalization and provisional unities, but the analysis of these group identities cannot be based on universalistic, ahistorical categories.

The Subject(s) of Power

This last section returns to an earlier point about the inherently political nature of feminist scholarship, and attempts to clarify my point about the possibility of detecting a colonialist move in the case of a hegemonic first–third world connection in scholarship. The nine texts in the Zed Press Women in the Third World series that I have discussed[12] focused on the following common areas in examining women's "status" within various societies: religion, family/kinship structures, the legal system, the sexual division of labor, education, and finally, political resistance. A large number of Western feminist writings on women in the third world focus on these themes. Of course the Zed texts have varying emphases. For instance, two of the studies, *Women of Palestine* (Downing 1982) and *Indian Women in Struggle* (Omvedt 1980), focus explicitly on female militance and political involvement, while *Women in Arab Society* (Minces 1980) deals with Arab women's legal, religious, and familial status. In addition, each text evidences a variety of methodologies and degrees of care in making generalizations. Interestingly enough, however, almost all the texts assume "women" as a category of analysis in the manner designated above.

Clearly this is an analytical strategy which is neither limited to these Zed Press publications nor symptomatic of Zed Press publications in general. However, each of the particular texts in question assumes "women" have a coherent group identity within the different cultures discussed, prior to their entry into social relations. Thus, Omvedt can talk about "Indian women" while referring to a particular group of women in the State of Maharashtra, Cutrufelli about "women of Africa," and Minces about "Arab women" as if these groups of women have some sort of obvious cultural coherence, distinct from men in these societies. The "status" or "position" of women is assumed to be self-evident, because women as an already constituted group are *placed* within religious, economic, familial, and legal structures. However, this focus whereby women are seen as a coherent group across contexts, regardless of class or ethnicity, structures the world in ultimately binary, dichotomous terms, where women are always seen in opposition to men, patriarchy is always necessarily male dominance, and the religious, legal, economic, and familial systems are implicitly assumed to be constructed by men. Thus, both men and women are always apparently constituted whole populations, and relations of dominance and exploitation are also posited in terms of whole peoples – wholes coming into exploitative relations. It is only when men and women are seen as different categories or groups possessing different *already constituted* categories of experience, cognition, and interests as *groups* that such a simplistic dichotomy is possible.

What does this imply about the structure and functioning of power relations? The setting up of the commonality of third world women's struggles across classes and cultures against a general notion of oppression (primarily the group in power – i.e., men) necessitates the assumption of what Michel Foucault (1980: 135–45) calls the "juridico-discursive" model of power, the principal features of which are "a negative relation" (limit and lack), an "insistence on the rule" (which forms a binary system), a "cycle of prohibition," the "logic of censorship," and a "uniformity" of the apparatus functioning at different levels. Feminist discourse on the third world which assumes a homogeneous category – or group – called women necessarily operates through the setting up of originary power divisions. Power relations are structured in terms of a unilateral and undifferentiated source of power and a cumulative reaction to power. Opposition is a generalized phenomenon created as a response to power – which, in turn, is possessed by certain groups of people.

The major problem with such a definition of power is that it locks all revolution-ary struggles into binary structures – possessing power versus being powerless. Women are powerless, unified groups. If the struggle for a just society is seen in terms of the move from powerless to powerful for women as a *group*, and this is the implication in feminist discourse which structures sexual difference in terms of the division between the sexes, then the new society would be structurally identical to the existing organization of power relations, constituting itself as a simple *inversion* of what exists. If relations of domination and exploitation are defined in terms of binary divisions – groups which dominate and groups which are dominated – surely the implication is that the accession to power of women as a group is sufficient to dismantle the existing organization of relations? But women as a group are not in some sense essentially superior or infallible. The crux of the problem lies in that initial assump-tion of women as a homogeneous group or category ("the oppressed"), a familiar assumption in Western radical and liberal feminisms.[13]

What happens when this assumption of "women as an oppressed group" is situated in the context of Western feminist writing about third world women? It is here that I locate the colonialist move. By contrasting the representation of women in the third world with what I referred to earlier as Western feminisms' self-presentation in the same context, we see how Western feminists alone become the true "subjects" of this counterhistory. Third world women, on the other hand, never rise above the debilitating generality of their "object" status.

While radical and liberal feminist assumptions of women as a sex class might elucidate (however inadequately) the autonomy of particular women's struggles in the West, the application of the notion of women as a homogeneous category to women in the third world colonizes and appropriates the pluralities of the simultane-ous location of different groups of women in social class and ethnic frameworks; in doing so it ultimately robs them of their historical and political *agency*. Similarly, many Zed Press authors who ground themselves in the basic analytic strategies of traditional Marxism also implicitly create a "unity" of women by substituting "women's activity" for "labor" as the primary theoretical determinant of women's situation. Here again, women are constituted as a coherent group not on the basis of "natural" qualities or needs but on the basis of the sociological "unity" of their role in domestic production and wage labor (see Haraway 1985, esp. p. 76). In other words, Western feminist discourse, by assuming women as a coherent, already constituted group which is placed in kinship, legal, and other structures, defines third world women as subjects *outside* social relations, instead of looking at the way women are constituted *through* these very structures.

Legal, economic, religious, and familial structures are treated as phenomena to be judged by Western standards. It is here that ethnocentric universality comes into play. When these structures are defined as "underdeveloped" or "developing" and women are placed within them, an implicit image of the "average third world woman" is produced. This is the transformation of the (implicitly Western) "oppressed woman" into the "oppressed third world woman." While the category of "oppressed woman" is generated through an exclusive focus on gender difference, "the oppressed third world woman" category has an additional attribute – the "third world difference!" The "third world difference" includes a paternalistic attitude toward women in the third world.[14] Since discussions of the various themes I identified earlier (kinship, education, religion, etc.) are conducted in the context of the relative "underdevelopment" of the third world (which is nothing less than unjustifiably confusing development with the separate path taken by the West in its development, as well as ignoring the directionality of the first–third world power relationship), third world women as a group or category are automatically and necessarily defined as religious (read "not progressive"), family-oriented (read "traditional"), legal minors (read "they-are-still-not-conscious-of-their-rights"), illiterate (read "ignorant"), domestic (read "backward"), and sometimes revolutionary (read "their-country-is-in-a-state-of-war; they-must-fight!"). This is how the "third world difference" is produced.

When the category of "sexually oppressed women" is located within particular systems in the third world which are defined on a scale which is normed through Eurocentric assumptions, not only are third world women defined in a particular way prior to their entry into social relations, but since no connections are made between first and third world power shifts, the assumption is reinforced that the third world just has not evolved to the extent that the West has. This mode of feminist analysis, by homogenizing and systematizing the experiences of different groups of women in these countries, erases all marginal and resistant modes and experiences.[15] It is significant that none of the texts I reviewed in the Zed Press series focuses on lesbian politics or the politics of ethnic and religious marginal organizations in third world women's groups. Resistance can thus be defined only as cumulatively reactive, not as something inherent in the operation of power. If power, as Michel Foucault has argued recently, can really be understood only in the context of resistance,[16] this misconceptualization is both analytically and strategically problematical. It limits theoretical analysis as well as reinforces Western cultural imperialism. For in the context of a first/third world-balance of power, feminist analyses which perpetrate and sustain the hegemony of the idea of the superiority of the West produce a corresponding set of universal images of the "third world woman," images such as the veiled woman, the powerful mother, the chaste virgin, the obedient wife, etc. These images exist in universal, ahistorical splendor, setting in motion a colonialist discourse which exercises a very specific power in defining, coding, and maintaining existing first/third world connections.

To conclude, then, let me suggest some disconcerting similarities between the typically authorizing signature of such Western feminist writings on women in the third world, and the authorizing signature of the project of humanism in general – humanism as a Western ideological and political project which involves the necessary recuperation of the "East" and "Woman" as Others. Many contemporary thinkers, including Foucault (1978, 1980), Derrida (1974), Kristeva (1980), Deleuze and Guattari (1977), and Said (1978), have written at length about the underlying anthropomorphism and ethnocentrism which constitute a hegemonic humanistic problematic that repeatedly confirms and legitimates (Western) Man's centrality. Feminist theorists such as Luce Irigaray (1981), Sarah Kofman (see Berg 1982), and Helene Cixous (1981) have also written about the recuperation and absence of woman/women within Western humanism. The focus of the work of all these thinkers can be stated simply as an uncovering of the political *interests* that underlie the binary logic of humanistic discourse and ideology whereby, as a valuable recent essay puts it, "the first (majority) term (Identity, Universality, Culture, Disinterested-ness, Truth, Sanity, Justice, etc.), which is, in fact, secondary and derivative (a con-struction), is privileged over and colonizes the second (minority) term (difference, temporality, anarchy, error, interestedness, insanity, deviance, etc.), which is in fact, primary and originative" (Spanos 1984). In other words, it is only insofar as "Woman/Women" and "the East" are defined as *Others*, or as peripheral, that (Western) Man/Humanism can represent him/itself as the center. If is not the center that determines the periphery, but the periphery that, in its boundedness, determines the center. Just as feminists such as Kristeva and Cixous deconstruct the latent anthro-pomorphism in Western discourse, I have suggested a parallel strategy in this essay in uncovering a latent ethnocentrism in particular feminist writings on women in the third world.[17]

As discussed earlier, a comparison between Western feminist self-presentation and Western feminist re-presentation of women in the third world yields significant results. Universal images of "the third world woman" (the veiled woman, chaste virgin, etc.), images constructed from adding the "third world difference" to "sexual difference," are predicated upon (and hence obviously bring into sharper focus) assumptions about Western women as secular, liberated, and having control over their own lives. This is not to suggest that Western women *are* secular, liberated, and in control of their own lives. I am referring to a *discursive* self-presentation, not necessarily to material reality. If this were a material reality, there would be no need for political movements in the West. Similarly, only from the vantage point of the West is it possible to define the "third world" as underdeveloped and economically dependent. Without the overdetermined discourse that creates the *third* world, there would be no (singular and privileged) first world. Without the "third world woman," the particular self-presentation of Western women mentioned above would be problematical. I am suggesting, then, that the one enables and sustains the other. This is not to say that the signature of Western feminist writings on the third world has the same authority as the project of Western humanism. However, in the con-text of the hegemony of the Western scholarly establishment in the production and dissemination of texts, and in the context of the legitimating imperative of human-istic and scientific discourse, the definition of "the third world woman" as a monolith might well tie into the larger economic and ideological praxis of "disinterested" scientific inquiry and pluralism which are the surface manifestations of a latent economic and cultural colonization of the "non-Western" world. It is time to move beyond the Marx who found it possible to say: They cannot represent themselves; they must be represented.

Notes

This essay would not have been possible without S. P. Mohanty's challenging and careful reading. I would also like to thank Biddy Martin for our numerous discussions about feminist theory and politics. They both helped me think through some of the arguments herein.

1 Terms such as *third* and *first world* are very problematic both in suggesting oversimplified similarities between and among countries labeled thus, and in implicitly reinforcing existing economic, cultural, and ideological hierarchies which are conjured up in using such terminology. I use the term "*third world*" with full awareness of its problems, only because this is the terminology available to us at the moment. The use of quotation marks is meant to suggest a continuous questioning of the designation. Even when I do not use quotation marks, I mean to use the term critically.

2 I am indebted to Teresa de Lauretis for this particular formulation of the project of feminist theorizing. See especially her introduction in de Lauretis, *Alice Doesn't: Feminism, Semiotics, Cinema* (Bloomington: Indiana University Press, 1984); see also Sylvia Wynter, "The Politics of Domination," unpublished manuscript.

3 This argument is similar to Homi Bhabha's definition of colonial discourse as strategically creating a space for a subject people through the production of knowledges and the exercise of power. The full quote reads: "[colonial discourse is] an apparatus of power. . . . an apparatus that turns on the recognition and disavowal of racial/cultural/historical differences. Its predominant strategic function is the creation of a space for a subject people through the production of knowledges in terms of which surveillance is exercised and a complex form of pleasure/unpleasure is incited. It (i.e. colonial discourse) seeks authorization for its strategies by the production of knowledges by coloniser and colonised which are stereotypical but antithetically evaluated" (1983: 23).

4 A number of documents and reports on the UN International Conferences on Women, Mexico City, 1975, and Copenhagen, 1980, as well as the 1976 Wellesley Conference on Women and Development, attest to this. Nawal el Saadawi, Fatima Mernissi, and Mallica Vajarathon (1978) characterize this conference as "American-planned and organized," situating third world participants as passive audiences. They focus especially on the lack of self-consciousness of Western women's implication in the effects of imperialism and racism in their assumption of an "international sisterhood." A recent essay by Valerie Amos and Pratibha Parmar (1984) characterizes as "imperial" Euro-American feminism which seeks to establish itself as the only legitimate feminism.

5 The Zed Press Women in the Third World series is unique in its conception. I choose to focus on it because it is the only contemporary series I have found which assumes that "women in the third world" are a legitimate and separate subject of study and research. Since 1985, when this essay was first written, numerous new titles have appeared in the Women in the Third World series. Thus, I suspect that Zed has come to occupy a rather privileged position in the dissemination and construction of discourses by and about third world women. A number of the books in this series are excellent, especially those which deal directly with women's resistance struggles. In addition, Zed Press consistently

publishes progressive feminist, antiracist, and antiimperialist texts. However, a number of the texts written by feminist sociologists, anthropologists, and journalists are symptomatic of the kind of Western feminist work on women in the third world that concerns me. Thus, an analysis of a few of these particular works in this series can serve as a representative point of entry into the discourse I am attempting to locate and define. My focus on these texts is therefore an attempt at an internal critique: I simply expect and demand more from this series. Needless to say, progressive publishing houses also carry their own authorizing signatures.

6   Elsewhere I have discussed this particular point in detail in a critique of Robin Morgan's construction of "women's herstory" in her introduction to *Sisterhood is Global: The International Women's Movement Anthology* (New York: Anchor Press/Doubleday, 1984). See my "Feminist Encounters: Locating the Politics of Experience," *Copyright* 1, "Fin de Siecle 2000," 30–44, especially 35–7.

7   Another example of this kind of analysis is Mary Daly's (1978) *Gyn/Ecology*. Daly's assumption in this text, that women as a group are sexually victimized, leads to her very problematic comparison between the attitudes toward women witches and healers in the West, Chinese footbinding, and the genital mutilation of women in Africa. According to Daly, women in Europe, China, and Africa constitute a homogeneous group as victims of male power. Not only does this label (sexual victims) eradicate the specific historical and material realities and contradictions which lead to and perpetuate practices such as witch hunting and genital mutilation, but it also obliterates the differences, complexities, and heterogeneities of the lives of, for example, women of different classes, religions, and nations in Africa. As Audre Lorde (1983) pointed out, women in Africa share a long tradition of healers and goddesses that perhaps binds them together more appropriately than their victim status. However, both Daly and Lorde fall prey to universalistic assumptions about "African women" (both negative and positive). What matters is the complex, historical range of power differences, commonalities, and resistances that exist among women in Africa which construct African women as "subjects" of their own politics.

8   See Eldhom, Harris, and Young (1977) for a good discussion of the necessity to theorize male violence within specific societal frameworks, rather than assume it as a universal fact.

9   These views can also be found in differing degrees in collections such as Wellesley Editorial Committee, ed., *Women and National Development: The Complexities of Change* (Chicago: University of Chicago Press, 1977), and *Signs*, Special Issue, "Development and the Sexual Division of Labor," 7, no. 2 (Winter 1981). For an excellent introduction of WID issues, see ISIS, *Women in Development: A Resource Guide for Organization and Action* (Philadelphia: New Society Publishers, 1984). For a politically focused discussion of feminism and development and the stakes for poor third world women, see Gita Sen and Caren Grown, *Development Crises and Alternative Visions: Third World Women's Perspectives* (New York: Monthly Review Press, 1987).

10 See essays by Vanessa Maher, Diane Elson and Ruth Pearson, and Maila Stevens in Kate Young, Carol Walkowitz, and Roslyn McCullagh, eds., *Of Marriage and the Market: Women's Subordination in International Perspective* (London: CSE Books, 1981); and essays by Vivian Mota and Michelle Mattelart in June Nash and Helen I. Safa, eds., *Sex and Class in Latin America: Women's Perspectives on Politics, Economics and the Family in the Third World* (South Hadley, Mass.: Bergin and Garvey, 1980). For examples of excellent, self-conscious work by feminists writing about women in their own historical and geographical locations, see Marnia Lazreg (1988) on Algerian women, Gayatri Chakravorty Spivak's "A Literary Representation of the Subaltern: A Woman's Text from the Third World," in her *In Other Worlds: Essays in Cultural Politics* (New York: Methuen,

1987), 241–68, and Lata Mani's essay "Contentious Traditions: The Debate on SATI in Colonial India," *Cultural Critique* 7 (Fall 1987), 119–56.

11   Olivia Harris, "Latin American Women – An Overview," in Harris, ed., *Latin American Women* (London: Minority Rights Group Report no. 57, 1983), 4–7. Other MRG Reports include Ann Deardon (1975) and Rounaq Jahan (1980).

12   List of Zed Press publications: Patricia Jeffery, *Frogs in a Well: Indian Women in Purdah* (1979); Latin American and Caribbean Women's Collective, *Slaves of Slaves: The Challenge of Latin American Women* (1980); Gail Omvedt, *We Shall Smash This Prison: Indian Women in Struggle* (1980); Juliette Minces, *The House of Obedience: Women in Arab Society* (1980); Bobby Siu, *Women of China: Imperialism and Women's Resistance, 1900–1949* (1981); Ingela Bendt and James Downing, *We Shall Return: Women in Palestine* (1982); Maria Rosa Cutrufelli, *Women of Africa: Roots of Oppression* (1983); Maria Mies, *The Lace Makers of Narsapur: Indian Housewives Produce for the World Market* (1982); Miranda Davis, ed., *Third World/Second Sex: Women's Struggles and National Liberation* (1983).

13   For succinct discussions of Western radical and liberal feminisms, see Hester Eisenstein, *Contemporary Feminist Thought* (Boston: G. K. Hall & Co., 1983), and Zillah Eisenstein, *The Radical Future of Liberal Feminism* (New York: Longman, 1981).

14   Amos and Parmar describe the cultural stereotypes present in Euro-American feminist thought: "The image is of the passive Asian woman subject to oppressive practices within the Asian family with an emphasis on wanting to 'help' Asian women liberate themselves from their role. Or there is the strong, dominant Afro-Caribbean woman, who despite her 'strength' is exploited by the 'sexism' which is seen as being a strong feature in relationships between Afro-Caribbean men and women" (9). These images illustrate the extent to which *paternalism* is an essential element of feminist thinking which incorporates the above stereotypes, a paternalism which can lead to the definition of priorities for women of color by Euro-American feminists.

15   I discuss the question of theorizing experience in my "Feminist Encounters" (1987) and in an essay coauthored with Biddy Martin, "Feminist politics: What's Home Got to Do with It?" in Teresa de Lauretis, ed., *Feminist Studies/Critical Studies* (Bloomington: Indiana University Press, 1986), 191–212.

16   This is one of M. Foucault's (1978, 1980) central points in his reconceptualization of the strategies and workings of power networks.

17   For an argument which demands a *new* conception of humanism in work on third world women, see Marnia Lazreg (1988). While Lazreg's position might appear to be diametrically opposed to mine, I see it as a provocative and potentially positive extension of some of the implications that follow from my arguments. In criticizing the feminist rejection of humanism in the name of "essential Man," Lazreg points to what she calls an "essentialism of difference" within these very feminist projects. She asks: "To what extent can Western feminism dispense with an ethics of responsibility when writing about different women? The point is neither to subsume other women under one's own experience nor to uphold a separate truth for them. Rather, it is to allow them to *be* while recognizing that what they are is just as meaningful, valid, and comprehensible as what we are. . . . Indeed, when feminists essentially deny other women the humanity they claim for themselves, they dispense with any ethical constraint. They engage in the act of splitting the social universe into us and them, subject and objects" (99–100).

This essay by Lazreg and an essay by S. P. Mohanty (1989) entitled "Us and Them: On the Philosophical Bases of Political Criticism" suggest positive directions for self-conscious cross-cultural analyses, analyses which move beyond the deconstructive to a fundamentally productive mode in designating overlapping areas for cross-cultural comparison. The latter essay calls not for a "humanism" but for a reconsideration of the question of the "human" in a posthumanist context. It argues that (1) there is no necessary "incompatibility between the deconstruction of Western humanism" and such "a positive elaboration" of the human, and moreover that (2) such an elaboration is essential if contemporary political-critical discourse is to avoid the incoherences and weaknesses of a relativist position.

References

Abdel-Malek, Anouar. 1981. *Social Dialectics: Nation and Revolution*. Albany: State University of New York Press.

Amin, Samir. 1977. *Imperialism and Unequal Development*. New York: Monthly Review Press.

Amos, Valerie, and Pratibha Parmar. 1984. "Challenging Imperial Feminism." *Feminist Review* 17: 3–19.

Baran, Paul A. 1962. *The Political Economy of Growth*. New York: Monthly Review Press.

Berg, Elizabeth. 1982. "The Third Woman." *Diacritics* (Summer): 11–20.

Bhabha, Homi. 1983. "The Other Question – The Stereotype and Colonial Discourse." *Screen* 24, no. 6: 23.

Boserup, Ester. 1970. *Women's Role in Economic Development*. New York: St. Martin's Press; London: Allen and Unwin.

Brown, Beverly. 1983. "Displacing the Difference – Review, *Nature, Culture and Gender*." *m/f* 8: 79–89.

Cixous, Helene. 1981. "The Laugh of the Medusa." In Marks and De Courtivron (1981).

Cowie, Elizabeth. 1978. "Woman as Sign." *m/f* 1: 49–63.

Cutrufelli, Maria Rosa. 1983. *Women of Africa: Roots of Oppression*. London: Zed Press.

Daly, Mary. 1978. *Gyn/Ecology: The Metaethics of Radical Feminism*. Boston: Beacon Press.

Deardon, Ann, ed. 1975. *Arab Women*. London: Minority Rights Group Report no. 27.

de Lauretis, Teresa. 1984. *Alice Doesn't: Feminism, Semiotics, Cinema*. Bloomington: Indiana University Press.

—— 1986. *Feminist Studies Critical Studies*. Bloomington: Indiana University Press.

Deleuze, Giles, and Felix Guattari. 1977. *Anti-Oedipus. Capitalism and Schizophrenia*. New York: Viking.

Derrida, Jacques. 1974. *Of Grammatology*. Baltimore, Johns Hopkins University Press.

Eisenstein, Hester. 1983. *Contemporary Feminist Thought*. Boston: G. K. Hall and Co.

Eisenstein, Zillah. 1981. *The Radical Future of Liberal Feminism*. New York: Longman.

Eldhom, Felicity, Olivia Harris, and Kate Young. 1977. "Conceptualising Women." *Critique of Anthropology: "Women's Issue"*, no. 3.

el Saadawi, Nawal, Fatima Mernissi, and Mallica Vajarathon. 1978. "A Critical Look at the Wellesley Conference." *Quest*, no. 2 (Winter): 101–7.

Foucault, Michel. 1978. *History of Sexuality: Volume One*. New York: Random House.

—— 1980. *Power/Knowledge*. New York: Pantheon.

Gunder-Frank, Andre. 1967. *Capitalism and Underdevelopment in Latin America*. New York: Monthly Review Press.

Haraway, Donna. 1985. "A Manifesto for Cyborgs: Science, Technology and Socialist Feminism in the 1980s." *Socialist Review* 80 (March/April): 65–108.

Harris, Olivia. 1983a. "Latin American Women – An Overview." In Harris (1983b).

420   Chandra Talpade Mohanty

—— 1983b. *Latin American Women*. London: Minority Rights Group Report no. 57.

Hosken, Fran. 1981. "Female Genital Mutilation and Human Rights." *Feminist Issues* 1, no. 3.

Huston, Perdita. 1979. *Third World Women Speak Out*. New York: Praeger.

Irigaray, Luce. 1981. "This Sex Which Is Not One" and "When the Goods Get Together." In Marks and De Courtivron (1981).

Jahan, Rounaq, ed. 1980. *Women in Asia*. London: Minority Rights Group Report no. 45.

Jeffery, Patricia. 1979. *Frogs in a Well: Indian Women in Purdah*. London: Zed Press.

Joseph, Gloria, and Jill Lewis. 1981. *Common Differences: Conflicts in Black and White Feminist Perspectives*. Boston: Beacon Press.

Kishwar, Madhu, and Ruth Vanita. 1984. *In Search of Answers: Indian Women's Voices from Manushi*. London: Zed Press.

Kristeva, Julia. 1980. *Desire in Language*. New York: Columbia University Press.

Lazreg, Marnia. 1988. "Feminism and Difference: The Perils of Writing as a Woman on Women in Algeria." *Feminist Issues* 14, no. 1 (Spring): 81–107.

Lindsay, Beverley, ed. 1983. *Comparative Perspectives of Third World Women: The Impact of Race, Sex and Class*. New York: Praeger.

Lorde, Audre. 1983. "An Open Letter to Mary Daly." In Moraga and Anzaldua (1983), 94–7.

Marks, Elaine, and Isabel De Courtivron. 1981. *New French Feminisms*. New York: Schocken Books.

Mies, Maria. 1982. *The Lace Makers of Narsapur: Indian Housewives Produce for the World Market*. London: Zed Press.

Minces, Juliette. 1980. *The House of Obedience: Women in Arab Society*. London: Zed Press.

Modares, Mina. 1981. "Women and Shi'ism in Iran." *m/f* 5 and 6: 61–82.

Mohanty, Chandra Talpade. 1987. "Feminist Encounters: Locating the Politics of Experience." *Copyright* 1, "Fin de Siecle 2000," 30–44.

Mohanty, Chandra Talpade, and Biddy Martin. 1986. "Feminist Politics: What's Home Got to Do with It?" In de Lauretis (1986).

Mohanty, S. P. 1989. "Us and Them: On the Philosophical Bases of Political Criticism." *Yale Journal of Criticism* 2 (March): 1–31.

Moraga, Cherríe. 1984. *Loving in the War Years*. Boston: South End Press.

—— and Gloria Anzaldúa, eds. 1983. *This Bridge Called My Back: Writings by Radical Women of Color*. New York: Kitchen Table Press.

Morgan, Robin, ed. 1984. *Sisterhood Is Global: The International Women's Movement Anthology*. New York: Anchor Press/Doubleday; Harmondsworth: Penguin.

Nash, June, and Helen I. Safa, eds. 1980. *Sex and Class in Latin America: Women's Perspectives on Politics, Economics and the Family in the Third World*. South Hadley, Mass.: Bergin and Garvey.

Rosaldo, M. A. 1980. "The Use and Abuse of Anthropology: Reflections on Feminism and Cross-Cultural Understanding." *Signs* 53: 389–417.

Said, Edward. 1978. *Orientalism*. New York: Random House.

Sen, Gita, and Caren Grown. 1987. *Development Crises and Alternative Visions: Third World Women's Perspectives*. New York: Monthly Review Press.

Smith, Barbara, ed. 1983. *Home Girls: A Black Feminist Anthology*. New York: Kitchen Table Press.

Spanos, William V. 1984. "Boundary 2 and the Polity of Interest: Humanism, the "Center Elsewhere" and Power." *Boundary* 2 12, no. 3/13, no. 1 (Spring/Fall).

Spivak, Gayatri Chakravorty. 1987. *In Other Worlds: Essays in Cultural Politics.* London and New York: Methuen.

Strathern, Marilyn, and Carol McCormack, eds. 1980. *Nature, Culture and Gender.* Cambridge: Cambridge University Press.

Tabari, Azar. 1980. "The Enigma of the Veiled Iranian Women." *Feminist Review* 5: 19–32.

Tinker, Irene, and Michelle Bo Bramsen, eds. 1972. *Women and World Development.* Washington, D.C.: Overseas Development Council.

Young, Kate, Carol Walkowitz, and Roslyn McCullagh, eds. 1981. *Of Marriage and the Market. Women's Subordination in International Perspective.* London: CSE Books.

27

Hybrid Cultures, Oblique Powers

Néstor García Canclini

From the Public Space to Teleparticipation

Perceiving that the cultural transformations generated by the latest technologies and by changes in symbolic production and circulation were not the exclusive responsibility of the communications media induced a search for more comprehensive notions. As the new processes were associated with urban growth, it was thought that the city could become the unity that would give coherence and analytical consistency to the studies.

Undoubtedly, urban expansion is one of the causes that intensified cultural hybridization. What does it mean for Latin American cultures that countries that had about 10 percent of their population in the cities at the beginning of the century now concentrate 60 to 70 percent in urban agglomerations? We have gone from societies dispersed in thousands of peasant communities with traditional, local, and homogeneous cultures – in some regions, with strong indigenous roots, with little communication with the rest of each nation – to a largely urban scheme with a heterogeneous symbolic offering renewed by a constant interaction of the local with national and transnational networks of communication.

Manuel Castells already observed in his book *La cuestión urbana* that the dizzying development of cities, in making visible under this name multiple dimensions of social change, made it comfortable to attribute to them the responsibility of vaster processes (Castells, 1973: 93). Something similar occurred to what happened with the mass media. The megalopolis was accused of engendering anonymity; it was imagined that neighborhoods produce solidarity, the suburbs crime, and that green spaces relax . . .

Urban ideologies attributed to *one* aspect of the transformation, produced by the intercrossing of many forces of modernity, the "explanation" of all its knots and crises. Since that book by Castells, much evidence has accumulated showing that "urban society" is not sharply opposed to the "rural world" and that the predominance of secondary relations over primary ones and of heterogeneity over homogeneity (or the opposite, according to the school) is not due only to the population concentration in the cities.

The urbanization predominant in contemporary societies is intertwined with serialization and anonymity in production, with restructurings of immaterial communication (from mass media to the telematic) that modify the connections between the private and public. How can we explain the fact that many changes in thinking and taste in urban life coincide with those in the peasantry, if not because the commercial interactions of the latter with the cities and the reception of electronic media in rural houses connects them daily with modern innovations?

Inversely, living in a big city does not imply becoming dissolved in the massive and the anonymous. The violence and public insecurity, the incomprehensibility of the city (who knows all the neighborhoods of a capital city?), lead us to search for selective forms of sociability in domestic intimacy and in trusting encounters. Popular groups seldom leave their spaces, whether peripheral or centrally located; middle- and upper-class sectors increase the bars on their windows and close and privatize the streets of their neighborhoods. For everyone radio and television, and for some the computer connected to basic services, bring them information and entertainment at home.

Living in cities, writes Norbert Lechner in his study on daily life in Santiago (1982), has become "isolating a space of one's own." In contrast to what Habermas observed in early periods of modernity, the public sphere is no longer the place of rational participation from which the social order is determined. It was like that, in part, in Latin America during the second half of the nineteenth century and the first half of the twentieth. It is enough to record the role of the "press, theater, and the patrician salons in conformity with a Creole elite"; first for restricted sectors, then broader ones, liberalism assumed that the public will should be constituted as "the result of the discussion and publicity of individual opinions" (Lechner, 1982: Part 2, 73–4).

Studies of the formation of popular neighborhoods in Buenos Aires in the first half of the century recorded that the microsocial structures of urbanism – the club, the café, the neighborhood society, the library, the political committee – organized the identity of the migrants and Creoles by linking immediate life with the global transformations that were being sought by society and the state. Reading and sports, militancy and neighborhood sociability were united in a utopian continuity with national political movements (Gutiérrez and Romero, 1985).

This is coming to an end, partly due to changes in the staging of politics; I am referring to the mix of bureaucratization and "mass mediatization." The masses, called upon since the 1960s to express themselves in the streets and to form unions, were being subordinated in many cases to bureaucratic formations. The last decade presents frequent caricatures of that movement: populist leaderships without economic

growth and without surplus to distribute, end up overwhelmed by a perverse mixture of reconversion and recession and sign tragic pacts with the speculators of the
economy (Alan García in Peru, Carlos Andrés Pérez in Venezuela, Carlos Menem
in Argentina). The massive use of the city for political theatricalization is reduced;
economic measures and requests for the collaboration of the people are announced
on television. Marches and rallies in streets and squares are occasional or have minor
effect. In the three countries cited, as in others, public demonstrations generated by
the impoverishment of the majority sometimes adopt the form of disarticulated
explosions, attacks on shops and supermarkets, on the margin of the organic paths
to political representation.

The city's loss of meaning is in direct relation to the difficulties of political parties
and unions in calling people to collective tasks that do not produce income or are of
doubtful economic gain. The lesser visibility of macrosocial structures, their subordination to nonmaterial and different circuits of communication that mediatize
personal and group interactions, is one of the causes for the decline in the credibility
of all-encompassing social movements, such as the parties that concentrated the
entirety of labor demands and civic representation. The emergence of multiple
demands, enlarged in part by the growth of cultural protests and those relating to
the quality of life, raises a diversified spectrum of organizations to speak for them:
urban, ethnic, youth, feminist, consumer, ecological movements, and so on. Social
mobilization, in the same way as the structure of the city, is fragmented in processes
that are more and more difficult to totalize.

The efficacy of these movements depends, in turn, on the reorganization of the
public space. Their actions have a low impact when they are limited to using traditional forms of communication (oral, of artisanal production, or in written texts that
circulate from person to person). Their power grows if they act in mass networks:
not only the urban presence of a demonstration of one or two hundred thousand
persons, but – even more – their capacity to interfere with the normal functioning of
a city and find support, for that very reason, in the electronic information media.
Then, sometimes, the sense of the urban is restored and the massive ceases to be a
vertical system of diffusion to become a larger expression of local powers, a comple-
menting of the fragments.

At a time when the city or the public sphere is occupied by actors that technically
calculate their decisions and technobureaucratically organize the attention to the
demands, according to criteria of revenue and efficiency, polemical subjectivity – or
simply subjectivity – retreats to the private sphere. The market reorders the public
world as a stage for consumption and dramatization of the signs of status. The
streets are saturated with cars, people rushing to fulfill work obligations or to a
programmed recreation activity, almost always according to its economic yield.

A separate organization of "free time," which turns it into a prolongation of work
and money, contributes to this reformulation of the public. From working breakfasts
to work, to business lunches, to work, to seeing what is on television at home, and
some days to socially productive dinners. The free time of the popular sectors,
compelled by underemployment and wage deterioration, is even less free in having
to be busy with a second or third job, or in looking for them.

Collective identities find their constitutive stage less and less in the city and in its history, whether distant or recent. Information about unforeseen social vicissitudes is received in the home and commented upon among family or with close friends. Almost all sociability, and reflection about it, is concentrated in intimate exchanges. Since information on price increases, what the governor did, and even the accidents that happened the previous day in our own city reach us through the media, these become the dominant constituents of the "public" meaning of the city, those that simulate integrating a disintegrated imaginary urban sphere.

Although this is the trend, it would be unjust not to point out that sometimes the mass media also contribute to overcoming fragmentation. To the degree they inform us about the common experiences of urban life – social conflicts, pollution, which streets have traffic jams at what hours – they establish networks of communication and make it possible to apprehend the social, collective meaning of what happens in the city. On a broader scale, it may be affirmed that radio and television, in placing in relation to each other diverse historical, ethnic, and regional patrimonies and diffusing them massively, coordinate the multiple temporalities of different spectators.

The investigations of these processes should articulate the integrating and disintegrating effects of television with other processes of unification and atomization generated by the recent changes in urban development and the economic crisis. The groups that get together now and then to analyze collective questions – parents at school, workers at their workplace, neighborhood organizations – tend to act and think as self-referential and often sectored groups because economic pressure forces them down the economic ladder. This has been studied chiefly by sociologists in the southern cone, where military dictatorships suspended political parties, unions, and other mechanisms of grouping, mobilization, and collective cooperation. The repression attempted to reshape the public space by reducing social participation to the insertion of each individual in the benefits of consumption and financial speculation.[1] Up to a point, the media became the great mediators and mediatizers, and therefore substitutes for other collective interactions.

The dictatorships made this transformation more radical. But in the last decade, when other Latin American governments have shared this neoconservative policy, its effects have been generalized. "To appear in public" is today to be seen by many people scattered in front of the family television set or reading the newspaper in their home. Political leaders and intellectuals accentuate their conditions as theatrical actors, their messages are distributed if they are "news," and "public opinion" is something measurable by opinion polls. The citizen becomes a client, a "public consumer."

"Urban culture" is restructured by giving up its leading role in the public space to electronic technologies. Given that almost everything in the city "happens" thanks to the fact that the media say so, and in seeming to occur the way the media want it to, there is an accentuation of social mediatization and of the weight of the stagings, and political actions are constituted as so many images of the political. Thus Eliseo Verón (1985), pushing things to the extreme, asserts that participating today means having relations with an "audiovisual democracy" in which the real is produced by the images created in the media.

I would put it in somewhat different terms. More than an absolute substitution of urban life by the audiovisual media, I perceive a *game of echoes*. The commercial advertising and political slogans that we see on television are those that we reencounter in the streets, and vice versa: the ones are echoed in the others. To this circularity of the communicational and the urban are subordinated the testimonies of history and the public meaning constructed in longtime experiences.

Historical Memory and Urban Conflicts

From mass culture to technoculture, from urban space to teleparticipation. In observing this trend, we run the risk of relapsing into the linear historical perspective and suggesting that communicational technologies *substitute for* the inheritance of the past and public interactions.

It is necessary to reintroduce the question of the modern and postmodern uses of history. I am going to do so with the most challenging and apparently most solemn reference: monuments. What meaning do they conserve or renew in the midst of the transformations of the city and in competition with transitory phenomena like advertising, graffiti, and political demonstrations?

There was a time when monuments, along with schools and museums, were a legitimizing stage of the traditional cultured. Their gigantic size or distinguished placement contributed to exalting them. "Why are there no statues in short sleeves?" the Argentine television program *La noticia rebelde* asked the architect Osvaldo Giesso, director of the Cultural Center of the city of Buenos Aires. To give a long, drawn-out response would require considering the statues together with the rhetoric of textbooks, the ritualism of civic ceremonies, and the other self-consecrating liturgies of power. One would also have to analyze how the monumentalist aesthetic that governs most historic spaces in Latin America was initiated as an expression of authoritarian social systems in the pre-Columbian world. Spanish and Portuguese colonial expansionism was superimposed on them because of the need to compete with the grandiloquence of indigenous architecture by means of neo-classical giganticism and baroque exuberance. Finally, it would be necessary to analyze how the processes of independence and construction of our nations engendered enormous buildings and murals, portraits of heroes, and calendars of historical events, all designed to establish an iconography representative of the size of the utopias.

What do monuments claim to say within contemporary urban symbolism? In re-volutionary processes with broad popular participation, public rites and monumental constructions express the historic impulse of mass movements. They are part of the struggle for a new visual culture in the midst of the stubborn persistence of signs of the old order, such as occurred with the first postrevolutionary Mexican muralism and with Russian graphic art in the twenties and Cuban graphic art in the sixties. But when the new movement becomes the system, the projects for change follow the route of bureaucratic planning more than that of participative mobilization. When social organization is stabilized, ritualism becomes sclerotic.

To show the type of tensions that are established between historical memory and the visual scheme of modern cities, I will analyze a group of monuments. It is a small selection from the abundant documentation on monuments of Mexico assembled by Paolo Gori and Helen Escobedo (1989).[2] I am going to begin with a group of sculptures that represent the founding of Tenochtitlán and are located a short distance from the Zócalo in Mexico City.

These examples suffice to show the changes the most solid commemorations of patrimony suffer. Monuments often contain several styles and references to diverse historical and artistic periods. Another hybridization is added later in interacting with urban growth, advertising, graffiti, and modern social movements. The iconography of national traditions (Juárez) is used as a resource for struggling against those who, in the name of other traditions (those of Catholicism that condemn abortion), oppose modernity.

These images suggest diverse ways in which traditions and the monuments that consecrate them are reutilized today. Certain heroes of the past survive in the middle of conflicts that unfold in any modern city between systems of political and commercial signs, traffic signals, and social movements.

Modern development attempted to distribute objects and signs in specific places: commodities in current use, in shops; objects of the past, in history museums; those that claim to be valuable for their aesthetic meaning, in art museums. At the same time, the messages emitted by commodities, historical works, and artistic works, and those that indicate how to use them, circulate through schools and the mass media. A rigorous classification of *things* and of the *languages* that speak about them sustains the systematic organization of the social *spaces* in which they should be consumed. This order structures the life of consumers and prescribes behaviors and modes of perceiving that are appropriate for each situation. To be cultured in a modern city consists in knowing how to distinguish between what is purchased for use, what is commemorated, and what is enjoyed symbolically. The social system requires living in a compartmentalized way.

Nevertheless, urban life transgresses this order all the time. In the movement of the city, commercial interests are crossed with historical, aesthetic, and communicational ones. The semantic struggles to neutralize each other, to perturb the message of the others or change its meaning, and to subordinate the rest to its own logic are stagings of the conflicts between social forces: between the market, history, the state, advertising, and the popular struggle for survival.

While historical objects in museums are removed from history and their intrinsic meaning is frozen in an eternity where nothing will ever happen, monuments open to the urban dynamic facilitate the interaction of memory with change and the revitalization of heroes thanks to propaganda or transit: they continue struggling with the social movements that survive them. In Mexico's museums, the heroes of independence are distinguished by their relation to those of the Reform and the revolution; in the street their meaning is renewed in dialoguing with present contradictions. Without display windows or guards to protect them, urban monuments are happily exposed to their being inserted into contemporary life by graffiti or a popular demonstration. Although sculptors resist abandoning the formulas of classical realism in representing the past or making heroes in short sleeves, monuments are kept up-to-date by the "irreverences" of the citizens.

Graffiti, commercial posters, social and political demonstrations, monuments – languages that represent the main forces operating in the city. Monuments are almost always works with which political power consecrates the founding persons and events of the state. Commercial posters seek to synchronize daily life with the interests of economic power. Graffiti (like the posters and political events of the oppositions) express popular criticism of the imposed order. That is why the publicity announcements that hide or contradict the monuments, and the graffiti written over other graffiti, are so significant. At times the proliferation of announcements drowns out historical identity and dissolves memory in the anxious perception of the novelties that are incessantly renewed by advertising. On the other hand, the authors of spontaneous legends are saying that monuments are inadequate for expressing how the city moves. Is not the need to politically reinscribe monuments evidence of the distance between a state and a people, or between history and the present?

Decollecting

This difficulty in including what we earlier totalized under the formula "urban culture," or with the notions of cultured, popular, and massive, presents the problem of whether the organization of culture can be explained by reference to *collections* of symbolic goods. The disarticulation of the urban also puts into doubt the possibility of cultural systems finding their key in the relations of the population with a certain type of *territory* and history that would, in a peculiar sense, prefigure the behaviors of each group. The next step in this analysis must be to work with the (combined) processes of *decollecting* and *deterritorialization*.

The formation of specialized collections of high art and folklore was a device in modern Europe, and later in Latin America, for ordering symbolic goods in separate groups and hierarchizing them. A certain type of paintings, music, and books belonged to those who were cultured, even though they did not have them in their houses and even though it was through access to museums, concert halls, and libraries. To know their order was already a way of possessing them that distinguished them from those who did not know how to relate to that order.

The history of art and literature was formed on the basis of collections that were housed in museums and libraries when these were buildings for keeping, exhibiting, and consulting collections. Today art museums exhibit Rembrandt and Bacon in one room, popular objects and industrial design in the following ones, and beyond those are happenings, performances, installations, and body art by artists who no longer believe in the works and refuse to produce collectible objects. Public libraries continue to exist in a more traditional mode, but any intellectual or student works much more in his or her private library, where books are mixed with journals, newspaper clippings, fragmentary bits of information that will be moved often from one shelf to another and whose use requires them to be spread out on several tables and on the floor. The situation of the cultural worker today is what Benjamin glimpsed in that pioneering text in which he described the sensations of moving and unpacking his library among the disorder of the boxes, "the floor strewn with scattered papers," the loss of the order that connected those objects with a history of knowledge, making him feel that the mania of collecting "is no longer of our time" (Benjamin, 1969: 59–66).

On the other hand, there was a repertory of folklore, of the objects of peoples or classes that had different customs and therefore other collections. Folklore was born from collecting, as we saw in an earlier chapter. It was formed when collectors and folklorists moved to archaic societies, investigated and preserved the containers used for cooking, the clothing, and the masks used in ritual dancing, and then gathered them together in museums. The containers, masks, and textiles are now found equalized under the name of "handicrafts" in urban markets. If we want to buy the best designs, we no longer go to the mountains or the forests where the Indians who produce them live, because the pieces of diverse ethnic groups are mixed together in shops in the cities.

The aggregate of works and messages that used to structure visual culture and provide the grammar of reading the city diminished their efficacy in the urban space as well. There is no homogeneous architectural system and the distinguishing pro-files of neighborhoods are being lost. The lack of urban regulation, and the cultural hybridity of buildings and users intermix styles from various eras in a single street. The interaction of the monuments with advertising and political messages situates the organization of memory and visual order in heteroclite networks.

The agony of collections is the clearest symptom of how the classifications that used to distinguish the cultured from the popular, and both from the massive, are disappearing. Cultures no longer are grouped in fixed and stable wholes, and there-fore the possibility disappears of being cultured by knowing the repertory of "the great works," or of being popular because one manages the meaning of the objects and messages produced by a more or less closed community (an ethnic group, a neighbor-hood, a class). Now these collections renew their composition and their hierarchy with the fashions; they are crossed all the time and, to top it all off, each user can make his or her own collection. The technologies of reproduction permit each person to set up a repertory of records and cassettes in his or her home that combine the cultured with the popular, including those who already do this in the structure of their works: Piazzola, who mixes the tango with jazz and classical music, and Caetano Veloso and Chico Buarque, who appropriate at once the experimentation of the concrete poets, Afro-Brazilian traditions, and post-Webernian musical experimentation.

In addition, there is a proliferation of reproduction devices that we cannot define as either cultured or popular. In them collections are lost, and images and contexts – along with the semantic and historical references that used to bind together their meanings – are destructed.

Photocopiers. Books are unbound; anthologies approach authors incapable of being dealt with in symposia; new bindings group together chapters of diverse volumes following the logic not of intellectual production but of their uses: to prepare for an exam, to follow the tastes of a professor, to pursue sinuous itineraries absent in the routine classifications of bookstores and libraries. This fragmentary relation with books leads us to lose the structure in which the chapters are inserted; we descend, Monsiváis once wrote, into the "Xerox grade of reading." It is also true that the freer handling of texts, their reduction to notes, as desacralized as the tape-recorded class – which sometimes never passes to the written page because it is transferred directly to the screen of a computer – induces more fluid links among the texts and among students and knowledge.

Videocassette recorders. One forms his or her personal collection by mixing football games and Fassbinder films, North American series, Brazilian soap operas, and a debate over the foreign debt – what the channels broadcast when we are watching them, when we are working, or when we are sleeping. The recording may be immediate or delayed and with the possibility of erasing, rerecording, and verifying how it turned out. The video recorder resembles television and the library, says Jean Franco: "it permits the juxtaposition of very different topics starting from an arbi-trary system and directed to communities that transcend the limits between races, classes, and sexes" (1987: 56). In truth, the video recorder goes farther than the library. It reorders a series of traditional or modern oppositions: between the national and the foreign, leisure and work, news and entertainment, politics and fiction. It also intervenes in sociability by allowing us to not miss a social or family gathering because we are watching a program and by promoting networks for borrowing and exchanging cassettes.

Videos. This is the most intrinsically postmodern genre. Intergenre: it mixes music, image, and text. Transtemporal: it gathers together melodies and images of various epochs and freely cites deeds out of context; it takes up what was done by Magritte and Duchamp, but for mass audiences. Some works take advantage of the versatility of video to create works that are brief but dense and systematic: *Fotoromanza* by Antonioni, *Thriller* by John Landis, *All Night Long* by Bob Rafelson, for example. But in most cases all action is given in fragments; it does not ask us to concentrate or to look for a continuity. There is no history to speak of. Not even art history or the media matter: images are plundered from everywhere and in any order. In a two-minute video, the German singer Falco summarizes the story of *The Black Vampire* by Fritz Lang; Madonna dresses like Marilyn Monroe, copying the choreography of *Gentleman Prefer Blondes* and the facial expressions of Betty Boop: "Those who remember love the homage and the nostalgia. Those who have no memory of it or who were not born yet also love it as their eyes follow the treat that is being sold to them as something brand-new" (McAllister, 1989: 21–3). There is no interest in indicating what is new and what comes from before. To be a good spectator one has to abandon oneself to the rhythm and enjoy the ephemeral sights. Even the videos that present a story downplay or ironize it by means of parodying montages and abrupt accelerations. This training in a fleeting perception of the real has had so much success that it is not limited to discotheques or a few entertainment programs on television; in the United States and Europe there are channels that broadcast them twenty-four hours a day. There are business, political, music, advertising, and educational videos that are replacing the business manual, the pamphlet, the theatrical spectacle, and the more or less reasoned staging of politics in electoral meetings. They are cold, indirect dramatizations that do not require the personal presence of interlocutors. The world is seen as a discontinuous effervescence of images, art as fast food. This ready-to-think culture allows us to de-think historical events without worrying about understanding them. In one of his films Woody Allen made fun of what he had understood by speed-reading *War and Peace:* "It talks about Russia," he concluded. *Le Nouvel Observateur* says seriously that it finds a new way of reinterpreting the student revolts of 1968 using this aesthetic: they were a "revolt clip: hot montage of shock images, rupture of rhythm, cutoff ending" (1987: 43).

Video games. These are like the participative version of videos. When they take the place of movies – not only in the public's free time but in the space of the movie theaters that close for lack of viewers – the operation of cultural displacement is clear. From contemporary cinema they take the most violent aspects: war scenes, car and motorcycle races, karate and boxing matches. They familiarize directly with the sensuality and efficacy of technology; they provide a mirror-screen where power itself and the fascination of battling with the big forces of the world are staged by taking advantage of the latest techniques and without the risk of direct confrontations. They dematerialize and disembody danger, giving us only the pleasure of winning out over others, or the possibility, in being defeated, that the only thing lost is coins in a machine.

As studies on the effects of television established long ago, these new technological resources are not neutral, nor are they omnipotent. Their simple formal innovation implies cultural changes, but the final sign depends on the uses different actors assign to them. We cite them here because they crack the orders that used to classify and distinguish cultural traditions; they weaken historical meaning and the macrostructural conceptions to the benefit of intense and sporadic relations with isolated objects, with their signs and images. Some postmodern theorists argue that this predominance of immediate and dehistoricized relations is coherent with the collapse of the great metaphysical narratives.

Actually, there are no reasons to lament the decomposition of rigid collections that, by separating the cultured, the popular, and the massive, promoted inequalities. Nor do we think that there are prospects for restoring the classic order of modernity. We see in the irreverent crossings occasions for relativizing religious, political, national, ethnic, and artistic fundamentalisms that absolutize certain patrimonies and discriminate against the rest. But we wonder if extreme discontinuity as a perceptive habit, the diminution of opportunities for understanding the reelaboration of the subsistent meanings of some traditions and for intervening in their change, do not reinforce the unconsulted power of those who continue to be concerned with understanding and managing the great networks of objects and meanings; the transnationals and the states.

Among the decollecting and dehierarchizing strategies of the cultural technologies must be included the existing asymmetry in production and use between the central and the dependent countries and between consumers of different classes within the same society. The possibilities for taking advantage of technological innovations and adapting them to their own productive and communicational needs are unequal in the central countries – generators of inventions, with high investment in renovating their industries, goods, and services – and in Latin America, where investments are frozen because of the debt and austerity policies, where scientists and technicians work with ridiculous budgets or have to emigrate, and where control of the more modern cultural media is highly concentrated and depends a great deal on outside programming.

Of course it is not a question of returning to the paranoid denunciations and conspiratorial conceptions of history that accused the modernization of quotidian and mass culture of being an instrument of the powerful in order to better exploit. The question is to understand how the dynamic itself of technological development remodels society and coincides with or contradicts social movements. There are different kinds of technologies, each with various possibilities for development and articulation with the others. There are social sectors with diverse cultural capitals and dispositions for appropriating them with different meanings: decollecting and hybridization are not the same for the adolescents from the popular classes who go to public video-game parlors as they are for those from the middle and upper classes who have the games at home. The meanings of the technologies are constructed according to the ways they are institutionalized and socialized.

The technological remodeling of social practices does not always contradict traditional cultures and modern arts. It has extended, for example, the use of patrimonial goods and the field of creativity. Just as video games trivialize historical battles and some videos trivialize experimental art trends, computers and other uses of video make it easy to obtain data, visualize graphics and innovate them, simulate the use of pieces and information, and reduce the distance between conception and execution, knowledge and application, information and decision. This multiple appropriation of cultural patrimonies opens up original possibilities for experimentation and communication with democratizing uses, as is appreciated in the use some popular movements make of video.

But new technologies not only promote creativity and innovation; they also reproduce known structures. The three most frequent uses of video – consumption of commercial movies, porno films, and the recording of family events – repeat audiovisual practices initiated by photography and the Super 8. On the other hand, video art – explored mainly by painters, musicians, and poets – reaffirms the difference and the hermetism in a way similar to that of art galleries and movie clubs.

The coexistence of these contradictory uses reveals that the interactions of new technologies with previous culture makes them part of a much bigger project than the one they unleashed or the one they manage. One of these changes of long standing that technological intervention makes more evident is the reorganization of the links between groups and symbolic systems; the decollections and hybridizations no longer permit a rigid linking of social classes to cultural strata. Although many works remain within the minority or popular circuits for which they were made, the prevailing trend is for all sectors to mix into their tastes objects whose points of origin were previously separated. I do not want to say that this more fluid and complex circulation has evaporated class differences. I am only saying that the reorganization of the cultural stagings and the constant crossings of identities require that we ask ourselves in a different way about the orders that systematize the material and symbolic relations among groups.

Deterritorializing

The most radical inquiries into what it means to be entering and leaving modernity are by those who assume the tensions between deterritorialization and reterritorialization. With this I am referring to two processes: the loss of the "natural" relation of culture to geographical and social territories and, at the same time, certain relative, partial territorial relocalizations of old and new symbolic productions.

In order to document this transformation of contemporary cultures I will analyze first the transnationalization of symbolic markets and migrations. Then I propose to explore the aesthetic meaning of this change by following the strategies of some impure arts.

1.   There was a method of associating the popular with the national that, as we noted in earlier chapters, nourished the modernization of Latin American cultures. Carried out first in the form of colonial domination, then as industrialization and urbanization under metropolitan models, modernity seemed to be organized in politicoeconomic and cultural antagonisms: colonizers versus colonized, cosmopolitanism versus nationalism. The last pair of opposites was the one handled by dependency theory, according to which everything was explained by the confrontation between imperialism and national popular cultures.

Studies of economic and cultural imperialism served to get to know some devices used by the international centers of scientific, artistic, and communicational production that conditioned, and still condition, our development. But this model is insufficient for understanding current power relations. It does not explain the planetary functioning of an industrial, technological, financial, and cultural system whose headquarters is not in a single nation but in a dense network of economic and ideological structures. Nor does it take into account the need of metropolitan nations to make their borders flexible and integrate their economies and their educational, technological, and cultural systems, as is occurring in Europe and North America.

The persistent inequality between what the dependency theorists called the First and the Third Worlds maintains with relative effect some of their postulates. But although the decisions and benefits of the exchanges may be concentrated in the bourgeoisie of the metropolises, new processes make the asymmetry more complex: the decentralization of corporations, the planetary simultaneity of information, and the adaptation of certain international forms of knowledge and images to the knowledge and habits of each community. The delocalization of symbolic products by electronics and telematics, and the use of satellites and computers in cultural diffusion, also impede our continuing to see the confrontations of peripheral countries as frontal combats with geographically defined nations.

The Manichaeism of those oppositions becomes even less realistic in the eighties and nineties when several dependent countries are registering a notable increase in their cultural exports. In Brazil, the advance of massification and industrialization of culture did not imply – contrary to what tended to be said – a greater dependency on foreign production. Statistics reveal that in the last several years its cinematography and the proportion of national films on the screens grew: from 13.9 percent in 1971 to 35 percent in 1982. Books by Brazilian authors, which accounted for 54 percent of publishing production in 1973, rose to 70 percent in 1981. Also, more national records and cassettes are listened to, while imported music declines. In 1972, 60 percent of television programming was foreign; in 1983, it fell to 30 percent. At the same time that this trend toward nationalization and autonomy is occurring in cultural production, Brazil is becoming a very active agent in the Latin American market of symbolic goods by exporting soap operas. As it also succeeds in broadly penetrating the central countries, it became the seventh world producer of television and advertising, and the sixth in records. Renato Ortiz, from whom I take these data, concludes that they went "from defense of the national popular to exportation of the international popular" (1988: 182–206).

Although this trend does not occur in the same way in all Latin American countries, there are similar aspects in those of more modern cultural development that reestablish the articulations between the national and the foreign. Such changes do not eliminate the question of how distinct classes benefit from and are represented in the culture produced in each country, but the radical alteration of the stagings of production and consumption – as well as the character of the goods that are presented – questions the "natural" association of the popular with the national and the equally a priori opposition with the international.

2.   Multidirectional migrations are the other factor that relativizes the binary and polar paradigm in the analysis of intercultural relations. Latin American internationalization is accentuated in the last few decades, when migrations not only include writers, artists, and exiled politicians as happened since last century, but settlers from all social layers. How do we include in the one-directional schema of imperialist domination the new flows of cultural circulation opened up by the transplants of Latin Americans to the United States and Europe, from the least-developed countries to the most prosperous ones of our continent, from poor regions to urban centers? Are there two million South Americans who, according to the most conservative statistics, left Argentina, Chile, Brazil, and Uruguay in the seventies because of ideological persecution and economic suffering? It is not accidental that the most innovative reflection on deterritorialization is unfolding in the principal area of migrations on the continent – the border between Mexico and the United States.

From both sides of that border, intercultural movements show their painful face: the underemployment and uprooting of peasants and indigenous people who had to leave their lands in order to survive. But a very dynamic cultural production is also growing there. If there are more than 250 Spanish-language radio and television stations in the United States, more than fifteen hundred publications in Spanish, and a high interest in Latin American literature and music, it is not only because there is a market of twenty million "Hispanics," or 8 percent of the US population (38 percent in New Mexico, 25 percent in Texas, and 23 percent in California). It is also due to the fact that so-called Latin culture produces films like *Zoot Suit* and *La Bamba*, the songs of Rubén Blades and Los Lobos, aesthetically and culturally advanced theaters like that of Luis Valdez, and visual artists whose quality and aptitude for making popular culture interact with modern and postmodern symbolism incorporates them into the North American mainstream.[3]

Whoever is familiar with these artistic movements knows that many are rooted in the everyday experiences of the popular sectors. So that no doubts remain about the transclass extent of the phenomenon of deterritorialization, it is useful to refer to the anthropological investigations on migrants. Roger Rouse studied the inhabitants of Aguililla, a rural town in southwestern Michoacán, apparently only accessible by a dirt road. Its two main activities continue to be agriculture and raising livestock for subsistence, but the emigration that began in the forties was such an incentive that almost all families there now have members who live or have lived abroad. The declining local economy is sustained by the flow of dollars sent from California, especially from Redwood City, that nucleus of microelectronics and post-industrial North American culture in Silicon Valley, where the Michoacanos work as laborers and in services. Most stay for brief periods in the United States, and those who remain longer maintain constant relations with their place of origin. There are so many outside of Aguililla, and so frequent are their connections with those who remain there, that one can no longer conceive of the two wholes as separate communities:

> Through the constant migration back and forth and the growing use of telephones, the residents of Aguililla tend to be reproducing their links with people that are two thousand miles away as actively as they maintain their relations with their immediate neighbors. Still more, and more generally, through the continuous circulation of people, money, commodities, and information, the diverse settlements have intermingled with such force that they are probably better understood as forming only one community dispersed in a variety of places. (Rouse, 1988: 1–2)

Two conventional notions of social theory collapse in the face of these "crossed economies, meaning systems that intersect, and fragmented personalities." One of these is that of "community," employed both for isolated peasant populations and for expressing the abstract cohesion of a compact national state, in both cases definable by relation to a specific territory. It was assumed that the links between the members of those communities would be more intense inside than outside of their space, and that the members treat the community as the principal medium to which they adjust their actions. The second image is the one that opposes center and periphery, also an "abstract expression of an idealized imperial system," in which the gradations of power and wealth would be distributed concentrically: most in the center and a progressive decrease as we move toward surrounding zones. The world functions less and less in this way, says Rouse; we need "an alternative cartography of social space" based instead on the notions of "circuit" and "border."

It also should not be assumed, he adds, that this reordering only includes those on the margins. He notes a similar disarticulation in the economy of the United States, previously dominated by autonomous blocks of capital. In the central area of Los Angeles, 75 percent of the buildings now belong to foreign capital; in all urban centers combined, 40 percent of the population consists of ethnic minorities from Asia and Latin America, and "it is calculated that this number will approach 60 percent in the year 2010" (Rouse, 1988: 2). There is an "implosion of the third world in the first," according to Renato Rosaldo (n.d.: 9); "the notion of an authentic culture as an autonomous internally coherent universe is no longer sustainable" in either of these two worlds, "except perhaps as a 'useful fiction' or a revealing distortion" (Rosaldo, 1989: 217).

When, in the last few years of his life, Michel de Certeau taught in San Diego, he used to say that in California the mix of immigrants from Mexico, Colombia, Norway, Russia, Italy, and the eastern United States made him think that "life consists of constantly crossing borders." Roles are taken and changed with the same versatility as cars and houses:

> This mobility rests on the postulate that one is not identified either by birth, by family, by professional status, by friendships or love relationships, or by property. It seems as if all identity defined by status and place (of origin, of work, of residence, etc.) were reduced, if not swept away, by the velocity of all movements. It is known that there is no identity document in the United States; it is replaced by the driver's license and the credit card, that is, by the capacity to cross space and by participation in a game of fiduciary contracts between North American citizens. (Certeau, 1981: 10–18)[4]

During the two periods during which I studied the intercultural conflicts on the Mexican side of the border, in Tijuana, in 1985 and 1988, several times I thought that this city is, along with New York, one of the biggest laboratories of postmodernity.[5] In 1950 it had no more than sixty thousand inhabitants; today there are more than a million, with migrants from almost all regions of Mexico (mainly Oaxaca, Puebla, Michoacán, and the Federal District) who have settled there over the years. Some go daily into the United States to work; others cross the border during the planting and harvesting seasons. Even those who stay in Tijuana are linked to commercial exchanges between the two countries, to North American *maquiladoras* located on the Mexican border, or to tourist services for the three or four million people from the United States who arrive in this city every year.

From the beginning of this century until fifteen years ago, Tijuana was known for a casino (abolished during the Cárdenas government), cabarets, dance halls, and liquor stores where North Americans came to elude their country's prohibitions on sex, gambling, and alcohol. The recent installation of factories, modern hotels, cultural centers, and access to wide-ranging international information has made it into a modern, contradictory, cosmopolitan city with a strong definition of itself.

In interviews we did of primary, secondary, and university students, and of artists and cultural promoters from all social layers, there was no theme more central for their self-definition than border life and intercultural contacts. One of our research techniques was to ask them to name the most representative places of life and culture in Tijuana in order to photograph them later; we also took pictures of other scenes that seemed to condense the city's meaning (publicity posters, casual encounters, graffiti) and selected fifty photos to show to fourteen groups from various economic and cultural levels. Two-thirds of the images they judged most representative of the city, and about which they spoke with the greatest emphasis, were those that linked Tijuana with what lies beyond it: Revolution Avenue, its shops and tourist centers, the minaret that bears witness to where the casino was, the parabolic antennas, the legal and illegal passages on the border, the neighborhoods where those from different parts of the country are concentrated, the tomb of the Unknown Soldier, "lord of the émigrés," to whom they go to ask that he arrange their "papers" or to thank him for their not having been caught by *la migra* (or Immigration).

The multicultural character of the city is expressed in the use of Spanish, English, and also indigenous languages in the neighborhoods and *maquiladoras*, or among those who sell crafts downtown. This pluralism diminishes when we move from private interactions to public languages, that is, those of radio, television, and urban advertising, where English and Spanish predominate and coexist "naturally."

Along with the poster that recommends the disco club and the radio station that plays "rock in your language," another announces a Mexican liqueur in English. Music and alcoholic beverages – two symbols of Tijuana – coexist under this linguistic duality. "The other choice" is explicitly the liqueur, but the contiguity of the messages makes it possible that it also refers to rock in Spanish. The ambivalence of the image, which the interviewees considered analogous to life in the city, also allows us to conclude – following the order of reading – that the other choice is English.

The uncertainty generated by the bilingual, bicultural, and binational oscillations has its equivalence in the relations with its own history. Some of the photos were chosen precisely because they allude to the simulated character of a good portion of Tijuana culture. The Hot Water Tower, burned in the 1960s with the intention of forgetting the casino it represented, was rebuilt a few years ago and now is exhibited with pride on magazine covers and in advertising; but in pointing out to the interviewees that the current tower is in a different location than the original one, they argue that the change is a way of displacing and relocating the past.

On several corners of Revolution Avenue there are zebras. In reality they are painted burros. They are there so that North American tourists can be photographed with a landscape behind them in which images from various regions of Mexico are crowded together: volcanoes, Aztec figures, cacti, the eagle with the serpent. "Faced with the lack of other types of things, as there are in the south where there are pyramids, there is none of that here . . . as if something had to be invented for the gringos," they said in one of the groups. In another group, they pointed out that "it also refers to the myth that North Americans bring with them, that it has something to do with crossing the border into the past, into the wilderness, into the idea of being able to ride horseback."

One interviewee told us: "The wire that separates Mexico from the United States could be the main monument of culture on the border."

In arriving at the beach "the line" falls and leaves a transit zone, used at times by undocumented migrants. Every Sunday the fragmented families on both sides of the border gather for picnics.

Where the borders move, they can be rigid or fallen; where buildings are evoked in another place than the one they represent, every day the spectacular invention of the city itself is renewed and expanded. The simulacrum comes to be a central category of culture. Not only is the "authentic" relativized. The obvious, ostentatious illusion – like the zebras that everyone knows are fake or the hiding games of illegal migrants that are "tolerated" by the United States police – becomes a resource for defining identity and communicating with others.

To these hybrid and simulated products, border artists and writers add their own intercultural laboratory. The following is from a radio interview with Guillermo Gómez-Peña, editor of the bilingual journal *La línea quebrada/The broken line*, with offices in Tijuana and San Diego:

> REPORTER: If you love our country so much, as you say you do, why do you
>   live in California?
> GÓMEZ-PEÑA: I am de-Mexicanizing myself in order to Mexicomprehend
>   myself . . .
> REPORTER: What do you consider yourself, then?
> GÓMEZ-PEÑA: Post-Mexica, pre-Chicano, pan-Latino, land-crossed, Art American
>   . . . it depends on the day of the week or the project in question.

Several Tijuana periodicals are dedicated to reworking the definitions of identity and culture taking the border experience as their starting point. *La línea quebrada*, which is the most radical, says that it expresses a generation that grew up "watching *charro* and science-fiction movies, listening to cumbias and Moody Blues songs, building altars and filming in Super 8, reading *El Corno Emplumado* and *Art Forum*." Since they live in the interval, "in the crack between the two worlds," and since they are "the ones who didn't go because we didn't fit, the ones who still don't arrive or don't know where to arrive," they decide to assume all possible identities:

> When they ask me my nationality or ethnic identity, I cannot respond with one word, since my "identity" has multiple repertories: I am Mexican but also Chicano and Latin American. On the border they call me "chilango" or "mexiquillo"; in the capital "pocho" or "norteño," and in Europe "sudaca." Anglo-Saxons call me "Hispanic" or "Latino," and Germans have more than once confused me with being Turkish or Italian.

With a phrase that would please a migrant as much as a young rocker, Gómez-Peña explains that "our deepest generational feeling is that of the loss that arises from the departure." But there are also things that they have gained: "a view of culture that is more experimental, that is, multifocal and tolerant" (Gómez-Peña, 1987: 3–5).[6]

Other artists and writers from Tijuana question the euphemized view of the contradictions and the uprooting they perceive in the *La línea quebrada* group. They reject the celebration of the migrations often caused by poverty in the place from which people migrate, and which is repeated in their new destination. There is no lack of those who, despite not having been born in Tijuana, contest this parodic and detached insolence in the name of their fifteen or twenty years in the city: "people who have arrived recently and want to discover us and tell us who we are."

Both in this polemic and in other manifestations of strong emotions in referring to the photos of Tijuana, we saw a complex movement that we would call *reterritorialization*. The same people who praise the city for being open and cosmopolitan want to fix signs of identification and rituals that differentiate them from those who are just passing through, who are tourists, or . . . anthropologists curious to understand intercultural crossings.

The editors of the other Tijuana journal, *Esquina baja*, devoted a long time to explaining to us why they wanted, in addition to having an organ in which to express themselves,

> to generate an audience of readers, a local journal of quality in all aspects, such as design and presentation . . . in order to counteract a bit that centrist trend that exists in the country, because what there is in the provinces does not succeed in transcending, and is minimized, if it does not first pass through the fine sieve of the Federal District.

We find something similar in the vehemence with which everyone rejected the "missionary" criteria for cultural activities favored by the central government. Against the national programs designed to "affirm Mexican identity" on the northern border, Baja Californians argue that they are as Mexican as the rest, though in a different way. About the "threat of North American cultural penetration" they say that, in spite of the geographic and communicational proximity to the United States, the daily commercial and cultural exchanges make them live inequality intensely and therefore have a less idealized image of those who receive a similar influence in the capital via television messages and imported consumer goods.

Deterritorialization and reterritorialization. In the exchanges of traditional symbols with international communications circuits, culture industries, and migrations, questions about identity and the national, the defense of sovereignty, and the unequal appropriation of knowledge and art do not disappear. The conflicts are not erased, as neoconservative postmodernism claims. They are placed in a different register, one that is multifocal and more tolerant, and the autonomy of each culture is rethought – sometimes – with smaller fundamentalist risks. Nevertheless, the chauvinist critiques of "those from the center" sometimes engender violent conflicts: acts of aggression against recently arrived migrants and discrimination in school and at work.

The intense crossings and the instability of traditions, bases of the valorizing opening, may also be – in conditions of labor competition – a source of prejudice and confrontation. Therefore, the analysis of the advantages or inconveniences of deterritorialization should not be reduced to the movements of ideas or cultural codes, as is frequently the case in the bibliography on postmodernity. Their meaning is also constructed in connection with social and economic practices, in struggles for local power, and in the competition to benefit from alliances with external powers.

Oblique Powers

This crossing of some postmodern transformations of the symbolic market and of everyday culture contributes to understanding the failure of certain ways of doing politics that are based on two principles of modernity: the autonomy of symbolic processes and the democratic renewal of the cultured and the popular. Likewise, it can help us explain the generalized success of neoconservative politics and the lack of socializing or more democratic alternatives adapted to the level of technological development and the complexity of the social crisis. In addition to the economic advantages of the neoconservative groups, their action is facilitated by their having better captured the sociocultural meaning of the new structures of power.

Starting from what we have been analyzing, a key question returns: the cultural reorganization of power. It is a question of analyzing *what the political consequences are of moving from a vertical and bipolar conception of sociopolitical relations to one that is decentered and multidetermined.*

It is understandable that there is resistance to this displacement. The Manichaean and conspiratorial representations of power find partial justification in some contemporary processes. The central countries use technological innovations to accentuate the asymmetry and inequality between them and the dependent countries. The hegemonic classes take advantage of industrial reconversion to reduce workers' employment, cut back the power of the unions, and commercialize goods – among which are educational and cultural ones – about which, after historic struggles, agreement had been reached that they were public services. It would seem that the big groups in which power is concentrated are the ones that subordinate art and culture to the market, the ones that discipline work and daily life.

A broader view allows us to see other economic and political transformations, supported by long-lasting cultural changes, that are giving a different structure to the conflicts. The crossings between the cultured and the popular render obsolete the polar representation between both modalities of symbolic development, and therefore revitalize the political opposition between hegemonics and subalterns, conceived as if it were a question of totally distinct and always opposed groups. What we know today about the intercultural operations of the mass media and new technologies, and about the reappropriation that makes of them diverse receivers, distances us from the theses about the omnipotent manipulation of the big metropolitan consortia. The classic paradigms with which domination was explained are incapable of taking into account the dissemination of the centers, the multipolarity of social initiatives, the plurality of references – taken from diverse territories – with which artists, artisans, and the mass media assemble their works.

The increase in processes of hybridization makes it evident that we understand very little about power if we only examine confrontations and vertical actions. Power would not function if it were exercised only by bourgeoisie over proletarians, whites over indigenous people, parents over children, the media over receivers. Since all these relations are *interwoven* with each other, each one achieves an effectiveness that it would never be able to by itself. But it is not simply a question of some forms of domination being superimposed on others and thereby being strengthened. What gives them their efficacy is the obliqueness that is established in the fabric. How can we discern where ethnic power ends and where family power begins, or the borders between political and economic power? Sometimes it is possible, but what is most important is the shrewdness with which the cables are mixed, and secret orders passed and responded to affirmatively.

Hegemonic, subaltern: heavy words that helped us to name the divisions between people but not to include movements of affection and participation in solidary or complicit activities in which hegemonic and subaltern groups are needed. Those who work on the border in constant relation with the tourism, factories, and language of the United States look strangely at those who consider them to be absorbed by the empire. For the protagonists of those relations, the interferences of English in their speech (to a certain extent equivalent to the infiltration of Spanish in the South of the United States) express the indispensable transactions in which everyday exchanges happen.

It is not necessary to look at those transactions as phenomena exclusive to zones of dense interculturalism. The ideological dramatization of social relations tends to exalt so much the oppositions that it ends by not seeing the rites that unite and connect them; it is a sociology of gratings, not of what is said through them or when they are not there. The most rebellious popular sectors and the most combative leaders satisfy their basic needs by participating in a system of consumption that they do not choose. They cannot invent the place where they work, the transportation that brings them there, nor the school where they educate their children, nor their food, nor their clothes, nor the media that supply them with daily information. Even protests against that order are made using a language they do not choose and demonstrating in streets or squares that were made by others. However many transgressive uses they make of the language, the streets, and the squares, the resignification is temporary and does not cancel the weight of the habits whereby we reproduce the sociocultural order, inside and outside of ourselves.

These realities – so obvious, but usually omitted in the ideological dramatization of conflicts – become clearer when nonpolitical behaviors are observed. Why do the popular sectors support those who oppress them? Medical anthropologists observe that in the face of health problems, the usual conduct of subaltern groups is not to attack the exploitation that makes it difficult for them to receive adequate care, but rather to accommodate themselves to the uses of the illness by private medicine or to take advantage as much as possible of deficient state services. This is not due to a lack of consciousness about their health needs, about the oppression that weighs them down, nor about the inadequacy or speculative cost of the services. Even when radical means of action are available for confronting inequality, they opt for intermediate solutions. The same thing happens in other scenarios. In the face of the economic crisis, they demand better salaries and at the same time limit their own consumption. Against political hegemony, the transaction consists, for example, in accepting personal relations in order to obtain individual benefits; in the ideological realm, in incorporating and positively valuing elements produced outside of their own group (criteria of prestige, hierarchies, designs, and functions of objects). The same combination of scientific and traditional practices – going to the doctor or to the healer – is a transactional way of taking advantage of the resources of both medicines, whereby the users reveal a conception that is more flexible than that of the modern medical system, so attached to allopathy, and of many anthropologists and folklorists who idealize the autonomy of traditional practices. From the perspective of the users, both therapeutic modalities are complementary and function as repertoires of resources starting from which they effect transactions between hegemonic and popular knowledge.[9]

The hybridizations described throughout this book bring us to the conclusion that today all cultures are border cultures. All the arts develop in relation to other arts: handicrafts migrate from the countryside to the city; movies, videos, and songs that recount events of one people are interchanged with others. Thus cultures lose the exclusive relation with their territory, but they gain in communication and knowledge.

There is yet another way in which the obliquity of the symbolic circuits allows us to rethink the links between culture and power. The search for mediations and diagonal ways for managing conflicts gives cultural relations a prominent place in political development. When we do not succeed in changing whoever governs, we satirize him or her in Carnival dances, journalistic humor, and graffiti. Against the impossibility of constructing a different order, we establish masked challenges in myths, literature, and comic strips. The struggle between classes or ethnic groups is, most of the time, a metaphorical struggle. Sometimes, starting from metaphors, new transformative practices slowly or unexpectedly invade the picture.

At every border there are rigid wires and fallen wires. Exemplary actions, cultural rodeos, rites are ways of going beyond the limits wherever possible. I think of the cunning of undocumented migrants in the United States, of the parodic rebelliousness of Colombian and Argentine graffiti. I remember the Mothers of the Plaza de Mayo walking every Thursday in a cyclical ritualism, holding photos of their disappeared children like icons, until they succeeded years later in having some of the guilty condemned to prison.

But the frustrations of human rights organizations make us reflect also on the role of culture as a symbolic expression for sustaining a demand when political paths are closed. The day the Argentine Congress approved the Law of Ending (Ley de Punto Final), which absolved hundreds of torturers and murderers, two formerly disappeared persons put themselves into narrow booths, handcuffed and blindfolded, in front of the legislative palace, with posters that said "The end means returning to this" – the ritual repetition of disappearance and confinement as the only way of preserving memory of them when political failure seemed to eliminate them from the social horizon.

This limited symbolic effectiveness leads to that fundamental distinction for defining relations between the cultural and political fields that we analyzed in the preceding chapter: the difference between *action* and *acting*. A chronic difficulty in the political valorization of cultural practices is to understand them as actions – that is, as effective interventions in the material structures of society. Certain sociologizing readings also measure the utility of a mural or a film by its capacity to perform and generate immediate and verifiable modifications. It is hoped that the spectators respond to the supposed "conscientizing" actions with " consciousness-raising" and "real changes" in their conduct. As this almost never happens, one reaches pessimistic conclusions about the efficacy of artistic messages.

Cultural practices are performances more than actions. They represent and simulate social actions but only sometimes operate as an action. This happens not only in cultural activities that are expressly organized and acknowledged as such; ordinary behaviors too, whether grouped in institutions or not, employ simulated action and symbolic performance. Presidential discourses in the face of a conflict that cannot be resolved with the available resources, the criticism of governmental performance by political organizations without the power to reverse it, and, of course, the verbal rebellions of the common citizen are performances that are more understandable for the theatrical gaze than for that of "pure" politics. Anthropology informs us that this is not due to the distance that crises put between ideals and acts but to the constitutive structure of the articulation between the political and the cultural in any society. Perhaps the greatest interest for politics in taking into account the symbolic problematic lies not in the sure efficacy of certain goods or messages but in the fact that the theatrical and ritual aspects of the social make evident what there is of the oblique, the simulated, and the deferred in any interaction.

Notes

1 On Chile, see Lechner's *Notas sobre la vida cotidiana* and Brunner's *Un espejo trizado Ensayos sobre cultura y politicas*, especially the first part. With respect to Argentina, see Landi (1984).
2 The photos of this series of monuments were taken by Paolò Gori. The book that he did with Helen Escobedo is entitled *Mexican Monuments: Strange Encounters* (1980). A more extensive analysis of the problems treated here can be found in my article "Monuments, Billboards, and Graffiti," included in that volume. I am grateful to the Institute of Aesthetic Research of the National University of Mexico for having facilitated my access to photos by Gori that were not included in the book, and that were donated by the author to that institution.
3 Two historians of Chicano art, Shifra M. Goldman and Tomás Ybarra-Frausto, have documented this cultural production and reflected upon it in an original way (1985). See, for example, the introductions to their book *Arte Chicago: A Comprehensive Annotated Bibliography of Chicago Art, 1965–1981*: see also the articles by both of them in Rodriguez Prampolini.
4 It should be clarified that the conception of life as a constant crossing of borders, although it remains adequate, is not as easy as Michel de Certeau pronounces it when it is a question of "second-class" North American citizens – for example, blacks, Puerto Ricans, and Chicanos.
5 The report of this investigation can be read in García Canclini and Safa, *Tijuana: la also de toda la genri*: photos by Lourdes Grobet. Jennifer Metcalfe, Federico Rosas, and Ernesto Bermejillo collaborated in the study.
6 With respect to the intercultural hybridization among rockers, *cholos*, and punks who produce magazines, records, and cassettes with information and music from various continents – see Valenzuela (1998).
7 The second slogan involves a play on words that does not translate into English without losing the effect of the original Spanish: "Dios no cumple. Ni años." But the free translation given here captures more or less the sentiment of the original. – *Trans.*
8 This affirmation, like others I cite from Fontanarrosa, was obtained in a personal interview with him in Rosario, Argentina, on 18 March 1988.
9 I am using here the investigations carried out by Menéndez and Módena, who extensively analyze the practices of transaction.

References

Baudrillard, Jean (1981) *For a Critique of the Political Economy of the Sign*, trans. Charles Levin. St. Louis, Mo.: Telos Press.

Benjamin, Walter (1969) "Unpacking My Library: A Talk about Book Collecting." In *Illuminations*, trans. Harry Zohn. New York: Schocken Books.

Brunner, José Joaquín (1988) *Un espejo trizado. Ensayos sobre cultura y políticas culturales.* Santiago: FLACSO.

Castells, Manuel (1973) *La cuestión urbana*, 2nd edn. Mexico: Siglo.

Certeau, Michel de (1981) "Californie, un théâtre de passants," *Autrement*, 31 (April).

Franco, Jean (1987) "Recibir a los bárbaros: ética y cultura de masas," *Nexos*, 115 (July), Mexico.

Goldman, Shifra M., and Tomás Ybarra-Frausto (1985) *Arte Chicano: A Comprehensive Annotated Bibliography of Chicano Art, 1965–1981*. Berkeley: Chicano Studies Library and Publications Unit, University of California.

Gómez-Peña, Guillermo (1987) "Wacha ese border, son," *La Jornada Semanal*, 162 (October 27).

Gori, Paolo, and Helen Escobedo (eds.) (1989) *Mexican Monuments: Strange Encounters.* New York: Abbeville Press.

Gutiérrez, Leandro H., and Luis Alberto Romero (1985) "La cultura de los sectores populares porteños," *Espacios* 2. Universidad de Buenos Aires.

Landi, Oscar (1984) "Cultura y política en la transición democrática." In *Proceso, crisis y transición democrática*, vol. 1, ed. Oskar Oszlak. Buenos Aires: Centro Editor de América Latina.

Le Nouvel Observateur (1987), January 9–15: 43.

Lechner, Norbert (1982) *Notas sobre la vida cotidiana: habitar, trabajar, consumir*, vol. 1, part 1. Santiago: FLACSO.

Lyotard, Jean-François (1993) *The Postmodern Explained: Correspondence 1982–1985*, translation edited by Julian Pefanis and Morgan Thomas. Minneapolis: University of Minnesota Press.

McAllister, Ricardo (1989) "Videoclips. La estética del parpadeo," *Crisis*, Mexico: 67 (January–February), Buenos Aires.

Menéndez, Eduardo (1981) *Poder, estratificación y salud*. Mexico: Ediciones de la Casa Chata.

Módena, María Eugenia (1990) *Madres, médicos y curanderos: diferencia cultural e identidad ideológica*. Mexico: CIESAS.

Ortiz, Renato (1988) *A moderna tradição brasileira*. São Paulo: Brasiliense.

Rosaldo, Renato (1989) *Culture and Truth: The Remaking of Social Analysis*. Boston, Mass.: Beacon Press.

—— (n.d.) *Ideology, Place, and People without Culture*. Stanford University, Department of Anthropology.

Rouse, Roger (1988) "Mexicano, Chicano, Pocho. La migración mexicana y el espacio social del posmodernismo," *Página Uno*, supplement to *Unomásuno* (December 31).

Sarlo, Beatriz (1988) *Una modernidad periférica: Buenos Aires 1920 y 1930*. Buenos Aires: Nueva Visión.

Valenzuela, José Manuel (1988) *A la brava ese! Cholos, punks, chavos banda*. Tijuana: Colegio de la Frontera Norte.

Verón, Eliseo (1985) "Discurso político y estrategia de la imagen. Entrevista de Rodolfo Fogwill," *Espacios*, 3 (December): 59–65.

Part V

The Postmodern Turn
and New Media

Introduction to Part V

Postmodernism lives. Legions of detractors and years of intellectual debate have done nothing to arrest its expansion or reduce its impact, and scores of usurpers have failed miserably in stultifying its scope. Despite or because of being profanely ambivalent and ambiguous, rejoicing in consumption and celebrating obsessions, ignoring consistency and avoiding stability, favoring illusions and pleasure, postmodernism is the only possible contemporary answer to a century worn out by the rise and fall of modern ideologies, the pervasion of capitalism, and an unprecedented sense of personal responsibility and individual impotence.

– Celeste Olalquiaga

The essays in this section represent positions on the contested and complex terrain of the "postmodern." The term is diverse and contradictory, and the essays in this section offer often conflicting interpretations of postmodern culture and media.[1] Ranging from Baudrillard's vision of a fragmented and hyperreal society of simulation to Jameson's Marxist analysis of postmodernism as the cultural logic of capitalism, these essays advance differing perspectives on a cultural and theoretical turn that has significantly transformed the ways we think about media, culture, and society.

French theorist Jean Baudrillard was one of the first to theorize a postmodern break in history.[2] In his studies of simulations and simulacra, which we excerpt from below, he distinguishes between modernity as an era of history organized around production, opposed to postmodernity as an era organized around simulations – by which he means models or images, as when situation comedies on television simulate real families and life, or virtual-reality games simulate the real.

For Baudrillard, the relationship implicit in the modernist idea of an original and a copy becomes transposed and disrupted in a postmodern era where referents and signifiers are no longer logically linked; rather, duplications represent the "real" in the postmodern world. On Baudrillard's definition, a "simulacrum," a copy without an original, is manifested in Disneyland, which he discusses as a simulation of an idealized America. On his reading, Disneyland provides a hyperreal model of the United States that is more-real-than-real, generating role models, ideals, and an image of a perfect world. Disneyland is also for Baudrillard a replica of a fantasy that serves to draw attention away from the Disneylike character of the rest of

America. Likewise, he claims that the Watergate scandal, which was not a scandal but rather, in his view, a normal outcome of the "monstrous unprincipled enterprise" of contemporary American politics, serves to deflect attention from the fact that American political life is itself corrupt to the core, that Watergate is not the exception but the rule.

The Baudrillardian simulacrum displaces and renders obsolete the idea of an "original." This society of simulacra is hyperreal – more real than any original could be – modeled on simulations and ideals that are then reproduced in actual existence; hence, the simulation or model comes to structure and constitute everyday life. In this original situation, simulations in the postmodern world replace and become reality, so that women undergo extensive cosmetic surgery to emulate the airbrushed and digitally manipulated models in the pages of magazines, and televised reenactments of crimes are accepted as news stories. This is a world in which power is not ideological but simulated, created through signs and models; it is a world in which there is no "subject," but rather a vortex of simulation created by constant implosions of images, information, and messages.

Fredric Jameson, in his highly influential article "Postmodernism, or the Cultural Logic of Late Capitalism," from which we excerpt here, interprets postmodernism as a type of cultural form appropriate to the contemporary stage of global capitalism.[3] In his ground-breaking essay, Jameson claims that postmodern culture manifests "the emergence of a new kind of flatness or depthlessness, a new kind of superficiality in the most literal sense – perhaps the supreme formal feature of all the postmodernisms" (1991, p. 9). Existentially, he identifies the "waning of affect" within fragmented postmodern selves devoid of the expressive energies characteristic of modernism. Such one-dimensional postmodern texts and selves put in question the continued relevance of hermeneutic depth models such as the Marxian model of essence and appearance, true and false consciousness; the Freudian model of latent and manifest meanings; the existentialist model of authentic and inauthentic existence; and the semiotic model of signifier and signified.

The models of postmodernity and postmodern culture advanced by Baudrillard and Jameson have been immensely influential in cultural studies. One version involves an appropriation of the collapse of high into low culture, of depth onto surface, and the audience into the text, such that distinctions within media culture and between texts, audiences, and contexts are increasingly difficult to make; in its more extreme versions, the postmodern turn in cultural studies excludes the very possibility of progressive or critical encoding or decoding of cultural texts, or production of alternative cultures. This version of postmodern cultural criticism thus signifies the death of hermeneutics: in place of what Paul Ricoeur (1970) termed a "hermeneutics of suspicion" and the interpretive reading of cultural symbols and texts, emerges a postmodern view that there is nothing behind the surface of texts, no depth or multiplicity of meanings for critical inquiry to discover and explicate. This version of postmodern cultural criticism thus renounces hermeneutics and tends to privilege the medium over the message, style over substance, and form over content. For postmodern theorists like Baudrillard, as for McLuhan, "the medium is the message" and the rise to cultural dominance of media culture is symptomatic of far-reaching social and cultural changes.

A more affirmative version of postmodern cultural theory and media theory celebrates the new culture in emphasis on the appearance, look, style, variety, and diversity of contemporary culture. Other theorists see potential for promoting new oppositional types of cultural analysis and politics in the field of the postmodern. Hal Foster (1983) distinguishes between a conservative postmodernism of quotation and pastiche of past cultural forms, contrasted to a postmodernism of resistance which champions art works that engage in social criticism and subversion. Indeed, many feminists, people of color, gays and lesbians, multiculturalists, postcolonialists, and others have developed diverse forms of postmodern cultural studies which stress otherness and marginality, valorizing the culture and practices of individuals and groups excluded from mainstream culture, and thus generating a cultural studies of the margins and oppositional voices. Néstor García Canclini (1995), for instance, describes the "hybrid cultures" and "oblique powers" of forms of popular art in Latin America, including monuments, graffiti, comic books, and songs, while Jésus Martín-Barbero describes how local groups and individuals assimilate media culture to construct their own popular forms.

Other theorists see potential for promoting innovative types of cultural analysis and politics in the field of the postmodern. Henry Jenkins's analysis of fan films in the digital age illustrates the creative aesthetic potential in the parodic, fantastic, often erotic, reworkings of mainstream commercial products such as the "Star Wars" films and spin-offs. He asserts that the proliferation of amateur cultural artifacts created by fans of mainstream texts is part of "a grassroots dialogue with mass culture," functioning in an interstice between commercial and alternative media. The "Do-It-Yourself" (DIY) movement and the availability of technologies that make media production easy and accessible to ordinary people (camcorders, digital editing, the Web) shift the terrain of media culture to include a welter of narratives and images, many of which appropriate and transform the iconography of the commercial. In Jenkins's view, this has allowed for a populist participatory culture that speaks back to the hegemonic limitations and restrictions brought about by media convergence and consolidated ownership of the culture industry. As he notes, the traditional theoretical oppositions between political economy and cultural studies cannot adequately address the multiple, dynamic, and complex relationships between media convergence and participatory culture that have been opened up by new modes of amateur production and distribution. The widespread public circulation of these quasi-commercial creations have opened up a "third space" of culture production which is at the heart of the legal and philosophical battles over intellectual property that mark the twenty-first-century media environment.

Angela McRobbie, in an essay "Feminism, Postmodernism and the 'Real Me'," wants to appropriate postmodernism for an activist feminist theory. She begins by noting that there are three approaches to postmodernism in today's conjuncture: those who simply affirm and celebrate it; those who completely reject it; and those who wish to avoid the excesses of a completely affirmative and highly rhetorical postmodernism for a "remorseless critique of modernity" combined with "a looking to those accounts of postmodernity as a way of finding a place from which to speak and a space from which to develop that critique of the places and the spaces of exclusion inside modernity." Herself a major participant in the development of British cultural studies, McRobbie cites Stuart Hall as a positive example of a productive appropriation of postmodernism. She emphasizes Hall's positioning of himself on "the other side of modernity," seeing "turbulence and savagery" while others perceive order and reason. From this perspective, the postmodern turn validates the discourses of those marginalized or oppressed within modern societies to speak and articulate experiences, positions, and perspectives suppressed in the canonical culture and master theories of the modern era.

McRobbie herself wants to use postmodernism for feminism, arguing that postmodern discourses put in question notions of "the real me," essentialist notions of the self that suggest there is a natural, unified, and hidden essence to the self that we should discover and realize. Such notions, McRobbie suggests, smuggle in conventional concepts of conformity and fixity, and cover over the ability to create more hybridized, complex, and unconventional selves that should be seen as contingent, flexible, and subject to further change and development. Such conceptions, McRobbie suggests, help women – and others! – to question the standard models of femininity (or masculinity, we would add), and to construct novel conceptions of their potential and possible lives.

In a study of "Postmodern Virtualities," Mark Poster highlights the importance of perceiving the implications of new media, communication, and information technologies. A scholar of French postmodern theory and new technologies, Poster proposes theorizing how new communication media are producing novel forms of culture and subjectivity. Citing the proliferation of information and communication technology, Poster argues against limited understanding of these phenomena as mere instruments that can be used by existing subjects and institutions. Rather, for Poster, the new media and technology are novel environments that create new realms of experience like virtual reality and innovative forms of communication and subjectivity. Just as books created an individual rational subject in the modern era of print culture, in the multimedia era, Poster claims, novel forms of cultural identity and experience are emerging in the virtual communities, cyberspaces, and relations of the emergent cyberculture.

For Poster and other theorists such as Sherry Turkle, proliferating computer technologies thus create novel identities, social relations, and realms of experience such as cyberspace, as well as fresh forms of communication within the emergent technoculture. Many postmodern theorists, such as Baudrillard and Poster, however, arguably exaggerate the rupture with the past, failing to note continuities, and the ways that the novelties they evoke are rooted in the dynamics of modernity (e.g. that the new technoculture is a part of a new stage of capitalism and integrally connected with globalization). Poster argues in his earlier book *Mode of Information* (1990), for example, that the mode of production is now transcended in importance by the mode of information as a fundamental principle of organizing society, just as Baudrillard argues that simulation is now the organizing principle of contemporary society and not political economy. We would argue, however, that the modes of production and information are intertwined within a new stage of capitalism and that we need both cultural analysis and political economy to make sense of this situation. Hence, while Poster highlights the importance of perceiving the connection of postmodernity with new media and new subjectivity, he does not link these phenomena with the restructuring of capital and globalization, and thus severs linkage between cultural analysis and political economy.

There is in fact a type of technological determinism in many variants of postmodern theory. Baudrillard and Poster both erase political economy and are overly determinist in descriptions of the forms of subjectivity and culture that the new technologies are producing. For Baudrillard, we are thrown into a novel world of simulation and hyperreality where the modern subject dissolves and implodes in a precession of simulacra. Reality, meaning, identity, and other modern categories dissolve for Baudrillard in what he describes as a "catastrophe of modernity." Poster and others see more positive potential in the new technologies, as well as the need for innovative cultural and political practices to promote a more democratic and egalitarian future. But there is a covert determinism in assuming that new media automatically generate new subjectivities and identities. It is for us too linear and reductive to claim that modern technology and culture produce one type of (rational, autonomous, centered, and stable) subject, while the new cyberculture produces multiple, hybridized, and flexible subjects. While Poster claims that the "second media age" of more interactive computer technology is responsible for generating the new subjectivity he valorizes, in fact earlier media such as film, radio, and television were already producing more fragmented, decentered, and hybridized subjects and presumably, we would argue, the features of a critical and autonomous rational modern subjectivity are still possible and valuable today.

Furthermore, just as there is extremely affirmative and celebratory embracing of postmodern theory, contrasted to passionate critiques and denunciations, so too are there positive and affirmative celebrations of the new media and technologies, as well as skeptical and critical perspectives. Hence, while Poster, Turkle, and myriad champions of the cyberculture see promising developments within new media and cultural spaces, some critics are skeptical, resisting claims concerning the emancipatory or novel features of new media and stressing by contrast the ways that capitalism is colonizing and controlling new media and how they are new sources of profitability, domination, and social control (see Golding 1998; Robins and Webster 1999; and Schiller 1999).

We would propose that there are both democratizing and empowering aspects and uses of new technologies, as well as more troubling features, such as threats to privacy and democracy and the empowering of corporations over individuals. Moreover, there are both continuities and discontinuities with previous technologies and modes of social organization. On the whole, we would maintain that we are in a novel cultural space between the modern and the postmodern, with highly complex conflicts between emergent and previous forms of culture, technology, and subjectivity. While we would agree that technological revolution and the global restructuring of capitalism are dramatically transforming our world, we believe that older modern theories and methods, as well as emergent postmodern ones, are valuable in helping us meet the challenges and changes of the contemporary era, and that there are negative and positive features in this turbulent transformation.

In any case, media and culture are more important than ever today, and so the contemporary student and citizen needs to become media and computer literate – indeed multimedia literate with new literacies for the present age (see Kellner 1998; Hammer and Kellner 1999). The texts we have assembled in this section provide some access to the brave new cultural and techno-logical worlds that we are inhabiting and dramatize the need for new understandings and approaches to culture and society if we are to survive the exigencies of the new millennium.

Notes

1   For an overview of postmodern theory and debates, see Best and Kellner (1991, 1997, and 2001).
2   See Baudrillard (1983a, 1983b, 1993, and 1994); for an overview of Baudrillard see Kellner (1989 and 2000).
3   On Jameson, see the essays collected in Kellner (1989c); Homer (1998); and Homer and Kellner (2004).

References

Baudrillard, Jean (1983a) *Simulations*. New York: Semiotext(e).
—— (1983b) *In the Shadow of the Silent Majorities*. New York: Semiotext(e).
—— (1983c) "The Ecstacy of Communication," in *The Anti-Aesthetic*, ed. Hal Foster. Washington: Bay Press.
—— (1993) *Symbolic Exchange and Death*. London: Sage.
—— (1994) *Simulacra and Simulation*. Ann Arbor: University of Michigan Press.
Best, Steven and Kellner, Douglas (1987) "(Re)Watching Television: Notes Toward a Political Criticism," *Diacritics* (Summer): 97–113.
—— (1991) *Postmodern Theory: Critical Interrogations*. London and New York: Macmillan and Guilford Press.
—— (1997) *The Postmodern Turn*. New York: Guilford Press.
—— (2001) *The Postmodern Adventure*. New York: Guilford Press.
Foster, Hal (1983) *The Anti-Aesthetic: Essays on Postmodern Culture*. Seattle: Bay Press.
García Canclini, Néstor (1995) *Hybrid Cultures: Strategies for Entering and Leaving Modernity*, trans. C. L. Chiappari and S. S. Lopes. Minneapolis: University of Minnesota Press.

Golding, Peter (1998) "Worldwide Wedge: Division and Contradiction in the Global Information Infrastructure," in *Electronic Empires: Global Media and Local Resistance*, ed. Daya Kishan Thussu. London: Arnold.

Hammer, Rhonda and Kellner, Douglas (1999) "Multimedia Pedagogical Curriculum for the New Millennium," *Journal of Adolescent & Adult Literacy* 42(7) (April): 522–6.

Homer, Sean (1998) *Fredric Jameson: Marxism, Hermeneutics, Postmodernism*. Cambridge: Polity Press.

Homer, Sean and Kellner, Douglas (2004) *Fredric Jameson: A Critical Reader*. London and New York: Palgrave Macmillan.

Jameson, Fredric (1984) "Postmodernism, or The Cultural Logic of Late Capitalism," *New Left Review* 146 (July–Aug.): 53–92.

Kellner, Douglas (1989b) *Jean Baudrillard: From Marxism to Postmodernism and Beyond*. Cambridge and Palo Alto: Polity Press and Stanford University Press.

—— (ed.) (1989c) *Postmodernism/Jameson/Critique*. Washington, DC: Maisonneuve.

—— (1998) "Multiple Literacies and Critical Pedagogy in a Multicultural Society," *Educational Theory* 48(1): 103–22.

Olalquiaga, Celeste (1992) "Prologue," in *Megalopolis*. Minneapolis: University of Minnesota Press, xi–xxi.

Poster, Mark (1990) *Mode of Information*. Palo Alto: Stanford University Press.

—— (1995) "Postmodern Virtualities," in *Cyberspace, Cyberbodies, Cyberpunk*, eds. Mike Featherstone and Rogers Burrows. London: Sage, 79–95.

Robins, Kevin and Webster, Frank (1999) *Times of the Technoculture*. New York: Routledge.

Ricoeur, Paul (1970) *Freud and Philosophy: An Essay on Interpretation*. New Haven: Yale University Press.

Schiller, Dan (1999) *Digital Capitalism*. Cambridge, MA: MIT Press.

Turkle, Sherry (1995) *Life on the Screen: Identity in the Age of the Internet*. New York: Simon & Schuster.

28

The Precession
of Simulacra

Jean Baudrillard

The simulacrum is never what hides the truth – it is truth that hides the fact that there is none.
The simulacrum is true.

– Ecclesiastes

If once we were able to view the Borges fable in which the cartographers of the Empire draw up a map so detailed that it ends up covering the territory exactly (the decline of the Empire witnesses the fraying of this map, little by little, and its fall into ruins, though some shreds are still discernible in the deserts – the metaphysical beauty of this ruined abstraction testifying to a pride equal to the Empire and rotting like a carcass, returning to the substance of the soil, a bit as the double ends by being confused with the real through aging) – as the most beautiful allegory of simulation, this fable has now come full circle for us, and possesses nothing but the discrete charm of second-order simulacra.[1]

Today abstraction is no longer that of the map, the double, the mirror, or the concept. Simulation is no longer that of a territory, a referential being, or a substance. It is the generation by models of a real without origin or reality: a hyperreal. The territory no longer precedes the map, nor does it survive it. It is nevertheless the map that precedes the territory – *precession of simulacra* – that engenders the territory, and if one must return to the fable, today it is the territory whose shreds slowly rot across the extent of the map. It is the real, and not the map, whose vestiges persist here and there in the deserts that are no longer those of the Empire, but ours. *The desert of the real itself.*

In fact, even inverted, Borges's fable is unusable. Only the allegory of the Empire, perhaps, remains. Because it is with this same imperialism that present-day simulators attempt to make the real, all of the real, coincide with their models of simulation.

From Jean Baudrillard, "The precession of simulacra." In *Simulacra and Simulation*, pp. 1–42. Translated by Sheila Faria Glaser. Ann Arbor: University of Michigan Press, 1994.

But it is no longer a question of either maps or territories. Something has disappeared: the sovereign difference, between one and the other, that constituted the charm of abstraction. Because it is difference that constitutes the poetry of the map and the charm of the territory, the magic of the concept and the charm of the real. This imaginary of representation, which simultaneously culminates in and is engulfed by the cartographer's mad project of the ideal coextensivity of map and territory, disappears in the simulation whose operation is nuclear and genetic, no longer at all specular or discursive. It is all of metaphysics that is lost. No more mirror of being and appearances, of the real and its concept. No more imaginary coextensivity: it is genetic miniaturization that is the dimension of simulation. The real is produced from miniaturized cells, matrices, and memory banks, models of control – and it can be reproduced an indefinite number of times from these. It no longer needs to be rational, because it no longer measures itself against either an ideal or negative instance. It is no longer anything but operational. In fact, it is no longer really the real, because no imaginary envelops it anymore. It is a hyperreal, produced from a radiating synthesis of combinatory models in a hyperspace without atmosphere.

By crossing into a space whose curvature is no longer that of the real, nor that of truth, the era of simulation is inaugurated by a liquidation of all referentials – worse: with their artificial resurrection in the systems of signs, a material more malleable than meaning, in that it lends itself to all systems of equivalences, to all binary oppositions, to all combinatory algebra. It is no longer a question of imitation, nor duplication, nor even parody. It is a question of substituting the signs of the real for the real, that is to say of an operation of deterring every real process via its operational double, a programmatic, metastable, perfectly descriptive machine that offers all the signs of the real and short-circuits all its vicissitudes. Never again will the real have the chance to produce itself – such is the vital function of the model in a system of death, or rather of anticipated resurrection, that no longer even gives the event of death a chance. A hyperreal henceforth sheltered from the imaginary, and from any distinction between the real and the imaginary, leaving room only for the orbital recurrence of models and for the simulated generation of differences.

The Divine Irreference of Images

To dissimulate is to pretend not to have what one has. To simulate is to feign to have what one doesn't have. One implies a presence, the other an absence. But it is more complicated than that because simulating is not pretending: "Whoever fakes an illness can simply stay in bed and make everyone believe he is ill. Whoever simulates an illness produces in himself some of the symptoms" (Littré). Therefore, pretending, or dissimulating, leaves the principle of reality intact: the difference is always clear, it is simply masked, whereas simulation threatens the difference between the "true" and the "false," the "real" and the "imaginary." Is the simulator sick or not, given that he produces "true" symptoms? Objectively one cannot treat him as being either ill or not ill. Psychology and medicine stop at this point, forestalled by the illness's henceforth undiscoverable truth. For if any symptom can be "produced," and can no longer be taken as a fact of nature, then every illness can be considered as simulatable and simulated, and medicine loses its meaning since it only knows how to treat "real" illnesses according to their objective causes. Psychosomatics evolves in a dubious manner at the borders of the principle of illness. As to psychoanalysis, it transfers the symptom of the organic order to the unconscious order: the latter is new and taken for "real" more real than the other – but why would simulation be at the gates of the unconscious? Why couldn't the "work" of the unconscious be "produced" in the same way as any old symptom of classical medicine? Dreams already are.

Certainly, the psychiatrist purports that "for every form of mental alienation there is a particular order in the succession of symptoms of which the simulator is ignorant and in the absence of which the psychiatrist would not be deceived." This (which dates from 1865) in order to safeguard the principle of a truth at all costs and to escape the interrogation posed by simulation – the knowledge that truth, reference, objective cause have ceased to exist. Now, what can medicine do with what floats on either side of illness, on either side of health, with the duplication of illness in a discourse that is no longer either true or false? What can psychoanalysis do with the duplication of the discourse of the unconscious in the discourse of simulation that can never again be unmasked, since it is not false either?[2]

What can the army do about simulators? Traditionally it unmasks them and punishes them, according to a clear principle of identification. Today it can discharge a very good simulator as exactly equivalent to a "real" homosexual, a heart patient, or a madman. Even military psychology draws back from Cartesian certainties and hesitates to make the distinction between true and false, between the "produced" and the authentic symptom. "If he is this good at acting crazy, it's because he is." Nor is military psychology mistaken in this regard: in this sense, all crazy people simulate, and this lack of distinction is the worst kind of subversion. It is against this lack of distinction that classical reason armed itself in all its categories. But it is what today again outflanks them, submerging the principle of truth.

Beyond medicine and the army, favored terrains of simulation, the question returns to religion and the simulacrum of divinity: "I forbade that there be any simulacra in the temples because the divinity that animates nature can never be represented." Indeed it can be. But what becomes of the divinity when it reveals itself in icons, when it is multiplied in simulacra? Does it remain the supreme power that is simply incarnated in images as a visible theology? Or does it volatilize itself in the simulacra that, alone, deploy their power and pomp of fascination – the visible machinery of icons substituted for the pure and intelligible Idea of God? This is precisely what was feared by Iconoclasts, whose millennial quarrel is still with us today.[3] This is precisely because they predicted this omnipotence of simulacra, the faculty simulacra have of effacing God from the conscience of man, and the destructive, annihilating truth that they allow to appear – that deep down God never existed, that only the simulacrum ever existed, even that God himself was never anything but his own simulacrum – from this came their urge to destroy the images. If they could have believed that these images only obfuscated or masked the Platonic Idea of God, there would have been no reason to destroy them. One can live with the idea of distorted truth. But their metaphysical despair came from the idea that the image didn't conceal anything at all, and that these images were in essence not images, such as an original model would have made them, but perfect simulacra, forever radiant with their own fascination. Thus this death of the divine referential must be exorcised at all costs.

One can see that the iconoclasts, whom one accuses of disdaining and negating images, were those who accorded them their true value, in contrast to the iconolaters who only saw reflections in them and were content to venerate a filigree God. On the other hand, one can say that the icon worshipers were the most modern minds, the most adventurous, because, in the guise of having God become apparent in the mirror of images, they were already enacting his death and his disappearance in the epiphany of his representations (which, perhaps, they already knew no longer represented anything, that they were purely a game, but that it was therein the great game lay – knowing also that it is dangerous to unmask images, since they dissimulate the fact that there is nothing behind them).

This was the approach of the Jesuits, who founded their politics on the virtual disappearance of God and on the worldly and spectacular manipulation of consciences – the evanescence of God in the epiphany of power – the end of transcendence, which now only serves as an alibi for a strategy altogether free of influences and signs. Behind the baroqueness of images hides the éminence grise of politics.

This way the stake will always have been the murderous power of images, murderers of the real, murderers of their own model, as the Byzantine icons could be those of divine identity. To this murderous power is opposed that of representations as a dialectical power, the visible and intelligible mediation of the Real. All Western faith and good faith became engaged in this wager on representation: that a sign could refer to the depth of meaning, that a sign could be exchanged for meaning and that something could guarantee this exchange – God of course. But what if God himself can be simulated, that is to say can be reduced to the signs that constitute faith? Then the whole system becomes weightless, it is no longer itself anything but a gigantic simulacrum – not unreal, but a simulacrum, that is to say never exchanged for the real, but exchanged for itself, in an uninterrupted circuit without reference or circumference.

Such is simulation, insofar as it is opposed to representation. Representation stems from the principle of the equivalence of the sign and of the real (even if this equivalence is utopian, it is a fundamental axiom). Simulation, on the contrary, stems from the utopia of the principle of equivalence, *from the radical negation of the sign as value*, from the sign as the reversion and death sentence of every reference. Whereas representation attempts to absorb simulation by interpreting it as a false representation, simulation envelops the whole edifice of representation itself as a simulacrum.

Such would be the successive phases of the image:

it is the reflection of a profound reality;
it masks and denatures a profound reality;
it masks the *absence* of a profound reality;
it has no relation to any reality whatsoever: it is its own pure simulacrum.

In the first case, the image is a *good* appearance – representation is of the sacramental order. In the second, it is an evil appearance – it is of the order of maleficence. In the third, it plays at being an appearance – it is of the order of sorcery. In the fourth, it is no longer of the order of appearances, but of simulation.

The transition from signs that dissimulate something to signs that dissimulate that there is nothing marks a decisive turning point. The first reflects a theology of truth and secrecy (to which the notion of ideology still belongs). The second inaugurates the era of simulacra and of simulation, in which there is no longer a God to recognize his own, no longer a Last Judgment to separate the false from the true, the real from its artificial resurrection, as everything is already dead and resurrected in advance.

When the real is no longer what it was, nostalgia assumes its full meaning. There is a plethora of myths of origin and of signs of reality – a plethora of truth, of secondary objectivity, and authenticity. Escalation of the true, of lived experience, resurrection of the figurative where the object and substance have disappeared. Panic-stricken production of the real and of the referential, parallel to and greater than the panic of material production: this is how simulation appears in the phase that concerns us – a strategy of the real, of the neoreal and the hyperreal that everywhere is the double of a strategy of deterrence.

Ramses, or the Rosy-Colored Resurrection

Ethnology brushed up against its paradoxical death in 1971, the day when the Philippine government decided to return the few dozen Tasaday who had just been discovered in the depths of the jungle, where they had lived for eight centuries without any contact with the rest of the species, to their primitive state, out of the reach of colonizers, tourists, and ethnologists. This at the suggestion of the anthropologists themselves, who were seeing the indigenous people disintegrate immediately upon contact, like mummies in the open air.

In order for ethnology to live, its object must die; by dying, the object takes its revenge for being "discovered" and with its death defies the science that wants to grasp it.

Doesn't all science live on this paradoxical slope to which it is doomed by the evanescence of its object in its very apprehension, and by the pitiless reversal that the dead object exerts on it? Like Orpheus, it always turns around too soon, and, like Eurydice, its object falls back into Hades.

It is against this hell of the paradox that the ethnologists wished to protect themselves by cordoning off the Tasaday with virgin forest. No one can touch them anymore: as in a mine the vein is closed down. Science loses precious capital there, but the object will be safe, lost to science, but intact in its "virginity." It is not a question of sacrifice (science never sacrifices itself, it is always murderous), but of the simulated sacrifice of its object in order to save its reality principle. The Tasaday, frozen in their natural element, will provide a perfect alibi, an eternal guarantee. Here begins an antiethnology that will never end and to which Jaulin, Castaneda,

Clastres are various witnesses. In any case, the logical evolution of a science is to distance itself increasingly from its object, until it dispenses with it entirely: its autonomy is only rendered even more fantastic – it attains its pure form.

The Indian thus returned to the ghetto, in the glass coffin of the virgin forest, again becomes the model of simulation of all the possible Indians *from before ethnology*. This model thus grants itself the luxury to incarnate itself beyond itself in the "brute" reality of these Indians it has entirely reinvented – Savages who are indebted to ethnology for still being Savages: what a turn of events, what a triumph for this science that seemed dedicated to their destruction!

Of course, these savages are posthumous: frozen, cryogenized, sterilized, protected *to death*, they have become referential simulacra, and science itself has become pure simulation. The same holds true at Cruesot, at the level of the "open" museum where one museumified in situ, as "historical" witnesses of their period, entire working-class neighborhoods, living metallurgic zones, an entire culture, men, women, and children included – gestures, languages, customs fossilized alive as in a snapshot. The museum, instead of being circumscribed as a geometric site, is everywhere now, like a dimension of life. Thus ethnology, rather than circumscribing itself as an objective science, will today, liberated from its object, be applied to all living things and make itself invisible, like an omnipresent fourth dimension, that of the simulacrum. *We are all Tasadays*, Indians who have again become what they were – simulacral Indians who at last proclaim the universal truth of ethnology.

We have all become living specimens in the spectral light of ethnology, or of antiethnology, which is nothing but the pure form of triumphal ethnology, under the sign of dead differences, and of the resurrection of differences. It is thus very naive to look for ethnology in the Savages or in some Third World – it is here, everywhere, in the metropolises, in the White community, in a world completely cataloged and analyzed, then *artificially resurrected under the auspices of the real*, in a world of simulation, of the hallucination of truth, of the blackmail of the real, of the murder of every symbolic form and of its hysterical, historical retrospection – a murder of which the Savages, noblesse oblige, were the first victims, but that for a long time has extended to all Western societies.

But in the same breath ethnology grants us its only and final lesson, the secret that kills it (and which the Savages knew better than it did): the vengeance of the dead.

The confinement of the scientific object is equal to the confinement of the mad and the dead. And just as all of society is irremediably contaminated by this mirror of madness that it has held up to itself, science can't help but die contaminated by the death of this object that is its inverse mirror. It is science that masters the objects, but it is the objects that invest it with depth, according to an unconscious reversion, which only gives a dead and circular response to a dead and circular interrogation.

Nothing changes when society breaks the mirror of madness (abolishes the asylums, gives speech back to the insane, etc.) nor when science seems to break the mirror of its objectivity (effacing itself before its object, as in Castaneda, etc.) and to bend down before the "differences." The form produced by confinement is followed by an innumerable, diffracted, slowed-down mechanism. As ethnology collapses in its classical institution, it survives in an antiethnology whose task it is to reinject the difference fiction, the Savage fiction everywhere, to conceal that it is this world, ours, which has again become savage in its way, that is to say, which is devastated by difference and by death.

In the same way, with the pretext of saving the original, one forbade visitors to enter the Lascaux caves, but an exact replica was constructed five hundred meters from it, so that everyone could see them (one glances through a peephole at the authentic cave, and then one visits the reconstituted whole). It is possible that the memory of the original grottoes is itself stamped in the minds of future generations, but from now on there is no longer any difference: the duplication suffices to render both artificial.

In the same way science and technology were recently mobilized to save the mummy of Ramses II, after it was left to rot for several dozen years in the depths of a museum. The West is seized with panic at the thought of not being able to save what the symbolic order had been able to conserve for forty centuries, but out of sight and far from the light of day. Ramses does not signify anything for us, only the mummy is of an inestimable worth because it is what guarantees that accumulation has meaning. Our entire linear and accumulative culture collapses if we cannot stockpile the past in plain view. To this end the pharaohs must be brought out of their tomb and the mummies out of their silence. To this end they must be exhumed and given military honors. They are prey to both science and worms. Only absolute secrecy assured them this millennial power – the mastery over putrefaction that signified the mastery of the complete cycle of exchanges with death. *We* only know how to place our science in service of *repairing* the mummy, that is to say restoring a *visible* order, whereas embalming was a mythical effort that strove to immortalize a *hidden* dimension.

We require a visible past, a visible continuum, a visible myth of origin, which reassures us about our end. Because finally we have never believed in them. Whence this historic scene of the reception of the mummy at the Orly airport. Why? Because Ramses was a great despotic and military figure? Certainly. But mostly because our culture dreams, behind this defunct power that it tries to annex, of an order that would have had nothing to do with it, and it dreams of it because it exterminated it by exhuming it *as its own past*.

We are fascinated by Ramses as Renaissance Christians were by the American Indians, those (human?) beings who had never known the word of Christ. Thus, at the beginning of colonization, there was a moment of stupor and bewilderment before the very possibility of escaping the universal law of the Gospel. There were two possible responses: either admit that this Law was not universal, or exterminate the Indians to efface the evidence. In general, one contented oneself with converting them, or even simply discovering them, which would suffice to slowly exterminate them.

Thus it would have been enough to exhume Ramses to ensure his extermination by museumification. Because mummies don't rot from worms: they die from being transplanted from a slow order of the symbolic, master over putrefaction and death, to an order of history, science, and museums, our order, which no longer masters anything, which only knows how to condemn what preceded it to decay and death and subsequently to try to revive it with science. Irreparable violence toward all secrets, the violence of a civilization without secrets, hatred of a whole civilization for its own foundation.

And just as with ethnology, which plays at extricating itself from its object to better secure itself in its pure form, *demuseumification* is nothing but another spiral in artificiality. Witness the cloister of Saint-Michel de Cuxa, which one will repatriate at great cost from the Cloisters in New York to reinstall it in "its original site." And everyone is supposed to applaud this restitution (as they did "the experimental campaign to take back the sidewalks" on the Champs Elysees!). Well, if the exportation of the cornices was in effect an arbitrary act, if the Cloisters in New York are an artificial mosaic of all cultures (following a logic of the capitalist centralization of value), their reimportation to the original site is even more artificial: it is a total simulacrum that links up with "reality" through a complete circumvolution.

The cloister should have stayed in New York in its simulated environment, which at least fooled no one. Repatriating it is nothing but a supplementary subterfuge, acting as if nothing had happened and indulging in retrospective hallucination.

In the same way, Americans flatter themselves for having brought the population of Indians back to pre-Conquest levels. One effaces everything and starts over. They even flatter themselves for doing better, for exceeding the original number. This is presented as proof of the superiority of civilization: it will produce more Indians than they themselves were able to do. (With sinister derision, this overproduction is again a means of destroying them: for Indian culture, like all tribal culture, rests on the limitation of the group and the refusal of any "unlimited" increase, as can be seen in Ishi's case. In this way, their demographic "promotion" is just another step toward symbolic extermination.)

Everywhere we live in a universe strangely similar to the original – things are doubled by their own scenario. But this doubling does not signify, as it did traditionally, the imminence of their death – they are already purged of their death, and better than when they were alive; more cheerful, more authentic, in the light of their model, like the faces in funeral homes.

The Hyperreal and the Imaginary

Disneyland is a perfect model of all the entangled orders of simulacra. It is first of all a play of illusions and phantasms: the Pirates, the Frontier, the Future World, etc. This imaginary world is supposed to ensure the success of the operation. But what attracts the crowds the most is without a doubt the social microcosm, the *religious*, miniaturized pleasure of real America, of its constraints and joys. One parks outside and stands in line inside, one is altogether abandoned at the exit. The only phantasmagoria in this imaginary world lies in the tenderness and warmth of the crowd, and in the sufficient and excessive number of gadgets necessary to create the multitudinous effect. The contrast with the absolute solitude of the parking lot – a veritable concentration camp – is total. Or, rather: inside, a whole panoply of gadgets magnetizes the crowd in directed flows – outside, solitude is directed at a single gadget: the automobile. By an extraordinary coincidence (but this derives without a doubt from the enchantment inherent to this universe), this frozen, childlike world is found to have been conceived and realized by a man who is himself now cryogenized: Walt Disney, who awaits his resurrection through an increase of 180 degrees centigrade.

Thus, everywhere in Disneyland the objective profile of America, down to the morphology of individuals and of the crowd, is drawn. All its values are exalted by the miniature and the comic strip. Embalmed and pacified. Whence the possibility of an ideological analysis of Disneyland (L. Marin did it very well in *Utopiques, jeux d'espace* [Utopias, plays of space]): digest of the American way of life, panegyric of American values, idealized transposition of a contradictory reality. Certainly. But this masks something else and this "ideological" blanket functions as a cover for a *simulation of the third order*: Disneyland exists in order to hide that it is the "real" country, all of "real" America that *is* Disneyland (a bit like prisons are there to hide that it is the social in its entirety, in its banal omnipresence, that is carceral). Disneyland is presented as imaginary in order to make us believe that the rest is real, whereas all of Los Angeles and the America that surrounds it are no longer real, but belong to the hyperreal order and to the order of simulation. It is no longer a question of a false representation of reality (ideology) but of concealing the fact that the real is no longer real, and thus of saving the reality principle.

The imaginary of Disneyland is neither true nor false, it is a deterrence machine set up in order to rejuvenate the fiction of the real in the opposite camp. Whence the debility of this imaginary, its infantile degeneration. This world wants to be childish in order to make us believe that the adults are elsewhere, in the "real" world, and to conceal the fact that true childishness is everywhere – that it is that of the adults themselves who come here to act the child in order to foster illusions as to their real childishness.

Disneyland is not the only one, however. Enchanted Village, Magic Mountain, Marine World: Los Angeles is surrounded by these imaginary stations that feed reality, the energy of the real to a city whose mystery is precisely that of no longer being anything but a network of incessant, unreal circulation – a city of incredible proportions but without space, without dimension. As much as electrical and atomic power stations, as much as cinema studios, this city, which is no longer anything but an immense scenario and a perpetual pan shot, needs this old imaginary like a sympathetic nervous system made up of childhood signals and faked phantasms.

Disneyland: a space of the regeneration of the imaginary as waste-treatment plants are elsewhere, and even here. Everywhere today one must recycle waste, and the dreams, the phantasms, the historical, fairylike, legendary imaginary of children and adults is a waste product, the first great toxic excrement of a hyperreal civilization. On a mental level, Disneyland is the prototype of this new function. But all the sexual, psychic, somatic recycling institutes, which proliferate in California, belong to the same order. People no longer look at each other, but there are institutes for that. They no longer touch each other, but there is contactotherapy. They no longer walk, but they go jogging, etc. Everywhere one recycles lost faculties, or lost bodies, or lost sociality, or the lost taste for food. One reinvents penury, asceticism, vanished savage naturalness: natural food, health food, yoga. Marshall Sahlins's idea that it is the economy of the market, and not of nature at all, that secretes penury, is verified, but at a secondary level: here, in the sophisticated confines of a triumphal market economy is reinvented a penury/sign, a penury/simulacrum, a simulated behavior of the underdeveloped (including the adoption of Marxist tenets) that, in the guise of ecology, of energy crises and the critique of capital, adds a final esoteric aureole to the triumph of an esoteric culture. Nevertheless, maybe a mental catastrophe, a mental implosion and involution without precedent lies in wait for a system of this kind, whose visible signs would be those of this strange obesity, or the incredible coexistence of the most bizarre theories and practices, which correspond to the improbable coalition of luxury, heaven, and money, to the improbable luxurious materialization of life and to undiscoverable contradictions.

Political Incantation

Watergate. The same scenario as in Disneyland (effect of the imaginary concealing that reality no more exists outside than inside the limits of the artificial perimeter): here the scandal effect hiding that there is no difference between the facts and their denunciation (identical methods on the part of the CIA and of the *Washington Post* journalists). Same operation, tending to regenerate through scandal a moral and political principle, through the imaginary, a sinking reality principle.

The denunciation of scandal is always an homage to the law. And Watergate in particular succeeded in imposing the idea that Watergate *was* a scandal – in this sense it was a prodigious operation of intoxication. A large dose of political morality reinjected on a world scale. One could say along with Bourdieu: "The essence of every relation of force is to dissimulate itself as such and to acquire all its force only because it dissimulates itself as such," understood as follows: capital, immoral and without scruples, can only function behind a moral superstructure, and whoever revives this public morality (through indignation, denunciation, etc.) works spontaneously for the order of capital. This is what the journalists of the *Washington Post* did.

But this would be nothing but the formula of ideology, and when Bourdieu states it, he takes the "relation of force" for the *truth* of capitalist domination, and he himself *denounces* this relation of force as *scandal* – he is thus in the same deterministic and moralistic position as the *Washington Post* journalists are. He does the same work of purging and reviving moral order, an order of truth in which the veritable symbolic violence of the social order is engendered, well beyond all the relations of force, which are only its shifting and indifferent configuration in the moral and political consciences of men.

All that capital asks of us is to receive it as rational *or* to combat it in the name of rationality, to receive it as moral *or* to combat it in the name of morality. Because *these are the same*, which *can be thought of in another way:* formerly one worked to dissimulate scandal – today one works to conceal that there is none.

Watergate is not a scandal, this is what must be said at all costs, because it is what everyone is busy concealing, this dissimulation masking a strengthening of morality, of a moral panic as one approaches the primitive (*mise en*) *scène* of capital: its instantaneous cruelty, its incomprehensible ferocity, its fundamental immorality – that is what is scandalous, unacceptable to the system of moral and economic equivalence that is the axiom of leftist thought, from the theories of the Enlightenment up to Communism. One imputes this thinking to the contract of capital, but it doesn't give a damn – it is a monstrous unprincipled enterprise, nothing more. It is "enlightened" thought that seeks to control it by imposing rules on it. And all the recrimination that replaces revolutionary thought today comes back to incriminate capital for not following the rules of the game. "Power is unjust, its justice is a class justice, capital exploits us, etc." – as if capital were linked by a contract to the society it rules. It is the Left that holds out the mirror of equivalence to capital hoping that it will comply, comply with this phantasmagoria of the social contract and fulfill its obligations to the whole of society (by the same token, no need for revolution: it suffices that capital accommodate itself to the rational formula of exchange).

Capital, in fact, was never linked by a contract to the society that it dominates. It is a sorcery of social relations, it is a *challenge to society,* and it must be responded to as such. It is not a scandal to be denounced according to moral or economic rationality, but a challenge to take up according to symbolic law.

Möbius-Spiraling Negativity

Watergate was thus nothing but a lure held out by the system to catch its adversaries – a simulation of scandal for regenerative ends. In the film, this is embodied by the character of "Deep Throat," who was said to be the éminence grise of the Republicans, manipulating the left-wing journalists in order to get rid of Nixon – and why not? All hypotheses are possible, but this one is superfluous: the Left itself does a perfectly good job, and spontaneously, of doing the work of the Right. Besides, it would be naive to see an embittered good conscience at work here. Because manipulation is a wavering causality in which positivity and negativity are engendered and overlap, in which there is no longer either an active or a passive. It is through the *arbitrary* cessation of this spiraling causality that a principle of political reality can be saved. It is through the *simulation* of a narrow, conventional field of perspective in which the premises and the consequences of an act or of an event can be calculated, that a political credibility can be maintained (and of course "objective" analysis, the struggle, etc.). If one envisions the entire cycle of any act or event in a system where linear continuity and dialectical polarity no longer exist, in a field *unhinged by simulation,* all determination evaporates, every act is terminated at the end of the cycle having benefited everyone and having been scattered in all directions.

Is any given bombing in Italy the work of leftist extremists, or extreme-right provocation, or a centrist *mise-en-scène* to discredit all extreme terrorists and to shore up its own failing power, or again, is it a police-inspired scenario and a form of blackmail to public security? All of this is simultaneously true, and the search for proof, indeed the objectivity of the facts does not put an end to this vertigo of interpretation. That is, we are in a logic of simulation, which no longer has anything to do with a logic of facts and an order of reason. Simulation is characterized by a *precession of the model*, of all the models based on the merest fact – the models come first, their circulation, orbital like that of the bomb, constitutes the genuine magnetic field of the event. The facts no longer have a specific trajectory, they are born at the intersection of models, a single fact can be engendered by all the models at once. This anticipation, this precession, this short circuit, this confusion of the fact with its model (no more divergence of meaning, no more dialectical polarity, no more negative electricity, implosion of antagonistic poles), is what allows each time for all possible interpretations, even the most contradictory – all true, in the sense that their truth is to be exchanged, in the image of the models from which they derive, in a generalized cycle.

The Communists attack the Socialist Party as if they wished to shatter the union of the Left. They give credence to the idea that these resistances would come from a more radical political need. In fact, it is because they no longer want power. But do they not want power at this juncture, one unfavorable to the Left in general, or unfavorable to them within the Union of the Left – or do they no longer want it, by definition? When Berlinguer declares: "There is no need to be afraid to see the Communists take power in Italy," it simultaneously signifies:

that there is no need to be afraid, since the Communists, if they come to power, will change nothing of its fundamental capitalist mechanism;
that there is no risk that they will ever come to power (because they don't want to) – and even if they occupy the seat of power, they will never exercise it except by proxy;
that in fact, power, genuine power no longer exists, and thus there is no risk whoever seizes power or seizes it again;
but further: I, Berlinguer, am not afraid to see the Communists take power in Italy – which may seem self-evident, but not as much as you might think, because
it could mean the opposite (no need for psychoanalysis here): *I am afraid* to see the Communists take power (and there are good reasons for that, even for a Communist).

All of this is simultaneously true. It is the secret of a discourse that is no longer simply ambiguous, as political discourses can be, but that conveys the impossibility of a determined position of power, the impossibility of a determined discursive position. And this logic is neither that of one party nor of another. It traverses all discourses without them wanting it to.

Who will unravel this imbroglio? The Gordian knot can at least be cut. The Möbius strip, if one divides it, results in a supplementary spiral without the reversibility of surfaces being resolved (here the reversible continuity of hypotheses). Hell of simulation, which is no longer one of torture, but of the subtle, maleficent, elusive twisting of meaning[4] – where even the condemned at Burgos are still a gift from Franco to Western democracy, which seizes the occasion to regenerate its own flagging humanism and whose indignant protest in turn consolidates Franco's regime by uniting the Spanish masses against this foreign intervention? Where is the truth of all that, when such collusions admirably knot themselves together without the knowledge of their authors?

Conjunction of the system and of its extreme alternative like the two sides of a curved mirror, a "vicious" curvature of a political space that is henceforth magnetized, circularized, reversibilized from the right to the left, a torsion that is like that of the evil spirit of commutation, the whole system, the infinity of capital folded back on its own surface: transfinite? And is it not the same for desire and the libidinal space? Conjunction of desire and value, of desire and capital. Conjunction of desire and the law, the final pleasure as the metamorphosis of the law (which is why it is so widely the order of the day): only capital takes pleasure, said Lyotard, before thinking that *we* now take pleasure in capital. Overwhelming versatility of desire in Deleuze, an enigmatic reversal that brings desire "revolutionary in itself, and as if involuntarily, wanting what it wants," to desire its own repression and to invest in paranoid and fascist systems? A malign torsion that returns this revolution of desire to the same fundamental ambiguity as the other, the historical revolution.

All the referentials combine their discourses in a circular, Möbian compulsion. Not so long ago, sex and work were fiercely opposed terms; today both are dissolved in the same type of demand. Formerly the discourse on history derived its power from violently opposing itself to that of nature, the discourse of desire to that of power – today they exchange their signifiers and their scenarios.

It would take too long to traverse the entire range of the operational negativity of all those scenarios of deterrence, which, like Watergate, try to regenerate a moribund principle through simulated scandal, phantasm, and murder – a sort of hormonal treatment through negativity and crisis. It is always a question of proving the real through the imaginary, proving truth through scandal, proving the law through transgression, proving work through striking, proving the system through crisis, and capital through revolution, as it is elsewhere (the Tasaday) of proving ethnology through the dispossession of its object – without taking into account:

the proof of theater through antitheater;
the proof of art through antiart;
the proof of pedagogy through antipedagogy;
the proof of psychiatry through antipsychiatry, etc.

Everything is metamorphosed into its opposite to perpetuate itself in its expurgated form. All the powers, all the institutions speak of themselves through denial, in order to attempt, by simulating death, to escape their real death throes. Power can stage its own murder to rediscover a glimmer of existence and legitimacy. Such was the case with some American presidents: the Kennedys were murdered because they still had a political dimension. The others, Johnson, Nixon, Ford, only had the right to phantom attempts, to simulated murders. But this aura of an artificial menace was still necessary to conceal that they were no longer anything but the mannequins of power. Formerly, the king (also the god) had to die, therein lay his power. Today, he is miserably forced to feign death, in order to preserve the *blessing* of power. But it is lost.

To seek new blood in its own death, to renew the cycle through the mirror of crisis, negativity, and antipower: this is the only solution-alibi of every power, of every institution attempting to break the vicious circle of its irresponsibility and of its fundamental nonexistence, of its already seen and of its already dead.

The Strategy of the Real

The impossibility of rediscovering an absolute level of the real is of the same order as the impossibility of staging illusion. Illusion is no longer possible, because the real is no longer possible. It is the whole *political* problem of parody, of hypersimulation or offensive simulation, that is posed here.

For example: it would be interesting to see whether the repressive apparatus would not react more violently to a simulated holdup than to a real holdup. Because the latter does nothing but disturb the order of things, the right to property, whereas the former attacks the reality principle itself. Transgression and violence are less serious because they only contest the *distribution* of the real. Simulation is infinitely more dangerous because it always leaves open to supposition that, above and beyond its object, *law and order themselves might be nothing but simulation.*

But the difficulty is proportional to the danger. How to feign a violation and put it to the test? Simulate a robbery in a large store: how to persuade security that it is a simulated robbery? There is no "objective" difference: the gestures, the signs are the same as for a real robbery, the signs do not lean to one side or another. To the established order they are always of the order of the real.

Organize a fake holdup. Verify that your weapons are harmless, and take the most trustworthy hostage, so that no human life will be in danger (or one lapses into the criminal). Demand a ransom, and make it so that the operation creates as much commotion as possible – in short, remain close to the "truth," in order to test the reaction of the apparatus to a perfect simulacrum. You won't be able to do it: the network of artificial signs will become inextricably mixed up with real elements (a policeman will really fire on sight; a client of the bank will faint and die of a heart attack; one will actually pay you the phony ransom), in short, you will immediately find yourself once again, without wishing it, in the real, one of whose functions is precisely to devour any attempt at simulation, to reduce everything to the real – that is, to the established order itself, well before institutions and justice come into play.

It is necessary to see in this impossibility of isolating the process of simulation the weight of an order that cannot see and conceive of anything but the real, because it cannot function anywhere else. The simulation of an offense, if it is established as such, will either be punished less severely (because it has no "consequences") or punished as an offense against the judicial system (for example if one sets in motion a police operation "for nothing") – but *never as simulation* since it is precisely as such that no equivalence with the real is possible, and hence no repression either. The challenge of simulation is never admitted by power. How can the simulation of virtue be punished? However, as such it is as serious as the simulation of crime. Parody renders submission and transgression equivalent, and that is the most serious crime, because it *cancels out the difference upon which the law is based*. The established order can do nothing against it, because the law is a simulacrum of the second order, whereas simulation is of the third order, beyond true and false, beyond equivalences, beyond rational distinctions upon which the whole of the social and power depend. Thus, *lacking the real*, it is there that we must aim at order.

This is certainly why order always opts for the real. When in doubt, it always prefers this hypothesis (as in the army one prefers to take the simulator for a real madman). But this becomes more and more difficult, because if it is practically impossible to isolate the process of simulation, through the force of inertia of the real that surrounds us, the opposite is also true (and this reversibility itself is part of the apparatus of simulation and the impotence of power): namely, it is *now impossible to isolate the process of the real*, or to prove the real.

This is how all the holdups, airplane hijackings, etc. are now in some sense simulation holdups in that they are already inscribed in the decoding and orchestration rituals of the media, anticipated in their presentation and their possible consequences. In short, where they function as a group of signs dedicated exclusively to their recurrence as signs, and no longer at all to their "real" end. But this does not make them harmless. On the contrary, it is as hyperreal events, no longer with a specific content or end, but indefinitely refracted by each other (just like so-called historical events: strikes, demonstrations, crises, etc.),[5] it is in this sense that they cannot be controlled by an order that can only exert itself on the real and the rational, on causes and ends, a referential order that can only reign over the referential, a determined power that can only reign over a determined world, but that cannot do anything against this indefinite recurrence of simulation, against this nebula whose weight no longer obeys the laws of gravitation of the real, power itself ends by being dismantled in this space and becoming a simulation of power (disconnected from its ends and its objectives, and dedicated to the *effects of power* and mass simulation).

The only weapon of power, its only strategy against this defection, is to reinject the real and the referential everywhere, to persuade us of the reality of the social, of the gravity of the economy and the finalities of production. To this end it prefers the discourse of crisis, but also, why not? that of desire. "Take your desires for reality!" can be understood as the ultimate slogan of power since in a nonreferential world, even the confusion of the reality principle and the principle of desire is less dangerous than contagious hyperreality. One remains among principles, and among those power is always in the right.

Hyperreality and simulation are deterrents of every principle and every objective, they turn against power the deterrent that it used so well for such a long time. Because in the end, throughout its history it was capital that first fed on the destructuration of every referential, of every human objective, that shattered every ideal distinction between true and false, good and evil, in order to establish a radical law of equivalence and exchange, the iron law of its power. Capital was the first to play at deterrence, abstraction, disconnection, deterritorialization, etc., and if it is the one that fostered reality, the reality principle, it was also the first to liquidate it by exterminating all use value, all real equivalence of production and wealth, in the very sense we have of the unreality of the stakes and the omnipotence of manipulation. Well, today it is this same logic that is even more set against capital. And as soon as it wishes to combat this disastrous spiral by secreting a last glimmer of reality, on which to establish a last glimmer of power, it does nothing but multiply the *signs* and accelerate the play of simulation.

As long as the historical threat came at it from the real, power played at deterrence and simulation, disintegrating all the contradictions by dint of producing equivalent signs. Today when the danger comes at it from simulation (that of being dissolved in the play of signs), power plays at the real, plays at crisis, plays at remanufacturing artificial, social, economic, and political stakes. For power, it is a question of life and death. But it is too late.

Whence the characteristic hysteria of our times: that of the production and reproduction of the real. The other production, that of values and commodities, that of the belle epoque of political economy, has for a long time had no specific meaning. What every society looks for in continuing to produce, and to overproduce, is to restore the real that escapes it. That is why *today this "material" production is that of the hyperreal itself.* It retains all the features, the whole discourse of traditional production, but it is no longer anything but its scaled-down refraction (thus hyperrealists fix a real from which all meaning and charm, all depth and energy of representation have vanished in a hallucinatory resemblance). Thus everywhere the hyperrealism of simulation is translated by the hallucinatory resemblance of the real to itself.

Power itself has for a long time produced nothing but the signs of its resemblance. And at the same time, another figure of power comes into play: that of a collective demand for *signs* of power – a holy union that is reconstructed around its disappearance. The whole world adheres to it more or less in terror of the collapse of the political. And in the end the game of power becomes nothing but the *critical* obsession with power – obsession with its death, obsession with its survival, which increases as it disappears. When it has totally disappeared, we will logically be under the total hallucination of power – a haunting memory that is already in evidence everywhere, expressing at once the compulsion to get rid of it (no one wants it anymore, everyone unloads it on everyone else) and the panicked nostalgia over its loss. The melancholy of societies without power: this has already stirred up fascism, that overdose of a strong referential in a society that cannot terminate its mourning.

With the extenuation of the political sphere, the president comes increasingly to resemble that *Puppet of Power* who is the head of primitive societies (Clastres).

All previous presidents pay for and continue to pay for Kennedy's murder as if they were the ones who had suppressed it – which is true phantasmatically, if not in fact. They must efface this defect and this complicity with their simulated murder. Because, now it can only be simulated. Presidents Johnson and Ford were both the object of failed assassination attempts which, if they were not staged, were at least perpetrated by simulation. The Kennedys died because they incarnated something: the political, political substance, whereas the new presidents are nothing but caricatures and fake film – curiously, Johnson, Nixon, Ford, all have this simian mug, the monkeys of power.

Death is never an absolute criterion, but in this case it is significant: the era of James Dean, Marilyn Monroe, and the Kennedys, of those who really died simply because they had a mythic dimension that implies death (not for romantic reasons, but because of the fundamental principle of reversal and exchange) – this era is long gone. It is now the era of murder by simulation, of the generalized aesthetic of simulation, of the murder-alibi – the allegorical resurrection of death, which is only there to sanction the institution of power, without which it no longer has any substance or an autonomous reality.

These staged presidential assassinations are revealing because they signal the status of all negativity in the West: political opposition, the "Left," critical discourse, etc. – a simulacral contrast through which power attempts to break the vicious circle of its nonexistence, of its fundamental irresponsibility, of its "suspension." Power floats like money, like language, like theory. Criticism and negativity alone still secrete a phantom of the reality of power. If they become weak for one reason or another, power has no other recourse but to artificially revive and hallucinate them.

It is in this way that the Spanish executions still serve as a stimulant to Western liberal democracy, to a dying system of democratic values. Fresh blood, but for how much longer? The deterioration of all power is irresistibly pursued: it is not so much the "revolutionary forces" that accelerate this process (often it is quite the opposite), it is the system itself that deploys against its own structures this violence that annuls all substance and all finality. One must not resist this process by trying to confront the system and destroy it, because this system that is dying from being dispossessed of its death expects nothing but that from us: that we give the system back its death, that we revive it through the negative. End of revolutionary praxis, end of the dialectic. Curiously, Nixon, who was not even found worthy of dying at the hands of the most insignificant, chance, unbalanced person (and though it is perhaps true that presidents are assassinated by unbalanced types, this changes *nothing*: the leftist penchant for detecting a rightist conspiracy beneath this brings out a false problem – the function of bringing death to, or the prophecy, etc., against power has always been fulfilled, from primitive societies to the present, by demented people, crazy people, or neurotics, who nonetheless carry out a social function as fundamental as that of presidents), was nevertheless ritually put to death by Watergate. Watergate is still a mechanism for the ritual murder of power (the American institution of the presidency is much more thrilling in this regard than the European: it surrounds itself with all the violence and vicissitudes of primitive powers, of savage rituals). But already impeachment is no longer assassination: it happens via the Constitution. Nixon has nevertheless arrived at the goal of which all power dreams: to be taken seriously enough, to constitute a mortal enough danger to the group to be one day relieved of his duties, denounced, and liquidated. Ford doesn't even have this opportunity anymore: a simulacrum of an already dead power, he can only accumulate against himself the signs of reversion through murder – in fact, he is immunized by his impotence, which infuriates him.

In contrast to the primitive rite, which foresees the official and sacrificial death of the king (the king or the chief is nothing without the promise of his sacrifice), the modern political imaginary goes increasingly in the direction of delaying, of concealing for as long as possible, the death of the head of state. This obsession has accumulated since the era of revolutions and of charismatic leaders: Hitler, Franco, Mao, having no "legitimate" heirs, no filiation of power, see themselves forced to perpetuate themselves indefinitely – popular myth never wishes to believe them dead. The pharaohs already did this: it was always one and the same person who incarnated the successive pharaohs.

Everything happens as if Mao or Franco had already died several times and had been replaced by his double. From a political point of view, that a head of state remains the same or is someone else doesn't strictly change anything, so long as they resemble each other. For a long time now a head of state – *no matter which one* – is nothing but the simulacrum of himself, and *only that gives him the power and the quality to govern*. No one would grant the least consent, the least devotion to a *real* person. It is to his double, he being always already *dead*, to which allegiance is given. This myth does nothing but translate the persistence, and at the same time the deception, of the necessity of the king's sacrificial death.

We are still in the same boat: no society knows how to mourn the real, power, the *social itself*, which is implicated in the same loss. And it is through an artificial revitalization of all this that we try to escape this fact. *This situation will no doubt end up giving rise to socialism.* Through an unforeseen turn of events and via an irony that is no longer that of history, it is from the death of the social that socialism will emerge, as it is from the death of God that religions emerge. A twisted advent, a perverse event, an unintelligible reversion to the logic of reason. As is the fact that power is in essence no longer present except to conceal that there is no more power. A simulation that can last indefinitely, because, as distinct from "true" power – which is, or was, a structure, a strategy, a relation of force, a stake – it is nothing but the object of a social *demand*, and thus as the object of the law of supply and demand, it is no longer subject to violence and death. Completely purged of a *political* dimension, it, like any other commodity, is dependent on mass production and consumption. Its spark has disappeared, only the fiction of a political universe remains.

The same holds true for work. The spark of production, the violence of its stakes no longer exist. The whole world still produces, and increasingly, but subtly work has become something else: a need (as Marx ideally envisioned it but not in the same sense), the object of a social "demand," like leisure, to which it is equivalent in the course of everyday life. A demand exactly proportional to the loss of a stake in the work process.[6] Same change in fortune as for power: the *scenario* of work is there to conceal that the real of work, the real of production, has disappeared. And the real of the strike as well, which is no longer a work stoppage, but its alternate pole in the ritual scansion of the social calendar. Everything occurs as if each person had, after declaring a strike, "occupied" his place and work station and recommenced production, as is the norm in a "self-managed" occupation, exactly in the same terms as before, all while declaring himself (and in virtually being) permanently on strike.

This is not a dream out of science fiction: everywhere it is a question of doubling the process of work. And of a doubling of the process of going on strike – striking incorporated just as obsolescence is in objects, just as crisis is in production. So, there is no longer striking, nor work, but both simultaneously, that is to say something else: a *magic of work*, a trompe l'oeil, a scenodrama (so as not to say a melodrama) of production, a collective dramaturgy on the empty stage of the social.

It is no longer a question of the ideology of work – the traditional ethic that would obscure the "real" process of work and the "objective" process of exploitation – but of the scenario of work. In the same way, it is no longer a question of the ideology of power, but of the *scenario* of power. Ideology only corresponds to a corruption of reality through signs; simulation corresponds to a short circuit of reality and to its duplication through signs. It is always the goal of the ideological analysis to restore the objective process, it is always a false problem to wish to restore the truth beneath the simulacrum.

This is why in the end power is so much in tune with ideological discourses and discourses on ideology, that is they are discourses of *truth* – always good for countering the mortal blows of simulation, even and especially if they are revolutionary.

The End of the Panopticon

It is still to this ideology of lived experience – exhumation of the real in its fundamental banality, in its radical authenticity – that the American TV verité experiment attempted on the Loud family in 1971 refers: seven months of uninterrupted shooting, three hundred hours of nonstop broadcasting, without a script or a screenplay, the odyssey of a family, its dramas, its joys, its unexpected events, nonstop – in short, a "raw" historical document, and the "greatest television performance, comparable, on the scale of our day-to-day life, to the footage of our landing on the moon." It becomes more complicated because this family fell apart during the filming: a crisis erupted, the Louds separated, etc. Whence that insoluble controversy: was TV itself responsible? What would have happened *if TV hadn't been there*?

More interesting is the illusion of filming the Louds *as if TV weren't there*. The producer's triumph was to say: "They lived as if we were not there." An absurd, paradoxical formula – neither true nor false: utopian. The "as if *we* were not there" being equal to "as if *you* were there." It is this utopia, this paradox that fascinated the twenty million viewers, much more than did the "perverse" pleasure of violating someone's privacy. In the "verité" experience it is not a question of secrecy or perversion, but of a sort of frisson of the real, or of an aesthetics of the hyperreal, a frisson of vertiginous and phony exactitude, a frisson of simultaneous distancing and magnification, of distortion of scale, of an excessive transparency. The pleasure of an excess of meaning, when the bar of the sign falls below the usual waterline of meaning: the nonsignifier is exalted by the camera angle. There one sees what the real never was (but "as if you were there"), without the distance that gives us perspectival space and depth vision (but "more real than nature"). Pleasure in the microscopic simulation that allows the real to pass into the hyperreal. (This is also somewhat the case in porno, which is fascinating more on a metaphysical than on a sexual level.)

Besides, this family was already hyperreal by the very nature of its selection: a typical ideal American family, California home, three garages, five children, assured social and professional status, decorative housewife, upper-middle-class standing. In a way it is this statistical perfection that dooms it to death. Ideal heroine of the American way of life, it is, as in ancient sacrifices, chosen in order to be glorified and to die beneath the flames of the medium, a modern *fatum*. Because heavenly fire no longer falls on corrupted cities, it is the camera lens that, like a laser, comes to pierce lived reality in order to put it to death. "The Louds: simply a family who agreed to deliver themselves into the hands of television, and to die by it," the director will say. Thus it is a question of a sacrificial process, of a sacrificial spectacle offered to twenty million Americans. The liturgical drama of a mass society.

TV verité. A term admirable in its ambiguity, does it refer to the truth of this family or to the truth of TV? In fact, it is TV that is the truth of the Louds, it is TV that is true, it is TV that renders true. Truth that is no longer the reflexive truth of the mirror, nor the perspectival truth of the panoptic system and of the gaze, but the manipulative truth of the test that sounds out and interrogates, of the laser that touches and pierces, of computer cards that retain your preferred sequences, of the genetic code that controls your combinations, of cells that inform your sensory universe. It is to this truth that the Loud family was subjected by the medium of TV, and in this sense it amounts to a death sentence (but is it still a question of truth?).

End of the panoptic system. The eye of TV is no longer the source of an absolute gaze, and the ideal of control is no longer that of transparency. This still presupposes an objective space (that of the Renaissance) and the omnipotence of the despotic gaze. It is still, if not a system of confinement, at least a system of mapping. More subtly, but always externally, playing on the opposition of seeing and being seen, even if the panoptic focal point may be blind.

Something else in regard to the Louds. "You no longer watch TV, it is TV that watches you (live)," or again: "You are no longer listening to Don't Panic, it is Don't Panic that is listening to you" – a switch from the panoptic mechanism of surveillance (*Discipline and Punish* [Surveiller et punir]) to a system of deterrence, in which the distinction between the passive and the active is abolished. There is no longer any imperative of submission to the model, or to the gaze "YOU are the model!" "YOU are the majority!" Such is the watershed of a hyperreal sociality, in which the real is confused with the model, as in the statistical operation, or with the medium, as in the Louds' operation. Such is the last stage of the social relation, ours, which is no longer one of persuasion (the classical age of propaganda, of ideology, of publicity, etc.) but one of deterrence: "YOU are information, you are the social, you are the event, you are involved, you have the word, etc." An about-face through which it becomes impossible to locate one instance of the model, of power, of the gaze, of the medium itself, because *you* are always already on the other side. No more subject, no more focal point, no more center or periphery: pure flexion or circular inflexion. No more violence or surveillance: only "information," secret virulence, chain reaction, slow implosion, and simulacra of spaces in which the effect of the real again comes into play.

We are witnessing the end of perspectival and panoptic space (which remains a moral hypothesis bound up with all the classical analyses on the "objective" essence of power), and thus to the *very abolition of the spectacular*. Television, for example in the case of the Louds, is no longer a spectacular medium. We are no longer in the society of the spectacle, of which the situationists spoke, nor in the specific kinds of alienation and repression that it implied. The medium itself is no longer identifiable as such, and the confusion of the medium and the message (McLuhan)[7] is the first great formula of this new era. There is no longer a medium in the literal sense: it is now intangible, diffused, and diffracted in the real, and one can no longer even say that the medium is altered by it.

Such a blending, such a viral, endemic, chronic, alarming presence of the medium, without the possibility of isolating the effects – spectralized, like these advertising laser sculptures in the empty space of the event filtered by the medium – dissolution of TV in life, dissolution of life in TV – indiscernible chemical solution: we are all Louds doomed not to invasion, to pressure, to violence and blackmail by the media and the models, but to their induction, to their infiltration, to their illegible violence.

But one must watch out for the negative turn that discourse imposes: it is a question neither of disease nor of a viral infection. One must think instead of the media as if they were, in outer orbit, a kind of genetic code that directs the mutation of the real into the hyperreal, just as the other micromolecular code controls the passage from a representative sphere of meaning to the genetic one of the programmed signal.

It is the whole traditional world of causality that is in question: the perspectival, determinist mode, the "active," critical mode, the analytic mode – the distinction between cause and effect, between active and passive, between subject and object, between the end and the means. It is in this sense that one can say: TV is watching us, TV alienates us, TV manipulates us, TV informs us . . . In all this, one remains dependent on the analytical conception of the media, on an external active and effective agent, on "perspectival" information with the horizon of the real and of meaning as the vanishing point.

Now, one must conceive of TV along the lines of DNA as an effect in which the opposing poles of determination vanish, according to a nuclear contraction, retraction, of the old polar schema that always maintained a minimal distance between cause and effect, between subject and object: precisely the distance of meaning, the gap, the difference, the smallest possible gap (PPEP!),[8] irreducible under pain of reabsorption into an aleatory and indeterminate process whose discourse can no longer account for it, because it is itself a determined order.

It is this gap that vanishes in the process of genetic coding, in which indeterminacy is not so much a question of molecular randomness as of the abolition, pure and simple, of the *relation*. In the process of molecular control, which "goes" from the DNA nucleus to the "substance" that it "informs," there is no longer the traversal of an effect, of an energy, of a determination, of a message. "Order, signal, impulse, message": all of these attempt to render the thing intelligible to us, but by analogy, retranscribing in terms of inscription, of a vector, of decoding, a dimension of which we know nothing – it is no longer even a "dimension," or perhaps it is the fourth (which is defined, however, in Einsteinian relativity by the absorption of the distinct poles of space and time). In fact, this whole process can only be understood in its negative form: nothing separates one pole from another anymore, the beginning from the end; there is a kind of contraction of one over the other, a fantastic telescoping, a collapse of the two traditional poles into each other: *implosion* – an absorption of the radiating mode of causality, of the differential mode of determination, with its positive and negative charge – an implosion of meaning. *That is where simulation begins.*

Everywhere, in no matter what domain – political, biological, psychological, mediatized – in which the distinction between these two poles can no longer be maintained, one enters into simulation, and thus into absolute manipulation – not into passivity, but into *the indifferentiation of the active and the passive.* DNA realizes this aleatory reduction at the level of living matter. Television, in the case of the Louds, also reaches this *indefinite* limit in which, vis-à-vis TV, they are neither more nor less active or passive than a living substance is vis-à-vis its molecular code. Here and there, a single nebula whose simple elements are indecipherable, whose truth is indecipherable.

The Orbital and the Nuclear

The apotheosis of simulation: the nuclear. However, the balance of terror is never anything but the spectacular slope of a system of deterrence that has insinuated itself from *the inside* into all the cracks of daily life. Nuclear suspension only serves to seal the trivialized system of deterrence that is at the heart of the media, of the violence without consequences that reigns throughout the world, of the aleatory apparatus of all the choices that are made for us. The most insignificant of our behaviors is regulated by neutralized, indifferent, equivalent signs, by zero-sum signs like those that regulate the "strategy of games" (but the true equation is elsewhere, and the unknown is precisely that variable of simulation which makes of the atomic arsenal itself a hyperreal form, a simulacrum that dominates everything and reduces all "ground-level" events to being nothing but ephemeral scenarios, transforming the life left us into survival, into a stake without stakes – not even into a life insurance policy: into a policy that already has no value).

It is not the direct threat of atomic destruction that paralyzes our lives, it is deterrence that gives them leukemia. And this deterrence comes from that fact that *even the real atomic clash is precluded* – precluded like the eventuality of the real in a system of signs. The whole world pretends to believe in the reality of this threat (this is understandable on the part of the military, the gravity of their exercise and the discourse of their "strategy" are at stake), but it is precisely at this level that there are no strategic stakes. The whole originality of the situation lies in the improbability of destruction.

Deterrence precludes war – the archaic violence of expanding systems. Deterrence itself is the neutral, implosive violence of metastable systems or systems in involution.

There is no longer a subject of deterrence, nor an adversary nor a strategy – it is a planetary structure of the annihilation of stakes. Atomic war, like the Trojan War, will not take place. The risk of nuclear annihilation only serves as a pretext, through the sophistication of weapons (a sophistication that surpasses any possible objective to such an extent that it is itself a symptom of nullity), for installing a universal security system, a universal lockup and control system whose deterrent effect is not at all aimed at an atomic clash (which was never in question, except without a doubt in the very initial stages of the cold war, when one still confused the nuclear apparatus with conventional war) but, rather, at the much greater probability of any real event, of anything that would be an event in the general system and upset its balance. The balance of terror is the terror of balance.

Deterrence is not a strategy, it circulates and is exchanged between nuclear protagonists exactly as is international capital in the orbital zone of monetary speculation whose fluctuations suffice to control all global exchanges. Thus the *money of destruction* (without any reference to *real* destruction, any more than floating capital has a real referent of production) that circulates in nuclear orbit suffices to control all the violence and potential conflicts around the world.

What is hatched in the shadow of this mechanism with the pretext of a maximal, "objective," threat, and thanks to Damocles' nuclear sword, is the perfection of the best system of control that has ever existed. And the progressive satellization of the whole planet through this hypermodel of security.

The same goes for *peaceful* nuclear power stations. Pacification does not distinguish between the civil and the military: everywhere where irreversible apparatuses of control are elaborated, everywhere where the notion of security becomes omnipotent, everywhere where the *norm* replaces the old arsenal of laws and violence (including war), it is the system of deterrence that grows, and around it grows the historical, social, and political desert. A gigantic involution that makes every conflict, every finality, every confrontation contract in proportion to this blackmail that interrupts, neutralizes, freezes them all. No longer can any revolt, any story be deployed according to its own logic because it risks annihilation. No strategy is possible any longer, and escalation is only a puerile game given over to the military. The political stake is dead, only simulacra of conflicts and carefully circumscribed stakes remain.

The "space race" played exactly the same role as nuclear escalation. This is why the space program was so easily able to replace it in the 1960s (Kennedy/Khrushchev), or to develop concurrently as a form of "peaceful coexistence." Because what, ultimately, is the function of the space program, of the conquest of the moon, of the launching of satellites if not the institution of a model of universal gravitation, of satellization of which the lunar module is the perfect embryo? Programmed microcosm, where *nothing can be left to chance*. Trajectory, energy, calculation, physiology, psychology, environment – nothing can be left to contingencies, this is the total universe of the norm – the Law no longer exists, it is the operational immanence of every detail that is law. A universe purged of all threat of meaning, in a state of asepsis and weightlessness – it is this very perfection that is fascinating. The exaltation of the crowds was not a response to the event of landing on the moon or of sending a man into space (this would be, rather, the fulfillment of an earlier dream), rather, we are dumbfounded by the perfection of the programming and the technical manipulation, by the immanent wonder of the programmed unfolding of events. Eascination with the maximal norm and the mastery of probability. Vertigo of the model, which unites with the model of death, but without fear or drive. Because if the law, with its aura of transgression, if order, with its aura of violence, still taps a perverse imaginary, the norm fixes, fascinates, stupefies, and makes every imaginary involute. One no longer fantasizes about the minutiae of a program. Just watching it produces vertigo. The vertigo of a world without flaws.

Now, it is the same model of programmatic infallibility, of maximum security and deterrence that today controls the spread of the social. There lies the true nuclear fallout: the meticulous operation of technology serves as a model for the meticulous operation of the social. Here as well, *nothing will be left to chance*, moreover this is the essence of socialization, which began centuries ago, but which has now entered its accelerated phase, toward a limit that one believed would be explosive (revolution), but which for the moment is translated by an inverse, *implosive*, irreversible process: the generalized deterrence of chance, of accident, of transversality, of finality, of contradiction, rupture, or complexity in a sociality illuminated by the norm, doomed to the descriptive transparency of mechanisms of information. In fact, the spatial and nuclear models do not have their own ends: neither the discovery of the moon, nor military and strategic superiority. Their truth is to be the models of simulation, the model vectors of a system of planetary control (where even the superpowers of this scenario are not free – the whole world is satellized).[9]

Resist the evidence: in satellization, he who is satellized is not who one might think. Through the orbital inscription of a spatial object, it is the planet earth that becomes a satellite, it is the terrestrial principle of reality that becomes eccentric, hyperreal, and insignificant. Through the orbital instantiation of a system of control like peaceful coexistence, all the terrestrial microsystems are satellized and lose their autonomy. All energy, all events are absorbed by this eccentric gravitation, everything condenses and implodes toward the only micromodel of control (the orbital satellite), as conversely, in the other, biological, dimension, everything converges and implodes on the molecular micromodel of the genetic code. Between the two, in this forking of the nuclear and the genetic, in the simultaneous assumption of the two fundamental codes of deterrence, every principle of meaning is absorbed, every deployment of the real is impossible.

The simultaneity of two events in the month of July 1975 illustrated this in a striking manner: the linkup in space of the two American and Soviet supersatellites, apotheosis of peaceful coexistence – the suppression by the Chinese of ideogrammatic writing and conversion to the Roman alphabet. The latter signifies the "orbital" instantiation of an abstract and modelized system of signs, into whose orbit all the once unique forms of style and writing will be reabsorbed. The satellization of language: the means for the Chinese to enter the system of peaceful coexistence, which is inscribed in their heavens at precisely the same time by the linkup of the two satellites. Orbital flight of the Big Two, neutralization and homogenization of everyone else on earth.

Yet, despite this deterrence by the orbital power – the nuclear or molecular code – events continue at ground level, misfortunes are even more numerous, given the global process of the contiguity and simultaneity of data. But, subtly, they no longer have any meaning, they are no longer anything but the duplex effect of simulation at the summit. The best example can only be that of the war in Vietnam, because it took place at the intersection of a maximum historical and "revolutionary" stake, and of the installation of this deterrent authority. What meaning did this war have, and wasn't its unfolding a means of sealing the end of history in the decisive and culminating historic event of our era?

Why did this war, so hard, so long, so ferocious, vanish from one day to the next as if by magic?

Why did this American defeat (the largest reversal in the history of the USA) have no internal repercussions in America? If it had really signified the failure of the planetary strategy of the United States, it would necessarily have completely disrupted its internal balance and the American political system. Nothing of the sort occurred.

Something else, then, took place. This war, at bottom, was nothing but a crucial episode of peaceful coexistence. It marked the arrival of China to peaceful coexistence. The nonintervention of China obtained and secured after many years, China's apprenticeship to a global modus vivendi, the shift from a global strategy of revolution to one of shared forces and empires, the transition from a radical alternative to political alternation in a system now essentially regulated (the normalization of Peking–Washington relations): this was what was at stake in the war in Vietnam, and in this sense, the USA pulled out of Vietnam but won the war.

And the war ended "spontaneously" when this objective was achieved. That is why it was deescalated, demobilized so easily.

This same reduction of forces can be seen on the field. The war lasted as long as elements irreducible to a healthy politics and discipline of power, even a Communist one, remained unliquidated. When at last the war had passed into the hands of regular troops in the North and escaped that of the resistance, the war could stop: it had attained its objective. The stake is thus that of a political relay. As soon as the Vietnamese had proved that they were no longer the carriers of an unpredictable subversion, one could let them take over. That theirs is a Communist order is not serious in the end: it had proved itself, it could be trusted. It is even more effective than capitalism in the liquidation of "savage" and archaic precapitalist structures.

Same scenario in the Algerian war.

The other aspect of this war and of all wars today: behind the armed violence, the murderous antagonism of the adversaries – which seems a matter of life and death, which is played out as such (or else one could never send people to get themselves killed in this kind of thing), behind this simulacrum of fighting to the death and of ruthless global stakes, the two adversaries are fundamentally in solidarity against something else, unnamed, never spoken, but whose objective outcome in war, with the equal complicity of the two adversaries, is total liquidation. Tribal, communitarian, precapitalist structures, every form of exchange, of language, of symbolic organization, that is what must be abolished, that is the object of murder in war – and war itself, in its immense, spectacular death apparatus, is nothing but the medium of this process of the terrorist rationalization of the social – the murder on which sociality will be founded, whatever its allegiance, Communist or capitalist. Total complicity, or division of labor between two adversaries (who may even consent to enormous sacrifices for it) for the very end of reshaping and domesticating social relations.

"The North Vietnamese were advised to countenance a scenario for liquidating the American presence in the course of which, of course, one must save face."

This scenario: the extremely harsh bombardments of Hanoi. Their untenable character must not conceal the fact that they were nothing but a simulacrum to enable the Vietnamese to seem to countenance a compromise and for Nixon to make the Americans swallow the withdrawal of their troops. The game was already won, nothing was objectively at stake but the verisimilitude of the final montage.

The moralists of war, the holders of high wartime values should not be too discouraged: the war is no less atrocious for being only a simulacrum – the flesh suffers just the same, and the dead and former combatants are worth the same as in other wars. This objective is always fulfilled, just like that of the charting of territories and of disciplinary sociality. What no longer exists is the adversity of the adversaries, the reality of antagonistic causes, the ideological seriousness of war. And also the reality of victory or defeat, war being a process that triumphs well beyond these appearances.

In any case, the pacification (or the deterrence) that dominates us today is beyond war and peace, it is that at every moment war and peace are equivalent. "War is peace," said Orwell. There also, the two differential poles implode into each other, or recycle one another – a simultaneity of contradictions that is at once the parody and the end of every dialectic. Thus one can completely miss the truth of a war: namely, that it was finished well before it started, that there was an end to war at the heart of the war itself, and that perhaps it never started. Many other events (the oil crisis, etc.) *never started*, never existed, except as artificial occurrences – abstract, ersatz, and as artifacts of history, catastrophes and crises destined to maintain a historical investment under hypnosis. The media and the official *news service* are only there to maintain the illusion of an actuality, of the reality of the stakes, of the objectivity of facts. All the events are to be read backward, or one becomes aware (as with the Communists "in power" in Italy, the retro, posthumous rediscovery of the gulags and Soviet dissidents like the almost contemporary discovery, by a moribund ethnology, of the lost "difference" of Savages) that all these things arrived too late, with a history of delay, a spiral of delay, that they long ago exhausted their meaning and only live from an artificial effervescence of signs, that all these events succeed each other without logic, in the most contradictory, complete equivalence, in a profound indifference to their consequences (but this is because there are none: they exhaust themselves in their spectacular promotion) – all "newsreel" footage thus gives the sinister impression of kitsch, of retro and porno at the same time – doubtless everyone knows this, and no one really accepts it. The reality of simulation is unbearable – crueler than Artaud's Theater of Cruelty, which was still an attempt to create a dramaturgy of life, the last gasp of an ideality of the body, of blood, of violence in a system that was already taking it away, toward a reabsorption of all the stakes without a trace of blood. For us the trick has been played. All dramaturgy, and even all real writing of cruelty has disappeared. Simulation is the master, and we only have a right to the retro, to the phantom, parodic rehabilitation of all lost referentials. Everything still unfolds around us, in the cold light of deterrence (including Artaud, who has the right like everything else to his revival, to a second existence as the *referential* of cruelty).

This is why nuclear proliferation does not increase the risk of either an atomic clash or an accident – save in the interval when the "young" powers could be tempted to make a nondeterrent, "real" use of it (as the Americans did in Hiroshima – but precisely only they had a right to this "use value" of the bomb, all of those who have acquired it since will be deterred from using it by the very fact of possessing it). Entry into the atomic club, so prettily named, very quickly effaces (as unionization does in the working world) any inclination toward violent intervention. Responsibility, control, censure, self-deterrence always grow more rapidly than the forces or the weapons at our disposal: this is the secret of the social order. Thus the very possibility of paralyzing a whole country by flicking a switch *makes* it so that the electrical engineers will never use this weapon: the whole myth of the total and revolutionary strike crumbles at the very moment when the means are available – but alas *precisely because* those means are available. Therein lies the whole process of deterrence.

It is thus perfectly probable that one day we will see nuclear powers export atomic reactors, weapons, and bombs to every latitude. Control by threat will be replaced by the more effective strategy of pacification through the bomb and through the possession of the bomb. The "little" powers, believing that they are buying their independent striking force, will buy the virus of deterrence, of their own deterrence. The same goes for the atomic reactors that we have already sent them: so many neutron bombs knocking out all historical virulence, all risk of explosion. In this sense, the nuclear everywhere inaugurates an accelerated process of *implosion*, it freezes everything around it, it absorbs all living energy.

The nuclear is at once the culminating point of available energy and the maximization of energy control systems. Lockdown and control increase in direct proportion to (and undoubtedly even faster than) liberating potentialities. This was already the aporia of the modern revolution. It is still the absolute paradox of the nuclear. Energies freeze in their own fire, they deter themselves. One can no longer imagine what project, what power, what strategy, what subject could exist behind this enclosure, this vast saturation of a system by its own forces, now neutralized, unusable, unintelligible, nonexplosive – except for the possibility of *an explosion toward the center*, of an *implosion* where all these energies would be abolished in a catastrophic process (in the literal sense, that is to say in the sense of a reversion of the whole cycle toward a minimal point, of a reversion of energies toward a minimal threshold).

Notes

1   Cf. J. Baudrillard, "L'ordre des simulacres" (The order of simulacra), in *L'échange symbolique et la mort* (Symbolic exchange and death) (Paris: Gallimard, 1976).
2   A discourse that is itself not susceptible to being resolved in transference. It is the entanglement of these two discourses that renders psychoanalysis interminable.
3   Cf. M. Perniola, *Icônes, visions, simulacres* (Icons, visions, simulacra), 39.
4   This does not necessarily result in despairing of meaning, but just as much in the improvisation of meaning, of nonmeaning, of many simultaneous meanings that destroy each other.
5   Taken together, the energy crisis and the ecological *mise-en-scène* are themselves a *disaster movie*, in the same style (and with the same value) as those that currently comprise the golden days of Hollywood. It is useless to laboriously interpret these films in terms of their relation to an "objective" social crisis or even to an "objective" phantasm of disaster. It is in another sense that it must be said that it is *the social itself that,* in contemporary discourse, *is organized along the lines of a disaster-movie script.* (Cf. M. Makarius, *La stratégie de la catastrophe* [The strategy of disaster], 115.)
6   To this flagging investment in work corresponds a parallel decline in the investment in consumption. Goodbye to use value or to the prestige of the automobile, goodbye amorous discourses that neatly opposed the object of enjoyment to the object of work. Another discourse takes hold that is a *discourse of work on the object of consumption* aiming for an active, constraining, puritan reinvestment (use less gas, watch out for your safety, you've gone over the speed limit, etc.) to which the characteristics of automobiles pretend to adapt. Rediscovering a stake through the transposition of these two poles. Work becomes the object of a need, the car becomes the object of work. There is no better proof of the lack of differentiation among all the stakes. It is through the same slippage between the "right" to vote and electoral "duty" that the divestment of the political sphere is signaled.
7   The medium/message confusion is certainly a corollary of that between the sender and the receiver, thus sealing the disappearance of all dual, polar structures that formed the discursive organization of language, of all determined articulation of meaning reflecting Jakobson's famous grid of functions. That discourse "circulates" is to be taken literally: that is, it no longer goes from one point to another, but it traverses a cycle that *without distinction* includes the positions of transmitter and receiver, now unlocatable as such. Thus there is no instance of power, no instance of transmission – power is something that circulates and whose source can no longer be located, a cycle in which the positions of the dominator and the dominated are exchanged in an endless reversion that is also the end of power in its classical definition. The circularization of power, of knowledge, of discourse puts an end to any localization of instances and poles. In the psychoanalytic interpretation itself, the "power" of the interpreter does not come from any outside instance but from the interpreted himself. This changes everything, because one can always ask of the traditional holders of power where they get their power from. Who made you duke? The king. Who made you king? God. Only God no longer answers. But to the question: who made you a psychoanalyst? the analyst can well reply: You. Thus is expressed, by an inverse simulation, the passage from the "analyzed" to the "analysand," from passive to active, which simply describes the spiraling effect of the shifting of poles, the effect of circularity in which power is lost, is dissolved, is resolved in perfect manipulation (it is no longer of the order of directive power and of the gaze, but of the order of tactility and commutation). See also the state/family circularity assured by the fluctuation and metastatic regulation of

the images of the social and the private (J. Donzelot, *La police des familles* [The policing of families]).

Impossible now to pose the famous question: "From what position do you speak?" – "How do you know?" "From where do you get your power?" without hearing the immediate response: "But it is *of* you (from you) that I speak" – meaning, it is you who are speaking, you who know, you who are the power. Gigantic circumvolution, circumlocution of the spoken word, which is equal to a blackmail with no end, to a deterrence that cannot be appealed of the subject presumed to speak, leaving him without a reply, because to the question that he poses one ineluctably replies: but *you are* the answer, or: your question is already an answer, etc. – the whole strangulatory sophistication of intercepting speech, of the forced confession in the guise of freedom of expression, of trapping the subject in his own interrogation, of the precession of the reply to the question (all the violence of interpretation lies there, as well as that of the conscious or unconscious management of the "spoken word" [*parole*]).

This simulacrum of the inversion or the involution of poles, this clever subterfuge, which is the secret of the whole discourse of manipulation and thus, today, in every domain, the secret of any new power in the erasure of the scene of power, in the assumption of all words from which has resulted this fantastic silent majority characteristic of our time – all of this started without a doubt in the political sphere with the democractic simulacrum, which today is the substitution for the power of God with the power of the people as the source of power, and of power as *emanation* with power as *representation*. Anti-Copernican revolution: no transcendental instance either of the sun or of the luminous sources of power and knowledge – everything comes from the people and everything returns to them. It is with this magnificent recycling that the universal simulacrum of manipulation, from the scenario of mass suffrage to the present-day phantoms of opinion polls, begins to be put in place.

8 PPEP is an acronym for smallest possible gap, or "plus petit écart possible." – [Trans.]
9 Paradox: all bombs are clean: their only pollution is the system of security and of control they radiate *as long as they don't explode*.

29

Postmodernism, or the Cultural Logic of Late Capitalism

Fredric Jameson

The last few years have been marked by an inverted millennarianism, in which premonitions of the future, catastrophic or redemptive, have been replaced by senses of the end of this or that (the end of ideology, art, or social class; the "crisis" of Leninism, social democracy, or the welfare state, etc., etc.): taken together, all of these perhaps constitute what is increasingly called postmodernism. The case for its existence depends on the hypothesis of some radical break or *coupure*, generally traced back to the end of the 1950s or the early 1960s. As the word itself suggests, this break is most often related to notions of the waning or extinction of the hundred-year-old modern movement (or to its ideological or aesthetic repudiation). Thus, abstract expressionism in painting, existentialism in philosophy, the final forms of representation in the novel, the films of the great *auteurs*, or the modernist school of poetry (as institutionalized and canonized in the works of Wallace Stevens): all these are now seen as the final, extraordinary flowering of a high modernist impulse which is spent and exhausted with them. The enumeration of what follows then at once becomes empirical, chaotic, and heterogeneous: Andy Warhol and pop art, but also photorealism, and beyond it, the "new expressionism"; the moment, in music, of John Cage, but also the synthesis of classical and "popular" styles found in composers like Phil Glass and Terry Riley, and also punk and new wave rock (the Beatles and the Stones now standing as the high-modernist moment of that more recent and rapidly evolving tradition); in film, Godard, post-Godard and experimental cinema and video, but also a whole new type of commercial film (about which more below); Burroughs, Pynchon, or Ishmael Reed, on the one hand, and the French *nouveau roman* and its succession on the other, along with alarming new kinds of literary criticism, based on some new aesthetic of textuality or *écriture* . . . The list might be extended indefinitely; but does it imply any more fundamental change or

From Fredric Jameson, "Postmodernism, or The cultural logic of late capitalism." *New Left Review* 146 (July–Aug. 1984), pp. 53–92.

break than the periodic style- and fashion-changes determined by an older high-modernist imperative of stylistic innovation?[1]

The Rise of Aesthetic Populism

It is in the realm of architecture, however, that modifications in aesthetic production are most dramatically visible, and that their theoretical problems have been most centrally raised and articulated; it was indeed from architectural debates that my own conception of postmodernism – as it will be outlined in the following pages – initially began to emerge. More decisively than in the other arts or media, postmodernist positions in architecture have been inseparable from an implacable critique of architectural high modernism and of the so-called International Style (Frank Lloyd Wright, Le Corbusier, Mies), where formal criticism and analysis (of the high-modernist transformation of the building into a virtual sculpture, or monumental "duck", as Robert Venturi puts it) are at one with reconsiderations on the level of urbanism and of the aesthetic institution. High modernism is thus credited with the destruction of the fabric of the traditional city and of its older neighbourhood culture (by way of the radical disjunction of the new Utopian high-modernist building from its surrounding context); while the prophetic elitism and authoritarianism of the modern movement are remorselessly denounced in the imperious gesture of the charismatic Master.

Postmodernism in architecture will then logically enough stage itself as a kind of aesthetic populism, as the very title of Venturi's influential manifesto, *Learning from Las Vegas*, suggests. However we may ultimately wish to evaluate this populist rhetoric, it has at least the merit of drawing our attention to one fundamental feature of all the postmodernisms enumerated above: namely, the effacement in them of the older (essentially high-modernist) frontier between high culture and so-called mass or commercial culture, and the emergence of new kinds of texts infused with the forms, categories and contents of that very Culture Industry so passionately denounced by all the ideologues of the modern, from Leavis and the American New Criticism all the way to Adorno and the Frankfurt School. The postmodernisms have in fact been fascinated precisely by this whole "degraded" landscape of schlock and kitsch, of TV series and Reader's Digest culture, of advertising and motels, of the late show and the grade-B Hollywood film, of so-called paraliterature with its airport paperback categories of the gothic and the romance, the popular biography, the murder mystery and science-fiction or fantasy novel: materials they no longer simply "quote", as a Joyce or a Mahler might have done, but incorporate into their very substance.

Nor should the break in question be thought of as a purely cultural affair: indeed, theories of the postmodern – whether celebratory or couched in the language of moral revulsion and denunciation – bear a strong family resemblance to all those more ambitious sociological generalizations which, at much the same time, bring us the news of the arrival and inauguration of a whole new type of society, most famously baptized "post-industrial society" (Daniel Bell), but often also designated consumer society, media society, information society, electronic society or "high tech", and the like. Such theories have the obvious ideological mission of demonstrating, to their own relief, that the new social formation in question no longer obeys the laws of classical capitalism, namely the primacy of industrial production and the omnipresence of class struggle. The Marxist tradition has therefore resisted them with vehemence, with the signal exception of the economist Ernest Mandel, whose book *Late Capitalism* sets out not merely to anatomize the historic originality of this new society (which he sees as a third stage or moment in the evolution of capital), but also to demonstrate that it is, if anything, a *purer* stage of capitalism than any of the moments that preceded it. I will return to this argument later; suffice it for the moment to emphasize a point I have defended in greater detail elsewhere,[2] namely that every position on postmodernism in culture – whether apologia or stigmatization – is also at one and the same time, and *necessarily*, an implicitly or explicitly political stance on the nature of multinational capitalism today.

Postmodernism as Cultural Dominant

A last preliminary word on method: what follows is not to be read as stylistic description, as the account of one cultural style or movement among others. I have rather meant to offer a periodizing hypothesis, and that at a moment in which the very conception of historical periodization has come to seem most problematical indeed. I have argued elsewhere that all isolated or discrete cultural analysis always involves a buried or repressed theory of historical periodization; in any case, the conception of the "genealogy" largely lays to rest traditional theoretical worries about so-called linear history, theories of "stages", and teleological historiography. In the present context, however, lengthier theoretical discussion of such (very real) issues can perhaps be replaced by a few substantive remarks.

One of the concerns frequently aroused by periodizing hypotheses is that these tend to obliterate difference, and to project an idea of the historical period as massive homogeneity (bounded on either side by inexplicable "chronological" metamorphoses and punctuation marks). This is, however, precisely why it seems to me essential to grasp "postmodernism" not as a style, but rather as a cultural dominant: a conception which allows for the presence and coexistence of a range of very different, yet subordinate features.

Consider, for example, the powerful alternative position that postmodernism is itself little more than one more stage of modernism proper (if not, indeed, of the even older romanticism); it may indeed be conceded that all of the features of postmodernism I am about to enumerate can be detected, full-blown, in this or that preceding modernism (including such astonishing genealogical precursors as Gertrude Stein, Raymond Roussel, or Marcel Duchamp, who may be considered outright postmodernists, *avant la lettre*). What has not been taken into account by this view is, however, the social position of the older modernism, or better still, its passionate repudiation by an older Victorian and post-Victorian bourgeoisie, for whom its forms and ethos are received as being variously ugly, dissonant, obscure, scandalous, immoral, subversive and generally "anti-social". It will be argued here that a mutation in the sphere of culture has rendered such attitudes archaic. Not only are Picasso and Joyce no longer ugly; they now strike us, on the whole, as rather "realistic"; and this is the result of a canonization and an academic institutionalization of the modern movement generally, which can be traced to the late 1950s. This is indeed surely one of the most plausible explanations for the emergence of postmodernism itself, since the younger generation of the 1960s will now confront the formerly oppositional modern movement as a set of dead classics, which "weigh like a nightmare on the brains of the living", as Marx once said in a different context.

As for the postmodern revolt against all that, however, it must equally be stressed that its own offensive features – from obscurity and sexually explicit material to psychological squalor and overt expressions of social and political defiance, which transcend anything that might have been imagined at the most extreme moments of high modernism – no longer scandalize anyone and are not only received with the greatest complacency but have themselves become institutionalized and are at one with the official culture of Western society.

What has happened is that aesthetic production today has become integrated into commodity production generally: the frantic economic urgency of producing fresh waves of ever more novel-seeming goods (from clothing to airplanes), at ever greater rates of turnover, now assigns an increasingly essential structural function and position to aesthetic innovation and experimentation. Such economic necessities then find recognition in the institutional support of all kinds available for the newer art, from foundations and grants to museums and other forms of patronage. Architecture is, however, of all the arts that closest constitutively to the economic, with which, in the form of commissions and land values, it has a virtually unmediated relationship: it will therefore not be surprising to find the extraordinary flowering of the new postmodern architecture grounded in the patronage of multinational business, whose expansion and development is strictly contemporaneous with it. That these two new phenomena have an even deeper dialectical interrelationship than the simple one-to-one financing of this or that individual project we will try to suggest later on. Yet this is the point at which we must remind the reader of the obvious, namely that this whole global, yet American, postmodern culture is the internal and superstructural expression of a whole new wave of American military and economic domination throughout the world: in this sense, as throughout class history, the underside of culture is blood, torture, death and horror.

The first point to be made about the conception of periodization in dominance, therefore, is that even if all the constitutive features of postmodernism were identical and continuous with those of an older modernism – a position I feel to be demonstrably erroneous but which only an even lengthier analysis of modernism proper could dispel – the two phenomena would still remain utterly distinct in their meaning and social function, owing to the very different positioning of postmodernism in the economic system of late capital, and beyond that, to the transformation of the very sphere of culture in contemporary society.

More on this point at the conclusion of the present essay. I must now briefly address a different kind of objection to periodization, a different kind of concern about its possible obliteration of heterogeneity, which one finds most often on the Left. And it is certain that there is a strange quasi-Sartrean irony – a "winner loses" logic – which tends to surround any effort to describe a "system", a totalizing dynamic, as these are detected in the movement of contemporary society. What happens is that the more powerful the vision of some increasingly total system or logic – the Foucault of the prisons book is the obvious example – the more power-less the reader comes to feel. Insofar as the theorist wins, therefore, by constructing an increasingly closed and terrifying machine, to that very degree he loses, since the critical capacity of his work is thereby paralysed, and the impulses of negation and revolt, not to speak of those of social transformation, are increasingly perceived as vain and trivial in the face of the model itself.

I have felt, however, that it was only in the light of some conception of a dominant cultural logic or hegemonic norm that genuine difference could be meas-ured and assessed. I am very far from feeling that all cultural production today is "postmodern" in the broad sense I will be conferring on this term. The postmodern is however the force field in which very different kinds of cultural impulses – what Raymond Williams has usefully termed "residual" and "emergent" forms of cultural production – must make their way. If we do not achieve some general sense of a cultural dominant, then we fall back into a view of present history as sheer hetero-geneity, random difference, a coexistence of a host of distinct forces whose effectivity is undecidable. This has been at any rate the political spirit in which the following analysis was devised: to project some conception of a new systemic cultural norm and its reproduction, in order to reflect more adequately on the most effective forms of any radical cultural politics today.

The exposition will take up in turn the following constitutive features of the postmodern: a new depthlessness, which finds its prolongation both in contem-porary "theory" and in a whole new culture of the image or the simulacrum; a consequent weakening of historicity, both in our relationship to public History and in the new forms of our private temporality, whose "schizophrenic" structure (following Lacan) will determine new types of syntax or syntagmatic relationships in the more temporal arts; a whole new type of emotional ground tone – what I will call "intensities" – which can best be grasped by a return to older theories of the sublime; the deep constitutive relationships of all this to a whole new technology, which is itself a figure for a whole new economic world system; and, after a brief account of postmodernist mutations in the lived experience of built space itself, some reflections on the mission of political art in the bewildering new world space of late multinational capital.

The Deconstruction of Expression

"Peasant Shoes"

We will begin with one of the canonical works of high modernism in visual art, Van Gogh's well-known painting of the peasant shoes, an example which as you can imagine has not been innocently or randomly chosen. I want to propose two ways of reading this painting, both of which in some fashion reconstruct the reception of the work in a two-stage or double-level process.

I first want to suggest that if this copiously reproduced image is not to sink to the level of sheer decoration, it requires us to reconstruct some initial situation out of which the finished work emerges. Unless that situation – which has vanished into the past – is somehow mentally restored, the painting will remain an inert object, a reified end-product, and be unable to be grasped as a symbolic act in its own right, as praxis and as production.

This last term suggests that one way of reconstructing the initial situation to which the work is somehow a response is by stressing the raw materials, the initial content, which it confronts and which it reworks, transforms, and appropriates. In Van Gogh, that content, those initial raw materials, are, I will suggest, to be grasped simply as the whole object world of agricultural misery, of stark rural poverty, and the whole rudimentary human world of backbreaking peasant toil, a world reduced to its most brutal and menaced, primitive and marginalized state.

Fruit trees in this world are ancient and exhausted sticks coming out of poor soil; the people of the village are worn down to their skulls, caricatures of some ultimate grotesque typology of basic human feature types. How is it then that in Van Gogh such things as apple trees explode into a hallucinatory surface of colour, while his village stereotypes are suddenly and garishly overlaid with hues of red and green? I will briefly suggest, in this first interpretative option, that the willed and violent transformation of a drab peasant object world into the most glorious materialization of pure colour in oil paint is to be seen as a Utopian gesture: as an act of compensation which ends up producing a whole new Utopian realm of the senses, or at least of that supreme sense – sight, the visual, the eye – which it now reconstitutes for us as a semi-autonomous space in its own right – part of some new division of labour in the body of capital, some new fragmentation of the emergent sensorium which replicates the specializations and divisions of capitalist life at the same time that it seeks in precisely such fragmentation a desperate Utopian compensation for them.

There is, to be sure, a second reading of Van Gogh which can hardly be ignored when we gaze at this particular painting, and that is Heidegger's central analysis in *Der Ursprung des Kunstwerkes*, which is organized around the idea that the work of art emerges within the gap between Earth and World, or what I would prefer to translate as the meaningless materiality of the body and nature and the meaning-endowment of history and of the social. We will return to that particular gap or rift later on; suffice it here to recall some of the famous phrases, which model the process whereby these henceforth illustrious peasant shoes slowly recreate about themselves the whole missing object-world which was once their lived context. "In them,' says Heidegger, "there vibrates the silent call of the earth, its quiet gift of ripening corn and its enigmatic self-refusal in the fallow desolation of the wintry field." "This equipment," he goes on, "belongs to the *earth* and it is protected in the *world* of the peasant woman . . . Van Gogh's painting is the disclosure of what the equipment, the pair of peasant shoes, *is* in truth . . . This entity emerges into the unconcealment of its being", by way of the mediation of the work of art, which draws the whole absent world and earth into revelation around itself, along with the heavy tread of the peasant woman, the loneliness of the field path, the hut in the clearing, the worn and broken instruments of labour in the furrows and at the hearth. Heidegger's account needs to be completed by insistence on the renewed materiality of the work, on the transformation of one form of materiality – the earth itself and its paths and physical objects – into that other materiality of oil paint affirmed and foregrounded in its own right and for its own visual pleasures; but has nonetheless a satisfying plausibility.

"Diamond Dust Shoes"

At any rate, both of these readings may be described as *hermeneutical*, in the sense in which the work in its inert, objectal form, is taken as a clue or a symptom for some vaster reality which replaces it as its ultimate truth. Now we need to look at some shoes of a different kind, and it is pleasant to be able to draw for such an image on the recent work of the central figure in contemporary visual art. Andy Warhol's *Diamond Dust Shoes* evidently no longer speaks to us with any of the immediacy of Van Gogh's footgear: indeed, I am tempted to say that it does not really speak to us at all. Nothing in this painting organizes even a minimal place for the viewer, who confronts it at the turning of a museum corridor or gallery with all the contingency of some inexplicable natural object. On the level of the content, we have to do with what are now far more clearly fetishes, both in the Freudian and in the Marxian sense (Derrida remarks, somewhere, about the Heideggerian *Paar Bauernschube*, that the Van Gogh footgear are a heterosexual pair, which allows neither for perversion nor for fetishization). Here, however, we have a random collection of dead objects, hanging together on the canvas like so many turnips, as shorn of their earlier life-world as the pile of shoes left over from Auschwitz, or the remainders and tokens of some incomprehensible and tragic fire in a packed dancehall. There is therefore in Warhol no way to complete the hermeneutic gesture, and to restore to these oddments that whole larger lived context of the dance hall or the ball, the world of jetset fashion or of glamour magazines. Yet this is even more paradoxical in the light of biographical information: Warhol began his artistic career as a commercial illustrator for shoe fashions and a designer of display windows in which various pumps and slippers figured prominently. Indeed, one is tempted to raise here – far too prematurely – one of the central issues about postmodernism itself and its possible political dimensions: Andy Warhol's work in fact turns centrally around commodification, and the great billboard images of the Coca-Cola bottle or the Campbell's Soup can, which explicitly foreground the commodity fetishism of a transition to late capital, *ought* to be powerful and critical political statements. If they are not that, then one would surely want to know why, and one would want to begin to wonder a little more seriously about the possibilities of political or critical art in the postmodern period of late capital.

But there are some other significant differences between the high modernist and the postmodernist moment, between the shoes of Van Gogh and the shoes of Andy Warhol, on which we must now very briefly dwell. The first and most evident is the emergence of a new kind of flatness or depthlessness, a new kind of superficiality in the most literal sense – perhaps the supreme formal feature of all the postmodernisms to which we will have occasion to return in a number of other contexts.

Then we must surely come to terms with the role of photography and the photographic/negative in contemporary art of this kind: and it is this indeed which confers its deathly quality on the Warhol image, whose glacéd x-ray elegance mortifies the reified eye of the viewer in a way that would seem to have nothing to do with death or the death obsession or the death anxiety on the level of content. It is indeed as though we had here to do with the inversion of Van Gogh's Utopian gesture: in the earlier work, a stricken world is by some Nietzschean fiat and act of the will transformed into the stridency of Utopian colour. Here, on the contrary, it is as though the external and coloured surface of things – debased and contaminated in advance by their assimilation to glossy advertising images – has been stripped away to reveal the deathly black-and-white substratum of the photographic negative which subtends them. Although this kind of death of the world of appearance becomes thematized in certain of Warhol's pieces – most notably, the traffic accidents or the electric chair series – this is not, I think, a matter of content any longer but of some more fundamental mutation both in the object world itself – now become a set of texts or simulacra – and in the disposition of the subject.

The Waning of Affect

All of which brings me to the third feature I had in mind to develop here briefly, namely what I will call the waning of affect in postmodern culture. Of course, it would be inaccurate to suggest that all affect, all feeling or emotion, all subjectivity, has vanished from the newer image. Indeed, there is a kind of return of the repressed in *Diamond Dust Shoes*, a strange compensatory decorative exhilaration, explicitly designated by the title itself although perhaps more difficult to observe in the reproduction. This is the glitter of gold dust, the spangling of gilt sand, which seals the surface of the painting and yet continues to glint at us. Think, however, of Rimbaud's magical flowers "that look back at you", or of the august premonitory eye-flashes of Rilke's archaic Greek torso which warn the bourgeois subject to change his life: nothing of that sort here, in the gratuitous frivolity of this final decorative overlay.

The waning of affect is, however, perhaps best initially approached by way of the human figure, and it is obvious that what we have said about the commodification of objects holds as strongly for Warhol's human subjects, stars – like Marilyn Monroe – who are themselves commodified and transformed into their own images. And here too a certain brutal return to the older period of high modernism offers a dramatic shorthand parable of the transformation in question. Edvard Munch's painting *The Scream* is of course a canonical expression of the great modernist thematics of alienation, anomie, solitude and social fragmentation and isolation, a virtually programmatic emblem of what used to be called the age of anxiety. It will here be read not merely as an embodiment of the expression of that kind of affect, but even more as a virtual deconstruction of the very aesthetic of expression itself, which seems to have dominated much of what we call high modernism, but to have vanished away – for both practical and theoretical reasons – in the world of the postmodern. The very concept of expression presupposes indeed some separation within the subject, and along with that a whole metaphysics of the inside and the outside, of the wordless pain within the monad and the moment in which, often cathartically, that "emotion" is then projected out and externalized, as gesture or cry, as desperate communication and the outward dramatization of inward feeling. And this is perhaps the moment to say something about contemporary theory, which has among other things been committed to the mission of criticizing and discrediting this very hermeneutic model of the inside and the outside and of stigmatizing such models as ideological and metaphysical. But what is today called contemporary theory – or better still, theoretical discourse – is also, I would want to argue, itself very precisely a postmodernist phenomenon. It would therefore be inconsistent to defend the truth of its theoretical insights in a situation in which the very concept of "truth" itself is part of the metaphysical baggage which poststructuralism seeks to abandon. What we can at least suggest is that the poststructuralist critique of the hermeneutic, of what I will shortly call the depth model, is useful for us as a very significant symptom of the very postmodernist culture which is our subject here.

Overhastily, we can say that besides the hermeneutic model of inside and outside which Munch's painting develops, there are at least four other fundamental depth models which have generally been repudiated in contemporary theory: the dialectical one of essence and appearance (along with a whole range of concepts of ideology or false consciousness which tend to accompany it); the Freudian model of latent and manifest, or of repression (which is of course the target of Michel Foucault's programmatic and symptomatic pamphlet *La Volonté de savoir*); the existential model of authenticity and inauthenticity, whose heroic or tragic thematics are closely related to that other great opposition between alienation and disalienation, itself equally a casualty of the poststructural or postmodern period; and finally, latest in time, the great semiotic opposition between signifier and signified, which was itself rapidly unravelled and deconstructed during its brief heyday in the 1960s and 70s. What replaces these various depth models is for the most part a conception of practices, discourses and textual play, whose new syntagmatic structures we will examine later on: suffice it merely to observe that here too depth is replaced by surface, or by multiple surfaces (what is often called intertextuality is in that sense no longer a matter of depth).

Nor is this depthlessness merely metaphorical: it can be experienced physically and literally by anyone who, mounting what used to be Raymond Chandler's Beacon Hill from the great Chicano markets on Broadway and 4th St. in downtown Los Angeles, suddenly confronts the great free-standing wall of the Crocker Bank Center (Skidmore, Owings and Merrill) – a surface which seems to be unsupported by any volume, or whose putative volume (rectangular, trapezoidal?) is ocularly quite undecidable. This great sheet of windows, with its gravity-defying two-dimensionality, momentarily transforms the solid ground on which we climb into the contents of a stereopticon, pasteboard shapes profiling themselves here and there around us. From all sides, the visual effect is the same: as fateful as the great monolith in Kubrick's *2001* which confronts its viewers like an enigmatic destiny, a call to evolutionary mutation. If this new multinational downtown (to which we will return later in another context) effectively abolished the older ruined city fabric which it violently replaced, cannot something similar be said about the way in which this strange new surface in its own peremptory way renders our older systems of perception of the city somehow archaic and aimless, without offering another in their place?

Euphoria and Self-Annihilation

Returning now for one last moment to Munch's painting, it seems evident that *The Scream* subtly but elaborately deconstructs its own aesthetic of expression, all the while remaining imprisoned within it. Its gestural content already underscores its own failure, since the realm of the sonorous, the cry, the raw vibrations of the human throat, are incompatible with its medium (something underscored within the work by the homunculus' lack of ears). Yet the absent scream returns more closely towards that even more absent experience of atrocious solitude and anxiety which the scream was itself to "express". Such loops inscribe themselves on the painted surface in the form of those great concentric circles in which sonorous vibration becomes ultimately visible, as on the surface of a sheet of water – in an infinite regress which fans out from the sufferer to become the very geography of a universe in which pain itself now speaks and vibrates through the material sunset and the landscape. The visible world now becomes the wall of the monad on which this "scream running through nature" (Munch's words) is recorded and transcribed: one thinks of that character of Lautréamont who, growing up inside a scaled and silent membrane, on sight of the monstrousness of the deity, ruptures it with his own scream and thereby rejoins the world of sound and suffering.

All of which suggests some more general historical hypothesis: namely, that concepts such as anxiety and alienation (and the experiences to which they correspond, as in *The Scream*) are no longer appropriate in the world of the postmodern. The great Warhol figures – Marilyn herself, or Edie Sedgewick – the notorious burn-out and self-destruction cases of the ending 1960s, and the great dominant experiences of drugs and schizophrenia – these would seem to have little enough in common anymore, either with the hysterics and neurotics of Freud's own day, or with those canonical experiences of radical isolation and solitude, anomie, private revolt, Van Gogh-type madness, which dominated the period of high modernism. This shift in the dynamics of cultural pathology can be characterized as one in which the alienation of the subject is displaced by the fragmentation of the subject.

Such terms inevitably recall one of the more fashionable themes in contemporary theory – that of the "death" of the subject itself = the end of the autonomous bourgeois monad or ego or individual – and the accompanying stress, whether as some new moral ideal or as empirical description, on the *decentring* of that formerly centred subject or psyche. (Of the two possible formulations of this notion – the historicist one, that a once-existing centred subject, in the period of classical capitalism and the nuclear family, has today in the world of organizational bureaucracy dissolved; and the more radical poststructuralist position for which such a subject never existed in the first place but constituted something like an ideological mirage – I obviously incline towards the former; the latter must in any case take into account something like a "reality of the appearance".)

We must add that the problem of expression is itself closely linked to some conception of the subject as a monad-like container, within which things are felt which are then expressed by projection outwards. What we must now stress, however, is the degree to which the high-modernist conception of a unique *style*, along with the accompanying collective ideals of an artistic or political vanguard or *avant-garde*, themselves stand or fall along with that older notion (or experience) of the so-called centred subject.

Here too Munch's painting stands as a complex reflexion on this complicated situation: it shows us that expression requires the category of the individual monad, but it also shows us the heavy price to be paid for that precondition, dramatizing the unhappy paradox that when you constitute your individual subjectivity as a self-sufficient field and a closed realm in its own right, you thereby also shut yourself off from everything else and condemn yourself to the windless solitude of the monad, buried alive and condemned to a prison-cell without egress.

Postmodernism will presumably signal the end of this dilemma, which it replaces with a new one. The end of the bourgeois ego or monad no doubt brings with it the end of the psychopathologies of that ego as well – what I have generally here been calling the waning of affect. But it means the end of much more – the end for example of style, in the sense of the unique and the personal, the end of the distinctive individual brushstroke (as symbolized by the emergent primacy of mechanical reproduction). As for expression and feelings or emotions, the liberation, in contemporary society, from the older *anomie* of the centred subject may also mean, not merely a liberation from anxiety, but a liberation from every other kind of feeling as well, since there is no longer a self present to do the feeling. This is not to say that the cultural products of the postmodern era are utterly devoid of feeling, but rather that such feelings – which it may be better and more accurate to call "intensities" – are now free-floating and impersonal, and tend to be dominated by a peculiar kind of euphoria to which I will want to return at the end of this essay.

The waning of affect, however, might also have been characterized, in the narrower context of literary criticism, as the waning of the great high-modernist thematics of time and temporality, the elegiac mysteries of *durée* and of memory (something to be understood fully as a category of literary criticism associated as much with high modernism as with the works themselves). We have often been told, however, that we now inhabit the synchronic rather than the diachronic, and I think it is at least empirically arguable that our daily life, our psychic experience, our cultural languages, are today dominated by categories of space rather than by categories of time, as in the preceding period of high modernism proper.

The Postmodern and the Past

Pastiche Eclipses Parody

The disappearance of the individual subject, along with its formal consequence, the increasing unavailability of the personal *style,* engender the well-nigh universal practice today of what may be called pastiche. This concept, which we owe to Thomas Mann (in *Doktor Faustus*), who owed it in turn to Adorno's great work on the two paths of advanced musical experimentation (Schoenberg's innovative planification, Stravinsky's irrational eclecticism), is to be sharply distinguished from the more readily received idea of parody.

This last found, to be sure, a fertile area in the idiosyncracies of the moderns and their "inimitable" styles: the Faulknerian long sentence with its breathless gerundives, Lawrentian nature imagery punctuated by testy colloquialism, Wallace Stevens' inveterate hypostasis of nonsubstantive parts of speech ("the intricate evasions of as"), the fateful, but finally predictable, swoops in Mahler from high orchestral pathos into village accordeon sentiment, Heidegger's meditative-solemn practice of the false etymology as a mode of "proof" . . . All these strike one as somehow "characteristic", insofar as they ostentatiously deviate from a norm which then reasserts itself, in a not necessarily unfriendly way, by a systematic mimicry of their deliberate eccentricities.

Yet, in the dialectical leap from quantity to quality, the explosion of modern literature into a host of distinct private styles and mannerisms has been followed by a linguistic fragmentation of social life itself to the point where the norm itself is eclipsed: reduced to a neutral and reified media speech (far enough from the Utopian aspirations of the inventors of Esperanto or Basic English), which itself then becomes but one more idiolect among many. Modernist styles thereby become postmodernist codes: and that the stupendous proliferation of social codes today into professional and disciplinary jargons, but also into the badges of affirmation of ethnic, gender, race, religious, and class-fraction adhesion, is also a political phenomenon, the problem of micropolitics sufficiently demonstrates. If the ideas of a ruling class were once the dominant (or hegemonic) ideology of bourgeois society, the advanced capitalist countries today are now a field of stylistic and discursive heterogeneity without a norm. Faceless masters continue to inflect the economic strategies which constrain our existences, but no longer need to impose their speech (or are henceforth unable to); and the postliteracy of the late capitalist world reflects, not only the absence of any great collective project, but also the unavailability of the older national language itself.

In this situation, parody finds itself without a vocation; it has lived, and that strange new thing pastiche slowly comes to take its place. Pastiche is, like parody, the imitation of a peculiar mask, speech in a dead language: but it is a neutral practice of such mimicry, without any of parody's ulterior motives, amputated of the satiric impulse, devoid of laughter and of any conviction that alongside the abnormal tongue you have momentarily borrowed, some healthy linguistic normality still exists. Pastiche is thus blank parody, a statue with blind eyeballs: it is to parody what that other interesting and historically original modern thing, the practice of a kind of blank irony, is to what Wayne Booth calls the "stable ironies" of the 18th century.

It would therefore begin to seem that Adorno's prophetic diagnosis has been realized, albeit in a negative way: not Schoenberg (the sterility of whose achieved system he already glimpsed) but Stravinsky is the true precursor of the postmodern cultural production. For with the collapse of the high-modernist ideology of style – what is as unique and unmistakable as your own fingerprints, as incomparable as your own body (the very source, for an early Roland Barthes, of stylistic invention and innovation) – the producers of culture have nowhere to turn but to the past: the imitation of dead styles, speech through all the masks and voices stored up in the imaginary museum of a now global culture.

"Historicism" Effaces History

This situation evidently determines what the architecture historians call "historicism", namely the random cannibalization of all the styles of the past, the play of random stylistic allusion, and in general what Henri Lefebvre has called the increasing primacy of the "neo". This omnipresence of pastiche is, however, not incompatible with a certain humour (nor is it innocent of all passion) or at least with addiction – with a whole historically original consumers' appetite for a world transformed into sheer images of itself and for pseudo-events and "spectacles" (the term of the Situationists). It is for such objects that we may reserve Plato's conception of the "simulacrum" – the identical copy for which no original has ever existed. Appropriately enough, the culture of the simulacrum comes to *life* in a society where exchange-value has been generalized to the point at which the very memory of use-value is effaced, a society of which Guy Debord has observed, in an extraordinary phrase, that in it "the image has become the final form of commodity reification" (*The Society of the Spectacle*).

The new spatial logic of the simulacrum can now be expected to have a momentous effect on what used to be historical time.

The past is thereby itself modified: what was once, in the historical novel as Lukács defines it, the organic genealogy of the bourgeois collective project – what is still, for the redemptive historiography of an E. P. Thompson or of American "oral history", for the resurrection of the dead of anonymous and silenced generations, the retrospective dimension indispensable to any vital reorientation of our collective future – has meanwhile itself become a vast collection of images, a multitudinous photographic simulacrum. Guy Debord's powerful slogan is now even more apt for the "prehistory" of a society bereft of all historicity, whose own putative past is little more than a set of dusty spectacles. In faithful conformity to poststructuralist linguistic theory, the past as "referent" finds itself gradually bracketed, and then effaced altogether, leaving us with nothing but texts.

The Nostalgia Mode

Yet it should not be thought that this process is accompanied by indifference: on the contrary, the remarkable current intensification of an addiction to the photographic image is itself a tangible symptom of an omnipresent, omnivorous and well-nigh libidinal historicism. The architects use this (exceedingly polysemous) word for the complacent eclecticism of postmodern architecture, which randomly and without principle but with gusto cannibalizes all the architectural styles of the past and combines them in overstimulating ensembles. Nostalgia does not strike one as an altogether satisfactory word for such fascination (particularly when one thinks of the pain of a properly modernist nostalgia with a past beyond all but aesthetic retrieval), yet it directs our attention to what is a culturally far more generalized manifestation of the process in commercial art and taste, namely the so-called "nostalgia film" (or what the French call "la mode rétro").

These restructure the whole issue of pastiche and project it onto a collective and social level, where the desperate attempt to appropriate a missing past is now refracted through the iron law of fashion change and the emergent ideology of the "generation". *American Graffiti* (1973) set out to recapture, as so many films have attempted since, the henceforth mesmerizing lost reality of the Eisenhower era: and one tends to feel that for Americans at least, the 1950s remain the privileged lost object of desire – not merely the stability and prosperity of a pax Americana, but also the first naive innocence of the countercultural impulses of early rock-and-roll and youth gangs (Coppola's *Rumble Fish* will then be the contemporary dirge that laments their passing, itself, however, still contradictorily filmed in genuine "nostalgia film" style). With this initial breakthrough, other generational periods open up for aesthetic colonization: as witness the stylistic recuperation of the American and the Italian 1930s, in Polanski's *Chinatown* and Bertolluci's *Il Conformista* respectively. What is more interesting, and more problematical, are the ultimate attempts, through this new discourse, to lay siege either to our own present and immediate past, or to a more distant history that escapes individual existential memory.

Faced with these ultimate objects – our social, historical and existential present, and the past as "referent" – the incompatibility of a postmodernist "nostalgia" art language with genuine historicity becomes dramatically apparent. The contraction propels this model, however, into complex and interesting new formal inventiveness: it being understood that the nostalgia film was never a matter of some old-fashioned "representation" of historical content, but approached the "past" through stylistic connotation, conveying "pastness" by the glossy qualities of the image, and "1930s-ness" or "1950s-ness" by the attributes of fashion (therein following the prescription of the Barthes of *Mythologies*, who saw connotation as the purveying of imaginary and stereotypical idealities, "Sinité", for example, as some Disney-EPCOT "concept" of China).

The insensible colonization of the present by the nostalgia mode can be observed in Lawrence Kazdan's elegant film, *Body Heat*, a distant "affluent society" remake of James M. Cain's *The Postman Always Rings Twice*, set in a contemporary Florida small town not far from Miami. The word "remake" is, however, anachronistic to the degree to which our awareness of the pre-existence of other versions, previous films of the novel as well as the novel itself, is now a constitutive and essential part of the film's structure: we are now, in other words, in "intertextuality" as a deliberate, built-in feature of the aesthetic effect, and as the operator of a new connotation of "pastness" and pseudo-historical depth, in which the history of aesthetic styles displaces "real" history.

Yet from the outset a whole battery of aesthetic signs begin to distance the officially contemporary image from us in time: the art deco scripting of the credits, for example, serves at once to programme the spectator for the appropriate "nostalgia" mode of reception (art deco quotation has much the same function in contemporary architecture, as in Toronto's remarkable Eaton Centre). Meanwhile, a somewhat different play of connotations is activated by complex (but purely formal) allusions to the institutions of the star system itself. The protagonist, William Hurt, is one of a new generation of film "stars" whose status is markedly distinct from that of the preceding generation of male superstars, such as Steve McQueen or Jack Nicholson (or even, more distantly, Brando), let alone of earlier moments in the evolution of the institutions of the star. The immediately preceding generation projected its various roles through, and by way of, well-known "off-screen" personalities, who often connoted rebellion and non-conformism. The latest generation of starring actors continues to assure the conventional functions of stardom (most notably, sexuality) but in the utter absence of "personality" in the older sense, and with something of the anonymity of character acting (which in actors like Hurt reaches virtuouso proportions, yet of a very different kind from the virtuosity of the older Brando or Olivier). This "death of the subject" in the institution of the star, however, opens up the possibility of a play of historical allusions to much older roles – in this case to those associated with Clark Gable – so that the very style of the acting can now also serve as a "connotator" of the past.

Finally, the setting has been strategically framed, with great ingenuity, to eschew most of the signals that normally convey the contemporaneity of the United States in its multinational era: the small-town setting allows the camera to elude the high-rise landscape of the 1970s and 80s (even though a key episode in the narrative involves the fatal destruction of older buildings by land speculators); while the object world of the present-day – artifacts and appliances, even automobiles, whose styling would at once serve to date the image – is elaborately edited out. Everything in the film, therefore, conspires to blur its official contemporaneity and to make it possible for you to receive the narrative as though it were set in some eternal Thirties, beyond real historical time. The approach to the present by way of the art language of the simulacrum, or of the pastiche of the stereotypical past, endows present reality and the openness of present history with the spell and distance of a glossy mirage. But this mesmerizing new aesthetic mode itself emerged as an elaborated symptom of the waning of our historicity, of our lived possibility of experiencing history in some active way: it cannot therefore be said to produce this strange occultation of the present by its own formal power, but merely to demonstrate, through these inner contradictions, the enormity of a situation in which we seem increasingly incapable of fashioning representations of our own current experience.

The Fate of "Real History"

As for "real history" itself – the traditional object, however it may be defined, of what used to be the historical novel – it will be more revealing now to turn back to that older form and medium and to read its postmodern fate in the work of one of the few serious and innovative Left novelists at work in the United States today, whose books are nourished with history in the more traditional sense, and seem, so far, to stake out successive generational moments in the "epic" of American history. E. L. Doctorow's *Ragtime* gives itself officially as a panorama of the first two decades of the century; his most recent novel, *Loon Lake*, addresses the Thirties and the Great Depression; while *The Book of Daniel* holds up before us, in painful juxtaposition, the two great moments of the Old Left and the New Left, of Thirties and Forties Communism and the radicalism of the 1960s (even his early Western may be said to fit into this scheme and to designate in a less articulated and formally self-conscious way the end of the frontier of the late nineteenth century).

The Book of Daniel is not the only one of these three major historical novels to establish an explicit narrative link between the reader's and the writer's present and the older historical reality which is the subject of the work; the astonishing last page of *Loon Lake*, which I will not disclose, also does this in a very different way; while it is a matter of some interest to note that the first sentence of the first version of *Ragtime* positions us explicitly in our own present, in the novelist's house in New Rochelle, New York, which will then at once become the scene of its own (imaginary) past in the 1900s. This detail has been suppressed from the published text, symbolically cutting its moorings and freeing the novel to float in some new world of past historical time whose relationship to us is problematical indeed. The authenticity of the gesture, however, may be measured by the evident existential fact of life that there no longer does seem to be any organic relationship between the American history we learn from the schoolbooks and the lived experience of the current multinational, high-rise, stagflated city of the newspapers and of our own daily life.

A crisis in historicity, however, inscribes itself symptomally in several other curious formal features within this text. Its official subject is the transition from a pre-World-War I radical and working-class politics (the great strikes) to the technological invention and new commodity production of the 1920s (the rise of Hollywood and of the image as commodity): the interpolated version of Kleist's *Michael Kohlhaas*, the strange tragic episode of the Black protagonist's revolt, may be thought to be a moment related to this process. My point, however, is not some hypothesis as to the thematic coherence of this decentred narrative; but rather just the opposite, namely the way in which the kind of reading this novel imposes makes it virtually impossible for us to reach and to thematize those official "subjects" which float above the text but cannot be integrated into our reading of the sentences. In that sense, not only does the novel resist interpretation, it is organized systematically and formally to short-circuit an older type of social and historical interpretation which it perpetually holds out and withdraws. When we remember that the theoretical critique and repudiation of interpretation as such is a fundamental component of poststructuralist theory, it is difficult not to conclude that Doctorow has somehow deliberately built this very tension, this very contradiction, into the flow of his sentences.

As is well known, the book is crowded with real historical figures – from Teddy Roosevelt to Emma Goldman, from Harry K. Thaw and Sandford White to J. Pierpont Morgan and Henry Ford, not to speak of the more central role of Houdini – who interact with a fictive family, simply designated as Father, Mother, Older Brother, and so forth. All historical novels, beginning with Scott himself, no doubt in one way or another involve a mobilization of previous historical knowledge, generally acquired through the schoolbook history manuals devised for whatever legitimizing purpose by this or that national tradition – thereafter instituting a narrative dialectic between what we already "know" about The Pretender, say, and what he is then seen to be concretely in the pages of the novel. But Doctorow's procedure seems much more extreme than this; and I would argue that the designation of both types of characters – historical names or capitalized family roles – operates powerfully and systematically to reify all these characters and to make it impossible for us to receive their representation without the prior interception of already-acquired knowledge or doxa – something which lends the text an extraordinary sense of déjà-vu and a peculiar familiarity one is tempted to associate with Freud's "return of the repressed" in "The Uncanny", rather than with any solid historiographic formation on the reader's part.

Loss of the Radical Past

Meanwhile, the sentences in which all this is happening have their own specificity, which will allow us a little more concretely to distinguish the moderns' elaboration of a personal style from this new kind of linguistic innovation, which is no longer personal at all but has its family kinship rather with what Barthes long ago called "white writing". In this particular novel, Doctorow has imposed upon himself a rigorous principle of selection in which only simple declarative sentences (predominantly mobilized by the verb "to be") are received. The effect is, however, not really one of the condescending simplification and symbolic carefulness of children's literature, but rather something more disturbing, the sense of some profound subterranean violence done to American English which cannot, however, be detected empirically in any of the perfectly grammatical sentences with which this work is formed. Yet other more visible technical "innovations" may supply a clue to what is happening in the language of *Ragtime*: it is for example well known that the source of many of the characteristic effects of Camus' novel *L'Etranger* can be traced back to that author's wilful decision to substitute, throughout, the French tense of the "passé composé" for the other past tenses more normally employed in narration in that language. 1 will suggest that it is *as if* something of that sort were at work here (without committing myself further to what is obviously an outrageous leap): it is, I say, *as though* Doctorow had set out systematically to produce the effect or the equivalent, in his language, of a verbal past tense we do not possess in English, namely the French preterite (or *passé simple*), whose "perfective" movement, as Émile Benveniste taught us, serves to separate events from the present of enunciation and to transform the stream of time and action into so many finished, complete, and isolated punctual event-objects which find themselves sundered from any present situation (even that of the act of storytelling or enunciation).

E. L. Doctorow is the epic poet of the disappearance of the American radical past, of the suppression of older traditions and moments of the American radical tradition: no one with left sympathies can read these splendid novels without a poignant distress which is an authentic way of confronting our own current political dilemmas in the present. What is culturally interesting, however, is that he has had to convey this great theme formally (since the waning of the content is very precisely his sub-ject), and, more than that, has had to elaborate his work by way of that very cultural logic of the postmodern which is itself the mark and symptom of his dilemma. *Loon Lake* much more obviously deploys the strategies of the pastiche (most notably in its reinvention of Dos Passos); but *Ragtime* remains the most peculiar and stunning monument to the aesthetic situation engendered by the disappearance of the his-torical referent. This historical novel can no longer set out to represent the historical past; it can only "represent" our ideas and stereotypes about that past (which thereby at once becomes "pop history"). Cultural production is thereby driven back inside a mental space which is no longer that of the old monadic subject, but rather that of some degraded collective "objective spirit": it can no longer gaze directly on some putative real world, at some reconstruction of a past history which was once itself a present; rather, as in Plato's cave, it must trace our mental images of that past upon its confining walls. If there is any realism left here, therefore, it is a "realism" which is meant to derive from the shock of grasping that confinement, and of slowly becoming aware of a new and original historical situation in which we are condemned to seek History by way of our own pop images and simulacra of that history, which itself remains forever out of reach.

The Breakdown of the Signifying Chain

The crisis in historicity now dictates a return, in a new way, to the question of temporal organization in general in the postmodern force field, and indeed, to the problem of the form that time, temporality and the syntagmatic will be able to take in a culture increasingly dominated by space and spatial logic. If, indeed, the sub-ject has lost its capacity actively to extend its pro-tensions and re-tensions across the temporal manifold, and to organize its past and future into coherent experi-ence, it becomes difficult enough to see how the cultural productions of such a subject could result in anything but "heaps of fragments" and in a practice of the randomly heterogeneous and fragmentary and the aleatory. These are, however, very precisely some of the privileged terms in which postmodernist cultural pro-duction has been analysed (and even defended, by its own apologists). Yet they are still privative features; the more substantive formulations bear such names as textuality, *écriture*, or schizophrenic writing, and it is to these that we must now briefly turn.

I have found Lacan's account of schizophrenia useful here, not because I have any way of knowing whether it has clinical accuracy, but chiefly because – as description rather than diagnosis – it seems to me to offer a suggestive aesthetic model. (I am obviously very far from thinking that any of the most significant postmodernist artists – Cage, Ashbery, Sollers, Robert Wilson, Ishmael Reed, Michael Snow, Warhol or even Beckett himself – are schizophrenics in any clinical sense.) Nor is the point some culture-and-personality diagnosis of our society and its art, as in culture critiques of the type of Christopher Lasch's influential *The Culture of Narcissism*, from which

I am concerned radically to distance the spirit and the methodology of the present remarks: there are, one would think, far more damaging things to be said about our social system than are available through the use of psychological categories.

Very briefly, Lacan describes schizophrenia as a breakdown in the signifying chain, that is, the interlocking syntagmatic series of signifiers which constitutes an utterance or a meaning. I must omit the familial or more orthodox psychoanalytic background to this situation, which Lacan transcodes into language by describing the Oedipal rivalry in terms, not so much of the biological individual who is your rival for the mother's attention, but rather of what he calls the Name-of-the-Father, paternal authority now considered as a linguistic function. His conception of the signifying chain essentially presupposes one of the basic principles (and one of the great discoveries) of Saussurean structuralism, namely the proposition that meaning is not a one-to-one relationship between signifier and signified, between the materiality of language, between a word or a name, and its referent or concept. Meaning on the new view is generated by the movement from Signifier to Signifier: what we generally call the Signified – the meaning or conceptual content of an utterance – is now rather to be seen as a meaning-effect, as that objective mirage of signification generated and projected by the relationship of Signifiers among each other. When that relationship breaks down, when the links of the signifying chain snap, then we have schizophrenia in the form of a rubble of distinct and unrelated signifiers. The connection between this kind of linguistic malfunction and the psyche of the schizophrenic may then be grasped by way of a two-fold proposition: first, that personal identity is itself the effect of a certain temporal unification of past and future with the present before me; and second, that such active temporal unification is itself a function of language, or better still of the sentence, as it moves along its hermeneutic circle through time. If we are unable to unify the past, present and future of the sentence, then we are similarly unable to unify the past, present and future of our own biographical experience or psychic life.

With the breakdown of the signifying chain, therefore, the schizophrenic is reduced to an experience of pure material Signifiers, or in other words of a series of pure and unrelated presents in time. We will want to ask questions about the aesthetic or cultural results of such a situation in a moment; let us first see what it feels like: "I remember very well the day it happened. We were staying in the country and I had gone for a walk alone as I did now and then. Suddenly, as I was passing the school, I heard a German song; the children were having a singing lesson. I stopped to listen, and at that instant a strange feeling came over me, a feeling hard to analyse but akin to something I was to know too well later – a disturbing sense of unreality. It seemed to me that I no longer recognized the school, it had become as large as a barracks; the singing children were prisoners, compelled to sing. It was as though the school and the children's song were set apart from the rest of the world. At the same time my eye encountered a field of wheat whose limits I could not see. The yellow vastness, dazzling in the sun, bound up with the song of the children imprisoned in the smooth stone school-barracks, filled me with such anxiety that I broke into sobs. I ran home to our garden and began to play "to make things seem as they usually were," that is, to return to reality. It was the first appearance of those elements which were always present in later sensations of unreality: illimitable vastness, brilliant light, and the gloss and smoothness of material things."[3]

In our present context, this experience suggests the following remarks: first, the breakdown of temporality suddenly releases this present of time from all the activities and the intentionalities that might focus it and make it a space of praxis; thereby isolated, that present suddenly engulfs the subject with undescribable vividness, a materiality of perception properly overwhelming, which effectively dramatizes the power of the material – or better still, the literal – Signifier in isolation. This present of the world or material signifier comes before the subject with heightened intensity, bearing a mysterious charge of affect, here described in the negative terms of anxiety and loss of reality, but which one could just as well imagine in the positive terms of euphoria, the high, the intoxicatory or hallucinogenic intensity.

"China"

What will happen in textuality or schizophrenic art is strikingly illuminated by such clinical accounts, although in the cultural text, the isolated Signifier is no longer an enigmatic state of the world or an incomprehensible yet mesmerizing fragment of language, but rather something closer to a sentence in free-standing isolation. Think, for example, of the experience of John Cage's music, in which a cluster of material sounds (on the prepared piano for example) is followed by a silence so intolerable that you cannot imagine another sonorous chord coming into existence, and cannot imagine remembering the previous one well enough to make any connection with it if it does. Some of Beckett's narratives are also of this order, most notably *Watt*, where a primacy of the present sentence in time ruthlessly disintegrates the narrative fabric that attempts to reform around it. My example will, however, be a less sombre one, a text by a younger San Francisco poet whose group or school – so-called Language Poetry or the New Sentence – seems to have adopted schizophrenic fragmentation as its fundamental aesthetic.

China

We live on the third world from the sun. Number three. Nobody tells us what to do
The people who taught us to count were being very kind.
It's always time to leave.
If it rains, you either have your umbrella or you don't.
The wind blows your hat off.
The sun rises also.
I'd rather the stars didn't describe us to each other; I'd rather we do it for ourselves.
Run in front of your shadow.
A sister who points to the sky at least once a decade is a good sister.
The landscape is motorized.
The train takes you where it goes.
Bridges among water.
Folks straggling along vast stretches of concrete, heading into the plane.
Don't forget what your hat and shoes will look like when you are nowhere to
    be found.

Even the words floating in air make blue shadows.
If it tastes good we eat it.
The leaves are falling. Point things out.
Pick up the right things.
Hey guess what? What? *I've learned how to talk.* Great.
The person whose head was incomplete burst into tears.
As it fell, what could the doll do? Nothing.
Go to sleep.
You look great in shorts. And the flag looks great too.
Everyone enjoyed the explosions.
Time to wake up.
But better get used to dreams.

(Bob Perelman from *Primer*, This Press, Berkeley)

Many things could be said about this interesting exercise in discontinuities: not the least paradoxical is the reemergence here across these disjoined sentences of some more unified global meaning. Indeed, insofar as this is in some curious and secret way a political poem, it does seem to capture something of the excitement of the immense, unfinished social experiment of the New China – unparalleled in world history – the unexpected emergence, between the two super-powers, of "number three", the freshness of a whole new object world produced by human beings in some new control over their collective destiny, the signal event, above all, of a collectivity which has become a new "subject of history" and which, after the long subjection of feudalism and imperialism, again speaks in its own voice, for itself as though for the first time.

I mainly wanted to show, however, the way in which what I have been calling schizophrenic disjunction or *écriture*, when it becomes generalized as a cultural style, ceases to entertain a necessary relationship to the morbid content we associate with terms like schizophrenia, and becomes available for more joyous intensities, for precisely that euphoria which we saw displacing the older affects of anxiety and alienation.

Consider, for example, Jean-Paul Sartre's account of a similar tendency in Flaubert: "His sentence" (Sartre tells us about Flaubert) "closes in on the object, seizes it, immobilizes it, and breaks its back, wraps itself around it, changes into stone and petrifies its object along with itself. It is blind and deaf, bloodless, not a breath of life; a deep silence separates it from the sentence which follows; it falls into the void, eternally, and drags its prey down into that infinite fall. Any reality, once described, is struck off the inventory." (*What is Literature?*)

Yet I am tempted to see this reading as a kind of optical illusion (or photographic enlargement) of an unwittingly genealogical type: in which certain latent or sub-ordinate, properly postmodernist features of Flaubert's style are anachronistically foregrounded. Yet it affords another interesting lesson in periodization, and in the dialectical restructuring of cultural dominants and subordinates. For these features, in Flaubert, were symptoms and strategies in that whole posthumous life and resentment of praxis which is denounced (with increasing sympathy) throughout the three thousand pages of Sartre's *Family Idiot*. When such features become themselves the cultural norm, they shed all such forms of negative affect and become available for other, more decorative uses.

But we have thereby not fully exhausted the structural secrets of Perelman's poem, which turns out to have little enough to do with that referent called China. The author has in fact related how, strolling through Chinatown, he came across a book of photographs whose idiogrammatic captions remained a dead letter to him (or perhaps one should say, a material signifier). The sentences of the poem in question are then Perelman's own captions to those pictures, their referents another image, another absent text; and the unity of the poem is no longer to be found within its language, but outside itself, in the bound unity of another, absent book. There is here a striking parallel to the dynamics of so-called photorealism, which looked like a return to representation and figuration after the long hegemony of the aesthetics of abstraction, until it became clear that its objects were not to be found in the "real world' either, but were themselves photographs of that real world, this last now transformed into images, of which the "realism" of the photorealist painting is now the simulacrum.

Collage and Radical Difference

This account of schizophrenia and temporal organization might, however, have been formulated in a different way, which brings us back to Heidegger's notion of a gap or rift, albeit in a fashion that would have horrified him. I would like, indeed, to characterize the postmodernist experience of form with what will seem, I hope, a paradoxical slogan: namely the proposition that "difference relates". Our own recent criticism, from Macherey on, has been concerned to stress the heterogeneity and profound discontinuities of the work of art, no longer unified or organic, but now virtual grab-bag or lumber room of disjoined subsystems and random raw materials and impulses of all kinds. The former work of art, in other words, has now turned out to be a text, whose reading proceeds by differentiation rather than by unification. Theories of difference, however, have tended to stress disjunction to the point at which the materials of the text, including its words and sentences, tend to fall apart into random and inert passivity, into a set of elements which entertain purely external separations from one another.

In the most interesting postmodernist works, however, one can detect a more positive conception of relationship which restores its proper tension to the notion of differences itself. This new mode of relationship through difference may sometimes be an achieved new and original way of thinking and perceiving; more often it takes the form of an impossible imperative to achieve that new mutation in what can perhaps no longer be called consciousness. I believe that the most striking emblem of this new mode of thinking relationships can be found in the work of Nam June Paik, whose stacked or scattered television screens, positioned at intervals within lush vegetation, or winking down at us from a ceiling of strange new video stars, recapitulate over and over again prearranged sequences or loops of images which return at dysynchronous moments on the various screens. The older aesthetic is then practised by viewers, who, bewildered by this discontinuous variety, decide to-concentrate on a single screen, as though the relatively worthless image sequence to be followed there had some organic value in its own right. The postmodernist viewer, however, is called upon to do the impossible, namely to see all the screens at once, in their radical and random difference; such a viewer is asked to follow the evolutionary mutation of David Bowie in *The Man Who Fell to Earth*, and to rise somehow to a level at which the vivid perception of radical difference is in and of itself a new mode of grasping what used to be called relationship: something for which the word *collage* is still only a very feeble name.

The Hysterical Sublime

Now we need to complete this exploratory account of postmodernist space and time with a final analysis of that euphoria or those intensities which seem so often to characterize the newer cultural experience. Let us stress again the enormity of a transition which leaves behind it the desolation of Hopper's buildings or the stark Midwest syntax of Sheeler's forms, replacing them with the extraordinary surfaces of the photorealist cityscape, where even the automobile wrecks gleam with some new hallucinatory splendour. The exhilaration of these new surfaces is all the more paradoxical in that their essential content – the city itself – has deteriorated or disintegrated to a degree surely still inconceivable in the early years of the 20th century, let alone in the previous era. How urban squalor can be a delight to the eyes, when expressed in commodification, and how an unparalleled quantum leap in the alienation of daily life in the city can now be experienced in the form of a strange new hallucinatory exhilaration – these are some of the questions that confront us in this moment of our inquiry. Nor should the human figure be exempted from investigation, although it seems clear that for the newer aesthetic the representation of space itself has come to be felt as incompatible with the representation of the body: a kind of aesthetic division of labour far more pronounced than in any of the earlier generic conceptions of landscape, and a most ominous symptom indeed. The privileged space of the newer art is radically anti-anthropomorphic, as in the empty bathrooms of Doug Bond's work. The ultimate contemporary fetishization of the human body, however, takes a very different direction in the statues of Duane Hanson – what I have already called the simulacrum, whose peculiar function lies in what Sartre would have called the *derealization* of the whole surrounding world of everyday reality. Your moment of doubt and hesitation as to the breath and warmth of these polyester figures, in other words, tends to return upon the real human beings moving about you in the museum, and to transform them also for the briefest instant into so many dead and flesh-coloured simulacra in their own right. The world thereby momentarily loses its depth and threatens to become a glossy skin, a stereoscopic illusion, a rush of filmic images without density. But is this now a terrifying or an exhilarating experience?

It has proved fruitful to think such experience in terms of what Susan Sontag once, in an influential statement, isolated as "camp". I propose a somewhat different cross-flight on it, drawing on the equally fashionable current theme of the "sublime", as it has been rediscovered in the works of Edmund Burke and Kant; or perhaps, indeed, one might well want to yoke the two notions together in the form of something like a camp or "hysterical" sublime. The sublime was for Burke, as you will recall, an experience bordering on terror, the fitful glimpse, in astonishment, stupor and awe, of what was so enormous as to crush human life altogether: a description then refined by Kant to include the question of representation itself – so that the object of the sublime is now not only a matter of sheer power and of the physical incommensurability of the human organism with Nature, but also of the limits of figuration and the incapacity of the human mind to give representation to such enormous forces. Such forces Burke, in his historical moment at the dawn of the modern bourgeois state, was only able to conceptualize in terms of the divine; while even Heidegger continues to entertain a fantasmatic relationship with some organic precapitalist peasant landscape and village society, which is the final form of the image of Nature in our own time.

Today, however, it may be possible to think all this in a different way, at the moment of a radical eclipse of Nature itself: Heidegger's "field path" is after all irredeemably and irrevocably destroyed by late capital, by the green revolution, by neocolonialism and the megalopolis, which runs its superhighways over the older fields and vacant lots, and turns Heidegger's "house of being" into condominiums, if not the most miserable unheated rat-infested tenement buildings. The *other* of our society is in that sense no longer Nature at all, as it was in precapitalist societies, but something else which we must now identify.

The Apotheosis of Capitalism

I am anxious that this other thing should not overhastily be grasped as technology per se, since I will want to show that technology is here itself a figure for something else. Yet technology may well serve as adequate shorthand to designate that enormous properly human and anti-natural power of dead human labour stored up in our machinery, an alienated power, what Sartre calls the counterfinality of the practico-inert, which turns back on and against us in unrecognizable forms and seems to con-stitute the massive dystopian horizon of our collective as well as our individual praxis.

Technology is, however, on the Marxist view the result of the development of capital, rather than some primal cause in its own right. It will therefore be appropriate to distinguish several generations of machine power, several stages of technological revolution within capital itself. I here follow Ernest Mandel who outlines three such fundamental breaks or quantum leaps in the evolution of machinery under capital: "The fundamental revolutions in power technology – the technology of the produc-tion of motive machines by machines – thus appears as the determinant moment in revolutions of technology as a whole. Machine production of steam-driven motors since 1848; machine production of electric and combustion motors since the 90s of the 19th century; machine production of electronic and nuclear-powered appara-tuses since the 40s of the 20th century – these are the three general revolutions in technology engendered by the capitalist mode of production since the 'original' industrial revolution of the later 18th century" (*Late Capitalism*, p. 18).

The periodization underscores the general thesis of Mandel's book *Late Capitalism*, namely that there have been three fundamental moments in capitalism, each one marking a dialectical expansion over the previous stage: these are market capitalism, the monopoly stage or the stage of imperialism, and our own – wrongly called postindustrial, but what might better be termed multinational capital. I have already pointed out that Mandel's intervention in the postindustrial involves the proposition that late or multinational or consumer capitalism, far from being inconsistent with Marx's great 19th-century analysis, constitutes on the contrary the purest form of capital yet to have emerged, a prodigious expansion of capital into hitherto uncommodified areas. This purer capitalism of our own time thus eliminates the enclaves of precapitalist organization it had hitherto tolerated and exploited in a tributary way: one is tempted to speak in this connection of a new and historically original penetration and colonization of Nature and the Unconscious: that is, the destruction of precapitalist third world agriculture by the Green Revolution, and the rise of the media and the advertising industry. At any rate, it will also have been clear that my own cultural periodization of the stages of realism, modernism and postmodernism is both inspired and confirmed by Mandel's tripartite scheme.

We may speak therefore of our own age as the Third (or even Fourth) Machine Age; and it is at this point that we must reintroduce the problem of aesthetic representation already explicitly developed in Kant's earlier analysis of the sublime – since it would seem only logical that the relationship to, and representation of, the machine could be expected to shift dialectically with each of these qualitatively different stages of technological development.

It is appropriate therefore to recall the excitement of machinery in the preceding moment of capital, the exhilaration of futurism most notably, and of Marinetti's celebration of the machine gun and the motor car. These are still visible emblems, sculptural nodes of energy which give tangibility and figuration to the motive energies of that earlier moment of modernization. The prestige of these great streamlined shapes can be measured by their metaphorical presence in Le Corbusier's buildings, vast Utopian structures which ride like so many gigantic steamshipliners upon the urban scenery of an older fallen earth. Machinery exerts another kind of fascination in artists like Picabia and Duchamp, whom we have no time to consider here; but let me mention, for the sake of completeness, the ways in which revolutionary or communist artists of the 1930s also sought to reappropriate this excitement of machine energy for a Promethean reconstruction of human society as a whole, as in Fernand Leger and Diego Rivera.

What must then immediately be observed is that the technology of our own moment no longer possesses this same capacity for representation: not the turbine, nor even Sheeler's grain elevators or smokestacks, not the baroque elaboration of pipes and conveyor belts nor even the streamlined profile of the railroad train – all vehicles of speed still concentrated at rest – but rather the computer, whose outer shell has no emblematic or visual power, or even the casings of the various media themselves, as with that home appliance called television which articulates nothing but rather implodes, carrying its flattened image surface within itself.

Such machines are indeed machines of reproduction rather than of production, and they make very different demands on our capacity for aesthetic representation than did the relatively mimetic idolatry of the older machinery of the futurist moment, of some older speed-and-energy sculpture. Here we have less to do with kinetic energy than with all kinds of new reproductive processes; and in the weaker productions of postmodernism the aesthetic embodiment of such processes often tends to slip back more comfortably into a mere thematic representation of content – into narratives which are *about* the processes of reproduction, and include movie cameras, video, tape recorders, the whole technology of the production and reproduction of the simulacrum. (The shift from Antonioni's modernist *Blowup* to DePalma's postmod-ernist *Blowout* is here paradigmatic.) When Japanese architects, for example, model a building on the decorative imitation of stacks of cassettes, then the solution is at best a thematic and allusive, although often humorous, one.

Yet something else does tend to emerge in the most energetic postmodernist texts, and it is the sense that beyond all thematics or content the work seems somehow to tap the networks of reproductive process and thereby to afford us some glimpse into a post-modern or technological sublime, whose power or authenticity is documented by the success of such works in evoking a whole new postmodern space in emergence around us. Architecture therefore remains in this sense the privileged aesthetic language; and the distorting and fragmenting reflexions of one enormous glass surface to the other call be taken as paradigmatic of the central role of process and reproduction in postmodernist culture.

As I have said, however, I want to avoid the implication that technology is in any way the "ultimately determining instance" either of our present-day social life or of our cultural production: such a thesis is of course ultimately at one with the post-Marxist notion of a "post-industrialist" society. Rather, I want to suggest that our faulty representations of some immense communicational and computer network are themselves but a distorted figuration of something even deeper, namely the whole world system of present-day multinational capitalism. The technology of contemporary society is therefore mesmerizing and fascinating, not so much in its own right, but because it seems to offer some privileged representational shorthand for grasping a network of power and control even more difficult for our minds and imaginations to grasp – namely the whole new decentred global network of the third stage of capital itself. This is a figural process presently best observed in a whole mode of contemporary entertainment literature, which one is tempted to characterize as "high tech paranoia", in which the circuits and networks of some putative global computer hook-up are narratively mobilized by labyrinthine conspiracies of autonomous but deadly interlocking and competing information agencies in a complexity often beyond the capacity of the normal reading mind. Yet conspiracy theory (and its garish narrative manifestations) must be seen as a degraded attempt – through the figuration of advanced technology – to think the impossible totality of the contemporary world system. It is therefore in terms of that enormous and threatening, yet only dimly perceivable, other reality of economic and social institutions that in my opinion the postmodern sublime can alone be adequately theorized.

Postmodernism and the City

Now, before I try to offer a somewhat more positive conclusion, I want to sketch the analysis of a full-blown postmodern building – a work which is in many ways uncharacteristic of that postmodern architecture whose principal names are Robert Venturi, Charles Moore, Michael Graves, and more recently Frank Gehry, but which to my mind offers some very striking lessons about the originality of postmodernist space. Let me amplify the figure which has run through the preceding remarks, and make it even more explicit: I am proposing the motion that we are here in the presence of something like a mutation in built space itself. My implication is that we ourselves, the human subjects who happen into this new space, have not kept pace with that evolution; there has been a mutation in the object, unaccompanied as yet by any equivalent mutation in the subject; we do not yet possess the perceptual equipment to match this new hyperspace, as I will call it, in part because our perceptual habits were formed in that older kind of space I have called the space of high modernism. The newer architecture therefore – like many of the other cultural products I have evoked in the preceding remarks – stands as something like an imperative to grow new organs, to expand our sensorium and our body to some new, as yet unimaginable, perhaps ultimately impossible, dimensions.

The Bonaventura Hotel

The building whose features I will very rapidly enumerate in the next few moments is the Bonaventura Hotel, built in the new Los Angeles downtown by the architect and developer John Portman, whose other works include the various Hyatt Regencies, the Peachtree Center in Atlanta, and the Renaissance Center in Detroit. I have mentioned the populist aspect of the rhetorical defence of postmodernism against the elite (and Utopian) austerities of the great architectural modernisms: it is generally affirmed, in other words, that these newer buildings are popular works on the one hand; and that they respect the vernacular of the American city fabric on the other, that is to say, that they no longer attempt, as did the masterworks and monuments of high modernism, to insert a different, a distinct, an elevated, a new Utopian language into the tawdry and commercial sign-system of the surrounding city, but rather, on the contrary, seek to speak that very language, using its lexicon and syntax as that has been emblematically "learned from Las Vegas".

On the first of these counts, Portman's *Bonaventura* fully confirms the claim: it is a popular building, visited with enthusiasm by locals and tourists alike (although Portman's other buildings are even more successful in this respect). The populist insertion into the city fabric is, however, another matter, and it is with this that we will begin. There are three entrances to the *Bonaventura*, one from Figueroa, and the other two by way of elevated gardens on the other side of the hotel, which is built into the remaining slope of the former Beacon Hill. None of these is anything like the old hotel marquee, or the monumental porte-cochère with which the sumptuous buildings of yesteryear were wont to stage your passage from city street to the older interior. The entryways of the *Bonaventura* are as it were lateral and rather backdoor affairs: the gardens in the back admit you to the sixth floor of the towers, and even there you must walk down one flight to find the elevator by which you gain access to the lobby. Meanwhile, what one is still tempted to think of as the front entry, on Figueroa, admits you, baggage and all, onto the second-storey shopping balcony, from which you must take an escalator down to the main registration desk. More about these elevators and escalators in a moment. What I first want to suggest about these curiously unmarked ways-in is that they seem to have been imposed by some new category of closure governing the inner space of the hotel itself (and this over and above the material constraints under which Portman had to work). I believe that, with a certain number of other characteristic postmodern buildings, such as the *Beaubourg* in Paris, or the Eaton Centre in Toronto, the *Bonaventura* aspires to being a total space, a complete world, a kind of miniature city (and I would want to add that to this new total space corresponds a new collective practice, a new mode in which individuals move and congregate, something like the practice of a new and historically original kind of hyper-crowd). In this sense, then, ideally the mini-city of Portman's *Bonaventura* ought not to have entrances at all, since the entryway is always the seam that links the building to the rest of the city that surrounds it: for it does not wish to be a part of the city, but rather its equivalent and its replacement or substitute. That is, however, obviously not possible or practical, whence the deliberate downplaying and reduction of the entrance function to its bare minimum. But this disjunction from the surrounding city is very different from that of the great monuments of the International Style: there, the act of disjunction was violent, visible, and had a very real symbolic significance – as in Le Corbusier's great *pilotis* whose gesture radically separates the new Utopian space of the modern from the degraded and fallen city fabric which it thereby explicitly repudiates (although the gamble of the modern was that this new Utopian space, in the virulence of its Novum, would fan out and transform that eventually by the very power of its new spatial language). The *Bonaventura*, however, is content to "let the fallen city fabric continue to be in its being" (to parody Heidegger); no further effect, no larger protopolitical Utopian transformation, is either expected or desired.

This diagnosis is to my mind confirmed by the great reflective glass skin of the *Bonaventura*, whose function I will now interpret rather differently than I did a moment ago when I saw the phenomenon of reflexion generally as developing a thematics of reproductive technology (the two readings are however not incompatible). Now one would want rather to stress the way in which the glass skin repels the city outside; a repulsion for which we have analogies in those reflector sunglasses which make it impossible for your interlocutor to see your own eyes and thereby achieve a certain aggressivity towards and power over the Other. In a similar way, the glass skin achieves a peculiar and placeless dissociation of the *Bonaventura* from its neighbourhood: it is not even an exterior, inasmuch as when you seek to look at the hotel's outer walls you cannot see the hotel itself, but only the distorted images of everything that surrounds it.

Now I want to say a few words about escalators and elevators: given their very real pleasures in Portman, particularly these last, which the artist has termed "gigantic kinetic sculptures" and which certainly account for much of the spectacle and the excitement of the hotel interior, particularly in the Hyatts, where like great Japanese lanterns or gondolas they ceaselessly rise and fall – given such a deliberate marking and foregrounding in their own right, I believe one has to see such "people movers" (Portman's own term, adapted from Disney) as something a little more than mere functions and engineering components. We know in any case that recent architectural theory has begun to borrow from narrative analysis in other fields, and to attempt to see our physical trajectories through such buildings as virtual narratives or stories, as dynamic paths and narrative paradigms which we as visitors are asked to fulfil and to complete with our own bodies and movements. In the *Bonaventura*, however, we find a dialectical heightening of this process: it seems to me that the escalators and elevators here henceforth replace movement but also and above all designate themselves as new reflexive signs and emblems of movement proper (something which will become evident when we come to the whole question of what remains of older forms of movement in this building, most notably walking itself). Here the narrative stroll has been underscored, symbolized, reified and replaced by a transportation machine which becomes the allegorical signifier of that older promenade we are no longer allowed to conduct on our own: and this is a dialectical intensification of the auto-referentiality of all modern culture, which tends to turn upon itself and designate its own cultural production as its content.

I am more at a loss when it comes to conveying the thing itself, the experience of space you undergo when you step off such allegorical devices into the lobby or atrium, with its great central column, surrounded by a miniature lake, the whole positioned between the four symmetrical residential towers with their elevators, and surrounded by rising balconies capped by a kind of greenhouse roof at the sixth level. I am tempted to say that such space makes it impossible for us to use the language of volume or volumes any longer, since these last are impossible to seize. Hanging streamers indeed suffuse this empty space in such a way as to distract systematically and deliberately from whatever form it might be supposed to have; while a constant busyness gives the feeling that emptiness is here absolutely packed, that it is an element within which you yourself are immersed, without any of that distance that formerly enabled the perception of perspective or volume. You are in this hyperspace up to your eyes and your body; and if it seemed to you before that that suppression of depth I spoke of in postmodern painting or literature would necessarily be difficult to achieve in architecture itself, perhaps you may now be willing to see this bewildering immersion as the formal equivalent in the new medium.

Yet escalator and elevator are also in this context dialectical opposites; and we may suggest that the glorious movement of the elevator gondolas is also a dialectical compensation for this filled space of the atrium – it gives us the chance at a radically different, but complementary, spatial experience, that of rapidly shooting up through the ceiling and outside, along one of the four symmetrical towers, with the referent, Los Angeles itself, spread out breathtakingly and even alarmingly before us. But even this vertical movement is contained: the elevator lifts you to one of those revolving cocktail lounges, in which you, seated, are again passively rotated about and offered a contemplative spectacle of the city itself, now transformed into its own images by the glass windows through which you view it.

Let me quickly conclude all this by returning to the central space of the lobby itself (with the passing observation that the hotel rooms are visibly marginalized: the corridors in the residential sections are low-ceilinged and dark, most depressingly functional indeed; while one understands that the rooms are in the worst of taste). The descent is dramatic enough, plummeting back down through the roof to splash down in the lake; what happens when you get there is something else, which I can only try to characterize as milling confusion, something like the vengeance this space takes on those who still seek to walk through it. Given the absolute symmetry of the four towers, it is quite impossible to get your bearings in this lobby; recently, colour coding and directional signals have been added in a pitiful and revealing, rather desperate attempt to restore the coordinates of an older space. I will take as the most dramatic practical result of this spatial mutation the notorious dilemma of the shopkeepers on the various balconies: it has been obvious, since the very opening of the hotel in 1977, that nobody could ever find any of these stores, and even if you located the appropriate boutique, you would be most unlikely to be as fortunate a second time; as a consequence, the commercial tenants are in despair and all the merchandise is marked down to bargain prices. When you recall that Portman is a businessman as well as an architect, and a millionaire developer, an artist who is at one and the same time a capitalist in his own right, one cannot but feel that here too something of a "return of the repressed" is involved.

So I come finally to my principal point here, that this latest mutation in space – postmodern hyperspace – has finally succeeded in transcending the capacities of the individual human body to locate itself, to organize its immediate surroundings perceptually, and cognitively to map its position in a mappable external world. And I have already suggested that this alarming disjunction point between the body and its built environment – which is to the initial bewilderment of the older modernism as the velocities of space craft are to those of the automobile – can itself stand as the symbol and analogue of that even sharper dilemma which is the incapacity of our minds, at least at present, to map the great global multinational and decentred communicational network in which we find ourselves caught as individual subjects.

The New Machine

But as I am anxious that Portman's space not be perceived as something either exceptional or seemingly marginalized and leisure-specialized on the order of Disneyland, I would like in passing to juxtapose this complacent and entertaining (although bewildering) leisure-time space with its analogue in a very different area, namely the space of postmodern warfare, in particular as Michael Herr evokes it in his great book on the experience of Vietnam, called *Dispatches*. The extraordinary linguistic innovations of this work may still be considered postmodern, in the eclectic way in which its language impersonally fuses a whole range of contemporary collective idiolects, most notably rock language and Black language: but the fusion is dictated by problems of content. This first terrible postmodernist war cannot be told in any of the traditional paradigms of the war novel or movie – indeed that breakdown of all previous narrative paradigms is, along with the breakdown of any shared language through which a veteran might convey such experience, among the principal subjects of the book and may be said to open up the place of a whole new reflexivity. Benjamin's account of Baudelaire, and of the emergence of modernism from a new experience of city technology which transcends all the older habits of bodily perception, is both singularly relevant here, and singularly antiquated, in the light of this new and virtually unimaginable quantum leap in technological alienation: "He was a moving-target-survivor subscriber, a true child of the war, because except for the rare times when you were pinned or stranded the system was geared to keep you mobile, if that was what you thought you wanted. As a technique for staying alive it seemed to make as much sense as anything, given naturally that you were there to begin with and wanted to see it close; it started out sound and straight but it formed a cone as it progressed, because the more you moved the more you saw, the more you saw the more besides death and mutilation you risked, and the more you risked of that the more you would have to let go of one day as a "survivor". Some of us moved around the war like crazy people until we couldn't see which way the run was taking us anymore, only the war all over its surface with occasional, unexpected penetration. As long as we could have choppers like taxis it took real exhaustion or depression near shock or a dozen pipes of opium to keep us even apparently quiet, we'd still be running around inside our skins like something was after us, ha ha, La Vida Loca. In the months after I got back the hundreds of helicopters I'd flown in began to draw together until they'd formed a collective metachopper, and in my mind it was the sexiest thing going; saver-destroyer, provider-waster, right hand-left hand, nimble, fluent, canny and human; hot steel, grease, jungle-saturated canvas webbing, sweat cooling and warming up again, cassette rock and roll in one ear and door-gun fire in the other, fuel, heat, vitality and death, death itself, hardly an intruder."[4]

In this new machine, which does not, like the older modernist machinery of the locomotive or the airplane, represent motion, but which can only be represented *in motion*, something of the mystery of the new postmodernist space is concentrated.

The Abolition of Critical Distance

The conception of postmodernism outlined here is a historical rather than a merely stylistic one. I cannot stress too greatly the radical distinction between a view for which the postmodern is one (optional) style among many others available, and one which seeks to grasp it as the cultural dominant of the logic of late capitalism: the two approaches in fact generate two very different ways of conceptualizing the phenomenon as a whole, on the one hand moral judgements (about which it is indifferent whether they are positive or negative), and on the other a genuinely dialectical attempt to think our present of time in History.

Of some positive moral evaluation of postmodernism little needs to be said: the complacent (yet delirious) camp-following celebration of this aesthetic new world (including its social and economic dimension, greeted with equal enthusiasm under the slogan of "post-industrial society") is surely unacceptable – although it may be somewhat less obvious the degree to which current fantasies about the salvational nature of high technology, from chips to robots – fantasies entertained not only by left as well as right governments in distress but also by many intellectuals – are essentially of a piece with more vulgar apologies for postmodernism.

But in that case it is also logical to reject moralizing condemnations of the postmodern and of its essential triviality, when juxtaposed against the Utopian "high seriousness" of the great modernisms: these are also judgements one finds both on the Left and on the radical Right. And no doubt the logic of the simulacrum, with its transformation of older realities into television images, does more than merely replicate the logic of late capitalism; it reinforces and intensifies it. Meanwhile, for political groups which seek actively to intervene in history and to modify its other-wise passive momentum (whether with a view towards channeling it into a socialist transformation of society or diverting it into the regressive reestablishment of some simpler fantasy past), there cannot but be much that is deplorable and reprehensible in a cultural form of image addiction which, by transforming the past visual mirages, stereotypes or texts, effectively abolishes any practical sense of the future and of the collective project, thereby abandoning the thinking of future change to fantasies of sheer catastrophe and inexplicable cataclysm – from visions of "terrorism" on the social level to those of cancer on the personal. Yet if postmodernism is a historical phenomenon, then the attempt to conceptualize it in terms of moral or moralizing judgements must finally be identified as a category-mistake. All of which becomes more obvious when we interrogate the position of the cultural critic and moralist: this last, along with all the rest of us, is now so deeply immersed in postmodernist space, so deeply suffused and infected by its new cultural categories, that the luxury of the oldfashioned ideological critique, the indignant moral denunciation of the other, becomes unavailable.

The distinction I am proposing here knows one canonical form in Hegel's differ-entiation of the thinking of individual morality or moralizing (*Moralität*) from that whole very different realm of collective social values and practices (*Sittlichkeit*). But it finds its definitive form in Marx's demonstration of the materialist dialectic, most notably in those classic pages of the *Manifesto* which teach the hard lesson of some more genuinely dialectical way to think historical development and change. The topic of the lesson is, of course, the historical development of capitalism itself and the deployment of a specific bourgeois culture. In a well-known passage, Marx powerfully urges us to do the impossible, namely to think this development positively *and* negatively all at once; to achieve, in other words, a type of thinking that would be capable of grasping the demonstrably baleful features of capitalism along with its extraordinary and liberating dynamism simultaneously, within a single thought, and without attenuating any of the force of either judgement. We are, somehow, to lift our minds to a point at which it is possible to understand that capitalism is at one and the same time the best thing that has ever happened to the human race, and the worst. The lapse from this austere dialectical imperative into the more comfortable stance of the taking of moral positions is inveterate and all too human: still, the urgency of the subject demands that we make at least some effort to think the cul-tural evolution of late capitalism dialectically, as catastrophe and progress all together.

Such an effort suggests two immediate questions, with which we will conclude these reflexions. Can we in fact identify some "moment of truth" within the more evident "moments of falsehood" of postmodern culture? And, even if we can do so, is there not something ultimately paralysing in the dialectical view of historical development proposed above; does it not tend to demobilize us and to surrender us to passivity and helplessness, by systematically obliterating possibilities of action under the impenetrable fog of historical inevitability? It will be appropriate to discuss these two (related) issues in terms of current possibilities for some effective contemporary cultural politics and for the construction of a genuine political culture.

To focus the problem in this way is of course immediately to raise the more genuine issue of the fate of culture generally, and of the function of culture specifically, as one social level or instance, in the postmodern era. Everything in the previous discussion suggests that what we have been calling postmodernism is inseparable from, and unthinkable without the hypothesis of, some fundamental mutation of the sphere of culture in the world of late capitalism, which includes a momentous modification of its social function. Older discussions of the space, function or sphere of culture (most notably Herbert Marcuse's classic essay on "The Affirmative Character of Culture") have insisted on what a different language would call the "semi-autonomy" of the cultural realm: its ghostly, yet Utopian, existence, for good or ill, above the practical world of the existent, whose mirror image it throws back in forms which vary from the legitimations of flattering resemblance to the contestatory indictments of critical satire or Utopian pain.

What we must now ask ourselves is whether it is not precisely this "semi-autonomy" of the cultural sphere which has been destroyed by the logic of late capitalism. Yet to argue that culture is today no longer endowed with the relative autonomy it once enjoyed as one level among others in earlier moments of capitalism (let alone in precapitalist societies), is not necessarily to imply its disappearance or extinction. On the contrary: we must go on to affirm that the dissolution of an autonomous sphere of culture is rather to be imagined in terms of an explosion: a prodigious expansion of culture throughout the social realm, to the point at which everything in our social life – from economic value and state power to practices and to the very structure of the psyche itself – can be said to have become "cultural" in some original and as yet untheorized sense. This perhaps startling proposition is, however, substantively quite consistent with the previous diagnosis of a society of the image or the simulacrum, and a transformation of the "real" into so many pseudo-events.

It also suggests that some of our most cherished and time-honoured radical conceptions about the nature of cultural politics may thereby find themselves outmoded. However distinct those conceptions may have been – which range from slogans of negativity, opposition, and subversion to critique and reflexivity – they all shared a single, fundamentally spatial, presupposition, which may be resumed in the equally time-honoured formula of "critical distance". No theory of cultural politics current on the Left today has been able to do without one notion or another of a certain minimal aesthetic distance, of the possibility of the positioning of the cultural act outside the massive Being of capital, which then serves as an Archimedean point from which to assault this last. What the burden of our preceding demonstration suggests, however, is that distance in general (including "critical distance" in particu- lar) has very precisely been abolished in the new space of postmodernism. We are submerged in its henceforth filled and suffused volumes to the point where our now postmodern bodies are bereft of spatial coordinates and practically (let alone theoret- ically) incapable of distantiation; meanwhile, it has already been observed how the prodigious new expansion of multinational capital ends up penetrating and coloniz- ing those very pre-capitalist enclaves (Nature and the Unconscious) which offered extraterritorial and Archimedean footholds for critical effectivity. The short-hand language of "cooptation" is for this reason omnipresent on the Left; but offers a most inadequate theoretical basis for understanding a situation in which we all, in one way or another, dimly feel that not only punctual and local countercultural forms of cultural resistance and guerrilla warfare, but also even overtly political interven- tions like those of *The Clash*, are all somehow secretly disarmed and reabsorbed by a system of which they themselves might well be considered a part, since they can achieve no distance from it.

What we must now affirm is that it is precisely this whole extraordinarily demor- alizing and depressing original new global space which is the "moment of truth" of postmodernism. What has been called the postmodernist "sublime" is only the moment in which this content has become most explicit, has moved the closest to the surface of consciousness, as a coherent new type of space in its own right – even though a certain figural concealment or disguise is still at work here, most notably in the high-technological thematics in which the new spatial content is still dramatized and articulated. Yet the earlier features of the postmodern which were enumerated above can all now be seen as themselves partial (yet constitutive) aspects of the same general spatial object.

The argument for a certain authenticity in these otherwise patently ideological productions depends on the prior proposition that what we have now been calling postmodern (or multinational) space is not merely a cultural ideology or fantasy, but has genuine historical (and socio-economic) reality as a third great original expansion of capitalism around the globe (after the earlier expansions of the national market and the older imperialist system, which each had their own cultural specificity and generated new types of space appropriate to their dynamics). The distorted and unreflexive attempts of newer cultural production to explore and to express this new space must then also, in their own fashion, be considered as so many approaches to the representation of (a new) reality (to use a more antiquated language). As para- doxical as the terms may seem, they may thus, following a classic interpretive option, be read as peculiar new forms of realism (or at least of the mimesis of reality), at the same time that they can equally well be analysed as so many attempts to distract and to divert us from that reality or to disguise its contradictions and resolve them in the guise of various formal mystifications.

As for that reality itself, however – the as yet untheorized original space of some new "world system" of multinational or late capitalism (a space whose negative or baleful aspects are only too obvious), the dialectic requires us to hold equally to a positive or "progressive" evaluation of its emergence, as Marx did for the newly unified space of the national markets, or as Lenin did for the older imperialist global network. For neither Marx nor Lenin was socialism a matter of returning to small (and thereby less repressive and comprehensive) systems of social organization; rather, the dimensions attained by capital in their own times were grasped as the promise, the framework, and the precondition for the achievement of some new and more comprehensive socialism. How much the more is this not the case with the even more global and totalizing space of the new world system, which demands the invention and elaboration of an internationalism of a radically new type? The disastrous realignment of socialist revolution with the older nationalisms (not only in Southeast Asia), whose results have necessarily aroused much serious recent Left reflexion, can be adduced in support of this position.

The Need for Maps

But if all this is so, then at least one possible form of a new radical cultural politics becomes evident: with a final aesthetic proviso that must quickly be noted. Left cultural producers and theorists – particularly those formed by bourgeois cultural traditions issuing from romanticism and valorizing spontaneous, instinctive or unconscious forms of "genius" – but also for very obvious historical reasons such as Zhdanovism and the sorry consequences of political and party interventions in the arts – have often by reaction allowed themselves to be unduly intimidated by the repudiation, in bourgeois aesthetics and most notably in high modernism, of one of the age-old functions of art – namely the pedagogical and the didactic. The teaching function of art was, however, always stressed in classical times (even though it there mainly took the form of *moral* lessons); while the prodigious and still imperfectly understood work of Brecht reaffirms, in a new and formally innovative and original way, for the moment of modernism proper, a complex new conception of the relationship between culture and pedagogy. The cultural model I will propose similarly foregrounds the cognitive and pedagogical dimensions of political art and culture, dimensions stressed in very different ways by *both* Lukács *and* Brecht (for the distinct moments of realism and modernism, respectively).

We cannot, however, return to aesthetic practices elaborated on the basis of historical situations and dilemmas which are no longer ours. Meanwhile, the conception of space that has been developed here suggests that a model of political culture appropriate to our own situation will necessarily have to raise spatial issues as its fundamental organizing concern. I will therefore provisionally define the aesthetic of such new (and hypothetical) cultural form as an aesthetic of *cognitive mapping*.

In a classic work, *The Image of the City*, Kevin Lynch taught us that the alienated city is above all a space in which people are unable to map (in their minds) either their own positions or the urban totality in which they find themselves: grids such as those of Jersey City, in which none of the traditional markers (monuments, nodes, natural boundaries, built perspectives) obtain, are the most obvious examples. Disalienation in the traditional city, then, involves the practical reconquest of a sense of place, and the construction or reconstruction of an articulated ensemble which can be retained in memory and which the individual subject can map and remap along the moments of mobile, alternative trajectories. Lynch's own work is limited by the deliberate restriction of his topic to the problems of the city form as such; yet it becomes extraordinarily suggestive when projected outwards onto some of the larger national and global spaces we have touched on here. Nor should it be too hastily assumed that his model – while it clearly raises very central issues of representation as such – is in any way easily vitiated by the conventional poststructuralist critiques of the "ideology of representation" or mimesis. The cognitive map is not exactly mimetic, in that older sense; indeed the theoretical issues it poses allow us to renew the analysis of representation on a higher and much more complex level.

There is, for one thing, a most interesting convergence between the empirical problems studied by Lynch in terms of city space and the great Althusserian (and Lacanian) redefinition of ideology as "the representation of the subject's *Imaginary* relationship to his or her *Real* conditions of existence". Surely this is exactly what the cognitive map is called upon to do, in the narrower framework of daily life in the physical city: to enable a situational representation on the part of the individual subject to that vaster and properly unrepresentable totality which is the ensemble of the city's structure as a whole.

Yet Lynch's work also suggests a further line of development insofar as cartography itself constitutes its key mediatory instance. A return to the history of this science (which is also an art) shows us that Lynch's model does not yet in fact really correspond to what will become map-making. Rather, Lynch's subjects are clearly involved in pre-cartographic operations whose results traditionally are described as itineraries rather than as maps; diagrams organized around the still subject-centred or existential journey of the traveller, along which various significant key features are marked – oases, mountain ranges, rivers, monuments and the like. The most highly developed form of such diagrams is the nautical itinerary, the sea chart or *portulans*, where coastal features are noted for the use of Mediterranean navigators who rarely venture out into the open sea.

Yet the compass at once introduces a new dimension into sea charts, a dimension that will utterly transform the problematic of the itinerary and allow us to pose the problem of a genuine cognitive mapping in a far more complex way. For the new instruments – compass, sextant and theodolite – do not merely correspond to new geographic and navigational problems (the difficult matter of determining longitude, particularly on the curving surface of the planet, as opposed to the simpler matter of latitude, which European navigators can still empirically determine by ocular inspection of the African coast); they also introduce a whole new coordinate – that of relationship to the totality, particularly as it is mediated by the stars and by new operations like that of triangulation. At this point, cognitive mapping in the broader sense comes to require the coordination of existential data (the empirical position of the subject) with unlived, abstract conceptions of the geographic totality.

Finally, with the first globe (1490) and the invention of the Mercator projection around the same period, yet a third dimension of cartography emerges, which at once involves what we would today call the nature of representational codes, the intrinsic structures of the various media, the intervention, into more naive mimetic conceptions of mapping, of the whole new fundamental question of the languages of representation itself: and in particular the unresolvable (well-nigh Heisenbergian) dilemma of the transfer of curved space to flat charts; at which point it becomes clear that there can be no true maps (at the same time in which it also becomes clear that there can be scientific progress, or better still, a dialectical advance, in the various historical moments of map-making).

Social Cartography and Symbol

Transcoding all this now into the very different problematic of the Althusserian definition of ideology, one would want to make two points. The first is that the Althusserian concept now allows us to rethink these specialized geographical and cartographic issues in terms of social space, in terms, for example, of social class and national or international context, in terms of the ways in which we all necessarily *also* cognitively map our individual social relationship to local, national and international class realities. Yet to reformulate the problem in this way is also to come starkly up against those very difficulties in mapping which are posed in heightened and original ways by that very global space of the postmodernist or multinational moment which has been under discussion here. These are not merely theoretical issues, but have urgent practical political consequences: as is evident from the conventional feelings of First World subjects that existentially (or "empirically") they really do inhabit a "postindustrial society", from which traditional production has disappeared and in which social classes of the classical type no longer exist – a conviction which has immediate effects on political praxis.

The second observation to be proposed is that a return to the Lacanian underpinnings of Althusser's theory can afford some useful and suggestive methodological enrichments. Althusser's formulation remobilizes an older and henceforth classical Marxian distinction between science and ideology, which is still not without value for us. The existential – the positioning of the individual subject, the experience of daily life, the monadic "point of view" on the world to which we are necessarily, as biological subjects, restricted – is in Althusser's formula implicitly opposed to the realm of abstract knowledge, a realm which as Lacan reminds us is never positioned in or actualized by any concrete subject but rather by that structural void called "le sujet supposé savoir", "the subject supposed to know", a subject-place of knowledge; what is affirmed is not that we cannot know the world and its totality in some abstract or "scientific" way – Marxian "science" provides just such a way of knowing and conceptualizing the world abstractly, in the sense in which, e.g. Mandel's great book offers a rich and elaborated *knowledge* of that global world system, of which it has never been said here that it was unknowable, but merely that it was unrepresentable, which is a very different matter. The Althusserian formula in other words designates a gap, a rift, between existential experience and scientific knowledge: ideology has then the function of somehow inventing a way of articulating those two distinct dimensions with each other. What a historicist view of this "definition" would want to add is that such coordination, the production of functioning and living ideologies, is distinct in different historical situations, but above all, that there may be historical situations in which it is not possible at all – and this would seem to be our situation in the current crisis.

But the Lacanian system is three-fold and not dualistic. To the Marxian-Althusserian opposition of ideology and science correspond only two of Lacan's tripartite functions, the Imaginary and the Real, respectively. Our digression on cartography, however, with its final revelation of a properly representational dialectic of the codes and capacities of individual languages or media, reminds us that what has until now been omitted was the dimension of the Lacanian Symbolic itself.

An aesthetic of cognitive mapping – a pedagogical political culture which seeks to endow the individual subject with some new heightened sense of its place in the global system – will necessarily have to respect this now enormously complex representational dialectic and to invent radically new forms in order to do it justice. This is not, then, clearly a call for a return to some older kind of machinery, some older and more transparent national space, or some more traditional and reassuring perspectival or mimetic enclave: the new political art – if it is indeed possible at all – will have to hold to the truth of postmodernism, that is to say, to its fundamental object – the world space of multinational capital – at the same time at which it achieves a breakthrough to some as yet unimaginable new mode of representing this last, in which we may again begin to grasp our positioning as individual and collective subjects and regain a capacity to act and struggle which is at present neutralized by our spatial as well as our social confusion. The political form of postmodernism, if there ever is any, will have as its vocation the invention and projection of a global cognitive mapping, on a social as well as a spatial scale.

Notes

1 The present essay draws on lectures and on material previously published in *The Anti-Aesthetic*, edited by Hal Foster (Port Townsend, Washington: Bay Press, 1983) and in *Amerika Studien/American Studies* 29/1 (1984).

2 In "The Politics of Theory", *New German Critique*, 32, Spring/Summer 1984.

3 Marguerite Séchehaye, *Autobiography of a Schizophrenic Girl*, trans. by G. Rubin-Rabson, New York, 1968, p. 19.

4 Michael Herr, *Dispatches*, New York, 1978, pp. 8–9

30

Feminism, Postmodernism and the "Real Me"

Angela McRobbie

A three-way split has developed recently around postmodernism. There are those who refuse to admit that postmodernism engages with anything that modernism is not better able to explain and who also defend the values of modernism as they relate to both intellectual work and political analysis. This grouping has established itself as a counterbalance to those others who from such a "reasonable" standpoint display what are viewed as the excesses of postmodernism. Allowing even for predictable negative typecasting in a debate which has become as heated as this, the image of these postmodernists remains particularly flimsy and marked by what Butler (1992) describes as a kind of slur of infantilism or at least youthful aberration. The third path is occupied by the postcolonialists and there is in this work both a notion of what Gilroy (1993), drawing on Bauman, labels "the counter-cultures of modernity" and at the same time a remorseless critique of modernity and a looking to those accounts of postmodernity as a way of finding a place from which to speak and a space from which to develop that critique of the places and the spaces of exclusion inside modernity.

The question which will be asked in this chapter is what does this three-way divide mean for women? And how does feminism define itself in an intellectual world now characterized by shifting borders, boundaries and identities? To begin to answer this question it is necessary to look first at how two strands of this debate, the pro-modernist and the postcolonialist, put on the agenda quite separate issues as central to our understanding of contemporary society. These usefully set a framework for going on to consider the place of feminism in this new conceptualization of the social. But in engaging with the feminists who have taken up a strongly postmodernist position, the reader should be warned that these writers have been criticized for "taking leave of their senses". To enter their discourse is therefore to display a willingness to consciously explore the other side, the under-side of

From Angela McRobbie, "Feminism, postmodernism and the 'real me.'" In *Postmodernism and Popular Culture*, pp. 61–74. New York and London: Routledge, 1985.

contemporary critical theory, a realm of thinking which is frequently charged with the abandonment not just of reason, but also of the subject, good sense and politics. In this process of searching around in the landscape of post-feminism, as well as postmodernism and postcoloniality, the question of who "we" intellectuals are these days and what role we have to play in feminist politics is constantly forced into prominence.

Postmodernists: Guilty of Playing with Politics

My starting-point is to suggest that the provocative stance adopted in language by a figure like Lyotard (1984), which results in his being charged with playfulness, is a deliberate strategy, a way of positioning himself within a certain kind of rhetorical mode which allows him to develop his critique. Gregor McLennan (1992a: 18) has recently expressed his antipathy to this way of thinking as follows: "The contemporary world, in spite of patches of surface civilisation, remains too ravaged by oppression, ignorance and malnutrition for privileged intellectuals to trade in seriousness for the sparkling interplay of language games." Contrary to this position it can be argued that postmodernism represents neither an absence of seriousness, nor a kind of political immorality or irresponsibility. It works as a critique because it forces precisely this kind of response, either urgently (and perhaps defensively) to redefine and defend the political and intellectual formation of modernity, or else, having subjected to scrutiny the great pillars of thinking which have supported the project of modernity, to stand back and ask "What's going on?" (as the great soul singer Marvin Gaye put it).

Postmodernism is a concept for understanding social change. It seems feeble to suggest it, but maybe the reason for the hostility to the concept in Britain lies at least partly in the abysmal fate of social science research and intellectual work in general in the UK during and after the Thatcher years, where the nature of these constraints inevitably produced defensive political and intellectual responses. Sociology as well as "society" itself became such redundant categories that there was little opportunity to investigate what the new theoretical vocabulary might look like in practice. Thus while there has been a debate about "new ways of living" and about post-Fordism as well as one on fragmentation and identity, there has been little opportunity to examine in any depth the lived "condition of postmodernity". As a result the really engaged debate on how best to understand this refiguring of society was never able to take place. What happened instead was either a rejection and retrenchment which none the less involved re-examining the premises and the assumptions upon which the intellectual edifice of modernity was based, or else a process of translating some of the categories of French or American postmodernism into the cultural politics of contemporary Britain. This latter can best be seen in the emergence of "New Times" (Hall and Jacques, 1989) politics in the late 1980s and early 1990s with its interest in consumerism, identity, ethnicity, and with the critique of essentialism, be it in relation to gender (Riley, 1988), class (Laclau, 1991) or ethnicity (McRobbie, 1985; Bhabha, 1990).

Finding the "Real Me"

The notion of the "real me" suggests the fictive unity of the self and the essentialism entailed in the search for such a person. What is being questioned in this phrase as used by Stuart Hall (1992) is the possibility of ever finding a "real me". One of the issues that will be explored here is what remains when we do away with the real me. How do we construct what I would define as a sufficiently focused "social self" in order to be effective in politics? And who can such a politics now claim to represent? Who, therefore, is the discursive "I" which speaks or writes, to whom and with what purpose? This question will be returned to in the final part of this chapter. But, for the moment, I would want to signal postmodernity as marking a convergence of a number of discourses each of which opens up new possibilities for positioning the self. Many would argue that feelings of dislocation or turbulence, and experiences of fragmentation and crises of identity were as much part of the experience of modernity as they now are of postmodernity (Berman, 1984). But what is distinctive about the discourses considered in the following pages is the respect for difference which they display, not, as some might see it, a "simple" celebration of difference, but rather a rigorous thinking through of what "living with difference" (Mercer, 1990) might entail. In addition I think there is a brave and necessary inclusion in the new intellectual agenda of difference, a different kind of language, one which insists on the interplay between intellectual boundaries and borders and also one which recognizes the importance of what have been the hidden dimensions of subjectivity, those which arise from positionalities which, within modernism, had no legitimate place, i.e. that of the black woman, that of the mother, the daughter, that of the feminist intellectual, the feminist teacher.

This kind of work is reflected in Carolyn Steedman's *Landscape for a Good Woman* (1985) which pulls together strands of social history and personal psychoanalysis producing a remarkable text where the oblique search for the "real me" through the joint guidance of history and psychoanalysis produces instead a layered, mysterious, unresolved self, a fictive daughter, whose positionality as daughter within a particular configuration of class, culture and family, has required that "she" produce "this" book. Feminism, in Steedman's case, also requires a necessary interdisciplinarity of intellectual work which problematizes its own foundations. It may well be that it is this which makes such work, as well as that produced by postcolonialist writers including Trinh T. Min-ha (1989), Homi Bhabha (1990) and Gayatri Chakravorty Spivak (1992), appear unruly and truculent and poetically disrespectful of the boundaries which have guarded and guaranteed the old rules of academia. It is partly this "game" of academic convention and the defence of disciplinary boundaries as guarantors of academic authorship and identity, which underpins recent altercations between those who defend modernity and those who move in some "other" direction.

In the recent volume which is part of the new Open University social science course, *Modernity and Its Futures*, we find an interesting version of the debate for and against postmodernism being played out by Gregor McLennan (1992b) and Stuart Hall (1992). Neither author wholly defends one against the other. But as

McLennan veers towards modernity, Stuart Hall leans towards the exploration of fragmented subjectivity. In the following pages a reading of these debates will be suggested as a means of establishing a framework for considering recent work in feminist theory.

Critical Embrace: Modernity and its Critique

In some ways the embracing of modernity as a critical concept in contemporary political thinking is a way of decentring Marxism by showing it to belong to a broader philosophical project. Thus, while Stuart Hall shows how modernity and its focus on "man" and the unified subject was itself undermined by Freud (the unconscious), by Marx himself (production and labour rather than exchange, the market and free will), later by structuralism (which opposed the transparency of meaning) and more recently by the social movements (including those of gender, sexual identity and ethnicity), so also could we say that the interest in modernity can be seen as a way of both relocating Marx in a less universalistic mode (a kind of process of downgrading or relativizing) and of looking to find something in modernity which can be used to ward off the encroaching chaos of postmodernity. Feminist intellectuals (with a few exceptions) have tended either to argue for the necessity of some of those great modernist values: truth, objectivity, reason (Nicholson, 1990), or else they have argued against the assumed invisibility of women found in much of the recent writing on modernity (Bowlby, 1992; Nava, 1992).

Gregor McLennan reminds us that the Enlightenment gave rise to the idea of social betterment, of improving and making better the society in which we live. The development of the social sciences was part of this project. Are these "foundations of modern thought" now obsolete? Or do they only need to be revised? The first of these questions implies that postmodernity blows everything away, the second that the existing vocabulary merely needs updating. McLennan opts for modifying modernity. He pitches the "overhauling" Lyotard against the more "reasonable" Habermas (1985). For Lyotard the Enlightenment promised science as pure knowledge and as narrative-free practice, but that picture of pure knowledge was in itself part of a very powerful story which helped legitimize capitalist exploitation. Therefore, beware of the meta-narratives. Knowledge is not pure or in the mind but moves in a game. Habermas, in contrast, sees the Enlightenment as an ideal not a reality. It poses questions of morality, science and art as separate from myth and primitivity. To abandon the commitment to reason and rationality is to embrace despair and conservatism. We can retain hope of objectivity in universals (the good life, the better society) without having "naive expectations". Enter the theory of communicative action/reason.

For McLennan relativism is the issue. Does cultural relativism lead to cognitive relativism, that is, we cannot understand therefore we give up and go home? Relativism encourages indifference, he suggests. It means that arguments about what is good and true cannot be engaged in and across cultures. Critics of this position (the rest, the others) would, McLennan agrees, say that what is being defended here "is the culture and society of western science and philosophy". He says in defence of this position that some values can be shared cross-culturally. And if this is not possible and if knowledge has such little import then why carry on doing academic work at all? Modernity did not promise one kind of progress but many. There was always a radicalized strand within modernity.

McLennan argues his position on the grounds that there is communicative action across cultures. There are still universals; for example, the possibility of democracy. One problem is that he takes the postmodernity critique as a kind of intellectual earthquake. He responds truculently. It is one or the other. If there is no logic, no reason, then we all shut up shop or embrace mysticism or unreason or madness. But this mode of argumentation based on pitching two binary opposites against each other need not always be the most useful way of proceeding. The tendency is to feel the necessity of coming down strongly in favour of one or the other, or, as McLennan does in a later piece, more measuredly, to bring together the "better elements of Enlightenment sociology" with "the undoubted insights of 'post' currents. Not . . . in order to form some bland and convenient theoretical convergence but rather to generate a series of productive and taxing tensions" (McLennan, 1992a: 20). What this restrained mode cannot afford to do is to look beyond the "reasonable" frame of reference within which the debate is conducted. Why not? What happens when we challenge this kind of management of reason, when we suggest that the tensions are more usefully explored when they remain aggressively outside and deeply uncomfortable with this kind of "convergence"?

Stuart Hall: Working in a World of Shifting Boundaries

Stuart Hall travels down a different road. What he is interested in exploring are the new worldly identities which have come into being, sweeping away, as capitalism itself does, the old nation-states which were the bearers of modernity and the givers of identity and "nationality". Instead we live in a world of moving boundaries, a world in which borders are crossed, new sub-nationalisms and transnationalisms are embraced. For Hall it is the struggle to explain which is important. What he turns his attention to are those aspects of modernity which incorporated subjection and subordination in the language of social advance, exploration, development, civilization. This more open-ended approach avoids the either/ors which define the terms of McLennan's argument. Instead it adopts a strategy of unsettlement and an embracing of the idea of difference and hybridity. What is also unsettled and differentiated is the "real me". This approach is also quite different from Jameson's (1984) and Harvey's (1989), as well as McLennan's, in that we see no sign of a return to the values or ethics of modernism being proposed. It is focused around the "new ethnicities" and it looks out for the connections among subjugated people which emerge from within the tracks of the metacommunications networks of the new global order.

Hall's contribution is significant also in that it does not prioritize an exclusively academic mode as the means of producing knowledge and understanding.

Postcolonialist writing acknowledges the work found in and produced by the inter-section of art and popular culture. Culture is a broad site of learning, and perhaps we learn best and are most open to ideas when the barriers between the discipline and the academy and the experiences of everyday life are broken down. There is a sense in which Stuart Hall is here speaking from the other side, from the space of difference. Where those who espoused modernity and its ideals saw vision and order and reason and achievement he sees turbulence and savagery. Included in Hall's essay is a quote from Salman Rushdie responding to the review of his book *The Satanic Verses*, "A bit of this and a bit of that is how newness enters the world. It is the great possibility that mass migration gives the world" (Hall, 1992: 311; quoting Rushdie). If, therefore, postcolonialist experience shares anything in common with the postmodern experience, then it must be a postmodernism which is much more than an overstylized posture adopted by those who can afford to abandon politics. Instead it is a way of marking out a new set of convergences and divergences round certain critical questions about the society in which we live.

Towards a Feminist Postmodernism

In her contribution to *Beyond Equality and Difference*, Rosi Braidotti (1992) rejects the defence of theoretical reason, the unity of the subject and even of equality (equal to whom, she asks?) as "domination", Enlightenment concepts, which have been part of an apparatus of regulation and subordination hidden under the great achievements of rationality and knowledge. This marks her out immediately as a postmodern feminist. The question that has to be asked, she suggests, is that of how we think, what is it to think? What does it mean if reason and truth are unsettled from their secure places in the foundationalist discipline of philosophy? She thus opens up for debate not only the possibility of other ways of thinking, but also the question of on whose behalf do we think as critical feminist intellectuals? What is the responsibility of the feminist intellectual? Is it not, in part, to think about think-ing and thus to unveil some of the power relations caught up in the category of knowledge?

These questions which she is asking from a feminist viewpoint, happen to coincide with the critique of western thinking by subaltern discourses. So the whole status of thinking and of thought is called into question. Let us move out of a dualistic logic, she continues: male versus female, women equal to men. "Feminists propose that reason does not sum up the totality of or even what is best in the human capacity for thinking" (Braidotti, 1992: 181). Do we therefore learn to think differently as a "female feminist subject"? The postmodern subject, argues Braidotti, is a subject in process, organized by a will to know and a desire to speak. The crisis of subjectivity produced by postmodernity "offers many positive openings" (Braidotti, 1992: 183). This crisis emerged in the dying moments of modernity through Freud, for example, with his insistence of the non-coincidence of the subject with consciousness, and then later with Foucault's account of the self as the product of discourse. Much thought, she reminds us, following Freud, is pre-rational, unconscious matter. Rationality rests on premises about thinking which are themselves nonrational. And desire "is that which being the a-priori condition for thinking is in excess of the thinking process itself" (Braidotti, 1992: 184). For Braidotti the enunciation of a philosophical stance rests, therefore, on a non-philosophical disposition to represent the self, to inscribe the subject in language. How then do we rethink subjectivity and the body as an "interface of will with desire", that is, the will to know and the desire to say?

Such an emphasis on desire inevitably runs the risk of positing desire as the source of a new essentialism. This is particularly the case when desire coincides not just with language but also with sexuality which is then taken, as Foucault (1984) has pointed out, as representing the truth of the body and of the self. Or is it rather, as Braidotti argues, that in western culture the sexed body dominates over the other levels of experience? It is how we are known, how we come to know. In language we are sexed and this process of being sexed is one of the key modalities of power inscribed in each of our bodies: "Sexuality is the dominant discourse of power in the West" (Braidotti, 1992: 185).

It is therefore a point of contestation. What, the feminist critic might ask, *is* the female body, what is it for, for whom? And to follow in this vein the feminist cultural critic might ask, is it because Madonna constructs herself exactly along this axis of *all body* that she unnerves and disrupts the axis of power which prefers to remain hidden? She pulls it all off the top shelf of the newsagent's, brings it – sex, power, pornography, the body – to the surface and leaves us to respond. It could be suggested that by placing her body on precisely those lines of classification, for example, as the site of sex, as the truth of femininity, and also as the property of the female self, something that can and does give pleasure quite autonomously from the regulative discourses within which it is more traditionally placed, the image of Madonna is disruptive. It is too much about sexuality to exist comfortably within the commercial machine, even where that machine is already linked with excessive sexual imagery (i.e. pop), or where it is licensed to shock. Instead of simply rejecting the essentialism which equates woman with body, Braidotti argues that (like Madonna) we must revisit the sites of assumed essentialism and work through them. We should explore the boundaries by going back to them.

But if we no longer know what woman is, if we are all good anti-essentialists, and if we take into account the critique by black feminists of white feminism's universalism, how do we move from analysing the implications for power of the borders and boundaries, to actively redefining the bonds through which a politics remains viable? Like all of the postmodern feminists being considered here, Braidotti puts the possibility of a communicative bond between women as the basis for politics on the agenda. This takes the form for feminist intellectuals of a kind of accountability, a recognition of the relations of responsibility between a writer and her readers and, it could be added, between a teacher and her students. Feminist thinking should, then, attempt to represent and analyse what it is to be female. In one decisive way, this breaks down the barriers between art, fiction, culture and the academic disciplines in much the way that Stuart Hall suggests (Hall, 1992). By far the most visible example of this force for breaking down barriers is the success and achievement of black women's writing over the last few years, not just for the community of women it brings into being as readers, but also because it *is* simultaneously art, history, literature, sociology, politics, biography, autobiography and also popular culture. At the opposite end of the same spectrum but "doing" in her own theoretical work very much the same kind of thing, we could also place Gayatri Chakravorty Spivak. Coming from the high end of deconstruction, and bringing to this practice a feminist postcolonialist critique, Spivak works within the discourse of theory but so transforms it as to make it an entirely different kind of practice. It becomes an interrogative, interweaving, reflective poetics. For Spivak the community of women can only come after the recognition of difference between women, and after the raising of some key questions about who is talking to whom, and why, all points which she returns to in her contribution to *Feminists Theorise the Political* (Spivak, 1992).

This is a similar position to that described by Judith Butler, who also engages with a notion of the community of women. In articulating women, from a feminist perspective, such a category is immediately broken and it is the breaking that is the important point (Butler, 1992). Who is not spoken to in feminism? In addition, who was the "subject" of feminism, but is no more? How has feminism opened itself out to speak to many female subjects and yet still engages with only a few? Butler sees these as crucial questions and illustrates them by referring to the old centrality of the mother as one of the primary stable subjects of feminist discourse. But this figure of the mother is not a biologically defined and stable category. She herself shifts and changes, just as feminism also does. As her children grow up and move away she no longer defines herself primarily through that particular mode of subjectivity. So the subjects of feminism change, feminism itself changes, particularly as it becomes subject to criticism by black women and, as the society within which feminism exists also undergoes quite dramatic changes, this too has an impact on what feminism is and can be. We could also add to Butler's questions the important one of how under such conditions feminism, or what remains of it, can hope to reproduce itself among a generation of younger women? What space away from feminism do young women need in order to disconnect from the historical experience of their mothers or their teachers and then find their own way towards feminism, redefining it in the process for themselves? These questions of how feminism continues and seeks to extend itself while recognizing different histories, experiences and identities are therefore crucial. Can it continue, can it still call itself feminism? What must it do to be able to legitimately address women?

As well as laying the ground for developing post-feminism theoretically, Judith Butler also takes issue with the slightly ridiculing tones frequently adopted to make light of postmodernism. As though in direct engagement with Gregor McLennan she disputes the assumption that there "must" be a foundation and a stable subject to have a politics. She sees this as authoritarian, the use of the "must" clause. Postmodernism does not mean that we have to do away with the subject but rather we ask after the process of its construction. The value of postmodernism therefore is that, like deconstruction, it shows clearly how arguments bury opposition. Its disorderly force is rude and impertinent in that it shows where power resides, hidden and quiet and displeased at being exposed. Demonstrating these ruses does not mean descending into unruly chaos. Rather it allows for open debate and dispute about boundaries and disciplines and what constitutes a study, what is knowledge. "A social theory committed to democratic contestation within a post-colonialist horizon needs to find a way to bring into question the foundations it is compelled to lay down" (Butler, 1992: 8).

Thus even minimal foundations need scrutinizing. Within feminism there is a need to speak as and for women but no sooner is this done than it is objected to. This is the point at which things move. Women then become "an undesignatable field of wills". The dispute *is* the ground of feminist theory. The category of women has to be released from the anchoring which feminism felt it needed. "What women signify has been taken for granted too long. . . . We have to instead break from the list of meanings and expand the possibilities of what it is to be a woman" (Butler, 1992: 16). Sex imposes a uniformity on bodies for the purposes of reproductive sexuality. This is also an act of violence. Therefore there must be a redefining, an invention of new categories. (We could add to this the question of whether this is already happening, with the emergence of the "single mother" as a sign of these expanded possibilities of being female, a category which marks a changed society and a changed mode of familial organization.)

Jane Flax (1992a) completes the assault on the male modernists who defend reason by saying how comforting it is to believe that reason will triumph and bail us all out. How often has it? Admittedly, it is frightening to think that without truth, pure power might prevail. Feminists are as prone to this wishful thinking that reason will win through as anybody else. But, says Flax, this failure to face up to the limits of reason, truth and knowledge is predicted on fear of letting go and of thinking outside the safety of inherited assumptions about thought. "They fear what will emerge in disrupted places if they are not in feminist control. They believe innocent clean knowledge is available somewhere for our discovery and use" (Flax, 1992b: 457). Flax prefers desire, fantasy and power. "What we really want is power in the world not an innocent truth" (1992b: 458). Many feminists are fearful of losing what they have gained by embracing or being seen to embrace postmodernity. But this being made insecure is productive and it coincides with being made insecure by the critique of women of colour. "At its best postmodernity invites us to engage in a continual process of dis-illusionment with the grandiose fantasies that have brought us to the brink of annihilation" (Flax, 1992b: 460). Feminist postmodernism does not eliminate the subject or the self but finds it in operation as a series of bit parts in the concrete field of social relations. Politics must therefore imply subjectivities in process, interacting and debating.

This idea of, as Stuart Hall puts it, becoming rather than being, continues the mode of argument that all of these feminist writers adopt, that is, to avoid binary oppositions and to dispute the value of terms like equality, and relativism, as the other of a discourse of absolutism (men, universalism) which they are committed to questioning. What emerges from this work is a desire to hold on to the notion of a meaningful feminist politics by interrogating rather than assuming the relations between who is talking to whom. In subjecting some of the big questions and concepts to critical scrutiny these feminist writers are not taking leave of their senses but rather are asking questions about how we learn, how we think and write. This has the effect of realigning the disciplines, rearranging the furniture of intellectual life. It allows for a certain interdisciplinary licence.

In the absence of a "real me", what I would describe as a social self (the female feminist subject as Braidotti labels her) none the less emerges, marked by a set of constraints and dispositions. This social self participates in intimacy, in communality and communication. She also uses desire and will in order to understand the process of subjection. The feminist social self, it might be suggested, is an amalgam of fragmented identities formed in discourse and history and called into being both by the experiences of femininity and by the existence and availability of a feminist discourse whether that comes in the form of books, education, mass media, or through friends, politics and community. This, I think, is what Butler and the other feminist writers discussed here mean by the communicative aspect of female experience.

Unmasking the "Real Me"

But while little work has been done on what is left behind when the myth of the "real me" is revealed, deconstructing the "real me" has involved showing it to be a social and political requirement, a form of enforcement, a means of regulating legitimate ways of being, legitimate ways of understanding the self and the world. The "real 'respectable' me" is also the product of a certain kind of psychoanalytical violence where desire is also constrained and endlessly defined in culture around the tropes of heterosexuality. Not being at one with this "real me" has produced much pain and suffering and has required, on the part of gay men and lesbian women, enormous effort to construct different kinds of subjectivity. But if the "real me" is a mask, a fiction which transcends discourse as an essence, how then, once we have dislodged this kind of self, can we talk about women, about identity, or indeed of feminism as mobilizing political categories? Once again Gayatri Spivak shows how, for white western feminists, there is still instant recourse to a language where feminism is pursued unalert to the limits of its efficacy and unwilling to be constantly interrogating who is the subject of its address. It is her attentiveness to the consequences of being designated a subaltern subject as she moves with her passport through the boundaries and barriers of nation-states and is inevitably questioned as to her professional status as teacher, as a person "here" to give a paper, that makes her ever alert to the question of power. In her contribution to *Feminists Theorise the Political* Spivak (1992: 56) asks, "What is it to write for you? What is it to teach? What is it to learn? What is it to assume that one already knows the meaning of the words 'something is taught by me and something is learned by others'?"

The value of the work of these feminist writers lies in their interrogating of the ground rules, the boundaries and the barriers which define feminist theory and politics and which simultaneously have to be broken, have to be trespassed on. In this postmodern field what we find is not, however, a scene of catastrophe, the cost of questioning reason, the punishment for risking rationality. The riposte to white feminists that they were not speaking and could not speak on behalf of "all women", has prompted a reassessment of the feminist self and who she is, and is speaking to and about. At the same time this particular fragmentation of the feminist subject is confirmed through the global and postmodern critique of the European Enlightenment. It is not so much a question of what is left behind, what fragments of the disassembled self can be picked up and put together again, but rather how might the continual process of putting oneself together be transformed to produce the empowerment of subordinate groups and social categories. This might mean living with fragmentation, with the reality of inventing the self rather than endlessly searching for the self. But abandoning the "real me" need not mean resignation, despair, or simply being reconciled to the loss of wholeness.

Living along the fault-lines of the postmodern condition might also give us some reasons to feel cheerful. We might modestly be aware of our limited successes, in putting feminism (with all the limits that word implies) into the webs of popular discourses about gender and sexuality. The appearance of new feminist discourses, not just in the academy but also in women's magazines, for example, and in some other spaces within the commercial mass media, tells us that feminism now has some control over constructions of the feminine, as Charlotte Brunsdon has recently suggested (1992). But this fact should not be viewed as unproblematic success. There remains the question of what sort of feminism is found in these spaces and to whom is it speaking?

This kind of question challenges, by necessity, the process of reproducing feminism. Just as a feminist "real me" was perhaps a necessary fiction in the early 1970s, so also was it necessary then to believe in the reproduction of feminism as part of the process of politicization. That such an attempt can backfire is not just about "backlash" but more productively about other younger women (like black women) disputing their being represented by feminists, just as much as they might take issue with their being represented in advertising, or in popular culture, or in the tabloid press. Thus, once again, politics occurs in the act of breaking away from the claim to be represented. New, emergent or otherwise excluded identities emerge from this discourse of rejection and repudiation. "This is not us", they are saying. And in saying so there is also a question of who indeed "they" are.

While this might create a crisis for the (white) feminist movement and for the feminist intellectuals who came into being in the 1970s, such a crisis is no bad thing. In the process of being challenged, older feminist identities are also revised. And what remains is remembered, perhaps even in a "passion of remembrance" (Blackwood and Julien, 1985).

The passage of feminism into the 1990s should not be seen, in conclusion, as a process of political dismemberment, leaving behind a sadly dispersed band of individuals dotted about the globe but found mostly in the universities of the western world and defining themselves as "feminist writers" or "feminist intellectuals". Nor should it be understood, after postmodernism, as a politics of difference based simply on pluralism, on everyone going their own way. In short the strength of feminism lies in its ability to create discourse, to dispute, to negotiate the boundaries and the barriers, and also to take issue with the various feminisms which have sprung into being. The value of the contribution to new feminist theory by Butler and Scott in *Feminists Theorise the Political*, Bock and James in *Beyond Equality and Difference*, and Hall, Held and McGrew in *Modernity and Its Futures* (all 1992) lies first in their rejection that there could be or should be "one voice", second in their willingness to take risks by exploring the relatively unnavigated political continent which lies "beyond equality and difference", third in their engagement with the politics of difference as characterized not by pluralism but by lines of connection and of disconnection, and fourth by their abandonment of the search for the "real me" in favour, to use Judith Butler's words again, "of expanding the possibilities of what it means to be a woman".

References

Berman, Marshall (1984) *All That Is Solid Melts into Air: The Experience of Modernity*, London: Verso.

Bhabha, Homi (1990) "DissemiNation: time, narrative and the margins of the modern nation", in H. Bhabha (ed.) *Nation and Narration*, London: Routledge, pp. 15–48.

Blackwood, Maureen and Julien, Isaac (dirs) (1985) *The Passion of Remembrance*, Sankofa Films.

Bowlby, Rachel (1992) *Still Crazy After All These Years*, London: Routledge.

Braidotti, Rosi (1992) "On the feminist female subject or from she-self to she-other", in G. Bock and S. James (eds.) *Beyond Equality and Difference: Citizenship, Feminist Politics and Female Subjectivity*, London: Routledge, pp. 176–92.

Brunsdon, Charlotte (1992) "Pedagogies of the feminine: feminist teaching and women's genres", *Screen* 32, 4: 364–82.

Butler, Judith (1992) "Contingent foundations: feminism and the question of 'postmodernism'", in J. Butler and J. W. Scott (eds.) *Feminists Theorise the Political*, London: Routledge, pp. 3–22.

Flax, Jane (1992a) "Beyond equality: gender, justice and difference", in G. Bock and S. James (eds.) *Beyond Equality and Difference: Citizenship, Feminist Politics and Female Subjectivity*, London: Routledge, pp. 192–209.

Flax, Jane (1992b) "The end of innocence", in J. Butler and J. W. Scott (eds.) *Feminists Theorise the Political*, London: Routledge, pp. 445–64.

Foucault, Michel (1984) *The History of Sexuality*, vol. 1, Harmondsworth, Mx: Penguin.

Gilroy, Paul (1993) *The Black Atlantic*, London: Verso.

Habermas, Jürgen (1985) "Modernity: an incomplete project", in H. Foster (ed.) *Postmodern Culture*, London: Pluto Press, pp. 3–15.

Hall, Stuart (1992) "The question of cultural identity", in S. Hall, D. Held and D. McGrew (eds.) *Modernity and Its Futures*, Oxford: Polity Press, pp. 273–327.

Hall, Stuart and Jacques, Martin (1989) *New Times: The Changing Face of Politics in the 1990s*, London: Lawrence & Wishart.

Harvey, David (1989) *The Condition of Postmodernity*, Oxford: Blackwell.

Jameson, Fredric (1984) "Postmodernism, or the cultural logic of capital", *New Left Review* 146: 53–92.

Laclau, Ernesto (1991) *Reflections on the New Revolutions of Our Times*, London: Verso.

Lyotard, Jean-François (1984) *The Postmodern Condition*, Manchester: Manchester University Press.

McLennan, Gregor (1992a) "Sociology after postmodernism", inaugural address, Faculty of Social Sciences Occasional Papers, Massey University, Palmers Bag, New Zealand, pp. 1–22.

McLennan, Gregor (1992b) "The Enlightenment project, revisited", in S. Hall, D. Held and D. McGrew (eds.) *Modernity and Its Futures*, Oxford: Polity Press, pp. 327–79.

McRobbie, Angela (1985) "Strategies of vigilance: an interview with Gayatri Chakravorty Spivak", *Block* 10: 5–9.

Mercer, Kobena (1990) "Welcome to the jungle", in J. Rutherford (ed.) *Identity*, London: Lawrence & Wishart, pp. 43–71.

Min-ha, Trinh T. (1989) *Woman, Native, Other*, Bloomington, IN: Indiana University Press.

Nava, Mica (1992) *Changing Cultures: Feminism, Youth, Consumerism*, London: Sage.

Nicholson, Linda J. (ed.) (1990) *Feminism/Postmodernism*, New York: Routledge.

Riley, Denise (1988) *"Am I That Name": Feminism and the Category of "Women" in History*, London: Macmillan.

Spivak, Gayatri Chakravorty (1992) "French feminism revisited", in J. Butler and J. W. Scott (eds.) *Feminists Theorise the Political*, London: Routledge, pp. 54–86.

Steedman, Carolyn (1985) *Landscape for a Good Woman*, London: Virago.

31

Postmodern Virtualities

Mark Poster

Introduction

On the eve of the 21st century there have been two innovative discussions about the general conditions of life: one concerns a possible "postmodern" culture and even society; the other concerns broad, massive changes in communications systems. Postmodern culture is often presented as an alternative to existing society which is pictured as structurally limited or fundamentally flawed. New communications systems are often presented as a hopeful key to a better life and a more equitable society. The discussion of postmodern culture focuses to a great extent on an emerging new individual identity or subject position, one that abandons what may in retrospect be the narrow scope of the modern individual with its claims to rationality and autonomy. The discourse surrounding the new communications systems attends more to the imminent technical increase in information exchange and the ways this advantage will redound to already existing individuals and already existing institutions.

My purpose in this essay is to bring these two discussions together, to enact a confrontation between them so that the advantages of each may redound to the other, while the limitations of each may be revealed and discarded. My contention is that a critical understanding of the new communications systems requires an evaluation of the type of subject it encourages, while a viable articulation of postmodernity must include an elaboration of its relation to new technologies of communication.

For what is at stake in these technical innovations, I contend, is not simply an increased "efficiency" of interchange, enabling new avenues of investment, increased productivity at work and new domains of leisure and consumption, but a broad and extensive change in the culture, in the way identities are structured. If I may be allowed a historical analogy: the technically advanced societies are at a point in their history similar to that of the emergence of an urban, merchant culture in the midst

From Mark Poster, "Postmodern virtualities." In Mike Featherstone and Roger Burrows (eds.), *Cyberspace/Cyberbodies/Cyberpunk*, pp. 79–95. Thousand Oaks, CA: Sage, 1995.

of feudal society in the Middle Ages. At that point practices of the exchange of commodities required individuals to act and speak in new ways,[1] ways drastically different from the aristocratic code of honor with its face-to-face encounters based on trust for one's word and its hierarchical bonds of interdependency. Interacting with total strangers, sometimes at great distances, the merchants required written documents guaranteeing spoken promises and an "arm's length distance" attitude even when face-to-face with the other, so as to afford a "space" for calculations of self-interest. A new identity was constructed, gradually and in a most circuitous path to be sure, among the merchants, in which a coherent, stable sense of individuality was grounded in independent, cognitive abilities. In this way the cultural basis for the modern world was begun, one that eventually would rely upon print media to encourage and disseminate these urban forms of identity.

In the 20th century, electronic media are supporting an equally profound transformation of cultural identity. Telephone, radio, film, television, the computer and now their integration as "multimedia" reconfigure words, sounds and images so as to cultivate new configurations of individuality. If modern society may be said to foster an individual who is rational, autonomous, centered and stable (the "reasonable man" of the law, the educated citizen of representative democracy, the calculating "economic man" of capitalism, the grade-defined student of public education), then perhaps a postmodern society is emerging which nurtures forms of identity different from, even opposite to those of modernity. And electronic communications technologies significantly enhance these postmodern possibilities. Discussions of these technologies, as we shall see, tend often to miss precisely this crucial level of analysis, treating them as enhancements for already formed individuals to deploy to their advantage or disadvantage.[2]

The Communications "Superhighway"

One may regard the media from a purely technical point of view, to the extent that is possible, evaluating them in relation to their ability to transmit units of information. The question to ask then is how much information with how little noise may be transmitted at what speed and over what distance to how many locations? Until the late 1980s technical constraints limited the media's ability in these terms. To transmit a high quality image over existing (twisted pair copper wire) phone lines took about ten minutes using a 2,400-baud modem or two minutes using a 9,600-baud modem. Given these specifications it was not possible to send "real time" "moving" images over the phone lines. The great limitation, then, of the first electronic media age is that images could only be transmitted from a small number of centers to a large number of receivers, either by air or by coaxial cable. Until the end of the 1980s an "economic" scarcity existed in the media highways that encouraged and justified, without much thought or consideration, the capitalist or nation-state exploitation of image transmission. Since senders needed to build their own information roads by broadcasting at a given frequency or by constructing (coaxial) wire networks, there were necessarily few distributors of images. The same economies of technology, it might be noted in passing, applied to processes of information production.

Critical theorists such as Benjamin, Enzensberger and McLuhan[3] envisioned the democratic potential of the increased communication capacity of radio, film and television. While there is some truth to their position, the practical model for a more radical communications potential during the first media age was rather the telephone. What distinguishes the telephone from the other great media is its decentralized quality and its universal exchangeability of the positions of sender and receiver. Anyone can "produce" and send a message to anyone else in the system and, in the advanced industrial societies, almost everyone is in the system. These unique qualities were recognized early on by both defenders and detractors of the telephone.

In the recent past the only technology that imitates the telephone's democratic structure is the Internet, the government funded electronic mail, database and general communication system.[4] Until the 1990s, even this facility has been largely restricted to government, research and education institutions, some private industry and individuals who enroll in private services (Compuserve, Prodigy) which are connected to it. In the last few years Internet has gained enormously in popularity and by the mid-1990s boasts 30 million users around the world (Cooke and Lehrer, 1993). But Internet and its segments use the phone lines, suffering their inherent technical limitations. Technical innovations in the late 1980s and early 1990s, however, are making possible the drastic reduction of earlier constraints. The digital encoding of sound, text and image, the introduction of fiber-optic lines replacing copper wire, the ability to transmit digitally encoded images and the subsequent ability to compress this information, the vast expansion of the frequency range for wireless transmission, innovations in switching technology and a number of other advances have so enlarged the quantity and types of information that may soon be able to be transmitted that a qualitative change, to allude to Engels' dialectical formula, in the culture may also be imminent.

Information superhighways are being constructed that will enable a vast increase in the flow of communications. The telephone and cable companies are estimating the change to be from a limit of 60 or so one-way video/audio channels to one of 500 with limited bidirectionality. But this kind of calculation badly misses the point. The increase in transmission capacity (both wired and wireless) will be so great that it will be possible to transmit any type of information (audio, video or text) from any point in the network to any other point or points, and to do so in "real time", in other words quickly enough so that the receiver will see or record at least 24 frames of video per second with an accompanying audio frequency range of 20 to 20,000 Hertz. The metaphor of the "superhighway" only attends to the movement of information, leaving out the various kinds of cyberspace on the Internet, meeting places, work areas and electronic cafés in which this vast transmission of images and words becomes places of communicative relation. The question that needs to be raised is "will this technological change provide the stimulus for the installation of new media different enough from what we now have to warrant the periodizing judgment of a second electronic media age?" If that is the case, how is the change to be understood?

A discourse on the new communications technology is in process of formation, one which is largely limited by the vision of modernity. The importance of the information superhighway is now widely recognized, with articles appearing in periodicals from the specialized zines (*Wired* and *Mondo 2000*) to general journals (*Time*, *Forbes* and *The Nation*). Essays on the new technology vary from breathless enthusiasm to wary caution to skepticism. Writing in *Time*, Philip Elmer-Dewitt (1993: 52) forecasts: "The same switches used to send a TV show to your home can also be used to send a video from your home to any other – paving the way for video phones. . . . The same system will allow anybody with a camcorder to distribute videos to the world . . .'. Key to the new media system are not only the technical advances mentioned above but also the merger of existing communication technologies. Elmer-Dewitt continues, ". . . the new technology will force the merger of television, telecommunications, computers, consumer electronics, publishing and information services into a single interactive information industry" (1993: 52–3). Other observers emphasize the prospects of wireless technology. Writing in *Forbes*, George Gilder (1993: 107) predicts the spread of this system:

> . . . the new minicell replaces a rigid structure of giant analog mainframes with a system of wireless local area networks . . . these wide and weak [replacing broadcasting based on "long and strong"] radios can handle voice, data and even video at the same time . . . the system fulfills the promise of the computer revolution as a spectrum multiplier . . . [the new system will] banish once and for all the concept of spectrum scarcity.

Whether future communications media employ wired, wireless or some combination of the two, the same picture emerges of profound transformation.

Faced with this gigantic combination of new technology, integration of older technologies, creation of new industries and expansion of older ones, commentators have not missed the political implications. In *Tikkun*, David Bollier underlines the need for a new set of policies to govern and regulate the second media age in the public interest. President Bill Clinton and Vice-President Al Gore have already drawn attention to the problem, stressing the need for broad access to the superhighway, but also indicating their willingness to make the new developments safe for the profit motive. For them the main issue at stake is the strength of the United States in relation to other nations (read especially Japan) and the health of the industries involved. Bollier (1993: 22) points to wider concerns, such as strengthening community life, supporting families and invigorating the democratic process.[5] At this point I want to note that Bollier understands the new media entirely within the framework of *modern* social institutions. The "information superhighway" is for him a transparent tool that brings new efficiencies but by itself changes nothing. The media merely redound to the benefit of or detract from familiar institutions – the family, the community, the state.

If Bollier presents a liberal or left-liberal agenda for politics confronted by the second media age, Mitchell Kapor, former developer of Lotus 1–2–3, offers a more radical interpretation. He understands better than Bollier that the information superhighway opens qualitatively new political opportunities because it creates new loci of speech:

> the crucial political question is "Who controls the switches?" There are two extreme choices. Users may have indirect, or limited control over when, what, why, and from whom they get information and to whom they send it. That's the broadcast model today, and it seems to breed consumerism, passivity, crassness, and mediocrity. Or, users may have decentralized, distributed, direct control over when, what, why, and with whom they exchange information. That's the Internet model today, and it seems to breed critical thinking, activism, democracy, and quality. We have an opportunity to choose now. (Kapor, 1993: 5)

With Kapor, the interpretation of the new media returns to the position of Enzensberger: socialist or radical democratic control of the media results in more freedom, more enlightenment, more rationality; capitalist or centralist control results in oppression, passivity, irrationality. Kapor's reading of the information superhighway remains within the binaries of modernity. No new cultural formations of the self are imagined or even thought possible. While the political questions raised by Bollier and Kapor are valid and raise the level of debate well beyond its current formation, they remain limited to the terms of discussion that are familiar in the landscape of modernity.

The political implications of the Internet for the fate of the nation-state and the development of a global community also requires attention. The dominant use of English on the Internet suggests the extension of American power as does the fact that e-mail addresses in the US alone do not require a country code. The Internet normalizes American users. But the issue is more complex. In Singapore, English serves to *enable* conversations between hostile ethnic groups, being a neutral "other". Of course, vast inequalities of use exist, changing the democratic structure of the Internet into an occasion for further wrongs to the poorer populations. Even within the high-use nations, wealthy white males are disproportionate users. Yet technologies sometimes spread quickly and the Internet is relatively cheap. Only grassroots political mobilization on this issue will ensure wide access (Tehranian, forthcoming).

In some ways the Internet undermines the territoriality of the nation-state: messages in cyberspace are not easily delimited in Newtonian space, rendering borders ineffective. In the Teale–Homolka trial of early 1994, a case of multiple murders including sexual assault and mutilation, the Canadian government was unable to enforce an information blackout because of Usenet postings in the United States being available in Canada (Turner, 1994). In order to combat communicative acts that are defined by one state as illegal, nations are being compelled to coordinate their laws, putting their vaunted "sovereignty" in question. So desperate are national governments, confronted by the disorder of the Internet, that schemes to monitor all messages are afoot, such as the American government's idea to monopolize encryption with a "Clipper Chip" or the FBI's insistence on building surveillance mechanisms into the structure of the information superhighway (Hotz, 1993: 22). Nation-states are at a loss when faced with a global communication network. Technology has taken a turn that defines the character of power of modern governments.

The effortless reproduction and distribution of information is greeted by modern economic organizations, the corporations, with the same anxiety that plagues nation-states. Audio taping was resisted by the moguls of the music industry; video taping by Hollywood; modems by the telephone industry giants. Property rights are put in doubt when information is set free of its material integument to move and to multiply in cyberspace with few constraints. The response of our captains of industry is the absurd one of attempting vastly to extend the principle of property by pro-mulgating new "intellectual property laws", flying in the face of the advance in the technologies of transmission and dissemination. The problem for capitalism is how to contain the word and the image, to bind them to proper names and logos when they flit about at the speed of light and procreate with indecent rapidity, not arborially, to use the terms of Deleuze and Guattari, as in a centralized factory, but rhyzomically, at any decentered location. If that were not enough to daunt defenders of modern notions of property, First Amendment issues are equally at risk. Who, for example, "owns" the rights to and is thereby responsible for the text on Internet bulletin boards: the author, the system operator, the community of participants? Does freedom of speech extend to cyberspace, as it does to print? How easy will it be to assess damages and mete out blame in a communicative world whose contours are quite different from those of face-to-face speech and print? These and numerous other fundamental questions are raised by Internet communications for institutions, laws and habits that developed in the very different context of modernity.

Reality Problematized

Before turning to the issue of the cultural interpretation of the second media age, we need to consider a further new technology, that of virtual reality. The term "virtual" was used in computer jargon to refer to situations that were near substitutes. For example, virtual memory means the use of a section of a hard disk to act as some-thing else, in this case, random access memory. "Virtual reality" is a more dangerous term since it suggests that reality may be multiple or take many forms.[6] The phrase is close to that of "real time", which arose in the audio recording field when splicing, multiple-track recording and multiple-speed recording made possible "other times" to that of clock time or phenomenological time. In this case, the normal or conventional sense of "time" had to be preserved by the modifier "real". But again the use of the modifier only draws attention to non-"reality" of clock time, its non-exclusivity, its insubstantiality, its lack of foundation. The terms "virtual reality" and "real time" attest to the force of the second media age in constituting a simulational culture. The mediation has become so intense that the things mediated can no longer even pretend to be unaffected. The culture is increasingly simulational in the sense that the media often changes the things that it treats, transforming the identity of originals and referentialities. In the second media age "reality" becomes multiple.

Virtual reality is a computer-generated "place" which is "viewed" by the participant through "goggles" but which responds to stimuli from the participant or particip-ants. A participant may "walk" through a house that is being designed for him or her to get a feel for it before it is built. Or she may "walk" through a "museum" or "city" whose paintings or streets are computer-generated but the position of the individual is relative to their actual movement, not to a predetermined computer program or "movie". In addition, more than one individual may experience the same virtual reality at the same time, with both persons' "movements" affecting the same "space". What is more, these individuals need not be in the same physical location but may be communicating information to the computer from distant points through modems. Further "movements" in virtual reality are not quite the same as movements in "old reality": for example, one can fly or go through walls since the material constraints of earth need not apply. While still in their infancy, virtual reality programs attest to the increasing "duplication", if I may use this term, of reality by technology. But the duplication incurs an alternation: virtual realities are fanciful imaginings that, in their difference from real reality, evoke play and discovery, instituting a new level of imagination. Virtual reality takes the imaginary of the word and the imaginary of the film or video image one step farther by placing the individual "inside" alternative worlds. By directly tinkering with reality, a simulational practice is set in place which alters forever the conditions under which the identity of the self is formed.

Already transitional forms of virtual reality are in use on the Internet. MUDs or Multi User Domains have a devoted following. These are conferences of sorts in which participants adopt roles in a neo-medieval adventure game. Although the game is played textually, that is, moves are typed as sentences, it is highly "visual" in the sense that complex locations, characters and objects interact continuously. In a variant of a MUD, LambdaMOO, a database contains "objects" as "built" by participants to improve upon the sense of reality. As a result, a quasi-virtual reality is created by the players. What is more, each player adopts a fictional role that may be different from their actual gender and indeed this gender may change in the course of the game, drastically calling into question the gender system of the dominant culture as a fixed binary. At least during the fictional game, individuals explore imaginary subject positions while in communication with others. In LambdaMOO, a series of violent "rapes" by one character caused a crisis among the participants, one that led to special conferences devoted to the issue of punishing the offender and thereby better defining the nature of the community space of the conference. This experience also cautions against depictions of cyberspace as utopia: the wounds of modernity are borne with us when we enter this new arena and in some cases are even exacerbated. Nonetheless, the makings of a new cultural space are also at work in the MUDs. One participant argues that continuous participation in the game leads to a sense of involvement that is somewhere between ordinary reality and fiction (Dibbell, 1993).[7] The effect of new media such as the Internet and virtual reality, then, is to multiply the kinds of "realities" one encounters in society.

The Postmodern Subject

The information superhighway and virtual reality are communications media that enrich existing forms of consumer culture. But they also depart or may depart from what we have known as the mass media or the "culture industry" in a number of crucial ways. I said "may depart" because neither of these technologies has been fully constituted as cultural practices; they are emergent communication systems whose features are yet to be specified with some permanence or finality. One purpose of this essay is to suggest the importance of some form of political concern about how these technologies are being actualized. The technical characteristics of the information superhighway and virtual reality are clear enough to call attention to their potential for new cultural formations. It is conceivable that the information superhighway will be restricted in the way the broadcast system is. In that case, the term "second media age" is unjustified. But the potential of a decentralized communications system is so great that it is certainly worthy of recognition. Examples from the history of the installation and dissemination of communications technologies are instructive. Carolyn Marvin points out that the telephone was, at the outset, by no means the universal, decentralized network it became. The phone company was happy to restrict the use of the instrument to those who registered. It did not understand the social or political importance of the universality of participation, being interested mainly in income from services provided. Also the example of Telefon Hirmondó, a telephone system in Budapest in the period before the First World War, is worth recalling. The Hungarians used the telephone as a broadcast system, with a published schedule of programming. They also restricted narrowly the dissemination of the technology to the ruling class. The process by which the telephone was instituted as a universally disseminated network in which anyone is able to call anyone else occurred in a complex, multi-leveled historical articulation in which the technology, the economic structure, the political institutions, the political culture and the mass of the population each played interacting roles (Marvin, 1988: 222ff). A similarly complex history will no doubt accompany the institution of the information superhighway and virtual reality.

In *The Mode of Information* (Poster, 1990) I argued that electronic communications constitute the subject in ways other than that of the major modern institutions. If modernity or the mode of production signifies patterned practices that elicit identities as autonomous and (instrumentally) rational, postmodernity or the mode of information indicates communication practices that constitute subjects as unstable, multiple and diffuse. The information superhighway and virtual reality will extend the mode of information to still further applications, greatly amplifying its diffusion by bringing more practices and more individuals within its pattern of formation. No doubt many modern institutions and practices continue to exist and indeed dominate social space. The mode of information is an emergent phenomenon that affects small but important aspects of everyday life. It certainly does not blanket the advanced industrial societies and has even less presence in less developed nations. The information superhighway and virtual reality may be interpreted through the poststructuralist lens I have used here in relation to the cultural issue of subject constitution. If that is done, the question of the mass media is seen not simply as that of sender/receiver, producer/consumer, ruler/ruled. The shift to a decentralized network of communications makes senders receivers, producers consumers, rulers ruled, upsetting the logic of understanding of the first media age. The step I am suggesting is at least temporarily to abandon that logic and adopt a poststructuralist cultural analysis of modes of subject constitution. This does not answer all the questions opened by the second media age, especially the political ones which at the moment are extremely difficult. But it permits the recognition of an emergent postmodernity and a tentative approach to a political analysis of that cultural system; it permits the beginning of a line of thought that confronts the possibility of a new age, avoiding the continued, limiting, exclusive repetition of the logics of modernity.

Subject constitution in the second media age occurs through the mechanism of interactivity. A technical term referring to two-way communications, "interactivity" has become, by dint of the advertising campaigns of telecommunications corporations, desirable as an end in itself so that its usage can float and be applied in countless contexts having little to do with telecommunications. Yet the phenomenon of communicating at a distance through one's computer, of sending and receiving digitally encoded messages, of being "interactive" has been the most popular application of the Internet. Far more than making purchases or obtaining information electronically, communicating by computer claims the intense interest of countless thousands (Dery, 1993). The use of the Internet to simulate communities far outstrips its function as retail store or reference work. In the words of Howard Rheingold (1993: 61), an enthusiastic Internet user, "I can attest that I and thousands of other cybernauts know that what we are looking for, and finding in some surprising ways, is not just information but instant access to ongoing relationships with a large number of other people." Rheingold terms the network of relations that come into existence on Internet bulletin boards "virtual communities". Places for "meeting" on the Internet, such as "the Well" frequented by Rheingold, provide "areas" for "public" messages, which all subscribers may read, and private "mailbox" services for individual exchanges.

The understanding of these communications is limited by modern categories of analysis. For example, many have interpreted the success of "virtual communities" as an indication that "real" communities are in decline. Internet provides an alternative, these critics contend, to the real thing (Rheingold, 1993: 62). But the opposition "virtual" and "real" community contains serious difficulties. In the case of the nation, generally regarded as the strongest group identification in the modern period and thus perhaps the most "real" community of this era, the role of the imaginary has been fundamental (Anderson, 1983). Pre-electronic media like the newspaper were instrumental in disseminating the sign of the nation and interpellating the subject in relation to it. In even earlier types of community, such as the village, kinship and residence were salient factors of determination. But identification of an individual or family with a specific group was never automatic, natural or given, always turning, as Jean-Luc Nancy (1991: xxxviii) argues, on the production of an "essence" which reduces multiplicity into fixity, obscuring the political process in which "community" is constructed: ". . . the thinking of community as essence . . . is in effect the closure of the political".[8] He rephrases the term community by asking the following question: "How can we be receptive to the *meaning* of our multiple, dispersed, mortally fragmented existences, which nonetheless only make sense by existing in common?" (1991: xi). Community for him then is paradoxically the absence of "community". It is rather the matrix of fragmented identities, each pointing toward the other, which he chooses to term "writing".

Nancy's critique of community in the older sense is crucial to the understanding of the construction of self in the Internet. For his part, Nancy has chosen to deny the significance of new communications technologies, as well as new subaltern subject positions in his understanding of community:

> The emergence and our increasing consciousness of decolonized communities has not profoundly modified [the givens of community], nor has today's growth of unprecedented forms of being-in-common – through channels of information as well as through what is called the "multiracial society" – triggered any genuine renewal of the question of community. (Nancy, 1991: 22)

Nancy denies the relation I am drawing between a postmodern constitution of the subject and bidirectional communications media. The important point however is that in order to do so he first posits the subject as "multiple, dispersed, mortally fragmented" in an ontological statement. To this extent he removes the question of community from the arena of history and politics, the exact purpose of his critique of the essentialist community in the first place. While presenting an effective critique of the essentialist community Nancy reinstates the problem at the level of the subject by ontologizing its inessentialism. My preference is rather to specify the historical emergence of the decentered subject and explore its links with new communications situations.

We may now return to the question of the Internet and its relation to a "virtual community". To restate the issue: the Internet and virtual reality open the possibility of new kinds of interactivity such that the idea of an opposition of real and unreal community is not adequate to specify the differences between modes of bonding, serving instead to obscure the manner of the historical construction of forms of community. In particular, this opposition prevents asking the question of the forms of identity prevalent in various types of community. The notion of a real community, as Nancy shows, presupposes the fixed, stable identities of its members, the exact assumption that Internet communities put into question. Observers of participants in Internet "virtual communities" repeat in near unanimity that long or intense experience with computer-mediated electronic communication is associated with a certain fluidity of identity. Rheingold foresees huge cultural changes as the effect of Internet use on the individual: ". . . are relationships and commitments as we know them even possible in a place where identities are fluid? . . . We reduce and encode our identities as words on a screen, decode and unpack the identities of others" (1993: 61). In bulletin boards like the Well, people connect with strangers without much of the social baggage that divides and alienates. Without visual cues about gender, age, ethnicity and social status, conversations open up in directions that otherwise might be avoided. Participants in these virtual communities often express themselves with little inhibition and dialogues flourish and develop quickly. Yet Rheingold attributes the conviviality of the Well and the extravagant identity transformations of MUDs to "the hunger for community that has followed the disintegration of traditional communities around the world" (1991: 62). Even for this advocate of new communications technologies the concept of a real community regulates his understanding of the new interactivity. While there may be some truth to a perspective that sees "virtual communities" as compensations for the loss of real communities, I prefer to explore the new territory and define its possibilities.

Another aspect to understanding identity in virtual communities is provided by Stone. Her studies of electronic communication systems suggest that participants code "virtual" reality through categories of "normal" reality. They do so by communicating to each other as if they were in physical common space, as if this space were inhabited by bodies, were mappable by Cartesian perspective, and by regarding the interactions as events, as fully significant for the participants' personal histories (Stone, 1992: 618). While treatment of new media by categories developed in relation to earlier ones is hardly new, in this case the overlap serves to draw closer together the two types of ontological status. Virtual communities derive some of their verisimilitude from being treated as if they were plain communities, allowing members to experience communications in cyberspace as if they were embodied social interactions. Just as virtual communities are understood as having the attributes of "real" communities, so "real" communities can be seen to depend on the imaginary: what makes a community vital to its members is their treatment of the communications as meaningful and important. Virtual and real communities mirror each other in chiasmic juxtaposition.

Narratives in Cyberspace

Electronic mail services and bulletin boards are inundated by stories. Individuals appear to enjoy relating narratives to those they have never met and probably never will meet. These narratives often seem to emerge directly from peoples' lives but many no doubt are inventions. The appeal is strong to tell one's tale to others, to many, many others. One observer suggests the novelty of the situation:

> technology is breaking down the notion of few-to-many communications. Some communicators will always be more powerful than others, but the big idea behind cyber-tales is that for the first time the many are talking to the many. Every day, those who can afford the computer equipment and the telephone bills can be their own producers, agents, editors and audiences. Their stories are becoming more and more idiosyncratic, interactive and individualistic, told in different forums to diverse audiences in different ways. (Katz, 1994)

This explosion of narrativity depends upon a technology that is unlike print and unlike the electronic media of the first age: it is cheap, flexible, readily available, quick. It combines the decentralized model of the telephone and its numerous "producers" of messages with the broadcast model's advantage of numerous receivers. Audio (Internet Talk Radio) and video (the World-Wide Web using Mosaic) are being added to text, enhancing considerably the potentials of the new narratives. There is now a "World-Wide Web" which allows the simultaneous transmission of text, images and sound, providing hypertext links as well. The implications of the Web are astounding: film clips and voice readings may be included in "texts" and "authors" may indicate their links as "texts". In addition, other related technologies produce similar decentralizing effects. Such phenomena as "desktop broadcasting", widespread citizen camcorder "reporting", and digital film-making are transgressing the constraints of broadcast oligopolies (*Mondo 2000*, 1993: 34 and 106).

The question of narrative position has been central to the discussion of postmodernity. Jean-François Lyotard has analyzed the change in narrative legitimation structures of the premodern, modern and postmodern epochs. Lyotard (1984) defines the postmodern as an "incredulity" toward metanarratives, especially that of progress and its variants deriving from the Enlightenment. He advocates a turn to the "little story" which validates difference, extols the "unpresentable" and escapes the overbearing logic of instrumentality that derives from the metanarrative of progress. Any effort to relate second media age technologies with the concept of the postmodern must confront Lyotard's skepticism about technology. For Lyotard, it must be recalled, technology itself is fully complicit with *modern* narrativity. For example, he warns of the dangers of "a generalized computerization of society" in which the availability of knowledge is politically dangerous:

> The performativity of an utterance . . . increases proportionally to the amount of information about its referent one has at one's disposal. Thus the growth of power, and its self-legitimation, are now taking the route of data storage and accessibility, and the operativity of information. (Lyotard, 1984: 47)

Information technologies are thus complicit with new tendencies toward totalitarian control, not toward a decentralized, multiple "little narrativity" of postmodern culture.

The question may be raised, then, of the narrative structure of second media age communications: does it or is it likely to promote the proliferation of little narratives or does it invigorate a developing authoritarian technocracy? Lyotard describes the narrative structure of tribal, premodern society as stories that first legitimate institutions, second contain many different forms of language, third are transmitted by senders who are part of the narrative and have heard it before and listeners who are possible senders, fourth construct a nonlinear temporality that foreshortens the past and the present, rendering each repetition of the story strangely concurrent and, most importantly, fifth authorize everyone as a narrator. Modern society, Lyotard argues derives its legitimacy from narratives about science. Within science, language first does not legitimate institutions, second contains the single language form of denotation, third does not confirm addressee as possible sender, fourth gains no validity by being reported, and fifth constructs "diachronic" temporality. These contrasting characteristics may serve, as Lyotard wishes, to indicate the "pragmatics" of language. It would be interesting to analyze the role of technologies in the premodern and modern cases, and especially the change, within the modern, from print to broadcast media.

In any case, for Lyotard, the postmodern little narrative refunctions the pre-modern language game but only in limited ways. Like the tribal myth, the little narrative insists on "the heteromorphous nature of language games" (1984: 66); in short, it validates difference. Unlike older narrative forms, the little narrative emphasizes the role of invention, the indication of the unknown and the unexpected. Lyotard looks to certain developments in the natural sciences for his examples of such postmodern narratives, but we may turn to the Internet and to the developing technology of virtual reality. As we have seen, the Internet seems to encourage the proliferation of stories, local narratives without any totalizing gestures and it places senders and addressees in symmetrical relations. Moreover, these stories and their performance consolidate the "social bond" of the Internet "community", much like the premodern narrative. But invention is central to the Internet, especially in MUDs and virtual reality: the production of the unknown or paralogy, in Lyotard's term, is central to second media age communications. In particular the relation of the utterance to representation is not limited to denotation as in the modern language game of science, and indeed the technology encourages a lightening of the weight of the referent. This is an important basis for the instability of identity in electronic communications, leading to the insertion of the question of the subject and its construction. In this spirit, Katherine Hayles (1993a: 175) defines the "revolutionary potential" of virtual reality as follows: "to expose the presuppositions underlying the social formations of late capitalism and to open new fields of play where the dynamics have not yet rigidified and new kinds of moves are possible".

For the new technologies install the "interface", the face between the faces; the face that insists that we remember that we have "faces", that we have sides that are present at the moment of utterance, that we are not present in any simple or immediate way. The interface has become critical to the success of the Internet. To attain wide appeal, the Internet must not simply be efficient, useful or entertaining: it must present itself in an agreeable manner. The enormous problem for interface design is the fear and hostility humans nourish toward machines and toward a dim recognition of a changing relation toward them, a sharing of space and an inter-dependence (Springer, 1991). The Internet interface must somehow appear "transparent", that is to say, appear not to be an interface, not to come between two alien beings and also seem fascinating, announcing its novelty and encouraging an exploration of the difference of the machinic. The problem of the Internet then is not simply "technological" but para-machinic: to construct a boundary between the human and the machinic that draws the human into the technology, transforming the technology into "used equipment" and the human into a "cyborg", into one meshing with machines.[9]

In Wim Wenders' recent film, *Until the End of the World* (1991), several characters view their own dreams on videotape, becoming so absorbed in what they see that they forget to eat and sleep. The characters sit transfixed before their viewing devices, ignoring everyone around them, disregarding all relations and affairs. Limited to the microworld of their own dreams, the characters are lost in a narcissistic stupor. And yet their total absorption is compelling. Visual representations of the unconscious – no doubt Wenders has film itself in mind – are irresistible compared to everyday reality, a kind of hyperreality.

One can imagine that virtual reality devices will become as compelling as the dream videos in Wenders' film. Virtual reality machines should be able to allow the participant to enter imagined worlds with convincing verisimilitude, releasing immense potentials for fantasy, self-discovery and self-construction. When groups of individuals are able to interact in the same virtual space the possibilities are even more difficult to conceive. One hesitates to suggest that these experiences are commensurate with something that has been termed community. Yet there is every reason to think that virtual reality technologies will develop rapidly and will eventually enable participation through the Internet. Connected to one's home computer one will experience an audiovisual "world" generated from a node somewhere in the Internet and this will include other participants in the same way that today one can communicate with others on bulletin boards in videotext. If such experiences become commonplace, just as viewing television is today, then surely reality will have been multiplied. The continued Western quest for making tools may at that point retrospectively be reinterpreted in relation to its culmination in virtual reality. From the club that extends and replaces the arm to virtual reality in cyberspace, technology has evolved to mime and to multiply, to multiplex and to improve upon the real.

Notes

1   See Agnew (1986) for an analysis of the formation of this subject position and its particular relation to the theater. Habermas (1989) offers a "public sphere" of coffee houses, salons and other agora-like locations, as the arena of the modern subject, while Weber (1958) looks to Calvinist religion for the roots of the same phenomenon.

2   See, for example, the discussion of new "interactive" technologies in the *New York Times* on 19 December 1993. In "The Uncertain Promises of Interactivity", Calvin Sims restricts future innovations to movies on demand, on-line information services, interactive shopping, "participatory programming", video games and conferencing systems for business. He omits electronic mail and its possible expansion to sound and image in networked virtual reality systems.

3   I have not discussed the work of Marshall McLuhan simply for lack of space and also because it is not as directly related to traditions of critical social theory as is Benjamin's, Enzensberger's and Baudrillard's. Also of interest is Kittler (1990a, 1990b).

4   For an excellent essay on the economics of the Internet and its basic structural features see Hal Varian, "Economic FAQs About the Internet", which is available on the Internet at listserver@essential.org (send message: subscribe tap-info [your name]).

5   See also the cautionary tone of Herbert Schiller (1993).

6   Many writers prefer the term "artificial reality" precisely because they want to underscore the privilege of real reality. Needless to say this substitution will not cure the problem.

7   I am indebted to Rob King for making me aware of this piece.

8   See also the response by Blanchot (1988).

9   Hayles (1993b: 60–91) interprets these "different configurations of embodiment, technology and culture" through the binary pattern/randomness rather than presence/absence.

References

Agnew, J. C. (1986) *Worlds Apart: The Market and the Theatre in Anglo-American Thought, 1550–1750*. New York: Cambridge University Press.

Anderson, B. (1983) *Imagined Communities: Reflections on the Origin and Spread of Nationalism*. New York: Verso.

Blanchot, M. (1988) *The Unavowable Community*, trans. Pierre Joris. Barrytown, NY: Station Hill Press.

Bollier, D. (1993) "The Information Superhighway: Roadmap for Renewed Public Purpose", *Tikkun* 8(4): 20–2.

Cooke, K. and D. Lehrer (1993) "The Whole World is Talking", *The Nation* 12 July: 89–90.

Dery, M. (ed.) (1993) "Flame Wars: The Discourse of Cyberculture", *South Atlantic Quarterly* 92(4).

Dibbell, J. (1993) "A Rape in Cyberspace", *The Village Voice* 21 December: 36–42.

Elmer-Dewitt, P. (1993) "Take a Trip into the Future on the Electronic Superhighway", *Time* 12 April: 50–8.

Gilder, G. (1993) "Telecosm: The New Rule of Wireless", *Forbes ASAP29* March: 96, 98–104, 106–9.

Habermas, J. (1989) *The Structural Transformation of the Public Sphere*, trans. Thomas Burger. Cambridge, MA: MIT Press.

Hayles, K. (1993a) "The Seductions of Cyberspace", in V. Conley (ed.) *Rethinking Technologies*. Minneapolis: University of Minnesota Press.

Hayles, K. (1993b) "Virtual Bodies and Flickering Signifiers", *October* 66: 69–91.

Hotz, R. L. (1993) "Computer Code's Security Worries Privacy Watchdogs", *Los Angeles Times* 4 October: A3, A22.

Kapor, M. (1993) "Where Is the Digital Highway Really Heading?: The Case for a Jeffersonian Information Policy", *Wired* 1(3): 53–9, 94.

Katz, J. (1994) "The Tales They Tell in Cyber-Space Are a Whole Other Story", *Los Angeles Times* 23 January: A1, A30.

Kittler, F. (1990a) "Gramophone, Film, Typewriter", *October* 41: 101–18.

Kittler, F. (1990b) *Discourse Networks: 1800/1900*, trans. Michael Metteer. Stanford: Stanford University Press.

Lyotard, J. F. (1984) *The Postmodern Condition: A Report on Knowledge*, trans. Geoff Bennington and Brian Massumi. Minneapolis: University of Minnesota Press.

Marvin, C. (1988) *When Old Technologies Were New: Thinking About Electric Communication in the Late Nineteenth Century*. New York: Oxford.

Mondo 2000 (1993) No. 11.

Nancy, J. L. (1991) *The Inoperative Community*, trans. Peter Conner et al. Minneapolis: University of Minnesota Press.

Poster, M. (1990) *The Mode of Information*. Oxford: Polity Press.

Rheingold, H. (1993) "A Slice of Life in My Virtual Community", in L. Harasim (ed.) *Global Networks: Computers and International Communication*. Cambridge: MIT Press.

Schiller, H. (1993) "The 'Information Highway': Public Way or Private Road?", *The Nation* July 12.

Springer, C. (1991) "The Pleasure of the Interface", *Screen* 32(3): 303–23.

Stone, A. R. (1992) "Virtual Systems", in *Incorporations*, ed. Jonathan Crary and Stanford K. Winter. Cambridge: MIT Press.

Tehranian, M. (forthcoming) "World With/Out Wars: Moral Spaces and the Ethics of Transnational Communication", *The Public* (Ljubljana).

Turner, C. (1994) "Courts Gag Media at Sensational Canada Trial", *Los Angeles Times* May 15: A4.

Weber, M. (1958) *The Protestant Ethic and the Spirit of Capitalism*, trans. Talcott Parsons. New York: Macmillan.

32

Quentin Tarantino's Star Wars?: Digital Cinema, Media Convergence, and Participatory Culture

Henry Jenkins

For me the great hope is now that 8mm video recorders are coming out, people who normally wouldn't make movies are going to be making them. And that one day a little fat girl in Ohio is going be the new Mozart and make a beautiful film with her father's camcorder. For once the so-called professionalism about movies will be destroyed and it will really become an art form.
– Francis Ford Coppola

We're going to empower a writer, somewhere in the world, who doesn't have filmmaking resources at his or her disposal. This is the future of cinema – Star Wars is the catalyst.
– Jason Wishnow, maker of the digital film *Tatooine or Bust*

Maybe you received this digital postcard (figure 32.1) from someone you know during the height of the Monica Lewinsky scandals. Like so much that circulates on the Net, it came without any clear-cut attribution of authorship. The same image now appears on a variety of websites without much indication of its origins. Given such an image's decentralized circulation, we have no way of knowing whether it was seen by more or fewer people than saw the Elian Gonzales spoof of the "Whazzup" commercials or the image of Bill Gates as a Borg from *Star Trek: The Next Generation*. Yet, few of us could be ignorant of the source material it parodies

Figure 32.1 A *Star Wars* poster, modified after the Lewinsky scandal

– the Brothers Hildebrant's famous poster for the original release of *Star Wars*. In this contemporary and somewhat off-color version, Bill Clinton thrusts his power cigar skyward as a scantily clad Monica clings to his leg, her black thong undies barely visible through her translucent white robe. The sinister face of Ken Starr looms ominously in the background. Hillary shields Chelsea's eyes from this frightful spectacle.

This grassroots appropriation of *Star Wars* became part of the huge media phenomenon that surrounded first the release of the digitally enhanced original *Star Wars* trilogy in 1997 and the subsequent release of *The Phantom Menace* in 1999. Spoofs and parodies of *Star Wars* were omnipresent the summer of 1999. The trailer for *Austin Powers II: The Spy Who Shagged Me* toyed with trigger-happy audiences eagerly anticipating their first glimpse of *The Phantom Menace* preview reel. It opened with ominous music, heavy breathing, and a spaceship interior, as a voiceover narrator explained, "Years ago, a battle was fought and an empire was destroyed. Now the saga will continue." The chair revolves around to reveal not the anticipated Darth Vader (or his latter-day counterpart, Darth Maul), but Doctor Evil, who shrugs and says, "You were expecting someone else?" Bowing before the media phenomenon, *Austin Powers* was released with the slogan, "If you see only one movie this summer, see . . . *Star Wars*. If you see two movies, see *Austin Powers*." *Doonesbury* did a series of cartoons depicting the "refuge camps" awaiting entry into the *Star Wars* films. Weird Al Yankovich, who had previously been successful with a music video, "Yoda," offered his own prequel with "The Saga Begins." *Mad TV* ran two spoofs – one which imagined Randy Newman composing feel-good music for the film, while another featured George Lucas as an obnoxious, overweight fan boy who seeks inspiration by dressing in an Ewok costume and who hopes to introduce Jar Jar's aunt "Jar-Jar-Mina" in his next release. David Letterman proposed casting smooth-voiced singer Barry White as Darth Vader. Accepting Harvard's Hasty Pudding Award, Samuel L. Jackson offered his own imitation of how Yoda might have delivered his lines from *Pulp Fiction*. Almost all of us can add many more entries to the list of mass-market spoofs, parodies, and appropriations of the *Star Wars* saga – some aimed at the film's director, some at its fans, others at the content of the series itself, with Jar Jar Binks bashing becoming the order of the day.

I begin with reference to these various commercial spoofs of *Star Wars* as a reminder that such creative reworkings of science fiction film and television are no longer, and perhaps never were, restricted to fan culture, but have become an increasingly central aspect of how contemporary popular culture operates. Too often, fan appropriation and transformation of media content gets marginalized or exoticized, treated as something that people do when they have too much time on their hands. The assumption seems to be made that anyone who would invest so much creative and emotional energy into the products of mass culture must surely have something wrong with them. In this essay, I will take a very different perspective – seeing media fans as active participants within the current media revolution, seeing their cultural products as an important aspect of the digital cinema movement. If many advocates of digital cinema have sought to democratize the means of cultural production, to foster grassroots creativity by opening up the tools of media production and distribution to a broader segment of the general public, then the rapid proliferation of fan-produced *Star Wars* films may represent a significant early success story for that movement. Force Flicks, one of several databases for fan film production, lists almost 300 amateur-produced *Star Wars* films currently in circulation on the web, and identifies an even larger number of such works as "in production." There is a tremendous diversity of theme, approach, and quality represented in this sample of the current state of amateur digital filmmaking. Some of the films have developed enormous cult followings. Amazon.com, the online bookseller, reports that sales of *George Lucas in Love* was outselling *The Phantom Menace* among their video customers, while *Troops* (which offers a Cops-style behind the scene look at the routine experience of stormtroopers serving their hitch on Tatooine) was featured in a two-page spread in *Entertainment Weekly*, and its director, Kevin Rubio, was reported to have attracted offers of production contracts from major studios.

In this essay, I will explore how and why *Star Wars* became, in Jason Wishnow's words, a "catalyst" for amateur digital filmmaking, and what this case study suggests about the future directions popular culture may take. *Star Wars* fan films represent the intersection of two significant cultural trends – the corporate movement towards media convergence and the unleashing of significant new tools which enable the grassroots archiving, annotation, appropriation, and recirculation of media content. These fan films build on longstanding practices of the fan community, but they also reflect the influence of this changed technological environment that has dramatically lowered the costs of film production and distribution. I will argue that this new production and distribution context profoundly alters our understanding of what amateur cinema is and how it intersects with the commercial film industry. In the end, I want to propose the fan-film aesthetic as a significant middle ground between the commercial focus of the new "dot-coms" and the avant-garde aesthetics of the "low-res" film movement, an approach which facilitates grassroots cultural production by building upon our investments in mainstream culture.

Media in Transition: Two Models

Media Convergence

As media critics such as Robert McChesney have noted, the current trend within the entertainment industry has been toward the increased concentration of media ownership into the hands of a smaller and smaller number of transmedia and transnational conglomerates. Horizontal integration, that is, the consolidation of holdings across multiple industries, has displaced the old vertical integration of the Hollywood studios. Companies, such as Viacom and Warners Communication, maintain interests in film, cable, and network television; video, newspapers, and magazines; book publishing and digital media. What emerged are new strategies of content development and distribution designed to increase the "synergy" between the different divisions of the same company. Studios seek content that can move fluidly across media channels. According to the "high concept" logic which has dominated the

American cinema since the 1970s, production decisions privileged films with presold content based on material from other media ("books"); simple, easily summarized narrative "hooks"; and distinctive "looks," broadly defined characters, striking icons, and highly quotable lines.

Initially, this "books, hooks, and looks" approach required the ability to construct ancillary markets for a successful film or television program. Increasingly, however, it becomes difficult to determine which markets are ancillary and which are core to the success of a media narrative. The process may start with any media channel, but a successful product will flow across media until it becomes pervasive within the culture at large – comics into computer games, television shows into films, and so forth. Marsha Kinder has proposed the term "entertainment supersystem" to refer to the series of intertextual references and promotions spawned by any successful product. The industry increasingly refers to *Star Trek* or *Star Wars* as "franchises," using a term that makes clear the commercial stakes in these transactions. This new "franchise" system actively encourages viewers to pursue their interests in media content across various transmission channels, to be alert to the potential for new experiences offered by these various tie-ins.

As a consequence of these new patterns of media ownership and production, there is increasing pressure toward the technological integration of the various content delivery systems, what industry analysts refer to as convergence. Technological convergence is attractive to the media industries because it will open multiple entry points into the consumption process and at the same time, enable consumers to more quickly locate new manifestations of a popular narrative. One may be able to move from watching a television drama to ordering the soundtrack, purchasing videos, or buying products that have been effectively "placed" within the narrative universe.

Such an approach requires the constant development of media content that can provoke strong audience engagement and investment. For this synergy-based strategy to be successful, media audiences must not simply buy an isolated product or experience but rather must buy into a prolonged relationship with a particular narrative universe, which is rich enough and complex enough to sustain their interest over time and thus motivate a succession of consumer choices. This approach encourages studios to be more attentive to audience interests, and studios are using the Net and the Web to directly solicit feedback as well as to monitor unsolicited fan responses to their products.

The strength of this new style of popular culture is that it enables multiple points of entry into the consumption process; the vulnerability is that if audiences fail to engage with the particular content on offer, then that choice has a ripple effect across all of the divisions of the media conglomerate. For every *Batman* that demonstrates the enormous potential of this franchising process, there is a *Dick Tracy* that just about takes the producing company down with it. In such a world, intellectual property, which has proven popular with mass audiences, has enormous economic value, and companies seek to tightly regulate its flow in order to maximize profits and minimize the risk of diluting their trademark and copyright holdings.

Star Wars is, in many ways, the prime example of media convergence at work. Lucas's decision to defer salary for the first *Star Wars* film in favor of maintaining a share of ancillary profits has been widely cited as a turning point in the emergence of this new strategy of media production and distribution. Lucas made a ton of money and Twentieth Century Fox learned a valuable lesson. Kenner's *Star Wars* action figures are thought to have been key in reestablishing the value of media tie-in products in the toy industry, and John Williams's score helped to revitalize the market for soundtrack albums. The rich narrative universe of the *Star Wars* saga provided countless images, icons, and artifacts that could be reproduced in a wide variety of forms and sold to diverse groups of consumers. The serialized structures of the films helped to sustain audience interest across a broad span of time and to provide an opportunity to revitalize it as each new sequel or prequel is released. Despite an almost two-decade gap between the release dates for *Return of the Jedi* and *The Phantom Menace*, Lucasfilm continued to generate profits from its *Star Wars* franchise through the production of original novels and comic books, the distribution of videotapes and audiotapes, the continued marketing of *Star Wars* toys and merchandise, and the maintenance of an elaborate publicity apparatus, including a monthly glossy newsletter for *Star Wars* fans. The careful licensing of the *Star Wars* iconography enabled Lucasfilm to form strategic alliances with a multitude of corporate partners, including fast-food franchises and soft drink bottlers, which sought to both exploit and enlarge public interest in their forthcoming release. As a consequence, by spring 1999, it was impossible to go anywhere without finding yourself face to face with the distinctive personas of Darth Maul, Queen Amidala, or Jar Jar Binks.

This climate of heightened expectations also fostered the production of the various commercial *Star Wars* parodies mentioned earlier, as other media producers sought to "poke fun" at the hype surrounding *Star Wars* phenomenon while tapping into audience awareness of the film's impending release. Letterman's spoofs of *Star Wars* were as much a part of the publicity campaign for the movie as were the appearance of Nathalie Portman or the other film stars on his program. The good-natured trailer of *Austin Powers* played with audience anticipation of the *Star Wars* trailer and became itself a vehicle for creating media buzz about both works.

Participatory Culture

Patterns of media consumption have been profoundly altered by a succession of new media technologies which enable average citizens to participate in the archiving, annotation, appropriation, transformation, and recirculation of media content. Participatory culture refers to the new style of consumerism that emerges in this environment. If media convergence is to become a viable corporate strategy, it will be because consumers have learned new ways to interact with media content. Not surprisingly, participatory culture is running ahead of the technological developments necessary to sustain industrial visions of media convergence and thus making demands on popular culture which the studios are not yet, and perhaps never will be, able to satisfy. The first and foremost demand consumers make is the right to participate in the creation and distribution of media narratives. Media consumers want to become media producers, while media producers want to maintain their traditional dominance over media content.

A history of participatory culture might well start with the photocopier, which quickly became "the people's printing press," paving the way for a broad range of subcultural communities to publish and circulate their perspectives on contemporary society. The videocassette recorder (VCR) enabled consumers to bring the broadcast signal more fully under their control, to build large libraries of personally meaningful media content, and increasingly, gave them tools which facilitated amateur media production. By the early 1990s, media fans were using the VCR to re-edit footage of their favorite television programs to provide raw materials for the production of music videos which enabled them to comment on the relationships between program characters. The availability of low-cost camcorders and, more recently, digital cameras has empowered more and more people to begin to enter directly into the filmmaking process; the power of the camcorder as a means of documentary production was aptly illustrated by the Rodney King video which placed the issue of police brutality in Los Angeles onto the national agenda. Portable technologies, such as the walkman and cell phone, enabled us to carry our media with us from place to place, to create our own "soundtracks" for our real-world experiences, and to see ourselves more and more connected within a networked communications environment. Computer and video games encouraged us to see ourselves as active participants in the world of fiction, to "fight like a Jedi" or to "outshoot Clint Eastwood." Digital photography and audio sampling technologies made it easy to manipulate and rework the sights and sounds of our contemporary media environment, paving the way for new forms of cultural expression, ranging from Photoshop collages to music sampling. These technologies do not simply alter the ways that media are produced or consumed; they also help to break down barriers of entry into the media marketplace. The Net opened up new space for public discussions of media content and the Web became an important showcase for grassroots cultural production. On one of my favorite websites, known as the Refrigerator, parents can scan in their children's artwork and place them on global display. In many ways, the Web has become the digital refrigerator for the "Do-It-Yourself" ("DIY") movement. Prior to the Web, amateurs might write stories, compose music, or make movies, but they had no venue where they could exhibit their works beyond their immediate circles of family and friends. For example, among those "digital movies" indexed by the various *Star Wars* fan websites were Super-8 productions dating back to the original release of *A New Hope* (such as *Star Wars Remake*) but only now reaching a broader audience because of their online circulation. The Web made it possible for alternative media productions of all kinds to gain greater visibility and to move beyond localized publics into much broader circulation.

This ability to exhibit grassroots cultural productions has in turn fostered a new excitement about self-expression and creativity. For some, these grassroots cultural productions are understood as offering a radical alternative to dominant media content, providing space for various minority groups to tell their own stories or to question hegemonic representations of their culture. Groups such as the Goths or the Riot Grrls have been quick to explore these political uses of the Web, as have a variety of racial and ethnic groups. Culture jammers seek to use the power of digital media to call into question the consumerist logic of mass media. Others employ the

Web as a means of getting greater visibility, of attracting public notice as a prelude for entering directly into the commercial media world. The Web has become an important showcase for productions of film school students, for example. Still others understand their cultural productions in the context of building social ties within a "virtual community" defined around shared interests. The pervasiveness of popular culture content has made it a particularly rich basis for forming social ties within the geographically dispersed population of the internet. People who may not ever meet face to face and thus have few real-world connections with each other can tap into the shared framework of popular culture to facilitate communication. Fans were early adopters of all of these media technologies, and as a consequence, their aesthetics and cultural politics have been highly influential in shaping public understanding of the relationship between dominant and grassroots media. Such groups seek not to shut down the corporate apparatus of the mass media but rather to build on their enjoyment of particular media products, to claim affiliation with specific films or television programs, and to use them as inspiration for their own cultural production, social interaction, and intellectual exchange.

As more and more amateur works have entered into circulation via the Web, the result has been a turn back toward a more folk-culture understanding of creativity. Historically, our culture evolved through a collective process of collaboration and elaboration. Folktales, legends, myths, and ballads were built up over time as people added elements that made them more meaningful to their own contexts. The Industrial Revolution resulted in the privatization of culture and the emergence of a concept of intellectual property that assumes that cultural value originates from the original contributions of individual authors. In practice, of course, any act of cultural creation builds on what has come before, borrowing genre conventions and cultural archetypes, if nothing else. The ability of corporations to control their "intellectual property" has had a devastating impact upon the production and circulation of cultural materials, meaning that the general population has come to see themselves primarily as consumers of – rather than participants within – their culture. The mass production of culture has largely displaced the old folk culture, but we have lost the possibility for cultural myths to accrue new meanings and associations over time, resulting in single authorized versions (or at best, corporately controlled efforts to rewrite and "update" the myths of our popular heroes). Our emotional and social investments in culture have not shifted, but new structures of ownership diminish our ability to participate in the creation and interpretation of that culture.

Fans respond to this situation of an increasingly privatized culture by applying the traditional practices of a folk culture to mass culture, treating film or television as if it offered them raw materials for telling their own stories and resources for forging their own communities. Just as the American folk songs of the nineteenth century were often related to issues of work, the American folk culture of the twentieth century speaks to issues of leisure and consumption. Fan culture, thus, represents a participatory culture through which fans explore and question the ideologies of mass culture, speaking from a position sometimes inside and sometimes outside the cultural logic of commercial entertainment. The key difference between fan culture and traditional folk culture doesn't have to do with fan actions but with corporate reactions. Robin Hood, Pecos Bill, John Henry, Coyote, and Br'er Rabbit belonged to the folk. Kirk and Spock, Scully and Mulder, Hans and Chewbacca, or Xena and Gabrielle belong to corporations.

Fan fiction repairs some of the damage caused by the privatization of culture, allowing these potentially rich cultural archetypes to speak to and for a much broader range of social and political visions. Fan fiction helps to broaden the potential interest in a series by pulling its content toward fantasies that are unlikely to gain widespread distribution, tailoring it to cultural niches underrepresented within and underserved by the aired material. In theory, such efforts could increase the commercial value of media products by opening them to new audiences, though producers rarely understand them in those terms.

Consider, for example, this statement made by a fan:

> What I love about fandom is the freedom we have allowed ourselves to create and recreate our characters over and over again. Fanfic rarely sits still. It's like a living, evolving thing, taking on its own life, one story building on another, each writer's reality bouncing off another's and maybe even melding together to form a whole new creation. . . . I find that fandom can be extremely creative because we have the ability to keep changing our characters and giving them a new life over and over. We can kill and resurrect them as often as we like. We can change their personalities and how they react to situations. We can take a character and make him charming and sweet or cold-blooded and cruel. We can give them an infinite, always-changing life rather than the single life of their original creation.

Fans reject the idea of a definitive version produced, authorized, and regulated by some media conglomerate. Instead, fans envision a world where all of us can participate in the creation and circulation of central cultural myths. What is most striking about the quote above is that the right to participate actively in the culture is assumed to be "the freedom we have allowed ourselves," not a privilege granted by a benevolent company. Fans also reject the studio's assumption that intellectual property is a "limited good," to be tightly controlled lest it dilute its value. Instead, they embrace an understanding of intellectual property as "shareware," something that accrues value as it moves across different contexts, gets retold in various ways, attracts multiple audiences, and opens itself up to a proliferation of alternative meanings. Giving up absolute control over intellectual property, they argue, increases its cultural value (if not its economic worth) by encouraging new, creative input and thus enabling us to see familiar characters and plots from fresh perspectives. Media conglomerates often respond to these new forms of participatory culture by seeking to shut them down or reigning in their free play with cultural material. If the media industries understand the new cultural and technological environment as demanding greater audience participation within what one media analyst calls the "experience economy," they seek to tightly structure the terms by which we may interact with their intellectual property, preferring the preprogrammed activities offered by computer games or commercial websites, to the free-form participation represented by fan culture. The conflict between these two paradigms – the corporate-based concept of media convergence and the grassroots-based concept of participatory culture

– will determine the long-term cultural consequences of our current moment of media in transition.

If *Star Wars* was an important ur-text for the new corporate strategy of media convergence, *Star Wars* has also been the focal point of an enormous quantity of grassroots media production, becoming the very embodiment of the new participatory culture. Fans began to write original fiction based on the *Star Wars* characters within a few months of the first film's release, building on an infrastructure for the production and distribution of fanzines that had first grown up around *Star Trek*. Fan writers sustained the production of original *Star Wars* stories throughout the "dark years" when Lucas had seemingly turned his back on his own mythology; and the release of *The Phantom Menace* provoked an enormous wave of new fan stories on the Web.

Grassroots appropriation and transformation of *Star Wars* has not, however, been restricted to media fandom *per se* but has spread across many other sectors of the new DIY culture. Will Brooker, for example, notes the persistence of *Star Wars* references in punk and techno music, British underground comics, novels like Douglas Coupland's *Microserfs*, films like Kevin Smith's *Clerks*, and various punk, thrasher, and slacker zines. Brooker argues that the rebellion depicted in the *Star Wars* films provides a useful model for thinking about the coalition-based cultural politics which define this whole DIY movement. The Empire, Brooker argues, is a "colonizing force" which seeks to impose top-down regimentation and demand conformity to its dictates. The Rebellion is a ragtag coalition of different races and cultures, a temporary alliance based on constant flux and movement from base to base, and dependent upon often decentralized and democratic forms of decision-making.

Encouraged by Lucas's romantic myth about grassroots resistance to controlling institutions, these fans have actively resisted efforts by Lucasfilm to tighten its control over intellectual property. Through the years, Lucasfilm has been one of the most aggressive corporate groups in trying to halt fan cultural production. As early as 1981, Lucasfilm had issued legal notices and warnings to fans who published zines containing sexually explicit stories, while implicitly giving permission to publish non-erotic stories about the characters: "Since all of the *Star Wars* Saga is PG-Rated, any story those publishers print should also be PG. Lucasfilm does not produce any X-Rated *Star Wars* episodes, so why should we be placed in a light where people think we do?" Many fans felt that Lucasfilm was claiming the right to ideologically police their shared "fantasies." Much of the writing of fan erotica was pushed underground by this policy, though it continued to circulate informally. In fall 1997, the Usenet discussion group devoted to *Star Wars* responded to increased traffic sparked by the re-release of the "digitally-enhanced" versions of the original films, creating a separate newsgroup where fans could post and critique original fiction set in the *Star Wars* universe. In a rare action, the Usenet hierarchy vetoed the plan, not even allowing it to be presented for a formal vote, claiming that it promoted "illegal activities," i.e., that net discussions of fan fiction encouraged the violation of Lucasfilm's copyright. Many believe that they made this decision based on a series of "cease and desist" letters issued by Lucasfilm attorneys aimed at shutting down *Star Wars* fan websites or blocking the circulation of fanzines.

Controversy erupted again when, in a shift of position which some felt was more encouraging to fans, Lucasfilm offered *Star Wars* fans free Web space and unique content for their sites, but only under the condition that whatever they created would become the studio's intellectual property. Fan activists were sharply critical of these arrangements, both on political grounds (insisting that it set a precedent which went directly against their own argument that fan fiction constituted a legitimate exercise of their "fair use" rights) and on economic grounds (concerned that such arrangements would make it impossible for them to profit in the future from their creative efforts, noting that some *Star Trek* fan writers had been able to turn their fan fiction into the basis for professional novels).

Yet if studio legal departments still encourage the rigorous enforcement of intellectual property law as a means of regulating the flow of media materials, their creative departments often display a rather different understanding of the intersection between media convergence and participatory culture. The culture industry has its own reasons for encouraging active, rather than passive, modes of consumption. They seek consumers who are mobile, who move between different media channels, and make meaningful links between different manifestations of the same story. Contemporary popular culture has absorbed many aspects of "fan culture" which would have seemed marginal a decade ago. Media producers are consciously building into their texts opportunities for fan elaboration and collaboration – codes to be deciphered, enigmas to be resolved, loose ends to be woven together, teasers and spoilers for upcoming developments – and they leak information to the media which sparks controversy and speculation. Media producers also actively monitor and, in some cases, directly participate in the fan discussions on the Web as a way of measuring grassroots response to their productions. The products which are emerging within this new media culture, then, are more complex in their reliance on back story and foreshadowing, more dependent on audience member's familiarity with character history, more open to serialization, genre-mixing, crossovers between different fictional universes, and more playful in their reliance on in-joke references or spoofing of other media content. As such, these media producers rely on audience access to an archive of episodes on videotape and the informational infrastructure provided by various fan-generated websites and databases. The most adept producers in this new media environment are, in fact, using the Web to reinforce or expand on the information contained in the commercial material.

The old either/or oppositions (co-optation vs. resistance) which have long dominated debates between political economy and cultural studies approaches to media simply do not do justice to the multiple, dynamic, and often contradictory relationships between media convergence and participatory culture. Approaches derived from the study of political economy may, perhaps, provide the best vocabulary for discussing media convergence, while cultural studies language has historically framed our understanding of participatory culture. Neither theoretical tradition, however, can truly speak to what happens at the intersection between the two. The result may be conflict (as in ongoing legal battles for access to or regulation over intellectual property rights), critique (as in the political activism of culture jammers who use participatory culture to break down the dominance of the media industries), challenge (as occurs with the blurring of the lines between professional and amateur products which may now compete for viewer interest if not revenues), collaboration (as in various plans for the incorporation of viewer-generated materials), or recruitment (as when commercial producers use the amateur media as a training ground or testing ground for emerging ideas and talent). In some cases, amateur media draws direct and explicit inspiration from mainstream media content, while in others, commercial culture seeks to absorb or mimic the appropriative aesthetic of participatory culture to reach hip, media-savvy consumers. These complex interrelationships provide the context for public awareness and response to amateur digital cinema production around *Star Wars*. In the next section, I will explore more fully the ways that *Star Wars* fan filmmakers have negotiated a place for themselves somewhere between these two competing trends, trying to co-exist with the mainstream media, while opening up an arena for grassroots creativity.

"Dude, we're gonna be Jedi!"

Maru pays homage to *Star Wars* and is intended to demonstrate to everyone who spent their entire childhood dreaming of wielding a light saber that inspired personal visions can now be realized using tools that are readily available to all of us. Maru was made using a camcorder and a PC with a budget of about $500. . . . Technology and the new media facilitate the articulation and exchange of ideas in ways never before imagined, and we hope that others will harness the power of these tools as we have in order to share their dreams with the world.

– amateur filmmakers Adam Dorr, Erik Benson,
Hien Nguyen, Jon Jones

George Lucas in Love, perhaps the best known of the *Star Wars* parodies, depicts the future media mastermind as a singularly clueless USC film student who can't quite come up with a good idea for his production assignment, despite the fact that he inhabits a realm rich with narrative possibilities. His stoner roommate emerges from behind the hood of his dressing gown and lectures Lucas on "this giant cosmic force, an energy field created by all living things." His sinister next-door neighbor, an arch rival, dresses all in black and breathes with an asthmatic wheeze as he proclaims, "My script is complete. Soon I will rule the entertainment universe." As Lucas races to class, he encounters a brash young friend who brags about his souped-up sports car and his furry-faced sidekick who growls when he hits his head on the hood while trying to do some basic repairs. His professor, a smallish man, babbles cryptic advice, but all of this adds up to little until Lucas meets and falls madly for a beautiful young woman with buns on both sides of her head. Alas, the romance leads to naught as he eventually discovers that she is his long-lost sister.

George Lucas in Love is, of course, a spoof of *Shakespeare in Love* as well as a tribute from one generation of USC film students to another. As co-director Joseph

Levy, a 24-year-old recent graduate from Lucas's Alma Mater, explained, "Lucas is definitely the god of USC. . . . We shot our screening-room scene in the George Lucas Instructional Building – which we're sitting in right now. Lucas is incredibly supportive of student filmmakers and developing their careers and providing facilities for them to be caught up to technology." Yet what makes this film so endearing is the way that it pulls Lucas down to the same level of countless other amateur filmmakers and in so doing, helps to blur the line between the fantastical realm of space opera ("A long, long time ago in a galaxy far, far away") and the familiar realm of everyday life (the world of stoner roommates, snotty neighbors, and incomprehensible professors). Its protagonist is hapless in love, clueless at filmmaking, yet somehow he manages to pull it all together and produce one of the top-grossing motion pictures of all time. *George Lucas in Love* offers us a portrait of the artist as a young geek.

One might contrast this rather down-to-earth representation of Lucas – the auteur as amateur – with the way fan filmmaker Evan Mather's website constructs the amateur as an emergent auteur. Along one column of the site can be found a filmography, listing all of Mather's productions going back to high school, as well as a listing of the various newspapers, magazines, websites, television and radio stations which have covered his work – *La Republica*, *Le Monde*, the *New York Times*, *Wired*, *Entertainment Weekly*, *CNN*, *NPR*, and so forth. Another sidebar provides up-to-the-moment information about his works in progress. Elsewhere, you can see news of the various film festival screenings of his films and whatever awards they have won. A tongue-in-cheek manifesto outlines his views on digital filmmaking: "... *no dialogue* ... *no narration* ... *soundtrack must be monaural* ... *length of credits may not exceed 1/20 the length of the film* ... *nonverbal human or animal utterances are permitted* ... *nonsense sounds whilst permitted are discouraged* ... *all credits and captions must be in both English and French whilst the type size of the French title may be no greater in height than 1/3 the height of the English* ..." More than 19 digital films are featured with photographs, descriptions, and links that enable you to download them in multiple formats. Another link allows you to call up a PDF file reproducing a glossy full-color, professionally-designed brochure documenting the making of his most recent work, *Les Pantless Menace*, which includes close-ups of various props and settings, reproductions of stills, score sheets, and storyboards, and detailed explanations of how he was able to do the special effects, soundtrack, and editing for the film. We learn, for example, that some of the dialogue was taken directly from Commtech chips that were embedded within Hasbro *Star Wars* toys. A biography provides some background: "Evan Mather spent much of his childhood running around south Louisiana with an eight-millimeter silent camera staging hitchhikings and assorted buggery. . . . As a landscape architect, Mr. Mather spends his days designing a variety of urban and park environments in the Seattle area. By night, Mr. Mather explores the realm of digital cinema and is the renowned creator of short films which fuse traditional hand drawn and stop motion animation techniques with the flexibility and realism of computer generated special effects."

The self-promotional aspects of Mather's site are far from unique. The Force. Net Fan Theater, for example, offers amateur directors a chance to offer their own commentary on the production and thematic ambitions of their movies. The creators of *When Senators Attack IV*, for example, give "comprehensive scene-by-scene commentary" on their film: "Over the next 90 pages or so, you'll receive an insight into what we were thinking when we made a particular shot, what methods we used, explanations to some of the more puzzling scenes, and anything else that comes to mind." Such materials often constitute a conscious parodying of the tendency of recent DVD releases to include alternative scenes, cut footage, storyboards, and director's commentary. Many of the websites provide information about fan films under production or may even include preliminary footage, storyboards, and trailers for films that may never be completed. Almost all of the amateur filmmakers have developed their own posters and advertising images for their productions, taking advantage of new Pagemaker and Photoshop software packages that make it easy to manipulate and rearrange images using the home computer. In many cases, the fan filmmakers often produce elaborate trailers, complete with advertising catchphrases.

Some of these materials serve useful functions within amateur film culture. The Making-of articles which are found on so many of the fan websites enable a sharing of technical advice; trading such information helps to improve the overall quality of work within the community. The trailers also respond to the specific challenges of the Web as a distribution channel: it can take hours to download relatively long digital movies, and as a consequence, the shorter, lower-resolution trailers (often distributed in a streaming video format) allow would-be viewers a chance to glimpse the work and determine if it is worth the effort. Yet, these mechanisms of self-promotion move beyond what would be required to support a functional network for amateur film distribution, suggesting that the fans, too, have come to understand that the art of "high concept" filmmaking (and the franchise system it supports) depends as much on the art of advertising and marketing as on the art of storytelling.

Many of the fans, after all, got their first glimpse of footage from *The Phantom Menace* by downloading the much-publicized trailer. In many cases, fan parodies of the trailer started to appear in the months during which fans were eagerly awaiting a chance to see the film itself. In some early examples, fans simply redubbed the original trailer with alternative soundtracks; in other cases, they remade the trailer shot-by-shot. For example, downloading the trailer inspired Ayaz Asif to produce a parody employing characters taken from *South Park*. When an acquaintance, Ted Bracewell, sent him a wallpaper he had drawn depicting *South Park* characters in *Star Wars* garb, the two decided to collaborate, resulting in a quickly made trailer for *Park Wars: The Little Menace*, then for a more elaborately-made "special edition," and then for a series of other shorts based on the *Star Wars* version of the *South Park* characters. The production received such media interest, including an interview with Asif during a Sci-Fi Channel documentary, that the young filmmakers were ultimately invited to air it on Comedy Central, the same network which produced Trey Parker and Matt Stone's series.

Trailervision.com pushes fan cinema's fascination with the trailer format to its logical extreme, releasing a trailer each Monday for a non-existent film. In some cases, these trailers for spoof commercial films which hit the theaters that same week, including *The Jar Jar Binks Project*, *I Know What You'll Want to Do Next Summer*, *The*

Wimp Club, *Scam 3*, and *American Booty*. These spoof trailers are, in some senses, the perfect genre for the current state of digital cinema – short, pithy, reflecting the amateur filmmaker's self-conscious relationship to commercial media, and recognizable by a mass audience who can be assumed to be familiar with the material that inspired them. These spoof trailers enable amateur and aspiring filmmakers to surf the publicity generated by a current release and thus to get media coverage (as was the case with a surprising number of the *Star Wars* spoofs) or to draw audiences already worked up about the commercial product.

All of this publicity surrounding the *Star Wars* parodies serves as a reminder of what is one of the most distinctive qualities of these amateur films – the fact that they are so public. Mather, for example, reports, "Since I started keeping track in February 1998, this site has been visited by over a half-million people from all seven continents, including such faraway places as Antarctica, Iran, San Marino . . . and Canada." The idea that amateur filmmakers could develop such a global following runs counter to the historical marginalization of grassroots media production.

In her book *Reel Families: A Social History of Amateur Film*, Patricia R. Zimmerman offers a compelling history of amateur filmmaking in the United States, examining the intersection between nonprofessional film production and the Hollywood entertainment system. As Zimmerman notes, a variety of critics and theorists, including Harry Potempkin in the 1920s, Maya Deren in the 1950s, Jonas Mekas and George Kuchar in the 1960s, and Hans Magnus Enzensberger in the 1970s, had identified a radical potential in broadening popular access to the cinematic apparatus, fostering a new public consciousness about how media images are constructed and opening a space for alternative experimentation and personal expression outside of the industrial context of the studio system. Amateur film production emerged alongside the first moving pictures. Tom Gunning has argued that the Lumière Brothers's shorts were best understood within a context of amateur photography in France, while Zimmerman points to the ways that amateur theater movements in the United States, as well as a prevailing entrepreneurial spirit, provided a base of support of amateur filmmaking efforts in the 1910s. However, the amateur film has remained, first and foremost, the "home movie," in several senses of the term: first, amateur films were exhibited primarily in private (and most often, domestic) spaces lacking any viable channel of distribution to a larger public; second, amateur films were most often documentaries of domestic and family life rather than attempts to make fictional or avant-garde films; and third, amateur films were perceived to be technically flawed and of marginal interest beyond the immediate family. Jokes and cartoons about the painfulness of being subjected to someone else's home movies are pervasive in our culture and represent a devaluing of the potential for an amateur cinema movement. Zimmerman cites a range of different critical appraisals which stressed the artlessness and spontaneity of amateur film in contrast with the technical polish and aesthetic sophistication of commercial films. She concludes, "[Amateur film] was gradually squeezed into the nuclear family. Technical standards, aesthetic norms, socialization pressures and political goals derailed its cultural construction into a privatized, almost silly, hobby." Writing in the early 1990s, Zimmerman saw little reason to believe that the camcorder and the VCR would significantly alter this situation, suggesting that the medium's technical limitations made it hard for amateurs to edit their films and that the only public means of exhibition were controlled by commercial media-makers (as in programs such as *America's Funniest Home Videos*).

Digital filmmaking alters many of the conditions which Zimmerman felt had led to the marginalization of previous amateur filmmaking efforts – the Web provides an exhibition outlet which moves amateur filmmaking from private into public space; digital editing is far simpler than editing Super-8 or video and thus opens up a space for amateur artists to more directly reshape their material; the home PC has even enabled the amateur filmmaker to directly mimic the special effects associated with Hollywood blockbusters like *Star Wars*. As a consequence, digital cinema consti-tutes a new chapter in the complex history of interactions between amateur filmmakers and the commercial media. These films remain amateur, in the sense that they are made on low budgets, produced and distributed in noncommercial contexts, and generated by nonprofessional filmmakers (albeit often by people who want entry into the professional sphere), yet, many of the other classic markers of amateur film production have disappeared. No longer home movies, these films are public movies – public in that from the start, they are intended for audiences beyond the filmmaker's immediate circle of friends and acquaintances; public in their content, which involves the reworking of personal concerns into the shared cultural framework provided by popular mythologies; and public in their aesthetic focus on existing in dialogue with the commercial cinema (rather than existing outside of the Hollywood system altogether).

Digital filmmakers tackled the challenge of making *Star Wars* movies for many different reasons. *Kid Wars* director Dana Smith is a 14-year-old who had recently acquired a camcorder and decided to stage scenes from *Star Wars* involving his younger brother and his friends, who armed themselves for battle with squirt guns and Nerf weapons. *The Jedi Who Loves Me* was shot by the members of a wedding party and intended as a tribute to the bride and groom, who were *Star Wars* fans. Some films – such as *Macbeth* – were school projects. Two high-school students – Bievenido Concepcion and Don Fitz-Roy – shot the film, which creatively blurs the lines between Lucas and Shakespeare, for their high-school advanced-placement English class. They staged light saber battles down the school hallway, though the principal was concerned about potential damage to lockers; the Millennium Falcon lifted off from the gym, though they had to composite it over the cheerleaders who were rehearsing the day they shot that particular sequence. Still other films emerged as collective projects for various *Star Wars* fan clubs. *Boba Fett: Bounty Trail*, for example, was filmed for a competition hosted by a Melbourne, Australia, Lucasfilm convention. Each cast member made their own costumes, building on previous experience with science fiction masquerades and costume contests. The film's stiffest competition came from *Dark Redemption*, a production of the Sydney fan com-munity, which featured a light-saber-waving female protagonist, Mara Jade. Their personal motives for making such films are of secondary interest, however, once they are distributed on the Web. If such films are attracting worldwide interest, it is not because we all care whether or not Bievenido Concepcion and Don Fitz-Roy made a good grade on their Shakespeare assignment; we are unlikely to know any of the members of the wedding party that made *The Jedi That Loved Me*. Rather, what motivates faraway viewers to watch such films is our shared investments in the *Star Wars* universe. These amateur filmmakers have reframed their personal experiences or interests within the context of a popular culture mythology that is known around the world.

In a very tangible sense, digital filmmaking has blurred the line between amateur and professional, with films made for minuscule budgets duplicating special effects which had cost a small fortune to generate only a decade earlier. Amateur filmmakers can make pod racers skim along the surface of the ocean or landspeeders scatter dust as they zoom across the desert. They can make laser beams shoot out of ships and explode things before our eyes. Several fans tried their hands at duplicating Jar Jar's character animation and inserting him into their own movies with varying degrees of success. (One filmmaker spoofed the defects of his own work, having Jar Jar explain that he took on a different accent for his part in Lucas's movie and suggesting that he had recently undergone a nose job.) The light saber battle, however, has become the gold standard of amateur filmmaking, with almost every filmmaker compelled to demonstrate his or her ability to achieve this particular effect. Many of the *Star Wars* shorts, in fact, consist of little more than light saber battles staged in Suburban rec-rooms and basements, in empty lots, in the hallways of local schools, inside shopping malls or more exotically against the backdrop of medieval ruins (shot during vacations).

As amateur filmmakers are quick to note, Lucas and Steven Spielberg both made Super-8 fiction films as teenagers and saw this experience as a major influence on their subsequent work. Although these films have not been made available to the general public, some of them have been discussed in detail in various biographies and magazine profiles. These "movie brat" filmmakers have been quick to embrace the potentials of digital filmmaking, not simply as a means of lowering production costs for their own films, but also as a training ground for new talent. Lucas, for example, told *Wired* magazine, "Some of the special effects that we redid for *Star Wars* were done on a Macintosh, on a laptop, in a couple of hours. . . . I could have very easily shot the *Young Indy* TV series on Hi-8. . . . So you can get a Hi-8 camera for a few thousand bucks, more for the software and the computer for less than $10,000 you have a movie studio. There's nothing to stop you from doing something provocative and significant in that medium." Elsewhere, he has paid tribute to several of the fan filmmakers, including Kevin Rubio (the director of *Troops*) and Joe Nussbaum (the director of *George Lucas in Love*).

Lucas's rhetoric about the potentials of digital filmmaking seems to have captured the imaginations of amateur filmmakers and they are struggling to confront the master on his own ground, to use digital cinema to create a far more vivid version of their childhood fantasies. As Clay Kronke, a Texas A&M University undergraduate who made *The New World*, explained, "This film has been a labor of love. A venture into a new medium. . . . I've always loved light sabers and the mythos of the Jedi and after getting my hands on some software that would allow me to actually become what I had once only admired at a distance, a vague idea soon started becoming a reality. . . . Dude, we're gonna be Jedi." Kronke openly celebrates the fact that he made the film on a $26.79 budget with most of the props and costumes part of their preexisting collections of *Star Wars* paraphernalia, that the biggest problem they faced on the set was that their plastic light sabers kept breaking after they clashed them together too often, and that those sound effects he wasn't able to borrow from a *Phantom Menace* PC game were "follied around my apartment, including the sound of a coat hanger against a metal flashlight, my microwave door, and myself falling on the floor several times."

The amateur's pride in recreating professional-quality special effects always seems to compete with a recognition of the enormous gap between their own productions and the big-budget Hollywood film they are mimicking. Scholars and critics writing about third-world filmmaking have productively described those films as an "imperfect cinema," noting the ways that filmmakers have had to deal with low budgets and limited access to high-tech production facilities, making it impossible to compete with Hollywood on its own terms. Instead, these filmmakers have made a virtue out of their limitations, often spoofing or parodying Hollywood genre conventions and stylistic norms through films that are intentionally crude or ragged in style. The abruptness in editing, the roughness of camera movement, the grittiness of film stock, and the unevenness of lighting have become markers of authenticity, a kind of direct challenge to the polished look of a big-budget screen production. These amateur filmmakers have also recognized and made their peace with the fact that digital cinema is, in some senses, an "imperfect cinema," with the small and grainy images a poor substitute for the larger-than-life qualities of Lucas's original films when projected on a big screen with Dolby Surroundsound. The trailer for the *Battle of the Bedroom* promises "lots of dodgy special effects," while the team that made *When Senators Attack* chose to call themselves Ultracheese Ltd. In some cases, the films are truly slapdash, relishing their sloppy special effects, embarrassing delivery, and salvage-store costumes. *The Throne Room*, for example, brags that it was shot and edited in only 30 minutes, and it shows. Two hammy adolescents cut up in-home movie footage clearly shot in their living room and inserted into the *Throne Room* material from *A New Hope* to suggest their flirtation with Princess Leia. In others, the productions are quite polished, but the filmmakers still take pleasure in showing the seams. Setting its story "a long, long time ago in a galaxy far cheaper than this one," Keri Llewellyn's technically-accomplished *Star Wars* reproduces the assault on the Death Star, using origami-folded paper TIE fighters and a basketball painted white as a stand-in for the Death Star. As the Death Star bursts into flames, we hear a loud boink as the elastic string holding it in space snaps and it falls out of the frame.

If the third-world filmmakers saw "imperfect cinema" as the basis for an implicit, and often very explicit, critique of the ideologies and market forces behind the Hollywood Blockbuster, and saw their parodies of American genre films as helping to "destroy the very toys of mystification," no such radical goal governs the production of these amateur films. They have, indeed, turned toward parody as the most effective genre for negotiating between these competing desires to reproduce, not to destroy, the special effects at the heart of the contemporary blockbuster and to acknowledge their own amateur status. Yet, their parody is almost always affectionate and rarely attempts to make an explicit political statement.

A notable exception may be *Tie-Tanic*, which directly references the huge corporate apparatus behind *Star Wars*'s success and calls into question the franchising of contemporary popular culture. The filmmaker, John Bunt, redubbed a sequence from the original *Star Wars* film depicting a conference between Darth Vader, Grand Moff Tarkin, and other imperial forces so that it now represented a Lucasfilm marketing meeting as corporate executives plot to rob consumers of their entertainment dollars. During a period of "nostalgic consumption" the *Star Wars* trilogy has regained its bid to be the highest grossing box-office success of all time, but remains potentially vulnerable to challenge while the producers are nervously awaiting the completion of the prequels. The slow deployment of trailers can only hold the audience's attention for so long in an environment of competing blockbusters. While the studio executives are convinced that "talking pigs will hold the mouse-lovers in mind," the real point of vulnerability is teenage girls: "If the rebels arouse sympathy and pathos in adolescent girls, it is possible – however unlikely – that they might find a market and exploit it." Darth Vader warns them that "the ability to control the medium for twenty years is insignificant next to the power of a good chick flick," only to be dismissed, "don't try to frighten us with your demographic ways, Lord Vader." Yet, Grand Moff Tarkin heeds his advice and dispatches him to deal with all challenges to this market segment. In a spectacular finale, which mixes and matches footage, sometimes within the same composite image, from *Star Wars* and *Titanic*, Vader's stormtroopers and TIE fighters open fire on the luxury liner. In several remarkable shots, we see R2D2, C-3PO, and a flaming Ewok among the terrified passengers flying from the sinking ship, and watch a TIE fighter swoop down and blow up one of the escaping lifeboats. Rarely has the cutthroat competition between media conglomerates been depicted with such vivid and witty images! Yet, such an overt – and still pretty tame – critique of market forces is the exception rather than the rule.

More often, these amateur filmmakers see themselves as actively promoting media texts that they admire. For example, *Shadows of the Empire* is an unauthorized fan-made adaptation of Steve Perry's commercial *Star Wars* novel. Perry's original novel explored events that occurred between the end of *Empire Strikes Back* and the opening moments of *Return of the Jedi*. *Shadows of the Empire* has proven especially popular with *Star Wars* fans because it pays significant attention to the bounty hunter, Boba Fett, a character relatively marginal to the original films but central to the fan culture. Frustrated that this novel had never been adapted to the screen, fan filmmakers Jeff Hendrich and Bob Branch created their own serialization of the story: "We pooled every *Star Wars* action-figure and toy that we could beg, borrow or steal to make up the cast of the film. The occasional special guest toy stands in for the characters we just couldn't find and as extras in the crowd scenes." Though the adaptation was unauthorized, it nevertheless follows the logic of the franchise system itself.

The Qui-Gon Show aptly suggests the blurring between professional and fan efforts which occurs in this context. The script emerged as part of AtomFilms.com's "Makin'

Wookie" competition, a commercially-sponsored contest which attracted more than 300 amateur and semi-professional entries, including such promising titles as *Mos Angeles*, *The Real World – Tatooine*, *Springer Wars*, *Star Wars: Close Encounters*, and *Wookie Nights*. Atomfilms then provided a budget for several of the more acclaimed fan filmmakers, including Jason Wishnow and Evan Mather, to produce a short based on Robert Fyvolent's contest-winning script. As with *The Qui-Gon Show*, many of the films have been distributed through the new commercial sites devoted to digital cinema, and in several notable cases have been released on commercial video.

Even in the absence of such direct commercial connections, the mass marketing of *Star Wars* inadvertently provided many of the resources needed to support these productions. The amateur filmmakers often make use of commercially available costumes and props, sample music from the soundtrack album and sounds of *Star Wars* videos or computer games, and draw advice on special effects techniques from television documentaries and mass-market magazines. For example, the makers of *Duel* described the sources for their soundtrack: "We sampled most of the light saber sounds from the *Empire Strikes Back* Special Edition laserdisc, and a few from *A New Hope*. Jedi was mostly useless to us, as the light saber battles in the film are always accompanied by music. The kicking sounds are really punch sounds from *Raiders of the Lost Ark*, and there's one sound – hideous running across the sand – that we got from *Lawrence of Arabia*. Music, of course, comes from the *Phantom Menace* soundtrack." By contrast, some filmmakers made use of images from the films themselves, but added soundtracks from other sources. *Stooge Wars*, for example, juxtaposes footage of Darth Vader and the stormtroopers with sounds and dialogue sampled from *I'll Never Heil Again*, a Three Stooges short which featured Moe as Hitler.

More broadly, the availability of these various ancillary products has encouraged these filmmakers, since childhood, to construct their own fantasies within the *Star Wars* universe. As one fan critic explained, "Odds are if you were a kid in the seventies, you probably fought in schoolyards over who would play Han, lost a Wookie action figure in your backyard and dreamed of firing that last shot on the Death Star. And probably your daydreams and conversations weren't about William Wallace, Robin Hood or Odysseus, but, instead, light saber battles, frozen men and forgotten fathers. In other words, we talked about our legend." Lucasfilm and Kenner may have initially understood the *Star Wars* action figures as commodities, but their cultural effects go much deeper. The action figures provided this generation with some of their earliest avatars, encouraging them to assume the role of a Jedi Knight or an intergalactic bounty hunter, enabling them to physically manipulate the characters and props in order to construct their own stories. Fans, for example, note that the Boba Fett action figure, far more than the character's small role in the trilogy, helped to make this character a favorite among digital filmmakers. The fans, as children, had fleshed out Boba Fett's intentionally murky character, giving him (or her) a personality, motives, goals, and conflicts, which helped to inspire the plots of a number of the amateur movies.

Not surprisingly, a significant number of filmmakers in their late teens and early twenties have turned toward those action figures as resources for their first production efforts. *Toy Wars* producers Aaron Halon and Jason VandenBerghe have launched an ambitious plan to produce a shot-by-shot remake of *Star Wars: The New Hope* cast entirely with action figures. Other filmmakers mix and match action figures from multiple fictional universes to create new works. For example, *Battle of the Bedroom* (Scott Middlebrook) teams Princess Leia and *Tomb Raider*'s Lara Croft against the Imperial stormtroopers in a battle that rocks a suburban home to its foundation. The Enterprise arrives with a well-timed message of peace, provoking combatants on both sides to open fire and blast the federation starship out of the skies. Other filmmakers have made films using the Lego *Star Wars* construction kits, though these materials have proven less flexible in their movements and thus narrow the range of narrative options. To date, most Lego movies have been short light saber battles. The Lego blocks, however, have proven to be extremely useful for building sets and other props.

These action figure movies require constant resourcefulness on the part of the amateur filmmakers. Damon Wellner and Sebastian O'Brien, two self-proclaimed "action figure nerds" from Cambridge, MA, formed Probot Productions with the goal of "making toys as alive as they seemed in childhood." Probot has made several action figure movies, including the 40-minute-long *Star Wars* epic, *Prequel: Revenge of the Snaggletooth* (which they bill as an "homage to the franchise that redefined Movie Merchandi$ing") and *Aliens 5* ("In space, no one can hear you playing with toys"). The Probot website offers this explanation of their production process:

> The first thing you need to know about Probot Productions is that we're broke. We spend all our $$$ on toys. This leaves a very small budget for special effects, so we literally have to work with what we can find in the garbage. You may be surprised at what you can create with a video camera and some simple household items. . . . If you have seen Aliens 5, you may remember Ripley and Bishop running down the computer-generated hallways of the space ship. . . . This effect was done simply by placing the camera directly in front of a TV, having one person holding the action figures up in front of the screen and another person playing the Alien vs. Predator video game. Any *Doom*-type 3/D environment game would work for this effect. It works so well because the video game is a "virtual-set," a HUGE 3/D environment in which you can easily shoot from any angle, and even mock complex camera movements. And video game graphics are just getting better and better! . . . We used a lot of pyrotechnics in the film, and had a fire extinguisher on the set at all times. . . . We used pump-action hairspray (not aerosol!!) and a lighter to create our flame-thrower effect. Please don't burn your house down making your movie. . . . For sets we used a breadbox, a ventilation tube from a dryer, cardboard boxes, a discarded piece from a vending machine, and milk crates. Large Styrofoam pieces from stereo component boxes work very well to create spaceship-like environments!

Despite such primitive working conditions, Probot has been able to mimic the original film's light saber battles, space weaponry, and holographic images.

No digital filmmaker has pushed the aesthetics of the action figure as far as Evan Mather. Mather's films, such as *Godzilla Versus Disco Lando*, *Kung-Fu Kenobi's Big Adventure*, and *Quentin Tarantino's Star Wars*, represent a no-holds-barred romp through contemporary popular culture. The rock-'em sock-'em action of *Kung-Fu Kenobi's Big Adventure* takes place against the backdrop of settings sampled from the film, drawn by hand, or built from Lego blocks, with the eclectic and evocative soundtrack borrowed from Neil Diamond, *Mission Impossible, Pee-Wee's Big Adventure*, and *Charlie Brown's Christmas Special*. Dialogue in Mather's movies is often sampled from the original films or elsewhere in popular culture. *Disco Lando* puts the moves on everyone from Admiral Ackbar to Jabba's blue-skinned dancing girl, and all of his pick-up lines come from the soundtrack of *The Empire Strikes Back*. Mace Windu "gets medieval" on the Jedi Council, delivering Samuel L. Jackson's lines from *Pulp Fiction* before shooting up the place. The camera focuses on the bald head of a dying Darth Vader as he gasps "rosebud." Rebels and stormtroopers battle it out on the snowy landscape of Hoth while cheery yuletide music plays in the background.

Literary critic Lois Rostow Kuznets has discussed the recurrent motif of toys coming to life across several centuries of children's literature, noting that such stories provide a variety of functions for their readers and authors: "Toy characters embody the secrets of the night: they inhabit a secret, sexual, sensual world, one that exists in closed toy shops, under Christmas trees, and behind the doors of dollhouses – and those of our parents' bedrooms. This is an uncanny (in Freudian terms) world of adult mysteries and domestic intrigue. It can be a marginal, liminal, potentially carnival world." Mather and the other action figure filmmakers explore the secrets of the night, blurring the boundaries between different fictional universes, playfully transgressing the family values of the original *Star Wars* films, to encourage our carnivalesque play with their molded plastic protagonists. The humor is often scatological. Yoda eats too many Banta Beans and farts repeatedly in Obi-Wan's face. A naked Barbie spews green vomit into a commode. His characters belch, fart, and barf with total abandon, as they punch, kick, and pummel each other with little or no provocation. *Disco Lando* climaxes with a bloody fistfight between Godzilla and the Virgin Mary. And, Mather loves to insinuate tabloid-style secret lives for the various characters. Obi-Wan wakes up in bed snuggling with Lobot. Luke Skywalker enjoys dressing in Princess Leia's skimpy slavegirl costume. As for Leia, Mather shows her smooching with her brother Luke, and then pulls back to show a whole lineup of panting aliens waiting their turn for the Princess.

Apart from their anarchic humor and rapid-fire pace, Mather's films stand out because of their visual sophistication. In some cases, Mather deftly pastiches the visual styles of contemporary filmmakers, especially Tarantino. Moreover, Mather's own frenetic style has become increasingly distinguished across the body of his works, constantly experimenting with different forms of animation, flashing or masked images, and dynamic camera movements. Mather has made a virtue of his materials, using the plastic qualities of the action figures to justify a movement into a brightly colored and totally surreal *mise-en-scène*.

Yet, if the action figure filmmakers have developed an aesthetic based on their appropriation of materials from the mainstream media, then the mainstream media has been quick to imitate that aesthetic. Nickelodeon's *Action League Now*, for example, has a regular cast of characters consisting of mismatched dolls and mutilated action figures. In some cases, their faces have been melted or mangled through inappropriate play. One protagonist has no clothes. They come in various size scales, suggesting the collision of the different narrative universes that characterize children's action figure play. Recurring gags involve the smashing of brittle characters or dogs gnawing on and mutilating the protagonists, situations all too common in domestic play. MTV's *Celebrity Death Match* creates its action figures using claymation, staging World Wrestling Federation-style bouts between various celebrities, some likely (Monica Lewinsky against Hillary Clinton), some simply bizarre (the rock star formerly known as Prince against Prince Charles). Screenwriter/Director Steve Oedekerk (*Ace Ventura 2*, *The Nutty Professor*, *Patch Adams*) produced *ThumbWars* using thumbs, dressed in elaborate costumes, as his primary performers, and then digitally adding on facial features and expressions. UPN aired the decisively low-tech and low-humor result the week the *Star Wars* prequel opened in the theaters. It is in the context of such unlikely cult television productions that it becomes plausible to see the creation of a high-quality fan film for Web distribution as a "try-out" for gaining access into the media industries.

We are witnessing the emergence of an elaborate feedback loop between the emerging "DIY" aesthetics of participatory culture and the mainstream industry. The Web represents a site of experimentation and innovation, where amateurs test the waters, developing new practices, themes, and generating materials which may well attract cult followings on their own terms. The most commercially viable of those practices are then absorbed into the mainstream media, either directly through the hiring of new talent or the development of television, video, or big-screen works based on those materials, or indirectly, through a second-order imitation of the same aesthetic and thematic qualities. In return, the mainstream media materials may provide inspiration for subsequent amateur efforts, which, in turn, push popular culture in new directions. In such a world, fan works can no longer be understood as simply derivative of mainstream materials but must be understood as themselves open to appropriation and reworking by the media industries.

This process is aptly illustrated by considering the work of popular artists like Kevin Smith, Quentin Tarantino, Mike Judge, Matt Groening, and Kevin Williamson, whose films and television series reflect this mainstreaming of fan aesthetics and politics. Their works often deal explicitly with the process of forming one's own mythology using images borrowed from the mass media. One of the protagonists of *Pulp Fiction*, for example, decides at the end that he wants to "wander the earth" like Kane in television's *Kung Fu*. *Reservoir Dogs* opens with a five-minute discussion of the erotic connotations of Madonna's "Like A Virgin," defining the characters first and foremost through their relationships to popular culture. Characters in *Chasing Amy* engage in animated debates and speculations about the sexuality of the various teens in the *Archie* comics, while *Dazed and Confused* opens with the scene of high-school students trying to recall as many different episodes of *Gilligan's Island* as they can, before one of the women offers a devastating critique of how the series builds upon the iconography of male pornography. Kevin Smith's films make recurring in-joke references to *Star Wars*, including a debate about the ethical obligations of the independent contractors who worked on the Death Star (*Clerks*), a comic episode when Silent Bob becomes convinced that he can actually perform Jedi mind tricks (*Mall Rats*), and a long rant about the "blackness" of Darth Vader (*Chasing Amy*); Smith devotes an entire issue of his *Clerks* comic-book to various characters's attempts to corner the market on collectible *Star Wars* action figures.

The protagonist of Williamson's television series, *Dawson's Creek*, decorates his room with posters for Steven Spielberg films, routinely discusses and critiques classic and contemporary films with the other characters on the series, and draws inspiration from them for the creation of his own videos. Tarantino's whole aesthetic seems to have emerged from his formative experiences working at a video store. In such an environment, older and newer films are more or less equally accessible; some movie is always playing on the monitor and providing a background for everyday interactions. These video store experiences encourage a somewhat scrambled but aesthetically productive relationship to film history. Tarantino, Smith, Williamson, and their contemporaries make films that attract the interests of other video store habitués, much as earlier generations of filmmakers – the French New Wave or the American Movie Brats – made movies for other cinéastes. Much as the cinéaste filmmakers set scenes in movie theaters or made whole movies centering around their protagonist's obsessions with the filmgoing experience, these newer filmmakers frequently cast video store clerks as protagonists (*Clerks*, *Scream*), celebrating their expertise about genre conventions or their insightful speculations about popular films. This video store aesthetic mixes and matches elements from different genres, different artistic movements, and different periods with absolute abandon. Tarantino's tendency toward quotation runs riot in the famous Jack Flash restaurant sequence in *Pulp Fiction*, where all of the service personnel are impersonating iconic figures of the 1950s and the menu uses different comedy teams to designate different shake flavors. As the John Travolta character explains, "It's like a wax museum with a pulse," a phrase which might describe Tarantino's whole approach to filmmaking. Even his casting decisions, such as the use of *Medium Cool*'s Robert Forrester and blaxploitation star Pam Greers in *Jackie Brown*, constitute quotations and appropriations from earlier film classics.

Not surprisingly, the works of these "video store filmmakers" have been deeply influential on the emerging generation of amateur digital filmmakers – almost as influential in fact as *Star Wars* itself. Jeff Allen, a 27-year-old "HTML monkey" for an Atlanta-based internet company, for example, made *Trooperclerks*, a spoof of the trailer for *Clerks*, which deals with the drab routine confronted by the stormtroopers who work in convenience stores and video rental outlets onboard the Death Star. The short spoof, which was immediately embraced and promoted by Kevin Smith's *View Askew*, was later followed by a half-hour animated film based on the same premise, made in response to the news that *Clerks* was being adapted into an animated network series. Allen's focus on *Clerks* came only after he considered and rejected the thought of doing a *Star Wars* parody based on Tarantino's *Reservoir Dogs*. Similarly, Allen Smith heads a team that is producing a feature-length animated film, *Pulp Phantom*, which offers a scene-by-scene spoof of *Pulp Fiction*, recast with characters from *Star Wars*. At writing, the team has produced more than 10 episodes for the Web, taking the story up to the point where paid assassin Darth Maul races the overdosing Princess Amadala to the home of drug dealer, Han Solo, frantic lest he get into trouble with her jealous gangland husband, Darth Vader. In a particularly inspired bit of casting, Jar Jar Binks plays the geeky college student who, in a still to be anticipated installment, Maul accidentally blows away in the back of Boba Fett's vehicle. "Fan boy" filmmakers like Smith and Tarantino are thus inspiring the efforts of the next generation of amateur filmmakers, who are, in turn, developing cult followings that may ultimately gain them access to the commercial mainstream. *The Pulp Phantom* website, for example, includes a mechanism where loyal fans can receive email each time a new installment of the series gets posted.

This cyclical process has only accelerated since the box office success of *The Blair Witch Project*, which presented itself as an amateur digital film (albeit one which got commercial distribution and challenged *Phantom Menace* at the box office in the Summer of 1999) and had built public interest through its sophisticated use of the Web. *The Blair Witch Project*, in turn, has inspired countless Web-based amateur parodies (including *The Jar Jar Binks Project* and *The Wicked Witch Project*) and has sparked increased public and industry interest in the search for subsequent amateurs who can break into the mainstream, while the bigger-budget sequel to *The Blair Witch Project* takes as its central image the explosion of amateur filmmakers who have come to Birkerts, Maryland, in hopes of making their own documentaries on the mysterious deaths.

Conclusion

I personally find the opportunity to explore this new form of entertainment and creative expression both stimulating and liberating. While much of what we have learned throughout our careers will apply, I am also certain that new and unusual aesthetic values will quickly evolve – shaped by the medium itself, the public and the creative collaborations which this company will encourage.

– Ron Howard

Just as MTV introduced a new entertainment form for music videos, we think this new enterprise will offer a new form of entertainment for the rapidly growing population of Internet users. POP.com has the capability not only to offer a variety of entertainment options, but to tap into an as-yet-undiscovered talent pool that is as global as the Internet itself.

– Jeffrey Katzenberg

What is the future of digital cinema? One position sees digital cinema as an extension of avant-garde filmmaking practices, opening a new space for formal experimentation and alternative cultural politics, and offering experimental artists access to a broader public than can be attracted to screenings of their works at film festivals, museums, or university classes. Another position, represented by the founders of Pop.com above, sees the digital cinema as a potential new site for commercial developments, an extension of the logic of media convergence, a kind of MTV for the twenty-first century. In this vision, established filmmakers, such as Steven Spielberg or Tim Burton, can produce shorter and riskier works, emerging talents can develop their production skills, and works may move fluidly back and forth between the Web, television, film, and computer games. Interestingly, both groups want to tap into the hipness of "DIY" culture, promoting their particular vision of the future of digital cinema in terms of democratic participation and amateur self-expression, pinning their hopes, as Coppola suggests, on the prospect that a "little fat girl" from the mid-west will become the "Mozart" of digital filmmaking. Both visions have inherent limitations: the "low-res" movement's appeals to avant-garde aesthetics and its language of manifestos and its focus on film festival screenings may well prove as elitist as the earlier film movements it seeks to supplant, while the new commercial version of the digital cinema may reinscribe the same cultural gatekeepers who have narrowed the potential diversity of network television or Hollywood cinema.

The *Star Wars* fan films discussed here represent a potentially important third space between the two. Shaped by the intersection between contemporary trends toward media convergence and participatory culture, these fan films are hybrid by nature – neither fully commercial nor fully alternative, existing as part of a grassroots dialogue with mass culture. We are witnessing the transformation of amateur film culture from a focus on home movies toward a focus on public movies, from a focus on local audiences toward a focus on a potential global audience, from a focus on mastering the technology toward a focus on mastering the mechanisms for publicity and promotion, and from a focus on self-documentation toward a focus on an aesthetic based on appropriation, parody, and the dialogic. Coppola's "little fat girl" has found a way to talk back to the dominant media culture, to express herself not simply within an ideolect but within a shared language constructed through the powerful images and narratives that constitute contemporary popular culture. She will find ways to tap into the mythology of *Star Wars* and use it as a resource for the production of her own stories, stories which are broadly accessible to a popular audience and which, in turn, inspire others to create their own works, much as Lucas created *Star Wars*, through the clever appropriation and transformation of various popular culture influences (ranging from Laurel and Hardy to *Battleship Yomamoto* and *The Hidden Fortress*).

This third space will survive, however, only if we maintain a vigorous and effective defense of the principle of "fair use," only if we recognize the rights of consumers to participate fully, actively, and creatively within their own culture, and only if we hold in check the desires of the culture industries to tighten their control over their own intellectual property in response to the economic opportunities posed by an era of media convergence. At the moment, we are on a collision course between a new economic and legal culture which encourages monopoly power over cultural mythologies, and new technologies which empower consumers to archive, annotate, appropriate, and recirculate media images. The recent legal disputes around Napster represent only a skirmish in what is likely to be a decade-long war over intellectual property, a war which will determine not simply the future direction of digital cinema but the nature of creative expression in the twenty-first century.

Digital Filmmography

Alien 5 (Damon Wellner and Sebastian O'Brien) http://home.earthlink.net/~bsplendor/index.htm

American Booty (Albert Nerenberg) http://www.trailervision.com/trailerPages/booty_choose.html

Battle of the Bedroom (Scott Middlebrook) http://www.geocities.com/Hollywood/Video/6351/botb/botb1.html

Boba Fett: Bounty Trail (Justin Dix) http://theforce.net/theater/shortfilms/bountytrail/index.shtml

Dark Redemption (Warren Duxbury, Peter Mether) http://theforce.net/theater/shortfilms/darkredemption/index.shtml

Duel (Mark Thomas and Dave Macomber) http://theforce.net/theater/shortfilms/duel/index.shtml

George Lucas in Love (Joe Nussbaum and Joseph Levy) http://www1.mediatrip.com/per/House_Picks/George_Lucas_In_Love1media.html

Godzilla versus Disco Lando (Evan Mather) http://www.evanmather.com

I Know What You Want Next Summer (Albert Nerenberg) http://www.trailervision.com/trailerPages/want.htm

Jar Jar Binks Project, The (Albert Nerenberg) http://www.trailervision.com/trailerPages/jarjar_1.htm

Jedi Who Loves Me, The (Henry Burrows and Adam Ahmad) http://saturn.spaceports.com/~jedi/

Kid Wars (Dana Smith) http://members.xoom.com/ip_president/

Kung-Fu Kenobi's Big Adventure (Evan Mather) http://www.evanmather.com

Les Pantless Menace (Evan Mather) http://www.evanmather.com

MacBeth (Students of Glenn Ridge High School) http://www.glenridge.org/macbeth/mainpage.htm

Maru (Adam Dorr, Erik Benson, Hien Nguyen, Jon Jones) http://theforce.net/theater/shortfilms/maru/index.shtml

New World, The (Clay Kronke) http://theforce.net/theater/shortfilms/newworld/index.shtml

Park Wars: The Little Menace (Ted Bracewell, Ayaz A. Asif) http://www.parkwars.com/

Prequel: Revenge of Tall Snaggletooth (Damon Wellner) http://home.earthlink.net/~bsplendor/about.htm

Pulp Phantom (Allen Smith, Dustin Resch, Brian Snook) http://www.pulpphantom.com/

Quenton Tarantino's Star Wars (Evan Mather) http:/www.evanmather.com

The Qui-Gon Show (Robert Fyvolent, Evan Mather, John Stavopoulos, Jason Wishnow) http://www.evanmather.com

Scam 3 (Albert Nerenberg) http://www.trailervision.com/trailerPages/scam3.html

Shadows of the Empire (Jeff Hendricks, Bob Branch)

Star Wars Remake (Jim Longsma, John Longsma, and Gary Baker) http://home.earthlink.net/~jimjongsma/StarWarsRemake/Page001.html

Star Wras (Ceri Llewellyn) http://www.theforce.net/theater/animation/starwras/index.shtml

Stooge Wars (Matt Spease) http://members.xoom.com/Matt_Spease/stoogewars.html

Tatooine or Bust (Jason Wishnow) http://www.wishnow.com/production/index.html

Throne Room (Steve Latham, Ben Latham) http://homepages.go.com/~lathamfilm/movies.html

Thumb Wars (Steve Oedekirk) http://www.thumbtv.com/thumbwars/index.html

Tie-Tantic (Tri Studio Productions) http://www.tie_tanic.com/

Toy Wars (Jason VandenBerghe, Aaron Halon) http://www.toywars.org/

Trooper Clerks (Jeff Allen) http://www.studiocreations.com/trooperclerks/

Trooper Clerks: The Animated One-Shot (Jeff Allen) http://www.studiocreations.com/trooperclerks/

Troops (Kevin Rubio) http://www.theforce.net/troops/

When Senators Attack IV (Ryan Mannion, Daniel Hawley) http://theforce.net/theater/animation/wsa4/index.shtml

Wicked Witch Project, The (Joe Barlow) http://www.wickedwitchproject.com/

Wimp Club (Albert Nerenberg) http://trailervision.com/trailerPages/wimpclub.htm

Part VI

Globalization and Social Movements

Introduction to Part VI

Globalization has been one of the most hotly contested phenomena of the past two decades. It has been a primary attractor of books, articles, and heated debate, just as postmodernism was the most fashionable and disputed topic of the 1980s. A wide and diverse range of theorists have argued that today's world is organized by accelerating globalization, which is strengthening the dominance of a world capitalist economic system, supplanting the primacy of the nation-state by transnational corporations and organizations, and eroding local cultures and traditions through a global culture. Contemporary theorists from diverse political and theoretical positions are converging on the position that globalization is a distinguishing trend of the present moment, but there are hot debates concerning its nature, effects, and future.[1]

Advocates of a postmodern break in history argue that developments in transnational capitalism are producing a new global historical configuration of post-Fordism, or postmodernism as an emergent cultural logic of capitalism (Harvey, 1989; Soja, 1989; Jameson, 1991). Others define the emergent global economy and culture as a "network society" grounded in new communications and information technology (Castells, 1996, 1997, and 1998). For its defenders, globalization marks the triumph of capitalism and its market economy (see apologists such as Fukuyama, 1992; Gates, 1995; and Friedman, 1999, who perceive this process as positive), while its critics portray globalization as negative (see, for example, Eisenstein, 1998; and Robins and Webster, 1999). Some theorists see the emergence of a new transnational ruling elite and the universalization of consumerism (Sklair, 2001), while others stress global fragmentation of "the clash of civilizations" (Huntington, 1996). Driving "post" discourses into novel realms of theory and politics, Hardt and Negri (2000) present the emergence of "Empire" as producing evolving forms of sovereignty, economy, culture, and political struggle that unleash an unforeseeable and unpredictable flow of novelties, surprises, and upheavals.

Discourses of globalization initially were polarized into pro or con celebrations or attacks. For critics, the term provides a cover concept for global capitalism and imperialism, and is accordingly condemned as another form of the imposition of the logic of capital and the market on ever more regions of the world and spheres of life. For defenders, globalization is the continuation of modernization and a force of progress, increased wealth, freedom, democracy, and happiness. Its champions present globalization as beneficial, generating fresh economic opportunities, political democratization, cultural diversity, and the opening to an exciting new world. Its detractors see globalization as harmful, bringing about increased domination and control by the wealthier overdeveloped nations over the poor underdeveloped countries, thus increasing the hegemony of the "haves" over the "have-nots." In addition, supplementing the negative view, globalization critics assert that globalization produces an undermining of democracy, a cultural homogenization, and increased destruction of natural species and the environment.[2] Some imagine the globalization project – whether viewed positively or negatively – as inevitable and beyond human control and intervention, whereas others view it as generating new conflicts and new spaces for struggle, distinguishing between globalization from above and globalization from below (see Brecher, Costello, and Smith 2000).

One question that underpins these debates is whether "globalization" is simply a synonym of "Westernization" or a more intricate and multidirectional process than is indicated by such a direct correlation. For Arjun Appadurai, the politics of globalization turn on fears of homogenization, but the cultural impositions are not necessarily only from the West. As he points out, in Korea, "Japanization" may be more of a threat than Americanization. For Appadurai, the United States "is only one node of a complex transnational construction of imaginary landscapes" (1996, p. 31). Appadurai sees globalization as a fluid and dynamic phenomenon tied to worldwide migrations (both voluntary and involuntary) and the dissemination of images and texts via electronic media. In a postcolonial and media-saturated environment, new forms of desire and subjectivity have been unleashed. Drawing on poststructuralist conceptions, Appadurai envisions the globe as crosscut by flows that he refers to as "scapes," which frame the constantly reconfigured worlds of the new global landscape.

Annabelle Sreberny Mohammadi theorizes the ways that the global and the local interact in international communications. Focusing on the centrality of the media in global communication, she argues that media in developing countries display an ambivalent role: they can be both "instruments of social control and agencies of emancipation, an expression of global western power and a means by which local identities are revitalized." Attacking monolithic conceptions of globalization and myths of harmony and unity, Mohammadi stresses the conflicts, contradictions, and struggles that run through globalization today. In her study, Mohammadi documents globalization of media forms and firms, notes the complexity of global media flows, and points to new forms of media localization.

Jésus Martín-Barbero also challenges totalizing conceptions of Western hegemony by stressing the active and processual mediations in which media are lived and experienced by the people, producing meanings, identities, and participation in national cultures. Focusing on a Latin American context, Martín-Barbero analyzes how the Mexican cinema, creole circus, radio theater, black music, and the popular press contributed to the emergence of national cultures and identities. In more recent times, Martín-Barbero notes that in an age of globalization, national and traditional cultures intersected with global cultures, but had their distinctive mediations and forms. While he recognizes that technologies are not tools that can be employed by anyone, he conceives of them as the materialization of power hierarchies, and offers a notion of the potential for subversion in communication technologies. Concluding his study with an important discussion of "the contradictions between technologies and uses," he argues that all communication technology, from loudspeakers to computers, can be reconstructed and used to meet people's needs and to create distinctive cultural forms.

Jan Nederveen Pieterse has written extensively on globalization, and in the selection reprinted here, he expands on his previous work on global cultures. As he points out, most theories of globalization focus almost exclusively on the economic and political aspects of the process, particularly engaging with neoliberalism and the spread of capitalist market relations. But globalization is a multidimensional process, encompassing a wide variety of human practices and social, political, and cultural arenas. Taking a long view, Pieterse examines the historical trajectory of globalization, critiquing the study of globalization in terms of modernization, which he argues is a Western-centric approach to a decentralized problem. Instead, he presents a theory of globalization that hinges on the concept of hybridity. He argues that globalization occurs through structural and cultural hybridizations, giving rise to new forms of social organization and creolized cultural forms. Pieterse differentiates among these hybridities, recognizing that an unproblematic valorization of such mixings can sustain neocolonial hegemonies. Instead he posits a continuum of hybridizations, some of which are assimilationist and hegemonic, others of which are subversive and counterhegemonic.

Joseph Straubhaar explores the ways that national television and national identity can be reasserted against the global, regional, and local levels of world television. Noting how discussions of globalization are becoming more complex, Straubhaar proposes developing a multilevel approach to global flows of television and culture that explores global, national, regional, and local flows of culture and forms of production and reception. Attacking the myth that globalization creates massification and homogenization, Straubhaar explores both the ways that globalizing forces of television traverse the world and are bound up with the expansion of market capitalism, and how forms of cultural hybridity proliferate through national, regional, and local appropriations of global forms. The result is a picture of globalization that is more complex, historically nuanced, and open to appropriation, transformation, and opposition.

Richard Kahn and Douglas Kellner argue that the continued growth of the internet, both as a form of mainstream media and as a tool for organizing democratic social interactions, requires that internet politics be retheorized from a standpoint that is both critical and reconstructive. Their approach is critical of corporate forms and hegemonic uses of the internet, but traces oppositional deployments made by a wide variety of groups in the cause of progressive cultural and political struggle. In addition, they show how new software developments such as blogs and wikis can democratize media and further oppositional movements and politics. In this regard, the internet has facilitated the worldwide emergence of the antiglobalization, antiwar, and anticapitalism movements, even as it has coalesced local communities and groups. Hence, internet politics must be thought dialectically as both global and local. The authors note the relevance of the ideas of Guy Debord, with his focus on the construction of situations, the use of technology, media of communication, and cultural forms to promote a revolution of everyday life. Indeed, Debord and the Situationist International have had a remarkable aftermath on the internet, where much of their work is available.

The present moment is characterized by the proliferation of new media and global forms of culture, as well as global political movements. Since the "Battle of Seattle" in 1999, a variety of global social movements have arisen that have opposed forms of corporate globalization from above while valorizing a wealth of social movements ranging from human rights, to struggles around labor, women, minority groups, the environment, and peace. These movements are increasingly using global forms of communication like the internet and new technology and helping produce a more complex, contested, and diverse global world.

A critical cultural studies is thus necessarily global in scope and engages planetary forms of culture, exploring different forms of cultural domination, hybridization, and struggle. Throughout the world, cultural studies has engaged local and national cultures, global flows of culture, and the impact of globalization on specific cultural sites and identities. As many argue, a new virtual culture is on the horizon and will increase both the dematerialization of culture and its globalization. New forms of media culture require new modes of theoretical analysis, hence we anticipate continued turbulence and contestation in media and cultural studies as we proceed into a new millennium.

Notes

1   Attempts to chart the globalization of capital, decline of the nation-state, and rise of a new global culture include the essays in Featherstone (1990); Giddens (1990); Robertson (1991); Arrighi (1994); Wark (1994); Held (1995); Cvetkovich and Kellner (1997); Friedman (1999); Held et al. (1999); Hardt and Negri (2000); Steger (2002); Stiglitz (2002); and Kellner (2002).

2   What now appears at the first stage of academic and popular discourses of globalization in the 1990s tended to be dichotomized into celebratory globophilia and dismissive globophobia. There was also a tendency in some theorists to exaggerate the novelties of globalization and others to dismiss these claims by arguing that globalization has been going on for centuries and there is not that much that is new and different. For a delineation and critique of academic discourses on globalization, see Steger (2002).

References

Appadurai, Arjun (1996) *Modernity at Large*. Minneapolis: University of Minnesota Press.

Arrighi, Giovanni (1994) *The Long Twentieth Century*. London and New York: Verso.

Barber, Benjamin R. (1995) *Jihad vs. McWorld*. New York: Ballatine Books.

Brecher, Jeremy, Costello, Tim and Smith, Brendan (2000) *Globalization From Below*. Boston: South End Press.

Burbach, Roger (2001) *Globalization and Postmodern Politics: From Zapatistas to High Tech Robber Barons*. London: Pluto Press.

Castells, Manuel (1996) *The Rise of the Network Society*. Oxford: Blackwell.

—— (1997) *The Power of Identity*. Oxford: Blackwell.

—— (1998) *End of Millennium*. Oxford: Blackwell.

Cvetkovich, Ann and Kellner, Douglas (1997) *Articulating the Global and the Local:. Globalization and Cultural Studies*. Boulder, CO: Westview.

Eisenstein, Zillah (1998) *Global Obscenities: Patriarchy, Capitalism, and the Lure of Cyberfantasy*. New York: New York University Press.

Featherstone, Mike (ed.) (1990) *Global Culture: Nationalism, Globalization and Modernity*. London: Sage.

Friedman, Thomas (1999) *The Lexus and the Olive Tree*. New York: Farrar, Straus, Giroux.

Fukuyama, Francis (1992) *The End of History*. New York: Avon.

Gates, Bill (1995) *The Road Ahead*. New York: Viking.

Giddens, Anthony (1990) *Consequences of Modernity*. Cambridge and Palo Alto: Polity and Stanford University Press.

Hardt, Michael and Negri, Antonio (2000) *Empire*. Cambridge, MA: Harvard University Press.

Harvey, David (1989) *The Condition of Postmodernity*. Oxford: Blackwell.

Held, David (1995) *Democracy and the Global Order*. Cambridge and Palo Alto: Polity Press and Stanford University Press.

—— McGrew, Anthony, Goldblatt, David, & Perraton, Jonathan (1999) *Global Transformations*. Cambridge and Palo Alto: Polity Press and Stanford University Press.

Huntington, Samuel (1996) *The Clash of Civilizations and the Remaking of World Order*. New York: Touchstone Books.

Jameson, Fredric (1991) *Postmodernism, or the Cultural Logic of Late Capitalism*. Durham, NC: Duke University Press.

Kellner, Douglas (2002) "Theorizing Globalization," *Sociological Theory* 20(3): 285–305.

Ritzer, George (1993; rev. ed. 1996) *The McDonaldization of Society*. Thousand Oaks, CA: Pine Forge Press.

Robertson, Roland (1991) *Globalization*. London: Sage.

Robins, Kevin and Webster, Frank (1999) *Times of the Technoculture*. London and New York: Routledge.

Sklair, Leslie (2001) *The Transnational Capitalist Class*. Oxford: Blackwell.

Soja, Edward (1989) *Postmodern Geographies*. London: Verso.

Steger, Manfred (2002) *Globalism: The New Market Ideology*. Lanham, MD: Rowman and Littlefield.

Stiglitz, Joseph E. (2002) *Globalization and Its Discontents*. New York: Norton.

Wark, McKenzie (1994) *Virtual Geography: Living With Global Media Events*. Bloomington and Indianapolis: Indiana University Press.

33

Disjuncture and Difference in the Global Cultural Economy

Arjun Appadurai

It takes only the merest acquaintance with the facts of the modern world to note that it is now an interactive system in a sense that is strikingly new. Historians and sociologists, especially those concerned with translocal processes (Hodgson 1974) and the world systems associated with capitalism (Abu-Lughod 1989; Braudel 1981–4; Curtin 1984; Wallerstein 1974; Wolf 1982), have long been aware that the world has been a congeries of large-scale interactions for many centuries. Yet today's world involves interactions of a new order and intensity. Cultural transactions be-tween social groups in the past have generally been restricted, sometimes by the facts of geography and ecology, and at other times by active resistance to interactions with the Other (as in China for much of its history and in Japan before the Meiji Restoration). Where there have been sustained cultural transactions across large parts of the globe, they have usually involved the long-distance journey of commodities (and of the merchants most concerned with them) and of travelers and explorers of every type (Helms 1988; Schafer 1963). The two main forces for sustained cultural interaction before this century have been warfare (and the large-scale political sys-tems sometimes generated by it) and religions of conversion, which have sometimes, as in the case of Islam, taken warfare as one of the legitimate instruments of their expansion. Thus, between travelers and merchants, pilgrims and conquerors, the world has seen much long-distance (and long-term) cultural traffic. This much seems self-evident.

But few will deny that given the problems of time, distance, and limited techno-logies for the command of resources across vast spaces, cultural dealings between socially and spatially separated groups have, until the past few centuries, been bridged at great cost and sustained over time only with great effort. The forces of cultural gravity seemed always to pull away from the formation of large-scale ecumenes,

From Arjun Appadurai, "Disjuncture and difference in the global cultural economy." In *Public Culture*, 2:2 (1990). © 1990 by Arjun Appadurai. Reprinted by permission of the author.

whether religious, commercial, or political, toward smaller-scale accretions of intimacy and interest.

Sometime in the past few centuries, the nature of this gravitational field seems to have changed. Partly because of the spirit of the expansion of Western maritime interests after 1,500, and partly because of the relatively autonomous developments of large and aggressive social formations in the Americas (such as the Aztecs and the Incas), in Eurasia (such as the Mongols and their descendants, the Mughals and Ottomans), in island Southeast Asia (such as the Buginese), and in the kingdoms of precolonial Africa (such as Dahomey), an overlapping set of ecumenes began to emerge, in which congeries of money, commerce, conquest, and migration began to create durable cross-societal bonds. This process was accelerated by the technology transfers and innovations of the late eighteenth and nineteenth centuries (e.g., Bayly 1989), which created complex colonial orders centered on European capitals and spread throughout the non-European world. This intricate and overlapping set of Eurocolonial worlds (first Spanish and Portuguese, later principally English, French, and Dutch) set the basis for a permanent traffic in ideas of peoplehood and selfhood, which created the imagined communities (Anderson 1983) of recent nationalisms throughout the world.

With what Benedict Anderson has called "print capitalism," a new power was unleashed in the world, the power of mass literacy and its attendant large-scale production of projects of ethnic affinity that were remarkably free of the need for face-to-face communication or even of indirect communication between persons and groups. The act of reading things together set the stage for movements based on a paradox – the paradox of constructed primordialism. There is, of course, a great deal else that is involved in the story of colonialism and its dialectically generated nationalisms (Chatterjee 1986), but the issue of constructed ethnicities is surely a crucial strand in this tale.

But the revolution of print capitalism and the cultural affinities and dialogues unleashed by it were only modest precursors to the world we live in now. For in the past century, there has been a technological explosion, largely in the domain of transportation and information, that makes the interactions of a print-dominated world seem as hard-won and as easily erased as the print revolution made earlier forms of cultural traffic appear. For with the advent of the steamship, the automobile, the airplane, the camera, the computer, and the telephone, we have entered into an altogether new condition of neighborliness, even with those most distant from ourselves. Marshall McLuhan, among others, sought to theorize about this world as a "global village," but theories such as McLuhan's appear to have overestimated the communitarian implications of the new media order (McLuhan and Powers 1989). We are now aware that with media, each time we are tempted to speak of the global village, we must be reminded that media create communities with "no sense of place" (Meyrowitz 1985). The world we live in now seems rhizomic (Deleuze and Guattari 1987), even schizophrenic, calling for theories of rootlessness, alienation, and psychological distance between individuals and groups on the one hand, and fantasies (or nightmares) of electronic propinquity on the other. Here, we are close to the central problematic of cultural processes in today's world.

Thus, the curiosity that recently drove Pico Iyer to Asia (1988) is in some ways the product of a confusion between some ineffable McDonaldization of the world and the much subtler play of indigenous trajectories of desire and fear with global flows of people and things. Indeed, Iyer's own impressions are testimony to the fact that, if *a* global cultural system is emerging, it is filled with ironies and resistances, sometimes camouflaged as passivity and a bottomless appetite in the Asian world for things Western.

Iyer's own account of the uncanny Philippine affinity for American popular music is rich testimony to the global culture of the hyperreal, for somehow Philippine renditions of American popular songs are both more widespread in the Philippines, and more disturbingly faithful to their originals, than they are in the United States today. An entire nation seems to have learned to mimic Kenny Rogers and the Lennon sisters, like a vast Asian Motown chorus. But *Americanization* is certainly a pallid term to apply to such a situation, for not only are there more Filipinos singing perfect renditions of some American songs (often from the American past) than there are Americans doing so, there is also, of course, the fact that the rest of their lives is not in complete synchrony with the referential world that first gave birth to these songs.

In a further globalizing twist on what Fredric Jameson has recently called "nostalgia for the present" (1989), these Filipinos look back to a world they have never lost. This is one of the central ironies of the politics of global cultural flows, especially in the arena of entertainment and leisure. It plays havoc with the hegemony of Eurochronology. American nostalgia feeds on Filipino desire represented as a hyper-competent reproduction. Here, we have nostalgia without memory. The paradox, of course, has its explanations, and they are historical; unpacked, they lay bare the story of the American missionization and political rape of the Philippines, one result of which has been the creation of a nation of make-believe Americans, who tolerated for so long a leading lady who played the piano while the slums of Manila expanded and decayed. Perhaps the most radical postmodernists would argue that this is hardly surprising because in the peculiar chronicities of late capitalism, pastiche and nostalgia are central modes of image production and reception. Americans themselves are hardly in the present anymore as they stumble into the megatechnologies of the twenty first century garbed in the film-noir scenarios of sixties' chills, fifties' diners, forties' clothing, thirties' houses, twenties' dances, and so on ad infinitum.

As far as the United States is concerned, one might suggest that the issue is no longer one of nostalgia but of a social *imaginaire* built largely around reruns. Jameson was bold to link the politics of nostalgia to the postmodern commodity sensibility, and surely he was right (1983). The drug wars in Colombia recapitulate the tropical sweat of Vietnam, with Ollie North and his succession of masks – Jimmy Stewart concealing John Wayne concealing Spiro Agnew and all of them transmogrifying into Sylvester Stallone, who wins in Afghanistan – thus simultaneously fulfilling the secret American envy of Soviet imperialism and the rerun (this time with a happy ending) of the Vietnam War. The Rolling Stones, approaching their fifties, gyrate before eighteen-year-olds who do not appear to need the machinery of nostalgia to be sold on their parents' heroes. Paul McCartney is selling the Beatles to a new audience by hitching his oblique nostalgia to their desire for the new that smacks of the old. *Dragnet* is back in nineties' drag, and so is *Adam-12*, not to speak of *Batman* and *Mission Impossible*, all dressed up technologically but remarkably faithful to the atmospherics of their originals.

The past is now not a land to return to in a simple politics of memory. It has become a synchronic warehouse of cultural scenarios, a kind of temporal central casting, to which recourse can be taken as appropriate, depending on the movie to be made, the scene to be enacted, the hostages to be rescued. All this is par for the course, if you follow Jean Baudrillard or Jean-François Lyotard into a world of signs wholly unmoored from their social signifiers (all the world's a Disneyland). But I would like to suggest that the apparent increasing substitutability of whole periods and postures for one another, in the cultural styles of advanced capitalism, is tied to larger global forces, which have done much to show Americans that the past is usually another country. If your present is their future (as in much modernization theory and in many self-satisfied tourist fantasies), and their future is your past (as in the case of the Filipino virtuosos of American popular music), then your own past can be made to appear as simply a normalized modality of your present. Thus, although some anthropologists may continue to relegate their Others to temporal spaces that they do not themselves occupy (Fabian 1983), postindustrial cultural productions have entered a postnostalgic phase.

The crucial point, however, is that the United States is no longer the puppeteer of a world system of images but is only one node of a complex transnational construction of imaginary landscapes. The world we live in today is characterized by a new role for the imagination in social life. To grasp this new role, we need to bring together the old idea of images, especially mechanically produced images (in the Frankfurt School sense); the idea of the imagined community (in Anderson's sense); and the French idea of the imaginary (*imaginaire*) as a constructed landscape of collective aspirations, which is no more and no less real than the collective representations of Émile Durkheim, now mediated through the complex prism of modern media.

The image, the imagined, the imaginary – these are all terms that direct us to something critical and new in global cultural processes: *the imagination as a social practice*. No longer mere fantasy (opium for the masses whose real work is elsewhere), no longer simple escape (from a world defined principally by more concrete purposes and structures), no longer elite pastime (thus not relevant to the lives of ordinary people), and no longer mere contemplation (irrelevant for new forms of desire and subjectivity), the imagination has become an organized field of social practices, a form of work (in the sense of both labor and culturally organized practice), and a form of negotiation between sites of agency (individuals) and globally defined fields of possibility. This unleashing of the imagination links the play of pastiche (in some settings) to the terror and coercion of states and their competitors. The imagination is now central to all forms of agency, is itself a social fact, and is the key component of the new global order. But to make this claim meaningful, we must address some other issues.

Homogenization and Heterogenization

The central problem of today's global interactions is the tension between cultural homogenization and cultural heterogenization. A vast array of empirical facts could be brought to bear on the side of the homogenization argument, and much of it has come from the left end of the spectrum of media studies (Hamelink 1983; Mattelart 1983; Schiller 1976), and some from other perspectives (Gans 1985; Iyer 1988). Most often, the homogenization argument subspeciates into either an argument about Americanization or an argument about commoditization, and very often the two arguments are closely linked. What these arguments fail to consider is that at least as rapidly as forces from various metropolises are brought into new societies they tend to become indigenized in one or another way: this is true of music and housing styles as much as it is true of science and terrorism, spectacles and con- stitutions. The dynamics of such indigenization have just begun to be explored systemically (Barber 1987; Feld 1988; Hannerz 1987, 1989; Ivy 1988; Nicoll 1989; Yoshimoto 1989), and much more needs to be done. But it is worth noticing that for the people of Irian Jaya, Indonesianization may be more worrisome than Americanization, as Japanization may be for Koreans, Indianization for Sri Lankans, Vietnamization for the Cambodians, and Russianization for the people of Soviet Armenia and the Baltic republics. Such a list of alternative fears to Americanization could be greatly expanded, but it is not a shapeless inventory: for polities of smaller scale, there is always a fear of cultural absorption by polities of larger scale, especially those that are nearby. One man's imagined community is another man's political prison.

This scalar dynamic, which has widespread global manifestations, is also tied to the relationship between nations and states, to which I shall return later. For the moment let us note that the simplification of these many forces (and fears) of homo- genization can also be exploited by nation-states in relation to their own minorities, by posing global commoditization (or capitalism, or some other such external enemy) as more real than the threat of its own hegemonic strategies.

The new global cultural economy has to be seen as a complex, overlapping, dis- junctive order that cannot any longer be understood in terms of existing center– periphery models (even those that might account for multiple centers and peripheries). Nor is it susceptible to simple models of push and pull (in terms of migration theory), or of surpluses and deficits (as in traditional models of balance of trade), or of consumers and producers (as in most neo-Marxist theories of development). Even the most complex and flexible theories of global development that have come out of the Marxist tradition (Amin 1980; Mandel 1978; Wallerstein 1974; Wolf 1982) are inadequately quirky and have failed to come to terms with what Scott Lash and John Urry have called disorganized capitalism (1987). The complexity of the current global economy has to do with certain fundamental disjunctures between economy, culture, and politics that we have only begun to theorize.[1]

I propose that an elementary framework for exploring such disjunctures is to look at the relationship among five dimensions of global cultural flows that can be termed

(a) *ethnoscapes*, (b) *mediascapes*, (c) *technoscapes*, (d) *financescapes*, and (e) *ideoscapes*.[2] The suffix *-scape* allows us to point to the fluid, irregular shapes of these landscapes, shapes that characterize international capital as deeply as they do international clothing styles. These terms with the common suffix *-scape* also indicate that these are not objectively given relations that look the same from every angle of vision but, rather, that they are deeply perspectival constructs, inflected by the historical, linguistic, and political situatedness of different sorts of actors: nation-states, multinationals, diasporic communities, as well as subnational groupings and movements (whether religious, political, or economic), and even intimate face-to-face groups, such as villages, neighborhoods, and families. Indeed, the individual actor is the last locus of this perspectival set of landscapes, for these landscapes are eventually navigated by agents who both experience and constitute larger formations, in part from their own sense of what these landscapes offer.

These landscapes thus are the building blocks of what (extending Benedict Anderson) I would like to call *imagined worlds*, that is, the multiple worlds that are constituted by the historically situated imaginations of persons and groups spread around the globe. An important fact of the world we live in today is that many persons on the globe live in such imagined worlds (and not just in imagined communities) and thus are able to contest and sometimes even subvert the imagined worlds of the official mind and of the entrepreneurial mentality that surround them.

By *ethnoscape*, I mean the landscape of persons who constitute the shifting world in which we live: tourists, immigrants, refugees, exiles, guest workers, and other moving groups and individuals constitute an essential feature of the world and appear to affect the politics of (and between) nations to a hitherto unprecedented degree. This is not to say that there are no relatively stable communities and networks of kinship, friendship, work, and leisure, as well as of birth, residence, and other filial forms. But it is to say that the warp of these stabilities is everywhere shot through with the woof of human motion, as more persons and groups deal with the realities of having to move or the fantasies of wanting to move. What is more, both these realities and fantasies now function on larger scales, as men and women from villages in India think not just of moving to Poona or Madras but of moving to Dubai and Houston, and refugees from Sri Lanka find themselves in South India as well as in Switzerland, just as the Hmong are driven to London as well as to Philadelphia. And as international capital shifts its needs, as production and technology generate different needs, as nation-states shift their policies on refugee populations, these moving groups can never afford to let their imaginations rest too long, even if they wish to.

By *technoscape*, I mean the global configuration, also ever fluid, of technology and the fact that technology, both high and low, both mechanical and informational, now moves at high speeds across various kinds of previously impervious boundaries. Many countries now are the roots of multinational enterprise: a huge steel complex in Libya may involve interests from India, China, Russia, and Japan, providing different components of new technological configurations. The odd distribution of technologies, and thus the peculiarities of these technoscapes, are increasingly driven not by any obvious economies of scale, of political control, or of market rationality but by increasingly complex relationships among money flows, political possibilities, and the availability of both un- and highly skilled labor. So, while India exports waiters and chauffeurs to Dubai and Sharjah, it also exports software engineers to the United States – indentured briefly to Tata-Burroughs or the World Bank, then laundered through the State Department to become wealthy resident aliens, who are in turn objects of seductive messages to invest their money and know-how in federal and state projects in India.

The global economy can still be described in terms of traditional indicators (as the World Bank continues to do) and studied in terms of traditional comparisons (as in Project Link at the University of Pennsylvania), but the complicated technoscapes (and the shifting ethnoscapes) that underlie these indicators and comparisons are further out of the reach of the queen of social sciences than ever before. How is one to make a meaningful comparison of wages in Japan and the United States or of real-estate costs in New York and Tokyo, without taking sophisticated account of the very complex fiscal and investment flows that link the two economies through a global grid of currency speculation and capital transfer?

Thus it is useful to speak as well of *financescapes*, as the disposition of global capital is now a more mysterious, rapid, and difficult landscape to follow than ever before as currency markets, national stock exchanges, and commodity speculations move megamonies through national turnstiles at blinding speed, with vast, absolute implications for small differences in percentage points and time units. But the critical point is that the global relationship among ethnoscapes, technoscapes, and financescapes is deeply disjunctive and profoundly unpredictable because each of these landscapes is subject to its own constraints and incentives (some political, some informational, and some technoenvironmental), at the same time as each acts as a constraint and a parameter for movements in the others. Thus, even an elementary model of global political economy must take into account the deeply disjunctive relationships among human movement, technological flow, and financial transfers.

Further refracting these disjunctures (which hardly form a simple, mechanical global infrastructure in any case) are what I call *mediascapes* and *ideoscapes*, which are closely related landscapes of images. *Mediascapes* refer both to the distribution of the electronic capabilities to produce and disseminate information (newspapers, magazines, television stations, and film-production studios), which are now available to a growing number of private and public interests throughout the world, and to the images of the world created by these media. These images involve many complicated inflections, depending on their mode (documentary or entertainment), their hardware (electronic or preelectronic), their audiences (local, national, or transnational), and the interests of those who own and control them. What is most important about these mediascapes is that they provide (especially in their television, film, and cassette forms) large and complex repertoires of images, narratives, and ethnoscapes to viewers throughout the world, in which the world of commodities and the world of news and politics are profoundly mixed. What this means is that many audiences around the world experience the media themselves as a complicated and interconnected repertoire of print, celluloid, electronic screens, and billboards. The lines between the realistic and the fictional landscapes they see are blurred, so that the farther away these audiences are from the direct experiences of metropolitan life, the more likely they are to construct imagined worlds that are chimerical, aesthetic, even fantastic objects, particularly if assessed by the criteria of some other perspective, some other imagined world.

Mediascapes, whether produced by private or state interests, tend to be image-centered, narrative-based accounts of strips of reality, and what they offer to those who experience and transform them is a series of elements (such as characters, plots, and textual forms) out of which scripts can be formed of imagined lives, their own as well as those of others living in other places. These scripts can and do get disaggregated into complex sets of metaphors by which people live (Lakoff and Johnson 1980) as they help to constitute narratives of the Other and protonarratives of possible lives, fantasies that could become prolegomena to the desire for acquisition and movement.

Ideoscapes are also concatenations of images, but they are often directly political and frequently have to do with the ideologies of states and the counterideologies of movements explicitly oriented to capturing state power or a piece of it. These ideoscapes are composed of elements of the Enlightenment worldview, which consists of a chain of ideas, terms, and images, including *freedom, welfare, rights, sovereignty, representation*, and the master term *democracy*. The master narrative of the Enlightenment (and its many variants in Britain France, and the United States) was constructed with a certain internal logic and presupposed a certain relationship between reading, representation, and the public sphere. (For the dynamics of this process in the early history of the United States, see Warner 1990.) But the diaspora of these terms and images across the world, especially since the nineteenth century, has loosened the internal coherence that held them together in a Euro-American master narrative and provided instead a loosely structured synopticon of politics, in which different nation-states, as part of their evolution, have organized their political cultures around different keywords (e.g., Williams 1976).

As a result of the differential diaspora of these keywords, the political narratives that govern communication between elites and followers in different parts of the world involve problems of both a semantic and pragmatic nature: semantic to the extent that words (and their lexical equivalents) require careful translation from context to context in their global movements, and pragmatic to the extent that the use of these words by political actors and their audiences may be subject to very different sets of contextual conventions that mediate their translation into public politics. Such conventions are not only matters of the nature of political rhetoric: for example, what does the aging Chinese leadership mean when it refers to the dangers of hooliganism? What does the South Korean leadership mean when it speaks of discipline as the key to democratic industrial growth?

These conventions also involve the far more subtle question of what sets of communicative genres are valued in what way (newspapers versus cinema, for example) and what sorts of pragmatic genre conventions govern the collective readings of different kinds of text. So, while an Indian audience may be attentive to the resonances of a political speech in terms of some keywords and phrases reminiscent of Hindi cinema, a Korean audience may respond to the subtle codings of Buddhist or neo-Confucian rhetoric encoded in a political document. The very relationship of reading to hearing and seeing may vary in important ways that determine the morphology of these different ideoscapes as they shape themselves in different national and transnational contexts. This globally variable synaesthesia has hardly even been noted, but it demands urgent analysis. Thus *democracy* has clearly become a master term, with powerful echoes from Haiti and Poland to the former Soviet Union and China, but it sits at the center of a variety of ideoscapes, composed of distinctive pragmatic configurations of rough translations of other central terms from the vocabulary of the Enlightenment. This creates ever new terminological kaleidoscopes, as states (and the groups that seek to capture them) seek to pacify populations whose own ethnoscapes are in motion and whose mediascapes may create severe problems for the ideoscapes with which they are presented. The fluidity of ideoscapes is complicated in particular by the growing diasporas (both voluntary and involuntary) of intellectuals who continuously inject new meaning-streams into the discourse of democracy in different parts of the world.

This extended terminological discussion of the five terms I have coined sets the basis for a tentative formulation about the conditions under which current global flows occur: they occur in and through the growing disjunctures among ethnoscapes, technoscapes, financescapes, mediascapes, and ideoscapes. This formulation, the core of my model of global cultural flow, needs some explanation. First, people, machinery, money, images, and ideas now follow increasingly nonisomorphic paths; of course, at all periods in human history, there have been some disjunctures in the flows of these things, but the sheer speed, scale, and volume of each of these flows are now so great that the disjunctures have become central to the politics of global culture. The Japanese are notoriously hospitable to ideas and are stereotyped as inclined to export (all) and import (some) goods, but they are also notoriously closed to immigration, like the Swiss, the Swedes, and the Saudis. Yet the Swiss and the Saudis accept populations of guest workers, thus creating labor diasporas of Turks, Italians, and other circum-Mediterranean groups. Some such guest-worker groups maintain continuous contact with their home nations, like the Turks, but others, like high-level South Asian migrants, tend to desire lives in their new homes, raising anew the problem of reproduction in a deterritorialized context.

Deterritorialization, in general, is one of the central forces of the modern world because it brings laboring populations into the lower-class sectors and spaces of relatively wealthy societies, while sometimes creating exaggerated and intensified senses of criticism or attachment to politics in the home state. Deterritorialization, whether of Hindus, Sikhs, Palestinians, or Ukrainians, is now at the core of a variety of global fundamentalisms, including Islamic and Hindu fundamentalism. In the Hindu case, for example, it is clear that the overseas movement of Indians has been exploited by a variety of interests both within and outside India to create a complicated network of finances and religious identifications, by which the problem of cultural reproduction for Hindus abroad has become tied to the politics of Hindu fundamentalism at home.

At the same time, deterritorialization creates new markets for film companies, art impresarios, and travel agencies, which thrive on the need of the deterritorialized population for contact with its homeland. Naturally, these invented homelands,

which constitute the mediascapes of deterritorialized groups, can often become sufficiently fantastic and one-sided that they provide the material for new ideoscapes
in which ethnic conflicts can begin to erupt. The creation of Khalistan, an invented
homeland of the deterritorialized Sikh population of England, Canada, and the
United States, is one example of the bloody potential in such mediascapes as they
interact with the internal colonialisms of the nation-state (e.g., Hechter 1975).
The West Bank, Namibia, and Eritrea are other theaters for the enactment of the
bloody negotiation between existing nation-states and various deterritorialized
groupings.

It is in the fertile ground of deterritorialization, in which money, commodities,
and persons are involved in ceaselessly chasing each other around the world, that the
mediascapes and ideoscapes of the modern world find their fractured and fragmented counterpart. For the ideas and images produced by mass media often are
only partial guides to the goods and experiences that deterritorialized populations
transfer to one another. In Mira Nair's brilliant film *India Cabaret*, we see the
multiple loops of this fractured deterritorialization as young women, barely competent in Bombay's metropolitan glitz, come to seek their fortunes as cabaret dancers
and prostitutes in Bombay, entertaining men in clubs with dance formats derived
wholly from the prurient dance sequences of Hindi films. These scenes in turn cater
to ideas about Western and foreign women and their looseness, while they provide
tawdry career alibis for these women. Some of these women come from Kerala,
where cabaret clubs and the pornographic film industry have blossomed, partly in
response to the purses and tastes of Keralites returned from the Middle East,
where their diasporic lives away from women distort their very sense of what the
relations between men and women might be. These tragedies of displacement
could certainly be replayed in a more detailed analysis of the relations between the
Japanese and German sex tours to Thailand and the tragedies of the sex trade in
Bangkok, and in other similar loops that tie together fantasies about the Other, the
conveniences and seductions of travel, the economics of global trade, and the brutal
mobility fantasies that dominate gender politics in many parts of Asia and the world
at large.

While far more could be said about the cultural politics of deterritorialization and
the larger sociology of displacement that it expresses, it is appropriate at this juncture to bring in the role of the nation-state in the disjunctive global economy of
culture today. The relationship between states and nations is everywhere an embattled one. It is possible to say that in many societies the nation and the state have
become one another's projects. That is, while nations (or more properly groups with
ideas about nationhood) seek to capture or co-opt states and state power, states
simultaneously seek to capture and monopolize ideas about nationhood (Baruah
1986; Chatterjee 1986; Nandy 1989). In general, separatist transnational movements, including those that have included terror in their methods, exemplify nations
in search of states. Sikhs, Tamil Sri Lankans, Basques, Moros, Québecois – each
of these represents imagined communities that seek to create states of their own
or carve pieces out of existing states. States, on the other hand, are everywhere
seeking to monopolize the moral resources of community, either by flatly claiming

perfect coevality between nation and state, or by systematically museumizing and representing all the groups within them in a variety of heritage politics that seems remarkably uniform throughout the world (Handler 1988; Herzfeld 1982; McQueen 1988).

Here, national and international mediascapes are exploited by nation-states to pacify separatists or even the potential fissiparousness of all ideas of difference. Typically, contemporary nation-states do this by exercising taxonomic control over difference, by creating various kinds of international spectacle to domesticate difference, and by seducing small groups with the fantasy of self-display on some sort of global or cosmopolitan stage. One important new feature of global cultural politics, tied to the disjunctive relationships among the various landscapes discussed earlier, is that state and nation are at each other's throats, and the hyphen that links them is now less an icon of conjuncture than an index of disjuncture. This disjunctive relationship between nation and state has two levels: at the level of any given nation-state, it means that there is a battle of the imagination, with state and nation seeking to cannibalize one another. Here is the seedbed of brutal separatisms – majoritarianisms that seem to have appeared from nowhere and microidentities that have become political projects within the nation-state. At another level, this disjunctive relationship is deeply entangled with the global disjunctures discussed throughout this chapter: ideas of nationhood appear to be steadily increasing in scale and regularly crossing existing state boundaries, sometimes, as with the Kurds, because previous identities stretched across vast national spaces or, as with the Tamils in Sri Lanka, the dormant threads of a transnational diaspora have been activated to ignite the micropolitics of a nation-state.

In discussing the cultural politics that have subverted the hyphen that links the nation to the state, it is especially important not to forget the mooring of such politics in the irregularities that now characterize disorganized capital (Kothari 1989; Lash and Urry 1987). Because labor, finance, and technology are now so widely separated, the volatilities that underlie movements for nationhood (as large as transnational Islam on the one hand, or as small as the movement of the Gurkhas for a separate state in Northeast India) grind against the vulnerabilities that characterize the relationships between states. States find themselves pressed to stay open by the forces of media, technology, and travel that have fueled consumerism throughout the world and have increased the craving, even in the non-Western world, for new commodities and spectacles. On the other hand, these very cravings can become caught up in new ethnoscapes, mediascapes, and, eventually, ideoscapes, such as democracy in China, that the state cannot tolerate as threats to its own control over ideas of nationhood and peoplehood. States throughout the world are under siege, especially where contests over the ideoscapes of democracy are fierce and fundamental, and where there are radical disjunctures between ideoscapes and technoscapes (as in the case of very small countries that lack contemporary technologies of production and information); or between ideoscapes and financescapes (as in countries such as Mexico or Brazil, where international lending influences national politics to a very large degree); or between ideoscapes and ethnoscapes (as in Beirut where diasporic, local, and translocal filiations are suicidally at battle); or between ideoscapes and mediascapes (as in many countries in the Middle East and Asia) where the lifestyles represented on both national and international TV and cinema completely overwhelm and undermine the rhetoric of national politics. In the Indian case, the myth of the law-breaking hero has emerged to mediate this naked struggle between the pieties and realities of Indian politics, which has grown increasingly brutalized and corrupt (Vachani 1989).

The transnational movement of the martial arts, particularly through Asia, as mediated by the Hollywood and Hong Kong film industries (Zarilli 1995) is a rich illustration of the ways in which long-standing martial arts traditions, reformulated to meet the fantasies of contemporary (sometimes lumpen) youth populations, create new cultures of masculinity and violence, which are in turn the fuel for increased violence in national and international politics. Such violence is in turn the spur to an increasingly rapid and amoral arms trade that penetrates the entire world. The worldwide spread of the AK-47 and the Uzi, in films, in corporate and state security, in terror, and in police and military activity, is a reminder that apparently simple technical uniformities often conceal an increasingly complex set of loops, linking images of violence to aspirations for community in some imagined world.

Returning then to the ethnoscapes with which I began, the central paradox of ethnic politics in today's world is that primordia (whether of language or skin color or neighborhood or kinship) have become globalized. That is, sentiments, whose greatest force is in their ability to ignite intimacy into a political state and turn locality into a staging ground for identity, have become spread over vast and irregular spaces as groups move yet stay linked to one another through sophisticated media capabilities. This is not to deny that such primordia are often the product of invented traditions (Hobsbawm and Ranger 1983) or retrospective affiliations, but to emphasize that because of the disjunctive and unstable interplay of commerce, media, national policies, and consumer fantasies, ethnicity, once a genie contained in the bottle of some sort of locality (however large), has now become a global force, forever slipping in and through the cracks between states and borders.

But the relationship between the cultural and economic levels of this new set of global disjunctures is not a simple one-way street in which the terms of global cultural politics are set wholly by, or confined wholly within, the vicissitudes of international flows of technology, labor, and finance, demanding only a modest modification of existing neo-Marxist models of uneven development and state formation. There is a deeper change, itself driven by the disjunctures among all the landscapes I have discussed and constituted by their continuously fluid and uncertain interplay, that concerns the relationship between production and consumption in today's global economy. Here, I begin with Marx's famous (and often mined) view of the fetishism of the commodity and suggest that this fetishism has been replaced in the world at large (now seeing the world as one large, interactive system, composed of many complex subsystems) by two mutually supportive descendants, the first of which I call production fetishism and the second, the fetishism of the consumer.

By *production fetishism* I mean an illusion created by contemporary transnational production loci that masks translocal capital, transnational earning flows, global management, and often faraway workers (engaged in various kinds of high-tech putting-out operations) in the idiom and spectacle of local (sometimes even worker) control, national productivity, and territorial sovereignty. To the extent that various kinds of free-trade zones have become the models for production at large, especially of high-tech commodities, production has itself become a fetish, obscuring not social relations as such but the relations of production, which are increasingly transnational. The locality (both in the sense of the local factory or site of production and in the extended sense of the nation-state) becomes a fetish that disguises the globally dispersed forces that actually drive the production process. This generates alienation (in Marx's sense) twice intensified, for its social sense is now compounded by a complicated spatial dynamic that is increasingly global.

As for the *fetishism of the consumer*, I mean to indicate here that the consumer has been transformed through commodity flows (and the mediascapes, especially of advertising, that accompany them) into a sign, both in Baudrillard's sense of a simulacrum that only asymptotically approaches the form of a real social agent, and in the sense of a mask for the real seat of agency, which is not the consumer but the producer and the many forces that constitute production. Global advertising is the key technology for the worldwide dissemination of a plethora of creative and cultur-ally well-chosen ideas of consumer agency. These images of agency are increasingly distortions of a world of merchandising so subtle that the consumer is consistently helped to believe that he or she is an actor, where in fact he or she is at best a chooser.

The globalization of culture is not the same as its homogenization, but globalization involves the use of a variety of instruments of homogenization (armaments, advertising techniques, language hegemonies, and clothing styles) that are absorbed into local political and cultural economies, only to be repatriated as heterogeneous dialogues of national sovereignty, free enterprise, and fundamentalism in which the state plays an increasingly delicate role: too much openness to global flows, and the nation-state is threatened by revolt, as in the China syndrome; too little, and the state exits the international stage, as Burma, Albania, and North Korea in various ways have done. In general, the state has become the arbitrageur of this *repatriation of differ-ence* (in the form of goods, signs, slogans, and styles). But this repatriation or export of the designs and commodities of difference continuously exacerbates the internal politics of majoritarianism and homogenization, which is most frequently played out in debates over heritage.

Thus the central feature of global culture today is the politics of the mutual effort of sameness and difference to cannibalize one another and thereby proclaim their successful hijacking of the twin Enlightenment ideas of the triumphantly universal and the resiliently particular. This mutual cannibalization shows its ugly face in riots, refugee flows, state-sponsored torture, and ethnocide (with or without state sup-port). Its brighter side is in the expansion of many individual horizons of hope and fantasy, in the global spread of oral rehydration therapy and other low-tech instru-ments of well-being, in the susceptibility even of South Africa to the force of global opinion, in the inability of the Polish state to repress its own working classes, and in the growth of a wide range of progressive, transnational alliances. Examples of both sorts could be multiplied. The critical point is that both sides of the coin of global cultural process today are products of the infinitely varied mutual contest of sameness and difference on a stage characterized by radical disjunctures between different sorts of global flows and the uncertain landscapes created in and through these disjunctures.

The Work of Reproduction in an Age of Mechanical Art

I have inverted the key terms of the title of Walter Benjamin's famous essay (1969) to return this rather high-flying discussion to a more manageable level. There is a classic human problem that will not disappear however much global cultural processes might change their dynamics, and this is the problem today typically discussed under the rubric of reproduction (and traditionally referred to in terms of the transmission of culture). In either case, the question is, how do small groups, especially families, the classical loci of socialization, deal with these new global realities as they seek to reproduce themselves and, in so doing, by accident reproduce cultural forms themselves? In traditional anthropological terms, this could be phrased as the problem of enculturation in a period of rapid culture change. So the problem is hardly novel. But it does take on some novel dimensions under the global conditions discussed so far in this chapter.

First, the sort of transgenerational stability of knowledge that was presupposed in most theories of enculturation (or, in slightly broader terms, of socialization) can no longer be assumed. As families move to new locations, or as children move before older generations, or as grown sons and daughters return from time spent in strange parts of the world, family relationships can become volatile; new commodity patterns are negotiated, debts and obligations are recalibrated, and rumors and fantasies about the new setting are maneuvered into existing repertoires of knowledge and practice. Often, global labor diasporas involve immense strains on marriages in general and on women in particular, as marriages become the meeting points of historical patterns of socialization and new ideas of proper behavior. Generations easily divide, as ideas about property, propriety, and collective obligation wither under the siege of distance and time. Most important, the work of cultural reproduction in new settings is profoundly complicated by the politics of representing a family as normal (particularly for the young) to neighbors and peers in the new locale. All this is, of course, not new to the cultural study of immigration.

What is new is that this is a world in which both points of departure and points of arrival are in cultural flux, and thus the search for steady points of reference, as critical life choices are made, can be very difficult. It is in this atmosphere that the invention of tradition (and of ethnicity, kinship, and other identity markers) can become slippery, as the search for certainties is regularly frustrated by the fluidities of transnational communication. As group pasts become increasingly parts of museums, exhibits, and collections, both in national and transnational spectacles, culture becomes less what Pierre Bourdieu would have called a habitus (a tacit realm of reproducible practices and dispositions) and more an arena for conscious choice, justification, and representation, the latter often to multiple and spatially dislocated audiences.

The task of cultural reproduction, even in its most intimate arenas, such as husband–wife and parent–child relations, becomes both politicized and exposed to the traumas of deterritorialization as family members pool and negotiate their mutual understandings and aspirations in sometimes fractured spatial arrangements. At larger levels, such as community, neighborhood, and territory, this politicization is often the emotional fuel for more explicitly violent politics of identity, just as these larger politics sometimes penetrate and ignite domestic politics. When, for example, two offspring in a household split with their father on a key matter of political identification in a transnational setting, preexisting localized norms carry little force. Thus a son who has joined the Hezbollah group in Lebanon may no longer get along with parents or siblings who are affiliated with Amal or some other branch of Shah ethnic political identity in Lebanon. Women in particular bear the brunt of this sort of friction, for they become pawns in the heritage politics of the household and are often subject to the abuse and violence of men who are themselves torn about the relation between heritage and opportunity in shifting spatial and political formations.

The pains of cultural reproduction in a disjunctive global world are, of course, not eased by the effects of mechanical art (or mass media), for these media afford powerful resources for counternodes of identity that youth can project against parental wishes or desires. At larger levels of organization, there can be many forms of cultural politics within displaced populations (whether of refugees or of voluntary immigrants), all of which are inflected in important ways by media (and the mediascapes and ideoscapes they offer). A central link between the fragilities of cultural reproduction and the role of the mass media in today's world is the politics of gender and violence. As fantasies of gendered violence dominate the B-grade film industries that blanket the world, they both reflect and refine gendered violence at home and in the streets, as young men (in particular) are swayed by the macho politics of self-assertion in contexts where they are frequently denied real agency, and women are forced to enter the labor force in new ways on the one hand, and continue the maintenance of familial heritage on the other. Thus the honor of women becomes not just an armature of stable (if inhuman) systems of cultural reproduction but a new arena for the formation of sexual identity and family politics, as men and women face new pressures at work and new fantasies of leisure.

Because both work and leisure have lost none of their gendered qualities in this new global order but have acquired ever subtler fetishized representations, the honor of women becomes increasingly a surrogate for the identity of embattled communities of males, while their women in reality have to negotiate increasingly harsh conditions of work at home and in the nondomestic workplace. In short, deterritorialized communities and displaced populations, however much they may enjoy the fruits of new kinds of earning and new dispositions of capital and technology, have to play out the desires and fantasies of these new ethnoscapes, while striving to reproduce the family-as-microcosm of culture. As the shapes of cultures grow less bounded and tacit, more fluid and politicized, the work of cultural reproduction becomes a daily hazard. Far more could, and should, be said about the work of reproduction in an age of mechanical art: the preceding discussion is meant to indicate the contours of the problems that a new, globally informed theory of cultural reproduction will have to face.

Shape and Process in Global Cultural Formations

The deliberations of the arguments that I have made so far constitute the bare bones of an approach to a general theory of global cultural processes. Focusing on disjunctures, I have employed a set of terms (*ethnoscape, financescape, technoscape, mediascape,* and *ideoscape*) to stress different streams or flows along which cultural material may be seen to be moving across national boundaries. I have also sought to exemplify the ways in which these various flows (or landscapes, from the stabilizing perspectives of any given imagined world) are in fundamental disjuncture with respect to one another. What further steps can we take toward a general theory of global cultural processes based on these proposals?

The first is to note that our very models of cultural shape will have to alter, as configurations of people, place, and heritage lose all semblance of isomorphism. Recent work in anthropology has done much to free us of the shackles of highly localized, boundary-oriented, holistic, primordialist images of cultural form and substance (Hannerz 1989; Marcus and Fischer 1986; Thornton 1988). But not very much has been put in their place, except somewhat larger if less mechanical versions of these images, as in Eric Wolf's work on the relationship of Europe to the rest of the world (1982). What I would like to propose is that we begin to think of the configuration of cultural forms in today's world as fundamentally fractal, that is, as possessing no Euclidean boundaries, structures, or regularities. Second, I would suggest that these cultural forms, which we should strive to represent as fully fractal, are also overlapping in ways that have been discussed only in pure mathematics (in set theory, for example) and in biology (in the language of polythetic classifications). Thus we need to combine a fractal metaphor for the shape of cultures (in the plural) with a polythetic account of their overlaps and resemblances. Without this latter step, we shall remain mired in comparative work that relies on the clear separation of the entities to be compared before serious comparison can begin. How are we to compare fractally shaped cultural forms that are also polythetically overlapping in their coverage of terrestrial space?

Finally, in order for the theory of global cultural interactions predicated on disjunctive flows to have any force greater than that of a mechanical metaphor, it will have to move into something like a human version of the theory that some scientists are calling chaos theory. That is, we will need to ask not how these complex, overlapping, fractal shapes constitute a simple, stable (even if large-scale) system, but to ask what its dynamics are: Why do ethnic riots occur when and where they do? Why do states wither at greater rates in some places and times than in others? Why do some countries flout conventions of international debt repayment with so much less apparent worry than others? How are international arms flows driving ethnic battles and genocides? Why are some states exiting the global stage while others are clamoring to get in? Why do key events occur at a certain point in a certain place rather than in others? These are, of course, the great traditional questions of causality, contingency, and prediction in the human sciences, but in a world of disjunctive global flows, it is perhaps important to start asking them in a way that relies on images of flow and uncertainty, hence *chaos*, rather than on older images of order, stability, and systematicness. Otherwise, we will have gone far toward a theory of global cultural systems but thrown out process in the bargain. And that would make these notes part of a journey toward the kind of illusion of order that we can no longer afford to impose on a world that is so transparently volatile.

Whatever the directions in which we can push these macrometaphors (fractals, polythetic classifications, and chaos), we need to ask one other old-fashioned question out of the Marxist paradigm: is there some pre-given order to the relative determining force of these global flows? Because I have postulated the dynamics of global cultural systems as driven by the relationships among flows of persons, technologies, finance, information, and ideology, can we speak of some structural-causal order linking these flows by analogy to the role of the economic order in one version of the Marxist paradigm? Can we speak of some of these flows as being, for a priori structural or historical reasons, always prior to and formative of other flows? My own hypothesis, which can only be tentative at this point, is that the relationship of these various flows to one another as they constellate into particular events and social forms will be radically context-dependent. Thus, while labor flows and their loops with financial flows between Kerala and the Middle East may account for the shape of media flows and ideoscapes in Kerala, the reverse may be true of Silicon Valley in California, where intense specialization in a single technological sector (computers) and particular flows of capital may well profoundly determine the shape that ethnoscapes, ideoscapes, and mediascapes may take.

This does not mean that the causal-historical relationship among these various flows is random or meaninglessly contingent but that our current theories of cultural chaos are insufficiently developed to be even parsimonious models at this point, much less to be predictive theories, the golden fleeces of one kind of social science. What I have sought to provide in this chapter is a reasonably economical technical vocabulary and a rudimentary model of disjunctive flows, from which something like a decent global analysis might emerge. Without some such analysis, it will be difficult to construct what John Hinkson calls a "social theory of postmodernity" that is adequately global (1990, 84).

Notes

1   One major exception is Fredric Jameson, whose work on the relationship between postmodernism and late capitalism has in many ways inspired this essay. The debate between Jameson and Aijaz Ahmad in *Social Text*, however, shows that the creation of a globalizing Marxist narrative in cultural matters is difficult territory indeed (Jameson 1986; Ahmad

1987). My own effort in this context is to begin a restructuring of the Marxist narrative (by stressing lags and disjunctures) that many Marxists might find abhorrent. Such a restructuring has to avoid the dangers of obliterating difference within the Third World, eliding the social referent (as some French postmodernists seem inclined to do), and retaining the narrative authority of the Marxist tradition, in favor of greater attention to global fragmentation, uncertainty, and difference.

2 The idea of *ethnoscape* is more fully engaged in chap. 3 [of *Modernity at Large*].

References

Abu-Lughod, L. (1989) *Before European Hegemony: The World System A.D. 1250–1350*. New York: Oxford University Press.

Ahmad, A. (1987) Jameson's Rhetoric of Otherness and the "National Allegory," *Social Text* 17: 3–25.

Amin, S. (1980) *Class and Nation: Historically and in the Current Crisis*. New York and London: Monthly Review Press.

Anderson, B. (1983) *Imagined Communities: Reflections on the Origin and Spread of Nationalism*. London: Verso.

Barber, K. (1987) Popular Arts in Africa, *African Studies Review* 30 (3, September): 1–78.

Baruah, S. (1986) Immigration, Ethnic Conflict and Political Turmoil, Assam 1979–1985, *Asian Survey* 26 (11, November): 1184–1206.

Bayly, C. A. (1989) *Imperial Meridian: The British Empire and the World, 1780–1830*. London and New York: Longman.

Benjamin, W. ([1936] 1969) The Work of Art in the Age of Mechanical Reproduction. In H. Arendt (Ed.) *Illuminations*. H. Zohn (Trans.) New York: Schocken Books.

Braudel, F. (1981–4) *Civilization and Capitalism, 15th–18th Century* (3 vols.). London: Collins.

Chatterjee, P. (1986) *Nationalist Thought and the Colonial World: A Derivative Discourse?* London: Zed Books.

Curtin, P. (1984) *Cross-Cultural Trade in World History*. Cambridge: Cambridge University Press.

Deleuze, G., and F. Guattari (1987) *A Thousand Plateaus: Capitalism and Schizophrenia*. B. Massumi (Trans.) Minneapolis: University of Minnesota Press.

Fabian, J. (1983) *Time and the Other: How Anthropology Makes Its Object*. New York: Columbia University Press.

Feld, S. (1988) Notes on World Beat, *Public Culture* 1 (1): 31–7.

Gans, E. (1985) *The End of a Culture: Toward a Generative Anthropology*. Berkeley: University of California Press.

Hamelink, C. (1983) *Cultural Autonomy in Global Communications*. New York: Longman.

Handler, R. (1988) *Nationalism and the Politics of Culture in Quebec*. Madison: University of Wisconsin Press.

Hannerz, U. (1987) The World in Creolization, *Africa* 57 (4): 546–59.

——. (1989) Notes on the Global Ecumene, *Public Culture* 1 (2, Spring): 66–75.

Hechter, M. (1975) *Internal Colonialism: The Celtic Fringe in British National Development, 1536–1966*. Berkeley: University of California Press.

Helms, M. W. (1988) *Ulysses' Sail: An Ethnographic Odyssey of Power, Knowledge, and Geographical Distance*. Princeton, N.J.: Princeton University Press.

Herzfeld, M. (1982) *Ours Once More: Folklore, Ideology and the Making of Modern Greece*. Austin: University of Texas Press.

Hinkson, J. (1990) Postmodernism and Structural Change, *Public Culture* 2 (2, Spring): 82–101.

Hobsbawm, E., and T. Ranger (Eds.) (1983) *The Invention of Tradition*. New York: Columbia University Press.

Hodgson, M. (1974) *The Venture of Islam, Conscience and History in a World Civilization*. (3 vols.) Chicago: University of Chicago Press.

Ivy, M. (1988) Tradition and Difference in the Japanese Mass Media, *Public Culture* 1 (1): 21–9.

Iyer, P. (1988) *Video Night in Kathmandu*. New York: Knopf.

Jameson, F. (1983) Postmodernism and Consumer Society. In H. Foster (Ed.) *The Anti-Aesthetic: Essays on Postmodern Culture*. Port Townsend, Wash.: Bay Press, 111–25.

——. (1986) Third World Literature in the Era of Multi-National Capitalism, *Social Text* 15 (Fall): 65–88.

——. (1989) Nostalgia for the Present, *South Atlantic Quarterly* 88 (2, Spring): 517–37.

Kothari, R. (1989) *State against Democracy: In Search of Humane Governance*. New York: New Horizons.

Lakoff, G., and M. Johnson (1980) *Metaphors We Live By*. Chicago and London: University of Chicago Press.

Lash, S., and J. Urry (1987) *The End of Organized Capitalism*. Madison: University of Wisconsin Press.

Mandel, E. (1978) *Late Capitalism*. London: Verso.

Marcus, G., and M. Fischer (1986) *Anthropology as Cultural Critique: An Experimental Moment in the Human Sciences*. Chicago: University of Chicago Press.

Mattelart, A. (1983) *Transnationals and the Third World: The Struggle for Culture*. South Hadley, Mass.: Bergin and Garvey.

McLuhan M., and B. R. Powers (1989) *The Global Village: Transformations in World, Life and Media in the 21st Century*. New York: Oxford University Press.

McQueen, H. (1988) The Australian Stamp: Image, Design and Ideology, *Arena* 84 (Spring): 78–96.

Meyrowitz, J. (1985) *No Sense of Place: The Impact of Electronic Media on Social Behavior*. New York: Oxford University Press.

Nandy, A. (1989) The Political Culture of the Indian State, *Daedalus* 118 (4): 1–26.

Nicoll, F. (1989) My Trip to Alice, *Criticism, Heresy and Interpretation* 3: 21–32.

Schafer, E. (1963) *Golden Peaches of Samarkand: A Study of T'ang Exotics*. Berkeley: University of California Press.

Schiller, H. (1976) *Communication and Cultural Domination*. White Plains, N.Y.: International Arts and Sciences.

Thornton, R. (1988) The Rhetoric of Ethnographic Holism, *Cultural Anthropology* 3 (3, August): 285–303.

Vachani, L. (1989) Narrative, Pleasure and Ideology in the Hindi Film: An Analysis of the Outsider Formula. M. A. Thesis, Annenberg School of Communication, University of Pennsylvania.

Wallerstein, I. (1974) *The Modern World System*. (2 vols.). New York and London: Academic Press.

Warner, M. (1990) *The Letters of the Republic: Publication and the Public Sphere in Eighteenth-Century America*. Cambridge, Mass.: Harvard University Press.

Williams, R. (1976) *Keywords*. New York: Oxford University Press.

Wolf, E. (1982) *Europe and the People without History.* Berkeley: University of California Press.

Yoshimoto, M. (1989) The Postmodern and Mass Images in Japan, *Public Culture* 1 (2): 8–25.

Zarilli, P. (1995) Repositioning the Body: An Indian Martial Art and Its Pan-Asian Publics. In C. A. Breckenridge (Ed.) *Consuming Modernity: Public Culture in a South Asian World.* Minneapolis: University of Minnesota Press.

34

The Global and the Local in International Communications

Annabelle Sreberny

After three thousand years of explosion, by means of fragmentary and mechanical technologies, the Western world is imploding. During the mechanical ages we had extended our bodies in space. Today, after more than a century of electric technology, we have extended our central nervous system itself in a global embrace, abolishing both space and time as far as our planet is concerned. As electrically contracted, the globe is no more than a village.
– McLuhan, Understanding Media, 1964, 11–12

A Third World in every First World
A Third World in every Third World
And vice-versa
– Trinh Minh-ha, 1987

Contemporary rhetoric suggests that we live in a unitary world in which space and time have collapsed and the experience of distance imploded for ever. The antagonistic blocs of East and West are giving way to international markets, moneys and media. Germany is unified. A new and expanding "Europe" looms. The centrifugal force of "globalization" is the catchphrase of the 1990s. Yet at the very same time, in the same but different world, the centripetal forces of old and new tribalisms and nationalisms are at work and ethnic struggles are breaking out all over. Armenians confront Azarbaijanis, Serbs fight Croats, Mowhawk Indians confront Quebecois, there is violence between Umkatha and the ANC. Race-related violence increases in New York City, with a new Black-Asian dimension. The Soviet Union acts violently against Lithuania, putting perestroika in peril. Iraq invades and annexes Kuwait, and

From Annabelle Sreberny [Annabelle Sreberny-Mohammadi], "The Global and the Local in International Communications." In James Curran and Michael Gerevitch (eds.), *Mass Media and Society*. London: Edward Arnold, 1991. © 1991 by A. S. Mohammadi.

Arab-Americans fear discrimination, as do Muslims in Europe, and the world waits for "high noon" on January 15, 1991. Far from the "loss of the subject", identity seems to lie at the heart of politics in the late twentieth century.

Giddens (1990, p. 64) defines globalization as "the intensification of world-wide social relations which link distant localities in such a way that local happenings are shaped by events occurring many miles away and vice versa". For Giddens what he calls "time-space distanciation" (p. 64), a theme developed at length in Harvey (1989), helps to create "complex relations between *local involvements* (circumstances of co-presence) and *interaction across distance* (connections of presence and absence). In this stretching process of relations, there are numerous modes of connection between different regions and contexts. Appadurai (1990) has described five such "scapes" of interaction as the ethnoscape, the technoscape, the infoscape, the financescape and the mediascape which are interconnected, even overlapping.

Much theoretical debate centres on how the current situation should be conceived and labelled. Some argue that there is a discernibly "new" kind of economic-cultural structure to be called "post-modernity" (Harvey 1989) while others argue that the evident changes of the last fifteen years simply reflect the supreme development and natural extension of global capitalism and prefer to call this structure "late capitalism" (Mandel, Jameson 1990) or "high modernity" (Giddens 1990). What is significant throughout these debates is that the roles of communication and information have been finally and generally recognized as crucial elements in the new world order. Yet the role and shape of communications at the beginning of the 1990s is by no means very fixed or very clear, and neither are our theoretical models for explaining exploring communications on an international scale. The rapidity and complexity of change in the media environment as we enter the 1990s seems to require a newer set of terms and vantage points than are offered by older perspectives, which often seem frozen in a bygone era. This chapter explores the dynamic tension between the global and local levels of analysis, as suggested by Giddens, as a provocative and useful construct which can help us uncover the deeply contradictory dynamics of the current moment. In the twin yet opposing processes of globalization versus localization, media play a central role and reveal the tensions between the macro and micro levels of socio-economic structures, cultures, and development dynamics.

A Brief Reprise of Older Models in International Communication

Since the 1960s, the field of International Communication has been dominated by three successive intellectual paradigms: that of "communications and development" that of "cultural imperialism" and currently by a revisionist "cultural pluralism" which is still searching for a coherent theoretical shape. It will be argued here that this third construct is itself full of contradictions, and that the "global/local" model at least has the merits of putting "contradiction" at the core of its construct. A brief reprise of these models is useful, both as intellectual history and to understand the different theoretical bases and implications of the models for current understanding.

"Communications and Development" emerged out of developmentalist thinking in the early 1960s. After the Second World War, the emergence of independent national political systems such as India, Algeria, Ghana, out of the grip of varied European colonialisms, spawned debates among Western academics about the nature of "development" and the obstacles within such newly-independent nations to development. Some arguments focused on the lack of capital for investment, prompting such practical solutions as the World Bank and interest-bearing loans, under which results many developing nations are still groaning. Other arguments examined the lack of entrepreneurial vision and trained manpower, spawning education exchanges and training programs. The arguments developed by Daniel Lerner (1958) and Wilbur Schramm (1964) focused instead on the Weberian/Parsonian "mentalities" or conjeries of attitudes that were supportive or obstructive to change. They suggested that the traditional values of the developing world were the central obstacles to political participation and economic activity, the two key elements of the development process. The "solution" for their analysis was the promotion of the use of communications media to alter attitudes and values, embodied in "media indicators" (minimum numbers of cinema seats, radio and television receivers, and copies of daily newspapers as a ratio of population necessary for development), which were adopted by UNESCO and widely touted in the developing world. This perspective has been roundly criticized for its ethnocentrism, its historicity, its linearity, for conceiving of development in an evolutionary, endogenist fashion and for solutions which actually reinforced dependency rather than helping to overcome it.

The "dependency" paradigm, developing initially in Latin America and building on older critiques of imperialism (Gunder-Frank 1964) instead recognized the global structures and interrelationships conditioning the "development" of the Third World, particularly the multiple and diverse legacies of colonialism. It was particularly critical of the post-independence economic dynamics which kept Third World states in economic hock to the ex-imperial powers, and argued that "development" could not be mere mimicry of Western structures but had to be conceived as an autonomous, self-chosen path that built on the rich/ancient cultures of the Third World. From within this broad, critical framework, the specific model of "cultural imperialism" argued that, far from aiding Third World nations to develop, the international flows of technology transfer and media hardware coupled with the "software" flows of cultural products actually strengthened dependency and prevented true development. The great merit of the models of "cultural imperialism" (Schiller 1976, Matterlart, 1979) and "media imperialism" (Boyd-Barrett 1977) was their recognition of *global* dynamics and relationships, taking their cue from much older models of imperialism, and the suggested linkages between foreign policy interests, capitalist expansion and media infrastructures and contents. This theoretical model spawned a wide variety of empirical studies which documented the imbalanced flow of media products – from news (Galtung and Ruge 1965) to films (Guback and Varis 1982) to television programming (Varis 1974–84) – as well as the export of organizational structures (Katz and Wedell 1977) and professional values (Golding 1977) from the developed to the Third World. Behind its structuralist analysis and the descriptive mapping of international communications dynamics, a central assumption was that

Western cultural values (often conflated to "American" values) such as consumerism and individualism, expressed implicitly in a variety of media genre as well as directly through advertising, were being exported to and decisively altering Third World cultural milieux. Fears of "cultural homogenization" and "cultural synchronization" (Hamelink 1983) were voiced, and arguments made for Third World "cultural disassociation" along the lines of Samir Amin's "delinking" from the global capitalist system as the only way toward autonomous development and protection of indigenous cultures. Criticisms of this position have been made from quite divergent historical perspectives. One argument, looking back in time, suggests that the very term "cultural imperialism tends to obscure the many deep and diverse *cultural* effects of imperialism itself, including the export of religion, educational systems and values, European languages, and administrative practices, all of which have long ago and perhaps irretrievably altered the cultural milieux of the colonized (Sreberny-Mohammadi in Golding, forthcoming). Such an argument questions the utility of terms such as "authenticity" and "indigeneity" within a length history of cultural contact, absorption and recreation, and suggests that a cultural debate which focuses mainly on modern media neglects other much older and deeper structures which may embody "foreign" values but may also be the pillars of modernization.

Another strand of critique, looking forward to the new realities of the 1990s, suggests that, like the earlier arguments for "communications and development", the "cultural imperialism" model was based on a situation of comparative global media scarcity, limited global media players and embryonic media systems in much of the Third World. The speed-up of history, evidenced in the rapidity of changes in many areas of social life, is especially evident in the global spread of communication and information technologies and the advent of many new and diverse media actors over the past decade or so. In 1990, it is clear that the international media environment is far more complex than that suggested by the "cultural imperialism" model whose depiction of a hegemonic media pied piper leading the global media mice appears frozen in the realities of the 1970s, now a bygone era.

Empirically there is a more complex syncopation of voices and a more complicated media environment in which Western media domination has given way to multiple actors and flows of media products. More nations of the South are producing and exporting media materials, including film from India and Egypt, television programming from Mexico and Brazil. For example, *TV Globo*, the major Brazilian network, exports telenovelas to 128 countries, including Cuba, China, The Soviet Union, East Germany, earning export dollars for Brazil, and its productions outnumber those of any other station in the world (Tracy 1988). Indeed the flow of televisual materials from Brazil to Portugal is one example of how contemporary cultural flows reverse the historic roles of imperialism, while Latin American telenovelas on Spanish television channels in the United States has been called "reverse cultural imperialism" (Rogers and Antola). In another region and medium, the Indian film industry has an international reputation as the most productive – more than nine hundred films in 1985 – with an extensive export market (Dissanayeke 1988). India has also managed to keep a somewhat dualistic yet productive tension between high art film and a popular cinema, creating movies that reflect and reinforce different elements of India's rich cultural past as well as indigenizing invasive foreign elements into a distinctive Indian style (Binford, 1988). Television, too, has been successful at translating ancient Indian culture into popular contemporary televisual fare, the Hindu epic, the Ramayana, clearing urban streets and creating a huge demand for additional episodes over the 50 originally planned (Chatterji 1989). These Third World producers have become not only national producers but international exporters of cultural products, a process which revisionists claim has altered any one-way flow of Western material and the "hegemonic" model of cultural imperialism (McNeely and Soysal 1989). These "global pluralists" adopt an optimistic voice regarding the diversity of media producers and locales and the many loops of cultural flows that have merged (Tracey 1988, Boyd 1984). But the very rapidity of change on the international media scene makes it hard to discern long-term trends. The "global pluralists" are correct to note the coming of age of many Third World media producers and the localization of some media production. Yet at the same time even stronger tendencies toward greater globalization and conglomeratization can be discerned, which I will document shortly.

There is also a conceptual challenge to the "cultural imperialism" model, stemming from new modes of analyzing media effects which question the "international hypodermic needle" assumption preferred by the "hegemonic" model. Arguments about "the active audience" and "polysemy" (e.g. Fiske 1987) inserted into international communications debate suggest that diverse audiences bring their own interpretive frameworks and sets of meaning to media texts, thus resisting, reinterpreting and reinventing any foreign "hegemonic" cultural products, the details of which we will again explore later. The "global pluralism" model seems to suggest many independent and happy producers, somewhat evacuating issues of dominance, cultural appropriation and media effects. I think we need a fourth perspective, one that essentially recognizes and does justice to the dynamic tension between the global and the local, as suggested by Giddens, and the shifting terrains that they encompass. After Trinh Minh Ha (1987), I'll call this outlook "the global in the local, the local in the global" and use the rest of the chapter to explore some of the evident contradictions and tensions between these two poles in different contexts. We could divide globalization in the media sphere into four separable elements: the globalization of media forms, of media structures, of media flows and of media effects. I'll examine them in turn.

1   Globalization of Media Forms

It is claimed that more and more of the world is wired as a global audience with access to electronic media. The "success" of the spread of media distribution and reception systems is in evidence – by the end of the 1980s radio signals were globally available and transistors have overcome lack of infrastructure, while nationally-based television services have been established in all but the smallest and poorest of African and Asian countries. Globally, the number of television receivers rose from 192 million in 1965 to 710 million in 1986. There are antennae in the Amazon jungle. China is

Table 34.1   Television receivers, 1965–86

Continents, major areas and groups of countries	Total television receivers (in millions)			Television receivers per thousand inhabitants		
	1965	1975	1986	1965	1975	1986
World total	192.0	414.0	710.0	57.0	102.0	145.0
Africa	0.6	2.5	15.0	1.9	6.2	25.0
Americas	84.0	160.0	268.0	182.0	286.0	397.0
Asia	24.0	57.0	138.0	13.0	25.0	48.0
Europe (incl USSR)	81.0	189.0	280.0	120.0	260.0	362.0
Oceania	2.4	5.5	9.0	137.0	262.0	360.0
Developed countries	181.0	373.0	564.0	177.0	325.3	472.0
Developing countries	11.0	41.0	146.0	4.7	14.0	39.0
Africa (excl. Arab States)	0.1	0.6	5.7	0.4	2.0	13.0
Asia (excl. Arab States)	24.0	56.0	130.0	13.0	25.0	45.0
Arab States	0.9	3.4	17.0	8.4	24.0	85.0
North America	76.0	133.0	209.0	355.0	564.0	783.0
Latin America and the Caribbean	8.0	27.0	59.0	32.0	84.0	145.0

Source: *Unesco Statistical Yearbook*, 1988.

the third largest producer of television receivers. Beyond RTV reception, video players/recorders (vcrs) have *potential* global reach, although a volume entitled *Video World-Wide* actually examines only 22 countries as well as "the Gulf States", "West Africa" and "Southern and East Africa" and argues that there are only four truly "video rich" areas in the world, Japan and South-East Asia; the "Arab countries", Western Europe, and North America (Alvarado 1988; see also Boyd et al. 1989). Thus, at least in terms of national involvement in electronic media production and distribution of public access to communications infrastructure, there has been significant development over the past two decades.

However, distribution is still extremely unequal. The global "average" of 145 receivers per 1,000 population actually ranges from a high of 783 per thousand in North America to a low of 13 per thousand in the non-Arab states of Africa. The global trend is in place, yet by no means "achieved". Global still does not mean universal. (See table 34.1.)

2   Globalization of Media Firms

Central to any discussion of globalization has been the rise of a global market and the role of transnational corporations (TNCS) in adapting to, producing for and profiting from that. The media sphere has long had its global firms, which tend to become bigger and more powerful as the century winds to an end (Bagdikian 1993). Media moguls such as Rupert Murdoch, Sylvio Berlusconi and Henry Luce with the Warner Brothers have created corporate structures that span continents, combine holdings in broadcast, print and film production and also control distribution facilities such as satellites and cable networks. As an example, the merger in March, 1989, between Henry Luce and Harry and Jack Warner made Time Warner the largest media corporation in the world. It has an assessed value of $18 billion, a workforce approaching 340,000, a corporate base in the United States, with subsidiaries in Australia, Asia, Europe and Latin America (Time Warner Inc., 1990). 1989 revenues were over $10 billion during 1989 from activities in magazine and book publishing, music recording and publishing, film and video and cable television. Time Warner is thus a prime example of a growing global corporate structure which is highly vertically integrated – controlling the production process from the conception of a film idea to the building in which it will be shown, for example – and diversifying horizontally to have stakes in other related leisure and information holdings. By Time Warner's own analysis, vertical integration has numerous benefits, including "creative synergies" and economies of scope and scale; "optimal levels of promotion" which prevents separate companies having a "free ride" on the promotional activities of others', enables companies to "be responsive to the desires of consumers", and allows companies to accept greater financial risk than firms which operate individual industry segments, thus being able to support projects of questionable commercial value. Access to global markets essentially reinforce and multiply the economies of scale.

Time Warner's own material readily describes the company as "a vertically integrated global entity" (Time Warner 1990, p. 47). Indeed, large corporations have not been slow to recognize the positive public value attached to the notion of "globalization" as a unifying process of recognition of a common humanity, and coolly to adopt it for their own purposes. Thus, as part of its own selfmarketing, on Earth Day – April 22, 1990 – a day devoted to global awareness and ecological concern, Time Warner launched a new logo and a new motto: "The World is Our Audience". In similar fashion, Sony justifies its development of American-based holdings by appropriating a famous radical grassroots slogan "Think Globally, Act Locally" for its own purposes. Thus Sony USA writes "It is Sony's philosophy that global corporations have a responsibility to participate actively in the countries in which they operate, a philosophy of 'global localization'. This means thinking globally while acting locally – being sensitive to local requirements, cultures, traditions and attitudes" (Sony USA, p. 1). (Note that Sony employs 100,000 worldwide, enjoys an annual consolidated sales of about $16.3 billion, and has its stock sold in exchanges in ten countries.) These global giants clearly see themselves as part of a current phenomenon and are quick to point out the increasingly international activities of competitors.

Some try to debate the extent of this process of consolidating a few vertically-integrated global media giants and their power to control the creation, production and distribution of world-wide information and communication. Thus, Murdoch's News Corporation argues against the notion that the emergent, pattern is of

Table 34.2   Selected major information and communication groupings.
Total Media turnover – Top 15 Corporations out of 78 listed by UNESCO

Group	Country	Ranking media	Media sales	Press Publishing, recording (%)	Radio-TV motion pictures (%)	Period
Capital Cities/ABC	USA	1	4,440	23	77	
Time	USA	2	4,193	61	39	
Bertelsmann	Germany, Fed. Rep. of	3	3,689	54	18	June 87
News Corp	Australia	4	3,453	58	32	June 88
Warner Communi.	USA	5	3,404	49	51	
General Electric	USA	6	3,165		25	
Gannett	USA	7	3,079	88	12	
Times Mirror	USA	8	2,994	85	11	
Gulf + Western	USA	9	2,904	37	63	
Yomiuri Group	Japan	10	2,848	63	23	86
CBS	USA	11	2,762		100	
ARD	Germany, Fed. Rep. of	12	2,614		100	
NHK	Japan	13	2,541		100	March 88
Advance Publications	USA	14	2,397	92	8	
MCA	USA	15	2,052	8	92	

NB: Of the 78 firms listed by UNESCO *in the complete table* not one was based in the Third World

"international media holdings by relatively few media forms", by arguing that "multi-national media companies have emerged but they are too numerous to be characterized as "few" (NTIA, 1990, p. 5). But this appears nothing more than a quibble; of the thousands of corporations active in the media business worldwide, this group of global media moguls is clearly no more than a handful. While accurate and extensive comparative data is still hard to find, a UNESCO-compiled table for 78 firms listed for their total 1987 media turnover (including press and publishing, television, radio and cinema) shows that only seven had turnover of more than three billion dollars, with 15 having turnover of more than 2 billion dollars (UNESCO 1989, p. 104).

Of the 78 firms listed in the complete table, not one was based in the Third World. Forty-eight were US or Japanese, while the rest were Western European, Canadian or Australian. Already in 1988, the combined revenue of five such giants (Bertelsmann AG, News Corp; Hachette; and premerger Time inc. and Warner) was estimated at $45 billion, or 18 percent of the $250 billion worldwide information industry. (table 34.2.)

Many of these corporations are American, and for many sectors of the American culture industries, international sales are now a crucial source of income. In 1989 foreign revenues accounted for 38% of total revenues for the American motion picture industry and helped to keep the value gap between imported film and film exports at 3 billion dollars. Ted Turner's Cable News Network is received by the Kremlin and the Islamic Republic, and *Dallas* enjoys an international audience in over 90 countries, and US corporations have shown interest in cultural products being included in GATT talks and terms of trade (Time Warner 1990, p. 62).

Yet clearly by 1990 not all this global expansion is conducted by American or European-based firms, the usual assumption of the "cultural imperial" thesis. There is considerable inter-capitalist rivalry, and foreign interests have discovered both the lucrative domestic US market, still the single largest in the world, and the global resonance of American popular culture. A few recent examples would be the global-ization of Hollywood, involving the purchase of Columbia Pictures and Tri-Star Pictures by Sony, the Japanese giant which had already bought Columbia Records in 1988 (the context for the Sony America slogan discussed above); the purchase of MGM/United Artists by Pathe SA, an Italian company; the purchase of 20th Century Fox by Rupert Murdoch's Australian-based News Corporation, and in November 1990, the purchase of MCA Inc, which includes Universal Studios; Universal Pic-ture and MCA Records by the Japanese firm Matsushita.

The dynamic of foreign firms buying US media outlets extends well beyond film-making into many other media: Murdoch's News Corporation owns newspapers in Boston and San Antonio, Harper Row books, and Triangle Publications which pub-lishes *TV Guide*, the largest circulation magazine in the United States; International Thomson Group, based in Canada, owns 116 daily newspapers in the United States; the British-based Maxwell Communications owns Macmillan Books, Bertelsmann AG, the West German giant, owns RCA and Arista Records, while the Dutch firm NV Philips owns Polygram Island A&M Records.

The increasing complexity and transnationalization of global media markets has, somewhat tardily, become the focus of a recently launched study by the National Telecommunications and Information Administration (NTIA), a section of the US Department of Commerce in Washington, DC. Entitled *Comprehensive Study on the Globalization of Mass Media Firms*, in February 1990 it invited input in order to "better formulate US communications policy in a rapidly changing information environment" (NTIA 1990). Culling through the responses which NTIA has provided, and from which much of the above factual evidence is drawn, it rapidly becomes clear that the US-based media/culture corporations are concerned essentially with two phenomena that affect their access to international media markets. The first is the newly defined and instituted European cultural policy interpreted as a set of trade barriers to the free flow of American cultural products. The second is the problem of media piracy, significantly but not solely in the Third World. Yet it is abundantly clear that Europe is viewed as the most promising media market, with very little interest paid to or in media development in the Third World, other than chagrin at the media free ride that many Third World societies have enjoyed. Thus these frequently cited examples of media "globalization" actually reveal its very limited coverage. These processes involve corporate actors of the North, interested in Northern media products and audiences, with marginal amounts of the production or circula-tion occurring among the peoples of the South. It seems quite evident that the production and promotion strategies of these global media firms would do little to alleviate the global imbalance in media availability, and rather exacerbate the global imbalances between the media rich and the media poor.

3   Global Media Flows

Globalization has often been applied to the spread of Western mediated products across the globe, from which few places seem immune. There is much anecdotal evidence of the use of Western cultural products, sometimes in somewhat improbable and erstwhile "remote" places. Ouderkirk (1989) describes trekking up the highest Guatamalan mountains in search of some remote and authentic Qeche Indians and hearing some stirring music which as she approached turned out to be old Beatles tapes! Pico Iyer's (1989) travelogue talks about "video nights in Kathmandu" and elsewhere in Asia, encountering "Ike and Tuna Turner" sandwiches in the heart of the people's Republic of China, Burmese musicians playing songs by the Doors, as well as countless Asian remakes of Rambo movies. The film *Bye Bye Brasil* amusingly reflects on the public abandonment of traditional performing arts for television as it spread into the hinterland of Brazil. Recent visits to the Islamic Republic of Iran revealed considerable use of American videos such as *Robocop* and Maximum Overdrive and audiotapes of Madonna and Michael Jackson, all brought in via the black market from Dubai (Sreberny-Mohammadi and Mohammadi 1991).

As already mentioned much early work supportive of the cultural imperialism hypothesis provided descriptive mappings of unequal global flows, and much international debate in the 1970s–80s focused on this notion, as an indicator of global domination and threat to indigenous cultural survival. This culminated in the UNESCO mass media declaration, the report of the Macbride Commission and the formulation of a tenet of the New International Information Order as moving from a merely "free" flow to a "free and balanced" flow of communication (although no adequate empirical measures of such balance have ever been devised).

Trade Barriers and Piracy: Local Strategies vis-à-vis the Global

Two different strategies have been devised to deal with the imbalanced flow, one of which involves limitations and trade barriers to cultural imports. Limits on the amount of imported programming and vetting of imported materials exist in Brazil, India, Iran and elsewhere in the Third World. But now that Europe appears to be moving toward an albeit voluntary continental policy for 1992, transnational corporations are extremely worried. Time Warner argues that it faces formidable trade barriers, "some of which are clothed in the garb of 'cultural' measures ostensibly designed to protect the cultural sovereignty and artistic heritage of the country in question" (Time Warner 1990, p. 48). The corporation proclaims a certain sensitivity: "Although we must be sensitive to the cultural environment and needs of every locale in which we operate, trade barriers can only be justified to the limited extent that they are truly necessary to protect indigenous cultures that would otherwise be overwhelmed by the cultural products of other countries" but in the very next paragraph the tone changes: "The cultural issue is appearing with alarming frequency in the international marketplace, and must be roundly rejected" (Time Warner 1990, p. 48). Its main concern, shared by other media multinationals, is the new European initiative in the *Television without Frontiers* directive which suggests a 50 per cent quota on imported programming by October 1992 where possible (although this is non-binding) and defines a "European" television company, one where the production and control of production is in an EC state or as a majority of the total cost of production is borne by a producer or co-producer from the EC states or those states privy to the Council of Europe convention. Thus even the possibility of transnationals developing co-productions with Europeans is limited to a minority financial and creative capacity, a trade limitation in Time Warner's eyes. There are also European Community initiatives to promote the EC audiovisual industry and cultural uniqueness of member states as well as the development and standardization of hardware such as HDTV. While Koreans are chastized for putting live snakes in cinemas showing US-made films, and Brazil and Egypt are noted for developing policies promoting homemade cultural production, from the statements of Time Warner and other corporations it is evident that essentially they see Europe as the problem, not the Third World. The former presents an already well-developed media market with a substantial population possessing considerable disposable income, a market to which US-based firms want ready access. Thus a closer examination of corporate "globalization" strategies reveals highly preferred locales and areas of acute disinterest, depending on the already existing level of insertion of the populations within global capitalism.

The Third World is problematic to transnationals mainly because of its video piracy, an ingeniously literal understanding of the "free" flow concept. Yet while this means lost revenues to multinationals, such piracy often affects embryonic industries at home, and thus undermines alternative national cultural production. It is apparent that the still limited and unregulated media markets of the Third World are not especially attractive to transnational culture brokers, which perhaps ironically gives Third World media systems a chance to produce for themselves and escape the Western cultural net, a *force majeure* for delinking.

Media Localization: The Newest Argument

At the same time as these dynamics of globalization have been established, an opposing tendency is concurrently at work, as a consequence of, and often in reaction to, the former; that is the dynamic of localized production and the indigenization of cultural products already referred to above. The evidence about such trends is patchy and somewhat contradictory. Varis in his two studies of television flows in 1973 and 1984 concluded that few national systems had made major transitions to self-reliance in television programming. Increasing counter-evidence and counter-argument to the few "positive" cases is being advanced. At a Summer 1990 meeting of communication researchers in Brazil, Latin American researchers argued that despite the proliferation of media, television programming has become more North

American; that 99 percent of the films shown on Brazilian television are American, and that cheap packages of old movies and TV shows are "dumped" and thus flood the Latin American media scene (Osava 1990). Oliveira argues that Brazilian homemade television is even more commercial than American programming with "merchandising" of products a central part of telenovela content, encouraging a consumerist way of life of which the United States is the most advanced example (Oliveira 1990). The same can be said of Peruvian media. India's film industry is being severely challenged by the spread of VCRs and video piracy, the importation of Western movies and the closure of cinemas as running costs rise and audiences dwindle (Mohan 1990). Cross-fertilization between Western cinema and television – predominantly American and British – with the popular Indian cinema is creating more "hybrid" cultural forms, like a new film genre wryly described as the "curry eastern" (Jain 1990).

Evidence suggests that when a choice is available, domestic production is preferred over imported, as telenovelas garner larger audiences than imported American soaps not only in Brazil but elsewhere in Latin America (Rogers and Antola). But in such a process, fears of hybridization and creolization exist, that the "authenticity" of a culture is damaged and undermined in its contact with Western culture industries and its adoption of genres foreign to domestic cultural tradition. Some counter that the Latin telenovela is a truly indigenous and independent genre (Straubhaar 1981), building on internal cultural forms and breaking with the mimicry of Western genre that Tunstall forwarned. But Oliveira argues that this "indigenization' of media often seems to enhance not diversity but domination by corporate concerns. Tunstall in *The Media are American* (1978) pointed out that the importation of media systems to the Third World included not only media hardware but also Western forms and genres, which he suggested would lead to precisely such "hybrid" concoctions. But we must ask what is this pristine image of culture that lurks behind this argument? Human history is a history of cultural contact, influence and recombination, as is in evidence in language, music, visual arts, philosophical systems; perhaps media flows merely reinforce our mongrel statuses.

More to the point, evidence suggests that this "newer" model of cultural indigenization may have been severely overstated and certainly presented in a far too naive manner. Much of this so-called indigenous production is created by large corporations, and deeply infused with consumption values, one of the basic critiques of the "cultural imperialism" perspective. Another point of direct relevance to the "localism" claim, is that the level of this media production is at the level of the nation, either through state supported or national corporate networks. Thus in such arguments the "local" is really the "national", while the truly local (sub-cultural, grassroots, etc.) is ignored. This "national" culture may privilege urban lifestyles over rural, may barely represent minority languages and tastes, even disallowing such diversity in the name of "national unity"; it may produce mediated culture within a narrowly-defined ideological framework that fits the politics of the regime of the day. The case of Iran suggests that tradition required defending at the moment that it was already challenged, so Islam as "cultural identity" was constructed to oppose the Shah and the influx of foreign cultural values and products, only to be used after

616   Annabelle Sreberny

the revolution as an ideological weapon against all political opponents (Sreberny-Mohammadi 1990). National agendas are not coincidental with truly "local" agendas, and real concerns arise as to whether "national" media cultures adequately represent ethnic, religious, political and other kinds of diversity. In international relations, the "national" level may be local vis-à-vis the global level, but in domestic relations, the "national" is itself a site of struggle, with a variety of "local" identities and voices in contention.

Cultural Products in the Global Economy

The *new revisionism* also seems to have exaggerated the size/amount of this "localized" production, which is perhaps of financial significance for national economies in the Third World, but is barely yet reflected in international statistics. There are immense difficulties involved in cross-national calculations and comparisons of media, information and cultural production and flow statistics (Braman 1990). UNESCO has made a major effort to compile international data in its *World Communication Report* published in 1989. Taking this information for the moment at face value, it provides important indicators of the extent of the changes the "global pluralists" suggest. For example, information on "total turnover for information and communication" for selected major information and communications groupings which includes equipment, services, and cultural products, clearly shows the continuing dominance of US and Japanese firms. (See table 34.3.)

These comprise 67 percent of the top 25 companies, 66 percent of top 50 companies and 67 percent of the top 100 companies; European firms, by contrast, comprise 28 percent of top 25, and 26 percent of the top 50 (with Canada the only other nation included), and 26 percent of the top 100 companies. Other commonwealth countries begin to appear in the second fifty, while Korean and Brazilian companies appear at positions 83, 91 and 94. Of 304 organizations listed by UNESCO in a ranked table of major information and communication groupings, Globo placed 301. Thus the exemplar of *Rede Globo* and Brazilian cultural production as a counter to "cultural imperialism" as a net exporter of cultural products is cut to size. Simply summarized, the US, Japan and Western Europe dominate in this agglomerate category.

If hardware and software areas are parcelled out, does the picture look any different? Not significantly. The table for "total media turnover" for major information and communication groupings provides a remarkably similar picture to the above.

Half of the first 25 companies, of the first 50, and of the total of 78 companies for which statistics are presented, are US companies. (See table 34.2.) No Third World media corporation penetrates this "top 78". Now, of course, such figures represent the total dollar value of communications output, and say nothing specific about *export* dollar values, but they do dampen the optimistic hailing of major Third World cultural producers. While the map of global cultural flows is more complex in 1990, it is not as yet fundamentally realigned. But what about the question of "effects"?

Table 34.3 Selected major information and communication groupings.
Total turnover for information and communication

Group	Country	Ranking-information and communication	Information and communication sales	Total sales	Information and communications (%)	Period
1	2	3	4	5	6	7
IBM	USA	1	54,217	54,217	100	March 88
NTT	Japan	2	40,926	40,926	100	March 88
ATT	USA	3	37,458	33,598	111	
Matsushita	Japan	4	24,683	34,832	71	March 88
Deutsche Bundespost	Germany, Fed. Rep. of	5	20,185	28,960	70	March 88
NEC	Japan	6	19,622	19,622	100	March 88
Philips	Netherlands	7	19,253	26,023	74	
British Telecom	UK	8	17,344	17,344	100	March 88
France Telecom	France	9	16,650	16,650	100	March 88
Toshiba	Japan	10	16,106	17,824	90	March 88
Lucky Gold Star	Korea, Rep. of	83	2,791	11,474	24	86
CBS	USA	84	2,762	2,762	100	
TRW	USA	85	2,721	6,821	40	
Apple	USA	86	2,661	2,661	100	September 87
ARD	Germany, Fed. Rep. of	87	2,614	2,614	100	
US Sprint	USA	88	2,592	2,592	100	
TDK	Japan	89	2,586	2,586	100	November 87
Toppan Printing	Japan	90	2,584	3,800	68	May 87
Samsung	Korea, Rep. of	91	2,581	14,193	18	85
NHK	Japan	92	2,541	2,541	100	March 88
Ford Motor	USA	93	2,500	71,643	3	
IBL	UK	300	501	501	100	86
Globo	Brazil	301	500	500	100	86
Nippon Telecommunication Construction	Japan	302	500	500	100	March 87
Talt	USA	303	500	500	100	
JTAS (Jydske Telefon)	Denmark	304	500	500	100	

Groups 11–82 and 94–299 have not been included in this table.

4   Global Media Effects?

Media effects is one of the most disputed areas of domestic media research so there is no reason to expect any greater unanimity about effects at the international level. The "cultural imperialism" thesis did tend to suggest a "hypodermic needle" model of international effects, "American" values being injected into Third World hearts and minds. Recent work, building on reception theory and models of the active audience, is giving a more nuanced view of international effects as mediated by pre-existing cultural frameworks and interpretative scheme. Thus, despite their book's title (*The Export of Meaning*), Leibes and Katz (1990) argue that meaning is not exported in Western television programming but created by different cultural sectors of the audience in relation to their already-formed cultural attitudes and political perceptions. Others (Beltran, Oliveira) argue that it is not so much national American values that are exported but rather more generalized capitalist consumption values (which, of course, America best epitomizes) reinforced by advertising and prevailing development orientations. For them, globalization portends homogenization which, while useful for milk, produces a culture that tastes bland and is not even good for you!

What is often omitted from discussions on effects, are the deeper shifts in cultural orientations and patterns of sociability, in modes of perception and information-processing, that the advent of media create everywhere, albeit in different forms relative to the pre-existing local culture, that is to say it is the very "fact of television", as Cavell (1982) calls it, in our social lives, not so much its content, that is most often overlooked.

The arrival of media in Third World settings is finally being examined by anthropologists (although there is never an index listing for "media" or "television" in a cultural anthropology textbook, despite the fact that most Third World societies are now mediated in some way) and communications researchers' ethnographic studies are beginning to show the rich play between the pre-existing culture and the new quasi-international culture and the shifts in social relations that the latter may foster. In an ethnographic study conducted in various sites across Brazil, Kottak (1990) explored how television alters pattern of sociability, usage of time, creates conflicts within the family and alters the gender balance, themes also explored in the comparative work on family use of television compiled by Lull (1988). Kottak suggests the need to investigate media impact over time, finding in Brazil an early mesmerization with the television set with a later development of selectivity and critical distance, negative attitudes toward television increasing with higher income and years of exposure.

Other ethnographic work suggests the slippery boundaries of the "global" and "local". Abu-Lughod (1990) has studied the impact of what she calls "technologies of public culture" on the Awlad "Ali, the Western Desert Bedouin in Egypt. Although these bedouin have been quite marginal to mainstream Egyptian culture, they were by no means culturally or politically untouched before these technologies arrived; indeed, they often made their money from selling post-war scrap metal and from smuggling goods between pre-Qaddafi Libya and Egypt. Abu-Lughod examines the impact of tape-players, radios and television on Awlad "Ali life, saying that their use does not eliminate sociability but in fact brings people together for long periods of time. Such use does realign social relationships, mixing the sexes and tempering age differences at home, while video shows in local cafes kept young men away from the home and gave them greater exposure to media. In line with reception theory, she argues too that these technologies do not destroy distinctive cultures because "it is not just that people themselves seem to embrace the technologies and actively use them for their own purposes, but that they select, incorporate and redeploy what comes their way" (p. 8), although she notes that so far at least the amount of truly *foreign* programming available is extremely limited. If anything, new technologies such as cassettes have helped to revitalize Bedouin identity as distinct from Egyptian culture through recordings of poetry and song. The urban middle-class Egyptian lifestyles revealed on soap operas present a different set of options to Bedouin women, specially the possibility of marrying for love and living independent of the extended family, so that the dominant Egyptian mediated culture is used as a language of resistance against the authority of tribal elders. Also embedded in such programming are consumer values, for electronic durables as well as products for a newly sexualized femininity, drawing the Bedouin further into the Egyptian political economy. Yet at the same time, in a contradictory manner, Egyptian radio and television carries more transnational messages about Islam, which is gaining in popularity, and which provides an antidote both to capitalist urban Egyptian values as well as the local Bedouin identity (Abu-Lughod, p. 11).

Hannah Davis (1990) describes life in a small Moroccan agricultural town of 50,000 people and notes how "symbols from different worlds overlap: a picture of the king of Morocco hangs next to a poster of the Beatles. The sounds of a religious festival outside . . . mingle with the televised cheering of soccer fans . . . in the morning we watch a holy man curing a boy, then stop off at the fair where we see a woman doing motorcycle stunts; in the evening we watch an Indian fairy tale or a Brazilian soap opera or an Egyptian romance" (p. 13). She remarks it is not "the contrast between the elements that is striking, it is the lack of contrast, the clever and taken-for-granted integration" (p. 12). As in much of the Middle East (the world?!) public space is male space, and thus it is the women who gather round the television and VCR at night, watching Egyptian, Indian and "French" – here the generic term used for Western films. Egyptian films were romances that reduced the women to tears, while the Western films elicited "gasps of surprise, horrified hiding of the eyes, fascination or prurience", with American sexual shamelessness being both admired and feared, imitated and denigrated. The transcultural mix of symbols is apparent when one young girl organizes a traditional religious feast yet defiantly appears wearing a denim skirt and earrings; thus, such symbols may be used in personal struggles to "define, test or transform the boundaries" of local lives (p. 17).

Such examples reveal the complex (re)negotiation of identity(ies) vis-à-vis the "dominant" and the "foreign" cultures, both of which shift in focus depending on the specific locale of the actor. The above examples pose a number of different pairs of relations in which the site of the "local" and the image of the "global" are differently defined: rural/urban; Bedouin/Egyptian; Moroccan/Egyptian; Bedouin/ French; Moroccan/American and so forth. This work reveals again the post-modern "bricolage" of assorted cultural icons from different locations and time periods which circulate inside the non-industrialized world, yet invites no simple reading of the effects of these encounters. Iran is again a useful example of the way in which cultural icons can become deeply invested with one set of ideological connotations in one moment of political struggle, and invested with completely the opposite connotations at a subsequent but differently defined political moment. Thus religious language, traditional symbolism and mythology were popularly (re-)adopted as part of the revolutionary struggle against the Shah, but with the new repression of the Islamic Republic a popular cultural underground began to produce hard liquor and circulate Western videos as part of a new resistance (Sreberny-Mohammadi and Mohammadi, forthcoming). Thus a "sign" of resistance – the veil, for example at one point in time can become a "sign" of oppression at another. The detail of such anthropological/ethnographic work extends the "localist" focus, and shows the complexity and range of reactions to and uses of contemporary global cultural encounters. They warn us against generalized assumptions about media/cultural effects, that the "foreign" may emanate from the urban capital, a Western country other than the US and perhaps even from a Third World media producer of very different cultural background but whose depictions of social life in the process of development can reverberate across the South.

One other basic shift that the global flow of mediated products and the establishment of culture industries in the Third World creates, is that documented by Horkheimer and Adorno toward consumption of mass-produced culture. That is culture, from being local lived experience becomes media product, with the implicit danger that what is not reflected on television no longer has cultural worth. One last neglected "effect" is important to consider. It has been argued that media development in the West has moved through a set of "stages" during which one form of communication and its preferred modality of discourse has been dominant. These have been described by Ong as orality, chirography/typography and the period of the dominance of electronic media which he labels "secondary orality". Yet in the Third World there is evidence that the middle stage, at least as measured by mass literacy and circulation of printed materials, may be "jumped", with societies moving directly from a predominantly oral culture directly into the "secondary orality" of electronic media. We have paid little attention to this new and different kind of cultural formation. The "communications and development" model tended to collapse history, suggesting the development of newspapers, cinemas, radio and television all at once, while the "cultural imperialism" model has given most attention to electronic media. Yet if print is connected to the development of rational logical thinking (Ong), to the development of modern ideologies not linked to church or aristocracy (Gouldner), and the growth of a public sphere, open debate and active citizenry (Habermas), then the limited if non-existent development of this mode of communication in developing countries has profound political and social consequences which have barely been acknowledged. Analysis of the uses of

different media by class and gender in Third World societies, and the power relations which develop is another rather ignored area of research (Sreberny-Mohammadi
1991).

Conclusion

If nothing else, the chapter has shown the complexity of the global contemporary
media/culture spectrum at the start of the twenty-first century, and the range of
theoretical constructs that have been used to explain, and base policy on the international role of media, particularly in the "Third World". The "mood" of contemporary analysis can be quite varied. One position is that of the happy post-modernist
who sees that many kinds of cultural texts circulate internationally and that people
adopt them playfully and readily integrate them in creative ways into their own lives,
and that cultural bricolage is the prevailing experience as we enter the twenty-first
century. Another is the melancholy political economist who sees the all-pervasive
reach of the multinationals and wonders how long distinctive cultures can outlast
the onslaught of the western culture industries. Somewhere in between lies the
cautiously optimistic fourth-Worlder who sees in the spread of media the possibilities for revitalization of local identities (ethnic, religious class, etc.) and their use as
tools of political mobilization vis-à-vis both national and global forces. But we have
also seen the slippery nature of the linguistic terms used in international communications analysis: that "global" rarely means "universal" and often implies only the
actors of the North; that "local" is often really "national" which can be oppressive of
the "local"; that "indigenous" culture is often already "contaminated" through
older cultural contacts and exists as a political claim rather than a clean analytic
construct. The bi-polar model suggests either imbalance/domination, the political-
economy perspective or balance, the "global pluralist" perspective, whereas the real
world reveals far greater complexity.

Cultural boundaries are not etched in stone but have slippery divisions dependent on the self-adopted labels of groups. What seems clear is that, far from an end
to history, or the loss of the subject, identity politics and cultural preservation
are going to be amongst the hottest issues of the next century that will be fought
out internationally and intranationally, with profound political and economic consequences. The apparent triumph of late capitalism in 1989–90 and the demise of
the so-called second world of state socialism, suggest that ideological politics in the
classic sense is going to be less important than the revival of identity politics in the
future. Yet at the same time as the demise of a single master narrative of global
progress is trumpeted in some quarters, in others the old indicators of a single path
to "development" are still utilized, and even adopted with greater eagerness by
Third World societies yearning for "progress". It is likely that in the next decade we
shall see a revival of intense debate about development, and the unresolved role of
culture within that process, neo-Lernerian arguments for the positive role of media
systems as part of national development encountering arguments for more thoroughgoing Third World economic disassociation and delinking from the global capitalist

economy (Amin 1990), as well as fourth world/indigenist culture arguments for the maintenance of local identities (Verhelst 1990). These levels may themselves be in conflict, for a strong "national" position taken in relation to international economic and cultural forces may lead to repression of "local" forces and voices in relation to that "national" level. Inter-state relations are not coterminous with inter-cultural relations, and the political and conceptual agenda of the twenty-first century is going to be how to cope with these various levels of actors and processes. It is here that conceptual leakage in the global/local framework of analysis is most evident, high-lighted by the particularly complex set of issues raised by mediated cultural flows which poignantly reveal in their electronic presence the absence or porousness of boundaries. In the bipolar model it is the "national" level of analysis that becomes invisible. Yet it is national policy-making that helps define a cultural identity, pro-vides the regulatory framework for media organizations – the state providing direct funding and control in many Third World nations – and cultural trade policy, as well as defining the domestic public sphere and the extent to which diverse voices will or will not be heard. As Giddens himself underscores in much of his work, nation-states are the key political systems of the modern world, controlling the structures – legal, administrative, financial, military, surveillance, and informational – in which we all live and which are now involved in transnational dynamics – a capitalist world economy, the world military order, systems of inter-governmental organizations, transnational political movements, etc. – which both press in on and explode the meaning of national boundaries (Giddens 1985). Indeed, as Giddens argues, the world-wide system of nations states exists in constant tension with the global capital-ist economy.

It seems that we require a third-term, between the two terms of "global", and "local", that recognizes the separate level of "state" structures and national policy-making which is still the crucial level of political, economic and cultural decision-making. So much of current political cultural struggle centres precisely on (the memories of) the "imagined communities" of nations and their claims to be "states" (Anderson 1983). At issue in current political struggles – in the Soviet Union, Eastern Europe, the Middle East, Africa – is whether "nations" do/should constitute homogenous cultural/ethnic bases on be political structures which allow heterogeneity and civic rights to flourish. While the latter was the basis for modern nation-states (Hobsbaum 1990) we increasingly hear demands for the former, raising questions about the appropriate relation between cultural rights and national boundaries, and whether narrowly-conceived ethnic states are really progressive. A bi-polar model such as globalization and localization too readily implies either dominance or balance. A triangular model, with the "national" re-inserted, reflects the multiple and deeper tensions and contradictions that constitute the present world order.

Notes

1   UNESCO suggests that 39 countries and territories had not yet introduced a television service by 1988:

Africa: Botswana, Cameroon, Cape Verde, Central African Republic, Chad, Comoros, Gambia, Guinea-Bissau, Malawi, Rwanda, St Helena, Sao Tome and Principe, Western Sahara; North America: Anguila, Belize, Caymen Islands, Dominica, Saint Vincent and the Grenadines, Turks and Caicos Islands; South America: Malvinas, Guyana; Asia: Bhutan, East Timor; Europe: Holy See, Liechtenstein, San Marino; Oceania: Cook Islands; Fiji, Kiribati, Nauru, Niue, Norfolk Island, Papua New Guinea, Samoa, Solomon Islands; Tonga, Tuvalu, Vanuatu.

References

Abu-Lughod, Lila, "Bedouins, Cassettes and Technologies of Public Culture", *Middle East Report*, 159, 4, 7–12.

Alvarado, Manuel, (ed.), (1988): *Video World-Wide: An International Study*, London/Paris: Unesco/John Libbey.

Amin, Samir, (1990): *Delinking*, Monthly Review Press.

Anderson, Benedict, (1983): *Imagined Communities*, London: Verso.

Antola, L. and E. M. Rogers, (1984): "Television Flows in Latin America", *Communication Research*, 11, 2, pp. 183–202.

Appadurai, Arjun, Spring (1990): "Disjuncture and Difference in the Global Cultural Economy", *Public Culture*, 2, 2, pp. 1–24.

Bagdikin, Ben, "Lords of the Global Village", *The Nation*, 248, 23, pp. 805–20.

Binford, Mira Reym, (1988): "Innovation and Imitation in the Indian Cinema", in W. Dissanayeke (ed.) *Cinema and Cultural Identity*, Maryland: University Press of America.

Boyd, Douglas, (1984): "The Janus Effect? Imported Television, Entertainment Programming in Developing Countries, *Critical Studies in Mass Communication*, 1, pp. 379–91.

Boyd, D., J. D. Straubhaar and J. A. Lent, (eds.), (1989): *Videocassette Recorders in The Third World*, Longman.

Boyd-Barrett, Oliver, (1977): "Media Imperialism: towards an international framework for the analysis of media systems", in J. Curran, M. Gurevitch and J. Woollacott (eds.) *Mass Communication and Society*, London: Edward Arnold.

Cavell, Stanley, Fall (1982): "The Fact of Television", *Daedalus*, III, 4, pp. 75–96.

Chatterji, P. C., (1989): "The Ramayana TV serial and Indian secularism", *InterMedia*, 17, 5, pp. 32–4.

Davis, Hannah, "American Magic in a Moroccan Town", *Middle East Report*, 159: 19, 4, pp. 12–18.

Dissanayeke, Wimal, (1988): "Cultural Identity and Asian Cinema", in W. Dissanayeke (ed.) *Cinema and Cultural Identity*, Maryland: University Press of America.

Fabrikant, Geraldini, "Studios look to Foreign Markets", *New York Times*, March 7, 1990, Section DI.

Fiske, John, (1987): *Television Culture*, New York: Methuen.

Galtung, J. and Ruge, M., (1965): "The Structure of Foreign News", *Journal of Peace Research*, 1, pp. 64–90.

Giddens, Anthony, (1990): *The Consequences of Modernity*, Stanford University Press.

—— (1985): *The Nation-State and Violence*, Cambridge: Polity Press.

Golding, Peter, (1977): "Media Professionalism in the Third World: the transfer of an ideology", in J. Curran, M. Gurevitch and J. Woollacott (eds.) *Mass Communication and Society*, London: Edward Arnold/Open University.

Guback, Thomas and Tapio Varis, (1982): *Transnational Communication and Cultural Industries*. (Reports and Papers on Mass Communication No. 92), Paris: Unesco.

Gunder-Frank, André, (1964): "The Development of Underdevelopment", in *Capitalism and Underdevelopment in Latin America*, New York: Monthly Review Press.

Hamelink, Cees, (1983): *Finance and Information*, New Jersey: Ablex.

—— 1983: *Cultural Autonomy in Global Communications*, New York: Longman.

Harvey, David, (1989): *The Condition of Postmodernity*, Oxford: Blackwell.

Hobsbaum, Eric, (1990): *Nations and Nationalism since 1780*, Cambridge: Cambridge University Press.

Iyer, Pico, (1989): *Video Nights in Kathmandu*, New York: Vintage Press.

Jain, Madhu, Spring (1990): "The Curry Eastern Takeaway" *Public Culture* 2, 2.

Jameson, Frederic, (1984): "Postmodernism, on the cultural logic of late capitalism", *New Left Review*, 146, 53–92.

Katz, E. and Wedesl, G., (1977): *Broadcasting in the Third World*, Massachusetts: Harvard University Press.

Kottak, Conrad Phillip, (1990): *Prime Time Society: An Anthropological Analysis of Television and Culture*, California: Wadsworth.

Lerner, Daniel, (1958): *The Passing of Traditional Society*, New York: Free Press.

Liebes, T. and E. Katz, (1990): *The Export of Meaning*, Oxford University Press.

Lull, James, (ed.), (1988): *World Families Watch Television*, California: Sage Publications.

Mattelart, Armand, (1979): *Multinational Corporations and the Control of Culture*, England: Harvester Press and New Jersey: Humanities Press.

McLuhan, Marshall, (1964): *Understanding Media*, London: Routledge Kegan Paul.

McNeely, Connie and Yasemin Muhoglu Soysal, Fall (1989): "International Flows of Television Programming: A Revisionist Research Orientation", *Public Culture*, 2, 1, 136–145.

Mohan, Anjoo, Sept–Oct (1990): "Cinema fall prey to video pirates", *Development Forum*.

Minhha, Trinh, (1987): "Of other Peoples: Beyond the 'Salvage' Paradigm", in Hal Foster (ed.) *Discussions in Contemporary Culture Number One*, Seattle: Bay Press.

Ntia (National Telecommunications and Information Administration), US Department of Commerce 1990: *Comprehensive Study of the Globalization of Mass Media Firms*, February.

Oliveira, Omar Souki, June (1990): "The Three-Step Flow of Cultural Imperialism: A Study of Brazilian Elites", paper presented at ICA Conference, Dublin, Ireland.

—— June (1990): "Brazilian Soaps Outshine Hollywood: Is Cultural Imperialism Fading Away?", paper presented at ICA Conference, Dublin, Ireland.

Osava Mario May–June (1990): "Foreign domination of TV perplexes Latin Americans", *Development Forum*.

Ouderkirk, Herbert, July (1989): "Modern-day Mayans", *World Monitor*, 2, 7.

Schiller, Herbert, (1976): *Communication and Cultural Domination*, White Plains: International Arts and Science Press.

Schramm, Wilbur, (1964): *Mass Media and National Development*, California: Stanford University Press.

Sony USA, May 30 (1990): *Comments in Response to Notice of Inquiry on Globalization of Mass Media Firms*, NTIA/OPAD.

Sreberny-Mohammadi, Annabelle, (1991): "Media Integration in the Third World: An Ongian Look at Iran", in B. Gronbeck, T. Farell and P. Soukup (eds.) *Media, Consciousness and Culture*, California: Sage Publications, in press.

—— "The Many Faces of Cultural Imperialism", in P. Golding, P. Lewis, and N. Jayaweera (eds.) *Beyond Cultural Imperialism: The New World Information Order Debate in Context*, London: Sage Publications, forthcoming.

Sreberny-Mohammadi, A. and A. Mohammadi, (1991): "Hegemony and Resistance: Cultural Politics in the Islamic Republic of Iran", *Quarterly Review of Film and Video* (special issue on World Television), forthcoming.

Straubhaar, Josaph D., (1981): "Estimating the Impact of Imported versus National Television Programming in Brazil", in S. Thomas, ed., *Studies in Communication and Technology*, vol. 1, New Jersey: Ablex.

Time Warner Inc., May 30 (1990): *Comprehensive Study of the Globalization of Mass Media Firms*, Response to National Telecommunications and Information Administration Request for Comments, NTIA/OPAD.

Tracey, Michael, March (1988): "Popular Culture and the Economics of Global Television", *Intermedia*, 16, 2.

Tunstall, Jeremy, (1977): *The Media are American*, London: Constable.

Unesco, (1989): *World Communication Report*, Paris: Unesco.

Varis, Tapio, Winter (1984): "The International Flow of Television Programs" *Journal of Communication*, 143–62.

Verhelst, Thierry, (1990): *No Life Without Roots: Culture and Development*, London: Zed Press.

35

The Processes: From Nationalisms to Transnationalisms

Jésus Martín-Barbero

A Difference that is More than Underdevelopment

Any reference to a "Latin America" beyond the original unity imposed by the Spanish conquest and domination lies necessarily in the other "visible unification" that J. L. Romero, speaks of in his study of the region's incorporation into the processes of industrial modernization and international trade. Dispersion and fragmentation were the main forces at work in Latin America from the time of the struggles for independence to the reorganization of imperialism in the twentieth century. Because of internal conflicts and the stratagems of division encouraged by the new centres of empire, the fragile national formations were in a state of almost continual break-up. If it is true that the different Latin American nationalisms took different routes and rates of development, starting in the 1930s, this diversity of patterns, as a whole, began to undergo a profound transformation.

After the 1930s the possibility of "becoming a nation" in the *modern* sense of this term hinged on establishing a national market, something that, in turn, depended on adjusting to the needs and requirements of the international market. The fact that Latin America's access to modernization was through political-economic dependency revealed its processes of "unequal development", the basic inequality on which capitalist development rests. This dependency also revealed the contradictions of its "simultaneous discontinuities" in which Latin America lives and carries out its modernization (Lechner, 1981: 12). These discontinuities occur at three levels: firstly, the processes of becoming a state and a nation are often out of phase with each other so that some states become nations much later and some nations delay a long time in becoming a state; secondly, the "deviant" way in which the popular classes enter the political system and become part of the process of forming the nation state

From Jésus Martín-Barbero, "The processes: From nationalisms to transnationalisms." In *Communication, Culture and Hegemony: From the Media to Mediations*, pp. 150–86. Newbury Park, CA.: Sage, 1991.

– more as the result of the general crisis of the system, setting the popular classes in confrontation with the state, than as a product of the autonomous development of their own organizations; and, thirdly, the fact that the mass media play not just an ideological but a *political* role in the incorporation of the masses into the nation.

Before examining each of these levels in further detail, it is important to clarify the concept of discontinuity, that is, the nature of a "modernity which is not contemporary", in order to free the concept from misunderstandings that frequently limit its usefulness. The "non-contemporary" of which we speak must be clearly separated from the notion of constitutive backwardness, that is, the backwardness which is made the explanation of cultural differences. There are two versions of this conception of discontinuity as backwardness. One suggests that the originality of the Latin American countries and of Latin America as a whole has been constituted by factors which lie outside the logic of capitalist development. Another thinks of modernization as the recovery of lost time and therefore identifies development with the definitive leaving behind of what Latin America once was in order to become, at last, modern.

The conception of discontinuity which we propose implies a quite different line of thinking which allows us to break with both an ahistorical and culturalist model and with the paradigm of accumulative rationality with its pretensions of unifying and subsuming all cultural histories in one linear timeline. Our perspective enables us, firstly, to think of historical differences and backwardness not as lost time but as a backwardness which is *produced by historical circumstances* – children who are dying every day because of malnutrition or dysentery, the millions of illiterate people, the caloric deficit in the nutrition of the great majority, the low level of life expectancy, etc. Secondly, we are able to take into consideration cultural differences which are not related to backwardness: the multiplicity of cultural histories of the native Americans, the Afro-Americans, people of European descent and, above all, the cultural history which emerges from the *mestizaje* of all these races and their histories.

Only in the tensions of discontinuities are we able to conceive of a modernity which is not reduced to imitation and of cultural differences which are not identified with backwardness. This was the aim of Bolivar's struggle: to apply the political doctrines of his time to the "grammar of racial, geographical, and cultural diversity" of the Latin American countries; to adjust liberal ideals to the requirements of a new society where liberalism in the name of equality usually meant the rule of the mighty (Bolivar, 1972). Bolivar did not propose a type of nation based on the model of the European nation, but a type of state, which, in abolishing absolute power, would still be strong enough to defend the weak against the wealthy classes.

Martí continued Bolivar's line of thought and his struggle, arguing that the main obstacle in the construction of the Latin American nations is the lack of understanding "of the disorganized mix of elements from which the new nations were so hurriedly formed" (Martí, 1971). Mariátegui also resolutely insisted that the task of these nations was not to catch up with Europe but to rediscover the value of and the meaning of the Latin American myth. Latin America "must let loose its fantasies, liberate its storytelling capacities from old chains in order to discover its reality" (Mariátegui, 1978).

The Discontinuity between the State and the Nation

Beginning in the 1920s, most Latin American countries launched a process of reorganizing their economies and transforming their political institutions. Industrialization was carried out on the basis of import substitution, the formation of an internal market, and bringing manpower into an employed sector. Various forms of supportive intervention of the state and the state's investment in the transportation and communication infrastructure were crucial in this. Thus, even though the take off of industrialization responded to the general conditions of the international market, there were significant differences depending on the model and maturity of the "national project" formulated by the bourgeoisie of each country in the second half of the nineteenth century.

There is much debate as to whether we can speak of a "national bourgeoisie" existing in Latin America in the last century, and there is also a debate about their contradictory role in the formation of the nation states. But, as Malcolm Deas stated, "How could there have been a national politics and a national economy without the articulation of class interests at a national level" (Deas, 1983: 150). Certainly, the national bourgeoisie have had different degrees of power and capacity for strategic influence in countries as different, for example, as Brazil and Ecuador. These differences, however, were not at the level of the Darwinist, evolutionary conceptions that oriented modernization and national development but, rather, in the size of the countries which provided greater scope for action. All countries, however, shared similar experiences of urban growth and erosion of the traditional society. The explosive urbanization of Latin America was the result of population growth and migration from the countryside, augmented, in some countries such as Argentina, by the waves of immigration. These processes produced mass societies with classes and social groups in conflict with the dominant, normative sector of society.

Whether or not the hegemonic groups that appeared were, strictly speaking, a "national bourgeoisie", certainly there were in the various countries new bourgeoisie sectors which controlled both the worlds of business enterprise and politics, and these sectors were responsible for the growing interdependence of these two worlds (Romero, 1976: 268). What stimulated this interweaving of business and politics was not just the new economic take off, but the assumption by these bourgeoisie sectors in Latin America that modernization implied the unavoidable necessity of incorporating their countries into the way of life of the "modern countries". They believed that only one model of transformation could bring their countries out of the morass of backwardness: the path toward a Europeanized urban society. Therefore, the social philosophers and men of science thought it was quite legitimate, indeed, inevitable, to marginalize and exploit the "passive masses" and any other social group that constituted a delay or obstacle. Otherwise the very existence of the nation was in danger.

The new bourgeoisie profited from the old national project of the creoles, changing the meaning of this project even as they sought to carry it to completion.[1] It was through a process of elaborating and moving ahead this national project that the creole classes took on attributes of national scope and became national them-selves. "This continuing, prolonged enterprise of the creole class to construct the state and the nation came to be known as the national project" (Palacios, 1983: 16). The project failed in the nineteenth century, but the new project of constructing a modern nation was built upon the foundations of the old project and took on the same structure of internal power relations.

A new nationalism emerged, based on the idea of national culture which would be the synthesis of different cultural realities and a political unity bringing together cultural, ethnic and regional differences. The nation absorbed the people, "transform-ing the multiplicity of the diverse cultures into a single aspiration, namely the feeling of nationhood". Thus, the diversity legitimated the irreplaceable unity of the nation. To work for the nation means, above all, to work for unification, overcoming the fragmentation that generated the regional and federal wars of the nineteenth cen-tury. Unification through roads, railways, telegraph networks, telephones and radio broadcasting made possible communication between regions, but above all between the regions and the centre, the capital.

There were two schools of thought in this effort, although they shared many elements. One school identified national progress with the advance of the governing social class and with efforts toward rapid industrialization. Another, present in those countries with the sociocultural formation that Darcy Ribeiro has called "peoples of witness" (Ribeiro, 1971), attempted to fuse the new sense of nationhood with the conception which existed before and which comes from below. The goal of the first school of thought was to industrialize in order to join the ranks of civilized nations; in the second there was tension between the compulsive desire to industrialize and the awareness of their uniqueness as a nation. This tension gave rise to the debate in Peru at the end of the 1920s that brought into open confrontation the project of "the national problem" argued by Haya de la Torre and the project of "the indigenous problem" put forward by José Carlos Mariátegui.[2]

In Latin America as a whole, the idea of modernization which oriented the processes of change and which provided the nationalisms with a concrete agenda of action was more a movement of economic and cultural *adaptation* than a rein-forcement of independence. E. Squeff, referring to Brazilian nationalism, affirms, "We were able to achieve our modernization only by translating our raw materials into an expression that would gain recognition abroad" (Squeff and Wisnik, 1983: 55). Thus, the dynamics of cultural policies began to take shape around economic policies. This, however, did not mean the development of an internal market, but rather the introduction into national institutions of a dynamic of conformity to demands which came from outside. Latin American countries wanted to be nations in order to at last define their identities, but the achievement of that identity implied the translation of these identities into the modernizing discourse of the hegemonic countries, for only in terms of that discourse could the efforts and achievements of nationhood be evaluated and validated. The logic of developmentist ideology could not be otherwise for the fundamental orientations were already contained in the modernizing nationalisms of the 1930s – the prior and indispensable stage of later development.

The political structure required for the modernizing project emerged out of the centralizing and initiating role of the state. It was impossible to conceive of national unity without strengthening the "centre", that is, organizing the administration of the country around a central point of decision making. In some countries this centralization would have as its plan of action and justification the establishment of the basic mechanisms of a still non-existent state administration with the organization of systems of national accounts, taxation, and public records.[3] In other countries, where a public administration already existed, centralism meant not simply unification but introducing a homogenizing uniformity of rhythms of life, gestures and ways of speaking. The heterogeneous traditions from which the Latin American countries are composed became merely external ritual functions. Where there have been significant, unavoidable regional cultural differences, this local originality and uniqueness was projected upon the whole nation. Where the differences were not sufficiently great to constitute a national tradition, these were transformed into folklore and offered to foreigners as a curiosity. However, neither the national absorption of the differences nor the transformation into folklore were simply functional strategies of the centralizing policies. For a time, at least, as the prominence of the Indian nativist genre of novels indicates, these cultural differences were used as a means of manifesting "the consciousness of a new country", a form of affirming a national identity still in the process of formation.

Another pivotal point of nationalism in the 1930s is the protagonist role of the state. Although this will be treated in greater detail later when we analyse populism as a way of incorporating the masses into the nation, it is important to point out its significance. In some countries, such as Mexico, the initiative of the state was so strong that it made the state the "hegemonic agent par excellence" (S. Zermeño, in Lechner, 1981: 75). Contributing to this state hegemony in Mexico was the continually erupting "plebeian volcano", the country's civil and external wars, and the constant erosion of the power of the upper classes, requiring a strong state. All this tended to demand of the state an interventionism that translated into a paradox of overpoliticization and desocialization.

In Chile the strengthening of the protagonistic role of the state, at the expense of the institutions and class organizations of civil society, eventually made politics an autonomous process and led to an instrumentalist conception of democracy.[4] And it could not have been otherwise in Chile since the path to industralization was considered to be the exclusive work of the state.

> In Latin America, the "spirit of enterprise" that defines certain basic characteristics of the industrial bourgeoisie in developed capitalist countries was a characteristic of the state, especially in these decisive periods. Instead of the social class for which history clamored with small success, it was the government of the populist *caudillos* that embodied the nation and gave the masses political and economic access to the benefits of industrialization. (Galeano, 1973: 230)

And something similar happened in the cultural sphere. Coming back to the case of Mexico, for Vasconcelos the Revolution, rather than being the moment when the masses marched onto the stage of history, was the opportunity to civilize the masses under the direction of the state, the great educator. His conception was portrayed in the murals "Exalting the armies of Zapata and the international proletariat, but on the walls of government buildings".[5] The muralists added peasant armies and the international proletariat to the humanist and culturalist project of Vasconcelos, but "the state dictated the rules of nationhood and monopolized the historical sentiments and the national heritage of art and culture" (Monsiváis, 1981: 38).

Paradoxically, the growth of the Mexican state was a "conquest by the people", a popular revolution against the creole castes, private corporations and foreign threats. In this paradox lies the strength of the national culture in Mexico, a strength that continued even when the state abandoned its patronage in great part and passed this role to the culture industry. Even then, nationhood is not only what the state has identified and brought into existence but the way in which the masses have experienced once again the social legitimacy of their aspirations. If no other Latin American country has as strong a sense of nationalism as Mexico, the reasons for this must be sought in the fact that other countries have not had the kind of revolution which conferred on the Mexican state a popular representativeness that is not just formal. The absence of a revolution in other Latin American countries, even those with a strong state, explains why the national culture continues to be so disconnected from the real culture and why the concern of the state for cultural identity continues to sound like empty rhetoric.

Massification, Social Movements and Populism

If the 1930s were important years in Latin America for the economic processes of industrialization and modernization, politically they were even more important for the "irruption" of the masses in the cities. Just at the time that the cities begin to fill with people due to both the demographic increase and the rural exodus, there was a crisis of hegemony produced by the absence of a class which could assume the direction of society. This brought the state in many countries to seek its *national* legitimacy in the masses. The maintenance of power was impossible without assuming in some way the vindication of the demands of the urban masses. Populism became the form of a state which sought to strengthen its legitimacy by taking upon itself the popular aspirations. This was not a strategy from a position of power, but rather an organization of power which expressed concretely the contract between the masses and the state. The ambiguousness of this contract resulted both from the vacuum of power which the state was supposed to fill – with the paternalistic authoritarianism which this produces – and from the political reformism which the masses demanded. If we wish, however, to avoid the extremes of attributing to populism an effectiveness which it never had or on the other hand perceiving the masses as in a state of passive manipulation, which is also false, it is important to clarify the implications of the social presence of the masses and the process of massification which came into existence.

Migration and the new sources and types of work nurtured the hybridization of the popular classes, a new form of becoming present in the city. "There was a kind of explosion among the people, and it was impossible to measure exactly how much was due to their larger numbers and how much was the result of the decision of many to make themselves known and their presence felt".[6] The crisis of the 1930s unleashed an offensive of the country against the city and a recomposition of social groups. There was a quantitative and qualititative change in the popular classes as a result of the appearance of a *mass* which could no longer be defined within the traditional social structure and that "dismantled the traditional forms of participation and representation" (Falleto et al., 1982: 109). The presence of that mass would soon affect the whole of urban society, its way of life and thinking, and, eventually, the physiognomy of the city itself.

With the formation of the urban masses, not only was there a quantitative growth of the popular classes, but the appearance of a new mode of existence of the popular: "The disarticulation of the popular world, (constituting it) as the space of the Other, the space of the forces negating the mode of capitalist production" (Sunkel, 1985: 16). The insertion of the popular classes in the conditions of existence of a "mass society" pushed the popular movement toward a new strategy of alliances. The new social experience fashioned a new vision, a new conception of action less openly confrontational. "It was the vision of a society which could be reformed little by little, a society which could come to be more just" (Gutiérrez and Romero, 1981: 8).

For a time, the masses were marginal. Compared with the mainstream of society, the mass was heterogeneous and *mestizo*. The people coming from the country had to learn to cope with a host of strange ways. It was necessary to learn how to catch a bus, how to find one's way through the streets, how to apply for identification papers. The old society responded to the immigrants with a disdain that covered over not just repugnance but fear. More than an assault, the appearance of the masses meant that it was now impossible to continue maintaining the rigid hierarchical organization of differences that constituted the society. For this reason, the aggressiveness of the masses seemed non-violent yet equally dangerous; it was not the uprising of a social class but the freeing of an uncontrollable energy. The "proletariat formed a massive flood" (Romero, 1982: 54) which did not find its political expression in the traditional parties and organizations of the working class but whose manifestations of violence revealed the force of which it was capable.

The presence of the masses in the city slowly acquired more specific characteristics. The sheer numbers meant a shortage of housing, a transportation problem, a new way of living in the city, a different pattern of walking the streets, a distinct way of behaving. On the peripheries of the city there sprang up the *barrios* created by invasions, and in the centre there was a visible breakdown of the organization of urban planning. The city began to lose its centre. In the face of the formless spreading out of the city that the invasions on the periphery implied – the *favelas*, the *villas miseria*, the *callampas* – the rich responded by moving out to still another periphery. But the mass continued invading everywhere. For in the midst of the ignorance of the masses regarding the norms of the city and the way that their mere presence was challenging the order of this environment, there was a secret desire to get possession of the good life that the city represented. The masses wanted work, health, education and entertainment. But they could not claim their right to these goods without massifying everything. The revolution of expectations drove home the meaning of the paradox – subversion lies embedded in integration. Massification meant simultaneously the integration of the popular classes in society and the acceptance by society of the masses' right to everything, a right to the goods and services which, until then, were the privilege of a few. This society could not accept the newcomers without a profound transformation. This transformation, however, did not follow the patterns nor the directions that revolutionaries expected, and therefore the revolutionaries thought that no transformation had occurred.

Massification affected everyone, but not all perceived and experienced it in the same way. The upper classes quickly learned to separate the demands of the masses – with their measure of political threat but also the potential for stimulating economic growth – from the massive supply of material and cultural goods "without differentiating style". For this latter, the upper classes felt only disdain. Massification was especially painful for the middle classes, the petit bourgeoisie, who, as much as they desired, could not distance themselves from the masses. Massification "threatened their dream of interiority that was their characteristic, their jealously guarded individuality and their condition as differentiated persons" (Romero, 1976: 374).

For the popular classes, however, although they were more defenceless in the face of the new conditions, massification implied more gain than loss. Not only did they find better conditions for physical survival, but also the possibility of cultural access and ascent. The new mass culture began not only as a culture directed to the popular classes but a culture in which the masses found synthesized in the music and in the narratives of radio and film some of the basic forms of their own way of perceiving, experiencing and expressing their world.

We are indebted to José Luis Romero not only for one of the most original terms for mass culture, "alluvial folklore", but also for the first sociological and phenomenological characterization of this culture in Latin America (1982: 67ff). Like Benjamin, Romero views mass culture from the perspective of experiences that provide access to forms of expression rather than as simply manipulation. Romero, following the path of Arguedas, has been interested in the analysis of the culture of *mestizaje*, the process of cultural hybridization and the re-elaboration of various cultural sources in a new synthesis. It is an approach that destroys the myth of cultural purity and has no repugnance in using modern instruments in the rendition of traditional indigenous music or in broadcasting such music over the radio. It is a study of the transition from the folkloric to the popular (Arguedas, 1977: 124–5).

Mass culture is the hybrid of foreign and national, of popular informality and bourgeois concern with upward mobility. It is the hybrid of two classic types: those who try to look rich without the means to do so, "who imitate the eternal forms that characterize those 'better' than they are", and the opposite, those crushed by the hopelessness of the slums on the edges of the cities and in the underworld. Mass culture is essentially an urban culture which compensates its open materialism – the supreme values are economic success and social ascent – with a superabundance of the sentimental and the passionate.

From the perspective of the "official policies" of both the left and the right, the masses and mass culture are looked upon with suspicion. The right takes a defensive position, seeing in the masses a threat to their established social privileges and to the sacredness of the cultural borders that separate them from those without taste. The left sees in the masses a dead weight, a proletariat without class consciousness or vocation for social struggle. The mass is a cultural fact that does not fit into their social conceptions. It is a challenge and an obstacle to their essentially Enlightenment frame of reference. Only for the populists does the presence of the urban mass seem to offer a significant new political reality. The populists "drafted the principles of a new ideology that channelled the explosive tendencies of the masses within norms that ensured the preservation of the basic social structures" (Romero, 1976: 381).

Between 1930 and 1960, populism was the political strategy that characterized, with varying degrees of intensity, the social struggle in virtually all Latin American societies. "It was the first strategy that attempted to resolve the crisis of the state which began in the 1930s in much of the region" (Lechner, 1981: 304). Among the first of the great populist leaders was Getulio Vargas, who orchestrated the process that led to the destruction of the "oligarchic state" and the organization of the "New State". Beginning in 1930 the socio-economic conditions of mass society – the rapid industrial growth and the inability of the oligarchy to control it, the liberal-democratic aspirations of the urban middle classes, and the pressures from below of the immigrants pouring into the cities from the rural areas – created the setting for a political pact between the masses and the state that was the root of populism (Weffort, 1978). The state, assuming the role of referee between conflicting class interests, set aside the aspirations of the popular masses, and, through a dictatorship in the name of the people, exercised a direct manipulation of the masses and their economic ambitions. Only in 1945 were democratic tendencies finally able to introduce intermediaries between the state and the masses.

In 1934, Lázaro Cárdenas assumed the presidency of Mexico and proposed a programme of government which took up once again the objectives of the Revolution and attempted to give back to the masses their role as protagonists in the national political process. Supported by the achievements of the Revolution already legislated and legitimated, Cárdenas set forth for the first time a model of economic development based on a "third way" which made the capitalist class responsible for the increase in production and the popular classes the movers of social progress. The role of the state was to reconcile these two sets of interests. Evidence of Cárdenas' socially advanced conception of populism was his defence of the workers' right to strike and refusal of the capitalists' right to close their factories (Cordova, 1974). At the same time, the state, committed to an expensive programme of public works, assumed the burden of the high-risk industries, leaving the most lucrative activities for the private sector.

In Argentina, the outcries of the masses freed Perón from prison in Argentina in 1945 and elected him president in 1946, initiating the classic paradigm of populist government in Latin America. But it was also the regime that generated the most intense debate. Like the earlier populist leaders, Perón proposed a policy of economic development directed by the state, the only institution that could reconcile conflicting interests. By 1946, however, social conflicts had grown to such an extent that it became necessary to transform the nexus between the state and the masses into an "organic" relationship, and in this originated both the strength and the ambiguous role of the labour unions. Perón's populism also contained a larger measure of the symbolic force of the *caudillo* – and of a charismatic wife, Evita – than occurred with any other leader of these years. The mythic symbolism of Perón resided not just in his dramatic "gestures" but in the discourse he created and his capacity to re-semanticize the disparate themes of various social movements, thereby drawing their symbols into the official language. O. Landi has studied this cultural process basic to all Latin American populisms – an appeal to the working class masses, proposing "a new system of acknowledgement of the characteristics of the workers, giving a name to the worker in another form" (Landi, 1983: 30; see also de Ipola, 1982).

For a long period, social analysis cancelled the theme of populism from the subjects of current debate, and an overly simplistic Marxism identified populism as, in practice, the same as fascism. The 1980s, however, opened up the topic again, and suggested that the Marxist conceptions be reexamined. Here, we can only briefly point to three examples of this new line of thought. In the text of Ernest Laclau (1977), which has gained acceptance in the region as one of the most balanced in the Marxist renewal, a new understanding of the role of populism is central. In the 1980 seminar organized by the communication research institute, Desco, in Lima on the theme, "Democracy and Popular Movements", with some of the most representative social science researchers of Latin America present, populism was one of the key issues of the discussions (Moulian et al., 1981). The same year, "Populism and Communication" was the theme of the annual meeting of the Brazilian Association of Communication Researchers (Marquez de Melo, 1981).

What is important in this renewal of interest in populism is a profound change of historical perspective. The political processes from 1930 to 1960 now appear to have been greatly oversimplified by the dependency theory that considered the state to be merely a conduit for the interests of the hegemonic countries. This made it difficult to conceive of the "national problem" in terms of class relationships. Another evidence of how current events have a "contaminating" influence on developments of social theory is the interest in the energetic presence of popular movements. This change of perspective has been particularly well documented by J. C. Portantiero who sees the need to accept within social theory what can be called "The Latin American deviation". This is the view that the popular classes have become social actors, not by the classic route, but through the political crisis that accompanied the processes of industrialization in the 1930s, placing the popular classes in direct relation with the state and making them part of the political process before they became constituted as a social class and protagonists of the social transformations (Portantiero, 1981: 217–40).

This suggestion that the Latin American process was different has had two important consequences for the established schemas of social theory. The first is the development of a politicized labour movement that defines itself and its actions in relation to the state rather than in relation to industry because its fate is determined largely by government economic policy. That this is a deviation from the classical schema becomes even more clear when we note the insistence on defining the relationship between the "social process" and the "political process" not in terms of unions and political parties but as a relation of the labour movement with the movement toward nationhood. A second difference is to attribute to populism "an experience of social class which nationalizes the masses and gives them citizenship" (Portantiero, 1981: 234). This implies that even though populism as a state project might be a thing of the past, its influence as a "phase in which the popular sectors are established as a political force" persists.

Historical memory sometimes tricks the analyst, showing that the relation between the subordinated classes and the people is not always clear. There is a space of conflict that does not coincide entirely with the relationships of class and production. It is a different and specific form of contradiction situated at the level of social formations that put the people in conflict with those in power (Laclau, 1977). This is a "popular democratic" struggle which is characterized precisely by the historical continuity of popular traditions in contrast with the discontinuity which characterizes the structures of class.

The peculiarities of the way in which the Latin American masses have made themselves present as actors on the social scene are related, in the final analysis, with the double form of appeal which motivated the masses from the moment of the urban explosion: an appeal to a sense of class which is perceived only by a small minority and the popular-nationalistic appeal which affects the great majority. But, could this mass mobilization have been merely a manipulation of the people by the state with the aid of the mass media? Today we know that this was not the case. Populism's appeal to the "popular classes" did contain elements of manipulation – higher salaries, the right to organize, etc. – but, when projected through the mass media, this appeal was transformed into a discourse constituting the worker as a citizen in a national social formation. Here, with all its ambiguity, lay the effectiveness of the appeal to popular traditions and the construction of a national culture. Here also we find the specific role of the mass media, especially film and radio, that constructed their discourse on the continuous link of the imagination of the masses from the old narrative memory, with its vivid *mise-en-scène* and popular iconography, to the proposal of new images charged with nationalistic sensibility.

The Mass Media in the Formation of National Cultures

If we are to understand the discontinuities between the state and the nation and the twisted, tortured path by which the masses burst into and became part of Latin American politics we must accept a profound change of perspective regarding the history of the mass media. For, although the social and political demands of the underclasses made themselves heard through the national-popular movements, it was through the discourse of the mass society that the national-popular became a recognizable identity for the great majority of people. With some exceptions, historians of the mass media have studied only the economic structure and the ideological content of the mass media; few have given close attention to the mediations through which the media have acquired a concrete institutional form and become a reflection of the culture. Studies have oscillated between attributing to the media the dynamics of profound historical changes in Latin America or reducing the media to mere passive instruments in the hands of powerful class interests acting with almost absolute autonomy.

If the cultural and political mediations have not been recognized in the history of the mass media, it is without doubt due to the fact that much of the general history leaves out culture or reduces it to high culture in its manifestations of art and literature. In the same way, the political history of Latin America consists of the great moments and important figures and almost never the events and political culture of the popular classes. It was left to an English historian to ask the following kind of questions about Colombian history: "What was the popular impact of independence? What do we know about the political practices of the illiterate? What do we know about informal communication in politics or how local ideas about national politics are formed?" (see Deas, 1983: 151ff).

To introduce the analysis of the cultural sphere does not mean, however, that we add a new and separate theme, but that we focus on those aspects of the social process that articulate the *meaning* of the economic and the political. This would mean writing the history of the mass media from the perspective of cultural processes as articulators of the communication practices – hegemonic and subaltern – of social movements. Some studies have begun to work from this perspective, and their findings provide a starting point for understanding the mediations from which, for example, information technologies become the media of communication.

The focus on mediations and social movements has shown the necessity of distinguishing two quite different stages in the introduction of media institutions and the constitution of mass culture in Latin America. In the first stage, which stretches from the 1930s to the end of the 1950s, the efficacy and social significance of the mass media do not lie primarily in the industrial organization and the ideological content, but rather in the way the popular masses have appropriated the mass media and the way the masses have recognized their identity in the mass media. Of course, economics and ideology influence how the media functioned, but to discover the meaning and ideology of economic structure we must go deeper to the conflict which in that historical moment gave structure and dynamism to the social movements, namely, the conflict between the masses and the state and the resolution of this conflict in the nationalist populisms and populist nationalisms.

During this first stage, the decisive role of the mass media was their ability to convey the challenge and the appeal of populism, which transformed the mass into the people and the people into the nation.

This appeal came from the state, but it was effective only to the extent that the masses perceived in it some of their basic demands and forms of expression. The function of the *caudillos* and the mass media was to re-semanticize the masses' demands and expressions. This occurred not only in those countries that experienced the "dramatization" of populism, but also in other countries which, under forms, names and rhythms other than populism, experienced the crisis of hegemony, the birth of nationality and the beginnings of modernity. Film in many countries and radio in virtually all countries gave the people of the different regions and provinces their first taste of nation.[7]

This function of the media is acknowledged, although unfortunately only in the conclusions, by a recent history of radio in Colombia.

> Before the appearance and growth of radio, the country was a patchwork of regions, each separate and isolated. Before 1940, Colombia could very well call itself a country of countries rather than a nation. Hyperbole aside, radio allowed the country to experience an invisible national unity, a cultural identity shared simultaneously by the people of the coast, Antioquia, Pasto, Santander and Bogota. (Pareja, 1984: 177)

This observation puts us on the trail of another dimension of the formation of mass culture: transforming the political "idea" of nationhood into the daily experience and feeling of nationhood.

The second stage in the constitution of mass culture in Latin America began after 1960. When the model of import substitution "reached the limits of its coexistence with the archaic sectors of society" and populism could no longer be sustained without radicalizing the first social reforms, the myth and strategies of *development* with its technocratic solutions and encouragement of a consumer society began to replace the worn out populist policies (Intercom, 1981: 21). At this point, the political function of the media was removed and the economic function took over. The state continued to maintain the rhetoric that the air waves were a public, social service – as rhetorical as the social function of property – but, in fact, the state handed over the management of education and culture to the private sector. Ideology became the backbone of mass discourse whose function was to make the poor dream the same dreams as the rich. As Galeano has said, "The system spoke a surrealist language". Not only was the wealth of the land transformed into the poverty of mankind, but scarcity and mankind's basic aspirations were converted into consumerism. The logic of this transformation would not become fully apparent until some years later when the economic crisis of the 1980s revealed the worldwide crisis of capitalism. The crisis could be solved only by making the model and decisions of production transnational and by standardizing, or, at least, pretending to standardize world culture. But by then mass culture would be riddled with new tensions that had their origins in the different national representations of popular culture, the multiplicity of cultural matrices and the new conflicts and resistances mobilized by transnationalization.

A Cinema in the Image of the People

Let us begin our analysis of the role of media in the period from 1930 to the late 1950s with that media experience which is the clearest and most easily identifiable expression of Latin American nationalism and mass, popular culture: the cinema of Mexico. According to Edgar Morin, until 1950, film was the backbone of mass culture (1977); and Mexican film performed this function in a special way for the mass culture of Latin America. Film was the centre of gravity of the new culture because

> the Mexican and the Latin American public in general did not experience cinema as a specific artistic or industrial phenomenon. The fundamental reason for the success of film was structural and touched the centre of life. In films this public saw the possibility of experimenting, of adopting new habits and of seeing codes of daily life reiterated and dramatized by the voices they would like to have or hear. They did not go to the movies to dream; they went to learn. Watching the styles and fashions of the actors, the public learned to recognize and transform itself, finding solace, comfort and, secretly, exaltation. (Monsiváis, 1976b: 446)[8]

Note carefully this quote because it synthesizes so well our argument. A first interesting aspect is how the great majority of the public perceived and experienced these films. This experience, more than the talent of the actors or the commercial strategies of the entrepreneurs, was responsible for the success of films. Going to the movies was not a purely psychological event, but the point of encounter between the collective lived experience generated by the Revolution and the mediation which, even though it deformed this experience, gave it social legitimacy. Freud has made clear that there is no access to language without passing through the shaping structures of symbolism, and Gramsci has explained that there is no social legitimation without re-semantization through the hegemonic code. Cinema was the living, social mediation that constituted the new cultural experience, and cinema became the first language of the popular urban culture. Beyond the reactionary subject matter and the rigidity of its forms, film connected with the yearnings of the masses to make themselves socially visible. Film became part of the movement to give "national identity" an image and a voice. People went to the movies more to see themselves in a sequence of images that gave them gestures, faces, manners of speaking and walking, landscapes and colours than to identify with the plots.

In the process of permitting people to see themselves, film formed them into a national body; not in the sense of giving them a nationality but in the way they experienced being a single nation. Along with all of its mystifications and chauvinistic attitudes, film provided an identity for the urban masses which diminished the impact of cultural conflicts and enabled them for the first time to conceive of the country in their own image. Monsiváis sums up the ambiguity and force of this national image in five verbs: people *recognize* themselves in film with a recognition that is not passive but that *transforms* them; for a people coming from the Revolution, this meant to *pacify* and *resign* oneself, but also to secretly *move upwards*. In other words, it was an experience not only of consolation but of revenge.

Three mechanisms were at work in the new experience of nationalism that film provided. The first was theatrical – film as the dramatic staging and legitimation of peculiarly Mexican models of gestures, linguistic expressions and feeling. It was film which taught the people how to be Mexican in the national sense. The second mechanism was degradation. That is, in order for the people to recognize themselves, it was necessary to place nationhood within their reach. From then on, the national image is one of "being irresponsible, being filled with filial affection for one's mother, to be an idler, the drunk, the sentimental slob . . . the programmed humiliation of women, the religious fanaticism, the obsessive respect for private property" (Monsiváis, 1976a: 86). The third mechanism was modernization. Often the mixture of images contradicted the traditional plots and brought up to date old myths, introduced customs and new models of moral behaviour and gave public access to the new rebelliousness and forms of speaking. "Without an explicit message, film could not have entered where it did. Without the visible subversion, it could not have found the acceptance it did among a public that was at once so eager and so repressed. Film was the apparent guardian of the traditions it subverted" (Monsiváis, 1983: 29). Examples of this are the coherent incoherence which intertwines the bodily expressions of Cantinflas with his labyrinthine verbal locutions or the eroticism of prostitutes cutting across a message defending monogamy.

The keys to film's seduction, however, were the melodrama and the stars. The melodrama was the dramatic backbone of all the plots, bringing together social impotency and heroic aspirations, appealing to the popular world from a "familiar understanding of reality". The melodrama made it possible for film to weave together national epics and intimate drama, display eroticism under the pretext of condemning incest, and dissolve tragedy in a pool of tears, depoliticizing the social contradictions of daily life. The stars – María Félix, Dolores del Río, Pedro Armendariz, Jorge Negrete, Ninón Sevilla – provided the faces, bodies, voices and tones of expression for a people eager to see and hear themselves. Above and beyond the make-up and the commercial star industry, the movie stars who were truly stars for the people gathered their force from a secret pact that bonded their faces with the desires and obsessions of their publics.

Mexican film had three stages of development. Between 1920 and 1940 movies rewrote the popular legends. Pancho Villa was passed through the traditional models and myths of banditry which made cruelty a form of generosity. The Revolution appeared more as a backdrop than a storyline – the heroic death of the rebel, the assault on the rich hacienda, the march of the soldiers – appear again and again as the scene of the film action. The struggle against injustice was transformed from a fight for an ideal into a fight motivated by loyalty to the leader. This melodramatic transformation stripped the Revolution of its political meaning, but did not become reactionary until the second stage, after the 1930s, when the *ranchero* appeared, making *machismo* the expression of a nationalism that by now had become folklore. This was a *machismo* that was no longer a way that the people could understand and confront death but a compensatory mechanism for social inferiority. *Machismo* becomes the "excess that redeemed the original sin of poverty . . . a plaintive cry for recognition" (Monsiváis, 1977: 31–2).

After the 1940s, Mexican films began to diversify their subject matter. We find now the urban comedy in which the neighbourhood replaced the countryside as the place where the old values found refuge and where the personal relations cut off by the city could be re-created. Other films about the lives of show girls and prostitutes depicted the "adventures" and eroticism that challenged the traditional family. Both types of films were a bridge between a rural past and an urban present, films in which the city was essentially a place of confusion where memories were lost. In some ways the people projected on to and re-created memories in films that simultaneously degraded and elevated them, capitalizing on their weaknesses and their search for new signs of identity.

From the Creole Circus to Radio Theatre

In Latin America the Argentinians became the masters of radio drama. Mario Vargas Llosa describes this so vividly in his novel about radio and the people working in it in the years when radio was first launched in Latin America. Why Argentina? Perhaps it is due to the fact of the pioneering forms of radio there, as recent studies show. Another factor may have been the early commercial organization of radio with the creation of networks and the extremely rapid popular access to radio – from 1,000 receivers in 1922 to a million and a half in 1936. In 1928 there were already weekly magazines devoted to the world of radio (see Rivera, 1981; Terrero, 1981; Ford et al., 1985).

But the early development of a technical infrastructure in Argentina tells only half of the story. It attributes to the medium alone something that must be traced back to a sociocultural process and "connects" radio with the country's long tradition of popular cultural expressions. In Argentina, the "literary" country of Latin America *par excellence*, the disdain of writers for radio lasted many years and marked the "distance between a media filled with possibilities and a cultural structure riddled with surprising paradoxes" (Rivera, 1980c: 383). Radio became the domain of the popular, the realm of the oral. The world of minstrels and travelling circuses helped to build a bridge between gaucho novels, wandering comedians and the radio. From the beginning, radio in Argentina was filled with popular music, readings of poetry, football matches, and, starting in 1931, radio was above all drama. Argentine radio did not receive any "cultural recognition" until much later. In 1947, Peronism placed radio on the same level as other literary forms, awarding radio prizes and giving the medium other forms of recognition through the National Commission of Culture (Rivera, 1980c: 587).

The true importance of radio theatre in Argentina was its bridging role between the cultural traditions of the people and mass culture. Patricia Terrero views the function of Argentine radio theatre in terms of its continuity, examining "its proximity to certain expressions of the national, popular imagination and its relationship to mythification, popular beliefs, and the formation of the social and cultural identity of the popular sectors" (1983: 5). Terrero's analysis looks beyond the radio medium itself to the experiences of listeners and the strategies of reception. It means taking into consideration the presence of the audiences in the studios where the radio dramas were transmitted, the provincial road tours of theatre groups presenting summaries of the broadcast dramas, listeners' letters, etc. This approach to analysis of radio brings to the fore once again the relation of the forms of listening to radio and the way people collectively listened to reading which, for so long, was customary in the popular culture. Fernando Ortiz makes this relationship explicit in his study of the evolution from collective reading to radio listening in the tobacco factories (Ortiz, 1947).

The spill-over of the study of the media into the surrounding cultural context brings into relief the importance of the "creole circus", that unusual kind of circus that combines circus rings and the stage, acrobats and dramatic plays under the same tent (Seibel, 1984; Franco, 1981). When we examined the melodrama of the 1800s, it became clear that the roots of the modern popular spectacle of melodrama were in the circus and the travelling road shows. We find that, in Argentina, it was in the circus that a tradition of popular theatre was formed, gathering the memories of the minstrels and gaucho myths in the "histories" of *Juan Moreira*, *Juan Cuello*, *Hormiga Negra*, *Santos Vega* and *Martín Fierro*. The creole circus was the first to build a bridge between the narrative tradition of the serial and the road show. The panto-mime of *Juan Moreira* in the Podestá Circus (1884) adapted the serials of Eduardo Gutiérrez, published between 1879 and 1880, to the stage. The mixture of circus comedy and popular drama gave birth to a radio theatre with the same actors and the same relationship with the public. "Without asking anyone's permission, the popular theatre was born in the circus of the Podestá, grew up in the tours of the creole circus tents, and came of age in the theatre companies of the radio dramas" (Seibel, 1982: 12). This gave the Argentine radio theatre its particular characteristics and justified its name. In other countries without this tradition it was called the *radionovela*. The serial novel that became the theatre of the creole circus, later, in radio, continued to have strong ties with the theatre, not only because of radio's transmission of the play before a public in the studio, but because the theatre com-panies of the radio dramas travelled throughout the provinces, allowing the people to "see what they heard". The radio theatres' success owed less to the medium, radio, than to the mediation already established with a cultural tradition.

If the creole circus was the place of osmosis, the gaucho serials were the place of "origin" of the popular mythology that eventually found its way into radio. Of all the serials, those by Gutiérrez had the most prestige, shocking literary critics by bringing together the urban and rural worlds, popular and mass cultures, but pro-viding for the people the key to their access to national sentiments. The characters of the serials stepped out of the verses of the troubadours that had circulated in printed sheets, booklets and magazines, but they also stepped out of police files. The serials presented a new dramatic universe, "a frontier world" that, in its own way, registered the changes and the crises brought by the modernization of Argentina beginning at the end of the nineteenth century. "Eduardo Gutiérrez basically worked with a popular audience that began to form with the modernization of Argentine society" (Rivera, 1982: 9). He established a fundamental complicity with his audience, countering the heroes who broke with "a reinterpretation in the mass of readers and spectators that made possible the acknowledgement of the crisis and the discord it brought to society and their own lives" (Rivera, 1980b: 222).

The Argentine radio theatre had several stages of development.[9] In the first stage, dialogue was minimal, and presentations were built around songs, ballads and coun-try music. In a second stage, beginning after 1935, the radio theatre found its own form. The theatrical companies came together, music was used dramatically and as a function of the plot, and the plots used themes from the gaucho tradition or from history. Gaucho literature was represented mainly in the works of González Pulido who collected the legends, verses and stories in a mythology of the outlaw, with their models of social protest and demands. The historical themes, the work of Héctor Pedro Blomberg, were based on archetypal characters among which the *Amores célebres de América Latina*, portraying the lives of the heroines of the independence movement, were especially popular with the public. The production of the radio theatre diversified after the mid-1940s in a way similar to what occurred with Mexican films. Although the gaucho legends continued to be important, two new themes entered the repertoires: detective stories and children's stories, most of which were adaptations. "Love stories" appeared with enormous popular success. Most of these were produced in Argentina, but they already contain some of the characteristic stereotypes that would be used in the melodramas of the culture industry. An important aspect of this subgenre is that many of the producers were women. Studies carried out with women on the significance of radio theatre for its audience have revealed to what extent the interpretation by the public activates the keys to meaning which connect radio theatre with expressions of culture and elements of popular life. Before becoming Peronism, Argentine populism was a way of plugging mass culture into a wide family of existing expressions of popular culture. How significant it is that Evita became much more than just an actress through her role in a radio theatre company!

The Urban Legitimation of Black Music

"To firmly stabilize a music expression from a popular background as a means of getting control of a language that reconciles a nation horizontally across geography and vertically across classes".[10] With this phrase Mario de Andrade described the role of music in the nationalizing project of Brazil in the 1930s. Perhaps in no other country of Latin America did music express so strongly the secret link between the integrating "ethos" and the "pathos" in the universe of feeling as it did in Brazil. This link made music especially appropriate for populist uses. What happened in Brazil with black music, especially its aberrant, off-course path to social and cultural legitimation, reveals the inability of both intellectual and populist currents of thought to comprehend the web of contradictions and seductions forming the relationship between popular and mass, the urban beginnings of populism.

The path that led Brazilian music from the samba chorus – with this ritual space: the *terreiro de candomblé* – to the radio and to records, passes through a multiplicity of manifestations that can be organized in terms of two historical moments: the social incorporation of the productive physical "gestural style" of the black people and the cultural legitimation of the musical rhythm that this gesture contained. National populism accompanied and in some ways made possible the passage from one stage to the next. Populism, however, was overwhelmed by a process that was too big for its political framework, that defied both the authoritarian pedantry of the Enlightenment tradition and purist idealism of Romanticism.

At the historical point when political independence was attempting to gather strength by radically changing the economy, slave labour began to be less productive and less of an economic advantage than free labour. The opening up of the national

market to the whole population broke down the traditional isolation of the planta-
tion, revealing the productivity of the physical gestural style of the blacks at the
social and national level. The conclusion was reached that if black people produce as
much as the immigrant, then let us encourage their productivity by giving them
what they are worth. The physical gesture of the blacks, however, was not just an
external manifestation. The social incorporation of the black gestural style set in
motion a process at another level. "To the extent that the blacks survived exclusively
by physical labour, it was in the 'gesture', in the physical manifestation of their
humanity, that they imposed their culture" (Squeff and Wisnik, 1983: 43).

A link, unknown to whites, emerged between the gestures of physical work and
the rhythm of the dance, the symbiosis of work and rhythm that was the survival
strategy of the slave. Black people, using an almost hypnotic cadence, were able to
survive backbreaking work; fatigue and effort became less painful when trapped in
a frenetic rhythm. It was an intoxication without alcohol but heavy with fantasy
and dreams. This does not attempt to reduce all meaning of the dance to work, but
tries to reveal in the "indecency" of black gestures and movements not just an
"unabashed" relationship with sex but a process of work that is at the heart of the
dance, in its rhythm. The dialectic of this double indecency is what truly scandalized
"society". It did not, however, prevent this society from accepting the profitable
productivity of blacks, but this acceptance was kept on the economic level. For an
acceptance of blacks at a cultural level, a political crisis would be necessary.

In this analysis of the relationship between populism and the creation of mass
culture, it is important to note that the national crises of Latin America in these years,
especially in Brazil, were not simply a result of the worldwide economic depression
of 1929. It was also a crisis of internal hegemony that placed the masses in conflict
with the state. The state attempted to resolve this crisis by taking upon itself the title
of defender of the popular classes and, at the same time, the motor of the modernization of the country. But this strategy led the state into a series of contradictions:
the state attempted to achieve the independence of the nation by imitating the
nations it now depended on; and the state tried to respond to democratic demands
with authoritarian policies. The same contradictions that tore populism apart at the
political level revealed themselves even more forcefully in the cultural expressions.
The development of music reveals with striking clarity these cultural contradictions.

The nationalistic project in musical expression operated at an internal and external
level. Internally, a quarantine was placed around "good" popular music – folk music
from the rural areas – to separate and protect it from the "bad" popular music, that
is, the commercialized and foreign-influenced music made in the cities. The strategy
looking to the external image of the country determined that only the music resulting from the synthesis of the best of Brazilian folk and the best of classical European
music could be offered to the civilized world, a music that, while it clearly reflected
national characteristics, could be listened to without seeming strange or unusual. The
music of Villa-Lobos would be considered a splendid achievement of this project.

Nevertheless, this internal–external strategy turned out to be part of an ambiguous process and a cultural policy full of contradictions. "In an attempt to benefit the
whole nation, the policy stirred up the aspirations of popular culture while at the

same time it tried to control these aspirations" (Squeff and Wisnik, 1983: 173). In the end, this limited legitimation of popular music proved to be equally disconcerting to two quite opposed vanguards of cultural nationalism. For those in the elitist, more rationalistic Enlightenment tradition, it was a degrading remnant of the illiterate, superstitious and indolent masses. For the purists of the Romantic tradition, it awakened political aspirations, caused strikes and incited dirty tastes. The appeal of a unifying national sentiment was not able to cover over all of these tensions and social wounds that were brought into the open.

Nevertheless, populist nationalism was an essential stage of development because in this process "the state sought legitimation in the image of the popular masses and the popular masses sought citizenship in the official recognition of the state" (Squeff and Wisnik, 1983: 175). This mutual need made possible the emergence of a culture that was both urban and popular. By this time, however, the process was no longer led by the state but by the dynamics of the market for records, radio and the leaders of foreign tastes.

In order to become urban, black music had to cross two ideological barriers. The first of these barriers was the populist concept of culture which insisted that the only authentically popular culture was that which could be traced back in its essence and roots, not to the actual historically verified origins, but to an idealized origin in a rural, peasant context.[11] Because of this illusion, populism could never resolve the contradiction between its romantic notion of the people and the reality of the urban masses – rootless, politicized, bitterly resentful, with degraded tastes, cosmopolitan – characteristics and aspirations which populism was somehow supposed to assume as its own. A second quite contrary ideological barrier for black music was the intellectual tradition of the Enlightenment which identified culture with fine arts, an art which emphasized its distance and distinction, careful social limits and discipline to dramatize its difference from the new, undisciplined and unclassifiable musical manifestations of the city. Popular music could become art only when it was elevated, distanced from its immediate environment and put into the form, for example, of a sonata. The incorporation of popular culture is always dangerous for an "intelligentsia" who feel the permanent threat of confusion, the abolition of forms and rules defining the distances. For these reasons, it was the "dirty" culture industry and the dangerous artistic vanguard that ended up incorporating the black rhythms in the culture of the city and legitimating urban popular culture as culture – a new culture "which was created by polymorphous appropriation and the establishment of a musical market where popular music in transformation lived side-by-side with elements of international music and the influences of urban daily life" (Squeff and Wisnik, 1983: 148).

The black physical gesture, tearing itself loose from the myth of origins, became the base of the new culture. It was a culture which no longer merely supplied the roots the city dweller lacks, the same lack revealed in the urban use of folkcrafts "in which the nostalgic feelings of the past are evoked in order to provide greater depth to domestic intimacy stereotyped by industrially produced household appliances" (García Canclini, 1982: 156). The black physical gesture became the heart of popular, mass culture, that is, a field of contradictory affirmations of work and leisure, sex, religion and politics. The passage which started from the *candomblé* and, following a winding path, twisted and overlaid with other meanings, finally brought music to the record and the radio. It was a journey marked by the conflicts, subterfuges and strategies that have always filled the path to social recognition followed by the downtrodden. It was like the form of fighting which the Brazilian blacks call *capoeira*, the fusion of combat and play, combat and dance, charged with *mandinga*, with seduction and malice capable of "throwing the enemy off his chosen path" (Muñiz Sodré, 1983: 205). It was another kind of logic that would find its highest point of recognition, dislocation, and parody in the carnival (Da Matta, 1981). Black music had to achieve its citizenship, "sideways", so to speak, and "the contradictions contained in this voyage were considerable, but the voyage generalized and consummated one of the most important Brazilian cultural events, the modern, urban development of black music" (Squeff and Wisnik, 1983: 161).

The Birth of the Popular Mass Press

The media which we have examined so far – film, radio and especially music – were born "popular" precisely because they were accessible to illiterate and uneducated publics. The press, however, also played a role in granting citizenship to the urban masses. This occurred after the changes which dislodged the press from the circle of the literate and learned and tore it loose from the matrix of the dominant culture.

Of all the media the press has the most written history, not only because it is the oldest, but because it is where those who write about history receive cultural acknowledgement. The history of the press looks mainly at the "serious press". When it examines the sensationalist press, it does so almost exclusively in economic terms: the growth of circulation and advertising. According to this type of journalism history, it is impossible to speak of politics, much less of culture, when one is dealing with newspapers that are nothing more than a business and scandal-mongering, exploiting the ignorance and low passions of the masses. In contrast to this concept that denies the sensationalist press any political meaning, another type of historical analysis has begun to introduce questions from the sociology of culture and political science. In Europe, this line of research, represented by Raymond Williams and Theodore Zeldin, has acquired a certain importance.[12] In Latin America, Guillermo Sunkel has carried out a pioneering study on the mass popular media in Chile. The subtitle of his recent book reveals the new approach: *A Study of the Relationship between Popular Culture, Mass Culture and Political Culture* (Sunkel, 1985).

Sunkel begins his study with a historical event – the bringing together, beginning in the 1930s, of the life and struggle of the people with the conditions of existence of mass society. This has been accompanied by a profound theoretical reconceptualization of the people in the political culture of the Marxist left. We will leave the analysis of this theoretical and methodological proposal until later and turn now to the map of mediations that shaped the development of the popular mass press in Chile.

A process of political change beginning in the 1920s culminated in 1938 with the formation of the Popular Front and the participation of the parties of the left in the government. During these years the Chilean press changed radically. The workers' press became the left-wing newspapers, and the sensationalist daily papers appeared. The first change was basically a shift in the workers' papers from a purely local setting to an interest in national topics or a presentation of local topics in a national language. This implied at least a potential new group of followers for the left-wing discourse: the mass public. The form of discourse of these newspapers, however, remained within the constraining matrix of the rationalistic Enlightenment, performing a function of popular educational formation and political propaganda. The objectives continued to be the education of the populace – raising their political consciousness – and to represent the interests of the masses in relation to the state. But that representation was limited to those issues that the Marxist left considered political or potentially political. Their concept of politics – and therefore of popular representation – did not include other actors than the working class and employers. Such a political press was concerned only with the conflicts that emerged out of the relationships of production – the clash between labour and capital – and only with the factory and labour union. It was a heroic vision that ignored daily life, personal subjectivity and sexuality as well as the cultural practices of the people such as their story telling, their religious customs and the fund of knowledge of the people. All this was ignored or, worse still, stigmatized as sources of alienation and obstacles in political struggle.

Thus, the transformation of the left-wing press was largely the adoption of national-level themes and language as well as a concentration in a smaller number of papers. Of the more than one hundred labour newspapers which existed at one time or another between 1900 and 1920 – with their diversity of ideological positions along socialist, anarchist or radical lines – in 1929 only five continued to be published regularly. The official paper of the Communist Party, *El Siglo*, appeared in 1940, culminating a process beginning with the newspaper, *Frente Unico*, which circulated between 1934 and 1936, and *Frente Popular*, from 1936 to 1940.

In the United States and Europe the appearance of the sensationalist press is normally "explained" as a function of the development of printing technology and the competition between the big newspapers. In Latin America, when the sensationalist press is studied, it is to provide a clear example of the penetration of North American models that, by putting profits ahead of any other criteria, have corrupted the region's tradition of serious journalism. Sunkel looks at the history of the sensationalist press from another angle, and he finds within Chile itself the antecedent press discourses and forms that evolved into the Chilean sensationalist press.

Chile, like many other Latin American countries since the second half of the nineteenth century, has had a great many popular publications which, like the *gacetas* in Argentina (Rivera, 1980a) or the literature of the *cordel* in Brazil (Luyten, 1981), mixed together news, poetry, and popular narratives. In Chile, these were called *liras populares*, and after the First World War they began to gain in news value what they lost in the quality of their poetry. Thus, they began to "assume the functions of journalism at a historical moment when the experiences of popular culture were on the threshold of mass culture" (Sunkel, 1985: 80). In this prototype of popular journalism, written mainly for oral distribution, that is, to be read, declaimed or sung in public places such as the markets, the railway station or in the street, we find the beginnings of the sensationalist press. Already they have the large headlines calling attention to the main story, the prominent graphics illustrating the story, the melodramatization of a discourse gripped by violence and the macabre, and the exaggerated fascination with the stars of sports and entertainment.

From the 1920s, Chile had newspapers that began to adopt and develop the forms of the *liras populares*. In 1922, *Los Tiempos*, already in tabloid form, introduced a new style of journalism. Some years earlier, *Crítica* in Argentina had revolutionized journalism, breaking the solemnity and pomposity of the "serious press" and introducing new elements that explicitly employed manners of popular expression: the graphic reconstruction of the scene of the crime; a short verse commenting on the episode that appeared with the story; a street scene or description of local customs; and a phrase taken from the vocabulary of the thieves (Rivera, 1980c). The Chilean newspaper, *Los Tiempos*, was also characterized by its lively style and use of scandal and humour in reporting the news. *Las Noticias Gráficas* appeared in 1944, presenting itself as "the paper of the people" and printing the demands of people from the popular classes that were normally not represented or were ignored in the traditional political discourse: the interests of women, the retired people, the world of the jails and the reformatories, the problems of alcoholism and prostitution. This type of press put more emphasis on the police chronicles and took a more irreverent and scandalous tone, with a frequent use of local slang from popular ways of speaking. The new journalism found its best expression in *Clarin*, founded in 1954, where commercial criteria were always tied to and determined by political and cultural criteria. In *Clarin* it was clear that the change in journalistic language was not only a question of attracting the public but of searching out and incorporating other languages circulating at the margins of society. It is in this light that one must interpret the caricature of the forms of speech of different social groups and the transposition of the discourse of crime to political discussion.

The issue of sensationalism calls attention to traces in the discourse of the press of another cultural matrix, much more symbolic and dramatic, which have their origins in the practices and moulds of popular culture. This matrix does not operate on the basis of concepts and generalizations but expresses itself in images and concrete situations. Rejected by the world of official education and serious politics, it survives in the world of the culture industry, and from this base it continues to exercise a powerful appeal to the popular. It is, of course, much easier and less dangerous to continue to reduce sensationalism to a "bourgeois tool" of manipulation and alienation. It took courage to affirm that "behind the notion of sensationalism as the commercial exploitation of crime, pornography and vulgar language lies a purist vision of the popular world" (Sunkel, 1985: 115). Only by taking this risk, however, was it possible to discover the *cultural* connection between the melodramatic aesthetic and the forms of survival and revenge in the matrix pervading popular cultures. The melodramatic aesthetic dared to violate the rationalistic division between serious and frivolous themes, to treat political events as dramatic events, and break with "objectivity" by observing the situation from the perspective that appeals to the subjectivity of the readers.

Developmentalism and Transnationalization

The first Latin American version of modernity had at its centre the idea of the *Nation* – to become a modern nation. The second version, beginning in the 1960s, was associated with development, a new understanding of the idea of progress. Development was taken as an objective step forward that could be quantified both in terms of economic growth and in its "natural" consequence, political democratization. The flow of democratization from economic growth was considered natural because an increase in production would increase consumption, redistribute goods and thereby strengthen democracy. In this way, democracy was a "spin-off of modernization" (Faletto, 1982: 119); it depended on economic growth, the fruit of a reform of society in which the state was conceived "no longer as the incarnation of the personalized vote for a social contract but as a neutral technical body carrying out the directives of development" (Lechner, 1981: 306).

During the 1960s, the majority of the Latin American countries experienced a rapid growth and diversification of industry and an expansion of internal markets. But this was accompanied by the rise of almost insoluble contradictions. For the left, these contradictions simply made visible the incompatibility between capitalist accumulation and social change. For the right, the contradictions demonstrated the incompatibility of economic development with democracy. Brazil, the first to experience a right-wing coup, followed by Chile's election of a socialist government, raised misgivings about the "naturalness" of development. Within a few years, the takeover by military regimes in a majority of Latin American countries showed clearly that the interests of capital were the only truly quantifiable objective of development. Developmentalism also illustrated something even more fundamental to the model: "the failure of the political principle of generalized modernization" (Mendes et al., 1977: 139). Clear testimony to this failure were the spread of government by force in the 1970s, the oppressive growth of foreign debt in the 1980s, and, above all, the new meaning of transnationalization that "jumped" from an economic model to the internationalization of a political model in response to the crisis of hegemony. "What allows us to speak of a transnational phase is its political nature. The rupture of the dike of national borders in the face of capitalist concentration radically changed the nature and function of the state by diminishing its ability to play a role in the economy and the historical development of a country" (Roncagliolo, 1982: 27).

What is the role of the mass media in the new phase of Latin American modernization? What changes have occurred in the role media plays in the creation of a mass society and in relation to the masses themselves? To answer these questions it is necessary to differentiate between what happened during the years of euphoria, the years of the "miracles of development" in the early 1960s (and in some countries up to the mid-1970s), and what happened in the 1980s when the world crisis heightened the contradiction between the national character of the political structure and the transnational character of the economic structure.

A New Meaning of Massification

In contrast to what happened during the period of the populisms, when the "mass" meant the ambiguous political weight of the masses in the city and their explosive charge of social realism, in the years of developmentalism, mass came to connote exclusively the means for homogenization and control of the masses. Massification was felt even where there were no masses. The media, which formerly were mediators between the state and the masses, between the rural and the urban, between tradition and modernity, increasingly tended to become only a simulation or even the instrument of deactivation of these relationships. Although the media continued to "mediate", and although simulation was already at the root of their social role, something was beginning to change. It was not an abstract change in the sense that the media became the message. It was a change in the same direction as development, the schizophrenic growth of a society whose reality did not coincide with its demands. Only with such changes in meaning could communication be measured in the quantitative circulation of newspapers and the number of radio and television receivers. Indeed, measurement became the cornerstone of development. The experts of the Organization of American States could proclaim, "Without communication there is no development". Now the radio dial became saturated with stations in cities with no running water, and slums sprouted TV aerials. Indeed, the TV aerials were symptomatic of changes that had occurred in the concept of mass.

Marching hand in hand with the diffusion of innovations as the "motor" of development were two key dimensions of the new field of communications: the hegemonic role of television and the functional diversification of radio.

Television implied not only an escalation of the economic investment and complexity of industrial organization of the media, but also a qualitative refinement of the ideological influences. In the model of democratizing development in its most complete form, television achieves its central role in so far as there is unification of consumer demand, the only way to expand the hegemony of the market without subsidiaries resenting the expansion. If we are able to consume the same things that developed peoples consume, then, clearly, we have finally achieved development.[13] Looking beyond the percentages of programming imported from the United States and even the imitations of US programme formats, what most influenced Latin America was the importation of the North American *model* of television. This does not mean simply the privatization of the networks. There are some countries, such as Colombia, where television belongs to and is administered by the state in a way that is quite compatible with the dominant model. Rather, the heart of the model lies in the tendency to constitute, through television, a single public,[14] and to reabsorb the sociocultural differences of a country to the point that one can confuse a higher degree of communicability with a higher degree of economic profitability. Within a few years after the introduction of television the audience rating systems became standardized among the world's television systems, and something the model already logically implied became explicit: the tendency for television to constitute a discourse that, in order to speak to the largest number of people, had to reduce the differences to the minimum. This required of the audiences the least possible effort in decodification and posed the least possible conflict with the sociocultural prejudices of the majority.

The press, even after it became a mass medium, always reflected cultural and political differences. This was not only its need for "social distinction", but corresponded to the press's liberal model that attempted to give expression to the diversity of liberal society. Radio also, for the quite different reasons of its closeness to popular culture, placed an emphasis on social and cultural diversity from the very beginning. Television, on the other hand, tends to absorb differences as much as possible. I use the word "absorb" because this best describes the way television attempts to deny differences: showing such differences with all implicit conflict stripped away. No other medium has the potential for providing access to such a wide variety of human experiences, countries, cultures and situations. But no other medium has channelled cultural perceptions to such a degree that, instead of encouraging a collapse of nationalistic ethnocentrism, reinforces it. As the spectacle of daily life is channelled into television,[15] the hegemonic model of television reconstructs reality with a paradoxical control of differences. Television's mechanisms of proximity and familiarization, by capitalizing on surface similarities, end up convincing viewers that if they get close enough to a reproduction of reality, the "farthest away" in time and space is in fact no different from us. On the other hand, the mechanisms of distancing and making something exotic convert what is different into something totally and radically strange, without any relation to us and without any meaning in our world. Both sets of mechanisms make it impossible for differences to challenge the viewer and question or undermine the myth of development sustaining the world view that there is only one model of society compatible with progress and, therefore, with the future.

Radio experienced a transformation in the 1960s as a result of the complex changes imposed by developmentalism and the crisis of the radio medium set in motion by the domination of television. Radio reacted to the competition from television by exploiting the stamp of popular culture which it bears, that is, its special way of "capturing" the popular world, "the way radio works with its following and its system of appeals" (Alfaro, 1985b: 53). Its closeness to popular culture is also implied in its technical characteristics: all you have to do is listen; its limitation to voice and music allowing it to develop a particular form of colloquial expression; and its non-exclusive form of use making it compatible with simultaneous activities and time frames (Gutiérrez and Munizaga, 1983: 15ff). These technical–discursive factors allowed radio to "mediate with the popular" in a way no other medium could. They renewed radio as a privileged link between modernizing, informative–instrumental rationality and the expressive–symbolic mentality of the popular world. The modernization project becomes in radio an *educational project*, encouraging both the technical adaptation of the practices of the peasants to the requirements and objectives of development and an ideological readjustment – overcoming the religious superstitions hampering technological progress and the benefits of consumerism.[16]

On the other hand, radio responded to the hegemony of television by "diversifying" and attracting more varied publics. Diversification was compatible with the demands of the market, but it spoke of something else: "The homogenization of the consumer made it necessary to categorize the receiver producing a classification that transformed previous social identities into a society where the category of citizen broadened to include spectator, fan, youth, women, etc." (Gutiérrez and Munizaga, 1983: 20). At first, the segmentation of publics corresponded to a diversification of programming types or specific programmes within a radio station. Later, it became a specialization of stations for groups of publics or listeners appealing to different cultural sectors or generations. The crisis of identity of the traditional political parties and the absence of an effective appeal to the popular world by the political left, made it easy for the mass media and especially radio to form new social identities that responded more to an economic model than to a renovation of politics. The transnationalization of mass culture in the 1980s was supported internally by this political vacuum and by the integrating diversification of radio counterbalancing the unifying tendencies of television.

The Contradictions Between Technologies and Uses

Since the end of the 1980s the "new technologies" have been the protagonists of Latin American communications. Seen from the perspective of the technology-producing countries, the new communication technologies – satellites, cable, videotext, teletext, etc. – represent a new stage in the continuous process of the acceleration of modernity that now takes a qualitative leap from the industrial revolution to the electronic revolution. No country can afford, culturally or economically, not to be part of this leap ahead. The new technologies raise many questions in Latin America, questions that are not resolved by the old dilemma: a "yes" or a "no" to technology is a "yes" or "no" to development itself. For the questions shift the focus from the technologies themselves to the model of production which they imply and to the modes of access, acquisition and use of these technologies. The shift is from technology in the abstract to the processes of imposition, deformation and dependence the technologies imply, to domination but also to resistance, recycling and redesign. The appearance of new technologies in Latin America is part of the old schizophrenia between modernization and the likelihood of actually realizing the social and cultural appropriation of the tools with which to modernize. "Adapt to the information technologies, or die", is the slogan of a capitalism in crisis and in dire need of expanding consumption of new information technologies.

Marks of schizophrenia are apparent at many levels, from the most mundane to decisions involving enormous investments and changes in national policies. There is a "semantic hole" in the argument which pushes the daily consumption of technologies without any reference to the context in which they are produced, a hole most people end up filling with the language of magic or religion. Another sign of schizophrenic thinking about new technologies are decisions by governments or political parties to throw out of shape the existing policies of national investment and informatization with no reasonable consideration for the economic and social costs they imply. A recent study by Mattelart and Schmucler (1983) showed that the levels of technological expansion in the field of communications are very different in each country but the levels of fascination and seduction by the technologies are very similar. One finds an omnipresent compulsive need for microcomputers, VCRs, video games and videotext not only in the capital cities but in the provincial towns.

The new communication technologies in Latin America raise two questions from the perspective of culture. Firstly, as a result of the rationality they materialize and of the way they operate, these technologies produce a crisis in the "fiction of identity" on which national cultures rest in these countries. Secondly, sophisticated techno-logies carry to the extreme the simulation of rationality – or, in Baudrillard's terms, the "sham" of rationality – and make visible that remnant of Latin American society which cannot be pushed into the simulation of rationality, that which, because of its cultural otherness, resists the generalized homogenization. This remnant is not something strange or mysterious; it is the conflictive and dynamic presence in Latin America of the popular cultures.

The questions which the new technologies raise regarding cultural identities oper-ate at quite different levels that need to be clearly distinguished. One is the challenge to the attempts to seek refuge in the past, the old idealist temptation to postulate an identity whose meaning is in the remote origins, far back in history and out of sight, outside the historical dynamics of the present. Another challenge is the meaning new technologies acquire as the summit of human development (Muñiz Sodré, 1983: 32). This reactivation of evolutionist logic reduces, radically and without exception, all that lies outside a certain linear conception of history to the status of "backward-ness", making what remains of identity in the other cultures merely a "reflective" identity, that is, an identity which has no value except to reflect the differences with hegemonic culture. This is a negative identity, defining what we are not, emphasiz-ing our deficiencies. And the implied message is that what we "lack", what we most need today is the technology produced by the industrialized countries, the techno-logy that ultimately is going to allow us to make the definitive leap to modernity.

This is a fabulous paradox, if it were not so bloody. In the name of an electronic memory our countries are being asked to renounce the right to have and develop their own memory. In the dilemma of choice between underdevelopment and mod-ernization, cultural memory does not count and has no place. It cannot be opera-tionalized in terms of information and therefore it cannot be used. In contrast to instrumental memory, "cultural memory" does not work with pure information or as a process of linear accumulation. It is articulated through experience and events. Instead of simply accumulating, it filters and weighs. It is not a memory we can *use*, but the memory of which we are made. Cultural memory has nothing to do with nostalgia; its function in the community is not to talk of the past but to give con-tinuity to the ongoing construction of collective identity. The logic of cultural memory, however, operating for example in the popular narrative where the quality of com-munication is far from proportional to the quantity of information, resists analysis by the categories of informatics.

Equally tragic is the pillaging of this cultural memory, the narrative tradition of East and West, to give some "substance" to the fetishistic form of representation of the new technologies. The new technologies are made "stars" by science fiction movies and television series (Gubern, 1982). As we enter into the playful mood of the most popular genres – the epics, the adventures, the tales of terror – we are shown a future that distorts and dissolves the present. Technology is made to appear spectacular and innocent at the same time. From the robot who is always so pleasant and good natured, or at least working with "the good guys", we pass to the embellishment of war machines as beautiful as they are deadly. In the films with brilliant special effects and visual beauty or, in their cheapened version, in the thousand cartoons for television, the "image of the new technologies" educates the popular classes of Latin America in a way that is most convenient for the producers of the technologies, a fascination with the new fetishism.

A central chapter in the research on new technologies is their effect on culture. Starting with the concept of "effect", however, the relation between technology and culture brings us back to the old conception of media: one side has all the action and the other side is merely a passive receiver. The use of this concept is aggravated by the continuation of the idea of a single cultural identity at the base of all identity. Technologies are the many, culture is only one. In Latin America, at least, exactly the opposite is true. Technology, with its "logo-tecnica" is one of the strongest and most profound sources of standardization, while the differences, the cultural pluralism, unmask this standardization by bringing to light the "discontinuities" making up the cultural reality of the region. One of the novelties of the new communication technologies is the coordination between the tempo of production by the rich countries and the tempo of consumption by the poor. For the first time, we are not buying second-hand machinery! It is, however, a false coordination of tempos. It cloaks a lack of coordination between objects and practices, technologies and users, making it impossible to understand the historical meaning of the appropriation of technology.

This lack of contemporaneity occurs at the national level in the clash of tempos and the crisis which the technological transnationalization accelerates or sets in motion, for example, in the lack of cultural articulation in the national projects. It also occurs in popular culture, which, confronted by new technologies, feels forced to take refuge in concepts and practices rooted in nostalgia and a simplistic transparency of meaning. The view of technologies from the perspective of cultural differences has nothing to do with a yearning or restlessness in the face of technological complexity or the abstraction of the mass media. Nor does it have anything to do with a voluntarist overconfidence in the ultimate triumph of the good. Technologies are not transparent tools that can be used in any manner. They are the materialization of the rationality of a culture and of a "global model of organization of power" (Mattelart and Schmucler, 1983).

The redesign of technology, however, is possible, if not as a strategy, at least as a tactic in the definition given by de Certeau: a manner of fighting of the person who cannot fight on his own grounds and is obliged to fight on the grounds of his adversary (de Certeau, 1984). The key lies in taking the original imported technology as energy, as a potential to develop on the basis of the requirements of the national culture. This does not ignore the fact that at times the only way to actively take control of what is imposed on us is the tactic of the anti-design, a design which is a parody and involves technology in a game which denies it as a value in itself. In any event when the machinery itself cannot be redesigned, at least its function can.

In a poor slum of Lima, a group of women attempted to better organize the market place. In the market area, they found a tape recorder and some loudspeakers which were being used only occasionally by the administrator. With the help of a group from a communication centre, the women began to use the tape recorder to interview people of the neighbourhood as to what they thought about the market and to provide music and celebrations on festival days and other holidays. And so they continued until they were criticized by a person of higher status, a nun, who ridiculed the way they talked and condemned their audacity to speak over the loudspeakers "without knowing how to talk properly". This caused a crisis and for some weeks the women did not want to have anything more to do with the loud-speakers. But then some of the women went to the communication centre to announce dejectedly, "We discovered that the nun was right. We don't know how to talk and in this society those who don't know how to talk do not have the least possibility of defending themselves or doing anything. But we also have understood that with the help of this little machine – the recorder – we can learn how to speak." And from that day the women of the market decided to tell stories about their own lives. They no longer used the recorder just to listen to others but began to use it to learn how to speak (Alfaro, 1983).

Notes

1   Regarding the "origins" of that project, using Guatemala as an example, see *La patria del criollo* (Costa Rica, 1972).
2   For an analysis of this debate from a current perspective in Peru, see Cornejo et al. (1981).
3   Colombia appears to be a typical case of this. See Uribe Celis (1984).
4   This is the conclusion reached by M. A. Garretón in his analysis of the crisis of 1973. See "Prospecto nacional, una perspectiva socio-política", in Garretón et al. (1983).
5   See Monsiváis (1981: 35): Regarding the education project of Vasconcelos, see also Taboada (1982).
6   In these pages, the basic ideas are taken from Romero (1976: 318).
7   The media built on the groundwork laid by the education system in the provision of this daily experience of nationhood. A key text that provides a general framework for this process and some specific national case studies is Braslavsky and Tedesco (1982).
8   Monsiváis (1976b: 446). This analysis is based on the work of Monsiváis.
9   Here we are following studies cited by Terrero.
10   Squeff and Wisnik (1983: 148). In addition to this text, which seems basic, our analysis is based on the collective article "Questao popular" (Chaui et al., 1980).
11   This is the biological–telluric paradigm mentioned by N. García Canclini (1984).
12   These two authors are discussed in Part I of this book [see Martín-Barbero, *Communication, Culture and Hegemony*].
13   Beltrán and Fox (1980) provide data and measures of some of these changes.
14   Muñiz Sodré (1981) is one of the best sources regarding this.
15   The relationship between entertainment and daily life has been examined in detail in Part II [see Martín-Barbero, *Communication, Culture and Hegemony*].
16   A model of this modernizing education project was Radio Sutatenza with its network of training centres. See Pareja (1984).

References

Alfaro, R. M. (1983) "Del periódico al altoparlante", *Materiales para la Communicación Popular*, 1 (Lima).

—— (1985) "Modelos radiales y proceso de popularización de la radio", *Contratexto*, 1 (Lima).

Arguedas, J. M. (1977) *Formación de una Cultura Nacional Indoamericana*. Mexico: Siglo XXI.

Beltrán, L. R. and Fox, E. (1980) *Communicación Dominada: Estados Unidos en los Medios de América Latina*. Mexico: Nueva Imagen.

Bolivar, Simon (1972) "Carta de Jamaica", in *Escritos Políticos* (Madrid).

Braslavsky, C. and Tedesco, J. C. (1982) "Tendencias históricas de la educación popular como expresiones de los proyectos políticos de los estados latino-americanos". Investigaciones Educativas (Mexico).

Chaui, M. et al. (1980) "Questao popular", *Arte em Revista*, 3 (São Paulo).

Cordova, A. (1974) *La Política de Masas del Cardenismo* (Mexico).

Cornejo, A. et al. (1981) *Problema Nacional: Cultura y Clases Sociales*. Lima: Desco.

Da Matta, R. (1981) *Carnavais, Malandros e Heróis*. Rio de Janeiro: Zahar.

Deas, M. (1983) "La presencia de la política nacional en la vida provinciana, pueblerina y rural de Colombia". In Palacios, M. (ed.), *La Unidad Nacional en América Latina: del Regionalismo a la Nacionalidad*. Mexico: El Colegio de México.

de Certeau, M. (1984) *The Practice of Everyday Life*. Berkeley and London: University of California Press.

de Ipola, E. (1982) *Ideología y Discurso Populista*. Mexico: Folios.

Faletto, E. (1982) "Estilos alternativos de desarrollo y opciones políticas", in Faletto, E. et al., *América Latina: Desarrollo y Perspectivas Democráticas*. Costa Rica: Flacso.

Faletto, E. et al. (1982) *América Latina: Desarrollo y Perspectivas Democráticas*. Costa Rica: Flacso.

Ford, A., Rivera, J. B. and Romano, E. (1985) *Medios de Comunicación y Cultura Popular*. Buenos Aires.

Franco, L. (1981) *El Circo Criollo*. Buenos Aires: CE de América Latina.

Galeano, E. (1973) *Open Veins in Latin America: Five Centuries of the Pillage of a Continent*. New York: New York Monthly Review Press.

García Canclini, N. (1982) *Las Culturas Populares en el Capitalismo*. Mexico: Nueva Imagen.

—— (1984) "Las políticas culturales en América Latina", *Materiales para la Communicación Popular*, 1. Lima.

Garretón, M. A. et al. (1983) *La Cuestión Nacional: Perspectiva Democrática*. Santiago: ILET.

Gubern, R. (1982) "Fascinación tecnológica o apocalípsis de sociedad industrial", *Papeles de Comunicación*, 1 (Madrid).

Gutiérrez, L. H. and Romero, L. A. (1981) "Buenos Aires 1920–1945: Una propuesta para el estudio de la cultura de los sectores populares", mimeo (Buenos Aires).

Gutiérrez, P. and Munizaga, G. (1983) *Radio y Cultura Popular de Masas*. Santiago: Ceneca.

Intercom (1981) "Documento básico", in Márquez de Melo, J. (ed.), *Populismo e Comunicaçao*. São Paulo: Cortez.

Laclau, E. (1977) *Politics and Ideology in Marxist Theory: Capitalism, Fascism, Populism*. London: New Left Books.

Landi, O. (1983) *Crisis y Lenguajes Políticos*. Buenos Aires: Cedes.

Lechner, N. (ed.) (1981) *Estado y Política en América Latina*. Mexico: Siglo XXI.

Luyten, J. M. (1981) *A Literatura de Cordel em São Paulo*. São Paulo.

Mariátegui, J. C. (1978) *Signos y Obras*. Lima: Amauta.

Márquez de Melo, J. (ed.) (1981) *Populismo e Comunicaçao*. São Paulo: Cortez.

Martí, J. (1971) *Nuestra América*. Havana.

Mattelart, A. and Schmucler, H. (1983) *América Latina en la Encrucijada Telemática*. Barcelona: Paidós.

Mendes, C. et al. (1977) *El Mito del Desarrollo*. Barcelona: Kairos.

Monsiváis, C. (1976a) "Cultura urbana y creación intelectual", *Casa de las Américas*, 116 (Havana).

—— (1976b) "Notas sobre la cultura mexicana en el siglo XX", in *Historia General de México*, vol. IV. Mexico: El Colegio de México.

—— (1977) *Amor Perdido*. Mexico: Era.

—— (1981) "Notas sobre el estado, la cultura nacional y las culturas populares en México", *Cuadernos Políticos*, 30 (Mexico).

—— (1983) "La cultura popular en el ámbito urbano. El caso de México", mimeo (Mexico).

Morin, E. (1977) *O Espirito do Tempo, 2: Necrose*. Rio de Janeiro: Forense Universitária.

Moulian, T. et al. (1982) *Autoritarismo y Alternativas Populares en América Latina*. Costa Rica: Flasco.

Muñiz Sodré (1981) *O Monopolisa da Fala. Funçao e Linguagem da Televisao no Brasil*. Petrópolis: Vozes.

—— *A Verdade Seduzida. Por um Conceito de Cultura no Brasil*. Rio de Janeiro: Codecri.

Ortiz, F. (1947) *Cuban Counterpoint: Tobacco and Sugar*. New York: Knopf.

Palacios, M. (ed.) (1983) *La Unidad Nacional en América Latina: del Regionalismo a la Nacionalidad*. Mexico: El Colegio de México.

Pareja, R. (1984) *Historia de la Radio en Colombia*. Bogotá: SC de CS.

Portantiero, J. C. (1981) "Lo nacional-popular y la alternativa democrática en América Latina", in *América Latina 80: Democracia y Movimiento Popular*. Lima: Desco.

Ribeiro, D. (1971) *The Americas and Civilization*. London: Allen & Unwin.

Rivera, J. B. (1980a) *El Escritor y la Industria Cultural*. Buenos Aires: CE de AL.

—— (1980b) *El Folletín: Eduardo Gutiérrez*. Buenos Aires: CE de AL.

—— (1980c) *La Forja del Escritor Profesional*. Buenos Aires: CE de AL.

—— (1981) *El Auge de la Industria Cultural (1930–1955)*. Buenos Aires: Centro Editor de América Latina.

—— (1982) *El Folletín*. Buenos Aires: CE de AL.

Romero, J. L. (1976) *Latinoamérica: Las Ciudades y las Ideas*. Mexico: Siglo XXI.

—— (1982) *Las Ideologías de la Cultura Nacional*. Buenos Aires: CEDAL.

Romero Tobar, L. (1976) *La Novela Popular Española del Siglo XIX*. Barcelona: Ariel.

Roncagliolo, R. (1982) *Comunicación Transnacional: Conflicto Político y Cultural*. Lima: DESCO/Ilet.

Seibel, B. (1982) *Los Cómicos Ambulantes*. Buenos Aires: CE de AL.

—— (1984) *El Teatro "Bárbaro" del Interior*. Buenos Aires: De la Pluma.

Squeff, E. and Wisnik, J. M. (1983) *O Nacional e o Popular na Cultura Brasileira: Música*. São Paulo: Brasiliense.

Sunkel, G. (1985) *Razón y Pasión en la Prensa Popular*. Santiago: ILET.

Taboada, E. (1982) "Educación y lucha ideológicas en el México post-revolucionario: 1920–1940", *Cuadernos de Investigaciones Educativas*, 6, Mexico.

Terrero, P. (1981) *El Radioteatro*. Buenos Aires: CE de AL.

—— "Radioteatro y teleteatro", mimeo (Buenos Aires).

Uribe Celis, L. (1984) *Los Años Veinte en Colombia: Ideologia y Cultura*. Bogotá: Aurora.

Weffort, F. (1978) *O Populismo na Política Brasileira*. Rio de Janeiro.

36

Globalization as Hybridization

Jan Nederveen Pieterse

The most common interpretations of globalization are the idea that the world is becoming more uniform and standardized, through a technological, commercial, and cultural synchronization emanating from the West, and that globalization is tied up with modernity. These perspectives are interrelated, if only in that they are both variations on an underlying theme of globalization as westernization. The former is critical in intent while the latter is ambiguous. My argument takes issue with both these interpretations as narrow assessments of globalization and instead argues for viewing globalization as a process of hybridization that gives rise to a global mélange.

Globalizations Plural

Globalization, according to Albrow, "refers to all those processes by which the peoples of the world are incorporated into a single world society, global society" (1990: 9). Since these processes are plural, we may as well conceive of globalizations in the plural. Thus, in social science there are as many conceptualizations of globalization as there are disciplines. In economics, globalization refers to economic internationalization and the spread of capitalist market relations. "The global economy is the system generated by globalising production and global finance" (Cox 1992: 30). In international relations, the focus is on the increasing density of interstate relations and the development of global politics. In sociology, the concern is with increasing worldwide social densities and the emergence of "world society." In cultural studies, the focus is on global communications and worldwide cultural standardization, as in Coca-colonization and McDonaldization, and on postcolonial culture. In history, the concern is with conceptualizing "global history" (Mazlish and Buultjens 1993). *All* these approaches and themes are relevant if we view globalization as a

From Jan Nederveen Pieterse, "Globalization as hybridization." In *International Sociology*, 9:2 (1994). © 1994 by Sage Publications Ltd. Reprinted by permission of the publisher and author.

multidimensional process, which, like all significant social processes, unfolds in multiple realms of existence simultaneously. Accordingly, globalization may be understood in terms of an open-ended synthesis of several disciplinary approaches. This extends beyond social science – for instance, to ecological concerns, technology, and agricultural techniques. Another way to conceive of globalizations plural is that there are as many modes of globalization as there are globalizing agents and dynamics or impulses. Historically these range from long-distance cross-cultural trade, religious organizations, and knowledge networks to contemporary multinational corporations, banks, international institutions, technological exchange, and transnational social movements networks. We can further differentiate between globalization as policy and project, as in the case of Amnesty International, which is concerned with internationalizing human rights standards; or as unintended consequence, as in the case of the "globalizing panic" of AIDS. *Globalism* is the policy of furthering or managing (a particular mode of) globalization. In political economy, it refers to policies furthering economic internationalization or to the corporate globalism of transnational enterprises; and in foreign affairs, to the global stance in U.S. foreign policy, both in its initial postwar posture (Ambrose 1971) and its post-Cold War stance. These varied dimensions all point to the inherent fluidity, indeterminacy, and open-endedness of globalizations. If this is the point of departure it becomes less obvious to think of globalizations in terms of standardization and less likely that globalizations can be one-directional processes, either structurally or culturally.

Globalization and Modernity

Modernity is a keynote in reflections on globalization in sociology. In several prominent conceptualizations, globalization is the corollary of modernity (e.g., Giddens 1990).[1] It's not difficult to understand this trend. In conjunction with globalization, modernity provides a structure and periodization. In addition, this move reflects the general thematization of modernity in social science from Jürgen Habermas to Marshall Berman. Together globalization and modernity make up a ready-made package. Ready-made because it closely resembles the earlier, well-established conceptualization of globalization: the Marxist theme of the spread of the world market. The timing and pace are the same in both interpretations: the process starts in the 1500s and experiences its high tide from the late nineteenth century. The structures are the same: the nation state and individualization – vehicles of modernity or, in the Marxist paradigm, corollaries of the spread of the world market. In one view, universalism refers to the logic of the market and the law of value, and in the other, to modern values of achievement. World-system theory is the most well-known conceptualization of globalization in the Marxist lineage; its achievement has been to make "society" as the unit of analysis appear a narrow focus, while on the other hand it faithfully replicates the familiar constraints of Marxist determinism (Nederveen Pieterse 1987).

There are several problems associated with the modernity/globalization approach. In either conceptualization, whether centered on capitalism or modernity, globalization begins in and emanates from Europe and the West. In effect, it is a theory of westernization by another name, which replicates all the problems associated with Eurocentrism: a narrow window on the world, historically and culturally. With this agenda, it should be called westernization and not globalization. Another problem is that globalization theory turns into or becomes an annex of modernization theory. While modernization theory is a passed station in sociology and development theory it is making a comeback under the name of globalization – the 1950s and 1960s revisited under a wide global umbrella. Roland Robertson takes issue with the prioritization of modernity in Giddens' work (1992: 138–45). Robertson's approach to globalization is multidimensional with an emphasis on sociocultural processes. Yet his preoccupation with themes such as "global order" is, according to Arnason, "indicative of a Parsonian approach, transferred from an artificially isolated and unified society to the global condition" (1990: 222). The re-thematization of modernity (Tiryakian 1991) indicates the continuing interest in modernization thinking, but the problems remain. The tendency to focus on social structure produces an account from which the dark side of modernity is omitted. What of modernity in the light of Bauman's *Modernity and the Holocaust*? While the Marxist perspective involves a critical agenda, the thematization of modernity, whether or not it serves as a stand-in for capitalism, does not: "The ambiguities involved in this discourse are such that it is possible, within it, to lose any sense of cultural domination: to speak of modernity can be to speak of cultural change as 'cultural fate' in the strong sense of historical . . . inevitability. This would be to abandon any project of rational cultural critique" (Tomlinson 1991: 141).

Generally, questions of power are marginalized in both the capitalism and modernity perspectives. Another dimension that is conspicuously absent from modernity accounts is imperialism. Modernity accounts tend to be societally inward looking, in a rarefied sociological narrative, as if modernity precedes and conditions globalization, and not the other way round: globalization constituting one of the conditions for modernity. The implication of the modernity/globalization view is that the history of globalization begins with the history of the West. But is it not precisely the point of globalizations as a perspective that globalizations begin with world history? The modernity/globalization view is not only geographically narrow (westernization) but also historically shallow (1500 plus). The time frame of some of the relevant perspectives is as follows (table 36.1).

Table 36.1 Timing of Globalization

Author	Start	Theme
Marx	1500s	Modern capitalism
Wallerstein	1500s	Modern world-system
Robertson	1500s, 1870–1920s	Multidimensionalism
Giddens	1800s	Modernity
Tomlinson	1960s	Cultural planetarization

Apparently the broad heading of globalization accommodates some very different views. The basic understanding is usually a neutral formulation, such as "Globalization can thus be defined as the intensification of worldwide social relations which link distant localities in such a way that local happenings are shaped by events occurring many miles away and vice versa" (Giddens 1990: 64). The "intensification of world-wide social relations" can be thought of as a long-term process that finds its begin-nings in the first migrations of peoples and long distance trade connections, and subsequently accelerates under particular conditions (the spread of technologies, religions, literacy, empires, capitalism). Or, it can be thought of as consisting only of the later stages of this process, from the time of the accelerating formation of global social relations, and as a specifically global momentum associated with particular conditions (the development of a world market, western imperialism, modernity). It can be narrowed down further by regarding globalization as a particular epoch and formation – as in Tomlinson's view of globalization as the successor to imperialism (rather than imperialism being a mode of globalization), Jameson's view of the new cultural space created by late capitalism, and David Harvey's argument that associ-ates globalization with the postmodern condition of time-space compression and flexible accumulation. But, whichever the emphasis, globalization as the "intensifica-tion of worldwide social relations" presumes the prior existence of "worldwide social relations," so that globalization is the conceptualization of a *phase* following an existing condition of *globality* and part of an ongoing process of the formation of worldwide social relations. This recognition of historical depth brings globalizations back to world history and beyond the radius of modernity/westernization.

One way around the problem of modernization/westernization is the idea of multiple *paths* of modernization, which avoids the onus of Eurocentrism and provides an angle for reproblematizing western development. Benjamin Nelson advances this as part of his concern with "inter-civilizational encounters" (1981). The idea that "all societies create their own modernity," or at any rate of alternative modernities is now a salient theme (Gaonkar 2001; Eisenstadt 2002).

The modernizations plural approach matches the notion of the *historicity* of mod-ernization, which is common in South and East Asia (Singh 1989). That Japanese modernization has followed a different path from that of the West is a cliché in Japanese sociology (Tominaga 1990) and well established in Taiwan and China (Li 1989; Sonoda 1990). It results in an outlook that resembles the argument of poly-centrism and multiple paths of development (Amin 1990). But this remains a static and one-dimensional representation: the multiplication of centers still hinges on centrism. It's not much use to make up for Eurocentrism and occidental narcissism by opting for other centrisms such as Sinocentrism, Indocentrism, Afrocentrism, or polycentrism. In effect, this echoes the turn of the century Pan-movements: Pan-Slavism, Pan-Islamism, Pan-Arabism, Pan-Turkism, Pan-Europeanism, Pan-Africanism, and so forth, in which the logic of nineteenth-century racial classifications is carried further under the heading of civilizational provinces turned into political projects. This may sub-stitute one centrism and parochialism for another and miss the fundamental point of the "globalization of diversity," of the mélange effect pervading everywhere, from the heartlands to the extremities and vice versa.

Structural Hybridization

With respect to cultural forms, hybridization is defined as "the ways in which forms become separated from existing practices and recombine with new forms in new practices" (Rowe and Schelling 1991: 231). This principle also applies to structural forms of social organization.

It is by now a familiar argument that nation state formation is an expression and function of globalization and not a process contrary to it (Greenfield 1992). At the same time it is apparent that the present phase of globalization involves the relative weakening of nation states – as in the weakening of the "national economy" in the context of economic globalism and, culturally, the decline of patriotism. But this too is not simply a one-directional process. Thus, the migration movements that make up demographic globalization can engender absentee patriotism and long-distance nationalism, as in the political affinities of Irish, Jewish, and Palestinian diasporas and émigré or exiled Sikhs in Toronto, Tamils in London, Kurds in Germany, Tibetans in India (Anderson 1992).

Globalization can mean the reinforcement of or go together with localism, as in "Think globally, act locally." This kind of tandem operation of local/global dynamics, or glocalization, is at work in the case of minorities who appeal to transnational human rights standards beyond state authorities, or indigenous peoples who find support for local demands from transnational networks. The upsurge of ethnic identity politics and religious revival movements can also be viewed in the light of globalization. "Identity patterns are becoming more complex, as people assert local loyalties but want to share in global values and lifestyles" (Ken Booth quoted in Lipschutz 1992: 396). *Particularity*, notes Robertson, is a *global* value and what is taking place is a "universalization of particularism" or "the global valorization of particular identities" (1992: 130).

Global dynamics such as the fluctuations of commodity prices on the world market can result in the reconstruction of ethnic identities, as occurred in Africa in the 1980s (Shaw 1986). State development policies can engender a backlash of ethnic movements (Kothari 1988). Thus "globalisation can engender an awareness of political difference as much as an awareness of common identity; enhanced international communications can highlight conflicts of interest and ideology, and not merely remove obstacles to mutual understanding" (Held 1992: 32).

Globalization can mean the reinforcement of both supranational and subnational regionalism. The European Union is a case in point. Formed in response to economic challenges from Japan and the United States, it represents more than the internal market and is becoming an administrative, legal, political, and cultural formation, involving multiple Europes: a Europe of the nations, the regions, "European civilization," Christianities, and so on. The dialectics of unification mean, for instance, that constituencies in Northern Ireland can appeal to the European Court of Human Rights in Strasbourg on decisions of the British courts, or that Catalonia can outflank Madrid and Brittany outmaneuver Paris by appealing to Brussels or by establishing links with other regions (e.g., between Catalonia and the Ruhr area). Again, there is an ongoing flow or cascade of globalization–regionalism–subregionalism. Or, "Globalization encourages macro-regionalism, which, in turn, encourages micro-regionalism" (Cox 1992: 34).

> Micro-regionalism in poor areas will be a means not only of affirming cultural identities but of claiming pay-offs at the macro-regional level for maintaining political stability and economic good behaviour. The issues of redistribution are thereby raised from the sovereign state level to the macro-regional level, while the manner in which redistributed wealth is used becomes decentralised to the micro-regional level. (ibid.: 35)

What globalization means in structural terms, then, is the *increase in the available modes of organization*: transnational, international, macroregional, national, microregional, municipal, local. This ladder of administrative levels is being crisscrossed by *functional networks* of corporations, international organizations, nongovernmental organizations, as well as professionals and computer users. This approximates Rosenau's "postinternational politics," made up of two interactive worlds with overlapping memberships: a state-centric world, in which the primary actors are national, and a multicentric world of diverse actors such as corporations, international organizations, ethnic groups, churches (1990). These multicentric functional networks in turn are nested within broader sprawling "scapes," such as finanscapes, ethnoscapes (Appadurai 1990). Furthermore, not only these modes of organization are important but also the informal spaces that are created in between, the interstices. Inhabited by diasporas, migrants, exiles, refugees, nomads, these are sites of what the sociologist Michael Mann (1986) calls "interstitial emergence" and identifies as important sources of social renewal.

Also in political economy, we can identify a wide range of hybrid formations. The articulation of modes of production follows a principle of hybridization. The dual economy argument saw neatly divided economic sectors whilst the articulation argument sees interactive sectors giving rise to mélange effects, such as "semi-proletarians" who have one foot in the agrarian subsistence sector. Counterposed to the idea of the dual economy split in traditional/modern and feudal/capitalist sectors, the articulation argument holds that what has been taking place is an interpenetration of modes of production. Uneven articulation in turn gives rise to asymmetric integration (Terhal 1987). Dependency theory may be read as a theory of structural hybridization in which dependent capitalism is a mélange category in which the logics of capitalism and imperialism have merged. Recognition of this hybrid condition is what distinguishes neo-Marxism from classical Marxism (in which capital was regarded as a "permanently revolutionizing force"): that is, regular capitalism makes for development but dependent capitalism makes for the "development of underdevelopment." The contested notion of semi-periphery may also be viewed as a hybrid formation.[2] In a wider context, the mixed economy, the informal sector, and the "third sector" of the "social economy," comprising cooperative and nonprofit organizations, may be viewed as hybrid economic formations. Social capital, civic entrepreneurship, and corporate citizenship – all themes of our times – are thoroughly hybrid in character.

Hybrid formations constituted by the interpenetration of diverse logics manifest themselves in *hybrid sites* and spaces. Thus, urbanization amidst the fusion of pre-capitalist and capitalist modes of production, as in parts of Latin America, may give rise to "cities of peasants" (Roberts 1978). Border zones are the meeting places of different organizational modes – such as free enterprise zones and offshore banking facilities (hybrid meeting places of state sovereignty and transnational enterprise), overseas military facilities, and surveillance stations (Enloe 1989). Borderlands generally are a significant topos (Anzaldúa 1987). The blurring and reworking of public and private spaces is a familiar theme (Helly and Reverby 1992). Global cities and ethnic mélange neighborhoods within them (such as Jackson Heights in Queens, New York) are other hybrid spaces in the global landscape. The use of information technology in supranational financial transactions (Wachtel 1990) gives rise to a hyper-space of capital.

Another dimension of hybridity concerns the experience of time, as in the notion of *mixed times* (tiempos mixtos) common in Latin America, where it refers to the coexistence and interspersion of premodernity, modernity, and postmodernity (Caldéron 1988; Vargas 1992). A similar point is that "intrinsic asynchrony" is a "general characteristic of Third World cultures" (Hösle 1992: 237).

Globalization, then, increases the range of organizational options, all of which are in operation simultaneously. Each or a combination of these may be relevant in specific social, institutional, legal, political, economic, or cultural spheres. What matters is that no single mode has a necessary overall priority or monopoly. This is one of the salient differences between the present phase of globalization and the preceding era from the 1840s to the 1960s, the great age of nationalism when by and large the nation state was the single dominant organizational option. While the spread of the nation state has been an expression of globalization, the dynamic has not stopped there.

The overall tendency towards increasing global density and interdependence, or globalization, translates, then, into the pluralization of organizational forms. Structural hybridization and the mélange of diverse modes of organization give rise to a pluralization of forms of cooperation and competition as well as to novel mixed forms of cooperation. This is the structural corollary to flexible specialization and just-in-time capitalism and, on the other hand, to cultural hybridization and multiple identities. Multiple identities and the decentering of the social subject are grounded in the ability of individuals to avail themselves of several organizational options at the same time. Thus globalization is the framework for the diversification and amplification of "sources of the self."

A different concern is the scope and depth of the historical field. The westernization/modernity views on globalization only permit a global momentum with a short memory. Globalization taken widely however refers to the formation of a worldwide historical field and involves the development of global memory, arising from shared global experiences. Such shared global experiences range from intercivilizational encounters such as long-distance trade and migration to slavery, conquest, war, imperialism, colonialism. It has been argued that the latter would be irrelevant to global culture:

Unlike national cultures, a global culture is essentially memoryless. When the "nation" can be constructed so as to draw upon and revive latent popular experiences and needs, a "global culture" answers to no living needs, no identity-in-the-making. . . . There are no "world memories" that can be used to *unite* humanity; the most global experiences to date – colonialism and the World Wars – can only serve to remind us of our historic cleavages. (Smith 1990: 180)

If, however, conflict, conquest, and oppression would *only* divide people, then nations themselves would merely be artifacts of division for they too were mostly born out of conflict (e.g., Hechter 1975). Likewise, on the larger canvas, it would be shallow and erroneous to argue that the experiences of conflict merely divide humanity: they also unite humankind, even if in painful ways and producing an ambivalent kind of unity (Abdel-Malek 1981; Nederveen Pieterse 1989). Unity emerging out of antagonism and conflict is the ABC of dialectics. It is a recurrent theme in postcolonial literature, for example, *The Intimate Enemy* (Nandy 1983). The intimacy constituted by repression and resistance is not an uncommon notion either, as hinted in the title of the Israeli author Uri Avneri's book about Palestinians, *My Friend the Enemy* (1986). A conflictual unity bonded by common political and cultural experiences, including the experience of domination, has been part of the make-up of hybrid postcolonial cultures. Thus, the former British Empire remains in many ways a unitary space featuring a common language, common elements in legal and political systems, infrastructure, traffic rules, an imperial architecture that is in many ways the same in India as in South Africa, along with the legacy of the Commonwealth (King 1990).

Robertson makes reference to the deep history of globality, particularly in relation to the spread of world religions, but reserves the notion of globalization for later periods, starting in the 1500s, considering that what changes over time is "the scope and depth of consciousness of the world as a single place." In his view, "contemporary globalization" also refers to "cultural and subjective matters" and involves *awareness* of the global human condition, a global consciousness that carries reflexive connotations (1992: 183). No doubt this reflexivity is significant, also because it signals the potential capability to act upon the global human condition. On the other hand, there is no good reason why such reflexivity should halt at the gates of the West and not also arise from and be cognizant of the deep history of inter-civilizational connections including the influence of the world religions.

Global Mélange

How do we come to terms with phenomena such as Thai boxing by Moroccan girls in Amsterdam, Asian rap in London, Irish bagels, Chinese tacos, and Mardi Gras Indians in the United States, or "Mexican schoolgirls dressed in Greek togas dancing in the style of Isadora Duncan" (Rowe and Schelling 1991: 161)? How do we interpret Peter Brook directing the Mahabharata, or Ariane Mnouchkine staging a Shakespeare play in Japanese Kabuki style for a Paris audience in the Théâtre Soleil?

Cultural experiences, past or present, have not been simply moving in the direction of cultural uniformity and standardization. This is not to say that the notion of global cultural synchronization (Schiller 1989) is irrelevant, on the contrary, but it is fundamentally incomplete. It overlooks the countercurrents – the impact non-western cultures have been making on the West. It downplays the ambivalence of the globalizing momentum and ignores the role of local reception of western culture – for example, the indigenization of western elements. It fails to see the influence nonwestern cultures have been exercising on one another. It has no room for crossover culture, as in the development of "third cultures" such as world music. It overrates the homogeneity of western culture and overlooks the fact that many of the standards exported by the West and its cultural industries themselves turn out to be of culturally mixed character if we examine their cultural lineages. Centuries of South–North cultural osmosis have resulted in intercontinental cross-over culture. European and western culture are *part* of this global mélange. This is an obvious case if we reckon that Europe until the fourteenth century was invariably the recipient of cultural influences from the "Orient."[3] The hegemony of the West dates only from very recent time, from 1800 and, arguably, from industrialization.

One of the terms offered to describe this interplay is the *creolization* of global culture (Hannerz 1987). This approach is derived from Creole languages and linguistics. Creolization is itself an odd, hybrid term. In the Caribbean and North America it stands for the mixture of African and European (the Creole cuisine of New Orleans, etc.), while in Latin America *criollo* originally denotes those of European descent born on the continent.[4] "Creolization" means a Caribbean window on the world. Part of its appeal is that it goes against the grain of nineteenth-century racism and the accompanying abhorrence of métissage as miscegenation, as in the view that race mixture leads to decadence and decay for in every mixture the lower element is bound to predominate. The doctrine of racial purity involves the fear of and *dédain* for the half-caste. By stressing and foregrounding the *mestizo* factor, the mixed and in-between, creolization highlights what has been hidden and valorizes boundary crossing. It also implies an argument with westernization: the West itself may be viewed as a mixture and western culture as a Creole culture.

The Latin American term *mestizaje* also refers to boundary crossing mixture. Since the early 1900s, however, this has served as a hegemonic élite ideology, which refers to "whitening" or Europeanization as the overall project for Latin American countries: the European element is supposed to maintain the upper hand and through the gradual "whitening" of the population and culture, Latin America is supposed to achieve modernity (Graham 1990; Whitten and Torres 1992). A limitation of both creolization and mestizaje is that they are confined to the experience of the post-sixteenth-century Americas.

Another terminology is the "orientalization of the world," which is referred to as "a distinct global process" (Featherstone 1990). In Duke Ellington's words, "We are all becoming a little Oriental" (quoted in Fischer 1992: 32). It is reminiscent of the theme of "East wind prevails over West wind" that runs through Sultan Galiev, Mao, and Abdel-Malek. In the setting of the rise of China and the Asian newly industrialized countries, it evokes the twenty-first century as an "Asian century" and the Asian Renaissance (Park 1985, Ibrahim 1996).

Each of these terms – creolization, mestizaje, orientalization – opens a different window on the global mélange. In the United States, *crossover* culture denotes the adoption of black cultural characteristics by European Americans and of white elements by African Americans. As a general notion, crossover culture may aptly describe long-term global intercultural osmosis and global mélange. Still what are not clarified are the *terms* under which cultural interplay and crossover take place. In terms such as global mélange, what is missing is acknowledgment of the actual unevenness, asymmetry, and inequality in global relations.

Theorizing Hybridity

Given the backdrop of nineteenth-century discourse, it's no wonder that those arguments that acknowledge hybridity often do so on a note of regret and loss – loss of purity, wholeness, authenticity. Thus according to the sociologist Hisham Sharabi, neopatriarchical society in the contemporary Arab world is "a new, hybrid sort of society/culture," "neither modern nor traditional" (1988: 4). The "neopatriarchal petty bourgeoisie" is likewise characterized as a "hybrid class" (1988: 6). This argument is based on an analysis of "the political and economic conditions of distorted, dependent capitalism" in the Arab world (1988: 5), in other words, it is derived from the framework of dependency theory.

In arguments such as these hybridity functions as a negative trope, in line with the nineteenth-century paradigm according to which hybridity, mixture, mutation are negative developments that detract from prelapsarian purity – in society and culture as in biology. Since the development of Mendelian genetics in the 1870s and subsequently in early twentieth-century biology, however, a revaluation has taken place according to which crossbreeding and polygenic inheritance have come to be positively valued as enrichments of gene pools. Gradually this has been seeping through in wider circles; the work of the anthropologist Gregory Bateson (1972), as one of the few to connect the natural sciences and the social sciences, has been influential in this regard.

In poststructuralist and postmodern analysis, hybridity and syncretism have become keywords. Thus, hybridity is the antidote to essentialist notions of identity and ethnicity (Lowe 1991). Cultural syncretism refers to the methodology of montage and collage, to "cross-cultural plots of music, clothing, behaviour, advertising, theatre, body language, or . . . visual communication, spreading multi-ethnic and multi-centric patterns" (Canevacci 1993: 3; 1992). Interculturalism, rather than multiculturalism, is a keynote of this kind of perspective. But it also raises different problems. What is the political portée of the celebration of hybridity? Is it merely another sign of perplexity turned into virtue by those grouped on the consumer end of social change? According to Ella Shohat, "A celebration of syncretism and hybridity per se, if not articulated in conjunction with questions of hegemony and neo-colonial power relations, runs the risk of appearing to sanctify the *fait accompli* of colonial violence" (1992: 109). Hence, a further step is not merely to celebrate but to theorize hybridity.

A theory of hybridity would be attractive. We are so used to theories that are concerned with establishing boundaries and demarcations among phenomena – units or processes that are as neatly as possible set apart from other units or processes – that a theory that instead would focus on fuzziness and mélange, cut'n'mix, criss-cross and crossover, might well be a relief in itself. Yet, ironically, of course, it would have to prove itself by giving as neat as possible a version of messiness, or an unhybrid categorization of hybridities.

By what yardstick would we differentiate hybridities? One consideration is in what context hybridity functions. At a general level, hybridity concerns the mixture of phenomena that are held to be different, separate; hybridization then refers to a *cross-category* process. Thus with the linguist Bakhtin (1968) hybridization refers to sites, such as fairs, that bring together the exotic and the familiar, villagers and townspeople, performers and observers. The categories can also be cultures, nations, ethnicities, status groups, classes, genres, and hybridity by its very existence blurs the distinctions among them. Hybridity functions, next, as part of a power relationship between center and margin, hegemony and minority, and indicates a blurring, destabilization or subversion of that hierarchical relationship.

One of the original notions of hybridity is *syncretism*, the fusion of religious forms. Here we can distinguish syncretism as *mimicry* – as in Santería, Candomblé, Vodûn, in which Catholic saints serve as masks behind which non-Christian forms of worship are practiced (Thompson 1984). The Virgin of Guadeloupe as a mask for Pacha Mama is another example. On the other hand, we find syncretism as a mélange not only of forms but also of beliefs, a merger in which both religions, Christian and native, have changed and a "third religion" has developed (as in Kimbangism in the Congo).

Another phenomenon is hybridity as migration mélange. A common observation is that second generation immigrants, in the West and elsewhere, display mixed cultural traits – a separation between and, next, a mix of a home culture and language (matching the culture of origin) and an outdoor culture (matching the culture of residence), as in the combination "Muslim in the daytime, disco in the evening" (Feddema 1992).

In postcolonial literature, hybridity is a familiar and ambivalent trope. Homi Bhabha (1990) refers to hybrids as intercultural brokers in the interstices between nation and empire, producing counternarratives from the nation's margins to the "totalizing boundaries" of the nation. At the same time, refusing nostalgic models of precolonial purity, hybrids, by way of mimicry, may conform to the "hegemonized rewriting of the Eurocentre." Hybridity, in this perspective, can be a condition tantamount to alienation, a state of homelessness. Smadar Lavie comments: "This is a response-oriented model of hybridity. It lacks agency, by not empowering the hybrid. The result is a fragmented Otherness in the hybrid" (1992: 92). In the work of Gloria Anzaldúa and others, she recognizes, on the other hand, a community-oriented mode of hybridity, and notes that "reworking the past exposes its hybridity, and to recognize and acknowledge this hybrid past in terms of the present empowers the community and gives it agency" (ibid.).

An ironical case of hybridity as intercultural crossover is mentioned by Michael Bérubé, interviewing the African American literary critic Houston Baker, Jr.: "That reminds me of your article in *Technoculture*, where you write that when a bunch of Columbia-graduate white boys known as Third Bass attack Hammer for not being black enough or strong enough . . . *that's* the moment of hybridity" (1992: 551).

Taking in these lines of thought, we can construct a *continuum of hybridities*: on one end, an assimilationist hybridity that leans over towards the center, adopts the canon and mimics hegemony and, at the other end, a destabilizing hybridity that blurs the canon, reverses the current, subverts the center. Hybridities, then, may be differentiated according to the components in the mélange: an assimilationist hybridity in which the center predominates – as in V.S. Naipaul, known for his trenchant observations such as there's no decent cup of coffee to be had in Trinidad; a posture that has given rise to the term Naipaulitis – and on the other hand, a hybridity that blurs (passive) or destabilizes (active) the canon and its categories. Perhaps this spectrum of hybridities can be summed up as ranging from Naipaul to Salman Rushdie (cf. Brennan 1989), Edward Said, and Subaltern Studies. Still what does it mean to destabilize the canon? It is worth reflecting on the politics of hybridity.

Politics of Hybridity

Relations of power and hegemony are inscribed and reproduced *within* hybridity for wherever we look closely enough we find the traces of asymmetry in culture, place, descent. Hence, hybridity raises the question of the *terms* of mixture, the conditions of mixing. At the same time, it's important to note the ways in which hegemony is not merely reproduced but *refigured* in the process of hybridization. Generally, what is the bearing of hybridity in relation to political engagement?

> At times, the anti-essentialist emphasis on hybrid identities comes dangerously close to dismissing all searches for communitarian origins as an archaeological excavation of an idealized, irretrievable past. Yet, on another level, while avoiding any nostalgia for a prelapsarian community, or for any unitary and transparent identity predating the "fall," we must also ask whether it is possible to forge a collective resistance without inscribing a communal past. (Shohat 1992: 109)

Isn't there a close relationship between political mobilization and collective memory? Isn't the remembrance of deeds past, the commemoration of collective itineraries, victories and defeats – such as the Matanza for the FMLN in El Salvador, Katipunan for the NPA in the Philippines, Heroes Day for the ANC – fundamental to the symbolism of resistance and the moral economy of mobilization? Still, this line of argument involves several problems. While there may be a link, there is no necessary symmetry between communal past/collective resistance. What is the basis of bonding in collective action – past or future, memory or project? While communal symbolism may be important, collective symbolism and discourse merging a heterogeneous collectivity in a common project may be more important. Thus while

Heroes Day is significant to the ANC (December 16 is the founding day of Umkhonto we Sizwe), the Freedom Charter and, specifically, the project of nonracial democracy (nonsexism has been added later) has been of much greater importance. These projects are not of a communal nature: their strength is precisely that they transcend communal boundaries. Generally, emancipations may be thought of in the plural, as an ensemble of projects that in itself is diverse, heterogeneous, multivocal.[5] The argument linking communal past/collective resistance imposes a unity and transparency which in effect reduces the space for critical engagement, for plurality *within* the movement, diversity within the process of emancipation. It privileges a communal view of collective action, a primordial view of identity, and ignores or downplays the importance of *intra*-group differences and conflicts over group representation, demands, and tactics, including reconstructions of the past. It argues as if the questions of whether demands should be for autonomy or inclusion, whether the group should be inward or outward looking, have already been settled, while in reality these are political dilemmas. The nexus between communal past/collective engagement is one strand in political mobilization, but so are the hybrid past/plural projects, and in everyday politics the point is how to negotiate these strands in roundtable politics. This involves going beyond a past to a future orientation – for what is the point of collective action without a future? The lure of community, powerful and prevalent in left as well as right politics, has been questioned often enough. In contrast, hybridity when thought through as a politics may be subversive of essentialism and homogeneity, disruptive of static spatial and political categories of center and periphery, high and low, class and ethnos, and in recognizing multiple identities, widen the space for critical engagement. Thus, the nostalgia paradigm of community politics has been contrasted to the landscape of the city, along with a reading of "politics as relations among strangers" (Young 1990).

What is the significance of this outlook in the context of global inequities and politics? Political theory on a global scale is relatively undeveloped. Traditionally political theory is concerned with the relations between sovereign and people, state and society. It's of little help to turn to the "great political theorists" from Locke to Mill for they are all essentially concerned with the state–society framework. International relations theory extrapolates from this core preoccupation with concepts such as national interest and balance of power. Strictly speaking, international relations theory, at any rate neorealist theory, precludes global political theory. In the absence of a "world society," how can there be a worldwide social contract or global democracy? This frontier has opened up through ideas such as global civil society and the transnational networks of nongovernmental organizations: "The growth of global civil society represents an ongoing project of civil society to reconstruct, re-imagine, or re-map world politics" (Lipschutz 1992: 391). While global society and post-international politics are relevant, a limitation to these reconceptualizations remains the absence of legal provisions that are globally binding rather than merely in interstate relations. Hence new initiatives such as the International Criminal Court and the Kyoto Protocol are particularly significant.

The question remains what kind of conceptual tools we can develop to address questions such as the double standards prevailing in global politics: perennial issues such as western countries practicing democracy at home and imperialism abroad; the edifying use of terms such as self-determination and sovereignty while the United States invades Panama, Grenada, or Iraq. The term *imperialism* may no longer be adequate to address the present situation. It may be adequate in relation to U.S. actions in Panama or Grenada, but less so to describe the Gulf War. Empire is the control exercised by a state over the domestic and foreign policy of another political society (Doyle 1986: 45), which is not an adequate terminology to characterize the Gulf War episode. If we consider that major actors in today's global circumstance are the IMF, World Bank, and World Trade Organization, transnational corporations, and regional investment banks, it is easy to acknowledge their influence on the domestic policies of countries from Brazil to the Philippines; but the situation differs from imperialism in two ways: the actors are not states and the foreign policy of the countries involved is not necessarily affected. The casual use of terms such as recolonization or neocolonialism to describe the impact of IMF conditionalities on African countries remains just that, casual. The situation has changed also since the emergence of regional blocs which can potentially exercise joint foreign policy (e.g., the European Union) or which within themselves contain two or more "worlds" (e.g., NAFTA, APEC). Both these situations differ from imperialism in the old sense. Literature in international political economy shows a shift from "imperialism" to "globalization." According to Tomlinson,

> the distribution of global power that we know as "imperialism" . . . characterised the modern period up to, say, the 1960s. What replaces "imperialism" is "globalisation." Globalisation may be distinguished from imperialism in that it is a far less coherent or culturally directed process. . . . The idea of "globalisation" suggests interconnection and interdependency of all global areas which happens in a less purposeful way. (1991: 175)

This is a particularly narrow interpretation in which globalization matches the epoch of late capitalism; still what is interesting is the observation that the present phase of globalization is less coherent and less purposeful than imperialism. Domination may be more dispersed, less orchestrated, more heterogeneous. To address global inequalities and develop global political theory a different kind of conceptualization is needed. We are not without points of reference but we lack a theory of global political action. The sociologist Alberto Melucci has discussed the "planetarization" of collective action (1989). Some of the implications of globalization for democracy have been examined by Held (1992). As regards the basics of a global political consensus, the UN Declaration of Human Rights, and its amendments by the Movement of Nonaligned Countries, may be a point of reference (Parekh 1992).[6]

Post-hybridity?

Cultural hybridization refers to the mixing of Asian, African, American, European cultures: hybridization is the making of global culture as a global mélange. As a category, hybridity serves a purpose based on the assumption of *difference* between the categories, forms, beliefs that go into the mixture. Yet the very process of hybridization shows the difference to be relative and, with a slight shift of perspective, the relationship can also be described in terms of an affirmation of *similarity*. Thus, the Catholic saints can be taken as icons of Christianity but can also be viewed as holdovers of pre-Christian paganism inscribed in the Christian canon. In that light, their use as masks for non-Christian gods is less quaint and rather intimates transcultural pagan affinities.

Ariane Mnouchkine's use of Kabuki style to stage a Shakespeare play leads to the question which Shakespeare play? The play is *Henry IV*, which is set in a context of European high feudalism. In that light, the use of Japanese feudal Samurai style to portray European feudalism (Kreidt 1987: 255) makes a point about transcultural historical affinities. "Mexican schoolgirls dressed in Greek togas dancing in the style of Isadora Duncan," mentioned before, reflects transnational bourgeois class affinities, mirroring themselves in classical European culture. Chinese tacos and Irish bagels reflect ethnic crossover in employment patterns in the American fast food sector. Asian rap refers to cross-cultural stylistic convergence in popular youth culture.

An episode that can serve to probe this more deeply is the influence of Japanese art on European painting. The impact of *Japonisme* is well known: it inspired impressionism, which in turn set the stage for modernism. The color woodcuts that made such a profound impression on Seurat, Manet, Van Gogh, Toulouse Lautrec, Whistler belonged to the Ukiyo school, a genre sponsored by the merchant class, that flourished in Japan between the seventeenth and nineteenth centuries. Ukiyo-e typically depicted urban scenes of ephemeral character, such as entertainments, theater, or prostitution, and landscapes. It was a popular art form that, unlike the high art of aristocracy, was readily available at reasonable prices in bookstores (rather than cloistered in courts or monasteries) and therefore also accessible to Europeans (Budde 1993). This episode, then, is not so much an exotic irruption in European culture, but rather reflects the fact that bourgeois sensibilities had found iconographic expression in Japan earlier than in Europe. In other words, Japanese popular art was modern before European art was. Thus, what from one angle appears as hybridity to the point of exoticism, from another angle, again, reflects transcultural class affinities in sensibilities vis-à-vis urban life and nature. In other words, the other side of cultural hybridity is transcultural compatibility.

What makes it difficult to discuss these issues is that two quite distinct concepts of *culture* are generally being used indiscriminately. The first concept of culture (culture 1) views culture as essentially territorial; it assumes that culture stems from a learning process that is, in the main, localized. This is culture in the sense of a *culture*, that is, the culture of a society or social group: a notion that goes back to nineteenth-century romanticism and that has been elaborated in twentieth-century anthropology, in particular cultural relativism – with the notion of cultures as a whole, a Gestalt, configuration. A related idea is the organic or "tree" model of culture.

A wider understanding of culture (culture 2) views culture as a general human "software" (Banuri 1990: 77), as in nature/culture arguments. This notion has been implicit in theories of evolution and diffusion, in which culture is viewed as, in the

Table 36.2   Assumptions about culture

Territorial Culture	*Translocal Culture*
endogenous	exogenous
orthogenetic	heterogenetic
societies, nations, empires	diasporas, migrations
locales, regions	crossroads, borders, interstices
community-based	networks, brokers, strangers
organic, unitary	diffusion, heterogeneity
authenticity	translation
inward looking	outward looking
community linguistics	contact linguistics
race	half-caste, half-breed, métis
ethnicity	new ethnicity
identity	identification, new identity

main, a *translocal* learning process. These understandings are not incompatible: culture 2 finds expression in culture 1; cultures are the vehicles of culture. But they do reflect different emphases in relation to historical processes of culture formation and hence generate markedly different assessments of cultural relations. Divergent meta-assumptions about culture underlie the varied vocabularies in which cultural relations are discussed (table 36.2).

Culture 2 or translocal culture is not without place (there is no culture without place), but it involves an *outward looking* sense of place, whereas culture 1 is based on an *inward looking* sense of place. Culture 2 involves what the geographer Doreen Massey calls "a global sense of place": "the specificity of place which derives from the fact that each place is the focus of a distinct *mixture* of wider and more local social relations" (1993: 240).

The general terminology of cultural pluralism, multicultural society, intercultural relations, and so on, does not clarify whether it refers to culture 1 or culture 2. Thus, relations among cultures can be viewed in a static fashion (in which cultures retain their separateness in interaction) or a fluid fashion (in which cultures interpenetrate) (table 36.3).

Hybridization as a perspective belongs to the fluid end of relations between cultures: the mixing of cultures and not their separateness is emphasized. At the same time, the underlying assumption about culture is that of culture/place. Cultural forms are called hybrid/syncretic/mixed/creolized because the elements in the mix derive from different cultural contexts. Thus, Hannerz defines Creole cultures as follows: "Creole cultures like creole languages are those which draw in some way on two or more historical sources, often originally widely different. They have had some time to develop and integrate, and to become elaborate and pervasive" (1987: 552). But in this sense would not every culture be a Creole culture? Can we identify any culture that is *not* Creole in the sense of drawing on one or more different

Table 36.3   Cultural relations

Static	Fluid
plural society (Furnivall)	pluralism, melting pot
multiculturalism (static)	multiculturalism (fluid), interculturalism
global mosaic	cultural flows in space (Hannerz)
clash of civilizations	third cultures

Table 36.4   Homogenization versus diversification

Globalization/homogenization	Globalization/diversification
cultural imperialism	cultural planetarization
cultural dependence	cultural interdependence
cultural hegemony	cultural interpenetration
autonomy	syncretism, synthesis, hybridity
modernity	modernities
westernization	global mélange
cultural convergence	creolization, crossover
world civilization	global ecumene

historical sources?[7] A scholar of music makes a similar point about world music: "All music is essentially world music" (Bor 1994: 2).

A further question is: Are cultural elements different merely because they originate from different cultures? More often, what may be at issue, as argued above, is the *similarity* of cultural elements when viewed from the point of class, status group, life style, or function. Hence, at some stage, toward the end of the story, the notion of cultural hybridity itself unravels or, at least, needs reworking. To explore what this means in the context of globalization, we can contrast the vocabularies and connotations of globalization-as-homogenization and globalization-as-hybridization (table 36.4).

What is common to some perspectives on both sides of the globalization/homogenization/heterogenization axis is a territorial view of culture. The territoriality of culture, however, itself is not constant over time. For some time we have entered a period of accelerated globalization and cultural mixing. This also involves an overall tendency towards the deterritorialization of culture, or an overall shift in orientation from culture 1 to culture 2. Introverted cultures, which have been prominent over a long stretch of history and overshadowed translocal culture, are gradually receding into the background, while translocal culture made up of diverse elements is coming to the foreground. This transition and the hybridization processes themselves unleash intense and dramatic nostalgia politics, of which ethnic upsurges, ethnicization of nations, and religious revivalism form part.

Hybridization refers not only to the crisscrossing of cultures (culture 1) but also and by the same token to a transition from the provenance of culture 1 to culture 2. Another aspect of this transition is that due to advancing information technology and biotechnology different *modes* of hybridity emerge on the horizon: in the light of hybrid forms such as cyborgs, virtual reality and electronic simulation, intercultural differences may begin to pale to relative insignificance – although of great local intensity. Biotechnology opens up the perspective of "merged evolution," in the sense of the merger of the evolutionary streams of genetics, cultural evolution, and information technology and the near prospect of humans intervening in genetic evolution, through the matrix of cultural evolution and information technologies (Goonatilake 1991).

Forward Moves

Globalization/hybridization makes, first, an empirical case: that processes of globalization, past and present, can be adequately described as processes of hybridization. Secondly, it is a critical argument: against viewing globalization in terms of homogenization, or of modernization/westernization, as empirically narrow and historically flat.

The career of sociology has been coterminous with the career of nation state formation and nationalism, and from this followed the constitution of the object of sociology as society and the equation of society with the nation. Culminating in structural functionalism and modernization theory, this career in the context of globalization is in for retooling. A global sociology is taking shape around notions such as social networks (rather than "societies"), border zones, boundary crossing, diaspora, and global society. In other words, a sociology conceived within the framework of nations/societies is making place for a post-inter/national sociology of hybrid formations, times, and spaces.

Structural hybridization, or the increase in the range of organizational options, and cultural hybridization, or the doors of erstwhile imagined communities opening up, are signs of an age of boundary crossing, not, surely, of the erasure of boundaries. Thus, state power remains strategic, but it is no longer the only game in town. The tide of globalization reduces the room of maneuver of states, while international institutions, transnational transactions, regional cooperation, subnational dynamics, and non-governmental organizations expand in impact and scope (Cooperrider and Dutton 1999).

In historical terms, writing diaspora histories of global culture may deepen this perspective. Due to nationalism as the dominant paradigm since the nineteenth century, cultural achievements have been routinely claimed for nations and culture has been "nationalized," territorialized. A different historical record can be constructed based on the contributions to culture formation and diffusion by diasporas, migrations, strangers, brokers. A related project would be histories of the hybridization of metropolitan cultures, that is, a counterhistory to the narrative of imperial history. Such historical inquiries may show that hybridization has been taking place all along but has been concealed by religious, national, imperial, and civilizational chauvinisms. Moreover, they may deepen our understanding of the temporalities of hybridization: how certain junctures witness downturns or upswings of hybridization, slowdowns or speedups. At the same time it follows that, if we accept that cultures have been hybrid *all along*, hybridization is in effect a tautology: contemporary accelerated globalization means the hybridization of hybrid cultures.

As such, the hybridization perspective remains meaningful only as a critique of essentialism. Essentialism will remain strategic as a mobilizational device as long as the units of nation, state, region, civilization, ethnicity remain strategic: and for just as long hybridization remains a relevant approach. Hybridity unsettles the introverted concept of culture that underlies romantic nationalism, racism, ethnicism, religious revivalism, civilizational chauvinism, and cultural essentialism. Hybridization, then, is a perspective that is meaningful as a counterweight to introverted notions of culture; at the same time, the very process of hybridization unsettles the introverted gaze, and accordingly, hybridization eventually ushers in post-hybridity, or transcultural cut-and-paste.

Hybridization is a factor in the reorganization of social spaces. Structural hybridization, or the emergence of new practices of social cooperation and competition, and cultural hybridization, or new translocal cultural expressions, are interdependent: new forms of cooperation require and evoke new cultural imaginaries. Hybridization is a contribution to a sociology of the in-between, a sociology from the interstices. This involves merging endogenous/exogenous understandings of culture. Significant perspectives include Hannerz' concern with mapping micro–macro linkages (1989) and contemporary work in geography and cultural studies (e.g., Bird et al. 1993).

In relation to the global human condition of inequality, the hybridization perspective releases reflection and engagement from the bounds of nation, community, ethnicity, or class. Fixities have become fragments as the kaleidoscope of collective experience is in motion. It has been in motion all along, and the fixities of nation, community, ethnicity, and class have been grids superimposed upon experiences more complex and subtle than reflexivity and organization could accommodate.

Notes

1   An equivalent view in international relations is Morse 1976. After arguing for globalizations in the plural, I will continue to use globalization singular because it matches conventional usage and there is no need to stress the point by way of inelegant grammar.
2   The mélange element comes across for instance in the definition of semiperiphery of Chase-Dunn and Hall (1993: 865–6): "(1) a semiperipheral region may be one that mixes both core and peripheral forms of organization; (2) a semiperipheral region may be spatially located between core and peripheral regions; (3) mediating activities between core and peripheral regions may be carried out in semiperipheral regions; (4) a semiperipheral area may be one in which institutional features are in some ways intermediate between those forms found in core and periphery." Interestingly, Chase-Dunn and Hall also destabilize the notions of core and periphery, pointing to situations "in which the 'periphery' systematically exploits the 'core'" (1993: 864). I am indebted to an anonymous reviewer

of *International Sociology* for alerting me to this source and the relevance of semiperiphery in this context.

3 I argue this case in Nederveen Pieterse 1994 and 1989: chapter 15.

4 As against *peninsulares*, born in the Iberian Peninsula, *indigenes*, or Native Americans, and *ladinos* and *cholos*, straddled betwixt those of European and Native American descent.

5 In *Pour Rushdie*, a collection of essays by Arab and Islamic intellectuals in support of freedom of expression, Paris is referred to as a "capitale Arabe." This evokes another notion of hybridity, one that claims a collective ground based on multiple subjectivities in the name of a universal value.

6 I use critical globalism as an approach to current configurations (Nederveen Pieterse 2001). This discussion of imperialism versus globalization is dated since in the wake of 9/11 has come a new imperial turn; this is taken up in a forthcoming book on *Globalization or Empire?* (Routledge, 2004).

7 Some of the "primitive isolates," the traditional study objects of anthropology, might be exceptions, although even this may be questioned in the long stretch of time.

References

Abdel-Malek, Anouar. *Civilizations and Social Theory*. 2 vols. London: Macmillan, 1981.

Albrow, Martin. "Introduction." In *Globalization, Knowledge and Society*, edited by M. Albrow and E. King. London: Sage, 1990.

Ambrose, Stephen E. *Rise to Globalism: American Foreign Policy since 1938*. London: Lane, 1971.

Amin, Samir. *Delinking: Towards a Polycentric World*. London: Zed, 1990.

Anderson, Benedict. "The New World Disorder." *New Left Review* 190 (1992): 3–14.

Anzaldúa, Gloria. *Borderland/La Frontera*. San Francisco: Spinsters/Ann Lute, 1987.

Appadurai, Arjun. "Disjuncture and Difference in the Global Political Economy." Pp. 295–310 in *Global Culture*, edited by Featherstone, 1990.

Arnason, Johann P. "Nationalism, Globalization and Modernity." Pp. 207–36 in *Global Culture*, edited by Featherstone, 1990.

Avneri, Uri. *My Friend the Enemy*. London: Zed, 1986.

Bakhtin, Mikhail. *Rabelais and His World*. Cambridge: MIT Press, 1968.

Banuri, Tariq. "Modernization and Its Discontents: A Cultural Perspective on Theories of Development." Pp. 73–101 in *Dominating Knowledge*, edited by F. Appfel-Marglin and S. A. Marglin. Oxford: Clarendon Press, 1990.

Bateson, Gregory. *Steps to an Ecology of Mind*. San Francisco: Chandler, 1972.

Bérubé, Michael. "Hybridity in the Center: An Interview with Houston A. Baker, Jr." *African American Review* 26, no. 4 (1992): 547–64.

Bhabha, Homi K. "Dissemination: Time, Narrative and the Margins of the Modern Nation." In *Nation and Narration*, edited by idem. London: Routledge, 1990.

Bird, Jon, Barry Curtis, Tim Putman, George Robertson, and Lisa Tickner, eds. *Mapping the Futures: Local Cultures, Global Change*. London: Routledge, 1993.

Bor, Joep. "Studying World Music: The Next Phase." Unpublished paper, 1994.

Brennan, Timothy. *Salman Rushdie and the Third World: Myths of the Nation*. New York: St. Martin's Press, 1989.

Budde, H. "Japanische Farbholzschnitte und Europäische Kunst: Maler und Sammler im 19. Jahrhundert." In *Japan und Europa 1543–1929*, edited by D. Croissant et al. Berlin: Berliner Festspiele/Argon, 1993.

Caldéron, F. "América Latina, Identitad y Tiempos Mixtos, O Cómo Pensar La Modernidad Sin Dejar De Ser Boliviano." Pp. 225–9 in *Imágenes Desconocidas*. Buenos Aires: Ed. CLACSO, 1988.

Canevacci, Massimo. "Fragmented Identity, Governmental Policy and Cultural Syncretism." Unpublished paper, 1993.

Chase-Dunn, Christopher, and Thomas D. Hall. "Comparing World-Systems: Concepts and Working Hypotheses." *Social Forces* 72, no. 1 (1993): 851–86.

Cooperrider, David L., and Jane E. Dutton, eds. *Organizational Dimensions of Global Change: No Limits to Cooperation*. London: Sage, 1999.

Cox, Robert W. "Global Perestroika." Pp. 26–43 in *New World Order? Socialist Register 1992*, edited by Ralph Miliband and Leo Panitch. London: Merlin Press, 1992.

Doyle, Michael W. *Empires*. Ithaca, NY: Cornell University Press, 1986.

Eisenstadt, Samuel N., ed. *Multiple Modernities*. New Brunswick, NJ: Transaction Books, 2002.

Enloe, Cynthia. *Bananas Beaches and Bases: Making Feminist Sense of International Politics*. Berkeley: University of California Press, 1989.

Featherstone, Mike, ed. *Global Culture: Nationalism, Globalization and Modernity*. London: Sage, 1990.

Feddema, R. 'Op Weg tussen Hoop en Vrees: De levensoriëntatie van jonge Turken en Marokkanen in Nederland." Utrecht University, Ph.D. diss., 1992.

Fischer, M. M. J. "Orientalizing America: Beginnings and Middle Passages." *Middle East Report* 22, no. 5 (1992): 32–7.

Gaonkar, Dilip P., ed. *Alternative Modernities*. Durham, NC: Duke University Press, 2001.

Giddens, Anthony. *The Consequences of Modernity*. Stanford, CA: Stanford University Press, 1990.

Goonatilake, Susantha. *The Evolution of Information: Lineages in Gene, Culture and Artifact*. London: Pinter, 1991.

Graham, R., ed. *The Idea of Race in Latin America, 1870–1940*. Austin: University of Texas Press, 1990.

Greenfield, L. *Nationalism: Five Roads to Modernity*. Cambridge, MA: Harvard University Press, 1992.

Hannerz, Ulf. "The World in Creolisation." *Africa* 57, no. 4 (1987): 546–59.

——. "Culture between Center and Periphery: Toward a Macroanthropology." *Ethnos* 54 (1989): 200–16.

Harvey, David. *The Condition of Postmodernity*. Oxford: Blackwell, 1989.

Hechter, Michael. *Internal Colonialism: The Celtic Fringe in British National Development, 1536–1966*. London: Routledge and Kegan Paul, 1975.

Held, David. "Democracy: From City-States to a Cosmopolitan Order?" Pp. 13–52 in *Prospects for Democracy*, edited by D. Held. Cambridge: Polity, 1992.

Helly, D. O., and S. M. Reverby, eds. *Gendered Domains: Rethinking Public and Private in Women's History*. Ithaca, NY: Cornell University Press, 1992.

Hösle, V. "The Third World As a Philosophical Problem." *Social Research* 59, no. 2 (1992): 227–62.

Ibrahim, Anwar. *The Asian Renaissance*. Singapore: Times Books, 1996.

Jameson, Fredric. *Postmodernism, or the Cultural Logic of Late Capitalism*. London: Verso, 1991.

Jameson, Fredric, and M. Miyoshi, eds. *The Cultures of Globalization*. Durham, NC: Duke University Press, 1998.

King, Anthony D. *Urbanism, Colonialism, and the World Economy: Cultural and Spatial Foundations of the World Urban System*. London: Routledge, 1990.

Kothari, Rajni. *Rethinking Development*. Delhi: Ajanta, 1988.

Kreidt, D. "Kann Uns Zum Vaterland die Fremde Werden? Exotismus im Schauspieltheater." Pp. 248–55 in *Exotische Welten, Europäische Phantasien*. Wurttemberg: Cantz, 1987.

Lavie, Smadar. "Blow-ups in the Borderzones: Third World Israeli Authors' Gropings for Home." *New Formations* 18 (1992): 84–106.

Li, Liu. "Theoretical Theses on 'Social Modernization.'" *International Sociology* 4, no. 4 (1989): 365–78.

Lipschutz, Ronald D. "Reconstructing World Politics: The Emergence of Global Civil Society." *Millennium* 21, no. 3 (1992): 389–420.

Lowe, Lisa. "Heterogeneity, Hybridity, Multiplicity: Marking Asian American Differences." *Diaspora* 1, no. 1 (1991): 24–44.

Mann, Michael. *The Sources of Social Power*. Cambridge: Cambridge University Press, 1986.

Massey, Doreen. "A Global Sense of Place." Pp. 232–40 in *Studying Culture*, edited by A. Gray and J. McGuigan. London: Edward Arnold, 1993.

Mazlish, Bruce, and Ralph Buultjens, eds. *Conceptualizing Global History*. Boulder, CO: Westview Press, 1993.

Melucci, Alberto. *Nomads of the Present*. London: Hutchinson Radius, 1989.

Nandy, Ashis. *The Intimate Enemy: Loss and Recovery of Self under Colonialism*. New Delhi: Oxford University Press, 1983.

Nederveen Pieterse, Jan P. "A Critique of World-System Theory." *International Sociology* 3, no. 3 (1987): 251–66.

——. *Empire and Emancipation: Power and Liberation on a World Scale*. New York: Praeger, 1989.

——. "Unpacking the West: How European Is Europe?" Pp. 129–49 in *Racism, Modernity, Identity*, edited by A. Rattansi and S. Westwood. Cambridge: Polity Press, 1994.

——. *Development Theory: Deconstructions/Reconstructions*. London: Sage, 2001.

Nelson, Benjamin. *On the Roads to Modernity*, edited by T. E. Huff. Totowa, NJ: Rowman & Littlefield, 1981.

Parekh, Bhikhu. "The Cultural Particularity of Liberal Democracy." Pp. 156–75 in *Prospects for Democracy*, edited by Held, 1992.

Park, Sung-Jo, ed. *The 21st Century – The Asian Century?* Berlin: EXpress Edition, 1985.

Roberts, B. *Cities of Peasants: The Political Economy of Urbanization in the Third World*. London: Edward Arnold, 1978.

Robertson, Roland. *Globalization: Social Theory and Global Culture*. London: Sage, 1992.

Rosenau, James N. *Turbulence in World Politics*. Brighton: Harvester, 1990.

Rowe, William, and Vivian Schelling. *Memory and Modernity: Popular Culture in Latin America*. London: Verso, 1991.

Schiller, Herbert I. *Culture Inc*. New York: Oxford University Press, 1989.

Sharabi, Hisham. *Neopatriarchy: A Theory of Distorted Change in Arab Society*. New York: Oxford University Press, 1988.

Shaw, Timothy. "Ethnicity As the Resilient Paradigm for Africa: From the 1960s to the 1980s." *Development and Change* 17, no. 4 (1986): 587–606.

Shohat, Ella. "Notes on the 'Post-Colonial.'" *Social Text* 31/32, (1992): 99–113.

Singh, Yogendra. *Essays on Modernization in India*. New Delhi: Manohar, 1989.

Smith, Anthony D. "Towards a Global Culture?" Pp. 171–92 in *Global Culture*, edited by Featherstone, 1990.

Sonoda, S. "Modernization of Asian Countries As a Process of 'Overcoming their Backwardness': the Case of Modernization in China." Paper presented at the Twelfth World Congress of International Sociological Association, Madrid, 1990.

Terhal, P. H. J. J. *World Inequality and Evolutionary Convergence*. Delft: Eburon, 1987.

Thompson, Robert Faris. *Flash of the Spirit: African and Afro-American Art and Philosophy*. New York: Vintage, 1984.

Tiryakian, Edward A. "Modernization: Exhumetur in Pace." *International Sociology* 6, no. 2 (1991): 165–80.

Tominaga, K. "A Theory of Modernization of Non-Western Societies: Toward a Generalization from Historical Experiences of Japan." Paper presented at the Twelfth World Congress of International Sociological Association, Madrid, 1990.

Tomlinson, John. *Cultural Imperialism*. Baltimore, MD: Johns Hopkins University Press, 1991.

Vargas, Virginia. "The Feminist Movement in Latin America: Between Hope and Disenchantment." Pp. 195–214 in *Emancipations, Modern and Postmodern*, edited by J. Nederveen Pieterse. London: Sage, 1992.

Wachtel, Howard M. *The Money Mandarins: The Making of a Supranational Economic Order*. Armonk, NY: M. E. Sharpe, 1990.

Whitten, Jr., N. E., and A. Torres. "Blackness in the Americas." *Report on the Americas* 25, no. 4 (1992): 16–22.

Young, Iris Marion. *Justice and the Politics of Difference*. Princeton, NJ: Princeton University Press, 1990.

37

(Re)Asserting National Television And National Identity Against the Global, Regional, and Local Levels of World Television

Joseph Straubhaar

Globalization of television is clearest at two levels. There is a strong globalization of media operations toward the advertising-based commercial market paradigm. That is accompanied by a systematic shift in the forms or genres of programs that are produced, so globalized content models or patterns tend to spread. They are, however, adapted to local cultures and circumstances, a process described by Robertson (1992, 1995) as glocalization. This process in turn is driven and bounded by audience desire for cultural proximity and relevance. Within these new structural boundaries, regional, national, and local producers also receive new resources to work with, both material (finance and technology) and symbolic (ideas and models). This interplay between globalizing structures and regional, national, and local producers's agency in content can be looked at in terms of structuration (Giddens, 1984).

Globalization theorists sometimes underestimate the continuing power of the nation-state to structure the circumstances within which most media industries still operate, even though these national producers now have to compete with global, cultural-linguistic regional, and local producers as well. This chapter offers some theoretical analysis of the relations between the global, regional, and national levels of television production, flow, and consumption.

From Cultural Imperialism to Globalization

One of the enduring problems in international communication has been how to theorize and explain the international flow and impact of television across cultures. Critical scholars in the 1960s to 1980s often analyzed problems of unequal television flows and structural inequalities of television production in the world in terms of media imperialism (Lee, 1980) and dependency (Fox, 1992), but more recently these approaches have fallen under critique as overly simplistic. In seeing the major industrialized countries as dominant and Third World countries as dependent, these theories have missed much of the complexity of change in industries, genres, and audience reception in the developing or peripheral nations.

The current discussion tends to focus on the globalization of cultures within a world capitalist economy (Featherstone, 1990; Wallerstein, 1991). The globalization approach originally posited that the world is becoming a single world society, "more uniform and standardized, through a technological, commercial and cultural synchronization emanating from the West, and that globalization is tied up with modernity" (Pieterse, 1995, p. 45). There has been a great deal of discussion about the globalization of television, particularly as it is driven by the spread of satellite and cable television technologies around the world. There is a fear of a renewed cycle of one-way television flows out from the United States, adding complete US television channels, such as CNN, MTV, Nickelodeon, and the Cartoon Channel to the already large export of US film, television programs, and music.

The discussion on globalization is becoming more complex. Increasingly it focuses less on dominant and dependent nation-states, more on globalized cultural actors, corporations, and governments, as well as globalized audiences. Still, most analyses of globalization diminish too much the continuing importance of national governments, national producers, and national identity among communication audiences in selecting and interpreting cultural products and messages. In much of the world, such as Eastern Europe or the Middle East, we currently see a rise of ethnic nationalism that reflects a search for identity and seems to extend to cultural consumption. The globalization discussion also often overlooks the rise of a new level of television flow and impact, that within regions of the world. A number of national/local television networks, like Brazil, Egypt, Hong Kong, India, and Mexico, export to surrounding regions, similar or proximate in culture and language. More rarely, some operations, like Star TV, produce for a supranational region, like Greater China, defined by culture and language.

Multilevel Approach

This chapter will focus on television within a world system that includes several levels of operation, investment, production, flow, and impact. There is a level that is truly global, one that is supranational regional or geolinguistic, one that is national, and others that are subnational or "regional" (within the nation), and even local. In fact, some of the most current theorizations of globalization recognize that "what globalization means in structural terms, then, is the *increase in the available modes of organization*: transnational, international, macro-regional, national, micro-regional, municipal, local" (Pieterse, 1995, p. 50, emphases in original). These levels correspond to levels of official government interactions, international organizations and nongovernmental organizations, international media and other firms, and cultural flows and interactions as well. These levels are not necessarily in conflict. Pieterse (1995, p. 50) observes that "Globalization can mean the reinforcement of both supranational and sub-national regionalism." While the main argument of this paper is that the role of geocultural regions need to be emphasized more, that can be fit into the more sophisticated interpretations of globalization that are emerging, such as Pieterse (1995). However, this chapter argues that it is clearer to think of television within a world system in which the term global is reserved for phenomena that are truly global, distinguishing those that are regional, national, and local within the world system.

The global level of analysis is in fact increasingly crucial. There are several kinds of globalization relevant to television. Some cable and satellite channels, such as CNN or the Cartoon Channel, take the same content to worldwide audiences, although some "global" channels are creating regionally or locally adapted versions. Quite a few television programs, such as *Dallas* or *Baywatch*, still are syndicated to flow globally to be broadcast nationally or locally. Quite a few national and local productions derive from formats or genres that have spread globally beyond their places of origin. Even more basically, models for broadcasting are being spread globally as private, commercial, entertainment-oriented stations and networks continue to spread into more nations.

Ferguson's excellent discussion of the myths of globalization raises several key problems: the idea that the world is becoming one homogeneous culture, largely fed by the US culture industries; that big cultural industries, like those of the US, have an automatic advantage due to economies of scale and the polish of their products; and that differences of time, space, and geography are eroded by technology (1992). This chapter will critique the ideas of globalization such as the worldwide homogenization of television, the erosion of national and cultural differences, and domination of all by US productions.

At the level of reception and audience impacts of television, some audiences do primarily watch globalized channels. We argue that those audiences are most often upper-middle and upper-class elites, since access to new channels is often limited by economic capital and interest in them limited by cultural capital. However, almost all audiences are touched by some aspect of globalization, at the level of program flow, genre, or broadcast model.

We propose that, in terms of media and media flows, a phenomenon equally significant to globalization, *per se*, may well be "regionalization" of television into multicountry markets linked by geography, language, and culture. These might more accurately be called the geocultural or cultural-linguistic (Wilkinson, 1995) markets, rather than regional markets, since not all these linked populations, markets and cultures are geographically contiguous.

For example, the US is clearly still the main media exporter in the world. The US dominates certain kinds of production, like feature films, which require huge investments, and certain kinds of television genres, like action-adventure, which also require big budgets and don't require a great deal of cultural capital or sophistication to understand. However, the "global" flow of television outward from the US is probably strongest among the Anglophone nations of the world, such as the UK, Anglophone Canada, Australia, and the English-speaking Caribbean, where US television exports tend to be most popular and best understood (Straubhaar et al., 1992). These are also among the few countries which manage to export television, film, or music back to the Anglophone US market. Within this geocultural sphere, Canada and the English-speaking Caribbean are most closely tied to the US by geographic proximity, notably being under the direct reach or footprint of US television satellites, but also by migration, by language, and, at least in the case of Canada, very strong cultural similarities or cultural proximities (Straubhaar, 1991).

There are a number of other geocultural markets emerging: Western Europe, where the European Community has been trying to create a region-wide cultural market; Latin America, linked also to other "Latin"-based language markets in Italy and France; a Francophone market linking France and its former colonies; an Arabic world market; a Chinese market; and a Hindi or South Asian market.

While globalization increasingly dominates current discussion of television flows and impacts, Tomlinson (1991) observes that most of the media imperialism and cultural imperialism discussion assumes that the primary actors are nations. Many of the studies done on media flows, media models, etc., are national case studies. Until the recent discussion of globalization, few studies focused on anything larger (or smaller) than the nation-state. Nearly all of the policy discussion about these issues has taken place within national governments, by academics speaking to national governments, or by national government representatives to institutions like UNESCO where much of the international debate has taken place (McPhail, 1989). Through frequency licensing, satellite orbit controls, market definition, financial incentives, cultural policy and advertising, and other financial controls, national governments still define the primary market realities of television. Even "regional" actors like Star TV, even within relatively coherent cultural regions, like Greater China, still find their audiences defined and to some degree controlled by the national governments of China, Taiwan, Singapore, etc. (Chan, 1994).

However, the view of the nation as a cultural unit is changing. Very few nations are ethnically homogenous – Portugal, Greece, Iceland, Norway, Malta, and perhaps, Germany and Japan. Most have fairly large minorities (Smith, 1981). If language is a primary characteristic of culture, then most nations are multilingual and not homogenous nation-states (Schlesinger, 1987). This opens up a large area of interest in media, including television in many areas, which address media audiences of smaller than national scope. Many local audiences would like to see programming in their own languages, addressing their own cultures. If this local audience shares a language, like the Chinese minority in Malaysia, with a larger geolinguistic group, then they might import programming in their language and culture, as did the Malaysian Chinese, first with VCRs, then DBS, particularly Star TV (Chan, 1994; McDaniel, 1994).

In many countries, broadcast television has been seen as too expensive to direct toward groups smaller than nations. Even countries like Brazil, a large middle-income country with an extensive commercialized television system, have only recently begun to address television programs toward regional and local audiences.

Structuring World Television Systems

This chapter proposes an analytical structure for understanding global, regional, national, and provincial systems, in this case, those of television. At all levels, it is useful to distinguish the structural from the cultural. Television, for example, has both structural and cultural components. The main structural elements, at least for television, are economic frameworks, technological bases, and institutional forms of organization and operation. These structural elements form boundaries within which cultural agents like television producers operate. The structures of television frame or limit what is possible. For example, commercial television systems tend to produce few documentaries, educational programs, or one-episode dramas. However, within those boundaries, the same structures do also provide resources to cultural forces and agents to create and consume television and other cultural products. As Giddens argues, institutional structures provide both rules/boundaries and resources to those who work within them (1984).

Structuration theory is Gidden's effort to reconcile the effects of structures and institutions upon society with the existence of agency exercised by individuals and groups, which often seem to go against the determining effects of the structures (Giddens, 1984). "Giddens proposes that we consider structure as a duality including constraining rules and enabling resources" (Mosco, 1996, p. 11). Working within constraining rules or boundaries imposed by structures and institutions, but with enabling resources and guiding patterns often provided by those same structures, individuals and groups produce cultural products like television, move them around the globe, and make meaning of them within other patterns provided by culture.

The chief structural factors are technological, economic, and political/institutional. These forces do tend to both enable and constrain social and cultural actions, products, and meanings. This gets us beyond the narrow issue of determinism. For example, technology tends to enable new developments, such as satellites's ability to let television broadcasts cross borders. It can also present constraints, but the result over time tends to be a layering, additive effect of new possibilities. New technologies, such as broadcast or satellite television, don't necessarily eliminate other options based on earlier technologies. For example, although VCRs and satellite/cable television bring in the possibility of many new US movies and programs for Latin Americans, only relatively small proportions have access to these technologies and many of them don't necessarily use them to watch the "new" US content. Several recent studies in Brazil, for example, show many, if not most, users of satellite dishes use them to get better reception of national channels, not to import channels from Galaxy (Hughes), Sky Latin America (Fox, Televisa, and Globo) or other international channels (LaPastina, Straubhaar, & Buarque de Almeida, 1999).

Technological forces sometimes seem the most revolutionary because they can sometimes enable very rapid changes. As a part of globalization, technologies such as ships, airplanes, telecommunications, and broadcasting can facilitate the rapid spatial extension of empires and political, economic, and military systems across nations and regions. The rapid recent expansion of satellite television broadcasting is to many people a somewhat terrifying example of this kind of technological potential. However, while technology can extend the reach of an idea or a system, its actual impact depends on economic, cultural, and political factors as well.

Economic conditions shape the actual development of technological possibilities. Economic factors both enable and limit cultural developments. Economic relations with other countries and economic growth can enable new possibilities, such as bringing television broadcasting into a country. However, economic patterns can limit possibilities. For example, advertising as an economic system for financing television broadcasts both enables and limits the possibilities of the medium. Advertising tends to enable by increasing the money available for production. It also tends to limit broadcast program genres to certain types, predominantly entertainment, which often puts other kinds of programming, like development education, high culture, and extensive information programming, out of bounds. For another example, poor income distribution can limit the number of people who can actually afford DBS television or the internet, hence restricting those technologies to national elites or upper middle classes.

At the political or institutional level, the dominant structure is still the nation-state, although globalization analysts like to point out its decline relative to other more global actors, like multinational corporations. Nation-states still structure most ground rules of media, such as national market structures, ownership rules, production incentives and subsidies, financial rules, frequency assignments, technical standards, and content rules. Recently, some regional groups are beginning to exercise power, and in certain policy arenas, like economic restructuring, international organizations like the World Bank, International Monetary Fund, and World Trade Organization can exercise considerable power as well.

At the cultural level, this chapter focuses on the formation of language and cultural communities and the creation and flow of media, particularly television, within and across those communities. The key elements in the formation of communities are their own historical dynamics, particularly the development of language and cultural themes, the creation and maintenance of group cultural identities as a locus of meaning, and cross-cultural interpersonal interactions such as travel and migration between communities. The media, the main focus of this chapter, build on, reinforce and, by dint of the agency of both media producers and consumers, sometimes contradict both this cultural context and the larger structural context of economics, technology, and institutions. Structuration emphasizes that human agency and even aggregate social forces are sometimes hard to predict from structural or even cultural forces.

Culture is clearly not just a force acted upon by technologies like television, institutions like the nation-state, and economic patterns like advertising. This chapter explores this cultural process as hybridization, the synthesis of local cultures with the imported elements of culture brought in by globalization, through specific processes like electronic media, migration, inflow of genres and models, and entrepreneurial action of global or regional companies.

Globalizing Forces

In much recent work on globalization, there has been a tendency to try to more fully consider both temporal and spatial aspects of international change (Giddens, 1991), including culture and media (Friedman, 1994). Several theorists, including Giddens (1991), Friedman (1994), and Robertson (1995), have raised the need to consider modernity as a crucial aspect of globalization. Tomlinson (1991) relates the media imperialism and globalization theorizations of media flows. He observes that much of the discussion of media imperialism had to do with spatial relationships, particularly US domination of other nations or cultural spaces, versus temporal relationships or change over time, in which modernization replaces tradition and may itself be replaced by postmodernity (Tomlinson, 1991, p. 69). "One way to attempt to simplify the level of complexity which the intensification of global flows is introducing in the figuration of competing nation-states and blocs, is to regard globalization as an outcome of the universal logic of modernity" (Featherstone & Lash, 1995, p. 2).

Globalization can be seen as both spatial, the outward geographic spread of ideas and forms, particularly those related to capitalism, and temporal, changes over time within many locales. This chapter will examine the concept of cultural hybridization as a temporal or historical aspect of modernization of culture. Over time cultures adapt via hybridization to a series of spatial extensions of technological and economic change emanating out from centers of global activity to the peripheries of the global system. Currently, we can see satellite and computer technologies and modern capitalism as rapid, recent spatial extensions of new forces of modernity, to which regional, national and local cultures must adapt.

Hybridization, which is treated at length below, is also a structuring process. It is an historical, temporal, reflexive cultural structuring process. Over time, cultures interact, mediated by technology, migration, and institutional and economic forms. Frequently, those cultures hybridize, with local elements and imported ones combining to create new forms of culture, like Latin Americans fusing local culture into the imported soap opera to create the *telenovela*. Sometimes, the result of interaction is less than hybridization, with local cultures only slightly adapting to foreign elements. Many times, the impact goes beyond hybridization, with local cultures and languages being essentially extinguished. "By the most reliable estimates, more than half of the world's 6,500 languages may be extinct by the end of this century" (Hotz, 2000).

In terms of structuration (Giddens, 1984), actors in a culture are reflexive in several ways that may produce hybridization. Some hybridization processes are very conscious, as when a television station deliberately copies a foreign genre, like a specific game show, from videotapes and mixes it together with local cultural specifics.

Some are relatively conscious, as when someone chooses to watch an imported television channel in English in order to practice their language skills. Some processes are less conscious but still reflexive, as when people slowly adapt elements seen on national television into their daily, local lives.

Global Spread of Market Capitalism

For many writers from the neo-Marxist and dependency traditions, globalization is essentially the worldwide spread, over both time and space, of a world capitalist market, or in Wallerstein's formulation, a world capitalist system (1979). Economically, globalization is seen as the spread of capitalism as a system, of consumerism and commercialism as social ethics (often referred to as McDonaldization or CocaColalization), and of the growing penetration and power of international corporations. Culturally, it is still seen by many as Westernization, a variation on or updating of the idea of cultural imperialism and synchronization (Tomlinson, 1991). While economics are a basic issue, various critics of globalization see overly simplistic assumptions being made about the causality of economics, particularly the global spread of capitalism, in globalization, and fear a new wave of economic reductionism which might over-simplify cultural phenomena (Boyne, 1990; Ferguson, 1992).

For many writers on globalization of television, foreign models for television are one major form of media imperialism (Lee, 1980). This line of analysis tends to focus on the importation of system level models, such as commercial versus public service broadcasting organizational forms. To use a concept found in structuration theory (Giddens, 1984), systemic changes like shifting towards a more commercial, advertising-driven basis of financing broadcasting redraw the boundaries of what is possible within that system.

Commercial broadcasting is proliferating across the globe. The increasingly global commercial system pattern for television is reinforced by several factors. Perhaps most powerfully, more and more countries are being drawn into a world capitalist or market economy (Herman & McChesney, 1997; Wallerstein, 1979). Within this global market economy, both national and global firms pressure broadcasters to allow – indeed, rely on – advertising (Fox, 1975; Herman & McChesney, 1997). Janus (1981) and Mattelart (1991) argue that multinational firms have pushed particularly hard to commercialize systems and introduce advertising, since they have become used to promoting goods with advertising in other markets. Viewing publics also tend to push for more programming choices, as with British television in the 1950s, which is often met by allowing in more commercial channels.

Commercial television systems, like commercial film studios before them, require that cultural products succeed in drawing a large, profitable audience. In television, like film before it, these demands for commercial success lead to the emergence and standardization of certain successful formulas (Schatz, 1981). If we consider both the production companies and the genre formulas as social structures, then Giddens (1984) would remind us that structures both bound and enable the agency of those who act within them. More specifically, commercial film studios and commercial television networks essentially require cultural producers to work within the boundaries of certain successful genres or formulas. However, within those structural boundaries, producers find not only constraints but also resources.

Cultural Hybridization and Modernization

Within certain increasingly global economic constraints and influenced by successful global patterns, regional and national cultures still tend to assert their own content very strongly over time. What emerges is often a strongly localized or hybridized adaptation of what is considered current or modern in global patterns. Robertson goes so far as to call the process of hybridizing the local and global together "glocalization" (Robertson, 1995). This chapter argues that hybridization is essentially the dominant pattern of cultural interaction over time. It is the temporal reflection of the local, national, and regional absorption and adaptation of global patterns of modernity in culture. As new patterns borne by technological and economic forces enter cultures, they interact with what is already there, producing a new pattern best characterized at this moment as hybrid (Bhahba, 1994; García Canclini, 1997).

For example, there is much current discussion of an Asian approach to modernity. Iwabuchi, interviewing Taiwanese young people, finds that they are more likely to choose and identify with popular music and television from Japan than from China because the Japanese material is seen as being more modern while still recognizably familiar within an Asian context. He argues that Japanese popular culture successfully adapts or Asianizes US popular culture genres into more localized or regionalized forms (Iwabuchi, 1997).

One useful theorization is to reconsider globalization as a set of regionally differentiated patterns of modernization. Japanese popular culture and its cultural industry represent a transformation from what was perceived in the 1970s, that "The media are American" (Tunstall, 1977), into globalized and regionalized patterns of modernity that build on, but also transform, patterns of modernity that seemed so specifically "American" in the first wave of US television program export dominance in the 1960s and 1970s. For example, Iwabuchi in the "Sweet Scent of Asian Modernity," describes the Japanese adaptation of cultural industry globalization as de-Westernized modernization (Iwabuchi, 1997). This is a hybrid localization or nationalization of a "global" pattern.

Hybridity and Globalization

Cutting across levels such as global, regional, national, and local is the notion of hybridization of cultures across levels. "Post-colonial theory, in so far as it addresses complex, multilayered identities, has proliferated in terms of terms having to do with cultural mixing: religious (syncretism); biological (hybridity); human-genetic (*mestizaje*); and linguistic (creolization) . . . while the themes are old – 'syncretism,' 'hybridity,' *créolité*, and *mestizaje* had already been invoked decades ago by diverse

Latin American modernisms – the historical moment is new" (Shohat & Stam, 1994, p. 41). For instance, in the 1920s and 1930s, Brazilian intellectuals created a project of indigenizing modern art by absorbing international influences into a base of indigenous and African culture, which they called cultural cannibalism or cultural anthropophagy (*anthropofagia cultural*) (Karp, 1994).

Latin American cultures are essentially syncretic or hybrid by definition. They have been created by the fusion of ethnic, religious, cultural, and even linguistic traditions from indigenous peoples, Europeans, and Africans (García Canclini, 1995). In contemporary terms, postcolonial theory deals with the cultural contradictions generated by the global circulation of peoples and cultural goods in a mediated and interconnected world, resulting in a kind of commodified or mass-mediated syncretism (Shohat & Stam, 1994, pp. 41–2). Current hybridity results from both the physical movement and mixture of peoples and the media-based flow of cultural products and representation of cultures.

Global Processes, National and Local Identities

In television and in other cultural industries as well, people use globally distributed forms to create cultural products which define and redefine what the national and the local are. Robertson observes that "globalization has involved the reconstruction, in a sense the production, of 'home,' 'community' and 'locality'" (1995, p. 30). Cultural producers use forms and genres that have spread globally to express ideas of what home is like. There is a subtle interplay between the global and local in television form and content. Robertson (1992), as we've seen, calls this "glocalization." This chapter sees it as one aspect of the historical, temporal process of hybridization.

For example, the soap opera has distinct roots in both English and French serial novels, which were carried over time in magazines and newspapers. US radio and, later, television took this idea and developed a particular form of soap opera, to entertain and draw loyal audiences over time, but explicitly also to sell soap. In fact, for quite a long time, the shows were produced for radio and television networks by advertising agencies on behalf of soap manufacturers. Soap companies and advertising agencies took this successful genre abroad, particularly to Latin America. Latin American radio and television producers adapted the genre to their cultures and needs, moving it into prime time, aiming it at both men and women, changing the form of storytelling, and using local motifs, characters, humor, etc.

In a sense, then, a global form is being localized, both for purposes of global capitalist development and for expression of local identity. The soap opera genre is still used to sell soap and, even more basically, to show local people an ethic or goal of consumption. For example, in one Brazilian soap opera in the late 1970s (Fernandes, 1982), a high point in the plot came when a man asked his wife if she would like a refrigerator and she burst into tears of joy. This consumption ethic is itself localized, with a refrigerator being an almost supreme ambition for lower-class

Brazilians, compared to something like an automobile in more developed countries. The consumption ethic is also met by local conditions of audience reception. A series of about 30 in-depth interviews by the author with working class and poor television viewers in São Paulo in 1989–90 showed that they were not generally frustrated by being exposed to advertising for consumer goods that they could not have, but had fairly specific, limited, and realistic consumer ambitions. They varied considerably in terms of how important consumption of goods had become to them; they were not uniformly permeated by a consumer ethic, although some were. This is a process over time, however. Interviewing in 1995–6 by Hamburger (in progress) in a São Paulo slum indicated that people were fairly rapidly being swept into consumer society, both by media exposure and by personal, daily life exposure to consumption in city life around them.

While a local soap opera such as the Brazilian one with the man, his wife, and the refrigerator is delivering an adapted underlying global message about joining the lower ranks of an emerging global consumer economy, it is primarily carrying messages about the local culture. In fact, in Brazil and India, among others, the soap opera became a prime vehicle for creating elements of a "national" culture and spreading them among localized and regionalized audiences that had not always shared a great deal of common culture between them despite being with common national boundaries (Fadul, 1993; Mitra, 1993). In Brazil, a study in various regions showed that television, in particular the local adaptation of the soap opera, the *telenovela*, has created a focus on common national holidays versus local ones, and has liberalized views on race and women's roles (Kottak, 1990). In India, nationally broadcast soap operas about Hindu religious myths have created more standardized versions of those myths around the diverse parts of India (Mitra, 1993).

In this example, the local adaptation of an increasingly global form of television illustrates that "the concept of globalization has involved the simultaneity of what are conventionally called the global and the local" (Robertson, 1995, p. 30). In particular, we see a diffusion of some basic global forms related to the expansion of the world economy, but those globalized forms co-exist with and even promote local adaptations with the expression of unique local content. Interviews by the author with advertising executives in Brazil in 1977–80 indicated that multinational advertisers had begun to prefer putting their ads in local productions with localized cultural content because the audience clearly preferred them. While cultural forms, particularly those related to consumption within capitalist societies, diffuse globally, they tend to be adapted locally. In fact, global diffusion of certain elements of consumer culture may well be more effective when those consumer elements are cast in local terms and adapted to local economic realities.

There is also a process of active resistance to globalization in some places. The example of popular rejection of cultural Westernization, mobilized effectively by Islamic clerics, in Iran was one of the first clear signals that not all cultures were going to easily adapt Western cultural elements. Barber speaks of two opposing trends, a "McWorld" of global homogenization versus the "Jihad world" of localizing or particularizing "lebanonization" (1992).

US Cultural Export Hegemony

A number of studies have described the twentieth-century domination of world culture flows by the United States (Guback & Varis, 1986; Nordenstreng & Varis, 1974; Schiller, 1971). Starting with films, popular music, and then television, the US has been the major exporter to the global market, even though its relative dominance is, we shall argue, declining.

Another way to look at the US position in global flows is an interesting pilot case in both globalization and hybridization of culture and cultural industries. While the US partakes of an Anglo-European cultural base, much of what makes its audiovisual products so successful in global markets is their hybridization of those cultural roots with the other cultures represented in late nineteenth- and twentieth-century immigration into the US by Arabs, Latin Americans, Eastern European Jews, and Asians. American media drew on these diverse cultures and, even more importantly, had to appeal to all of them to succeed in the American national cultural marketplace (Read, 1976). Read and others note that US cultural products were then well situated to succeed as exports because they had already achieved a kind of universalization by the absorption of various elements and the need to appeal to very diverse audiences. Tomlinson notes that fear of Americanization assumes a homogeneity to American culture that it probably does not have (1991).

Hollywood used this initial cultural advantage relatively well. Producers there developed interesting genres of film, music, and television. They began to draw in much of the world's talent, film directors, actors, writers, and singers from Europe and even Latin America (Read, 1976). This again heightened a certain type of universalism based on hybridization of "American" and other cultural elements.

The US also capitalized on an emerging English linguistic hegemony, drawing on the global penetration of English under the British Empire as well as the twentieth-century of the United States itself. As Hoskins and Mirus (1988) and others have pointed out, the fact of production in English gave the US an export advantage in the global market of the twentieth century. The US also has the advantage of having several wealthy media markets – the US itself, Canada, Great Britain, and Australia – as part of a narrower English-speaking geolinguistic market, in which the US is even more dominant than in other markets where language and culture present greater barriers to popular acceptance of American cultural products.

From Exporting Television Programs to Exporting Genres

A 1972 study for the UN Educational, Scientific, and Cultural Organization found that over half of the countries studied imported over half of their television, mostly entertainment and mostly from the US (Nordenstreng & Varis, 1974). There is now some debate and questioning about whether US dominance is slipping in world television markets. American television exports are increasing fairly rapidly in their dollar values, and exports represent a steadily increasing share of television producers's profits (Hoskins & Mirus, 1988; Wildman & Siwek, 1988). Many shows now make more overseas than in the US, and a number of American producers are beginning to shape their programs to anticipate and maximize overseas sales. However, American television programs are also facing increased competition at a variety of levels: regional, national, and local. More countries are also competing to sell programs to others. Some like Brazil and Hong Kong compete worldwide (Marques de Melo, 1988). American programs remain attractive to world audiences; this seems particularly true of better educated audiences, who are likely to be more cosmopolitan in their tastes and previous exposure (Straubhaar, 1991). Still, it seems that people more frequently look for television programming that is closer to their own languages, cultures, histories, religious values, etc. – more culturally proximate or close to them (Straubhaar, 1991).

What has happened to replace American programming in a number of countries is the local adaptation of the American commercial model and American television program formats (Oliveira, 1990). In the process of diffusion, the "American" model has been generalized and adapted in a global model for commercial media. This fits the model of Robertson (1995) and others that a number of current transformations may be described as glocalization, the oftentimes deliberate adaptation of a foreign or global model to fit national circumstances. Robertson observes that Japan is in some ways the prototype for this approach, and that Japan in fact developed the term "glocalization," which Robertson has popularized within globalization theory.

Regional Media and Cultures

A major trend of the last 20 years has been the "regionalization" of television into multicountry markets linked by geography, language, and culture. These might more accurately be called the geocultural or cultural linguistic markets, rather than regional markets, since not all these linked populations, markets, and cultures are geographically contiguous (Wilkinson, 1995).

Efforts to define cultural markets, particularly for television, by geographic regions have met very mixed success. There is the hope that for some regions that old common cultural traditions will bind diverse nations into a common cultural region that would welcome common television programming. Huntington (1993) has hypothesized that there are a limited number of "civilizations" based on underlying religious, language, and cultural divisions, which create what he calls civilizations. If his analysis extends to culture as represented on television, then we might expect to see the Chinese market broaden to a "Confucian" cultural influence area market, the Arabic language market broaden to an Islamic market, and a Slavic-Orthodox market emerging out of the former USSR and Eastern Europe (Huntington, 1993).

Government policymakers and some industry programmers have proceeded along lines similar to Huntington's analysis. In Europe, for example, the EEC has made an assumption that "Beneath the surface diversity of languages, tastes and artistic styles, there is a likeness, a kinship, a European dimension or identity based on a common cultural heritage" (Commission of the European Communities, cited in Schlesinger,

1991, p. 139). Some of the initial DBS (satellite) efforts to target all of Asia, like Star TV, seem to have similar assumptions about a common culture underlying the apparent diversity of Asian cultures.

Critics such as Schlesinger (1991) think that success for the EEC efforts is unlikely because what they are attempting to define as "European" is in fact an uneasy geographical alliance of several very distinct language and cultural groups, such as the English-speaking, the German-speaking, and the French-speaking groups which comprise both countries and subpopulations within other countries.

Geocultural markets are unified by language (even though different accents and dialects may divide countries somewhat). However, they go beyond language to include history, religion, ethnicity (in some cases), and culture in several senses: shared identity, gestures, and nonverbal communication; what is considered funny or serious or even sacred; clothing styles; living patterns; climate influences and other relationships with the environment. Geocultural markets are often centered in a geographic region, hence the tendency to call them regional markets, but they have also been spread globally by colonization, slavery, and migration.

There are waves or creation of regional or geolinguistic cultures and effects on local cultural identity from early recorded history (and before). They reflect a long history of cultural development and hybridization within earlier empires before the current European-dominated world system. These empires had very strong impacts, often spreading religion and culture beyond the reach of any boundaries of conquest, as with the spread of Buddhism well beyond India into much of Asia, or with the spread of Chinese customs through much of Asia. In a discussion of cultural imperialism, several Asian graduate students once joked with the author that current Western influence on Asia was nothing compared to earlier Chinese cultural imperialism.

However, current geolinguistic cultures such as the Arab world or the widespread Chinese population have formed in part in interaction with and reaction to the Western culture spread by European colonization. The indigenous peoples of North America were displaced by a primarily European civilization, although Mexico produced a *mestizo* or mixed ethnicity and culture of indigenous and European roots, which has substantial impact on the US. In much of Latin America, a similarly mixed or hybrid civilization arose from indigenous, European, and African cultures and peoples (García Canclini, 1990).

These cultural similarities and common histories come together to define cultural markets to which television responds. Populations defined by these kinds of characteristics tend to seek out cultural products, like television programs or music, which are most similar or proximate to them. Whereas some scholars used to fear that the intrinsic attraction of US cultural products would result in "wall-to-wall *Dallas*" around the world (Collins, 1986), it seems more likely that most audiences are really looking for cultural proximity (Straubhaar, 1991), to see people and styles they recognize, jokes that are funny without explanation, etc. To use another framework, people acquire a cultural capital based on their experience, family background, and education which enables them to understand things (Bourdieu, 1984). When confronted with unfamiliar cultural products, people are likely to apply a cultural discount to them (Hoskins & Mirus, 1988), to reject them in favor of things that are more familiar, more amusing, and more easily understood.

Regional Television Markets

Since the benchmark study of television flow by Nordenstreng and Varis in 1972, more nations at virtually all levels of wealth are doing more of their own television programming. Production technology costs are much lower, production groups of experienced technicians and artists have been trained by now in most places (Santoro, 1990), and a number of low-cost program forms or genres have been developed, such as talk, variety, live music, etc. Some countries which have slowed their film production down, rapidly continue to produce quite a bit of television programming. As ratings in many countries reflect, audiences usually tend to prefer local programming when they can get it.

Major regional TV markets are developing in Spanish, Arabic, Chinese, Hindi, English, and French. These are often called regional because they are focused around a world region tied together by common language, culture, religion, and a history of being colonized by the same country (usually Great Britain, France, or Spain). Increasingly, though, these cultural markets extend beyond neighboring countries to follow populations that have migrated throughout a larger region or even the world. For instance, the Chinese audience is centered on China and nations near it (Hong Kong, Singapore, and Taiwan) but extends slightly further away to Chinese populations mixed in with others (Singapore, Malaysia) and even further to Chinese speakers around the world. Such world-spanning populations are not so much "regional" as they are defined by language and culture. They are reached and united through a variety of new technologies: video, satellite television, and cable TV. For instance, Turkish television is following Turkish guest workers into a number of Western European countries by satellite – those people are a major and profitable target of Turkish satellite television channels. Similarly, Arabs in Europe are a major target for the MBC Arabic satellite channel.

National Forces

Concern with both globalization and cultural-linguistic regionalization should not obscure the fact, that, as this chapter will demonstrate, television remains a primarily national phenomenon. Most television is watched via national systems. States as diverse as China and Brazil work to protect the national market for national broadcast television. Many states in Asia (Chan, 1994; McDaniel, 1994) and the Mid-East (Boyd, 1993) specifically restrict international DBS. Others, like Brazil, focus on providing incentives to national broadcasters to ensure their competitiveness (Straubhaar, 1991).

Further, unlike the situation observed in the early 1970s by Nordenstreng and Varis (1974), much if not most of that television, particularly in the primetime hours when most people watch, is produced at the national level (see table 37.1).

Table 37.1   Percentage of nationally produced programming in primetime and total broadcast day

	1962		1972		1982		1991	
	Prime	*Total*	*Prime*	*Total*	*Prime*	*Total*	*Prime*	*Total*
Asia								
Japan	81%	92%	95%	90%	96%	95%	92%	94%
South Korea	73	76	80	79	89	87	89	86
Hong Kong	23	26	64	62	92	79	95	83
India			98	80	89	88	97	78
Latin Am.								
Dominican R	38	45	33	55	21	32		
Chile	63	65	54	52	58	48	58	44
Brazil	70	69	86	55	64	63	72	64
Colombia	65	77	81	75	83	66		
Hispanic US			3	66	14	43	0	43
Mexico	63	56	68	62	58	57	46	67
Anglo US	99	98	98	98	98	93	98	99
Mid-East								
Israel			63	69	72	71	67	57
Lebanon	66	60	46	38	37	34	34	24
Caribbean								
Trinidad	26	24	46	42	31	18		
Jamaica	17	30	30	29	37	20		
Barbados	16	16	13	51	10	16		

Note: This table is based on samples of one week of programming for each year, which was categorized by expert coders from each country by genres and country or region or origin.

However, much of this national programming is produced using regionalized or globalized genres or formats, an interesting contradiction which echoes Robertson's idea that we are increasingly using globalized forms to produce the local (Robertson, 1995).

There are a number of crucial structural conditions which make national media production more likely. These structural conditions enable national cultural producers to resist the contrasting advantages of global and regional producers. Some of these are inherent to the size and type of economy in question, which are structural conditions that limit or enable the state itself to act in regulating or structuring media industries. *Market size* is a crucial boundary or limit to whether national industry grows. Very few small countries produce a great deal of television, even in Europe. Conversely, almost all large developing countries eventually become significant producers of television because the size of the market supports greater production. *Wealth* of a market is also a crucial boundary. As noted for cultural-linguistic markets above, it can compensate for market size, *per se*, if the market, like Japan, Taiwan, or Hong Kong, is wealthy enough.

Some structural conditions are the result of interaction between global economic forces and national governments. While the global market pushes for certain kinds of commercial or financial structures (Herman & McChesney, 1997), the nation-state can still make certain decisions about how media institutions or industries are to be structured.

National commercial structure bounds or limits what kind of media products will be produced. If commercial success in a market is imperative, the most commercially successful program models will be adopted, local or foreign.

The *national financial base* likewise places boundaries around what kind of programming will be produced. Reliance on advertising tends to constrain programming options to those which are commercially successful – i.e., those that draw the largest or most economically attractive audiences. Government finance tends to give greater control over programming to government institutions and ruling political parties. License fees, like in Britain or Japan, tend to insulate programming more against both government and commercial pressures.

Competition among media in a national, regional, or global market may sponsor creativity but also tends to disperse resources among a number of competitors. Growth in national or regional television industries, particularly in their infancy, is sometimes enhanced by limiting the number of competing stations or networks.

Government policies are crucial for shaping industries and enabling them to act independently of foreign pressure, but style of government involvement may limit industry growth. The state can be a media actor on its own. It can be a facilitating or obstructive regulator and can create favorable conditions, such as subsidies for construction, R&D, or other needs.

Other cultural industries can support or limit television industries. Television draws heavily on the strength of related local cultural industries (film, music, theater, recordings). If those are underdeveloped, too, that places another boundary to television production.

Within the boundaries placed by these political economy structures, developments tend to be nonlinear and hard to predict, but we do see patterns among the groups of actors involved. The key groups of people involved are those involved in the management and direction of television, the entrepreneurs; those involved in the actual program planning and production, the producers; and the receivers or audiences.

Producer behavior follows commercial imperatives but will tend to follow the demands of the domestic market or audience when resources allow. Entrepreneurial behavior likewise will tailor operations to the programming interests of domestic (or regional or global) audiences and to domestic and foreign business needs and markets, with considerable differentiation among larger markets/systems. National cultures vary in their appeal to domestic audiences, although this tends to be a crucial local advantage. National media's ability to compete with foreign imports varies depending on homogeneity and acceptance of local culture.

Over time, the patterns of action and behavior by these kinds of actors tend to stabilize and form culturally defined boundaries. Among industry professionals, those tend to take the form of "the way we do things here," and among audiences, they tend to take the form of preferences for certain kinds of programming. Theoretically, these are both forms of reflexive cultural structuring (Giddens, 1984) and hybridization (García Canclini, 1995).

National Television Markets as "Imagined Communities"

Nations are "imagined political communities," according to Anderson (1983, p. 15), who says, "It is imagined because members of even the smallest nation will never know most of their fellow-members, meet them, or even hear of them, yet in the minds of each lives the image of their communion." Similarly, other levels of community can also be imagined: globe-spanning views of a rock-music youth culture, geolinguistic identification with Chinese culture even if one lives in Montreal, civilizations, à la Huntington, in which one's identity as Christian or Muslim may be more important than being Guatemalan or Indonesian, membership in a tribe which lives in a remote place in the Amazon barely aware of the other levels, including the "nations" of Brazil or Venezuela whose borders they might routinely cross. Anderson agrees that all levels of community larger than the village of face-to-face contact are imagined (1983, p. 15), and Tomlinson observes that "all cultural identities – be they national, regional, local – are, in one way, of the same order. They are all representations of belonging.... Where people think beyond the immediate presence of others, which is today almost everywhere, they 'imagine a community' to which they belong" (1991, p. 81).

Tomlinson (1991, pp. 81–2) notes that for Anderson, imagining a national community comes only with modernity, with the technological and economic changes that lead traditional people to be contacted by outside forces. For Anderson, the essential modernizing medium has been the national newspaper. Schlesinger (1987) criticizes Anderson, in fact, for not seeing that broadcast media easily flow across borders, leading to less clearly national "imagined communities."

National Television Production

Television genres have developed remarkably over the last 20 to 30 years, however. For example, a number of people have remarked on the changes the soap opera/ serial/*telenovela* has experienced over time and the variety of forms it has taken in various settings (Allen, 1995). More importantly, in some ways, is that a number of very low-cost genres have evolved which can be produced almost anywhere with the simplest and cheapest of equipment: news, talk, variety, live music, and games. More and more nations are producing an increasing proportion of their own programming using such genres. Table 37.1 shows that a significant number of countries are doing over half of their own programming, both in the total broadcast day and during primetime, where audience viewing is concentrated and the most popular programs are usually placed.

Conclusions

Current formulations of globalization show less economic reductionism, less tendency to assume a monolithic and homogenizing globalization, more awareness that there is an active interplay between global, national, and local (Friedman, 1994; Robertson, 1995). Recent work more often recognizes the existence of separate layers of global, supranational/regional, national, subnational/regional, and local (Featherstone & Lash, 1995; Pieterse, 1995). Robertson (1995) asserts, with some logic and evidence, that most of the cultures we now think of as national or local have been touched and often partially shaped over the centuries by contact with other cultures at "national," regional, and global levels. He argues that there is a certain pattern now of what we expect national and local cultures to look like that is an aspect of what he calls glocalization. We can extend that same analysis to geolinguistic or cultural-linguistic regions. Certainly in television production, there is good evidence that regional productions of major genres are influenced by global developments in those genres, such as the global evolution of the soap opera, in which global, regional, and national experiences interplay.

One of the strengths of the new globalization theorization is that it is more historically nuanced than much of the cultural imperialism debate. As Tomlinson (1991) pointed out, the cultural imperialism debate was often primarily concerned with the current geographic or spatial spread of media exports, which sometimes had the effect of neglecting complex histories of development prior to the advent of the medium under discussion. Tomlinson and others (Featherstone & Lash, 1995; Pieterse, 1995; Robertson, 1995) observe that it is necessary to add a historical dimension, which has been manifested as an analysis of modernity as part of globalization and vice versa. This chapter also places that historical dimension for cultures as a tendency to hybridity between global and other outside elements and the local or national. Theoretically, this makes it easier to see how countries may have very distinct developments of certain kinds of "modern" television genres, like the soap opera or the variety show. Even more basically, it helps us understand that a commercial network employing modern advertising and cultivating audiences as consumers may be operating within a distinct capitalist modernity of their own.

The media imperialism and cultural synchronization theories assumed an epochal change in the power of media to affect cultures. Earlier generations of anthropologists had seen change in cultures from contact with other cultures as constant and normal. Friedman (1994), for example, documents a long history of empires, migrations, and other strong forms of contact leading to cultural change. Current globalization theorists seem to be reverting more to this mode of thinking, seeing mass media as one recent wave in a very long series of cultural interactions on a global or nearly global scale (Friedman, 1994; Robertson, 1995).

Overall, within an increasingly internationalized world of television, we find a fairly compelling argument for looking at global, regional, and national levels fairly equally. Much of the change from the 1970s to the 1990s has been the development of more national production by almost all countries. However, in several regions, particularly Latin America and the Arab world, regional trade in television has grown rapidly as well. Now the new technologies of cable and satellite television present a new level of globalization, simultaneous global exposure to some channels delivered by satellite. These media also present an equal if not larger opportunity for a new level of regionalization, channels targeted at geolinguistic groups across national borders. Both these new global and new regional channels will have an impact on nation-states's sovereignty and control, but perhaps no more than earlier waves of cultural change that preceded most of the current nation-states and will be absorbed by local cultures in much the same way.

The analysis of globalization can be strengthened by theorizing it in terms of structuration (Giddens, 1984). Structuration helps clarify the role of various institutional and cultural structures in refashioning the boundaries of possibility for various cultural producers, in some cases expanding them, in others imposing severe limits. Some early, even premodern, forces, such as colonization, migration, and racial and cultural hybridization, have created social structures that still define boundaries of cultural production. At the current global level, cultural production boundaries are being most powerfully changed by the expansion of capitalist market economy forms into almost all nations. This places limits on certain forms of culture while enabling social actors to create others. Institutional and cultural forms of modernity tend to accompany capitalist globalization, but have their own logic. (This century has seen influential forms of socialist modernization and public or governmental/institutional modernization, as well.) Migration, driven by political and economic forces, also is powerful in redrawing social and cultural boundaries.

Regional and national structures can and do sometimes counter certain forces of globalization. Linguistic and cultural borders dating to both ancient and recent empires define supranational markets which are either an aspect of or a competitor of global actors and markets, depending on just how broadly one defines globalization. Perhaps most importantly, nation-states still have the power to define crucial structures for media production. States employ political power, define aspects of cultures, license broadcasters, create market incentives, limit imports through quotas, and counteract global actors who wish to penetrate national cultural space.

References

Allen, R. C. (1995) *To be continued–: Soap Operas Around the World*. London and New York: Routledge.

Anderson, B. (1983) *Imagined Communities: Reflections on the Origin and Spread of Nationalism*. New York: Verso.

Barber, R. R. (1992) "Jihad vs. McWorld," *The Atlantic*, 269: 3.

Bhahba, H. (1994) *The Location of Culture*. New York: Routledge.

Bourdieu, P. (1984) *Distinction: A Social Critique of the Judgement of Taste*. Cambridge, MA: Harvard University Press.

Boyd, D. (1993) *Broadcasting in the Arab World: A Survey of the Electronic Media in the Middle East* (2nd ed.). Ames, IA: Iowa State University Press.

Boyne, R. (1990) "Culture and the World System," *Theory, Culture and Society* 7: 57–62.

Chan, J. M. (1994) "National Responses and Accessibility to STAR TV in Asia," *Journal of Communication* 44(3): 70–88.

Collins, R. (1986) "Wall-to-wall Dallas? The US–UK Trade in Television," *Screen*, May–Aug.: 66–77.

Commission of the European Communities (1985) *The European Community and Culture.* Commission of the European Communities, Brussels.

Fadul, A. (1993) *Serial Fiction in TV: The Latin American Telenovelas.* São Paulo, Brazil: Escola de Comunicações e Artes, University of São Paulo.

Featherstone, M. (1990) *Global Culture: Nationalism, Globalization and Modernity.* Newbury Park, CA: Sage Publications.

—— & Lash, S. (1995) "An Introduction," in M. Featherstone, S. Lash, & R. Robertson (eds.), *Global Modernities.* Thousand Oaks, CA: Sage.

Ferguson, M. (1992) "The Mythology about Globalization," *European Journal of Communication* 7: 69–93.

Fernandes, I. (1982) *Memoria da telenovela brasileira.* Sao Paulo: Proposta Editorial.

Fox, E. (1975) "Multinational Television," *Journal of Communication* 25(2): 122–7.

—— (1992) "Cultural Dependency Thrice Revisited." Paper presented at the International Association for Mass Communication Research, Guarujá, Brazil.

Friedman, J. (1994) *Cultural Identity and Global Process.* Thousand Oaks, CA: Sage.

García Canclini, N. (1990) *Culturas hibridas: estrategias para entrar y salir de la modernidad.* Mexico, DF, Grijalbo: Consejo Nacional para la Cultura y las Artes.

—— (1995) *Hybrid Cultures: Strategies for Entering and Leaving Modernity.* Minneapolis: University of Minnesota Press.

—— (1997) "Hybrid Cultures and Communicative Strategies," *Media Development* 44(1): 22–9.

Giddens, A. (1984) *The Constitution of Society: Outline of a Theory of Structuration.* Berkeley, CA: University of California Press.

—— (1991) *Modernity and Self-identity.* Oxford: Polity.

Guback, T. & Varis, T. (1986) *Transnational Communication and Cultural Industries.* New York: UNESCO.

Herman, E. S. & McChesney, R. (1997) *The Global Media: The New Missionaries of Global Capitalism.* Washington, DC: Cassell.

Hoskins, C. & Mirus, R. (1988) "Reasons for the U.S. Dominance of the International Trade in Television Programs," *Media, Culture and Society* 10: 499–515.

Hotz, R. L. (2000) "The Struggle to Save Dying Languages," *Los Angeles Times*, Jan. 13: A1, 14–15.

Huntington, S. (1993) "The Clash of Civilizations," *Foreign Affairs* 72(3): 22–9.

Iwabuchi, K. (1997) "The Sweet Scent of Asian Modernity: The Japanese Presence in the Asian Audiovisual Market." Paper presented at the Fifth International Symposium on Film, Television and Video – Media Globalization the Asia-Pacific Region, Taipei.

Janus, N. (1981) "Advertising and the Mass Media in the Era of the Global Corporations," in E. McAnany & J. Schnitman (eds.), *Communication and Social Structure: Critical Studies in Mass Media Research.* New York: Praeger.

Karp, J. (1994) "Cast of Thousands," Far Eastern Economic Review, Jan. 27: 46–53.

Kottak, C. P. (1990) *Prime Time Society – An Anthropological Analysis of Television and Culture.* Belmont, CA: Wadsworth.

LaPastina, A., Straubhaar, J., and Buarque de Almeida, H. (1999) "Producers, Audiences and the Limits of Social Marketing on Television: The Case of O Rei do Gado, a Telenovela about Land Reform in Brazil." Paper presented at the International Communication Association, San Francisco.

Lee, C. (1980) *Media Imperialism Reconsidered.* Beverly Hills, CA: Sage Publications.

Marques de Melo, J. (1988) *As telenovelas da Globo: Produção e Exportação.* São Paulo: Summus.

Mattelart, A. (1991) *Advertising International: The Privatization of Public Space.* New York: Routledge.

McDaniel, D. O. (1994) *Broadcasting in the Malay World.* Norwood, NJ: Ablex.

McPhail, T. (1989) *Electronic Colonialism.* Newbury Park, CA: Sage.

Mitra, A. (1993) *Television and Popular Culture in India: A Study of the Mahabharat.* New Delhi: Sage.

Mosco, V. (1996) *The Political Economy of Communication: Rethinking and Renewal.* Thousand Oaks, CA: Sage.

Nordenstreng, K. & Varis, T. (1974) *Television Traffic: A One-Way Street.* Paris: UNESCO.

Oliveira, O. S. (1990) "Brazilian Soaps Outshine Hollywood: Is Cultural Imperialism Fading Out?" Paper presented at the International Communication Association, Dublin.

Pieterse, J. N. (1995) "Globalization as Hybridization," in M. Featherstone, S. Lash, & R. Robertson (eds.), *Global Modernities.* Thousand Oaks, CA: Sage.

Read, W. H. (1976) *America's Mass Media Merchants.* Baltimore, MD: Johns Hopkins University Press.

Robertson, R. (1992) "Globality and Modernity," *Theory, Culture and Society* 9(2).

—— (1995) "Glocalization: Time-Space and Homogeneity-Heterogeneity," in M. Featherstone, S. Lash, & R. Robertson (eds.), *Global Modernities.* Thousand Oaks, CA: Sage.

Santoro, L. F. (1990) Interview with the author, Professor, University of Sao Paulo. Co-Director, TV dos Trabalhadores.

Schatz, T. (1981) *Hollywood Genres.* New York: Random House.

Schiller, H. I. (1971) *Mass Communication and American Empire.* Boston: Beacon.

Schlesinger, P. (1987) "On National Identity: Some Conceptions and Misconceptions Criticized," *Social Science Information* 26(2): 219–64.

—— (1991) *Media, State and Nation.* London: Sage.

Shohat, E. & Stam, R. (1994) *Unthinking Eurocentrism: Multiculturalism and the Media.* New York: Routledge.

Sinclair, J., Jacka, E., & Cunningham, S. (1996) *Peripheral Vision: New Patterns in Global Television.* New York: Oxford University Press.

Smith, A. D. (1981) *The Ethnic Revival in the Modern World.* Cambridge: Cambridge University Press.

Straubhaar, J. D. (1991) "Beyond Media Imperialism: Asymmetrical Interdependence and Cultural Proximity," *Critical Studies in Mass Communication* 8: 1–11.

—— (1991) "Class, Genre and the Regionalization of the Television Market in Latin America," *Journal of Communication* 41(1): 53–69.

——, Campbell, C., Youn, S. N., Champagnie, K., Ha, L., Shrikhande, S., Elasmar, M., and Castellon, L. (1992) "The Emergence of a Latin American Market for Television Programs." Paper presented at the International Communication Association, Miami.

Tomlinson, J. (1991) *Cultural Imperialism.* Baltimore, MD: Johns Hopkins Press.

Tunstall, J. (1977) *The Media Are American.* New York: Columbia University Press.

Wallerstein, I. (1979) *The Capitalist World Economy.* Cambridge: Cambridge University Press.

—— (1991) *Geopolitics and Geoculture: Essays on the Changing World System.* Cambridge: Cambridge University Press.

Wildman, S. & Siwek, S. (1988) *International Trade in Films and Television Programs.* Cambridge, MA: Ballinger.

Wilkinson, K. (1995) *Where Culture, Language and Communication Converge: The Latin-American Cultural Linguistic Market.* Austin: University of Texas.

38

Oppositional Politics and the Internet: A Critical/ Reconstructive Approach

Richard Kahn and Douglas M. Kellner

It has been just over a decade since the blossoming of hypertext and the emergence of the utopian rhetoric of cyberdemocracy and personal liberation that accompanied the growth of the online communities that formed the nascent World Wide Web. While the initial cyberoptimism of many ideologues and theorists of the "virtual community" now seems partisan and dated, debates continue to rage over the social nature, cultural effects, and political possibilities of the internet and the related new media technologies with which it interfaces.[1] Some critics claim that the internet is producing a cyberbalkanization of "daily me" news feeds and fragmented communities,[2] while other theorists like Jodi Dean have argued that the internet might appropriately be likened to the circulation of noise and effectless content in a new stage of "communicative capitalism."[3]

In our view, the continued growth of the internet as a tool for organizing novel forms of information and social interaction requires that internet politics be continually retheorized from a standpoint that is both critical and reconstructive. By this, we intend an approach that is both critical of corporate and mainstream forms and uses of technology and that advocates reconstruction of technologies to further the projects of progressive social and political struggle. Recognizing the limitations of internet politics, we want also to engage in dialectical critique of how emergent information–communication technologies (ICTs) have facilitated oppositional cultural and political movements and provided possibilities for the sort of progressive sociopolitical change and struggle that is an important dimension of contemporary cultural politics.

To begin, the internet constitutes a dynamic and complex space in which people can construct and experiment with identity, culture, and social practices.[4] It also makes more information available to a greater number of people, more easily, and from a wider array of sources, than any instrument of information and communication in history.[5] On the other hand ICTs have been shown to retard face-to-face relationships,[6] threaten traditional conceptions of the commons,[7] and extend structures of Western imperialism and advanced capitalism to the ends of the earth.[8] The challenge at hand is to begin to conceive the political reality of new media, such as the internet, as a complex series of places dynamically embodying reconstructed models of citizenship and new forms of political activism, even as it is recognized that the internet itself reproduces logics of capital and is continually co-opted by hegemonic forces. In this sense, we should look to how emergent technologies and communities are interacting as tentative forms of self-determination and control "from below" – recognizing that as today's internet citizen-activists organize politically around issues of access to information, capitalist globalization, imperialist war, ecological devastation, and other forms of oppression, they represent important oppositional forms of agency in the ongoing struggle for social justice and a more participatory democracy.[9]

In contradistinction, since George W. Bush ascended to the presidency in a highly contested election in 2000, the lived ideal and forms of democracy have taken a terrible beating.[10] The Bush administration arguably used the events of 9/11 to proclaim and help produce an epoch of Terror War, responding to the 9/11 terror attacks to invade, conquer, and occupy both Afghanistan and Iraq and to promote a new geopolitical doctrine of preemptive war.[11] In this context, the threat of constant terrorism has been used to limit the public sphere, curtail information and communication, legitimate government surveillance of electronic exchange, and to cut back on civil liberties. Likewise, a panoply of neoliberal economic policies have been invoked and made law under the guise of promoting patriotism, supporting the war effort, and advancing domestic security. With democracy under attack on multiple fronts, progressive groups and individuals face the challenge of developing modes of communication and organization to oppose militarism, terrorism, and the threats to democracy and social justice.

The Rise of Internet Activism

Since the internet's inception, "hackers" have creatively reconstructed the internet through the creation of programs and code that facilitate the sharing of research material, communication, and the formation of communities. Today, "hacker" has ominous connotations of illegal activity, but it is important to note that it initially arose as a positive term defining a person of high technical literacy who could make socially beneficial improvements to computer software and hardware. Largely through corporate, state, and media co-optation of the term, however, "hacking" eventually came to suggest a mode of "terrorism" whereby malicious computer nerds either invade and disrupt closed computer systems or proliferate computer codes known as viruses and worms that attempt to disable computers and networks. While hackers certainly are engaged in such activities, often with no clear social good in mind, we argue below that a relatively unknown "hactivist" movement has also continued to develop which uses ICTs for progressive political ends.

In terms of the prehistory of internet activism, we should also mention the community media movement that from the 1960s through the present has promoted alternative media such as public access television, community and low-power radio, and public use of new information and communication technologies. As early as 1986, when French students coordinated a national strike over the internet-like Minitel system, there have been numerous examples of people redeploying information technology for their own political ends, thereby actualizing a more participatory society and alternative forms of social organization.[12] Since the mid-1990s, there have been growing discussions of internet activism and how new media have been used effectively by a variety of political movements, especially to further participatory democracy and social justice.[13]

On the one hand, much of the initial discussion of internet politics centered on issues internal to the techies and groups that constructed the code, architecture, and social relations of the technoculture. Thus, internet sites like Wired (www.wired.com) and Slashdot (www.slashdot.org) have provided multi-user locations for posts and discussion mixing tech, politics, and culture, as well as places for promoting and circulating open source software, while criticizing corporate forces like Microsoft. Yet, on the other hand, politicized techno-subcultures, such as the anarchist community that frequents Infoshop (www.infoshop.org), have increasingly used the internet to inform, generate solidarity, propagandize, and contest hegemonic forces and power.

In this respect, while mainstream media in the United States have tended to promote Bush's militarism, economic and political agenda, and "war on terrorism," a wide array of citizens, activists, and oppositional political groups have attempted to develop alternative organs of information and communication. In so doing, we believe that there has now been a new cycle of internet politics, which has consisted of the implosion of media and politics into popular culture, with the result being unprecedented numbers of people using the internet and other technologies to produce original instruments and modes of democracy. Further, it is our contention here that in the wake of the September 11 terror attacks and US military interventions in Iraq and Afghanistan, a tide of political activism has risen, with the internet playing an important and increasingly central role.[14]

In late 2002 and early 2003, global antiwar movements began to emerge as significant challenges to Bush administration policies against Iraq and the growing threats of war. Reaching out to broad audiences, political groups like MoveOn (www.moveon.org), ANSWER (www.internationalanswer.org), and United for Peace & Justice (www.unitedforpeace.org) used the internet to circulate antiwar information, organize demonstrations, and promote a wide diversity of antiwar activities. February 15, 2003's unprecedented public demonstration of millions around the world calling for peace in unison revealed that technopolitics help to define, coalesce, and extend the contemporary struggle for peace and democracy across the world. Indeed, after using the internet and wireless technologies to successfully organize a wide range of antiwar/globalization demonstrations, activists (including many young people) are now continuing to build a kind of "virtual bloc" that monitors, critiques, and fights against the aggressive versions of Western capitalism and imperialism being promoted by Bush, Blair, and their G8 counterparts.

In the US, Howard Dean's team of internet activists used the internet to raise funds for his presidential campaign, recruit activists and organizers, and produce local "meet ups" where like-minded people could connect and become active in various political groups and activities. Although Dean's campaign collapsed dramatically after intensely negative mainstream media presentations of controversial statements and endless replay of an electronically magnified Dean shout to his followers after he lost the Iowa caucuses, Dean's anti-Bush and anti-Iraq discourses circulated through other Democratic party campaigns and the mainstream media. Further, Dean's use of the internet showed that it could generate political enthusiasm amongst the youth, connect people around issues, and articulate with struggles in the real world. The Dean experiment demonstrated that internet politics was not just a matter of circulating discourse in a self-contained cybersphere but a force that could intervene in the political battles of the contemporary era of media culture.

Technopolitics likewise played a crucial role in the March 2004 Spanish election, where the socialist party candidate upset the conservative party Prime Minister who had been predicted to win easily after a series of terrorist bombings killed approximately 200 people days before the election. At first, in a self-serving manner, the government insisted that the Basque nationalist separatist group ETA was responsible. However, information leaked out that the bombing did not have the signature of ETA, but was more typical of an Al Qaeda attack, and that intelligence agencies themselves pointed in this direction. Consequently, the Spanish people used the internet, cell phones and text messaging,[15] and other modes of technological communication to mobilize people for massive antigovernment, anti-occupation demonstrations (see figure 38.1).[16] These protests denounced the alleged lies by the existing regime concerning the Madrid terrorist attacks and called for the end of Spain's involvement in Bush's "coalition of the willing" which had Spanish military troops occupying Iraq. The media spectacle of a lying government, massive numbers of people demonstrating against it, and the use of alternative modes of information and communication developed a spike of support for the antigovernment candidate. Millions of young people, and others who had never voted but who felt deeply that Spain's presence in Iraq was wrong, went to the polls, and a political upset with truly global consequences was achieved.

Groups and individuals excluded from mainstream politics and cultural production have also been active in the construction of internet technopolitics and culture. While early internet culture tended to be male and geek dominated, today women circulate information through media like Women's eNews (womensenews.org), which sends emails to thousands of women and collects progressive gender-informed stories on its website. Likewise, scores of feminist organizations deploy internet politics through their web portals, and increasing numbers of women are active in blogging and other cutting-edge cyberculture. Communities of color, gay and lesbian groups, and many other underrepresented or marginal political communities have set up their own email lists, websites, blogs and are now a thriving and self-empowered force online.

¡Passa-ho!
a les 6 a Génova

NI RÀDIOS NI TELES. **L**A PROTESTA DEL 13-M DAVANT LA SEU DEL PP ES VA FER VIA INTERNET I SMS. **D**UES ARMES QUE VAN PROVAR LA SEVA CAPACITAT DE CONVOCATÒRIA.

LUZ SANCHIS
MADRID

Les acusacions de Rajoy van ser tan eficaces per mobilitzar com els SMS

La convocatòria que sí que es va gestar a Génova per SMS va ser 'A las diez, en Sol'

Figure 38.1 Spanish text message mobilization

708   Richard Kahn and Douglas M. Kellner

According to the PEW internet and American Life Project (www.pewinternet.org), 44 percent of internet users have created content for the World Wide Web through building or posting websites, creating blogs, or sharing files; the numbers of Americans over 65 who are using the internet has jumped by 47 percent since 2000, making them the fastest-growing group to embrace the online world, and youth continue to be extremely active in producing new forms and content in many dimensions of internet life.

Of course, we do not mean to imply that the internet is essentially (or only) a participatory and democratic media, as we recognize major commercial interests are fundamentally at play and that the internet has been developed by a range of competing groups existing on the political spectrum from right to left. In addition, decisive issues exist from public participation in hardware design and online access to how individuals and groups are permitted to use and configure information and communication technologies.[17] Hence, while it is required that the progressive political uses of the internet be enumerated, we recognize that this does not absolve its being criticized and theorized as a tool and extension of global technocapitalism.[18]

Accepting this, our point here is that the internet and other new media represent "contested terrains" in which alternative subcultural forces and progressive political groups are being articulated in opposition to more reactionary, conservative, and dominant forces. It is not that today's internet is either a wholly emancipatory or oppressive technology, but rather that its future meaning is constituted by an ongoing struggle that contains contradictory forces. Thus, as the social critic Ivan Illich has pointed out, while it is significant to criticize the ways in which mainstream technologies can serve as one-dimensionalizing instruments, it is equally necessary to examine the ways in which everyday people subvert the intended uses of these technologies towards their own needs and uses.[19]

Moreover, it is important to articulate internet politics with actually existing political struggles to make technopolitics a major instrument of political action. Today's internet activism is thus arguably an increasingly important domain of current political struggles that is creating the base and the basis for an unprecedented worldwide antiwar/pro-peace and social justice movement during a time of terrorism, war, and intense political contestation. Correspondingly, the internet itself has undergone significant transformations during this time toward becoming a more participatory and democratic type of medium. Innovative forms of communicative design, such as blogs, wikis, and social networking portals, have emerged as central developments of the net's hypertextual architecture, and online phenomena such as hacker culture and web militancy are no longer the elite and marginal technocultures of a decade ago.[20]

Contemporary internet subcultures are potentially involved in a radically democratic social and educational project that amounts to a massive circulation and politicization of information and culture. Thus, it is our belief that many emergent online political and cultural projects today are moving toward reconfiguring what participatory and democratic global citizenship will look like in the global/local future, even as more reactionary and hegemonic political forces attempt to do the same. We will accordingly focus on how oppositional groups and movements use ICTs to promote democracy and social justice on local and global scales in the following sections.

Globalization and Net Politics

The internet today has become a complex assemblage of a variety of groups and movements, both mainstream and oppositional, reactionary and democratic, global and local. However, after the massive hi-tech sector bust at the start of the new millennium, and with economic sectors generally down across the board due to the transnational economic recession, the Terror War erupting in 2001, and the disastrous effects of Bushonomics, much of the corporate hype and colonization of so-called "new media" has waned. If the late 1990s represented the heyday for the commercialization of the net, the Bush years have found the internet more overtly politicized beyond the attempt to grow the production, consumption, and efficiency of online commerce alone.

Since 9/11, oppositional groups have been forming around the online rights to freedom of use and information, as well as user privacy, that groups such as the Electronic Frontier Foundation (EFF), Computer Professionals for Social Responsibility (CPSR), and the Center for Democracy and Technology (CDT) have long touted.[21] When it emerged in late 2002 that the Bush administration was developing a Total Information Awareness project that would compile a government database on every individual with material collected from a diversity of sources, intense online debate erupted and the Bush administration was forced to make concessions to critics concerned about privacy and Big Brother surveillance.[22] Examples such as this demonstrate the manner in which technopolitics have been generated within online subcultural groups and communities, many of whom did not previously have an obvious political agenda, getting them to critically transform their identities towards speaking out against the security policies of government.

Alongside these shifts from online consumers to technocitizens, internet corporations have attempted to court the middle ground – sometimes appearing to side with the users they court as customers (such as when internet Service Provider UUNET instituted a zero-tolerance spam policy) or with the political administrations that could regulate them (such as Microsoft's antitrust battle under the Clinton administration and then again under Bush). The general case of internet corporations is perhaps best exemplified by a company like Yahoo, which has quietly fought legislation that would demand that companies notify users of attempts to subpoena information about their on- and offline personages. Even the supposedly progressive company, Google, has recently been criticized for not being forthcoming about its attempt to assemble and proliferate user information (for sale or otherwise) of all those who sign up for its new "Gmail" application. As the internet has become more highly politicized, however, it has become harder for corporations to portray themselves simply as neutral cultural forces mediating electronic disputes between citizens and states, being in service to one but not the other.

Using the state and corporate developed internet towards advancing state and corporate-wary agendas, those now involved in progressive technopolitics are beginning to develop and voice a critical awareness that perceives how corporate and governmental behavior are intertwined in the name of "globalization." As part of the backlash against corporate globalization over the past years, a wide range of theorists have argued that the proliferation of difference and the shift to more local discourses and practices define significant alternatives. In this view, theory and politics should swing from the level of globalization and its accompanying, often totalizing, macrodimensions in order to focus on the local, the specific, the particular, the heterogeneous, and the microlevel of everyday experience. An array of discourses associated with poststructuralism, postmodernism, feminism, and multiculturalism focus on difference, otherness, marginality, hybridity, the personal, the particular, and the concrete over more general theory and politics that aim at more global or universal conditions. Likewise, a broad spectrum of internet subcultures of resistance have focused their attention on the local level, organizing struggles around a seemingly endless variety of social, cultural, and political issues.

However, it can be argued that such dichotomies as those between the global and the local express contradictions and tensions between key constitutive forces of the present moment, and that it is therefore a mistake to reject a focus on one side in favor of an exclusive concern with the other.[23] Hence, an important challenge for developing a critical theory of globalization, from the perspective of contemporary technopolitics, is to think through the relationships between the global and the local by observing how global forces influence and even structure an increasing number of local situations. This in turn requires analysis of how local forces mediate the global, inflect global forces to diverse ends and conditions, and produce unique configurations of the local and the global as the matrix for thought and action in everyday life.[24]

Globalization is thus necessarily complex and challenging to both critical theories and radical democratic politics. But many people these days operate with binary concepts of the global and the local, and promote one or the other side of the equation as the solution to the world's problems. For globalists, globalization is the solution, and underdevelopment, backwardness, and provincialism are the problem. For localists, the globalized eradication of traditions, cultures, and places is the problem and localization is the solution. Yet often, it is the mix that matters, and whether global or local solutions are most fitting depends upon the conditions in the distinctive context that one is addressing and the particular solutions and policies proposed.

Specific locations and practices of a plurality of online groups and movements constitute perhaps what is most interesting now about oppositional, subcultural activities at work within the context of the global internet. Much more than other contemporary subcultures like boarders, punks, or even New Agers, internet activists have taken up the questions of local and global politics and are attempting to construct answers both locally and globally in response. Importantly, this can be done due to the very nature of the medium in which they exist. Therefore, while the internet can and has been used to promote capitalist globalization, many groups and movements are constructing ways in which the global network can be diverted and used in the struggle against it.

The use of the internet as an instrument of political struggle by groups such as Mexico's EZLN Zapatista movement to the internet's role in organizing the anti-corporate globalization demonstrations, from the "Battle of Seattle" up to the present, has been well-documented.[25] Initially, the incipient antiglobalization movement was precisely that: against globalization. The movement itself, however, became increasingly global, linking together a diversity of movements into networks of affinity and using the internet and instruments of globalization to advance its struggles in this behalf. Thus, it would be more accurate to say that the movement embodies a globalization-from-below and alternative globalizations that defend social justice, equality, labor, civil liberties, universal human rights, and a healthy planet on which to live safely from the ravages of an uncontrolled neoliberal strategy.[26] Accordingly, the anticapitalist globalization movements began advocating common values and visions and started defining themselves in positive terms such as the global justice movement.

Internet politics has thus become part and parcel of the mushrooming global movement for peace, justice, and democracy that has continued to grow through the present and shows no sign of ending. The emergent movements against capitalist globalization have thus placed the issue of whether participatory democracy can be meaningfully realized squarely before us. Although the mainstream media had failed to vigorously debate or even report on globalization until the eruption of a vigorous anticapitalist globalization movement, and rarely, if ever, critically discussed the activities of the WTO, World Bank, and IMF, there is now a widely circulating critical discourse and controversy over these institutions. Whereas prior to the rise of the recent antiwar/pro-democracy movements average citizens were unlikely to question a presidential decision to go to war, now people do question, and not only question, but protest publicly. While such protest has not prevented war, or successfully turned back globalized development, it has continued to evoke the potential for a participatory democracy that can be actualized when publics reclaim and reconstruct technology, information, and the spaces in which they live and work.

Alternative Globalizations: Global/Local Technopolitics

To capital's globalization-from-above, subcultures of cyberactivists have been attempting to carry out alternative globalizations, developing networks of solidarity and propagating oppositional ideas and movements throughout the planet.[27] Against the capitalist organization of neoliberal globalization, a Fifth International, to use Waterman's phrase (1992), of computer-mediated activism is emerging that is qualitatively different from the party-based socialist and communist Internationals of the past. As the virtual community theorist Howard Rheingold notes, advances in personal, mobile informational technology are rapidly providing the structural elements for the existence of fresh kinds of highly informed, autonomous communities that coalesce around local lifestyle choices, global political demands, and everything in between.[28]

These multiple networks of connected citizens and activists transform the "dumb mobs" of totalitarian states into "smart mobs" of socially active personages linked by notebook computers, PDA devices, internet cell phones, pagers, and global positioning systems (GPS). As noted, these technologies were put to use in the March

2004 mobilization in Spain that at the last moment organized the population to vote out the existing conservative government. Thus, while emergent mobile technology provides yet another impetus toward experimental identity construction and identity politics, such networking also links diverse communities such as labor, feminist, ecological, peace, and various anticapitalist groups, providing the basis for a democratic politics of alliance and solidarity to overcome the limitations of postmodern identity politics.[29]

Of course, rightwing and reactionary forces can and have used the internet to promote their political agendas as well. In a short time, one can easily access an exotic witch's brew of websites maintained by the Ku Klux Klan and myriad neo-Nazi assemblages, including the Aryan Nation and various militia groups. Internet discussion lists also disperse these views and rightwing extremists are aggressively active on many computer forums.[30] These organizations are hardly harmless, having carried out terrorism of various sorts extending from church burnings to the bombings of public buildings. Adopting quasi-Leninist discourse and tactics for ultraright causes, these groups have been successful in recruiting working-class members devastated by the developments of global capitalism, which has resulted in widespread unemployment for traditional forms of industrial, agricultural, and unskilled labor. Moreover, extremist websites have influenced alienated middle-class youth as well (a 1999 HBO documentary, "Hate on the internet," provides a disturbing number of examples of how extremist websites influenced disaffected youth to commit hate crimes). An additional twist in the saga of technopolitics seems to be that allegedly "terrorist" groups are now increasingly using the internet and websites to organize and promote their causes (www.alneda.com).[31]

Post-9/11 internet extremism led to dangerous policy changes on the part of the Bush administration that legalized new federal surveillance of the internet and even allowed for the outright closing of websites which authorities believe condone terror.[32] Despite the expectation that any governmental administration would seek to target and disarm the information channels of its enemy, it is exactly the extreme reaction by the Bush administration to the perceived threats posed by the internet that have the subtechnocultural forces associated with the battle against globalization-from-above fighting in opposition to US internet policies. Drawing upon the expertise of computer "hacktivists,"[33] people are progressively more informed about the risks involved in online communications, including threats to their privacy posed by monitoring government agencies such as the Office of Homeland Security, and this has led in turn to a wider, more populist opposition to internet policing generally. This technical wing has become allied to those fighting for alternative globalizations with groups such as Cult of the Dead Cow (www.cultdeadcow.com), Cryptome (www.cryptome.org), and the hacker journal *2600* (www.2600.org) serving as figureheads for a broad movement of exceptionally computer-literate individuals who group together under the banner of HOPE (Hackers On Planet Earth) and who practice a politics called "hacktivism."

Hacktivists have involved themselves in creating open source software programs that can be used freely to circumvent attempts by government and corporations to control the internet experience. Notably, and somewhat scandalously, hackers have released programs such as Six/Four (after Tiananmen Square) that combine the peer-to-peer capabilities of Napster with a virtual private networking protocol that makes user identity anonymous, and Camera/Shy, a powerful Web browser stenography application that allegedly allows anyone to engage in the type of secret information storage and retrieval that groups such as Al Qaeda have used against the Pentagon. Moreover, associated with the hacktivist cause are the "crackers" who create "warez," pirated versions of commercial software or passwords. While anathema to Bill Gates, there is apparently no software beyond the reach of the pirate-crackers, and to the delight of the alternative internet subculture, otherwise expensive programs are often freely traded and shared over the web and peer-to-peer networks across the globe. Hackers also support the Open Source movement, in which noncorporate software is freely and legally traded, collectively improved upon, and available for general use by a public that agrees not to sell their improvements for profit in the future. Free competitors to Microsoft, such as the operating system Linux (www.linux.org) and the word-processing suite OpenOffice (www.openoffice.org), provide powerful and economically palatable alternatives to the PC hegemon.

Another hacker ploy is the monitoring and exploitation for social gain of the booming wireless, wide-area internet market (called Wi-Fi, WAN, or WLAN). Wi-Fi, besides offering institutions, corporations, and homes the luxury of internet connectivity and organizational access for any and all users within the area covered by the local network, also potentially offers such freedoms to nearby neighbors and wireless pedestrians if such networks are not made secure. In fact, as then acting US cybersecurity czar Richard Clarke noted in December 2002, an astounding number of Wi-Fi networks are unprotected and available for hacking. This led the Office of Homeland Security to label wireless networking a terrorist threat.[34] Particularly demonized by the government is the activist technique of "wardriving," in which hackers equipped with computers and basic wireless antennae drive through communities searching for insecure network access nodes.[35] Many hackers had been wardriving around Washington DC, thereby gaining valuable federal information and server access, prompting the government contractor Science Applications International Corporation (SAIC) to begin monitoring drive-by hacks in the summer of 2002.[36]

But not all war drivers are interested in sensitive information, and many more are simply interested in proliferating information about what amounts to free broadband internet access points – a form of internet connectivity that otherwise comes at a premium cost.[37] Thus, wireless network hackers are often deploying their skills toward developing a database of "free networks" that, if not always free of costs, represent real opportunities for local communities to share connections and corporate fees. Such freenets represent inclusive resources that are developed by communities for their own needs and involve values like conviviality and culture, education, economic equity, and sustainability that have been found to be progressive hallmarks of online communities generally.[38] Needless to say, corporate internet service providers are outraged by this anticapitalist development, and are seeking government legislation favoring prosecution of this mode of gift economy activism.

Hacktivists are also directly involved in the immediate political battles played out around the dynamically globalized world. Hacktivists such as the Mixter, from Germany, who authored the program Tribe Floodnet that shut down the website for the World Economic Forum in January 2002, routinely use their hacking skills to cause disruption of governmental and corporate presences online. In March 2003, another hacker successfully broke into the server of Diebold Corp., manufacturer of much-maligned electronic voting machines, and downloaded a 1.8-gigabyte file worth of internal memoranda that appeared to contain information that confirmed activists's fears that the machines could be subject to tampering. On July 12, 2002, the homepage for the *USA Today* website was hacked and altered content was presented to the public, leaving *USA Today* to join such other media magnets as the *New York Times* and Yahoo! as the corporate victims of a media hack. In February 2003, immediately following the destruction of the Space Shuttle Columbia, a group calling themselves Trippin Smurfs hacked NASA's servers for the third time in three months. In each case, security was compromised and the web servers were defaced with antiwar political messages. Another repeated victim of hacks is the Recording Industry Association of America (RIAA), who because of its attempt to legislate P2P (peer to peer) music trading has become anathema to internet hacktivists. A sixth attack upon the RIAA website in January 2003 posted bogus press releases and even provided music files for free downloading.

Indeed, hactivist programs to share music, film, television, and other media files have driven the culture industries into offensive movements against the techno-culture that are currently being played out in the media, courts, and government. While there is nothing inherently oppositional about P2P file trading, Napster gained notoriety when major entertainment firms sued the company and the government passed laws making file-sharing more difficult. P2P networks like Gnutella and Kazaa continue to be popular sites for trading files of all sorts of material, and millions of people participate in this activity. It highlights an alternative principle of symbolic economy whereby the internet subverts the logic of commodification and helps generate the model of a gift economy in which individuals freely circulate material on websites, engage in file sharing, and produce new forms of texts like blogs and wikis outside of the commodity culture of capitalism.

The related activist practice of "culture jamming" has emerged as another important global form of oppositional activity. Mark Dery (1993) attributes the term to the experimental band Negativland and many have valorized the subversion of advertising and corporate culture in the Canadian journal *Adbusters* (www.adbusters.org) and RTMark (www.rtmark.com), while drawing upon online resources like the Culture Jammers Encyclopedia (www.sniggle.net) and Subvertise (www.subvertise.org) to further their own projects. Internet jammers have attacked and defaced major corporate websites, but they have also produced playful and subversive critical appropriations of the symbols of the capitalist status quo. Thus, in the hands of the hacker-jammers, McDonald's becomes McGrease, featuring sleazy images of clown Ronald McDonald, Starbucks becomes Fourbucks, satirizing the high price for a cup of coffee, and George W. Bush is morphed onto the Sauron character and shown wearing the evil ring of power featured in the *Lord of the Rings* trilogy. Additionally,

Nike, Coca Cola, the Barbie doll, and other icons of establishment corporate and political culture have been tarnished with subversive and sometimes obscene animations.

Blogs, Wikis, and Social Networking

While hacker technopolitics such as the movement for freely shared community internet bandwidth are promising, cheap internet connectivity in itself does not guarantee social benefit if its only use is the sort of e-commerce typical of E-bay. Importantly, however, emergent interactive forms of internet media, such as blogs and wikis have become widely popular communication tools alongside the ultimate "killer app" of email. The mushrooming internet community that has erupted around blogging is particularly deserving of analysis here, as bloggers have demonstrated themselves as technoactivists favoring not only democratic self-expression and networking, but also global media critique and journalistic sociopolitical intervention.

Blogs, short for "web logs," are partly successful because they are relatively easy to create and maintain – even for nontechnical web users. Combining the hypertext of webpages, the multi-user discussion of messageboards and listservs, and the mass syndication ability of RSS and Atom platforms (as well as email), blogs are popular because they represent the next evolution of web-based experience. If the WWW was about forming a global network of interlocking, informative websites, blogs make the idea of a dynamic network of ongoing debate, dialogue, and commentary come alive, and so emphasize the interpretation and dissemination of alternative information to a heightened degree. While the initial mainstream coverage of blogs tended to portray them as narcissistic domains for one's own individual opinion, many group blogs exist, such as American Samizdat (www.drmenlo.com/samizdat), Metafilter (www.metafilter.com), and BoingBoing (www.boingboing.net), in which teams of contributors post and comment upon stories. The ever-expanding series of international Indymedia (www.indymedia.org) sites, erected by activists for the public domain to inform one another both locally and globally are especially promising. But even for the hundreds of thousands of purely individual blogs, connecting up with groups of fellow blog readers and publishers is the netiquette norm, and blog posts inherently tend to reference (and link) to online affinity groups and peers to an impressive degree.

A controversial article in the *New York Times* by Katie Hafner, "For Some, the Blogging Never Stops" (May 27, 2004), cited a blog-tracking service, Technorati, which claimed that there are currently 2.5 million blogs active. Hafner also referenced a Jupiter Research estimate that only 4 percent of online users read blogs, while bloggers were quick to counter with a PEW study that claimed 11 percent of internet users read blogs regularly. Although Hafner's article was itself largely dismissive, it documented the passionate expansion of blogging amongst internet users, and the voluminous blogger response to the article showed an aggressive activism within the so-called "blogosphere."

One result of bloggers's fascination with networks of links has been the sub-cultural phenomenon known as "Google Bombing." Documented in early 2002, it was revealed that the popular search engine Google had a special affinity for blogs because of its tendency to favor highly linked, recently updated web content in its site ranking system. With this in mind, bloggers began campaigns to get large numbers of fellow bloggers to post links to specific postings designed to include the desirable keywords that Google users might normally search. A successful Google Bomb, then, would rocket the initial blog that began the campaign up Google's rankings to number one for each and every one of those keywords – whether the blog itself had important substantive material on them or not.

While those in the blog culture often abused this trick for personal gain (to get their own name and blog placed at the top of Google's most popular search terms), many in the blog subculture began using the Google Bomb as a tool for political subversion. Known as a "justice bomb," this use of blogs served to link a particularly distasteful corporation or entity to a series of keywords that either spoof or criticize the same. Hence, thanks to a Google Bomb, Google users typing in "McDonald's" might very well get pointed to a much-linked blog post titled "McDonald's Lies about Their Fries" as the top entry. Another group carried out a campaign to link Bush to "miserable failure" so that when one typed this phrase into Google one was directed to George W. Bush's official presidential website. While Google continues to favor blogs in its rankings, amidst the controversy surrounding the so-called clogging of search engine results by blogs, it has recently taken steps to deemphasize blogs in its rating system and may soon remove blogs to their own search subsection altogether – this despite blogs accounting for only an estimated 0.03 percent of Google's indexed web content.[39]

Google or not, many blogs are increasingly political in the scope of their commentary. A plethora of leftist-oriented blogs have been created and organized in networks of interlinking solidarity, so as to contest the more conservative and moderate blog opinions of mainstream media favorites like Glenn Reynolds (www.instapundit.com). Post-9/11, with the wars on Afghanistan and Iraq, the phenomenon of Warblogging arose amongst leftist blogs to become an important and noted genre in its own right. Blogs, such as our own BlogLeft (www.gseis.ucla.edu/courses/ed253a/blogger.php), have provided a broad range of critical alternative views concerning the objectives of the Bush administration and Pentagon and the corporate media spin surrounding them. One blogger, the now famous Iraqi Salam Pax (www.dear_raed.blogspot.com), gave outsiders a dose of the larger unexpurgated reality as the bombs exploded overhead in Baghdad. Meanwhile, in Iran, journalist Sina Mottallebi became the first blogger to be jailed for "undermining national security through cultural activities."[40] And after the 2004 election in Iran, boycotted by significant groups of reformers after government repression, dozens of new websites popped up to circulate news and organize political opposition. In response to the need for anonymous and untraceable blogging (as in countries where freedom of speech is in doubt), open-source software like invisiblog (www.invisiblog.com) has been developed to protect online citizens's and journalists's identities. Recent news that the FBI now actively monitors blogs in order to gain information on citizens suggests a need for US activist-bloggers to implement the software themselves, just as many use PGP (Pretty Good Privacy) code keys for their email and anonymity cloaking services for their web surfing (www.anonymizer.com).

On another note, political bloggers have played a significant role in US politics, beginning in 2003 with the focus of attention upon the racist remarks made by Speaker of the House Trent Lott and then the creation of a media uproar over the dishonest reporting exposed at the *New York Times*. Lott's remarks had been buried in the back of the *Washington Post* until communities of bloggers began publicizing them, generating public and media interest that then led to his removal. In the *New York Times* example, bloggers again rabidly set upon the newsprint giant, whipping up so much controversy and hostile journalistic opinion that the *Times*'s executive and managing editors were forced to resign in disgrace. Also disgraced was veteran CBS newsanchor Dan Rather when rabid rightwing bloggers undermined a story of his on *60 Minutes* in which memos were brought forward that appeared to confirm that then Texas Air National Guardsman George W. Bush was delinquent and AWOL in his military duties. Within an hour, blogs heated up the story that the memos were faked which led to Rather's public apology a week later.

Bloggers also made their own intervention in the campaign against Diebold computerized voting machines. While the mainstream media neglected this story, bloggers constantly discussed how the company was run by Republican activists, how the machines were unreliable and could be easily hacked, and how paper ballots were necessary to guarantee a fair election. After the widespread failure of the machines in 2003 elections, and a wave of blog discussion, the mainstream media finally picked up on the story and the state of California in turn cancelled their contract with the company.

Taking note of blogs's ability to organize and proliferate groups around issues, the campaign for Howard Dean became an early blog adopter (www.blogforamerica.com) and his blog undoubtedly helped to successfully catalyze his grassroots campaign. In turn, blogs became *de rigueur* for all political candidates and have been sites for discussing the policies and platforms of various candidates, interfacing with local and national support offices, and in some cases speaking directly to the presidential hopefuls themselves.[41]

Another momentous media spectacle, fueled by intense blog discussion, emerged in May 2004 with the television and internet circulation of a panorama of images of US prisoner abuse of Iraqis and the quest to pin responsibility on the soldiers and higher US military and political authorities. Evoking universal disgust and repugnance, the images of young American soldiers humiliating Iraqis circulated with satellite-driven speed through broadcasting channels and print media, but it was the manner in which they were proliferated and archived on blogs that may help make them stand as some of the most influential images of all time.

Bloggers should not be judged, however, simply by their ability to generate political and media spectacle. As alluded to earlier, bloggers are cumulatively expanding the notion of what the internet is and how it can be used, as well as questioning conventional journalism, its frames and limitations. A genre of "Watchblogs" (www.watchblog.com) has emerged that focuses upon specific news media, or even reporters, dissecting their every inflection, uncovering their spin, and attacking their errors. Many believe that a young and inexperienced White House press corps was overly hypercritical of Al Gore in the 2000 election, while basically giving George W. Bush a pass; by now, however, the major media political correspondents are being minutely dissected for their biases, omissions, and slants.

Increasingly, bloggers are not tied to their desktops, writing in virtual alienation from the world, but are posting pictures, text, audio, and video on the fly from PDA devices and cell phones as part of a movement of mobloggers (i.e. mobile bloggers; see www.mobloggers.com). Large political events, such as the World Summit for Sustainable Development, the World Social Forum, and the G8 forums, all now have wireless bloggers providing real-time alternative coverage, and a new genre of confblogs (i.e., conference blogs) has emerged.[42] One environmental activist, a tree-sitter named Remedy, even broadcast a wireless account of her battle against the Pacific Lumber Company from her blog (www.contrast.org/treesit), 130 feet atop an old growth redwood. She has since been forcefully removed, but continues blogging in defense of a sustainable world in which new technologies can coexist with wilderness and other species.[43]

In fact, there are increasingly all manner of blogging communities. Milbloggers (i.e., military bloggers) provide detailed commentary on the action of US and other troops throughout the world, sometimes providing critical commentary that eludes mainstream media. And in a more cultural turn, blog-types are emerging that are less textual, supported by audio bloggers, video bloggers, and photo bloggers, with the three often meshing as an on-the-fly multimedia experience. Blogging has also become important within education circles (www.ebn.weblogger.com), and people are forming university blogging networks (blogs.law.harvard.edu) just as they previously created city-wide blogging portals (www.nycbloggers.com).

While the overt participatory politics of bloggers, as well as their sheer numbers, makes the exciting new media tool called the wiki secondary to this discussion, the inherent participatory, collective, and democratic design of wikis have many people believing that they represent the coming evolution of the hypertextual web. Taken from the Hawaiian word for "quick," wikis are popular innovative forms of group databases and hypertextual archives that work on the principle of open editing, meaning that any online user can not only change the content of the database (add, edit, or delete), but also its organization (the way in which material links together and networks). Wikis have been coded such that they come with a built-in failsafe that automatically saves and logs each previous version of the archive. This makes them highly flexible because users are then freed to transform the archive as they see fit, as no version of the previous information is ever lost beyond recall. The result, then, is not only of an information-rich databank, but one that can be examined as *in process*, with viewers able to trace and investigate how the archive has grown over time, which users have made changes, and what exactly they have contributed.

Although initially conceived as a simple, informal, and free-form alternative to more highly structured and complex groupware products such as IBM's Lotus Notes, wikis can be used for a variety of purposes beyond organizational admin-istration.[44] To the degree that wikis could easily come to supplant the basic model of the website, which is designed privately, placed online, and then is mostly a static experience beyond following preprogrammed links, wikis deserve investigation by technology theorists as the next development of the emerging democratic internet.

Two interesting wiki projects are the dKosopedia (www.dkosopedia.com) and the Golem's Wiki (www.g0lem.net/PhpWiki/), which are providing valuable cultural resources and learning environments through their syntheses and analyses of the connections behind today's political happenings. Perhaps the preeminent example of wiki power, though, is the impressive Wikipedia (www.wikipedia.org), a free, globally collaborative encyclopedia project based on wiki protocol that would have made Diderot and his fellow *philosophes* proud. Beginning on January 15, 2001, the Wikipedia has quickly grown to include approximately 162,000 always-evolving articles in English (with over 138,000 in other languages), and the database grows with each passing day. With over 5,000 vigilant contributors worldwide creating, updating, and deleting information in the archive daily, the charge against wikis is that such unmoderated and asynchronous archives must descend into chaos and not information. However, as required by the growth of the project, so-called Wikipedians have gathered together and developed their own loose norms regarding what constitutes helpful and contributive actions on the site. Disagreements, which do occur, are settled online by Wikipedians as a whole in what resembles a form of virtualized Athenian democracy wherein all contributors have both a voice and vote.

Blogs and wikis are both emerging examples of the trend in internet development towards "social software" that networks people around similar interests or other semantic connections. As mentioned earlier, Howard Dean's campaign use of internet "meet ups" generated a new paradigm for grassroots electoral politics enthusiasm, and people are using online social networking to gather around all manner of topics and issues (www.meetup.com). Social software has moved to incorporate a quasi "six degrees of separation" model into its mix, with portals like Friendster (www.friendster.com), LinkedIn (www.linkedin.com), Ryze (www.ryze.com), Orkut (www.orkut.com), and FriendFan (www.friendfan.com) allowing groups to form around common interests, while also creating linkages and testimonials between friends and family members. This has allowed for a greater amount of trust in actually allowing virtual relationships to flourish offline, while also allowing a new friendship to quickly expand into the preexisting communities of interest and caring that each user brings to the site.

While all of these examples are reason to hope that the internet can be a tool for the strengthening of community and democracy amongst its users, it must be stressed again that we do not conclude that either blogs or wikis or social networking software, alone or altogether, are congruent with strong democratic practices and emancipatory anticapitalist politics. For all the interesting developments we are chronicling here, there are also the shopping blogs, behind-the-firewall corporate wikis, and all-in-one business platforms such as Microsoft's planned Wallop application. It remains a problem that most blogs, while providing the possibility for public voice for most citizens, are unable to be found by most users, thus resulting in the cyberbalkinization of so-called "nanoaudiences." Further, that a great many of the millions of blogs have an extremely high turnover rate, falling into silence as quickly as they rise into voice, and that huge amounts of users remain captivated by the individualistic diary form of the "daily me," means that the logic of capitalism is here too apparent.

However, while recognizing that internet politics can serve as a "soft activism" that provides an illusion of political action through typing on a computer, we argue for a critical/reconstructive approach that sharply criticizes mainstream media institutions and the use of technologies like the internet, but that valorizes approaches that break with the logic of capital and that advance oppositional politics. We have stressed how internet politics can be connected to projects of political activism, and provided examples of how ICTs have been used to promote ongoing political struggles. While there are no guarantees that social software will ignite a new phase in democratic life, it does appear that there are examples and trends that it is our job as critical theorists to recognize and engage.

In Conclusion: Situating Oppositional Technopolitics

The analyses in this chapter suggest how rapidly evolving media developments in technoculture make possible a reconfiguring of politics and culture and a refocusing of participatory democratic politics for everyday life. In this conjuncture, the ideas of Guy Debord and the Situationist International are especially relevant, with their stress on the construction of situations, the use of technology, media of communication, and cultural forms to promote a revolution of everyday life, and to increase the realm of freedom, community, and empowerment.[45] To a meaningful extent, then, the new information and communication technologies *are* revolutionary and constitute a dramatic transformation of everyday life in the direction of more participatory and democratic potentials. Yet it must be admitted that this progressive dimension coevolves with processes that also promote and disseminate the capitalist consumer society, individual, and competition, and that have involved emergent modes of fetishism, alienation, and domination yet to be clearly perceived and theorized.[46]

The internet is thus a contested terrain, used by left, right, and center of both dominant cultures and subcultures to promote their own agendas and interests. The political battles of the future may well be fought in the streets, factories, parliaments, and other sites of past struggle, but politics is already mediated by broadcast, computer, and information technologies and will increasingly be so in the future. Our belief is that this is at least in part a positive development that opens radical possibilities for a greater range of opinion, novel modes of virtual and actual political communities, and original forms of direct political action. Those interested in the politics and culture of the future should therefore be clear on the important role of the alternative public spheres and intervene accordingly, while critical cultural theorists and activists have the responsibility of educating students around the literacies that ultimately amount to the skills that will enable them to participate in the ongoing struggle inherent in cultural politics.[47]

Online activist subcultures and political groups have thus materialized as a vital oppositional space of politics and culture in which a wide diversity of individuals and groups have used emergent technologies to help produce creative social relations and forms of democratic political possibility. Many of these subcultures and groups may become appropriated into the mainstream, but no doubt novel oppositional cultures and different alternative voices and practices will continue to appear as we navigate the increasingly complex present toward the ever-receding future. The internet provides the possibility of an alternative symbolic economy, forms of culture and politics, and instruments of political struggle. It is up to oppositional groups that utilize the internet to develop the forms of technopolitics that can produce a freer and happier world and which can liberate humanity and nature from the tyrannical and oppressive forces that currently constitute much of our global and local reality.

Notes

1   See Howard Rheingold, *The Virtual Community: Homesteading on the Electronic Frontier* (Reading, MA: Addison-Wesley, 1993); John Perry Barlow, "A Declaration of the Independence of Cyberspace," available at www.eff.org/~barlow/Declaration-Final.html, 1996 (accessed July 2003); Bill Gates, *The Road Ahead* (New York: Penguin Books, 1996); Kevin Kelly, *New Rules for the New Economy* (New York: Viking Press, 1998). By "technopolitics" we mean politics that is mediated by technologies such as broadcasting media or the internet. Thus, internet politics and a myriad of other forms of media politics are contained under the more general concept of "technopolitics," which describes the proliferation of technologies that are engaged in political struggle. On technopolitics, see Douglas Kellner, "Intellectuals, the New Public Spheres, and Technopolitics," *New Political Science* 41–2 (Fall 1997): 169–88; Steven Best and Douglas Kellner, *The Postmodern Adventure* (New York and London: Guilford Press and Routledge, 2001); and J. Armitage, ed., Special Issue on Machinic Modulations: New Cultural Theory and Technopolitics, *Angelaki: Journal of the Theoretical Humanities* 4, no. 2 (Sept. 1999). For an early history of internet politics, see Jim Walch, *In the Net. An Internet Guide for Activists* (London and New York: Zed Books, 1999).
2   See Cass Sunstein, *Republic.com* (Princeton, NJ: Princeton University Press, 2002) and M. Van Alstyne & E. Brynjolfsson, "Electronic Communities: Global Village or Cyberbalkans?" *Proceedings of the International Conference on Information Systems* (1996), available at aisel.isworld.org/password.asp?Vpath=ICIS/1996&PDFpath=paper06.pdf.
3   Jodi Dean, *Publicity's Secret: How Technoculture Capitalizes on Democracy* (Ithaca: Cornell University Press, 2002).
4   Mark Poster, "Cyberdemocracy: The internet and the Public Sphere" in *Internet Culture*, ed. D. Porter (New York: Routledge, 1997); Sherry Turkle, *Life on the Screen: Identity in the Age of the Internet* (New York: Touchstone Press, 1997).
5   Douglas Kellner, "The Media and the Crisis of Democracy in the Age of Bush2," *Communication and Critical/Cultural Studies*, 1, no. 1 (March 2004).
6   N. H. Nie and L. Ebring, *Internet and Society: A Preliminary Report* (Stanford: The Institute for the Quantitative Study of Society, 2000).
7   C. A. Bowers, *Educating for Eco-Justice and Community* (Athens: University of Georgia Press, 2001).

8   D. Trend, *Welcome to Cyberschool: Education at the Crossroads in the Information Age* (Lanham, MD: Rowman & Littlefield, 2001).

9   Herbert Marcuse, *Towards a Critical Theory of Society: Collected Papers of Herbert Marcuse,Vol. II*, ed. D. Kellner (New York: Routledge, 2001), 180–2.

10   Douglas Kellner, *Grand Theft 2000: Media Spectacle and a Stolen Election* (Lanham, MD: Rowman & Littlefield, 2001).

11   Douglas Kellner, *From 9/11 to Terror War: Dangers of the Bush Legacy* (Lanham, MD: Rowman & Littlefield, 2003).

12   See Andrew Feenberg, *Alternative Modernity* (Los Angeles: University of California Press, 1995), 144–66; Nick Couldry and James Curran, eds., *Contesting Media Power: Alternative Media in a Networked World* (Lanham, MD: Rowman & Littlefield, 2003); and Best and Kellner, *Postmodern Adventure*. For a pre-internet example of the subversion of an informational medium, in this case, public access television, see Douglas Kellner, "Public Access Television: Alternative Views" available at www.gseis.ucla.edu/courses/ed253a/MCkellner/ACCESS.html (accessed Jan. 30, 2004). Selected episodes are freely available for viewing as streaming videos at www.gseis.ucla.edu/faculty/kellner (accessed June 30, 2005).

13   See Graham Meikle, *Future Active: Media Activism and the Internet* (London: Taylor & Francis, 2002).

14   Kellner, *From 9/11 to Terror War*.

15   So-called "texting" has been important in a number of political circumstances. Notably, in 2001, some 700,000 protestors organized via text messaging in Manilla to demand the ouster of Joseph Estrada, then President of the Phillipines, which led to his resignation. It has also been used to effect oppositional politics in China, India, and Hong Kong (see "U Say U Want a Revolution," Jacob Adelman, *Time Asia* at: http://www.time.com/time/asia/magazine/printout/0,13675,501040712-660984,00.html). The use of texting was also central to 2004 demonstrations in Boston for the Democratic National Convention and in New York for the Republican National Convention. United States activists utilized the Textmob website (www.txtmob.com) and Dodgeball (dodgeball.com), as documented by the *Wall Street Journal* (Aug 31, 2004), "Get the Word Out" by Carl Bialik. While the use of cell phones by activists for progressive ends is an important new tactic, it should also be pointed out that the technology has been used for opposite purposes. Thus, in Madrid, the terrorist bombing of the subway station was itself ignited by a wireless phone that was used as a triggering device. In another less violent example, during the massive protests outside the Republican National Convention, conservative delegates often coordinated their activities via cell phone, so as not to be disrupted by activists.

16   The advertisement roughly translates (thanks to Lola Calderon for assistance with this): "An Event at 6 Genova Street! No radios, no TVs, the protest of March 13th in front of the party headquarters of the Popular/People's party is going to be organized via the internet and SMS (i.e. text messaging). Our arms (i.e. the cell phones) will prove our capacity to convocate." The text message within the cell phone reads: "A concentration – At the People's Party headquarters – Pass it along."

17   Andrew Feenberg, *Questioning Technology* (New York: Routledge, 1999); C. Luke, "Cyber-schooling and Technological Change: Multiliteracies for New Times" in *Multiliteracies: Literacy, Learning, and the Design of Social Futures*, eds. B. Cope and M. Kalantzis (Australia: Macmillan, 2000), 69–105; Langdon Winner, "Citizen Virtues in a Technological Order" in *Controlling Technology*, eds. E. Katz, A. Light, and W. Thompson (Amherst, NY: Prometheus Books, 2003), 383–402.

18 Best and Kellner, *Postmodern Adventure*.

19 Illich's "learning webs" (1971) and "tools for conviviality" (1973) anticipate the internet and how it might provide resources, interactivity, and communities that could help revolutionize education. For Illich, science and technology can either serve as instruments of domination or progressive ends. Hence, whereas big systems of computers promote modern bureaucracy and industry, personalized computers made accessible to the public might be constructed to provide tools that can be used to enhance learning. Thus, Illich was aware of how technologies like computers could either enhance or distort education depending on how they were fit into a well-balanced ecology of learning. See Ivan Illich, *Tools for Conviviality* (New York: Harper and Row, 1973) and *Deschooling Society* (New York: Harper and Row, 1971). See also Richard Kahn and Douglas Kellner (forthcoming), "Paulo Freire and Ivan Illich: Technology, Politics and the Reconstruction of Education" in Carlos Alberto Torres, ed., *Paulo Freire and the Possible Dream* (Urbana-Champaign: University of Illinois Press).

20 "Blogs" are hypertextual web logs that people use for new forms of journaling, self-publishing, and media/news critique, as we discuss in detail below. It was estimated that there were some 500,000 blogs in January 2003, while six months later the estimated number was claimed to be between 2.4 and 2.9 million, with a 2005 projection of 10 million; see www.blogcensus.net for current figures. For examples, see our two blogs: BlogLeft, www.gseis.ucla.edu/courses/ed253a/blogger.php, and Vegan Blog: The (Eco)Logical Weblog, www.getvegan.com/blog/blogger.php. "Wikis" are popular new forms of group databases and hypertextual archives, covered in more depth later in this paper.

21 The internet has equally played a major role in the global environmental "right to know" movement that seeks to give citizens information about chemical, biological, and radiological threats to their health and safety. For examples of links, see www.mapcruzin.com/globalchem.htm.

22 Recently, a subversive initiative has been formed by a team at the MIT Media Lab to monitor politicians and governmental agents via a web databank provided by global users. See Government Information Awareness at: http://18.85.1.51.

23 A. Cvetkovich and D. Kellner, *Articulating the Global and the Local: Globalization and Cultural Studies* (Boulder, CO: Westview, 1997); Manuel Castells, "Flows, Networks, and Identities: A Critical Theory of the Informational Society" in *Critical Education in the New Information Age*, ed. D. Macedo (Lanham, MD: Rowman & Littlefield, 1999), 37–64.

24 A. Luke and C. Luke, "A Situated Perspective on Cultural Globalization" in *Globalization and Education*, eds. N. Burbules and C. Torres (New York: Routledge, 2000).

25 Best and Kellner, *Postmodern Adventure*.

26 J. Brecher, T. Costello, and B. Smith, *Globalization from Below* (Boston: South End Press, 2000); M. Steger, *Globalism: The New Market Ideology* (Lanham, MD: Rowman & Littlefield, 2002); and M. Hardt and A. Negri, *Empire* (Cambridge, MA: Harvard University Press, 2000). Hardt and Negri present contradictions within globalization in terms of an imperializing logic of "Empire" and an assortment of struggles by the Multitude, creating a contradictory and tension-full situation. Like Hardt and Negri, we see globalization as a complex process that involves a multidimensional mixture of expansions of the global economy and capitalist market system, new technologies and media, expanded judicial and legal modes of governance, and emergent modes of power, sovereignty, and resistance. While we do not find the dialectic of Empire vs. the Multitude to be an adequate substitute for theories of global capital and analyses of

contradictions and resistance, we share Hardt and Negri's quest to find new agents and movements of struggle and to use the instruments of technology and the networked society to advance progressive movements.

27 On globalization, see Best and Kellner, *Postmodern Adventure*; Douglas Kellner, "Globalization and the Postmodern Turn" in *Globalization and Europe*, ed. R. Axtmann (London: Cassells, 1998); and Douglas Kellner, "Theorizing Globalization," *Sociological Theory* 20, no. 3 (Nov. 2002): 285–305.

28 Howard Rheingold, *The Virtual Community: Homesteading on the Electronic Frontier* (Reading, MA : Addison-Wesley, 1993).

29 See Nick Dyer-Witheford, *Cyber-Marx: Cycles and Circuits of Struggle in High-Technology Capitalism* (Urbana, IL: University of Illinois Press, 1999); Best and Kellner, *Postmodern Adventure*; and R. Burbach, *Globalization and Postmodern Politics: From Zapatistas to High-Tech Robber Barons* (London: Pluto Press, 2001).

30 Extreme rightwing material is also found in other media, such as radio programs and stations, public access television programs, fax campaigns, video and even rock music productions.

31 Kellner, *From 9/11 to Terror War*.

32 For example, the FBI closed down www.raisethefist.com and www.iraradio.com as part of its post-9/11 terror concerns.

33 On the origins of hacker culture, see S. Levy, *Hackers* (New York: Dell Books, 1984) and K. Hafner and J. Markoff, *Cyberpunk: Outlaws and Hackers on the Computer Frontier* (New York: Simon and Schuster). For more recent analysis, see P. Taylor, *Hackers: Crime and the Digital Sublime* (New York: Routledge, 1999); and P. Himanen, *The Hacker Ethic* (New York: Random House, 2001).

34 See www.wired.com/news/wireless/0,1382,56742,00.html (accessed Feb. 2, 2004).

35 See www.wardriving.com (accessed Feb. 2, 2004) and www.azwardriving.com (accessed Feb. 2, 2004). Related to wardriving is "warspying" in which hactivists search a city looking for the wireless video signals being sent by all manner of hidden digital cameras. For more on this, see www.securityfocus.com/news/7931 (accessed Feb. 2, 2004).

36 See www.securityfocus.com/news/552 (accessed Feb. 2, 2004).

37 See www.freenetworks.org (accessed Feb. 2, 2004).

38 Doug Schuler, *New Community Networks: Wired for Change* (Reading, MA: ACM Press and Addison-Wesley, 1996).

39 See Andrew Orlowski, "Google to Fix Blog Noise Problem," *The Register* (May 9, 2003) available at www.theregister.co.uk/content/6/30621.html (accessed Feb. 2, 2004).

40 See Michelle Delio, "Blogs opening Iranian Society?" *Wired News*, May 28, 2003. Another Iranian blogger, Hossein Derakhshan, living in exile in Toronto, develops software for Iranian and other bloggers and has a popular website of his own. Hoder, as he is called, worked with the blogging community to launch a worldwide blogging protest on July 9, 2003, to commemorate the crackdown by the Iranian state against student protests on that day in 1999 and to call for democratic change once again in the country. See his blog at http://hoder.com/weblog. On recent political blogging in Iran, see Luke Thomas, "Blogging Toward Freedom" (*Salon*, Feb. 28, 2004).

41 See www.dailykos.com (accessed Feb. 2, 2004) for an example.

42 See http://www.iht.com/articles/126768.html (accessed March 31, 2004) for an example on how the World Economic Forum, while held in increasingly secure and remote areas, has been penetrated by bloggers.

43 See www.contrast.org/treesit (accessed Feb. 2, 2004).

44 B. Leuf and W. Cunningham, *The Wiki Way: Collaboration and Sharing on the Internet* (Boston: Addison-Wesley, 2001).

45 On the importance of the ideas of Debord and the Situationist International to make sense of the present conjuncture, see S. Best and D. Kellner, *The Postmodern Turn* (New York and London: Guilford Press and Routledge, 1997), chap. 3; and on the new forms of the interactive consumer society, see Best and Kellner, *Postmodern Adventure*.

46 See Best and Kellner, *Postmodern Adventure*.

47 Douglas Kellner, "Technological Revolution, Multiple Literacies, and the Restructuring of Education" *in Silicon Literacies*, ed. Ilana Snyder (New York: Routledge, 2002), 154–69.

Acknowledgments

The editors and publisher gratefully acknowledge the permission granted to reproduce the copyright material in this book:

1. Karl Marx and Friedrich Engels, "The ruling class and the ruling ideas." In *Karl Marx, Friedrich Engels: Collected Works*, vol. 5, pp. 59–62. Translated by Richard Dixon. New York: International Publishers, 1976.

2 (i and ii). Antonio Gramsci, "History of the subaltern classes" and "The concept of 'ideology.'" In Quintin Hoare and Geoffrey Nowell Smith (eds. and trans.), *Selections from the Prison Notebooks of Antonio Gramsci*, pp. 52–3, 57–8, and 375–7. New York: International Publishers, 1971.

2 (iii). Antonio Gramsci, "Cultural themes: Ideological material." In David Forgacs and Geoffrey Nowell-Smith (eds.), *Antonio Gramsci: Selections from Cultural Writings*, pp. 389–90. Translated by William Boelhower. London: Lawrence and Wishart, 1985. © 1985 by Lawrence and Wishart.

3. Walter Benjamin, "The work of art in the age of mechanical reproduction." In *Illuminations*, pp. 217–51. New York: Schocken Books, 1969.

4. Max Horkheimer and Theodor W. Adorno, "The culture industry: Enlightenment as mass deception." In Gunzelin Schmid Noerr (ed.), *Dialectic of Enlightenment: Philosophical Fragments*, pp. 94–136. Translated by Edmund Jephcott. Stanford, CA: Stanford University Press, 2002. Original German version © 1944 by Social Studies Association, NY; new edition © 1969 by S. Fischer Verlag GmbH, Frankfurt am Main. English translation © 2002 by Board of Trustees of Leland Stanford Jr. University. All rights reserved. Used with the permission of Stanford University Press, www.sup.org.

5. Jürgen Habermas, "The public sphere: An encyclopedia article." In Stephen Eric Bronner and Douglas M. Kellner (eds.), *Critical Theory and Society: A Reader*, pp. 136–42. Translated by Sara Lennox and Frank Lennox. New York and London: Routledge, 1989.

6. Louis Althusser, "Ideology and ideological state apparatuses (Notes towards an investigation)." In *Lenin and Philosophy and Other Essays*, pp. 142–7, 166–76. Translated by Ben Brewster. New York and London: Monthly Review Press, 1971. © 1971 by Monthly Review Press. Reprinted by permission of Monthly Review Press.

7. Roland Barthes, "Operation margarine" and "Myth today." In *Mythologies*, pp. 41–2 and 150–9. Translated by Annette Lavers. New York: Hill and Wang, 1983.

8. Marshall McLuhan, "The medium is the message." In *Understanding Media: The Extensions of Man*, pp. 23–35, 63–7. New York: Signet, 1964.

9. Guy Debord, "The commodity as spectacle." In *Society of the Spectacle*, Revised Edition, paras. 1–18 and 42. Detroit: Black & Red Books, 1977.

10. Ariel Dorfman and Armand Mattelart, "Introduction: Instructions on how to become a general in the Disneyland Club." In *How to Read Donald Duck*, pp. 25–32. New York: International General, 1971.

11. Raymond Williams, "Base and superstructure in Marxist cultural theory." In *Problems in Materialism and Culture: Selected Essays*, pp. 31–49. London: Verso and NLB, 1980.

12. Dick Hebdige, "From culture to hegemony" and "Subculture: The unnatural break." In *Subculture: The Meaning of Style*, pp. 5–19 and 90–9. New York and London: Routledge, 1979.

13. Stuart Hall, "Encoding/decoding." In Stuart Hall, Dorothy Hobson, Andrew Love, and Paul Willis (eds.), *Culture, Media, Language*, pp. 128–38. London: Hutchinson, 1980.

14. Ien Ang, "On the politics of empirical audience research." In *Living Room Wars: Rethinking Media Audiences for a Postmodern World*, pp. 35–52. New York and London: Routledge, 1991.

15. Nicholas Garnham, "Contribution to a political economy of mass-communication." In Richard Collins, et al. (eds.), *Media, Culture & Society: A Critical Reader*, pp. 9–32. London: Sage. 1986.

16. Dallas W. Smythe, "On the audience commodity and its work." In *Dependency Road: Communications, Capitalism, Consciousness, and Canada*, pp. 22–51. Norwood, NJ: Ablex, 1981.

17. Edward Herman and Noam Chomsky, "A propaganda model." In *Manufacturing Consent: The Political Economy of the Mass Media*, pp. 1–35. New York: Pantheon, 1988.

18. Herbert I. Schiller, "Not yet the post-imperialist era." In *Critical Studies in Mass Communication*, 8 (1991), pp. 13–28. © 1991 by the National Communications Association.

19. Eileen R. Meehan, "Gendering the commodity audience: Critical media research, feminism, and political economy." In Eileen R. Meehan and Ellen Riordan (eds.),

Sex and Money: Feminism and Political Economy in the Media, pp. 209–22. Minneapolis: University of Minnesota Press, 2002. © 2002 by University of Minnesota Press. Reprinted by permission of the publisher.

20. Pierre Bourdieu, "Introduction" and "The aristocracy of culture." In *Distinction: A Social Critique of the Judgement of Taste*, pp. 1–3, 5–7, and 11–13. Translated by Richard Nice. Cambridge, Mass.: Harvard University Press, 1984. © 1984 by the President and Fellows of Harvard College and Routledge and Kegan Paul, Ltd. Reprinted by permission of Harvard University Press, Taylor & Francis Books Ltd, Georges Borchardt, Inc and Les Editions de Minuit.

21. Pierre Bourdieu, *On Television*, pp. 44–56 and 66–7. Translated by Priscilla Parkhurst Ferguson. New York: The New Press, 1998. © 1998 by Pierre Bourdieu.

22. Laura Mulvey, "Visual pleasure and narrative cinema." In *The Sexual Subject: A Screen Reader in Sexuality*, pp. 22–34. New York and London: Routledge, 1992.

23. Richard Dyer, "Stereotyping." In *Gays and Film*, pp. 27–39. New York: Zoetrope, 1984. © 1984 by Richard Dyer. Reprinted by permission of the author.

24. bell hooks, "Eating the other: Desire and resistance." In *Black Looks: Race and Representation*, pp. 21–39. Boston: South End Press, 1992.

25. Paul Gilroy, "British cultural studies and the pitfalls of identity." In James Curran, David Morley, and Valerie Walkerdine (eds.), *Cultural Studies and Communications*, pp. 35–49. London: Arnold, 1996. © 1996 by Paul Gilroy. Reprinted by permission of the author.

26. Chandra Talpade Mohanty, "Under Western eyes: Feminist scholarship and colonial discourse." In Chandra Talpade Mohanty, Ann Russo, and Lourdes Torres (eds.), *Third World Women and the Politics of Feminism*, pp. 51–80. Bloomington: Indiana University Press, 1991.

27. Néstor García Canclini, "Hybrid cultures, oblique powers." In *Hybrid Cultures: Strategies for Entering and Leaving Modernity*, pp. 207–49, 258–63. Translated by Christopher L. Chiappari and Silvia L. Lopez. Minneapolis: University of Minnesota Press, 1995. © 1995 by University of Minnesota Press. Reprinted by permission of the publisher.

28. Jean Baudrillard, "The precession of simulacra." In *Simulacra and Simulation*, pp. 1–42. Translated by Sheila Faria Glaser. Ann Arbor: University of Michigan Press, 1994.

29. Fredric Jameson, "Postmodernism, or The cultural logic of late capitalism." *New Left Review* 146 (July–Aug. 1984), pp. 53–92.

30. Angela McRobbie, "Feminism, postmodernism and the 'real me.'" In *Postmodernism and Popular Culture*, pp. 61–74. New York and London: Routledge, 1985.

31. Mark Poster, "Postmodern virtualities." In Mike Featherstone and Roger Burrows (eds.), *Cyberspace/Cyberbodies/Cyberpunk*, pp. 79–95. Thousand Oaks, CA: Sage, 1995.

32. Henry Jenkins, "Quentin Tarantino's Star Wars?: Digital Cinema, Media Convergence, and Participatory Culture." In David Thorburn and Henry Jenkins (eds.), *Rethinking Media Change: The Aesthetics of Transition*. Cambridge: MIT Press, 2003. © 2003 by The MIT Press. Reprinted by permission of the publisher.

33. Arjun Appadurai, "Disjuncture and difference in the global cultural economy." In *Public Culture*, 2:2 (1990). © 1990 by Arjun Appadurai. Reprinted by permission of the author.

34. Annabelle Sreberny [Annabelle Sreberny-Mohammadi], "The Global and the Local in International Communications." In James Curran and Michael Gerevitch (eds.), *Mass Media and Society*. London: Edward Arnold. 1991. © 1991 by A. S. Mohammadi.

35. Jésus Martín-Barbero, "The processes: From nationalisms to transnationalisms." In *Communication, Culture and Hegemony: From the Media to Mediations*, pp. 150–86. Newbury Park, CA.: Sage, 1991.

36. Jan Nederveen Pieterse, "Globalization as hybridization." In *International Sociology*, 9:2 (1994). © 1994 by Sage Publications Ltd. Reprinted by permission of the publisher and author.

37. Joseph Straubhaar, "(Re)asserting national television and national identity against the global, regional, and local levels of world television." In Joseph M. Chan and Bryce T. McIntyre (eds.), *In Search of Boundaries: Communication, Nation-States, and Cultural Identities*. Westport, CN: Ablex Publishing, 2002. © 2002 by Greenwood Publishing Group, Inc. Reprinted by permission of the publisher.

38. Richard Kahn and Douglas M. Kellner, "Oppositional politics and the internet: A critical/reconstructive approach." In *Cultural Politics*, 1:1. Oxford and New York: Berg Publishers, 2005. www.bergpublishers.com. © 2005 by Richard Kahn and Douglas Kellner. Reprinted by permission of the authors.

The publisher apologizes for any errors or omissions in the above list and would be grateful if notified of any corrections that should be incorporated in future reprints or editions of this book.

Index

NOTE: Page numbers in bold indicate a text by an author.

gays and lesbians: stereotyping and film, 353–65

gaze: male gaze and film, 346–52

gender: audience research differences, 186–8; and commodity audience, 199, 311, 312–13, 316–20; film and visual pleasure, 339, 344–52; gendered violence in media, 598; and hegemony, xv; *see also* feminism; patriarchy; sexual difference; women

Genet, Jean, 152

genital mutilation, 401–2

geo-cultural media markets, 683–4, 693–5, 699

George Lucas in Love (amateur film), 560–1

Georgetown Center for Strategic and International Studies (CSIS), 274

Geraghty, Christine, 361

Gerbner, George, 166, 311

Germany: culture industry, 49, 66–71; *see also* Frankfurt school

gesture: black music in Brazil, 643–6

Gibbon, Edward, 112

Giddens, Anthony, 605, 608, 622, 660, 661, 687; structuration theory, 681, 685, 687–8, 688–9, 700

Gide, André, 329

Giesso, Osvaldo, 426

gift economy and internet, 713, 714

Gilder, George, 536

Gilroy, Paul, 340, 341, **381–95**, 520

global capital, 590

global capitalism, xxxiv–xxxv, 96, 579

global memory, 664–5

global pluralism, 605, 608, 616, 664

global products, xxiii

global sociology, 675

"global village," 585

globalization, xxx, xxxv–xxxvi, 579–83, 584–601; ambiguity of, xxxvi; conceptualizations of, 658–9, 661, 671; and cultural imperialism, xxxi, 199, 298, 299, 301, 302–4, 580, 586, 587, 588, 605, 606–8; and cultural reproduction, 597–9; fractal cultural forms, 599–600; global media flows, 613–17, 683–4; homogenization and heterogenization, 588–97, 607, 666, 674, 683; and

hybridity, 580–1, 662–77, 687–8, 689–90; and ideology, xiv, 579–80; and internet activism, 709–20; and local, 580, 614–16, 621–2, 662; media effects, 618–21, 654; of media forms, 608–9; mélange effect, 661, 663, 665–7; and modernity, 659–61, 687; negative views of, 579–80; and postmodernism, 579; scapes of global cultural economy, 588–95, 599, 600, 605, 663; of television, 681–700; *see also* cultural imperialism; global cultural flows

glocalization, 662, 689, 693, 699

Gloucester, Duke of, 112

Godelier, M., 147–8

Golding, Peter, 197, 210–11, 232, 293*n*

Gombrich, E. H., 110

Gómez-Peña, Guillermo, 438

Google, 709; Google Bombing, 716

Gori, Paolo, 427

graffiti on monuments, 428

Gramsci, Antonio, xv–xvi, xix, xxiv, 3, 80, 150, 151, 393, 639; and demand management, 232; Williams on, 134–5, 139

grassroots culture *see* participatory culture

gratifications research, 176, 178–81, 185, 186

Great Dictator, The (film), 59–60

Greeks: production of art, 19

Greene, Graham, 99

Grimme, Hubert, 36*n*

Groening, Matt, 571

Grossberg, Larry, 175, 183, 184, 190*n*

Guattari, Félix, 415, 538

guest-workers, 592, 695

Gunning, Tom, 563

Gurevitch, Michael, 178, 312

Gutiérrez, Eduardo, 642

Gutiérrez, L. H., 632

Gwertzman, Bernard, 280

Habermas, Jürgen, xv, xviii–xix, 5, **73–8**, 232, 423, 523

habitus, 327*n*, 597

hackers/"hacktivism," 704–5, 712–15

Hafner, Katie, 715

hailing, 86

Hairspray (film), 378

selective perception, 170
self: "real me" in postmodern discourse,
   522–3, 524–5, 529–31; *see also* identity;
   subjectivity
Selye, Hans, 109
semiology/semiotics, xxii, 6, 70, 94,
   166, 178; and subcultures, 146–7, 149,
   151; *see also* Barthes, Roland; signs and
   signification
semi-periphery, 663
sensationalism, 14
sensationalist press in Latin America, 646–8
sense perceptions, 21–2
sensibility, 141
separation and spectacle, 93, 117, 118, 121
separatist movements, 593–4
Séverin-Mars, 25
Sex Pistols, 154, 160–1*n*
sexism, xiv, xxv, 199, 401; and commodity
   audiences, 318–19, 320
sexual difference: "third world women"
   construction, 398, 407, 414
sexual division of labor and "third world
   women," 410–11
sexuality: and Other, 366, 367–8;
   postmodern feminism, 526;
   psychoanalysis and film, 342–52;
   representations of "third world women,"
   401–2, 404, 409–10; repression and
   culture industry, 53–5; stereotyping and
   film, 353–65
Shadows of the Empire (amateur film), 567
Shakespeare, William: on new media,
   108–9
Sharabi, Hisham, 667
shareware, 713, 714
Shevchenko, Arkady, 274
Shohat, Ella, 667–8, 669
signs and signification: encoding/
   decoding, 166–73; signifying chain and
   postmodern, 499–501; and simulation,
   456–7; and spectacle, 118; *see also*
   semiology/semiotics
Simon, Julian L., 234, 238
simulation and simulacra, xxxiv, 447–8,
   450, 453–81; fetishism of the consumer,
   596; and postmodernism, 494, 503, 504,
   507, 513; and virtual reality, 538
Sistine Madonna (Raphael), 36–7*n*

Situationist International, 92–3, 494, 581,
   720
slave labor in Brazil, 643–4
slave mentality, 116
Smith, Adam, xi
Smith, Allen, 572–3
Smith, Anthony D., 665
Smith, Dana, 564
Smith, Kevin, 571–2
Smythe, Dallas W., 197, 198, 211,
   230–56, 313–14, 316
Snow, C. P., 113–14
soap operas, 42, 317, 690; from Brazil,
   304–5, 434, 690–1
social class: base and superstructure model,
   138–41; in British cultural studies, xxiv;
   class struggle and State Ideological
   Apparatus, 81; creole class in Latin
   America, 628–9; and cultural capital,
   200, 215, 322–6; identity and
   cultural studies, 388–94; and mass
   communications, 209, 216–17;
   massification in Latin America, 631–6;
   national bourgeoisie in Latin America,
   628–9; and sign, 151; *see also* ruling
   class; working classes
social life and cultural studies, xxi–xxvi,
   91–7
social movements: in Latin America, 631–6,
   637–8; oppositional politics and internet,
   xxxvi, 581, 709–20
social networking portals, 708, 715–20
social self: feminism and postmodernism,
   529
social software, 719–20
social transformation, xxiv
social types, 355, 363
social welfare state and public sphere, 77–8
socialism, 515–16
society of the spectacle, xxii–xxiii, 92–3,
   117–21
sociology: Bourdieu on, 334–5; global
   sociology, 675
soft power, 300, 305
solidarity and identity, 387, 388, 389
Some of my Best Friends Are . . . (film),
   363–4
Sontag, Susan, 504
Sorel, Georges, 17*n*